D1313823

ECONOMICS

CANADA IN THE GLOBAL ENVIRONMENT

Michael Parkin

University of Western Ontario

Robin Bade

University of Western Ontario

ADDISON-WESLEY PUBLISHERS LIMITED

*Don Mills, Ontario • Reading, Massachusetts
Menlo Park, California • New York • Wokingham,
England • Amsterdam • Bonn • Sydney
Singapore • Tokyo • Madrid • San Juan*

Canadian Cataloguing in Publication Data

Parkin, Michael, 1939–

Economics

ISBN 0–201–19564–X

1. Economics. I. Bade, Robin. II. Title.

HB171.5.P37 1991 330 C90-094975-9

ISBN 0–201–19564–X

A B C D E F –DON– 96 95 94 93 92 91

SPONSORING EDITOR: Shannon Bailey
PROJECT EDITOR: Shirley Tessier
TYPESET AND LAYOUT: Tony Gordon Limited
TEXT FORMATTING: Cindy Kantor
PROOFREADER: Karen Rolfe
PERMISSIONS EDITOR: Gail Copeland
COVER AND INTERIOR DESIGN: Pronk&Associates
TECHNICAL ART: Artplus Design Consultants
COVER ART: Calvin Nichols Paper Sculpture
MANUFACTURING SUPERVISOR: Roberta Dick
PRINTER: R.R. Donnelley & Sons

Text and photo credits appear on p. I-15, which constitutes a continuation of the copyright page.

ABOUT THE AUTHORS

MICHAEL PARKIN was educated at the University of Leicester. Currently in the Department of Economics at the University of Western Ontario, Professor Parkin has held faculty appointments at the Universities of Sheffield, Leicester, Essex, and Manchester and has lectured extensively throughout Canada, the United States, Europe, Australia, and Japan. He has served as managing editor of the *Canadian Journal of Economics* and on the editorial boards of the *American Economic Review* and the *Journal of Monetary Economics.* Professor Parkin's research on macroeconomics, monetary economics, and international economics has resulted in 160 publications in the *American Economic Review*, the *Journal of Political Economy*, the *Review of Economic Studies*, the *Journal of Monetary Economics*, the *Journal of Money, Credit and Banking*, and dozens of other journals and edited volumes.

ROBIN BADE teaches at the University of Western Ontario. She earned degrees in mathematics and economics at the University of Queensland and her Ph.D at the Australian National University. She has held faculty appointments in the business school at the University of Edinburgh and in the economics departments at the University of Manitoba and the University of Toronto. Her research on international capital flows appears in the *International Economic Review* and the *Economic Record.*

Professor Parkin and Dr. Bade are joint authors of *Modern Macroeconomics* (Prentice-Hall), an intermediate text, and have collaborated on many research and textbook writing projects. They are both experienced and dedicated teachers of introductory economics.

To Our Students

PREFACE

To change the way students see the world: this is our goal in teaching economics and in writing this book.

Economics teaches students to use the economist's lens to view the world more clearly. At every point in the writing, development, and production of this book, we have tried to put ourselves in the student's place. We have repeatedly recalled our own early struggles to master this discipline and drawn on the learning experiences of the several thousand principles students whom we have been privileged to teach over the past twenty-five years.

Three assumptions (or are they facts?) about students have been our guiding principles in determining the content, organization, features, and visual appearance of this book. First, students are eager to learn, but they are overwhelmed by the seemingly endless claims on their time, interests, and energy. As a result, they want to be told — and in a convincing way — just *why* they are being asked to study a particular body of material. They want to be motivated by a demonstration of its relevance to their everyday experience. Second, once motivated, students want to be presented with a thoughtful, clear, and logical explanation, so that they can understand and begin to apply what they have learned. They do not want to be handed loosely related facts and anecdotes. Third, students are more interested in the present and future than in the past. They want to learn the economics of the 1990s so that, as they enter the twenty-first century, they will be equipped with the most up-to-date tools available to guide them.

Content and Organization

This book seeks to be truly modern and accurate and, at the same time, to respect and reflect the heritage of timeless principles that have been distilled from the scholarship of economists over the past two centuries.

The core of the principles course has been around for more than one hundred years and other important elements, especially parts of the theory of the firm and Keynesian macroeconomics, have been with us for more than fifty years. But economics has also been developing and changing rapidly during the past few decades. Although all principles texts pay some attention to these more recent developments, they have not succeeded in integrating the new and the traditional. They have created a patchwork quilt rather than a seamless web. We have worked hard to avoid this patchwork approach and to present new ideas in a new way, incorporating them into the body of timeless principles so as to weave a coherent pattern.

Among the many recent developments that you will find in this book are rational expectations, efficient markets, game theory, the principal-agent problem, public choice theory, aggregate demand and aggregate supply, and real business cycle theory. Yet the presence of modern topics does not translate into "high level." Nor does it translate into "bias." The presentation has been crafted to make recent developments in economics thoroughly accessible to the beginning student. Furthermore, where these modern theories are controversial, the more traditional theories that they are seeking to replace are also presented and the two (or more) approaches are evaluated and compared. Thus, for example, in macroeconomics, all the alternative "schools" — Keynesian, monetarist, rational expectations, and real business cycle — are given an even-handed treatment.

But this book does have a point of view. It is that economics is a serious, lively, and evolving science — a science that seeks to develop a body of theory powerful enough to explain the economic world around us and that pursues its task by building, testing, and rejecting economic models. In some areas the science has succeeded in its task, but in others it has some way to go and controversy persists. Where matters are settled, we present what we know in the clearest possible light; where controversy persists, we present the alternative viewpoints.

The existence of controversy and disagreement has implications for the organization of the principles course. As a consequence, we have paid special attention to ensuring that this book can be used in a wide variety of ways.

Flexibility

There is legitimate disagreement about how best to teach the principles of economics. Most fundamentally, there is disagreement about the best order in which to present microeconomics and macroeconomics. We have chosen to do microeconomics first, but the book has been written to accommodate courses that are sequenced in either order. The microeconomics and macroeconomics chapters do not depend on each other; concepts and terms are defined and ideas are developed independently in each of the two halves.

We have accommodated a wide range of teaching approaches by building flexibility into the book. In addition to the techniques mentioned below, there are several optional chapter sections, which are indicated with an asterisk (*) on the section title and in the table of contents. These sections may be omitted with no loss of continuity.

Microeconomics This book permits consumer theory to be taught using either the marginal utility approach (Chapter 7) or the indifference curve approach (Chapter 8) or both. In other words, the indifference curve chapter may be treated as a complement of or a substitute for the marginal utility chapter and for those using both, there is an appendix showing how they fit together.

The theory of production and costs is presented in a traditional way but there is also an optional chapter on isoquants (Chapter 11). We have provided a full chapter rather than an appendix on this topic because it is our firm belief that more difficult ideas need a more gentle and thoughtful treatment than relatively easy material. Our own teaching experiences have led us to the conclusion that books that place more difficult material in short appendixes render that material almost unteachable.

Because many instructors run out of time when they get to factor markets, the first chapter (Chapter 15) in this part contains the core material, and the remaining chapters may be treated as optional.

We have placed all the material on the economic behaviour of government in a single part (Chapters 19, 20, and 21). However, these chapters may be read before those on factor markets (Chapters 15, 16, 17, and 18). This means that competition policy (Chapter 21) may be studied immediately following competition, monopoly, monopolistic competition and oligopoly (Chapters 12, 13, and 14).

Macroeconomics In recognition of the diversity in approaches to teaching macroeconomics — and believing strongly that diversity is appropriate in unsettled parts of the discipline — we have paid special attention to writing these chapters so that they can be used in a variety of ways. We think that the most natural way to teach macroeconomics is as it is presented here. But several other sequences also work well.

We have long been puzzled by the way principles texts present the aggregate demand and aggregate supply model. *Aggregate* demand and *aggregate* supply analysis is more difficult than demand and supply analysis. Yet most books devote a full and thoughtful chapter to the demand and supply model and then present the aggregate demand and aggregate model in a scant few pages. We have recognized the inherently more difficult nature of the aggregate model and have tried to present an equally careful development of that model in Chapter 24, which parallels our development of the microeconomic demand and supply model in Chapter 4.

Chapter 24 on aggregate demand and aggregate supply serves as an overview of the rest of the macroeconomics material. Alternatively, it can be read as a synthesis of the individual components of aggregate demand and aggregate supply and can be studied after Chapter 31.

For those instructors who like to teach the *IS–LM* model, it is presented in an appendix, but one that is longer, more gentle, and (we hope) more teachable than is commonly found.

Special Features

Art Program

One of the most important tools for economists is graphical analysis, yet students often find this method of analysis extremely challenging and even a stumbling block. Recognizing this fact and always keeping it in mind, we and the developmental and art editors at Addison-Wesley have taken extraordinary care in developing the art program.

We began by observing a distinction between diagrams that represent models and those that display data. Model-based diagrams emphasize analysis and abstraction, whereas empirical graphs emphasize shapes, patterns, and visual correlations. It makes good pedagogical sense to differentiate these two kinds of figures in order to help students work with them. As a signal to students, we set our model-based diagrams on a white background, and the empirical graphs on a manila background.

Our goal in the model-based art (see the adjacent sample figure) is to show clearly "where the economic action is." To achieve this, we observe a consistent protocol in style, notation, and use of colour which includes:

- Highlighting shifted curves, points of equilibrium, and the most important features in red.
- Using arrows in conjunction with colour to lend directional movement to what are usually static presentations.
- Pairing graphs with data tables from which the curves have been plotted.
- Using colour consistently to underscore the content, and referring to such colour in the text and captions.
- Labelling key pieces of information in graphs with boxed notes.
- Rendering each piece electronically, so that precision is achieved.

The entire art program has been developed with the study and review needs of the student in mind. We have included the following features:

- Marking the most important figures and tables with a red "key" and listing them at the end of the chapter as "Key Figures and Tables."
- Using complete, informative captions that encapsulate the major points in the graph, so that students can preview or review the chapter by skimming through the art.

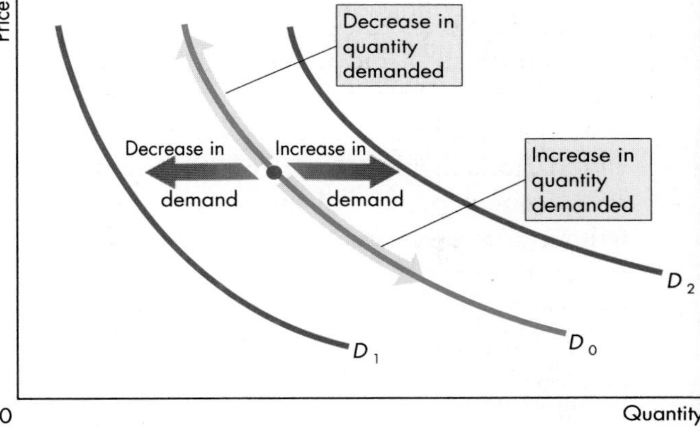

We undertook extensive tests of the quality of our art program. For example, we had two art reviewers evaluate every graph. Once a style had been developed, we also conducted informal discussions on the use of colour and on the rendering technique. And since the accuracy of illustrations and their in-text references are vital, we engaged five economists as accuracy reviewers of the manuscript. These economists assisted the publisher's in-house developmental editors and proofreaders, who checked every line, point, label, and cross-reference for clarity and accuracy.

The Interviews

An important goal of the principles course is to develop, in students, the ability to reason like economists. To aid this process, this book enables students to eavesdrop on a series of conversations that we conducted with fourteen eminent contributors to economics or to the formation and execution of economic policy. These interviews open each of the book's parts. It has been a great joy to learn from these creators or users of economics something of how they view their area of specialization, of their unique contributions to economics, and also of their general insights which are relevant to beginning students.

Each interview has been carefully edited to be self-contained and the necessary concepts and terms are defined informally within each one. Since each interview discusses topics that are introduced formally in the following group of chapters, students can use it as a preview to some of the issues they are about to encounter. A more careful reading afterwards will give students a fuller appreciation of the discussion. Finally, the whole series of interviews can be approached as an informal symposium on the subject matter of economics as it is practiced today.

Reading Between the Lines

Another common goal of the principles course is to develop the student's ability to use economics to analyze current events reported in the media. Recognizing this need, we have developed a feature that may, we hope, be a fruitful model. Each "Reading Between the Lines" spread contains three passes at a story. It begins with a facsimile of an actual (usually abbreviated) newspaper or magazine article. It then presents a digest of the article's essential points. Finally, it provides an economic analysis of the news story. We believe that students, using this feature, will learn how to do more than just notice the relevance of economics to modern life. We hope that they will also develop the ability to ask good questions, to evaluate the quality of information presented in the media, and to use economic models to deepen their understanding of the economic world around them.

Our Advancing Knowledge

Another group of special essays reveals the birth and development of economic ideas, not just as abstract models, but as intimately tied to the people and circumstances that formed them.

Learning Aids

We have developed a careful pedagogical plan to ensure that this book complements and reinforces classroom learning. Each chapter contains the following pedagogical elements:

- *Objectives.* A list of chapter objectives that enables students to set their goals before embarking on a chapter.
- *Chapter openers.* Economic vignettes, questions, puzzles, or metaphors that motivate the analysis and that are resolved in the chapter.
- *Highlighted in-text reviews.* Succinct summaries at the end of many main sections.
- *Key terms.* Highlighted within the text, these concepts form the first part of a three-tiered review of economic vocabulary. These terms are repeated, with page references, at chapter ends and compiled in the end-of-book glossary.
- *Key figures and tables.* Identified with a "key" logo and listed at chapter ends.
- *End-of-chapter study material.* Summaries organized around major headings; lists of key terms with page references; lists of key figures and tables with page references; review questions; and problems. We have worked hard to make the problems interesting, challenging, and useful for students.

Design

The design has an important place in the overall pedagogical plan. Our mission with the design of special features was to evoke the colourful feeling of nontextbook print media, notably magazines and annual reports, thus reinforcing the connection of economics to the real world. In the text itself, we strove for a scrupulously clear and honest look that would let the models being presented speak for themselves.

The Teaching and Learning Package

In conjunction with the authors of the supplements and Addison-Wesley we have put a tremendous amount of effort into ensuring that each component of the package will help students and instructors derive the maximum benefit from the textbook.

Study Guide Prepared by Avi Cohen of York University, and Harvey King of the University of Regina, the Study Guide has been carefully coordinated with the main textbook. Each chapter contains: Chapter in Perspective; Learning Objectives; Helpful Hints; Self-Test (concepts review; true/false, multiple-choice, short-answer questions, and problems) and Answers to Self-Test; and Key Figures and Tables.

Test Item File Prepared by Harvey King of the University of Regina, this file offers over 4,000 multiple-choice questions. Each chapter includes a separate section of questions directly from the Study Guide and a section of questions that parallel those in the Study Guide.

Computerized Test Item File This software for qualified adopters is available for IBM-PC and compatible microcomputers and Macintosh microcomputers.

Instructor's Manual Prepared by Sharon Pearson of the University of Alberta, the Instructor's Manual includes detailed chapter outlines and teaching suggestions, a list of acetates, answers to all review questions and problems in the textbook, and a flexibility guide prepared by the authors.

Acetates/Transparency Masters Reproductions of the text's key figures are available to qualified adopters of the textbook by contacting Addison-Wesley.

Graph Package Key graphs from the text are reproduced in a consumable format. This inexpensive supplement will allow the student to concentrate on the content of the lecture rather than redrawing the instructor's overhead material.

Graphecon II Software This software for IBM-PC and compatible microcomputers, prepared by Cols. James R. Golden and L. Donne Olvey of the United States Military Academy at West Point, are menu-driven interactive tutorial and quizzing programs that allow students to work with economic graphs.

Student Edition Software Full-function versions of leading software adapted for educational use are available from Addison-Wesley, including Student Edition Software for Lotus® 1-2-3®, release 2.2, MathCAD®, and MINITAB® 2.0.

Acknowledgements

One of the great pleasures of writing an introductory text is the opportunity it affords to learn from so many generous friends and colleagues. Although the extent of our debts cannot be fully acknowledged here, it is nevertheless a joy to record our gratitude to the many people who have helped, some without realizing just how helpful they were.

We want to thank Valerie Bencevenga, Gerhard Illing, Lawrence Leger, Gordon Myers, and Sharon Pearson, our colleagues at the University of Western Ontario who used this book in manuscript form, and who gave us invaluable feedback on areas needing improvement. We also want to thank those of our colleagues who have taught us so much of what can be found in these pages: Ig Horstmann and Phil Reny on game theory and its applications (Chapter 14); Jim Davies on income and wealth distribution (Chapter 18); Chris Robinson on labour markets (Chapters 15 and 16); Jeremy

Greenwood, Peter Howitt, Greg Huffman, and David Laidler, on macroeconomics (Chapters 22 through 35); and John Whalley and Ron Wonnacott on international issues (Chapter 36). We want to extend a special thanks to Glenn MacDonald whose constant involvement with this project has been a great source of inspiration and help throughout the past five years. He has read and commented in detail on all the microeconomics chapters and has helped us to conceive some of the book's most innovative pedagogical features.

It is a pleasure to acknowledge our debt to those who have had a profound influence on our whole view of and approach to economics and whose influence we can see in these pages. Although we never sat in their classrooms, they are in a very real sense our teachers. We are especially grateful to John Carlson (Purdue University), Carl Christ (John Hopkins University), Robert Clower (University of South Carolina), Ed Feige (University of Wisconsin at Madison), Herschel Grossman (Brown University), Ronald Jones (University of Rochester), Richard Lipsey (Simon Fraser University), and Sam Wu (University of Iowa). We also want to place on record our enormous debt to the late Karl Brunner. The energy, drive, and entrepreneurship of this outstanding economist provided us and our generation of economists with incredible opportunities to interact and learn from each other in a wide variety of conference settings both in North America and in Europe.

It is also a pleasure to acknowledge our debt to the several thousand students to whom we have been privileged to teach introductory economics. The instant feedback that comes from that look of puzzlement or enlightenment has taught us, more than anything else, how to teach economics. We are especially grateful to the more than 6,000 students who have used this book in successive manuscript stages between 1985 and 1990 in Economics 020 at the University of Western Ontario. The enthusiasm and care with which they have used the book in its manuscript form has been an inspiration to us and we have benefitted immeasurably from their comments, criticisms, and suggestions. We dedicate this book to them.

This is a "made in Canada" book. It was written and developed at the University of Western Ontario, class tested with Canadian students, and wherever possible, uses Canadian issues and problems to illustrate economic concepts. Nevertheless, the enterprise on which we embarked in 1985 when we began writing was and has remained a truly international one. At the same time as this book was being written, a United States edition was produced from it. Also, working with co-authors, we are producing European and Australian editions.

Producing a text such as this is a team effort and the members of the Addison-Wesley *Economics* team, both here in Canada and in the United States, are genuine co-producers of this book. We are especially grateful to George MacD. Bryson, Chairman of the Board of Addison-Wesley Canada until September 1989, for his instant enthusiasm, support, and encouragement and for the role he played in ensuring this book's multinational dimension. We are also especially grateful to and have been truly inspired by Barbara Rifkind, the Sponsoring Editor of the United States edition. Barbara came onto the project when Addison-Wesley had already designed the book and when we thought we had finished writing it. Barbara liked what she saw, but saw more in its potential than in its realization. She coaxed us into rewriting much of the manuscript and coaxed Addison-Wesley into yet another complete overhaul of the design. It is also a pleasure to acknowledge our debt to Shannon Bailey, our Sponsoring Editor in Canada, who has had an important influence on both this book and its U.S. counterpart; to Sue Gleason who, as Development Editor, has had an enormous influence on both the words and the art program; to Shirley Tessier, who as Project Editor has coordinated the entire editorial team and production process — a process that has tested previously untried technologies — keeping us all on track and coping cheerfully with our numerous and sometimes outrageous demands; to Ron Doleman, Addison-Wesley's Editorial Director, who has pioneered the application of the new technologies that have made it economically feasible to produce a book of this size and quality given the size of the Canadian market; to John More, Director and Vice-President of Addison-Wesley's college division, for his constant attention to this project, his insistence that a full colour book could and should be produced for this market, and for his vigilant reading of the Canadian press, coast-to-coast, in search of news items for Reading Between the Lines; to Gord Pronk, who has designed many of the books features; to Joe Swan, Cindy Kantor, Roberta Dick, Trish Hall, and Bob McGough; and to the economists (whose names appear separately) who have acted as reviewers and whose work has been of enormous value to us. We thank Jane McAndrew, the librarian in the Department of Economics at the University of Western Ontario, for her creative help in tracking down sources, no matter how obscure—see "Our Advancing Knowledge" on page 85 for example—and for taking care of couriers, fax messages, and a host of other details. Next we want to thank the many secretaries who have helped at various stages of this book, tirelessly and cheerfully typing and retyping its countless drafts and redrafts. They are Yvonne Adams, Lynda Sollazzo, Kendra McKague, and most recently, Barbara Craig.

We have left until last three people to whom we want to give special thanks: Catherine, Richard, and Ann Parkin. Through the years that we have been developing and writing this work, they have been going through various stages of high school and college. They have helped us in a large number of concrete ways, working as research assistants, secretaries, reviewers and critics, and sounding boards. They have enabled and forced us to write a book that they can understand and find interesting.

The empirical test of this textbook's value will be made in the classroom. We would appreciate hearing from instructors and students about how we might improve the book in future editions.

Michael Parkin
Robin Bade
Department of Economics,
University of Western Ontario,
London, Ontario, N6A 5C2

Reviewers

Syed Ashan, *Concordia University*
Ronald Bodkin, *University of Ottawa*
Paul Booth, *University of Alberta*
John Brander, *University of New Brunswick*
Emanuel Carvalho, *University of Waterloo*
Robert Cherneff, *University of Victoria*
Louis Christofides, *University of Guelph*
Avi Cohen, *York University*
Michael Hare, *University of Toronto*
Arnold Paus-Jennessen, *University of Saskatchewan*
Robin Neill, *Carleton University*
Scott Lynch, *Memorial University*
Balbir Sahni, *Concordia University*
Brian Scarfe, *University of Regina*
Stan Shedd, *University of Calgary*

BRIEF CONTENTS

TABLE OF CONTENTS

* Summary, Key Elements, Review Questions, and Problems appear at the end of each chapter.

PART 5 MARKETS FOR GOODS AND SERVICES

PART 7 MARKETS AND GOVERNMENT

PART 8 INTRODUCTION TO MACROECONOMICS

CHAPTER 26 *Expenditure and Income* 683

PART 10 MONEY, INTEREST, AND THE DOLLAR

CHAPTER 27 *Money, Banking, and Prices* 717

PART 11 MACROECONOMIC PROBLEMS

PART 12 MACROECONOMIC POLICY

PART 14 GROWTH, DEVELOPMENT, AND COMPARATIVE SYSTEMS

PART 1

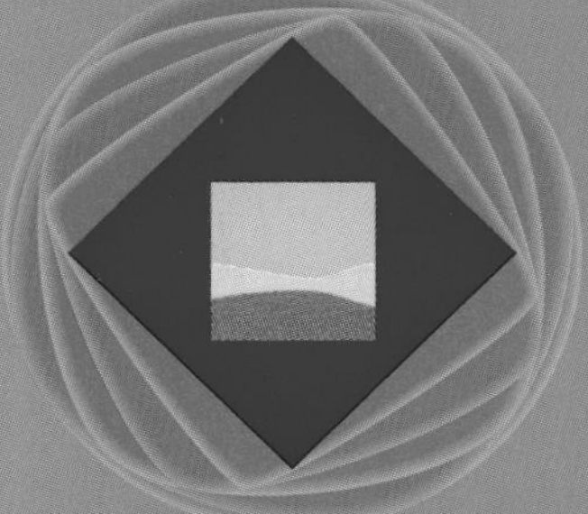

Introduction

TALKING WITH

ASSAR LINDBECK

Assar Lindbeck is a professor of economics and director of the Institute for International Economic Studies at the University of Stockholm. He has been a visiting professor at Columbia University, the University of Michigan, and Yale University. Since 1981, he has been chairman of the committee that annually awards the Nobel Prize for economic science. Michael Parkin talked with Professor Lindbeck about the nature of economics, the economic landscape of the 1990s, and the way economists do their work.

"I wonder if we aren't straining out young people with creativity by forcing them into elaborate technical analysis."

Professor Lindbeck, how did you decide to become an economist?

My father was a politican in northern Sweden, so I was interested myself in studying political science at college. After three semesters, I decided to learn economics as a background. The problem is that I never finished learning economics!

What was it about economics that was so compelling?

I discovered that political science dealt mainly with the forms of political events, the way political decisions are made. But it dealt very little with the consequences of political decisions. Economics, on the other hand, does just that, by looking at how political decisions and economic policy actually affect families, businesses, or nations.

What makes economics different from political science or the other social sciences?

First, economics asks different questions. Questions about employment; output; the allocation of resources, including labour; the distribution of income. Next, economics has been able to build up a general analytical structure. We don't need a special kind of economics to discuss housing or agriculture or education. We apply the same economic principles to each different field. Other social sciences tend to build specific theories for each issue or field. Family sociology is different from criminal sociology, for example. Finally, economics can use narrower assumptions to produce reasonably good predictions. For instance, if you ask me about factors that influence the demand for butter or margarine, I don't have to go into philosophical issues about the basis for human behaviour.

Do microeconomics and macroeconomics, the two traditional branches of economics, use the same principles?

Well, there has been a discontinuity between microeconomics and macroeconomics. Macroeconomics is based on the idea that there are systematic movements of broad aggregates—total output, national economic growth, unemployment, or inflation—and that we can explain one aggregate by another, as a kind of short cut. You don't have to explain all relative prices and the allocation of resources to be able to explain a recession. But it is important that what you're saying about these aggregate movements should be consistent with the microeconomic assumptions you would make about the behaviour of individual firms or consumers. Milton Friedman, Franco Modigliani, James Tobin, and others started this approach in the 1950s because they were dissatisfied with the absence of microecomic foundations for the empirical generalizations that characterized macroeconomics at the time.

If you want to talk about "the economy," you need to work with aggregate concepts because the human brain is just too small to consider all the variables at one time. For economics to be useful to you as an individual, you have to be able to play with the model in your head. You should be able to read the newspaper or watch the TV news and process it mentally. For economics to be useful to society, an economist must be able to talk with journalists and politicians, or to draw diagrams on the blackboard for students. If you cannot transform your thinking into broad categories, you can never communicate outside a group of specialists.

You've been chairman of the committee that awards the Nobel Prize for economic science. What characterizes the great economists?

The Prize Committee—and economists in general—recognize the value both of people who have influential ideas, even if they haven't formalized them into complete models, and of people who formalize ideas borrowed partly from others. There are very few people with both bright ideas and the ability or opportunity to formalize them. I think that today economists with interesting and realistic visions are scarcer than technical economists. I have always been a strong advocate for rigorous training, but I sometimes wonder if we aren't straining out some young people with common sense and creativity by forcing them into elaborate technical analysis.

What do you see as the most important economic issue facing us in the 1990s?

Let me begin by looking back at some of the events that have led us to where we are today. The 25 years after World War II are regarded now as a golden age—expanding world trade, low unemployment, rapid growth, and prosperity. Unique historical events contributed to that era—workers were available to move from agriculture to industry; prewar trade protectionism gave way; there were great advances in technology after years of stagnation. In the 1960s and 1970s, politicians started to believe, however, that economic growth and prosperity were manna from heaven. And we began to consume the very source of our economic success—by tampering with the efficiency of our market economies. In the 1970s, the OPEC oil shocks came, and, at least in Europe, great explosions in wages. There were also extraordinary policy efforts to squeeze out inflation, which was a basic reason for the depths of the recessions in the 1970s and 1980s. The late 1980s were a period of recovery from the turmoil of the previous decade. The growth rate has started to improve, unemployment has fallen in the United States and England. What is happening? There's a distinct possibility that we're finally returning the strength of the market to market economies.

And in the future?

I see the issue of the 1990s as how far deregulation can go without interest groups protesting—many people feel the pinch of deregulation. In global terms, with the European Economic Community, how much control will any national government give up to international market forces? Will a government be willing to say that they can't do anything about a problem because they've deregulated both the domestic economy and its foreign economic relations? Can a government do that without its domestic population throwing them out of office?

"I see the issue of the 1990s as how far deregulation can go without interest groups protesting."

"We cannot make economic forecasts without forecasting policies."

In addressing such difficult issues, can economists really separate scientific analysis from passionate advocacy of policy?

If someone asks an economist what will be the effects of a tax on imported oil, the answer should be completely independent of his or her opinion about whether those effects are good or bad. A liberal or a conservative economist should give the same answer if they've each used the same type of economic model. So why don't they always? Perhaps because they have inadvertently been influenced by their political beliefs to choose a model that tends to support a certain political value or world view.

The purpose of science, of economic science, is to discriminate correctly among different models in order to produce an honest assessment. It's never easy to do this, but it's critical to the justification of economics as a positive science.

You've tried in some of your writing to apply positive economics to explain the policy choices made by politicans—what is called "public choice." Why is this an important area of economic research and what progress have we made in understanding political decison making?

This is a vital area of research. We cannot make economic forecasts without forecasting policies. And we cannot forecast policies without having a theory that predicts how politicians will react to new economic events in the future. But so far, I think that there are few generally solid results—because politicians naturally have a very complex pattern of behaviour that we can't yet really explain. For example, there are often conflicts between the policy agenda that politicians believe they should pursue and the policy decisions they may have to make in order to stay in office. The chief result of research in this area, so far, is that economists have become much more aware of how complicated it really is to give good advice on policy.

What have been the guiding principles that have helped you as an economist and as a person concerned with economic policy?

I'd like to be inspired by real-world problems. I want to look around and see something that puzzles me, something I don't understand, and try to find a plausible explanation. Next, I sit down at my desk and try to write the problem down. I try to make sense of it in both ordinary words and formal terms, with graphs and equations. I often find out that the answer was different from what I had expected.

What advice would you give to a student in the first weeks of a principles of economics course?

Try to understand the principles intuitively and not just mechanically. Try to understand the common sense, if there is any, of the examples your teachers and textbooks provide. If you only memorize the facts, after two years you'll have forgotten it all. But if you learn economics with your intuition backing you up, you'll keep something of great value.

CHAPTER 1

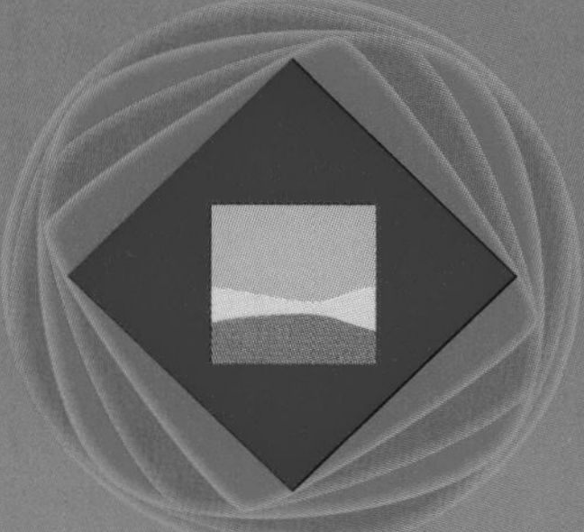

What Is Economics?

After studying this chapter, you will be able to:

- State the kinds of questions that economics tries to answer.
- Explain why all economic questions and economic activity arise from scarcity.
- Explain why scarcity forces people to make choices.
- Define opportunity cost.
- Describe the function and the working parts of an economy.
- Distinguish between positive and normative statements.
- Explain what is meant by an economic theory and how economic theories are developed by building and testing economic models.

Seven Big Questions

WHAT IS ECONOMICS about? A good way to begin to answer this question is to ask some further questions. Let's examine seven of the big questions that economics tries to answer.

Production, Consumption, and Technological Change

If you wanted to watch a movie in your home in 1975, you had to rent a movie projector and a screen — as well as the movie itself. The cost of such entertainment was as high as that faced by a theatre showing the movie to several hundred people. Only the rich chose to watch movies in the comfort of their own homes. ■ In 1976, the video cassette recorder became available to consumers. Its typical price was $2,000 (which in today's dollars would translate into about $4,000). Since that time, the price of VCRs has steadily fallen, so that today you can buy a reliable machine for $200. A video can be rented for a few dollars a day and can be bought for less than $30. In just a few years, watching a movie at home has changed from a luxury available to the richest few to an event enjoyed by millions. ■ Advances in technology affect the way we consume. We now watch far more movies at home than we did a decade ago because new technologies have lowered the cost. ■ New technologies also affect the way we *produce* things. Johnny Wilder, Jr., was a successful popular musician in the 1970s with such hits as "Boogie Nights" and "Always and Forever." A car accident in 1979 left Wilder paralysed from the neck down. Today, Wilder again produces music but with a Macintosh computer and synthesizers controlled by his breath and by beams of light. ■ We hear a great deal these days about lasers. They scan prices at the supermarket checkout. They create holograms on credit cards, making them harder to forge. Neurosurgeons and eye surgeons use them in our hospitals. ■ These examples show how new technologies affect the way that we produce goods and services and give rise to the first big economic question:

How do people choose *what* to consume and *how* to produce, and how are these choices affected by the discovery of new ways of doing things — of new technologies?

Wages and Earnings

On a crisp, bright winter day on the ski slopes at Banff, a bronzed 23-year-old instructs some beginning skiers in the snowplough turn. For this pleasant and uncomplicated work, the young man, who quit school after grade 11, is paid $10 an hour.

In a lawyer's office in the centre of Vancouver, a 23-year-old secretary handles a large volume of correspondence, filing, scheduling, and meetings. She arrives home most evenings exhausted. She has a bachelor's degree in English and has taken night courses in computer science and word processing. She receives $8 an hour for her work.

On July 9, 1989, Steffi Graf and Martina Navratilova played a stunning tennis match in the final at Wimbledon. At the end of the close and hard-fought match, the winner, Graf, received $331,278; Navratilova collected only half that amount. A similar phenomenon can be seen in the headquarters of large companies. Chief executive officers who work no harder (and in some cases, even less hard) than the people immediately beneath them receive far higher salaries than their subordinates.

Situations like these raise the second big economic question:

What determines people's incomes and why do some people receive much larger rewards than others whose efforts appear to be similar?

Unemployment

During the worst years of the Great Depression, from 1929 to 1933, unemployment afflicted almost one-fifth of the labour force in the industrial world. For months and in some cases years on end, many families had no income other than meagre payments from the government or from private charities. In the 1950s and 1960s, unemployment rates stayed below 5 percent in most countries and in some — for example, Japan and Britain — below 2 percent. During the 1970s, unemployment steadily increased so that by the early 1980s more than 10 percent of the Canadian labour force was looking for work. But in 1989, the Canadian unemployment rate had fallen to 7.7 percent.

Unemployment hurts different groups unequally. When the average unemployment rate in Canada is 5 percent, the unemployment rate among young people 16 to 19 years old is close to 20 percent. The unemployment rate has a large regional variation as well, being especially high in Newfoundland and the Maritimes.

These facts about unemployment raise the third big economic question:

What are the causes of unemployment and why are some groups more severely affected than others?

Inflation

Between August 1945 and July 1946, prices in Hungary rose by an average of 20,000 percent per month. In the worst month, July 1946, they rose 419 quadrillion percent (a quadrillion is the number 1 followed by 15 zeros).

In 1985, the cost of living in Bolivia rose by 11,750 percent. This meant that in downtown La Paz a McDonald's hamburger that cost 20 bolivianos on January 1 cost 2370 bolivianos by the end of the year. That same year, prices rose only 2.9 percent in Canada. But in the late 1970s, prices in Canada were rising at a rate in excess of 10 percent a year.

These facts about inflation raise the fourth big economic question:

Why do prices rise, and why do some countries sometimes experience rapid price increases while others have stable prices?

Government

Government touches many aspects of life. The government of Canada provides pensions for our grandparents, a basic income for the unemployed, grants to the provinces to equalize living standards across our nation, and maintains the Canadian Armed Forces for our national defence. The federal, provincial, and municipal governments provide law enforcement, health care, insurance, and education. Their agencies regulate food and drug production, nuclear energy, and agriculture.

The cost of government has increased dramatically over the years. In 1867, the year of Confederation, the federal government collected $14 million in revenue, almost all from customs and excise duties. Expressed in terms of today's prices, that amounted to $66 per person — or less than a penny on every dollar earned. In 1987, the average Canadian family paid taxes equivalent to 34 cents on every dollar of income. Until recently, the federal and provincial governments usually had balanced budgets. But throughout the 1980s the federal government has been spending close to $30 billion in excess of its revenue each year. This amounts to more than $1,000 for every Canadian.

These facts about government raise the fifth big economic question:

How do government spending and taxes influence economic life and what happens when the government has a deficit, as it does at the present time?

International Trade

In the 1960s, almost all the cars and trucks on the highways of Canada and the United States were Fords, Chevrolets, and Chryslers. By the 1980s, Toyotas, Hondas, Volkswagens, and BMWs were also a common sight. As a matter of fact, by 1985 one-third of all new cars sold in North America were imported; in the mid-1950s, less than 1 percent were. Cars are not exceptional. The same can be said of television sets, clothing, and computers.

Governments regulate international trade in cars and in many other commodities. They impose taxes on imports, called tariffs, and also establish quotas, which restrict the quantities that may be imported. Recently, the federal government negotiated a major agreement with the United States that will eventually eliminate most of the restrictions on international trade between the two countries — the Canada – United States Free Trade Agreement.

These facts about international trade raise the sixth big economic question:

What determines the pattern and the volume of trade between nations, and what are the effects of tariffs and quotas on international trade?

Wealth and Poverty

At the mouth of the Canton River in southeast China is a small rocky peninsula and a group of islands with virtually no natural resources. But this bare land supports more than 5 million people who, though not excessively rich, live in rapidly growing abundance. They produce much of the world's fashion goods and electronic components. They are the people of Hong Kong.

On the eastern edge of Africa bordering the Red Sea, a tract of land more than a thousand times larger supports a population of 34 million people — only seven times that of Hong Kong. The region suffers such abject poverty that in 1985 rock singers from Europe and North America organized one of the most spectacular worldwide fund-raising efforts ever seen — Live Aid — to help them. These are the desperate and dying people of Ethiopia.

Hong Kong and Ethiopia, two extremes in income and wealth, are not isolated examples. The poorest two-thirds of the world's population consumes less than one-fifth of all the goods and services produced. Middle income groups account for almost one-fifth of the world's population and consume almost one-fifth of the world's output. The rest of the world's population — living in high income countries such as Canada, the United States, Western Europe, Japan, Australia, and New Zealand — consumes almost two-thirds of the world's output.

These facts about income and wealth raise the seventh big economic question:

What causes differences in living standards among nations, making the people in some countries rich and in others poor?

Big Questions with No Easy Answers

These seven big questions provide an overview of economics. They are *big* questions for two reasons. First, they have an enormous effect on the quality of human life. Second, they are hard questions to answer. They generate passionate argument and debate, and just about everybody has an opinion about them. Self-appointed experts abound. One of the hardest things for students of economics, whether beginners or seasoned practitioners, is to stand clear of the passion and emotion, and to approach their work with the detachment, rigour, and objectivity of a scientist.

Later in this chapter, we will explain how economists try to find answers to economic questions. But before doing that, let's go back to the seven big questions. What do these questions have in common? What distinguishes them from noneconomic questions?

Scarcity

All economic questions arise from a single and inescapable fact: you can't always get what you want. We live in a world of scarcity. An economist defines **scarcity** to mean that wants always exceed the resources available to satisfy them. A child wants a 75-cent can of soft drink and a 50-cent pack of gum but has only $1 in her pocket. She experiences scarcity. A student wants to go to a party on Thursday night but also wants to spend that same night catching up on late assignments. He also experiences scarcity. The rich and the poor alike face scarcity. The government of Canada with its $120 billion budget faces scarcity. The total amount that the government wants to spend on defence, health, education, welfare, and other services far exceeds what it is able to borrow and collect in taxes. Even parrots face scarcity — there just aren't enough crackers to go around.

Wants do not simply exceed resources; they are unlimited. In contrast, resources are limited, or finite. People want good health and a long life, material comfort, security, physical and mental recreation, and, finally, an awareness and understanding of themselves and their environment.

None of these wants are satisfied for everyone — everyone has some unsatisfied wants. Although many Canadians have all the material comfort they want, many do not. No one feels entirely secure, especially in this nuclear age, and not even the wealthiest person has the time to enjoy all the travel, vacations, and art that he or she would like. Not even the wisest and most knowledgeable philosopher or scientist knows as much as he or she would like to know.

We can imagine a world that satisfies people's wants for material comfort and, perhaps, even security. But we cannot imagine a world in which people have all the time, energy, and resources to enjoy all the sports, travel, vacations, and art that they would like. Nor can we imagine a world in which everyone has all the health care services they want, or is satisfied with our efforts to protect such vital resources as the atmosphere, forests, rivers, and lakes. Natural resources and human resources — in the form of time, muscle-power, and brain-power — as well as all the dams, highways, buildings, machinery, tools, and other equipment that have been built by past human efforts amount to an enormous heritage, but they are limited. Our unlimited wants will always outstrip the resources available to satisfy them.

"Not only do I want a cracker—we all want a cracker!"

Economic Activity

The confrontation of unlimited wants with limited resources results in economic activity. **Economic activity** is what people do to cope with scarcity. **Economics**, then, is the study of how people use their limited resources to try to satisfy unlimited wants. Defined in this way, economic activity and economics deal with a wide range of issues and problems. The seven big questions posed earlier are examples of the more important problems economists study. Let's see how those questions could not arise if resources were infinitely abundant and scarcity did not exist.

With unlimited resources, there would be no need to devise better ways of producing more goods. Studying how we all spend our time and effort would not be interesting because we would simply do what we enjoyed without restriction. There would be no wages. We would do only the things that we enjoyed because there would be enough goods and services to satisfy everyone without effort. Unemployment would not be an issue because no one would work — except people who wanted to work simply for the pleasure that it gave them. Inflation — rising prices — would not be a problem because everything would be free. Questions about government intervention in economic life would not arise because there would be no need for government-provided goods and no taxes. We would simply take whatever we wanted from the infinite resources available. There would be no international trade since, with complete abundance, it would be pointless to transport goods from one place to another. Finally, differences in wealth among nations would not arise because we would all have as much as we wanted. There would be no such thing as rich and poor countries — all countries would be infinitely wealthy.

You can see that this science fiction world of complete abundance would have no economic problems. It is the universal fact of scarcity that produces economic problems.

Choice

Faced with scarcity, people must make choices. When we cannot have everything that we want, we have to choose among the available alternatives. Because scarcity forces us to choose, economics is sometimes called the science of choice — the science that explains the choices that people make and predicts how changes in circumstances affect their choices.

To make a choice, we balance the benefits of having more of some things against the costs of having less of something else. Balancing benefits against costs and doing the best within the limits of what is possible is called **optimizing**. There is another word that has a similar meaning — *economizing*. **Economizing** is making the best possible use of the resources available. Once people have made a choice and have optimized, they cannot have more of *everything*. To get more of one thing means having less of something else. Expressed in another way: in making choices, we face costs. Whatever we choose to do, we could always have chosen to do something else instead.

Opportunity Cost

Economists use the term "opportunity cost" to emphasize that making choices in the face of scarcity implies a cost. The **opportunity cost** of any action is the best alternative forgone. If you cannot have everything that you want, you have to choose among the alternatives. The best action that you choose not to do — the alternative forgone — is the cost of what you choose to do. This is the meaning of opportunity cost. We must be careful to measure opportunity cost accurately. To understand how to do this, let's examine a familiar situation.

You are supposed to attend a lecture at 8:30 on a Monday morning. There are two alternatives to attending this lecture: to stay in bed for an hour or to go jogging for an hour. The opportunity cost of attending the lecture is not the loss of an hour in bed *and* the benefits derived from jogging for an hour. If these are the only two alternatives that you would contemplate, you have to decide which one you would do if you did not go to the lecture. The opportunity cost of attending a lecture for a jogger is an hour of exercise; the opportunity cost of attending a lecture for a late sleeper is an hour in bed.

Suppose you always spend $1.50 on a muffin and a cup of coffee for breakfast. On the day that you go to your lecture, you pick these items up in the school's cafeteria on your way to class. If you did not spend $1.50 every day on your breakfast, you would go to the movies more often than you are now able to afford. The movies that you forgo are the opportunity cost of your breakfast. But they are not part of the opportunity cost of going to class — you spend $1.50 on your breakfast every day, whether or not you attend your class.

Not all the opportunity costs that you incur are the result of your own choices. Sometimes others make choices that impose opportunity costs on you. For example, when you cannot get onto a bus at rush hour, you have to bear the cost of the choices made by all the other people who filled the bus.

Every choice involves an opportunity cost. In choosing one activity, an individual decides that the cost of that activity — the best alternative forgone — is worth paying. Scarcity not only implies cost; it implies one other fundamental feature of human life — competition.

Competition and Cooperation

Competition If wants exceed resources, wants must compete against each other for what is available. **Competition** is a contest for command over scarce resources. In the case of the child with $1 in pocket money who wants a soft drink and gum that add up to $1.25, the soft drink and gum compete for the $1 in her pocket. For the student who has allowed assignments to accumulate, the party and the assignments compete with each other for Thursday night. For the government, defence and social services compete with each other for limited tax dollars.

Scarcity also implies competition between people. If it is not possible to have everything that you want, you must compete with others for what is available. All societies have developed rules that organize and restrain competition. The evolution of rules is itself a direct response to the problem of scarcity. Not all societies, even modern societies, employ identical rules to govern competition. For example, the way that economic life is organized in Canada differs greatly from that in the Soviet Union. In

Chapter 39, we examine these differences and compare alternative economic systems. For now, we will restrict our attention to the rules that govern competition in Canada.

A key rule of competition is that people own what they have acquired through voluntary exchange. People can compete with each other by offering more favourable exchanges — for example, by lowering the price of the good they are selling or by bidding up the price of the good they are buying. But they cannot compete with each other by simply taking something from someone else.

Cooperation Perhaps you are thinking that scarcity does not make competition inevitable and that cooperation would better solve economic problems. **Cooperation** means working with others to achieve a common end. If we cooperated instead of competing with each other, wouldn't that eliminate economic problems? This line of reasoning is appealing because it emphasizes the possibility that we might be able to solve our economic problems by using reason. Examples of solving economic problems through cooperation abound. We cooperate when we agree to rules of the game that limit competition to avoid violence. Most forms of business entail cooperation: workers cooperate with each other on the production line; members of a management team cooperate with each other to design, produce, and market their products; management and workers cooperate. Marriage partners cooperate.

Common as it is, cooperative behaviour neither solves the economic problem nor eliminates competition. Almost all cooperative behaviour implies some prior competition to find the best individuals with whom to cooperate. Marriage provides a good example. Although marriage is a cooperative affair, unmarried people compete intensely to find marriage partners. Similarly, although workers and management cooperate with each other, firms compete for the best workers and workers compete for the best employers. Professionals such as lawyers and doctors compete with each other for the best business partners.

Competition does not end when a partner has been found. Groups of people who cooperate together compete with other groups. For example, although a group of lawyers may have formed a partnership and may work together, they are in competition with other lawyers.

R E V I E W

Economics studies the activities arising from scarcity. Scarcity forces people to make choices. Economists try to understand the choices that people make. To make choices, people optimize. To optimize, they evaluate the costs of alternative actions. We call these opportunity costs, to emphasize that doing one thing removes the opportunity to do something else. Scarcity also implies that people must compete with each other. ■

You now know the types of questions that economists try to answer and that all economic questions and economic activity arise from scarcity. In the following chapters, we are going to study economic activity and discover how a modern economy, such as Canada's, works. But before we do that, we need to stand back and take an overview of our economy. What exactly do we mean by "the economy"?

The Economy

What is an economy? How does an economy work? Rather than trying to answer these questions directly, let's begin by asking similar questions on a more familiar subject. What is an airplane? How does an airplane work?

Without delving into the detail that would satisfy an aeronautical engineer, most of us could take a shot at answering these two questions. We would describe an airplane as a flying machine that transports people and cargo. To explain how an airplane works, we would describe its key components — fuselage (or body), wings, and engines and also perhaps its flaps, rudder, and control and navigation systems. We would also explain that as powerful engines move the machine forward, its wings create an imbalance in air pressure that lifts it into the air.

This example nicely illustrates four things. First, it is hard to explain what something is without saying what it does. To say that an airplane is a machine does not tell us much. We have to go beyond that and say what the machine is for and how it works.

Second, it is hard to explain how something works without being able to divide it into components. Once we have described something in terms of its components, we can explain how those components work and how they interact with each other.

Third, it is hard to explain how something works without leaving out some details. Notice that we did not describe an airplane in all its detail. Instead, we isolated the most important parts in order to explain how the whole works. We did not emphasize the in-flight movie system, the seat belts, or the colour of the paint on the wings. We supposed that these things were largely, or even totally, irrelevant to an explanation of how an airplane works.

Fourth and finally, there are different levels of understanding how something works. We gave a superficial account of how an airplane works. An aeronautical engineer would have given a deeper explanation, and experts in the individual components — engines, navigation systems, control system, and so on — would have given an even more detailed and precise explanation than a general engineer.

Now let's return to questions about the economy. What is an economy? How does it work?

What is an Economy?

An **economy** is a mechanism that allocates scarce resources among competing uses. This mechanism achieves three things that can be summarized in three words:

- What
- How
- For whom

1 *What* goods and services will be produced and in *what* quantities? How many VCRs will be made and how many movie theatres will be built? Will young professionals vacation in Europe or live in large houses? How many high performance cars will be built, and how many trucks and station wagons?

2 *How* will the various goods and services be produced? Will a supermarket operate with three checkout lines and clerks using laser scanners or six checkout lines and clerks keying in prices by hand? Will workers weld station wagons by hand or will robots do the job? Will farmers keep track of their livestock feeding schedules and inventories by using paper and pencil records or personal computers? Will credit card companies use computers to read charge slips in Toronto or ship paper records to Barbados for hand processing?

3 *For whom* will the various goods and services be produced? The distribution of economic benefits depends on the distribution of income and wealth. People with high incomes and great wealth consume more goods and services than those with low incomes and little wealth. Who gets to consume what thus depends on income and wealth. Will the ski instructor consume more than the lawyer's secretary? Will the people of Hong Kong get to consume more than the people of Ethiopia?

The Economy's Working Parts

To understand how an economy works, we must identify its major working parts and see how they interact with each other. The working parts of an economy and the interrelations between them are illustrated in Fig. 1.1. The working parts of the economy fall into two categories:

- **Decision makers** — any person or organized group of persons who make choices
- **Coordination mechanisms** — arrangements that make the choices of one person or group compatible with the choices of others.

Decision Makers Decision makers fall into three groups:

- Households
- Firms
- Governments

A **household** is any group of people living together as a decision-making unit. Every individual in the economy belongs to a household. Some households consist of a single person while others consist of families or of groups of unrelated individuals, such as two or three students sharing an apartment.

A **firm** is an organization that produces goods and services. All producers are called firms, no matter how big or small they are. Automobile manufacturers, banks and insurance companies, farmers and babysitters are all examples of firms.

A **government** is an organization that has two functions: the provision of goods and services to households and firms and the redistribution of income and wealth. Examples of the goods and services supplied by government are law enforcement, national defence, public health, and education.

Figure 1.1 A Picture of the Economy

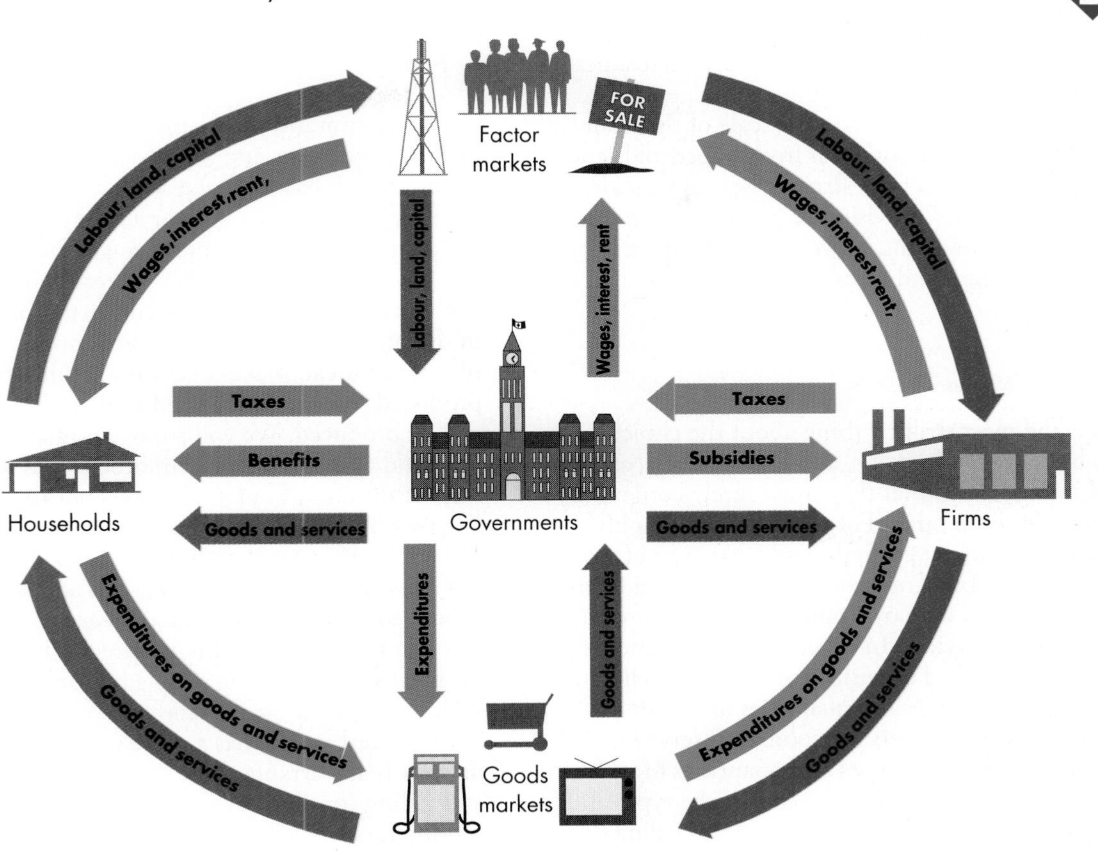

The economy has three groups of decision makers: households, firms, and governments. It also has two groups of markets: factor markets and goods markets. Households supply factors of production to both firms and governments through the factor markets. Firms supply goods and services to households through the goods markets. Governments provide goods and services directly to households and firms. These flows are shown by the red arrows. Firms and governments pay households wages, interest, and rent in exchange for the services of factors of production. Households and governments pay firms for goods and services. Households and firms pay taxes to governments, and governments provide subsidies and benefits to firms and households. These flows are shown by the green arrows.

You can see these three groups of decision-makers in Fig. 1.1. You can also see in this figure the decisions that they make. Households supply factors of production to firms and governments. **Factors of production** are the economy's productive resources, usually classified under three headings:

- Labour
- Land
- Capital

Labour is the brain-power and muscle-power of human beings; **land** is natural resources of all kinds; **capital** is all the equipment, buildings, tools, and other manufactured goods that can be used in production. Households sell or rent factors of production to firms and governments and receive an income in payment for their supply. Households also receive benefits from governments and pay taxes to them. With what is left, households buy goods and services produced by firms.

Firms hire factors of production from households and choose how to use them to produce goods and services. They also decide what goods and services to produce and in what quantities. Expenditures by households and governments on goods and services are received by firms. Firms use these receipts to make payments to households for the factors of production they supply. Firms also receive subsidies from, and pay taxes to, governments.

Governments decide on the scale of their purchases of factors of production from households and of goods and services from firms. They also decide on the scale of their provision of goods and services to households and firms, as well as on the rates of benefits, subsidies, and taxes.

Coordination Mechanisms

Perhaps the most striking thing about the choices made by households, firms, and governments, as illustrated in Fig. 1.1, is that they must surely come into conflict with each other. For example, households choose how much work to do and what type of work to specialize in, but firms choose the types and quantities of labour to employ in the production of various goods and services. In other words, households choose the types and quantities of labour to sell and firms choose the types and quantities of labour to buy. Similarly, in markets for goods and services, households choose the types and quantities of goods and services to buy, while firms choose the types and quantities to sell. Government choices regarding taxes, benefits, subsidies, and the provision of goods and services also enter the picture. Taxes taken by governments affect the amount of income that households and firms have available for spending and saving. Also, decisions by firms and households depend on the types and quantities of goods and services governments make available. For example, if governments provide excellent highways but a dilapidated railway system, households will allocate more of their income to buying motor vehicles and less to buying train rides.

How is it possible for the millions of individual decisions taken by households, firms, and governments to be consistent with each other? What makes households want to sell the same types and quantities of labour that firms want to buy? What happens if the number of households wanting to work as economics professors exceeds the number that universities want to hire? How do firms know what to produce so that households will buy their output? What happens if firms want to sell more hamburgers than households want to buy?

There are two mechanisms that can achieve a coordination of individual economic choices:

- Command mechanism
- Market mechanism

A **command mechanism** is a method of determining *what, how,* and *for whom* goods and services are produced, based on the authority of a ruler or ruling body — such as a king or a ruling political party. Although undergoing rapid change, the economies of the U.S.S.R. and some other Eastern European countries are the best examples of command mechanisms in the modern world. In those economies, a central planning bureau makes decisions about *what* will be produced, *how* it will be produced, and *for whom* it will be produced. We will study command economies and compare them with other types of economies at the end of our study of economics, in Chapter 39.

A **market mechanism** is a method of determining *what, how,* and *for whom* goods and services are produced, based on individual choices coordinated through markets. In ordinary speech, the word *market* means a place where people buy and sell goods such as fish, meat, fruits, and vegetables. In economics, the word *market* has a more general meaning. A **market** is any arrangement that facilitates the buying and selling (trading) of a good, service, or factor of production.

As an example of a market, consider that in which oil is bought and sold — the world oil market. The world oil market is not a place. It is all the many different institutions, buyers, sellers, brokers, and so on who buy and sell oil. The market is a coordination mechanism because it pools together the separate plans of all the individual decision-makers who try to buy and sell any particular good. Decision-makers do not have to meet in a physical sense. In the modern world, telecommunications have replaced direct contact as the main link between buyers and sellers.

Markets are classified according to the types of things traded in them. Figure 1.1 shows the two types of market. The markets in which goods and services are traded are called **goods markets**. The markets in which factors of production are traded — markets for labour, land, and capital — are called **factor markets**. These markets enable the plans of individual households, firms, and governments to be coordinated and made consistent with each other.

The Canadian economy relies extensively on

the market as the mechanism for coordinating the plans of individual households and firms. There is, though, an element of command in the Canadian economy. Markets do not operate in isolation of the legal framework established and enforced by the government sector of the economy. In recognition of the role played by both command and market mechanisms, modern economies are referred to as mixed economies. A **mixed economy** is one that uses both market and command mechanisms to coordinate economic activity.

The Canadian economy is a mixed economy but one that relies much more heavily on the market than on a command mechanism. However, actions taken by the government sector modify the allocation of scarce resources, changing *what*, *how*, and *for whom* the various goods and services are produced.

How Market Coordination Works The market coordinates individual decisions through price adjustments. To see how, think about the market for hamburgers in your local area. Suppose that the quantity of hamburgers being offered for sale is less than the quantity that people would like to buy. Some people who want to buy hamburgers will not be able to do so. To make the choices of buyers and sellers compatible, buyers will have to cut back on their hamburger consumption and more hamburgers will have to be offered for sale. An increase in the price of hamburgers will produce this outcome. A higher price will encourage producers to offer more hamburgers for sale. It will also change some people's lunch plans. People will buy fewer hamburgers and more hot dogs (or some other alternative). More hamburgers (and more hot dogs) will be offered for sale.

Now imagine the opposite situation. More hamburgers are available than people want to buy. In this case, the price is too high. A lower price will discourage the production and sale of hamburgers and encourage their purchase and consumption. Decisions to produce and sell and to buy and consume are continuously adjusted and kept in balance with each other by adjustments in prices.

In some cases, prices get stuck or fixed. When this happens, some other adjustment is necessary to make the plans and choices of individuals consistent. Customers waiting in lines and stocks of inventories will operate as temporary safety valves when the market price is stuck. If people want to buy more than the quantity that firms have decided to sell and if the price is temporarily fixed, one of two things will have to happen. Firms will wind up selling more than they would like and their inventories will shrink, or lines of customers will develop and only those who get to the head of the line before the goods run out will be able to make a purchase. The longer the line or the bigger the decline in inventories, the more prices will eventually have to adjust to keep buying and selling decisions in balance.

We have now seen how the market solves the question of *what* quantity to produce — how many hamburgers to make. The market solves the question of *how* to produce in a similar fashion. For example, hamburger producers can use gas, electric power, or charcoal to cook their hamburgers. Which fuel is used depends in part on the flavour that the producer wants to achieve and in part on the cost of the different fuels. If a fuel becomes very expensive, as did oil in the 1970s, less of it will be used and more of other fuels will be used in its place. By substituting one fuel for another as the costs of the different fuels change, the market solves the question of how to produce.

Finally, the market helps solve the question of *for whom* to produce. Skills, talents, and resources that are in very short supply will command a higher price than those in greater abundance. The owners of rare resources and skills will obtain a larger share of the output of the economy than the owners of those resources in abundant supply.

Closed and Open Economies

The economy depicted in Fig. 1.1 is a closed one. A **closed economy** is one that has no links with any other economy. The only truly closed economy is that of the entire world. The Canadian economy is an open economy. An **open economy** is one that has economic links with other economies. Firms in an open economy export some of their production to other countries, rather than selling only to households within their own country. Firms, households, and governments in an open economy also buy some of the goods and services that they use from firms in other countries. These imports and exports of goods and services are illustrated in Fig. 1.2. The total values of exports and imports are not necessarily equal to each other. The difference between those two values is the net amount that a country lends to or borrows from the rest of the world.

Figure 1.2 International Linkages

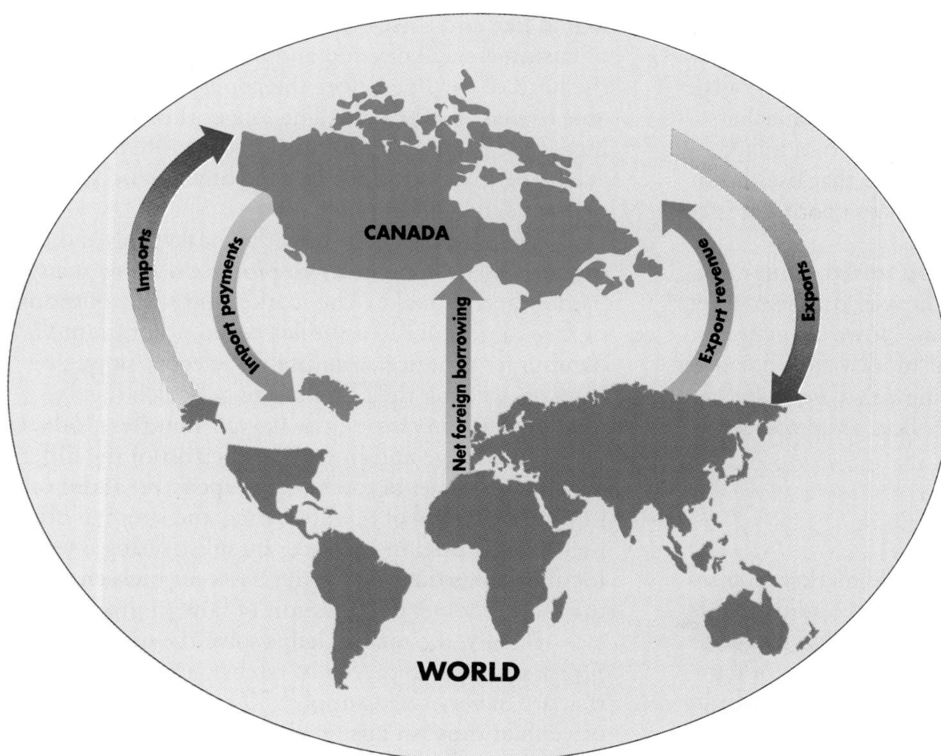

The Canadian economy exports and imports goods and services. It receives a flow of revenue from its exports of goods and services and makes payments for its imports. The difference between these two flows is the country's net foreign borrowing or lending. In recent years, Canada has been a net borrower. In the late 1980s, Canadians spent $10 billion a year more on their imports of goods and services from the rest of the world than they earned from their export sales. As a consequence, Canada is a net borrower from — not a net lender to — the rest of the world.

REVIEW

An economy is a mechanism that allocates scarce resources. It determines what is produced, how it is produced, and for whom it is produced. In the Canadian economy, these choices are made by households, firms, and governments, and they are coordinated through markets. Governments influence these choices by taxing, subsidizing, regulating, and lawmaking. The Canadian economy is an open economy, having extensive links with other economies. ■

We have now described an economy in about as much detail as we described an airplane. But we're about to become the economic equivalent of aeronautical engineers! We're going to build economies that fly! To do that, we have to understand the principles of economics as thoroughly as aeronautical engineers understand the principles of flight. To discover these principles, economists approach their work with the rigour and objectivity of natural scientists — they do economic science.

Economic Science

Economic science, like the natural sciences (such as physics and biology) and the other social sciences (such as political science, psychology, and sociology), is an attempt to find a body of laws. All sciences have two components:

- Careful and systematic observation and measurement
- Development of a body of theory to direct and interpret observations

All sciences are careful to distinguish between two types of statements:

- Statements about what *is*
- Statements about what *ought* to be

What Is and What Ought to Be

Statements about what *is* are **positive statements.** Statements about what *ought* to be are **normative statements.** Let's illustrate the distinction between positive and normative statements with two examples.

First, consider the controversy over acid rain. The question "*is it possible* to design and operate factories that do not pollute the atmosphere with chemicals that cause acid rain?"is positive. The question "*ought* we to build such factories?" is normative. Second, consider the economic controversy over the Canada – United States Free Trade Agreement. The question "*will* the Free Trade Agreement lead to increased international trade and lower costs?" is positive. The question "*should* we enter into such an agreement?" is normative.

Science — whether natural, social, or economic — tries to discover and catalogue positive statements that are consistent with what we observe in the world. Science is silent on normative questions. It is not that such questions are unimportant. On the contrary, they are often the most important questions. Nor is it that scientists do not have opinions on such questions. It is simply that science cannot settle a normative matter and the possession of scientific knowledge does not equip a person with superior moral precepts or norms. A difference of opinion on a positive matter can ultimately be settled by careful observation and measurement. A difference of opinion on a normative matter cannot be settled in that way. In fact, there are no well-defined rules for settling a normative dispute, and sometimes reasonable people simply have to agree to disagree. When they cannot, political and judicial institutions intervene in order for decisions to be made. We settle normative disagreements in the political, not the scientific, arena. The scientific community can, and often does, contribute to the normative debates of political life. But science is a distinct activity. Even though scientists have opinions about what ought to be, those opinions have no part in science itself.

Now let's see how economists attempt to discover and catalogue positive statements that are consistent with their observations and that enable them to answer economic questions such as the seven big questions that we studied earlier.

Observation and Measurement

Economic phenomena can be observed and measured in great detail. For example, we can catalogue the amounts and locations of natural and human resources. We can describe who does what kind of work, for how many hours, and how they are paid. We can catalogue the goods and services that people produce, consume, and store and their prices. We can describe in detail who borrows and who lends and at what interest rates. We can also catalogue the things that the government taxes and at what rate, as well as the programs it finances and at what cost.

Our list is not exhaustive. It gives a sample, though, of the array of things that economists can describe through careful observation and measurement of economic activity.

In today's world, computers have given us access to an enormous volume of economic description. Government agencies around the world, national statistical bureaus, private economic consultants, banks, investment advisors, and research economists working in universities generate an astonishing amount of information about economic behaviour.

But economists do more than observe and measure economic activity, crucial as that is. Describing something is not the same as understanding it. You can describe your digital watch in great detail, but that does not mean you can explain what makes it work. Understanding what makes things work requires the discovery of laws. That is the main task of economists — the discovery of laws governing economic behaviour. How do economists go about this task?

Economic Theory

We can describe in great detail the ups and downs, or cycles, in unemployment, but can we explain *why* unemployment fluctuates? We can describe the fall in the price of a VCR or a pocket calculator and the dramatic increase in its use, but can we explain the low price and popularity of such items? Did the fall in the price lead more people to use pocket calculators, or did their popularity lower the costs of production and make it possible to lower the price? Or did something else cause both the fall in the price and the increase in use?

Questions like these can be answered only by developing a body of economic theory. An **economic theory** is a reliable generalization that enables us to understand and predict the economic choices that people make. We develop economic theories by building and testing economic models. What is an economic model?

Economic Model

You have just seen an economic model. To answer the question "what is an economy and how does it work?", we built a model of an economy. We did not describe in detail all the economic actions that take place in Canada. We concentrated our attention only on those features that seemed important for understanding economic choices, and ignored everything else. You will perhaps better appreciate what we mean by an economic model if you think about more familiar models.

We have all seen model trains, cars, and airplanes. Although we do not usually call dolls and stuffed animals models, we can think of them in this way. Architects make models of buildings, and biologists make models of DNA (the double helix carrier of the genetic code).

A model is usually smaller than the real thing that it represents. But models are not always smaller in scale (for example, the biologist's model of the components of cells) and, in any case, the scale of a model is not its most important feature. A model also shows less detail than its counterpart in reality. For example, all the models we have mentioned resemble the real thing in appearance, but they are not usually made of the same substance nor do they work like the real thing that they represent. The architect's model of a new high-rise shows us what the building will look like and how it will conform with the buildings around it — but it does not contain plumbing, telephone cables, elevator shafts, air conditioning, plants, or other interior workings.

All the models that we have discussed (including those that are typically used as toys) represent something that is real, but they lack some of the features of the real thing. The model abstracts from the detail of the real thing. It includes only those features needed for the purpose at hand. It leaves out the nonessential or unnecessary. What a model includes and what it leaves out is not arbitrary; it results from a conscious and careful decision.

The models that we have just considered are all "physical" models. We can see the real thing and we can see the model. Indeed, the purpose of those models is to enable us to "visualize" the real thing. Some models, including economic models, are not physical. We cannot look at the real thing and look at the model and simply decide whether the model is a good or bad representation of the real thing. But the idea of a model as an abstraction from reality still applies to an economic model.

An **economic model** is an artificial or imaginary economy or part of an economy. An economic model has two components:

- Assumptions
- Implications

Assumptions form the foundation on which a model is built. They are propositions about what is important and what can be ignored, about what can be treated as being constant and, can therefore, be reliably used to make predictions.

Implications are the outcome of a model. The link between a model's assumptions and its implications is a process of logical deduction.

Let's illustrate these components of a model by building a simple model of your daily journey to school. The model has three assumptions:

1 Class begins at 8:30 a.m.

2 The bus ride takes 30 minutes.

3 The walk from the bus to class takes five minutes.

The implication of this model is that to be in class on time, you have to be on the bus by 7:55 a.m.

The assumptions of a model depend on its purpose. The purpose of an economic model is to understand how people make choices in the face of scarcity. Thus in building an economic model, we abstract from the rich detail of human life and focus only on behaviour that is relevant for coping with scarcity. Everything else is ignored. Economists know that people fall in love and form deep friendships, that they experience great joy and security or great pain and anxiety. But economists assume that in seeking to understand economic behaviour, they may build models that ignore many aspects of life. They focus on one and only one feature of the world: people have wants that exceed their resources and so, by their choices, have to make the best of things.

Assumptions of an Economic Model Economic models are based on four key assumptions:

1 *People have preferences.* Economists use the term **preferences** to denote likes and dislikes and the intensity of those likes and dislikes. People can judge whether one situation is better, worse, or just as good as another one. For example, you can judge whether for you, one loaf of bread and no cheese is better, worse, or just as good as half a loaf of bread and 100 grams of cheese.

2 *People are endowed with a fixed amount of resources and a technology that can transform those resources into goods and services.* Economists use the term **endowment** to refer to the amount of resources that people have and the term **technology** to describe the methods of converting those endowments into goods and services.

3 *People economize.* They choose how to use their endowments and technologies in order to make themselves as well-off as possible. Such a choice is called a rational choice. A **rational choice** is the best possible course of action from the point of view of the person making the choice. In an economic model, each choice, no matter what it is or how foolish it may seem to an observer, is interpreted as a rational choice.

Choices are made on the basis of the information available. With hindsight and with more information, people may well feel that some of their past choices were bad ones. This fact does not make such choices irrational. Again, a rational choice is the best possible course of action from the point of view of the person making the choice, given that person's preferences and *given the information available when the choice is made.*

4 *People's choices are coordinated.* One person's choice to buy something must be matched by another person's choice to sell that same thing. One person's choice to work at a particular job must be matched by another person's choice to hire someone to do that job. The coordination of individual choices is made by either a market mechanism or a command mechanism.

Implications of an Economic Model The implications of an economic model are the equilibrium values of various prices and quantities. An **equilibrium** is a situation in which everyone has economized — that is, all individuals have made the best possible choices in the light of their own preferences and given their endowments, technologies, and information — and in which those choices have been coordinated and made compatible with the choices of everyone else. Equilibrium is the solution or outcome of an economic model.

The term equilibrium conjures up the picture of a balance of opposing forces. For example, a balance scale can be said to be in equilibrium if a kilogram of cheese is placed on one side of the balance and a one-kilogram weight is placed on the other side. The two weights exactly equal each other and so offset each other, leaving the balance arm horizontal. A soap bubble provides another excellent physical illustration of equilibrium. The delicate spherical film of soap is held in place by a balance of forces of the air inside the sphere and the air outside it.

This second physical analogy illustrates a further important feature of an equilibrium. An equilibrium is not necessarily static; it may be dynamic — constantly changing. By squeezing or stretching the bubble, you can change its shape, but its shape at each point in time is determined by the balance of the forces acting upon it (including the forces that you exert upon it).

An economic equilibrium has a great deal in common with the soap bubble. First, it is in a constant state of motion. At each point in time, each person makes the best possible choice, given the endowments and actions of others. But changing circumstances alter those choices. For example, on a busy day in New York City, there are more cars looking for parking spaces than the number of spaces available. In this situation, the equilibrium number of free spaces is zero. But people do get to park. Individual cars are leaving and arriving at a steady pace. As soon as one car vacates a parking space, another instantly fills it. Being in equilibrium does not mean that everyone gets to park instantly. There is an equilibrium amount of time spent finding a vacant space. People hunting for a space are frustrated and experience rising blood pressure and increased anger. But there is still an equilibrium in the hunt for available parking spaces. Similarly, an economic equilibrium does not mean that everyone is experiencing economic prosperity. Some people may be very poor. Nevertheless, given individuals' preferences and

"And now a traffic update: A parking space has become available on Sixty-fifth Street between Second and Third. Hold it! A bulletin has just been handed me. That space has been taken."

Adam Smith and the Birth of Economic Science

Adam Smith

In the year that colonists in far-off America revolted against Britain, a Scottish thinker touched off a different kind of revolution. It was in 1776 that Adam Smith published *An Inquiry into the Nature and Causes of the Wealth of Nations*, the book that began economics as a science. Even today, more than two hundred years after its publication, the book is reprinted, reinterpreted, and reread repeatedly.

Smith led a quiet, scholarly life. He was born in 1723 in Kirkcaldy, Scotland, a small community near Edinburgh where he spent his first 14 years. At the remarkably early age of 14, he became a student at the University of Glasgow. He graduated at 17 and then went on to Oxford University, where he spent the next six years. His first major academic appointment, at age 28, was as professor of logic, and subsequently as professor of logic and moral philosophy, at Glasgow. After 13 years at Glasgow, Smith became a tutor to a wealthy Scottish duke who lived in France. After Smith spent two years in that position, the duke gave him a pension—an income for the rest of his life—of £300 a year. (An income of this size would have bought a great deal in the eighteenth century, when the average wage was about £30 a year.)

With the financial security provided by his pension, Smith devoted the next ten years of his life—from 1766 to 1776—to his great treatise. He was writing his *Wealth of Nations* at a time when the British economy was undergoing what came to be called the Industrial Revolution. New technologies were being invented and applied to the manufacture of cotton and wool, iron, transportation, and agriculture. The prevailing intellectual climate held that Britain needed to be protected from cheap foreign imports so that the nation could build up its stock of gold and finance its continuing process of industrialization.

Smith scoffed at this idea and developed a massive case against protection and in favour of "free trade." *The Wealth of Nations* argued that when each person makes the best economic choice possible, that choice leads, as if by "an invisible hand," to the best economic outcome for society as a whole. This best possible social outcome arises not because people pay attention to the needs of others but from self-interest. Said Smith, "It is not from the benevolence of the butcher, the brewer, or the baker, that we can expect our dinner, but from their regard to their own interest." [1]

The Wealth of Nations proposed that all economic behaviour can be understood as the rational pursuit of self-interest. The book begins much like the one that you are now studying, but much more profoundly, for Smith's was the first systematic treatment of these ideas. Smith explained how specialization, exchange, and the development of money lead to massive increases in goods and services. He applied his basic theory to a sweep of human history, starting from the fall of the Roman Empire. He explained the rise and progress of towns and cities, how commerce between towns and farmlands benefits both, and why free international trade leads to improved living standards. He also applied the theory of rational self-interest to explain why the universities of the eighteenth century were organized not for the benefit of the students but, as he put it, "for the ease of the professors." He even used his theory to explain the proliferation of new religions.

Many thinkers had written earlier on economic questions, but Smith was the first to make a science of economics.

> "It was Smith who provided so broad and authoritative an account of the known economic doctrine that henceforth it was no longer permissible for any subsequent writer on economics to advance his own ideas while ignoring the state of general knowledge. A science consists of interacting practitioners, and henceforth no one could decently ignore Smith's own work and in due time the work of Malthus, Ricardo, and the galaxy of economists who populated the first half of the nineteenth century." [2]

This first essay on our advancing knowledge in economic science has been devoted to Adam Smith, who stands alone as the founder of this discipline. Subsequent essays in this series will give you a taste of how various branches of the subject have advanced from this founding father through to the present. The goal is to enable you to see how the science of economics advances and perhaps even to inspire you to become one of that community of scholars seeking to deepen our understanding of economic phenomena.

---

[1] Adam Smith, *An Inquiry into the Nature and Causes of the Wealth of Nations*, ed. Edwin Cannan, with a new preface by George J. Stigler (Chicago: University of Chicago Press, 1976), 18.

[2] George J. Stigler, "Nobel Lecture: The Process and Progress of Economics," *Journal of Political Economy* 91 (August 1983): 529-45.

endowments, the available technologies, and the actions of everyone else, each person has made the best possible choice and sees no advantage in modifying his or her current action.

Microeconomic and Macroeconomic Models

Economic models fall into two categories: microeconomic and macroeconomic. **Microeconomics** is the branch of economics that studies the decisions of individual households and firms. Microeconomics also studies the way that individual markets work and the detailed way that government regulation and taxes affect the allocation of labour and of goods and services.

Macroeconomics is the branch of economics that studies the economy as a whole. It seeks to understand the big picture rather than detailed individual choices. In particular, it studies the determination of the overall level of economic activity — of unemployment, aggregate income, average prices, and inflation.

Of the seven big questions, those dealing with technological change, production and consumption, and wages and earnings are microeconomic. Those dealing with unemployment, inflation, and differences in wealth among nations are macroeconomic.

Model, Theory, and Reality

People who build models often get carried away and start talking as if their model *is* the real world — as if their model is reality. No matter how useful it is, there is no sense in which a model can be said to be reality.

A model is an abstract entity. It lists assumptions and their implications. When economists talk about people who have made themselves as well-off as possible, they are not talking about real people. They are talking about artificial people in an economic model. Do not lose sight of this important but easily misunderstood fact.

Economic theory bridges the gap between an economic model and the real world. Economic theory proposes that the economic behaviour of people in actual economies can be understood and predicted by using models in which people who make rational choices interact with each other in an equilibrium. Economics develops models based on this idea to explain all aspects of economic behaviour. But economic models have to be tested.

Figure 1.3 How Theories Are Developed

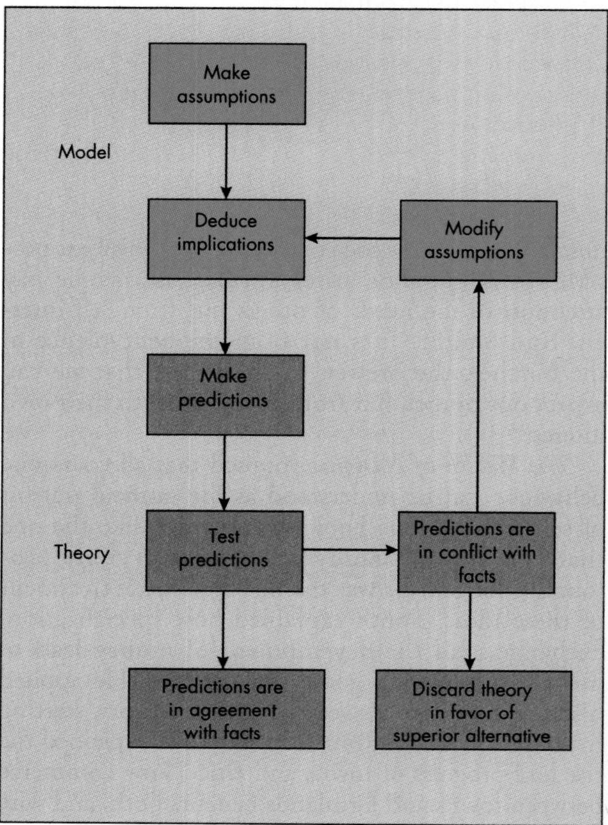

Economic theories are developed by building and testing economic models. An economic model is a set of *assumptions* about what is important and what can be ignored and the *implications* of those assumptions. The implications of a model form the basis of *predictions* about the world. These predictions are tested by being checked against the facts. If the predictions are in conflict with the facts, either the theory is discarded in favour of a superior alternative or the model-building process begins anew with modified assumptions. It is only when predictions are in agreement with the facts that a useful theory has been developed.

To test an economic model, its implications are matched against actual events in the real world. That is, the model is used to make predictions about the real world. The model's predictions may correspond to or be in conflict with the facts. By comparing its predictions with the facts, we are able to test a model. The process of using models to develop economic theories is illustrated in Fig. 1.3. We begin by building a model. Its implications are used to generate predictions about the world. These predictions and their tests form the basis of a theory. When predictions are in conflict with the facts, either a theory is discarded in favour of a superior alternative or we return to the model-building stage, modifying our assumptions and creating a new model. Economics itself provides guidance on how we might discover a better model. It prompts us to look for some aspect of preferences, endowments, technology, or the coordination mechanism that has been overlooked.

Economics is a young science. Its birth can be dated fairly precisely in the eighteenth century with the publication of Adam Smith's *The Wealth of Nations* (see Our Advancing Knowledge, pp. 20-21). In the closing years of the twentieth century, economic science has managed to discover a sizeable number of useful generalizations. In many areas, however, we are still going around the loop shown in Fig. 1.3 — changing assumptions, performing new logical deductions, generating new predictions, and getting wrong answers yet again. The gradual accumulation of correct answers gives most practitioners some faith that their methods will eventually provide usable answers to all the big economic questions.

As we make progress, more and more things become clearer and seem to fit together. Theoretical advances lead to deeper understanding. This feature of economics is shared with scientists in all fields. As Albert Einstein, the great physicist, said: "Creating a new theory is not like destroying an old barn and erecting a skyscraper in its place. It is rather like climbing a mountain, gaining new and wider views, discovering new connections between our starting point and its rich environment. But the point from which we started still exists and can be seen, although it appears smaller and forms a tiny part of our broad view gained by the mastery of the obstacles on our adventurous way up."[1]

■ In the next chapter, we will study some of the tools that economists use to build economic models. Then, in Chapter 3, we will build an economic model and use that model to understand the world around us and to start to answer some of the seven big economic questions.

[1] These words are attributed to Einstein in a letter by Oliver Sacks to *The Listener* 88, 2279 (November 30, 1972): 756.

SUMMARY

Seven Big Questions

Economics tries to answer difficult questions that affect our daily lives. These questions concern the production and consumption of goods and services; wages and earnings; unemployment; inflation; government spending, taxation, and regulation; international trade; and the distribution of wealth and poverty in Canada and throughout the world. There are no easy answers to the big economic questions, which must be approached in a scientific manner. (pp. 6-8)

Scarcity

All economic questions arise from the fundamental fact of scarcity. Scarcity means that wants exceed resources. Human wants are effectively unlimited, but the resources available to satisfy them are finite.

Economic activity is what people do to cope with scarcity. Scarcity forces people to make choices. Making the best choice possible from what is available is called optimizing. In order to make the best possible choice, a person weighs the costs and benefits of the alternatives.

Opportunity cost is the cost of one choice in terms of the best alternative forgone. The opportunity cost of any action is the best alternative action that could have been undertaken in its place.

Scarcity forces people to compete with each other for scarce resources. People may cooperate in certain areas, but all economic activity ultimately results in competition among individuals acting alone or in groups. (pp. 9-11)

The Economy

The economy is a mechanism that allocates scarce resources among competing uses, determining *what*, *how*, and *for whom* the various goods and services will be produced.

The economy's working parts are divided into two categories: decision makers and coordination mechanisms. Economic decision makers are households, firms, and governments. Households decide how much of their factors of production to sell to firms and governments and what goods and services to buy from firms. Firms decide what factors of production to hire and which goods and services to produce. Governments decide on the scale of their purchases of factors of production from households and of goods and services from firms. They also decide on the scale of their provision of goods and services to households and firms, as well as on the rates of benefits and subsidies and taxes.

There are two types of coordination mechanisms: the command mechanism and the market mechanism. The Canadian economy relies mainly on the market mechanism, but the actions taken by the government sector do modify the allocation of scarce resources. The Canadian economy is, therefore, a mixed economy. (pp. 11-16)

Economic Science

Economic science, like the natural sciences and the other social sciences, attempts to find a body of laws. Economic science seeks to understand what *is* and is silent about what *ought* to be. Economists try to find economic laws by developing a body of economic theory, and economic theory, in turn, is developed by building and testing economic models. Economic models are abstract, logical constructions that contain two components: assumptions and implications. An economic model has four key assumptions:

1 People have preferences.

2 People have a given endowment of resources and technology.

3 People economize.

4 Peoples' choices are coordinated through market or command mechanisms.

The implications of an economic model are the equilibrium values of various prices and quantities that result from each individual doing the best that is possible, given his or her preferences and endowments, the available technology and information, and the coordination mechanism. (pp. 16-23)

KEY ELEMENTS

Key Terms

Key Figure 

REVIEW QUESTIONS

1 Illustrate each of the seven big economic questions with your own examples.

2 Why does scarcity force us to make choices?

3 What do we mean by "rational choice"? Give examples of rational and irrational choices.

4 Why does scarcity force us to optimize?

5 Why does optimization require us to calculate costs?

6 Why does scarcity imply competition?

7 Why can't we solve economic problems by cooperating with each other?

8 Who are the main economic decision makers?

9 List the economic decisions made by households, firms, and governments.

10 What is the difference between a command mechanism and a market mechanism?

11 Distinguish between positive and normative statements by listing three examples of each type of statement.

12 What are the four key assumptions of an economic model?

13 Explain the difference between a model and a theory.

PROBLEMS

1 Which of the following are part of your opportunity cost of attending school? Explain why they are or are not.

   a) The money you spend on haircuts
   b) The vacation you would have taken if you had been working rather than being in school
   c) The tapes and compact discs that you don't have because you've had to spend so much on economics textbooks
   d) The amount you pay for your lunch in your school's cafeteria each week
   e) The $20,000 annual salary you could have made in your Uncle Fred's store

2 List some examples of opportunity costs that you have incurred today.

3 Give some examples of opportunity costs you have incurred that were the result of someone else's actions. Give some examples of opportunity costs incurred by someone else that were the result of your actions.

4 Which of the following statements are positive and which are normative?

   a) Low rents will restrict the supply of housing.
   b) High interest rates lower the demand for mortgages and new homes.
   c) Housing costs too much.
   d) Owners of apartment buildings ought to be free to charge whatever rent they like.
   e) The government should restrict the rents that apartment owners are allowed to charge.

5 You have been hired by a company that makes and markets tapes, records, and compact discs (CDs). Your employer is going to start selling these products in a new market that has a population of 20 million people. A survey has revealed that 40 percent of this market buys only popular music and 5 percent of it buys only classical music. No one buys both types of music. The average income of the pop music fan is $10,000 a year and that of the classical fan is $50,000 a year. It has also been discovered that people with low incomes spend one-quarter of 1 percent of their income on tapes, records, and CDs while those with high incomes spend 2 percent of theirs. You have been asked to predict how much is likely to be spent in this market on pop music and classical music in one year.

Build a model to answer that question. List your assumptions and work out their implications. Draw attention to the potential for unreliability in your answers. Why might your model give incorrect answers?

CHAPTER 2

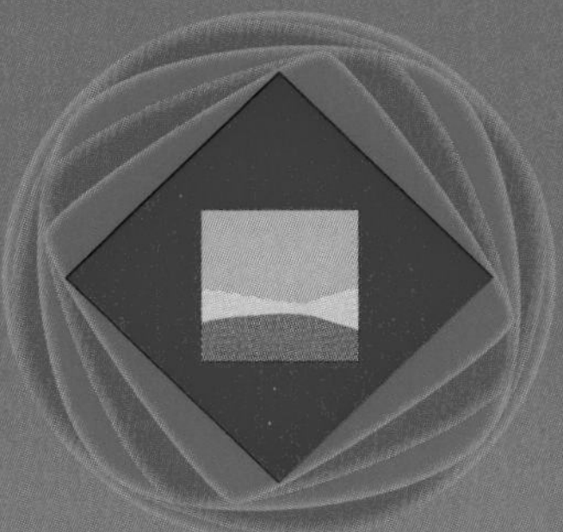

Making and Using Graphs

After studying this chapter, you will be able to:

- Make and interpret a time-series graph and a scatter diagram.
- Distinguish between linear and nonlinear relationships and between relationships that have a maximum and a minimum.
- Define and calculate the slope of a line.
- Graph relationships among more than two variables.

Three Kinds of Lies

BENJAMIN DISRAELI, BRITISH prime minister in the late nineteenth century, is reputed to have said that there are three kinds of lies: lies, damned lies, and statistics. One of the most powerful ways of conveying statistical information is in the form of a picture — a graph. Graphs too can tell lies. But the right graph does not lie. Indeed, it reveals data and helps its viewer to see and think about relationships that would otherwise be obscure. ■ Graphs are a surprisingly modern invention. They first appeared in the late eighteenth century, long after the discovery of mathematically sophisticated ideas such as logarithms and calculus. But today, especially in the age of the personal computer and the video display, graphs have become almost more important than words. The ability to make and use graphs is as important as the ability to read and write. ■ How do economists use graphs? What are the different types of graphs that economists use? What do economic graphs reveal and what can they hide? What are the main pitfalls that can result in a graph that lies? ■ It will be clear to you from the seven big questions you saw in Chapter 1 that the problems that economics seeks to solve are difficult ones. You will also suspect, and rightly so, that hardly anything in economics has a single cause. Variations in the quantity of ice cream consumed are not caused merely by variations in the air temperature or in the price of cream but by at least these two factors and probably several others as well. How can we draw graphs of relationships that involve several variables all of which vary simultaneously? How can we interpret such relationships?

■ In this chapter, we are going to look at the different kinds of graphs that are used in economics. We are going to learn how to read them and make them. ■ We are going to look at examples of useful graphs as well as misleading graphs. We are also going to study how we can calculate the strength of the effect of one variable on another.

There are no graphs or techniques used in this book that are more complicated than those explained and described in this chapter. If you are already familiar with graphs, you may want to skip or only skim this chapter. Whether you study this chapter thoroughly or give it a quick pass, you may find it a handy reference to which you can return if you feel that you need additional help understanding the graphs that you encounter in your study of economics.

Graphing Data

Graphs enable us to see patterns in data. They do so by representing quantities as distances on scales. The simplest graph shows just one variable. Let's begin with this type of graph.

Graphing a Single Variable

Figure 2.1 shows two examples of graphing a single variable. Part (a) shows temperature, measured in degrees Celsius, as the distance on a scale. Movements from left to right represent increases in temperature. Movements from right to left represent decreases in temperature. The point marked zero represents zero degrees Celsius. To the right of zero, the temperatures are positive. To the left of zero, the temperatures are negative (as indicated by the minus sign in front of the numbers).

Figure 2.1(b) provides another example. This time altitude, or height, is measured in thousands of metres above sea level. The point marked zero represents sea level. Points to the right of zero represent metres above sea level. Points to the left of zero (indicated by a minus sign) represent depths below sea level.

There are no rigid rules about the scale for a graph. The scale is determined by the range of the variable being graphed and the space available for the graph.

The two graphs in Fig. 2.1 show just a single variable. Marking a point on either of the two scales indicates a particular temperature or a particular height. Thus the point marked *a* represents 100°C, the boiling point of water. The point marked *b* represents 6,194 metres, the height of Mount McKinley, the highest mountain in North America.

Graphing a single variable as we have done does not usually reveal much. Graphs become more powerful when they show how two variables are related to each other.

Figure 2.1 Graphing a Single Variable

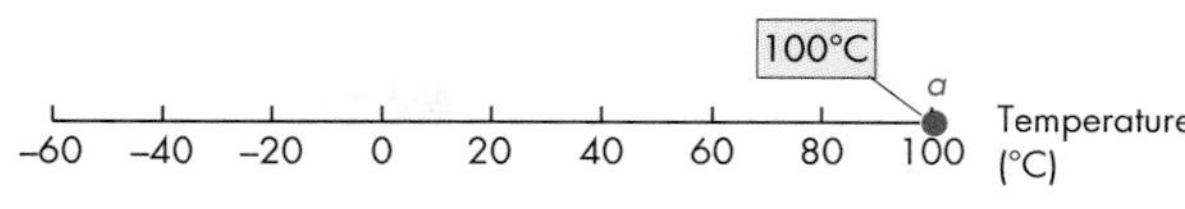

(a) Temperature

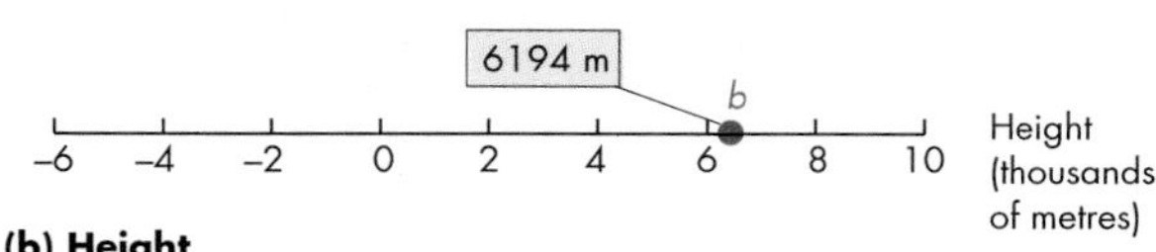

(b) Height

All graphs have a scale that measures quantity as a distance. The two scales here measure temperature and height. Numbers to the right of zero are positive. Numbers to the left of zero are negative.

Two-Variable Graphs

To construct a two-variable graph, we set two scales perpendicular to each other. Let's continue to use the same two variables as those in Fig. 2.1. We will measure temperature in exactly the same way, but we will turn the height scale to a vertical position. Thus temperature is measured exactly as it was before but height is now represented by movements up and down a vertical scale.

The two scale lines in Fig. 2.2 are called **axes.** The vertical line is called the **y-axis** and the horizontal line is called the **x-axis**. The letters y and x appear on the axes of Fig. 2.2. Each axis has a zero point shared by the two axes. The zero point, common to both axes, is called the **origin**.

To represent something in a two-variable graph, we need two pieces of information. For example, Mount McKinley is 6,194 metres high and, on a particular day, the temperature at its peak is –20°C. We can represent this information in Fig. 2.2 by marking the height of the mountain on the y-axis at 6,194 metres and the temperature on the x-axis at –20°C. We can now identify the values of the two variables that appear on the axes by marking point c.

Two lines, called coordinates, can be drawn from point c. **Coordinates** are lines running from a point on a graph perpendicularly to its axes. The line running from c to the x-axis is the ***y*-coordinate**, because its length is the same as the value marked off on the y-axis. Similarly, the line running from c to

Figure 2.2 Graphing Two Variables

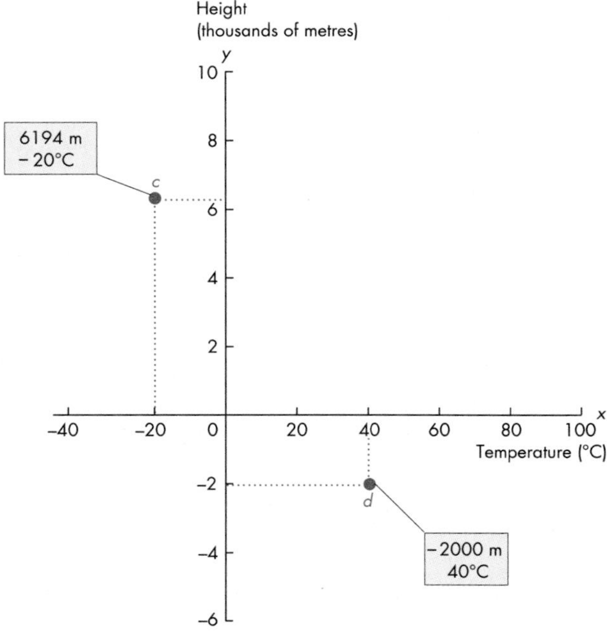

The relationship between two variables is graphed by forming two axes perpendicular to each other. Height is measured here on the *y*-axis and temperature on the *x*-axis. Point *c* represents the top of Mt. McKinley, 6,194 metres above sea level (measured on the *y*-axis), with a temperature of –20°C (measured on the *x*-axis). Point *d* represents the inside temperature in a submarine, 40°C, exploring the depths of an ocean, 2,000 metres below the sea.

the vertical axis is the ***x*-coordinate**, because its length is the same as the value marked off on the *x*-axis.

Now let's leave the top of Mount McKinley, at 6,194 metres and –20°C, and take a trip in a submarine. You are exploring the depths of the ocean, 2,000 metres below the sea at a sweltering 40°C. You are at the point marked *d* in the figure. Your *y*-coordinate is –2,000 metres and your *x*-coordinate is 40°C. Economists use graphs similar to this one in a variety of ways. Let's look at two examples.

Time-Series Graphs

One of the most common and powerful graphs used in economics is the time-series graph. A **time-series graph** measures time (for example, in years or months) on the *x*-axis and the variable or variables in which we are interested on the *y*-axis.

Figure 2.3 illustrates a time-series graph. Time is measured in years on the *x*-axis. The variable that we are interested in — the Canadian unemployment rate (the percentage of the labour force unemployed) — is measured on the *y*-axis. The time-series graph conveys an enormous amount of information quickly and easily:

1 It tells us the *level* of the unemployment rate — when it is *high* and when it is *low*. When the line is a long way from the *x*-axis, the unemployment rate is high. When the line is close to the *x*-axis, the unemployment rate is low.

2 It tells us how the unemployment rate *changes* — whether it *rises* or *falls*. When the line slopes upward, as in the early 1930s, the unemployment rate is rising. When the line slopes downward, as in the early 1940s, the unemployment rate is falling.

3 It tells us the *speed* with which the unemployment rate is *changing* — whether it is rising or falling *quickly* or *slowly*. If the line rises or falls very steeply, the unemployment rate is changing quickly. If the line is not steep, the unemployment rate is rising or falling slowly. For example, the unemployment rate rose sharply between 1930 and 1932. It went up again in 1933 but more slowly. Similarly, when the unemployment rate was falling in the 1960s, it fell quickly between 1961 and 1962, but then it began to fall more slowly in 1963 and 1964.

A time-series graph can also be used to depict a trend. A **trend** is a general tendency for a variable to rise or fall. You can see that the unemployment rate had a general tendency to rise from the mid-1940s to the mid-1980s. That is, although there were ups and downs in the unemployment rate, there was an upward trend.

Graphs also allow us to compare different periods quickly. It is apparent, for example, that the 1930s were different from any other period in the twentieth century because of exceptionally high unemployment.

We can thus see that not only does Fig. 2.3 convey a wealth of information, it does so in a much smaller space than we have used to describe only some of its features.

Misleading Time-Series Graphs Although time-series graphs are powerful devices for conveying a large

Figure 2.3 A Time-Series Graph

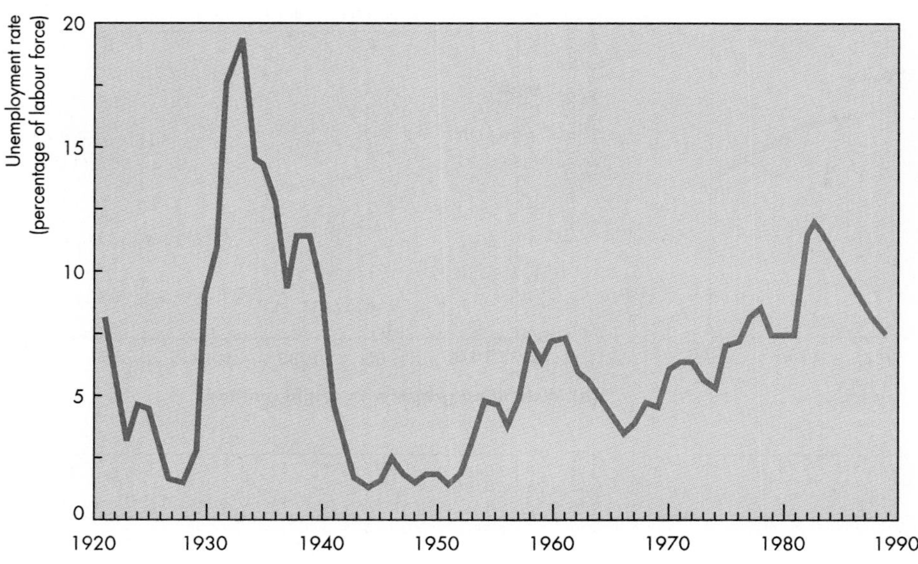

A time-series graph plots the level of a variable on the *y*-axis against time (days, weeks, months, or years) on the *x*-axis. This graph shows the Canadian unemployment rate each year from 1921 to 1989.

amount of information, they can also be used to create a misleading picture.

One common way of misleading is to place, side by side, two graphs that have different scales. Figure 2.4 provides an illustration. This figure contains exactly the same information as Fig. 2.3, but the information is packaged in a different way. In part (a), the scale on the *y*-axis has been compressed; in part (b), it has been expanded. When we look at these two parts together, they suggest that the unemployment rate was pretty stable from 1921 to 1955 but that it has trended upward dramatically in the last 33 years.

Figure 2.4 Misleading Graphs: Squeezing and Stretching Scales

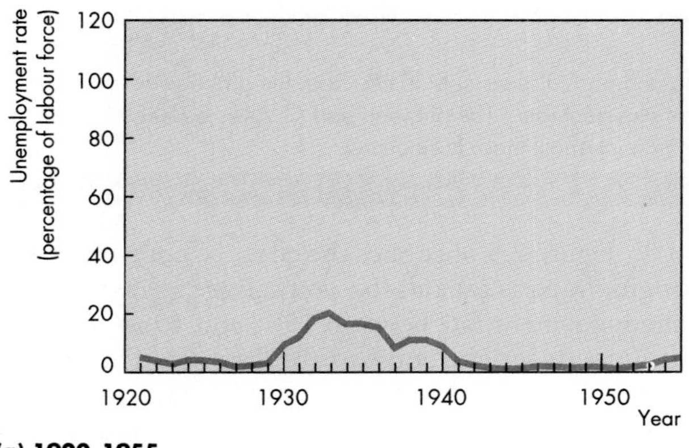

(a) 1920–1955

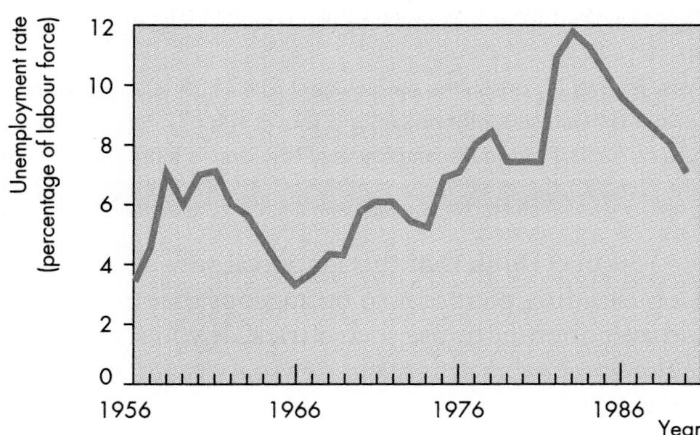

(b) 1956–1989

Graphs can mislead by squeezing and stretching the scales. These two graphs show exactly the same data as Fig. 2.3 — the Canadian unemployment rate from 1921 to 1989. Part (a) has squeezed the *y*-axis, while part (b) has stretched that axis. The result appears to be a low and stable unemployment rate before 1955 and a rising, highly volatile unemployment rate after that date. Contrast the lie of Fig. 2.4 with the truth of Fig. 2.3.

Figure 2.5 Omitting the Origin

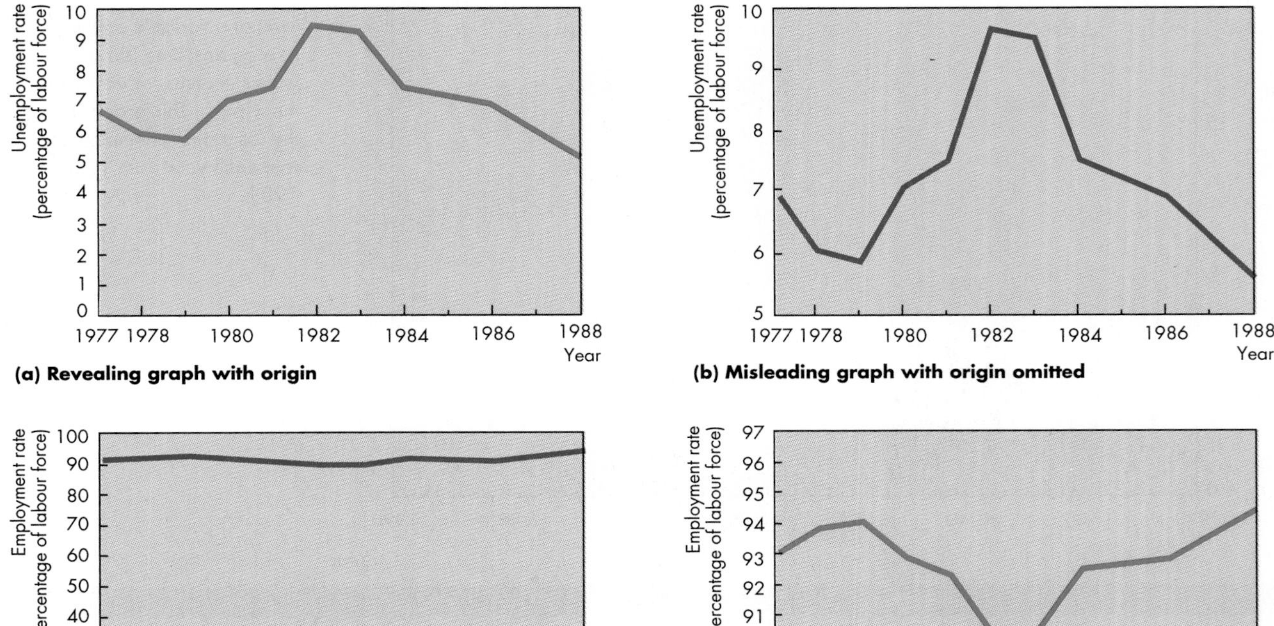

(a) Revealing graph with origin

(b) Misleading graph with origin omitted

(c) Uninformative graph with origin

(d) Revealing graph with origin omitted

Sometimes the origin is omitted from a graph. This practice can be either revealing or misleading, depending on how it is used. Parts (a) and (b) graph the Canadian unemployment rate between 1977 and 1988. Part (a) is graphed with the origin, and part (b) without it. Part (a) reveals a large amount of information about the level and changes in the unemployment rate over this time period. Part (b) overdramatizes the rises and falls in the unemployment rate and gives no direct visual information about its level.

Parts (c) and (d) graph the employment rate. Part (c) contains an origin, and part (d) does not. In this case, the graph with the origin is much less informative and shows virtually no variation in the employment rate. The graph in part (d) gives a clear picture of fluctuations in the employment rate and is more informative than part (c) about those fluctuations.

You may think that this graphical way of creating a misleading picture is so outrageous that no one could ever attempt to use such a trick. If you scrutinize the graphs that you see in newspapers and magazines, you will be surprised how common this device is.

Omitting the Origin Sometimes a graph is drawn with the origin (0 on the axis) omitted. There are times when omitting the origin is precisely the correct thing to do, as it enables the graph to reveal its information. But there are also times when omitting the origin is misleading.

Figure 2.5 illustrates the effect of omitting the origin. In parts (a) and (b), you can see a graph of the unemployment rate between 1977 and 1988. Part (a) includes the origin, and part (b) does not. The graph in part (a) provides a clear account of what happened to unemployment over the time period in question. You can use that graph in the same way that we used Fig. 2.3 to describe all the features of unemployment during that time period. But the graph in part (b) is less revealing and distorts the picture. It fails to reveal the *level* of the unemployment rate. It focuses only on, and exaggerates the magnitude of, the increases and decreases. In particular, the increases in the unemployment rate in the late 1970s and early 1980s look enormous when compared with the increases that appear in part (a). With the origin omitted, small percentage changes in the unemployment rate look like many hundredfold changes. This device is often used in the press and an example can be found in Reading Between the Lines, pp. 34-35.

Parts (c) and (d) of Fig. 2.5 graph the employment rate — the percentage of the labour force employed. Part (c) includes the origin, and part (d) omits it. As you can see, the graph in part (c) reveals very little about movements in the employment rate. It seems to suggest that the employment rate was pretty constant. The main feature of part (c) is an enormous amount of empty space — an inefficient use of the space available. Part (d) shows the same information but with the origin omitted. The scale begins at 87 percent. In this case, we can see very clearly the ups and downs in the employment rate. This graph does not provide a visual impression of the *level* of the employment rate, but it does provide a clear picture of its variations.

The decision to include or exclude the origin of the graph depends on what the graph is designed to reveal. To convey information about the levels of the employment and unemployment rates and their variations, the graphs in parts (a) and (d) of Fig. 2.5 are almost equally revealing. By comparison, the graphs in parts (b) and (c) convey almost no information.

Comparing Two Time-Series Sometimes we want to use a time-series graph to compare two different variables. For example, suppose you wanted to know how the balance of the federal government's budget — its surplus or deficit — fluctuated and how those fluctuations compared with fluctuations in the unemployment rate. You can examine two such series by drawing a graph of each of them in the manner shown in Fig. 2.6(a). The scale for the unemployment rate appears on the left side of the figure, and the scale for the federal government's budget surplus appears on the right. The red line shows unemployment and the blue line shows the budget surplus. You will probably agree that it is pretty hard work figuring out from Fig. 2.6(a) just what the relationship is between the unemployment rate and the budget. But it does look as if there is a tendency for the budget to go into a bigger deficit (the blue line goes downward) when the unemployment rate increases (the red line goes upward). In other words, it seems as if these two variables have a tendency to move in opposite directions.

In a situation such as this, it is often more revealing to flip the scale of one of the variables over, and graph it upside-down. Figure 2.6(b) does this. The unemployment rate in part (b) is graphed in exactly the same way as in part (a), but the federal government's budget has been flipped over. Now, instead of measuring the surplus (a positive number) in the up direction and the deficit (a negative number) in the down direction, we measure the surplus downward and the deficit upward. You can now see very clearly the relationship between these two variables. There is indeed a tendency for the federal government's deficit to get bigger when the unemployment rate gets higher. But the relationship is by no means an exact one, and there have been significant periods, clearly revealed in the graph, when the deficit and the unemployment rate moved apart. You can see these periods as those in which the distance between the two lines widens.

Time-series graphs, whether simple ones with a single variable or more complex ones such as those in Fig. 2.6 that show two variables, enable us to see how variables change over time. But sometimes we are more interested in how variables relate to each other than in how they move over time. To study such relationships, we use a scatter diagram.

Scatter Diagrams

A **scatter diagram** plots the value of one economic variable associated with the value of another. It measures one of the variables on the x-axis and the other variable on the y-axis.

Figure 2.7 illustrates three scatter diagrams. Part (a) shows the relationship between consumption and income. The x-axis measures average family income and the y-axis measures average family consumption. Each point represents average consumption and average income in Canada from 1968 to 1988. For example, the point marked 71 tells us that in 1971 average consumption was $5,800 and average income was $10,800. The pattern formed by the points in Fig. 2.7(a) tells us that when income rises, consumption also rises.

In Fig 2.7(b), the x-axis shows the percentage of households that own a video cassette recorder and the vertical axis shows its average price. Each point represents the price and the percentage of households that own a VCR in a particular year. For example, the point marked 81 tells us that the average price of a VCR in 1981 was $600 and that VCRs were owned by

Misleading Graphics

Fewer tipplers dry up hotels

Albertans' declining thirst for liquor is hurting the hospitality industry, especially hotels in rural parts of the province, say concerned industry spokesmen.

They attribute falling sales of alcohol in Alberta to several factors: more and more people are saying no to booze, the success of groups condemning drinking and driving, designated driver programs and tougher laws against drinking and driving.

"It's devastating. Many hotels are on the brink of bankruptcy," said Randall Williams, president of the Calgary Hotel Association, in an interview Monday.

The association also blames low liquor sales on a proliferation of liquor licences to places like small eateries and pizza parlors.

Restaurants and other food service establishments are also reeling from slumping sales, said Susan Costello, president of the Alberta Restaurant and Foodservices Association.

"We've noticed a steady decline in the past two years. If most of your sales come from liquor, you can feel anywhere between a five to 15-per-cent drop in consumption," said Costello.

"Because liquor sales have dropped so dramatically, up to 70 per cent of Alberta hotels — mostly smaller, family-run operations in rural areas — are facing bankruptcy or are barely breaking even", said Williams.

Jim Hansen, executive vice-president of the Alberta Hotel Association, said declining liquor sales contributed to 106 Alberta hotels going into receivership between 1983 and 1988. With 400 members, the group represents 70 per cent of all hotels in the province. Williams estimated that sales of alcohol, including hard liquor, wine and beer, now account for an average of 25 per cent of hotel revenues. Ten to 15 years ago, they accounted for 35 per cent to 40 per cent.

And smaller rural hotels draw as much as 75 per cent of their revenues from liquor consumption, said Hansen.

The Alberta Liquor Control Board says it sold 213.5 million litres of alcohol in 1988, the latest year for which figures are available, down from 221.5 million litres in 1984. The figures include sales of all types of beer, wine and liquor.

***The Calgary Herald,* January 16, 1990**
By Claudia Catteano

The Essence of the Story

- Between 1984 and 1988, Alberta alcoholic beverages sales fell from 221.5 to 213.5 million litres.
- In the graph, 1984 sales are represented by a full glass which is less than one-third full in 1988.
- Because of declining liquor sales:
  - 106 Alberta hotels have gone out of business between 1983 and 1988 (Jim Hansen, Alberta Hotel Association).
  - Up to 70 percent of Alberta hotels are facing bankruptcy or are barely breaking even (Randall Williams Calgary Hotel Association).
- Declining liquor sales have been caused by:
  - "more people say no to booze"
  - anti-drinking, driving campaigns
  - tougher laws against drunk driving

Background and analysis

- Figure (a) gives two views of declining liquor sales in Alberta.
- In part (i) the decline looks tiny but in part (ii) it looks large—like the graph in the news story.
- A 3.6 per cent decline is shown in both figures. A false impression of a large decline is created by omitting the origin.
- Figure (b) (i) shows that the dollar value of liquor sales increased but taxes increased even more.
- If liquor sales declined by only 3.6 per cent, why all the fuss? The next figure answers this question.
- In part (ii) the effects of inflation are removed and the source of the fuss is revealed. Higher taxes and a falling value of money left those in the liquor retail business with a fall in the after-tax value of sales.

(a) Two views of declining liquor sales in Alberta

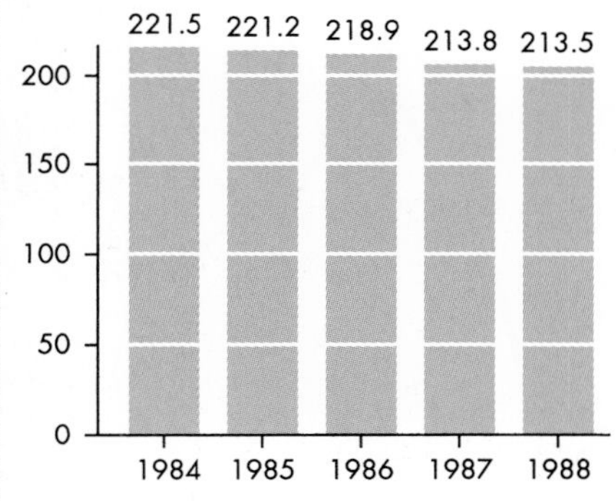

(i) Graph with origin

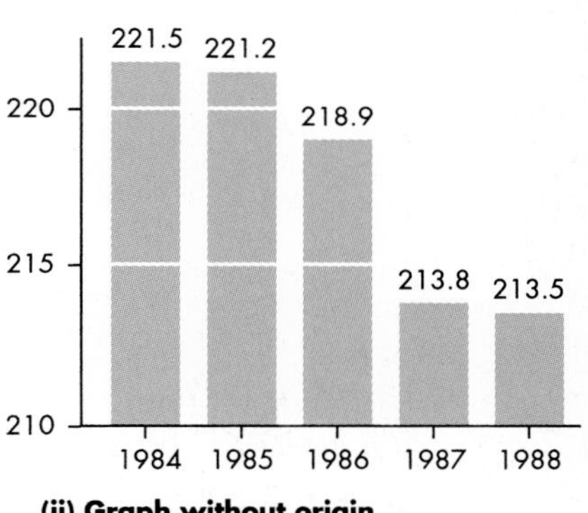

(ii) Graph without origin

(b) A closer look at liquor sales in Alberta

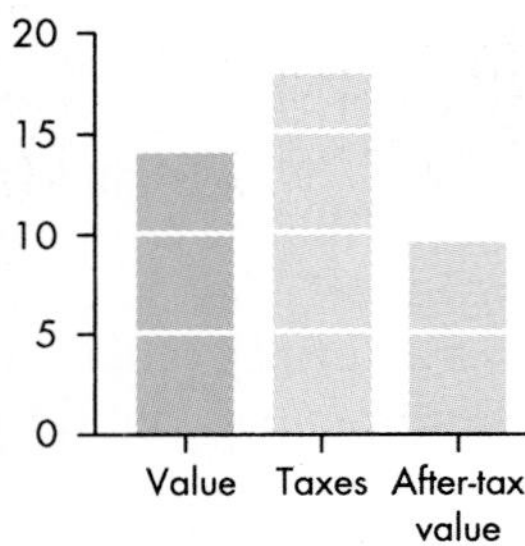

(i) Dollar amounts

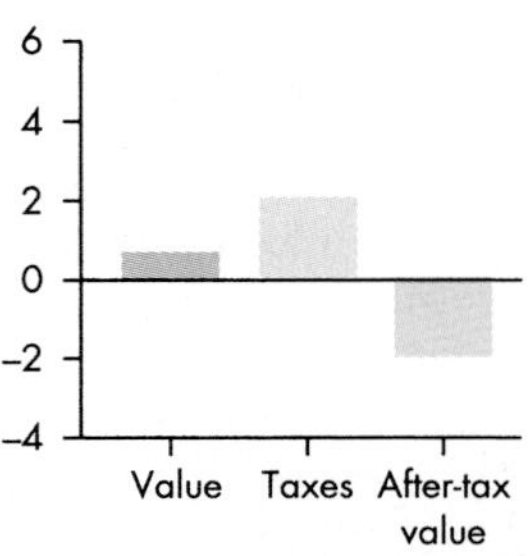

(ii) After removing effects of inflation

Figure 2.6 Seeing Relationships in Time-Series Graphs

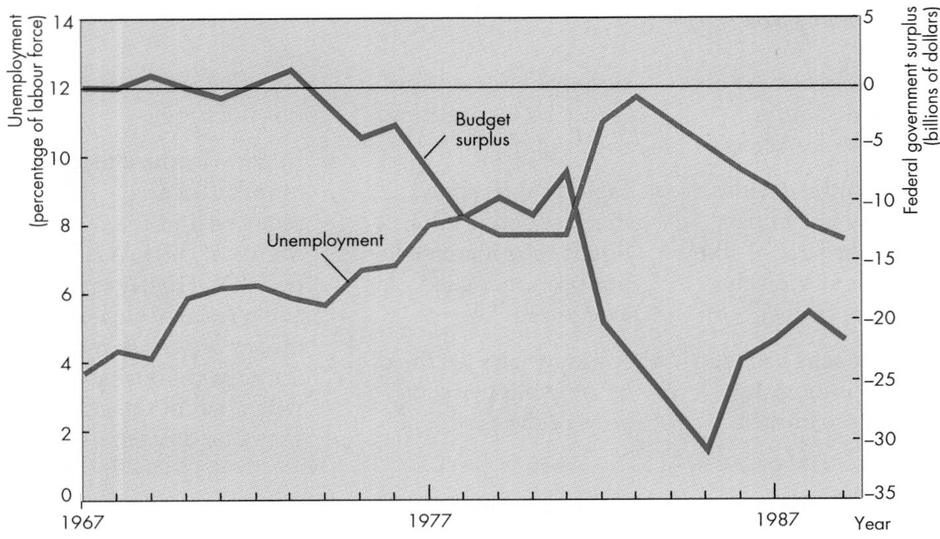

(a) Unemployment and budget surplus

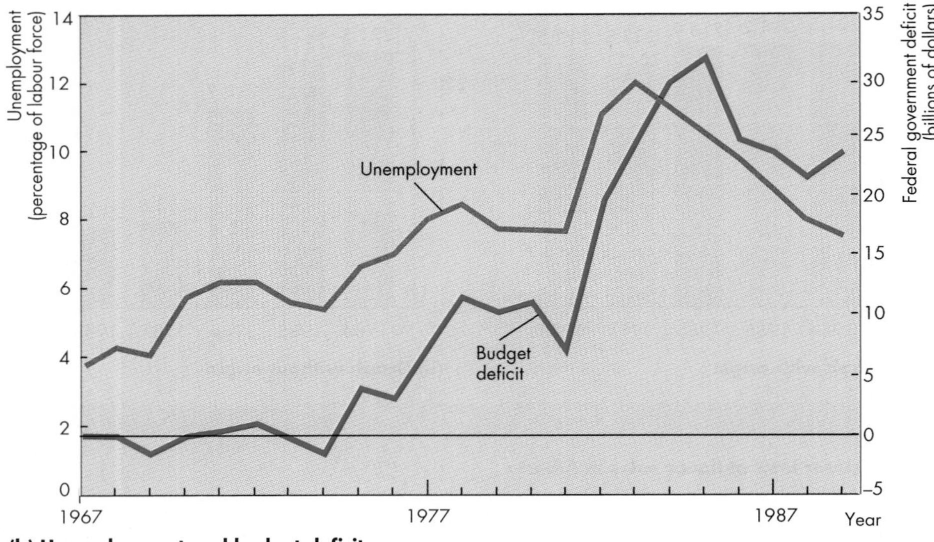

(b) Unemployment and budget deficit

A time-series graph can be used to reveal relationships between two variables. The two graphs here show the unemployment rate and the balance of the federal government's budget between 1967 and 1989. The unemployment line is identical in the two parts. In part (a), the budget balance is shown measuring surpluses upward and deficits downward (as negative numbers) on the right scale. It looks as if the budget goes into a bigger deficit when the unemployment rate rises, but not much else is shown by part (a). Part (b) inverts the scale on which the budget is measured. Now a deficit is measured in the up direction and a surplus in the down direction on the right scale. The relationship between the budget deficit and the unemployment rate is now clearer. There is a tendency for the unemployment rate and the budget deficit to move together.

20 percent of all households. The pattern formed by the points in Fig 2.7(b) tells us that as the price of a VCR falls, more people own one.

Figure 2.7(c) is another scatter diagram. Its x-axis measures Canadian unemployment and its y-axis measures inflation. Each point represents the unemployment rate and inflation rate in a particular year. For example, the point marked 82 tells us that in 1982 unemployment was 11 percent and inflation was 9 percent. The pattern formed by the points in Fig. 2.7(c) does not reveal a clear relationship — upward-sloping or downward-sloping — between the two variables. The graph thus informs us, by its lack of a distinct pattern, that there is no systematic relationship between these two variables.

Now that we have seen how we can use graphs in economics to represent economic data and to show the relationship between variables, let us examine how economists use graphs in a more abstract way to construct and analyse economic models.

Figure 2.7 Scatter Diagrams

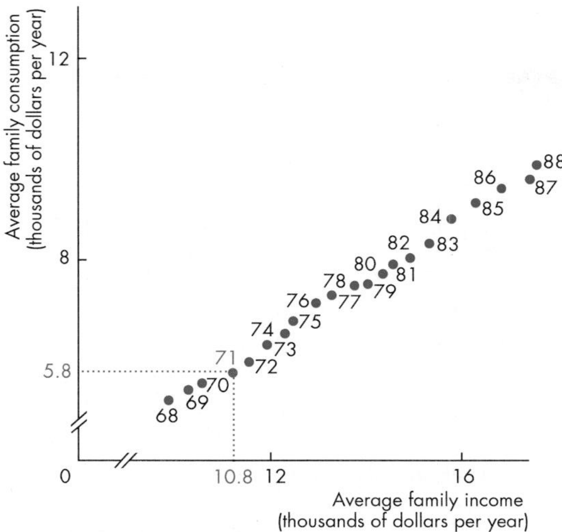

(a) Consumption and income

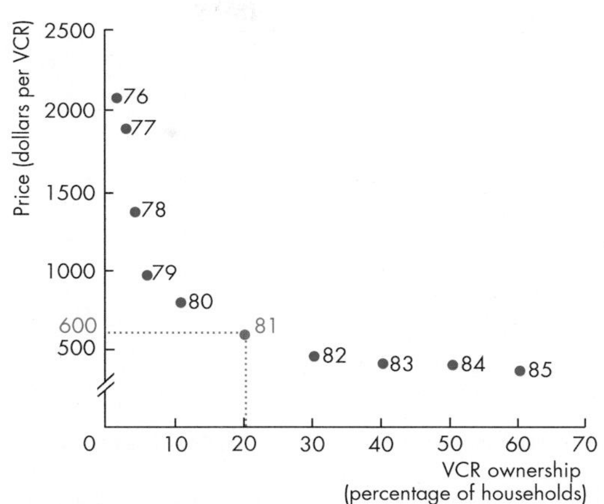

(b) VCR ownership and price

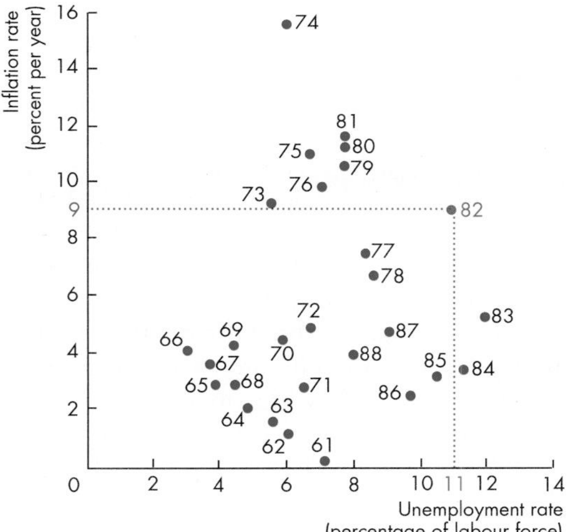

(c) Unemployment and inflation

A scatter diagram shows a relationship between two variables. Each point on these scatter diagrams represents an observation of two variables in a specific year. Part (a) shows that as average family income increases, so does average family consumption. Part (b) shows that as the price of a VCR falls, the number of VCRs owned increases. Part (c) shows that there is no relationship between inflation and unemployment.

Graphs Used in Economic Models

Although you will encounter many different kinds of graphs in economics, there are some patterns that, once you have learned to recognize them, will instantly convey to you the meaning of a graph. There are graphs that show each of the following:

- Variables that go up and down together
- Variables that move in opposite directions
- Variables that are not related to each other at all
- Relationships that have a maximum or a minimum

Let's look at these four cases.

Variables That Go Up and Down Together

Graphs that show the relationship between two variables that move up and down together are shown in Fig. 2.8. The relationship between two variables that

Figure 2.8 Positive Relationships

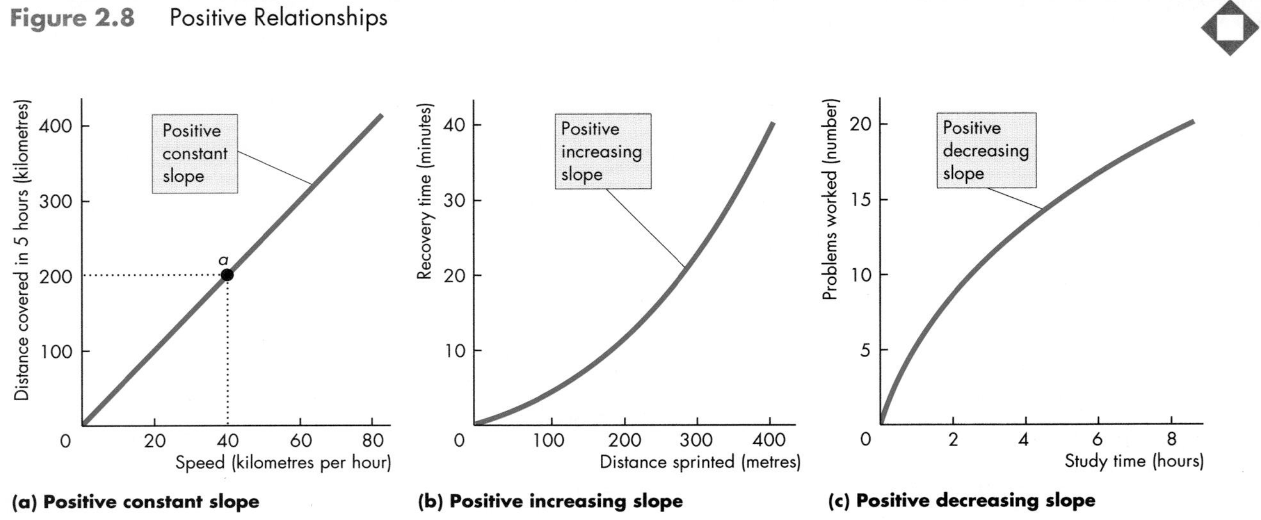

Each part of this figure shows a positive relationship between two variables. That is, as the value of the variable measured on the x-axis increases, so does the value of the variable measured on the y-axis. Part (a) illustrates a linear relationship — a relationship whose slope is constant as we move along the curve. Part (b) illustrates a positive relationship whose slope becomes steeper as we move along the curve away from the origin. It is a positive relationship with an increasing slope. Part (c) shows a positive relationship, whose slope becomes flatter as we move away from the origin. It is a positive relationship with a decreasing slope.

move in the same direction is called a **positive relationship**. Such a relationship is shown by a line that slopes upward.

Figure 2.8(a) shows the relationship between the number of kilometres travelled in 5 hours and speed. For example, the point marked *a* tells us that we will travel 200 kilometres in 5 hours if our speed is 40 kilometres per hour. If we double our speed and travel at 80 kilometres per hour, we will cover a distance of 400 kilometres. The relationship between the number of kilometres travelled in 5 hours and speed is represented by an upward-sloping straight line. A relationship depicted by a straight line is called a **linear relationship**. A linear relationship is one that has a constant slope.

Figure 2.8(b) shows the relationship between distance sprinted and exhaustion (exhaustion being measured by the time it takes the heart rate to return to normal). This relationship is an upward-sloping one depicted by a curved line that starts out with a gentle slope but then becomes steeper.

Figure 2.8(c) shows the relationship between the number of problems worked by a student and the amount of study time. This relationship is illustrated by an upward-sloping curved line that starts out with a steep slope but then becomes more gentle.

The graphs in Fig. 2.8 show three types of upward-sloping lines, one straight and two curved. But they are all called curves. Any line on a graph — no matter whether it is straight or curved — is called a **curve**.

Variables That Move in Opposite Directions

Figure 2.9 shows relationships between variables that move in opposite directions. A relationship between variables that move in opposite directions is called a **negative relationship**.

Figure 2.9(a) shows the relationship between the number of hours available for playing squash and the number of hours for playing tennis when five hours are available for leisure time. One extra hour spent playing tennis means one hour less playing squash and vice versa. This relationship is both negative and linear.

Figure 2.9(b) shows the relationship between the cost per kilometre travelled and the length of a

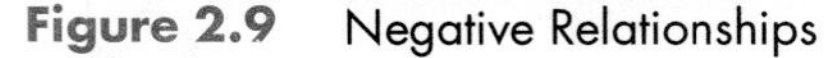

Figure 2.9 Negative Relationships

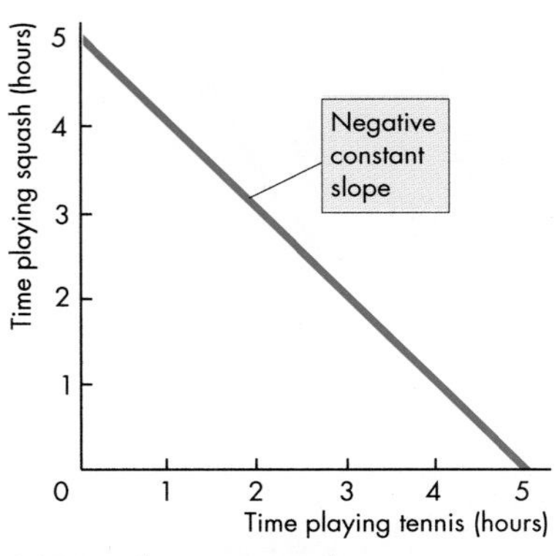

(a) Negative constant slope

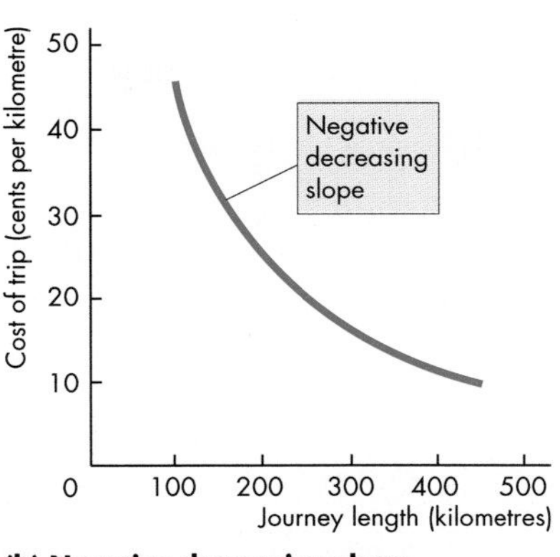

(b) Negative decreasing slope

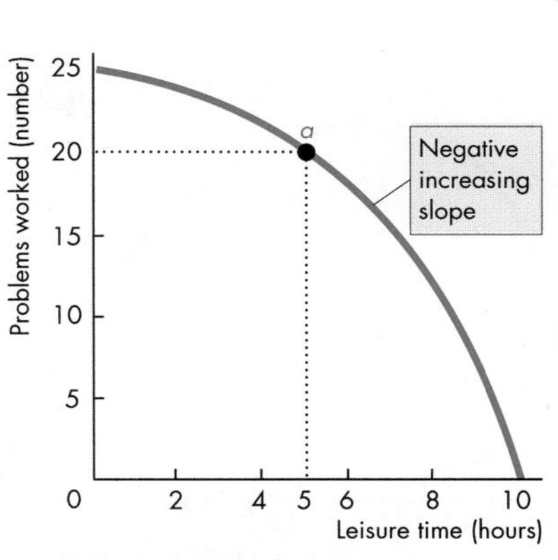

(c) Negative increasing slope

Each part of this figure shows a negative relationship between two variables. Part (a) shows a linear relationship — a relationship whose slope is constant as we travel along the curve. Part (b) shows a negative relationship with a decreasing slope. That is, the slope of the relationship gets less steep as we travel along the curve from left to right. Part (c) shows a negative relationship with an increasing slope. That is, the slope becomes steeper as we travel along the curve from left to right.

journey. The longer the journey, the lower the cost per kilometre. But as the journey length increases, the cost per kilometre falls at a decreasing rate. This feature of the relationship is illustrated by the fact that the curve slopes downward, starting out steep at a short journey length and then becoming flatter as the journey length increases.

Figure 2.9(c) shows the relationship between the amount of leisure time a student takes and the number of problems he or she works. If the student takes no leisure time, 25 problems can be worked in eight hours. If the student takes 5 hours of leisure, only 20 problems can be worked (point *a*). Increasing leisure time beyond 5 hours produces a large reduction in the number of problems worked, and if the student takes 10 hours of leisure a day, no problems are worked. This relationship is a negative one that starts out with a gentle slope at a low number of leisure hours and becomes increasingly steep as leisure hours increase.

Relationships That Have a Maximum and a Minimum

Economics is about optimizing, or doing the best with limited resources. Making the highest possible profit and achieving the lowest possible cost of production are examples of optimizing. Economists make frequent use of graphs depicting relationships that have a maximum or a minimum. Figure 2.10 illustrates such relationships.

Figure 2.10(a) shows the relationship between rainfall and wheat yield. When there is no rainfall, wheat will not grow, so the yield is zero. As the rainfall increases up to 10 days a month, the wheat yield also increases. With 10 rainy days each month, the wheat yield reaches its maximum at 20 bushels per hectare (point *a*). Rain in excess of 10 days a month starts to lower the yield of wheat. If every day is rainy, the wheat suffers from a lack of sunshine and the yield falls back almost to zero. This relationship is one that starts out positive, reaches a maximum, and then becomes negative.

Figure 2.10(b) shows the reverse case — a relationship that begins with a negative slope, falls to a minimum, and then becomes positive. An example of such a relationship is the gasoline cost per kilometre as the speed of travel varies. At low speeds, the car is creeping along in a traffic snarl-up. The number of kilometres per litre is low, so the gasoline cost per kilometre is high. At very high speeds, the car is operated beyond its most efficient rate, and, again, the number of kilometres per litre is low and the

Figure 2.10 Maximum and Minimum Points

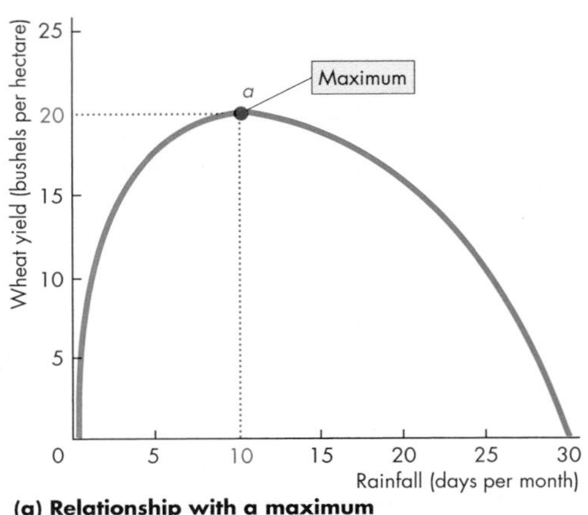

(a) Relationship with a maximum

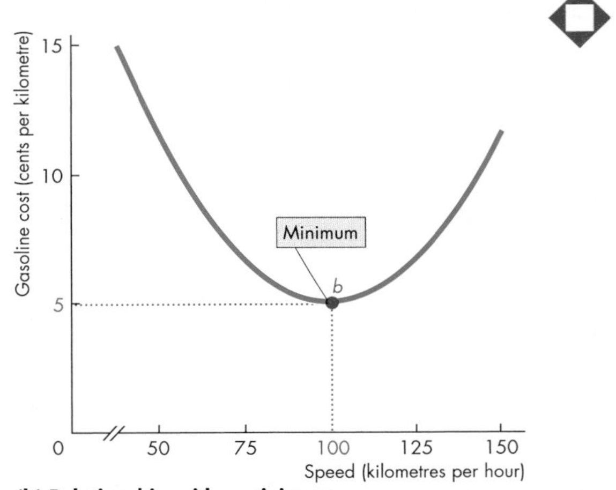

(b) Relationship with a minimum

Part (a) shows a relationship that has a maximum point, *a*. The curve rises at first, reaches its highest point, and then falls. Part (b) shows a relationship with a minimum point, *b*. The curve falls to its minimum and then rises.

gasoline cost per kilometre is high. At a speed of 100 kilometres per hour, the gasoline cost per kilometre travelled is at its minimum (point *b*).

Variables That Are Independent

There are many situations in which one variable is independent of another. No matter what happens to the value of one variable, the other variable remains constant. Sometimes we want to show the independence between two variables in a graph. Figure 2.11 shows two ways of achieving this. In part (a), your grade in economics is shown on the vertical axis against the price of bananas on the horizontal axis. Your grade (75 percent in this example) does not depend on the price of bananas. The absence of a relationship between these two variables is shown by a horizontal straight line. In part (b), the output of French wine is shown on the horizontal axis and the number of rainy days a month in British Columbia is shown on the vertical axis. Again, the output of French wine (15 billion litres a year in this example) does not change when the number of rainy days in British Columbia changes. The absence of a relationship between these two variables is shown by a vertical straight line.

Figures 2.8 through 2.11 illustrate ten different shapes of graphs that we will encounter in economic models. In describing these graphs, we have talked about curves that slope upward or downward and slopes that are steep or gentle. The concept of slope is an important one. Let's spend a little time discussing exactly what we mean by slope.

The Slope of a Relationship

The Definition of Slope

The **slope** of a relationship is the change in the value of the variable measured on the y-axis divided by the change in the value of the variable measured on the x-axis. We use the Greek letter Δ to represent "change in." Thus Δy means the change in the value of the variable on the y-axis and Δx means the change in the value of the variable on the x-axis. The slope of the relationship between x and y is

$$\frac{\Delta y}{\Delta x}.$$

If a large Δy is associated with a small Δx, the slope is large and the curve is steep. If a small Δy is associated with a large Δx, the slope is small and the curve is flat.

Figure 2.11 Variables with No Relationship

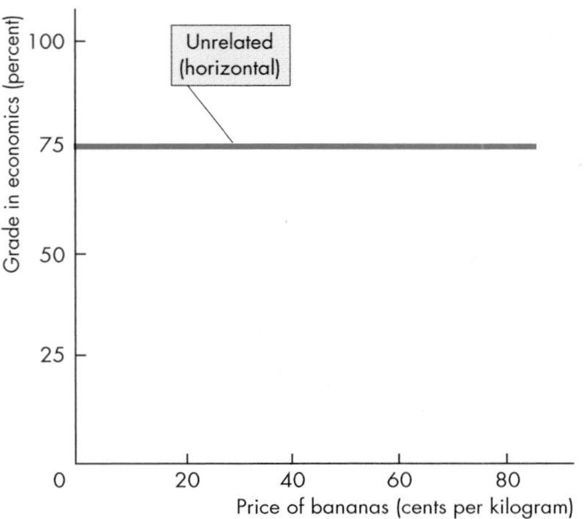

(a) Unrelated: horizontal

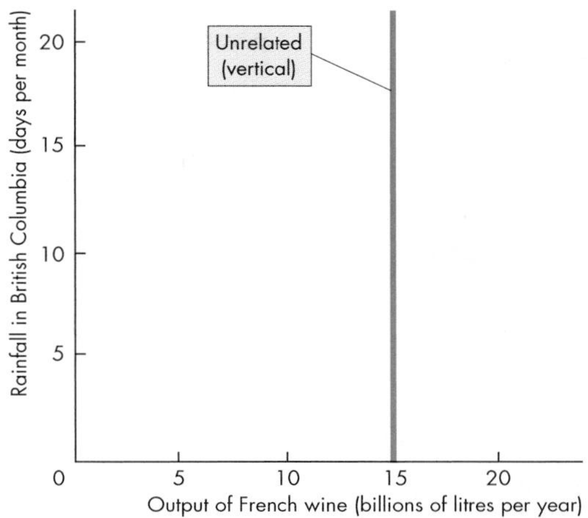

(b) Unrelated: vertical

This figure shows how we can graph two variables that are unrelated to each other. In part (a), a student's grade in economics is plotted at 75 percent regardless of the price of bananas on the *x*-axis. In part (b), the output of the vineyards of France does not vary with the rainfall in British Columbia.

We can make the idea of slope clearer by doing some calculations.

Calculating Slope

A Straight Line The slope of a straight line is the same regardless of where on the line you calculate it. Thus the slope of a straight line is constant. Let's calculate the slopes of the lines in Fig. 2.12. In part (a), when x increases from 2 to 6, y increases from 3 to 6. The change in x is +4 — that is, Δx is +4. The change in y is +3 — that is, Δy is +3. The slope of that line is

$$\frac{\Delta y}{\Delta x} = \frac{3}{4}.$$

In part (b), when x increases from 2 to 6, y decreases from 6 to 3. The change in x is *plus* 4 — that is Δx is +4. The change in y is *minus* 3 — that is Δy is -3. The slope of the curve is

$$\frac{\Delta y}{\Delta x} = \frac{-3}{4}.$$

Notice that the two slopes have the same magnitude ($3/4$), but the slope of the line in Fig 2.12(a) is positive ($+3/+4 = 3/4$), while that in Fig 2.12(b) is negative ($-3/+4 = -3/4$). The slope of a positive relationship is positive; the slope of a negative relationship is negative.

A Curved Line Calculating the slope of a curved line is more difficult. The slope of a curved line is not constant. Its slope depends on where on the line we calculate it. There are two ways to calculate the slope of a curved line: you can calculate the slope at a point on the line, or you can calculate the slope across an arc of the line. Let's look at the two alternatives.

Slope at a point To calculate the slope at a point on a curved line, you need to construct a straight line that has the same slope as the curve at the point in question. Figure 2.13 shows how such a calculation is made. Suppose you want to calculate the slope of the curve at the point marked *a.* Place a ruler on the graph so that it touches point *a* and no other point on the curve and then draw a straight line along the edge of the ruler. Such a straight line is called a tangent.

Figure 2.12 The Slope of a Straight Line

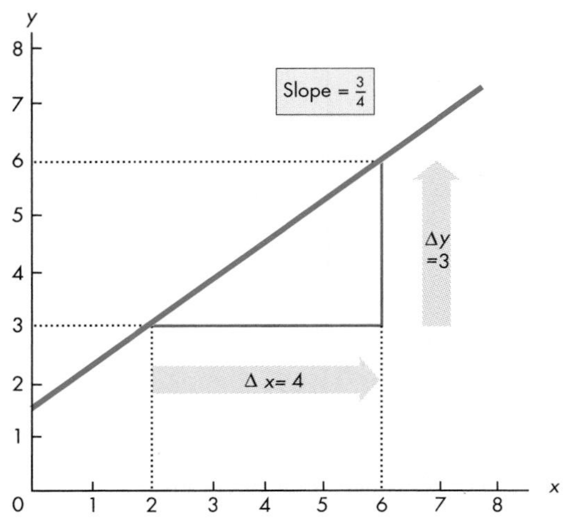

(a) Positive slope

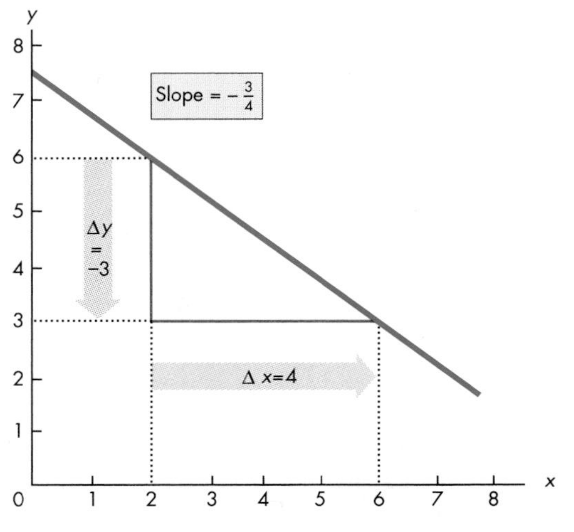

(b) Negative slope

To calculate the slope of a straight line, we divide the change in the value of y by the change in the value of x. Part (a) shows the calculation of a positive slope — where both x and y go up together. When x goes up from 2 to 6, the change in x is 4 — that is, Δx equals 4. That change in x brings about an increase in y from 3 to 6, so that Δy equals 3. The slope ($\Delta y/\Delta x$) equals 3⁄4. Part (b) shows a negative slope (when x goes up, y goes down). When x goes up from 2 to 6, Δx equals 4. That change in x brings about a decrease in y from 6 to 3, so that Δy equals −3. The slope ($\Delta y/\Delta x$) equals −3⁄4.

The straight line in Fig 2.13(a) is such a line. If the ruler touches the curve only at point *a*, then the slope of the curve at point a must be the same as the slope of the edge of the ruler. If the curve and the ruler do not have the same slope, the line along the edge of the ruler will cut the curve instead of just touching it — it will not be a tangent.

Having now found a straight line with the same slope as the curve at point *a*, you can calculate the slope of the curve at point *a* by calculating the slope of the straight line. We already know how to calculate the slope of a straight line, so the task is straightforward. In this case, as x increases from 0 to 8 ($\Delta x = 8$), y decreases from 6 to 0 ($\Delta y = -6$). Therefore the slope of the straight line is

$$\frac{\Delta y}{\Delta x} = \frac{-6}{+8} = \frac{-3}{4}.$$

Thus the slope of the curve at point *a* is – 3⁄4.

Slope across an arc To calculate the slope across an arc of a curve, you need to construct a straight line joining two points on the curve and then calculate the slope of that straight line. Figure 2.13(b) illustrates this method. In this figure, we are looking at the same curve as in Fig. 2.13(a) but instead of calculating the slope at point *a*, we calculate the slope for a change in x from 3 to 5. As x increases from 3 to 5, y decreases from 4 to 2½. The change in y is −1½ ($\Delta y = -1\frac{1}{2}$). The change in x is +2 ($\Delta x = 2$). Therefore the slope of the line is

$$\frac{\Delta y}{\Delta x} = \frac{-1\frac{1}{2}}{2} = \frac{-3}{4}.$$

This calculation gives us the slope of the line between points *b* and *c*. In this particular example, the slope of the arc *bc* is identical to the slope of the curve at point *a* in Fig. 2.13(a). Calculating the slope across an arc does not always work out so neatly. You might have some fun constructing other examples that do not give such an outcome.

Figure 2.13 The Slope of a Curve

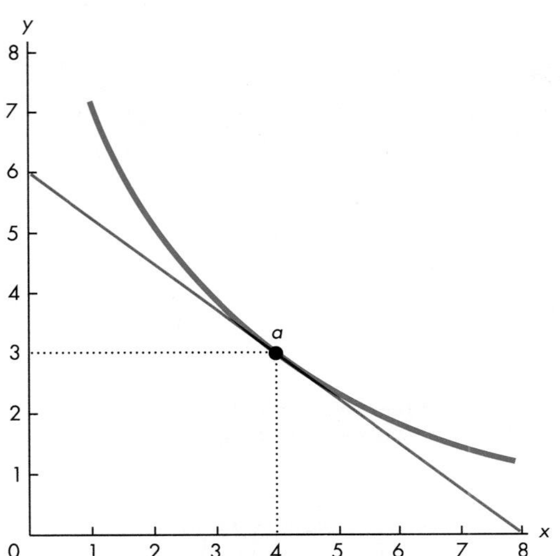

(a) Slope at a point

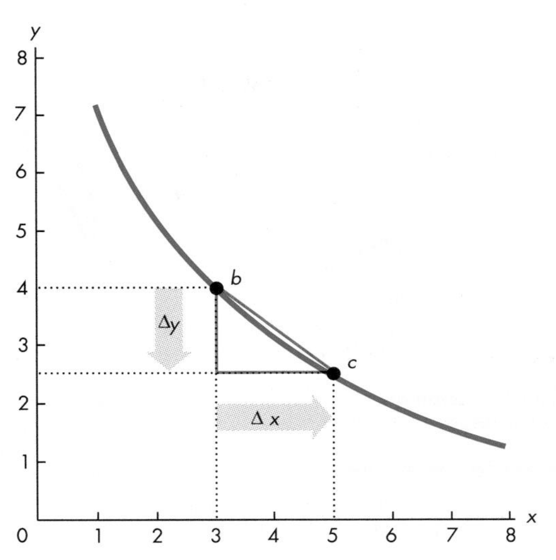

(b) Slope across an arc

The slope of a curve can be calculated either at a point, as in part (a), or across an arc, as in part (b). The slope at a point is calculated by finding the slope of a line that touches the curve at that point — the tangent to the curve at that point. The tangent to point *a* is shown. The slope of that tangent is calculated by dividing the change in *y* by the change in *x*. When *x* increases from 0 to 8, Δx equals 8. That change in *x* is associated with a fall in *y* from 6 to 0, so Δy equals -6. The slope of the line is $-\frac{6}{8}$ or $-\frac{3}{4}$.

To calculate the slope across an arc, we place a straight line across the curve from one point to another and then calculate the slope of that straight line. One such line is that from *b* to *c* in part (b). The slope of the straight line *bc* is calculated by dividing the change in *y* by the change in *x*. In moving from *b* to *c*, *x* goes up by 2, so Δx equals 2, and *y* goes down by $1\frac{1}{2}$, so Δy equals $-1\frac{1}{2}$. The slope of the line *bc* is $-1\frac{1}{2}$ divided by 2, or $-\frac{3}{4}$.

Graphing Relationships Between More Than Two Variables

We have seen that we can graph a single variable as a point on a straight line, and we can graph the relationship between two variables as a point formed by the *x*- and *y*-coordinates in a two-dimensional graph. You may be suspecting that although a two-dimensional graph is informative, most of the things in which you are likely to be interested involve relationships between not just two variables but many.

Examples of relationships between more than two variables abound. For example, consider the relationship between the price of ice cream, the air temperature, and the amount of ice cream eaten. If ice cream is expensive and the temperature is low, people eat much less ice cream than when ice cream is inexpensive and the temperature is high. For any given price of ice cream, the quantity consumed varies with the temperature, and for any given temperature, the quantity of ice cream consumed varies with its price.

Other Things Being Equal

Figure 2.14 illustrates such a situation. The table shows the number of litres of ice cream that will be eaten each day at various temperatures and ice cream prices. How can we graph all these numbers? To graph a relationship that involves more than two variables, we consider what happens if all but two of the variables are held constant. This device is called ceteris paribus. ***Ceteris paribus*** is a Latin phrase that means "other things being equal." For example, in

Figure 2.14 Graphing a Relationship Between Three Variables

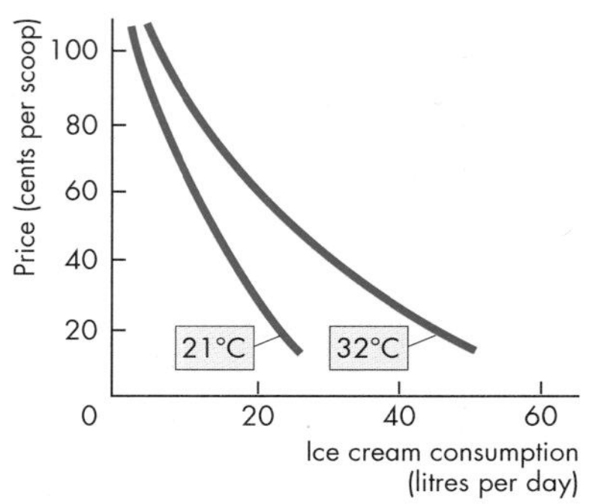

(a) Price and consumption at a given temperature

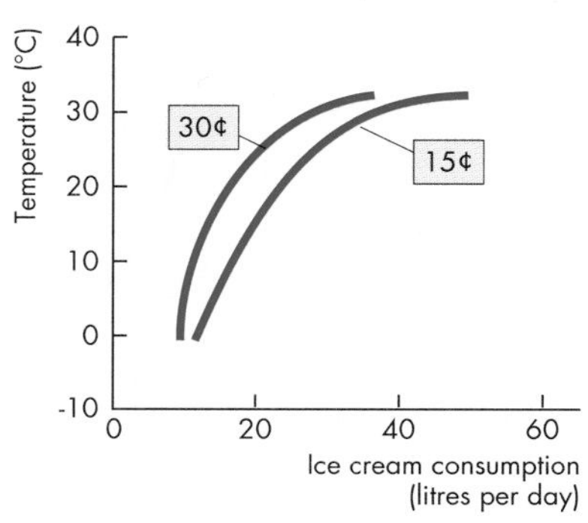

(b) Temperature and consumption at a given price

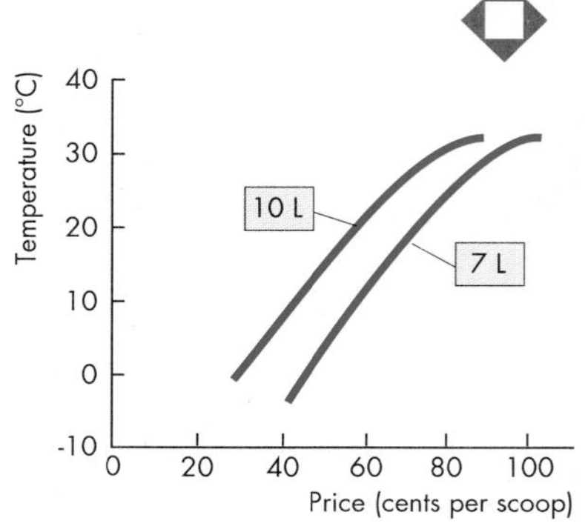

(c) Temperature and price at a given consumption

Price (cents per scoop)	Ice cream consumption (litres per day)			
	-1°C	10°C	21°C	32°C
15	12	18	25	50
30	10	12	18	37
45	7	10	13	27
60	5	7	10	20
75	3	5	7	14
90	2	3	5	10
105	1	2	3	6

The quantity of ice cream consumed (one variable) depends on its price (a second variable) and the air temperature (a third variable). The table provides some hypothetical numbers that tell us how many litres of ice cream are consumed each day at different prices and different temperatures. For example, if the price is 45 cents per scoop and the temperature is 10°C, 10 litres of ice cream will be consumed. In order to graph a relationship between three variables, the value of one variable must be held constant. Part (a) shows the relationship between price and consumption, holding temperature constant. One curve holds temperature constant at 32°C and the other at 21°C. Part (b) shows the relationship between temperature and consumption, holding price constant. One curve holds the price at 30 cents and the other at 15 cents. Part (c) shows the relationship between temperature and price, holding consumption constant. One curve holds consumption constant at 10 litres and the other at 7 litres.

Fig. 2.14(a) you can see what happens to the quantity of ice cream consumed when the price of ice cream varies while the temperature is held constant. The line labelled 21°C shows the relationship between ice cream consumption and the price of ice cream when the temperature stays at 21°C. The numbers used to plot that line are those in the third column of the table in Fig. 2.14. The curve labelled 32°C shows the consumption of ice cream when the price varies and the temperature is 32°C.

Alternatively, we can show the relationship between ice cream consumption and temperature while holding the price of ice cream constant, as is shown in Fig. 2.14(b). The curve labelled 30 cents shows how the consumption of ice cream varies with the temperature when ice cream costs 30 cents, and a second curve shows the relationship when ice cream costs 15 cents. Figure 2.14(c) shows the combinations of temperature and price that result in a constant consumption of ice cream. One curve shows the combination that results in the consumption of 10 litres of ice cream a day, and the other shows the combination that results in the consumption of 7 litres of ice cream a day. A high price and a high temperature lead to the same consumption as a lower price and a lower temperature. For example, 7 litres are consumed at -1°C and 45 cents a scoop and at 21°C and 75 cents a scoop.

■ With what you have now learned about graphs, you can move forward with your study of economics. There are no graphs in this book that are more complicated than those that have been explained here.

SUMMARY

Graphing Data

There are two main types of graphs used to represent economic data: time-series graphs and scatter diagrams. A time-series graph plots the value of one or more economic variables on the vertical axis (y-axis) and time on the horizontal axis (x-axis). A well-constructed time-series graph quickly reveals the level, direction of change, and speed of change of a variable. It also reveals trends. Graphs sometimes mislead, especially when scales are stretched or squeezed to exaggerate or understate a variation.

Scatter diagrams plot the value of one economic variable associated with the value of another. These diagrams reveal whether or not there is a relationship between two variables, and if there is a relationship, its nature. (pp. 29-36)

Graphs Used in Economic Models

Graphs are used in economic models to illustrate positive relationships, negative relationships, relationships that have a maximum or a minimum, and variables that are not related to each other. Examples of these different types of relationships are summarized in Fig. 2.8 through 2.11. (pp. 37-40)

The Slope of a Relationship

The slope of a relationship is calculated as the change in the value of the variable on the y-axis divided by the change in the value of the variable on the x-axis — $\Delta y/\Delta x$. A straight line has a constant slope, but a curved line has a varying slope. To calculate the slope of a curved line, we either calculate the slope at a point or across an arc of the curve. (pp. 40-43)

Graphing Relationships Between More Than Two Variables

To graph a relationship between more than two variables, we hold constant the values of all the variables except two. We then plot the value of one of the variables against the value of another. Holding constant all the variables but two is called the *ceteris paribus* assumption — other things being equal. (pp. 43-44)

KEY ELEMENTS

Key Terms

Axes, 29
Ceteris paribus, 43
Coordinates, 29
Curve, 38
Linear relationship, 38
Negative relationship, 38
Origin, 29
Positive relationship, 38
Scatter diagram, 33
Slope, 40
Time-series graph, 30
Trend, 30
x-axis, 29
x-coordinate, 30
y-axis, 29
y-coordinate, 29

Key Figures 

REVIEW QUESTIONS

1 Why do we use graphs?

2 What are the two scale lines on a graph called?

3 What is the origin on a graph?

4 What do we mean by the y-coordinate and the x-coordinate?

5 What is a time-series graph?

6 List three things that a time-series graph shows quickly and easily.

7 What do we mean by trend?

8 What is a scatter diagram?

9 Sketch some graphs to illustrate:

a) Two variables that move up and down together.

b) Two variables that move in opposite directions.

c) A relationship between two variables that has a maximum.

d) A relationship between two variables that has a minimum.

10 Which of the relationships in question 9 is a positive relationship and which is a negative relationship?

11 What is the definition of the slope of a relationship?

12 What are the two ways of calculating the slope of a curved line?

13 How do we graph relationships between more than two variables?

PROBLEMS

1 The inflation rate in Canada between 1977 and 1989 was as follows:

Year	Inflation rate
1977	6.2
1978	6.0
1979	10.0
1980	10.6
1981	10.8
1982	8.7
1983	5.0
1984	3.1
1985	2.9
1986	2.5
1987	4.3
1988	3.4
1989	5.4

Draw a time-series graph of these data. Then use your graph to answer the following questions:

a) In which year was inflation highest?

b) In which year was inflation lowest?

c) In which years did inflation rise?

d) In which years did inflation fall?

e) In which year did inflation rise or fall the fastest?

f) In which year did inflation rise or fall the slowest?

g) What have been the main trends in inflation?

2 Interest rates on Government of Canada treasury bills between 1977 and 1989 were as follows:

Year	Interest rate
1977	7.4
1978	8.6
1979	11.6
1980	12.8
1981	17.8
1982	13.8
1983	9.3
1984	11.1
1985	9.4
1986	9.0
1987	8.2
1988	9.3
1989	12.1

Use these data together with those in problem 1 to draw a scatter diagram showing the relationship between inflation and the interest rate. Use this diagram to determine whether there is a relationship between inflation and the interest rate and whether it is positive or negative.

3 Use the following information to draw a graph showing the relationship between x and y:

x	0	1	2	3	4	5	6	7	8
y	0	1	4	9	16	25	36	49	64

a) Is the relationship between x and y positive or negative?

b) Does the slope of the relationship rise or fall as the value of x rises?

4 Using the data in problem 3:

a) Calculate the slope of the relationship between x and y when x equals 4.

b) Calculate the slope of the arc when x rises from 3 to 4.

c) Calculate the slope of the arc when x rises from 4 to 5.

d) Calculate the slope of the arc when x rises from 3 to 5.

e) What do you notice that is interesting about your answers to (b), (c), and (d), compared with your answer to (a)?

5 Calculate the slopes of the following two relationships between x and y:

a)

x	0	2	4	6	8	10
y	20	16	12	8	4	0

b)

x	0	2	4	6	8	10
y	0	8	16	24	32	40

6 Draw a graph showing the following relationship between x and y:

x	0	1	2	3	4	5	6	7	8	9
y	0	2	4	6	8	10	8	6	4	2

a) Is the slope positive or negative when x is less than 5?

b) Is the slope positive or negative when x is greater than 5?

c) What is the slope of this relationship when x equals 5?

d) Is y at a maximum or at a minimum when x equals 5?

7 Draw a graph showing the following relationship between x and y:

x	0	1	2	3	4	5	6	7	8	9
y	10	8	6	4	2	0	2	4	6	8

a) Is the slope positive or negative when x is less than 5?

b) Is the slope positive or negative when x is greater than 5?

c) What is the slope of this relationship when x equals 5?

d) Is y at a maximum or at a minimum when x equals 5?

CHAPTER 3

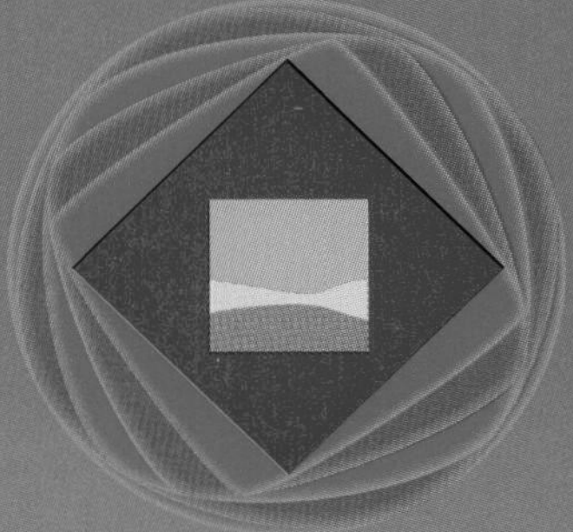

Production, Specialization, and Exchange

After studying this chapter, you will be able to:

- Define the production possibility frontier.
- Calculate opportunity cost.
- Explain why economic growth and technical change do not provide free gifts.
- Explain comparative advantage.
- Explain why people specialize and how they gain from trade.
- Explain why property rights and money have evolved.

Making the Most of It

WE LIVE IN A STYLE that most of our grandparents could not even have imagined. Medicine has cured diseases that terrified them. Most of us live in better and more spacious homes. We eat more, we grow taller, we are even born larger than they were. Our parents are amazed at the matter-of-fact way we handle computers. We casually use products — microwave ovens, graphite tennis rackets, digital watches — that didn't exist in their youth. Economic growth has made us richer than our parents and grandparents. ■ Yet economic growth and technical change, and the wealth they bestow, have not liberated us from scarcity. Why not? Why, despite our incredibly high living standards, do we still have to face costs? Why are there no "free lunches"? ■ We see an enormous amount of specialization and trading in the modern world. Each one of us specializes in one or two particular jobs — lawyer, car maker, homemaker. Countries and regions also specialize — Alberta and Saskatchewan in wheat, Prince Edward Island in potatoes, Oshawa and Windsor in cars, Montreal and Toronto in banking and finance, and Ottawa in computer-related products. We have become so specialized that the output of one farm worker can feed 100 people. Only one in five Canadians works in manufacturing. More than half of all Canadians work in wholesale and retail trade, banking and finance, government and other services. ■ Why do we specialize? How do we benefit from specialization and exchange? How do money and the legal institution of private property extend our ability to specialize and increase production?

■ In this Chapter we will begin to answer this question by making the idea of scarcity more precise. Then we will go on to see how we can measure opportunity cost. We will also see how, when each individual tries to get the most out of scarce resources, specialization and exchange occur. That is, people specialize in doing what they do best and exchange their products with other specialists. We are also going to see why such social arrangements as private property and money exist and how these arrangements spring from people's attempts to make the most of their limited resources.

The Production Possibility Frontier

What do we mean by production? **Production** is the conversion of *land, labour,* and *capital* into goods and services. We defined the factors of production, land, labour, and capital in Chapter 1. Let us briefly recall what they are.

Land is all the gifts of nature. It includes the air, the water, and the land surface, as well as the minerals that lie beneath the surface of the earth. *Labour* is all the muscle-power and brain-power of human beings. The voices and artistry of singers and actors, the strength and coordination of athletes, the daring of astronauts, and the political skill of diplomats, as well as the physical and mental skills of the many millions of people who make cars and cola, gum and glue, wallpaper and watering cans are included in this category. *Capital* is all the goods that have been produced and can now be used in the production of other goods and services. Examples include the Trans-Canada highway system, the Saddledome and the Skydome, dams and power projects, airports and jumbo jets, car production lines, shirt factories and cookie shops. A special kind of capital is called human capital. **Human capital** is the accumulated skill and knowledge of human beings which arise from their training and education.

Goods and services are all the valuable things that people produce. Goods are tangible — cars, spoons, VCRs, and bread. Services are intangible — haircuts, amusement park rides, and telephone calls. There are two types of goods: capital goods and consumption goods. **Capital goods** are goods that can be used many times before they eventually wear out. Examples of capital goods are buildings, plants and equipment, automobiles, and telephones. **Consumption goods** are goods that can be used just once. Examples are dill pickles and toothpaste. **Consumption** is the process of using up goods and services.

The amount that we can produce is limited by our resources and the technologies available for transforming those resources into goods and services. That limit is described by the production possibility frontier. The **production possibility frontier** marks the boundary between production levels that can and cannot be attained. It is important to understand the production possibility frontier in the real world but in order to achieve that goal more easily, we will first study an economy — a model economy — that is simpler than the one in which we live.

A Model Economy

Instead of looking at the real world economy with all its complexity and detail, we will build a model of an economy. The model will have features that are essential to understanding the real economy, but we will ignore most of reality's immense detail. Our model economy will be simpler in three important ways:

1 For now, we will suppose that everything that is produced is also consumed. This simplification means that, in our model, capital resources neither grow nor shrink. Later we will examine what happens if we consume less than we produce and add to capital resources.

2 Although in the real world we use our scarce resources to produce countless goods and services, in our model economy there will be just two goods.

3 Although there are approximately five billion people living on this planet, our model economy will initially have just one person, Jane, who lives on a deserted island and has no dealings with other people.

Let's suppose that all the resources of Jane's island economy can be used to produce two goods, corn and cloth. Assume also that Jane can work 10 hours each day. The amount of corn and cloth that Jane can produce will depend on how many hours she devotes to producing them. Table 3.1 sets out Jane's production possibilities for corn and cloth. If she does no work, she produces nothing. Two hours a day devoted to corn farming produces 6 kilograms of corn a month. Devoting more hours to corn increases the output of corn, but the extra corn obtained from each extra hour of effort declines. The reason for this decline is that Jane has to use increasingly unsuitable land for growing corn. At first, she plants on a lush, flat plain. Eventually, when she has used all the arable land, she has to start planting on the rocky hills and the edge of the beach. The numbers in the second column of Table 3.1 show how the output of corn rises as the hours devoted to cultivating it rise.

To produce cloth, Jane gathers wool from the

Table 3.1 Jane's Production Possibilities

Hours worked per day		Corn grown (kilograms per month)		Cloth produced (metres per month)
0	either	0	or	0
2	either	6	or	1
4	either	11	or	2
6	either	15	or	3
8	either	18	or	4
10	either	20	or	5

If Jane does no work, she produces no corn or cloth. If she works for 2 hours per day and spends the entire amount of time on corn production, she produces 6 kilograms of corn per month. If that same time is used for cloth production, 1 metre of cloth is produced but no corn. The last four rows of the table show the amounts of corn or cloth that can be produced per month as more hours are devoted to each activity.

sheep that live on the island. Some of the sheep are tame, so the first few hours she works produce a large amount of cloth. As she devotes more hours to collecting wool and making cloth, her output rises but, as in the case of corn, each additional hour produces less wool. To make more wool Jane has to find and catch less friendly sheep.

If Jane devotes all her time to growing corn, she can produce 20 kilograms of corn in a month. In that case, however, she cannot produce any cloth. Conversely, if she devotes all her time to making cloth, she can produce 5 metres a month but will have no time left for growing corn. Jane can devote some of her time to corn and some to cloth but not more than 10 hours a day in total. Thus she can spend 2 hours growing corn and 8 hours making cloth or 6 hours on one and 4 hours on the other (or any other combination of hours that add up to 10 hours).

We have defined the production possibility frontier as the boundary between what is feasible and what is not feasible. You can calculate Jane's production possibility frontier by using the information in Table 3.1. These calculations are summarized in the table in Fig. 3.1 and graphed in that figure as Jane's production possibility frontier. To see how we calculated that frontier, let's concentrate first on the table in Fig. 3.1.

Possibility *a* shows Jane devoting no time to cloth and her entire 10-hour working day to corn. In this case, she can produce 20 kilograms of corn a month and no cloth. For possibility *b*, she spends 2 hours a day making cloth and 8 hours growing corn, to produce a total of 18 kilograms of corn and 1 metre of cloth a month. The pattern continues on to possibility *f*, where she devotes 10 hours a day to cloth and no time to corn. The same numbers are plotted in the graph shown in Fig. 3.1. Metres of cloth are measured on the horizontal axis and kilograms of corn on the vertical axis. Points *a*, *b*, *c*, *d*, *e*, and *f* represent the numbers in the corresponding row of the table.

Of course, Jane does not have to work in blocks of 2 hours, as in our example. She can work 1 hour or 1 hour and 10 minutes growing corn and devote the rest of her 10 hours to making cloth. All these other feasible allocations of Jane's 10 hours will result in a series of production possibilities represented by the line that joins points *a*, *b*, *c*, *d*, *e*, and *f*. This line shows Jane's production possibility frontier. She can produce at any point on the frontier or inside it. All these points are attainable. Points outside the frontier are unattainable. To produce at points beyond the frontier, Jane needs more time than she has — more than 10 hours a day. By working 10 hours a day producing corn and cloth, Jane can choose any point she wishes on the frontier. By working less than 10 hours a day, she produces at a point inside the frontier.

On the Frontier Is Best

Jane produces corn and cloth not for the fun of it but so that she can eat and keep warm. The larger the quantities of corn and cloth she produces, the more she can consume. And she prefers a high level of consumption of both goods to a low one. But the best that she can do is to produce (and consume) at a point *on* her production possibility frontier. To see why, consider a point such as *z* in the attainable region. At point *z*, Jane can improve her situation by moving to a point such as *b* or *d* or to a point on the frontier between *b* and *d*, such as point *c*. Jane can have more goods on the frontier than at points inside it. At point *b*, she can consume more corn and no less cloth than at point *z*. At point *d*, she can consume more cloth and no less corn than at point *z*. At point *c*, she can consume more corn and more cloth than at point *z*. Jane will never choose points such as

Figure 3.1 Jane's Production Possibility Frontier

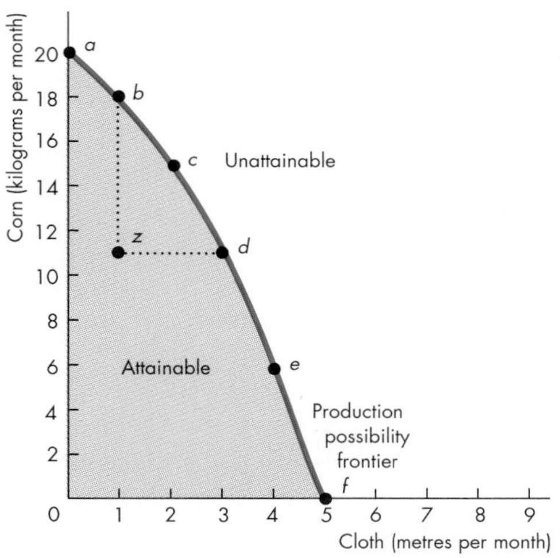

Possibility	Corn (kilograms per month)		Cloth (metres per month)
a	20	and	0
b	18	and	1
c	15	and	2
d	11	and	3
e	6	and	4
f	0	and	5

The table lists six points on Jane's production possibility frontier. Row *e* tells us that if Jane produces 6 kilograms of corn, the maximum cloth production that is possible is 4 metres. These same points are graphed as points *a*, *b*, *c*, *d*, *e*, and *f* in the figure. The line passing through these points is Jane's production possibility frontier, which separates the attainable from the unattainable. The orange attainable area contains all the possible production points. Jane can produce anywhere inside this area or on the production possibility frontier. Points outside the frontier are unattainable. Jane prefers points on the frontier to any point inside. Points between *b* and *d* on the frontier are better than point *z* inside the frontier because they give Jane more of both goods.

z because better choices, such as *b*, *c*, and *d* are available. That is, some point on the frontier is always better than a point inside the frontier.

We have just seen that Jane wants to produce at some point on her production possibility frontier, but she is still faced with the problem of choosing the best point. In choosing between one point and another, Jane is confronted with opportunity costs. At point *c*, for example, she has less cloth and more corn than at point *d*. If she chooses point *d*, she does so because she figures that the extra cloth is worth the corn forgone. Let's go on to explore opportunity cost more closely and see how we can measure it.

Opportunity Cost

We've defined opportunity cost as the best alternative forgone: For a late sleeper, the opportunity cost of attending an early morning class is an hour in bed; for a jogger, it is an hour of exercise. The concept of opportunity cost can be made more precise by using a production possibility frontier such as the one shown in Fig. 3.1. Let's see what that curve tells us.

The Best Alternative Forgone

The production possibility frontier in Fig. 3.1 traces the boundary between attainable and unattainable combinations of corn and cloth. Since there are only two goods, there is no difficulty in working out what is the best alternative forgone. More corn can be grown only by paying the price of having less cloth, and more cloth can be made only by bearing the cost of having less corn. Thus the opportunity cost of producing an additional metre of cloth is the amount of corn forgone, and the opportunity cost of producing an additional kilogram of corn is the amount of cloth forgone. Let's put numerical values on the opportunity costs of corn and cloth.

Measuring Opportunity Cost

We are going to measure opportunity cost by using Jane's production possibility frontier. We will calculate how much cloth she has to give up to get more

Figure 3.2 Jane's Opportunity Cost of Cloth

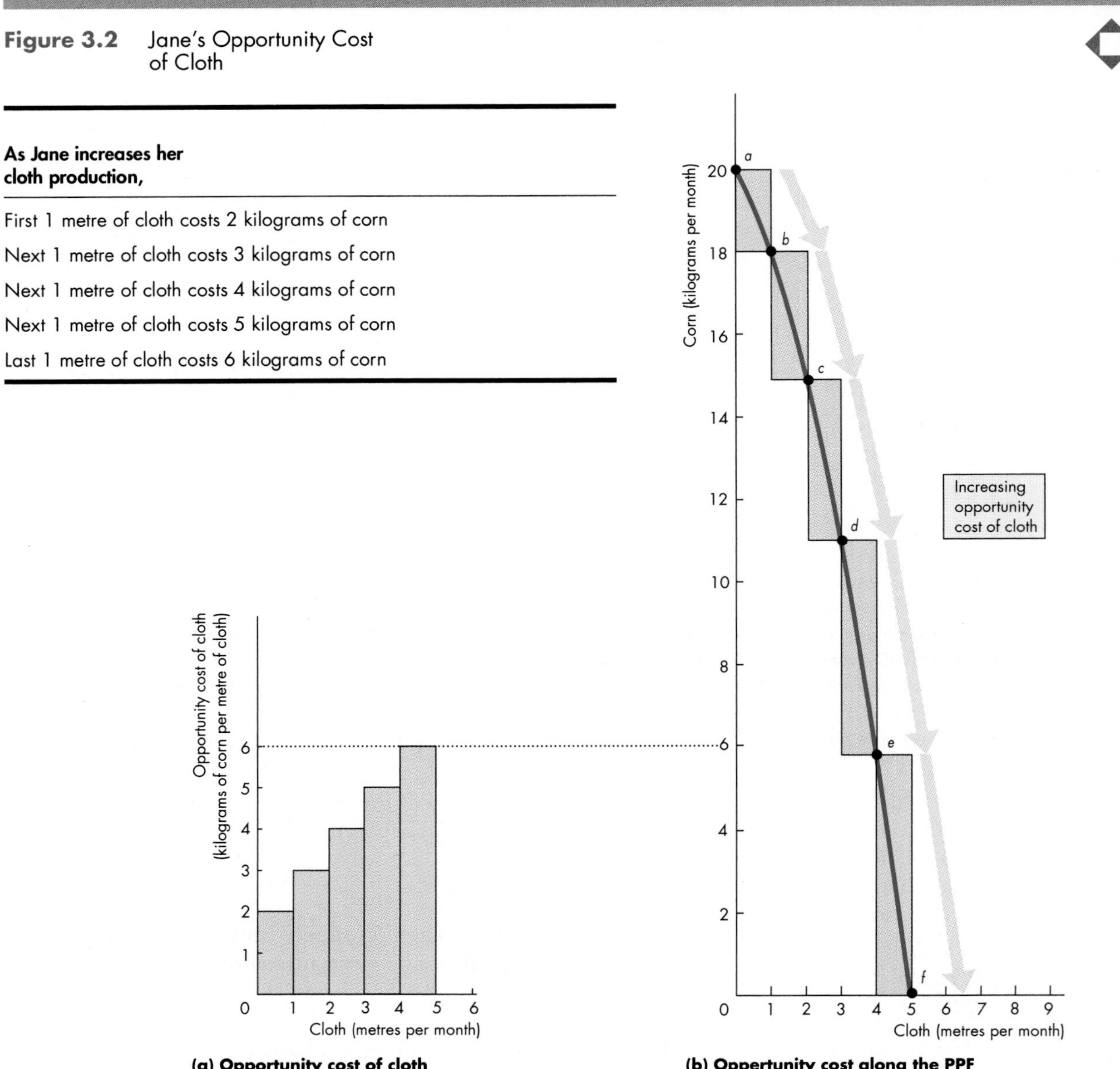

The table records Jane's opportunity cost of cloth. The first metre of cloth costs 2 kilograms of corn. The next metre of cloth costs 3 kilograms of corn. The opportunity cost of cloth rises as Jane produces more cloth, with the last metre of cloth costing 6 kilograms of corn. Part (a) of the figure shows the increasing opportunity cost of cloth, and part (b) shows increasing opportunity cost as Jane moves along her outward-bowed production possibility frontier increasing her production of cloth and decreasing her production of corn.

corn and how much corn she has to give up to get more cloth.

If all Jane's time is used to produce corn, she produces 20 kilograms of corn and no cloth. If she decides to produce 1 metre of cloth, how much corn does she have to give up? You can see the answer in Fig. 3.2. To produce 1 metre of cloth Jane moves from *a* to *b* and gives up 2 kilograms of corn. Thus the opportunity cost of the first metre of cloth is 2 kilograms of corn. If she decides to produce an additional metre of cloth, how much corn does she gives up? The answer can be seen in Fig. 3.2. This time, Jane moves from *b* to *c* and gives up 3 kilograms of corn to produce the second metre of cloth.

These opportunity cost calculations are set out in the table of Fig. 3.2 and illustrated in that figure. The first two rows of the table sets out the opportunity costs that we have just calculated. The table also lists the opportunity costs of moving between points *c*, *d*, *e* and *f* on Jane's production possibility frontier of Fig. 3.1. You may want to work out another example on your own to be sure that you understand what is going on. Calculate Jane's opportunity cost of moving from point *e* to *f*.

Increasing Opportunity Cost

As you can see, opportunity cost varies with the quantity produced. The first metre of cloth costs 2 kilograms of corn. The next metre of cloth costs 3 kilograms of corn. The last metre of cloth costs 6 kilograms of corn. Thus the opportunity cost of cloth increases as Jane produces more cloth. Figure 3.2(a) illustrates the increasing opportunity cost of cloth.

The Shape of the Frontier

Pay special attention to the shape of the production possibility frontier in Fig. 3.1. When a large amount of corn and not much cloth is produced — between points *a* and *b* — the production possibility frontier has a gentle slope. When a large amount of cloth and not much corn is produced — between points *e* and *f* — the frontier is steep. The whole frontier bows outward — it is concave to the origin. These features of the production possibility frontier are a reflection of increasing opportunity cost. You can see the connection between increasing opportunity cost and the shape of the production possibility frontier in Fig. 3.2(b). Between points *a* and *b*, 1 metre of cloth can be obtained by giving up a small amount of corn, so the opportunity cost of cloth is low and the opportunity cost of corn is high. Between points *e* and *f*, a large amount of corn must be given up to produce 1 extra metre of cloth. In this region, the opportunity cost of cloth is high and the opportunity cost of corn is low.

Everything Has an Increasing Opportunity Cost

We've just worked out the opportunity cost of cloth. But what about the oportunity cost of corn? Does it also increase as more of it is produced? You can see the answer in Fig. 3.2. By giving up 1 metre of cloth to produce some corn, Jane moves from *f* to *e* and produces 6 kilograms of corn. Thus the opportunity cost of the first 6 kilograms of corn is 1 metre of cloth. Moving from *e* to *d* you can see that the next 5 kilograms of corn cost 1 metre of cloth. Thus the opportunity cost of corn also increases as Jane makes more corn.

Increasing opportunity cost and the outward bow of the production possibility frontier arise from the fact that scarce resources are not equally useful in all activities. For instance, some of the land on Jane's island is extremely fertile and produces a high crop yield, while other land is rocky and barren. The friendliest sheep on the island, however, prefer the rocky, barren land.

Jane uses the most fertile land for growing corn and gathers wool from the friendliest sheep, which occupy the most barren areas. Only if she wants a larger amount of corn does she try to cultivate relatively barren areas, and only if she wants a larger amount of wool does she pursue less friendly sheep. If she uses all her time to grow corn, she has to use some very unsuitable, low-yielding land. Devoting some time to making cloth, and reducing the time spent growing corn by the same amount, produces a small drop in corn production but a large increase in the output of cloth. Conversely, if Jane uses all her time to make cloth, a small reduction in wool-gathering yields a large increase in corn production.

Production Possibilities in the Real World

Jane's island is dramatically different from the world that we live in. The fundamental lesson it teaches us, however, applies to the real world. The world has a fixed number of people endowed with a given amount of human capital and with a limited amount of time to spend producing goods and services. The world also has a fixed amount of land and capital equipment. Thus there is a limit to the goods and services that can be produced — a boundary between what is attainable and what is not attainable. That boundary is the real-world economy's production possibility frontier. Producing more of any one good requires producing less of some other good or goods.

For example, if the federal government makes available more child-care services, it must at the same time cut the scale of spending on other programs, increase taxes, or borrow more. Higher taxes and more government borrowing mean less money left over for vacations and other consumption goods and services. The cost of more child-care services is less of other goods. On a smaller scale but equally important, each time you decide to rent a video you decide not to use your limited income to buy pizza, popcorn, or some other good. The cost of one more video is one less slice of pizza.

On Jane's island, we saw that the opportunity cost of a good increased as the output of the good increased. Opportunity costs in the real world increase for the same reasons that Jane's opportunity costs increase. Consider, for example, two goods vital to our well being — food and health care. In allocating our scarce resources, we use the most fertile land and the most skillful farmers to produce food. We use the best doctors and the least fertile land for health care. If we shift fertile land and tractors away from farming and ask farmers to do surgery, the production of food drops drastically and the increase in the production of health-care services is small. The opportunity cost of health-care services rises. Similarly, if we shift our resources away from health-care towards farming, we have to use more doctors and nurses as farmers and more hospitals as hydroponic cucumber factories. The drop in health-care services is large, but the increase in food production is small. The opportunity cost of producing more food rises.

This example is extreme and unlikely, but the same considerations apply to any pair of goods that you can imagine: guns and butter; housing for the needy and Cadillacs for the rich; wheelchairs and golf carts; television programs and breakfast cereals. We cannot escape from scarcity and opportunity cost. More of one good always means less of some other good or service, and the more of anything that we produce, the higher is its opportunity cost.

R E V I E W

The production possibility frontier is the boundary between what is attainable and what is unattainable. There is always a point on the frontier that is better than any point inside it. Moving from one point to another on the frontier means having less of one good or service to get more of another. The frontier is bowed outward; equivalently, the opportunity cost of a good increases as more of it is produced. ■

Changing Production Possibilities

Although the production possibility frontier defines the boundary between what is attainable and what is unattainable, that boundary is not static. It is constantly changing. Sometimes the production possibility frontier shifts inward, reducing our production possibilities. For example, droughts or other extreme climatic conditions shift the frontier inward. Sometimes the frontier moves outward. For example, excellent growing and harvest conditions have this effect. Sometimes the frontier shifts outward because we get a new idea. It suddenly occurs to us that there is a better way of doing something that we never before imagined possible — we reinvent the wheel.

Over the years, our production possibilities have undergone enormous expansion. The persistent expansion of our production possibilities is called **economic growth**. As a consequence of economic growth, we can now produce much more than we could 100 years ago and quite a bit more than even 10 years ago. By the mid-1990s, if the same pace of growth continues, our production possibilities will be even greater. Are we not pushing out the frontier of what is possible? And by pushing out the frontier, can we avoid the constraints imposed on us by our limited resources? That is, can we get our free lunch after all?

The Cost of Shifting the Frontier

We are going to discover that although we can and do shift the production possibility frontier outward over time, we cannot increase the pace at which we do so without incurring costs. The faster the pace of economic growth, the less we can consume at the present time. Let's investigate the costs of growth by examining why economies grow.

Two activities generate economic growth: capital accumulation and technological progress. **Capital accumulation** is the growth of capital resources. **Technological progress** is the development of new and better ways of producing goods and services. As a consequence of capital accumulation and technological progress, we have an enormous quantity of cars and airplanes that enable us to produce more transportation than when we only had horses and carriages; we also have satellites that make transcontinental communications possible on a scale much larger than that produced by the earlier cable technology. But accumulating capital and developing new technology is costly. To see why, let's go back to Jane's island economy.

Capital Accumulation and Technological Change

We know that if Jane spends her entire 10 hours of working time each day producing corn and cloth, she will be somewhere on the production possibility frontier illustrated in Fig. 3.1. If Jane produces at a point on the frontier, she cannot devote any time to making tools or equipment that can be used to grow corn or to make cloth. Her production possibilities for next year will be the same as this year. She will have no more capital and no better technology in the future than she has now. To expand her future production, Jane must produce less corn and cloth today and devote resources to making tools or developing better methods of growing corn and making cloth. The cut in her output of corn and cloth today will be the opportunity cost of expanding her production in the future.

Figure 3.3 provides a more concrete example. The table sets out Jane's production possibilities for producing tools as well as corn and cloth. If she devotes all her working hours to corn and cloth production (row *e*), she produces no tools. If she devotes enough time to produce 1 tool per month (row *d*), her corn and cloth production is cut back to 90 percent of its maximum possible level. She can devote still more time to toolmaking, and as she does so, her corn and cloth production falls by successively larger amounts.

The numbers in the table are graphed in the figure. Each point, *a* through *e*, represents a row of the table. Notice the similarity between Figs. 3.3 and 3.1. Each shows a production possibility frontier. In the case of Fig. 3.3, the frontier is that between producing tools and producing current consumption goods — corn and cloth. If Jane produces at point *e* in Fig. 3.3, she produces no tools and remains stuck on the production possibility frontier for corn and cloth shown in Fig. 3.1. If she moves to point *d* in Fig. 3.3, she can produce 1 tool each month. But to do so, Jane must reduce her production of corn and cloth to 90 percent of what she can produce if all her time is devoted to those activities.

By lowering her production of corn and cloth and producing tools, Jane is able to increase her production possibilities. She will have an increasing stock of tools, which she can use to become more productive at growing corn and making cloth. She can even use tools to make better tools. As a consequence, Jane's production possibility frontier shifts outward — she experiences economic growth. The

Figure 3.3 Jane's Tool Production Possibilities 

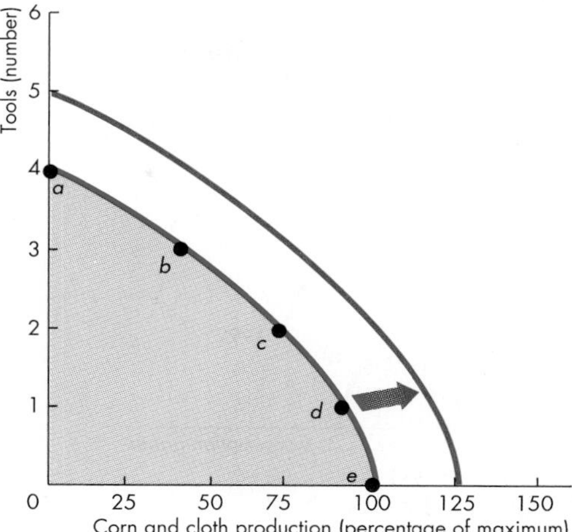

Possibility	Tools (number)	Corn and cloth production (percent)
a	4	0
b	3	40
c	2	70
d	1	90
e	0	100

If Jane devotes all her time to corn and cloth production, she produces no tools (row *e* of the table). As she devotes more time to tool production, she can produce successively smaller amounts of corn and cloth. If all her time is devoted to tool production (possibility *a*), no corn and cloth and 4 tools are produced. In the figure, the curve *abcde* is Jane's production possibility frontier for tools and consumption goods (corn and cloth). If Jane produces at point *e* (producing no tools), her production possibility frontier remains fixed at *abcde*. If she cuts her production of corn and cloth and makes one tool (producing at point *d*), her future production possibility frontier shifts outward as shown in the figure. The more tools and the less corn and cloth Jane produces, the farther out the frontier shifts. The reduced output of corn and cloth is the opportunity cost of increasing future production possibilities.

Figure 3.4 Economic Growth in Canada and Japan

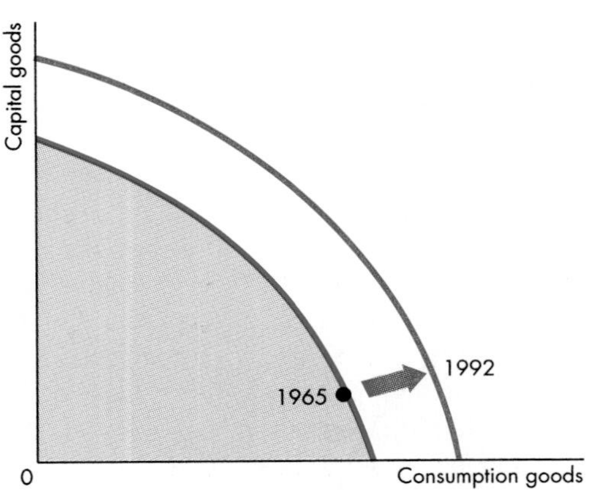

(a) Canada

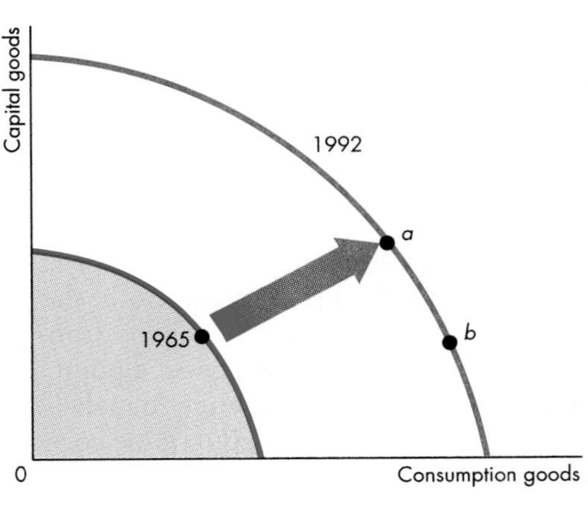

(b) Japan

In 1965, the production possibilities per capita in Canada, part (a), were much larger than those in Japan, part (b). But Japan devoted one-third of its resources to producing capital goods, while Canada devoted only one-fifth. Japan's more rapid increase in capital equipment shifted its production possibility frontier out more quickly than did Canada's. The two countries' production possibilities per capita in 1992 are similar. If Japan produces at point *a* on its 1992 frontier, it will continue to grow more quickly than Canada. If Japan increases consumption and produces at point *b* on its 1992 frontier, its growth rate will slow down to that of Canada.

amount by which the frontier shifts out depends on how much time she devotes to toolmaking. If she devotes no time to making tools, the frontier remains at *abcde*— the original production possibility frontier. If she cuts back on the production of corn and cloth and produces one tool (at point *d*), her frontier moves out by the amount shown in the figure. The less time she devotes to corn and cloth production and the more time to toolmaking, the farther out the frontier shifts. But economic growth is not a free gift for Jane. To make it happen, she has to devote more time to producing tools and less to producing corn and cloth. Economic growth is no magic formula for abolishing scarcity.

The Real World Again

The ideas that we have explored in the setting of Jane's island apply with equal force to our real world economy. If we devote all our resources to producing food, clothing, housing, vacations, and the many other consumer goods that we enjoy and devote no resources to research, development, and the accumulation of capital, we will have no more capital and no better technologies in the future than we have at present. Our production possibilities in the future will be exactly the same as those today. If we are to expand our production possibilities in the future, we must produce fewer consumption goods today. The resources we free up today will enable us to accumulate capital and to develop better technologies for producing consumption goods in the future. The reduction in the output of consumption goods today is the opportunity cost of economic growth.

The recent experience of Canada and Japan provides a striking example of the effects of our choices on the rate of economic growth. In 1965, the production possibilities (per capita) in Canada were much larger than those in Japan (see Fig. 3.4). Canada devoted one-fifth of its resources to producing capital goods and the other four-fifths to producing consumption goods, as illustrated by the point marked 1965 in Fig. 3.4(a). But Japan devoted one-third of its resources to producing capital goods and only two-thirds to producing consumption goods, as illustrated by the point marked 1965 in Fig. 3.4(b). Both countries experienced economic growth, but the growth in Japan was much more rapid than the growth in Canada. Because Japan devoted a bigger fraction of its resources to producing capital goods, its stock of capital equipment grew more quickly than ours, and its production possibilities expanded more quickly. As a result, Japanese production possibilities per capita are now so close to those of Canada that it is hard to say which country has the larger per capita production possibilities. If Japan continues to devote a third of its resources to producing capital goods (at point *a* on its 1992 production possibility frontier), it will continue to grow much more rapidly than Canada and its frontier will move out beyond our own. If Japan increases its production of consumption goods and reduces its production of capital goods (moving to point *b* on its 1992 production possibility frontier), its rate of economic expansion will slow down to that of our own.

R E V I E W

Economic growth results from the accumulation of capital and the development of better technologies. To achieve economic growth, we must incur the cost of fewer goods and services for current consumption. By cutting the current output of consumption goods, we can devote more resources to accumulating capital and to the research and development that lead to technological change — the engines of economic growth. Thus economic growth does not provide a free lunch. It has an opportunity cost — the fall in the current output of consumption goods. ■

Gains From Trade

Different individuals in different situations have different opportunity costs of producing various goods. Such differences give rise to comparative advantage. A person has a **comparative advantage** in producing a particular good if that person can produce the good at a lower opportunity cost than anyone else.

People can produce for themselves all the goods that they consume, or they can concentrate on producing one good (or perhaps a few goods) and then exchange some of their own products for the output of others. Concentrating on the production of only one good or a few goods is called **specialization**. We are going to discover how people can gain by specializing in that good at which they have a comparative advantage and then trading their output with others.

Comparative Advantage: Jane Meets Joe

Let's return again to our island economy. Suppose that Jane has discovered another island that is very close to her own and that, like her island, has just one inhabitant — Joe. Jane and Joe each have access to a simple boat that is adequate for transporting themselves and their goods between the two islands.

Joe's island, too, can produce only corn and cloth, but its terrain differs from that on Jane's island. While Jane's island has a lot of fertile corn-growing land and a small sheep population, Joe's island has little fertile corn-growing land and plenty of hilly land and friendly sheep. This important difference between the two islands means that Joe's production possibility frontier differs from Jane's. Figure 3.5 illustrates these production possibility frontiers. Jane's frontier is labelled "Jane's PPF" and Joe's frontier is labelled "Joe's PPF."

Jane and Joe can be self-sufficient in corn and cloth. **Self-sufficiency** is a state that occurs when each individual consumes only what he or she produces. Suppose that Jane and Joe are each self-sufficient. Jane chooses to produce and consume 3 metres of cloth and 11 kilograms of corn a month. Joe chooses to produce and consume 2 metres of cloth and 7 kilograms of corn a month. These choices are identified on their respective production possibility frontiers in Fig. 3.5. (Each could have chosen any other point on his or her own production possibility frontier.) The total production of corn and cloth is the sum of Jane's and Joe's production: 18 kilograms of corn and 5 metres of cloth a month. Point *n* in the figure represents this total production.

Jane's Comparative Advantage In which of the two goods does Jane have a comparative advantage? We have defined comparative advantage as a situation in which one person's opportunity cost of producing a good is lower than another person's opportunity cost of producing that same good. Jane, then, has a comparative advantage in producing whichever good she produces at a lower opportunity cost than Joe. What is that good?

You can answer the question by looking at the production possibility frontiers for Jane and Joe in Fig. 3.5. At the points at which they are producing and consuming Jane's production possibility frontier is much steeper than Joe's. To produce one more kilogram of corn, Jane gives up less cloth than Joe. Hence, Jane's opportunity cost of a kilogram of corn is lower than Joe's. This means that Jane has a comparative advantage in producing corn.

Joe's Comparative Advantage Joe's comparative advantage is in producing cloth. His production possibility frontier at his consumption point is flatter than Jane's. This means that Joe has to give up less corn to produce one more metre of cloth than Jane does. Joe's opportunity cost of a metre of cloth is lower than Jane's, so Joe has a comparative advantage in cloth production.

Achieving the Gains from Trade

Can Jane and Joe each do better than be self-sufficient? In particular, what happens if Jane and Joe each specialize in producing the good at which he or she has a comparative advantage and then trade with each other?

If Jane, who has a comparative advantage in corn production, puts all her time into growing corn, she can grow 20 kilograms. If Joe, who has a comparative advantage in cloth production, puts all his time into making cloth, he can make 9 metres. By specializing, Jane and Joe together can produce 20 kilograms of corn and 9 metres of cloth (the amount labelled *s* in Fig. 3.5). Point *s* shows the production of 20 kilograms of corn (all produced by Jane) and 9 metres of cloth (all produced by Joe). Clearly, Jane and Joe produce more cloth and corn at point *s* than they were producing at point *n*, when each took care only of his or her own requirements. Point *s* is better than *n* because, between them, Jane and Joe have more of both corn and cloth at point *s* than at point *n*.

To obtain the gains from trade, Jane and Joe must do more than specialize in producing the good at which each has a comparative advantage. They must exchange the fruits of their specialized production. Suppose that Jane and Joe agree to exchange 5 metres of cloth for 8 kilograms of corn. Jane has 20 kilograms of corn and Joe has 9 metres of cloth before any exchange takes place. After the exchange, Joe consumes 8 kilograms of corn and Jane 12 kilograms of corn; Joe consumes 4 metres of cloth and Jane 5 metres of cloth. Compared to the time when they were each self-sufficient, Jane now has 1 extra kilogram of corn and 2 extra metres of cloth, and Joe has 1 extra kilogram of corn and 2 extra metres of cloth. The gains from trade are represented by the increase in consumption of both goods that each person obtains.

Figure 3.5 The Gains from Specialization and Exchange

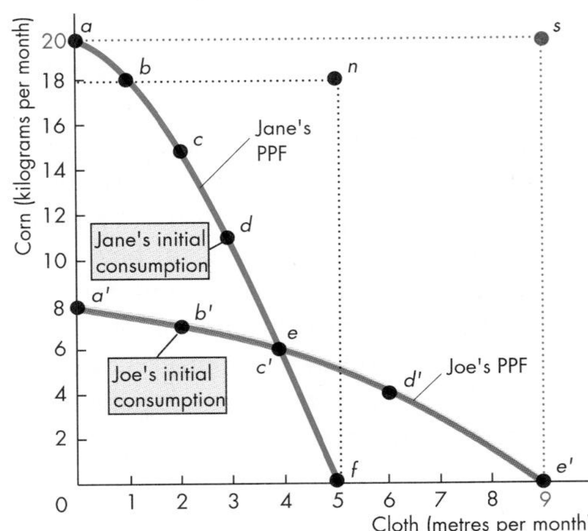

The figure shows Jane's and Joe's production frontiers. Joe's consumption point is 7 kilograms of corn and 2 metres of cloth (point *b'*), and Jane's consumption point is 11 kilograms of corn and 3 metres of cloth (point *d*). Their total production is at point *n*. Joe and Jane can do better by specialization and exchange. Jane has a lower opportunity cost of producing corn than Joe, and Joe has a lower opportunity cost of producing cloth than Jane. Jane has a comparative advantage in corn production. If she specializes in corn production, she produces 20 kilograms of corn and no cloth. Joe has a comparative advantage in cloth production. If he specializes in that activity, he produces 9 metres of cloth and no corn. Total production is then 20 kilograms of corn and 9 metres of cloth (point *s*). If Jane exchanges some of her corn for Joe's cloth and Joe exchanges some of his cloth for Jane's corn, each can consume more corn and cloth than they can in a state of self-sufficiency. If they exchange 8 kilograms of corn for 5 metres of cloth, Jane and Joe can each consume an extra kilogram of corn and 2 extra metres of cloth than when they are self-sufficient. Both Jane and Joe gain from specialization and trade.

Productivity and Absolute Advantage

Productivity is defined as the amount of output produced per unit of input used to produce it. For example, Jane's productivity in making cloth is measured as the amount of cloth she makes per hour of work.

If one person has greater productivity than another in the production of all goods, that person is said to have an **absolute advantage**. In our example, neither Jane nor Joe has an absolute advantage. Jane is more productive than Joe in growing corn, and Joe is more productive than Jane in making cloth.

It is often suggested that people and countries that have an absolute advantage can outcompete others in the production of all goods. For example, it is said that Canada cannot compete with Japan because the Japanese are more productive than we are. This conclusion is wrong, as you are about to discover. To see why, let's look again at Jane and Joe.

Suppose that a volcano engulfs Jane's island, forcing her to search for a new one. And suppose further that this disaster leads to fortune. Jane stumbles on a new island that is much more productive than the original one, enabling her to produce twice as much of either corn or cloth with each hour of her labour. Jane's new production possibilities appear in Table 3.2. Notice that she now has an absolute advantage.

We have already worked out that the gains from trade arise when each person specializes in producing that good with the lower opportunity cost. Joe's opportunity costs remain exactly the same as they were before. What has happened to Jane's opportunity costs now that her time has become twice as productive?

You can work out Jane's opportunity costs by using exactly the same calculation that was used in the table of Fig. 3.2. Start by looking at Jane's opportunity cost of corn. The first 12 kilograms of corn that Jane grows cost her 2 metres of cloth. So the opportunity cost of 1 kilogram of corn is ⅙ of a metre of cloth — the same as Jane's original opportunity cost of corn. If you calculate Jane's opportunity costs of corn for each of her production possibilities *a* through *e*, you will discover that they have remained the same.

Table 3.2 Jane's New Production Possibilities

Possibility	Corn (kilograms per month)		Cloth (metres per month)
a	40	and	0
b	36	and	2
c	30	and	4
d	22	and	6
e	12	and	8
f	0	and	10

Since the opportunity cost of cloth is the inverse of the opportunity cost of corn, Jane's opportunity costs of cloth also have remained unchanged. Let's work through one example. If Jane moves from *a* to *b* to make 2 metres of cloth, she has to reduce her corn production by 4 kilograms — from 40 to 36 kilograms. Thus the first 2 metres of cloth cost 4 kilograms of corn. The cost of 1 metre of cloth is, therefore, 2 kilograms of corn — exactly the same as before.

When Jane becomes twice as productive as she was, each hour of her time produces more output, but her opportunity costs remain the same. One more unit of corn costs the same in terms of cloth forgone as it did previously. Since Jane's opportunity costs have not changed and since Joe's have not changed, Joe continues to have a comparative advantage in producing cloth. Both Jane and Joe can have more of both goods if Jane specializes in corn production and Joe in cloth production.

The key point to recognize is that it is *not* possible for a person having an absolute advantage to have a comparative advantage in everything.

R E V I E W

Gains from trade come from comparative advantage. Unless two individuals have the same opportunity costs, each has a comparative advantage in some activity. Differences in opportunity costs provide the basis for comparative advantage and the gains from specialization and exchange. Even a person with an absolute advantage gains from specialization and exchange. ■

Exchange in the Real World

In the real world, where there are billions of people specializing in millions of different activities, gains from specialization and trade exist, but they are harder to achieve. Trade has to be organized. To organize trade, people have developed rules of conduct and mechanisms for enforcing those rules. One such mechanism is private property rights. Another is money. In the island economy of Jane and Joe, direct exchange of one good with another is feasible. In the real world economy, direct exchange of one good for another would be very cumbersome. To lubricate the wheels of exchange, societies have created money — a medium that enables exchange of goods for money and money for goods. Let's examine these two aspects of exchange in more detail.

Property Rights

Property rights are social arrangements that govern the ownership, use, and disposal of property. **Property** is anything of value that is owned. It includes land and buildings, which are the items we call *property* in ordinary speech. It also includes stocks and bonds, durable goods, plant and equipment. Finally, it includes **intellectual property** — the intangible products of creative efforts. This type of property is protected by copyrights on books, music, and computer programs and by patents on inventions of all kinds.

What if property rights did not exist? What would such a world be like?

A World Without Property Rights Without property rights, people could take possession of whatever they had the strength to obtain for themselves. In such a world, people would have to devote a good deal of their time, energy, and resources to protecting what they had produced or acquired.

In a world without property rights, it would be impossible to reap any gains from specialization and exchange. People would have no incentive to specialize in producing those goods at which they had a comparative advantage. If a person could take the goods of others without giving up something in exchange, there would be no point in specializing in producing something for exchange. Also, the more of a particular good someone produced, the greater the chance that others would simply help themselves to it. In a world without property rights, no one would enjoy the gains from specialization and exchange, and everyone would specialize only in unproductive acts of piracy.

It is to overcome the problems we have just described that property rights have evolved. Let's examine these property rights as they operate to govern economic life in Canada today.

Property Rights in Private Enterprise Capitalism The Canadian economy operates for the most part on the principles of private enterprise capitalism. **Private enterprise** is an economic system that permits individuals to decide on their own economic activities. **Capitalism** is an economic system that permits private individuals to own the capital resources used in production.

Under the property rights in such an economic system, individuals own what they have made, acquired in voluntary exchange with others, or been given. Any attempt to remove the property of someone against that person's will is considered theft, a crime punished by a penalty sufficiently severe to deter most people from becoming thieves.

It is easy to see that property rights based on these ideas make gainful trade possible. People can specialize in producing those goods that, for them, have the least opportunity cost. Some people will specialize in enforcing and maintaining property rights (for example, politicians, judges, and police officers), and all individuals will have the incentive to trade with others, each offering the good in which he or she has a comparative advantage in exchange for the goods produced by others.

Although the Canadian economic system is based on a system of private property with voluntary exchange, property rights even in this country have limits. Let's look at some of them.

Taxes Limit Private Property Rights The most important and pervasive limit on people's rights to private property comes from taxes. All of us have to pay taxes to federal, provincial, and municipal governments. Taxing part of the property that people have created limits their efforts to create more property and reduces their gain from specialized production.

Even though taxes constitute an intrusion into private property rights, the taxes themselves are not arbitrary. Everyone faces the same rules and can calculate the effects of their own actions on the taxes for which they will be liable.

Regulation Limits Private Property Rights Other restrictions on private property rights prohibit certain kinds of voluntary exchange. For example, drug manufacturers cannot place a product on the market without first obtaining approval from a government agency. The government controls or prohibits the sale of many types of chemicals. It also restricts trading in human beings and their component parts — that is, it prohibits the selling of slaves, children, and human organs.

These restrictions on the extent of private property and on the legitimacy of voluntary exchange, though important, do not for the most part seriously impede specialization and gainful trade. Most people take the view that the benefits of regulation — for example, prohibiting the sale of dangerous drugs — far outweigh the costs imposed on the sellers.

Let's now turn to the other social mechanism that permits specialization and exchange — the development of an efficient means of exchange.

Money

We have seen that when well-defined property rights exist, voluntary exchange allows individuals to specialize and to gain through trading their output with each other. In our island economy, we studied only two people and two goods. Exchange in such a situation was a simple matter. In the real world, however, how can billions of people exchange the millions of goods that are the fruits of their specialized labour?

Barter Goods can be simply exchanged for goods. This system is known as **barter**. However, exchanging goods only through the barter system severely limits the amount of trading that can take place. Imagine that you have roosters but you want to get roses. The first thing you do is to look for someone with roses who wants roosters. Economists call this a **double coincidence of wants** — person A wants to sell exactly what person B wants to buy, and person B wants to sell exactly what person A wants to buy. As the term implies, such occurrences are coincidences and do not arise frequently. If you fail to find a rose grower looking for roosters, you must embark on a sequence of barter exchanges. You exchange your roosters for apples, apples for oranges, oranges for plums, plums for pomegranates, pomegranates for pineapples, and then eventually pineapples for roses.

Cumbersome though it is, quite a large amount of barter trade does take place. For example, when British rock star Rod Stewart played in Budapest, Hungary, in August 1986, he received part of his $30,000 compensation in Hungarian sound equipment, electrical cable, and the use of a forklift truck. Hairdressers in Warsaw, Poland, obtain their barbershop equipment from England in exchange for hair clippings that they supply to London wigmakers.

Although barter exchange does occur, a better alternative has been invented — an alternative that we use for most of our trading activity.

Monetary Exchange An alternative to barter is **monetary exchange** — a system in which some commodity or token serves as the medium of exchange. A **medium of exchange** is anything that is generally acceptable in exchange for goods and services. **Money** is a medium of exchange — something that can be passed on to others in exchange for goods and services. In a monetary exchange system, people exchange money for goods and services (including the labour services of others) and exchange goods and services (including their own labour services) for money, but they do not directly exchange goods and services for other goods and services. Metals such as gold, silver, and copper have long served as money, most commonly, by being stamped as coins. Primitive societies have traditionally used various commodities, such as sea shells, as money. Prisoners of war in German camps in World War II used cigarettes as money. Even in recent times in Bucharest, Romania, people have used cigarettes as money (see Reading Between the Lines pp. 64-65). Using cigarettes as a medium of exchange should not be confused with barter. Under barter, the apple farmer exchanges apples for the services of the mechanic who fixes his tractor; the mechanic exchanges the apples that he has received for meat; the butcher exchanges the apples that he has received for dinner in a packed restaurant; the maitre d' uses the apples to pay his doctor; and the doctor eats the apples — if they have not, by now, gone off! When cigarettes are used as money they circulate as the medium of exchange.

In modern societies, governments provide paper money. The banking system also provides money in the form of chequing accounts. Chequing accounts can be used for settling debts simply by writing an instruction — writing a cheque — to the bank requesting that funds be transferred to another chequing account. Electronic links between bank accounts, now becoming more widespread, enable direct transfers between different accounts without writing any cheques.

■ You have now begun to see how economists go about the job of trying to answer some important questions. The simple fact of scarcity and the associated concept of opportunity cost allow us to understand why people specialize, why they trade with each other, why they have social conventions that define and enforce private property rights, and why they use money. One simple idea — scarcity and its direct implication, opportunity cost — explains so much!

Overcoming Obstacles To The Gains From Trade

In Romania, smoking a Kent cigarette is like burning money

It isn't true that Romania, a hard-core Communist country, doesn't operate on the market principle. It does. Call it the farmers' market principle, and this is how it works:

As dawn breaks, a crowing rooster on sale at the downtown market signals the opening of an intense round of barter trading. Apples will get you peppers. Cauliflower will get you beets. Turnips will get you garlic. And Kent cigarettes will get you everything.

"Psssst. Mister. With the Kents," whispers a young farmer rushing from behind his fruit and vegetable stand to pursue someone who has just flashed a pack of Kents. Never mind the line of customers at the stand. They can wait; they have only *lei*, the official Romanian currency. The other guy has Kents.

"You sell?" asks the farmer, now being joined by four fellow farmers. He presents his left palm and begins writing on it. "Twenty-five," he writes. That is 25 *lei*, or about $2.20, for one pack of Kents. The man with the Kents sells two packs for 50 *lei* and inquires about the apples on sale.

"You want apples?" asks the farmer. He pulls out a bag hidden at the bottom of the pile. These aren't the yellow apples for the regular customers—the ones with *lei*. These are red apples for the man with the Kents.

Under the farmers' market principle, the fruit and vegetable farmer perhaps will trade away his Kents to get his tractor fixed. The mechanic will use the Kents to get a rare and relatively good cut of meat at the butcher shop. The butcher will pass on the Kents to get a table at a packed restaurant. The maitre d' will use the Kents to pay his doctor. The doctor will flash the Kents at the farmers' market to get some attention. And some farmer, writing on his hand, will come running.

"In Romania, Kents are the ultimate affirmation of the market theory," says a Western diplomat here. "You've heard of the gold standard. Well this is the Kent standard. Everyone in this country wants Kents. And only Kents. Winston, Marlboro, Pall Mall won't do."

Want to be a big shot in Romania? Flash a pack of Kents. Want a taxi? Wave some Kents. (With the distinctive gold box used for the European Kents, they can be spotted at surprising distances.) Want to get past a troublesome passport officer at the airport? A couple of packs of Kents will do. Kents will open most every door in this country, including the door to the outside world.

The Wall Street Journal,
January 3, 1986
By Roger Thurow

The Essence of the Story

- In Romania, people buy and sell goods in three ways:
  - By barter—exchanging apples for peppers and cauliflower for beets
  - By using their official currency—giving and receiving lei in exchange for goods and services
  - By using Kents—giving and receiving packs of Kent cigarettes in exchange for goods and services
- People offering Kents get a better deal than people offering lei. Kents circulate as a medium of exchange:
  - The "man with the Kents" buys apples.
  - The farmer uses Kents to get his tractor fixed.
  - The mechanic uses Kents to buy meat.
  - The butcher uses Kents at a restaurant.
  - The head waiter uses Kents to get medical treatment.
  - The doctor uses Kents to buy apples—and so on.
- Kents thus allow people to undertake a wide variety of trades (or exchanges).

Background and Analysis

- Romania is a socialist country in Eastern Europe. Private property rights are restricted and the government controls most aspects of economic life. Some examples of what the government dictates:
  - What people may produce
  - The quantities that may be produced
  - The prices at which goods may be sold
- Romanians specialize in producing the things at which they have a comparative advantage. If they sell their output at the prices fixed by the government, they often receive less than the opportunity cost of production.

  For this reason, people try to evade the government's controlled prices by direct barter or by using Kent cigarettes as money. Because people widely accept Kents as a means of payment, these cigarettes have come to serve as a medium of exchange—as money.

Conclusion

- The people of Romania have invented the social contract of using Kents as money. By so doing, they have lessened the severity of restricted property rights and removed, at least partly, a major obstacle to achieving the gains from specialization and exchange.

SUMMARY

The Production Possibility Frontier

The production possibility frontier is the boundary between what is attainable and what is not attainable. Production can take place at any point inside or on the production possibility frontier. But it is not possible to produce outside the frontier. There is always a point on the production possibility frontier that is better than a point inside it. (pp. 51-53)

Opportunity Cost

The opportunity cost of any action is the best alternative forgone. The opportunity cost of acquiring one good is equivalent to the amount of another good that must be given up. The opportunity cost of a good increases as the quantity of it produced increases. (pp. 53-56)

Changing Production Possibilities

Although the production possibility frontier marks the boundary between the attainable and the unattainable, that boundary does not remain fixed. It changes, partly because of natural forces (changes in climate and the accumulation of ideas about better ways of producing) and partly because of the choices we make. If we use some of today's resources for producing capital goods and for research and development, we will be able to produce more goods and services in the future. The economy will grow. But growth cannot take place without incurring costs. The opportunity cost of consuming more goods and services in the future is fewer goods and services today. (pp. 56-59)

Gains From Trade

When people have different opportunity costs, they can gain from specialization and exchange. Each person specializes in producing the good for which his or her opportunity cost is lower than everyone else's — the good in which he or she has a comparative advantage. They then exchange part of their output with each other. As a result, everyone's consumption increases. (pp. 59-61)

Exchange in the Real World

Property rights and a system of monetary exchange enable people to specialize, exchanging their labour for money and their money for goods, thereby reaping the gains from trade. (pp. 61-63)

KEY ELEMENTS

Key Terms

Key Figures 

REVIEW QUESTIONS

1 How does the production possibility curve illustrate scarcity?

2 How does the production possibility curve illustrate opportunity cost?

3 Explain what shifts the production possibility frontier outward and what shifts it inward.

4 Explain how our choices influence economic growth. What is the cost of economic growth?

5 Why does it pay people to specialize and trade with each other?

6 What are the gains from trade between individuals? How do these gains arise?

7 Why do social contracts such as property rights and money become necessary?

8 Why is monetary exchange more efficient than barter?

PROBLEMS

1 Suppose that a change in the weather conditions on Jane's island makes the corn yields much higher. This enables Jane to produce the following amounts of corn:

Hours worked per day	Corn (kilograms per month)
0	0
2	60
4	100
6	120
8	130
10	140
12	150

Her cloth production possibilities are the same as those that appeared in Table 3.1.

a) What are five points on Jane's new production possibility frontier?

b) What are Jane's opportunity costs of corn and cloth? List them at each of the five levels of output.

c) Compare Jane's opportunity cost of corn with that in the table of Fig. 3.2.

d) Has her opportunity cost of corn gone up, down, or remained the same? Explain why.

2 Suppose that Joe has the following production possibilities:

Corn (kilograms per month)		Cloth (metres per month)
6	and	0.0
5	and	0.5
4	and	1.0
3	and	1.5
2	and	2.0
1	and	2.5
0	and	3.0

Jane has the following production possibilities:

Corn (kilograms per month)		Cloth (metres per month)
3.0	and	0
2.5	and	1
2.0	and	2
1.5	and	3
1.0	and	4
0.5	and	5
0.0	and	6

Find the maximum quantity of corn and cloth that Jane and Joe can produce if each specializes in the activity at which he or she has the lower opportunity cost.

3 Suppose that Jane has become twice as productive as in problem 2, so she can now produce the following quantities:

Corn (kilograms per month)		Cloth (metres per month)
6	and	0
5	and	2
4	and	4
3	and	6
2	and	8
1	and	10
0	and	12

a) Show the effect of Jane's increased productivity on her production possibility frontier.

b) Now that Jane is twice as productive as before, will it still pay her to specialize and trade with Joe? Explain why or why not.

c) Will it still pay Joe to trade with Jane? Explain why or why not.

CHAPTER 4

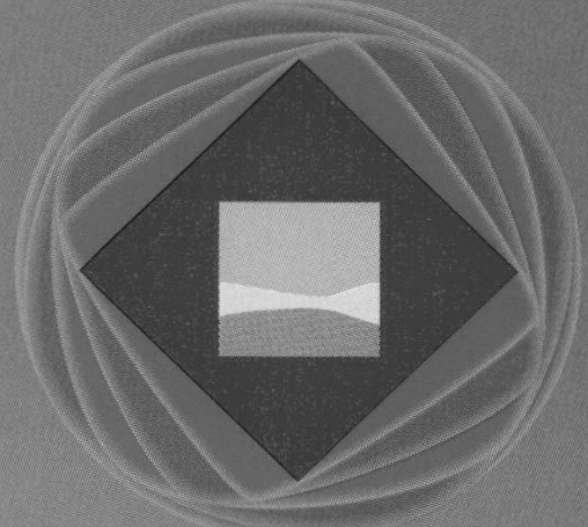

Demand and Supply

After studying this chapter, you will be able to:

- Explain how prices are determined.
- Explain why some prices rise, some fall, and some fluctuate.
- Explain how quantities bought and sold are determined.
- Construct a demand schedule and a demand curve.
- Construct a supply schedule and a supply curve.
- Make predictions about price changes using the demand and supply model.

Slide, Rocket, And Rollercoaster

RIDES AT CANADA'S WONDERLAND? No. Commonly used descriptions of the behaviour of prices. ■ There are lots of examples of price slides. One particular example is probably very familiar to you. In 1979, Sony began to market a pocket-sized cassette player that delivered its sound through tiny earphones. Sony named its new product the Walkman and gave it a price tag of about $300 — more than $500 in today's money. Today Sony has been joined by many other producers of Walkman clones and you can buy a Walkman (or its equivalent) that's even better than the 1979 prototype for less than one-tenth of the original price. During the time that the Walkman has been with us, the quantity bought has increased steadily each year. Why has there been a long and steady slide in the price of the Walkman? Why hasn't the increase in the quantity bought kept its price high? ■ Rocketing prices are also a familiar phenomenon. An important recent example is that of rents paid for apartments and houses, especially in central locations in big cities. Large increases in rents and house prices have not deterred people from living in the centres of cities — on the contrary, their numbers have increased slightly in recent years. Why do people continue to seek housing in city centres when rents have rocketed so sharply? ■ There are lots of price rollercoasters — cases in which prices rise or fall from season to season or year to year. Prices of coffee, strawberries, and many other agricultural commodities fit this pattern. Why does the price of coffee fluctuate even when people's taste for coffee hardly changes at all? ■ Though amusement park rides provide a vivid description of the behaviour of prices, many of the goods that we buy have remarkably steady prices. The audiocassette tapes that we play in a Walkman are an example. The price of a tape has barely changed over the past ten years. Nevertheless, the number of tapes bought has risen steadily year after year. Why do firms sell more and more tapes, even though they're not able to get higher prices for them, and why do people willingly buy more tapes, even though their price is no lower than it was a decade ago?

■ We will discover the answers to these and similar questions by studying demand and supply. We are first going to discover what determines the demand for different goods and the supply of them. Then we are going to discover how demand and supply together determine price. This powerful theory enables us to analyse many important economic events that affect our lives and even to make predictions about future prices.

Demand

The **quantity demanded** of a good or service is the amount that consumers plan to buy in a given period of time at a particular price. Demands are different from wants. **Wants** are the unlimited desires or wishes that people have for goods and services. How many times have you thought that you would like something "if only you could afford it" or "if it weren't so expensive"? Scarcity guarantees that many of our wants will never be satisfied. Demand reflects a decision about which wants to satisfy. If you demand something, then you've made a plan to buy it.

The quantity demanded is not necessarily the same amount as the quantity actually bought. The quantity that people actually buy and sell is called the **quantity traded**. Sometimes the quantity demanded is greater than the amount of goods available, so the quantity traded is less than the quantity demanded.

The quantity demanded is measured as an amount per unit of time. For example, suppose a person consumes one cup of coffee per day. The quantity of coffee demanded by that person can be expressed as 1 cup per day or 7 cups a week or 365 cups a year. Without a time dimension, we cannot tell whether a particular quantity demanded is large or small.

What Determines the Quantity Demanded?

The amount that consumers plan to buy of any particular good or service depends on many factors. Among the more important ones are:

- The price of the good
- The prices of other goods
- Income
- Population
- Preferences

The theory of demand and supply makes predictions about the prices at which goods are traded and the quantities bought and sold. Our first focus, therefore, is on the relationship between the quantity demanded and the price of a good. To study this relationship, we hold constant all other influences on consumers' planned purchases. We can then ask: how does the quantity demanded of the good vary as its price varies?

The Law of Demand

The law of demand states:

Other things being equal, the higher the price of a good, the lower is the quantity demanded.

Why does a higher price reduce the quantity demanded? The answer is that each good can usually be replaced by some other good. As the price of a good climbs higher, people buy less of that good and more of some substitute that serves almost as well.

Let's consider an example — blank audiocassette tapes, which we'll refer to as "tapes." Many different goods provide a service similar to that of a tape; for example, records, compact discs, prerecorded tapes, radio and television broadcasts, and live concerts. Tapes sell for about $3 each. If the price of a tape doubles to $6 while the prices of all the other goods remain constant, the quantity of tapes demanded will fall dramatically. People will buy more records and prerecorded tapes and fewer blank tapes. If the price of a tape falls to $1 while the prices of all the other goods stay constant, the quantity of tapes demanded will rise and the quantity of records, compact discs, and prerecorded tapes demanded will fall dramatically.

Demand Schedule and Demand Curve

A **demand schedule** lists the quantity demanded at each different price, when all other influences on consumers' planned purchases — such as the prices of other goods, income, population, and preferences — are held constant.

The table in Fig. 4.1 sets out a demand schedule for tapes. For example, if the price of a tape is $1, the quantity demanded is 9 million tapes a week. If the price of a tape is $5, the quantity demanded is 2 million tapes a week. The other rows of the table show us the quantities demanded at prices between $2 and $4.

A demand schedule can be illustrated by drawing a demand curve. A **demand curve** graphs the relationship between the quantity demanded of a good and its price, holding constant all other influences on consumers' planned purchases. The graph in Fig. 4.1 illustrates the demand curve for tapes. Conventionally, the quantity demanded is always measured on the horizontal axis and the price is measured on the vertical axis. The points on the demand curve labelled *a* through *e* represent the rows of the demand schedule. For example, point *a* on the graph represents a quantity demanded of 9 million tapes a week at a price of $1 a tape.

The term **demand** refers to the entire relationship between the quantity demanded and the price of a good. The demand for tapes is described by both the demand schedule and the demand curve in Fig. 4.1.

Figure 4.1 The Demand Schedule and the Demand Curve

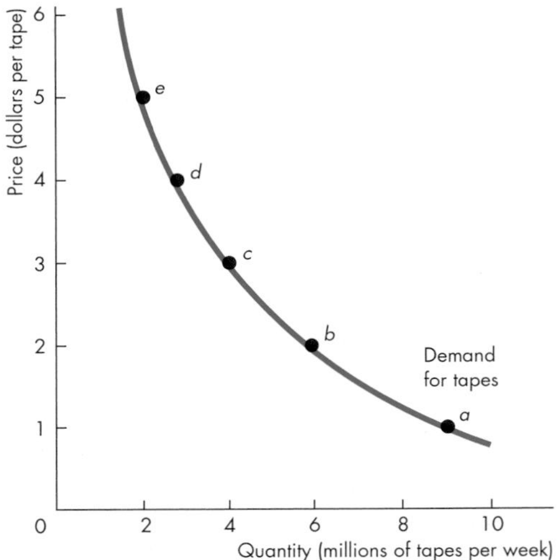

	Price (dollars per tape)	Quantity (millions of tapes per week)
a	1	9
b	2	6
c	3	4
d	4	3
e	5	2

The table shows a demand schedule listing the quantity of tapes demanded at each price if all other influences on buyers' plans are held constant. At a price of $1 per tape, 9 million tapes per week are demanded; at a price of $3 per tape, 4 million tapes per week are demanded. The demand curve shows the relationship between quantity demanded and price, holding everything else constant. The demand curve slopes downward: as price decreases, the quantity demanded increases. The demand curve can be read two ways. For a given price, it tells us the quantity that people plan to buy. For example, at a price of $3 per tape, the quantity demanded is 4 million tapes per week. For a given quantity, the demand curve tells us the maximum price that consumers are willing to pay for the last tape bought. For example, the maximum price that consumers will pay for the 6 millionth tape is $2.

Willingness to Pay

There is another way of looking at the demand curve: it shows the highest price that people are willing to pay for the last unit bought. If a large quantity is available, that price is low, but if only a small quantity is available, that price is high. For example, if 9 million tapes are available each week, the highest price that consumers are willing to pay for the 9 millionth tape is $1. But if only 2 million tapes are available each week, consumers are willing to pay $5 for the last tape available.

This view of the demand curve may become clearer if you think about your own demand for tapes. If you are given a list of possible prices of tapes, you can write down alongside each price your planned weekly purchase of tapes. On the other hand, if you are told that there is just one tape available each week, you can say how much you are willing to pay for it. If you are then told that there is one more tape available, you can say the maximum price that you are willing to pay for that second tape. This process can continue, — you are told that there is one more tape available and you say how much you are willing to pay for each extra tape. The schedule of prices and quantities arrived at is your demand schedule.

A Change in Demand

To construct a demand schedule and demand curve, we hold constant all other influences on consumers' buying plans. But what are the effects of each of those other influences?

1. Prices of Other Goods. The quantity of tapes that consumers plan to buy does not depend only on the price of tapes. It also depends in part on the prices of other relevant goods. These other goods fall into two categories: substitutes and complements.

A **substitute** is a good that can be used in place of another good. For example, a bus ride substitutes for a train ride; a hamburger substitutes for a hot dog; a pear substitutes for an apple. As we have seen, tapes have many substitutes — records, prerecorded tapes, compact discs, radio and television broadcasts, and live concerts. If the price of one of these substitutes increases, people economize on its use and buy more tapes. For example, if the price of records doubles, fewer records are bought and the demand for tapes increases — there is much more taping of other people's records. Conversely, if the price of one of these substitutes decreases, people use the now cheaper good in larger quantities and buy fewer tapes. For example, if the price of prerecorded tapes decreases, people buy more prerecorded tapes and make fewer of their own tapes — the demand for blank tapes falls.

The effects of a change in the price of a substitute occur no matter what the price of a tape. Whether tapes have a high or a low price, a change in the price of a substitute encourages people to make the substitutions that we've just described. As a consequence, a change in the price of a substitute changes the entire demand schedule for tapes and shifts the demand curve.

A **complement** is a good consumed in conjunction with another good. Some examples of complements are hamburgers and french fries, party snacks and drinks, spaghetti and meat sauce, running shoes and jogging pants. Tapes also have their complements: Walkmans, tape recorders, and stereo tape decks. If the price of one of these complements increases, people buy fewer tapes. For example, if the price of a Walkman doubles, fewer Walkmans are bought, and as a consequence, fewer people are interested in buying tapes — the demand for tapes decreases. Conversely, if the price of one of these complements decreases, people buy more tapes. For example, if the price of the Walkman is halved, more Walkmans are bought, and a larger number of people buy tapes — the demand for tapes increases.

2. Income. Another influence on demand is consumer income. When income increases, consumers demand more of most goods. When income decreases, consumers demand less of most goods.

Although an increase in income leads to an increase in the demand for most goods, it does not lead to an increase in the demand for all goods. Goods for which demand increases as income increases are called **normal goods**. Examples of normal goods are restaurant meals, clothing, housing, art, vacations, and entertainment. Goods for which demand decreases when income increases are called **inferior goods**. Examples of inferior goods are rice and potatoes. These two goods are a major part of the diet of people with very low incomes. As incomes increase, the demand for these goods declines because more expensive meat and dairy products are substituted for them.

3. Population. Demand also depends on the size of the population. The larger the population, the greater is the demand for all goods and services. The smaller the population, the less is the demand for all goods and services.

4. Preferences. Finally, demand depends on preferences. *Preferences* are an individual's attitude toward goods and services. For example, a rock music fanatic has a much greater preference for tapes than does a tone-deaf workaholic. As a consequence, even if the two have the same incomes, their demands for tapes will be very different.

There is a fundamental difference between preferences and all the other influences on demand. Preferences cannot be directly observed. We can observe the price of a good and the price of its substitutes and complements. We can observe income and population size. But we cannot observe people's preferences. Economists assume that preferences do not change or that they change only slowly and that they are independent of all the other influences on demand.

A summary of influences on demand and the direction of those influences is presented in Table 4.1.

Movement Along Versus a Shift in the Demand Curve

Changes in the influences on buyers' plans cause either a movement along the demand curve or a shift in it. Let's discuss each case in turn.

Movement Along the Demand Curve If the price of a good changes but everything else remains the same, we say that the quantity demanded of that good has

Table 4.1 The Demand for Tapes

The law of demand

The quantity of tapes demanded

Falls if	*Rises if*
• The price of a tape rises	• The price of a tape falls

Changes in demand

The demand for tapes

Falls if	*Rises if*
• The price of a substitute falls	• The price of a substitute rises
• The price of a complement rises	• The price of a complement falls
• Income falls*	• Income rises*
• The population decreases	• The population increases

*A tape is a normal good

changed. We illustrate the effect as a movement along the demand curve. For example, if the price of a tape increases from $3 to $5, the result is a movement along the demand curve, from point *c* to point *e* in Fig. 4.1.

A Shift in the Demand Curve If the price of a good remains constant but another influence on buyers' plans changes, we say that there is a change in demand for that good. We illustrate the change in demand as a shift in the demand curve. For example, a dramatic fall in the price of the Walkman — a complement of tapes — increases the demand for tapes. We illustrate this increase in demand for tapes with a new demand schedule and a new demand curve. Consumers demand a larger quantity of tapes at each and every price.

The table in Fig. 4.2 provides some hypothetical numbers that illustrate such a shift. The table sets out the original demand schedule and the new demand schedule resulting from a fall in the price of a Walkman. These numbers record the change in the demand schedule. The graph in Fig. 4.2 illustrates the corresponding shift in the demand curve. When the price of the Walkman falls, the demand curve for tapes shifts to the right.

A Change in Demand Versus a Change in the Quantity Demanded The quantity demanded at a given price is shown by a point on a demand curve. The entire demand curve shows demand. A **change in demand** is a shift in the entire demand curve. A movement along a demand curve is a **change in the quantity demanded**. Fig. 4.3 illustrates these distinctions. If the price of a good falls but nothing else changes, there is an increase in the quantity demanded of that good (a movement down the demand curve D_0). If the price rises, but nothing else changes, there is a decrease in the quantity demanded (a movement up the demand curve D_0). When any other influence on buyers' planned purchases changes, the demand curve shifts and there is a change (an increase or a decrease) in demand. A rise in income (for a normal good), in population, or in the price of a substitute or a fall in the price of a complement shifts the demand curve to the right (from D_0 to D_2). This represents an increase in demand. A fall in income (for a normal good), in population, in the price of a substitute or a rise in the price of a complement shifts the demand curve to the left (from D_0 to D_1). This represents a decrease in demand.

R E V I E W

The quantity demanded of a good is the amount of the good that consumers plan to buy in a given period of time at a particular price. Other things being equal, the quantity demanded of a good increases if its price falls. Demand can be represented by a schedule or curve that sets out the quantity demanded at each price. Demand describes the quantity that consumers plan to buy at each possible price, or the highest price that consumers are willing to pay for the last unit bought. Demand increases if the price of a substitute rises, if the price of a complement falls, or if the population increases. Demand decreases if the price of a substitute falls, if the price of a complement rises, or if the population decreases.

For a normal good, demand increases if income rises and decreases if income falls. For an inferior good, demand decreases if income rises and increases if income falls.

If the price of a good changes but all other influences on buyers' plans are held constant, there is a change in the quantity demanded and a movement along the demand curve. All other influences on buyers' plans shift the demand curve. ■

Figure 4.2 A Change in the Demand Schedule and a Shift in the Demand Curve

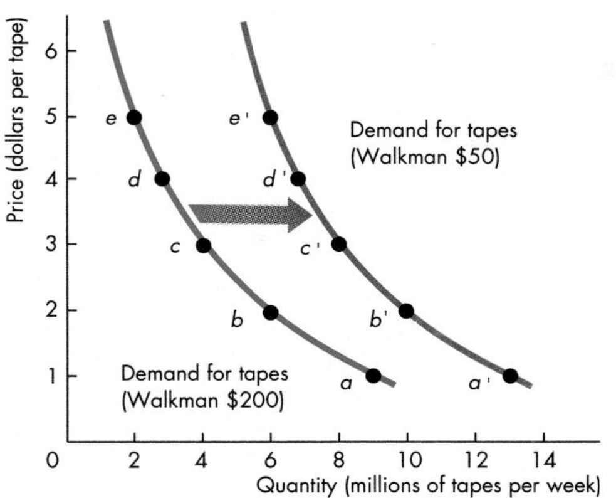

A change in any influence on buyers other than the price of the good itself results in a new demand schedule and a shift in the demand curve. Here, a fall in the price of a Walkman — a complement of tapes — increases the demand for tapes. At a price of $3 per tape (row *c* of the table), 4 million tapes a week are demanded when the Walkman costs $200 and 8 million tapes per week are demanded when the Walkman costs only $50. The demand curve shifts to the right, as shown by the shift arrow and the resulting red curve.

	Original Demand Schedule (Walkman $200)			**New Demand Schedule (Walkman $50)**	
	Price (dollars per tape)	**Quantity (millions of tapes per week)**		**Price (dollars per tape)**	**Quantity (millions of tapes per week)**
a	1	9	*a'*	1	13
b	2	6	*b'*	2	10
c	3	4	*c'*	3	8
d	4	3	*d'*	4	7
e	5	2	*e'*	5	6

Figure 4.3 A Change in Demand Versus a Change in the Quantity Demanded

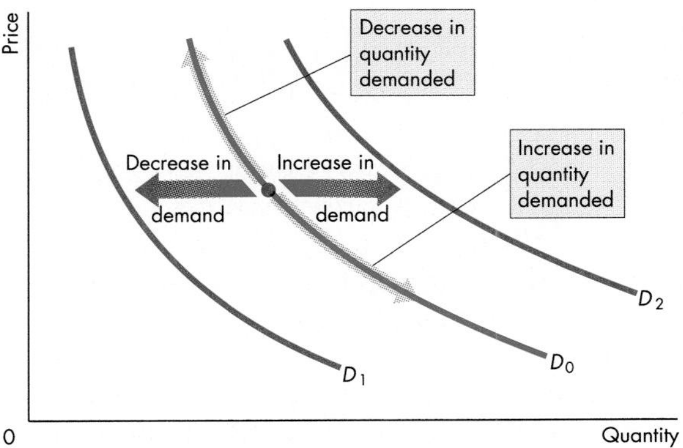

When the price of a good changes, there is a movement along the demand curve and *a change in the quantity of the good demanded.* For example, if the demand curve is D_0, a rise in the price of the good produces a decrease in the quantity demanded and a fall in the price of the good produces an increase in the quantity demanded. The arrows on demand curve D_0 represent these movements along the demand curve. If some other influence on demand changes, which increases the quantity that people plan to buy, there is a shift in the demand curve to the right (from D_0 to D_2) and an *increase in demand.* If some other influence on demand changes, which reduces the quantity people plan to buy, there is a shift in the demand curve to the left (from D_0 to D_1) and a *decrease in demand.*

Supply

The **quantity supplied** of a good is the amount that producers plan to sell in a given period of time at a particular price. The quantity supplied is not the amount that firms would like to sell but the amount they definitely plan to sell. However, the quantity supplied is not necessarily the same amount as the quantity actually sold, or traded. If consumers do not want to buy the quantity that firms plan to sell, then firms' sales plans will be frustrated. Like quantity demanded, the quantity supplied is expressed as an amount per unit of time.

What Determines the Quantity Supplied?

The quantity supplied depends on the number of firms supplying a good and the plans of each firm. The amount of any good that each firm plans to supply depends on many factors. Among the more important ones are:

- The price of the good
- The prices of other goods
- The prices of the factors of production used to produce the good
- Technology

Since the theory of demand and supply makes predictions about prices and quantities traded, we will focus first on the relationship between the price of a good and the quantity supplied. In order to study this relationship, we will hold constant all the other influences on the quantity supplied. We ask, how does the quantity supplied of a good vary as its price varies?

The Law of Supply

The law of supply states:

Other things being equal, the higher the price of a good, the greater is the quantity supplied.

Why does a higher price lead to a greater quantity supplied of a good? The answer is profitability. If the prices of the factors of production used to produce a good are held constant, a higher price for the good means a higher profit for the producer. Higher profits encourage existing producers to increase the quantity they supply. Higher profits also attract additional producers.

The Supply Schedule and the Supply Curve

A **supply schedule** lists the quantities supplied at each different price, when all other influences on the amount firms plan to sell are held constant. Let's construct a supply schedule. To do so, we examine how the quantity supplied of a good varies as its price varies, holding constant the prices of other goods, the prices of the factors of production used to produce it, and the state of technology.

The table in Fig. 4.4 sets out a supply schedule for tapes. It shows the quantity of tapes supplied at each possible price. For example, if the price of a tape is $1, no tapes are supplied. If the price of a tape is $4, then 5 million tapes are supplied each week.

A supply schedule can be illustrated by drawing a supply curve. A **supply curve** graphs the relationship between the quantity supplied and the price of a good, holding everything else constant. Using the same numbers listed in the table, the graph in Fig. 4.4 illustrates the supply curve for tapes. For example, point *d* represents a quantity supplied of 5 million tapes a week at a price of $4 a tape.

Minimum Supply Price

Just as the demand curve has two interpretations, so does the supply curve. So far we have thought about the supply curve and the supply schedule as showing the quantity that firms will supply at each possible price. But we can also think about the supply curve as showing the minimum price at which the last unit will be supplied. Looking at the supply schedule in this way, we ask: what is the minimum price that brings forth a given quantity supplied? For firms to supply the 3 millionth tape each week, the price has to be at least $2 a tape. For firms to supply the 5 millionth tape each week, they have to get at least $4 a tape.

A Change in Supply

The term **supply** refers to the entire relationship between the quantity supplied of a good and its price. The supply of tapes is described by both the supply schedule and the supply curve in Fig. 4.4. To construct a supply schedule and supply curve, we hold constant all the other influences on suppliers' plans. Let's now consider these other influences.

Figure 4.4 The Supply Schedule and the Supply Curve

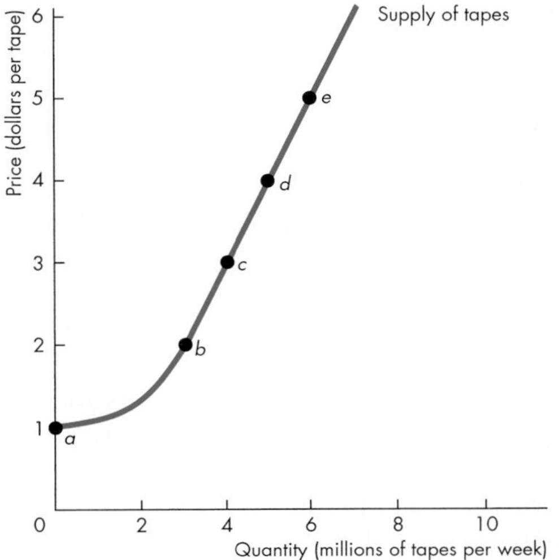

	Price (dollars per tape)	Quantity (millions of tapes per week)
a	1	0
b	2	3
c	3	4
d	4	5
e	5	6

The table shows the supply schedule of tapes. For example, at $2 per tape, 3 million tapes per week are supplied; at $5 per tape, 6 million tapes per week are supplied. The supply curve shows the relationship between the quantity supplied and price, holding everything else constant. The supply curve usually slopes upward: as the price of a good increases, so does the quantity supplied. A supply curve can be read in two ways. For a given price, it tells us the quantity that producers plan to sell. For example, at a price of $3 per tape, producers plan to sell 4 million tapes per week. The supply curve also tells us the minimum price at which a given quantity will be offered for sale. For example, the minimum price that will bring forth a supply of 4 million tapes per week is $3 per tape.

1. Prices of Other Goods. The supply of a good can be influenced by the prices of other goods. For example, if an automobile assembly line can produce either sports cars or sedans, the quantity of sedans produced will depend on the price of sports cars and the quantity of sports cars produced will depend on the price of sedans. These two goods are substitutes in production. An increase in the price of a substitute in production decreases the supply of the good. Goods can also be complements in production.

Complements in production arise when two things are, of necessity, produced together. There are many examples of complements in production, especially in the chemicals industry. A particularly clear example is that of extracting chemicals from coal. This process produces coke, coal tar, nylon and a host of other chemical products. An increase in the price of any one of these byproducts of coal increases the supplies of the other byproducts.

Tapes have no obvious complements in production, but they do have substitutes: prerecorded tapes. An increase in the price of prerecorded tapes will decrease the supply of blank tapes.

2. Prices of Factors of Production. The prices of the factors of production used to produce a good will exert an important influence on its supply. For example, an increase in the prices of the labour and the capital resources used to produce tapes decreases the supply of tapes.

3. Technology. New technologies which enable producers to use fewer or less costly inputs lower the cost of production and increase supply. For example, the development of a new technology for tape production by companies such as Sony and Minnesota Mining and Manufacturing (3M) has lowered the cost of producing tapes and increased their supply.

A summary of influences on supply and the directions of those influences is presented in Table 4.2.

Movement Along Versus a Shift in the Supply Curve

Changes in the influences on producers cause either a movement along the supply curve or a shift in it.

Movement Along the Supply Curve If the price of a good changes but everything else influencing

Table 4.2 The Supply of Tapes

The law of supply

The quantity of tapes supplied

Falls if	*Rises if*
• The price of a tape falls	• The price of a tape rises

Changes in supply

The supply of tapes

Falls if	*Rises if*
• The price of a substitute in production rises	• The price of a substitute in production falls
• The price of a complement in production falls	• The price of a complement in production rises
• The price of a factor of production used to produce tapes increases	• The price of a factor of production used to produce tapes decreases
	• More efficient technologies for producing tapes are discovered

suppliers' planned sales remains constant, there is a movement along the supply curve. For example, if the price of tapes increases from $3 to $5 a tape, there is a movement along the supply curve from point *c* (4 million tapes a week) to point *e* (6 million tapes a week) in Fig. 4.4.

A Shift in the Supply Curve If the price of a good remains constant but another influence on suppliers' planned sales changes, there is a change in supply and a shift in the supply curve. For example, as we have already noted, technological advances lower the cost of producing tapes and increase their supply. As a result, the supply schedule changes. The table in Fig. 4.5 provides some hypothetical numbers that illustrate such a change. The table contains two supply schedules: the original, based on "old" technology, and another based on "new" technology. With the new technology, the quantity of tapes supplied increases at each price. The graph in Fig. 4.5 illustrates the resulting shift in the supply curve. When tape-producing technology improves, the supply curve of tapes shifts to the right.

A Change in Supply Versus a Change in the Quantity Supplied

The quantity supplied at a given price is shown by a point on a supply curve. The entire supply curve shows supply. A **change in supply** occurs whenever there is a shift in the supply curve. A **change in the quantity supplied** occurs when there is a movement along the supply curve.

Figure 4.6 illustrates and summarizes these distinctions. If the price of a good falls but nothing else changes, there is a decrease in the quantity supplied of that good (a movement down the supply curve S_0). If the price of a good rises but nothing else changes, there is an increase in the quantity supplied (a movement up the supply curve S_0). When any other influence on sellers changes, the supply curve shifts and there is a *change in supply.* If the supply curve is S_0 and there is a technological change that reduces the amounts of the factors of production needed to produce the good, then supply increases and the supply curve shifts to S_2. If production costs rise, supply decreases and the supply curve also shifts to S_1.

R E V I E W

The quantity supplied is the amount of a good that producers plan to sell in a given period of time at a particular price. Other things being equal, the quantity supplied of a good increases if its price rises. Supply can be represented by a schedule or a curve that shows the relationship between the quantity supplied of a good and its price. Supply describes the quantity that will be supplied at each possible price or the lowest price at which producers will supply the last unit. Supply increases if the price of a substitute in production falls, if the price of a complement in production rises, if the prices of the factors of production used to produce the good fall, or if technological advances lower the cost of production. If the price of a good changes but all other influences on producers' plans are held constant, there is a change in the quantity supplied and a movement along the supply curve. A change in any other influence on producers' plans shifts the supply curve. Changes in the prices of substitutes and complements in production, changes in the prices of factors of production, or improvements in technology shift the supply curve and are said to change supply. ■

Figure 4.5 A Change in the Supply Schedule and a Shift in the Supply Curve

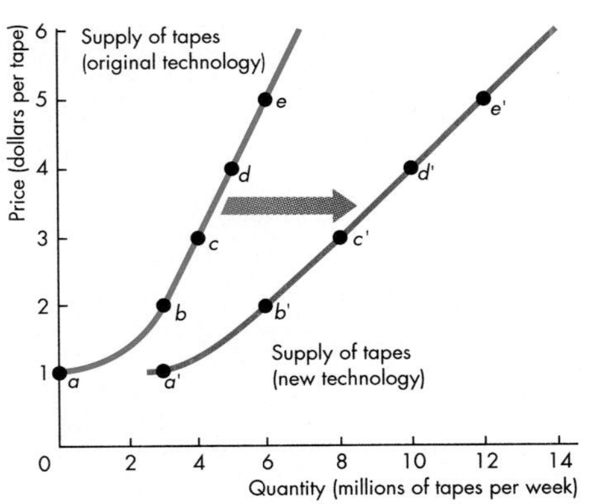

	Original technology			New technology	
	Price (dollars per tape)	Quantity (millions of tapes per week)		Price (dollars per tape)	Quantity (millions of tapes per week)
a	1	0	*a′*	1	3
b	2	3	*b′*	2	6
c	3	4	*c′*	3	8
d	4	5	*d′*	4	10
e	5	6	*e′*	5	12

If the price of a good remains constant but another influence on its supply changes, there will be a new supply schedule and the supply curve will shift. For example, if Sony and 3M invent a new, cost-saving technology for producing tapes, the supply schedule changes, as shown in the table. At $3 per tape, producers plan to sell 4 million tapes per week with the original technology and 8 million tapes per week with the new technology. Improved technology increases the supply of tapes and shifts the supply curve of tapes to the right.

Figure 4.6 A Change in Supply Versus a Change in the Quantity Supplied

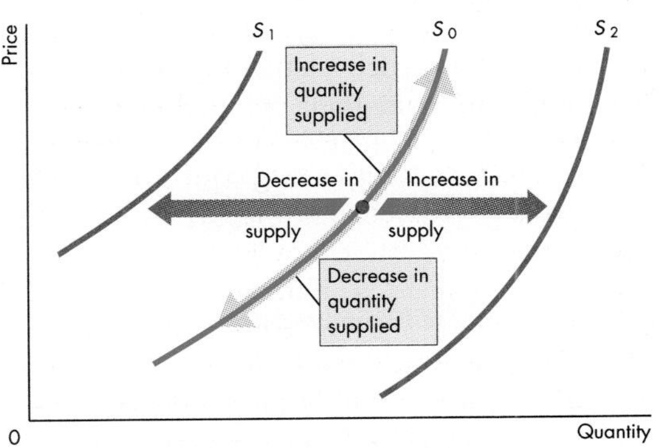

When the price of a good changes, there is a movement along the supply curve and a change in the quantity of the good supplied. For example, if the supply curve is S_0, a rise in the price of the good produces an increase in the quantity supplied, and a fall in the price produces a decrease in the quantity supplied. The arrows on curve S_0 represent these movements along the supply curve. If some other influence on supply changes, so that the quantity that producers plan to sell increases, there is a shift in the supply curve to the right (from S_0 to S_2) and an *increase in supply*. If some other influence on supply changes, so that the quantity the producers plan to sell decreases, there is a shift to the left in the supply curve (from S_0 to S_1) and a *decrease in supply*.

Now that we have studied demand and supply, let's bring these two concepts together and see how prices are determined.

Price Determination

We have seen that when the price of a good rises, the quantity demanded decreases and the quantity supplied increases. We are now going to see how adjustments in price achieve an equality between the quantities demanded and supplied.

Price as a Regulator

The price of a good regulates the quantities demanded and supplied. If the price is too high, the quantity supplied exceeds the quantity demanded. If the price is too low, the quantity demanded exceeds the quantity supplied. There is only one price, at which the quantity demanded equals the quantity supplied. We are going to work out what that price is. We are also going to discover that natural forces operating in a market move the price toward the level that makes the quantity demanded equal the quantity supplied.

The demand schedule shown in the table in Fig. 4.1 and the supply schedule shown in the table in Fig. 4.4 appear together in the table in Fig. 4.7. If the price of a tape is $1, the quantity demanded is 9 million tapes a week but the quantity produced is zero. The quantity demanded exceeds the quantity supplied by 9 million tapes a week. In other words, at a price of $1 a tape, there is a shortage of 9 million tapes a week. This shortage is shown in the final column of the table. At a price of $2 a tape, there is still a shortage but only of 3 million tapes a week. If the price of a tape is $4, the quantity supplied exceeds the quantity demanded. The quantity supplied is 5 million tapes a week, but the quantity demanded is only 3 million. There is a surplus of 2 million tapes a week. There is only one price at which there is neither a shortage nor a surplus. That price is $3 a tape. At that price the quantity demanded is equal to the quantity supplied — 4 million tapes a week. That quantity is also the quantity traded.

The market for tapes is illustrated in the graph in Fig. 4.7. The graph shows both the demand curve of Fig. 4.1 and the supply curve of Fig. 4.4. The demand curve and the supply curve intersect when the price is $3 a tape. The quantity traded is 4 million tapes a week. At each price above $3 a tape, the quantity supplied exceeds the quantity demanded. That is, there is a surplus of tapes. At $4 a tape, the surplus is 2 million tapes a week, as shown by the labelled arrow in the figure. At each price below $3 a tape, the quantity demanded exceeds the quantity supplied. At $2 a tape, the shortage is 3 million tapes a week, as shown by the labelled arrow in the figure.

Equilibrium

We defined *equilibrium* in Chapter 1 as a situation in which opposing forces exactly balance each other and in which no one is able to make a better choice given the available resources and actions of others. So, in an equilibrium, the price is such that opposing forces exactly balance each other. The **equilibrium price** is the price at which the quantity demanded equals the quantity supplied. To see why this situation is an equilibrium, we need to examine the behaviour of buyers and sellers a bit more closely. First, let's look at the behaviour of buyers.

The Demand Curve and the Willingness to Pay Suppose that the price of a tape is $2. In such a situation, producers plan to sell 3 million tapes a week. Consumers cannot force producers to sell more than they want to sell, so the quantity sold is also 3 million tapes a week. What is the highest price that buyers are willing to pay for the 3 millionth tape each week? The answer can be found on the demand curve in Fig. 4.7 — it is $4 a tape.

If the price remains at $2 a tape, the quantity of tapes demanded is 6 million tapes a week — 3 million more than are available. In such a situation, the price of a tape does not remain at $2. Because people want more tapes than are available at that price and because they are willing to pay up to $4 a tape, the price rises. If the quantity supplied stays at 3 million tapes a week, the price will rise all the way to $4 a tape.

In fact, the price does not have to rise by such a large amount because at higher prices the quantity supplied increases. The price will rise from $2 a tape to $3 a tape. At that price, the quantity supplied is 4 million tapes a week, and $3 a tape is the highest price that consumers are willing to pay. At $3 a tape, buyers are able to make their planned purchases and producers are able to make their planned sales. Therefore no one has an incentive to bid the price higher.

The Supply Curve and the Minimum Supply Price Suppose that the price of a tape is $4. In such a situation, the quantity demanded is 3 million tapes a week. Producers cannot force consumers to buy more than they want, so the quantity bought is 3 million tapes a week. Producers are willing to sell 3 million tapes a week for a price lower than $4 a tape. In fact, you can see on the supply curve in Fig. 4.7 that suppliers are willing to sell the 3 millionth tape each week at a price of $2. At $4 a tape, they would like to sell 5 million tapes each week. Because they want to sell more than 3 million tapes a week at $4 a tape, and because they would be willing to sell the 3 millionth tape for as little as $2, they will continuously undercut each other in order to get a bigger share of the market. They will cut their price all the way to $2 a tape if only 3 million tapes a week can be sold.

Figure 4.7 Equilibrium

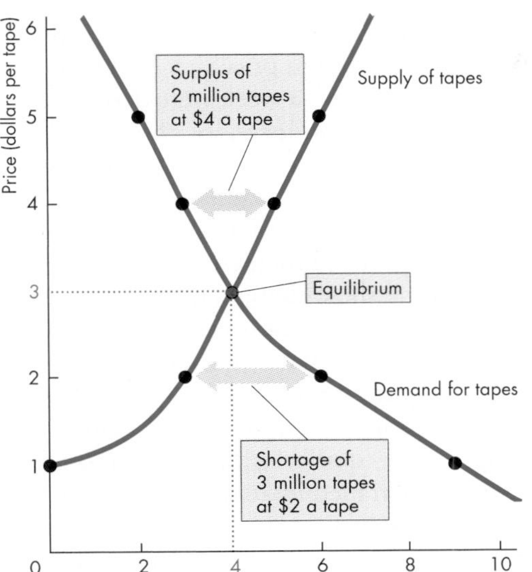

The table lists the quantities demanded and quantities supplied as well as the shortage or surplus of tapes at each price. (Note that the numbers in the final column of the table represent the shortages as negative numbers and the surpluses as positive numbers.) If the price of a tape is $2, 6 million tapes per week are demanded and 3 million are supplied. There is a shortage of 3 million tapes per week and the price rises. If the price of a tape is $4, 3 million tapes per week are demanded but 5 million are supplied. There is a surplus of 2 million tapes per week and the price falls. If the price of a tape is $3, 4 million tapes per week are demanded and 4 million are supplied. There is neither a shortage nor a surplus. Neither buyers nor sellers have any incentive to change the price. The price at which the quantity demanded equals the quantity supplied is the equilibrium price.

Price (dollars per tape)	Quantity demanded (millions of tapes per week)	Quantity supplied (millions of tapes per week)	Shortage (–) or surplus (+) (millions of tapes per week)
1	9	0	–9
2	6	3	–3
3	4	4	0
4	3	5	+2
5	2	6	+4

In fact, producers don't have to cut their price to $2 a tape because the lower price brings forth an increase in the quantity demanded. When the price falls to $3, the quantity demanded is 4 million tapes a week, which is exactly the quantity that producers want to sell at that price. So when the price reaches $3 a tape, producers have no incentive to cut the price any further.

The Best Deal Available for Buyers and Sellers Both situations we have just examined result in price changes. In the first case, the price starts at $2 and is bid upward. In the second case, the price starts at $4 and producers undercut each other. In both cases, the price changes until it hits $3 a tape. At that price, the quantity demanded and the quantity supplied are equal and no one has any incentive to do business at a different price. Consumers are paying the highest acceptable price and producers are selling at the lowest acceptable price.

When people can freely make bids and offers and when they seek to buy at the lowest price and sell at the highest price, the price at which they trade is the equilibrium price — the quantity demanded equals the quantity supplied.

R E V I E W

The equilibrium price is the price at which the plans of buyers and sellers match each other — the price at which the quantity demanded equals the quantity supplied. If the price is below equilibrium, the quantity demanded exceeds the quantity supplied, buyers offer higher prices, sellers ask for higher prices, and the price rises. If the price is above equilibrium, the quantity supplied exceeds the quantity demanded, buyers offer lower prices, sellers ask for lower prices, and the price falls. Only when the price is such that the quantity demanded and the quantity supplied are equal are there no forces acting on the price to make it change. Therefore that price is the equilibrium price. At that price, the quantity traded is also equal to the quantity demanded and the quantity supplied. ■

The theory of demand and supply that you have just studied is now a central part of economics. But that was not always so. Only 100 years ago, the best economists of the day were quite confused about these matters, which today even students in introductory courses find relatively easy to get right (see Our Advancing Knowledge on pp. 84-85).

You'll discover in the rest of this chapter that the theory of demand and supply enables us to understand and make predictions about changes in prices — including the price slides, rockets, and rollercoasters described in the chapter opener.

Predicting Changes in Price and Quantity Traded

The theory we have just studied provides us with a powerful way of analysing influences on prices and quantities traded. According to the theory, a change in price stems from either a change in demand or a change in supply. Let's look first at the effects of a change in demand.

A Change in Demand

What happens to the price of tapes and the quantity traded if the demand for tapes increases? We can answer this question with a specific example. If the price of a Walkman (a complement) falls from $200 to $50, the demand for tapes increases as is shown in the table in Fig. 4.8. The original demand schedule and the new one are set out in the first three columns of the table. The table also shows the supply schedule.

The original equilibrium price was $3 a tape. At that price, 4 million tapes a week were demanded and supplied. When demand increases, the price that makes the quantity demanded equal the quantity supplied is $5 a tape. At this price, 6 million tapes are traded each week. When demand increases, the price rises and the quantity traded increases.

We can illustrate these changes in the graph in Fig. 4.8. The graph shows the original demand for and supply of tapes. The original equilibrium price is $3 a tape and the quantity traded is 4 million tapes a week. When demand increases, the demand curve shifts to the right. The equilibrium price rises to $5 a tape and the quantity traded increases to 6 million tapes a week, as highlighted in the figure.

The exercise we've just conducted can easily be reversed. If we start at a price of $5 a tape, trading 6 million tapes a week, we can then work out what happens if demand decreases to its original level. You will see that a decrease in demand lowers price and decreases the quantity traded. We can now make our first two predictions:

- When demand increases, the price rises and the quantity traded increases.
- When demand decreases, the price falls and the quantity traded decreases.

Reading Between the Lines (pp. 88-89) provides further illustration of demand and supply in action. It explains what happened when a massive but temporary rise in demand for boat rides around Liberty Island for the illumination of the refurbished Statue of Liberty occurred on July 4, 1986.

A Change in Supply

Let's see what happens if supply changes. Again, we'll start out with a price of $3 a tape and 4 million tapes a week being traded. Suppose that Sony and 3M have just introduced a new cost-saving technology for producing tapes. The new technology shifts the supply schedule and the supply curve. The new supply schedule (the same one that was shown in Fig. 4.5) is presented in the table in Fig. 4.9. What is the new

Figure 4.8 The Effect of a Change in Demand

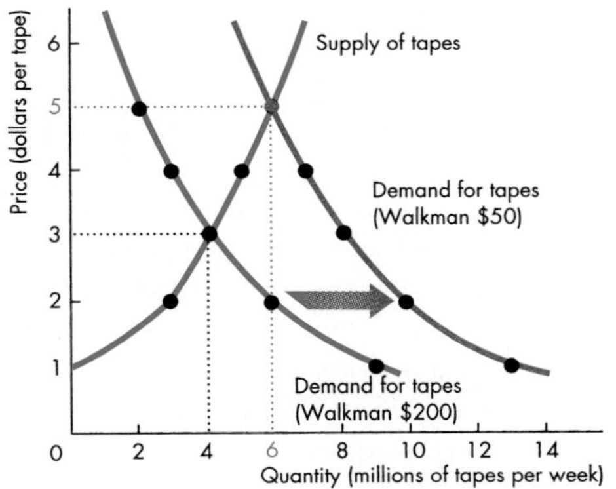

If the price of a Walkman is $200, the quantity of tapes demanded and the quantity traded is 4 million tapes per week at a price of $3 per tape. If the price of a Walkman falls from $200 to $50, the quantity of tapes demanded at a price of $3 is 8 million tapes per week. If the price stays at $3, there is a shortage of 4 million tapes per week. The quantities of tapes demanded and supplied are equal when the price is $5 per tape and the quantity traded is 6 million tapes per week. The increase in demand raises the equilibrium price by $2 and raises the quantity traded by 2 million tapes per week.

Price (dollars per tape)	Quantity demanded (millions of tapes per week)		Quantity supplied (millions of tapes per week)
	Walkman $200	Walkman $50	
1	9	13	0
2	6	10	3
3	4	8	4
4	3	7	5
5	2	6	6

equilibrium price and quantity traded? The answer is highlighted in the table: the price falls to $2 a tape and the number of tapes traded rises to 6 million a week. You can see why by looking at the quantities demanded and supplied at the old price of $3 a tape. The quantity supplied at that price is 8 million tapes a week and there is a surplus of tapes. The price falls. Only when the price is $2 a tape is the quantity supplied equal to the quantity demanded.

The graph in Fig. 4.9 illustrates the effect of an increase in supply. The graph shows the demand curve for tapes and the original and new supply curves. The initial equilibrium price is $3 a tape and the original quantity traded is 4 million tapes a week. When the supply increases, the supply curve shifts to the right. The new equilibrium price is $2 a tape and the quantity traded is 6 million tapes a week, as highlighted in the figure.

The exercise that we've just conducted can easily be reversed. If we start out at a price of $2 a tape with 6 million tapes a week being traded, we can work out what happens if the supply curve shifts back to its original position. You can see that the decrease in supply increases the equilibrium price to $3 a tape and decreases the quantity traded to 4 million tapes a week. Such a decrease in supply could arise from an increase in the cost of labour or raw materials. We can now make two more predictions:

- When supply increases, the quantity traded increases and the price falls.
- When supply decreases, the quantity traded decreases and the price rises.

Reading Between the Lines (pp. 90-91) shows the effects of changes in demand and supply in the market for oats.

OUR ADVANCING • KNOWLEDGE •

Discovering the Laws of Demand and Supply

Antoine-Augustin Cournot

Alfred Marshall

How are the prices of goods and services determined? Why are some vital-to-life resources, such as the air that we breathe and the water that we drink, virtually free, while luxurious but inessential commodities such as diamonds are so expensive? For centuries, people puzzled over these and similar questions. They were finally answered when the theories of demand, supply, and equilibrium price, which you have been studying in this chapter, were discovered and refined. But this discovery was not completed until the 1890s.

Let's transport ourselves back in time to the early part of the nineteenth century. We are planning to make a sizeable investment in railways and we are using the prevailing theory of prices to guide our decision. Economists believe that prices are determined by costs of production. So we predict that the price of railway transportation will stay in line with production costs and that a reasonable rate of return will be made on our investment. As a result, we (and millions of others) invest heavily in this new mode of transportation. Rates of return turn out to be much lower than we predicted. Why? What went wrong? Ignorant of the laws of demand and supply, we failed to realize that a massive increase in the supply of railway transportation services would drive their prices down and therefore lower the return on investing in them. Let's look at the main milestones on the road to the discovery of the theory of demand and supply.

The road begins with the work of Antoine-Augustin Cournot. Cournot (1801-1877) was born near Dijon, France. In 1834, he became professor of mathematics at the University of Lyon. Four years later he published a book entitled *Recherches sur les principes mathématiques de la théorie des richesses (The Mathematical Principles of the Theory of Wealth).* In that book, Cournot wrote down the law of demand. But he wrote it in abstract mathematical language. Cournot's book was a work of amazing clarity, but because it was written in mathematical language unfamiliar at that time to most students of economics, it did not have much influence until many years later.

The first person to draw a demand curve was Arsène-Jules-Émile Juvenal Dupuit (1804-1866). Like Cournot, Dupuit was also French. He made profound contributions both as an engineer and economic theorist. Dupuit's demand curve, which he called "the curve of consumption" (courbe de consommation), appeared in 1844.

The law of demand was independently discovered a few years later and given its first practical application by Dionysius Lardner (1793-1859), an Irishman who was professor of philosophy at the University of London. In his book *Railway Economy*, published in 1850, Lardner drew and used a demand curve for transportation services.

The first person to a draw demand curve and a supply curve together and to use demand and supply theory to determine price was Fleeming Jenkin (1833-1885), an Englishman who was also a professor of philosophy at the University of London. Jenkin's demand and supply curves appeared in a paper entitled "The Graphic Representation of the Laws of Supply and Demand," published in 1870. Jenkin also was the first to use the theories of demand and supply to make predictions about the effects of taxes, in a paper entitled "On the Principles Which Regulate the Incidence of Taxes," published in 1872.

Many others had a hand in the refinement of the theory of demand and supply, but the first thorough and complete statement of the theory, in terms sufficiently modern for it to be recognized as the same theory that you have studied in this chapter, was provided by Alfred Marshall (1842-1924). Marshall was a professor of political economy at the University of Cambridge, and in 1890, he published a monumental treatise — *Principles of Economics.* Marshall's *Principles* was the textbook on this subject for almost half a century. In the preface to the *Principles,* Marshall acknowledged his own debt to Cournot. He also expressed his view that the theory of demand and supply provides a unifying analysis applicable to all aspects of economics.

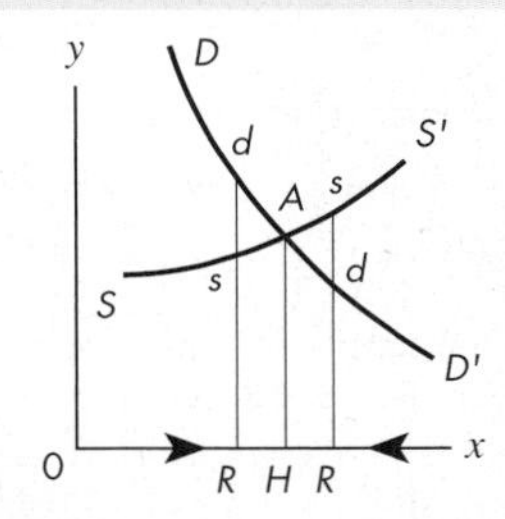

Although Marshall was an outstanding mathematician, he kept mathematics and even diagrams in the background. His own supply and demand diagram and discussion of how the equilibrium price arises appears only in a footnote. It is reproduced here. Although Marshall was an outstanding mathematician, he kept mathematics and even diagrams in the background. His own supply and demand diagram and discussion of how the equilibrium price arises appears only in a footnote. It is reproduced here. Although Marshall's diagram is far less striking than those you have been studying, note the strong similarities it has to Fig. 4.7.

Figure 4.9 The Effect of a Change in Supply

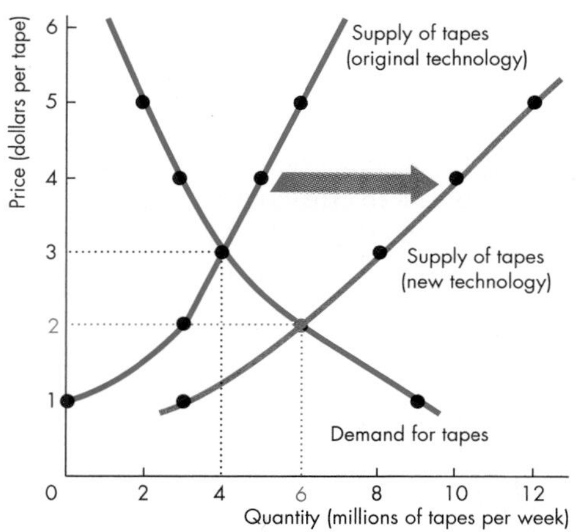

Price (dollars per tape)	Quantity demanded (millions of tapes per week)	Quantity supplied (millions of tapes per week) Original technology	New technology
1	9	0	3
2	6	3	6
3	4	4	8
4	3	5	10
5	2	6	12

When the supply schedule changes as a result of introducing a new technology, the quantity of tapes supplied at $3 per tape exceeds the quantity demanded at that price. The quantity supplied is 8 million tapes at a price of $3. The table shows that the quantity demanded equals the quantity supplied when the price of tapes falls to $2. At this price, 6 million tapes are demanded and supplied each week. The new technology results in a shift in the supply curve to the right. The original technology supply curve intersects the demand curve at a price of $3 and a quantity traded of 4 million tapes per week. The new technology supply curve intersects the demand curve at a price of $2 and a quantity traded of 6 million tapes per week. The increase in supply lowers the price of tapes by $1 and raises the quantity traded by 2 million tapes per week.

Changes in Both Supply and Demand

In the exercises above, we changed either demand or supply but only one at a time. If we change just one of these, we can predict the direction of change of the price and the quantity traded. If we change both demand and supply, we cannot always say what will happen to both the price and the quantity traded. For example, if both demand and supply increase, we know that the quantity traded increases, but we cannot predict whether the price rises or falls. To make such a prediction, we need to know the relative importance of the increases in demand and supply. If demand increases and supply decreases, we know that the price rises, but we cannot predict whether the quantity traded increases or decreases. Again, to be able to make a prediction about the quantity traded, we need to know the relative magnitudes of the changes in demand and supply.

As an example of a change in both supply and demand, let's take one final look at the market for tapes. We've seen how demand and supply determine the price and quantity of tapes traded; and how an increase in demand resulting from a fall in the price of a Walkman both raises the price of tapes and increases the quantity traded; and how an increase in the supply of tapes resulting from an improved technology lowers the price of tapes and increases the quantity traded. Let's now examine what happens when both of these changes — a fall in the price of a Walkman (which increases the demand for tapes) and an improved production technology (which increases the supply of tapes) — occur together.

The table in Fig. 4.10 brings together the numbers that describe the original quantities demanded and supplied and the new quantities demanded and supplied after the fall in the price of the Walkman and the improved tape production technology. These same numbers are illustrated in the graph. The original supply and demand curves intersect at a price of $3 a tape and a quantity traded of 4 million tapes a

Figure 4.10 The Effect of a Change in Both Demand and Supply

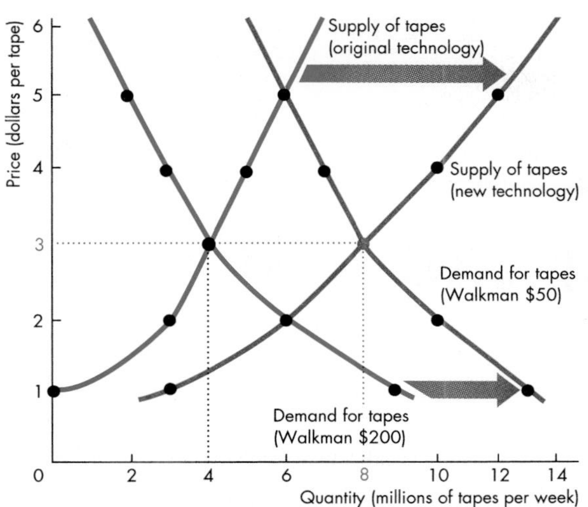

When a Walkman costs $200, the price of a tape is $3 and the quantity traded is 4 million tapes per week. A fall in the price of a Walkman increases the demand for tapes, and improved technology increases the supply of tapes. The new technology supply curve intersects the new demand curve at $3, the same price as before, but at a higher quantity traded of 8 million tapes per week. This simultaneous increase in both demand and supply increases the quantity traded but leaves the price unchanged.

Price (dollars per tape)	Original quantities (millions of tapes per week)		New quantities (millions of tapes per week)	
	Quantity demanded (Walkman $200)	**Quantity supplied (Original technology)**	**Quantity demanded (Walkman $50)**	**Quantity supplied (New technology)**
1	9	0	13	3
2	6	3	10	6
3	4	4	8	8
4	3	5	7	10
5	2	6	6	12

week. The new demand and supply curves also intersect at a price of $3 a tape but at a quantity traded of 8 million tapes a week. In this example, the increase in supply and demand are such that the rise in price brought about by the increase in demand is offset by the fall in price brought about by the increase in supply. So the price does not change. An increase in either supply or demand increases the quantity traded. Therefore when both supply and demand increase, so does the quantity traded. Note that if demand had increased slightly more than shown in the figure, the price would have risen. If supply had increased slightly more than shown in the figure, the price would have fallen. But in both cases the quantity traded would have increased.

Walkmans, Apartments, and Coffee

At the beginning of this chapter, we looked at some facts about prices and quantities traded of Walkmans, apartments, and coffee. Let's use the theory of demand and supply that we have just studied to explain the movements in the prices and the quantities

Demand And Supply In Action: A Temporary Increase In Demand

Planning early for the 4th of July

Let others grouse about Christmas coming so early in the year. New Yorkers are frantically making plans for the Fourth of July.

The city's chronic scramble for space—space to walk, space to dine, space to rent—focuses now on finding a spot to view the historic, histrionic relighting of the Statue of Liberty on July 4 and related extravaganzas, Frank Sinatra and an armada of tall ships among them.

Some hotels and restaurants are already booked. Rudy Montgomery has been offered \$3,600— three times his monthly rent—to sublet his modest Brooklyn Heights apartment, a short walk from the Promenade and a view of the statue, for the four-day holiday weekend.

Boats that normally charge \$25 to \$50 per person for trips around the harbor have raised their fees to \$1,000 per person or more. Nieman Marcus has made a Fourth of July harbor excursion one of its extravagant Christmas catalogue items. And the scramble for a place at the bar at Windows On The World has begun....

One of the unanswered questions is: Is there enough water in the harbor? The Coast Guard estimates that there will be at least 25,000 private pleasure boats in the harbor to observe the flotilla and fireworks. "You will be able to walk across the hulls," said one boater. "It will be a bumper-boat situation."

"Everything that floats is being rented," said Bill Sills, another boater. "Some of the boats ain't much more than a piece of driftwood."

Marilyn Vogel, commodore of the Sebago Canoe Club of Brooklyn, said that a boat at the 79th Street Marina that doesn't even run was rented for the holiday weekend for \$7,000.

She said the canoe club receives requests to rent canoes for that weekend, and that the club is considering becoming part of the festivities. "It would be their last outing ... gridlock on the waters."

"The only thing they forgot," said Mr. O'Keefe [owner of the River Cafe] is that there is nowhere to embark and disembark. You figure 1,000 yachts minimum and maybe, just maybe, Manhattan's three marinas can service 15 extra boats, so what do the other 985 do?"

"This will be 10 times the colossal jam caused by the boats at the Brooklyn Bridge celebration," he said. "That was a New York party. This is national and international. I get five calls a day from Florida, Texas, the Caribbean and everywhere to tie up at our restaurant." "You will see launch services springing up to take people out to the boats," he said.

Captain Parker [of The Ethel] is leasing some dock space for \$2,500 for the weekend and plans to rent it out at high rates: about \$3,000 for a single 100-foot boat to pick up passengers. He will hire security guards to make sure only customers use the space. "Boats will be landing wherever they can," he said. "This will look like Dunkirk."

The New York Times,
November 6, 1985
By William E. Geist

The Essence of the Story

- In celebration of the United States' bicentennial, a unique and massive spectacular was held in the waters surrounding Liberty Island, New York, on the weekend of the Fourth of July in 1986. The refurbished Statue of Liberty was illuminated amidst fireworks, tall ships, and "related extravaganzas."
- The demand for space to view these events was extraordinarily high. Boats, restaurants, and any place with a view of the Liberty celebrations were demanded on a scale much larger than the demand for those same facilities on an ordinary day.
- The prices increased astronomically and the quantities available increased (to the point of total congestion).

Background and Analysis

- The events of this weekend illustrate the effects of a large temporary increase in the demand for boat rides. The figure shows what happened.
- The demand curve for boat rides and places with a view of the Liberty celebrations shifted to the right.
- The quantity of boat-rides and viewing places supplied increased but could not do so without limit.
- The increase in demand produced a large price rise (to P_{F0}) but only a small increase in the quantity of boat rides and viewing places traded (to Q_F).
- After the Fourth of July weekend, demand returned to its normal level and so did the price and the quantity traded—to P_N and Q_N.

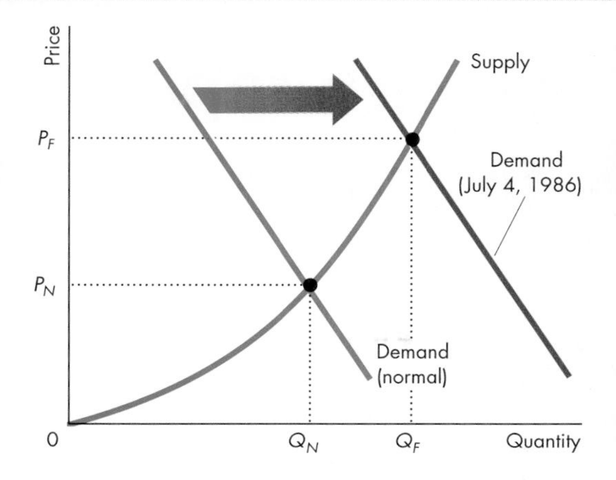

Demand and Supply In Action

Health reports send demand for oat products skyrocketing

While cereal makers delight in the popularity of oat bran on breakfast tables, farmers...are being hurt by overproduction and disappointing prices.

Fuelled by reports that oat bran reduces levels of cholesterol, which has been associated with heart disease, oat cereals and snack foods have enjoyed explosive sales growth in the past year....

Total oat product sales in the first four months of fiscal 1990 are up a healthy 25% and Jon Grant, president and chief executive officer of Quaker Oats Co. of Canada Ltd., sees no slackening in demand in the months ahead. "I don't see it as a fad. It's part of a trend back to good, healthy breakfast eating."...

Cal Kelly, manager of oat marketing for Regina-based grain company Can-Mar Grain Inc., agrees the consumer shift to oat products "is more or less permanent."

[But]...the price of oats fell drastically from last year's drought-fired record, down to US$1.40 a bushel at the Chicago Board of Trade from about US$4 a bushel. The price has managed a slight rebound in recent weeks to US$1.54 a bushel....

That is a big comedown for farmers who a year ago were predicting big things for their crop as a supply for the burgeoning oat-bran craze, especially in the U.S.

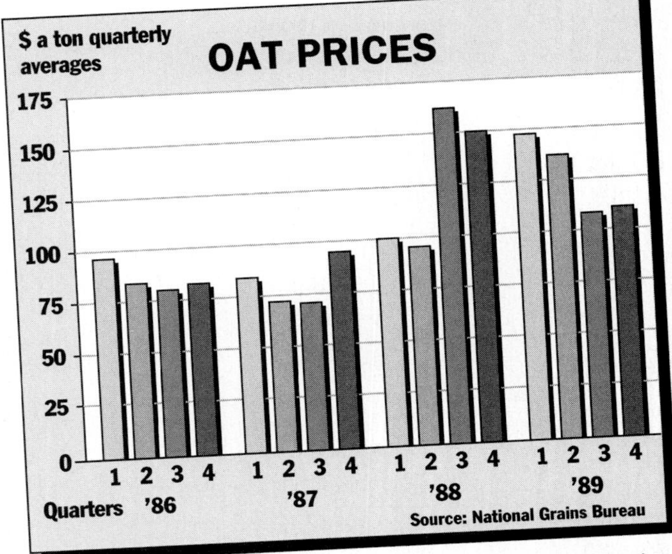

The frantic demand could not be met by U.S. farmers, who withdrew much of their land from oat production under federal programs designed to reduce the grain surplus that had driven down prices in the 1980s.

The situation was made worse by the drought, which hit the remaining production, and by poor harvests in Sweden and Finland, the other major oat suppliers to the U.S.

The supply crunch set the stage for Canada to capture a large share of the U.S. market, and farmers lifted their plantings last spring by 14% to meet it. Production should reach 3.7 million metric tons this year, up from 3 million in 1988.

But a hot summer and rainy harvest left most of it unfit for milling.

Meanwhile, this year's Scandinavian crop is excellent and Argentina and Australia have also entered the market. The oat boom has not gone unnoticed by U.S. farmers, either. They have boosted production a staggering 70% to 5.7 million metric tons. Predictably, prices took a nosedive.

***The Financial Post,* January 15, 1990**
By John Fox

The Essence of The Story

- In 1989, the quantity of oat cereals sold increased but the price of oats decreased.
- Increased sales are attributed to a permanent increase in demand resulting from reports that oat bran may reduce heart disease.
- The supply of oats decreased in 1988 because the U.S. government had encouraged farmers to cut production and there were poor harvests both in the United States and in Sweden and Finland.
- The price of oats increased in 1988 (see figure in news item).
- In 1989 there was an increase in oats production in Canada, Scandinavia, Argentina, Australia, and the United States.
- At the start of 1989, farmers had expected the price of oats to remain at its 1988 level. But the price decreased, disappointing the farmers.

Background and Analysis

- Some facts:

Year	Price (dollars per metric ton)	Quantity traded (millions of metric tons)
1987	80	44
1988	150	38
1989	110	42

- The news story does not distinguish between shifts of the demand and supply curves and movements along those curves, but to understand the story it is necessary to make those distinctions.
- In 1987, as illustrated in Fig. (a), the demand curve for oats was $D_{Original}$ and the supply curve was S_{1987}. The price of oats was $80 a metric ton and the quantity traded was 44 million metric tons.
- In 1988 the demand for oats increased *permanently* because of the newly perceived health benefits of oat bran. But only a small portion of total oats production is used for making oat bran and other oat cereals. The bulk of it is used for animal feed. As a consequence, the increase in the demand for oats was modest. The demand curve shifted to D_{New}.
- In 1988, there was a *temporary* decrease in the supply of oats resulting from U.S. government encouragement to curtail production and bad growing and harvesting conditions in many producing areas. The supply curve shifted to S_{1989}.
- The combined effects of the increase in demand and the decrease in supply, as illustrated in Fig. (a), were an increase in the price of oats to $150 a metric ton and a decrease in the quantity traded to 38 million metric tons.
- In 1989, demand remained at its new level but better growing and harvesting conditions resulted in an increase in supply. As illustrated in Fig. (b), the supply curve shifted to the right and there was a movement along the new demand curve: the price of oats decreased to $110 a metric ton and the quantity traded increased to 42 million metric tons.

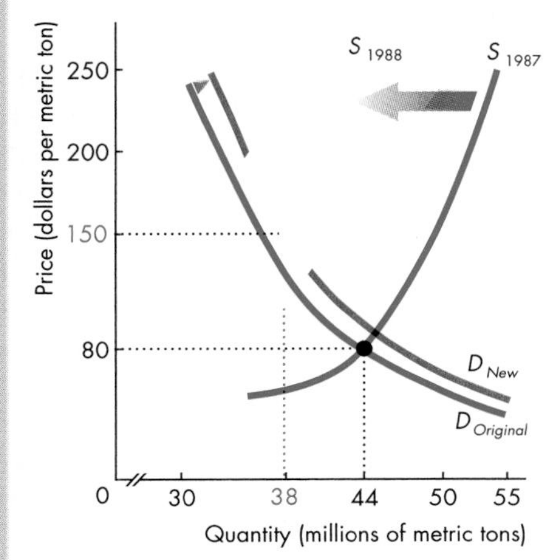

(a) The 1988 price rise

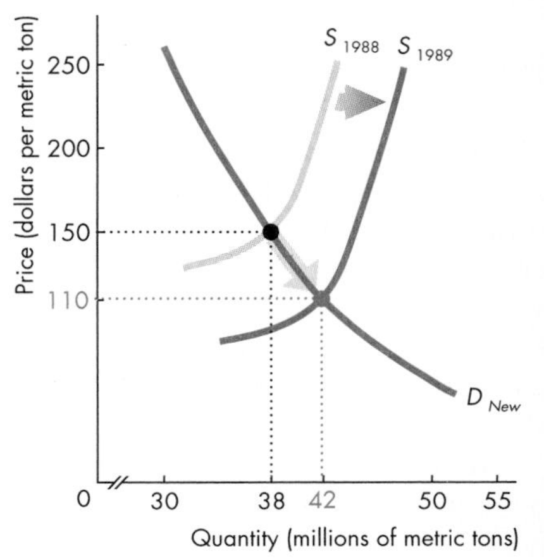

(b) The 1989 price decline

Figure 4.11 More Changes in Supply and Demand

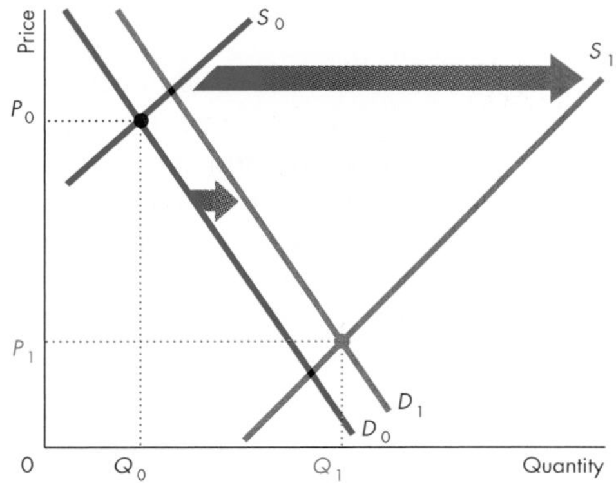

(a) Walkmans

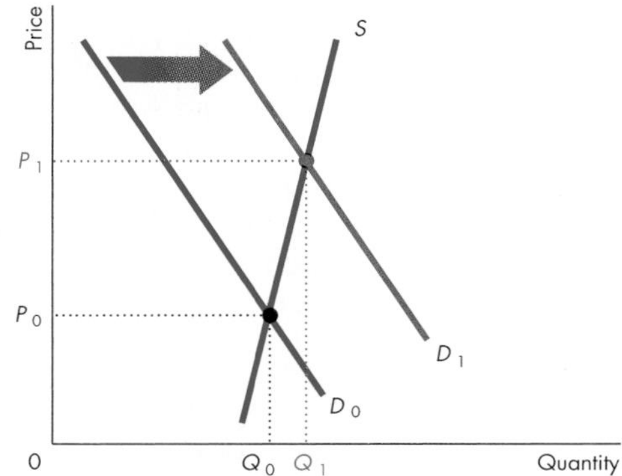

(b) Apartments

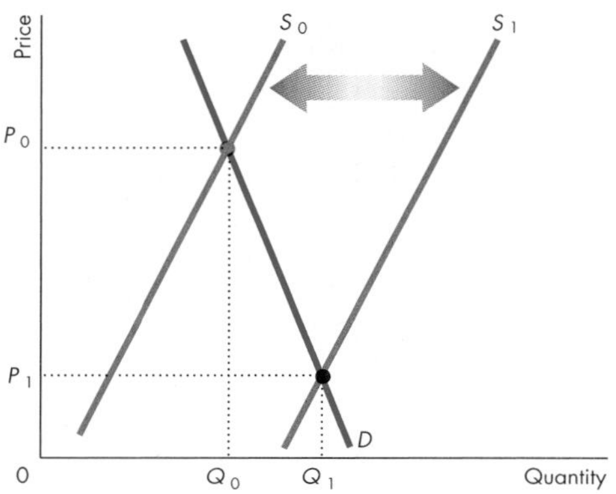

(c) Coffee

A large increase in the supply of Walkmans, from S_0 to S_1, combined with a small increase in demand, from D_0 to D_1, results in a fall in the price, from P_0 to P_1, and an increase in the quantity traded from Q_0 to Q_1 (part a). An increase in the demand for apartments produces a large increase in the price, from P_0 to P_1, but only a small increase in the quantity traded, from Q_0 to Q_1 (part b). Variations in the weather and in growing conditions lead to fluctuations in the supply of coffee, between S_0 and S_1, which produce fluctuations in the price of coffee, between P_0 and P_1, and in the quantity traded, be-

traded of those goods. Fig. 4.11 illustrates the analysis.

First, let's consider the Walkman, shown in Fig. 4.11(a). The supply of Walkmans in 1980 when the original technology was used for production, is described by the supply curve S_0. The 1980 demand curve is D_0. The quantities supplied and demanded in 1980 are equal at Q_0 and the price is P_0. Advances in technology and the building of additional production plants increase supply and shift the supply curve from S_0 to S_1. At the same time, increasing incomes increase the demand for Walkmans but not by nearly as much as the increase in supply. The demand curve shifts from D_0 to D_1. With the new demand curve D_1 and supply curve S_1, the equilibrium price is P_1 and the quantity traded is Q_1. The large increase in supply combined with a smaller increase in demand results in an increase in the quantity of Walkmans traded and a dramatic fall in their price.

Next, let's consider apartments in the centre of the city, as in Fig. 4.11(b). The supply of apartments is described by the supply curve *S*. The supply curve is steep, reflecting the fact that there is a fixed amount of urban land and a fixed number of apartment buildings. As the number of young professionals increases and the number of two-income families increases, the demand for urban apartments increases sharply. The demand curve shifts from D_0 to D_1. As a result, the price increases from P_0 to P_1 and the quantity traded also increases but not as dramatically as price.

Finally, let's consider the market for coffee, shown in Fig. 4.11(c). The demand for coffee is described by curve *D*. The supply of coffee fluctuates between S_0 and S_1. When growing conditions are good, the supply curve is S_1. When there are adverse growing conditions such as frost, the supply decreases and the supply curve is S_0. As a consequence of fluctuations in supply, the price of coffee fluctuates between P_0 (a high price) and P_1 (a low price). The quantity traded fluctuates between Q_0 and Q_1.

■ By using the theory of demand and supply, you will be able to explain past fluctuations in prices and quantities traded and also make predictions about future fluctuations. But you will want to do more than predict whether prices are going to rise or fall. You will want to predict by how much they will change when there is a change in demand or supply. To make such predictions, we need a quantitative measure of the relationship between the quantities demanded and supplied and the price. In the next chapter, we will study such a measure.

S U M M A R Y

Demand

The quantity demanded of a good or service is the amount that consumers plan to buy in a given period of time at a particular price. Demands are different from wants. Wants are unlimited, whereas demands reflect decisions to satisfy specific wants. The quantity that consumers plan to buy of any good depends on

- The price of the good.
- The prices of other goods — substitutes and complements.
- Income.
- Population.
- Preferences.

The demand schedule lists the quantities that will be demanded at each price, holding constant all other influences on consumers' planned purchases.

A demand curve graphs the quantity demanded at each price, holding everything else constant. A change in the price of a good produces a movement along the demand curve for that good. Such a movement is called a change in the quantity demanded. Changes in things other than the price of a good shift the demand curve. Such changes are said to change demand. (pp. 71-75)

Supply

The quantity supplied of a good or service is the amount that producers plan to sell in a given period of time at a particular price. The quantity that producers plan to sell of any good or service depends on

- The price of the good.
- The prices of other goods.
- The prices of the factors of production used to produce the good.
- Technology.

The supply schedule lists the quantities that will be supplied at each price, holding constant all other influences on producers' planned sales. The supply curve graphs that relationship. Changes in the price of the good produce movements along the supply curve of that good. Such movements are called changes in the quantity supplied. Changes in variables other than the price of the good shift the supply curve. Such shifts are called changes in supply. (pp. 76-79)

Price Determination

Price regulates the quantities supplied and demanded. The higher the price, the greater is the quantity supplied and the smaller is the quantity demanded. At high prices, there is a surplus — an excess of the quantity supplied over the quantity demanded. At low prices, there is a shortage — an excess of the quantity demanded over the quantity supplied. There is one price and only one price at which the quantity demanded equals the quantity supplied. That price is the equilibrium price. At that price, buyers have no incentive to offer a higher price and suppliers have no incentive to sell at a lower price. (pp. 79-82)

Predicting Changes In Price and Quantity Traded

Changes in demand and supply lead to changes in price and in the quantity traded. An increase in demand leads to a rise in the price and to an increase in the quantity traded. A decrease in demand leads to a fall in price and to a decrease in the quantity traded. An increase in supply leads to an increase in the quantity traded and to a fall in price. A decrease in supply leads to a decrease in the quantity traded and a rise in price. (pp. 82-93)

KEY ELEMENTS

Key Terms

Key Figures and Tables 

REVIEW QUESTIONS

1 Define the quantity demanded of a good or service.

2 Define the quantity supplied of a good or service.

3 Define the quantity traded and distinguish among the quantities demanded, supplied, and traded.

4 What determines the quantity demanded of a good? List the more important factors and say whether an increase in each of them increases or decreases the amount that consumers plan to buy.

5 What determines the quantity supplied? List the more important factors and say whether an increase in each of them increases or decreases the quantity that firms plan to sell.

6 State the law of demand and the law of supply.

7 The demand curve shows the quantity of a good demanded at each price. If a fixed amount of the good is available, what does the demand curve tell us about the price that consumers are willing to pay for that fixed quantity?

8 The supply curve shows the quantity supplied at each price. If consumers are willing to buy only a certain fixed quantity, what does the supply curve tell us about the price at which firms will supply that quantity?

9 Distinguish between

a) A change in demand and a change in the quantity demanded.

b) A change in supply and a change in the quantity supplied.

10 Why is the equilibrium price the price at which the quantity demanded equals the quantity supplied?

11 What happens to the price and the quantity traded of a good if

a) Demand increases?

b) Supply increases?

c) Both demand and supply increase?

d) Demand decreases?

e) Supply decreases?

f) Both demand and supply decrease?

PROBLEMS

1 Suppose that the following events occur one at a time:

a) The price of gasoline rises.

b) The price of gasoline falls.

c) All speed limits on highways are abolished.

d) A new fuel-effective engine that runs on cheap alcohol is invented.

e) The population doubles.

f) Robotic production plants lower the cost of producing cars.

g) A law banning car imports from outside North America is passed.

h) The rates for auto insurance double.

i) The national highway system is greatly improved.

j) The minimum age for drivers is increased to 19 years.

k) A massive and high-grade oil supply is discovered in Mexico.

l) The environmental lobby succeeds in closing down all nuclear power stations.

m) The price of cars rises.

n) The price of cars falls.

o) The summer temperature averages five degrees higher than normal and the winter temperature averages five degrees lower than normal.

p) GM stops making cars.

State which of these events will

1 Increase the quantity of gasoline demanded.

2 Decrease the quantity of gasoline demanded.

3 Increase the quantity of cars demanded.

4 Decrease the quantity of cars demanded.

5 Increase the quantity of gasoline supplied.

6 Decrease the quantity of gasoline supplied.

7 Increase the quantity of cars supplied.

8 Decrease the quantity of cars supplied.

9 Increase the demand for gasoline.

10 Decrease the demand for gasoline.

11 Increase the demand for cars.

12 Decrease the demand for cars.

13 Increase the supply of gasoline.

14 Decrease the supply of gasoline.

15 Increase the supply of cars.

16 Decrease the supply of cars.

17 Increase the price of gasoline.

18 Decrease the price of gasoline.

19 Increase the price of cars.

20 Decrease the price of cars.

21 Increase the quantity of gasoline purchased.

22 Decrease the quantity of gasoline purchased.

23 Increase the quantity of cars purchased.

24 Decrease the quantity of cars purchased.

2 The demand and supply schedules for gum are as follows:

Price (cents per week)	Quantity demanded	Quantity supplied
	(millions of packs per week)	
10	200	0
20	180	30
30	160	60
40	140	90
50	120	120
60	100	140
70	80	160
80	60	170
90	40	180

a) What is the equilibrium price of gum?

b) How much gum is bought and sold each week?

Suppose that a huge fire destroys one-half of the gum producing factories. Supply decreases to one-half of the amount shown in the above supply schedule.

c) What is the new equilibrium price of gum?

d) How much gum is now bought and sold each week?

e) Has there been a shift in or a movement along the supply curve of gum?

f) Has there been a shift in or a movement along the demand curve for gum?

g) As the gum factories destroyed by fire are rebuilt and gradually resume gum production, what will happen to

(i) the price of gum?
(ii) the quantity of gum traded?
(iii) the demand curve for gum?
(iv) the supply curve of gum?

PART 2

How Markets Work

TALKING WITH

MILTON FRIEDMAN

Milton Friedman spent most of his career at the University of Chicago, where he was one of the most forceful exponents of the Chicago view of economics. Currently a senior fellow at the Hoover Institution at Stanford University, he has made contributions to the theories of consumption, money, the functioning of markets, and comparative economic systems, and to the methods of scientific inquiry in economics. In 1977, Dr. Friedman was awarded the Nobel Prize in economic science.

"It always comes down to trying to understand the forces of demand and supply."

Professor Friedman, what brought you to economics?

I took my first courses in economics in 1930 and 1931, during the depths of the Depression. The choice for me was very easy, since the Depression was clearly the single most important issue facing the world.

What was your college experience in economics like?

I was lucky enough to study with two people who had a great influence on me: Homer Jones, a student of Frank Knight's and Arthur Burns, later chairman of the Fed. I took a seminar with Burns that was devoted entirely to poring over his Ph.D. thesis on U.S. production trends, sentence by sentence. It was probably the best research training I ever got!

Your lifetime contributions have spanned an enormous breadth. What is the unifying theme in all your work?

Most important is taking economics seriously. There are two ways to look at economics, I believe. One is to regard it as a game, a mathematical recreation judged by its elegance. Some of that is very impressive intellectually and contributes to our understanding of the world. The other approach descends from Alfred Marshall and his idea that economics is an engine for analyzing concrete problems. That's how I approach economics. In practice, it always comes down to trying to understand the forces of demand and supply, based on the idea of using scarce resources to achieve alternative goals. There is no major economic problem that ultimately does not reduce to this.

Can you give some examples that illustrate how economic problems of all sorts reduce to demand and supply?

When people decide what fraction of their income to consume, it's clear that they have scarce resources that they'd like to apply to alternative ends. In the realm of macroeconomics, when you're deciding how to conduct monetary policy, the paper on which currency is printed may be, in effect, unlimited, but the resources that they command are scarce. You have to decide how they should be applied. It's the same approach that Gary Becker originally used, in his dissertation, to study racial discrimination. People have scarce resources and can use them to discriminate against people. That's one goal—you may not like it, but that's a different question. So finally, my approach includes the belief that economics is capable in principle of being value-free. It's a technique of analysis, not a begging of the question of what's good or bad.

Your approach includes a methodology that some people have criticized—that you say that assumptions don't matter. Is this fair?

What I've said is that the crucial test of any hypothesis is found in its predictions, not in its assumptions. I'll give you an analogy from outside economics. I hypothesize, for example, that if I drop a ball from a building, it will hit the ground in an amount of time given by a certain formula. The formula only gives an accurate answer in a perfect vacuum. So am I actually assuming that there's a vacuum all around me as I drop the ball from the rooftop? No, of course not. I know there isn't a vacuum. But it doesn't make any difference. How do I know? There's only one way to tell. I predict that the ball will hit the ground in so much time. You tell me what range of error you'll permit. Then we drop the ball. If it hits the ground within the range you set, then I'm getting correct results by *assuming* that there is a vacuum.

Another use of assumptions is to let them stand in for a body of complex propositions. For example, I can predict the density of distribution of leaves on a tree by supposing that the leaves deliberately position themselves to get maximum sunlight. Now that gives me good predictions, but I obviously don't really believe that the leaves do this. In economics, we say that people in business behave as if they know what their production functions are. It's just a shorthand—a good one if it works.

By the way, the article in which I made these comments about assumptions has given rise to more comments and attacks than any other I've written. I never replied to any of them, because I decided that I'd rather spend my time doing economics than talking about how economics should be done.

You've studied the effectiveness of markets. What do we know about how markets work?

I always say that economists may not know much, but we know one thing very well, and that's how to create shortages and surpluses. Just tell us which you want! If you want a shortage, all we have to do is to set a price that's below the market price and I'll guarantee you a shortage. If you want a surplus, set a price too high and you'll have your surplus.

The contrast between the taxicab markets in New York and Washington, D.C., is a good example with many implications. In Washington, because government officials, who control the city, want cheap taxicab rides, entry into the taxicab industry is virtually free. Prices are fixed, but also elastic and responsive to change. In New York,

"The crucial test of any hypothesis is in its predictions, not its assumptions."

"What's true for the individual is the opposite of what's true for the society."

however, there is essentially a taxicab cartel, a limit on the number of taxicab medallions—a breakdown of the market. Therefore, these licenses have a very high value—somewhere over a hundred thousand dollars. One consequence is that it's often difficult to find a cab in New York, while there are almost always cabs available in Washington. But the most important effect, in my mind, is that the fraction of black and Latin cab drivers and owners is high in Washington but very low in New York. That's because many members of minority groups can't afford to break into the business. And that's a tragedy.

What have been the most important developments in economics of the past 20 years?

Let's divide that question into developments in the theoretical discipline and in the world of economics. In the discipline, I'd say the rational expectations revolution, the public choice approach, and the revival of money as an important factor in macroeconomics. In the world of economics, there's no doubt that the most important change is the complete loss of faith in socialism—the triumph of capitalism over socialism as an ideology, though not as an actual practice. In fact, there's been very little change in the practice, but there's been the enormous change whereby practically nobody believes that a centrally planned economy is the right way to get prosperity. Twenty years ago that wasn't true.

What advice would you share with a student studying economics for the first time?

Try to get a feel for the central principles of demand and supply, for how these two forces are reconciled with each other. Work to understand the function of prices and the price system. Don't worry about all the intricate details of the banking system or the institutions you're familiar with now. I'd also propose the statement that it's generally correct that what's true for the individual is the opposite of what's true for the society. Find out why that's so.

CHAPTER 5

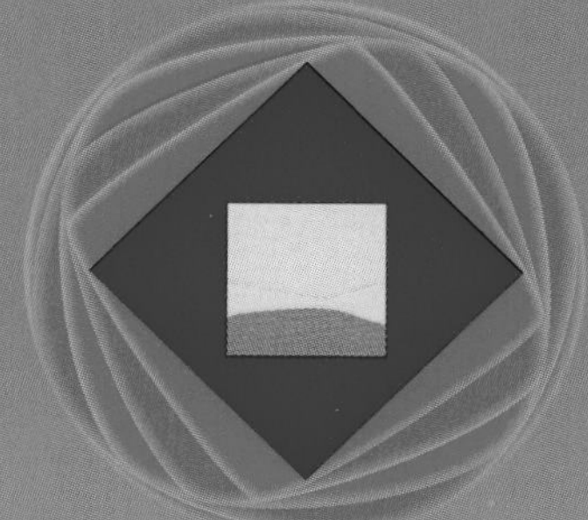

Elasticity

After studying this chapter, you will be able to:

- Define and calculate the price elasticity of demand.
- Explain what determines the elasticity of demand.
- Distinguish between short-run demand and long-run demand.
- Use elasticity to determine whether a price change will increase or decrease revenue.
- Define and calculate other elasticities of demand and supply.
- Distinguish between momentary supply, long-run supply, and short-run supply.

OPEC's Dilemma

IF THE SUPPLY OF A GOOD FALLS, its price rises. But by how much? To answer this question, you will have to don a flowing caftan: you have just been named chief economic strategist for OPEC — the Organization of Petroleum Exporting Countries. You want to bring more money into OPEC. Would you restrict the supply of oil to raise prices? Or would you produce more oil? ■ You know that a higher price will bring in more dollars per barrel, but lower production means that fewer barrels will be sold. Will the price rise high enough to offset the smaller quantity that OPEC will sell? ■ As OPEC's economic strategist, you need to know about the demand for oil in great detail. For example, as the world economy grows, how will that growth translate into an increasing demand for oil? What about substitutes for oil? Will we discover inexpensive methods to convert coal and tar sands into usable fuel? Will nuclear energy become safe and cheap enough to compete with oil?

■ In this chapter you will learn how to tackle questions such as the ones posed. You will learn how we can measure in a precise way the responsiveness of the quantities bought and sold to changes in prices and other influences on buyers or sellers.

Price Elasticity of Demand

Let's begin by looking a bit more closely at your task as OPEC's economic strategist. You are trying to decide whether to advise a cut in output to shift the supply curve to the left and raise the price of oil. To make this decision, you need to know how the quantity of oil demanded responds to a change in price. You also need some way to measure that response.

Two Possible Scenarios

To understand the importance of the responsiveness of the quantity of oil demanded to a change in its price, let's compare two possible (hypothetical) scenarios in the oil industry, shown in Fig. 5.1. In the two parts of the figure, the supply curves are identical, but the demand curves differ.

Focus first on the supply curve labelled S_0 in each part of the figure. This curve represents the initial supply of oil. Notice that this supply curve cuts the demand curve, in both cases, at a price of $10 a barrel and a quantity traded of 40 million barrels a day. Now suppose that you contemplate a cut in supply that shifts the supply curve from S_0 to S_1. In Fig. 5.1(a), the new supply curve S_1 cuts the demand curve D_a at a price of $30 a barrel and a quantity traded of 23 million barrels a day. In part (b), the supply curve shifts by the same amount, but the new supply curve S_1 cuts the demand curve D_b at a price of $15 a barrel and a quantity traded of 15 million barrels a day.

Figure 5.1 Demand, Supply, and Total Revenue

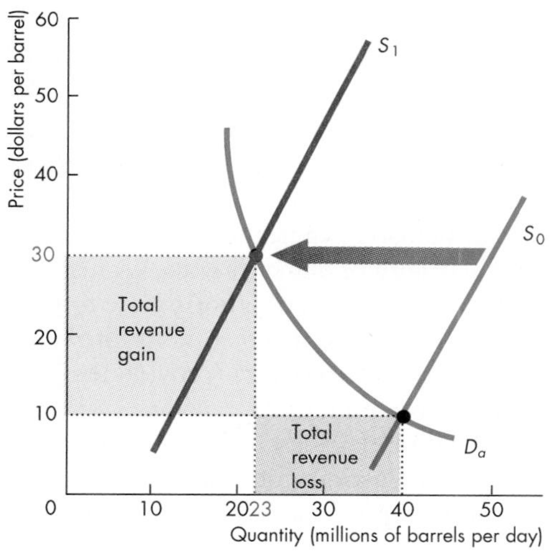

(a) More total revenue

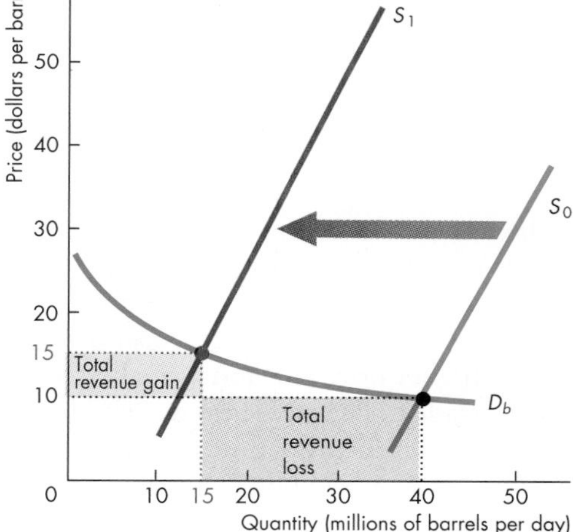

(b) Less total revenue

If supply decreases from S_0 to S_1, the price increases and the quantity traded decreases. In part (a), total revenue — the quantity traded multiplied by price — rises from $400 million to $690 million per day. The increase in total revenue from a higher price (blue area) exceeds the decrease in total revenue from lower sales (red area). In part (b), total revenue falls from $400 million to $225 million per day. The increase in total revenue from a higher price (blue area) is smaller than the decrease in total revenue from lower sales (red area). These two different responses in total revenue arise from different responses of the quantity demanded to a change in price. In the figure, total revenue increases when the demand curve is steep; it falls when the demand curve is flat. To compare the responsiveness of two demand curves, we must draw them on the same scale. Changing the scale or the units of measurement will change the slope of the demand curve, thus creating the illusion of a different degree of responsiveness.

You can see that in part (a) the price rises by more and the quantity traded falls by less than it does in part (b). What happens to the total revenue of the oil producers in these two cases? The **total revenue** from the sale of a good equals the price of the good multiplied by the quantity sold.

An increase in price has two opposing effects on total revenue. The higher price brings in more revenue on each unit sold (blue area) but the higher price leads to a decrease in the quantity sold, which in turn results in less total revenue (red area). In the case in Fig. 5.1(a), the first effect is larger (the blue area exceeds the red area), so total revenue rises. In the case in Fig. 5.1(b), the second effect is larger (the red area exceeds the blue area), so total revenue falls.

You can confirm these results by doing some multiplication. In both cases, the original total revenue was $400 million a day ($10 a barrel × 40 million barrels a day). What happens to the total revenue after the supply is reduced? In part (a), total revenue goes up to $690 million a day ($30 a barrel × 23 million barrels a day). In part (b), total revenue falls to $225 million a day ($15 a barrel × 15 million barrels a day).

Slope Depends on Units of Measurement

What differs in these two cases is how the quantity demanded responds to a change in the price of oil. Demand curve D_a is much steeper than demand curve D_b. For the same cut in supply, the steeper demand curve causes a higher price rise and a smaller drop in the quantity traded. The steepness of the demand curve is one way of measuring how the quantity demanded of a good is affected by its price. A steep demand curve means that the quantity demanded does not respond much to price changes. A relatively flat demand curve means that the quantity demanded responds greatly to price changes.

But the slope of a demand curve depends on the units that we put on the axes of the diagram. In Fig. 5.1, we use the same units in both parts so that we can compare the demand curves D_a and D_b. However, we can easily make the demand curve D_b look as steep as D_a by changing the units on the axes of the figure. If, in part (b), we measure quantity in hundreds of millions of barrels a day, the demand curve D_b will be almost vertical. It will look much steeper than demand curve D_a, but the appearance will be an illusion.

If, again in part (b), we measure the price in cents per barrel, the demand curve D_b will appear much steeper than the curve D_a. Again, the appearance will be an illusion.

Since we can influence the slope of a demand curve purely by our choice of the units in which we measure prices and quantities, we cannot hope to find a rule that tells us how total revenue responds to a price change that is based on only the slope of the demand curve. What we need is a measure of response that is independent of our units of measurement of prices and quantities. Price elasticity of demand is such a measure.

A Units-Free Measure of Response

Price elasticity of demand measures the responsiveness of the quantity demanded of a good to a change in its price. It measures responsiveness as the percentage change in the quantity demanded that results from a one percent change in price. Our main interest is in the *magnitude* or *absolute value* of the percentage change in the quantity demanded that results from a one percent change in price. When the price of a good *increases* along a demand curve, the quantity demanded *decreases*. If the percentage change in price is *positive*, then the percentage change in quantity demanded is *negative*. As a consequence, the price elasticity of demand is a negative number. Because the price elasticity of demand is always negative, we adopt the convention of ignoring the minus sign and speaking of the magnitude or absolute value of the elasticity. Also, for simplicity (provided no ambiguity will result), we often drop the word "price" and simply refer to the elasticity of demand. Whenever we use the term **elasticity of demand**, we mean the *absolute value* of the *price* elasticity of demand.

Let's calculate an elasticity of demand.

Calculating Elasticity

In order to calculate the elasticity of demand, we need to know the quantities demanded at different prices. We also need some reasonable assurance that when the price changes, nothing else that influences consumers' buying plans changes. As an example, let's assume we have the relevant data on prices and quantities demanded for the oil industry. The calculations that we will perform are summarized in Table 5.1. You can use the symbols and the formulas shown in the final column of the table to perform

Table 5.1 Calculating the Price Elasticity of Demand

	Numbers	Symbols and formulas*
Prices (dollars per barrel)		
Original price	9.50	P_0
New price	10.50	P_1
Change in price	1.00	$\Delta P = P_1 - P_0$
Average price	10.00	$P_{ave} = (P_0 + P_1)/2$
Percentage change in price	10 %	$(\Delta P/P_{ave}) \times 100$
Quantities (millions of barrels per day)		
Original quantity demanded	41	Q_0
New quantity demanded	39	Q_1
Change in quantity demanded	– 2	$\Delta Q = Q_1 - Q_0$
Average quantity demanded	40	$Q_{ave} = (Q_0 + Q_1)/2$
Percentage change in quantity demanded	– 5 %	$(\Delta Q/Q_{ave}) \times 100$
Percentage change in quantity demanded divided by percentage change in price	– 0.5	$(\Delta Q/Q_{ave})/(\Delta P/P_{ave})$
Price elasticity of demand	0.5	η

*The Greek letter *delta* (Δ) stands for "change in."

the same calculations on any set of numbers.

At \$9.50 a barrel, 41 million barrels a day are sold. As the price increases to \$10.50 a barrel, the quantity demanded decreases to 39 million barrels a day. When the price increases by \$1.00 a barrel, the quantity demanded decreases by 2 million barrels a day. To calculate the elasticity of demand, we have to express changes in price and quantity demanded as percentage changes. But there are two prices and two quantities — the original and the new. Which price and which quantity do we use for calculating the percentage change? By convention, we use the *average price* and the *average quantity*. The formula for calculating a percentage change (in either the price or the quantity) is:

$$\text{Percentage change} = \frac{\text{Change in value}}{\text{Average value}} \times 100.$$

Let's use this formula to calculate the percentage changes in price and quantity. The original price was \$9.50 and the new price is \$10.50, so the average price is \$10.00. When the price increases by \$1.00, it increases by 10 percent of the average price. The original quantity was 41 million barrels and the new quantity is 39 million barrels, so the average quantity demanded is 40 million barrels. When the quantity decreases by 2 million barrels a day, it decreases by 5 percent of the average quantity.

The percentage change in the quantity demanded divided by the percentage change in the price is:

$$-\frac{5\%}{10\%} = -0.5.$$

Remember, elasticity of demand (η) is the absolute

value of the ratio of the percentage change in the quantity demanded to the percentage change in the price. That is,

$$\eta = 0.5.$$

Notice two things about the calculation of the price elasticity of demand:

1 The changes in prices and quantities demanded are expressed as percentages of the *average* price and *average* quantity demanded. We do this to avoid the awkwardness of having two values for the elasticity of demand, depending on whether the price increases (from the original price to the new price) or the price decreases (from the new price back to the original price). The price and quantity demanded change by the same absolute amounts in each case — in our example, \$1.00 a barrel and 2 million barrels a day. But \$1.00 is 10.5 percent of \$9.50, whereas it is only 9.5 percent of \$10.50. Furthermore, 2 million barrels a day is 4.9 percent of 41 million barrels but 5.1 percent of 39 million barrels. If we use these numbers to calculate the elasticity, we get a value of – 0.54 for an increase in the price from \$9.50 to \$10.50 and – 0.47 for a decrease in the price from \$10.50 to \$9.50. By using the average price and average quantity demanded, we calculate an elasticity that is the same, – 0.5, regardless of whether the price increases or decreases.

2 Although it is convenient to think of elasticity as the ratio of the percentage change in the quantity demanded to the percentage change in the price, it is also, equivalently, the proportionate change in the quantity demanded divided by the proportionate change in the price. In Table 5.1, notice that although the formula multiplies both the proportionate change in price ($\Delta P / P_{ave}$) and the proportionate change in quantity demanded ($\Delta Q / Q_{ave}$) by 100 to create a percentage, those hundreds cancel when we divide.

R E V I E W

Elasticity is a units-free measure of response. The price elasticity of demand — or simply, the elasticity of demand — is calculated as the absolute value of the percentage change in the quantity demanded divided by the percentage change in price. ■

Elastic and Inelastic Demand

The elasticity that we have just calculated in our example is 0.5. Is that a large or a small value for an elasticity? The magnitude of the elasticity of demand can range between zero and infinity. The elasticity of demand is zero if the quantity demanded does not change when the price changes. You can see that by assuming that the percentage change in the quantity demanded is zero and then doing a little calculation. It doesn't matter what the percentage change in the price is because if we divide zero by any number, we get zero. An example of a good that has a very low elasticity of demand (perhaps zero) is insulin. This commodity is of such importance to many diabetics that they would buy the quantity they need for their health at almost any price.

When a price change causes a change in the quantity demanded, the magnitude of the elasticity of demand is greater than zero. If the percentage change in the quantity demanded is less than the percentage change in price, the elasticity is a fraction (the example that we calculated in Table 5.1 is such a case). If the percentage change in the quantity demanded exactly equals the percentage change in price, the elasticity of demand is 1. If the percentage change in the quantity demanded exceeds the percentage change in price, the elasticity of demand is greater than 1.

In an extreme case, the quantity demanded may be infinitely sensitive to price changes. At a particular price, people demand any quantity of a good, but if the price changes by 1 cent, the quantity demanded will drop to zero. In this case, an almost zero percentage change in the price produces an infinite percentage change in the quantity demanded, so the elasticity of demand is infinity. An example of a good that has a very high elasticity of demand (almost infinite) is Sealtest 2% milk. If the price of a litre of Sealtest 2% milk increases, while all other prices, including the prices of competing brands of 2% milk, remain constant, there will be an infinitely large decrease in the quantity of Sealtest milk consumed. Other brands of 2% milk are almost perfect substitutes for Sealtest.

For elasticities between zero and 1, demand is called **inelastic**. When the elasticity is greater than 1, demand is said to be **elastic**. The dividing line between inelastic and elastic demand is called **unit elastic demand**. When elasticity is equal to infinity, demand is called **perfectly elastic**; when elasticity is equal to zero, demand is called **perfectly inelastic**.

Table 5.2 Inelastic, Unit Elastic, and Elastic Demands: Effects of a 10 Percent Change in Price

	Original quantity demanded	New quantity demanded	Average quantity demanded	Change in quantity demanded	Percentage change in quantity demanded	Elasticity of demand
Inelastic	41	39	40	– 2	– 5	0.5
Unit elastic	42	38	40	– 4	–10	1.0
Elastic	50	30	40	–20	–50	5.0

Table 5.2 shows examples of inelastic, elastic, and unit elastic demands. We can see in this table the decreases in quantities demanded for a 10 percent increase in price. The first row simply reproduces the calculations that you worked through in Table 5.1. The second row shows the case of a unit elastic demand. The initial quantity demanded was 42 million barrels a day and the new quantity demanded is 38. Thus the average quantity demanded is 40 and the change in the quantity demanded is – 4. The percentage change in the quantity demanded is – 10 percent. Therefore the elasticity of demand is 1. The final case is one in which the original quantity demanded was 50 and the new quantity demanded is 30. The average quantity demanded is still 40 but the change in quantity demanded is now – 20. The percentage change in the quantity demanded is – 50 percent. In this case, the elasticity is 5.

Elasticity is not just a number calculated by economists. Whether demand is elastic or inelastic is of enormous importance to each of us. In the 1970s, when OPEC did in fact cut back on the supply of oil, North Americans discovered that their demand for oil was inelastic. Despite the lower supplies, we still demanded a lot of oil and gasoline, which led to cuts in spending on other goods and services — people took fewer vacations; huge companies were thrown into turmoil as they tried to adjust; people lowered their thermostats and formed car pools; speed restrictions were imposed; and angry car owners had to face the premature obsolescence of their gas guzzlers.

Elasticity and the Slope of the Demand Curve

Elasticity is not the same as slope, but the two are related. However, that connection is not entirely straightforward. To understand the relation better, we'll consider the elasticity along a demand curve that has a constant slope. Such a demand curve is a straight line.

Let's calculate the elasticity of the straight-line demand curve shown in Fig. 5.2. To do so, we first pick an initial price and quantity demanded. Next, we change the price and observe the change in the quantity demanded. Finally, we combine the information on prices and quantities to calculate elasticity by using the discarded formula.

Let's start with a price of $50 a barrel. What is the elasticity if we lower the price from $50 to $40? The decrease in the price is $10 and the average price is $45 (average of $50 and $40), which means that the proportionate decrease in price is

$$\Delta P / P_{ave} = 10/45.$$

The original quantity demanded was zero and the new quantity demanded is 10 million barrels a day, so the increase in the quantity demanded is 10 million barrels a day and the average quantity is 5 million barrels a day (the average of 10 million and zero). We can use these numbers to calculate the proportionate increase in the quantity demanded as

$$\Delta Q / Q_{ave} = 10/5.$$

To calculate the elasticity of demand, we divide the proportionate increase in the quantity demanded by the proportionate decrease in the price. That is

$$\eta = (\Delta Q/ Q_{ave})/(\Delta P/ P_{ave}) = (10/5)\,/(10/45) = 9.$$

Using the same method, we can calculate the elasticity of demand when the price of a barrel is cut repeatedly by $10 — from $45 to $35, from $40 to $30, from $35 to $25, and so on. You can verify the

Figure 5.2 Elasticity Along a Straight-Line Demand Curve

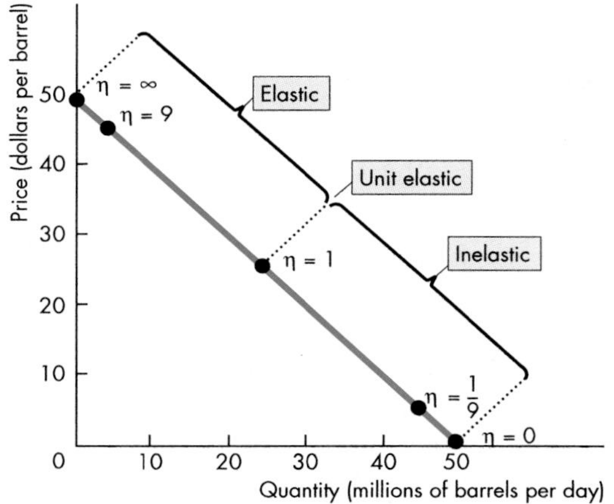

On a straight-line demand curve, elasticity falls as the price decreases and the quantity demanded increases. Demand is unit elastic at the midpoint of the demand curve (elasticity is 1). Above the midpoint, demand is elastic (elasticity is greater than 1); below the midpoint, demand is inelastic (elasticity is less than 1).

elasticity of demand at other points on the demand curve in Fig. 5.2. Notice that on a straight-line demand curve, the elasticity falls as the price decreases.

At the midpoint of the demand curve, where the price is $25 a barrel and the quantity demanded is 25 million barrels a day, elasticity is exactly 1. Above the midpoint, the elasticity is larger than 1, and it rises as the price rises. Below the midpoint, the elasticity is less than 1, and it falls as the price falls. Elasticity is infinity when the price is $50 a barrel and the quantity demanded is zero, and elasticity is zero when the quantity demanded is 50 million barrels a day and the price is zero. We can use the formula for elasticity of demand to verify these values.

But why does the elasticity along a straight-line demand curve decrease as the price decreases? In the example in Fig. 5.2, no matter what the average price and average quantity demanded, as the price decreases by $10 a barrel, the quantity demanded rises by 10 million barrels a day. At a high average price, the average quantity demanded is small, so the percentage change in the quantity demanded is larger than the percentage change in the price: the elasticity of demand is greater than 1. At a low average price, the average quantity demanded is large, so the percentage change in the quantity demanded is smaller than the percentage change in the price: the elasticity of demand is less than 1. At the midpoint, the average price and average quantity demanded are such that the percentage changes in the price and quantity demanded are equal: the elasticity of demand is 1.

Figure 5.3 Demand Curves with Constant Elasticity

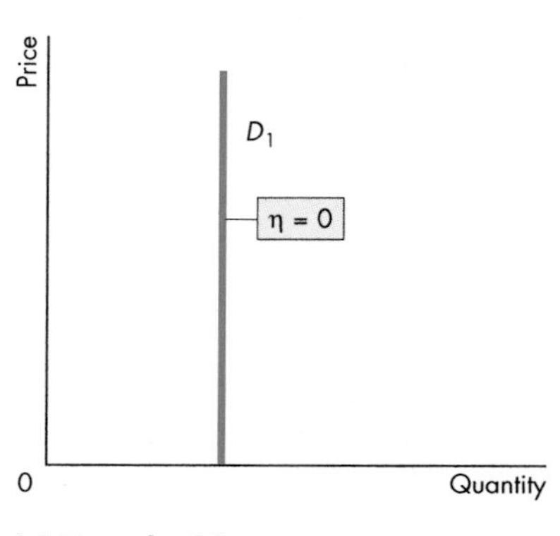

(a) Zero elasticity

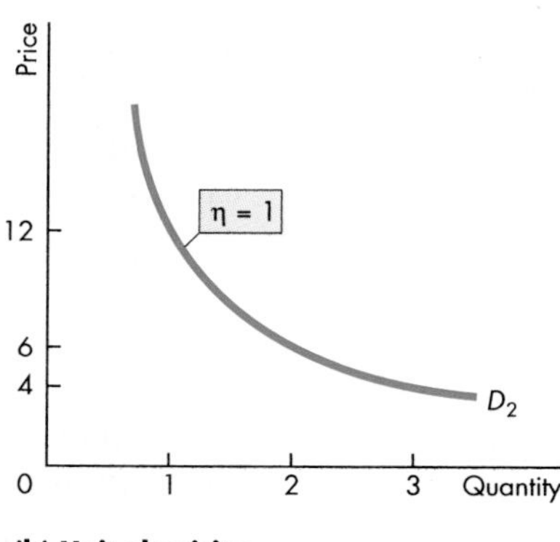

(b) Unit elasticity

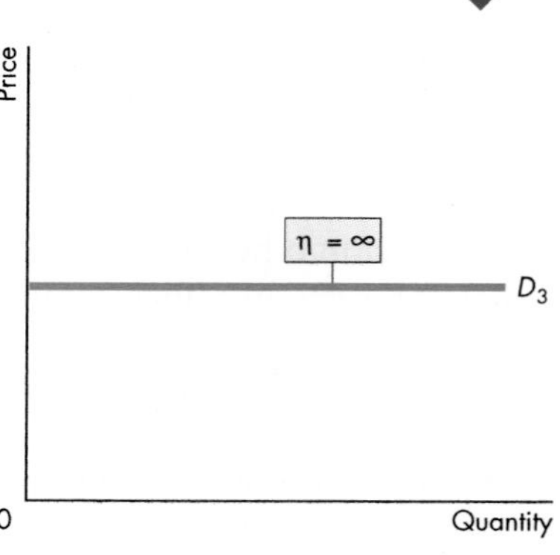

(c) Infinite elasticity

Each demand curve shown here has a constant elasticity. The demand curve in part (a) has zero elasticity. The demand curve in part (b) has unit elasticity. The demand curve in part (c) has infinite elasticity.

A demand curve can have a constant elasticity. A perfectly inelastic demand curve has a constant elasticity of zero ($\eta = 0$) and is vertical. A perfectly elastic demand curve has a constant elasticity of infinity ($\eta = \infty$) and is horizontal. Other constant elasticity demand curves are *curved.* Figure 5.3 illustrates three constant elasticity demand curves — the cases of zero, unity, and infinity.

The example we gave earlier of a good with very low elasticity of demand is insulin — shown as zero in Fig. 5.3(a). Regardless of the price, the quantity demanded remains constant. An example of a good whose elasticity is close to 1 is electricity — shown in Fig. 5.3(b). As its price increases, the quantity demanded decreases by the same percentage amount. The example we gave of a good whose elasticity is (almost) infinite is Sealtest 2% milk — shown in Fig. 5.3(c). Sealtest is bought only if its price equals that of identical competing brands. If the price of Sealtest milk exceeds the price of competing brands, the quantity of Sealtest demanded is zero. If the price of competing brands exceeds that of Sealtest, Sealtest is the only 2% milk bought. When the prices are equal, there is no unique quantity demanded.

Real-World Elasticities Values of elasticities of demand have been estimated from the average spending patterns of consumers. Some representative examples are set out in Table 5.3.

Table 5.3 Some Real-World Price Elasticities

Industry	Elasticity
Elastic Demand	
Metals	1.52
Electrical engineering products	1.39
Mechanical engineering products	1.30
Furniture	1.26
Motor vehicles	1.14
Instrument engineering products	1.10
Professional services	1.09
Transportation services	1.03
Inelastic Demand	
Gas, electricity, and water	0.92
Oil	0.91
Chemicals	0.89
Beverages (all types)	0.78
Tobacco	0.61
Food	0.58
Banking and insurance services	0.56
Housing services	0.55
Clothing	0.49
Agricultural and fish products	0.42
Books, magazines, and newspapers	0.34
Coal	0.32

Source: Ahsan Mansur and John Whalley, "Numerical Specification of Applied General Equilibrium Models: Estimation, Calibration, and Data," in *Applied General Equilibrium Analysis*, eds. Herbert E. Scarf and John B. Shoven (New York: Cambridge University Press, 1984), 109.

The Size of the Elasticity of Demand

What makes the demand for some goods elastic and the demand for others inelastic? Elasticity of demand depends on

- The ease with which one good can be substituted for another.
- The proportion of income spent on the good.
- The amount of time elapsed since the price change.

Substitutability Substitutability depends on the nature of the good itself. For example, oil is a good that certainly has substitutes but none that is very close (imagine a steam-driven, coal-fuelled car or a nuclear-powered jetliner). On the other hand, metals are goods that have very good substitutes in the form of plastics. The demand for metals is more elastic than the demand for oil.

The degree of substitutability between two goods depends on how narrowly (or broadly) we define them. For example, even though oil does not have a close substitute, different types of oil substitute for each other without much difficulty. Oils from different parts of the world differ in weight and chemical composition. Let's consider a particular kind of oil — called Saudi Arabian Light. Its elasticity of demand will be relevant if you happen to be the economic advisor to Saudi Arabia (as well as the OPEC economic strategist!). Suppose Saudi Arabia is contemplating a unilateral price rise, which means that prices of other types of oil will stay the same. Although Saudi Arabian Light has some unique characteristics, other oils can easily substitute for it, and most buyers are very sensitive to its price relative to the prices of other types of oil. As a result the demand for Saudi Arabian Light is highly elastic.

This example, which distinguishes between oil in general and different types of oil, has broad applications. For example, the demand for meat in general has a lower elasticity than the demand for beef, lamb, or pork. The demand for personal computers has a lower elasticity than the demand for IBM, Toshiba, or Apple computers.

Proportion of Income Spent on a Good Elasticity of demand is higher, other things being equal, the higher is the proportion of income spent on a good. If only a small fraction of income is spent on a good, a change in its price will have little impact on the consumer's overall budget. In contrast, even a small increase in the price of a good that commands a large part of a consumer's budget will induce the consumer to undertake a radical reappraisal of expenditures.

To appreciate the importance of the proportion of income spent on a good, consider the elasticity of demand for textbooks and chewing gum. If the price of textbooks doubles (increases 100 percent), there is an enormous decrease in the quantity of textbooks bought. There is an increase in sharing and in illegal photocopying. If the price of chewing gum doubles, also a 100 percent increase, there is almost no change in the quantity of gum demanded. Why the difference? Textbooks take a large proportion of a student's budget while gum takes only a tiny portion. You don't like either price increase, but you hardly notice the effects of the increased price of gum, while the increased price of textbooks blows you away!

Time Elasticity of demand also depends on the amount of time elapsed since the price change. In general, the greater the lapse of time, the higher is the elasticity of demand. The reason is substitutability. The greater the passage of time, the more it becomes possible to develop substitutes for the good whose price has increased. Thus at the moment of a price increase, consumers often have little choice but to continue consuming similar quantities of a good. However, given enough time, consumers find alternatives or cheaper substitutes and gradually cut their purchases of the item that has become more expensive.

REVIEW

The elasticity of demand ranges between zero and infinity. Goods for which there are close substitutes and on which a large proportion of income is spent have a higher elasticity of demand than goods for which there are no good substitutes and on which a small portion of income is spent. Elasticity is also higher, the longer is the time lapse since the price change. ■

Two Time Frames for Demand

To take account of the importance of time on the elasticity of demand, we distinguish between two time frames for demand — the short run and the long run. Let's examine them now.

Short-Run Demand

The **short-run demand curve** describes the initial response of buyers to a change in the price of a good. The short-run response depends on whether the price change is seen as permanent (or, at least, long-lasting) or temporary. A price change that is believed to be temporary produces a highly elastic buyer response. Why would you pay a higher price now if you can get the same thing for a lower price a few days from now? And if the price is temporarily low, why wouldn't you take advantage of it and buy a lot before the price goes up again?

Examples of temporary price changes abound. For example, you can make telephone calls at much lower rates during the evening than during the business day. The drop in price at 6:00 p.m. (and a further drop at 11:00 p.m.) and the rise in price at 9:00 a.m. produces a large change in the quantity demanded — demand is highly elastic. Of course, many calls are made during normal business hours, but the lower price in the evening induces a large switch from business-day calling to night-time calling. Other examples are seasonal variations in the prices of travel and certain fresh fruits and vegetables.

When a price change seems permanent, the quantity bought does not change much in the short run. That is, short-run demand is more inelastic. The reason is that people find it hard to change their buying habits. More important, they often have to adjust their consumption of other complementary goods, an expensive and time-consuming undertaking.

An example of a permanent or at least a long-lasting price change occurred in the market for oil in the early 1970s. At the end of 1973 and the beginning of 1974, the price of oil increased 400 percent, leading in turn to a sharp rise in the costs of home heating and of gasoline. Initially, consumers had little choice but to accept the price increases and maintain consumption at more or less their original levels. Home-heating equipment and cars may not have been the most energy-efficient, but there was nothing else available. Drivers could lower their average speed and economize on gasoline. Thermostats could be turned down but that too imposed costs — costs of discomfort. As a consequence, there were severe limits in the extent to which people felt it worthwhile cutting back on their consumption of the now much more costly fuel, oil, and gasoline. The short-run buyer response to this sharp price increase was inelastic.

Long-Run Demand

The **long-run demand curve** describes the response of buyers to a change in price after buyers have made all possible adjustments to their buying plans. Long-run demand is more elastic than short-run demand. The 1974 rise in the price of oil and gasoline produced a clear demonstration of the distinction between long-run and short-run demand. Initially, buyers responded to higher gasoline and oil prices by using their existing capital equipment — furnaces and gas guzzlers — in a way that economized on the more expensive fuel. With a longer time to respond, people bought more energy-efficient capital equipment. Cars became smaller and more fuel-efficient; car engines also became more efficient.

Two Demand Curves

The short-run and long-run demand curves for oil in 1974 appear in Fig. 5.4. The short-run demand curve (SD) shows the initial response of the quantity demanded to a permanent change in price. The long-run demand curve (LD) shows the change in the quantity demanded after buyers have made all possible adjustments.

The price of a barrel of oil in 1974 was $10, and the quantity of oil traded in that year was 40 million barrels a day. The two demand curves have been drawn to intersect at that price and quantity. At that point of intersection, the long-run demand curve is more elastic than the short-run demand curve.

In Chapter 6, we'll use the short-run and long-run demand curves to work out what happens in a market when supply changes.

Figure 5.4 Short-Run and Long-Run Demand

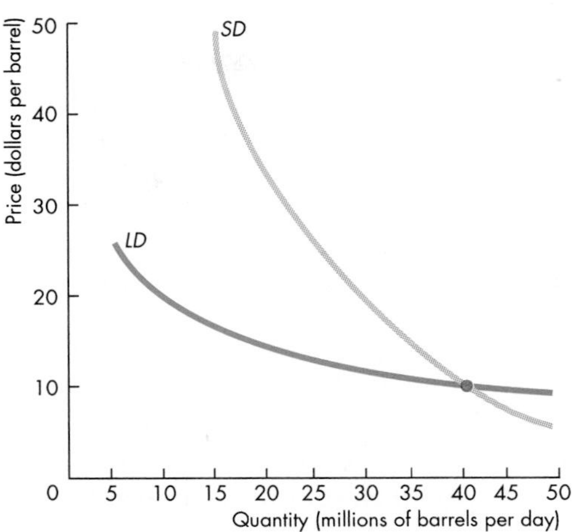

The short-run demand curve (*SD*) shows the initial response of the quantity demanded to a change in the price of a good, before buyers have had sufficient time to make all possible adjustments to their buying plans. The long-run demand curve (*LD*) shows how the quantity demanded varies with the price of a good when buyers have made all possible adjustments to their buying plans.

Elasticity, Total Revenue, and Total Expenditure

We've defined total revenue as the price of a good multiplied by the quantity sold. **Total expenditure** is the price of a good multiplied by the quantity *bought.* Thus, total revenue and total expenditure are two sides of the same coin — revenue is the sellers' receipts and expenditure is the buyers' outlays. When the price of a good rises along a demand curve, the quantity sold falls. What happens to total revenue (and total expenditure) depends on the extent to which the quantity sold decreases as the price increases. If a 1 percent increase in the price reduces the quantity sold by less than 1 percent, total revenue rises. If a 1 percent increase in price lowers the quantity sold by more than 1 percent, total revenue falls. If a 1 percent increase in price lowers the quantity sold by 1 percent, the price increase and the quantity decrease offset each other and total revenue stays constant. But we now have a precise way of linking the percentage change of the quantity sold to the percentage change in price — the elasticity of demand. When the price of a good increases, the size of the elasticity of demand determines whether total revenue rises or falls. Table 5.4 provides some examples based on the three cases in Table 5.2.

In case *a*, the elasticity of demand is 0.5. When the price goes up from $9.50 to $10.50, the quantity sold falls from 41 million to 39 million barrels a day. Total revenue, which is equal to price multiplied by quantity sold, was originally $9.50 multiplied by 41 million, which is $389.5 million a day. After the price increases, total revenue rises to $409.5 million a day. Thus an increase in the price leads to a *rise* in total revenue of $20 million a day.

In case *b*, the elasticity of demand is 1. As the price increases from $9.50 to $10.50, the quantity sold decreases from 42 million to 38 million barrels a day. Total revenue in this case is the same at each price, $399 million a day. Thus when the price changes and the elasticity of demand is 1, total revenue *does not change.*

In case *c*, the elasticity of demand is 5. When the price increases by $1, the quantity sold decreases from 50 million barrels a day to 30 million barrels a day. The original revenue was $475 million a day, but the new revenue is $315 million a day. Thus in this case, an increase in the price leads to a *fall* in total revenue of $160 million a day.

Elasticity and total revenue are closely connected. When the elasticity of demand is greater than 1, the percentage decrease in the quantity demanded exceeds the percentage increase in price. Therefore a price increase lowers total revenue. When the elasticity of demand is less than 1, the percentage decrease in the quantity demanded is less than the percentage increase in price. Therefore a price increase increases total revenue. When the elasticity of demand is 1, the percentage decrease in the quantity demanded equals the percentage increase in price. Total revenue remains constant as the price increases. The extra total revenue from a higher price is exactly offset by the loss in total revenue from the smaller quantities sold.

As we have seen, long-run demand curves are more elastic than short-run demand curves. It is possible, therefore, that an increase in price will result in an increase in total revenue in the short run but not in the long run. If the short-run elasticity is less than 1 but the long-run elasticity is greater than 1, this outcome will occur.

The price elasticity of demand that you have just learned to calculate and interpret is the most important of all the elasticities. Whenever economists refer to the elasticity of demand without qualification, they mean the price elasticity of demand. There are, however, some other elasticities of demand. Let's now turn our attention to them.

More Demand Elasticities

The quantity demanded of any good (or service or factor of production) is influenced by many things other than its price. It depends

Table 5.4 Elasticity of Demand, Total Revenue, and Total Expenditure

	Elasticity	Price (dollars per barrel)		Quantity demanded (millions of barrels per day)		Total revenue/ Total expenditure (millions of dollars per day)		
		Original	New	Original	New	Original	New	Change
a	0.5	9.50	10.50	41	39	389.5	409.5	+20
b	1.0	9.50	10.50	42	38	399.0	399.0	0
c	5.0	9.50	10.50	50	30	475.0	315.0	– 160

Figure 5.5 Income Elasticity of Demand

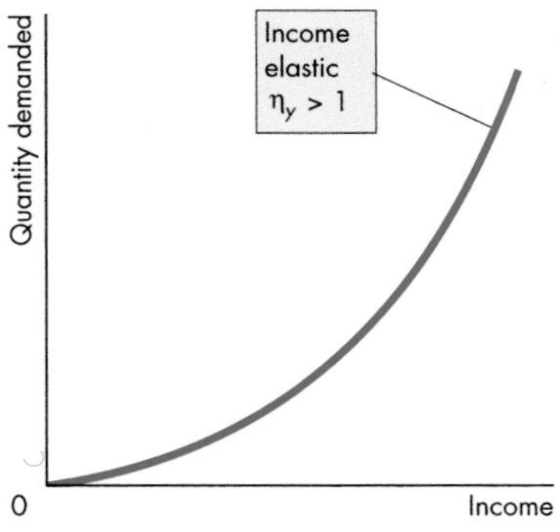

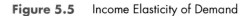

(a) Elasticity greater than 1

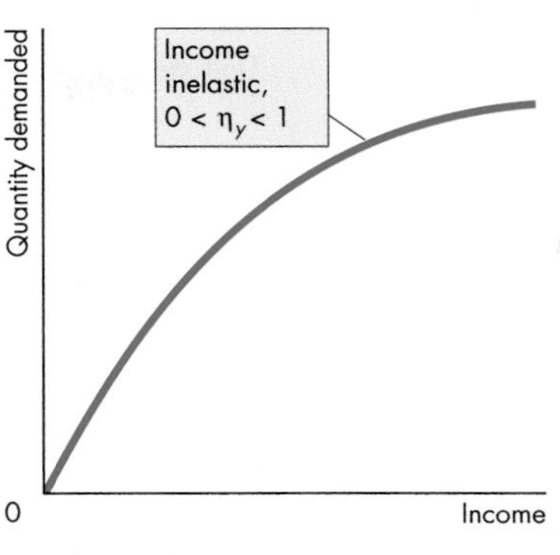

(b) Elasticity between zero and 1

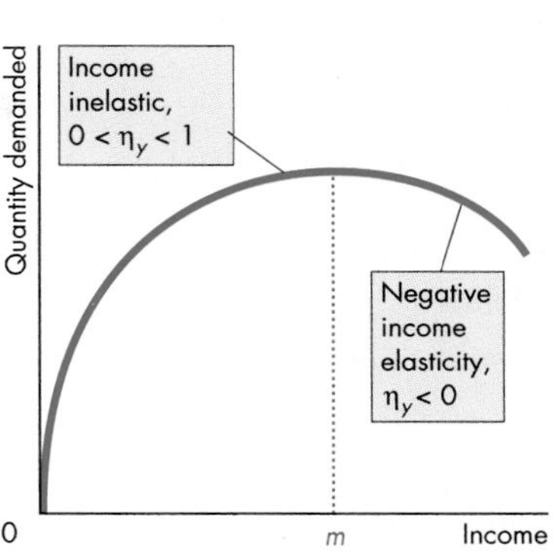

(c) Elasticity less than 1 and becomes negative

There are three ranges of values for income elasticity of demand. In part (a), income elasticity of demand is greater than 1. In this case, as income increases, the quantity demanded increases but by a bigger percentage than the increase in income. In part (b), income elasticity of demand is between zero and 1. In this case, as income increases, the quantity demanded increases but by a smaller percentage than the increase in income. In part (c), the income elasticity of demand is positive at low incomes but becomes negative as income rises above level *m*. Maximum consumption of the good occurs at the income *m*.

on, among other things, incomes and the prices of other goods. We can calculate elasticities of demand with respect to these other variables as well. Let's now examine some of these additional elasticities.

Income Elasticity of Demand

As income grows, how will the demand for a particular good change? The answer depends on the income elasticity of demand for the good. The **income elasticity of demand** is the percentage change in the quantity demanded divided by the percentage change in income. It is represented by η_y. That is

$$\eta_y = \frac{\text{Percentage change in quantity demanded}}{\text{Percentage change in income}}.$$

Income elasticities of demand can be positive or negative. However, there are three interesting ranges for the income elasticity of demand:

- Greater than 1 (income elastic)
- Between zero and 1 (income inelastic)
- Less than zero (negative income elasticity)

These three cases are illustrated in Fig. 5.5.

Part (a) shows an income elasticity of demand that is greater than 1. In this case, the quantity demanded increases as income rises, but the quantity demanded increases faster than income. The curve slopes upward and has an increasing slope. Goods that fall into this category include ocean cruises, custom clothing, international travel, jewellery, and works of art.

Figure 5.5(b) shows an income elasticity of demand that is between zero and 1. In this case, the quantity demanded increases as income rises, but income rises faster than the quantity demanded. The curve slopes upward, but the slope declines as income rises. Goods that fall into this category include basic food, clothing, housing, and local bus transportation.

The borderline between the income elastic example given in Fig. 5.5(a) and the income inelastic example given in Fig. 5.5(b) is a curve, starting at the origin, whose slope is constant — a linear relationship between the quantity demanded and income. In this case, the income elasticity equals 1 and demand is unit elastic with respect to income.

Figure 5.5(c) illustrates a third category of goods, one that is more complicated. For such a good, as income rises, the quantity demanded increases until it

Table 5.5 Some Real-World Income Elasticities of Demand

Elastic	
Airline travel	5.82
Movies	3.41
Foreign travel	3.08
Drugs and medicines	3.04
Housing services	2.45
Toys	2.01
Electricity	1.94
Intercity buses	1.89
Stationery	1.83
Restaurant meals	1.61
Books and maps	1.42
Local buses and trains	1.38
Gasoline and oil	1.36
Hair cutting	1.36
Car insurance	1.26
Household appliances	1.18
Taxicabs	1.15
Cars	1.07

Unit elastic	
Dentists' services	1.00

Inelastic	
Shoes and other footwear	0.94
Car repairs	0.90
Tobacco	0.86
China, glassware, and utensils	0.77
Shoe repairs	0.72
Alcoholic beverages	0.62
Water	0.59
Furniture	0.53
Clothing	0.51
Newspapers and magazines	0.38
Telephone	0.32

Source: H. S. Houthakker and Lester D. Taylor, *Consumer Demand in the United States* (Cambridge, Mass.: Harvard University Press, 1970).

reaches a maximum at income m. Beyond that point, as income continues to rise, the quantity demanded declines. The elasticity of demand is positive but less than 1 up to income m. Beyond income m, the income elasticity of demand is negative. Examples of goods in this category include one-speed bicycles, small motorbikes, potatoes, and rice. Low-income consumers buy most of these goods. At low income levels, the demand for such a good rises as income rises. Eventually, income reaches a level (point m) at which consumers replace the good with a superior alternative. For example, a small car replaces the motorbike; fruit, vegetables, and meat begin to appear in a diet that was heavy in rice or potatoes.

Goods whose income elasticities of demand are positive are called *normal goods.* Goods whose income elasticities of demand are negative are called *inferior goods.* They are "inferior" in the sense that as income increases they are replaced with "superior" but more expensive substitutes.

Let's now look at some estimates of real-world income elasticities of demand. Table 5.5 provides a summary. The various goods and services are listed in three groups. The first group lists goods and services whose income elasticity is greater than 1. The second group, in which there is just one example, has an income elasticity of 1. The third group lists goods whose income elasticity is less than 1 and whose demands are said to be income inelastic.

By using estimates of income elasticity of demand, we can translate projections of average income growth rates into growth rates of demand for particular goods and services. For example, if average incomes grow by 3 percent a year, the demand for gasoline and oil will grow by 4 percent a year (3 percent multiplied by the income elasticity of demand for gasoline and oil, which, as shown in Table 5.5, is 1.36).

Cross Elasticity of Demand

The quantity of any good demanded depends on the prices of its substitutes and complements. The

Table 5.6 A Compact Glossary of Elasticities of Demand

Price elasticities (η)

When η is	The relationship is	Which means that
Infinity	Perfectly elastic or infinitely elastic	The smallest possible increase (decrease) in price causes an infinitely large decrease (increase) in the quantity demanded
Less than infinity but greater than 1	Elastic	The percentage decrease (increase) in the quantity demanded exceeds the percentage increase (decrease) in price
1	Unit elastic	The percentage decrease (increase) in the quantity demanded equals the percentage increase (decrease) in price
Greater than zero but less than 1	Inelastic	The percentage decrease (increase) in the quantity demanded is less than the percentage increase (decrease) in price
Zero	Perfectly inelastic or completely inelastic	The quantity demanded is the same at all prices

Income elasticities (η_y)

When η_y is	The relationship is	Which means that
Greater than 1	Income elastic (normal good)	The percentage increase (decrease) in the quantity demanded is greater than the percentage increase (decrease) in income
Less than 1 but greater than zero	Income inelastic (normal good)	The percentage increase (decrease) in the quantity demanded is less than the percentage increase (decrease) in income
Less than zero (negative)	Negative income elastic (inferior good)	When income increases, quantity demanded decreases

Cross elasticities (η_x)

When η_x is	The relationship is	Which means that
Infinity	Perfect substitutes	The smallest possible increase (decrease) in the price of one good causes an infinitely large increase (decrease) in the quantity demanded of the other good
Positive, less than infinity	Substitutes	If the price of one good increases (decreases), the quantity demanded of the other good also increases (decreases)
Zero	Independent	The quantity demanded of one good remains constant regardless of the price of the other good
Less than zero (negative)	Complements	The quantity demanded of one good decreases (increases) when the price of the other good increases (decreases)

responsiveness of the quantity demanded of a particular good to a change in the price of one of its substitutes or complements is measured by **cross elasticity of demand**, which is represented by η_x. The cross elasticity of demand is calculated as the percentage change in the quantity demanded of one good divided by the percentage change in the price of another good (a substitute or a complement). That is,

$$\eta_x = \frac{\text{Percentage change in quantity demanded of one good}}{\text{Percentage change in the price of another good}}.$$

The cross elasticity of demand with respect to the price of a substitute is *positive*. The cross elasticity of demand with respect to the price of a complement is *negative*. Figure 5.6 explains why. When the price of coal (a substitute for oil) increases, the demand for oil increases. When the price of cars (a complement to oil) increases, the demand for oil decreases. The degree to which demand changes depends on how close the substitute or complement is. That is, the more easily coal and oil substitute for each other, the larger the cross elasticity of demand between them. The more complementary are cars and oil, the more negative the cross elasticity of demand for oil with respect to the price of a car.

Table 5.6 provides a compact summary of all the different kinds of demand elasticities you've just studied, and Reading Between the Lines, on pp. 118-119 gives an example of how these elasticities can be used in practical calculations.

Let us now turn our attention to the supply curve and study the concept of the elasticity of supply.

Figure 5.6 Cross Elasticities: Substitutes and Complements

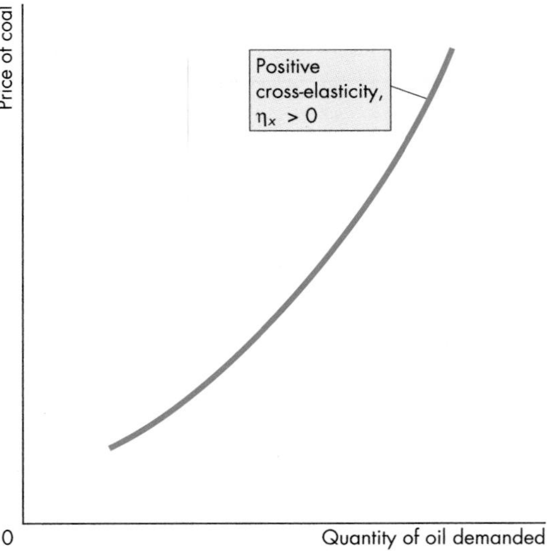

(a) Substitutes

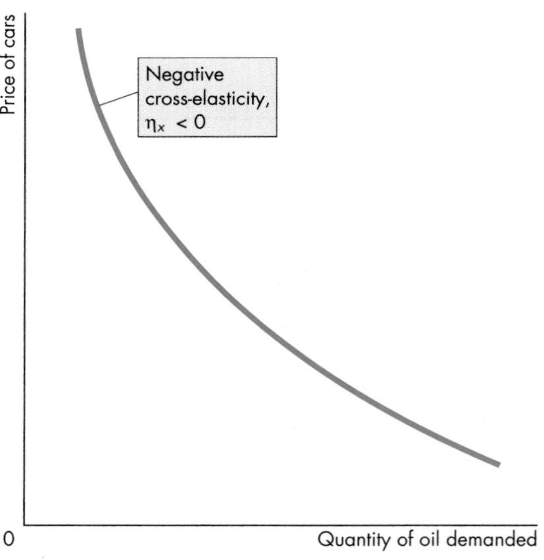

(b) Complements

Part (a) shows the cross elasticity of demand with respect to the price of a substitute. When the price of coal increases, the quantity of oil demanded also increases — the cross elasticity is positive. Part (b) shows the cross elasticity of demand with respect to the price of a complement. When the price of cars increases, the quantity of oil demanded decreases — the cross elasticity is negative.

Elasticity of Supply

We have seen that the concept of elasticity of demand may be used to determine the extent to which price and the quantity traded change when there is a change in supply. But suppose we want to predict the effects of a change in demand on price and the quantity traded. To make such a prediction, we need to know how responsive the quantity supplied is to the price of a good. That is, we need the concept of the elasticity of supply.

The **elasticity of supply** is the percentage change in the quantity supplied of a good divided by the percentage change in its price. It is represented by η_s. That is,

$$\eta_s = \frac{\text{Percentage change in quantity supplied}}{\text{Percentage change in price}}.$$

The supply curves that we have considered in this chapter (and those in Chapter 4) all slope upward. When the price increases, the quantity supplied increases. Upward-sloping supply curves have a positive elasticity of supply.

There are two interesting cases of the elasticity of supply. If the quantity supplied is fixed regardless of the price, the supply curve is vertical. In this case, the elasticity of supply is zero. An increase in price leads to no change in the quantity supplied. Alternatively, if the price is fixed regardless of the quantity supplied —that is, there is a price at which suppliers are willing to supply *any* quantity demanded and below which they are unwilling to supply anything — the supply curve is horizontal. In this case, the elasticity of supply is infinite. The small fall in price reduces the quantity supplied from an indefinitely large amount to zero.

The magnitude of the elasticity of supply depends on

- The technological conditions governing production.
- The amount of time elapsed since the price change.

The importance of technological conditions is best illustrated by considering two extreme examples. Some goods, such as a painting by Emily Carr, are unique. There is just one of each of her paintings. The supply curve of any one of her paintings is vertical, and its elasticity of supply is zero. At the other extreme, the supply of sand for making silicon chips is available in indefinitely large quantities at a virtually constant cost of production. Its supply curve is horizontal, and its elasticity of supply is infinitely large.

To study the influence of the length of time elapsed since a price change on the quantity supplied, we distinguish three time frames of supply: momentary, short run, and long run.

Momentary Supply

When the price of a good suddenly increases or decreases, we use the momentary supply curve to describe the initial change in the quantity supplied.

The **momentary supply curve** shows the response of the quantity supplied immediately following a price change.

For many goods, the momentary supply curve is perfectly inelastic — which means that the supply curve is vertical. Consider perishable fruits and vegetables. The amounts that can be supplied depend on crop-planting decisions made several months earlier. In the case of fruit such as apples, for example, the planting decisions have to be made many years in advance. All crops and animal products take some time to grow, and so the momentary supply curve for these goods is always perfectly inelastic.

Other goods have elastic momentary supply curves. One such good is electricity. If we all turn on our TV sets and air conditioners simultaneously, there is a big surge in the demand for electricity. If the supply of electricity were inelastic, this surge in demand would cause a sharp rise in price and no change in the quantity of electricity actually bought. Such rises do not happen. Surges in demand are common, but when they occur the quantity bought increases and the price remains constant. Electricity producers can usually anticipate fluctuations in demand and bring more generators into operation to ensure that the quantity supplied equals the quantity demanded without raising the price. (There is, of course, an upper limit to what can be produced, but normally increased output can meet the extra demand.) In this example, the momentary supply is perfectly elastic. But the momentary supply curve for most goods is inelastic, perhaps perfectly inelastic.

Let's now look at the other extreme — the long run.

Long-Run Supply

The **long-run supply curve** shows the response of the quantity supplied to a change in price after *all* the technologically possible adjustments to the production process have been made. In the case of apples, the long run is the time it takes new plantings to grow to full maturity — about eight years. In some cases, the long-run adjustment occurs only after a completely new production plant has been built and workers have been trained to operate it — typically a process that may take several years.

Between the momentary and the long-run time frames, there are many intermediate time frames. We call these the short run.

Warning: Travel With Care

Terrorism spurs U.S. tourists to change their vacation plans in droves

It is Eastertime in Rome, April in Paris, and the eve of Passover in Jerusalem. But suddenly, for millions of American tourists, this is chiefly the season for caution in making travel plans. In 1986, in sharp contrast to the overseas-travel surge of a year ago, Americans and their sought-after dollars are making themselves scarce in many parts of Western Europe and the Mediterranean. The phones of travel agents are as busy as ever, but many of the callers now want to change their vacation plans. Some are canceling their trips abroad entirely. Others are choosing more circuitous means and routes to reach their destinations, rather than having to pass through airports in Rome, Athens, and other cities along the Mediterranean littoral. The fear of terrorism has suddenly become an important factor in the $250 billion U.S. travel industry.

Many U.S. holidaymakers are hurriedly lining up presumably safer summer excursions, including Caribbean cruises and even charter tours to Moscow. But above all, Americans this year are deciding that they would rather take in the splendors of their own land, on motor-home jaunts to Disney World, camping trips to U.S. national parks, and surfing safaris to Hawaii. The travel industry expects a jump of 10% or more in domestic bookings this year. Says Harold Van Sumeren, president of the Chamber of Commerce in Traverse City, Mich., a boating and camping mecca: "We're really anticipating one of the biggest and finest summer seasons we've ever had."

The apprehension over travel to Europe and the Mediterranean is a direct result of the recent rash of bloody attacks directed against U.S. citizens in Italy and West Germany, of rioting in Egypt, and of random bombings in France. Last week travelers had further cause to be spooked by the harsh words and bellicose gestures flying between the U.S. and Libya. Reasons other than the terrorism scare, such as a sharp decline in the value of the U.S. dollar abroad and an abundance of cheap gasoline at home, are also involved in the shuffle of itineraries. Even so, says Sam Massell, an Atlanta travel agent, "if you're going on vacation, you want to start off happy. You're not supposed to go where you have to think about stress management."

The change in U.S. traveling patterns is already starting to have substantial effects. Until late last year, U.S. travel to Europe and the Mediterranean was setting records, thanks partly to the buying power of the strong dollar. Some 6.4 million Americans visited European countries in 1985, up from 5.8 million the previous year. Now the trade magazine *Travel Industry Monthly* expects European tourism by Americans to fall by about 25% in 1986.

***Time*,**
April 21, 1986
By Stephen Koepp,

The Essence of the Story

Facts

- In 1984, 5.8 million Americans visited Europe.
- In 1985, 6.4 million Americans visited Europe, a 10 percent increase.
- In April 1986, it was predicted that European tourism by Americans would fall by 25 percent of its 1985 level.
- In April 1986, the U.S. travel industry expected a rise of 10 percent in domestic business.
- In 1986, the U.S. dollar fell in value—that is, it bought fewer goods abroad than in 1985.
- In 1986, the price of gasoline fell.
- In the winter of 1985 and the spring of 1986, there was a wave of terrorism directed at U.S. citizens in several European and Mediterranean countries.

Alleged Explanation

- People switched from European to domestic vacations mainly because of the rise in anti-American terrorism and partly because of the drop in the value of the dollar and in the price of gasoline.

Background and Analysis

Prices

- A fall in the price of a good leads to an increase in the quantity demanded.
- An increase in the price of a substitute leads to an increase in demand.
- In 1985, the price of a European vacation fell by 1.8 percent. (The U.S. dollar cost of a European vacation rose by 1.7 percent, but U.S. prices rose by 3.5 percent, so that the relative price (opportunity cost) of a European vacation fell by the difference—1.8 percent.)
- In 1986, the price of a European vacation increased by 18.2 percent. In that year, the U.S. dollar fell in value, resulting in an increased U.S. dollar cost of a European vacation of 21.3 percent. U.S. prices rose by 3.1 percent so the relative price (opportunity cost) of a European vacation rose by the difference —18.2 percent.

Incomes

- In 1985, disposable income per head rose by 1 percent.
- In 1986, disposable income per head rose by 2 percent.

Elasticities

- The income elasticity of U.S. demand for foreign travel is estimated to be 3 (see Table 5.5, p. 114).
- The price elasticity of demand for European vacations is not known but is likely to be much bigger than 1 because vacations in Europe, Asia, Latin America, Canada, and the United States are close substitutes for each other.
- The formula used for predicting the percentage change in the quantity demanded of a good is:

  Price rise in quantity demanded =

  Price elasticity × percent fall in price +

  Income elasticity + percent rise in income.
- The table gives predicted percentage changes in the quantity of European vacations demanded by Americans for three values of the price elasticity of demand and for an income elasticity of demand of 3.

Price elasticity	in 1985	in 1986
1	+ 4.8%	− 12.2%
2	+ 6.6%	− 30.4%
3	+ 8.4%	− 48.6%
Actual	+ 10%	− 25%

- If the price elasticity is about 2, then the price and income changes in 1985 and 1986 come close to predicting the actual changes in U.S. travel.
- The rise in the quantity demanded in 1985 is slightly bigger than would have been predicted, but the fall in the quantity demanded in 1986 is smaller than predicted.
- The puzzle raised by the numbers in the table is not that European travel by Americans fell in 1986. Rather, it is that European travel fell by so little! It is thus possible that terrorism had no effect.
- But why would European travel fall by only 25 percent when the relative price had risen by 18 percent? Perhaps something else changed.
- Since vacations in Japan and the Far East are substitutes for vacations in Europe, a rise in the price of an Asian vacation would lead to a rise (or a smaller fall) in the demand for European vacations.
- Prices in Japan rose by 1.6 percent, but the U.S. dollar fell in value against the Japanese yen by 26.3 percent, so the U.S. dollar cost of a Japanese vacation rose by 27.9 percent.
- Since European travel costs, in U.S. dollars, rose by 18.2 percent, the price of a European vacation relative to that of a Japanese vacation *fell* by almost 10 percent.
- The rise in the cost of a Japanese vacation relative to that of a European vacation would moderate the fall in the quantity of European vacations demanded.

Conclusion

- The journalists reporting this story probably overemphasized the importance of terrorism and underemphasized the importance of price and income changes in explaining the changes in the vacation plans of Americans.

Short-Run supply

The **short-run supply curve** shows how the quantity supplied responds to a price change when only *some* of the technologically possible adjustments to the production process have been made. The first adjustment that is usually made is in the amount of labour employed. To increase output in the short-run, firms work their labour force overtime and perhaps hire additional workers. To decrease their output in the short run, firms lay off workers or reduce their hours of work. With the passage of more time, firms can make additional adjustments, perhaps training additional workers or buying additional tools and other equipment. The short-run response to a price change, unlike the momentary and long-run responses, is not a unique response but a sequence of adjustments.

Figure 5.7 Supply: Momentary, Short Run, and Long Run

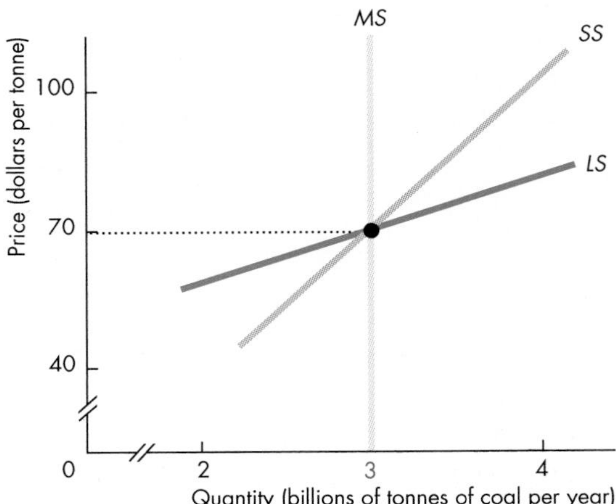

The momentary supply curve (*MS*) shows how quantity supplied responds to a price change the moment that it occurs. The very light blue momentary supply curve shown here is perfectly inelastic. The medium blue short-run supply curve (*SS*) shows how the quantity supplied responds to a price change after *some* adjustments to the production process have been made. The dark blue long-run supply curve (*LS*) shows how the quantity supplied responds to a price change when *all* the technologically possible adjustments to the production process have been made.

Three Supply Curves

Three supply curves corresponding to the three time frames are illustrated in Fig. 5.7. They are the supply curves in the world market for coal in a year in which the price is $70 a tonne and the quantity of coal produced is 3 billion tonnes. The three supply curves all pass through that point. The momentary supply curve (MS) is perfectly inelastic at 3 billion tonnes. The long-run supply curve (LS) is the most elastic of the three curves. The short-run supply curve (SS) lies between the other two curves. In fact, there is a series of successively more elastic short-run supply curves between the momentary and the long-run curves. As more time elapses following a price change, more changes can be made in the method of production to increase output. The short-run supply curve (SS) shown in Fig. 5.7 is an example of one of these short-run supply curves.

The momentary supply curve (MS) is vertical because, at a given moment in time, no matter what the change in the price of coal, producers are not able to change their output. They have a certain labour force and a certain amount of coal-mining equipment in place, and there is a given amount of output that can be produced. But as time elapses, coal-producing companies can increase their capacity. They can hire and train more miners and buy more equipment. In the long run, they can sink new mines, discover more accessible coal deposits, and increase the quantity supplied even more in response to a given price rise.

■ You have now studied the theory of demand and supply, and you have learned how to measure the responsiveness of the quantities demanded and supplied to changes in price and income. In the next chapters we are going to use what we have learned, to study some real world markets — markets in action.

SUMMARY

Price Elasticity of Demand

Price elasticity of demand is a precise measure of the responsiveness of the quantity demanded of a good to a change in its price. It enables us to calculate the effect of a change in supply on price, quantity traded, and total revenue. Price elasticity of demand (η) is the absolute value of the ratio of the percentage change in the quantity demanded of a good to the percentage change in its price. Price elasticity of demand (η) is calculated using the formula,

$$\eta = \frac{\text{Percentage change in quantity demanded}}{\text{Percentage change in price}}.$$

An *increase* in price always leads to a *decrease* in the quantity demanded and ε, the price elasticity of demand, is the absolute value of the above ratio. The elasticity can lie between zero and infinity. When elasticity is between zero and 1, demand is inelastic. When elasticity is 1, demand is unit elastic. When elasticity is greater than 1, demand is elastic.

Elasticity varies along a straight-line demand curve. The magnitude of the elasticity falls as the price falls and the quantity demanded rises.

The magnitude of the elasticity depends on how easily one good may serve as a substitute for another, on the proportion of income spent on the good, and on the time that has elapsed since the price change. (pp. 103-110)

Two Time Frames for Demand

We use two time frames to analyse demand: short run and long run. Short-run demand describes the initial response of buyers to a price change. Long-run demand describes the response of buyers to a price change after buyers have made all possible adjustments to their buying plans. Short-run demand is usually less elastic than long-run demand. (pp. 110-111)

Elasticity, Total Revenue, and Total Expenditure

If the elasticity of demand is less than 1, a decrease in supply leads to an increase in total revenue — the percentage increase in price is greater than the percentage decrease in the quantity traded. If the elasticity of demand is greater than 1, a decrease in supply leads to a decrease in total revenue — the percentage increase in price is less than the percentage decrease in the quantity traded. (pp. 111-112)

More Demand Elasticities

Income elasticity of demand measures the responsiveness of demand to a change in income. Income elasticity of demand is calculated as the percentage change in the quantity demanded divided by the percentage change in income. Income elasticities may be greater than 1 (income elastic), between zero and 1 (income inelastic), or less than zero (negative income elastic). Income elasticities are greater than 1 for items typically consumed by the rich. They are positive but less than 1 for more basic consumption items. Income elasticities are less than zero for inferior goods — goods that are consumed only at low incomes and that disappear from shopping lists as budgets increase.

Cross elasticity of demand measures the responsiveness of demand for one good to a change in the price of another good. Cross elasticity of demand is calculated as the percentage change in the quantity demanded of one good divided by the percentage change in the price of another good (a substitute or a complement). The cross elasticity of demand with respect to the price of a substitute is positive. The cross elasticity of demand with respect to the price of a complement is negative. (pp. 112-115)

Elasticity of Supply

The elasticity of supply measures the responsiveness of the quantity supplied to a change in price. Elasticity of supply is calculated as the percentage change in the quantity supplied of a good divided by the percentage change in its price. Supply elasticities are usually positive but range between zero (vertical supply curve) and infinity (horizontal supply curve).

We classify supply according to three different time frames: momentary, long run, and short run. Momentary supply refers to the response of the quantity supplied to a price change at the instant that it happens. Long-run supply refers to the response of the quantity supplied to a price change when all the technologically feasible adjustments to the production process have been made. Short-run supply refers to the response of the quantity supplied to a price change after only some adjustments to the production process have been made. For most goods, the momentary supply curve is perfectly inelastic. Supply becomes more elastic as suppliers have more time to respond to price changes. (pp. 115-120)

KEY ELEMENTS

Key Terms

Cross elasticity of demand, 116
Elastic demand, 106
Elasticity of demand, 104
Elasticity of supply, 115
Income elasticity of demand, 113
Inelastic demand, 106
Long-run demand curve, 111
Long-run supply curve, 117
Momentary supply curve, 117
Perfectly elastic demand, 106
Perfectly inelastic demand, 106
Price elasticity of demand, 104
Short-run demand curve, 110
Short-run supply curve, 120
Total expenditure, 111
Total revenue, 104
Unit elastic demand, 106

Key Figures and Tables 

Figure 5.2 Elasticity Along a Straight-Line Demand Curve, 108
Figure 5.3 Demand Curves with Constant Elasticity, 108
Figure 5.5 Income Elasticity of Demand, 113
Table 5.1 Calculating the Price Elasticity of Demand, 105
Table 5.6 A Compact Glossary of Elasticities of Demand, 115

REVIEW QUESTIONS

1 Define the price elasticity of demand.

2 Why is elasticity a more useful measure of responsiveness than slope?

3 Draw a graph of, or describe the shape of, a demand curve that along its whole length has an elasticity of

   a) Infinity.

   b) Zero.

   c) Unity.

4 What three factors determine the size of the elasticity of demand?

5 What do we mean by short-run demand and long-run demand?

6 Explain why the short-run demand curve is usually less elastic than the long-run demand curve.

7 What is the connection between elasticity and total revenue? If the elasticity of demand is 1, by how much does a 10 percent price increase change total revenue?

8 Define the income elasticity of demand.

9 Give an example of a good whose income elasticity is

   a) Greater than 1.

   b) Positive but less than 1.

   c) Less than zero.

10 Define the cross elasticity of demand. Is the cross elasticity of demand positive or negative?

11 Define the elasticity of supply. Is the elasticity of supply positive or negative?

12 Give an example of a good whose elasticity of supply is

   a) Zero.

   b) Positive but less than infinity.

   c) Infinity.

13 What do we mean by momentary, short-run, and long-run supply?

14 Why is the momentary supply curve perfectly inelastic for many goods?

15 Why is the long-run supply curve more elastic than the short-run supply curve?

PROBLEMS

1 The demand schedule for videotape rentals is

Price (dollars)	Quantity demanded per day
0	120
1	100
2	80
3	60
4	40
5	20
6	0

a) At what price is the elasticity of demand equal to

(i) 1?

(ii) Infinity?

(iii) Zero?

b) What price brings in the most total revenue per day?

c) Calculate the elasticity of demand for a rise in price from \$3 to \$4.

2 Assume that the demand for videotape rentals in problem 1 increases by 10 percent.

a) Draw the old and new demand curves.

b) Calculate the elasticity of demand for a rise in the rental price from \$3 to \$4. Compare your answer with that of problem 1(c).

3 Which item in each of the following pairs has the larger elasticity of demand:

a) Daily newspapers or the *The Vancouver Sun*?

b) Exercise equipment or rowing machines?

c) Pop or Diet Pepsi?

4 You have been hired as an economic consultant by OPEC and given the following schedule showing the world demand for oil.

Price (dollars per barrel)	Quantity demanded (millions of barrels per day)
10	35,000
20	30,000
30	25,000
40	20,000
50	15,000

Your advice is needed on the following questions:

a) If the supply of oil is cut back so that the price rises from \$10 to \$20 a barrel, will the total revenue from oil sales rise or fall?

b) What will happen to total revenue if the supply of oil is cut back further and the price rises to \$30 a barrel?

c) What will happen to total revenue if the supply of oil is cut back further still so that the price rises to \$40 a barrel?

d) What is the price that will achieve the highest total revenue?

e) What quantity of oil will be sold at the price that answers problem 4(d)?

f) What are the values of the price elasticity of demand for price changes of \$10 a barrel at average prices of \$15, \$25, \$35, and \$45 a barrel?

g) What is the elasticity of demand at the price that answers problem 4(d)?

5 For the following elasticities state whether positive or negative and, where possible, the range (less than 1, 1, greater than 1):

a) The price elasticity of demand for coal at the point of maximum total revenue

b) The cross elasticity of demand for coal with respect to the price of oil

c) The income elasticity of demand for diamonds

d) The income elasticity of demand for toothpaste

e) The elasticity of supply of B.C. salmon

f) The cross elasticity of demand for floppy discs with respect to the price of personal computers

6 The following table gives the demand schedule for chocolate chip cookies:

Price (cents per cookie)	Quantity demanded (thousands per day)	
	Short Run	**Long Run**
10	700	1000
20	500	500
30	200	0

Using 20 cents as the average price of a cookie and 500,000 cookies a day as the average quantity, calculate the elasticity of

a) Short-run demand.

b) Long-run demand.

7 The following table gives the supply schedule for chocolate chip cookies:

Price (cents per cookie)	Quantity supplied (thousands per day)		
	Momentary	**Short run**	**Long run**
10	500	200	0
20	500	500	500
30	500	700	10,000

Using 20 cents as the average price of a cookie and 500,000 cookies a day as the average quantity, calculate the elasticity of

a) Momentary supply.

b) Short-run supply.

c) Long-run supply.

CHAPTER 6

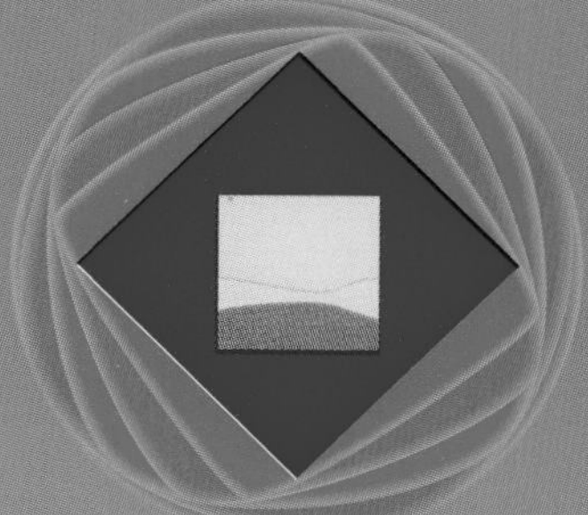

Markets in Action

After studying this chapter, you will be able to:

- Explain the short-run and long-run effects of a change in supply on price and the quantity traded.
- Explain the short-run and long-run effects of a change in demand on price and the quantity traded.
- Explain the effects of price controls.
- Explain why price controls can lead to black markets.
- Explain how people cope with uncertainty and make decisions in the face of unpredictable fluctuations in demand and supply.
- Explain how inventories and speculation limit price fluctuations.

Turbulent Times

ON APRIL 18, 1906, SAN FRANCISCO suffered a devastating earthquake. From April 18 to April 20, massive fires destroyed countless buildings on 3400 acres in the heart of the city. Despite the extreme destruction of property, fewer than 1000 people died. The remaining population somehow had to fit into a vastly smaller number of houses and apartments. How did the San Francisco housing market cope with this enormous shock? What happened to rents and to the quantity of housing services available? ■ Almost every day, people invent new machines and techniques that save labour and increase productivity. But the adoption of new technologies doesn't reduce the demand for labour — it changes its composition. The simplest tasks performed by the least skilled workers are the ones most easily mechanized. So the march of technological change brings a persistent decrease in the demand for the least skilled types of labour. But ever more sophisticated equipment needs ever more sophisticated management and maintenance. As a consequence, it brings a steady increase in the demand for more highly skilled types of labour. How do labour markets cope with the changing patterns in demand for labour and what happens to the wages of the unskilled in the process? Does falling demand make those wages fall lower and lower? ■ Wages and housing costs are the two most important items in the budget of every household. Because of this, politicians take great interest in the markets for housing and labour. If rents get too high, rent controls are introduced. If wages get too low, minimum wage laws are introduced. What are the effects of rent controls and minimum wage laws? How do rent controls affect the rents that people pay and the housing services that are available? How do minimum wages affect employment and wage prospects? ■ When the winter is severe and the summer is hot and humid, there is an increase in the number of days on which people run furnaces and air conditioners. The number of such days in the year has an important effect on the total demand for electricity and, in turn, for fuels used to generate electricity. As we know from experience, fluctuations in the weather cannot be forecast with any real accuracy — at least not a whole season ahead. We know the range of possibilities, but there is no way of predicting whether the coming winter will turn out to be mild or severe. Producers of electricity and of the fuels they use must devise ways of coping with the inherent unpredictability in the demand for their products. How do these producers cope with uncertainty about demand? What are the effects of unpredictable fluctuations in demand on prices and the quantities traded? ■ The weather also creates unpredictable fluctuations in supply. The output of virtually every agricultural product is subject to unpredictable fluctuations of weather conditions — the hours of sunshine, the amount of rainfall, and the average temperature. For example, in 1982 growing conditions were good and the grain yield was very high, but in 1988 yield was extremely low as crops were devastated by drought.

Fluctuations in demand and supply cause fluctuations in the price of a good and in the quantity traded. In some cases, the price fluctuates a great deal and the quantity traded hardly changes. In other cases, the quantity traded fluctuates dramatically and price changes very little. What determines the amount by which the price and quantity traded fluctuate?

Every day, the pages of any newspaper — from your local daily to the *Financial Post* — report the latest fortunes of the stock market. Attention focuses on various indexes, such as the TSE 300 — an average of the prices of 300 stocks that trade on the Toronto Stock Exchange. On one particular day — October 19, 1987 — a page in history was written. The TSE 300 average fell by more than 30 percent from its peak value. A movement of this magnitude is unusual. Nevertheless, stock prices do go up and down — and they do so much more than the prices of most of the ordinary goods and services we buy. Why are stock prices so volatile? Is it speculation that makes the stock market fluctuate so much?

■ In this chapter, we use the theory of demand and supply (see Chapter 4) and the concept of elasticity (see Chapter 5) to answer questions such as those we have just asked. We'll study how unregulated markets work, and we'll study government intervention to regulate prices. We'll see how such regulation can produce waiting lines, black markets, and unemployment. We'll extend the demand and supply model to take account of the fact that production decisions made today often do not affect output until a later date. For example, if a producer decides today to grow more apples, the actual supply of apples will not increase until the new apple trees mature — in about eight years. In a situation such as this, suppliers have to make today's production decisions on the basis of forecasts of future prices. We'll see how they go about making such forecasts. A final extension of the demand and supply model that we'll make takes account of the fact that many goods can be stored. We'll study the way in which inventories of goods, and changes in those inventories, affect the prices of goods and the quantities traded. We'll emerge from this chapter with a richer model of demand and supply that explains many features of the real world.

Let's begin by studying how a market responds to a severe supply shock in both the short run and the long run. We'll see how an unregulated market responds, and we'll also see what happens when the government intervenes in the market to limit price changes.

Housing Markets and Rent Ceilings

To see how an unregulated market copes with a massive supply shock, let's transport ourselves to San Francisco in April 1906, as the city is facing the effects of a massive earthquake and fire. You can sense the enormity of San Francisco's problems by reading some headlines from the *New York Times* on the first days of the crisis.

On April 19, 1906:

> *Over 500 Dead, $200,000,000 Lost in San Francisco Earthquake*
>
> *Nearly Half the City Is in Ruins and 50,000 Are Homeless*

On April 20, 1906:

> *Army of Homeless Fleeing from Devastated City*
>
> *200,000 Without Shelter and Facing Famine*

And again on April 21, 1906:

> *San Francisco's New Peril; Gale Drives Fire Ferryward*
>
> *Fighting Famine and Disease Among the 200,000 Refugees*
>
> *San Francisco Multitudes Camped Out Shelterless and in Want*

The commander of the federal troops in charge of the resulting emergency described the magnitude of the problem:

> Not a hotel of note or importance was left standing. The great apartment houses had vanished . . . two-hundred-and-twenty-five thousand people were . . . homeless.[1]

Almost overnight, more than half the people in a city of 400,000 had lost their homes. Temporary shelters and camps alleviated some of the problem, but it was also necessary to utilize the apartment buildings and houses left standing. The existing buildings had to accommodate 40 percent more people than they had before the earthquake.

The *San Francisco Chronicle* was not published for more than a month after the earthquake. When the newspaper reappeared on May 24, 1906, the city's housing shortage — presumably still a serious problem and therefore a major news item — was not mentioned. Milton Friedman and George Stigler describe the situation:

> *There is not a single mention of a housing shortage!* The classified advertisements listed sixty-four offers of flats and houses for rent, and nineteen of houses for sale, against five advertisements of flats or houses wanted. Then and thereafter a considerable number of all types of accommodation except hotel rooms were offered for rent.[2]

How did San Francisco cope with such a devastating reduction in the supply of housing?

The Market Response to an Earthquake

We can work out how the unregulated San Francisco housing market responded to the earthquake of 1906 by using the model of demand and supply that we studied in Chapters 4 and 5. Figure 6.1 analyses this market. Part (a) shows the situation before the earthquake, and parts (b) and (c), after the earthquake. The horizontal axis of each part measures the quantity of housing units, and the vertical axis measures the monthly rent of a unit of housing.

Look first at the situation before the earthquake (Fig 6.1a). The demand curve for housing is *D*. There are two supply curves: the short-run supply curve, which is labelled *SS*, and the long-run supply curve, which is labelled *LS*. The short-run supply curve shows how the quantity of housing supplied varies as the price (rent) varies, while the number of houses and apartment buildings remains constant. This supply response arises from a variation in the intensity with which existing buildings are used. The quantity of housing supplied increases as families rent out rooms or parts of their houses and apartments to others, and the quantity supplied decreases as families occupy a larger number of the rooms under their control.

The long-run supply curve shows how the quantity supplied varies after enough time has elapsed for new apartment buildings and houses to be erected or existing buildings to be destroyed. The long-run supply curve is shown as being perfectly elastic. We do not actually know that the long-run supply curve is perfectly elastic, but it is a reasonable assumption. It implies that the cost of building an apartment is pretty much the same regardless of whether there are 50,000, 100,000, or 150,000 apartments in existence.

The equilibrium price and quantity traded are determined at the point of intersection of the short-run supply curve and the demand curve. Before the earthquake, that equilibrium rent is $110 a month and the quantity of housing units traded is 100,000. In addition (but only because we are assuming it to be so), the housing market is on its long-run supply curve, *LS*. Let's now look at the situation immediately after the earthquake.

After the Earthquake

After the earthquake and the subsequent fires, 56 percent of the housing stock is destroyed. Figure 6.1(b)

---

[1] Reported in Milton Friedman and George J. Stigler, "Roofs or Ceilings? The Current Housing Problem," in *Popular Essays on Current Problems* 1, 2 (New York: Foundation for Economic Education, 1946) 3–15, 3.

[2] *Ibid.*, 3.

Figure 6.1 The San Francisco Housing Market in 1906

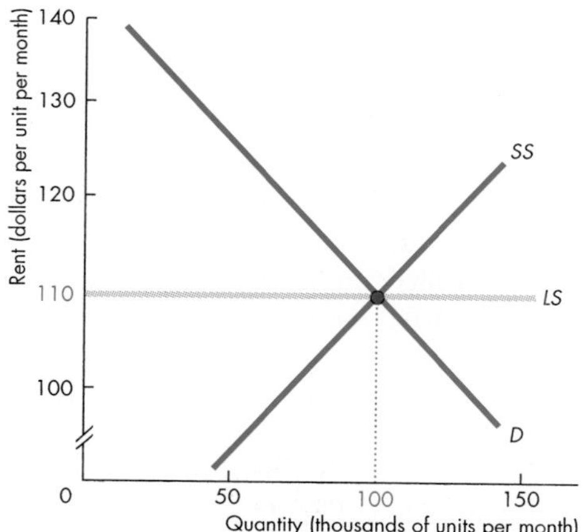

(a) Before earthquake

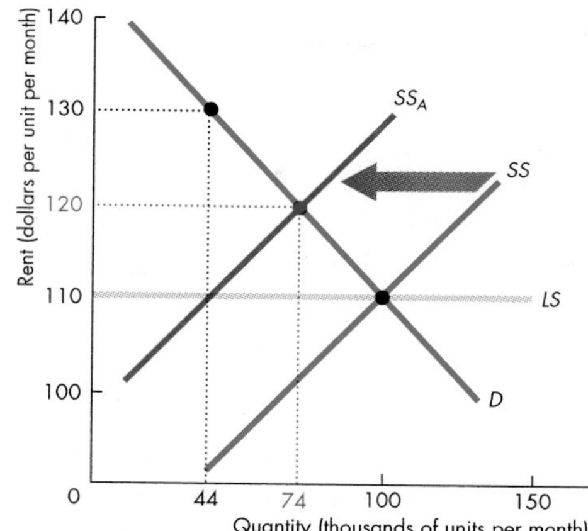

(b) After earthquake

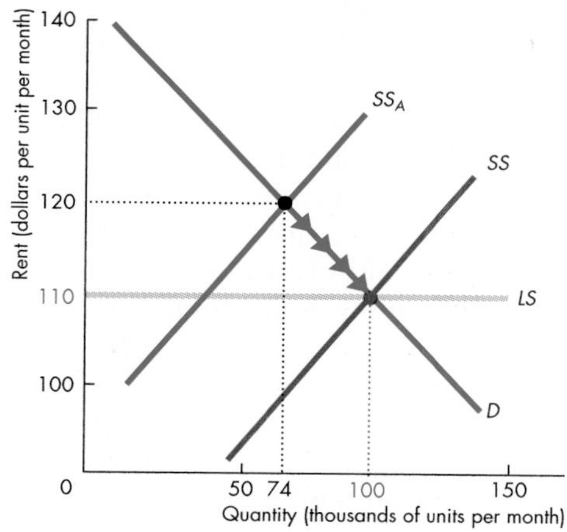

(c) Long-run adjustment

Before the earthquake, the San Francisco housing market is in equilibrium with 100,000 housing units being traded each month at an average rent of $110 per month. This equilibrium is at the intersection of demand curve *D*, short-run supply curve *SS*, and long-run supply curve *LS*. After the earthquake, the short-run supply curve shifts from *SS* to SS_A (part b). The equilibrium rent rises to $120 per month, and the number of housing units available falls to 74,000 per month. The rent rises because only 44,000 units of housing will be supplied at the old rent of $110 per month, and the price that demanders are willing to pay for the forty-four thousandth unit is $130 per month.

reflects the new situation by shifting the short-run supply curve *SS* to the left by 56,000 units, to become the short-run supply curve SS_A (*A* stands for "after the earthquake"). If people use the remaining housing units with the same intensity as before the earthquake and if the rent remains at $110 a month, only 44,000 units of housing are available.

But rents do not remain at $110. With only 44,000 units of housing available, the maximum rent that will willingly be paid for the last available apartment is $130 a month. Since people value the available housing more highly than the long-run price of $110 a month, they offer to pay higher rents. At higher rents, people with accommodations economize on their use of space and make their spare rooms, attics, and basements available to others. Thus the quantity of housing units supplied increases. The market achieves a new, short-run equilibrium at a rent of $120 a month, with 74,000 units of housing available. In this new short-run equilibrium, approximately 20 percent of the population have left the city and a further 6 percent have been housed in temporary camps.[3]

You've now seen how the housing market reacts, almost overnight, to a devastating shock. When supply decreases, the intersection point of the new short-run supply curve and the demand curve determines the price and the quantity traded. The price rises; those willing to pay the higher price find housing, and those with housing are willing to economize on its use. People who are unwilling or unable to pay the higher rents either leave the city or are housed in temporary shelters.

Long-Run Adjustments

The new equilibrium depicted in Fig. 6.1(b) is not the end of the story. The long-run supply curve tells us that with sufficient time for new apartment buildings and houses to be constructed, housing will be supplied at a rent of $110 a month. Since the current rent of $120 a month is higher than the long-run supply price of housing, there will be a rush to build and supply new apartments and houses. As time passes, more apartments and houses will be built, and the short-run supply curve will start moving gradually back to the right.

Figure 6.1(c) illustrates the long-run adjustment. As the short-run supply curve shifts back to the right, it intersects the demand curve at lower rents and higher quantities. The market follows the arrows down the demand curve. The process ends when there is no further profit in building new housing units. Such a situation occurs at the original rent of $110 a month and the original quantity of 100,000 units of housing.

REVIEW

An earthquake reduces the short-run supply of housing, raising rents and lowering the quantity traded. Higher rents immediately bring forth an increase in the quantity of housing supplied as people economize on their own use of space and make rooms available for rent to others. High rents also lead to increased building activity, which causes the short-run supply curve to shift gradually back to the right. As this process continues, the price of housing falls and the quantity traded rises. The original (pre-earthquake) equilibrium eventually is restored (because nothing has happened in the meantime to shift the long-run supply curve or the demand curve). ■

[3] *Ibid.*, 3.

A Regulated Housing Market

We've just seen how the housing market of San Francisco coped with a massive supply shock. One of the things that happened was that rents increased sharply. Let's now suppose that the San Francisco city government imposed a rent ceiling. A **rent ceiling** is a regulation making it illegal to charge a rent higher than a specified level. What would have happened if a rent ceiling of $110 a month — the rent before the earthquake — had been imposed? This question is answered in Fig. 6.2.

First let's work out what happens to the quantities supplied and demanded. The quantity supplied at the controlled rent of $110 a month is 44,000 units. The quantity demanded at that rent is 100,000 units. When the quantity demanded exceeds the quantity supplied, what determines the quantity actually bought and sold? The answer is the smaller of the quantities demanded and supplied. At a monthly rent of $110, the suppliers of housing want to supply only 44,000 units. They cannot be forced to supply more. The demanders would like to rent 100,000 units at that price, but they cannot do so. The difference between the quantity demanded and the quantity supplied is called the excess quantity demanded.

When a rent ceiling of $110 a month is imposed, the quantity of housing available falls to 44,000 units, but the quantity demanded remains constant at 100,000 units. There is an excess quantity demanded of 56,000 units. Is that the end of the story? Is this situation an equilibrium? To answer this question, we need to explore a bit more closely what the demanders are doing.

If the rent is controlled at $110 a month, a lot of people who would like to rent more housing will not be able to do so. Moreover, some people will be willing to pay much more than $110 a month to get an apartment. To understand why, recall that there are two ways of interpreting a demand curve. One interpretation is that the curve tells us the quantities demanded at each price. But the demand curve also tells us the highest price that demanders will pay for the last unit available. What is the highest price that people will pay for the last apartment available? The answer, which can be read from the demand curve, is $130 a month. Since the people who are not able to find housing are willing to pay more than the rent ceiling, the situation that we have just described is not an equilibrium. Two mechanisms come into play in an unbalanced situation such as this one to achieve equilibrium. They are search activity and black markets.

Search Activity

Even when the quantity demanded exceeds the quantity supplied, some suppliers have goods available. But many are sold out. In these circumstances, buyers spend time looking for a supplier with whom they can do business. The time and effort spent searching for someone with whom to do business is called **search activity**. Even in markets in which prices are permitted to fluctuate to bring equality between the quantities demanded and supplied, search activity takes place. But when price is regulated, search activity increases.

The time spent searching for available supplies imposes costs on buyers. Adjustments in the time spent searching bring about an equilibrium. You can see why by thinking about the total amount that the demanders are willing to pay for the last unit of housing available. With only 44,000 housing units available, demanders are willing to pay $130 a month. But the rent is restricted to $110. How does the buyer spend another $20? The answer is, by using $20 worth of time in the business of searching for an available apartment. That is, the total rental cost of housing — the price actually paid for housing obtained — is equal to the rent paid to the owner plus the opportunity cost of time spent searching for the available supply.

Black Markets

Opportunity cost (the best alternative forgone) enables us to predict *who* will search for available housing. Some people earn high wages and others earn low wages. If it takes one hour to find an apartment, the total price paid is higher for a high-wage earner than for a low-wage earner. Therefore the lowest paid people will be those who devote the most time to searching out available supplies. High-wage earners will devote time to search activity only if they place a much higher value on the good than low-wage earners.

A person with a high opportunity cost of time has another way of obtaining a good — buying it from someone whose opportunity cost of time is lower. The person with a low wage can devote time to searching out the available supplies and then resell to someone whose opportunity cost of searching is higher. Buying goods in this way is illegal and creates what is known as a black market. A **black market** is an illegal trading arrangement in which buyers and sellers do business at a price higher than the legally imposed price ceiling. A black market in housing may include the payment of "key money" or bribes, illegal sublets, and the "required" purchase of furniture and drapes not wanted by the tenant.

The functioning of a black market depends on how tightly the government polices its price regulations, the chances of being caught violating them, and on the scale of the penalties imposed for violations. At one extreme, the chance of being caught violating a rent ceiling is small. In this case, the black market will function similarly to an unregulated market, and the black market rent and quantity traded will be close to the unregulated equilibrium. At the other extreme, where policing is highly effective and where large penalties are imposed on violators, the rent ceiling will restrict the quantity traded to 44,000 units. The small number of black marketeers operating in the market will buy at the controlled rent of

Figure 6.2 A Rent Ceiling

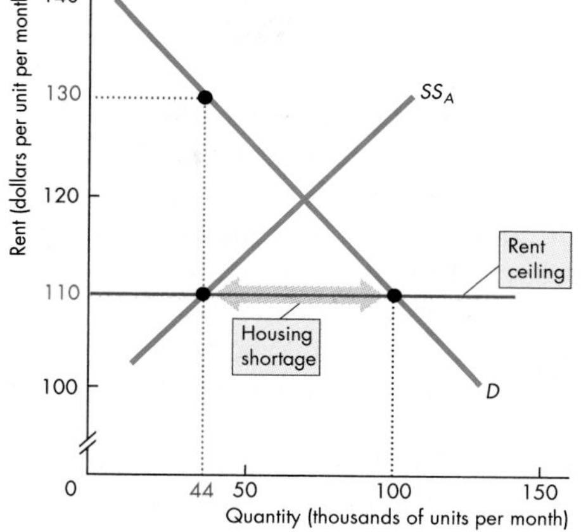

If there had been a rent ceiling of $110 a month following the earthquake, the quantity of housing supplied would have been stuck at 44,000 units. People would have willingly paid $130 a month for the forty-four thousandth unit. The difference between the rent ceiling and the maximum price willingly paid is the value of the time used up searching for an available apartment. The individuals doing the searching are those with the lowest opportunity cost of time. Those whose value of time is high avoid search costs by renting on an illegal black market.

$110 dollars a month and sell at $130 a month. The government will constantly try to detect and punish such people. The equilibrium in the black market will be such that anyone can obtain an apartment for $130 a month and the profit for the black marketeer is just sufficient compensation for the risk of being caught and punished.

There are many other regulated markets in which economic forces give rise to black market trading. One example is the market for bread in communist Romania and other Eastern European countries. (See Reading Between the Lines, pp. 134-135)

We've just looked at what would have happened in a hypothetical situation if there had been rent ceilings following the San Francisco earthquake. But San Francisco actually did have rent ceilings 45 years later — following World War II — so we can see how rent ceilings operated in practice. Let's take a look at that episode in the history of the San Francisco housing market.

Rent Ceilings in Practice

By 1940, a year before the United States entered the war, the population of San Francisco had increased to 635,000. At that time, only 93 percent of the city's houses and apartments were occupied — a 7 percent vacancy rate. The situation stayed much the same throughout World War II. Then, after the war, the population increased rapidly by 30 percent, but the number of houses and apartments increased by only 20 percent. As a result, each dwelling unit had to house 3 percent more people in 1946 than one year earlier — a 30 percent increase in the quantity demanded, minus a 20 percent increase in the quantity supplied, minus the 7 percent vacancy rate. The housing problems that San Francisco suffered in 1946 were less than one-tenth of the magnitude of the problems that followed the earthquake in 1906. Yet the 1946 housing shortage was a major political problem.

> On January 8 [1946] the California State Legislature was convened, and the Governor listed the housing shortage as "the most critical problem facing California." During the first five days of the year there were altogether only four advertisements offering houses or apartments for rent . . . [and] . . . there were thirty advertisements per day by persons wanting to rent houses or apartments.[4]

[4] *Ibid.*, 4.

The key difference between San Francisco in 1906 and in 1946 was the way in which scarce housing was rationed. In 1906, the scarce housing was allocated by an unregulated market. Rent increases achieved an equilibrium between the quantity of housing supplied and the quantity demanded and resulted in a steady increase in the quantity of housing available. In 1946, rent ceilings were in place. Scarce housing was allocated to those people who were willing to devote the largest amount of time and effort to searching out and to advertising for available houses and apartments. The actual cost of housing, taking account of the frustration and effort involved in finding accommodation, exceeded the controlled rent level and even exceeded the rents that would have prevailed in an unregulated market.

We've now studied the way in which a market responds, in both the short run and the long run, to a change in supply and how a regulated market works in the face of such a supply shock. Let's now study how a market responds, both in the short run and the long run, to a change in demand. We'll study how an unregulated market handles such a shock and the effects of government intervention to limit price movements.

The Labour Market and Minimum Wage Regulation

Labour-saving technology is constantly being invented, and, as a result, the demand for certain types of labour, usually the least skilled types, is constantly decreasing. How does the labour market cope with this continuous decrease in the demand for unskilled labour? Doesn't it mean that the wages of the unskilled are constantly falling? To study this question, let's examine the market for unskilled labour.

Figure 6.3(a) shows this market. The quantity of labour (millions of hours per year) is measured on the horizontal axis and the wage rate (dollars per hour) on the vertical axis. The demand curve for labour is *D*. There are two supply curves of labour: the short-run supply curve (*SS*) and the long-run supply curve (*LS*). In the labour market illustrated here, the long-run supply curve is perfectly elastic — a horizontal curve. In some labour markets, the long-run supply curve is upward sloping but more elastic than the short-run supply curve.

The short-run supply curve shows how the

hours of labour supplied by a given number of workers varies as the wage rate varies. To get workers to work longer hours, firms have to offer higher wages. The long-run supply curve shows the relationship between the quantity of labour supplied and the wage rate when the number of workers in the market varies. The number of people in this unskilled labour market depends on the wage in this market compared with other opportunities. If the wage is high enough, people will enter this market. If the wage is too low, people will leave this unskilled labour market and seek training to enter a different, more skilled market. The long-run supply curve tells us the conditions under which workers supply labour in this unskilled market after enough time has passed for people to have acquired new skills and moved to new types of jobs.

The labour market is initially in equilibrium at a wage rate of $4 an hour and with 30 million hours of labour being supplied. We're now going to analyse what happens in the labour market if the demand for this particular type of labour falls as a result of the invention of some labour-saving technology. Figure 6.3(b) shows the short-run effects of such a change. The demand curve before the new technology is introduced is labelled *D*. After the introduction

Figure 6.3 A Market for Unskilled Labour

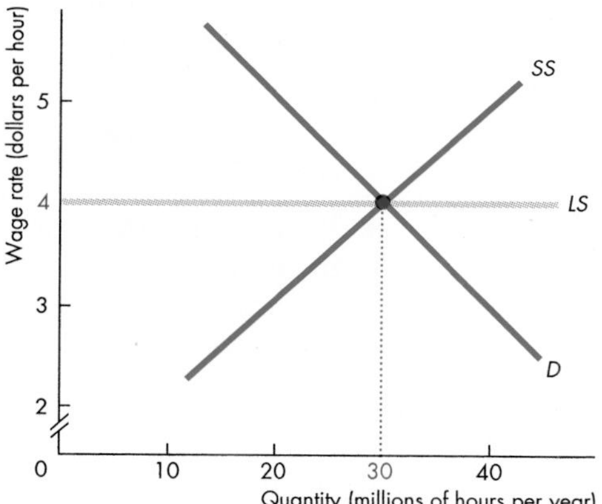

(a) Before invention

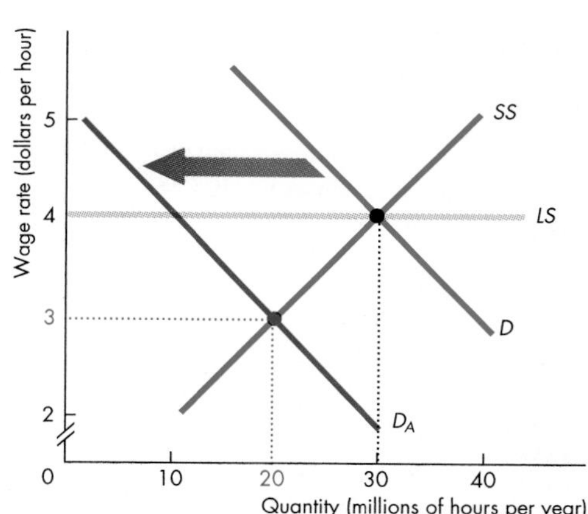

(b) After invention

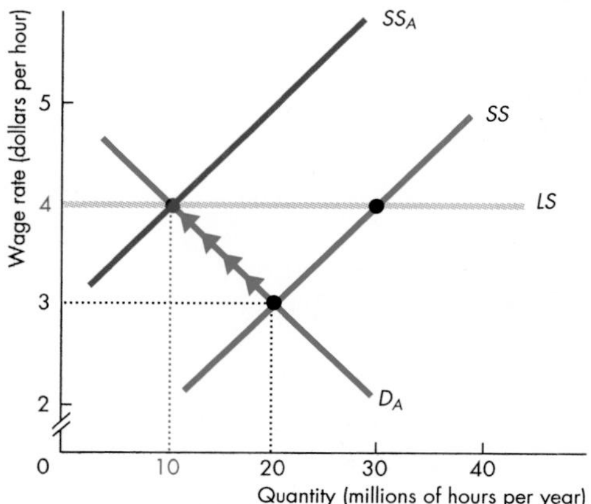

(c) Long-run adjustment

A market for unskilled labour is in equilibrium (part a) at a wage rate of $4 per hour with 30 million hours of labour per year being traded. The short-run supply curve (*SS*) slopes upward because employers have to pay a higher wage to get more hours out of a given number of workers. The long-run supply curve (*LS*) is perfectly elastic because workers will eventually enter this labour market if the wage rate is above $4 per hour or leave it if the wage rate is below $4 per hour. The invention of a labour-saving machine shifts the demand curve from *D* to D_A (part b). The wage rate falls to $3 per hour and employment falls to 20 million hours a year. With the lower wage, some workers begin to leave this market to undertake training for other types of work. As they do so, the short-run supply curve shifts to SS_A (part c). As the supply curve shifts, the wage rate gradually increases and the employment level decreases. Ultimately, wages return to $4 per hour and employment falls to 10 million hours a year.

Supply and Demand Returns in Eastern Europe

In Rumania, supply and demand redux

Pushing his long flat shovel deep into a coal-fired oven, Sachie Lazar draws out five crusty brown loaves, each weighing just over 4 lbs. He glazes them quickly with practiced brush-strokes and tips them into plastic containers, which fill up rapidly. Then the baker starts kneading and shaping a new batch of bread on a flour-dusted table, as a rivulet of perspiration makes its way down his forehead beneath a clean white cap.

Brushing away the sweat, Lazar acknowledges that his working hours at the village bakery in Buciumi (pop. 1900) have doubled since the overthrow of dictator Nicolae Ceausescu. But Lazar is not complaining. "I am now working with my heart as well as my hands," he says, a grin exploding across his thin face. Before the overthrow, rationing allowed a bit more than 8 oz. of bread per person per day. Even before the shooting stopped in Bucharest, Buciumi abandoned the system, and the tiny bakery's production doubled to 4,000 loaves a week. When asked who ordered the increase in production, Lazar grins again. "The revolution demanded it," he says. "I am producing as much as people want to buy."

For almost as long as anyone can remember, the laws of supply and demand were suspended in Buciumi, as in the rest of Rumania. Economics was governed by harsh dictates that affected everything from electricity consumption to local supplies of bread and meat. "How we suffered under Ceausescu, how we suffered," laments Gheorghe Moldovan, a Buciumi electrician. "It was better here than in the cities, but even here it was like living in the Middle Ages."

***Time*, January 15, 1990**

By John Borrell

The Essence of the Story

- In December 1989, the Rumanian people overthrew the socialist dictatorship of Nicolae Ceausescu.
- Under the Ceausescu regime, the government determined almost all aspects of economic life, down to how much electricity, bread, and meat people could consume.
- Life was likened to that in the Middle Ages.
- Within one month of the overthrow of Ceausescu, the laws of supply and demand had returned to Rumania.
- As an example, Sachie Lazar's bakery in Buciumi, a village of 1900 people, doubled its bread production and Sachie doubled his hours of work.

Background and Analysis

- Before December 1989, Rumania operated a socialist economy in which the quantities of goods and services produced and their prices were determined by the dictates of the government and not by the forces of supply and demand.

- But the forces of supply and demand cannot be eradicated. Even in a socialist dictatorship, the supply curve tells us the quantity that will be supplied at each price and the minimum price necessary to call forth a given quantity. The demand curve tells us the quantity that will be demanded at each price and the maximum price that people are willing to pay for a given quantity.

- The figure illustrates the bread market in Buciumi, Rumania. The demand curve *D* tells us the quantities of bread that people are willing to buy at various prices.

- At the price *P* Sachie Lazar can produce all the bread demanded in Buciumi. But if he raised his price above *P*, someone else would come into the market, undercut his price, and take his market. Thus someone is always willing to supply bread at the price *P*. In this market the supply curve *S* is horizontal: any quantity will be supplied provided the price is *P* and this price is the minimum one at which anyone will produce and sell bread.

- In the socialist economy, the government rationed the amount of bread produced in Buciumi to 2000 loaves a week. It probably enforced this ration by restricting the amount of flour and other ingredients that it made available to the bakery.

- The government also determined the price of bread in the socialist economy, but the news item does not tell us what the price was. The price could have been anything between *P* and P_{max}. *P* is the lowest price at which anyone would produce bread. P_{max} is the highest price that anyone would pay for the 2000th loaf each week.

- At a price of P_{max}, the quantity demanded would equal the quantity produced and there would be no waiting lines. At a price lower than P_{max}, the quantity demanded would exceed the quantity produced. A waiting line would form and a black market would develop.

- The government had to pay a price of *P* to the baker to bring forth any supply at all. The difference between this price and the price charged to consumers is a tax on bread—and a profit for the government.

- When the socialist dictatorship was abandoned, the forces of supply and demand began to operate. Those forces resulted in an equilibrium quantity of bread produced of 4000 loaves a week and a price of *P*. The baker worked longer hours to produce this larger output.

- The return of market forces eliminated the waiting line and the black market and lowered the price of bread.

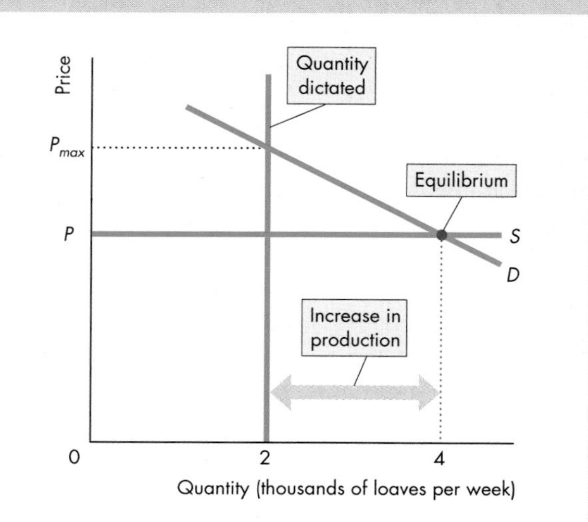

of the new technology, the demand curve shifts to the left, to D_A. The wage rate falls to $3 an hour, and the quantity of labour employed falls to 20 million hours. This short-run effect on wages and employment is not the end of the story.

People who are now earning only $3 an hour look for other opportunities. They see, for example, that the new labour-saving equipment doesn't always work properly and that when it breaks down, it is maintained by more highly paid, highly skilled workers. There are many other jobs (in markets for other types of skills) paying higher wages than $3 an hour. Some workers decide to quit this particular market for unskilled labour. They go back to school, or they take jobs that pay less but offer on-the-job training. As a result of these decisions, the short-run supply curve begins to shift to the left.

Figure 6.3(c) shows the long-run adjustment. As the short-run supply curve shifts to the left, it intersects the demand curve D_A at higher wage rates and lower levels of employment. In the long run, the short-run supply curve will have shifted all the way to SS_A. At this point, the wage has returned to $4 an hour, and the level of employment has fallen to 10 million hours.

Sometimes the adjustment process that we have just described will take place quickly. At other times, it will be a long, drawn-out affair. If the adjustment process is long and drawn out and wages remain low for a prolonged period, the government may be tempted to intervene in the market, setting a minimum wage to protect the incomes of the lowest-paid workers. What are the effects of imposing a minimum wage?

The Minimum Wage

Suppose that when the demand for labour decreases from D to D_A, as illustrated in Fig. 6.3(b), and the wage falls to $3 an hour, the government passes a minimum wage law. A **minimum wage law** is a regulation that makes trading labour below a specified wage illegal. In particular, suppose that the government declares that the minimum wage is $4 an hour. What are the effects of this law?

The answer can be found by studying Fig. 6.4. In that figure, the minimum wage is shown as the horizontal red line labelled "minimum wage." At the minimum wage, only 10 million hours of labour are demanded (point *a*). But there are 30 million hours of labour available at that wage (point *b*). Because the number of hours demanded is less than the number of hours supplied, 20 million hours of available labour go unemployed.

What are the workers doing with their unemployed hours? They are looking for work. It pays to spend a lot of time searching for work. With only 10 million hours of labour being employed, there are many people willing to supply their labour for wages much lower than the minimum wage. In fact, the 10-millionth hour of labour will be supplied for as little as $2. How do we know that there are people willing to work for as little as $2 an hour?

Look again at Fig. 6.4. As you can see, when there are only 10 million hours of work available, the lowest wage at which workers will supply that 10-millionth hour — read off from the supply curve — is $2. Someone who manages to find a job will earn $4 an hour — $2 an hour more than the lowest wage at which someone is willing to work. It pays the unemployed, therefore, to spend a considerable amount of time and effort looking for work. Even though workers actually find only 10 million hours of employment, each person will spend time and effort searching for one of the scarce jobs.

Figure 6.4 The Minimum Wage and Unemployment

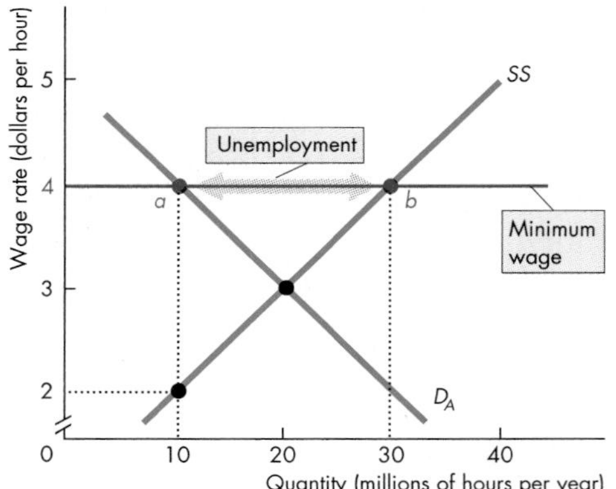

The demand curve for labour is D_A and the supply curve is SS. In an unregulated market, the wage rate is $3 per hour and 20 million hours of labour per year are employed. If a minimum wage of $4 per hour is imposed, only 10 million hours of labour are hired but 30 million hours are available. This results in unemployment — *ab* — of 20 million hours of labour per year. With only 10 million hours of labour being demanded, workers will willingly supply that 10-millionth hour for $2. It will pay such suppliers to spend the difference between the minimum wage and the wage for which they are willing to work — $2 per hour — in time and effort looking for a job.

The severity of the unemployment generated by a minimum wage depends on the demand and supply for labour. You can see that if the supply curve were farther to the left, unemployment would be less. In fact, if the supply curve cut the demand curve at point *a*, the minimum wage would be the same as the unregulated wage. In such a situation, there would be no unemployment. You can also see that if the demand curve for labour were farther to the right, unemployment would be less. If the demand curve cut the supply curve at point *b*, the minimum wage would be the same as the unregulated wage, and there would be no unemployment.

The Minimum Wage in Reality

Regulations and laws governing labour markets are matters under the jurisdiction of the provinces, and each province has its own minimum wage regulation that makes it illegal to hire a worker for less than a specified hourly rate. Economists do not agree on the effects of a minimum wage or on how much unemployment it causes. However, they do agree that a minimum wage bites hardest on the unskilled. Since there is a preponderance of unskilled workers among the young — the young have had less opportunity to obtain work experience and acquire skills — we would expect the minimum wage to cause more unemployment among young workers than among older workers. And that is exactly what happens. The unemployment for teenagers is more than twice the average rate. Although many factors other than the minimum wage influence unemployment among young people, it is almost certainly the case that part of the higher unemployment among the young arises from the impact of minimum wage laws.

R E V I E W

Governments intend minimum wages to protect the incomes of the lowest paid. But a minimum wage lowers the quantity of labour demanded and hired. Some people want to work, but they are unemployed and spend time searching for work. The young and the unskilled are hit hardest by the minimum wage. ■

We have now studied how changes in either supply or demand bring about changes — in the short run and the long run — in price and in the quantity traded. The examples that we've studied are of shocks that come like bolts from the blue — an earthquake lowers the supply of housing or a technological change lowers the demand for unskilled labour. But many changes in demand and supply are predictable. How do predictable changes in demand and supply affect prices and quantities traded? And how do people go about making predictions? Let's now study these questions.

Anticipating the Future

Producers are especially concerned about two uncertainties: the price at which they will be able to sell their product, and the conditions affecting how much of their product will be produced. Farmers provide a clear illustration of the importance of these two uncertainties. First, when farmers decide how many hectares of corn to plant, they do not know the price at which the corn will be sold. Knowing the price of corn today does not help them make decisions about how much seed to sow today. Today's planting becomes tomorrow's crop, so tomorrow's price determines how much total revenue farmers get from today's sowing decisions. Second, when farmers plant corn, they do not know what the growing conditions will turn out to be. Conditions may be excellent, producing a high yield and a bumper crop, or conditions such as drought and inadequate sunshine may lead to a low crop yield and perhaps disaster.

Uncertainty about the future price of a good can arise from uncertainty about its future demand or its future supply. We have just considered some uncertainties about supply. There are also many uncertainties about demand. We know that demand for a good depends on the prices of its substitutes and complements, income, population, and preferences. Demand varies as a result of fluctuations in all these influences on buyers' plans. Since these influences do fluctuate and are impossible to predict exactly, the level of future demand is always uncertain.

Uncertainties about future supply and demand also make future prices uncertain. But producers must make decisions today even though they do not know the price at which their output will be sold. In making such decisions, they have no choice but to rely on a forecast of the future price.

The higher the expected price, the greater is the amount that each producer will supply. The total market supply combines the supplies of all producers and it too depends on the expected future price. In Fig. 6.5, the market supply curve (*ES*) shows how the quantity supplied of a good one year in the future responds to producers' current expectations or forecasts of next year's price of that good — not to next year's actual price of that good. To determine what actions to take today to influence the quantity supplied next year, producers must first form expectations of next year's price. How do they do that?

Making Forecasts

The time and effort devoted to making forecasts varies considerably from one individual to another. Most people devote hardly any time to this activity at all. Instead, they follow rules of thumb that seem to work well most of the time. But in important matters that directly affect their incomes, people will try to do better than that. One way of doing better is simply to imitate the actions of others who have a track record of success. Another way of doing better is to buy forecasts from specialists. A large number of forecasting agencies exist — from investment advisors and stock and commodity brokers to professional economic forecasting agencies. Such agencies have a strong incentive to make their forecasts correct, at least on the average.

Figure 6.5 Supply and Expected Prices

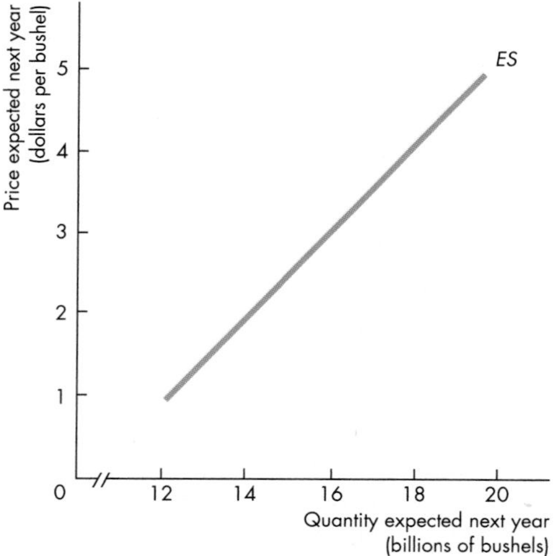

When the quantity supplied depends on past production decisions, the quantity supplied depends on the price expected at the time the production decision is made, rather than on the actual price. Expected supply is represented by the supply curve *ES*. The expected future quantity supplied rises as the expected future price rises.

The particular methods used to make forecasts are, of course, highly diverse, and our task is not to describe all of the actual methods used. Instead, our task is to build a model of forecasting. To build such a model, we use the fundamental assumption of economics — the assumption that people are seeking to get the most they can out of their scarce resources. In pursuit of that goal, forecasts will be correct on the average and forecasting errors will be as small as possible. If any information is available that can improve a forecast, that information will be used. The forecast that uses all of the relevant information available about past and present events and that has the least possible error is called a **rational expectation**.

How does an economist go about calculating a rational expectation? The answer is, by using an economic model. The economic model that explains prices is the model of demand and supply. Therefore we use the demand and supply model to forecast prices — to calculate a rational expectation of a future price. We know that the point at which next year's demand curve intersects next year's supply curve determines next year's price. But until next year arrives, we don't know where those demand and supply curves will be located. However we do know what factors determine their position, and by forecasting those factors we can forecast next year's demand and supply curves and thus forecast their point of intersection — next year's price. Let's work out a rational expectation of the future price of corn.

Expected Demand and Expected Supply

To forecast next years price of corn, we must forecast the positions of next year's demand and supply curves for corn. We learned earlier that the position of the demand curve for a good depends on the prices of its substitutes and complements, income, population, and preferences. The expected position of a demand curve, therefore, depends on the expected values of all these variables. In order to form an expectation about the future position of the demand curve of corn, it is necessary to forecast the future prices of corn's substitutes and complements, of income, of population, and of current trends that might influence preferences. By taking into account every conceivable piece of available information that helps forecast such variables, farmers — or the specialists from whom farmers buy forecasts — can form a rational expectation of next year's demand for corn.

We also learned earlier that the position of the supply curve of a good depends on the prices of its substitutes in production and complements in production, the prices of the resources used to produce the good, and technology. An important part of the technology of farming is the biological process that converts seed to crop. That process, of course, depends on the temperature, the amount of sunshine, and the amount of rain. Expected supply depends on the expected values of all these variables. In order to form an expectation about the future supply of corn, it is necessary to forecast the future prices of corn's substitutes and complements in production, and the prices of the resources used to produce the corn (the wages of farm workers and the prices of seed and fertilizers) as well as any current trends in weather patterns that might influence growing conditions. By taking into account every available piece of information that helps forecast such variables, people can form a rational expectation of the next year's corn supply.

Calculating a Rational Expectation

Figure 6.6 illustrates how to form a national expectation of next year's price of corn. The quantities measured on the two axes are expectations of next year's price and quantity. The curve labelled *ED* is the best forecast available of next year's demand for corn. The curve labelled *ES* is the best forecast available of next year's supply of corn.

What do people expect the price of corn to be next year? They expect it to be $3 a bushel. That is the price at which expected quantity demanded equals the expected quantity supplied. People can also forecast next year's quantity traded. That forecast is 16 billion bushels. The price of $3 a bushel is the rational expectation of next year's price of corn. It is the forecast of the price based on all the available relevant information. Producers use that forecast of the price to decide how many hectares of corn to plant.

R E V I E W

The rational expectation of a future price is the best forecast that can be made using all the available information. It is the price at which the expected quantity demanded equals the expected quantity supplied. Expected demand and expected supply are themselves the best forecasts available of the positions of the supply and demand curves. ■

We have seen how people form a rational expectation of a future price. What determines the actual future price?

Demand Fluctuations

Producers make the best forecast they can of future demand and future price — but almost certainly they will turn out to be wrong. The future hardly ever turns out to be exactly as expected. Let's suppose that the demand for corn fluctuates between a high level and a low level but that on the average it is *ED*, expected demand. These demand curves are shown in Fig. 6.7(a). Let's also suppose that it is impossible to forecast the fluctuations in demand. The best that people can do in forecasting demand is to suppose that demand will be at its average level. The rational expectation of this year's demand for corn is the demand curve *ED*. But this expectation was made last year. The curves D_0 and D_1 are possible actual demand curves for the current year.

We will be able to understand the effects of fluctuations in demand if we focus exclusively on that

Figure 6.6 Rational Expectation of Price 

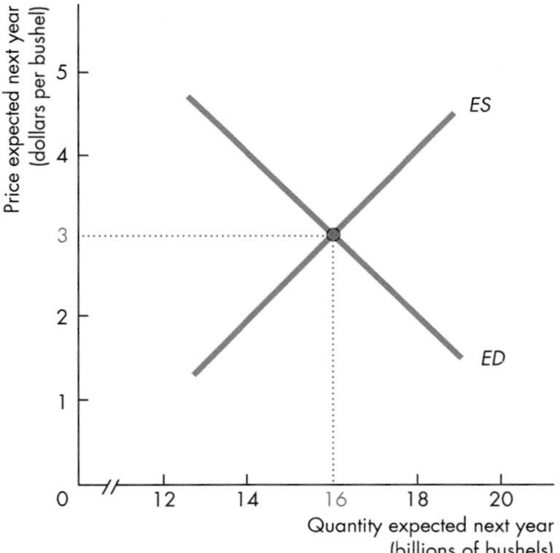

Since actual price is determined by actual supply and demand, expected price is determined by expected supply and expected demand. The point where expected demand (*ED*) cuts expected supply (*ES*) determines the rational expectation of the price, ($3 per bushel) and the expected quantity traded (16 billion bushels).

Figure 6.7 The Effects of Temporary Fluctuations in Demand

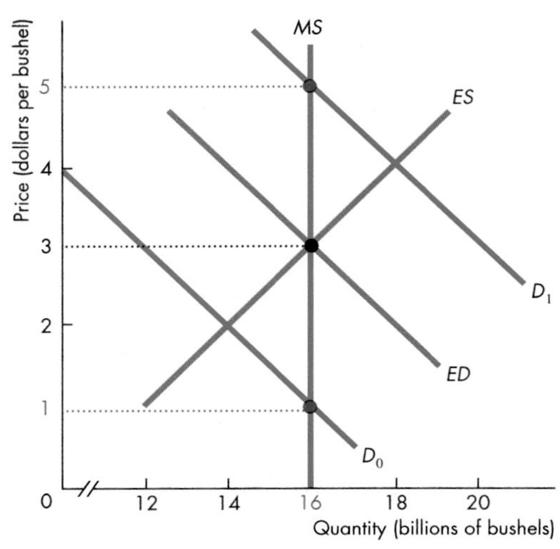

(a) Actual price fluctuations

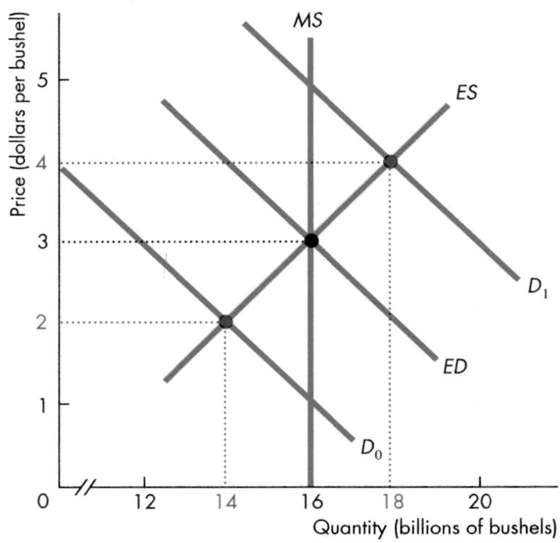

(b) With perfect forecasts

Demand fluctuates between D_0 and D_1, but on the average, demand is as expected, *ED*. Expected supply is *ES*. The rational expectation of the price is $3 per bushel. Producers plan to produce 16 billion bushels. The actual quantity supplied equals the planned quantity supplied and the momentary supply curve is *MS*. As demand fluctuates, the price fluctuates. In part (a) when demand is D_0, the price falls to $1 per bushel. When demand is D_1, the price rises to $5 per bushel. In part (b), if suppliers could anticipate the demand fluctuations correctly, the quantity supplied would fluctuate along the curve *ES* and price fluctuations would be less severe than those that actually occur. But because the future is uncertain, suppliers can do no better than produce 16 billion bushels and put up with the price fluctuations that result.

source of future uncertainty. To do that, let's suppose just for the moment that there is no uncertainty about supply. Expecting the price next year to be $3 a bushel, farmers plant enough hectares of corn for the actual output to equal the output they expected — 16 billion bushels. Growing conditions turn out to be exactly the same as they forecast, so they actually achieve their plan of producing 16 billion bushels. Since the quantity of corn actually produced is 16 billion bushels, the momentary supply curve of corn (*MS*) is completely inelastic.

Price Determination If demand turns out to be exactly as expected, the price of corn this year will be exactly the same as was forecast a year ago. That is, with this year's demand turning out to be *ED* and with this year's momentary supply curve *MS*, the quantity demanded equals the quantity supplied at a price of $3 a bushel — exactly the same price that was forecast a year ago and shown in Fig. 6.6.

Let's now look at the two other cases where demand is either higher or lower than expected, both shown in Fig. 6.7(a). First, suppose that demand is D_1. In this case, the demand and momentary supply curves intersect at a price of $5 a bushel. When demand is higher than expected, the price turns out to be higher than it was forecast to be. If demand is D_0, the demand and momentary supply curves intersect at a price of $1 a bushel. When demand is lower than expected, the price turns out to be lower than it was forecast to be.

It is interesting to note that suppliers are disappointed with the outcome whenever demand turns out to be different from its expected level. If demand is D_1, suppliers will regret that they did not sow more land to produce a bigger quantity. They would have liked, in this case, to have produced 18 billion bushels and sold them for $4 a bushel, as shown in Fig. 6.7(b). This point is where the demand curve D_1 intersects the expected supply curve *ES*. That is, if they could have correctly forecast demand at D_1, they would have forecast a price of $4 a bushel and produced 18 billion bushels. At a price of $5 a bushel, farmers have produced less than they would have liked to produce. But bygones are bygones. They couldn't do any better than forecast demand at *ED*, so, at the time they made their planting decision, they made the correct decision.

If demand turns out to be D_0, suppliers will regret that they did not sow a smaller amount of land, so that they would have produced 14 billion bushels of corn and sold at $2 a bushel, in Fig. 6.7(b). This quantity and price are at the point where the demand curve D_0 intersects the expected supply curve *ES*. That is, if farmers could have correctly forecast demand at D_0, they would have forecast a price of $2 a bushel and sown sufficient land to grow 14 billion bushels. At a price of $1 a bushel, farmers would have liked to produce less than they did. Again, bygones are bygones. They did the best they could at the time they had to make their decisions.

Figure 6.8 The Effects of Temporary Fluctuations in Supply

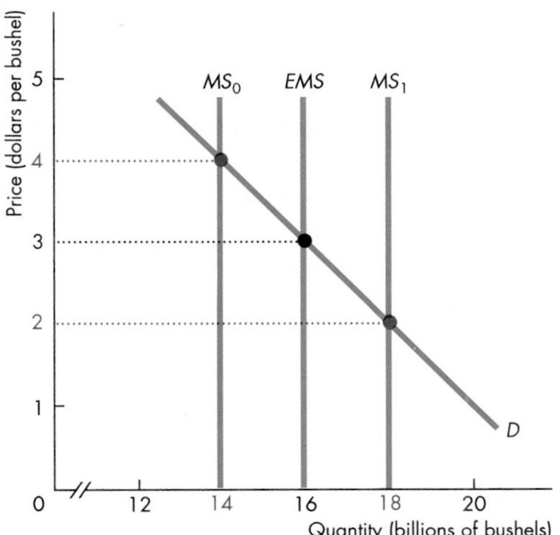

Growing conditions fluctuate and momentary supply fluctuates between MS_0 and MS_1. Expected momentary supply is *EMS*. Demand is expected to be and actually turns out to be *D*. The rational expectation of the price is $3 per bushel. When growing conditions are poor and 14 billion bushels are produced, supply is low (MS_0), and the price rises to $4 per bushel. When growing conditions are excellent and 18 billion bushels are produced, supply is high (MS_1), and the price falls to $2 per bushel.

Supply Fluctuations

Let's now study the effects of supply fluctuations on price and the quantity traded. We'll understand these effects more clearly if we isolate supply as the only source of uncertainty. To do this, let's suppose that demand is forecast correctly. The actual demand curve turns out to be the same one that was expected. What is uncertain now is the size of the crop.

There are three possibilities regarding growing conditions. First, they may turn out to be excellent, resulting in a bumper crop. Although ideal growing conditions do sometimes occur, farmers cannot forecast them. When they do happen, farmers grow more corn than they originally planned or expected. Second, growing conditions may turn out to be unusually poor, resulting in a crop yield much lower than expected. Third, growing conditions may turn out to be average, resulting in a crop yield equal to what was expected.

Figure 6.8 illustrates how each of these situations affects price. The demand curve *D* is the same as the demand curve that was forecast a year ago. The figure contains three momentary supply curves: the curve *EMS* arises if growing conditions are average; the curve MS_0 arises if there is a drought and a low crop yield results; the curve MS_1 describes the situation in which excellent growing conditions occur and a bumper crop results.

Price Determination The price is determined at the point of intersection of the momentary supply curve and the demand curve. In a drought, that price will be $4 a bushel; with a bumper crop, it will be $2 a bushel; and, on the average, when expectations are correct, it will be $3 a bushel.

Notice that when the quantity produced is correctly forecast, the actual price equals the forecast price. If the quantity produced turns out to be lower than its expected level, the price is higher than it was forecast to be. If the quantity produced turns out to be higher than its expected level, the price is lower than forecast.

In the examples that we've just worked through, momentary supply is perfectly inelastic, so price fluctuations have to do all of the work to achieve an equilibrium. What happens to these price fluctuations if corn is stored in inventories? We will now spend a bit of time examining this common situation.

Inventories

Many goods, including a wide variety of agricultural products, can be stored. These inventories provide a cushion between production and consumption. If demand increases or if production decreases, goods can be sold from inventory. If demand decreases or if production increases, goods can be put into inventory.

Inventory holders speculate. They try to buy at a low price and sell at a high price. That is, they try to buy goods and put them into inventory when the price is low and to sell them from inventory when the price is high. Their aim is to profit from the difference between their buying price and selling price, minus the cost of storage.[5] But how do inventory holders know when to buy and when to sell? How do they know whether the price is high or low? To decide whether a price is high or low and to make their buying and selling decisions, inventory holders have to forecast future prices. To do this, they form a rational expectation of the future price. If the price is above its expected future level, they sell goods from inventory. If the price is below its expected future level, they buy goods to put into inventory.

In a market that has inventories, we need to distinguish the producers' supply and the market supply. The quantity supplied to the market is the sum of the quantities supplied by both producers and inventory holders. Selling goods from inventory is equivalent to increasing the quantity supplied. Buying goods to put into inventory is equivalent to decreasing the quantity supplied. If the price is one penny above the inventory holders' rational expectation, goods will be supplied from inventory. If the price is one penny below the inventory holders' rational expectation, the quantity supplied to the market will be reduced as inventory holders put goods into inventory. This behaviour by inventory holders makes the market supply curve perfectly elastic at the inventory holders' rational expectation of the price.

Let's now work out what happens to the price and quantity traded when there are unexpected fluctuations in demand and in producers' supply in a market in which inventories are held. We'll study demand fluctuations first.

[5] We will suppose that the cost of storage is so small that we can ignore it. This assumption, though not essential, enables us to see more sharply the effects of inventory holders' decisions on prices.

Demand Fluctuations

Figure 6.9(a) illustrates the analysis of demand fluctuations. We'll suppose, for the moment, that the producers' supply of corn is perfectly inelastic and determined by the momentary supply curve *MS* at 16 billion bushels. The market supply curve is determined by the behaviour of inventory holders. Their supply is perfectly elastic at the rational expectation of the price. We determined the rational expectation of the price in Fig. 6.6 to be $3 a bushel. The market supply curve is perfectly elastic at that price, as illustrated by the supply curve *S*.

Demand fluctuates between D_0 and D_1. In the absence of inventories, the quantity traded stays fixed at 16 billion bushels and the price fluctuates to maintain equality between the quantity demanded and the fixed quantity supplied. For example, if demand is low (the curve D_0), the price falls to $2 a bushel. But things turn out very differently when there are inventory holders. Now if demand is low (D_0), the quantity bought by consumers falls to 14 billion bushels. Producers still supply 16 billion bushels. The difference between the quantity supplied by producers and the quantity demanded by consumers is taken off the market and put into inventory. Thus inventories increase by 2 billion bushels. If the demand is high (D_1), consumers buy 18 billion bushels. Farmers produce 16 billion bushels, and the additional 2 billion bushels come from inventory. Demand fluctuations lead to fluctuations in the quantity bought and to fluctuations in the size of inventory holdings, but the price stays constant at the inventory holder's rational expectation of its future level. The expectation of the future price becomes the actual price.

Now let's consider fluctuations in supply.

Supply Fluctuations

Supply fluctuations are analysed in Fig. 6.9(b). Here the demand curve is expected to be and actually turns out to be *D*. The rational expectation of the price level is $3, so the market supply curve (*S*) is perfectly elastic at that price. The producers' momentary supply now fluctuates between MS_0 and MS_1. Recall that when producers' supply fluctuates and there are no inventories, the price and the quantity traded fluctuate; the price falls when supply increases and rises when supply decreases. For example, if the quantity produced is 14 billion bushels, the price rises to $4 a bushel.

Figure 6.9 How Inventories Limit Price Changes

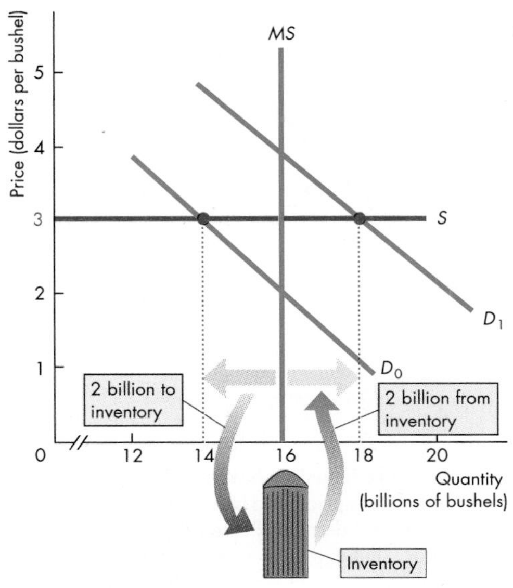

(a) Demand fluctuations

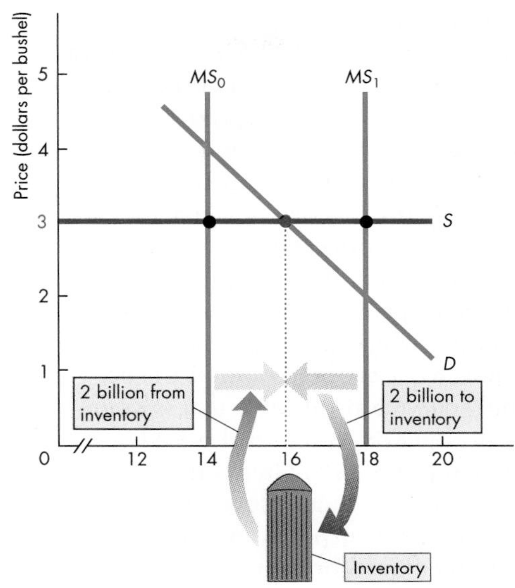

(b) Supply fluctuations

The rational expectation of the price is \$3 per bushel. Inventory holders supply from inventory if the price rises above \$3 per bushel and take goods into inventory if the price falls below \$3 per bushel. The market supply curve is the perfectly elastic curve *S* at the rationally expected price of \$3 per bushel. When demand fluctuates between D_0 and D_1, the price stays constant at \$3 per bushel, as shown in part (a). When demand is low (at D_0), production exceeds consumers' purchases by 2 billion bushels and that amount is taken into inventory. When demand is high (at D_1), consumers buy more than producers are supplying and the difference is made up from inventories. Fluctuations in supply lead the producers' momentary supply curve to fluctuate between MS_0 and MS_1, in part (b). The price stays constant at \$3 per bushel, and consumers buy a constant 16 billion bushels. When supply falls to 14 billion bushels, 2 billion bushels are supplied from inventory. When supply increases to 18 billion bushels, 2 billion bushels are taken into inventory.

With inventories, there are no price fluctuations. When producers' supply is low (at MS_0), the producers sell 14 billion bushels. The quantity bought remains 16 billion bushels and inventory holders supply the 2 billion bushels that make up the difference. When producers' supply is high (at MS_1), producers sell 18 billion bushels. Consumers continue to buy 16 billion bushels and 2 billion bushels are taken into inventory. Again the actual price is equal to the inventory holders' expectations of the future price.

The model of a market with inventories that we have reviewed is a simple one. It serves to show how inventories and inventory holders' expectations about future prices reduce price fluctuations. In the example above, the price fluctuations are entirely eliminated. When there are costs of carrying inventories and when inventories become almost depleted, some price fluctuations do occur, but they are much smaller than those occurring in a market without inventories.

People's holdings of stock are similar to holdings of inventories. They are also a good example of an inventory that does, in fact, have a zero (or almost zero) cost of storage — you can store shares in Northern Telecom or Bell Canada at virtually zero cost. Do inventories of stocks work like inventories of corn to reduce the range of price fluctuations? And if they do, why do the prices on the stock market fluctuate so dramatically?

The Stock Market

The stock market is the market in which the stocks of corporations are traded. Figure 6.10 illustrates how a stock price is determined. The horizontal axis measures the quantity expected next period. The vertical axis measures the price expected next period and the actual price this period. This period's expectations of next period's demand and supply are shown as the curves *ED* and *ES*. The intersection point of those curves determines the rational expectation of next period's price, *EP*. If the actual price rises a penny above that expected price, people will supply stocks from their inventories. If the price falls a penny below that price, people will put stocks into their inventory. Thus the market supply of stocks, taking into account inventory behaviour, is the perfectly elastic supply curve *S* at the price that is rationally expected for next period. The actual price (*P*) is equal to the expected price (*EP*). No matter how the demand and supply curves actually fluctuate, as long as the expected demand and expected supply curves are those shown in the figure, holders of stock will supply stock from inventory or take stock into inventory and, by so doing, keep the price at its expected level.

Figure 6.10 The Stock Market

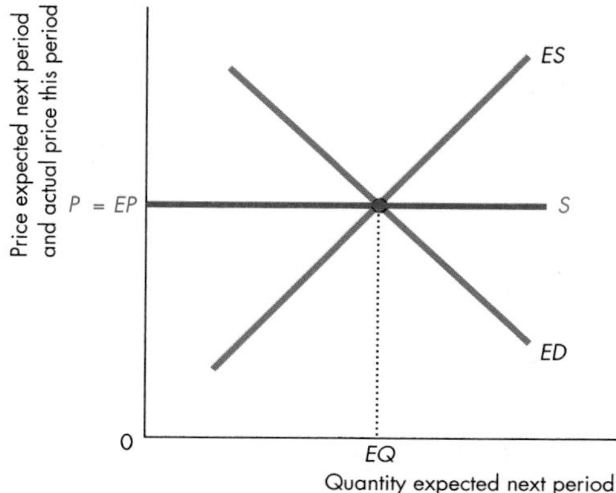

Holders of stocks behave like inventory holders. They form a rational expectation of the future price of a stock (*EP*) at the point of intersection of the expected demand curve (*ED*) and the expected supply curve (*ES*). If the price is a penny above their expectation of the future price, stockholders sell. If the price is a penny below their expectation of the future price, they buy. These transactions keep the actual price (*P*) equal to the expected future price. Such a market is called an efficient market. In an efficient market, it is not possible to forecast a future price change and profit from that forecast. A foreseen price change is acted on immediately, and the actual price adjusts to eliminate the profit opportunity.

We have seen that a rational expectation is an expectation that uses all the available information that is relevant for forecasting a future price. Since the actual stock price is equal to the rational expectation of the future stock price, that stock price also embodies all the relevant information that is available. A market in which the actual price embodies all currently available relevant information is called an **efficient market**. In an efficient market, it is impossible to forecast changes in price. Why? If your forecast is that the price is going to rise next period, you will buy now (since the price is low today compared with what you predict it is going to be in the future). Your action of buying today acts like an increase in demand today and increases today's price. It's true that your action — the action of a single trader — is not going to make much difference to a huge market such as the Toronto or New York exchanges. But if traders in general expect a higher price next period and they all act today on the basis of that expectation, then today's price will rise. It will keep on rising until it reaches the expected future price, for only at that price do traders see no profit in buying more stock today.

There is an apparent paradox about efficient markets. Markets are efficient because people try to make a profit. They seek a profit by buying at a low price and selling at a high price. But the very act of buying and selling to make a profit means that the market price moves to its expected future value. With the market price at its expected future value, no one can *predictably* make a profit. Every profit opportunity seen by a trader leads to an action that produces a price change that removes the profit opportunity for others.

Thus an efficient market has two features:

- Its price equals the expected future price and embodies all the available information.
- There are no forecastable profit opportunities available.

The key thing to understand about an efficient market such as the stock market is that if something can be anticipated, it will be, and the anticipation will be acted upon.

"Drat! I suppose the market has already discounted this, too."

Drawing by Lorenz; © 1986 The New Yorker Magazine, Inc.

Volatility in Stock Prices

If the price of a stock is always equal to its expected future price, why is the stock market so volatile? The answer must be that expectations themselves are subject to fluctuation. Expectations depend on the information available. As new information becomes available, stock traders form new expectations about the future state of the economy and, in turn, new expectations of future stock prices. Expectations about the economy are of crucial importance. Is the economy going to enjoy sustained rapid expansion? Or is it going to suffer a recession? The macroeconomic events that influence stock prices are described in Chapter 22. Individual stock prices are influenced by technological change, which, in turn, influences the supply of and demand for particular goods and services. Since new information is being accumulated daily about all these matters, expectations about the future price of a stock are constantly being re-evaluated. It is this process of re-evaluation that leads to high volatility in the stock market. As expectations change from being optimistic to pessimistic, the stock market can plunge many percentage points — as it did dramatically on October 19, 1987. On the other hand, a sustained period of increasing optimism can produce a long upswing in stock prices. The five-year run from mid-1982 to mid-1987 is an example of such stock market behaviour.[6]

■ We've now completed our study of demand and supply and its applications. You've seen how this powerful model enables us to make predictions about prices and quantities traded and also how it enables us to understand a wide variety of markets and situations.

We're now going to start digging a bit more deeply into people's economic choices, and in the next section, we'll study the economic choices of households.

[6]We will study the stock market in more detail in Chapter 17.

SUMMARY

Housing Markets and Rent Ceilings

A sudden decrease in the supply of housing shifts the short-run supply curve to the left. Rents increase. In the short run, higher rents bring forth an increase in the quantity of housing supplied (from the existing stock of houses and apartments) as people economize on the available space. In the long run, the higher rents stimulate building activity, resulting in a shift to the right of the short-run supply curve. Through this process, rents gradually decrease, and the quantity of housing available gradually increases.

If a rent ceiling prevents rents from increasing, the quantity of housing supplied is lower, in both the short run and the long run, than it would be in an unregulated market. There is no inducement for people to economize on space in the short run and no incentive to build new houses and apartments in the long run. People spend time searching for housing and the amount of time they spend increases so as to acheive an equilibrium. The total cost of housing, including the value of the time spent searching, exceeds the cost in an unregulated market. (pp. 127-132)

The Labour Market and Minimum Wage Regulations

A decrease in the demand for unskilled labour lowers wages and reduces employment in the short run. Low wages encourage people to quit a particular market, to acquire skills, and to seek different, more highly paid work. As they do so, the short-run supply curve for unskilled labour shifts to the left. As it does so, it intersects the demand curve for unskilled labour at higher wages and lower levels of employment. Eventually, the wage returns to its previous level but at a much lower employment level.

If the government imposes a minimum wage, a decrease in the demand for labour results in an increase in unemployment and an increase in the amount of time spent searching for a job. Minimum wages have the greatest effect on people who have the fewest skills, and such workers tend to be young people. The unemployment rate among such people is more than twice the average rate. (pp. 132-137)

Anticipating the Future

Producers have to make decisions about how much of a good to supply before they know the price at which they can sell it. In order to make supply decisions, producers form expectations about future prices. There is uncertainty about both demand and supply.

Producers form rational expectations about future prices based on their forecasts of future demand and supply. The actual price fluctuates around its expected level. Higher-than-expected demand produces a higher-than-expected price. Higher-than-expected supply produces a lower-than-expected price. (pp. 137-142)

Inventories

Goods that can be stored in inventory have smaller price fluctuations than those that cannot be stored. If demand or supply fluctuate, such goods can be put into or taken out of inventory. When goods are put into inventory, the supply to the market is reduced; when goods are taken out of inventory, the supply to the market is increased. Inventory holders try to buy at a low price and sell at a high price. To do so, they forecast the future price — they form a rational expectation — and sell when the price is above that expectation and buy when it is below it. Inventory holders' supply curves are perfectly elastic at their expected price (if we ignore the costs of holding inventories).

Actual prices are determined by inventory holders' rational expectations. Inventories fluctuate in response to fluctuations in both demand and producers' supply.

A rational expectation embodies all relevant information that is available. In a market in which the price equals its rational expectation, that price embodies all relevant information. Such a market is called an efficient market. Since the actual price equals the expected price, no systematic profit can be made in such a market. The actual price fluctuates in an efficient market because new information leads to a revision of the rational expectation of the price. (pp. 142-145)

K E Y   E L E M E N T S

Key Terms

Black market, 131
Efficient market, 144
Minimum wage law, 136
Rational expectation, 138
Rent ceiling, 130
Search activity, 131

Key Figures 

REVIEW QUESTIONS

1 Describe what happens to the rent and to the quantity of housing available if an earthquake suddenly and unexpectedly reduces the supply of housing. Trace the evolution of the rent and the quantity traded over time.

2 In the situation described in question 1, how will things be different if a rent ceiling is imposed?

3 Describe what happens to the price and quantity traded in a market in which there is a sudden increase in supply. Trace the evolution of the price and quantity traded in the market over time.

4 Describe what happens to the price and quantity traded in a market in which there is a sudden increase in demand. Trace the evolution of the price and quantity traded in the market over time.

5 Describe what happens to the wage rate and quantity of labour employed when there is a sudden increase in demand for labour. Trace the evolution of the wage rate and employment over time.

6 In the situation described in question 5, how are things different if a minimum wage is introduced?

7 When a government regulation prevents a price from changing, what forces come into operation to achieve an equilibrium?

8 What are the main uncertainties that producers face?

9 What is a rational expectation?

10 How are the price and quantity traded of a good determined in a market in which expectations are rational and the good cannot be stored in inventory?

11 How are the price and quantity traded of a good determined in a market in which expectations are rational and the good can be stored in inventory?

12 What determines the price per share of a corporation's stock? Why will the actual price always equal the expected price?

13 Why is the stock market so volatile?

PROBLEMS

You may find it easier to answer some of these problems by drawing the supply and demand curves on graph paper.

1 You have been given the following information about the market for rental housing in your town:

Rent (dollars per month)	Quantity demanded (per month)	Quantity supplied (per month)
100	20,000	0
200	15,000	5,000
300	10,000	10,000
400	5,000	15,000
500	2,500	20,000
600	1,500	25,000

a) What is the equilibrium rent?

b) What is the equilibrium quantity of housing traded?

2 Now suppose that a rent ceiling of $200 a month is imposed in the housing market described in problem 1.

a) What is the quantity of housing demanded?

b) What is the quantity of housing supplied?

c) What is the excess quantity of housing demanded?

d) What is the maximum price that demanders are willing to pay for the last unit available?

e) Suppose that the average wage rate is $10 per hour. How many hours a month will a person spend looking for housing?

3 Why does a minimum wage create unemployment?

4 The demand for and supply of teenage labour are as follows:

Wage rate (dollars per hour)	Hours demanded (per month)	Hours supplied (per month)
1	3,000	1,000
2	2,500	1,500
3	2,000	2,000
4	1,500	2,500
5	1,000	3,000

a) What is the equilibrium wage rate?

b) What is the level of employment?

c) What is the level of unemployment?

d) If the government imposes a minimum wage of $2.50 an hour for teenagers, how many hours do teenagers work?

e) If the government imposes a minimum wage of $3.50 an hour for teenagers, what are the employment and unemployment levels?

f) If there is a minimum wage of $3.50 an hour and demand increases by 500 hours, what is the level of unemployment?

5 The following table gives three supply schedules for train travel:

Price (cents per passenger kilometre)	Quantity supplied (billions of passenger kilometres)		
	Momentary	Short Run	Long Run
10	500	300	100
20	500	350	200
30	500	400	300
40	500	450	400
50	500	500	500
60	500	550	600
70	500	600	700
80	500	650	800
90	500	700	900
100	500	750	1,000

a) If the price is 50 cents per passenger kilometre, what is the quantity supplied

(i) In the long run?

(ii) In the short run?

b) Suppose that the price is initially 50 cents, but that it then rises to 70 cents. What will be the quantity supplied

(i) Immediately following the price rise?

(ii) In the short run?

(iii) In the long run?

6 Suppose that the supply of train travel is the same as in problem 5. The following table gives two demand schedules — original and new:

Price (cents per passenger kilometre)	Quantity demanded (billions of passenger kilometres)	
	Original	New
10	10,000	10,300
20	5,000	5,300
30	2,000	2,300
40	1,000	1,300
50	500	800
60	400	700
70	300	600
80	200	500
90	100	400
100	0	300

a) What is the original equilibrium price and quantity?

b) After the increase in demand has occurred, what is

(i) The momentary equilibrium price and quantity?

(ii) The short-run equilibrium price and quantity?

(iii) The long-run equilibrium price and quantity?

7 The short-run and long-run demand for train travel are as follows:

Price (cents per passenger kilometre)	Quantity demanded (billions of passenger kilometres)	
	Short Run	Long Run
10	700	10,000
20	650	5,000
30	600	2,000
40	550	1,000
50	500	500
60	450	400
70	400	300
80	350	200
90	300	100
100	250	0

The supply of train travel is the same as in problem 5.

a) What is the long-run equilibrium price and quantity of train travel?

b) Serious floods destroy one-fifth of the train tracks and rolling stock, and supply falls by 100 billion passenger kilometres. What happens to the price and the quantity of train travel

(i) In the short run?

(ii) In the long run?

8 Assume that wheat is not stored. The demand for wheat and the supply of wheat are expected to be as follows:

Price (dollars)	Expected Quantity demanded (per month)	Expected Quantity supplied (per month)
1	700	100
2	600	200
3	500	300
4	400	400
5	300	500
6	200	600
7	100	700

a) The average levels of demand and supply are expected to remain constant, and farmers expect no unusual events. What is their rational expectation of the price of wheat?

b) A drought occurs and wheat production is 100 units less than expected.

(i) What is the actual quantity of wheat traded?

(ii) What is the actual price of wheat at that quantity?

(iii) How much wheat will producers wish they had supplied if they had been able to forecast the drought accurately?

c) Growing conditions turn out to be exactly as expected, and the actual quantity grown equals its expected level. At the same time, a drought in the Soviet Union increases Soviet demand for Canadian wheat by 100 units.

(i) What is the actual price of wheat?

(ii) What is the actual quantity of wheat traded?

(iii) How much wheat will Canadian growers wish they had produced if they had been able to predict the increase in Soviet demand?

9 Assume that wheat *is* stored and that the average demand and supply described in problem 8 still apply.

a) If farmers expect the average levels of demand and supply and they forecast no unusual events, what is their rational expectation of the price of wheat?

b) A drought occurs and wheat production is 100 units less than expected.

(i) What is the actual price of wheat?

(ii) What is the actual quantity of wheat traded?

(iii) How much wheat will producers wish they had supplied if they had been able to forecast the drought accurately?

(iv) Is wheat added to inventories or taken out of inventories? By how much do inventories change?

c) Growing conditions turn out to be exactly as expected, and the actual production equals its expected level. At the same time, a drought in the Soviet Union increases Soviet demand for Canadian wheat by 100 units.

(i) What is the actual price of wheat?

(ii) What is the actual quantity of wheat traded?

(iii) How much wheat will Canadian growers wish they had produced if they had been able to predict the increase in Soviet demand?

(iv) Is wheat added to inventories or taken out of inventories? By how much does the inventory level change?

PART 3

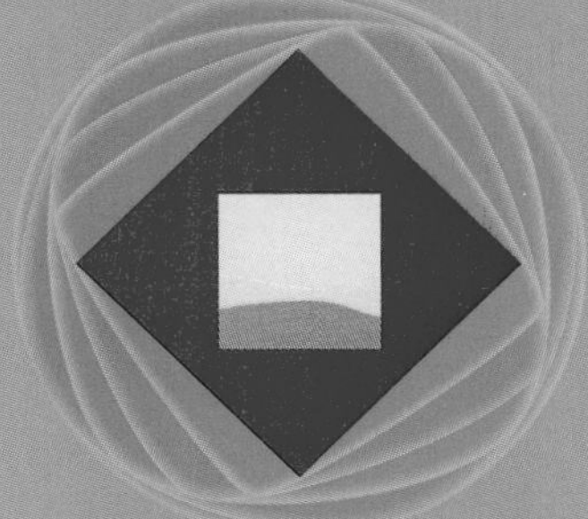

Households' Choices

TALKING WITH GARY BECKER

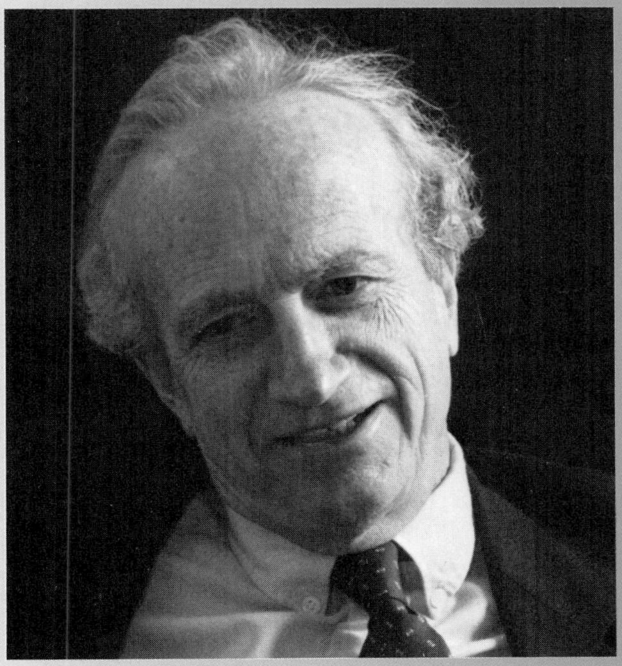

Gary Becker has devoted much of his lifetime research to applying the economic way of thinking to problems traditionally studied by sociologists. Professor Becker holds professorships in the departments of economics and sociology at the University of Chicago. Michael Parkin spoke with him about how the economics of human behaviour sheds light on social issues.

"I don't believe that people make rational choices sometimes and irrational choices other times."

Professor Becker, can we really hope to explain all human choices by using models that were invented to explain and predict choices about the allocation of income among alternative consumer goods?

All human decisions involve scarcity. Should I watch television or read a book? Should I go out on a date or drink beer with my friends? Should I get married now or remain single? In all these problems, I'm deciding how to allocate my money, my time, my effort, and my love among various uses. We live in a rich society, but we're not rich in time or energy. We're limited even in money. It's natural to ask, how do people make their choices? Do they make different types of choices when they decide what to watch on television than when they plan how to spend their money in a grocery store? Do they make different types of choices in deciding whether to get divorced or what job they should take? When I try to understand what people are doing, I do not believe that they make rational choices sometimes and at other times they make irrational choices. It's far more natural to suspect that they use the same criteria in making all their decisions. That's really the economic approach to choice, or what's called the rationality assumption.

Other social sciences consider social issues and problems. How do they differ from economics?

Economics is, uniquely I believe, a way of thinking about social issues. I think it's fair to say that economics is the most powerful of all the social sciences in providing a general organizing theory. In other respects, it's inferior to the other social sciences. Sociologists are more ingenious at conducting surveys. Anthropologists are wonderful observers and recorders of information. Psychologists are good experimenters. So all the social sciences contribute, but economics' main contribution is its analytical framework.

In this economic framework, which principles have been most fruitful for your own work?

I like to stress four principles. First, that people maximize—that's what economists sometimes associate with rational behaviour. People try to do the best they can given limited income or time. They want to use their time and resources effectively. Next, people's goals are stable over time and don't shift around. If people's goals changed readily, it would be very hard for us to talk about their behaviour. And third, people try to anticipate the adverse consequences of their behaviour. If I'm going to smoke, what's going to happen to me? I may still do it, but I try to anticipate the consequences. Finally, at the group level, these different individuals interact and end up with some aggregate solution, or what we call equilibrium. These are the basic principles. They sound simple, but it's a little more complicated to see all their implications.

What are the achievements of the economics of human behaviour? To what questions do we have convincing answers?

We have answers to many questions! For example, if we raise the tax on cigarettes, we can predict with confidence not only that the consumption of cigarettes will decline but by how much. If the price goes up, people consume less. Even those addicted to cigarettes will consume less. We can predict outcomes in labour markets, and say, for example, that when firms have to provide paid child care, the wages of women will fall. Or perhaps firms will try not to hire women.

I'm willing to say we also know a good deal about less conventional areas. We know that if you increase the likelihood that you'll catch criminals and stiffen their punishment, you get less crime. Lots of recent studies demonstrate that. We know that if you have unemployment you'll increase the amount of crime.

When you first suggested that children could be treated as durable consumer goods, the suggestion was treated with derision. Thirty years later, what are the concrete payoffs gained from making that assumption?

Thirty years later many more economists are taking this approach. And it's accepted not only by economists but by groups who didn't accept it then, by sociologists, demographers, and the like. Let me give you an example of its success. What would the economic approach emphasize in looking at the demand for children? It would naturally look at the benefits and costs of having children, including the value of the mother's time. You would predict with this approach that if the value of the mother's time went up, it would raise the cost of having children and mothers would have fewer children. Now some people would say, that's such a materialistic view. People have children because they love them. Well, of course people have children because of love. We wouldn't have any children with all the difficulties of raising kids if we didn't love them, but love has its price.

Now, if you're a skeptic, you'll want to see the evidence. And the evidence shows that as the value of the time women have goes up, they have fewer children, in every country that I know of. The theory also says that you might substitute. When people have fewer children, they give them more education, they may spend more time with each child. For example, China has had an official "one child policy" of family planning. There's much discussion now in Chinese newspapers about the so-called Emperor Child. The child who gets lots of toys, whose parents are pushing him to get him into the best nursery school. That's just what the theory predicts. The substitution between quantity and quality.

"As the value of the time women have goes up, they have fewer children."

"When people solve problems rationally, . . . they don't look at their marginal utility . . . any more than Orel Hershiser is Einstein."

Some people think it's immoral to reduce choices of a deeply personal nature to mere economic calculations. How do you respond to this objection?

First of all, when we use an economic approach, we don't concentrate on money alone. I never claim that people marry only according to how much money they're going to get out of it, or that when they have children, they reckon up each child as a profit or loss. That's ridiculous. Money is just a part of it. There have certainly been lots of family fights over money, but it's not the whole of life or any human behaviour. The economic approach doesn't say it's the whole of life. It just says that people maximize. What they're maximizing may include love toward children or a spouse. I think it's a great virtue to say, life is short and full of hardships, so let's try to get as much out of life as we can. Not the least, but the most.

Many people who are not economists don't believe that the "rationality assumption" should be taken seriously. They look inside themselves, examine their own behaviour, and don't find it rational. So how can you fairly assume that other people behave rationally?

I disagree with the premise of that question. I believe that, on reflection, people will say that a lot of things they do are in fact rational. Let me pose some simple question. You're a college student and you're thinking of going to the movies and a happy hour. You're worried about how much the evening will cost. Suppose there's no student discount and the movie will cost $6. Will you change your behaviour? Well if you don't think you can afford $6, you'll maybe go and watch television. Are you behaving rationally? Are you thinking about the consequences? Yes. That's rationality.

I'd ask more questions of this 19-year-old: How many beers are you going to have at the happy hour? Well, the legal drinking age is 21, but maybe you have a fake ID, so you get in under age. But suppose you're caught by campus security. You've got to spend the night in jail and get thrown out of school. Do you think you'd be willing to try to get in under age? Well, you might very well answer, what's my chance of being caught? And that's exactly a rational choice. Worrying about your chances of being caught and about the likely punishment.

But even if you don't actually analyze your actions in these terms doesn't mean you're acting irrationally. Let me give you another example. Orel Hershiser is a top baseball player. He effectively knows all the laws of motion, of eye and hand coordination, about the speed of the bat and the ball, and so on. He's in fact solving a complicated physics problem when he steps up to pitch, but obviously he doesn't have to know physics to do that. Likewise, I'm saying that when people solve problems rationally, they're really not thinking that, well, I have this budget and I look at my marginal utility or my indifference curve. They don't do that, but it doesn't mean they're not being rational any more than Orel Hershiser is Einstein.

CHAPTER 7

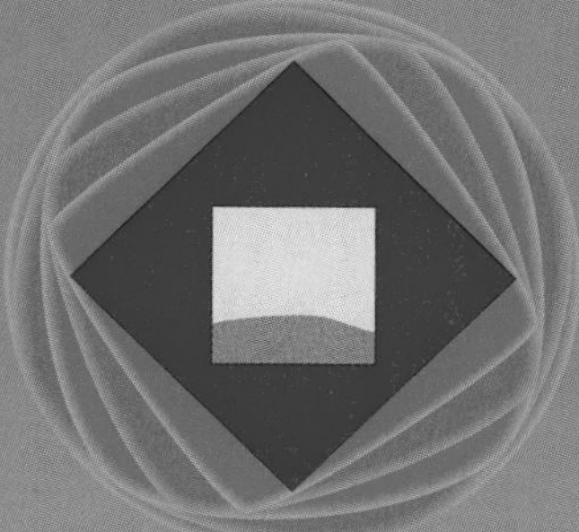

Utility and Demand

After studying this chapter, you will be able to:

- Explain the connection between individual demand and market demand.
- Define total utility and marginal utility.
- Explain the marginal utility theory of consumer choice.
- Use the marginal utility theory to predict the effects of changing prices.
- Use the marginal utility theory to predict the effects of changing income.
- Define and calculate consumer surplus.
- Explain the paradox of value.

Water, Water, Everywhere

WE NEED WATER TO LIVE. We don't need diamonds for much besides decoration. If the benefits of water far outweigh the benefits of diamonds, why, then, does water cost practically nothing while diamonds are terribly expensive? ■ When OPEC restricted its sale of oil in 1973, it created a dramatic rise in price, but people continued to use almost as much oil as they had before. Our demand for oil was inelastic. But why? ■ When Sony introduced the Walkman in 1979, it cost about $300, and at this price sales were not very brisk. Since then, the price has decreased dramatically, and people are buying them in enormous quantities. Our demand for portable audio headsets is elastic. But why? What makes the demand for some goods and services elastic while the demand for others is inelastic? ■ Over the past 40 years, there have been dramatic changes in the way we spend our incomes. Expenditure on automobiles has increased from 6.5 percent in 1948 to almost 16 percent of total expenditure today. Expenditure on food has fallen from 31 percent in 1948 to less than 20 percent of total expenditure today. Why, as incomes rise, does the proportion of income spent on some goods rise and on others fall?

■ In the last three chapters, we've seen that demand has an important effect on the price of a good. But we have not analysed what exactly shapes a person's demand. This chapter explains why demand is elastic for some goods and inelastic for others. It also explains why the prices of some goods, such as diamonds and water, are so out of proportion with their benefits.

Individual Demand And Market Demand

When we studied how demand and supply determine price and the quantity bought and sold, we used the concept of **market demand** — the relationship between the total quantity of a good demanded and its price, holding everything else constant. Yet it is individuals that buy goods and services. The relationship between the quantity demanded by a single individual and the price of a good, holding everything else constant, is called **individual demand**.

Obviously, there is a relationship between market demand and individual demand. In fact, market demand is the sum of all individual demands. The table in Fig. 7.1 illustrates the relationship between individual demand and market demand. In this example Lisa and Chuck are the only people. Therefore the market demand is the total demand of Lisa and Chuck. At $3 a movie, the quantity demanded by Lisa is 5 movies and by Chuck is 2 movies. Therefore at $3 a movie, the total quantity demanded by the market is 7 movies.

We can represent the relationship between individual and market demands in a diagram such as that in Fig. 7.1. Here Lisa's demand curve for movies appears in part (a) and Chuck's appears in part (b). The market demand curve, shown in part (c), adds Chuck's quantity demanded to Lisa's quantity demanded at each price.

The market demand curve is the sum of the quantities demanded by each individual at each price.

Let's now investigate an individual demand curve by studying how an individual household makes its consumption choices.

Figure 7.1 Individual and Market Demand Curves

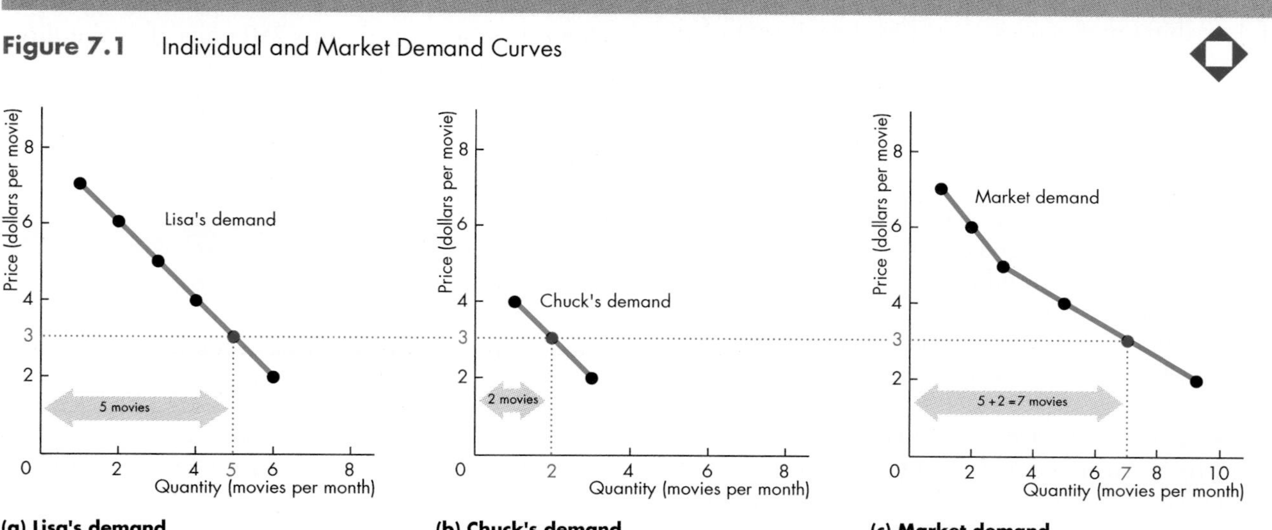

Price (dollars per movie)	Quantity of movies demanded		
	Lisa	Chuck	Market
7	1	0	1
6	2	0	2
5	3	0	3
4	4	1	5
3	5	2	7
2	6	3	9

The table and diagram illustrate how the quantity of movies demanded varies as the price of a movie varies. Lisa and Chuck are the only people in this economy. The market demand is the sum of demands by Lisa and Chuck. For example, at a price of $3, Lisa demands 5 movies and Chuck demands 2 movies, so the total quantity demanded in the market is 7 movies.

Household Consumption Choices

Suppose that a household has a certain amount of money to spend and that it cannot influence the prices of the goods and services that it buys. How does the household choose the consumption goods on which to spend its income? In answer to this question, you're about to study the marginal utility theory. It was invented almost 100 years ago by Alfred Marshall (see Our Advancing Knowledge on pp. 84-85).

To study the marginal utility theory, we'll examine Lisa's consumption choices. Lisa has a monthly income of $30 and spends all of it on only two goods — movies and pop. Movies cost $6 each and pop costs 50 cents a can or $3 for a six-pack. How does Lisa divide her $30 between these two goods? The answer depends on her likes and dislikes — on what economists call *preferences.* The marginal utility theory of consumption choice has a particular way of describing preferences — it uses the concept of utility.

Utility

The benefit or satisfaction that a person gets from the consumption of a good or service is called **utility**. What exactly is utility and in what units can we measure it? Utility is an abstract theoretical concept and units of utility are chosen arbitrarily, just like the units in which we measure temperature.

Temperature — An Analogy Temperature is a concept with which you are familiar. You know when you feel hot and you know when you feel cold. But you can't *observe* temperature. You can observe water turning to steam if it is hot enough or turning to ice if it is cold enough. You can construct an instrument, called a thermometer, that will enable you to predict when such changes of state will occur. The scale on the thermometer is what we call temperature. But the units in which we measure temperature are arbitrary. For example, we can accurately predict that when a Celsius thermometer shows a temperature of 0°, water will turn to ice. But the units of measurement do not matter because this same event will also occur when a Fahrenheit thermometer shows a temperature of 32°.

The concept of utility helps us make predictions about consumption choices in much the same way that the concept of temperature helps us make predictions about physical phenomena. It has to be admitted, though, that the marginal utility theory is not as precise as the theory that enables us to predict when water will turn to ice or steam.

Let's now see how we can use the concept of utility to describe preferences.

Total Utility and Consumption

Total utility is the total benefit or satisfaction that a person gets from the consumption of goods and services. The amount of total utility that a person gets depends on the person's level of consumption — more consumption gives more total utility. Table 7.1 gives an example of Lisa's total utility derived from consuming different quantities of movies and pop. If she sees no movies, she gets no utility from movies. If she sees 1 movie in a month, she gets 50 units of utility. As the number of movies she sees in a month increases, her total utility increases so that if she sees 10 movies a month, she gets 250 units of total utility. The other part of the table shows Lisa's total utility from pop. If she drinks no pop, she gets no utility. As the amount of pop she drinks rises, her total utility increases.

Table 7.1 Lisa's Total Utility from Movies and Pop

Movies		Pop	
Quantity per month	Total utility	Six-packs per month	Total utility
0	0	0	0
1	50	1	75
2	88	2	117
3	121	3	153
4	150	4	181
5	175	5	206
6	196	6	225
7	214	7	243
8	229	8	260
9	241	9	276
10	250	10	291

Figure 7.2 Total Utility and Marginal Utility

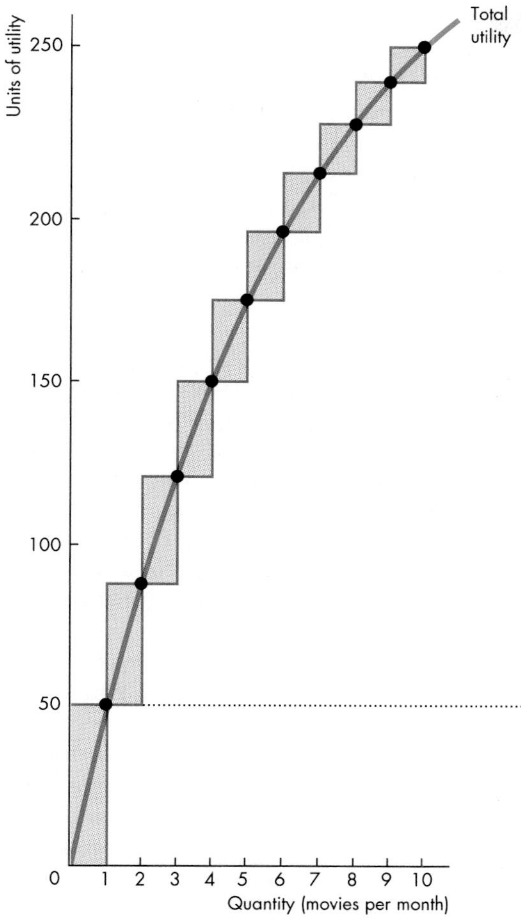

Quantity	Total utility	Marginal utility
0	0	
		50
1	50	
		38
2	88	
		33
3	121	
		29
4	150	
		25
5	175	
		21
6	196	
		18
7	214	
		15
8	229	
		12
9	241	
		9
10	250	

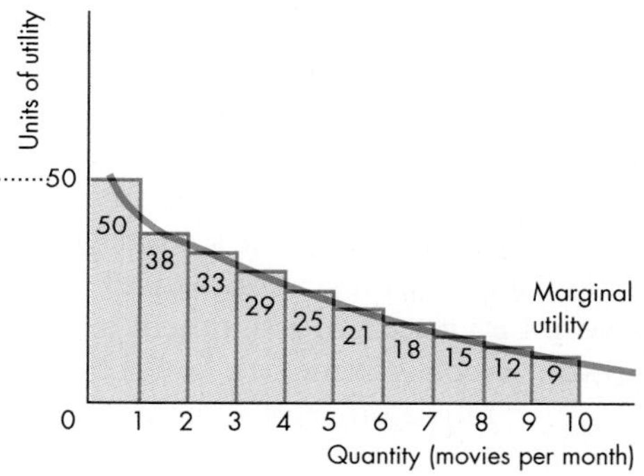

(a) Total Utility

(b) Marginal utility

The table shows that as Lisa's consumption of movies increases, so does the total utility she derives from movies. For example, 4 movies give 150 units of utility while 5 movies give 175 units. The table also shows her marginal utility — the change in total utility resulting from the last movie seen. Marginal utility declines as consumption increases. For example, the marginal utility from the fourth movie is 29 units while that from the fifth movie is 25 units. Lisa's total utility and marginal utility from movies are graphed in the figure. Part (a) shows the extra total utility gained from each additional movie as a bar. Part (b) shows the marginal utility of each new movie as a declining series of steps.

Marginal Utility

Marginal utility is the additional total utility derived from the last unit of a good consumed. We calculate marginal utility as the change in total utility that occurs when one more unit of a good is consumed.

Such a calculation is shown in the table in Fig. 7.2. When Lisa's consumption of movies increases from 4 to 5 movies a month, her total utility from movies increases from 150 units to 175 units. Thus Lisa's marginal utility of the fifth movie each month is 25 units. The table displays calculations of marginal utility for each level of movie consumption. Notice that the units of marginal utility appear midway between the quantities of consumption. It is the *change* in consumption from 4 to 5 movies that produces the *marginal* utility of 25 units.

Lisa's total utility and marginal utility can be illustrated in a graph. Figure 7.2(a) illustrates the total utility that Lisa gets from movies. As you can see, the more movies Lisa sees in a month, the more total utility she gets. Part (b) illustrates her marginal utility. This graph tells us that as Lisa sees more movies, the marginal utility that she gets from watching movies falls. For example, her marginal utility from the first movie is 50 units, from the second, 38 units, and from the third, 33 units. We call this decline in marginal utility as the consumption of a good increases the principle of **diminishing marginal utility**.

Marginal utility is positive but diminishes as the consumption of a good increases. Why does marginal utility have these two features? In Lisa's case, she likes movies, and the more she sees the better. That's why marginal utility is positive. The benefit that Lisa gets from the last movie seen is its marginal utility. To see why marginal utility diminishes, think about how you'd feel in the following two situations. In one, you've just been studying for 29 evenings in a row. An opportunity arises to see a movie. The utility that you get from that movie is the marginal utility from seeing one movie in a month. In the second situation, you've been on a movie binge. For the past 29 nights, you have not even seen an assignment or test. You are up to your eyeballs in movies. You are happy enough to go to a movie on yet one more night. But the kick that you get out of that thirtieth movie in 30 days is not very large. It is the marginal utility of the thirtieth movie in a month.

REVIEW

Lisa divides her income of $30 a month between movies that cost $6 each and pop that costs $3 a six-pack. Lisa's preferences are described by using the concept of utility: the more movies Lisa sees in a given month, the more total utility she gets; the more cans of pop she drinks in a month, the more total utility she gets. The increase in total utility that results from the last unit of a good consumed is called marginal utility. As the quantity of a good consumed increases, marginal utility decreases. ■

Utility Maximization

Utility maximization is the attainment of the greatest possible total utility. But a household's income and the prices that it faces limit the utility that it can obtain. We assume that a household consumes in a way that maximizes its total utility taking into consideration its income and the prices that it faces. In Lisa's case, we examine how she allocates her spending between movies and pop to maximize her utility, assuming that movies cost $6 each, pop costs $3 a six-pack, and Lisa has only $30 a month to spend. We will now discover a rule that always works to produce the highest attainable level of total utility.

The Utility-Maximizing Choice Let's calculate how Lisa spends her money to maximize her utility by constructing a table. Table 7.2 has two parts. Part (a) records Lisa's expenditure and part (b), her total utility. Part (a) shows six ways in which Lisa can allocate her $30 of income between movies and pop. For example, she can buy 2 movies at a cost of $12, in which case she will be able to buy 6 six-packs for a cost of $18. Each row in part (a) shows the combinations of movies and pop that exhaust her income.

Part (b) considers the same affordable combinations of movies and pop that are set out in part (a). Part (b) records three things: first, the number of movies consumed and the total utility derived from them (the left side of the table); second, the number of six-packs of pop consumed and the total utility derived from them (the right side of the table); and third, the total utility derived from both movies and pop (the middle column of the table).

Consider, for example, the first row. It shows Lisa watching no movies, getting no utility from them but getting 291 units of total utility from drinking 10 six-packs of pop. Her total utility from movies and pop, in this case, is 291 units.

Now consider the second row. Lisa watches 1 movie, getting 50 units of total utility from it, and drinks 8 six-packs of pop, getting another 260 units of total utility. In this case, her total utility from movies and pop is the sum of 50 units from movies and 260 units from pop, or 310 units. The rest of part (b) is constructed in exactly the same way.

Notice that Table 7.2 does not consider allocations in which Lisa consumes odd numbers of six-packs of pop (1, 3, 5, 7, or 9). The reason is that she cannot buy half a movie. She has to buy movies in whole numbers, and since movies cost $6, twice as much as a six-pack of pop, she can consume only 0,

Table 7.2 Lisa's Utility Maximizing Combinations of Movies and Pop

(a) Expenditure

Movies			Pop	
Quantity	Expenditure (dollars)	Total expenditure (dollars)	Expenditure (dollars)	Six-packs
0	0	30	30	10
1	6	30	24	8
2	12	30	18	6
3	18	30	12	4
4	24	30	6	2
5	30	30	0	0

(b) Total utility

Movies			Pop	
Quantity	Total utility	Total utility from movies and pop	Total utility	Six-packs
0	0	291	291	10
1	50	310	260	8
2	88	313	225	6
3	121	302	181	4
4	150	267	117	2
5	175	175	0	0

2, 4, 6, 8, or 10 six-packs of pop if she spends all her income on these two goods.

The consumption of movies and pop that maximizes Lisa's total utility is highlighted in Table 7.2(b). When Lisa consumes 2 movies and 6 six-packs of pop, she gets 313 units of total utility. This is the best Lisa can do given that she has only $30 to spend and given the prices of movies and six-packs. If she buys 8 six-packs of pop, she can see only 1 movie and gets 310 units of total utility, 3 less than the maximum attainable. If she sees 3 movies and drinks only 4 six-packs, she gets 302 units of total utility, 11 less than the maximum attainable. Thus Lisa can do no better than consume 2 movies and 6 six-packs — the allocation of her $30 that maximizes her utility, given the prices of movies and pop.

The situation that we've just described is a consumer equilibrium. A **consumer equilibrium** is a /situation in which a consumer has allocated his or her income in a manner that maximizes total utility. In calculating Lisa's consumer equilibrium, we have measured her total utility from the consumption of movies and pop. There is another, better way of determining a consumer equilibrium that does not involve measuring total utility at all. Let's look at this alternative.

Equalizing Marginal Utility per Dollar Spent

We can find out the allocation that maximizes a consumer's utility by making the marginal utility per dollar spent on each good equal for all goods. The **marginal utility per dollar spent** is the marginal utility obtained from the last unit of a good consumed divided by the price of the good. For example, Lisa's marginal utility from consuming the first movie is 50 units of utility. The price of a movie is \$6, which means that the marginal utility per dollar spent on movies is 50 units divided by \$6, or 8.33 units of utility per dollar.

Lisa maximizes utility when she spends all her income and consumes movies and pop such that

$$\frac{\text{Marginal utility from movies}}{\text{Price of movies}} = \frac{\text{Marginal utility from pop}}{\text{Price of pop}}.$$

Let's do some calculations to see how this formula delivers the utility-maximizing allocation of Lisa's income.

Table 7.3 sets out Lisa's marginal utilities per dollar spent for both movies and pop. Each row of the table represents an allocation of her income that uses up her \$30. You can see that Lisa's marginal utility per dollar spent on either good, like marginal utility itself, declines as consumption of the good rises. The marginal utility per dollar spent on movies falls from 8.33 for the first movie to 6.33 for the second to 4.16 for the fifth. The marginal utility per dollar spent on pop is 14.00 for 2 six-packs, 9.33 for 4 six-packs, 6.33 for 6 six-packs, and 5.00 for 10 six-packs.

Notice that when Lisa consumes 2 movies and 6 six-packs of pop, she gets the same marginal utility per dollar spent from movies as she does from pop. This allocation of her income maximizes her utility. It is the same allocation as we calculated in Table 7.2.

Utility is maximized when the marginal utility per dollar spent is equal for all goods.

In calculating the utility-maximizing allocation of income in Table 7.3, we have not used the concept of total utility at all. All the calculations have been performed using marginal utility and price. By making the marginal utility per dollar spent equal for both goods, we know that Lisa has maximized her utility, but we have not calculated what the maximum level of total utility is. As a matter of fact, we do not need to know what the level of total utility is. We only need to know that maximum total utility has been obtained. This way of viewing maximum utility is important; it means that the units in which utility is measured do not matter. We could double or halve all the numbers measuring utility, or multiply them by any other positive number, or square them, or take their square roots. None of these transformations of the units used to measure utility would change the utility-maximizing allocation of the consumer's income. Total utility is maximized when the marginal utility per dollar spent is equal for all goods. It is in this respect that utility is analogous to temperature. Our prediction about the freezing of water does not depend on the temperature scale; our prediction about maximizing utility does not depend on the units of utility.

Table 7.3 Maximizing Utility by Equalizing Marginal Utilities per Dollar Spent

Movies (\$6 each)			Pop (\$3 per six-pack)		
Quantity	Marginal utility	Marginal utility per dollar spent	Six-packs	Marginal utility	Marginal utility per dollar spent
0	0		10	15	5.00
1	50	8.33	8	17	5.67
2	38	6.33	6	19	6.33
3	33	5.50	4	28	9.33
4	29	4.83	2	42	14.00
5	25	4.16	0	0	

You can see why the rule "equalize marginal utility per dollar spent on all goods" works by considering what happens if Lisa spends differently. Suppose that instead of consuming 2 movies and 6 six-packs of pop, Lisa consumes 1 movie and 8 six-packs of pop (the second row of Table 7.3). She will then get 8.33 units of utility from the last dollar spent on movies and 5.67 units of utility from the last dollar spent on pop. It will pay Lisa to spend less on pop and more on movies. If she spends a dollar less on pop and a dollar more on movies, her total utility from pop falls by 5.67 units and her total utility from movies rises by 8.33 units. Lisa's total utility rises if she spends less on pop and more on movies.

Or suppose that Lisa consumes 3 movies and only 4 six-packs of pop (the fourth row of the table). In this situation, she gets 5.50 units of utility from the last dollar spent on movies and 9.33 units of utility from the last dollar spent on pop. Lisa can now get more total utility by cutting her spending on movies, at a cost of 5.50 units of utility per dollar, and raising her spending on pop, where she gets 9.33 units of utility per dollar. When Lisa's marginal utility per dollar spent on both goods is equal, she cannot get more total utility by spending differently. Her utility is maximized.

R E V I E W

Consumers maximize total utility. A consumer spends his or her income in order to make the marginal utility per dollar spent on each good equal. Once the marginal utilities per dollar spent are equal, the consumer cannot reallocate spending to get more total utility. The absolute level of utility is irrelevant — all that matters is its maximization. The units in which utility is measured are irrelevant — all that matters is that the marginal utility per dollar is equal for all goods. ■

Predictions of Marginal Utility Theory

Now let's go on to use marginal utility theory to make some predictions. In particular, let's see what happens to Lisa's consumption of movies and pop when their prices change and also when her income changes.

The Effects of Changes in Prices

First, we'll work out what happens to Lisa's consumption if the price of a movie is halved to \$3 but the price of pop is unchanged. Next, we'll work out what happens if the price of a movie stays at \$3 and the price of pop doubles to \$6 per six-pack.

A Fall in the Price of Movies Table 7.4 shows ways of consuming movies at \$3 each and pop at \$3 a six-pack. Once again, each row of the table shows quantities consumed that exactly use up the \$30 of income available. The marginal utility per dollar spent is the marginal utility of the good divided by its price. Marginal utility, which was shown in the table in Fig. 7.2, describes Lisa's preferences. Her preferences do not change when prices change, so her marginal utility schedule remains the same as that in Fig. 7.2. But now we divide her marginal utility from movies by \$3, the new price of a movie, to get the marginal utility per dollar spent on movies. You can see that Lisa's marginal utility per dollar spent on movies declines from 16.67 at 1 movie all the way down to 3.00 at 10 movies.

Table 7.4 How a Change in the Price of Movies Affects Lisa's Choices

Movies cost \$3.00 each
Pop costs \$3.00 a six-pack

Movies		Pop	
Quantity	Marginal utility per dollar spent	Six-pack	Marginal utility per dollar spent
0		10	5.00
1	16.67	9	5.33
2	12.67	8	5.67
3	11.00	7	6.00
4	9.67	6	6.33
5	8.33	5	8.33
6	7.00	4	9.33
7	6.00	3	12.00
8	5.00	2	14.00
9	4.00	1	25.00
10	3.00	0	

Figure 7.3 A Fall in the Price of Movies

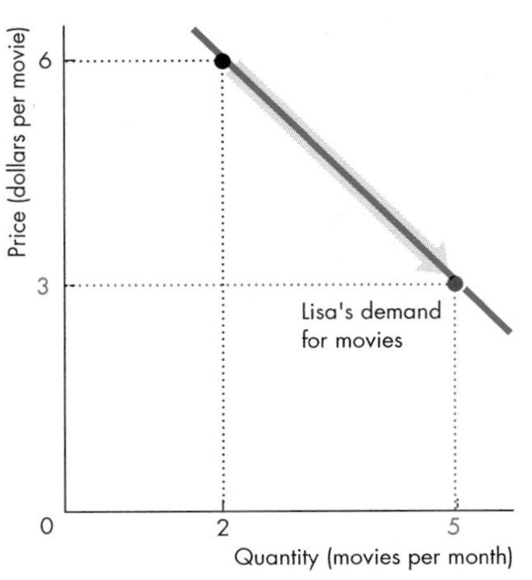

(a) Movies

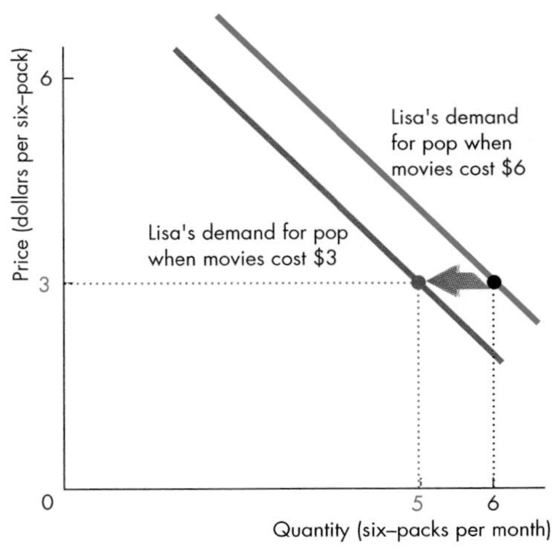

(b) Pop

When the price of movies falls and the price of pop remains constant, Lisa moves along her demand curve for movies (part a) and there is a shift in her demand for pop (part b).

Lisa's marginal utility per dollar spent on pop declines from 25.00 at 1 six-pack to 5.00 at 10 six-packs. The marginal utilities per dollar spent on movies and on pop are each equal to 8.33 when Lisa watches 5 movies and drinks 5 six-packs.

What has been the effect of the fall in the price of a movie on Lisa's consumption? You can find the answer by comparing Lisa's utility-maximizing allocation shown in Table 7.4 with her allocation in Table 7.3. As a result of the fall in the price of a movie, Lisa watches more movies (up from 2 to 5 a month) and she drinks less pop (down from 6 six-packs to 5 six-packs a month). That is, Lisa substitutes movies for pop when the price of a movie falls.

The effects that we've just analysed are illustrated in Fig. 7.3. In part (a) you can see the effect as a movement along Lisa's demand curve for movies and in part (b) as a shift in her demand curve for pop.

To determine the effects of changes in prices on consumption requires three steps. First, we need to determine the combinations of movies and pop that can be bought at the new prices. Second, we need to calculate the new marginal utilities per dollar spent. Third, we need to determine the consumption of each good that makes the marginal utility per dollar spent on each good equal and that just exhausts the money available for spending.

A Rise in the Price of Pop Let us now work out Lisa's consumption when the price of a movie stays at $3, but the price of pop doubles to $6 a six-pack. The rows of Table 7.5 show the possible ways of consuming

Table 7.5 How a Change in Price of Pop Affects Lisa's Choices

Movies cost $3.00 each
Pop costs $6.00 a six-pack

Movies		Pop	
Quantity	**Marginal utility per dollar spent**	**Six-pack**	**Marginal utility per dollar spent**
0		5	4.17
2	12.67	4	4.67
4	9.67	3	6.00
6	7.00	2	7.00
8	5.00	1	12.50
10	3.00	0	

Figure 7.4 A Rise in the Price of Pop

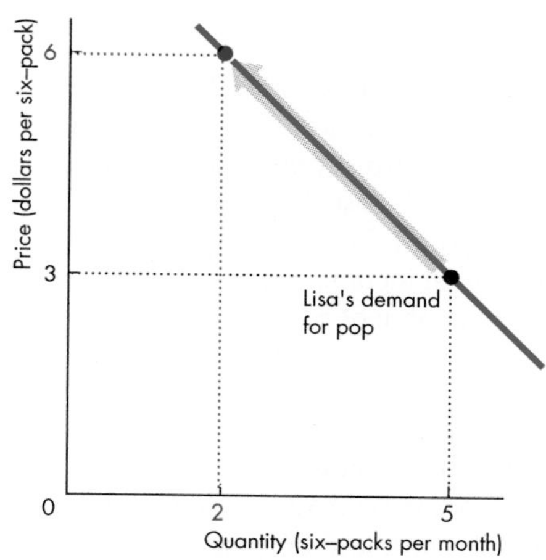

(a) Pop

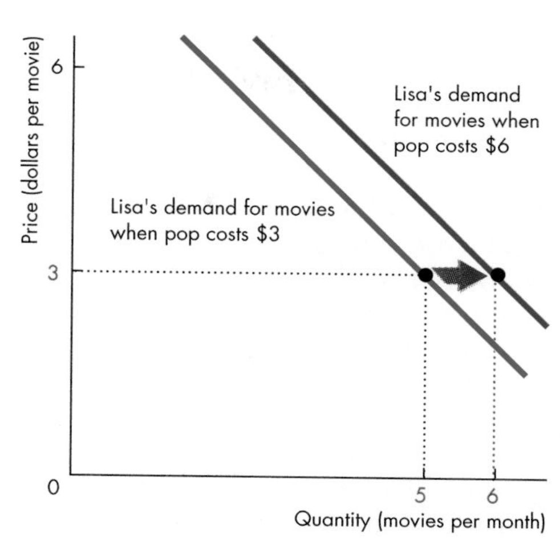

(b) Movies

When the price of pop rises and the price of movies remains constant, Lisa moves along her demand curve for pop and there is a shift in her demand curve for movies.

pop and movies at these new prices. Because pop now costs $6, Lisa cannot consume more than 5 six-packs. Five six-packs of pop cost $30, exactly the amount that she has available. Since we are assuming that a six-pack cannot be split into single cans, Lisa can consume only 0, 2, 4, 6, 8, or 10 movies. Because movies cost the same as in Table 7.4 the marginal utility per dollar spent on them remains the same. You can see that if Lisa sees 2 movies, her marginal utility per dollar spent on movies is 12.67 in both cases. If Lisa sees 10 movies, her marginal utility per dollar spent on movies is 3.00.

Lisa's marginal utility per dollar spent on pop is the marginal utility of pop divided by the new price of pop ($6). These marginal utilities per dollar spent are set out in Table 7.5. As you can see, the marginal utility per dollar spent on movies and on pop are equal when Lisa watches 6 movies and drinks 2 six-packs a month. You can calculate the effects of the rise in the price of pop on Lisa's consumption by comparing her choice in Table 7.5 with that in Table 7.4. Lisa's consumption of pop has fallen from 5 six-packs to 2 six-packs, and her consumption of movies has increased from 5 to 6 a month. For Lisa, pop and movies are substitutes. When there is a rise in the price of pop, Lisa substitutes movies for pop. She sees more movies and drinks less pop.

The effects that we've just analysed are illustrated in Fig. 7.4. In part (a) you can see the effect as a movement along Lisa's demand curve for pop and in part (b) as a shift in her demand curve for movies.

R E V I E W

When the price of a movie falls but the price of pop stays constant, Lisa increases her consumption of movies and reduces her consumption of pop. There is a movement along her demand curve for movies and a shift in her demand curve for pop. When the price of a movie stays constant but the price of pop increases, Lisa reduces her consumption of pop and increases her consumption of movies. There is a movement along her demand curve for pop and a shift in her demand curve for movies. If the price of a movie falls or the price of pop rises and Lisa does not change her consumption of movies and pop, her marginal utility per dollar spent on movies exceeds that of pop. To restore the equality of the marginal utility per dollar spent on each good, she must increase her consumption of movies and decrease her consumption of pop. ■

Marginal utility theory predicts these two results: if the price of a good rises, the quantity demanded of that good falls; if the price of one good rises, the demand for another good that can serve as a substitute increases. Does this sound familiar? It should. These predictions of marginal utility theory correspond to the assumptions that we made about consumer demand in Chapter 4. There we *assumed* that the demand curve for a good sloped downward, and we *assumed* that a rise in the price of a substitute increased demand. Marginal utility theory predicts these responses to price changes. In doing so it makes three assumptions. First, that consumers maximize utility. Second, that they get more utility as they consume more of a good. Third, as consumption increases, marginal utility declines.

Thus the assumption of diminishing marginal utility implies the law of demand. But this is not the only implication of diminishing marginal utility. It also has implications for the response of consumption to a change in income. Let's see the effects of a change in Lisa's income on her consumption.

The Effects of a Rise in Income

Let's suppose that Lisa gets a raise of $12 a month, which means that she now has $42 a month to spend on movies and pop. Let's also suppose that movies cost $3 each and a six-pack costs $3 (as in Table 7.4). We now want to compare Lisa's consumption of movies and pop at her original income of $30 with her consumption at her new income of $42. The calculations for such a comparison are presented in Table 7.6. Case 1 (which is identical to Table 7.4) shows Lisa's utility-maximizing consumption of movies and pop when she earns $30. Case 2 shows what happens when Lisa's income goes up to $42. With $42, Lisa can buy 14 movies a month and no pop or 14 six-packs a month and no movies or any combination of the two goods shown in the rows of Table 7.6.

Table 7.6 How a Change in Income Affects Lisa's Choices

Case 1: Income $30				*Case 2:* Income $42			
Movies ($3 each)		Pop ($3 per six-pack)		Movies ($3 each)		Pop ($3 per six-pack)	
Quantity	Marginal utility per dollar spent	Six-pack	Marginal utility per dollar spent	Quantity	Marginal utility per dollar spent	Six-pack	Marginal utility per dollar spent
0		10	5.00	0		14	
1	16.67	9	5.33	1	16.67	13	
2	12.67	8	5.67	2	12.67	12	
3	11.00	7	6.00	3	11.00	11	
4	9.67	6	6.33	4	9.67	10	5.00
5	8.33	5	8.33	5	8.33	9	5.33
6	7.00	4	9.33	6	7.00	8	5.67
7	6.00	3	12.00	7	6.00	7	6.00
8	5.00	2	14.00	8	5.00	6	6.33
9	4.00	1	25.00	9	4.00	5	8.33
10	3.00	0		10	3.00	4	9.33
				11		3	12.00
				12		2	14.00
				13		1	25.00
				14		0	

We can calculate the marginal utility per dollar spent on movies and pop in exactly the same way as we did before. Only now, because Lisa has more income, she can consume more pop for any given consumption of movies or, equivalently, more movies for any given consumption of pop. For example, Lisa can watch 1 movie and drink 13 six-packs of pop when she earns $42. When her income is $30, however, she can buy only 9 six-packs of pop if she sees 1 movie. Lisa maximizes her utility when the marginal utilities per dollar spent on movies and on pop are equal. At an income of $42 such a situation occurs when the marginal utility per dollar spent on each good is 6.00 units. Lisa watches 7 movies a month and drinks 7 six-packs of pop.

By comparing Case 2 with Case 1, we can see another important prediction of the marginal utility theory of consumption. When Lisa earns more income, she increases her consumption of both goods. In this particular example, Lisa increases her consumption of both goods by the same amount — 2 more six-packs and 2 more movies. This response arises from Lisa's preferences, as described by her marginal utilities. Different preferences produce different quantitative responses, but for normal goods, a higher income always brings a larger consumption of all goods.

For Lisa, pop and movies are normal goods. When her income rises, Lisa buys more of both goods. This prediction of the marginal utility theory corresponds to another assumption that we made when studying the theory of demand in Chapter 4. There we *assumed* that demand for a normal good rises when income rises. Here we have obtained that result as a prediction of marginal utility theory.

The marginal utility theory of consumption is summarized in Table 7.7. We can use the marginal utility theory of consumer behaviour to make sense of some of the features of the world described at the beginning of this chapter. For example, it explains why the demand for some goods, such as audio headsets, is elastic and for others, such as oil, is inelastic. It also explains why, as income increases, the proportion of income spent on some goods, such as automobiles, increases, while the proportion spent on other goods, such as food, decreases. These effects occur because of our preferences. The speed with which our marginal utility for each good diminishes as we increase our consumption of the good affects the way in which we reallocate our income in response to price changes and the way in which our spending responds to a change in income. The calculations that we've performed for Lisa illustrate these effects.

Table 7.7 Marginal Utility Theory

Assumptions

(a) A consumer derives utility from the goods consumed.

(b) Each additional unit of consumption yields additional total utility; marginal utility is positive.

Implication

The consumer's total utility is maximized when the marginal utility per dollar spent is equal for all goods.

Predictions

(a) Other things being equal, the higher the price of a good, the lower is the quantity bought (the law of demand).

(b) Other things being equal, the higher the price of a good, the higher is the consumption of substitutes for that good.

(c) Other things being equal, the higher the consumer's income, the greater is the quantity demanded of normal goods.

Criticisms of Marginal Utility Theory

Marginal utility theory helps us to understand the choices people make, but there are some criticisms of this theory. Let's look at them.

Utility Can't Be Observed or Measured

Agreed — we can't observe utility. But we do not need to observe it to use it. We can and do observe the quantities of goods and services that people consume, the prices of those goods and services, and people's incomes. Our goal is to understand the consumption choices that people make and to predict the effects of changes in prices and incomes on these choices. To make such predictions, we *assume* that people derive utility from their consumption, that more consumption yields more total utility, and that marginal utility diminishes. Given these assumptions, we can make predictions about the directions of change in consumption when prices and incomes change. As we've already seen, the actual numbers we use to express utility do not matter. Consumers maximize total utility by making the marginal utility per dollar spent on each good equal. As long as we use the same scale to express utility for all goods, we'll get the same answer regardless of the units on our scale. In this regard, utility is similar to temperature — water freezes when it's cold enough, and that occurs independently of the temperature scale used.

People Aren't That Smart

Some critics maintain that marginal utility theory assumes that people are supercomputers. It requires people to look at the marginal utility of every good at every different quantity they might consume, divide those numbers by the prices of the goods, and then calculate the quantities so as to equalize the marginal utility of each good divided by its price.

Such criticism of marginal utility theory confuses the actions of people in the real world with those of people in a model economy. A model economy is no more an actual economy than a model railway is an actual railway. The people in the model economy perform the calculations that we have just described. People in the real world just consume. We observe their consumption choices, not their mental gymnastics. The marginal utility theory proposes that the consumption patterns we observe in the real world are similar to those implied by the model economy in which people do compute the quantities of goods that maximize total utility. We test how closely the marginal utility model resembles reality by checking the predictions of the model against observed consumption choices.

Marginal utility theory also has some broader implications that provide an interesting way of testing its usefulness. Let's examine two of them.

Some Implications of Marginal Utility Theory

We all love bargains — paying less for something than its usual price. One implication of the marginal utility theory is that we almost *always* get a bargain when we buy something. That is, we place a higher total value on the things we buy than the amount that they cost us. Let's see why.

Consumer Surplus and the Gains from Trade

In Chapter 3, we saw how people can gain by specializing in producing the goods in which they have a comparative advantage and then trading with each other. Marginal utility theory provides a precise way of measuring the gains from trade.

When Lisa buys movies and pop, she exchanges her income for them. Does Lisa profit from this exchange? Are the dollars she has to give up worth more or less than the movies and pop are worth to her? As we are about to discover, the principle of diminishing marginal utility guarantees that Lisa gets more value from the goods she buys than the amount of money she gives up in exchange.

Calculating Consumer Surplus

The **value** a consumer places on a good is the maximum amount that person would be willing to pay for it. The amount actually paid for a good is its price. **Consumer surplus** is the difference between the value of a good and its price. The principle of diminishing marginal utility guarantees that there always is a consumer surplus. To understand why, let's look again at Lisa's consumption choices.

As before, let's assume that Lisa has $30 a month to spend, that movies cost $3 each, and that she watches 5 movies each month. Now let's look at Lisa's demand curve for movies, shown in Fig. 7.5. We can see from Lisa's demand curve that if she were able to watch only 1 movie a month, she would be willing to pay $7 to see it. She would be willing to pay $6 to see a second movie, $5 to see a third, and so on.

Luckily for Lisa, she has to pay only $3 for each movie she sees — the market price of a movie. Although she values the first movie she sees in a month at $7, she pays only $3, which is $4 less than she would be willing to pay. The second movie she sees in a month is worth $6 to her. The difference between the value she places on this movie and what she has to pay is $3. The third movie she sees in a month is worth $5 to her, which is $2 more than she has to pay for it, and the fourth movie is worth $4, which is $1 more than she has to pay for it. You can

Figure 7.5 Consumer Surplus

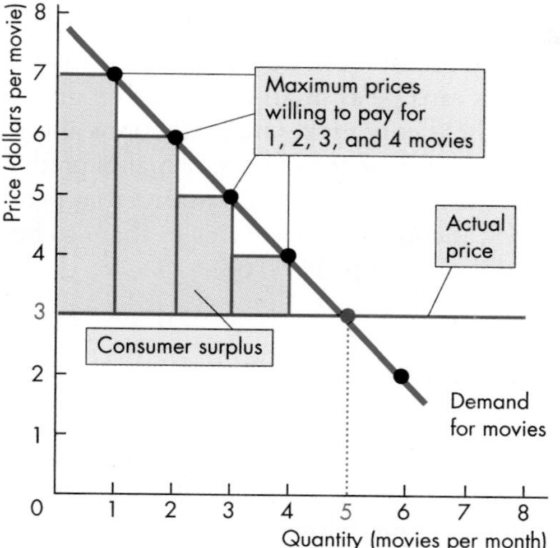

Lisa is willing to pay $7 to watch her first movie, $6 to watch her second, $5 to watch her third, and $4 to watch her fourth. She actually has to pay only $3 for each movie. At that price, she sees 5 movies. She has a consumer surplus on the first four movies equal to $10 — the difference between the highest price she is willing to pay and the price she actually pays ($4 + $3 + $2 + $1).

see this progression in Fig. 7.5, which highlights the difference between the price she pays ($3) and the higher value she places on the first, second, third, and fourth movies. These differences are a gain to Lisa. Let's calculate her total gain.

The total amount that Lisa is willing to pay for the 5 movies that she sees is $25 (the sum of $7, $6, $5, $4, and $3). She actually pays $15 (5 movies at $3 each). The extra value she receives from the movies is therefore $10. This amount is Lisa's consumer surplus. From watching 5 movies a month, she gets $10 worth of value in excess of what she has to spend to see them.

Let's now look at another implication of the marginal utility theory.

The Paradox of Value

More than 200 years ago, Adam Smith posed the paradox that we raised at the start of this chapter. Water, which is essential to life itself, costs little, but diamonds, which are useless compared to water, are expensive. Why? Adam Smith could not solve the paradox. Not until the theory of marginal utility had been invented could anyone give a satisfactory answer.

You can solve Adam Smith's puzzle by distinguishing between total utility and marginal utility. The total utility that we get from water is enormous. But remember, the more we consume of something, the smaller is its marginal utility. We use so much water that the marginal utility — the benefit we get from one more glass of water — diminishes to a tiny value. Diamonds, on the other hand, have a small total utility relative to water, but because we buy few diamonds, they have a high marginal utility.

Our theory also tells us that consumers spend in a way that makes the marginal utility from each good divided by its price equal for all goods. This also holds true for their spending on diamonds and water: diamonds have a high marginal utility divided by a high price, while water has a low marginal utility divided by a low price. In each case, the marginal utility per dollar spent is the same.

We've now completed our study of the marginal utility theory of consumption. We've used that theory to examine how Lisa allocates her income between the two goods that she consumes — movies and pop. We've also seen how the theory can be used to resolve the paradox of value. Furthermore, we've seen how the theory can be used to explain our real-world consumption choices.

In the next chapter, we're going to study an alternative theory of household behaviour. To help you see the connection between the marginal utility theory of this chapter and the more modern theory of consumer behaviour of the next chapter, we'll continue with the same example. We'll meet Lisa again and discover another way of understanding how she gets the most out of her $30 a month.

SUMMARY

Individual Demand and Market Demand

Individual demand represents the relationship between the price of a good and the quantity demanded by a single individual, other things being equal. Market demand is the sum of all individual demands. (pp. 157)

Household Consumption Choices

The marginal utility theory explains how people divide their spending between goods and services. The theory is based on a model that assumes certain characteristics about the consumer: the consumer derives utility from the goods consumed and the consumer's total utility rises as consumption of the good increases. The change in total utility resulting from a one-unit increase in the consumption of a good is called marginal utility. Marginal utility declines as consumption of the good rises. The consumer's goal is to maximize total utility, which occurs when the marginal utility per dollar spent on each good is equal. (pp. 158-163)

Predictions of Marginal Utility Theory

Marginal utility theory predicts how prices and income affect the amounts of each good consumed. First, it predicts the law of demand. That is, other things being equal, the higher the price of a good, the lower is the quantity demanded of that good. Second, it predicts that, other things being equal, the higher the consumer's income, the greater is the consumption of all normal goods. (pp. 163-167)

Criticisms of Marginal Utility Theory

Some people criticize marginal utility theory because utility cannot be observed or measured. However, the units of measurement of utility do not matter. All that matters is that the ratio of the marginal utility from each good to its price is equal for all goods. Any units of measure consistently applied will do. The concept of utility is analogous to the concept of temperature — it cannot be directly observed, but it can be used to make predictions about events that are observable.

Another criticism of marginal utility theory is that consumers can't be as smart as the theory implies. In fact, the theory makes no predictions about the thought processes of consumers. It makes predictions only about their actions and assumes that people spend their income in what seems to them to be the best possible way. (pp. 167-168)

Some Implications of Marginal Utility Theory

Marginal utility theory implies that every time we buy goods and services we get more value for our expenditure than the money we spend. We benefit from consumer surplus, which is equal to the difference between the maximum amount that we are willing to pay for a good and the price that we actually pay.

Marginal utility theory resolves the paradox of value. Water is extremely valuable but cheap, while diamonds are less valuable though expensive. When we talk loosely about value, we are thinking of total utility. The total utility of water is higher than the total utility of diamonds. The marginal utility of water, though, is lower than the marginal utility of diamonds. People choose the amount of water and diamonds to consume so as to maximize total utility. In maximizing total utility, they make the marginal utility per dollar spent the same for water as for diamonds. (pp. 168-169)

K E Y E L E M E N T S

Key Terms

Consumer equilibrium, 161
Consumer surplus, 168
Diminishing marginal utility, 160
Individual demand, 157
Marginal utility, 159
Marginal utility per dollar spent, 161
Market demand, 157
Total utility, 158
Utility, 158
Utility maximization, 160
Value, 168

Key Figures and Table 

Figure 7.1 Individual and Market Demand Curves, 157
Figure 7.2 Total Utility and Marginal Utility, 159
Figure 7.3 A Fall in the Price of Movies, 164
Figure 7.4 A Rise in the Price of Pop, 165
Figure 7.5 Consumer Surplus, 169
Table 7.7 Marginal Utility Theory, 167

REVIEW QUESTIONS

1 What is the relationship between individual demand and market demand?

2 How do we construct a market demand curve from individual demand curves?

3 What do we mean by total utility?

4 What is marginal utility?

5 How does marginal utility change as the level of consumption of a good changes?

6 Susan is a consumer. Is Susan's total utility maximized

a) When she has spent all her income?

b) When she has spent all her income and marginal utility is equal for all goods?

c) When she has spent all her income and the marginal utility per dollar spent is equal for all goods?

Explain your answers.

7 What does marginal utility theory predict about the effect of a change in price on the quantity of a good consumed?

8 What does marginal utility theory predict about the effect of a change in the price of one good on the consumption of another good?

9 What does marginal utility theory predict about the effect of a change in income on consumption?

10 How would you answer someone who says that marginal utility theory is useless because utility cannot be observed?

11 How would you respond to someone who tells you that marginal utility theory is useless because people are not smart enough to compute a consumer equilibrium in which the marginal utility per dollar spent is equal for all goods?

12 What is consumer surplus? How is consumer surplus calculated?

13 What is the paradox of value? How does marginal utility theory resolve it?

14 Calculate Lisa's marginal utility from pop from the numbers given in Table 7.1. Draw two graphs, one of her total utility and the other of her marginal utility from pop. Your graphs should look similar to those for movies in Fig. 7.2.

PROBLEMS

1 Shirley's demand for yogurt is given by the following:

Price (dollars per carton)	Quantity (cartons per week)
1	9
2	7
3	5
4	3
5	2

a) Draw a graph of Shirley's demand for yogurt.

Don also likes yogurt. His demand for yogurt is given by the following:

Price (dollars per carton)	Quantity (cartons per week)
1	5
2	4
3	3
4	2
5	1

b) Draw a graph of Don's demand curve.

c) If Shirley and Don are the only two individuals in the market, construct the market demand schedule for yogurt.

d) Draw a graph of the market demand for yogurt.

e) Draw a graph to show that the market demand curve is the horizontal sum of Shirley's demand curve and Don's demand curve.

2 Max enjoys windsurfing and snorkelling. He obtains the following total utility from each of these sports:

Half-hours per month	Total utility from windsurfing	Total utility from snorkelling
1	60	20
2	110	38
3	150	53
4	180	64
5	200	70
6	210	70

a) Draw graphs showing Max's total utility from windsurfing and from snorkelling.

b) Compare the two total utility graphs. Can you say anything about Max's preferences?

c) Draw graphs showing Max's marginal utility from windsurfing and from snorkelling.

d) Compare the two marginal utility graphs. Can you say anything about Max's preferences?

3 Max has $35 to spend. Equipment for windsurfing rents for $10 a half-hour while snorkelling equipment rents for $5 a half-hour. Use this information together with that given in problem 1 to answer the following questions:

a) What is the marginal utility per dollar spent on snorkelling if Max snorkels for

(i) One half hour?

(ii) One and a half hours?

b) What is the marginal utility per dollar spent on windsurfing if Max windsurfs for

(i) One half hour?

(ii) One hour?

c) How long can Max afford to snorkel if he windsurfs for

(i) One half hour?

(ii) One hour?

(iii) One and a half hours?

d) Will Max choose to snorkel for one hour and windsurf for one and a half hours?

e) Will he windsurf for more or less than one and a half hours?

f) How long will Max choose to windsurf and to snorkel?

4 Max's sister gives him $20 to spend on his leisure pursuits, so he now has $55 to spend. How long will Max now windsurf and snorkel?

5 If Max has only $35 to spend and the rent on windsurfing equipment doubles to $20 a half hour, how will Max now spend his time windsurfing and snorkelling?

6 Does Max's demand curve for windsurfing slope downward or upward?

7 Max takes a Club Med holiday, the cost of which includes unlimited sports activities — including windsurfing, snorkelling, and tennis. There is no extra charge for any equipment. Max decides to spend three hours each day on both windsurfing and snorkelling. How long does he windsurf? How long does he snorkel?

8 Sara also enjoys windsurfing, which costs $10 a half-hour. Her demand for windsurfing is given by:

Price (dollars per half hour)	Time windsurfing (half-hours per month)
2.50	8
5.00	7
7.50	6
10.00	5
12.50	4
15.00	3
17.50	2
20.00	1

a) If Sara windsurfs for a half an hour, what is her consumer surplus?

b) If Sara windsurfs for two and a half hours, what is her consumer surplus?

c) What is Sara's consumer surplus on the fifth half hour?

CHAPTER 8

Possibilities, Preferences, and Choices

After studying this chapter, you will be able to:

- Calculate and graph a household's budget line.
- Work out how the budget line changes when prices and income change.
- Make a map of preferences by using indifference curves.
- Calculate a household's optimal consumption plan.
- Predict the effects of price and income changes on the pattern of consumption.
- Explain why the work week gets shorter as wages rise.
- Explain how budget lines and indifference curves can be used to understand all household choices.

Subterranean Movements

THE PAST 40 YEARS have seen great changes in how we spend our incomes. Some goods, from home videos to microwave popcorn, that now regularly appear on our shopping lists didn't exist then. Other goods, such as 78 rpm phonograph records and blocks of ice for "ice boxes," have virtually disappeared. Yet other goods, such as miniskirts, appear, disappear, and reappear in cycles of fashion. ■ But the glittering surface of our consumption obscures deeper and slower changes in how we spend. In the last few years, we've seen a proliferation of gourmet food shops and designer clothing boutiques. Yet we spend a smaller percentage of our income today on food and clothing than we did 40 years ago. Over the same period, the percentage of our income spent on housing, transportation, and recreation has grown steadily. Like the continents floating on the earth's mantle, our spending patterns change steadily over time. Business empires rise and fall on such subterranean movements. Why does consumer spending change over the years? How do people react to changes in income and changes in the prices of the things they buy? ■ There are similar subterranean movements governing most aspects of household behaviour. For example, the average work week has fallen steadily from 70 hours a week in the nineteenth century to 35 hours a week today. Why has the average work week declined? Similarly, there have been steady trends in fertility, marriage, education, crime, and social interactions. Why do the habits and social mores of one generation become the old-fashioned ideas of another?

■ We're going to study a model of household behaviour that makes predictions about an enormous range of choices. We'll first use the model to study consumption choice. We'll learn how to predict the way in which people spend their income and how spending changes when income and prices change. Then we'll see how this same model helps us to understand people's choices of hours of work and leisure, borrowing and lending, and even such sociological matters as fertility and the incidence of crime.

Consumption Possibilities

How does a household divide its income among the goods and services available? We are going to study a model of household behaviour that can answer this question and that predicts how consumption patterns change when income and prices change. Our first step is to examine the constraint on the household's possible choices.

Constraint

A household's consumption choices are limited by the household's income and by the prices of the goods and services available. We're going to study a household that has a given amount of income to spend and that cannot influence the prices of the goods and services that it buys. It has to take those prices as given.

The limits to a household's consumption choices are described by its **budget line**. In order to make the concept of the household's budget line as clear as possible, we'll consider the example of Lisa, who has an income of $30 a month to spend[1]. She buys only two goods — movies and pop. Movies cost $6 each, and pop costs $3 a six-pack. If Lisa spends all of her income, she will reach the limits of her consumption of movies and pop.

In Fig. 8.1, each row of the table shows an affordable way for Lisa to consume movies and pop. Row *a* indicates that she can buy 10 six-packs of pop and see no movies. You can see that this combination

Figure 8.1 The Budget Line

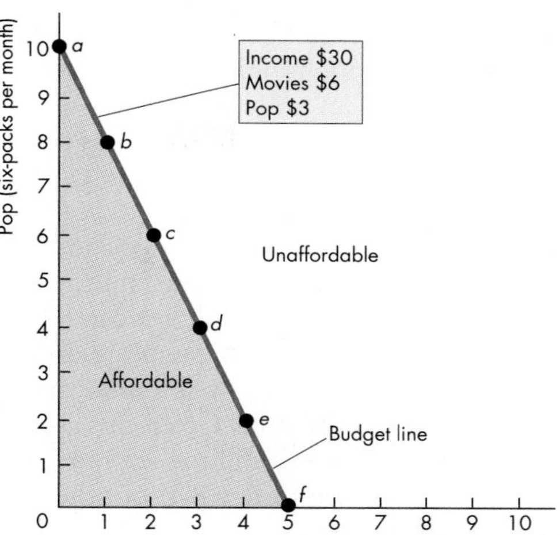

Consumption possibility	Movies (per month)	Pop (six-packs per month)
a	0	10
b	1	8
c	2	6
d	3	4
e	4	2
f	5	0

Lisa's budget line shows the boundary between what she can and cannot afford. The table lists Lisa's affordable combinations of movies and pop when she has an income of $30 and when pop costs $3 per six-pack and movies cost $6 each. For example, row *a* tells us that Lisa can buy 10 six-packs and see no movies — a combination that exhausts her $30 income. The figure graphs Lisa's budget line. Points *a* through *f* on the graph represent rows of the table. For divisible goods, the budget line is the continuous line *af*.

of movies and pop exhausts her monthly income of $30. Now look at row *f*. It says that Lisa can watch 5 movies and drink no pop — another combination that exhausts the $30 available. Each of the other rows in the table also exhausts Lisa's income. (Check that the costs in each of the other rows equal $30.) The numbers in the table define Lisa's consumption possibilities. We can graph Lisa's consumption possibilities as points *a* through *f* in Fig. 8.1.

[1]If you have read the preceding chapter on marginal utility theory, you have already met Lisa. This tale of her thirst for pop and zeal for movies will sound familiar to you — up to a point. But in this chapter, we're going to use a different method for representing preferences — one that does not require us to resort to the idea of utility. The appendix to this chapter explains the differences and the connections between the marginal utility approach and the approach of this chapter.

Divisible and Indivisible Goods Some goods can be bought in any quantity desired. Such goods are called divisible. Examples of divisible goods are gasoline and electricity, both of which can be bought in almost any quantity at all. Other goods — called indivisible goods — can be bought only in whole units. Movies are an example of an indivisible good. Although you can watch a fraction of a movie (as presumably you've done when you've picked a loser), you can buy movies only in whole units.

Although Lisa can consume at only one of the six points represented by each row of the table in our example, we'll develop the model so that it can deal with the more general case in which goods are divisible into any desired units. That is, we'll *assume* that the goods and services are divisible. Given this assumption, the consumption possibilities are not just the points *a* through *f* shown in Fig. 8.1, but those points plus all the intermediate points that form a continuous straight line running from *a* to *f*. Such a line is a budget line. Thus, if Lisa could buy movies by the minute and pop by the teaspoon, she could buy at any point along the line, consuming any fraction of a movie or a six-pack.

Lisa's budget line is a constraint on her choices. It marks the boundary between what is affordable and what is unaffordable. She can afford all the points on the line and inside it. She cannot afford points outside the line. The constraint on her consumption depends on prices and on her income, and the constraint changes when prices and her income change.

The Budget Equation

To discover how the constraint on consumption changes when prices and income change, we need to describe the budget line in the form of an equation. Such an equation is called the budget equation. The **budget equation** describes the relationship between the maximum quantities of goods and services that can be consumed from a given income at given prices. We're going to work out such an equation, and we'll summarize our calculations in Table 8.1.

The left side of the table works out the budget equation by using symbols that apply to any consumer; the right side of the table works out the equation by using numbers that describe Lisa's situation. The first section of the table lists the variables that affect a household's budget. Those variables are income, the prices of the goods consumed, and the quantities consumed. To make our calculations clear, we have assigned symbols to each of these variables. In Lisa's case, her income is \$30, the prices are \$6 for movies and \$3 for pop, and Lisa will choose the quantities of movies and pop to consume.

The consumer's budget is set out in the second section of the table. It states that expenditure (on the left side of the equation) equals income (on the right side of the equation). Look at the elements of expenditure. Expenditure is equal to the sum of the expenditure on each of the goods. Expenditure on any one good equals its price multiplied by the quantity consumed. In Lisa's case, income (on the right side) is \$30, and the most that she can spend (on the left side of the equation) is the amount of pop consumed (Q_p) multiplied by the price of pop (\$3) plus the number of movies consumed (Q_m) multiplied by their price (\$6).

The third section of the table shows you how to derive the budget equation from the consumer's budget equation. There are just two steps. First, divide both sides by the price of pop, P_p. Second, subtract $(P_m/P_p)Q_m$ from both sides of the resulting equation. The result is the budget equation shown in the last line of the table. This equation tells us how the consumption level of one good varies as consumption of the other good varies.

To interpret the equation, let's go back to the budget line of Fig. 8.1. First let's check that the budget equation we derived in Table 8.1 delivers the budget line in Fig. 8.1. Begin by setting Q_m equal to zero. In this case, the budget equation tells us that Q_p is 10. This combination of Q_p and Q_m is the same as that shown in row *a* of the table in Fig. 8.1. Setting Q_m equal to 5 makes Q_p equal to zero (row *f* of the table in Fig. 8.1). Check that you can derive the other rows of the table on Fig. 8.1.

The budget equation contains two variables under the control of the individual (Q_m and Q_p) and two numbers outside the individual's control (y/P_p and P_m/P_p). Let's look more closely at those two numbers outside the individual's control.

The first number, y/P_p, or 10 in Lisa's case, is the maximum number of six-packs that the consumer can buy. It is called real income in terms of pop. **Real income** is income expressed in units of goods or services. Real income in terms of a particular good is income divided by the price of that good. In Lisa's case, her real income in terms of pop is 10 six-packs. In Fig. 8.1, the budget line intersects the vertical axis at Lisa's real income in terms of pop. That is, if Lisa spends all her income on pop, she can buy 10 six-packs.

Table 8.1 Calculating the Budget Equation 

In general			In Lisa's case		
1. The variables					
Income	=	y	y	=	\$30
Price of movies	=	P_m	P_m	=	\$6
Price of pop	=	P_p	P_p	=	\$3
Quantity of movies	=	Q_m	Q_m	=	Lisa's choice
Quantity of pop	=	Q_p	Q_p	=	Lisa's choice
2. The budget					
$P_pQ_p + P_mQ_m = y$			$\$3Q_p + \$6Q_m = \$30$		
3. The calculation					
• Divide by Pp to obtain			• Divide by \$3 to obtain		
$Q_p + \frac{P_m}{P_p} Q_m = \frac{y}{P_p}$			$Q_p + 2Q_m = 10$		
• Subtract $(P_m/P_p)\,Q_m$ from both sides to obtain			• Subtract $2Q_m$ from both sides to obtain		
$Q_p = \frac{y}{P_p} - \frac{P_m}{P_p} Q_m$			$Q_p = 10 - 2Q_m$		

Let's now look at the second number in the budget equation that is outside the consumer's control, P_m/P_p, or 2 in Lisa's case. This number shows the relative price of the two goods. A **relative price** is the price of one good divided by the price of another good. In the equation, P_m/P_p is the relative price of movies in terms of pop. For Lisa, that relative price is 2. That is, in order to see one more movie, she has to give up 2 six-packs.

You can see the relative price of movies in terms of pop in Fig. 8.1 as the magnitude of the slope of the budget line. To calculate the slope of the budget line, recall the formula for slope from Chapter 2: the slope of a line equals the change in the variable measured on the y-axis divided by the change in the variable measured on the x-axis as we move along the line. In this case, the variable measured on the y-axis is the quantity of pop and on the x-axis is the quantity of movies. Along Lisa's budget line, as pop falls from 10 to 0, movies increase from 0 to 5. Therefore the slope of the budget line is –10/5, or –2. The flatter the budget line, the less expensive is the good measured on the horizontal axis relative to the good measured on the vertical axis. The steeper the line, the more expensive is the good measured on the horizontal axis relative to the one on the vertical axis. In other words, the magnitude of the slope of the budget line is the relative price of the good whose quantity appears on the horizontal axis.

The relative price of one good in terms of another is the opportunity cost of the first good in terms of the second. In Lisa's case, the opportunity cost of one movie is 2 six-packs of pop. Equivalently, the opportunity cost of 2 six-packs of pop is one movie.

Changes in Prices and Income

Let's now work out what happens to the budget line when prices and income change. We'll begin with a change in the price of one good.

A Change in the Price of Movies Suppose that the price of movies rises. What happens to Lisa's budget line? To make things clear, let's suppose that the price of movies halves to \$3 a movie. By working through the calculations in Table 8.1, you can find Lisa's budget line with the new price of movies. Recall that the budget equation is

$$Q_p = \frac{y}{P_p} - \frac{P_m}{P_p} Q_m .$$

Nothing has happened to income (y) or the price of pop (P_p). Lisa's real income in terms of pop remains 10. But the price of movies has fallen and is now equal to the price of pop. Therefore the relative price of movies P_m/P_p has decreased to 1. Lisa's new budget equation is

$$Q_p = 10 - Q_m .$$

Let's check that this new budget equation works. With movies costing \$3 each, Lisa can see as many as 10 movies with her income. Using Lisa's new budget equation, you can see that substituting 10 for Q_m results in zero for Q_p. You know that this answer is correct because if Lisa sees 10 movies, she spends all her income on movies and has nothing left to spend on pop.

Figure 8.2(a) shows how the fall in the price of movies affects the budget line. Because the price of

Figure 8.2 Prices, Income and the Budget Line

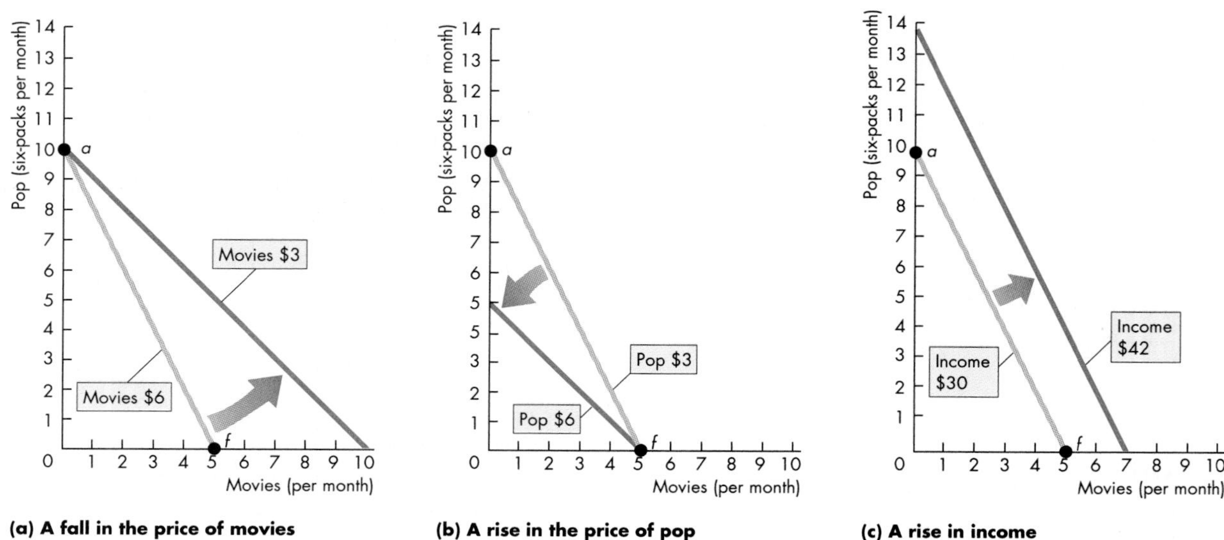

In part (a), the price of a movie falls from $6 to $3. In part (b), the price of a six-pack of pop increases from $3 to $6. In part (c), income increases from $30 to $42, but prices remain constant. The arrow in each part indicates the shift in the budget line.

movies has gone down, the new budget line is flatter than budget line *af.* But notice that point *a* has not changed. If Lisa spends all her income on pop, she can still buy 10 six-packs. In other words, Lisa's real income in terms of pop has not changed. Only the price of movies has changed. Movies have become cheaper in terms of pop. Previously, 1 movie was worth 2 six-packs. In the new situation, the relative price or opportunity cost of 1 movie is 1 six-pack.

Let's see what happens to the budget line when the price of pop changes.

A Change in the Price of Pop Let's go back to the original situation in which movies cost $6 each and pop $3 a six-pack. What happens to Lisa's budget line if the price of a six-pack rises? Let's suppose that the price goes up from $3 to $6. If Lisa spends all her income on pop, she can now buy 5 six-packs. Her real income in terms of pop has gone down. Since movies cost $6 each and pop costs $6 a six-pack, the relative price of movies is 1, the same as in the previous example. The opportunity cost of 1 movie is 1 six-pack of pop. We can work out the new budget line by using the budget equation:

$$Q_p = \frac{y}{P_p} - \frac{P_m}{P_p} Q_m .$$

The price of pop is now $6. Lisa's income is still $30 and the price of a movie is still $6. So Lisa's budget equation is

$$Q_p = \frac{30}{6} - \frac{6}{6} Q_m ;$$

$$\text{or} \quad Q_p = 5 - Q_m .$$

Figure 8.2(b) shows the new budget line. Notice that this time point *f* has not moved. If Lisa spends all her income on movies, she can still see only 5 movies. Her real income in terms of movies has not changed.

Look at the new budget lines in parts (a) and (b). In part (a), both movies and pop cost $3; in part (b), they both cost $6. Lisa earns $30 in both cases. Therefore in part (b), she can consume less of everything than in part (a). Notice that the new budget line in part (b) has the same slope as the new budget line in part (a). This means that movies have the same opportunity cost in the two cases — to see 1 more movie she must give up 1 six-pack of pop.

Let's now see what happens to the budget line when income changes.

A Change in Income If prices remain constant and income rises, a person can then consume more of all goods. Go back to the initial situation in which Lisa had an income of $30, a movie cost $6, and a six-pack cost $3. Keeping the prices of the two goods constant, let's work out what happens if Lisa's income goes up from $30 to $42. Again, recall the budget equation:

$$Q_p = \frac{y}{P_p} - \frac{P_m}{P_p} Q_m .$$

Let's work out Lisa's new budget equation. The price of pop (P_p) is $3 and the price of movies (P_m) is $6. Income ($y$) is $42. Putting these numbers into the equation gives

$$Q_p = \frac{42}{3} - \frac{6}{3} Q_m,$$

$$\text{or} \quad Q_p = 14 - 2Q_m .$$

Lisa's real income has gone up because her money income has gone up while the prices of movies and pop have stayed the same. Her real income in terms of pop has gone up from 10 to 14. That is, if she spends all her income on pop, she can now buy 14 six-packs. Her real income in terms of movies has also gone up. If she spends all her income on movies, she can see 7 movies.

The shift in Lisa's budget line is shown in Fig. 8.2(c). The initial budget line is the same one that we began with in parts (a) and (b) when Lisa's income was $30. The new budget line shows Lisa able to consume more of each good. The new line is parallel to the old one but farther out. The two budget lines are parallel — they have the same slope — because the relative price of movies in terms of pop is the same in both cases. With movies costing $6 each and a six-pack $3, Lisa must give up 2 six-packs to see 1 movie. The new budget line is farther out than the initial one because her real income has risen.

R E V I E W

The budget line describes the maximum amounts of consumption that a household can undertake given its income and the prices of the goods that it buys. A change in the price of one good changes the slope of the budget line. If the price of the good measured on the horizontal axis rises, the budget line gets steeper. A change in income makes the budget line shift, but its slope does not change. If income increases, the budget line shifts to the right; if income decreases, the budget line shifts to the left. ■

Let's now leave the budget line and look at the second ingredient in the model of consumer choice: preferences.

Preferences

Preferences are a person's likes and dislikes. There are three fundamental assumptions about preferences:

- Preferences do not depend on the prices of goods.
- Preferences do not depend on income.
- More of any good is preferred to less of that good.

The first two assumptions amount to the proposition that people's likes and dislikes do not depend on what they can afford to buy. This assumption does not mean that people's preferences do not change over time. Nor does it mean that their preferences are not influenced by the things that they have consumed and experienced. It *does* mean that just because income increases or the price of a good decreases, people do not, *for that reason*, suddenly decide that they like a particular good more than they did before.

The third assumption — more of any good is preferred to less of that good — is just a different way of saying that wants are unlimited. Of course, in reality, you can imagine having enough of any one good to want no more of it, but there is always something that you prefer to have more of rather than to have less of.

We are going to discover in this section a very neat device — that of drawing a map of a person's preferences.

Figure 8.3 Mapping Preferences

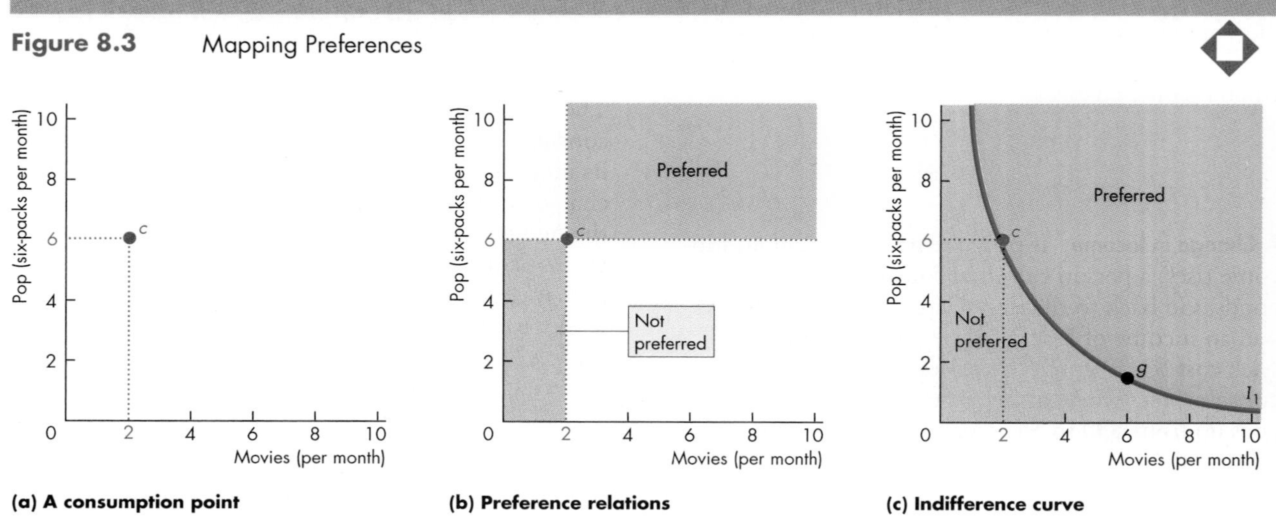

(a) A consumption point **(b) Preference relations** **(c) Indifference curve**

If Lisa consumes 6 six-packs of pop and 2 movies, she consumes at point *c* in part (a). Lisa prefers more goods to fewer goods. This fact is illustrated in part (b). She prefers any point at which she consumes more of both pop and movies to point *c* (all the points in the orange area). She prefers point *c* to any point at which fewer movies and six-packs are consumed (all the points in the grey area). Whether or not she prefers seeing more movies but having less pop than at point *c* depends on how many more movies and how much less pop. Similarly, if she consumes more pop and sees fewer movies than at point *c*, whether she prefers that situation to *c* depends on how much more pop and how many fewer movies she has. The boundary between points that she prefers to point *c* and those to which *c* is preferred is shown in part (c). That boundary is called an indifference curve. Lisa is indifferent between points such as *g* and *c* on the indifference curve. She prefers any point above the indifference curve (orange area) to any point on it, and she prefers any point on the indifference curve to any point below it (grey area).

A Preference Map

Let's see how we can draw a map of a person's preferences by constructing a map of Lisa's preferences for movies and pop. This map, which appears in Fig. 8.3, measures the number of movies seen on the horizontal axis and the number of six-packs consumed on the vertical axis. Let's start with Fig. 8.3(a) and focus on point *c*, where Lisa sees 2 movies and consumes 6 six-packs of pop. We will use this point as a reference and ask how Lisa likes all the other points in relation to point *c*.

Figure 8.3(b) takes us to the next step. It is divided into four areas. The area shaded orange has, at each point, more movies and more pop than at point *c*. Lisa prefers all the points in this area to point *c*. The area shaded grey has, at each point, fewer movies and less pop than at point *c*. She prefers point *c* to all the points in this area. Points in the two white areas have either more movies and less pop than point *c* or more pop and fewer movies than point *c*. How does Lisa rank points in these areas against point *c*? To answer this question, we need to take the final step in constructing a map of Lisa's preferences.

Figure 8.3(c) takes that final step. It contains a line passing through point *c* and through what were the two white areas. That line defines the boundary between points that Lisa prefers to point *c* and points she regards as inferior to point *c*. Lisa is indifferent between point *c* and the other points on line I_1 such as point *g*. The line itself is called an indifference curve. An **indifference curve** is a line that shows all combinations of two goods among which the consumer is indifferent. The indifference curve shown in Fig. 8.3(c) shows all the combinations of movies and pop among which Lisa is indifferent.

The indifference curve shown in Fig. 8.3(c) is just one of a whole family of such curves. This indifference curve appears again in Fig. 8.4. It is labelled I_1, and passes through points *c* and *g*. Two other indifference curves are I_0 and I_2. Lisa prefers any point on indifference curve I_2 to those on indifference curve I_1, and she prefers any point on I_1 to those on I_0. We refer to I_2 as being a higher indifference curve than I_1 and to I_1 as higher than I_0.

Indifference curves never intersect each other. To see why, consider indifference curves I_1 and I_2 in Fig. 8.4. We know that point *j* is preferred to point *c*. We also know that all points on indifference curve I_2 are preferred to all points on indifference curve I_1. If these indifference curves did intersect, the consumer would be indifferent between the combination of goods at the intersection point and combinations *c* and *j*. But we know that point *j* is preferred to point *c*, so such an intersection point cannot exist. Hence indifference curves never intersect.

A preference map consists of a series of indifference curves. The indifference curves shown in Fig. 8.4 are only a part of Lisa's preference map. Her entire map consists of an infinite number of indifference curves. An indifference curve joins points representing combinations of goods among which a consumer is indifferent in much the same way that contour lines on a map join points of equal height above sea level. By looking at the shape of the contour lines on a map, we can draw conclusions about the terrain. In the same way, by looking at the shape of a person's indifference curves we can draw conclusions about preferences. But interpreting a preference map requires a bit of work. It also requires some way of describing the shape of the indifference curves. In the next two sections we'll learn how to "read" a preference map.

Figure 8.4 A Preference Map

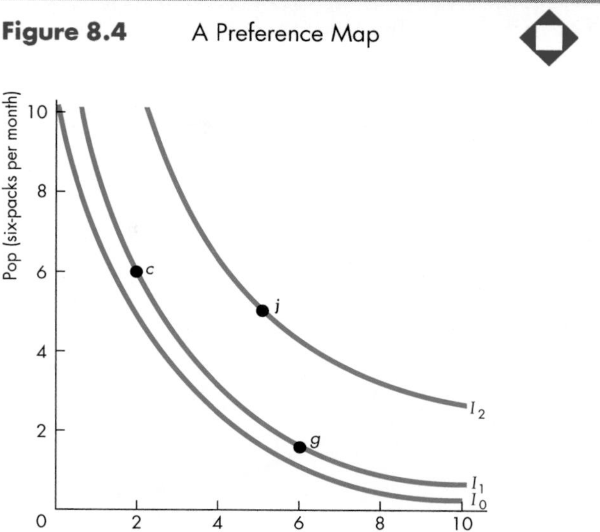

A preference map consists of an infinite number of indifference curves. Here, we show just three — I_0, I_1, and I_2 — that are part of Lisa's preference map. Each indifference curve shows points among which Lisa is indifferent. For example, she is indifferent between point *c* and point *g* on indifference curve I_1. But points on a higher indifference curve are preferred to points on a lower curve. For example, Lisa prefers all the points on indifference curve I_2 to all the points on indifference curve I_1; she prefers point *j* to point *c* or *g*.

Indifference Curves and Preferences

We use the concept of the marginal rate of substitution to describe the shape of an indifference curve. The **marginal rate of substitution** (or MRS) is the rate at which a person will give up one good in order to get more of another good and, at the same time, remain indifferent. The marginal rate of substitution is measured as the magnitude of the slope of an indifference curve. If the indifference curve is steep, the marginal rate of substitution is high. The person is willing to give up a large quantity of the good measured on the vertical axis in exchange for a small quantity of the good measured on the horizontal axis, while remaining indifferent. If the indifference curve is flat, the marginal rate of substitution is low. The person is willing to give up only a small amount of the good measured on the vertical axis and must be compensated with a large amount of the good measured on the horizontal axis to remain indifferent.

Let's work out the marginal rate of substitution in two cases, both illustrated in Fig. 8.5. The curve labelled I_1 is one of Lisa's indifference curves. Suppose that Lisa drinks 6 six-packs of pop and watches 2 movies (point *c* in the figure). What is her marginal rate of substitution at this point? It is calculated by measuring the magnitude of the slope of the indifference curve at that point. To measure the slope, place a straight line against, or tangential to, the indifference curve at that point. The slope of that line is the change in the quantity of pop divided by the change in the quantity of movies as we move along the line. For example, moving from 10 six-packs and no movies to 5 movies and no pop, pop consumption falls by 10 six-packs and movie consumption increases by 5. The slope of the tangential line is –2. Thus when Lisa consumes 2 movies and 6 six-packs of pop, her marginal rate of substitution is 2.

Figure 8.5 The Marginal Rate of Substitution

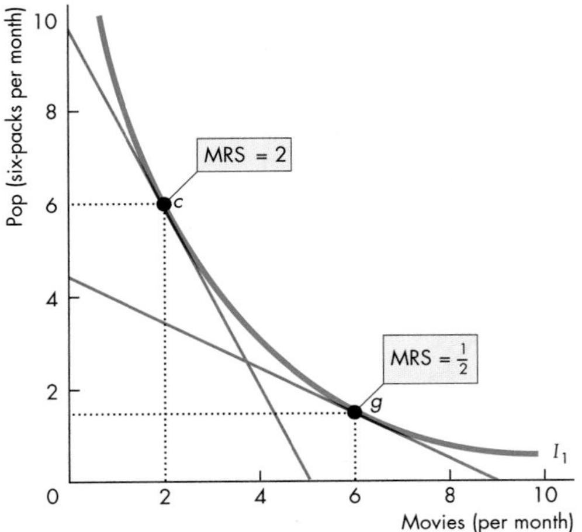

The magnitude of slope of an indifference curve measures the marginal rate of substitution, or MRS. The marginal rate of substitution tells us how much of one good a person is willing to give up to gain more of another good, while remaining indifferent. The marginal rate of substitution at point *c* is 2; at point *g* it is 1/2.

Now, suppose that Lisa consumes 6 movies and 1.5 six-packs (point *g* in Fig. 8.5). What is her marginal rate of substitution at this point? The answer is found by calculating the magnitude of the slope of the indifference curve at that point. That slope is the same as the slope of the straight line drawn tangential to the point. Here, for example, moving from 4.5 six-packs and no movies to 9 movies and no pop, pop consumption decreases by 4.5 six-packs and movie consumption increases by 9. Hence, the slope of the tangential line equals –½ and Lisa's marginal rate of substitution is ½. Thus when Lisa sees 6 movies and consumes 1.5 six-packs of pop a month, she is willing to substitute movies for pop at the rate of half a six-pack per movie while remaining indifferent.

Notice that if Lisa drinks a lot of pop and does not see many movies, her marginal rate of substitution is high. If she watches a lot of movies and does not drink much pop, her marginal rate of substitution is low. This feature of the marginal rate of substitution is the central assumption of the theory of consumer behaviour and is referred to as the diminishing marginal rate of substitution. A **diminishing marginal rate of substitution** is a general tendency for the marginal rate of substitution to diminish as the consumer moves along an indifference curve, increasing consumption of the good measured on the *x*-axis and decreasing consumption of the good measured on the *y*-axis.

You may be able to appreciate why we assume the principle of a diminishing marginal rate of substitution by thinking about your own preferences. Imagine two situations between which you are indifferent. In one, you watch 3 movies a night but have no pop. In the other, you have 6 six-packs of pop a night and watch no movies. In the first situation, you would probably willingly give up seeing 1 movie if you could get just a small amount of pop in exchange. In the second situation, you would probably be willing to give up quite a lot of pop to watch just 1 movie. That is, the more movies you see and the less pop you drink, the less pop you are willing to give up to see an extra movie, while remaining indifferent. Your preferences satisfy the principle of diminishing marginal rate of substitution.

The shape of the indifference curves incorporates the principle of the diminishing marginal rate of substitution because the curves are bowed towards the origin. The tightness of the bend of an indifference curve tells us how willing a person is to substitute one good for another, while remaining indifferent. Let's look at some examples to clarify this point.

Degree of Substitutability

Most of us would not regard movies and pop as being close substitutes for each other. We probably have some fairly clear ideas about how many movies we want to see each month and how many cans of pop we want to drink. Nevertheless, to some degree, we are willing to substitute between these two goods. No matter how big a pop freak you are, there is surely some increase in the number of movies you see that would compensate you for being deprived of a can of pop. Similarly, no matter how addicted you are to the movies, surely some number of cans of pop would compensate you for being deprived of seeing one movie. A person's indifference curves for movies and pop might look something like Lisa's, as shown in Fig. 8.6(a).

Close Substitutes Some goods substitute so easily for each other that most of us do not even notice which we are consuming. A good example concerns different

Figure 8.6 The Degree of Substitutability

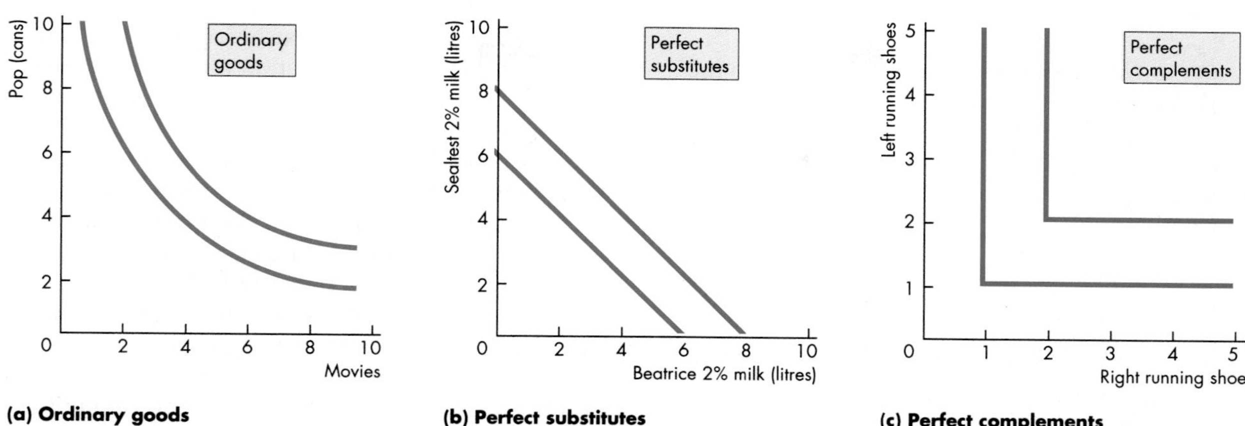

The shape of the indifference curves reveals the degree of substitutability between two goods. Part (a) shows the indifference curves for two ordinary goods: movies and pop. To remain indifferent as less pop is consumed, one must see more movies. The number of movies that compensates for a reduction in pop increases as less pop is consumed. Part (b) shows the indifference curves for two perfect substitutes. For the consumer to remain indifferent, one less litre of Sealtest 2% milk must be replaced by one extra litre of Beatrice 2% milk. Part (c) shows two perfect complements — goods that cannot be substituted for each other at all. The consumer is indifferent between two left running shoes with one right running shoe and one of each. But two of each is preferred to one of each.

brands of personal computers. Zenith, Compaq, and Tandy are all clones of the IBM PC — but most of us can't tell the difference between the clones and the IBM machine itself. The same holds true for 2% milk. Except for a few connoisseurs, most of us don't care whether we are drinking Sealtest or Beatrice 2% milk. When two goods are perfect substitutes for each other, their indifference curves are straight lines that slope downward, as illustrated in Fig. 8.6(b). The marginal rate of substitution between perfect substitutes is constant.

Complements Some goods cannot substitute for each other at all. Instead they are complements. The complements in Fig. 8.6(c) are left and right running shoes. Indifference curves of perfect complements are L-shaped. One left running shoe and one right running shoe are as good as one left shoe and two right ones. Two of each is preferred to one of each, but two of one and one of the other is no better than one of each.

The extreme cases of perfect substitutes and perfect complements shown here don't often happen in reality. They do, however, illustrate that the shape of the indifference curve shows the degree of substitutability between two goods. The more perfectly substitutable the two goods, the more nearly are their

"With the pork I'd recommend an Alsatian white or a Coke."

indifference curves straight lines and the less quickly does the marginal rate of substitution fall. Poor substitutes for each other have tightly curved indifference curves, approaching the shape of those shown in Fig. 8.6(c).

As you can see in the cartoon, according to the waiter's preferences, Coke and Alsatian white wine are perfect substitutes for each other and are each a complement to pork. We hope the customers agree with him.

R E V I E W

A person's preferences can be represented by a preference map. A preference map consists of a series of indifference curves. Indifference curves slope downward, bow towards the origin, and do not intersect each other. The magnitude of the slope of an indifference curve is called the marginal rate of substitution. The marginal rate of substitution falls as a person consumes less of the good measured on the y-axis and more of the good measured on the x-axis. The tightness of an indifference curve tells us how well two goods substitute for each other. Indifference curves that are almost straight lines indicate that the goods are close substitutes. Indifference curves that are tightly curved, approaching an L-shape, indicate that the two goods complement each other. ■

The two components of the model of consumer behaviour are now in place: the budget line and the preference map. We will now use these two components to work out the consumer's choice.

Choice

Recall that Lisa has $30 to spend and that she buys only two goods: movies (at $6 each) and pop (at $3 a six-pack). We've learned how to construct Lisa's budget line, which summarizes what she can buy, given her income and the prices of movies and pop (Fig. 8.1). We've also learned how to characterize Lisa's preferences in terms of her indifference curves (Fig. 8.4). We are now going to bring Lisa's budget line and indifference curves together and discover her best affordable consumption of movies and pop.

The analysis is summarized in Fig. 8.7, which combines the budget line from Fig. 8.1 and the indifference curves from Fig. 8.4. Let's first focus on point *h* on indifference curve I_0. That point is on Lisa's budget line, so we know that she can afford it. But does she prefer this combination of movies and pop over all the other affordable combinations? The answer is no. To see why not, consider point *c*, where she consumes 2 movies and 6 six-packs. Point *c* is on Lisa's budget line, so we know she can afford to consume at this point. But point *c* is on indifference curve I_1, a higher indifference curve than I_0. Therefore we know that Lisa prefers point *c* to point *h*.

Are there any affordable points that Lisa prefers to point *c*? The answer is that there are not. All Lisa's other affordable consumption points — all the other points on or below her budget line — lie on indifference curves that are lower than I_1. Indifference curve I_1 is the highest indifference curve on which Lisa can afford to consume. Let's look more closely at Lisa's best affordable choice.

Properties of the Best Affordable Point

The best affordable point — point *c* in this example — has two properties. It is *on*

- The budget line.
- The highest attainable indifference curve.

On the Budget Line The best affordable point is *on* the budget line. If Lisa chooses a point inside the budget line, she will have an affordable point on the budget line at which she can consume more of both goods. Lisa prefers that point to the one inside the budget line. The best affordable point cannot be outside the budget line because Lisa cannot afford such a point.

On the Highest Attainable Indifference Curve The chosen point is on the highest attainable indifference curve where that curve has the same slope as the budget line. Stated another way, the marginal rate of substitution between the two goods (the magnitude of the slope of the indifference curve) equals their relative price (the magnitude of the slope of the budget line).

To see why this condition describes the best affordable point, consider point *h*, which Lisa regards as inferior to point *c*. At point *h*, Lisa's marginal rate of substitution is less than the relative price — indifference

Figure 8.7 The Best Affordable Point

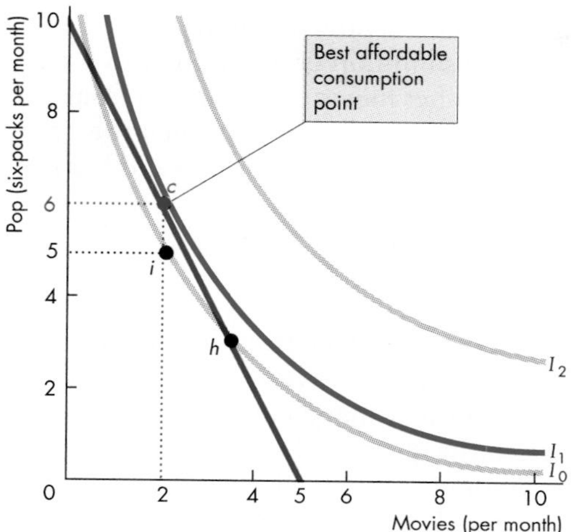

Lisa's best affordable point is *c*. At that point, she is on her budget line and so spends her entire income on the two goods. She is also on the highest attainable indifference curve, I_1. Higher indifference curves (such as I_2) do not touch her budget line, and so she cannot afford any point on them. At point *c*, the marginal rate of substitution (the magnitude of the slope of the indifference curve) equals the relative price of movies (the magnitude of the slope of the budget line). A point such as *h* on the budget line is not Lisa's best affordable point because at that point she is willing to give up more movies in exchange for pop than she has to. She can move to a point such as *i*, which she regards as being just as good as point *h* and which allows her to have some income left over. She can spend that income by moving to *c*, a point that she prefers to point *i*.

curve I_0 has a flatter slope than Lisa's budget line. As Lisa gives up movies for pop and moves up indifference curve I_0, she moves inside her budget line and has some money left over. She can move to point *i*, for example, where she consumes 2 movies and 5 six-packs and has $3 to spare. She is indifferent between the combination of goods at point *i* and at point *h*. But she prefers point *c* to point *i*, since at *c* she has more pop than at *i* and sees the same number of movies.

By moving along her budget line from point *h* toward point *c*, Lisa passes through a whole array of indifference curves (not shown in the figure) located between indifference curves I_0 and I_1. All of these indifference curves are higher than I_0, and therefore any point on them is preferred to point *h*. Once she gets to point *c*, Lisa has reached the highest attainable indifference curve. If she keeps moving along the budget line, she will now start to encounter indifference curves that are lower than I_1.

R E V I E W

The consumer has a given income and faces fixed prices. The consumer's problem is to allocate that fixed income in the best possible way. Affordable combinations of goods are described by the consumer's budget line. The consumer's preferences are represented by indifference curves. The consumer's best allocation of income occurs when all income is spent (on the budget line) and when the marginal rate of substitution (the magnitude of the slope of the indifference curve) equals the relative price (the magnitude of the slope of the budget line). ■

We will now use this model of consumer choice to make some predictions about changes in consumption patterns when income and prices change.

Predicting Consumer Behaviour

Let's examine how consumers respond to changes in prices and income. We'll start by looking at the effect of a change in price. By studying the effect of a change in price on a consumer's choice, holding all other effects constant, we can derive a consumer's demand curve.

A Change in Price

The effect of a change in price on the quantity of a good consumed is called the **price effect**. We will use Fig. 8.8 to work out the price effect of a fall in the price of movies. We start with movies costing $6 each, with pop costing $3 a six-pack, and with Lisa's income at $30 a month. In this situation, she consumes at point *c*, where her budget line is tangential to her highest attainable indifference curve, I_1. She consumes 6 six-packs and 2 movies a month.

Now suppose that the price of a movie falls to $3. We've already seen how a change in price (in Fig. 8.2a) affects the budget line. With a lower price of movies, the budget line moves outward and

Figure 8.8 The Price Effect and the Demand Curve

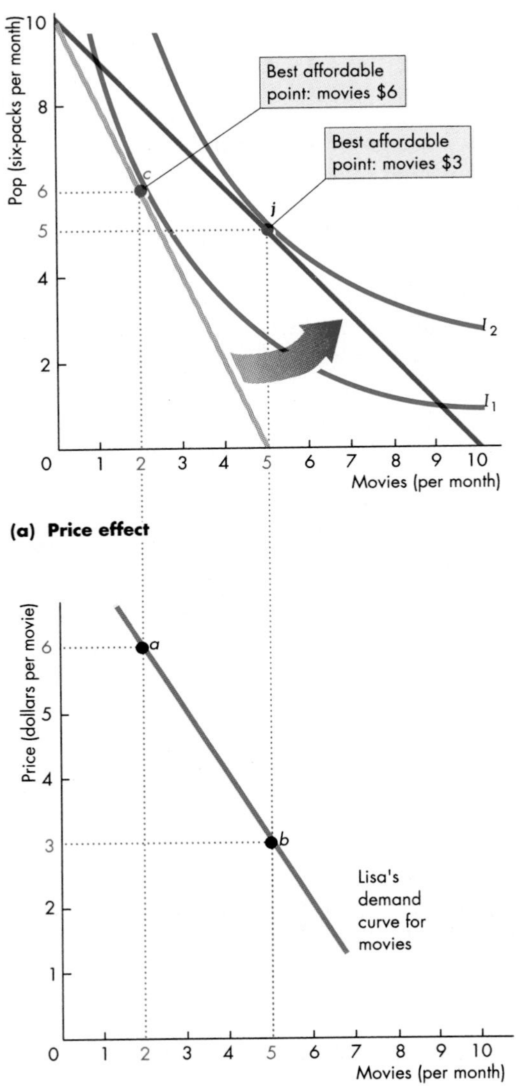

Initially, Lisa consumes at point *c* (part a). If the price of a movie falls from $6 to $3, she consumes at point *j*. The increase in the consumption of movies from 2 to 5 per month is the price effect. When the price of a movie falls, Lisa consumes more movies. She also consumes less pop. Lisa's demand curve for movies is shown in part (b). When the price of a movie is $6, she consumes 2 per month, at point *a*. When the price of a movie falls to $3, she consumes 5 per month, at point *b*. The demand curve is traced by varying the price of movies and calculating Lisa's best affordable consumption of movies for each different price.

becomes less steep. The new budget line is the dark red one in Fig. 8.8(a). Lisa's new best affordable point is *j*, where she consumes 5 movies and 5 six-packs of pop. As you can see, Lisa drinks less pop and watches more movies now that movies cost less. She reduces her consumption of pop from 6 to 5 six-packs, and increases her movie consumption from 2 to 5. Lisa substitutes movies for pop when the price of movies falls, and the price of pop and her income remain constant.

The Demand Curve

This analysis of the effect of a change in the price of movies enables us to derive Lisa's demand curve for movies. Recall that the demand curve graphs the relationship between the quantity demanded of a good and its price, holding constant all other influences on the quantity demanded. We can derive Lisa's demand curve by gradually lowering the price of movies and working out how many movies she sees by finding her best affordable point at each different price. Figure 8.8(b) highlights just two prices and two points that lie on Lisa's demand curve for movies. When the price of a movie is $6, Lisa consumes two movies a month at point *a*. When the price falls to $3, she increases her consumption to 5 movies a month at point *b*. The entire demand curve is made up of these two points plus all the other points that tell us Lisa's best affordable consumption of movies at each price — more than $6, between $6 and $3, and less than $3 — given the price of pop and Lisa's income. As you can see, Lisa's demand curve for movies slopes downward — the lower the price of a movie, the more movies she watches each month. This is the law of demand.

Next, let's examine what happens when Lisa's income changes.

A Change in Income

The effect of a change in income on consumption, holding all prices constant, is called the **income effect**. Let's work out the income effect by examining how consumption changes when income changes with constant prices. We've already seen, earlier in this chapter, how a change in income shifts the budget line. We worked out and illustrated (in Fig. 8.2c) that a rise in income shifts the budget line outward, with its slope unchanged.

It will be clear to you that as income rises, a person can consume more of all goods. But being able to consume more of all goods does not mean

Figure 8.9 The Income Effect

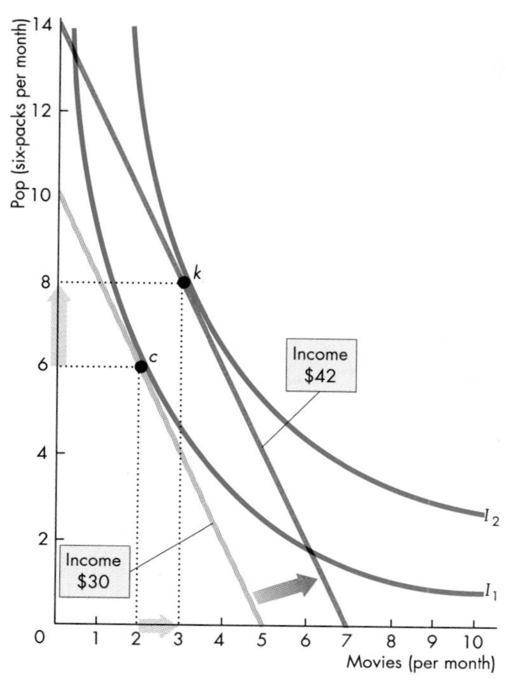

(a) Normal goods

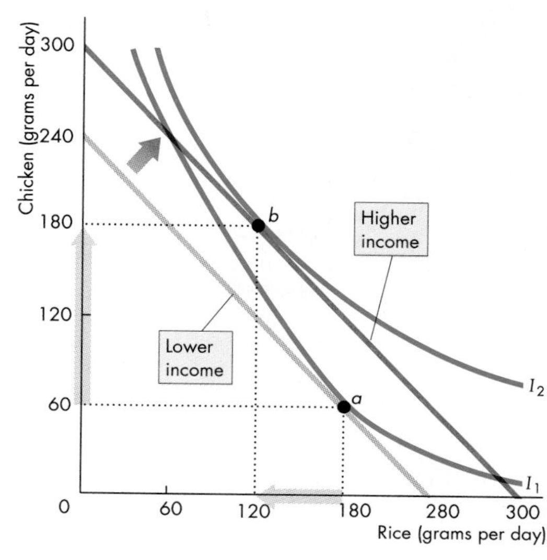

(b) Inferior goods

An increase in income increases the consumption of most goods. These goods are normal goods. In part (a), Lisa consumes more of both pop and movies (as shown by the orange arrows) as her income increases. Pop and movies are normal goods, but some goods are inferior goods. The consumption of inferior goods decreases as income increases. In part (b), as income increases, the consumption of rice decreases and more chicken is consumed (again shown by the orange arrows). For this consumer, rice is an inferior good.

that a person will do so. Goods are classified into two groups: normal goods and inferior goods. *Normal goods* are goods whose income effect is positive — consumption increases, as income increases. *Inferior goods* are goods whose income effect is negative — consumption decreases as income increases.

As the name implies, most goods are normal goods. A few examples of inferior goods, however, do exist. Rice and potatoes are perhaps the most obvious. People with low incomes have a heavy rice or potato component to their diet. As incomes rise, their consumption of chicken and beef — normal goods — increases, but that of rice and potatoes — inferior goods — decreases. In Lisa's case, both movies and pop are normal goods. Therefore as Lisa's income rises, she consumes more movies and more pop.

Figure 8.9 illustrates the two types of income effect. Part (a) shows the income effect for normal goods, using Lisa's consumption as an example. With an income of $30 and with movies costing $6 each and pop $3 a six-pack, she consumes at point *c* — 2 movies and 6 six-packs. If her income goes up to $42, she consumes at point *k* — 3 movies and 8 six-packs. Thus with a higher income Lisa consumes more of both goods. These income effects are marked on the axes of Fig. 8.9(a). As you can see, both income effects are positive. Figure 8.9(b) shows the income effect for an inferior good — rice. At the initial income level, the household consumes at point *a*, 60 grams of chicken and 180 grams of rice a day. When income increases, chicken consumption increases to 180 grams a day, but rice consumption decreases to 120 grams a day, at point *b*. The income effect for an inferior good is negative.

Figure 8.10 Price Effect, Substitution Effect, and Income Effect

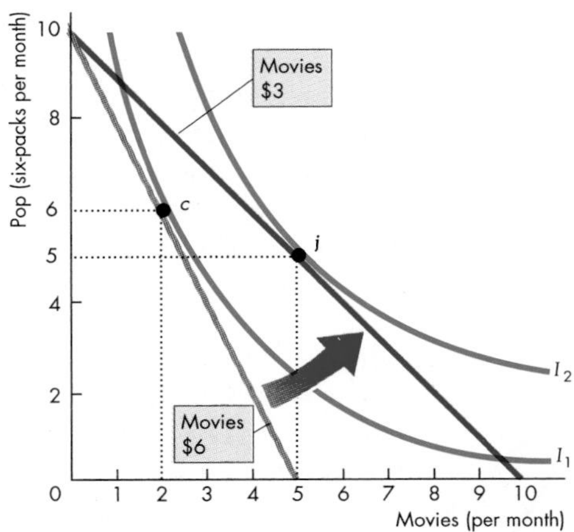

(a) Price effect

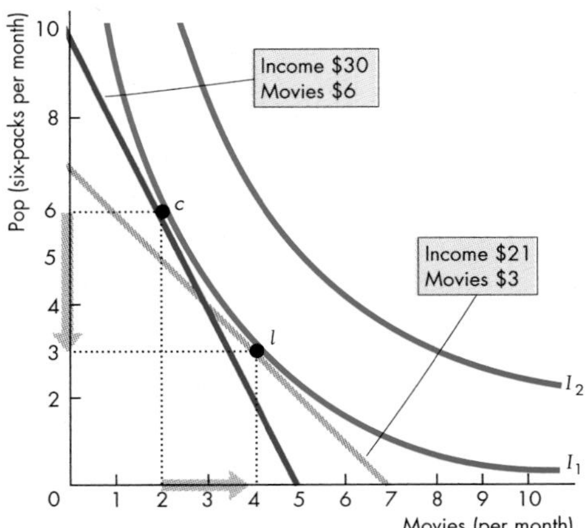

(b) Substitution effect

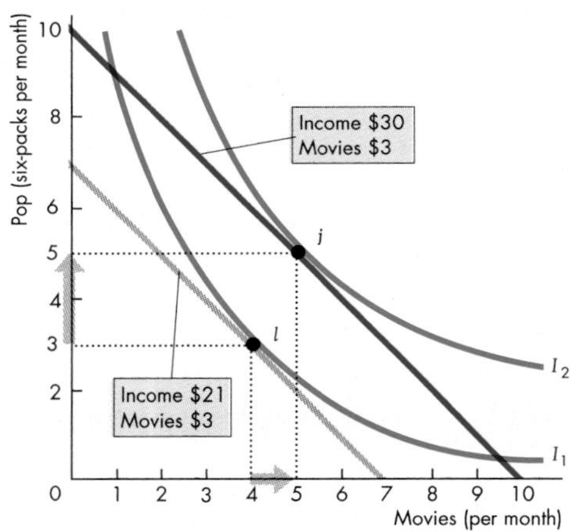

(c) Income effect

The price effect can be separated into substitution effect and an income effect. The price effect is shown in part (a) and is the same as that in Fig. 8.8(a).

The substitution effect in part (b) is calculated by imagining that Lisa's income falls at the same time as the fall in the price of a movie, so that when she chooses her best affordable point, she is indifferent between that point and the original situation. The move from *c* to *l* is the substitution effect. The substitution effect of a price change always results in more consumption of the good whose price has fallen. The orange arrows show the changes in consumption.

The income effect (part c) is calculated by reversing the imaginary pay cut. Income is increased and prices are held constant at their new level. The budget line moves outward and more of both goods are consumed, as shown by the orange arrows. The move from *l* to *j* is the income effect.

A Change in Price: Income and Substitution Effects

We've now worked out the effects of a change in the price of movies and the effects of a change in Lisa's income on the consumption of movies and pop. We've discovered that when her income increases, she increases her consumption of both goods. Movies and pop are normal goods. When the price of movies falls, Lisa increases her consumption of movies and decreases her consumption of pop. A fall in the price of a normal good leads to an increase in its consumption, as well as to a decrease in the consumption of its substitutes. In this example, a fall in the price of movies leads to an increase in the consumption of movies and to a decrease in the consumption of pop, a substitute for movies. To see why these changes in spending patterns occur when there is a change in price, we separate the effect of the price change into two parts. One part is called the substitution effect; the other part is called the income effect. The price effect and its separation into a substitution effect and an income effect are illustrated in Fig. 8.10. Part (a) shows the price effect that you already worked out in Fig. 8.8. Let's see how that price effect comes about, first by isolating the substitution effect.

The Substitution Effect The **substitution effect** is the effect of a change in price of one good on the quantities consumed when the consumer (hypothetically) remains indifferent between the original and the new combinations of goods consumed. To work out Lisa's substitution effect, we have to imagine that when the price of movies falls, Lisa's income also falls by an amount that is just enough to leave her best affordable point on the same indifference curve as before. The substitution effect is illustrated in Fig. 8.10(b). When the price of movies falls from \$6 to \$3, let's suppose that Lisa's income falls to \$21. What's special about \$21? It is the income that is just enough, at the new price of movies, to keep Lisa's best affordable point, on the same indifference curve as her initial consumption point *c*. Lisa's budget line in this situation is the light red line shown in Fig. 8.10(b). With the new price of movies and the new lower income, Lisa's best affordable consumption point is *l* on indifference curve I_1. The move from *c* to *l* isolates the substitution effect of a price change. The substitution effect of the fall in the price of movies is an increase in the consumption of movies from 2 to 4 and a decrease in the consumption of pop. The direction of the substitution effect never varies: when the relative price of a good falls, the consumer substitutes more of that good for the other good.

The Income Effect To calculate the substitution effect, we gave Lisa a \$9 pay cut. Now let's give Lisa her money back. This increase in income shifts Lisa's budget line, as shown in Fig. 8.10(c). That move does not involve any change in prices. The budget line moves outward, but its slope does not change. This change in the budget line is similar to the one that occurred in Fig. 8.9, where we studied the effect of income on consumption. As Lisa's budget line shifts outward, her consumption possibilities expand and her best affordable point becomes *j* on indifference curve I_2. The move from *l* to *j* isolates the income effect of a price change. In this example, the increase in income increases the consumption of both movies and pop; they are normal goods.

The Price Effect As Fig. 8.10 illustrates, we have separated the effect of a change in price in part (a) into two parts: part (b) keeps the consumer indifferent between the two situations (by making a hypothetical income change at the same time) and looks at the substitution effect of the price change; part (c) keeps prices constant and looks at the effect of (hypothetically) restoring the original income and looks at the income effect. The substitution effect always works in the same direction — the consumer buys more of the good whose price has fallen. The direction of the income effect depends on whether the good is normal or inferior. By definition, normal goods are ones whose consumption rises as income rises. In our example, movies and pop are normal goods because consumption of each of them rises as income rises.

The substitution and income effects of a price change are marked off on the axes in parts (b) and (c) of Fig. 8.10. The move from point *c* to point *l* determines the substitution effect, and the move from point *l* to point *j* determines the income effect. For movies, the income effect reinforces the substitution effect with the result that Lisa's consumption of movies increases. For pop, the substitution effect and the income effect work in opposite directions with the result that Lisa's consumption of pop decreases.

The example that we have just studied is that of a change in the price of a normal good. The effect of the change in price of an inferior good is different. Recall that an inferior good is one whose consumption falls as income increases. For an inferior good, the income effect is negative. Thus it is not always the case that lowering the price leads to an increase in the quantity demanded of an inferior good. The lower price has a substitution effect that tends to increase the quantity demanded. But the lower price has a negative income effect — lowering the demand for an inferior good. Thus the income effect offsets the substitution effect to some degree.[2]

---

[2]It has been suggested that the negative income effect for some goods is so large that it dominates the substitution effect. As a result, lowering the price for such a good leads to a decrease in the quantity demanded. Goods of this type are called "Giffen" goods, named after Sir Robert Giffen, an Irish economist. During a potato famine in Ireland in the nineteenth century, Giffen noticed that when the price of potatoes increased, the quantity of potatoes consumed also increased. Potatoes made up such a large part of the diets of these impoverished people that when the price of potatoes rose, consumers couldn't afford to buy meat or other substitutes, which were all even more expensive.

Though it is likely that there are many inferior goods, Giffen goods are very uncommon. Thus even though some goods do have a negative income effect, that effect is usually not large enough to offset the substitution effect. So the law of demand still operates — when the price of a good falls, the quantity of that good consumed rises.

Reading Between the Lines on pp. 192-193 takes a look at some recent real world examples of income and price changes and their effects on consumption patterns.

Model, Theory, and Reality

We have built a model of household behaviour that makes predictions about consumption choices and how those choices are affected by changes in income and prices. This model leads to a theory of consumer behaviour that helps us to understand past spending patterns and to predict future ones. Let's summarize this model.

The Model

All models begin with assumptions. By using logic, we work out the implications of those assumptions. Let's look at the assumptions and implications in the model of consumer choice.

Assumptions The assumptions of the model of household behaviour are as follows:

- A household has a fixed income to allocate among various goods.
- The prices of goods cannot be influenced by the household.
- The household has preferences and can compare alternative combinations of goods as preferred, not preferred, or indifferent.
- Preferences can be represented by indifference curves.
- Indifference curves bow towards the origin — the marginal rate of substitution falls as consumption of the good measured on the x-axis rises and consumption of the good measured on the y-axis falls.
- The household chooses its best affordable combination of goods.
- Preferences do not change when prices and incomes change. *Choices* change, but the new choices result from given preferences and changed constraints.

Implications The implications of the model of household behaviour are as follows:

- The chosen consumption point is affordable and is *on* the budget line.
- The chosen consumption point is on the highest attainable indifference curve.
- At the chosen consumption point, the slope of the indifference curve equals the slope of the budget line. Expressed in another way, the marginal rate of substitution equals the relative price of the two goods.
- For normal goods, a rise in income raises demand.
- For inferior goods, a rise in income lowers demand.
- For any good, a rise in its price has a substitution effect that lowers the quantity demanded of it.
- For a normal good, a rise in its price lowers the quantity demanded of it — the income effect and the substitution effect reinforce each other. This is the law of demand.
- For an inferior good, a rise in its price can lead to a rise in the quantity demanded of it if the income effect is bigger than the substitution effect.

The above is, in a nutshell, the model of consumer choice that we have studied in this chapter. That model provides a basis for developing a theory that explains the patterns of consumption.

The Theory

The theory of consumer choice can be summarized as follows:

- The choices made by real people resemble the choices made by the artificial people in the model economy.
- Spending patterns in the model look like the actual spending patterns in the real world.

What the Theory Is Not The theory of consumer choice does *not* say that people compute marginal rates of substitution and then set them equal to relative prices to decide how much of each good to buy. Economists do not have a theory about the mental processes people use to arrive at their choices.

Back to the Facts

We started this chapter by observing how consumer spending has changed over the years. The theory of consumption choice studied in this chapter can be used to explain those changes. Spending patterns are interpreted as being the best choices households can make, given their preferences and incomes and given the prices of the goods they consume. Changes in prices and in income lead to changes in the best possible choice — changes in consumption patterns.

Models based on the same ideas that you've studied here are used to explain the actual changes that occur and to measure the response of consumption to changes in prices and in income — the price and income elasticities of demand. You met some measures of these elasticities in Chapter 5. Most of those elasticities were measured by using models of exactly the same type that we've studied here (but models that have more than two goods).

But the model of household choice can do much more than explain consumption choices. It can be used to explain a wide range of other aspects of household behaviour. Let's look at some of them.

Other Household Choices

Households make many choices other than those concerning how to spend their income on the various goods and services available. There are two key choices that households must make:

- The type and amount of work to do
- How much to consume and how much to save

Time Allocation and Labour Supply

Every day, we have to allocate our 24 hours among leisure, working for ourselves, and working for someone else. When we work for someone else, we are supplying labour.

We can understand our labour supply decisions by using the theory of household choice. Supplying more labour is exactly the same thing as consuming less leisure. Leisure is a good, just like movies and pop. Other things being equal, a situation that has more leisure is preferred to one that has less leisure. We have indifference curves for leisure and consumption goods similar to those that we've already studied. For example, we can relabel the axes of Fig. 8.4 so that instead of pop, we measure all consumption goods on the vertical axis and instead of movies, we measure leisure on the horizontal axis.

We can't have as much leisure and consumption as we'd like. Our choices are constrained by the wages that we can earn. For a given hourly wage rate, increasing our consumption of goods and services is possible only if we decrease our leisure time and increase the quantity of labour we supply. The wage rate that we can earn determines how much extra consumption we can undertake by giving up an extra hour of leisure. The magnitude of the slope of our indifference curve tells us the marginal rate of substitution — the rate at which we are willing to give up consumption of goods and services to get one more hour of leisure while remaining indifferent. Our best choice of consumption and leisure has exactly the same properties as our best choice of movies and pop. We get onto the highest possible indifference curve by making the marginal rate of substitution between consumption and leisure equal to the wage rate relative to the prices of consumption goods.

Changes in wages affect the choice of consumption and leisure in a way similar to that in which a change in the price of movies affects the consumption of movies and pop. A higher wage rate makes leisure more expensive. There is a substitution effect encouraging the individual to take less leisure and work longer hours, thereby consuming more goods and services. But a higher wage rate also has an income effect. A higher wage leads to a higher income, and with a higher income we consume more of all normal goods. Leisure is a normal good. Other things being equal, the higher the person's income, the more leisure he or she takes.

People who can earn only a very low hourly wage rate tend to work fewer hours, or perhaps not at all. As the wage rate increases, the substitution effect encourages less leisure and more work to be undertaken. But as the wage rate keeps on increasing, the income effect eventually comes to dominate the substitution effect. The higher wage leads to higher consumption of goods and services and to additional leisure. It is the ultimately dominant role of the income effect that has resulted in a steadily shorter work week despite the fact that wages have increased.

Consumption and Saving

We don't have to spend all our income here and now. Nor are we constrained to consuming only our current income. We can consume less than our current income, saving the difference for future consumption. Or we can consume more than our current income, borrowing the difference and putting ourselves in a position in which we must later consume less in

Growing Pains at 40

As they approach midlife, baby boomers struggle to have it all

The generation that wanted to stay forever young is entering middle age. This year the leading edge of the Baby Boom, the 76 million Americans born in the fecund years between 1946 and 1964, reaches mid-life. Former White House Wunderkind David Stockman and Actor Sylvester Stallone (Rocky, Rambo) turn 40 in 1986. So do ex-Mouseketeer Carl ("Cubby") O'Brien, Arms Control and Disarmament Agency Director Kenneth Adelman, Real Estate Mogul Donald Trump.

The generation idealized by Madison Avenue for its superior muscle tone and free-spending habits is ruefully discovering that, contrary to the promise of the ads, it cannot have it all... Says Merv Wildcat, 30, ... "People want a home, two cars and all the new technologies, like VCRs, but it's hard to afford it all."...

The Baby Boom, says Richard C. Michel of the Urban Institute, was hit by a quadruple whammy: inflation, fierce competition for jobs, exorbitant housing costs and the recessions of the 70s and early '80s. "They grew up with the expectation that they would live better than their parents no matter what they did," says Michel. "The 1970s ended that. It was a time of tremendous economic disillusionment for many people." Between 1973 and 1983 the median real income of a typical young family headed by a person age 25 to 34 fell by 11.5%...

"If you can't afford a home, you want the best espresso machine you can buy," observes Psychologist Shelly Taylor, 39. Ad Executive Julianne Hastings, 39, wears designer clothes and jets off to the Caribbean for vacations. But she lives in an apartment "the same size as the bedroom I grew up in."

***Time*,**
May 19, 1986
By Evan Thomas,

The Essence of the Story

- No matter what our aspirations, there are limits to what we can consume. Scarcity is a fact of life for everyone.
- The following four negative factors have lowered consumption possibilities: inflation, a competitive job market, high housing prices, and recession.
- The net result of the four negative factors is a cut in real income of 11.5 percent for a typical family headed by a person aged 25 to 34.
- People would prefer to have avoided a fall in real income.
- Even for people whose real income has risen, the demand for housing has remained fairly constant while the demand for other goods—such as designer clothes, Caribbean vacations, VCRs and espresso machines—has increased.

Background and Analysis

- We can use the theory of consumer choice to analyse this article. The household's budget line defines the limit of the household's consumption possibilities. Points beyond that line are not attainable.
- Between 1973 and 1983, two things happened to the budget line of the median family: it shifted inward, and the relative price of housing increased.
- The top figure illustrates these changes. The horizontal axis measures the consumption of housing and the vertical axis measures the consumption of other goods such as VCRs, Caribbean vacations, designer clothes, and espresso machines.
- People prefer to be on the 1973 budget line rather than on the 1983 one.
- Income for some people increased between 1973 and 1983, but higher housing costs had to be faced. The bottom figure illustrates the situation facing such individuals (for example, Julianne Hastings in the story).
- In 1973, the budget line was the light red line; in 1983, it was the dark red line.
- In 1973, consumption of housing was H and of other goods V.
- A rise in income produces a rise in the demand for all goods.
- A rise in the price of housing produces a substitution effect away from housing towards other goods.
- For some people, the combination of a rise in the price of housing and a rise in income results in a larger quantity demanded of designer clothes and Caribbean vacations V' but not a change in the quantity of housing demanded H.

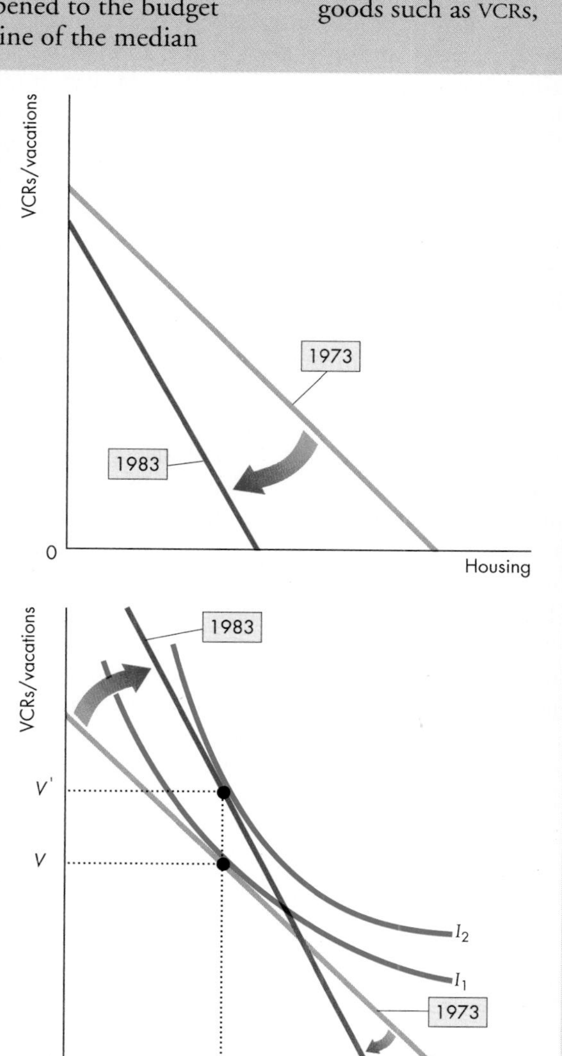

Conclusion

- "Growing Pains at 40" is an interesting and clear example of scarcity and how the behaviour of mid-life baby boomers can be predicted by an economic model of consumer choice.

Understanding Human Behaviour

Jeremy Bentham

The past 35 years have seen incredible advances in applying economic analysis to a wide range of aspects of human behaviour not normally thought of as falling within the traditional domain of economics. Although many people have made contributions to our advancing knowledge in this area, one person stands out: Gary Becker of the University of Chicago. (see "Talking with Gary Becker" pp. 151-154).

Becker's work on this broad area began in the 1950s with his pioneering study of discrimination—on the causes and effects of racial and gender discrimination. In the years since then he has applied the economic approach to political systems, crime, the allocation of time within the household, fertility and family size, marriage and divorce, and the demand for habit forming goods—drugs, alcohol, tobacco. He has also proposed an economic explanation for altruism, based on the value to the individual of social interaction that competes with the sociobiological genetic explanation.

But the economic approach to understanding human behaviour did not begin with Becker's work. Adam Smith (see Our Advancing Knowledge pp. 20-21) used economic analysis to understand political choices, religion, and the laziness and lack of concern for their students of eighteenth-century professors! The economic approach was also taken by one of Smith's contemporaries, Jeremy Bentham (1748-1832). Bentham believed that what he called the pleasure-pain calculus was applicable to all human behaviour: "Nature has placed mankind under the governance of two sovereign masters, *pain and pleasure*. It is for them alone to point out what we ought to do, as well as to determine what we shall do... They govern us in all we do, in all we say, in all we think." [1]

Many years passed between the writings of Bentham and Becker with little development in the economics of human behaviour. In the last 35 years, many scholars have worked to extend the economic approach to a variety of nontraditional problems. Here, we look at just three of the areas opened up by Becker.

- The economics of the family
- The economics of crime
- The economics of language

The Economics of the Family

The economics of the family have attracted a lot of attention and a good deal of controversy. The Chicago view (led by Becker) is that we must seek explanations of family behaviour as the outcome of given preferences and changing constraints. Chicago students of the economics of the family, such as Robert Michael and Robert J. Willis (both at the Universtiy of Chicago's National Opinion Research Center), have used this approach to conduct extensive studies of fertility designed to understand the postwar baby boom (and its subsequent bust).

A competing view, sometimes called the "Pennsylvania school," inspired primarily by Richard Easterlin of the University of Pennsylvania, assumes that preferences have changed in a systematic way to affect postwar fertility.

Canadian economists have done pioneering work on this topic. For example, Geoffrey Carliner, Chris Robinson, and Nigel Tomes (at the University of Western Ontario) have studied the interdependencies between fertility and female labour supply, finding that high-wage women — those with a high opportunity cost of their time — postpone having children and when they do have children, have fewer on the average than low-wage women; Alice and Masao Nakamura (University of Alberta) have done comparative studies of the labour force behaviour of married women in Canada and the United States; Barry Smith (York University) and Morton Steloner (Concordia University) have also studied female labour supply behaviour; and James Pesando and Morley Gunderson, (pp. 375-378) have studied the effects of pensions on retirement.

This research effort has given us a deeper understanding of how households allocate their time and make choices on the distribution of effort within the family.

The Economics of Crime

Among the more active investigators of the economics of crime are Isaac Ehrlich (State University of New York at Buffalo), Stephen Layson (University of North Carolina at Greensboro), Mitchell A. Polinsky (Stanford Law School), and Steven Shavell (Harvard Law School). These scholars are attempting to discover what might be called "supply of offenses" and "demand for enforcement of protection" curves that can be used to provide guidance on how to design a system of law and enforcement that balances the gains from low crime rates against the cost of achieving them.

One of the most important Canadian contributions to this area is Kenneth Avio's (University of Victoria) study of the deterrent effects of capital punishment, and his predictions of the effects of its abolition on homicide rates.

The Economics of Language

How valuable is the knowledge of a second language? And what determines the extent to which people choose to learn a second language? These questions are especially interesting and important in the Canadian context. Chris Robinson has studied the economic determinants and consequences of decisions to learn a second language or to endow one's children with English or French as their mother tongue.

The economic approach to the study of human behaviour is being refined and its range of application is continuously being extended. These are exciting times to study the economic approach to human behaviour.

---

[1] Quoted from Gary Becker, *The Economic Approach to Human Behaviour* (Chicago: University of Chicago Press, 1976), 8.

order to repay our loan. Choosing when to consume, how much to save, and how much to borrow can be understood by using the same theory of household choice that explained Lisa's allocation of her income to movies and pop.

Other things being equal, more consumption today is preferred to less. Also, other things being equal, more consumption in the future is preferred to less. As a consequence, we have indifference curves for consumption now and in the future that are similar to our indifference curves for any pair of goods. Of course, we cannot consume as much as we'd like to today or in the future. Our choices are constrained. The constraint on our choices depends on our income and the interest rate that we can earn on our savings or that we have to pay on our borrowings. The interest rate is a relative price — the relative price of consumption today versus consumption in the future. We choose the timing of consumption (and the amount of saving or borrowing to undertake) by making the marginal rate of substitution between current and future consumption equal to the interest rate. Thus high interest rates will discourage borrowing and lead to lower current consumption and higher future consumption.

Other Choices

Many other choices can be understood by using this same theory of household behaviour, choices about whether and when to marry, how many children to have and when to have them, whether to do legitimate work or illegal "work" — crime. The economic analysis of some of these choices is discussed in Our Advancing Knowledge on pp. 194-195.

■ We've now completed our study of household choices. We've seen how we can derive the law of demand from a model of household choice. We've also seen how that same model can be applied to a wide range of other choices, including the demand for leisure and the supply of labour.

In Part 4, we're going to study the choices made by firms. We'll see how, in the pursuit of profit, firms make choices governing the supply of goods and services and the demand for the factors of production (inputs).

After completing these chapters, we'll bring the analysis of households and firms back together again, studying their interactions in the markets for goods and services and factors of production.

SUMMARY

Consumption Possibilities

A household's budget line shows the limits to consumption, given the household's income and the prices of goods. Changes in prices and changes in income produce changes in the budget line, the boundary between what the consumer can and cannot afford. The magnitude of the slope of the budget line equals the relative price of the two goods. The point at which the budget line intersects each axis marks the consumer's real income in terms of the good measured on that axis. (pp. 175-179)

Preferences

A consumer's preferences can be represented by indifference curves. An indifference curve joins all the combinations of goods among which the consumer is indifferent. A consumer prefers points above an indifference curve to the points on it and points on an indifference curve to all points below it. Indifference curves bow towards the origin.

The magnitude of the slope of an indifference curve is called the marginal rate of substitution. A key assumption is that of a diminishing marginal rate of substitution. In other words, the marginal rate of substitution diminishes as the consumption of the good measured on the y-axis decreases and the consumption of the good measured on the x-axis increases. The more perfectly two goods substitute for each other, the straighter are the indifference curves. The less easily they substitute, the more tightly curved are the indifference curves. Goods that are always consumed together are complements and have L-shaped indifference curves. (pp. 179-184)

Choice

A household consumes at its best affordable point. Such a point is on the budget line and on the highest attainable indifference curve. At that point the indifference curve and the budget line have the same slope — the marginal rate of substitution equals the relative price. (pp. 184-185)

Predicting Consumer Behaviour

Goods are classified into two groups: normal goods and inferior goods. Most goods are normal. When income increases, a consumer buys more normal goods and fewer inferior goods. If prices are held constant, the change in consumption resulting from a change in income is called the income effect.

The change in consumption resulting from a change in the price of a good is called the price effect. The price effect can be divided into a substitution effect and an income effect. The substitution effect is calculated as the change in consumption resulting from the change in price accompanied by a (hypothetical) change in income that leaves the consumer indifferent between the initial situation and the new situation. The substitution effect of a price change always results in an increase in consumption of the good whose price has decreased. The income effect of a price change is the effect of (hypothetically) restoring the consumer's original income but keeping the price of the good constant at its new level. For a normal good, the income effect reinforces the substitution effect. For an inferior good, the income effect works in the opposite direction to the substitution effect. (pp. 185-190)

Model, Theory, and Reality

The model of household behaviour is based on the assumption that households' preferences can be represented by indifference curves that bow towards the origin (that have a diminishing marginal rate of substitution). The model has the implication that the household will choose to consume on its budget line at a point at which the marginal rate of substitution and relative price are equal. A change in price leads to a new choice that corresponds to the law of demand: when the price of a good falls, the quantity consumed increases.

The theory of consumer behaviour based on this model is that the choices made in the real world correspond to choices made in the model economy. Such a model is used to measure the response of consumption to changes in price and income — the price and income elasticities of demand that appeared in Chapter 5. (pp. 190-191)

Other Household Choices

The model of household behaviour also enables us to understand other household choices, such as the allocation of time between leisure and work, the allocation of consumption over time, and decisions regarding borrowing and saving. (pp. 191-196)

K E Y E L E M E N T S

Key Terms

Budget equation, 176
Budget line, 175
Diminishing marginal rate of substitution, 182
Income effect, 186
Indifference curve, 180
Marginal rate of substitution, 181
Price effect, 185
Real income, 176
Relative price, 177
Substitution effect, 189

Key Figures and Table 

REVIEW QUESTIONS

1 What determines the limits to a household's consumption choices?

2 What is the budget line?

3 What determines the intercept of the budget line on the vertical axis?

4 What determines the intercept of the budget line on the horizontal axis?

5 What determines the slope of the budget line?

6 What do all the points on an indifference curve have in common?

7 What is the marginal rate of substitution?

8 How can you tell how closely two goods substitute for each other according to the preferences of a consumer by looking at the consumer's indifference curves?

9 What two conditions are satisfied when a consumer makes the best possible consumption choice?

10 What is the effect of a change in income on consumption?

11 What is the effect of a change in price on consumption?

12 Define and distinguish between the income effect and the substitution effect of a price change.

PROBLEMS

1 Marc has an income of $20. Beer costs $1 a can, and chips cost 50 cents a bag.

a) What is Marc's real income in terms of beer?

b) What is his real income in terms of chips?

c) What is the relative price of beer in terms of chips?

d) What is the opportunity cost of a can of beer?

e) What is Marc's budget equation?

f) Calculate Marc's budget equation (placing cans of beer on the left side).

g) Draw a graph of Marc's budget line with chips on the horizontal axis.

2 Suppose that with the same income and prices as above, Marc chooses to consume 10 cans of beer and 20 bags of chips each month.

a) Is Marc on his budget line?

b) What is his marginal rate of substitution of beer for chips?

3 Now suppose that the price of beer rises to $1.50 a can and the price of chips falls to 25 cents a bag.

a) Can Marc still buy the same quantities of beer and chips as before if he wants to?

b) Will he want to?

c) If he changes his consumption, which good does he buy more of and which does he buy less of?

d) Which situation does Marc prefer: beer at $1 a can and chips at 50 cents a bag, or beer at $1.50 and chips at 25 cents?

e) When Marc changes his consumption in response to the new prices (beer up by 50 cents a can and chips down by 25 cents a bag), is there an income effect and a substitution effect, or just one of them at work? If only one effect is at work, which one is it?

4 Now suppose that the prices of beer and chips are at their original levels — $1 and 50 cents respectively. Marc gets a pay raise of $5. He now buys 16 cans of beer and 18 bags of chips. Which good is a normal good, and which is an inferior good?

Appendix to Chapter 8

Utility and Preferences

If you have studied both Chapters 7 and 8, you know that they both explain people's consumption choices. Each chapter presents a different model of consumer choice, but both do the same job. They even use the same example — Lisa and her consumption of movies and pop. This appendix deals with the connection between the two models. When you have read this appendix, you will be able to reinterpret each model in terms of the other.

Utility and Indifference Curves

A key element in each theory of choice is its way of describing the consumer's preferences. The marginal utility theory of Chapter 7 describes preferences in terms of the utility derived from consumption. In the indifference curve theory of Chapter 8, indifference curves represent preferences. You can understand how the two models relate to each other by thinking of an indifference curve as connecting points of equal total utility. Let's say that Lisa is indifferent between watching 3 movies and drinking 4 six-packs of pop and watching 2 movies and drinking 6 six-packs of pop. Another way of saying that she is indifferent is that she gets equal total utility from the two.

You can see the connection between total utility and indifference curves by looking at the two parts of Fig. A8.1. Part (a) of this figure has three dimensions: the quantity of pop consumed, the quantity of movies watched, and the level of utility. Part (b) has just two dimensions: the quantities of pop and movies consumed.

In part (a), the utility that Lisa gets from pop alone (with no movies) is the left-hand yellow line. It shows that as Lisa's consumption of pop rises, so does the total utility she gets from pop. Lisa's total utility from movies, which appeared in Fig. 7.2, appears here as the right-hand yellow line. It shows that as Lisa's consumption of movies increases, so does the total utility she gets from movies. Lisa's indifference curve for movies and pop is also visible in both parts of the figure. It appears as the blue line in part (b). It can also be seen in part (a). There it appears as a contour line on a map that shows the height of the terrain. Viewed in this way, an indifference curve is interpreted as a contour line that measures equal levels of total utility.

We can work either with total utility curves, as we did in Chapter 7, or with indifference curves, as we did in Chapter 8. They each give the same answers. There are, though, some interesting differences between the two theories.

Figure A8.1 Utility and Indifference Curves

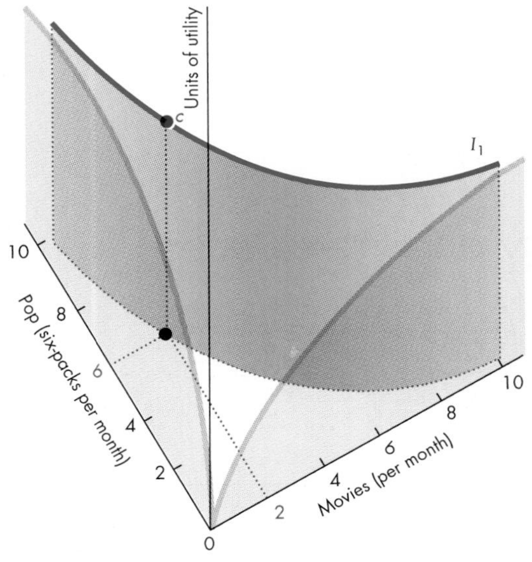

(a) Total utility from pop and movies

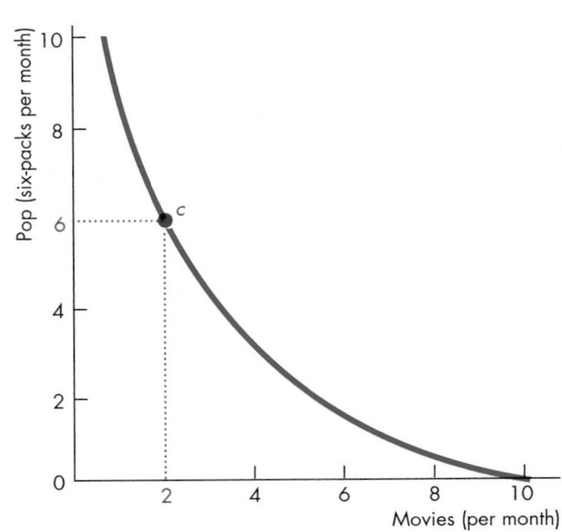

(b) Indifference curve for pop and movies

We can represent preferences in two ways: by using total utility curves or indifference curves. These two methods are different ways of looking at the same thing. Part (a) shows the total utility received from pop when no movies are consumed (the left-hand yellow curve) and the total utility received from movies when no pop is consumed (the right-hand yellow curve). It also shows an indifference curve that tells us the combinations of pop and movies that give equal (constant) total utility — the blue curve.

Part (b) shows an indifference curve for movies and pop. You can see that it is the same as the indifference curve in part (a). Point *c* in part (a) is exactly the same as point *c* in part (b). The indifference curve in part (b) is what you would see if you looked straight down on top of the three-dimensional diagram shown in part (a).

Maximizing Utility and Choosing the Best Affordable Point

According to marginal utility theory, the consumer maximizes utility by dividing the available income among different goods and services so that the marginal utility per dollar spent on each is equal. In Lisa's case, she maximizes utility by making the marginal utility of a dollar spent on movies equal to the marginal utility of a dollar spent on pop. Her choice of movies and pop satisfies the following equation:

$$\frac{\text{Marginal utility of movies}}{\text{Price of movies}} = \frac{\text{Marginal utility of pop}}{\text{Price of pop}}.$$

In the indifference curve theory, the best affordable point is chosen by making the marginal rate of substitution between the two goods equal to their relative price. In terms of our example, Lisa makes her marginal rate of substitution of movies for pop equal to the relative price of movies in terms of pop. That is, her choice of movies and pop satisfies the following equation:

$$\text{Marginal rate of substitution} = \frac{\text{Price of movies}}{\text{Price of pop}}.$$

In Chapter 8, we learned how to calculate the marginal rate of substitution as the magnitude of the slope of the indifference curve. The marginal rate of substitution is, therefore, the absolute value of the ratio of the change in the quantity of pop to the change in the quantity of movies, so that Lisa remains indifferent. "Indifference" in the indifference curve theory means the same thing as "constant total utility" in the marginal utility theory. The two situations that derive the same total utility are two situations between which Lisa is indifferent. The marginal rate of substitution, therefore, is the absolute value of the ratio of the change in the consumption of pop divided by the change in the consumption of movies, holding total utility constant. But, according to the utility theory, when consumption levels change, total utility changes. Total utility, in fact, changes in accordance with the following equation:

$$\begin{array}{c}\text{Change in} \\ \text{total utility}\end{array} = \begin{array}{c}\text{Marginal utility of movies} \times \Delta Q_m \\ + \text{Marginal utility of pop} \times \Delta Q_p\end{array}$$

where Δ stands for "change in." If Lisa is indifferent, the change in total utility must be zero, which means that

$$\begin{array}{c}\text{Marginal} \\ \text{utility of pop}\end{array} \times \Delta Q_p = \begin{array}{c}-\text{ Marginal utility} \\ \text{of movies}\end{array} \times \Delta Q_m .$$

If we divide both sides of the above equation by ΔQ_m, and also by the marginal utility of pop, we get

$$\frac{\Delta Q_p}{\Delta Q_m} = \frac{-\text{ Marginal utility of movies}}{\text{Marginal utility of pop}}.$$

We've just calculated the change in pop divided by the change in movies, while holding total utility constant or, equivalently, while staying on an indifference curve. Therefore the absolute value of this ratio is nothing other than the marginal rate of substitution. That is,

$$\begin{array}{c}\text{Marginal rate} \\ \text{of substitution}\end{array} = \frac{\text{Marginal utility of movies}}{\text{Marginal utility of pop}}.$$

You are now ready to see directly the connection between the two theories. The utility theory says that Lisa chooses her consumption of movies and pop to ensure that

$$\frac{\begin{array}{c}\text{Marginal utility} \\ \text{of movies}\end{array}}{\text{Price of movies}} = \frac{\text{Marginal utility of pop}}{\text{Price of pop}}.$$

The indifference curve theory says that Lisa chooses her consumption of movies and pop to ensure that

$$\begin{array}{c}\text{Marginal rate} \\ \text{of substitution}\end{array} = \frac{\text{Price of movies}}{\text{Price of pop}}.$$

Substituting for the marginal rate of substitution in terms of marginal utilities, we get

$$\frac{\text{Marginal utility of movies}}{\text{Marginal utility of pop}} = \frac{\text{Price of movies}}{\text{Price of pop}}.$$

All that you now have to do is to notice that you can manipulate the marginal utility condition by dividing both sides by the marginal utility of pop and multiplying both sides by the price of movies. Thus you wind up with exactly the same equation that the indifference curve theory uses to characterize the consumer's best affordable choice.

Equivalently, you can go the other way and start with the indifference curve equation. Multiply both sides by the marginal utility of pop and divide both sides by the price of a movie, and you arrive at the condition for maximizing utility. Thus the condition for maximizing utility, according to the marginal utility theory, and the condition for choosing the best affordable point, according to the indifference curve theory, are equivalent to each other.

Differences Between the Theories

The key difference between the two models of consumer choice is that the indifference curve approach does not require the concept of utility. We only have to say whether the consumer prefers one combination to another or is indifferent between the two combinations. We don't have to say anything about *how* the consumer makes such evaluations. Though the indifference curve theory does not require the concept of utility as we've seen, it is not inconsistent with marginal utility theory.

PART 4

Firms' Choices

TALKING WITH
CHRISTOPHER GREEN

Christopher Green earned his BA and MA from the University of Connecticut and his PhD from the University of Wisconsin. Since 1969 he has been a professor at McGill University and has become one of Canada's foremost experts on industrial organization and competition policy. Michael Parkin talked with Christopher Green about industrial and competition policy in Canada today.

"Learning to live with and rely on a set of rules of the game is important."

Professor Green, how did you get into economics?

I studied history as an undergraduate and then started graduate work in eighteenth-and nineteenth-century English history. But one of my teachers felt I wasn't made to be an historian because I was too interested in current issues. He said, "You ought to be a political scientist or an economist"—I don't think he really knew the difference between the two. I took an MA in economics thinking that would enable me to teach social sciences in a high school. But once I got into it, I decided to go on for a PhD and become a university professor.

What are the most important industrial policy issues facing Canada today?

First I'd list a couple of areas or general issues. One is competing in the world economy. Markets are becoming increasingly globalized, and even small firms are going to have to learn not simply to be located in their own domestic markets. Because the role of marketing is so important, investing in another market, carrying out some activities elsewhere, will become necessary. Canada has been heavily reliant on trade with the United States, yet there is a huge European market of relevance. In computer services, programming, and telecommunications equipment, ours is a world-leading country. But it's not likely that firms in high-tech areas can invade the European markets without having some presence there. This is an area, not a policy, in which governments can provide information—a public good—but that's about all.

Another important issue is that we're never going to be in a perfectly laissez-faire economy. Learning to live with and rely on a set of rules of the game is important. That's why the reform of competition policy was an important event for Canada.

The main *policy* issue that concerns me is the possibility of reregulation because of blind privatization. I was all for the privatization of some of our Crown corporations, but I am not happy about the privatization of others. There are circumstances in which public enterprise can be more efficient than regulated private enterprise.

Can you give an example?

Take privatizing Air Canada. Most of Air Canada's problems came from regulation, not public ownership. Studies showed that Air Canada was much less efficient than CP Air, with the source of inefficiency being excess capacity—having too much of the wrong sort of equipment. But those studies didn't prove anything; they used data from 1961 to 1982 when the government, not Air Canada, decided the equipment that the airline operated. Yet nothing requires government to interfere with the type of equipment used by a public enterprise. In fact, before Air Canada was privatized, one of the forms of deregulation was no longer telling any of the airlines what equipment to buy. In many cases public enterprise *is* less efficient than private enterprise especially when it's a public enterprise monopoly. But it's not so clear when you have a duopoly, when you've told the public firm to go out and compete.

I wouldn't have privatized Air Canada or Petro Can or CN. They were not working badly. And when there's public-private competition you presume firms aren't going to get into anything like price-fixing and other forms of collusion.

How can we make the Canadian telecommunication industry more competitive?

It won't be as easy as it was in the United States. Before the breakup of the U.S. Bell system long-distance rates subsidized local service, just as they do in Canada. But the structure of the American firms differed from the Canadian. AT&T owned shares in the Bell operating companies. It was easy to break off the AT&T long-distance from local operating companies, which were spread out in each region of the country. Now long-distance rates have come down as a result of competition and local rates have been raised. That type of divestiture does not appear to be possible in Canada where there's a firm in each province. There's no overall organization that can be split from the bottom. That means that if you introduce competition in long-distance service, the firm coming in to compete won't provide local service. So there's no apparent way of breaking up Bell Canada and the other telephone companies as was done in the United States. It's a structural problem—a matter of organization.

What is your assessment of Canada's new law on anti-competitive practices? Is it working?

One of the big areas of reform was abuse of dominant position. The first case has only now (April 1990) come to the Tribunal. That means the law is probably working; if the government doesn't bring too many cases in this area, that suggests to me that firms are being careful. One case is that of NutraSweet®, and it is going to be extremely controversial.

The issue arises from a swirl on diet pop cans. (Though the symbol didn't mean much to me, all my students knew of it). The swirl is a trademark for a sweetener whose generic name is aspartame. NutraSweet had a patent on the product that has now expired, and Japanese and Italian firms could sell aspartame at competitive prices. Coca Cola and Pepsi Cola would like to buy at these prices. But before the patent expired, NutraSweet signed exclusive contracts with all its users saying that if they want to use that swirl on their pop cans they must use only NutraSweet. Now the problem is not with NutraSweet's ownership of the swirl trademark. It's the exclusivity of the contracts that say it's all or nothing. Coca Cola and Pepsi Cola, which are providing evidence in the case, would like to buy aspartame, a homogenous product, from the lowest-price supplier. But NutraSweet has very neatly created in consumers' minds the idea that there's only *one* sweetener, NutraSweet, and the swirl identifies it on the can. But under the exclusive contracts, firms can't use part NutraSweet and part cheaper aspartame from another supplier and still put the swirl on their cans. No one cares about NutraSweet, it's the swirl that firms

"There's no apparent way of breaking up Bell Canada and the other telephone companies as was done in the United States. It's a structural problem—a matter of organization."

"Economic theory is a set of tools with which to look at an extremely rich and varied world."

want to use. An additional complication in this case is a constitutional issue. The Competition Tribunal is made up of federal court judges and lay members. Two weeks ago, a federal court in Québec ruled this composition a violation of the Charter of Rights. Non-judges may have biases that a judge would not; therefore the rights of people appearing before them may be jeopardized. NutraSweet is now appealing the hearing on that ground.

I'm not sure how the matter will turn out, and I'm not sure I know how it should turn out. One could make a case for NutraSweet: the law says the tribunal must consider the possibility of superior competitive performance, which is the basis of NutraSweet's defence. It is not clear whether superior competitive performance implies greater efficiency. On the other hand, it's very interesting that big buyers have actually joined in providing testimony. Also appearing are all sorts of potential suppliers who have waited 14 years to break into the field. It would be very unfortunate if the case is dropped for constitutional reasons. No matter how it ends, it will be a case study in product differentiation, vertical agreement, and the like.

What advice would you give young people interested in careers in public policy? Would you tell a student to get an economics degree? To seek a law degree? Or to study both?

Having an undergraduate degree in economics is very useful if you're going to go into law. If you're planning to do legal work, it's useful to sit in on an economics course that deals with competition policy or at least to study some of the cases. For anyone working in this area, it's important to keep an open mind, not to become methodologically rigid. For example, in public policy you can't assume that no policy is always the right thing. "No policy" is itself a policy. Economic theory is a set of tools with which to look at an extremely rich and varied world.

CHAPTER 9

Organizing Production

After studying this chapter, you will be able to:

- Explain what a firm is, and describe the economic problems that all firms face.
- Describe and distinguish among different types of business organization.
- Explain how firms raise the money to finance their operations.
- Define present value and explain its use in a firm's financing decisions.
- Calculate and distinguish between a firm's historical costs and its opportunity costs.
- Define technological efficiency and economic efficiency and distinguish between them.
- Explain why firms solve some economic problems and markets solve others.

Trees, Forests, and Apples

EVERY DAY TENS OF THOUSANDS of trees are harvested and new seedlings are planted to replace them. Billions of individual trees become one day older. The forest looks much the same from one day to the next, but the evolution of the birth and death of trees means that the individual trees that make up the forest are continuously changing. It is much the same with businesses. Every day thousands of new businesses are born and a similar number die. From one day to the next, the industries that produce the goods and services we consume look much the same, but the individual firms that make up those industries are constantly changing. ■ In the summer of 1971, Greig Clark, a student at the University of Western Ontario, realized that he was going to need $3,000 to pay his bills for the coming year of school. He hit on the idea of hiring other students as workers to paint houses in his home town of Thunder Bay, Ontario. Clark attacked his job with systematic professionalism and his approach worked. So was born College Pro Painters, a tiny new firm that today has grown into a serious enterprise, providing profits for its owners and work and income for thousands of students. By 1987, College Pro had more than 500 outlets across North America and sales of $35 million. ■ Another spectacular growth story from a tiny seedling to a giant member of the forest is that of Apple Computer. Apple began its life when Steven Jobs and Stephen Wozniak, two Stanford University students working out of a garage, bought a few components and produced the world's first commercially successful personal computer, the Apple. From that modest start, Apple Computer has grown into a giant, with revenue in 1987 of $2.7 billion. But neither founder now works at Apple. Both have left Apple and founded new companies. ■ As College Pro and Apple grew, they passed through several stages of organization, much as a growing tree passes from seed to sapling to maturity. Just as a tree needs nourishment to grow, so does a business. The main form of nourishment that encourages business growth is financial, and it is obtained from investors. Why do companies take different forms? How does a company get the money it needs to build plants and to do research? What do investors expect in return when they put money into a company? ■ At the same time that College Pro and Apple were growing, so were lots of other firms. Many fizzled! Sometimes disaster can follow hard on the heels of success. Worlds of Wonder, Inc., a toymaker that created a talking bear, was one of the fastest growing companies in history in 1986. In 1987, it filed for bankruptcy. How does an economist measure a firm's health? What happens to owners and investors of business organizations that die? ■ Economists call business organizations firms. Some 2 million firms operate in Canada today in a startling diversity of forms. They range from multinational giants, such as IBM, Exxon, and Sony, to small family businesses, such as painters, gardeners, and restaurants. Some types of business can be done in several forms: some bookstores have single owners, others belong to corporations. Three-quarters of all firms are operated by their owners, as College Pro and Apple once were. But corporations (such as College Pro and Apple today) account for 90 percent of all business sales. Why do owner-operated firms so dominate in number, but corporations dominate in sales? ■ We have learned that the market is an amazing instrument for coordinating the economic actions of millions of individuals. Firms are another type of instrument for coordinating individual activity. Why do we need firms to organize and coordinate activity? Why don't people simply buy everything they need from other individuals in markets?

■ In this chapter we are going to address the questions that have just been posed. Although we are going to learn about the many different types of firms, we will understand better the behaviour of all firms if we focus on what they have in common.

The Firm's Economic Problem

The close to 2 million firms in Canada differ enormously in size, in what they do, and in their survival power. What do they have in common? What is the distinguishing characteristic of a firm? What are the different ways in which firms are organized? Why are there different forms of organization? These are the questions that we will tackle first.

What Is a Firm?

A **firm** is an institution that buys or hires factors of production and *organizes* these resources to produce and sell goods and services. The important word in the definition of a firm is "organizes." Someone, or some hierarchy of managers, runs the firm.

What Firms Have in Common

Firms exist because of scarcity. We use firms to get as much as we can out of our scarce resources. Each firm has to solve its own economic problem. That is, each firm has to get the most it can out of the scarce resources under its control. To do so, a firm has to decide on the following:

- What to produce and in what quantities
- The techniques of production to use
- The quantities of each factor of production to employ
- Its organization and management structure
- Arrangements for compensating the factors of production

A firm's receipts from the sale of goods and services that it produces are called *total revenue.* The total payment made by a firm for the services of factors of production is called **total cost**. The difference between a firm's total revenue and total cost is its **profit** (if revenue exceeds cost) or its **loss** (if cost exceeds revenue). A firm's total revenue, total cost, and profits (or losses) are obviously affected by the choices that a firm makes to solve its economic problem. Though all firms face common problems, they do not solve those problems in the same way. In particular, the management arrangements and the arrangements for compensating factors of production vary and lead to different forms of business organization. Let's look at these different forms.

Forms of Business Organization

There are three main forms of business organization:

- Sole proprietorship
- Partnership
- Corporation

Which form a firm takes influences both its management structure and how it compensates factors of production. It also affects how much tax the firm and its owners have to pay. Finally, it affects who receives the firm's profits and who is liable for its debts in the event that it has to go out of business.

Sole Proprietorship Most firms are sole proprietorships. Corner stores, computer programmers, and freelance editors and artists are all examples of proprietorships. A **sole proprietorship** is a firm with a single owner — a sole proprietor — who has unlimited liability. **Unlimited liability** is the legal responsibility for all the debts of a firm up to an amount equal to the entire wealth of the owner. If a sole proprietorship cannot pay its debts, the personal property of the owner can be claimed by those to whom the firm owes money.

The management structure of a sole proprietorship is very simple. Its owner makes all the management decisions — what to produce, in what quantities, and with what techniques; what capital equipment to buy and how much labour to hire; how much money to put into the firm and how much to borrow from others. The sole proprietor is also the firm's only residual claimant. A firm's **residual claimant** is the agent or agents who receive the firm's profits and are responsible for its losses.

The profits of a sole proprietorship are treated as the income of the proprietor. They are simply added to any other income that he or she has and are taxed as personal income. The sole proprietorship does not pay taxes in its own right. Profits are taxed just once, when the owner receives them.

Partnership Partnerships are the second most common type of business organization. Most law firms and accounting firms are partnerships. A **partnership** is a firm with two or more owners who have unlimited liability. A partnership has a more complicated management structure than a sole proprietorship. The partners must agree on an appropriate management structure and how to run the firm. They also must agree on how to divide the firm's profits among themselves. As in a sole proprietorship, the profits of a partnership are taxed as the personal income of the owners. But each partner is legally liable for all the debts of the partnership (limited only by that individual's wealth). Liability for the full debts of the partnership is called **joint unlimited liability**.

Corporation Corporations are the best known types of business organizations, though they are not the most common. Canadian Pacific Ltd. and Bell Canada are examples of corporations. Many corporations, such as IBM, Exxon, and Sony are multinational giants.

A **corporation** is a firm owned by one or more limited liability shareholders. **Limited liability** means the owners have legal liability only for the value of their financial investment. Furthermore, the stock of a corporation is divided into shares. A **share** is a fraction of the stock of a corporation. Shares in some corporations are held privately and can be bought and sold only by mutual agreement between two people. Shares in other corporations can be bought and sold on stock markets such as the Toronto and Montreal stock exchanges. Only larger corporations, however, have shares traded on major stock exchanges. The shares of smaller corporations are handled by individual stockbrokers, in what is known as the over-the-counter market.

The management structures of corporations vary enormously. Some corporations are no bigger than a sole proprietorship and have just one effective owner. Such corporations are managed in exactly the same way as a sole proprietorship. Large corporations have elaborate management arrangements. Typically, they have an organization structure headed by a chief executive officer. Below that officer, there are usually senior vice-presidents responsible for such areas as production, finance, marketing, and perhaps research. These senior executives are in turn served by a series of specialists and subspecialists. Each layer in the management structure knows enough about what happens in the layer below to exercise control, but the entire management consists of specialists who concentrate on a narrow aspect of the corporation's activities.

The corporation receives much of its money from its owners — the shareholders. The shareholders' compensation comes in part from dividends and in part from changes in the market price of their shares. Corporations also raise money by issuing bonds. Bondholders are compensated by an agreed fixed interest payment.

As long as a corporation makes profits, the residual claimants to those profits are its shareholders. If a corporation incurs losses on such a scale that it becomes bankrupt, the residual loss is absorbed by the banks and other corporations to whom the troubled corporation is in debt. The shareholders themselves, by virtue of their limited liability, are responsible for the debt of the corporation only up to the value of their investment.

Government taxes the profits of a corporation independently of the incomes of the shareholders. Thus corporate profits are, in effect, taxed twice. After the corporation has paid tax on its profits, the shareholders themselves pay taxes on their dividend income at a rate determined by the shareholder's total income.

Other Types of Firms Although most firms are sole proprietorships, partnerships, or corporations, there are three other less common types of firms — not-for-profit firms, cooperatives, and Crown corporations.

A **not-for-profit firm** is an organization that either chooses or is required to have equal total costs and total revenue. Examples are universities and colleges, churches, and some insurance companies called mutual insurance companies. A **cooperative** is a firm owned by a group of people who have a common objective and who collectively bear the risks of the enterprise and share in its profits. Cooperatives are more common in western European countries than they are in Canada and in the nineteenth and early twentieth centuries organized much of the retail trade. The most common and successful type of cooperative in Canada is the credit union and mutual savings bank. Members often have close ties to each other and so cooperatives are able to borrow and to lend for small scale business and household purposes even more efficiently than can large, publicly owned financial institutions. A **Crown corporation** is a firm that is publicly owned and operated under government supervision. Two examples of Crown corporations are the Canadian Broadcasting Corporation and Canada Post.

What are the pros and cons of the various forms of business organization?

Table 9.1 Pros and Cons of Different Firm Types

Type of firm	Pros	Cons
Sole proprietorship	• Easy to set up • Simple decision making • Profits taxed only once as owner's income	• Bad decisions not checked by need for consensus • Owner's entire wealth at risk • Firm dies with owner • Capital is expensive • Labour is expensive
Partnership	• Easy to set up • Diversified decision making • Can survive withdrawal of partner • Profits taxed only once as owners' incomes	• Achieving consensus may be slow and expensive • Owners' entire wealth at risk • Withdrawal of partner may create capital shortage • Capital is expensive
Corporation	• Owners have limited liability • Large-scale, low-cost capital available • Professional management not restricted by ability of owners • Perpetual life • Long-term labour contracts cut labour costs	• Complex management structure can make decisions slow and expensive • Profits bear corporation tax, and dividends are not taxed as income of shareholders

Pros and Cons of Different Firm Types

Since each of the three main types of firms exists in large numbers, each type obviously has advantages in particular situations. Each type also has its disadvantages, which explains why it has not driven out the other two. Table 9.1 summarizes the pros and cons of each type of firm. Let's see how the advantages and disadvantages balance out for each type of business, beginning with a proprietorship.

Sole Proprietorship The pros and cons of a sole proprietorship balance out in favour of this form of business organization mainly for small operations in which the proprietor is an expert. Though the risk of a bad decision always exists, the expertise of the proprietor keeps mistakes to a minimum. For example, experienced computer programmers with a good grasp of their field often work as sole proprietors. The sole proprietorship also works well in businesses that require relatively low-skilled labour and that are not hurt in terms of efficiency by a high rate of labour turnover. Most farms, which require the expertise of the owners but which also use unskilled labour, are sole proprietorships.

A sole proprietorship is often a step on the way to becoming a corporation — the first step in the evolution of a firm. Sole proprietorships are, however, risky. Those with profitable ideas and expert abilities can earn a large income. Those whose ideas don't fly die quickly. The survivors, with the wealth coming from their success, may go on to create and manage corporations.

For example, the largest greeting card company in North America, Hallmark Cards, started out as a sole proprietorship. Its founder, Joyce Hall, kept his first greeting cards under a bed in his room at the YMCA in Kansas City. Today, Hallmark is a corporation with annual sales of more than $1 billion.

Partnership The partnership suits skilled professionals who share a body of knowledge and a discipline such as accounting, architecture, law, or medicine. The common viewpoint and background of a group of lawyers, for example, usually mean that they can reach a consensus easily. Partnerships have thrived in professions and are especially important in finance, insurance, and real estate, as well as in the service sector.

Corporation The corporation has many natural advantages, especially in the production of goods and services that benefit from large-scale production, and where specialized, professional management and skills acquired on the job are important. Because of their limited liability and, in principle at least, perpetual life, corporations can acquire large and complex production plants and can train and provide long-term incentives to management and other professional workers. Although large organizations require a complex management structure, which slows down decision-making, the costs associated with such a structure have proved to be well worth bearing. As a consequence, the corporation has become the dominant form of business organization in the modern economy.

R E V I E W

A firm is an institution that buys or hires factors of production and organizes them to produce goods and services. There are three main types of firm: sole proprietorships, partnerships, and corporations. Each has its advantages and each plays a role in every sector of the economy. The pros and cons of the different types of firm are summarized in Table 9.1. ■

Business Finance

Now let's look at some financial aspects of firms. First we will examine the ways in which firms raise money. Then we will see how we can measure their costs. And finally, we will look at the ways in which accountants measure costs and compare them with the economist's concept of cost — opportunity cost.

How Firms Raise Money

All firms get some of their money from their owner. The owner's stake in a business is called **equity** or **equity capital**. Sole proprietorships and partnerships raise additional money by borrowing from the bank or from friends. This limits the amount of money that they can raise. Corporations raise much more money than partnerships or sole proprietorships. An airline, for example, may raise hundreds of millions of dollars to buy a bigger fleet of jets. A steel manufacturer may raise hundreds of millions of dollars to build a new plant. The more permanent structure of

Figure 9.1 Selling Bonds

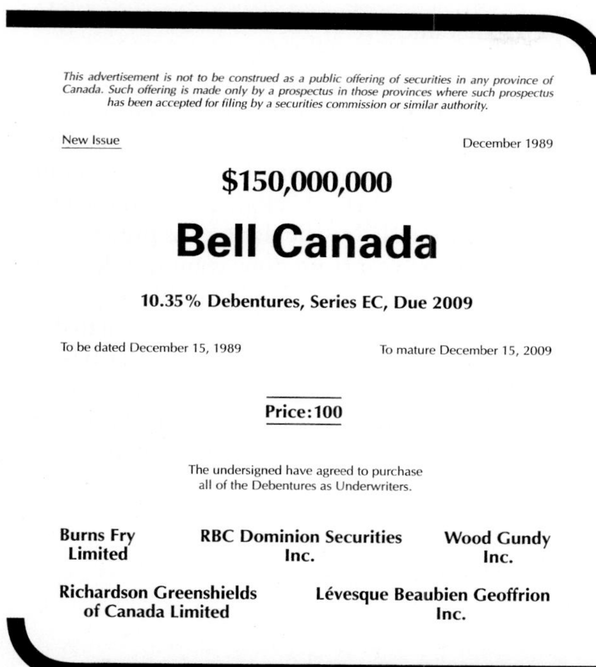
This advertisement is not to be construed as a public offering of securities in any province of Canada. Such offering is made only by a prospectus in those provinces where such prospectus has been accepted for filing by a securities commission or similar authority.

New Issue

December 1989

$150,000,000

Bell Canada

10.35% Debentures, Series EC, Due 2009

To be dated December 15, 1989

To mature December 15, 2009

Price: 100

The undersigned have agreed to purchase all of the Debentures as Underwriters.

Burns Fry Limited

RBC Dominion Securities Inc.

Wood Gundy Inc.

Richardson Greenshields of Canada Limited

Lévesque Beaubien Geoffrion Inc.

A bond is an obligation to make coupon payments and a redemption payment. Bell Canada issued bonds in 1989 promising to pay 10.35 percent each year for the following 20 years as a coupon payment and to redeem the bonds in 2,009.

corporations gives them two important ways of raising large sums of money that are not generally available to households and unincorporated businesses:

- Selling bonds
- Issuing stock

Let's look at these two ways in which corporations raise billions of dollars each year.

Selling Bonds

A **bond** is a legally enforceable obligation to pay specified sums of money at specified future dates. Usually a corporate bond specifies that a certain sum of money called the **redemption value** of the bond will be paid at a certain future date called the **redemption date**. In addition, another sum will be paid each year between the date of issue of the bond and the redemption date. The sum of money paid each year is called the **coupon payment.**

Let's look at the example shown in Fig. 9.1. On December 15, 1989, Bell Canada raised $150 million by selling bonds. On that day, Bell Canada obligated itself to make a payment on the redemption date, December 15, 2009, of $150 million plus the interest then owing. It also committed itself to making a coupon payment of 10.35 percent on December 15 each year.

The flow of cash between Bell Canada and its bondholders is set out in Table 9.2. As you can see, Bell received $150 million on December 15, 1989 and then makes coupon payments of $15,525,000 (10.35 percent of $150 million) each December 15 through 2008. Finally, in 2009 it will redeem the bonds for $150 million and make the final coupon payment for the last year, paying out a total of $165.525 million on that date. By that time, it will have paid out $310.5 million more than it received from the bondholders. In other words, Bell Canada received $150 million in 1989, and it contracted to pay back over the next 20 years that $150 million plus another $310.5 million.

On the face of it, this appears to be a terrible way of doing business. Why would Bell Canada

Table 9.2 Bell Canada Bonds: Cash Flow

Year	Cash received (millions of dollars)	Cash paid out (millions of dollars)
1989	150	
1990		15.525
1991		15.255
.		.
.		.
.		.
2008		15.525
2009		165.525
Total	150	460.500
Net cash paid out		310.500

have found that a worthwhile deal? To answer this question, we need to understand a fundamental principle of business (and indeed personal) finance.

Discounting and Present Value

We have seen that a bond is an obligation to make a series of *future* payments. Also, a bond is sold for a *current* receipt. Money flows into Bell Canada in 1989 and out in 1990 through 2009.

If you were given the choice between a dollar today and a dollar a year from today, you would choose a dollar today. The same is true for Bell Canada. A dollar in 1989 is worth more to Bell Canada than that same dollar in 1990 and even more still than that same dollar in 2009. A dollar today is worth more than a dollar in the future because today's dollar can be invested to earn interest.

The next two paragraphs contain a hefty load of calculations, but they are well worth sticking with. There are many situations in your own life where an understanding of this material will help you to make the right decisions — decisions about whether to rent or to buy a videotape or a VCR, whether to buy for cash or buy on credit, whether to buy in bulk or buy more frequently in smaller quantities. Any calculation that involves comparing a sum of money today with a different sum of money at a later date involves calculating a present value. Let's learn how to do such a calculation.

Calculating a Present Value Suppose that the interest rate is 10 percent a year. If $100 is invested this year at 10 percent, it produces $110 one year from now. We can turn the tables and say that $110 a year from now is worth $100 today. The **present value** of a future sum of money is the amount that, if invested today, will grow as large as that future sum, taking into account the interest that it will earn. Let's express this idea with an equation:

$$\text{Future sum} = \text{Present value} \times (1 + i).$$

If you have $100 today and the interest rate (i) is 10 percent a year ($i = 0.1$), one year from today you will have $110. Check that the above formula delivers that answer: $100 multiplied by 1.1 equals $110.

We have just used the formula to calculate a future sum from the present value and an interest rate. We can calculate the present value of a future sum of money by just working backward. Instead of multiplying the present value by $(1 + i)$, we divide the future sum by $(1 + i)$. That is,

$$\text{Present value} = \frac{\text{Future sum}}{(1 + i)}.$$

We can use this formula to calculate present value. Calculating present value is called discounting. **Discounting** is the conversion of a future sum of money to its present value. Let's check that we can use the present value formula by calculating the present value of $110 one year from now assuming the interest rate is 10 percent a year. You'll be able to guess that the answer is $100 because we just calculated that $100 invested today at 10 percent a year becomes $110 in one year. Thus it follows immediately that the present value of $110 in one year's time is $100. But let's use the formula. Putting the numbers into the above formula we have,

$$\begin{aligned}\text{Present value} &= \frac{\$110}{(1 + 0.1)} \\ &= \frac{\$110}{1.1} \\ &= \$100.\end{aligned}$$

Calculating the present value of a sum of money one year from now is the easiest case. But we can also calculate the present value of a sum any number of years in the future. As an example, let's see how we calculate the present value of a sum of money available two years from now.

Suppose that you invest $100 today for two years at an interest rate of 10 percent a year. The money will earn $10 in the first year, which means that by the end of the first year you will have $110. If the interest of $10 is invested, the interest earned in the second year will be a further $10 on the original $100 plus $1 on the $10 interest. Thus the total interest earned in the second year will be $11. Overall, the total interest earned will be $21 ($10 in the first year and $11 in the second year). After two years, you will have $121. From the definition of present value, you can see that at 10 percent the present value of $121 two years hence is $100. That is, $100 is the present sum that, if invested at 10 percent interest, will grow to $121 two years from now.

To calculate the present value of a sum of money two years in the future, we use the formula

$$\text{Present value} = \frac{\text{Sum of money two years in future}}{(1+i)^2}.$$

To see if the formula works, let's calculate the present value of \$121 two years in the future when the interest rate is 10 percent a year. Putting these numbers into the above formula gives:

$$\begin{aligned}\text{Present value} &= \frac{\$121}{(1+0.1)^2}\\ &= \frac{\$121}{(1.1)^2}\\ &= \frac{\$121}{1.21}\\ &= \$100.\end{aligned}$$

We can calculate the present value of a sum of money any number of years in the future by using a formula based on the two that we've already used. The general formula is:

$$\text{Present value} = \frac{\text{Money available } n \text{ years in future}}{(1+i)^n}.$$

For example, if the interest rate is 10 percent a year, \$100 received 10 years from now will have a present value of \$38.55. That is, if \$38.55 is invested today at an interest rate of 10 percent, it will accumulate to \$100 in 10 years. (You may want to check that calculation on your pocket calculator.)

Now that you understand and can calculate a present value, we can return to the main question: why does it pay Bell Canada to borrow \$150 million in 1989 and pay out \$460.5 million over the next 20 years?

The Present Value of a Bond First, Bell Canada isn't planning to pay out \$460.5 million on a \$150 million loan just for fun. It plans to use the money for its business. Let's suppose that Bell Canada plans to install \$150 million worth of computerized telephone-switching equipment and cables. It doesn't have \$150 million in its pocket to spare. It can borrow the money from the bank for 11 percent interest. Alternatively, it can sell the bonds that we have just been describing. Let's suppose it sells the bonds.

You know from what you have just learned about discounting that a sum of money paid two or five or ten years in the future is worth a smaller sum today. Discounting tells you that the money Bell Canada will pay in future years to its bondholders is worth less today. How much less? To find out, let's calculate the present value of the bond payments.

We will use the formulas that we have just learned. To begin, we need to list the sums of money that Bell Canada is going to receive and to pay out. Such a list appears in Table 9.3, in the column headed "Cash flow." A plus sign means that money flows into Bell Canada and a minus sign means that money flows out from it. In 1989, Bell Canada received \$150 million. Between 1990 and 2009, the company makes coupon payments of \$15.525 million each year. In 2009, the company makes a final coupon payment of \$15.525 million and redeems the bonds for \$150 million, so it makes a total payment of \$165.525 million. To calculate the present value of this stream of receipts and payments, we divide each item by $(1 + i)^n$. Recall that the variable n is the number of years in the future that the money is paid and i is the interest rate. Since Bell Canada could have borrowed the money that it needs from the bank for 11 percent, that is the interest rate that we will use for calculating the present value of a bond; in other words, $i = 0.11$.

The results of our calculations are set out in Table 9.3, in the column headed "Present value." The present value of a sum of money today is the sum itself. For Bell Canada, the relevant date for calculating the present value is December 15, 1989. Viewed from that date, the present value of the cash receipt in 1989 is \$150 million. The present value of \$15.525 million in 1990 — one year hence — is

Table 9.3 The Present Value of Bell Canada Bonds

Year	Cash flow (millions of dollars)	Present value at 11% per year (millions of dollars)
1989	+150.000	+150.000
1990	−15.525	−13.986
1991	−15.525	−12.600
.	.	.
.	.	.
.	.	.
2008	−15.525	−2.137
2009	−165.525	−20.531
Net	−310.500	+7.763

$13.986 million. How did we arrive at that figure? We used our formula:

$$\text{Present value} = \frac{15.525}{1 + 0.11}$$

$$= \frac{\$15.525}{1.11}$$

$$= \$13.986.$$

You can use your pocket calculator to verify this calculation. The further we go into the future, the smaller are the present values. For example, the present value of $15.525 million two years hence (in 1991) is $12.6 million. That is,

$$\text{Present value} = \frac{\$15.525}{(1.11)^2}$$

$$= \$12.600.$$

The present value 19 years hence (in 2008) is only $2.137 million. That is,

$$\text{Present value} = \frac{\$15.525}{(1.11)^{19}}$$

$$= \$2.137.$$

In the final year, when Bell Canada makes a payment of $165.525 to redeem the bonds plus the coupon payment for the last year, the present value of that payment is $20.531 million.

The sum of the present values is called the net present value. The **net present value** of a stream of future payments is the sum of the present values of the payments in each year. As you can see, the net present value of these bonds when the interest rate is 11 percent is $7.763 million. Expressed another way, the present value of the future payments Bell Canada will make is slightly less than the $150 million it borrowed in 1989.

Now you can see that Bell Canada was not so crazy to decide to take in $150 million in 1989 and pay out $460.5 million over the next 20 years. The present value of its future payments is far smaller than $460.5 million. In our example, we used an interest rate of 11 percent to calculate the present value. Using other interest rates yields different results. But if a bank loan at an interest rate of 11 percent is the alternative, issuing the bond is better than borrowing from the bank. The wisdom of borrowing at all will finally depend on the profits of the new phone equipment. Bell will want the equipment to earn enough profits to meet the payments on the bonds.

The Attractions of Bonds Bonds provide a corporation with predictable long-term financing at guaranteed cost. A large corporation usually sells some bonds every year or two and redeems others in sequence so that the firm has a fairly constant maturity structure of bonds outstanding. The **maturity structure** of bonds is the distribution of future dates on which bonds are to be redeemed. Bonds are attractive to purchasers because of the security they provide. Just as they give the corporation predictable interest costs, so do they provide the investor with predictable interest income.

Bonds are risky in the sense that if a corporation goes bankrupt it may not be able to pay the bondholders. Nevertheless, the bondholders get paid with any residual value of the corporation before shareholders get any payments. Though bondholders have a prior claim on the residual value of the company in the event of bankruptcy, they have less control over the company than shareholders do. They have no rights to choose the directors who oversee management or to choose the management that runs the corporation.

Issuing Stock

The second major way in which corporations raise money is by issuing stock. Money raised in this way is the corporation's *equity capital* because the shareholders of a corporation are its owners. They have bought shares of the corporation's stock.

There are three types of corporate stock:

- Common stock
- Preferred stock
- Convertible stock

Common stock entitles its holder to vote at shareholders' meetings and to participate in the election of directors. The holder of common stock is entitled to claim a dividend only if the directors vote to pay one. Such a dividend is paid at a variable rate, determined by the directors and varying according to the firm's profits.

Preferred stock gives no voting rights, but it gives a prior claim on dividends at a fixed rate, regardless of the profit level. The holders of preferred stock stand before those of common stock but after bondholders if the corporation cannot meet all its obligations.

Convertible stock is not quite a bond and not quite a stock. Its owner receives a fixed coupon payment, as a bondholder does, but has the privilege of being able to convert the bond into a fixed number of shares of common stock.

Corporations issue millions of shares of their stock, and these shares regularly trade on stock exchanges. A **stock exchange** is an organized market for trading in stock. Canada has four stock exchanges: Montreal, Toronto, Vancouver, and Alberta. With computers and advanced electronic communications, many Canadians also trade on the major stock exchanges in New York, London, Tokyo, and elsewhere.

The Price of a Share of Stock In August 1989, Royal Trust sold 11 million shares of common stock for $18.50 a share (see Fig. 9.2). What determined the price for the shares of Royal Trust's common stock? Why couldn't it get $20 a share? Why were people willing to pay more than $17 a share?

To answer these questions, we need to examine common stock as a financial investment. The holder of a share receives a dividend each year. That dividend may be zero. If the dividend is zero and is expected to be zero forever, the value of the stock will be exactly zero! Suppose that a corporation is expected to pay a dividend of $110 a share one year from now and nothing thereafter. What will such a share be worth? You probably guessed it: the share will be worth the present value of $110 one year from now. If the interest rate is 10 percent a year, the present value of $110 one year from now is $100. People will be willing to pay $100 for the share today. If the share sells for less than $100, there will be a strong demand for it since the expected return on the share will exceed 10 percent, the prevailing interest rate. For example, if you can buy that share for $90, and you receive $110 next year, you will have earned $20, or 22 percent, on your initial $90 investment. If someone tries to sell the share for more than $100, no one will buy it. No one will pay more than $100 for a claim to $110 one year from now if the interest rate is 10 percent. People can do better by simply putting $100 in the bank and collecting $110 in one year's time.

In general, the price of a share is the present value of its expected future dividends. To drive this fact home, let's consider another example. Suppose that investors expect a corporation to pay a dividend of $10 a share each and every year into the indefinite future. Suppose also that the interest rate is 10 percent a year. What will that corporate share be worth? The answer is $100. An investment of $100 in the share will produce $10 a year, or a return of 10 percent a year. That is the same as the interest rate available on other things. The net present value of $10 a year forever, discounted at a 10 percent interest rate, is $100.[1]

Investors can estimate future dividends, but they cannot know them for sure, and their estimates can change. These changing expectations cause share prices to fluctuate dramatically. Because corporations pay dividends out of their profits, news about a firm's profitability can change investors' expectations of its future dividends.

One number that investors pay attention to is called the price-earnings ratio. The **price-earnings ratio** is the current price of a share divided by the current profit per share. A high price-earnings ratio means that investors are willing to pay a high price for a share compared to the profits that the share is currently earning. Such a situation arises when the firm's future profits are expected to be high relative to

---

[1]If you are comfortable with algebra, you may find the following demonstration of this result helpful. The formula for the present value of $\$A$ a year forever at an interest rate of i per year is:

$$PV = \frac{\$A}{1+i} + \frac{\$A}{(1+i)^2} + \ldots \frac{\$A}{(1+i)^n} + \ldots\ldots$$

The dots stand for the years between year 2 and year n and the years beyond n. Next, divide this equation by $(1 + i)$ to give

$$\frac{PV}{(1+i)} = \frac{\$A}{(1+i)^2} + \frac{\$A}{(1+i)^3} + \ldots \frac{\$A}{(1+i)^{n+1}} + \ldots\ldots$$

Now subtract the second equation from the first to give

$$PV - \frac{PV}{(1+i)} = \frac{\$A}{(1+i)}.$$

Multiply both sides of this equation by $(1 + i)$ to give

$$(1+i)\,PV - PV = \$A,$$

and simplify the left-hand side as

$$iPV = \$A.$$

Finally, divide both sides of the previous equation by i to give

$$PV = \frac{\$A}{i}.$$

For example, if $\$A = \$10$, and $i = 0.1$ (that is, an interest rate of 10 percent a year),

$$PV = \frac{\$10}{0.1} = \$100.$$

So the present value of $10 a year forever at an interest rate of 10 percent a year is $100.

Figure 9.2 Issuing Stock

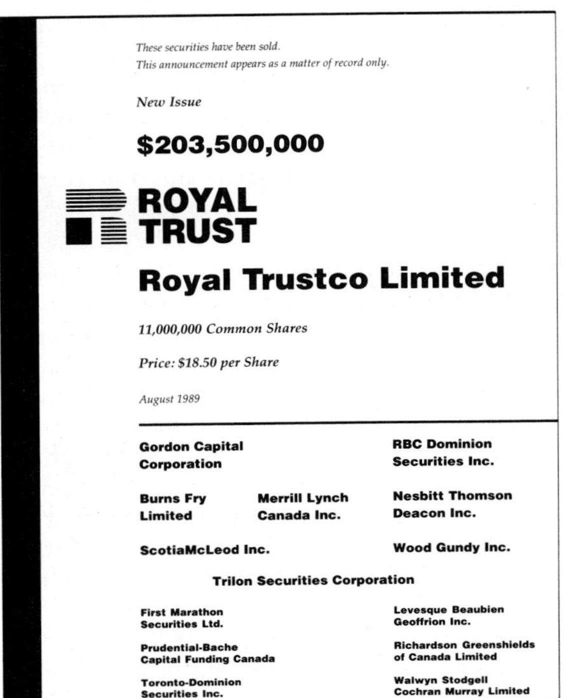

These securities have been sold.
This announcement appears as a matter of record only.

New Issue

$203,500,000

ROYAL TRUST

Royal Trustco Limited

11,000,000 Common Shares

Price: $18.50 per Share

August 1989

Gordon Capital Corporation **RBC Dominion Securities Inc.**

Burns Fry Limited **Merrill Lynch Canada Inc.** **Nesbitt Thomson Deacon Inc.**

ScotiaMcLeod Inc. **Wood Gundy Inc.**

Trilon Securities Corporation

First Marathon Securities Ltd. **Levesque Beaubien Geoffrion Inc.**

Prudential-Bache Capital Funding Canada **Richardson Greenshields of Canada Limited**

Toronto-Dominion Securities Inc. **Walwyn Stodgell Cochran Murray Limited**

Royal Trust (Royal Trustco Limited) issued 11 million shares in 1989 at $18.50 per share. The price of a share is determined as the present value of the expected future dividends, based on the company's expected future profits.

its current profits. A low price-earnings ratio means that investors are willing to pay only a low price for a share relative to its current earnings. This situation arises when future profits are expected to be low compared with current profits.

We have just worked out how the price of a share of common stock is determined. The prices of preferred stock and convertible stock are determined in a similar manner and depend on the expected future stream of payments that will be made to the holders of those stocks.

Cost and Profit

What is cost? Cost is the total payment made by a firm for the services of factors of production. There are two ways of measuring cost — the accountant's way and the economist's way.

Accountants measure historical cost. **Historical cost** values factors of production at the prices actually paid for them. Economists measure opportunity cost. Opportunity cost is the best alternative forgone. For example, the opportunity cost of an hour in the classroom is an hour of swimming, if that is the best alternative forgone.

Although opportunity cost is something real, it is convenient, when analysing the costs of firms, to talk about the dollar equivalent of opportunity cost. Thus we can ask how many dollars would we have had available to spend on a good if we had not produced some quantity of another good. Here we'll value opportunity cost in terms of dollars. But don't lose sight of the fact that such a measure is just a convenience. When we calculate the opportunity cost of producing something, we're really asking another question: what did we give up to produce this good? We're using dollars as a convenient unit of accounting.

In some cases, historical cost and opportunity cost measures are the same. In others, important differences arise. Let's look first at the cases where they are the same.

When Historical Cost Equals Opportunity Cost

Historical cost equals opportunity cost when a company uses up a factor of production soon after buying it. Historical cost is the money paid for that factor of production. The opportunity cost (expressed in dollars) is the same as the historical cost because the money could have bought other factors to produce something else or could have bought the goods directly from someone else. Labour is the most important factor of production whose historical cost typically equals its opportunity cost.

When Historical Cost and Opportunity Cost Differ

There are two main sources of difference between historical cost and opportunity cost:

- Durable input costs
- Costs of inputs not directly purchased

Durable inputs are factors of production that are not entirely used up in a single production period. They are bought in a lump and then used gradually over a prolonged period of time. A firm may spend a large sum of money on buildings, plant, and equipment in a single year and then spend nothing on them for another five years. Similarly, a firm may carry large inventories of raw materials and semifinished products that it does not use up completely in a single year. In production, the firm may use items that it bought a year or two earlier. What is the opportunity cost of using capital equipment bought several years earlier? What is the opportunity cost of taking inputs from inventory? We'll answer these questions below.

A second difference between historical cost and opportunity cost occurs when a firm uses inputs that it does not directly pay for. Examples are the time of the owner and the owner's reputation for reliable service.

Let's examine the differences by looking first at buildings, plant, and machinery costs, then at inventory costs, and finally at the costs of inputs not directly purchased.

Buildings, Plant, and Machinery Costs

The cost of buildings, plant, and machinery has two components:

- Depreciation
- Interest

We'll first examine the accountant's historical cost methods of determining these costs.

Depreciation The fall in the value of a durable input over a given period of time is **depreciation**. Accountants assess this fall in value by applying a conventional depreciation rate to the original purchase price. For buildings, the conventional depreciation allowance is 5 percent a year. Thus if a firm builds a factory for $100,000, an accountant regards 5 percent of that amount, $5,000, as a cost of production in the first year. At the end of the first year, the accountant records the value of the building as $95,000 (the original cost minus the 5 percent depreciation). In the next year, the accountant regards $4,750 as a cost of production (5 percent of the remaining $95,000 value of the building), and so on. The accountant uses different depreciation rates for different types of inputs. Fifteen percent is a common rate for plant and equipment.

Interest If a firm borrows money to buy a building, plant, or equipment, the accountant counts the interest on the borrowing as a cost of production. So, in this case, if the firm borrows the entire $100,000 and if the interest rate is 10 percent a year, the accountant treats the $10,000 interest payment as a cost of production. If the firm has not borrowed anything to build the factory but instead has used its own previously earned profits, the accountant regards the interest cost incurred in production as zero.

Next, let's see how economists determine these costs. Like accountants, economists also look at depreciation and interest costs to assess the cost of buildings, plant, and machinery, but they calculate both as opportunity costs. Let's see how.

Economic depreciation The change in the market price of a durable input over a given period is **economic depreciation**. For example, economic depreciation over a year is calculated as the market price of the input at the beginning of the year minus its market price at the end of the year. The original cost of the equipment is not directly relevant to this calculation. The equipment could have been sold at the beginning of the year for the market price then prevailing. The opportunity cost of hanging on to the equipment, therefore, is the value lost by not selling it. If a firm has kept the equipment for a year and used it, the difference between its market price at the beginning of the year and at the end of the year tells us how much of its value has been used up in production.

Sunk costs A situation sometimes arises in which a firm has bought some capital equipment and the equipment is in place and functioning well but has no resale value. The historical cost of buying that equipment is called a sunk cost. A **sunk cost** is the historical cost of buying plant and machinery that have no current resale value. The opportunity cost of using such equipment is zero.

Interest costs The other cost of using durable inputs is interest. Whether a firm borrows to buy its buildings, plant, and equipment or uses previously earned profits to pay for them makes no difference to the opportunity cost of the funds tied up in its productive assets. If the firm borrowed the money, it made an interest payment. (That's the payment the accountant picks up using the historical cost method.) If the firm uses its own funds, the opportunity cost is the amount that could have been earned by using those funds for something else. The firm could have sold the equipment at the beginning of the year and used the funds from the sale for some other purpose. At the very least, the firm could have put the money in the bank and earned interest. The interest forgone is the opportunity cost of the funds tied up in equipment, regardless of whether that money is borrowed or not. So the economist's measure of the interest cost of a durable resource — its opportunity cost — is the value of the input at the beginning of the year multiplied by the current year's interest rate.

Inflation Inflation complicates the calculation of opportunity cost. A change in prices that results purely from inflation — a rise in all prices — does not affect opportunity cost. To avoid being misled by inflation, we measure opportunity cost in terms of the prices prevailing in a single year. As a result of the high inflation rates experienced in the 1970s and early 1980s, accountants have also begun to pay attention to the distortions that inflation can cause in measuring historical cost and comparing costs between one year and another.

Implicit Rental Rate To measure the opportunity cost of using buildings, plant, and equipment, we calculate the sum of economic depreciation and interest costs. Another way of looking at this opportunity cost is as the income that the firm forgoes by not renting its assets out to another firm and instead renting the assets to itself. When a firm rents assets to itself, it pays an **implicit rental rate** for their use. You are familiar with the idea of renting equipment. People commonly rent houses, apartments, cars, televisions, VCRs, and videotapes; firms commonly rent earthmoving equipment, satellite launching services, and so on. When someone rents a piece of equipment, that person pays an *explicit* rent. When an owner uses a piece of equipment rather than renting it out, the economist notes that the owner could have rented the equipment out instead. By not doing so, owners *implicitly* rent from themselves. Another term that is sometimes used to describe an implicit cost or rent is imputed cost. An **imputed cost** is an opportunity cost that does not require an actual expenditure of cash.

Next, let's examine inventory costs.

Inventory Costs

Inventories are stocks of raw materials, semifinished goods, and finished goods held by firms. Some firms have small inventories or inventories that turn over very quickly. In such cases, the accountant's historical cost and the economist's opportunity cost are the same. When a production process requires inventories to be held for a long time, the two measurements differ, possibly in important ways.

Historical Cost Measures To measure the cost of using inventories, accountants use a historical cost method called FIFO, which stands for "First In, First Out." This method of pricing the use of inventories assumes, as a convenient fiction, that the first item placed into the inventory is literally the first one out. An alternative accountant's measure that is used in some cases is called LIFO, which stands for "Last In, First Out." This measure, though not quite opportunity cost, is close to it, for it measures the cost of an inventory item at the price most recently paid. If prices are constant, the price most recently paid is the same as the price that will have to be paid to replace the used item and, therefore, is precisely its opportunity cost.

Opportunity Cost Measures The opportunity cost of using inventories is their current replacement cost. If an item is taken out of inventory, it will have to be replaced by a new item. The cost of that new item is the opportunity cost of using the inventory. Again, we have to be careful to avoid contaminating our measure with the effects of inflation. If the cost of some inventory item has risen purely because the prices of all things have risen, then the higher dollar cost is not a higher opportunity cost.

Other Costs

Owners' Wages The owner of a firm often puts a great deal of time and effort into working for the firm but rarely takes an explicit wage payment for this work. Instead, the owner withdraws cash from the business to meet living expenses. Accountants regard such withdrawals of cash as part of the owner's profits from the business, rather than a measure of the cost of the owner's time. But the owner could have worked at some other activity and earned a wage. The opportunity cost of the owner's time is the income forgone by the owner by not working in the best alternative job.

Patents, Trademarks, and Names Many firms have patents, trademarks, or names that have come to be associated with reliability, service, or some other desirable characteristic. Sometimes firms have acquired these things by their own past efforts. In

Table 9.4 Rocky's Mountain Bikes' Revenue, Cost,and Profit Statement

The accountant		**The economist**	
Item	**Amount**	**Item**	**Amount**
Total revenue	$300,000	Total revenue	$300,000
Costs:		Costs:	
Wholesale cost of bikes	150,000	Wholesale cost of bikes	150,000
Utilities and other services	20,000	Utilities and other services	20,000
Wages	50,000	Wages	50,000
		Rocky's wages (imputed)[a]	40,000
Depreciation[b]	22,000	Economic depreciation[c]	10,000
Bank interest	12,000	Bank interest	12,000
		Interest on Rocky's money invested in firm (imputed)[d]	11,500
Total costs	$254,000	Total costs	$293,500
Profit	$46,000	Profit	$6,500

Notes

(a) Rocky worked 1,000 hours on the firm's business. He could have worked elsewhere for $40 per hour, which means that the opportunity cost of his time was $40,000.
(b) A percentage of the purchase price of the firm's assets determined by convention — in this example, 10 percent.
(c) Economic depreciation is the fall in the market value of the firm's assets. It is the opportunity cost of not selling the assets one year ago, and is part of the opportunity cost of using them for the year.
(d) Rocky has invested $115,000 in the firm. If the current rate of interest is 10 percent per year, the opportunity cost of those funds is $11,500.

other cases, they have bought them. A firm always has the option of selling its patents, trademarks, or name to other firms.

In calculating historical cost, these items are ignored unless the firm actually bought them. But they have an opportunity cost regardless of whether or not they were bought. The opportunity cost of a firm's patents, trademarks, or name used in this year's production is the change in their market value — the change in the best price for which they could be sold. If their value falls over the year, there is an additional opportunity cost of production. If their value rises, there is a negative opportunity cost, or a reduction in the opportunity cost of production.

The Bottom Line

What does all this add up to? Is the historical measure of cost higher or lower than the opportunity cost measure? And what about the bottom line — the profit or loss of the firm. Does the accountant come up with the same answer as the economist or is there a difference in the measurement of profit as well?

Profit is the difference between total revenue and total cost. There is no difference in the accountant's measure and the economist's measure of a firm's receipts or total revenue. However, the two measures of cost generally differ. Opportunity cost generally includes more things than historical cost, so the historical measure of cost understates the opportunity cost of production. Thus profit, as measured by economists, is generally lower than profit as measured by accountants.

To see how this works out, let's look at an example. Rocky owns a shop that sells mountain bikes. His total revenue, total costs, and profit appear in Table 9.4, with the historical view on the left-hand side and the economic view on the right-hand side.

Rocky sold $300,000 worth of bikes during the year. This amount appears as his total revenue. The wholesale cost of bikes was $150,000, he bought $20,000 worth of utilities and other services, and he paid out $50,000 in wages to his mechanic and sales clerk. Rocky also paid $12,000 in interest to the bank. All of the items just mentioned appear in both the accountant's and the economist's statement. The remaining items differ between the two statements; some notes at the foot of the table explain the differences. The only additional cost taken into account by the accountant is depreciation, which the accountant calculates as a fixed percentage of Rocky's assets. The economist imputes a cost to Rocky's time and money invested in the firm and also calculates economic depreciation. The historical cost method puts Rocky's cost at $254,000 and his profit at $46,000. In contrast, the opportunity cost of Rocky's year in business was $293,500 and his economic profit was $6,500.

REVIEW

A firm's economic profit is the difference between its total revenue and its opportunity cost of production. Opportunity cost differs from historical cost. Historical cost measures cost as the dollars spent to buy inputs. Opportunity cost measures cost as the value of the best alternative forgone. The most important differences between the two measures arise when assessing the cost of durable inputs and of inputs that the firm does not directly buy, such as the labour of the owner. ■

We are interested in measuring the opportunity cost of production not for its own sake but so that we can compare the efficiency of alternative methods of production. What do we mean by efficiency?

Economic Efficiency

Firms have to make decisions about *how* they will produce their output. There is almost always more than one way of making a product. For example, cars can be made on assembly lines that make extensive use of robots but use hardly any people. Cars can also be made with a larger number of workers and no robots. The first case uses more capital than the second but less labour.

How does a firm choose among alternative methods of production? What is the most efficient way of producing? There are two concepts of efficiency: technological efficiency and economic efficiency. **Technological efficiency** occurs when it is not possible to increase output without increasing inputs. Equivalently, if a firm is producing a given level of output, it cannot reduce its scale of input of one factor of production without increasing the scale of use of another factor of production. There are usually many different technologically efficient methods of production, some using a large amount of capital and a small amount of labour, and others using a large amount of labour and a small amount of capital. One of the technologically efficient methods of production will also be economically efficient. **Economic efficiency** occurs when the cost of producing a given output is as low as possible.

Technological efficiency is an engineering matter. Given what is technologically feasible, something can or cannot be done. Economic efficiency goes further than technological efficiency. It depends on the prices of inputs. Something that is technologically efficient may not be economically efficient. But something that is economically efficient is always technologically efficient.

Let's examine the differences and the connection between technological efficiency and economic efficiency by looking at an example.

Suppose that there are four ways of making TV sets:

- Method *a*: Robot assembly line. One person monitors the entire computer-driven assembly process.
- Method *b*: Human assembly line. Each person specializes in a small part of the job as the emerging TV set passes by.
- Method *c*: Human assembly line. Each person follows a TV set along the assembly line and performs

Table 9.5 Four Ways of Making 10 TV Sets a Day

		Quantities of inputs	
	Method	**Labour**	**Capital**
a	Robot assembly line	1	1,000
b	Human assembly line	10	10
c	Human assembly line	100	10
d	Hand-tooled assembly	1,000	1

Table 9.6 Costs of Four Ways of Making 10 TV Sets per Day

Method	Labour cost ($75 per day)		Capital cost ($250 per day)		Total cost	Cost per TV set
a	$75	+	$250,000	=	$250,075	$25,007.50
b	750	+	2,500	=	3,250	325.00
c	7,500	+	2,500	=	10,000	1,000.00
d	75,000	+	250	=	75,250	7,525.00

each and every task, using the appropriate piece of machinery as it is needed.

- Method *d*: Hand-tooled assembly. Each TV set is assembled completely by a single worker who uses just a few hand tools.

Table 9.5 sets out the amount of labour and capital required to make 10 TV sets a day by each of these four methods. Are all of these alternative methods technologically efficient? By inspecting the numbers in the table, you can see that method *c* is not technologically efficient. It requires 100 workers and 10 units of capital to produce 10 TV sets. Those same 10 TV sets can be produced by method *b* with the same 10 units of capital but only 10 workers. Therefore method *c* is not technologically efficient. It uses 90 more units of labour and the same 10 units of capital as does method *b* to produce 10 TV sets.

Are any of the other methods not technologically efficient? The answer is no: each of the other three methods is technologically efficient. Method *a* uses less labour and more capital than method *b*, and method *d* uses more labour and less capital than method *b*.

What about economic efficiency? Are all three methods economically efficient? To answer that question, we need to know the labour and capital costs. Let's suppose that labour costs $75 a person-day and that capital costs $250 a machine-day. Recall that economic efficiency occurs with the least expensive production process. Table 9.6 sets out the costs of using the four different methods of production. As you can see, the least expensive method of producing a TV set is *b*. Method *a* uses less labour but more capital. The combination of labour and capital used by method *a* winds up costing much more than that of method *b*. Method *d*, the other technologically efficient method, uses much more labour and hardly any capital. Like using method *a*, it costs far more to make a TV set using method *d* than method *b*.

Method *c* is technologically inefficient. It uses the same amount of capital as *b* but 10 times as much labour. It is interesting to notice that although *c* is technologically inefficient, it costs less to produce a TV set using method *c* than it does using methods *a* or *d*. But method *b* dominates method *c*. Because method c is not technologically efficient, there is always

Table 9.7 Costs of Three Ways of Making 10 TV Sets: High Labour Costs

Method	Labour cost ($150 per day)		Capital cost ($1 per day)		Total cost	Cost per TV set
a	$150	+	$1,000	=	$1,150	$115.00
b	1,500	+	10	=	1,510	151.00
d	150,000	+	1	=	150,001	15,000.10

Table 9.8 Costs of Three Ways of Making 10 TV Sets: High Capital Costs

Method	Labour cost ($1 per day)		Capital cost ($1000 per day)		Total cost	Cost per TV set
a	$1	+	$1,000,000	=	$1,000,001	$100,000.10
b	10	+	10,000	=	10,010	1,001.00
d	1,000	+	1,000	=	2,000	200.00

a lower cost method available. That is, a technologically inefficient method is never economically efficient.

Although *b* is the economically efficient method in this example, methods *a* or *d* could be economically efficient in other circumstances. Let's see when.

First, suppose that labour costs $150 a person-day and capital only $1 a machine-day. Table 9.7 now shows the costs of making a TV set. In this case, method *a* is economically efficient. Capital is now sufficiently cheap relative to labour so that the method using the most capital is the economically efficient method.

Now, suppose that labour costs only $1 a day while capital costs $1,000 a day. Table 9.8 shows the costs in this case. As you can see, method *d*, which uses a lot of labour and little capital, is now the economically efficient method.

A firm that does not use the economically efficient method of production makes a smaller profit. Natural selection favours firms that choose the economically efficient method of production and goes against firms that do not. In extreme cases, an inefficient firm may go bankrupt or be taken over by another firm that can see the possibilities for lower cost and greater profit. Efficient firms will be stronger and better able to survive temporary adversity than inefficient ones.

Firms and Markets

At the beginning of this chapter, we defined a firm as an institution that buys or hires factors of production and organizes these resources to produce and sell goods and services. In organizing production, firms coordinate the economic activities of many individuals. But a firm is not the only institution that coordinates economic activity. Coordination can also be achieved by using the market. In Chapter 1, we defined the market as a mechanism for coordinating people's buying and selling plans. By buying inputs and services in many individual markets, each one of us can organize the production of the goods and services that we consume. Consider, for example, two ways in which you might get your creaking car fixed.

- *Firm coordination*: You take the car to the garage. The garage owner coordinates the parts and tools as well as the automechanic's time, and your car gets fixed. You pay one bill for the entire job.
- *Market coordination*: You hire an automechanic who diagnoses the problems and makes a list of the parts and tools needed to fix them. You buy the parts from the local wrecker's yard and rent the tools from ABC Rentals. You hire the automechanic again to fix the problems. You return the tools and pay your bills — wages to the automechanic, rental to ABC, and the wrecker for the parts used.

What determines the method that you use? The answer is cost. Taking account of the opportunity cost of your own time as well as the costs of the other inputs that you'd have to buy, you will use the method that costs least. In other words, you will use the economically efficient method.

Firms coordinate economic activity when they can perform a task more efficiently than markets. In such a situation, it will pay someone to set up a firm. If markets can perform a task more efficiently than a firm, people will use markets and any attempt to set up a firm to replace such market coordination will be doomed to failure.

Why Firms?

There are three key reasons why, in many instances, firms are more efficient than markets as coordinators of economic activity. Firms achieve

- Lower transactions costs.
- Economies of scale.
- Economies of team production.

Transactions Costs The idea that firms exist because there are activities in which they are more efficient than markets was first suggested by Ronald Coase of the University of Chicago.[2] Coase focused on the firm's ability to reduce or eliminate transactions costs. **Transactions costs** are the costs arising from finding someone with whom to do business, of reaching an agreement about the price and other aspects of the exchange, and of ensuring that the terms of the agreement are fulfilled. Market transactions require buyers and sellers to get together and negotiate the terms and conditions of their trading. Sometimes lawyers have to be hired to draw up contracts. A broken contract leads to still more expenses. A firm can lower such transactions costs by reducing the number of individual transactions undertaken.

Consider, for example, the two ways of getting your car fixed that we've just described. The first method requires that you undertake only one transaction with one firm. It's true that the firm has to undertake several transactions — hiring the labour and buying the parts and tools required to do the job. But the firm doesn't have to undertake those transactions simply to fix your car. One set of such transactions enables the firm to fix hundreds of cars. Thus there is an enormous reduction in the number of individual transactions that take place if people get their cars fixed at the garage rather than going through the elaborate sequence of market transactions that we described above.

Economies of Scale When the cost of producing a unit of a good falls as its output rate increases, **economies of scale** exist. Many industries experience economies of scale — automobile and television manufacturing are two examples. Economies of scale can only be reaped by a large organization; thus they give rise to firm coordination rather than market coordination.

Team Production A production process in which each of a group of individuals specializes in mutually supportive tasks is **team production**. Sports provide the best examples of team activity. Some team members specialize in pitching and some in batting, some in defence and some in offence. The production of goods and services also offers many examples of team activity. For example, production lines in automobile and TV manufacturing plants work most efficiently when individuals work in teams, each specializing in a small task. You can also think of an entire firm as being a team. The team has buyers of raw material and other inputs, production workers, and salespersons. There are even subspecialists within these various groups. Each individual member of the team specializes, but the value of the output of the team and the profit that it earns depend on the coordinated activities of all the team's members.

The idea that firms arise as a consequence of the economies of team production was first suggested by Armen Alchian and Harold Demsetz of the University of California at Los Angeles.[3]

Because firms can economize on transactions costs, reap economies of scale, and organize efficient team production, it is firms rather than markets that coordinate most of our economic activity. There are, however, limits to the economic efficiency of firms. If firms become too big or too diversified in the things that they seek to do, the cost of management and monitoring per unit of output begins to rise, and at some point, the market becomes more efficient at coordinating the use of resources.

■ In the next two chapters, we are going to study the choices of firms. We will study their production decisions, how they minimize costs, and how they choose the amounts of the various inputs to employ.

[2]Ronald H. Coase, "The Nature of the Firm," *Economica* (November 1937): 386-405.

[3]Armen Alchian and Harold Demsetz, "Production, Information Costs, and Economic Organization," *American Economic Review* 57, 5 (December 1972): 777-95.

SUMMARY

The Firm's Economic Problem

A firm is an institution that organizes the production of goods and services. Firms and markets are alternative mechanisms for coordinating economic activity. All firms have to make certain decisions: what to produce and in what quantities; the techniques of production to use; the quantities of each factor of production to employ; their organization and management structure; and the arrangements for compensating the factors of production.

There are three main forms of business organization: sole proprietorship, partnership, and corporation. Each has its advantages and disadvantages. Sole proprietorships are easy to set up and face lower taxes than corporations, but they are risky and face higher costs of capital and labour. Partnerships can draw on diversified expertise, but they can also involve decision conflicts. Corporations have limited liability so they can obtain large-scale capital at relatively low cost. They can hire professional management. But complex management structures can slow down decisions. Corporations pay taxes on profits, and their shareholders pay taxes on dividends. Sole proprietorships are the most common form of business organization, but corporations account for most of the economy's production. (pp. 209-212)

Business Finance

Firms raise money to finance their purchases of capital — plant and equipment, and buildings — by selling bonds and issuing stock. When a firm issues bonds, it makes a promise to its bondholders of a fixed payment that is not dependent on the profitability of the firm's activities. As a consequence bondholders receive a guaranteed annual interest income. They face less risk than shareholders from fluctuating profits and face less risk from bankruptcy than do shareholders. When a firm issues stock, it is offering people an opportunity to become part owners of the firm. That is, the shareholders of a firm are its owners. The holders of common stock vote at meetings and elect directors. Their liability is limited. That is, they cannot be held personally liable for the debts of the firm and their liability is limited to the value of their initial purchase of shares. Common stock holders do not receive a dividend unless it is voted by the directors.

In deciding whether to raise money by issuing bonds, firms calculate the present value of the payments that they will obligate themselves to make to the bondholder and compare that present value with that of some alternative method of financing. The value of a firm's stock is determined on the stock market by the present value of the expected future stream of dividends that the firm will pay from its profits. The value of a firm's stock is *not* determined by its *current profit*, although, to the extent that current profit is an indicator of future profit, it is a relevant factor. For this reason, the price-earnings ratio of firms vary considerably. (pp. 212-218)

Cost and Profit

Business profit is calculated as the difference between total revenue and total cost. Accountants and economists measure cost in different ways. Accountants measure historical cost, while economists measure opportunity cost. Opportunity cost usually exceeds historical cost because it includes imputed costs not counted as part of historical cost. The different measures of cost lead to different measures of profit. Economic profit equals total revenue minus opportunity cost. (pp. 218-222)

Economic Efficiency

There are two concepts of efficiency: technological efficiency and economic efficiency. A method of production is technologically efficient when to produce a given output, it is not possible to use less of one factor of production without at the same time using more of another. A method of production is economically efficient when the cost of producing a given output is as low as possible. Economic efficiency requires technological efficiency. Economic efficiency also takes into account the relative prices of inputs. Economically efficient firms have a better chance of surviving than do inefficient ones. (pp. 222-224)

Firms and Markets

Firms coordinate economic activities when they are able to achieve lower costs than coordination through markets does. Firms are able to economize on transactions costs and to achieve the benefits of economies of scale and of team production. (pp. 224-225)

KEY ELEMENTS

Key Terms

Bond, 213
Common stock, 216
Convertible stock, 217
Cooperative, 211
Corporation, 210
Coupon payment, 213
Crown corporation, 211
Depreciation, 219
Discounting, 214
Durable inputs, 218
Economic depreciation, 219
Economic efficiency, 222
Economies of scale, 225
Equity or equity capital, 212
Firm, 209
Historical cost, 218
Implicit rental rate, 220
Imputed cost, 220
Inventories, 220
Joint unlimited liability, 210
Limited liability, 210
Loss, 209
Maturity structure, 216
Net present value, 216
Not-for-profit firm, 211
Partnership, 210
Preferred stock, 216
Present value, 214
Price-earnings ratio, 217
Profit, 209
Redemption date, 213
Redemption value, 213
Residual claimant, 210
Share, 210
Sole proprietorship, 210
Stock exchange, 217
Sunk cost, 219
Team production, 225
Technological efficiency, 222
Total cost, 209
Transactions costs, 225
Unlimited liability, 210

Key Tables 

Table 9.1 Pros and Cons of Different Firm Types, 211
Table 9.4 Rocky's Mountain Bikes' Revenue, Cost, and Profit Statement, 221
Table 9.6 Costs of Four Ways of Making 10 TV Sets per Day, 223

REVIEW QUESTIONS

1 What is a firm?

2 What are the economic problems that all firms face? List the main forms of business organization and the advantages and disadvantages of each.

3 What are the main ways in which firms can raise money?

4 What is a bond?

5 What is a share?

6 What do we mean by net present value?

7 What determines the value of a bond?

8 What determines the value of a share?

9 Distinguish between historical cost and opportunity cost. What are the main items of opportunity cost that don't get counted as part of historical cost?

10 Define economic efficiency.

11 Distinguish between economic efficiency and technological efficiency.

12 Why do firms, rather than markets, coordinate such a large amount of economic activity?

PROBLEMS

1 Soap Bubbles, Inc. has a bank loan of $1 million on which it is paying an interest rate of 10 percent a year. The firm's financial adviser suggests paying off the loan by selling bonds. To raise $1 million, Soap Bubbles will have to offer bonds with a redemption value two years in the future of $1,050,000 and with a coupon payment of 9 percent.

a) Does it pay Soap Bubbles to sell the bonds to repay the bank loan?

b) What is the present value of the profit or loss that would result from repaying the bank loan and selling the bonds?

2 One year ago, Jack and Jill set up a vinegar bottling firm called JJVB.

- Jack and Jill put $50,000 of their own money into the firm.
- They bought equipment for $30,000 and an inventory of bottles and vinegar for $15,000.
- They hired one employee to help them for an annual wage of $20,000.
- The sales of JJVB for the year were $100,000.
- Jack gave up his previous job, at which he earned $30,000, and spent all his time working for JJVB.
- Jill kept her old job, which pays $30 an hour, but gave up 10 hours of leisure each week (for 50 weeks) to work for JJVB.
- The cash expenses of JJVB were $10,000 for the year.
- The inventory at the end of the year was worth $20,000.
- The market value of the equipment at the end of the year was $28,000.
- The accountant for JJVB depreciated the equipment by 20 percent a year.

a) Construct JJVB's profit and loss account as recorded by its accountant.

b) Construct JJVB's profit and loss account based on opportunity cost rather than historical cost concepts.

3 You can use three methods for doing your tax return: a personal computer, a pocket calculator, or a pencil and paper. With a PC, you complete the job in an hour; with a pocket calculator, it takes 12 hours; and with a pencil and paper, it takes two days. The PC and its software cost $1,000, the pocket calculator costs $10, and the pencil and paper cost $1.

a) Which, if any, of the above methods are technologically efficient?

b) Suppose your wage rate is $5 an hour. Which of the above methods is economically efficient?

c) Suppose your wage rate is $50 an hour. Which of the above methods is economically efficient?

d) Suppose your wage rate is $500 an hour. Which of the above methods is economically efficient?

CHAPTER 10

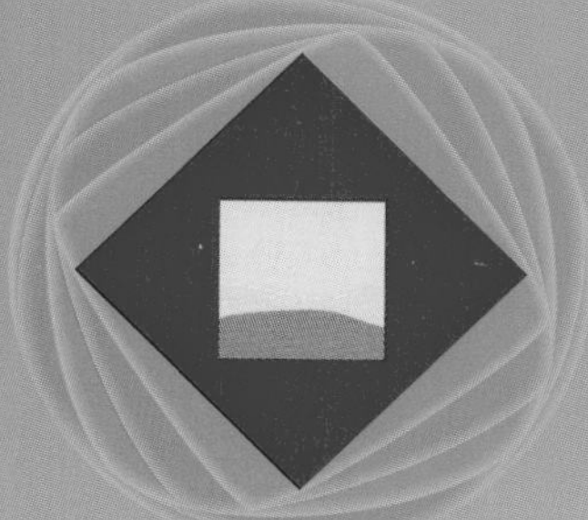

Output and Costs

After studying this chapter, you will be able to:

- Explain the objective of a firm.
- Explain what limits a firm's profitability.
- Explain the relationship between a firm's output and its costs.
- Derive a firm's short-run cost curves.
- Explain how cost changes when a firm's plant size changes.
- Explain long-run cost and derive a firm's long-run average cost curve.
- Explain why some firms operate with excess capacity and others overutilize their plants.

Survival of the Fittest

SIZE DOES NOT GUARANTEE success in business. True, the Hudson's Bay Company has been around a long time and has grown pretty large. But most of the giants of 50 years ago don't even exist today. Remember Studebaker cars? Marconi radios? Both giants in their day, but now almost forgotten. ■ What were these businesses striving for? If it was for size alone, it didn't ensure their survival. What goals do their successors set for themselves today? How do they decide how to produce and what resources to use? Does a pharmaceutical firm arrive at these decisions in the same way as a chain of discount stores or the corner pizza parlour? Or do such businesses have nothing in common except the earning of profits? ■ Every firm tries to keep its costs under control. So you would think that firms would want to keep their production plants fully utilized more or less all the time. But most car makers in Canada can produce far more cars than they can sell. Why do car makers have expensive equipment lying around that isn't fully used? In other industries, such as electric power production, there isn't always enough production equipment on hand to meet demand. Firms often have to buy power from other producers. Why don't such firms have bigger production plants so that they can supply the market themselves?

■ We are going to answer these and similar questions in this chapter. To do so, we are going to study the economic decisions that all firms make about how much to produce and how to keep their costs as low as possible. Although many firms are giants, we will make better progress if we concentrate our attention on a small, imaginary firm — Swanky Inc., a producer of knitted sweaters. The firm is owned and operated by Sidney. By studying Swanky's economic problems and the way Sidney solves them, we will be able to get a clear view of the key problems that face all firms — small ones such as Swanky as well as the giants.

Firms' Objectives and Constraints

To understand and predict the behaviour of firms, we will start by describing a firm's objectives — what it is trying to achieve.

The Objective: Profit Maximization

The firm that we will study has a single objective: profit maximization. **Profit maximization** means making the largest possible profit. As you know, the fundamental problem from which all economic activity springs is scarcity. Profit maximization is a direct consequence of scarcity. Seeking to make the best possible use of scarce resources is the same thing as trying to make the largest possible profit. A firm that does not try to maximize profit will not survive in a competitive environment. Firms have high birth and death rates. They also frequently get taken over. A firm that does not seek to maximize profits will either lose the competitive race to firms that do or be taken over by such a firm.

In studying Swanky, we will suppose that Sidney is constantly striving to make the largest possible profits. However, there are limits to, or constraints on, the profits that a firm can make. What are they?

Constraints

There are two types of constraints that limit the profits a firm can make: market constraints and technology constraints.

Market Constraints A firm's **market constraints** are the conditions under which it can buy its inputs and sell its output. On the output side, people have a limited demand for each good or service and will buy additional quantities only at lower prices. Firms have to recognize this constraint on how much they can sell. A small firm competing with many other firms in a large market has no choice but to sell its output at the same price as everyone else. It cannot, through its own actions, influence the market price. A large firm that dominates the market for a particular good can manipulate the price to its own advantage. But in so doing, it has to accept the fact that at higher prices it will sell lower quantities.

On the input side, people own limited amounts of factors of production, and they will supply additional quantities only at higher prices. Most firms, even large ones, compete with many other firms in the markets for factors of production and have no choice but to buy their inputs at the same prices as everyone else. Except in rare circumstances, firms cannot manipulate the market prices of their factors of production through their own actions.

We will study the output market constraints on firms more thoroughly in Chapters 12 through 14 and the input market constraints in Chapters 15 through 17. Swanky, the firm that we will study in this chapter, is small and cannot influence the prices at which it sells its sweaters or at which it buys the inputs used to make them.

Technology Constraints Firms use inputs to produce outputs. Any feasible way of converting inputs into output is called a **technique**. For example, one technique that Swanky can adopt to produce sweaters uses workers equipped with knitting needles. A second technique uses labour and hand-operated knitting machines. A third technique uses automated knitting machines that require a small amount of labour to set them in motion and to reset them for different sizes and styles of sweaters. A fourth technique uses robotic knitting machines controlled by computers that automatically adjust the size, type, and colour of the sweaters with human intervention only at the point of programming the computer. These different techniques use different amounts of labour and capital. But they are all capable of producing the same total output.

Some techniques are capital intensive and some are labour intensive. A **capital-intensive technique** uses a relatively large amount of capital and a relatively small amount of labour. A computer-controlled automated knitting machine is an example of a capital-intensive technique. A **labour-intensive technique** uses a relatively large amount of labour and a relatively small amount of capital. Knitting sweaters by hand — the only capital equipment used is knitting needles — is an example of a labour-intensive technique.

To maximize profit, a firm will choose a *technologically efficient* production method. Recall the definition of technological efficiency that you encountered in Chapter 9 — a state in which no more output can be produced without using more inputs. Technological efficiency does not necessarily require the use of up-to-date or sophisticated equipment. When knitters are working flat out, even if they are using only needles, sweaters are being produced in a technologically efficient way. To produce more sweaters will require more knitters. No resources are being wasted. Similarly, when a computerized automated knitting plant is operating flat out, sweaters are also being produced in a technologically efficient way.

A firm can do no better than to use an efficient technique. But it must determine which efficient technique to employ, for not all technologically efficient methods of production are economically efficient. Furthermore, the possibilities open to the firm will depend on the length of the planning period over which it is making its decisions. A firm that wants to change its output rate overnight has far fewer options than one that can plan ahead and change its output rate several months or even years in the future. In studying the way a firm's technology constrains its actions, we distinguish between two planning horizons — the short run and the long run.

The Short Run and the Long Run

The **short run** is a period of time in which the quantities of some inputs are fixed and others can be varied. The **long run** is a period of time in which the quantities of all inputs can be varied. Inputs whose quantity can be varied in the short run are called **variable inputs**. Inputs whose quantity cannot be varied in the short run are called **fixed inputs**.

There is no set amount of time that can be marked on the calendar to separate the short run from the long run. The distinction between the short run and long run varies from one industry to another. For example, if an electric power company decides that it needs a bigger production plant, it will take several years to implement its decision. The short run for an electric power company is several years in length because it cannot change its production plant in a shorter period. At the other extreme, a laundromat or a copying service has a short run of just a month or two. New premises can be acquired and new machines installed and made operational quickly.

Swanky has a fixed amount of capital equipment in the form of knitting machines, and to vary its output in the short run it has to vary the quantity of labour that it uses. For Swanky, labour is the variable input. The quantity of knitting machinery is fixed in the short run, so this equipment is Swanky's fixed input. In the long run, Swanky can vary the quantity of both knitting machines and labour employed.

Let's look a bit more closely at how Sidney makes his output decisions in the short run.

*The Short-Run Production Function

A firm's **short-run production function** describes how the maximum attainable output varies as the quantity of the variable input varies. Usually, and in the example that we'll study in this chapter, labour is the variable input and capital is the fixed input. In our example, Swanky can produce more sweaters with a given number of knitting machines if it employs more workers. The short-run production function for sweaters shows how the output rate of a fixed number of knitting machines varies as the number of workers varies. There are three ways of describing the short-run production function:

- Total product curve
- Marginal product curve
- Average product curve

Total, Marginal, and Average Product Curves

Swanky's short-run production function appears first in Fig. 10.1. The table shows us how the firm's total quantity produced — the number of sweaters that can be knitted in a day (output) — varies as the quantity of labour employed varies. As you can see, when employment is zero, no sweaters are knitted. As employment rises, so does the number of sweaters knitted. The total quantity produced is called **total product**.

Total product can be illustrated as a total product curve. The **total product curve** shows the maximum output available for each quantity of the variable input (usually the labour input). The total product curve for Swanky is graphed in Fig. 10.1 and labelled *TP*. Points *a* through *f* on the curve correspond to the same rows in the table. The total product curve separates the attainable output levels from the unattainable. All the points above the curve are unattainable. The points below the curve, in the orange area, are attainable, but they are inefficient.

---

*The reader who is anxious to move more quickly to a study of costs may omit this section and jump immediately to the section entitled "Short-run Cost."

Figure 10.1 Total Product

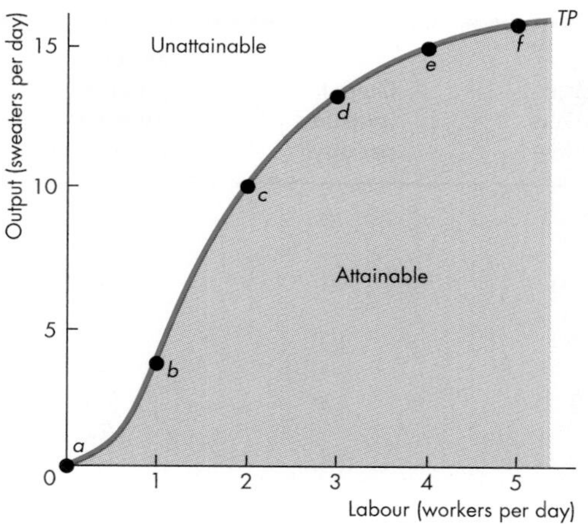

	Labour (workers per day)	Output (sweaters per day)
a	0	0
b	1	4
c	2	10
d	3	13
e	4	15
f	5	16

The numbers in the table show how, with one knitting machine, Swanky can vary the total output of sweaters by varying the amount of labour it employs. For example, 1 worker (row *b*) produces 4 sweaters per day; 2 workers (row *c*) produce 10 sweaters per day. The short-run production function is graphed here as the total product curve (*TP*). Points *a* through *f* on the curve correspond to the rows of the table. The total product curve separates the attainable output from the unattainable.

The **marginal product** of any input is the increase in total product resulting from an increase of one unit of that input. The **marginal product of labour** is the change in total product resulting from a one-unit increase in the quantity of labour employed, holding the quantity of capital constant. In Swanky's case, the marginal product of labour is the additional number of sweaters knitted each day that results from hiring one additional worker. The magnitude of that marginal product depends on how many workers Swanky is employing. Swanky's marginal product of labour is calculated in the table in Fig. 10.2. The first two columns of the table are the same as the table in Fig. 10.1. The last column shows the calculation of marginal product. For example, when the quantity of labour rises from 1 to 2 workers, total product rises from 4 to 10 sweaters. The change in total product — 6 sweaters — is the marginal product of the second worker.

Swanky's marginal product of labour is illustrated in the two parts of Fig. 10.2. Part (a) reproduces the total product curve that you saw in Fig. 10.1. Part (b) shows the marginal product curve, labelled *MP*. In part (a), the marginal product of labour is illustrated by the bars. The height of each bar measures marginal product. Marginal product is also measured by the slope of the total product curve in part (a). Recall that the slope of a curve is the change in the variable measured on the *y*-axis — output — divided by the change in the variable measured on the *x*-axis — labour input — as we move along the curve. A 1-unit rise in labour input, from 1 to 2 workers, increases output from 4 to 10 sweaters, so the slope from point *b* to point *c* is 6, exactly the same as the marginal product that we've just calculated.

Notice the relationship between the total and marginal product curves. The steeper the slope of the total product curve, the higher is the level of the marginal product curve. The total product curve in Fig. 10.2(a) shows that a rise in employment from 1 to 2 workers raises output from 4 to 10 sweaters (an increase of 6). The increase in output of 6 sweaters appears on the vertical axis of Fig 10.2(b) as the marginal product of the second worker. We plot that marginal product at the midpoint between 1 and 2 workers per day. Notice that marginal product shown in Fig. 10.2(b) reaches a peak at 1 unit of labour and at that point marginal product is more than 6. The peak occurs at 1 unit of labour because the total product curve is steepest at 1 unit of labour.

Average product is total product per unit of variable input. In Swanky's case, average product is the total number of sweaters produced each day divided by the number of workers employed. Swanky's average product is calculated in the table in Fig. 10.3. For example, 3 workers can knit 13 sweaters a day, so the average product is 13 divided by 3, which is 4.33 sweaters per worker.

Average product is illustrated in the two parts of Fig. 10.3. In part (a), average product can be measured as the slope of a line from the origin to a point on the total product curve. For example, at point *d* 3 workers knit 13 sweaters. The slope of the line from the origin to point *d* is equal to the output —

Figure 10.2 Total Product and Marginal Product

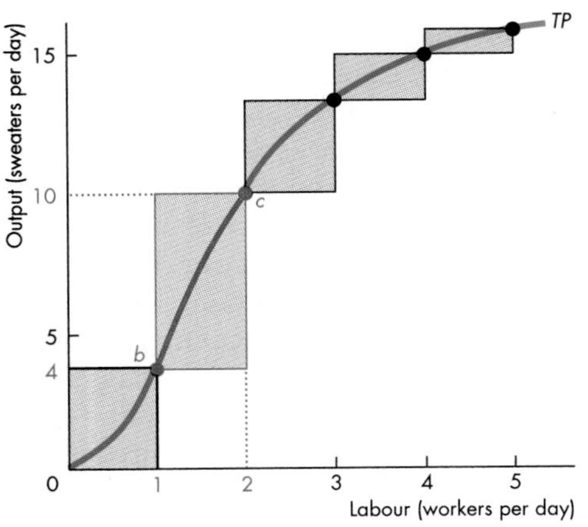

(a) Total product

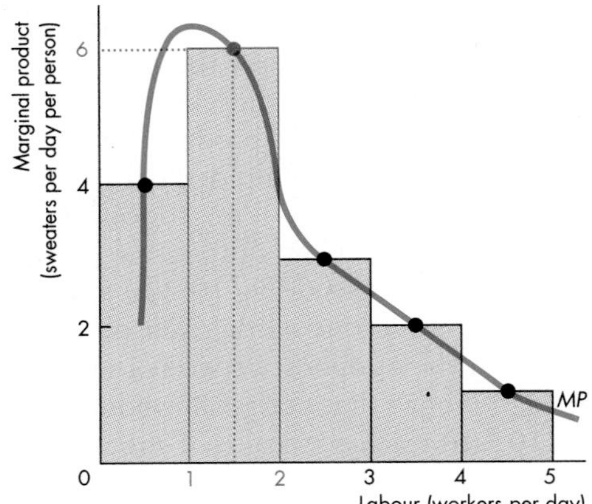

(b) Marginal product

	Labour (workers per day)	Output (sweaters per day)	Marginal product (sweaters per worker)
a	0	0	
			4
b	1	4	
			6
c	2	10	
			3
d	3	13	
			2
e	4	15	
			1
f	5	16	

The table calculates marginal product as the change in total product resulting from a one-unit increase in labour input. For example, when labour increases from 1 to 2 workers (row *b* to row *c*), total product increases from 4 to 10 sweaters per day, an increase of 3. Marginal product is 6 sweaters. (Marginal product is shown midway between the rows to emphasize that it is the result of *changing* inputs — moving from one row to the next.)

Marginal product is illustrated in both parts of the figure by the orange bars. The height of the bars indicates the size of the marginal product. For example, when labour increases from 1 to 2, marginal product is the highlighted orange bar whose height is 6 sweaters (visible in each part of the figure). The steeper the slope of the total product curve (*TP*) in part (a), the higher is marginal product (*MP*), in part (b). Marginal product rises to a maximum (when 1 worker is employed in this example) and then declines — diminishing marginal product.

13 sweaters — divided by the quantity of labour used — 3 workers. The result is an average product for 3 workers of 4.33 sweaters a day. You can use this method of calculating average product to check that point *c* is the point of maximum average product. The steepest line from the origin to a point on the total product curve touches it only at *c*. Place a ruler on the curve and check that. Since the slope of such a line measures average product and this line is steepest when 2 workers are employed, average product is at a maximum at that point.

Figure 10.3 (b) graphs the average product curve (*AP*) and also shows the relationship between average product and marginal product. Points *b* through *f* on the average product curve correspond to those same rows in the table. Average product rises from 1 to 2 workers (its maximum value at point *c*) but then falls as yet more workers are employed. Notice also that the highest average product occurs when average and marginal product are equal to each other. That is, the marginal product curve cuts the average product curve at the point of maximum

Figure 10.3 Total, Marginal, and Average Product

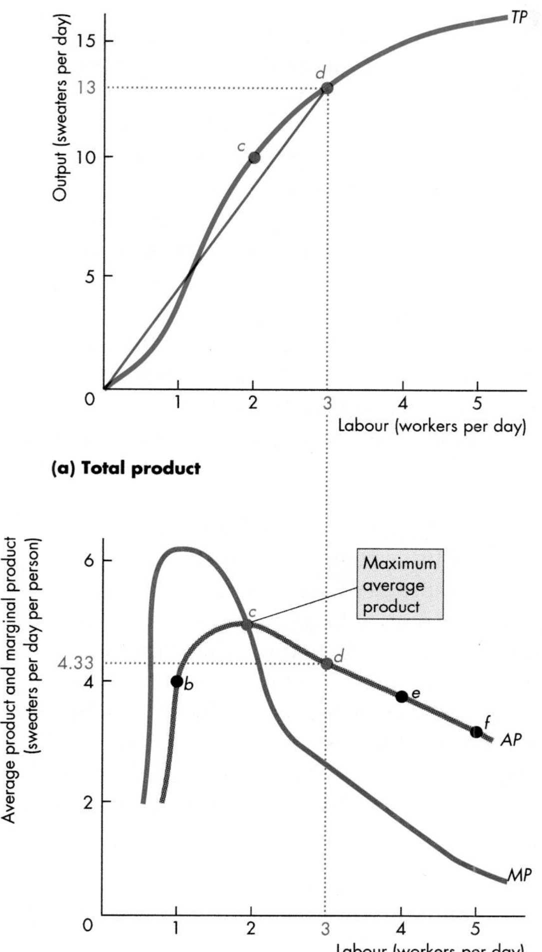

(a) Total product

(b) Marginal and average product

	Labour (workers per day)	Output (sweaters per day)	Average product (sweaters per day)
b	1	4	4.00
c	2	10	5.00
d	3	13	4.33
e	4	15	3.75
f	5	16	3.20

Average product — total product per unit of labour — is calculated in the table by dividing total product by the quantity of labour employed. For example, 3 workers produce 13 sweaters per day, so the average product of three workers is 4.33 sweaters per day. The two parts of the figure show two ways of representing average product on a graph. In part (a), average product is measured as the slope of a straight line from the origin to a point on the total product curve. The straight line to point *d* is such a line. The slope of that line is 4.33 (13 sweaters per day divided by 3 workers). Part (b) graphs average product. Points *b* through *f* on the average product curve (*AP*) correspond to the rows of the table.

Part (b) also shows the connection between the average product and marginal product curves. When marginal product exceeds average product, average product is rising, and when marginal product is less than average product, average product is falling. Average product and marginal product are equal at the maximum average product. Part (b) shows that marginal product increases from 0 to 1 worker and decreases thereafter and that average product increases from 0 to 2 workers and decreases thereafter.

average product. When marginal product exceeds average product, average product is rising. When marginal product is less than average product, average product is falling.

Why does Swanky care about diminishing marginal and average product? Because they have an important influence on the costs of producing sweaters and the way those costs vary as the production rate varies. We will examine these matters soon, but first we will take one more look at how marginal product and average product are related, for you will meet this type of relationship many times in your study of economics. You can also see it in your everyday life.

Relationship Between Marginal and Average Values We have seen, in Fig. 10.3, that when marginal product exceeds average product, average product is rising and when marginal product is less than average product, average product is falling. We have also seen that when marginal product equals average product, average product is neither rising nor falling — it is at its

Table 10.1 Average and Marginal Test Scores

Test	Test score	Aggregate score	Average score	Marginal score
Sidney				
1	55	55	55	
				65
2	65	120	60	
				75
3	75	195	65	
				85
4	85	280	70	
Steve				
1	85	85	85	
				75
2	75	160	80	
				65
3	65	225	75	
				55
4	55	280	70	
Sam				
1	70	70	70	
				70
2	70	140	70	
				70
3	70	210	70	
				70
4	70	280	70	

On the second test, Sidney scores 65 percent. After the first two tests, he has an average score of 60 percent. On the third test, Sidney scores 75 percent. His marginal score is the change in his aggregate score as the result of doing one more test. The marginal score after three tests is 75 percent (this score is located midway between the scores for the second and third tests to emphasize that it is associated with doing one more test). His marginal score now exceeds his previous average (60), so his average after three tests is higher (65 percent). Steve's marginal score is less than his average score, so his average falls. Sam's marginal score equals his average score, so his average remains constant.

peak, and it is constant. These relationships between average and marginal product are a general feature of the relationship between the average and marginal values of any variable. Let's look at a familiar example.

Sidney (the owner of Swanky) attends an introductory economics class with his friends Steve and Sam. During the first term, they each received a grade of 70 percent in the course, but the three achieved their marks in different ways. Table 10.1 illustrates how. They took four tests, each worth a quarter of the final mark. Sidney, preoccupied with managing Swanky, started out disastrously with 55 percent but then steadily improved. Steve started out brilliantly but then nose-dived, while Sam scored 70 percent on every test.

We can calculate the average and the marginal scores of these three students. The average score is simply the total marks obtained divided by the number of tests written. After two tests, Sidney has an aggregate score of 55 percent plus 65 percent, which is 120 percent, so his average score is 60 percent. A student's marginal score is the score on the last test written. After two tests, Sidney's marginal score is 65 percent.

Over the four tests, Sidney's marginal score rises, Steve's falls, and Sam's is constant. But notice what the average scores are doing. For Sidney, the average is rising. His marginal score is higher than his average score, so his average rises. For Steve, the marginal score falls. So too does his average. Steve's marginal score is always below his average score and pulls his average down. Sam's marginal score equals his average score, so his average stays constant.

These examples of an everyday relationship between marginal and average values agree with the relationship between marginal and average product that we have just discovered. Average product rises when marginal product exceeds average product (Sidney). Average product falls when marginal product is below average product (Steve). Average product is at a maximum and constant (it neither rises nor falls) when marginal product equals average product (Sam).

The Shape of the Short-Run Production Function

Now let's get back to studying production. The short-run production function, as described by the total, marginal, and average product curves, is different for different firms and different types of goods. Laura Secord's production function differs from that of Jim's burger stand, which, in turn, differs from that of Sidney's sweater factory. But the shape of their product curves is similar, because almost every production process incorporates two features:

- Increasing marginal returns initially
- Diminishing marginal returns eventually

Increasing Marginal Returns When the marginal product of an additional worker exceeds the marginal product of the previous worker, **increasing marginal**

returns occur. If Sidney hires just one worker at Swanky, that person has to learn all the different aspects of sweater production. Running the knitting machines, fixing breakdowns, packaging and mailing sweaters, buying and checking the type and colour of the wool: all these tasks have to be done by that one person. If Sidney hires a second person, each worker can specialize in different parts of the production process. As a result, two workers produce more than twice as much as one. This is the range over which marginal returns are increasing.

Diminishing Marginal Returns When the marginal product of an additional worker falls short of the marginal product of the previous worker, **diminishing marginal returns** occur. If Sidney hires a third worker, output increases but not by as much as it did when he added the second worker. With a third worker, the factory produces more sweaters, but the equipment is being operated closer to its limits. Furthermore, there are times when the third worker has nothing to do because the plant is running without the need for further attention. Adding yet more and more workers continues to increase output but by successively smaller amounts. This is the range over which marginal returns are diminishing. This phenomenon is such a pervasive one that it is called "the law of diminishing returns." The **law of diminishing returns** states:

As a firm uses more of a variable input, with the quantity of fixed inputs held constant, its marginal product eventually diminishes.

Because marginal product eventually diminishes, so does average product. Recall that average product falls when marginal product is below average product. If marginal product is falling, it must eventually fall below average product, and when it does so, average product begins to decline.

R E V I E W

The short-run production function shows how the output rate of a given plant varies as the quantity of labour input is varied. Three curves — total product, marginal product, and average product — describe the short-run production function. If the total labour input is small, average and marginal product rise as the quantity of labour input increases. If the total labour input is larger, average and marginal product fall as the quantity of labour input increases. Average product rises when marginal product exceeds average product. Average product falls when marginal product is less than average product. Marginal product and average product are equal at the point at which average product is a maximum. ■

Short-Run Cost

We have seen how a firm's output can be varied in the short run by varying its labour inputs. Let's now examine how a firm's costs vary as it varies its output. Swanky cannot influence the prices of its inputs; it has to pay the market price for them. Given the prices of its inputs, Swanky's lowest attainable cost of production for each output level is determined by its short-run production function. Let's see how.

Total, Marginal, and Average Cost

Total cost is the sum of the costs of all the inputs used in production. Total cost is divided into two categories: total fixed cost and total variable cost. A **fixed cost** is a cost that is independent of the output level. A **variable cost** is a cost that varies with the output level. **Total fixed cost** is the cost of the fixed inputs. **Total variable cost** is the cost of the variable inputs. We call total cost *TC*, total fixed cost *TFC*, and total variable cost *TVC*.

Swanky's total cost and its division into total fixed cost and total variable cost appears in the table of Fig. 10.4. The first two columns show the short-run production function from Fig. 10.1. Swanky has fixed inputs in the form of knitting machines and factory space. Let's suppose that the cost of these fixed inputs — total fixed cost — is $25 a day. Furthermore, let's suppose that a worker costs $25 a day (the wage rate). Total variable cost rises as the quantity of labour rises. For example, when Swanky employs 3 workers, total variable cost is $75 (3 × $25). Total cost is the sum of total fixed cost and total variable cost. For example, when Swanky employs 3 workers, total variable cost is $75, total fixed cost is $25, and total cost is $100.

Marginal cost is the increase in total cost resulting from a unit increase in output. To calculate marginal cost, we find the change in total cost and divide

Figure 10.4 Short-Run Costs

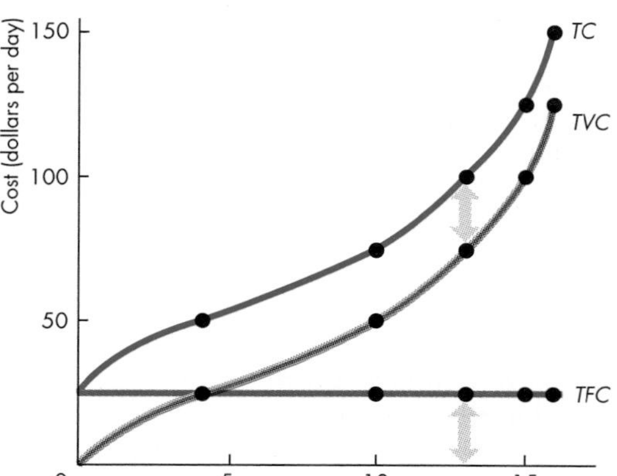

(a) Total costs

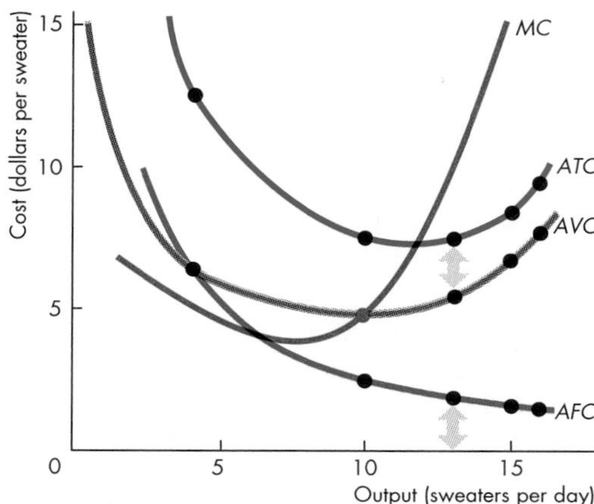

(b) Marginal and average costs

Labour (workers per day)	Output (sweaters per day)	Total fixed cost (*TFC*)	Total variable cost (*TVC*)	total cost (*TC*)	Marginal cost (MC) (change in dollars) per unit change in output	Average fixed cost (*AFC*)	Average variable cost (*AVC*)	Average total cost (ATC)
		(dollars per day)				(dollars per sweater)		
0	0	25	0	25		—	—	—
					6.25			
1	4	25	25	50		6.25	6.25	12.50
					4.17			
2	10	25	50	75		2.50	5.00	7.50
					8.33			
3	13	25	75	100		1.92	5.77	7.69
					12.50			
4	15	25	100	125		1.67	6.67	8.33
					25.00			
5	16	25	125	150		1.56	7.81	9.38

Short-run costs are calculated in the table and illustrated in the graphs. At each level of employment and output in the table, total variable cost (*TVC*) is added to total fixed cost (*TFC*) to give total cost (*TC*). The change in total cost per unit change in output gives marginal cost (*MC*). Average costs are calculated by dividing the total costs by output.

The firm's total cost curves are shown in part (a). Total cost (*TC*) increases as output increases. Total fixed cost (*TFC*) is constant — it graphs as a horizontal line — and total variable cost (*TVC*) increases in a similar way to total cost. The vertical distance between the (*TC*) and (*TVC*) curves equals total fixed cost (*TFC*) as illustrated by the arrows.

The average and marginal cost curves are shown in part (b). Average fixed cost (*AFC*) falls as the constant total fixed cost is divided by ever higher output levels. The curves showing average total cost (*ATC*) and average variable cost (*AVC*) are U-shaped. The vertical distance between them is equal to average fixed cost, which becomes smaller as output increases. The marginal cost curve (*MC*) is also U-shaped. It cuts the average variable cost curve and the average total cost curve at their minimum points.

it by the change in output. For example, when output (total product) increases from 4 to 10 sweaters, total cost rises from \$50 to \$75. The change in output is 6 sweaters, and the change in total cost is \$25. The marginal cost of one of those 6 sweaters is \$4.17 (\$25 ÷ 6).

Average cost is the cost per unit of output. There are three average costs:

- Average fixed cost
- Average variable cost
- Average total cost

Average fixed cost is total fixed cost per unit of output. **Average variable cost** is total variable cost per unit of output. **Average total cost** is total cost per unit of output. Average fixed cost plus average variable cost equals average total cost. For example, in the table of Fig. 10.4 when the output is 10 sweaters a day, average fixed cost is \$2.50 (\$25 ÷ 10), average variable cost is \$5.00 (\$50 ÷ 10), and average total cost is \$7.50 (\$75 ÷ 10, or, equivalently, average fixed cost plus average variable cost, \$2.50 + \$5.00).

Short-Run Cost Curves

We can illustrate Swanky's short-run costs as the short-run cost curves in Fig. 10.4(a). Swanky's total fixed cost of \$25 appears as the horizontal curve labelled *TFC*. Total variable cost and total cost both increase with output. They are graphed as the total variable cost curve (*TVC*) and the total cost curves (*TC*). The vertical distance between those two curves is equal to total fixed cost — as indicated by the arrows.

There is a close relationship between the total variable cost curve in Fig. 10.4(a) and the total product curve of Fig. 10.1. They both slope upward. But the more gently sloped the total product curve, the more steeply sloped is the total variable cost curve. The more gently sloped the total product curve, the slower output rises with a given increase in labour input. But cost and labour input changes are proportional, so the more gently sloped the total product curve, the faster total variable cost rises for a given rise in output and the more steeply sloped is the total variable cost curve.

The average cost curves appear in Fig. 10.4(b). The average fixed cost curve (*AFC*) slopes downward. As output rises, the same constant fixed cost is spread over a larger output: when Swanky produces only 4 sweaters, average fixed cost is \$6.25; when it produces 16 sweaters, average fixed cost is \$1.56.

The average total cost curve (*ATC*) and the average variable cost curve (*AVC*) are U-shaped curves. The vertical distance between the average total cost and average variable cost curves is equal to average fixed cost — as indicated by the arrows. That distance shrinks as output rises, since average fixed cost falls with rising output.

Figure 10.4(b) also illustrates the marginal cost curve, which is labelled *MC*. This curve is also U-shaped. It cuts both the average variable cost curve and the average total cost curve at their minimum points. That is, when marginal cost is less than average cost, average cost is falling, and when marginal cost exceeds average cost, average cost is rising. This relationship holds for both the *ATC* and *AVC* curves. You may wonder why the marginal cost curve cuts both the average total cost curve and the average variable cost curve at their minimum points. It does so because the source of the change in total cost, from which we calculate marginal cost, is variable cost. For average variable cost to fall, marginal cost must be less than average variable cost, and for average variable cost to rise, marginal cost must exceed average variable cost. Similarly, for average total cost to fall, marginal cost must be less than average total cost, and for average total cost to rise, marginal cost must exceed average total cost. This is exactly the same relationship that we found when studying students' grades in Table 10.1.

There is an interesting and important connection between the average and marginal product curves, shown in Fig. 10.3(b), and the average and marginal cost curves, shown in Fig. 10.4(b). The relationship between the average and marginal cost curves is like the flip side of the relationship between the average and marginal product curves. Average variable cost is at a minimum at the same output at which average product is at a maximum (10 sweaters). The output range over which average variable cost is decreasing is the same as that over which average product is increasing. Similarly, the output range over which average variable cost is increasing is the same as that over which average product is decreasing.

The product and cost concepts that we have just studied are summarized in Table 10.2.

Real World Short-Run Costs

Swanky's costs are a lot like the costs of a real world firm. Let's confirm this fact by looking at the costs of a real firm, Ontario Hydro. Ontario Hydro is an

Table 10.2 A Compact Glossary on Product and Cost

Term	Symbol	Equation	Definition
Fixed input			An input whose quantity used cannot be varied in the short run
Variable input	L		An input (labour in our examples) whose quantity used can be varied in the short run
Total product	TP		Output produced
Marginal product	MP	$MP = \Delta TP \div \Delta L$	Change in total product resulting from a unit rise in variable input (equals change in total product divided by change in variable factor)
Average product	AP	$AP = TP \div L$	Total product per unit of variable input (equals total product divided by number of units of variable factor)
Point of maximum average product			Output rate above which average product diminishes
Point of maximum marginal product			Output rate above which marginal product diminishes
Fixed cost			Cost that is independent of the output level
Variable cost			Cost that varies with the output level
Total fixed cost	TFC		Cost of the fixed inputs (equals their number multiplied by their unit price)
Total variable cost	TVC		Cost of the variable inputs (equals their number multiplied by their unit price)
Total cost	TC	$TC = TFC + TVC$	Cost of all inputs (equals fixed costs plus variable costs)
Marginal cost	MC	$MC = \Delta TC \div \Delta TP$	Change in total cost resulting from a unit rise in total product (equals the change in total cost divided by the change in total product)
Average fixed cost	AFC	$AFC = TFC \div TP$	Total fixed cost per unit of output (equals total fixed cost divided by total product)
Average variable cost	AVC	$AVC = TVC \div TP$	Total variable cost per unit of output (equals total variable cost divided by total product)
Average total cost	ATC	$ATC = AFC + AVC$	Total cost per unit of output (equals average fixed cost plus average variable cost)

electric power producer serving the more than 9 million people who live in Ontario. If Ontario Hydro works its production plants to their physical limits, it can generate about 24,000 megawatt-hours of electric power.

Ontario Hydro's actual production is never that high. It fluctuates between 15,000 and 23,000 megawatt-hours, depending partly on the time of day, partly on the day of the week, and partly on the temperature. To vary its output in the short run, Hydro

Figure 10.5 Ontario Hydro Output and Cost

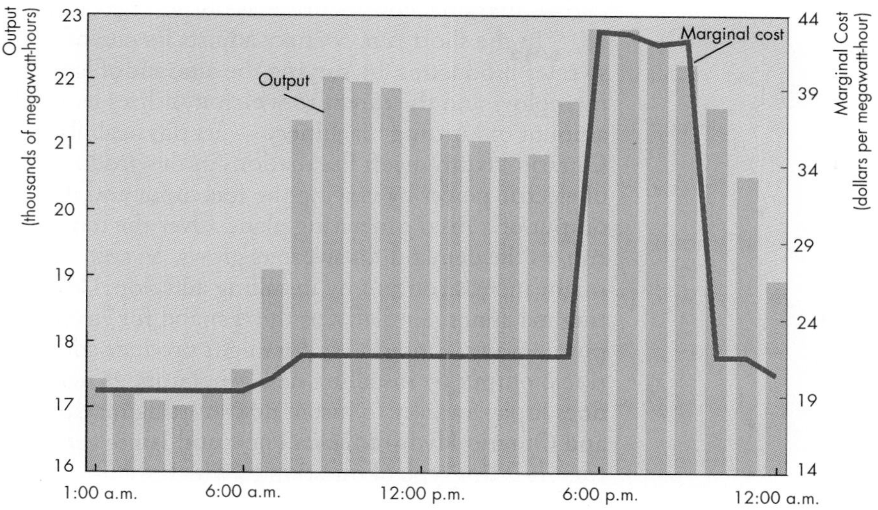

During the 24 hours of January 4, 1989, electric power production at Ontario Hydro fluctuated between 17,000 and almost 23,000 megawatt-hours. Over the same period, marginal cost fluctuated between $19 and $43 per megawatt-hour.

Source: Ontario Hydro.

varies the amount and type of fuel that it uses. Fuel is the main variable input of a power producer. The power source with the lowest fuel cost in the Ontario system is hydraulic, such as the water power of the Niagara Falls. Ontario Hydro rents water and the fuel cost of this source of power is less than $3 a megawatt hour. Nuclear generators at Pickering, Kincardine, Darlington, and Bruce Point also have low fuel costs — about $5 a megawatt hour. Large coal-burning generators come next — at a fuel cost of between $19 and $22 a megawatt hour. The power sources with the highest fuel cost are oil-burning generators and small gas-turbine generators that use the same kind of fuel as jet aircraft. These methods produce electricity at a fuel cost of more than $40 a megawatt hour.

Ontario Hydro engineers working in a master control centre in Etobicoke, equipped with powerful computers, make minute by minute decisions to turn power generators on and off in order to minimize the total cost of production. The engineers bring generators into operation to meet demand by choosing the remaining power source with the lowest fuel cost. That is, to increase the amount of electricity, the engineers tap into the power source with the lowest marginal cost. Only at the peak of demand do they use the generators with the highest marginal cost.

On January 4, 1989, a cold winter day, Ontario Hydro was hit with its peak demand for that winter. Its hour by hour production through that day is shown in Fig. 10.5. That figure also shows the hour by hour marginal cost of production. As you can see, electric power production has two cycles in a 24-hour period. From 1:00 a.m. to 6:00 a.m., output (shown by the orange bars) is between 17,000 and 17,600 megawatts-hours. Then between 6:00 a.m. and 7:00 a.m., output rises as we all turn on morning TV shows, toasters, and coffeemakers. Output reaches a peak at 9:00 a.m. and then falls off slightly during the day to a low point at 3:00 p.m. The daily peak occurs in the early evening, when there is another TV-viewing and meal-preparation period. Production then gradually falls through the evening as people go to bed.

The marginal cost of production follows a similar cycle, fluctuating between $19 a megawatt-hour at the trough and $43 a megawatt-hour at the peak.

A different way of looking at the relationship

Figure 10.6 Ontario Hydro Marginal Cost Curve

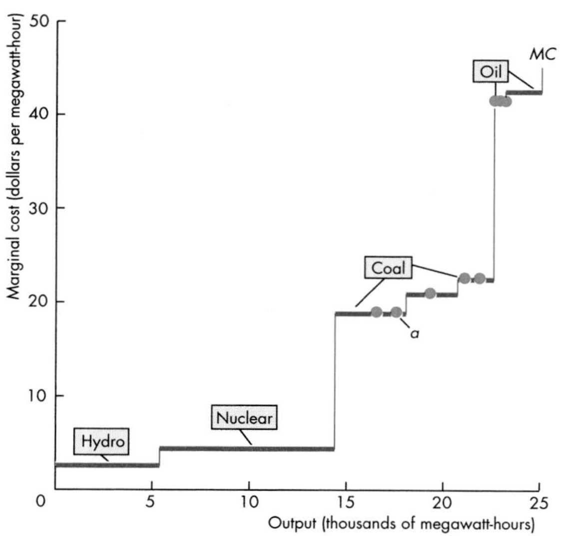

Each point in the figure represents Ontario Hydro's marginal cost at a particular hour on January 4, 1989. For example, point *a* represents a marginal cost of $19 per megawatt-hour and an output rate of 17,600 megawatt-hours. The marginal cost curve for electric power in Ontario is step-shaped because there are large jumps in the fuel costs of the different methods of generation employed. Marginal cost rises steeply as output approaches the physical limits of the generating plant.

Source: Ontario Hydro and our calculations.

between Ontario Hydro's output and marginal cost appears in Fig. 10.6, where the firm's marginal cost curve is shown. Each blue point in that figure represents the marginal cost and output at a particular hour of January 4, 1989. For example, you can see in Fig. 10.5 that at 6 a.m., 17,600 megawatt-hours were produced at a marginal cost of $19 a megawatt-hour. That output and marginal cost generate point *a* in Fig. 10.6. The stepped curve labelled *MC* is the marginal cost curve for Ontario Hydro.

Ontario Hydro's marginal cost curve shares an important feature with Swanky's marginal cost curve: both are upward sloping. But Swanky's curve is a smooth one, while Ontario Hydro's is shaped like a staircase. Why is Ontario Hydro's marginal cost curve step-shaped? It is because of the large jumps in fuel cost as different types of fuels and generators are brought into operation. These different types are highlighted in the figure.

Although there are some differences in Ontario Hydro and Swanky, all production processes have marginal cost curves that have the features of these two — marginal cost increases as output increases.

In the short run, Swanky adjusts its rate of sweater production by varying the amount of labour it employs and the extent to which it utilizes its fixed amount of knitting machinery — its physical plant. Ontario Hydro meets fluctuations in the production of electric power by varying the fuel input and the output of a fixed generating plant. Over the long run, as the demand for sweaters grows, Swanky might increase output by installing additional knitting machines. Similarly, as the demand for electric power grows, Ontario Hydro might produce additional output by installing new generators. When does it pay Swanky to install new knitting machines and Ontario Hydro to install new and larger generators? It is this type of question to which we now turn.

Plant Size, Cost, and Capacity

We have studied how the cost of production varies for a given sweater plant when different quantities of labour are used. The output rate at which a plant's average total cost is at a minimum is called the **capacity** of the plant. If a plant's output is less than that at the point of minimum average total cost — that is, if it produces a smaller amount than its capacity — it is said to have **excess capacity**. If a plant's output exceeds that at the point of minimum average total cost — that is, if it produces a greater amount than its capacity — it is said to have **overutilized capacity**.

The economist's use of the word "capacity" differs from the everyday use. It seems more natural to talk about a plant operating at capacity when it cannot produce any more. However, when we want to refer to the maximum output that a plant can produce, we call that output the **physical limits** of the plant.

The cost curves that were shown in Fig. 10.4 apply to a plant size of one knitting machine that has a fixed cost of $25. Each different plant size has a set of short-run cost curves like those shown in Fig. 10.4. In the short run, a firm is economically efficient if it produces at a point on the short-run average total cost curve for its given plant. In the long run, though, the firm may be able to do better. It can choose its plant size and therefore can create a different short-run average total cost curve on which it will operate.

The Capacity Utilization Puzzle

Ontario Hydro sometimes operates its plant at outputs above capacity and close to its physical limits. This situation is not uncommon. High-quality gardeners, plumbers, electricians, painters, and other suppliers of services often work so hard that they produce at an average total cost that is higher than their minimum average cost. To get the work done, they have to hire extra help at overtime wage rates and work evenings and weekends, thereby incurring high marginal costs of production.

Operating with increasing average total cost looks uneconomic. Why don't such firms buy more capital equipment and increase the scale of their business to meet the obvious high demand for their output? Is there an economic reason why they don't?

In contrast, it is not uncommon in many industries to have an almost permanent excess capacity. Steel production is an example. Excess capacity also occurs in the auto industry, in many mining operations, and in a host of other industries. These producers claim that they could increase their output if the demand for their product was higher and they, as a result, could produce at a lower average total cost.

It sounds as if these firms have invested in too big a production plant. It seems as if the steel producers and automakers would be better off if they had smaller plants so that they could produce closer to the point of minimum average total cost. Is this the case? Or is there some economic explanation for the fact that firms in such industries persistently have excess capacity? This section provides a large part of the answers to these questions.

You have already studied how a firm's costs change when it varies its use of labour, while holding constant the size of its production plant. This cost behaviour is described by the firm's short-run cost curves. Now we are going to study how a firm's costs vary when all its inputs vary — both labour and the scale of the production plant. These variations in costs are described by the firm's long-run cost curves.

Although we want to understand the behaviour of real firms, we will, as before, spend most of our time studying the long-run costs of our imaginary firm — Swanky Inc. We will then use the insights that we get from Sidney's sweater factory to make sense of the behaviour of real firms.

Short-Run and Long-Run Cost

Short-run cost is made up of the fixed cost of a fixed plant and the variable cost of labour. The behaviour of short-run cost depends on the short-run production function. **Long-run cost** is the cost of production when a firm uses the economically efficient plant size. The behaviour of long-run cost depends on the firm's production function. A **production function** is the relationship between the maximum output attainable and the quantities of inputs used.

The Production Function

Swanky's production function is shown in Fig. 10.7. In the table, we look at four different plant sizes and five different quantities of labour input. Perhaps you will recognize the numbers in the column for a plant size of one knitting machine. This is the sweater factory whose short-run product and cost curves we have just studied. With one knitting machine, output varies as the labour input is varied, as described by the numbers in that column. The table also shows three other plants sizes — two, three, and four times the size of the original one. If Sidney doubles the plant size (to two knitting machines), the various amounts of labour can produce the outputs shown in the second column of the table. The other two columns show the outputs of yet larger plants. Each of the columns of the table is a short-run production function. The production function itself is just the collection of all the short-run production functions.

The total product curves for these four different plant sizes appear in Fig. 10.7. As you can see, each total product curve has the same basic shape, but the bigger the sweater plant, the larger is the number of sweaters knitted each day by a given number of workers. One of the fundamental technological facts reflected in the shape of a total product curve is the law of diminishing returns.

Diminishing Returns

Diminishing returns occur in all four plants as the labour input increases. You can check that fact by doing, for the larger plants, similar calculations to those done in Fig. 10.2. Regardless of the size of the plant, the larger the labour input, the lower (eventually) is its marginal product.

Just as we can calculate the marginal product of labour for each plant size, we can also calculate the

Figure 10.7 The Production Function

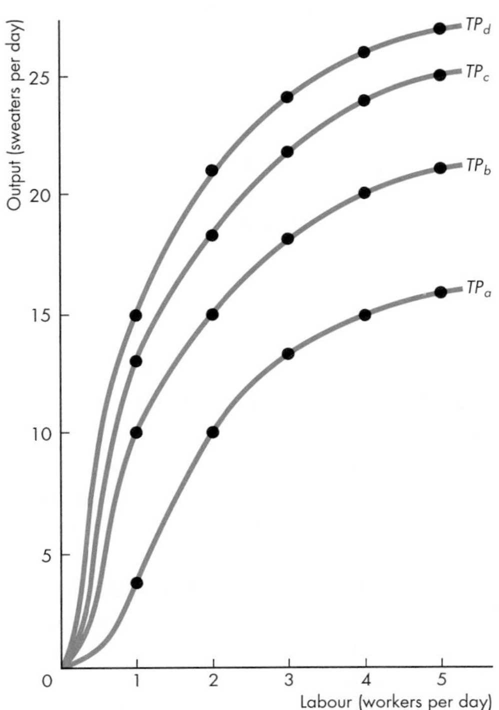

Labour (workers per day)	Plant size (number of knitting machines)			
	1	2	3	4
1	4	10	13	15
2	10	15	18	21
3	13	18	22	24
4	15	20	24	26
5	16	21	25	27

The table shows the short-run production function for each of four different plant sizes. These production functions are plotted in the graph and are labelled TP_a (1 knitting machine), TP_b (2 knitting machines), TP_c (3 knitting machines) and TP_d (4 knitting machines). Each total product curve displays diminishing marginal returns — for each plant, marginal product declines as more labour is employed. The bigger the plant, the larger is the total product for any given amount of labour employed. The highlighted numbers in the table show what happens as the firm changes its scale of production. Doubling the scale from 1 machine and 1 worker to 2 machines and 2 workers more than doubles the output — an example of increasing returns to scale. Increasing the scale again from 2 workers and 2 machines to 3 workers and 3 machines and to 4 workers and 4 machines increases output by a smaller percentage than the increase in inputs — an example of decreasing returns to scale.

marginal product of capital for each quantity of labour. The **marginal product of capital** is the change in total product resulting from a one-unit increase in the quantity of capital employed, holding the quantity of labour constant. It is calculated in a similar way to the marginal product of labour. Also, it behaves in a similar way to the marginal product of labour. That is, if the labour input is held constant as the capital input is increased, the marginal product of capital diminishes.

The law of diminishing returns tells us what happens to output when a firm changes one input, either labour or capital, and holds the other input constant. What happens to output if a firm changes both labour and equipment?

Returns to Scale

A change in scale occurs when there is an equal percentage change in the use of all the firm's inputs. For example, if Swanky has been employing one worker and one knitting machine and then doubles its use of both inputs (to two workers and two knitting machines), the scale of the firm will double. **Returns to scale** are the increase in output relative to the increase in inputs when all inputs are increased by the same percentage. There are three possible cases:

- Constant returns to scale
- Increasing returns to scale
- Decreasing returns to scale

Constant Returns to Scale When the percentage increase in a firm's output is equal to the percentage increase in its inputs, **constant returns to scale** occur. If constant returns to scale are present when a firm doubles all its inputs, its output exactly doubles. Constant returns to scale occur if a rise in output is achieved by replicating the original production process. For example, General Motors can double its production of Cavaliers by doubling its production facility for those cars. It can build an identical production line and hire an identical number of workers.

With the two identical production lines, GM will produce exactly twice as many cars.

Increasing Returns to Scale When the percentage increase in output exceeds the percentage increase in inputs, **increasing returns to scale** (also called **economies of scale**) occur. If economies of scale are present when a firm doubles all its inputs, its output more than doubles. Economies of scale occur in production processes in which increased output enables a firm to use a more productive technology. For example, if GM produces only 100 cars a week, it will not pay to install an automated assembly line. The cost per car will be lower if instead GM uses skilled but expensive workers equipped only with inexpensive hand tools. But at an output rate of several thousand cars a week, it will pay GM to install an automated assembly line. Each worker can specialize in a small number of tasks at which he or she will become highly proficient. General Motors may use a hundred times more capital and labour, but the number of cars it can make will increase much more than a hundred fold. It will experience increasing returns to scale.

Decreasing Returns to Scale When the percentage increase in output is less than the percentage change in inputs, **decreasing returns to scale** (also called **diseconomies of scale**) occur. For example, if inputs double and output increases by 50 percent, diseconomies of scale are present. Diseconomies of scale occur in all production processes at some output rate, but perhaps at a very high one. The most common source of diseconomies of scale is the increasingly complex management and organizational structure required to control a large firm. The larger the organization, the larger is the number of layers in the management pyramid and the greater are the costs of monitoring and maintaining control of all the various stages in the production and marketing process.

Scale Economies at Swanky Swanky's production possibilities, set out in Fig. 10.7, display both economies of scale and diseconomies of scale. If Sidney has 1 knitting machine and employs 1 worker, his factory produces 4 sweaters a day. If he doubles the firm's inputs to 2 knitting machines and 2 workers, the factory's output rises almost fourfold to 15 sweaters a day. If he increases his inputs another 50 percent to 3 knitting machines and 3 workers, output rises to 22 sweaters a day — an increase of less than 50 percent. Doubling the scale of Swanky from 1 to 2 units of each input gives rise to economies of scale, but the further increase from 2 to 3 units of each input gives rise to diseconomies of scale.

Whether a firm experiences increasing, constant, or decreasing returns to scale has an important effect on its long-run costs. Let's see how.

Plant Size and Cost

Earlier in this chapter, we worked out Swanky's short-run costs when it has a fixed amount of capital — one knitting machine — and a variable number of workers. We can also work out the short-run costs of different plant sizes. It takes longer to change the size of the production plant than to change the size of the plant's work force. That is why we speak of a short run for each different plant size. But Sidney can buy another knitting machine and put it into his existing factory. He will then have a different size of plant. He can vary the amount of labour employed in that plant, and as he does so, we can trace the short-run cost curves associated with those different levels of variable input.

Let's look at the short-run costs for different plants and see how plant size itself affects the short-run cost curves.

Four Different Plants

We've already studied the costs of a plant with 1 knitting machine. We'll call that plant *a*. The table in Fig. 10.8 sets out the costs for plant *a* and for three larger plants — which we'll call *b*, *c*, and *d*. Plant *b* has 2 knitting machines; plant *c* has 3 knitting machines; and plant *d* has 4 knitting machines.

The average total cost curves associated with the original plant and the three larger ones appear in Fig. 10.8(a). The average total cost curve for each of the four plant sizes has the same basic U-shape. Which of these cost curves Swanky operates on depends on its plant size. For example, if Swanky has plant *a*, its average total cost curve is ATC_a and it costs $7.69 per sweater to knit 13 sweaters a day. But Swanky can produce 13 sweaters a day with any of these 4 different plant sizes. If it uses plant *b*, the average total cost curve is ATC_b and the average total cost of a sweater will be $6.80. And if it uses plant *d*, the average total cost of a sweater will be $9.50. If Swanky wants to produce 13 sweaters a day, the best

Figure 10.8 Short-run and Long-run Costs

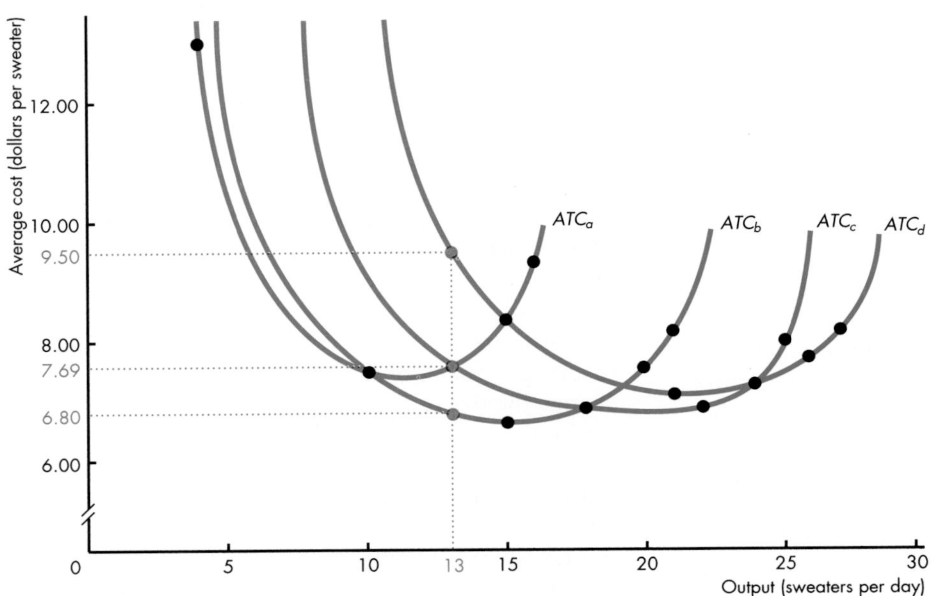

(a) Short-run average cost

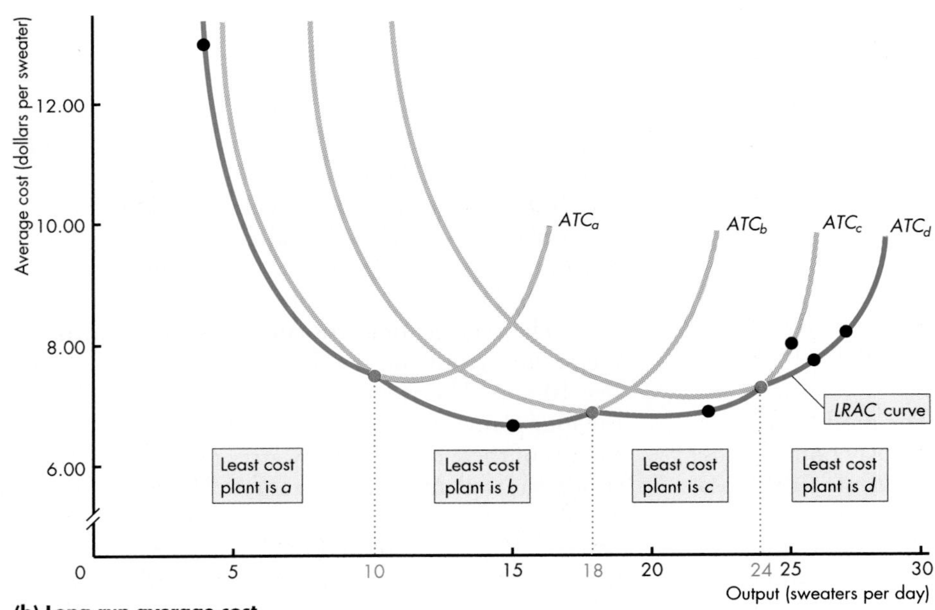

(b) Long-run average cost

The table (opposite page) shows the short-run costs of four different plants. Each plant has a different fixed cost. Plant *a* has 1 knitting machine and a fixed cost of $25; plant *b* has 2 knitting machines and a fixed cost of $50; plant *c* has 3 knitting machines and a fixed cost of $75; and plant *d* has 4 knitting machines and a fixed cost of $100. The short-run average total cost curve for each plant is graphed in part (a). Part (b) illustrates the construction of the long-run average cost curve. The curve traces the lowest attainable cost of production at each output when both the capital and labour inputs are varied. On the long-run average cost curve, Swanky uses plant *a* to produce up to 10 sweaters per day; plant *b* to produce between 11 and 18 sweaters per day; plant *c* to produce between 19 and 24 sweaters per day; and plant *d* to produce more than 24 sweaters per day.

Figure 10.8 (Continued)

Labour (workers per day)	Output (sweaters per day)	Total Fixed Cost	Total Variable Cost	Total Cost	Average Total Cost (dollars per sweater)
		(dollars per day)			
Plant *a* : 1 unit of capital — total cost of capital = $25					
1	4	25	25	50	12.50
2	10	25	50	75	7.50
3	13	25	75	100	7.69
4	15	25	100	125	8.33
5	16	25	125	150	9.38
Plant *b* : 2 units of capital — total cost of capital = $50					
1	10	50	25	75	7.50
2	15	50	50	100	6.67
3	18	50	75	125	6.94
4	20	50	100	150	7.50
5	21	50	125	175	8.33
Plant *c* : 3 units of capital — total cost of capital = $75					
1	13	75	25	100	7.69
2	18	75	50	125	6.94
3	22	75	75	150	6.82
4	24	75	100	175	7.29
5	25	75	125	200	8.00
Plant *d* : 4 units of capital — total cost of capital = $100					
1	15	100	25	125	8.33
2	21	100	50	150	7.14
3	24	100	75	175	7.29
4	26	100	100	200	7.69
5	27	100	125	225	8.33

plant is obviously plant *b*, the one with the lowest average total cost of production. That is the economically efficient plant.

The Long-Run Average Cost Curve

The **long-run average cost curve** traces the relationship between the lowest attainable average total cost and output when both capital and labour inputs can be varied. This curve is illustrated in Fig 10.8(b) as *LRAC.* It is derived directly from the four short-run average total cost curves that we reviewed in Fig. 10.8(a). As you can see in Fig. 10.8, from either part (a) or (b), plant *a* has the lowest average total cost for all output rates up to 10 sweaters a day. Plant *b* has the lowest average total cost for output rates between 10 and 18 sweaters a day. Between output rates of 18 and 24 sweaters a day, plant *c* has the lowest average total cost. Finally, for output rates of more than 24 sweaters a day, plant *d* has the lowest average total cost. The segments of the four average total cost curves for which each plant has the lowest

Figure 10.9 Returns to Scale

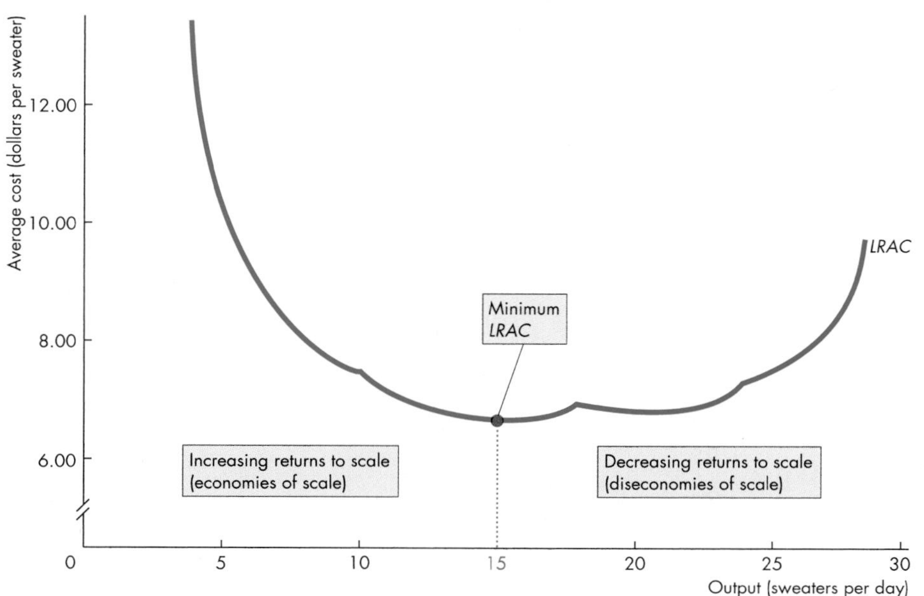

When the long-run average cost curve (*LRAC*) slopes downward, there are increasing returns to scale (or economies of scale). When the long-run average cost curve slopes upward, there are decreasing returns to scale (or diseconomies of scale).

average total cost are highlighted in Fig. 10.8(b). The scallop-shaped curve made up of these four segments is the long-run average cost curve.

Swanky will be on its long-run average cost curve if it does the following: to produce up to 10 sweaters a day, it uses 1 machine; to produce between 11 and 18 sweaters a day, it uses 2 machines; to produce between and 19 and 24 sweaters, it uses 3 machines; and finally, to produce more than 24 sweaters, it uses 4 machines. Within these ranges, it varies its output by varying the amount of labour employed.

Long-Run Cost and Returns to Scale Figure 10.9 shows the connection between the long-run average cost curve and returns to scale. When long-run average cost falls, there are increasing returns to scale (or economies of scale). When long-run average cost rises, there are decreasing returns to scale (or diseconomies of scale). At outputs up to 15 sweaters a day, Swanky experiences economies of scale; at 15 sweaters a day, long-run average cost is at a minimum. When output rises to more than 15 sweaters a day, Swanky experiences diseconomies of scale.

To see why this relationship arises, recall the definition of increasing returns to scale. Increasing returns to scale are present when the percentage increase in output exceeds the percentage increase in inputs. The percentage increase in total cost equals the percentage increase in the inputs. Hence, if the percentage increase in output exceeds the percentage increase in inputs, it also exceeds the percentage increase in total cost. Therefore average cost declines. When there are decreasing returns to scale, this chain of reasoning leads to the conclusion that as output increases, average cost rises.

The long-run average cost curve that we have derived for Swanky has two special features not always found in a firm's long-run cost curve. First, Swanky is able to adjust its plant size only in big jumps. We can imagine a firm with a type of plant that it can vary in tiny increments so that there are an infinite number of plant sizes. In such a situation, there are an infinite number of short-run average total cost curves, one for each plant. Second, Swanky's long-run average cost curve is either falling (economies of scale) or rising (diseconomies of scale).

Figure 10.10 Short-Run and Long-Run Average Costs

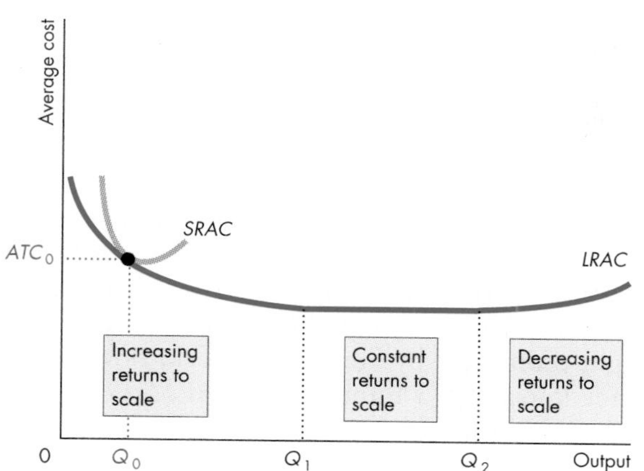

If the capital input can be varied in small units, there are not just four different plant sizes, as in Fig. 10.8, but an infinitely large number of them. There are also an infinitely large number of short-run average total cost curves. Each short-run average total cost curve touches the long-run average cost curve at a single point. For example, the short-run average total cost curve (*SRAC*) touches the long-run average cost curve (*LRAC*) at the output rate Q_0 and an average total cost of ATC_0. The short-run average total cost curve shown is representative of the infinite number of others, each with one point only tangential to the long-run average cost curve. The long-run average cost curve also illustrates the possibility of constant returns to scale. For outputs up to Q_1, there are increasing returns to scale; for outputs between Q_1 and Q_2, there are constant returns to scale; for outputs above Q_2, there are decreasing returns to scale.

Some production processes have constant returns to scale over some intermediate range of output.

Figure 10.10 illustrates this alternative situation in which there are an infinite number of plant sizes and output ranges over which returns to scale are increasing (up to Q_1), constant (between Q_1 and Q_2), and decreasing (above Q_2). For each plant size there is a short-run average total cost curve, and each short-run average total cost curve is tangential to the long-run average cost curve (*LRAC*) at a single point. Thus for each output, there is a unique, economically efficient plant size — that is, one plant size that will produce that output at the lowest average cost. To keep the figure clear, only one of the infinite number of short-run average total cost curves, labelled *SRAC*, is shown. The short-run average total cost curve shown in Fig. 10.10 is for the plant that can produce the output rate Q_0 at minimum average total cost, ATC_0.

The first time the long-run average cost curve appeared in print, it was drawn incorrectly. Take a look at Our Advancing Knowledge on pp. 250-251 to see why. You will understand the connection between short-run and long-run average cost curves more thoroughly after you have studied the material in that essay.

Long-Run Costs Are Total Costs When we examine short-run costs, we distinguish between fixed, variable, and total cost. We make no such distinctions for long-run costs. All inputs vary in the long run, so there are no long-run fixed costs. Since there are no long-run fixed costs, long-run total cost and long-run variable cost are the same thing.

There is a long-run marginal cost curve that goes with the long-run average cost curve. The relationship between the long-run average cost curve and the long-run marginal cost curve is similar to that between the short-run average cost curve and the short-run marginal cost curve. When long-run average cost is falling, long-run marginal cost is less than long-run average cost. When long-run average cost is rising, long-run marginal cost exceeds long-run average cost, and when long-run average cost is constant, long-run marginal cost is equal to long-run average cost.

Shifts in Cost Curves

Both short-run and long-run cost curves depend on two things: the production function and input prices. A change in technology shifts the production function and thus shifts the cost curves. Technological advances increase the output that can be produced from given inputs. They also shift the total product curve as well as the average and the marginal product curves upward, and they shift the cost curves downward. For example, advances in genetic engineering are making it possible to increase the milk production of a cow without increasing the amount of food that it eats — a technological advance that lowers the cost of milk production.

Resource or input prices also affect the cost curves. If the price of an input increases, it directly increases cost and shifts the cost curves upward.

Cost Curves

Jacob Viner

The cost curves that you have studied in this chapter were first expressed in their current form in 1931 by Jacob Viner in an article entitled "Cost Curves and Supply Curves."[1] Viner, the son of poor immigrant parents from Eastern Europe, was born in Montreal in 1892. He did his undergraduate studies at McGill University in Montreal, where he was taught economics by Stephen Leacock, now perhaps better known as a humorist. From McGill, Viner went to Harvard where he earned a Ph.D. in 1922. He became a full professor at the University of Chicago at the age of 32. In 1946, he left Chicago for Princeton, where he stayed until his death in 1970.

Viner wrote many important books and articles, mostly on international economic issues. It was his article on cost curves, though, that became his most widely known work. His analysis of cost and cost curves is now studied by every beginning student of economics.

Short-Run Cost Curves

Viner's account of the behaviour of short-run cost is so clear that it provides a beautifully compact review of what you have studied in this chapter. The following is the essence of Viner's own presentation:

- The short run is a period long enough to permit any desired change of output that is technologically possible without altering the scale of plant but not long enough to permit any adjustment of scale of plant.
- Inputs are classified in two groups—those necessarily fixed in amount in the short run and those freely variable.
- Scale of plant means the amount of the inputs that are fixed in the short run.
- Scale of plant is measured by the output that it produces when average total cost is a minimum.
- Costs associated with fixed factors are called fixed costs.
- Costs associated with variable factors are called variable costs.[2]

Viner's diagram of short-run cost curves is reproduced here.+

Viner pointed out the following features of the cost curves:

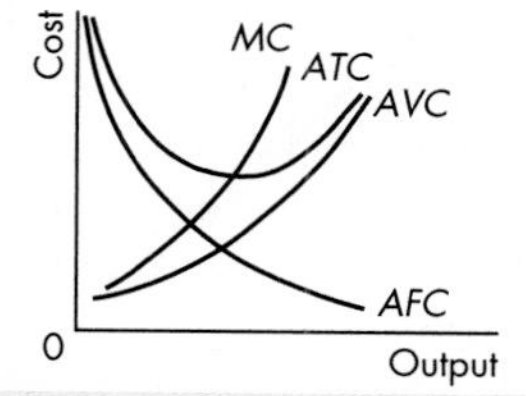

- Average fixed cost (*AFC*) declines as output rises.
- Average variable cost (*AVC*) rises as output rises.
- Marginal cost (*MC*) rises and equals average cost (*ATC*) at the lowest point of average total cost.
- Average cost is the vertical sum of average fixed cost and average variable cost and is necessarily U-shaped "for all industries having any substantial fixed costs."

Long-Run Cost Curves

Viner also showed how the short-run cost curves and long-run cost curves are related to each other. In this exercise, he made what has become a famous mistake — one that can reinforce your understanding of the long-run average cost curve. The figure below shows the relation between the long-run average cost curve (*LRAC*) and short-run average total cost curve (*SRAC*) in part (a) and Viner's version in part (b).

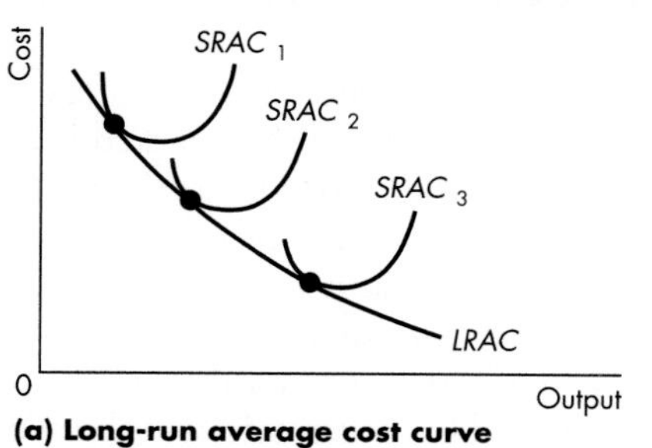

(a) Long-run average cost curve

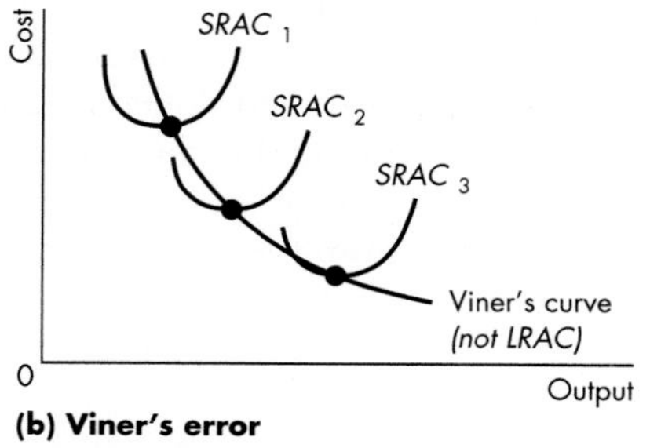

(b) Viner's error

When instructing his draftsman, a brilliant Chinese mathematician at the University of Chicago, Viner asked that the long-run average cost curve do two things:

- Pass through the minimum point of each *SRAC* curve
- Not rise above any *SRAC* curve at any point

Notice that in part (a) the *SRAC* is never below the *LRAC*. Part (a) thus satisfies Viner's second instruction — that the *LRAC* not rise above any *SRAC* at any point. But it does not satisfy Viner's first instruction — that the *LRAC* pass through the minimum points of each *SRAC*.

In part (b), you can see what purports to be a long-run average cost curve and that curve does pass through the minimum points of the *SRAC* curves. This curve satisfies Viner's first condition but not the second one.

Viner had given his draftsman what he subsequently called a "technically impossible and economically inappropriate assignment." It is possible to draw a curve that never rises above a *SRAC* curve and that does not pass through the points of minimum short-run average cost (part a), or it is possible to draw a curve that passes through the points of minimum short-run average cost and that does rise above the *SRAC* curve (part b), but it is not possible to draw a curve that does both of these things. The curve in part (a) is a long-run average cost curve and the curve in part (b) is not.

Such is the stuff of advancing knowledge. A great economist like Jacob Viner, struggling with a new idea, makes a mistake. Today, a student in an introductory economics course would feel embarrassed to make such an error.

---

[1] One of the most accessible sources of Viner's article is in Kenneth E. Boulding and George J. Stigler (eds.) *Readings in Price Theory*, (Chicago: Richard D. Irwin, 1952), 198-232. The brief Viner quotations that appear later in this essay are taken from this source. The article was first published in *Zeitschrift für Nationalökonomie*, 3 (1931): 23-46.

[2] Viner called variable costs "direct costs."

+ The figure shown here is a simplified version of the one that appeared in the orginal article.

Returns To Scale in Reality

Let's close this chapter by looking at some real world examples and see why there is a great deal of excess capacity in some industries while in others, firms are operating "flat out."

Excess Capacity

It has been estimated that one vacuum cleaner factory could produce more vacuum cleaners than the entire North American market buys, and it would still be operating on the falling section of its long-run average cost curve.[1] But North America has more than one vacuum cleaner factory, so each is operating at an output rate below that at which long-run average cost is at a minimum — with excess capacity . The situation also holds for the production of TV picture tubes, steel, cars, refined petroleum, cigarettes, semiconductors, and matches.

Figure 10.11 illustrates the situation prevailing in those industries that could lower their average production costs if the market were big enough to permit them to expand to their most efficient scale. Output, limited by the extent of the market, is Q_0. The firm is producing efficiently at an average total cost of ATC_0. But the firm has excess capacity. It could lower its costs to ATC_{min} even with its existing plant if output could be increased to Q_c, and it could lower its costs even more by switching to a bigger plant. But the firm can't sell more than Q_0. So, even when it is operating as efficiently as possible, the firm has excess capacity. The production of vacuum cleaners, TV picture tubes, steel, cars, and the other products mentioned above are examples of industries in which the situation shown in Fig. 10.11 prevails.

Figure 10.11 Excess Capacity

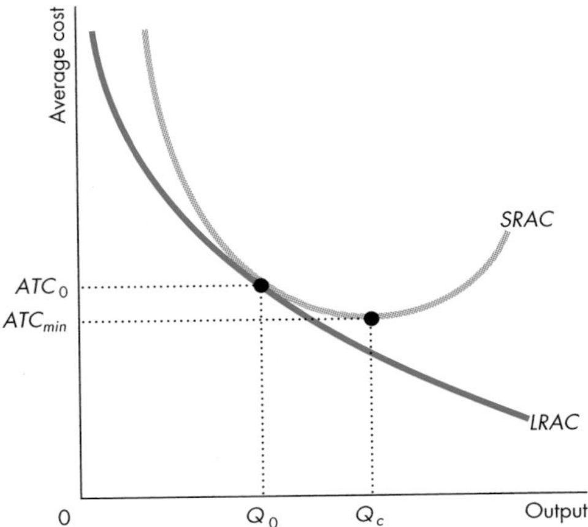

The size of the market limits a firm's output to Q_0. At output Q_0, the long-run average cost curve is downward sloping — there are economies of scale. To produce Q_0 at least cost, the firm installs a plant with a capacity of Q_c and operates the plant below capacity. This situation prevails in many industries, including those manufacturing vacuum cleaners, TV picture tubes, steel, cars, refined petroleum, typewriters, cigarettes, semiconductors, and matches.

Operating "Flat Out"

When we examined the short-run marginal cost of Ontario Hydro, we discovered that its marginal cost increases as it produces more power. As we saw in Fig. 10.6, Ontario Hydro's marginal cost becomes extremely high at output rates in excess of 22,000 megawatt hours. Why doesn't Ontario Hydro build additional plants? We can answer this question by applying the lessons that you've just learned about the relationship between short-run and long-run costs.

Figure 10.12 shows Ontario Hydro's short-run marginal cost curve (MC) as well as its short-run average total cost curve (ATC). Two points are marked on the output axis. Point C is Ontario Hydro's capacity. (The word "capacity" is being used here in its economic sense as the output rate that minimizes average total cost.) The other point marked is L, the physical limits of the output of the existing plant.

Ontario Hydro's marginal cost curve slopes upward very steeply because as its output approaches its physical limits, generators are brought into operation that use expensive oil, the most costly form of which is similar to that used by jet aircraft. But the average total cost curve has a much more gentle slope. Why? Because the bulk of Ontario Hydro's costs are fixed costs, not variable fuel costs. Ontario Hydro's fixed resources — capital equipment and skilled labour — cannot be varied to meet hourly shifts in demand for power. Because a large proportion of Ontario Hydro's total costs comes from the cost of these fixed resources, the firm's average total cost varies much less than marginal cost. Ontario Hydro's output fluctuates

[1]James V. Koch, *Industrial Organization and Prices*, 2nd ed. (Englewood Cliffs, N.J.: Prentice-Hall, 1980), 123-134.

Figure 10.12 Overutilizing Capacity

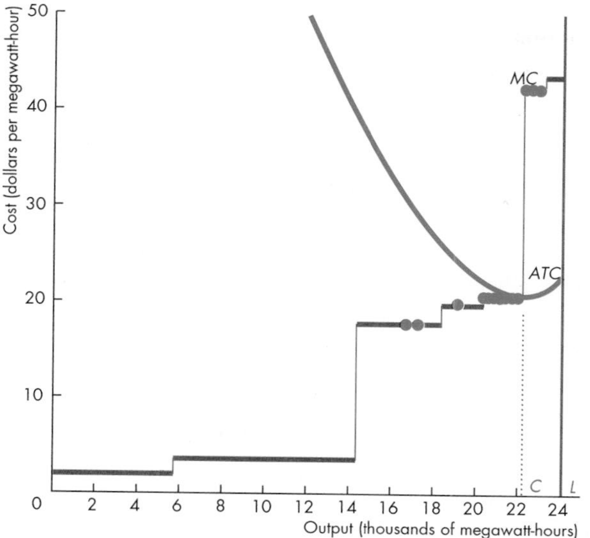

Although Ontario Hydro faces a steeply increasing marginal cost, its average total cost declines until it reaches output *C*. The capacity (minimum cost) of Ontario Hydro's plant is output *C*. Output *L* is the physical limit of its plant. Between *C* and *L*, average total cost rises. When demand increases so that Ontario Hydro is producing in the range between *C* and *L* for a significant amount of time, it will pay to increase its plant size to meet the additional demand. It would not pay to build a bigger plant to meet current demand even though at peak demand Ontario Hydro is operating flat out. Although marginal cost could be lowered with a larger plant, average total cost could not.

Source: Ontario Hydro and our calculations

between 15,000 and 23,000 megawatt-hours. Ontario Hydro operates on the rising part of the marginal cost curve, but it also operates, most of the time, on the falling part of its average total cost curve. Occasionally, output rises above capacity and therefore moves into the range in which average total cost rises. But such cases are rare — occurring only at the peak of demand for the year.

As the demand for electric power gradually increases, Ontario Hydro will be able to achieve lower average total cost by increasing its plant size. Currently, output fluctuates between 15,000 and 23,000 megawatt-hours. If output exceeded 22,000 megawatt hours for a significant part of each day, Ontario Hydro would be operating on the upward-sloping part of its short-run average total cost curve and it would frequently be necessary for the firm to operate "flat out" — at its physical limits — and to import power from neighbouring producers to meet the demand. In such a situation, it would pay Ontario Hydro to increase its production capacity to meet the additional demand.

It does not pay to increase capacity to meet demand fluctuations in the range shown in the figure. An increased plant would increase the fixed costs and shift the average cost curve upward. The new average total cost curve would only fall below the current one at higher output than can be sold.

■ We've now studied the way in which costs vary as a firm's inputs and output rate vary. We've seen how the fact that marginal product eventually diminishes gives rise to eventually increasing average and marginal cost. We've also seen how long-run cost curves take their shape from economies and diseconomies of scale — long-run average cost decreasing as output increases with economies of scale and long-run average cost increasing as output increases with diseconomies of scale.

In the next chapter, we're going to probe a firm's costs and input decisions more closely, studying the way in which its demands for inputs at a given output are affected by input prices. With this model, we'll be able to understand why we see variations in techniques employed and why some industries are much more capital intensive than others.

S U M M A R Y

Firms' Objectives and Constraints

Firms aim to maximize profit. Profit maximization stems directly from scarcity. Only firms that maximize profits can survive in a competitive environment.

The market and technology impose constraints on profit maximization. Some firms operate in such competitive markets that they have no choice but to sell their output at the going price. In other cases, the firm can choose the price at which to sell its output. However, at higher prices, they will sell less. Most firms are unable to influence the markets for their inputs and have to buy them at the going prices. Technology limits the production process of firms. If firms are technologically efficient, they can increase their output only by using more inputs.

In the short run, some inputs cannot be changed. In most cases, the capital input is fixed in the short run while labour can be varied. (pp. 231-232)

The Short-Run Production Function

The short-run production function describes the limits to output as a firm changes the quantity of a variable input such as labour. The short-run production function is described by the total, marginal, and average product curves. Total product is the output produced in a given period. Average product is total product per unit of variable input. Marginal product is the change in total product resulting from a one-unit increase in the variable input. As the variable input is increased, marginal and average product rise until they reach a peak, and thereafter they fall — diminishing returns begin. When average product rises, marginal product exceeds average product. When average product falls, marginal product is less than average product. When average product is at its maximum, marginal product equals average product. (pp. 232-237)

Short-Run Cost

Total cost is divided into total fixed cost and total variable cost. As output rises, total cost rises because total variable cost rises. Marginal cost is the additional cost of producing one more unit of output. Average total cost is the total cost per unit of output.

Costs depend on how much a firm produces. Average fixed cost falls as output rises. The average variable cost and average total cost curves are U-shaped. The marginal cost curve is also U-shaped. When average cost is falling, marginal cost is below average cost, and when average cost is rising, marginal cost exceeds average cost. When average product is at a maximum, average variable cost is at a minimum. When average product is rising, average variable cost is falling, and when average product is falling, average variable cost is rising. (pp. 237-242)

Plant Size, Cost, and Capacity

Plant capacity is the output rate with the lowest average total cost. Firms that produce an amount smaller than their capacity are said to have excess capacity; those that produce an amount larger than their capacity are said to have overutilized capacity.

Long-run cost is the cost of production when all inputs — labour as well as plant and equipment — have been adjusted to their economically efficient levels. The behaviour of long-run cost depends on the firm's production function. As a firm uses more labour while holding capital constant, it eventually experiences diminishing returns. When it uses more capital while holding labour constant, it also experiences diminishing returns. When it varies all its inputs in equal proportions, it experiences returns to scale. Returns to scale can be constant, increasing, or decreasing. (pp. 242-245)

Plant Size and Cost

Each different plant size has a set of short-run cost curves. There is one least-cost plant for each output. The higher the output, the larger is the plant that will minimize average total cost.

The long-run average cost curve traces the relationship between the lowest attainable average total cost and output when both capital and labour inputs can be varied. With increasing returns to scale, the long-run average cost curve slopes downward. With decreasing returns to scale, the long-run average cost curve slopes upward.

There is no distinction between fixed cost and variable cost in the long run. Since all inputs are variable, all costs are also variable.

Cost curves shift when either input prices or technology change. An improvement in technology raises the output from a given set of inputs and shifts the cost curves downward. A rise in input prices shifts the cost curves upward. (pp. 245-249)

Returns to Scale in Reality

Some firms, including those that make vacuum cleaners, TV picture tubes, and cars have increasing returns to scale (economies of scale). Usually economies of scale exist when the total market is too small to allow the efficient scale of production. In such industries, firms operate efficiently with excess capacity.

Some firms overutilize their plants, operating them at an output that exceeds capacity. Ontario

Hydro is a good example. Though the marginal cost of electric power rises as output rises, only rarely does Ontario Hydro produce so much power that it is operating on the upward-sloping section of its short-run average total cost curve. Only if a firm persistently operates on the upward-sloping part of its short-run average total cost curve will it be efficient to increase its plant size. (pp. 252-253)

KEY ELEMENTS

Key Terms

Average fixed cost, 239
Average product, 233
Average total cost, 239
Average variable cost, 239
Capacity, 242
Capital-intensive technique, 231
Constant returns to scale, 244
Decreasing returns to scale (diseconomies of scale), 245
Diminishing marginal returns, 237
Excess capacity, 242
Fixed cost, 237
Fixed inputs, 232
Increasing marginal returns, 236
Increasing returns to scale (economies of scale), 245
Labour-intensive technique, 231
Law of diminishing returns, 237
Long run, 232
Long-run average cost curve, 246
Long-run cost, 243
Marginal cost, 237
Marginal product, 233
Marginal product of capital, 244
Marginal product of labour, 233
Market constraints, 231
Overutilized capacity, 242
Physical limits, 242
Production function, 243
Profit maximization, 231
Returns to scale, 244
Short run, 232
Short-run production function, 232
Technique, 231
Total cost, 237
Total fixed cost, 237
Total product, 232
Total product curve, 232
Total variable cost, 237
Variable cost, 237
Variable inputs, 232

Key Figures and Table 

Figure 10.2 Total Product and Marginal Product, 234
Figure 10.3 Total, Marginal, and Average Product, 235
Figure 10.4 Short-Run Costs, 238
Figure 10.8 Short-Run and Long-Run Costs, 246
Figure 10.9 Returns to Scale, 248
Table 10.2 A Compact Glossary on Product and Cost, 240

REVIEW QUESTIONS

1 Why do we assume that firms maximize profit?

2 What are the main constraints on a firm's ability to maximize profit?

3 Distinguish between the short run and the long run.

4 Define total product, average product, and marginal product. What are the relationships between the total product curve, the average product curve, and the marginal product curve?

5 State the law of diminishing returns. What does this law imply about the shapes of the total, marginal, and average product curves?

6 Define total cost, total fixed cost, total variable cost, average total cost, average fixed cost, average variable cost, and marginal cost.

7 What are the relationships between the average

total cost curve, the average variable cost curve, and the marginal cost curve?

8 Define the long-run average cost curve. What is the relationship between the long-run average cost curve and the short-run average total cost curve?

9 What does the long-run average cost curve tell us?

10 Define economies of scale. What effects do economies of scale have on the shape of the long-run average cost curve?

11 When does the long-run average cost curve touch the minimum point of a short-run average total cost curve?

12 When does the long-run average cost curve touch a point on the short-run average total cost curve to the left of its minimum point?

13 When does the long-run average cost curve touch a point on the short-run average total cost curve to the right of its minimum point?

14 Why might long-run average cost decline? Why might long-run average cost rise?

15 What makes the short-run cost curves shift

a) upward?

b) downward?

PROBLEMS

1 The short-run production function of Rubber Duckies Inc., a firm making rubber boats, is described by the following:

Labour (number of persons employed per week)	Output (rubber boats per week)
1	1
2	2
3	4
4	7
5	11
6	14
7	16
8	17
9	18
10	18

a) Draw the total product curve.

b) Calculate average product and draw the average product curve.

c) Calculate marginal product and draw the marginal product curve.

d) What is the relationship between average product and marginal product at output rates of less than 16 boats per week? Why?

e) What is the relationship between average and marginal product at outputs of more than 16 boats per week? Why?

2 Suppose that the price of labour is $400 a week, total fixed costs are $10,000 a week, and the production possibilities are those presented in problem 1.

a) Calculate the firm's total cost, total variable cost, and total fixed costs for each of the outputs given.

b) Draw the total cost, total variable cost, and total fixed cost curves.

c) Calculate the firm's average total cost, average fixed cost, average variable cost, and marginal cost at each of the outputs given.

d) Draw the following cost curves: average total cost, average variable cost, average fixed cost, and marginal cost.

3 Suppose that Rubber Duckies' total fixed costs rise to $11,000 a week. How will this affect the firm's average total cost, average fixed cost, average variable cost, and marginal cost curves in problem 2?

4 Suppose that Rubber Duckies' total fixed costs remain at $10,000 a week but the price of labour rises to $450 a week. Using these new costs, rework problems 2(a) and 2(b) and draw the new cost curves.

CHAPTER 11

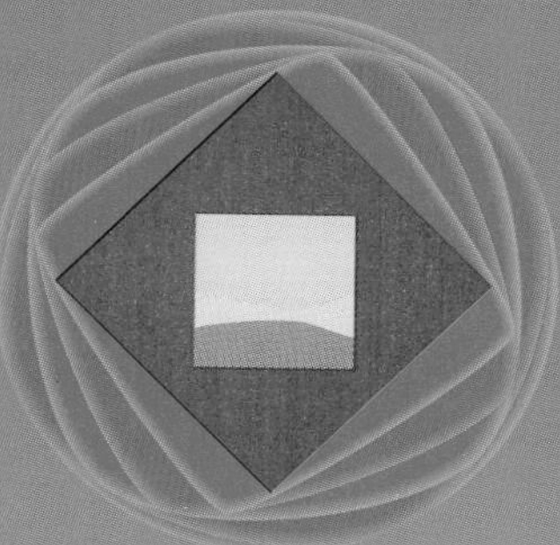

Producing at Least Cost

After studying this chapter, you will be able to:

- Define and calculate the marginal rate of substitution between two inputs.
- Explain what an isoquant measures.
- Explain what an isocost line measures.
- Calculate the least cost technique of production.
- Predict the effect of a change in input prices on the least-cost technique.
- Explain variations in capital intensity across industries and countries.

A Dollar a Day in Amazonia

IF YOU JOURNEY to the right part of Amazonia, deep in the interior of Brazil, you encounter a scene straight from medieval times. As you approach by helicopter, you see through the mist an enormous pit, many metres wide, dug into the earth. As you draw closer, you can see crude wooden ladders scaling the pit's terraces. Finally, you distinguish the muddy, exhausted shapes of thousands of men scaling the ladders with sacks of dirt on their backs. What you are watching is an enormous gold mine being dug largely by hand by labourers paid little more than a dollar a day. ■ The scene is quite different at a Canadian strip mine. There, far fewer workers, who receive far higher pay, operate earthmovers so large that they make ordinary cars and trucks look like toys. ■ Why do such differences exist? Why do gold mines in Amazonia employ such large numbers of people, risking their lives daily on rickety ladders? Why don't Brazilian mines use the efficient, labour-saving equipment of Canadian mines? ■ The capital equipment used by all the firms operating in Canada is worth close to $1 trillion — or $76,000 per person employed. The processed food industry, which produces packaged meat and frozen fruits and vegetables, uses about the average amount of capital per worker. Manufacturers of chemicals, especially of plastic materials and industrial gases, use eight times the average, while manufacturers of shirts and other clothing use about one-tenth the average amount of capital per person. Why don't shirtmakers use more machinery? Why do plastics makers use so much equipment? ■ Capital per person employed varies because different industries and even different countries use different techniques of production. The choice of production technique is a crucial decision for a firm.

■ This chapter examines the way in which firms make such decisions. It also introduces you to some powerful tools of analysis that are well worth the effort required to master them.

Input Substitution

You would be hard-pressed to think of many goods that can be produced in only one way. Just about every good and service can be produced by using a large amount of labour and a small amount of capital or a large amount of capital and a small amount of labour. For example, cars can be made with computer-controlled robotic assembly lines that use enormous amounts of capital and hardly any labour, or they can be built by skilled labour using only hand tools. Highways and dams can be built by a small amount of labour using giant earth-moving machines or by hordes of workers using picks, shovels, and wheelbarrows. A production technique that uses a lot of capital per worker is called a *capital-intensive technique.* One that uses a lot of labour and a little capital per worker is called a *labour-intensive technique.*

The technically feasible range of production possibilities is described by the production function. An example of a production function is shown in Fig. 11.1. This production function is that of Swanky Inc., the sweater factory owned by Sidney that was introduced in Chapter 10. The figure records the maximum daily output of sweaters that can be produced by using different combinations of labour and capital. For example, if Swanky has 3 knitting machines and employs 1 worker, it can produce 13 sweaters a day. With 3 knitting machines and 5 workers, it can produce 25 sweaters a day.

If you study the numbers in Fig. 11.1, you will see that it shows three ways of producing 15 sweaters a day. It also shows two ways of producing 10, 13, 16, 18, 21, 22, 24, 25, and 27 sweaters a day.

The production function in Fig. 11.1 can be used to calculate the marginal product of labour and the marginal product of capital. The *marginal product of labour* is the change in total product per unit change of labour, holding the amount of capital constant. The *marginal product of capital* is the change in total product per unit change in capital, holding the amount of labour constant. The law of diminishing returns applies to both labour and capital. That is, holding capital input constant, the marginal product of each additional unit of labour diminishes as the labour input increases, and holding labour input

Figure 11.1 Swanky's Production Function

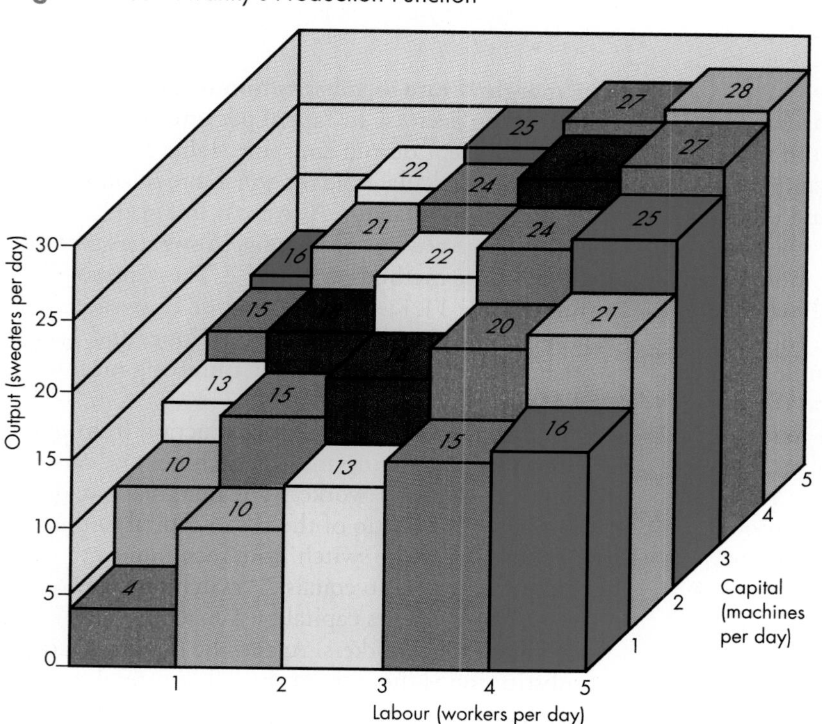

The figure shows how many sweaters can be produced per day with various combinations of labour and capital inputs. For example, by using 4 workers and 2 knitting machines, Swanky can produce 20 sweaters per day.

Table 11.1 Substituting Between Capital and Labour to Produce 15 Sweaters per Day

Method	Capital (K)	Labour (L)	Fall in Capital ($-\Delta K$)	Rise in Labour (ΔL)	Marginal rate of substitution of capital for labour ($-\Delta K/\Delta L$)
a	4	1			
			2	1	2
b	2	2			
			1	2	½
c	1	4			

Switching from method *a* to method *b* involves cutting capital ($-\Delta K$) by 2 machines and raising labour (ΔL) by 1 worker. The marginal rate of substitution of capital for labour — which is the ratio of the fall in capital (ΔK) to the rise in labour (ΔL) — is 2. Switching from method *b* to method *c* involves cutting capital by 1 machine and raising labour by 2 workers, which means that the marginal rate of substitution of capital for labour is ½.

constant, the marginal product of each additional unit of capital diminishes as the capital input increases.

It's easy to see why the law of diminishing returns applies to capital by imagining this scene in Swanky's knitting factory. Suppose that there is 1 worker and 1 machine. Output (as shown in Fig. 11.1) is 4 sweaters a day. If an extra machine is installed, the 1 worker can easily handle both machines and produce greater output. For example, one machine can be set to knit blue sweaters and the other red sweaters. There's no need to stop the machines to change the wool colour. Output more than doubles to 10 sweaters a day. But if a third machine is added, the single worker finds it hard to cope with the increasingly complex factory. For example, there are now three times as many breakdowns as there were with just 1 machine. The worker has to spend an increasing amount of time fixing problems. Output increases only to 13 sweaters a day.

Although all goods and services can be produced by using a variety of methods of production, the ease with which capital and labour can be substituted for each other varies from industry to industry. The production function reflects the ease with which inputs can be substituted for each other. Also, the production function can be used to calculate the degree of substitutability between inputs. Such a calculation involves a new concept — that of the marginal rate of substitution of capital for labour.

The Substitutability of Capital and Labour

The **marginal rate of substitution of capital for labour** is the decrease in capital per unit increase in labour that keeps output constant. Table 11.1 illustrates how to calculate the marginal rate of substitution of capital for labour. As we saw in Fig. 11.1, there are three ways of producing 15 sweaters a day. Let's call those methods *a*, *b*, and *c*. They appear again in Table 11.1. A daily output of 15 sweaters can be produced with 4 knitting machines and 1 worker, 2 units of each input, or 1 knitting machine and 4 workers.

Changing the method of production from *a* to *b* reduces the capital input by 2 machines and raises the labour input by 1 worker. The marginal rate of substitution is the ratio of the fall in capital to the rise in labour; for the switch from technique *a* to technique *b*, that ratio equals 2. Switching from method *b* to *c* reduces capital by 1 machine and raises labour by 2 workers. Again, the marginal rate of substitution is the ratio of the fall in capital to the rise in labour, so for the move from technique *b* to *c*, the marginal rate of substitution is ½.

The marginal rates of substitution that we have just calculated obey the **law of diminishing marginal rate of substitution**, which states:

The marginal rate of substitution of capital for labour falls as the amount of capital decreases and the amount of labour increases.

You can see that the law of diminishing marginal rate of substitution makes sense by considering Swanky's sweater factory. Suppose there is 1 worker racing between 4 knitting machines, desperately trying to keep them all operating, stopping the wool from tangling, and coping with breakdowns. Output can be held constant by getting rid of 1 machine and hiring only a small additional amount of labour. The marginal rate of substitution is high. At the other extreme, 4 workers are falling over each other to operate 1 machine. In this situation, output can be kept constant by laying off 2 workers and installing 1 additional machine. The marginal rate of substitution is low. The law of diminishing marginal rate of substitution applies to (almost) all production processes.

Figure 11.2 An Isoquant

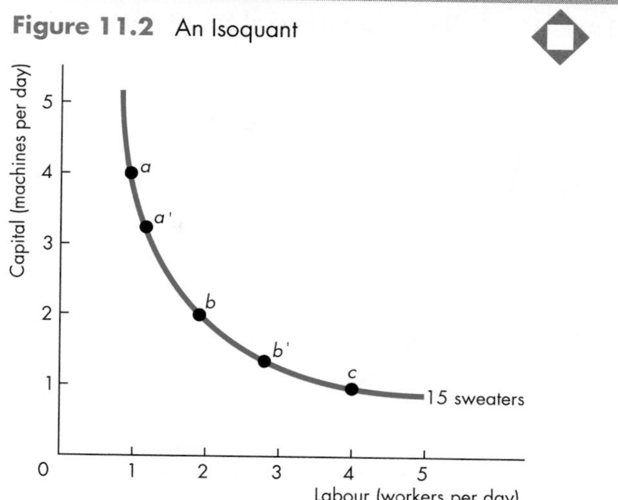

This isoquant shows the different techniques of production or combinations of capital and labour, required to produce 15 sweaters per day. For example, point *a* tells us that 4 machines and 1 worker can produce 15 sweaters per day. The same output level can be produced by 2 machines and 2 workers (point *b*) or 1 machine and 4 workers (point *c*). Each of these points can be found in Fig. 11.1. The isoquant also shows combinations not found in Fig. 11.1, such as *a′* and *b′*.

Isoquants

Suppose that we want to graph the different combinations of labour and capital that produce 15 sweaters a day. Such a graph is an isoquant. An **isoquant** is a curve that shows the different combinations of labour and capital required to produce a given quantity of output. (The word "isoquant" means *equal quantity* — "iso" meaning *equal* and "quant" meaning *quantity*.) Figure 11.2 illustrates an isoquant. Each point (*a*, *b*, and *c*) represents a technique of production — a combination of workers and knitting machines — that can produce 15 sweaters a day. These three techniques are the same as those that appear in Table 11.1 (and are extracted from Fig. 11.1).

The isoquant in Fig. 11.2 shows more than the three techniques of production set out in the table. It shows *all* the combinations of capital and labour capable of producing 15 sweaters a day. For example, between techniques *a* and *b* there is technique *a′* which combines 3.2 knitting machines with 1.2 workers to produce 15 sweaters a day. Between techniques *b* and *c* is technique *b′* which combines 1.4 units of capital and 2.8 units of labour to produce 15 units of output. (You might think it's strange to talk about fractions of knitting machines and workers. If so, think of Swanky as using three machines full time and another one-fifth of the time — 0.2 — so that 3.2 machines are used in total. Similarly, you can think of Swanky hiring one full-time worker and one part-time worker.)

Marginal Rate of Substitution and Isoquant

The marginal rate of substitution equals the magnitude of the slope of the isoquant. Figure 11.3 illustrates this relationship. The figure shows the isoquant for 13 sweaters a day. Let's pick any point on this isoquant and imagine increasing labour by the smallest conceivable amount and decreasing capital in order to keep output constant at 13 sweaters. As we lower the capital input and raise the labour input, we travel along the isoquant. If the isoquant is steep (as at point *a*), the capital input falls by a large amount relative to the rise in the labour input. The marginal rate of substitution is high. But if the isoquant has a gentle slope (as at point *b*), the fall in capital is small

Figure 11.3 The Marginal Rate of Substitution

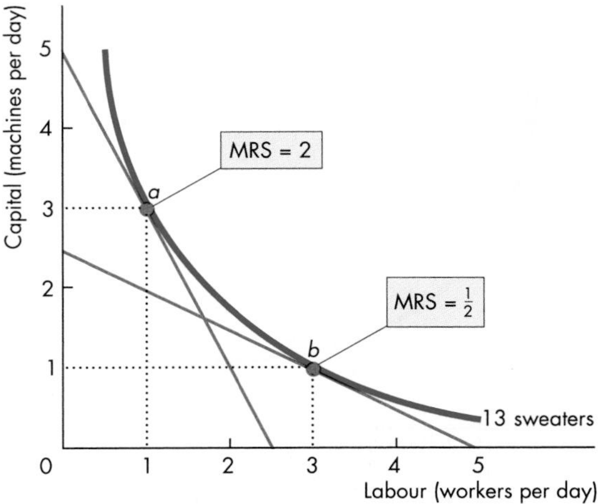

The marginal rate of substitution is measured by the magnitude of the slope of an isoquant. To calculate the marginal rate of substitution at point *a*, use the red line, which is tangential to the isoquant at point *a*. Calculate the slope of that line to find the slope of the isoquant at point *a*. The magnitude of the slope at point *a* is 2. Thus at point *a*, the marginal rate of substitution of capital for labour is 2. The marginal rate of substitution of capital for labour at point *b* is found from the slope of the line tangential to the isoquant at that point. That slope is ½. The marginal rate of substitution of capital for labour at point *b* is ½.

relative to the rise in labour, and the marginal rate of substitution of capital for labour is small.

The marginal rate of substitution at point *a* is the magnitude of the slope of the straight red line that is tangential to the isoquant at point *a*. The slope of the isoquant at point *a* is the same as the slope of the line. To calculate that slope, let's move along the red line from 5 knitting machines and no workers to 2.5 workers and no knitting machines. Capital falls by 5 knitting machines and labour rises by 2.5 workers. The magnitude of the slope is 5 divided by 2.5, which equals 2. Thus when using technique *a* to produce 13 sweaters a day, the marginal rate of substitution of capital for labour is 2.

The marginal rate of substitution at point *b* is the magnitude of the slope of the straight red line that is tangential to the isoquant at point *b*. This line has the same slope as the isoquant at point *b*. Along this red line, if capital falls by 2.5 knitting machines, labour increases by 5 workers. The magnitude of the slope is 2.5 divided by 5, which equals ½. Thus when using technique *b* to produce 13 sweaters a day, the marginal rate of substitution of capital for labour is ½.

You can now see that the principle of the diminishing marginal rate of substitution is embedded in the shape of the isoquant. When the capital input is large and the labour input is small, the isoquant is steep. As the capital input decreases and the labour input increases, the magnitude of the slope of the isoquant diminishes. Only curves that are bowed towards the origin have this feature; hence, isoquants are always bowed towards the origin.

The Isoquant Map

An **isoquant map** shows a series of isoquants, each for a different output. You have already seen two different isoquants in Figs. 11.2 and 11.3 (for 15 and 13 sweaters a day respectively). Figure 11.4(a) shows an isoquant map. It has three isoquants: one for 10 sweaters, one for 15 sweaters (the one that appears in Fig. 11.2), and one for 21 sweaters. Isoquants for higher outputs are farther from the origin. That is, to produce more output with a given capital input requires more labour, and to produce more output with a given labour input requires more capital. Thus if you start on any given isoquant and move to the right (more labour) or upward (more capital) or to the right and upward (more of both capital and labour), you get more output. Each of the isoquants shown in Fig. 11.4(a) is based on the production function presented in Fig. 11.1. But Fig. 11.4(a) does not show all the isoquants.

Let's make sure that we can see the relationship between the isoquant map in Fig. 11.4(a) and the numbers describing the production function in Fig. 11.1. Figure 11.4(b) is designed to help us do so. It extracts from Fig. 11.1 the three output levels shown by the isoquants in Fig. 11.4(a). Each output level, represented by a number in Fig. 11.4(b), corresponds to a point on an isoquant, and equal outputs are traced by curves that correspond to the isoquants. Let's identify two points on the isoquant map and find them in Fig. 11.4(b). First, consider point *a* on the isoquant for 10 sweaters a day. At point *a*, 2 knitting machines and 1 worker produce 10 sweaters. We can see that this same information appears in Fig. 11.4(b). Second, consider point *b* on the isoquant for 21 sweaters a day. At point *b*, 4 machines and 2 workers produce 21 sweaters a day. We can also see the same information in Fig. 11.4(b).

Figure 11.4 An Isoquant Map

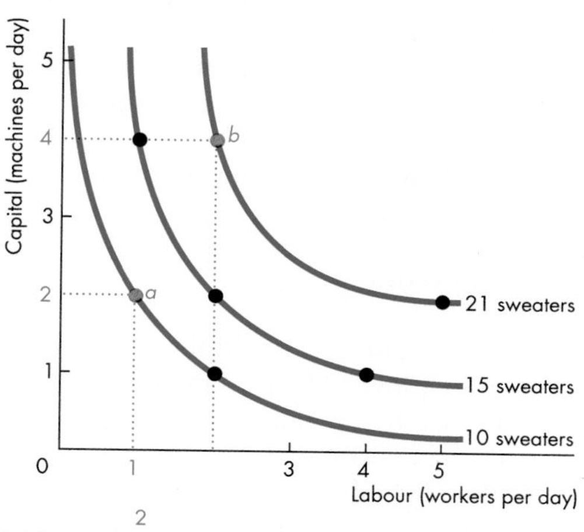

(a) Isoquants

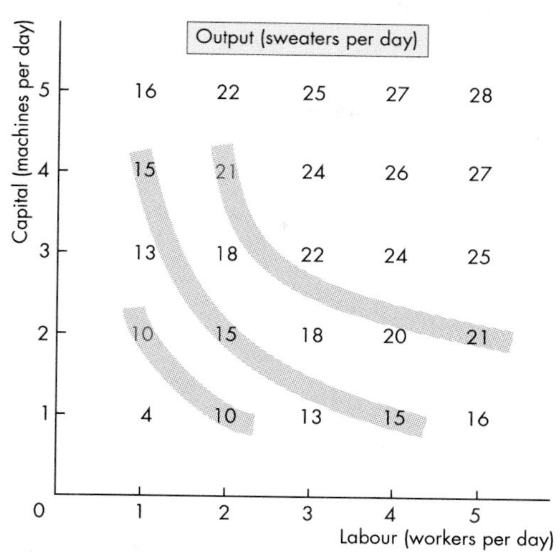

(b) Production function table

Part (a) is an isoquant map but one showing only 3 isoquants — those for 10, 15, and 21 sweaters a day. Part (b) highlights from Fig. 11.1 the different ways of producing these output levels. The different ways of producing a given output are connected in part (b) by the light blue curves. These curves correspond to the isoquants in part (a). Each of the points on the isoquants can be found in part (b). For example, point *a* uses 2 machines and 1 worker to produce 10 sweaters, and point *b* uses 4 machines and 2 workers to produce 21 sweaters.

R E V I E W

A firm's production function can be shown as an isoquant map. An isoquant shows all the alternative combinations of capital and labour required to produce a given level of output. The magnitude of the slope of an isoquant measures the marginal rate of substitution. The marginal rate of substitution of capital for labour diminishes as the capital input is decreased and the labour input is increased. There is a separate isoquant for each distinct level of output. Thus isoquants are bowed towards the origin. ■

Isoquants are very nice, you may be saying to yourself, but what do we do with them? The answer is that we use them to work out a firm's least-cost technique of production. But to do so, we need a way of illustrating the firm's costs in the same sort of diagram as that containing the isoquants.

Isocost Lines

An **isocost line** shows all the combinations of capital and labour that can be hired at given prices for a given total cost. To make the concept of the isocost line as clear as possible, we'll consider the following example. Swanky is going to spend a total of $100 a day producing sweaters. Knitting-machine operators can be hired for $25 a day. Knitting machines can be rented for $25 a day. (Later, we'll consider what happens when these input prices vary.) The table in Fig. 11.5 lists five possible combinations of labour and capital that Swanky can employ for a total cost of $100 a day. For example, row *b* shows that Swanky can use 3 machines (a cost of $75) and 1 worker (a cost of $25). The numbers in the table are graphed in the figure; each point, *a* through *e*, represents the corresponding row in the table. If Swanky can employ workers and machines for fractions of a day, then any of the combinations

Figure 11.5 Swanky's Input Possibilities

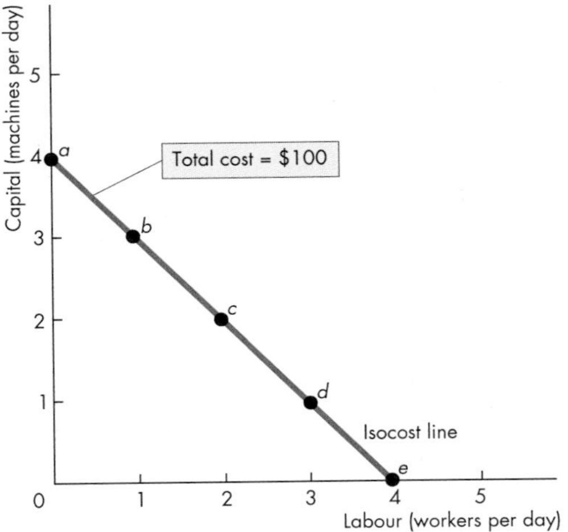

	Capital (Machines per day)	Labour (Workers per day)
a	4	0
b	3	1
c	2	2
d	1	3
e	0	4

For a given total cost, Swanky's input possibilities depend on input prices. If labour and capital each cost $25 per day, Swanky can employ for a total cost of $100 per day any of the combinations of capital and labour presented in the table. These combinations are graphed in the figure. The line passing through points *a* and *e* is an isocost line for a total cost of $100 per day.

along line *ae* can be employed for a total cost of $100. This line is Swanky's isocost line for a total cost of $100 a day.

The Isocost Equation

The isocost line can be described by an isocost equation. An **isocost equation** states the relationship between the quantities of inputs that can be hired at given input prices for a given total cost. Table 11.2 works out the isocost equation by using symbols that apply to any firm and numbers that describe Swanky's situation.

The first section of the table lists the variables that affect the firm's total cost: total cost itself, the prices of each input, and the quantity of each input employed. We have assigned a symbol to each of these variables. In Swanky's case, we're going to look at the amount of labour and capital that can be employed when a unit of either costs $25 a day and when total cost is $100.

The firm's total cost is set out in the second section of the table. It is

$$P_L L + P_K K = TC.$$

That is, the price of labour (P_L) multiplied by the quantity of labour employed (L) plus the price of capital (P_K) multiplied by the quantity of capital employed (K) equals total cost (TC). In Swanky's case, TC is $100 and the price of each of the inputs is $25.

The third section of the table shows you how to calculate the isocost equation. There are two steps.

Table 11.2 Calculating an Isocost Equation

In general		In Swanky's case
1. The variables		
Total cost	$= TC$	TC = $100
Price of labour (daily wage rate)	$= P_L$	P_L = $25
Price of capital (daily rental rate of machine)	$= P_K$	P_K = $25
Quantity of labour (number of knitting machine operators)	$= L$	L = Swanky's choice
Quantity of capital (number of knitting machines)	$= K$	K = Swanky's choice
2. Firm's total cost		
$P_L L + P_K K = TC$		$25*L* + $25*K* = $100
3. The calculation		
■ Divide by P_K to give $(P_L/P_K)L + K = TC/P_K$		■ Divide by P_K to give $L + K = 4$
■ Subtract $(P_L/P_K)L$ from both to give $K = TC/P_K - (P_L/P_K)L$		■ Subtract L from both sides to give $K = 4 - L$

First, divide the firm's total cost by the price of capital. Second, subtract (P_L / P_K) from both sides of the resulting equation. The result is the isocost equation:

$$K = TC / P_K - (P_L / P_K)\ L.$$

This equation tells us how the capital input varies as the labour input varies, holding total cost constant. You can check that Swanky's isocost equation corresponds to the isocost line graphed in Fig. 11.5. If L is 0, K is 4, which is point *a* in the figure. If L is 1, K is 3, which is point *b* in the figure, and so on.

The Effect of Input Prices

Along the isocost line that we have just calculated, capital and labour each cost $25 a day. Because these input prices are the same, in order to increase labour by 1 unit, the amount of capital used must be reduced by 1 unit to keep the total cost constant at $100. The isocost line shown in Fig. 11.5 has a slope of 1. That slope tells us that adding 1 unit of labour costs 1 unit of capital.

Next, let's consider some different prices, as shown in the table for Fig. 11.6. If the daily wage rate is $50 and the daily rental rate for knitting machines remains at $25, then 1 worker costs the same as 2 machines. To keep the total cost constant at $100, using 1 more worker now requires using 2 fewer machines. With the wage rate double that of the machine rental rate, the isocost line is line B in Fig. 11.6(a) and its slope is 2. That is, in order to hire 1 more worker and keep total cost constant, Swanky must give up 2 knitting machines.

If the daily wage rate remains at $25 and the daily rental rate of a knitting machine rises to $50,

Figure 11.6 Input Prices and the Isocost Line

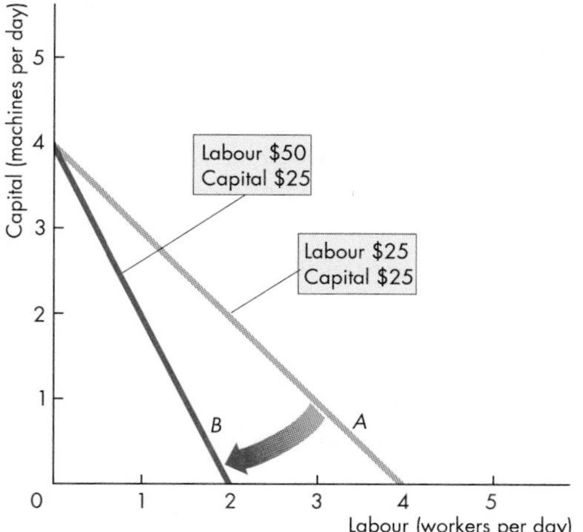

(a) An increase in the price of labour

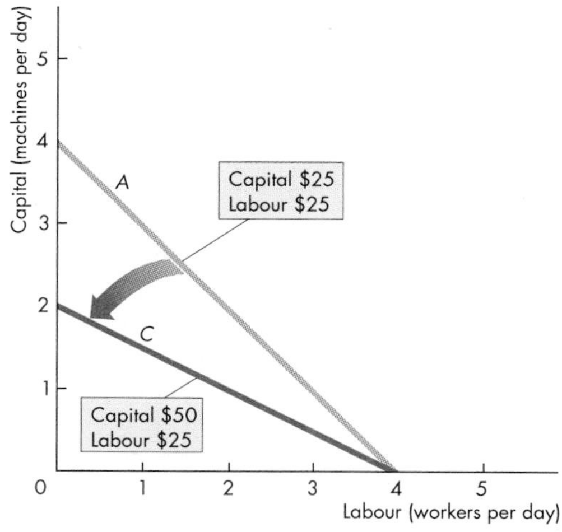

(b) An increase in the price of capital

Isocost line	Price of capital (rental rate per day)	Price of labour (wage per day)	Isocost equation
A	$25	25	$K = 4 - L$
B	$25	50	$K = 4 - 2L$
C	$50	25	$K = 2 - (1/2)L$

The slope of the isocost line depends on the relative input price. When all the inputs have the same price, the isocost line has a slope of 1. The line labelled A shows the isocost line for a total cost of $100 a day when capital and labour each cost $25 per day. If the price of labour doubles to $50 per day but the price of capital remains constant at $25 per day, the isocost line for a total cost of $100 per day is B in part (a). Its slope is twice that of isocost line A. If the price of capital doubles to $50 per day but the price of labour stays at $25 per day, the isocost line for a total cost of $100 per day is C in part (b). The slope of line C is half that of A.

then 2 workers cost the same as 1 machine. In this case, in order to get 1 more worker and keep total cost constant, Swanky must give up only half a knitting machine. The slope of the isocost line is now -½, as shown by line *C* in Fig. 11.6(b).

The higher the relative price of labour, the steeper is the slope of the isocost line. The magnitude of the slope of the isocost line measures the relative price of labour in terms of capital — that is, the price of labour divided by the price of capital.

The Isocost Map

An **isocost map** shows a series of isocost lines, each for a different level of total cost. Obviously, the higher the total cost, the larger the quantities of all inputs that can be employed. Figure 11.7 illustrates an isocost map. In that figure, the middle isocost line is the one that appeared in Fig. 11.5, showing a total cost of $100 when both capital and labour cost $25 a day each. The other two isocost lines in Fig. 11.7 are for a total cost of $125 and $75, with the prices of the inputs held constant at $25 each.

Figure 11.7 An Isocost Map

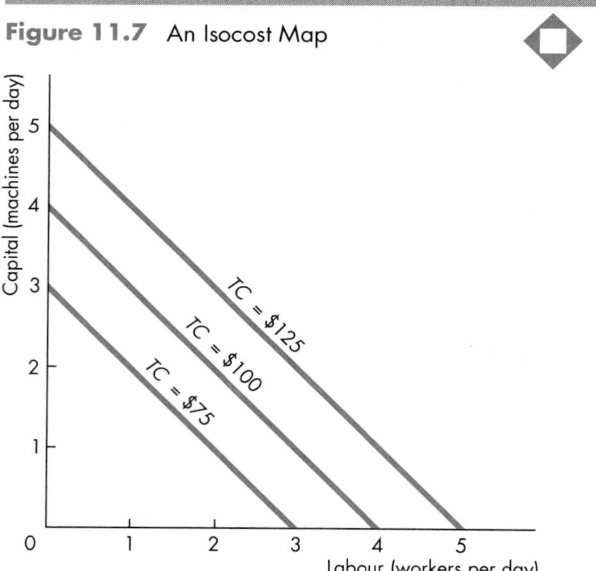

Each level of total cost has an isocost line. The three shown here are just a sample: one for a total cost of $75 per day, one for $100 per day, and one for $125 per day. For each isocost line, the prices of capital and labour are $25 per day each. The magnitude of the slope of the lines in an isocost map is the relative price of the two inputs — the price of labour divided by the price of capital. The higher the total cost, the further is the isocost line from the origin.

R E V I E W

An isocost line shows all the combinations of capital and labour that can be hired at given prices for the same total cost. The magnitude of the slope of an isocost line is the relative price of the two inputs — the price of labour divided by the price of capital. An isocost map shows a series of isocost lines, each for a different level of total cost. ■

We now have all the tools that we need to calculate the firm's least-cost technique of production.

The Least-Cost Technique

The **least-cost technique** is the combination of inputs that minimizes the total cost of producing a given output, given the input prices. Let's suppose that Swanky wants to produce 15 sweaters a day. What is the least-cost way of doing this? The answer can be seen in Fig. 11.8, which shows the isoquant for 15 sweaters. The three points on that isoquant (marked *a*, *b*, and *c*) illustrate the three techniques of producing 15 sweaters, as given in Fig. 11.1. Figure 11.8 also contains two isocost lines — each drawn for a price of capital and a price of labour of $25. One isocost line is for a total cost of $125 a day and the other for a total cost of $100 a day.

First, consider point *a*, which is on the isoquant for 15 sweaters a day and also on the isocost line with a total cost of $125 a day. Swanky can produce 15 sweaters at point *a* by using 1 worker and 4 machines. The total cost, using this technique of production, is $125. Point *c*, which uses 4 workers and 1 knitting machine, is similar to point *a*, except that it shows another technique by which the firm can produce 15 sweaters for a cost of $125.

Next look at point *b*. Swanky can produce 15 sweaters by using 2 machines and 2 workers. The total cost using this technique is $100. When knitting machines and workers each cost $25 a day, there is no way that Swanky can produce 15 sweaters for less than $100. Point *b* is the *least-cost technique* or the *economically efficient technique* for producing 15 sweaters at those input prices.

The least-cost technique, point *b*, has an important feature. At that point, the isocost line (for a total cost of $100) is tangential to the isoquant

Figure 11.8 The Least-Cost Technique of Production

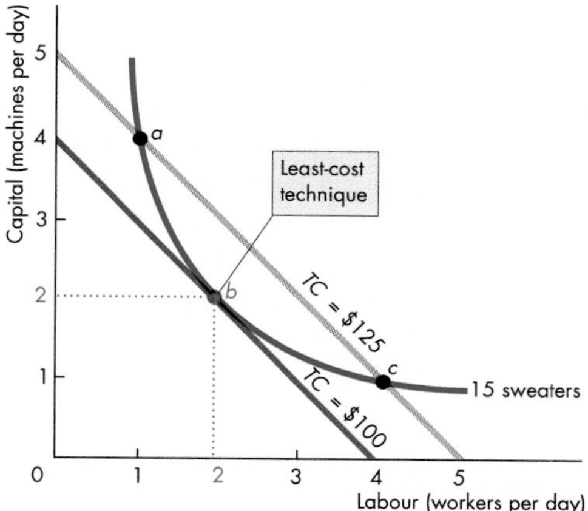

The least-cost technique of producing 15 sweaters per day uses 2 machines and 2 workers — at point *b*. An output of 15 sweaters can be produced with the technique illustrated by point *a* (4 machines and 1 worker) or the one illustrated by point *c* (1 machine and 4 workers). With either of these techniques, the total cost is $125 per day, which exceeds the total cost at *b* of $100 per day. At b, the isoquant for 15 sweaters is tangential to the isocost line for $100. The isocost line and the isoquant have the same slope. If the isoquant intersects the isocost line — for example at *a* and *c* — the least-cost technique has not been found. With the least-cost technique, the marginal rate of substitution (the magnitude of the slope of the isoquant) equals the relative price of the inputs (the magnitude of the slope of the isocost line).

(for 15 sweaters). The isoquant on which Swanky is producing (the isoquant for 15 sweaters) has a slope equal to that of the isocost line.

Notice that although there is only one way that Swanky can produce 15 sweaters for $100, there are several ways of producing 15 sweaters for more than $100. The techniques shown by points *a* and *c* are two examples. All the points between *a* and *b* and all the points between *b* and *c* are also ways of producing 15 sweaters for a cost that exceeds $100 but is less than $125. All of these ways of producing 15 sweaters are economically inefficient.

You can see that Swanky cannot produce 15 sweaters for less than $100 by imagining the isocost line for $99. It will not touch the isoquant for 15 sweaters. That is, the firm cannot produce 15 sweaters for $99. At $25 for a unit of each input, $99 will not buy the inputs required to produce 15 sweaters.

Marginal Rate of Substitution Equals Relative Input Price

When a firm is using the least-cost technique of production, the marginal rate of substitution between the inputs equals their relative price. Recall that the marginal rate of substitution is the magnitude of the slope of an isoquant. Relative input price equals the magnitude of the slope of the isocost line. We've just seen that producing at least cost means producing at a point where the isocost line is tangential to the isoquant. Since the two curves are tangential, their slopes are equal. Hence the marginal rate of substitution (the magnitude of the slope of isoquant) equals the relative input price (the magnitude of the slope of isocost line).

You will perhaps better appreciate the importance of relative input prices if we examine what happens to the least-cost technique when those input prices change.

Changes in Input Prices

The least-cost technique of production depends in an important way on the relative price of the inputs. In the case we've just studied, capital and labour each cost $25 a day. Let's look at two other cases: one in which capital costs twice as much as labour, and another in which labour costs twice as much as capital.

If knitting machines cost $25 a day and the wage paid increases to $50 a day, the isocost line becomes twice as steep as the one in Fig. 11.8. That is, to hire one more worker while holding total cost constant, Swanky has to operate two fewer knitting machines. Let's see how this change in the relative input price changes the least-cost production technique. In Fig. 11.9(a) you can see the isoquant for 15 sweaters a day and the initial least-cost technique of 2 knitting machines and 2 workers. When wages are $50 a day and knitting machines $25 a day, the isocost line becomes steeper. The least-cost method of producing 15 sweaters a day is now point *d*, where Swanky uses 3 machines and 1.3 workers per day. To continue producing 15 sweaters a day, total cost has to rise; that is, the minimum total cost of producing 15 sweaters is now higher than it was originally. The new, steeper isocost line in the figure shows the minimum total cost at which 15 sweaters can be produced at the new input prices. Along that isocost line, Swanky's total cost is $140. The total cost is calculated:
3 machines × $25 = $75, and 1.3 workers × $50 = $65; $75 + $65 = $140.

Figure 11.9 Changes in Input Prices

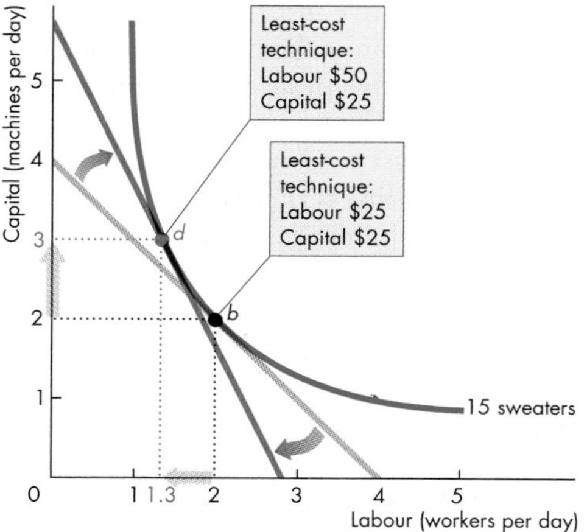

(a) An increase in wages

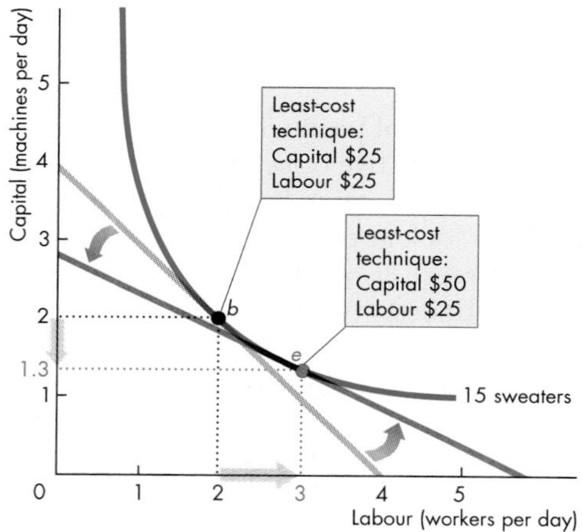

(b) An increase in the price of capital

If the price of labour doubles while the price of capital is held constant, the isocost line becomes twice as steep (part a). The least-cost method of producing 15 sweaters per day changes from *b* to *d*, using one more machine and 0.7 fewer workers per day. If the price of capital doubles while the price of labour is held constant, the isocost line becomes half as steep (part b). The least-cost method now changes from point *b* to point *e*, one additional worker is hired and 0.7 fewer machines are used.

Next, let's see what happens if wages stay constant but the cost of a machine increases. Suppose that knitting machines cost $50 a day while wages stay at $25 a day. In this case, the isocost line becomes less steep than the one in Fig. 11.8. Swanky now has to give up only half a worker to get one more machine. Figure 11.9(b) illustrates the effect of this change on the least-cost technique. Again, the initial isocost line and the least-cost technique are shown in the figure. When the cost of capital increases, the isocost line flattens. The least-cost method of producing 15 sweaters a day now uses 1.3 machines and 3 workers a day. This combination costs Swanky $140 a day, but it is the least-cost method of producing 15 sweaters a day when machines cost $50 and labour costs $25 a day.

A change in input prices leads to input substitution. To produce a given output level, firms use less of the input whose price has increased and more of the other input. The size of this substitution depends on the technology itself. If the inputs are very close substitutes for each other, the isoquants will be almost straight lines and the amount of substitution will be large. If the inputs are not close substitutes, the isoquants will curve very tightly and quite large changes in input prices will lead to only a small amount of substitution.

R E V I E W

The least-cost technique of producing a given output is the combination of inputs that minimizes total cost. With the least-cost technique,

- The slope of the isoquant equals the slope of the isocost line.
- The marginal rate of substitution of capital for labour equals the ratio of the price of labour to the price of capital.
- The higher the price of an input, the less of that input is used to produce a given output. ■

Let's now return to some of the questions with which this chapter opened and see how we can answer them using the ideas that you've studied in this chapter.

Real World Choice of Technique

The amount of capital used per unit of labour — capital intensity — varies enormously from one industry to another. Capital intensity also varies across countries. With the tools that you have just discovered, you can interpret these facts.

Industry Variations in Capital Intensity

Variations in capital intensity across industries in a given country arise because of differences in production functions. All firms buy their inputs in common markets, so they have to pay similar input prices. As a result, they face similar isocost lines. But production functions and the isoquants that describe technologies vary across industries. Figure 11.10 shows possible shapes of isoquants for three industries: plastics, frozen foods, and shirts. Although each industry faces a similar isocost line, the least-cost technique chosen varies considerably from one industry to another. In plastics, the chosen point is technique *a*, which uses a high capital-labour ratio. Faced with the same input prices, firms producing frozen foods choose technique *b*, with an average ratio. Faced with those same input prices, shirt producers choose technique *c*, with a low capital-labour ratio.

As input prices change, the least-cost technique changes. Throughout our industrial economic history, the most important such change has been a steady increase in the relative price of labour. As wages have increased over time, isocost lines have become steeper. As a consequence, firms have substituted capital for labour — they have chosen more capital-intensive techniques. This tendency to increased capital intensity has not occurred only in industries such as plastics. It has affected all industries.

Differences Across Countries

The differences in capital intensity across countries are explained mainly by differences in wages. In a high-wage country, the isocost lines are steep; in a low-wage country, they are gently sloped. Figure 11.11 shows two isocost lines — one for a country in which wages are high and the other for a country in which wages are low.

In contrast with wages, the two countries' isoquants are similar. That similarity arises from the fact that at a given point in time all firms, no matter where they are located, have access to the same technology. (This is true in most cases, although it may not be so if some techniques are protected by patents.) In general, the isoquants in a particular industry are therefore the same for both high-wage and low-wage countries. One such isoquant is shown in Fig. 11.11. For the high-wage country, the least-cost technique of production is at point *a*; for the

Figure 11.10 Variations in Capital and Labour Inputs Across Industries

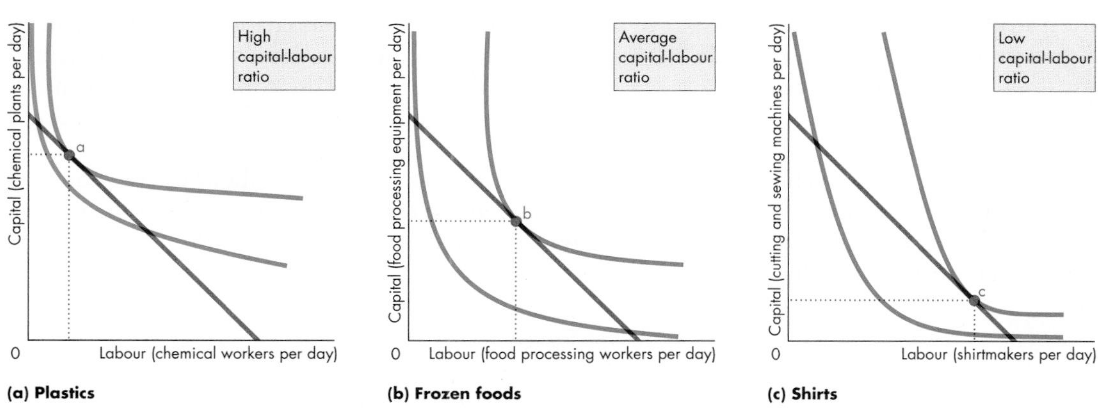

Variations in the relative amounts of capital and labour employed in different industries arise from differences in technologies. Industries face the same relative input prices (their isocost lines have the same slope) but have different isoquants. Isoquants for plastics (part a), frozen foods (part b), and shirts (part c) are shown in the figure. The least-cost technique for plastics (point *a*) uses a high capital-labour ratio; that for frozen food (point *b*) uses an average capital-labour ratio; and that for shirts (point *c*) uses a low capital-labour ratio.

Figure 11.11 Capital and Labour Inputs in High-Wage and Low-Wage Countries

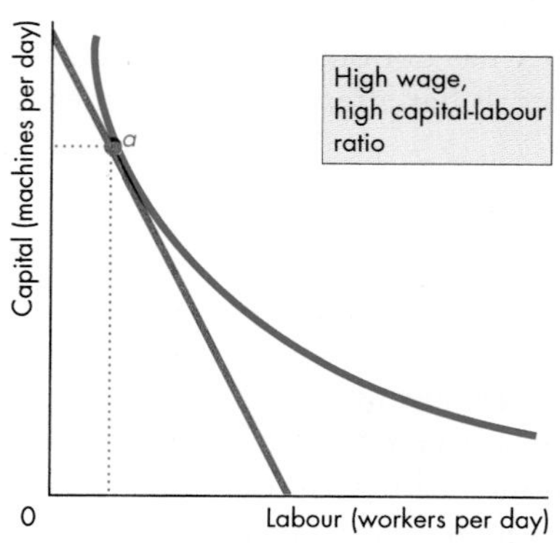

(a) High-wage country

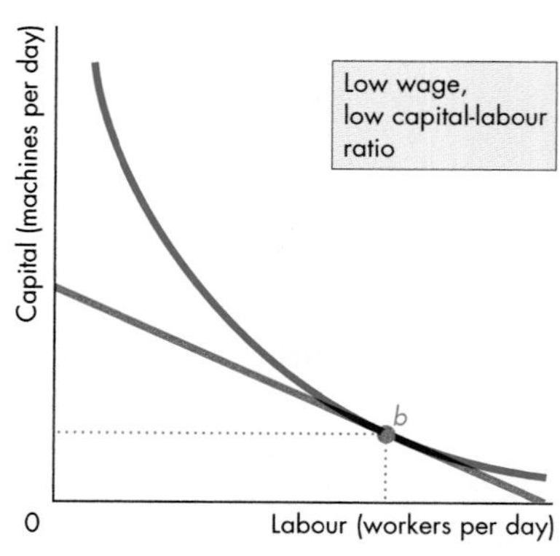

(b) Low-wage country

In high-wage countries, the isocost line is steep (part a). In low-wage countries, it is gentle (part b). The same technologies are available in all countries, so the isoquants are the same for both countries. The least-cost technique in the high-wage country (point *a*) uses a high capital-labour ratio. The least-cost technique in the low-wage country (point *b*) uses a low capital-labour ratio.

low-wage country, it is at point *b*. In low-wage countries, firms use a more labour-intensive technique than in high-wage countries, where a more capital-intensive technique is adopted. As wages rise in poorer countries, firms gradually slide along their isoquants and use a more capital-intensive technique of production. If wages in high-wage countries rise further relative to the cost of capital, firms in these countries will use an even more capital-intensive technique of production.

You can now see why gold mines in Amazonia look so different from strip mines in Canada. With low wages and a high cost of capital, it pays Brazilian gold mine operators to use a very labour-intensive production technique. With a high wage rate and a low cost of capital, it pays the mining companies of Canada to use a highly capital-intensive technique of production. As wages gradually rise in Brazil, more and more capital will be substituted for labour and those Amazonian gold mines will come to look like strip mines in Canada.

Marginal Product and Marginal Cost

When we studied short-run cost in Chapter 10, we learned about the connection between the marginal product curve of a variable input and the marginal cost curve. In the output range over which marginal product increases, marginal cost decreases; in the output range over which marginal product decreases, marginal cost increases. We also learned in Chapter 10 that it pays a firm to change its plant size if a different plant can produce the firm's desired output at a lower short-run cost than the existing plant. In this chapter, we have learned how to calculate the firm's cost-minimizing combination of capital (plant) and labour. The discussion of product curves and cost curves in Chapter 10 and of isocost lines, isoquants, and least-cost techniques of production in this chapter both deal with the same problem, but they look at it from different viewpoints. Let's examine the connection between these two approaches to the firm's cost-minimization problem.

First, we're going to learn about the relationship between the marginal rate of substitution and marginal product.

The Marginal Rate of Substitution and Marginal Product

The marginal rate of substitution and marginal product are linked together in a simple formula:

The marginal rate of substitution of capital for labour equals the marginal product of labour divided by the marginal product of capital.

That is,

$$MRS = MP_L / MP_K.$$

A few steps of reasoning are needed to establish this fact. First, we know that output changes when a firm changes the amounts of labour and capital employed. Furthermore, we know that the effect on output of a change in one of the inputs is determined by the marginal product of the input. It is equal to the change in the input multiplied by its marginal product. If both labour and capital inputs change, the change in output is given by the formula:

$$\text{Change in output} = \text{Marginal product of labour} \times \Delta L + \text{Marginal product of capital} \times \Delta K.$$

Suppose now that the firm wants to remain on a particular isoquant — that is, Swanky wants to produce the same number of sweaters when it changes its labour and capital inputs. To remain on an isoquant, the change in output must be zero. Making the change of output zero in the above equation and then rearranging it yields:

$$\begin{matrix}\text{Marginal} \\ \text{product} \\ \text{of labour}\end{matrix} \times \Delta L = - \begin{matrix}\text{Marginal} \\ \text{product} \\ \text{of capital}\end{matrix} \times \Delta K.$$

This equation tells us what must happen to the capital and labour inputs if Swanky is to stay on a particular isoquant. If the labour input rises, the capital input must fall. Equivalently, if the labour input falls, the capital input must rise. Thus we can write the equation in a slightly different way:

$$\begin{matrix}\text{Marginal} \\ \text{product} \\ \text{of labour}\end{matrix} \times \begin{matrix}\text{Rise in} \\ \text{labour} \\ \text{input}\end{matrix} = \begin{matrix}\text{Marginal} \\ \text{product} \\ \text{of capital}\end{matrix} \times \begin{matrix}\text{Fall in} \\ \text{capital} \\ \text{input}\end{matrix}.$$

If we divide both sides of the above equation by the rise in the labour input and also by the marginal product of capital, we get

$$\frac{\text{Fall in capital}}{\text{Rise in labour}} = \frac{\text{Marginal product of labour}}{\text{Marginal product of capital}}.$$

This equation tells us that when Swanky remains on an isoquant, the fall in its capital input divided by the rise in its labour input is equal to the marginal product of labour divided by the marginal product of capital. Now recall that we defined the marginal rate of substitution of capital for labour as the fall in capital divided by the rise in labour when the firm remains on a given isoquant. What we have discovered then is that the marginal rate of substitution of capital for labour is the ratio of the marginal product of labour to the marginal product of capital.

Marginal Cost

We can use the fact that we have just discovered — that the marginal rate of substitution of capital for labour equals the ratio of the marginal product of labour to the marginal product of capital — to work out an important implication of cost minimization. A few steps are needed, and Table 11.3 provides a guide to them.

Part (a) of Table 11.3 defines some symbols. Part (b) reminds us that the marginal rate of substitution of capital for labour is the magnitude of the slope of the isoquant, which in turn equals the ratio of the marginal product of labour (MP_L) to the marginal product of capital (MP_K). Part (b) also reminds us that the magnitude of the slope of the isocost line equals the ratio of the price of labour (P_L) to the price of capital (P_K). Part (c) of the table summarizes three propositions about a firm that is using the least-cost technique of production.

The first of these propositions is that when the least-cost technique is employed, the slope of the isoquant and the isocost line are the same. That is,

$$MP_L / MP_K = P_L / P_K.$$

The second proposition is that total cost is minimized when the marginal product per dollar spent on labour equals the marginal product per dollar spent on capital. To see why, just rearrange the above equation in the following way. First, multiply both sides by the marginal product of capital and then divide both sides by the price of labour. The result is

$$MP_L / P_L = MP_K / P_K.$$

This equation says that the marginal product of labour per dollar spent on labour is equal to the marginal product of capital per dollar spent on capital. In other words, the extra output from the last dollar spent on labour equals the extra output from the last dollar spent on capital. This makes sense. If the extra output from the last dollar spent on labour exceeds the extra output from the last dollar spent on capital, it will pay the firm to use less capital and more labour. By doing so, it can produce the same output at a lower total cost. Conversely, if the extra output from the last dollar spent on capital exceeds the

Table 11.3 The Least-Cost Technique

(a) Symbols

Marginal rate of substitution of capital for labour	MRS
Marginal product of labour	MP_L
Marginal product of capital	MP_K
Price of labour	P_L
Price of capital	P_K

(b) Definitions

Magnitude of the slope of the isoquant (MRS)	MP_L / MP_K
Magnitude of the slope of the isocost line	P_L / P_K

(c) The least-cost technique

Slope of the isoquant = Slope of the isocost line

Therefore:

$$MP_L / MP_K = P_L / P_K .$$

Equivalently:

$$MP_L / P_L = MP_K / P_K .$$

That is,

Total cost is minimized when the marginal product per dollar spent on labour equals the marginal product per dollar spent on capital.

Equivalently, flipping over the last equation:

$$P_L / MP_L = P_K / MP_K.$$

That is,

Marginal cost with capital fixed and labour varying equals marginal cost with labour fixed and capital varying.

extra output from the last dollar spent on labour, it will pay the firm to use less labour and more capital. Again, doing so lowers the cost of producing a given output. A firm achieves the least-cost technique of production only when the extra output from the last dollar spent on all the inputs is the same.

The third proposition is that marginal cost with capital fixed and labour varying equals marginal cost with labour fixed and capital varying. To see this proposition, simply flip over the last equation and write it as

$$P_L / MP_L = P_K / MP_K .$$

Expressed in words, this equation says that the price of labour divided by its marginal product must equal the price of capital divided by its marginal product. But what is the price of an input divided by its marginal product? The price of labour divided by the marginal product of labour is marginal cost when the capital input is held constant. To see why this is so, first recall the definition of *marginal cost:* the change in total cost resulting from a unit increase in output. If output rises because one more unit of labour is employed, total cost rises by the cost of the extra labour, and output rises by the marginal product of the labour. So marginal cost is the price of labour divided by the marginal product of labour. For example, if labour costs \$25 a day and the marginal product of labour is 2 sweaters, then the marginal cost of a sweater is \$12.50 (\$25 ÷ 2) ·

The price of capital divided by the marginal product of capital has a similar interpretation. The price of capital divided by the marginal product of capital is marginal cost when the labour input is constant. As you can see from the above equation, with the least-cost technique of production, marginal cost is the same regardless of whether the capital input is constant and more labour is used or the labour input is constant and more capital is used.

R E V I E W

If a firm wants to increase output, it looks at the various methods available for achieving that end. If one of the methods of increasing output adds less to cost than some other method does, then that method is used. Even if the firm doesn't want to increase output, if the marginal cost of production using one input exceeds that of using another, it will pay the firm to decrease its use of the input whose contribution to marginal cost is highest and increase the use of the input whose contribution to marginal cost is lowest. Only when all inputs have the same impact on marginal cost has the firm achieved the least-cost method of production. ■

■ We have now seen how firms minimize cost. Our next task is to study the interactions of firms and households in markets for goods and services to see how prices, output levels, and profits are determined.

SUMMARY

Input Substitution

A given amount of output can be produced by using a small amount of capital and a large amount of labour (labour-intensive technique) or a small amount of labour and a large amount of capital (capital-intensive technique). The production function describes the output produced by different combinations of capital and labour.

The marginal rate of substitution of capital for labour measures the decrease in capital needed per unit increase in labour to keep output constant. The marginal rate of substitution of capital for labour diminishes as the amount of labour used to produce a given output increases and the amount of capital used decreases. This general tendency is the law of diminishing marginal rate of substitution. (pp. 259-261)

Isoquants

An isoquant is a curve that shows the different combinations of inputs that can produce a fixed amount of output. The magnitude of the slope of the isoquant measures the marginal rate of substitution. An isoquant map shows a series of isoquants, each for a different level of output. The larger the level of output, the farther the isoquant is from the origin. (pp. 261-263)

Isocost Lines

An isocost line shows the combinations of capital and labour that can be hired at given prices for a given total cost. An isocost map shows a series of isocost lines, each for a different level of total cost. The magnitude of the slope of an isocost line is the ratio of the price of labour to the price of capital — the relative price of labour. (pp. 263-266)

The Least-Cost Technique

The least-cost technique of production is the least expensive combination of inputs that produces a given output at given factor prices. The least-cost technique occurs when the marginal rate of substitution of capital for labour equals the ratio of the price of labour to the price of capital. This situation is illustrated on a graph as the point at which the isocost line for the least possible cost is tangential to the isoquant for the given output level.

A change in input prices changes the least-cost production technique. The higher the price of an input, the smaller is the quantity of that input used in the least-cost technique. (pp. 266-268)

Real World Choice of Technique

Variations in capital intensity across industries occur because of differences in production functions. Some industries have isoquants that lead them to choose a capital-intensive technique as the least-cost technique of production. Others have isoquants that lead to a labour-intensive technique of production.

Capital intensity varies across different countries mainly because of differences in wages. In a high-wage country, the isocost lines are relatively steep; in a low-wage country, they are more gently sloped. Thus firms in high-wage countries use capital-intensive techniques while those in low-wage countries adopt labour-intensive techniques. (pp. 268-270)

Marginal Product and Marginal Cost

The marginal rate of substitution of capital for labour equals the ratio of the marginal product of labour to the marginal product of capital. When total cost is minimized, the ratio of the marginal product of labour to the marginal product of capital equals the ratio of the price of labour to the price of capital. This fact implies that when the least-cost technique of production is used, the marginal product of labour per dollar spent on labour is equal to the marginal product of capital per dollar spent on capital. It also implies that the marginal cost of increasing output is the same regardless of whether that increase is achieved by increasing the labour or the capital input. (pp. 270-272)

KEY ELEMENTS

Key Terms

Key Figures and Tables 

REVIEW QUESTIONS

1 What is a production function?

2 Define the marginal rate of substitution.

3 How is the marginal rate of substitution calculated?

4 What is an isoquant?

5 What does the slope of an isoquant measure?

6 What is an isocost line?

7 What does the slope of an isocost line measure?

8 Describe the conditions that are satisfied when a firm has chosen the least-cost technique for producing a given output.

9 How does the least-cost technique change when input prices change?

10 Why do we observe variations in capital intensity across industries in a given country?

11 Why do we observe variations in capital intensity across countries?

12 What is the relationship between the marginal rate of substitution and the marginal product of labour and of capital?

13 When costs are minimized, what is the relationship between the marginal cost of increasing output by using more capital and that from using more labour?

PROBLEMS

1 The following table shows the output per hour of a doughnut producer using alternative combinations of capital and labour:

Units of capital	**Units of labour** 1	2	3
3	280	430	490
2	190	280	320
1	100	160	190

Sketch the isoquants for 190 and 280 doughnuts an hour and identify two points on each isoquant.

2 Using the information in problem 1, calculate the marginal rate of substitution of capital for labour if the firm switches the method of production from

a) 1 unit of labour and 3 units of capital to 2 units of each.

b) 1 unit of labour and 2 units of capital to 3 units of labour and 1 unit of capital.

3 Suppose the doughnut producer in problem 1 finds that labour costs $10 an hour and capital rents for $15 an hour. Calculate the isocost equation.

4 Given the information in problems 1 and 3, what is the least-cost technique of producing

a) 190 doughnuts an hour?

b) 280 doughnuts an hour?
(Use only whole units, not fractions of units, of labour and capital.)

5 When the least-cost technique is being used in problem 4, what is the marginal cost of labour and of capital?

6 Suppose that the doughnut producer's labour costs rise to $15 an hour and the cost of capital equipment falls to $10 an hour. Calculate the isocost equation.

7 Given the information in problem 6, what is the doughnut producer's least-cost technique of producing

a) 190 doughnuts an hour?

b) 280 doughnuts an hour?
(Use only whole units, not fractions of units, of labour and capital.)

8 When the least-cost technique is being used in problem 7, what is the marginal cost of labour and of capital?

9 Compare your answers to problems 3 and 6. What do they tell you about the effect of the relative input price on the slope of the isocost line?

10 Compare your answers to problems 4 and 7. What do they tell you about the effects of the relative input price on the least-cost technique of production?

11 Compare the marginal cost of labour with the marginal cost of capital in problem 5. Do the same thing in problem 10. What can you say about these marginal costs and the least-cost technique of production?

PART 5

Markets For Goods and Services

TALKING WITH

CURTIS EATON

Curtis Eaton, who obtained his BA and PHD from the University of Colorado, has taught at the University of British Columbia, the University of Toronto, and Simon Fraser University. Professor Eaton specializes in microeconomic theory and, collaborating with Richard Lipsey, has made important advances in our understanding of the working of markets with monopolistic elements arising from product differentiation—monopolistic competition. With his wife, Diane Eaton, he is coauthor of *Microeconomics* (W. H. Freeman and Company), an intermediate text. Michael Parkin spoke with

Curtis Eaton about his work and about the role of theory and of mathematics in economics.

"Economics appealed to me because it had a unifying vision—a vision of individual behaviour driven by self-interest."

Professor Eaton, how and when did you get into economics?

In my last year of high school I had a devoted teacher who was also a social scientist. Listening to her, I decided I wanted to be a social scientist (I'm not sure I'd even heard of economics). In university I sampled all the social sciences. Economics appealed to me because it had a unifying vision—a vision of individual behaviour driven by self-interest. Economics also appealed to me because it appeared to enable one to do a lot of policy intervention. I think I got into economics to become a trust-buster. That was the first piece of public policy that made sense to me. (I remember writing an essay in the first year of university about the evils of monopoly and how we should make the world safe for consumers!)

Much of your work has been mathematical in nature, proving theorems about economic relationships in the manner that mathematicians prove theorems about more abstract relationships. Is economics unavoidably a mathematical subject?

It's essential to have a fair amount of mathematics to survive in economics—it's the language in which economists communicate with one another. But I don't think that economics is fundamentally mathematical. Most of the very good ideas in economic theory are very simple and nonmathematical.

The best example I can think of is the work of George Akerlof. He asked, "Why is it that when I buy a new car, the minute I drive it off the lot its market value drops by a significant percentage?" To answer that question, he asked another: "Why would someone who has only recently bought a new car want to sell it?" His answer was, "Perhaps in the time between buying and deciding to resell, the person discovered that the car is a lemon." He then generalized this simple insight, observing that if he could figure it out, so could the average buyer in the used-car market. Hence the average buyer would infer that a recent model on the used-car market had a high probability of being a lemon and hence was not worth the price of an apparently identical new car. From this thinking was born the economics of asymmetric information.

You're an economic theorist. What does an economic theorist do?

Economic theory is a body of knowledge whose purpose is to help us understand economic reality. Its central presumption is that people are motivated by what they perceive as their own self-interest. The role of the economic theorist is to spot anomalies—why the drop in value of a new car when it's driven off the lot?—and to construct explanations of them consistent with the overall vision of human behaviour driven by self-interest.

Can we talk about the role of assumptions in economic theory?

Economists tell what seems to be a joke against them. There are three people stranded on a desert island: an engineer, a physicist, and an economist. They have a can of beans but no canopener. "No problem," says the engineer, "I'll climb a tree and drop the can onto a rock. Its contents will splatter all over the rock, but at least we'll be able to eat them." "Hold it" says the physicist, "I can do better. I'll use a piece of broken glass to concentrate the sun's rays and burn a hole in the can. The beans will even be cooked when we get at them!" The economist is bemused by these proposed antics. "I've got the best solution of all," he says. "Let's assume that we have a can opener!" What is the place of assumptions in economics? Are they always unrealistic like the can opener assumption?

I don't think economists should apologize for their penchant for unrealistic assumptions. It's a natural part of building theory and it occurs in all sciences. Two very good economists working in Canada right now—Mukesh Eswaran and Russell Davidson—started out as theorists in physics, and both report two things: economic theory is as difficult to do as physics, and the use of unreal assumptions is pervasive in both sciences.

One reason we often find ourselves making assumptions that capture very little of reality is that economics is not an experimental science. We have this reality that we would like to understand, and it's difficult for us to tinker with it to find out directly what assumptions are appropriate. Ideally, we find a set of assumptions consistent with that reality and then explore their boundaries. But if you explore boundaries, sometimes you're going to jump over them and explore the implications of something that is not consistent with the reality—that is unreal.

Let's look at the two main economic models of markets: perfect competition and monopoly. The assumptions that characterize these two types of markets are extreme—they are beyond or at least at the boundary of what we see in real economies. Most real-world markets have both competitive and monopolistic elements. Are the models of perfect competition and monopoly nevertheless useful?

They're the most useful models we have, at least as pedagogical devices. They are extremely simple. They convey the basic insights of economics, and in tandem, they convey insights about what does and does not tend to give rise to efficiency in the allocation of resources. We don't have what it takes to construct simple models that are not monopolistic and/or competitive.

Can we talk about your own attempts to develop models that blend monopolistic and competitive elements? What are the anomolies that your work seeks to help us understand?

Go into a department store and try to find two products that

"I don't think economists should apologize for their penchant for unrealistic assumptions. It's a natural part of building theory."

"If I were an ambitious young person starting out today . . . I would embark on trying to construct an evolutionary theory of economics."

are identical but produced by different firms. It's virtually impossible to do so. Almost always, firms choose to produce products that are differentiated from one another. Why? That's one awkward fact that we'd like to explain.

Now imagine that a group of students bring their entire wardrobes into the classroom and search through them for identical products. We start out looking for identical wardrobes. There aren't any. Then we look for identical pieces in these wardrobes. We find a few, but not very many. Tastes are extremely diverse. That's another awkward fact.

A third interesting fact is that although the diversity of products allows us a fair amount of latitude to indulge our diverse tastes, it's almost always true that we can't get *exactly* what we want. We buy off-the-rack clothes, cars, and houses. That tells me that the degree of observed product differentiation is small relative to the degree of diversity of taste.

That set of facts leads to a question. What is it that limits our ability to indulge our diversity of tastes?

What's the answer—and its implications?

Part of the answer is the cost of product development. This cost is the single most important limit to the ability of markets to produce diversity and thus the single most important source of increasing returns to scale. In the microchip industry, for example, it's said that the resources that go into developing a new generation of chips are of the same order of magnitude as all of the resources that go into actually producing the chips.

So we've got this diversity of taste, and we've got increasing returns to scale. What follows is more or less ubiquitous market power. There's no invisible hand at work in this world as there is in Adam Smith's world, and there are no obvious institutions to get us an efficient allocation of resources (supposing that we can identify efficiency). But I don't think our role is to be social engineers (I've really changed my view on that since I was an undergraduate); rather, it is to understand the world.

If you were just embarking on your career as an economic theorist today, what would you study and why?

I perceive that at the frontiers of economic theory we are running up against the limits of the hypothesis that people pursue their self-interest in a rational, foresighted way. Two things happen when we get very sophisticated about the notion of informed, foresighted self-interest. One, the substance tends to dissipate in the sense that too many things are possible, and where not too many things are possible, it's extremely difficult to solve the problem. So we need to start exploring an alternative hypothesis. I believe that the most promising alternative is evolutionary theory. If I were an ambitious young person starting out today, I would study mathematical theories of evolution. I would invest a fair amount in the mathematics of stochastic processes and in the study of algorithms and in the acquisition of the skills necessary to do simulations. I would embark on trying to construct an evolutionary theory of economics.

CHAPTER 12

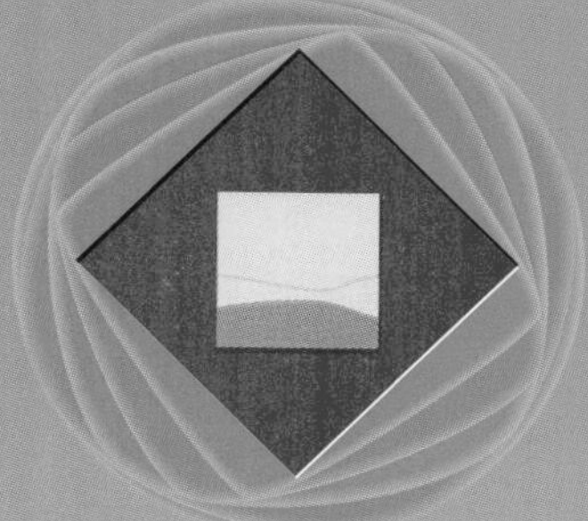

Competition

After studying this chapter, you will be able to:

- Define perfect competition.
- Explain why a perfectly competitive firm cannot influence the market price.
- Explain how a competitive industry's output changes when price changes.
- Explain why firms sometimes shut down temporarily and lay off workers.
- Explain why firms enter and leave an industry.
- Predict the effects on an industry and on a typical firm of a change in demand and of a technological advance.
- Explain why farmers have had such a bad time in recent years.
- Explain why perfect competition is efficient.

Collision Course in Car Repairs

IT IS MORNING RUSH HOUR and a six-vehicle pile-up snarls the traffic on Toronto's busiest section of Highway 401. Mercifully, human injuries are light, but the toll in damaged hardware is considerable. Dented car bodies, buckled wheels and damaged tires, and crushed mufflers litter two blocked lanes. And the competition to clean up the mess begins. ■ Within a 15-minute drive of the crash site there are no fewer than 50 towing companies competing for the initial stage of the clean-up. Then several hundred body shops, from national household names such as Maaco ("we've painted 4 million cars") to small operators such as Gary's Garage, are ready to compete for the job of replacing damaged panels and supplying new coats of paint. More than 20 brands of tires, sold by scores of dealers from national giants such as Canadian Tire and OK to small firms such as Tubby's Tire Service, compete to replace the damaged tires. Speedy, Midas, Mufflerman, and countless other small "mufflermen" such as George Noseworthy are at the ready to compete for the job of replacing the crushed mufflers. ■ Fixing cars is not the only competitive business activity. Whether you want your car fixed, a new lock installed, your TV repaired, your furniture moved, a new eyeglass prescription filled, or a pizza delivered, you have lots of choice about which of dozens, perhaps hundreds of firms to call. Just look in the Yellow Pages if you're not convinced! The firms supplying these and many other goods and services are locked together in fierce competition. Every day in such industries some firms disappear, squeezed out of business by the forces of competition, and new firms arrive on the scene to try their luck. ■ How does competition affect prices and profits? What causes some firms to leave an industry and others to enter it? What are the effects on profits and prices when new firms enter and old firms leave an industry? ■ In 1982 and 1983, more than one million people were unemployed. Of these, more than one-half were unemployed because they had lost their jobs. Some of these job-losers had worked for firms that went out of business. But many of them were laid off by firms that were seeking to trim their costs and thus avoid bankruptcy. Automobile producers, ice cream makers, computer manufacturers, and firms in almost every sector of the economy were laying off their workers on a massive scale. Those years were unusually harsh ones, but even in a typical year, more than one-quarter of a million people are unemployed as firms trim back the scale of their labour force. Why do firms lay off workers? When will a firm temporarily shut down, laying off all its workers? ■ Over the past few years, there has been a dramatic fall in the prices of all kinds of consumer goods, such as VCRs, Walkmans, pocket calculators, and personal computers. What exactly goes on in an industry when the price of its output falls dramatically? What causes the price to fall, and what happens to the profits of the firms that produce such goods? ■ Canadian farms have been in the news a great deal in recent years. Most farmers have fallen on very hard times. Many of them have gone out of business. What has been happening in the farm sector that has created such serious problems?

■ With what you learn in this chapter, you will be able to make sense of the questions just posed. To tackle these issues, we have to look beyond the individual firm standing in isolation and think about how firms interact with each other. Most goods are produced by more than one firm, so the firms compete with each other. Each tries to outdo its rivals by producing at a lower cost and by selling a larger output, thereby making the biggest possible profit. We will study markets in which firms are locked in such stiff competition with each other that the best one firm can do is to match its rivals in terms of quality and price. We will study other types of markets in the following two chapters. But what we learn in this chapter will help us to understand a wide variety of business situations, including the phenomena described above.

Perfect Competition

In order to study competitive markets, we are going to build a model of a market in which competition is as fierce and extreme as possible — even more extreme than in the examples just given. Economists call it perfect competition. **Perfect competition** occurs in a market where

- There are many firms, each selling an identical product.
- There are many buyers.
- There are no restrictions on entry into the industry.
- Firms already in the industry have no advantage over potential new entrants.
- Firms and buyers are completely informed about the prices of the products of each firm in the industry.

Under the conditions that characterize perfect competition, no single firm can exert a significant influence on the market price of a good. Firms in such markets are said to be price takers. A **price taker** is a firm that cannot influence the price of its product.

Perfect competition does not occur frequently in the real world, but competition in many industries is so fierce that the model of perfect competition that we are about to study is of enormous help in predicting the behaviour of the firms in these industries. Wreck towing, panel beating and fixing, muffler fixing, farming, fishing, wood pulping and paper milling, the manufacture of paper cups and plastic shopping bags, grocery retailing, photofinishing, lawn service, plumbing, painting, and dry cleaning and the provision of laundry services are all examples of industries that are highly competitive.

When a Firm Can't Influence Price

Perfectly competitive or, equivalently, price-taking behaviour occurs in markets in which a single firm produces a small fraction of the total output of a particular good. Imagine for a moment that you are a wheat farmer in Saskatchewan. You have 500 hectares under cultivation — which sounds like a lot. But then you go on a drive, first heading west. The flat lands turn into rolling hills as you head towards the Rocky Mountains, but everywhere you look you see thousands and thousands of hectares of wheat. The sun goes down in the west behind millions of hectares of golden plants. The next morning it rises in the east above the same scene. Driving east to Manitoba or south to the Dakotas reveals similar vistas. You also find unbroken stretches of wheat in other parts of the United States, Argentina, Australia, and the Soviet Union. Your 500 hectares is a drop in the bucket — to be accurate, it's a molecule in a bucket.

You are a price taker. Nothing makes your wheat any better than any other farmer's. If everybody else sells wheat for $3 a bushel and you want $3.10, why would people buy from you? They can simply go to the next farmer, and the one after that, and the next and buy all they need for $3. So at a price of $3.10, you sell nothing. The same is true for any price above $3. If you try to get more than the going market price for your product, you don't make any sales. And there is no point in cutting your price below $3 to try to increase your sales. If you did offer your wheat for less than $3, the whole world would be knocking on your door and you wouldn't be able to fill your orders. You can sell your entire output for $3, so why ask for less?

Industry and Firm Elasticity of Demand

A price-taking firm faces a demand curve that is perfectly elastic. To see why, let's consider an example. Suppose that there are 1,000 firms of equal size producing a good. Even if one firm doubles its output (a big change for an individual firm), industry output will rise by only 0.01 percent (which is another way of writing one one-thousandth). Suppose that the industry elasticity of demand for the good is 0.5; then this increase in industry output results in a 0.02 percent fall in price. To put things in perspective, a price change of this magnitude is a dollar on a $500 television set, 10 cents on a $50 dress, and a penny on a $5 movie ticket. But these price changes, although small, are much larger than the ones that result from output changes of a magnitude that a firm might actually make. Therefore when one firm changes its output rate, the effect of that change on price is tiny and the firm ignores it. The firm behaves as if its own actions have no effect on the market price.

Table 12.1 works through a real world example — the market for fish — and shows the relationship between the elasticity of demand facing an individual competitive fishery and the fish market as a whole. The market elasticity of demand for fish is 0.42 but the elasticity of demand facing an individual producer is almost 40,000.

When we studied the concept of elasticity in Chapter 5, we discovered that a horizontal demand curve has an elasticity of infinity. An elasticity of 40,000 is not quite infinity, but it is very large. A firm whose demand has such an elasticity has, for all practical purposes, an infinitely elastic demand. Such a firm's demand curve is horizontal. The firm is a price taker.

Table 12.1 A Fishery's Elasticity of Demand

(a) Data

- World output of fish is 76.8 billion kilograms per year.
- An average fishery produces 0.8 million kilograms per year.
- The average price of fish is 82.5 cents per kilogram.
- The coefficient of the elasticity of demand for fish and fish products (η_m) is 0.42.

(b) Effect on world price

- If an average fishery increases output by 100 percent, world output increases by 0.8 million kilograms — 0.00107 percent.
- To calculate the change in world price that results from this increase in output, use the formula:

$$\eta_m = \frac{\text{Percentage change in quantity demanded}}{\text{Percentage change in price}}.$$

In equilibrium, the change in the quantity demanded equals the change in the quantity supplied, which means that

$$\text{Percentage change in price} = \frac{\text{Percentage change in quantity}}{\eta_m}.$$

- To find the fall in price, use the formula:

$$\text{Percentage change in price} = 0.00107/0.42 = 0.00254 \text{ percent.}$$

- A price fall of 0.00254 percent is a fall of 0.0021 cents per kilogram.
- When a firm doubles its output, the price falls by 0.0021 cents per kilogram.

(c) Fishery's elasticity of demand

- The firm's elasticity of demand (η_f) is given by

$$\eta_f = \frac{\text{Percentage change in firm's output sold}}{\text{Percentage change in price}}.$$

$$= 100/0.00254$$

$$= 39{,}370.$$

Part (a) provides some data about the market for fish. Most fish is sold frozen and the market for fish is worldwide. Part (b) calculates the effects on the world market price if one fishery doubles its output. If one fishery doubles its output, world output rises by 0.8 million kilograms or changes by approximately 0.001 percent. As a result of this increase, the world price of fish falls by 0.00254 percent or 0.0021 cents per kilogram. Part (c) calculates the individual producer's elasticity of demand, η_f. That elasticity is almost 40,000!

Note: Quanity, price, and estimate of the elasticity of demand for fish products are for 1982 and have been taken from U.S. Bureau of the Census, *Statistical Abstract of the United States*: 1986, 106th ed. (Washington, DC, 1985): 681-9. Imperial measures in the source have been converted to metric, as appropriate.

Competition in Everyday Life

We have defined perfect competition as a situation in which a firm is a price taker. If the firm tries to charge a higher price, no one will buy its output; if it offers its goods for a lower price than that prevailing in the market, it will sell them, but since it can also sell them for the market price, there is no point in price cutting.

The inability of a perfectly competitive firm to compete by price cutting makes it seem as if a perfectly competitive market is not, in fact, very competitive at all. If firms don't compete on price, in what sense do they compete with each other?

Firms compete with each other in much the same way as athletes or football teams do. Firms try to find new approaches that will give them an edge over their competitors. Sometimes, though, the competition that they face is so stiff that they are left with little room to manoeuvre. This happens in sporting events, too. For example, when two wrestlers are closely matched, neither has much room to manoeuvre. They are locked in such fierce competition that the best they can do is to match each other's moves, try not to make a mistake, and accept the inevitable — that the outcome will be close and may even be a tie.

Like evenly matched athletes, firms in perfect competition are locked in such a fierce competitive struggle with each other that they have no choice other than to mimic each other's actions — producing a comparable quality good at a comparable price — and to put up with an outcome analogous to a tie.

Let's now study the behaviour of a perfectly competitive industry, beginning with an examination of the choices made by a typical firm in such an industry.

Firms' Choices in Perfect Competition

A perfectly competitive firm has to make three key decisions:

- Whether to stay in the industry or to leave it
- If the decision is to stay in the industry, whether to produce or temporarily shut down
- If the decision is to produce, how much to produce

In studying the competitive firm's choices, we will continue to look at a model firm whose single objective is to maximize its profit. We'll first consider a situation in which a firm decides to produce. We will then look at the other cases — firms that decide to shut down production temporarily or to leave the industry altogether.

Profit and Revenue

Profit is the difference between a firm's total revenue and its total cost. We defined and studied the behaviour of total cost in the last two chapters. But what is total revenue? Let's begin by looking at the concepts of revenue.

Total revenue is the value of a firm's sales. It equals the price of the firm's output multiplied by the number of units of output sold (price times quantity). **Average revenue** is total revenue divided by the total quantity sold — revenue per unit of output. Since total revenue is price times quantity sold, average revenue (total revenue divided by quantity sold) equals price. **Marginal revenue** is the change in total revenue resulting from a one-unit increase in the quantity sold. Since, in the case of perfect competition, the price remains constant when the quantity sold changes, the change in total revenue is equal to price multiplied by the change in quantity. In perfect competition, the change in total revenue resulting from a one-unit increase in the quantity sold is equal to the price. Therefore in perfect competition, marginal revenue equals price.

An example of these revenue concepts is set out for Swanky Inc. in Fig. 12.1. The table in the figure shows three different quantities of sweaters sold. For a price taker, as the quantity sold varies, the price stays constant — for Swanky, the price remains at $25. Total revenue is equal to price multiplied by quantity. For example, if Swanky sells 8 sweaters, total revenue is $200 (8 × $25). Average revenue is total revenue divided by quantity. Again, if Swanky sells 8 sweaters, average revenue is $25 ($200 ÷ 8). Marginal revenue is the change in total revenue for a unit change in the quantity sold. For example, when the quantity sold rises from 7 to 8 sweaters, total revenue rises from $175 to $200, so marginal revenue is $25. (Notice that in the table, marginal revenue appears *between* the lines for the quantities sold. This arrangement presents a visual reminder that marginal revenue results from the change in the quantity sold.)

Suppose that Swanky is one of a thousand similar

Figure 12.1 Demand, Price, and Revenue in Perfect Competition

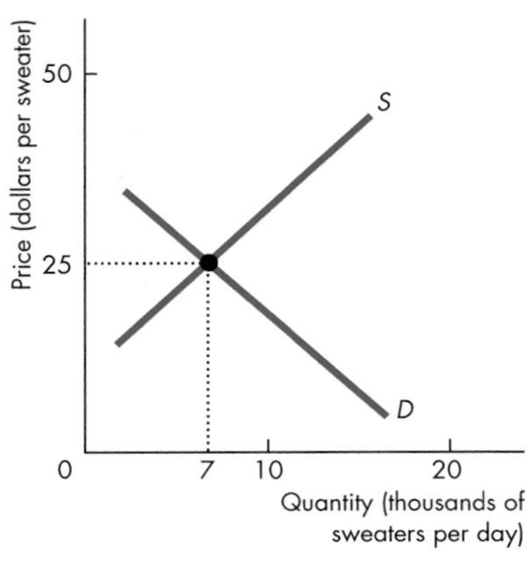

(a) Sweater industry

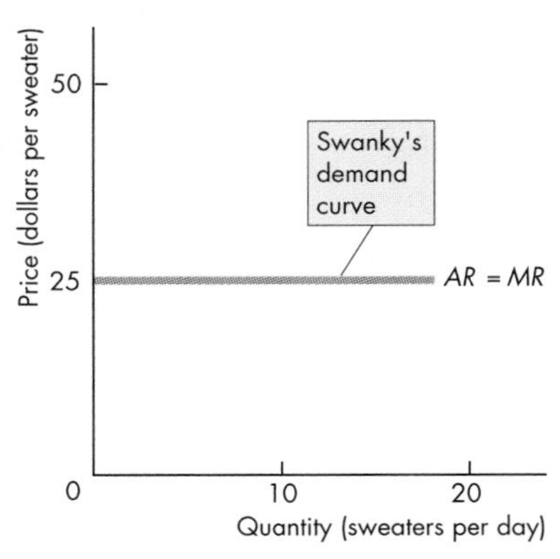

(b) Swanky's demand, average revenue, and marginal revenue

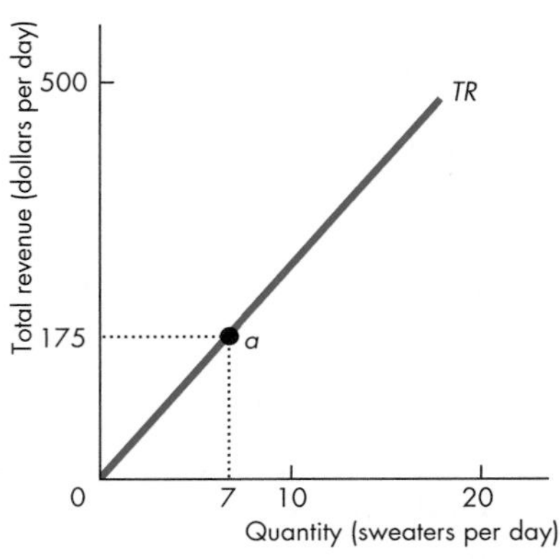

(c) Swanky's total revenue

Quantity sold (Q) (sweaters per day)	Price (P) (dollars per sweater)	Total revenue ($TR = P \times Q$) (dollars per day)	Average revenue ($AR = TR/Q$) (dollars per sweater)	Marginal revenue ($MR = \Delta TR/\Delta Q$) (dollars per sweater)
7	25	175	25	
				25
8	25	200	25	
				25
9	25	225	25	

In perfect competition, price is determined at the intersection point of the industry demand and supply curves. Such an equilibrium is illustrated in part (a), at the point where the price is $25 and 7,000 sweaters are bought and sold. Swanky, a perfectly competitive firm, faces a fixed price ($25 in this example) regardless of the quantity it produces. The table calculates Swanky's total, average, and marginal revenue. For example, when 7 sweaters are sold, total revenue is $175, and average revenue is $25. When sales increase from 7 sweaters to 8 sweaters, marginal revenue equals $25. The demand curve faced by Swanky is perfectly elastic at the market price, and is shown in part (b). Swanky's demand curve is also its average revenue curve and marginal revenue curve (*AR* = MR). Swanky's total revenue curve (*TR*) is shown in part (c). Point *a* on the total revenue curve corresponds to the first row of the table.

small producers of sweaters. The demand and supply curves for the entire sweater industry are shown in Fig. 12.1(a). Demand curve *D* intersects supply curve S at a price of $25 and a quantity of 7,000 sweaters a day. Figure 12.1(b) shows Swanky's demand curve. Since the firm is a price taker, its demand curve is perfectly elastic — it is the horizontal line at $25. The figure also illustrates Swanky's total, average, and marginal revenues. The average revenue curve and the marginal revenue curve are the same as the firm's demand curve. That is, the firm's demand curve tells us the revenue per sweater sold (average revenue) and the change in total revenue that results from selling one more sweater (marginal revenue).

Swanky's total revenue curve, in Fig. 12.1(c), shows the total revenue for each quantity sold. For example, when Swanky sells 7 sweaters, total revenue is $175 (point *a*). Since each additional sweater sold brings in a constant amount — $25 in this case — the total revenue curve is an upward-sloping straight line.

REVIEW

A firm in a perfectly competitive market is a price taker. The firm's demand curve is perfectly elastic at the market price. The firm's average revenue and marginal revenue are each equal to price so the marginal revenue and average revenue curves are the same as the firm's demand curve. Total revenue rises as the quantity sold rises. ■

Profit-Maximizing Output

Profit is the difference between a firm's total revenue and total cost. Maximizing profit is the same as maximizing the difference between total revenue and total cost. Even though a perfectly competitive firm cannot influence the price at which it sells its output, it can influence its profit by choosing its level of output. As we have just seen, a perfectly competitive firm's total revenue changes when its output changes. Also, as we discovered in Chapter 10, a firm's total cost varies as its output varies. By changing its inputs and its output, a firm can change its total cost. In the *short run*, a firm can change its output by changing its variable inputs and by changing the intensity with which it operates its fixed inputs. In the *long run*, a firm can vary all its inputs. Let's work out how a firm maximizes profit in the short run.

Total Revenue, Total Cost, and Profit Figure 12.2 shows Swanky's total revenue, total cost, and profit both as numbers (in the table) and as curves (in the graphs). Part (a) of the figure shows Swanky's total revenue and total cost curves. These curves are graphs of the numbers shown in the first three columns of the table. The total revenue curve (TR) is the same as that in Fig. 12.1(c). The total cost curve (TC) is similar to the one that you saw in Chapter 10. Notice that when output is zero, Swanky's total cost is $25. This amount is Swanky's total fixed cost — the cost the firm incurs even if it produces nothing. As output increases, so does total cost.

The difference between total revenue and total cost is profit. As you can see in Fig. 12.2(b), Swanky makes a profit at any output between 4 and 12 sweaters a day. At an output of fewer than 4 or more than 12, Swanky makes a loss. At an output of 4 or 12 sweaters, total cost equals total revenue. An output at which total cost equals total revenue is called a **break-even point**.

Swanky's profit, calculated in the final column of the table, is graphed in part (b) of Fig. 12.2. Notice the relationship between the total revenue and total cost curves and the profit curve. Profit is measured by the vertical gap between the total revenue and total cost curves. When the total revenue curve in Fig. 12.2 (a) is above the total cost curve (between 4 and 12 sweaters), the firm is making a profit and the profit curve in Fig. 12.2 (b) is above the horizontal axis. At the break-even point, where the total cost and total revenue curves intersect, the profit curve cuts the horizontal axis. When the profit curve is at its highest, the gap between the total revenue and total cost curves is greatest. In this example, profit maximization occurs at an output of 9 sweaters a day. At this output, profit is $40 a day.

Marginal Calculations

In working out Swanky's profit-maximizing output, we examined its total cost and total revenue schedules, and from all the possibilities, we picked out the point at which profit is at a maximum. There is a quicker, neater, and more powerful way of figuring out the profit-maximizing output. All Swanky has to do is to calculate its marginal cost and marginal revenue and compare the two. If marginal revenue exceeds marginal cost, it pays to produce more. If marginal revenue is less than marginal cost, it pays to produce less. When marginal revenue and marginal cost are equal, profit is maximized.

Let's convince ourselves that this rule works. Look at the table in Fig. 12.3. It records Swanky's marginal cost and marginal revenue. Recall that marginal cost is the change in total cost per unit change in output. For example, when output rises from 7 to 8 sweaters, total cost rises from $144 to $163, a rise of $19, which is the marginal cost of changing the output rate from 7 to 8 sweaters a day. Marginal revenue is the change in total revenue per unit change in the quantity sold and is, for a perfectly competitive firm, the same as price. In this case, marginal revenue is $25. Figure 12.3(a) illustrates Swanky's marginal cost and marginal revenue curves.

Now focus on the highlighted row of the table. When output rises from 8 to 9 sweaters, marginal cost is $22. Marginal revenue is $25, so the rise in total revenue exceeds the rise in total cost. Profit goes up by the difference — $3. By looking at the last column of the table, you can see that profit does indeed rise by $3. Because marginal revenue exceeds marginal cost, it pays to expand output from 8 to 9 sweaters. At 8 sweaters a day, profit is $37 and at 9 sweaters a day it is $40 — $3 more.

Suppose that output is expanded further to 10 sweaters a day. Marginal revenue is still $25, but marginal cost is now $27. Marginal cost exceeds marginal revenue by $2, so the increase in output from

Figure 12.2 Total Revenue, Total Cost, and Profit

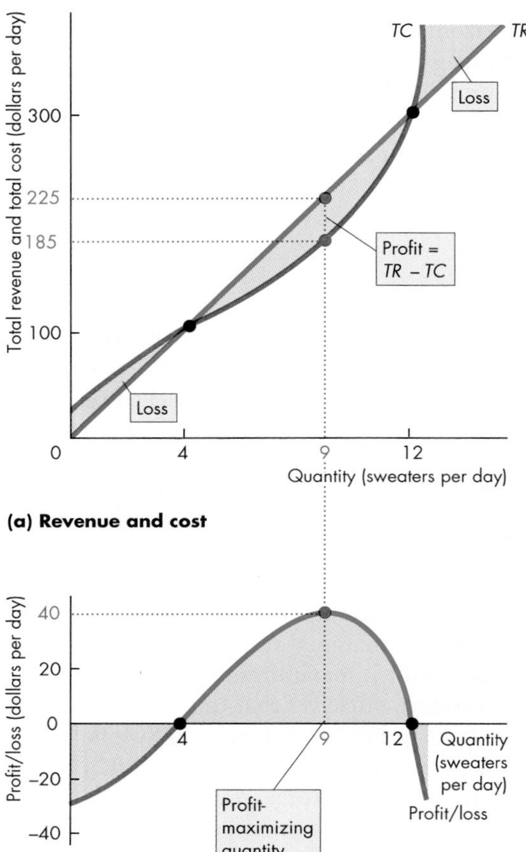

(a) Revenue and cost

(b) Profit and loss

Quantity (*Q*) (sweaters per day)	Total revenue (*TR*)	Total cost (*TC*)	Profit (*TR* − *TC*)
	(dollars per day)		
0	0	25	−25
1	25	49	−24
2	50	69	−19
3	75	86	−11
4	100	100	0
5	125	114	11
6	150	128	22
7	175	144	31
8	200	163	37
9	225	185	40
10	250	212	38
11	275	246	29
12	300	300	0
13	325	360	−35

The table lists Swanky's total revenue, total cost, and profit. Part (a) graphs the total revenue and total cost curves; profit equals the vertical gap between the total cost and total revenue curves. At outputs between 4 and 12 sweaters per day, Swanky makes a profit. The maximum profit, $40 per day, occurs when 9 sweaters are produced — the point at which the vertical gap between the total revenue and total cost curves is at its largest. At outputs of 4 sweaters per day and 12 sweaters per day, Swanky makes zero profit — these are break-even points. At outputs of less than 4 and more than 12 sweaters per day, Swanky makes a loss. Part (b) shows Swanky's profit curve. It is at its highest when profit is at a maximum. It cuts the horizontal axis at the break-even points.

9 to 10 sweaters increases total cost by $2 more than total revenue. Profit falls by $2.

So, to maximize profit, all Swanky has to do is to compare marginal cost and marginal revenue. As long as marginal revenue exceeds marginal cost, it pays to increase output. Swanky keeps increasing output until the cost of producing one more sweater equals the price at which the sweater can be sold. At that point the firm is making maximum profit. If Swanky makes one more sweater, that sweater will cost more to produce than the revenue it will bring back in, so Swanky will not produce it.

Profit in the Short Run

We've just seen that we can calculate a firm's profit-maximizing output by comparing marginal revenue with marginal cost. But maximizing profit is not the

Figure 12.3 Marginal Revenue, Marginal Cost, and Profit-Maximizing Output

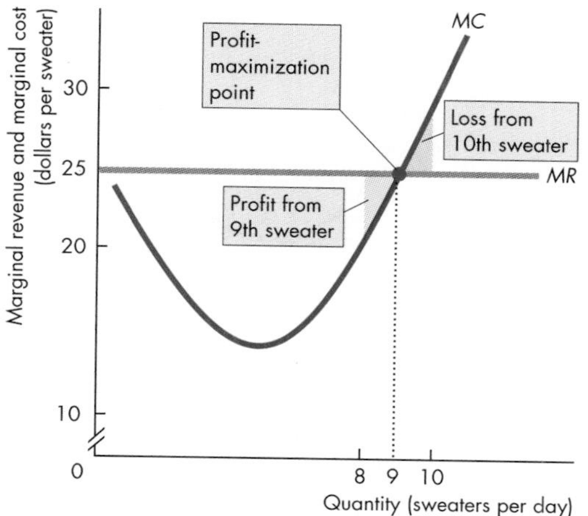

Another way of finding the profit-maximizing output is to determine the output at which marginal revenue equals marginal cost. The table shows that if output rises from 8 to 9 sweaters, marginal cost is $22, which is less than the marginal revenue of $25. If output rises from 9 to 10 sweaters, marginal cost is $27, which exceeds the marginal revenue of $25. The figure shows that marginal cost and marginal revenue are equal when Swanky produces 9 sweaters per day. If marginal revenue exceeds marginal cost, an increase in output increases profit. If marginal revenue is less than marginal cost, an increase in output lowers profit. If marginal revenue equals marginal cost, profit is maximized.

Quantity (*Q*) (sweaters per day)	Total revenue (*TR*) (dollars per day)	Marginal revenue (*MR*) (dollars per sweater)	Total cost (*TC*) (dollars per day)	Marginal cost (*MC*) (dollars per sweater)	Profit (*TR* – *TC*) (dollars per day)
0	0		25		–25
		25		24	
1	25		49		–24
		25		20	
2	50		69		–19
		25		17	
3	75		86		–11
		25		14	
4	100		100		0
		25		14	
5	125		114		11
		25		14	
6	150		128		22
		25		16	
7	175		144		31
		25		19	
8	200		163		37
		25		22	
9	225		185		40
		25		27	
10	250		212		38
		25		34	
11	275		246		29
		25		54	
12	300		300		0
		25		60	
13	325		360		–35

same thing as *making* a profit. Maximizing profit can mean minimizing loss. Simply comparing marginal revenue and marginal cost cannot tell us whether a firm is actually making a profit. To check whether it is, we need to look at total revenue and total cost, as we did before, or we need to compare average total cost

Figure 12.4 Three Possible Profit Outcomes

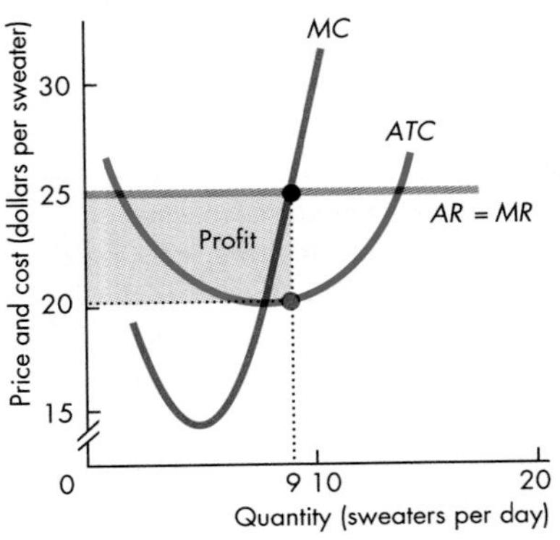

(a) Economic profit

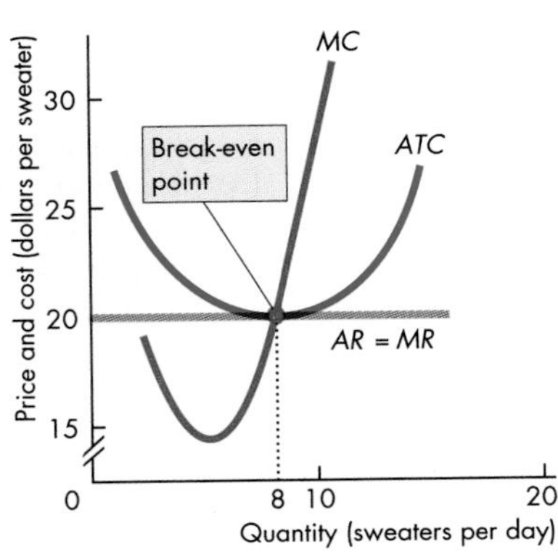

(b) Zero economic profit

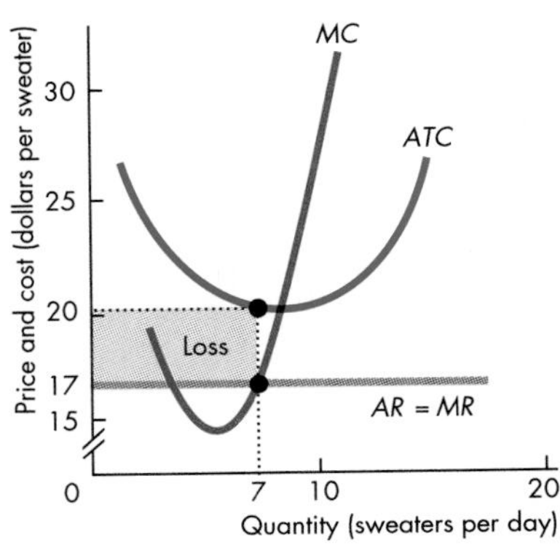

(c) Economic loss

In the short run, a firm's economic profit may be positive, zero (a break-even), or negative (a loss). If the market price is greater than the average total cost of producing the profit-maximizing output, the firm makes a profit (part a). If price equals minimum average total cost, the firm breaks even (part b). If price is below average total cost the firm makes a loss (part c). The firm's profit is shown as the blue rectangle and the firm's loss is the red rectangle.

with price. When a firm is making a profit, average total cost is lower than price. If average total cost exceeds price, the firm is making a loss. When average total cost equals price, the firm is breaking even.

The three possible profit outcomes are illustrated in Fig. 12.4. In part (a), Swanky is making an economic profit. At a price of $25, average revenue and marginal revenue are also $25 and the profit-maximizing output is 9 sweaters a day. Average total cost is lower than the market price, and economic profit is represented by the blue rectangle. The height of that rectangle is the gap between price and average total cost, or the economic profit per sweater. Its length represents the quantity of sweaters produced. So the rectangle's area measures Swanky's economic profit: profit per sweater (its height, $4.44 a sweater) multiplied by the number of sweaters produced (its length, 9 sweaters) equals total profit (its area, $40).

In Fig. 12.4(b), Swanky breaks even. In this case, the market price is $20, the same as the minimum average total cost and the maximum profit that Swanky can make is zero.

In Fig. 12.4(c), Swanky incurs an economic loss. At a market price of $17, the profit-maximizing output is 7 sweaters a day. At that output, average total cost is $20.57, so the firm is losing $3.57 a sweater, a total loss of $25.

Temporary Plant Shutdown

In some situations, the firm's profit-maximizing decision is to shut down temporarily, lay off its workers, and produce nothing. Such a situation arises when the price is so low that total revenue is not even enough to cover the variable costs of production. A firm cannot escape its fixed costs; they are incurred even at a zero output. A firm that shuts down and produces no output makes an economic loss equal to its total fixed cost. But this loss is the maximum loss that the firm will make. If the firm produces and the price just equals the average variable cost of production, total revenue equals total variable cost and its loss equals total fixed cost. But if it produces at a price below average variable cost, total revenue does not even cover total variable cost and the loss exceeds total fixed cost. It is in such a situation that the firm minimizes its losses by shutting down, incurring a loss equal to its total fixed cost.

The **shutdown point** is the point at which a firm's maximum profit is the same regardless of whether it produces a positive amount of output or produces nothing — shuts down temporarily. The shutdown point is reached when the market price falls to a level equal to minimum average variable cost. The shutdown point occurs at the minimum

Table 12.2 The Shutdown Point

(a) Swanky keeps on producing

Output (sweaters per day)	Total fixed cost (dollars per day)	Total variable cost (dollars per day)	Total cost (dollars per day)	Average variable cost (dollars per sweater)	Marginal cost (dollars per sweater)	Price (dollars per sweater)	Total revenue (dollars per day)	Marginal revenue (dollars per sweater)	Profit (+) or loss (−) (dollars per day)
6	25	103	128	17.17		17	102		−26
					16			17	
7	25	119	144	17.00		17	119		−25
					19			17	
8	25	138	163	17.25		17	136		−27

(b) Swanky shuts down

Output (sweaters per day)	Total fixed cost (dollars per day)	Total variable cost (dollars per day)	Total cost (dollars per day)	Average variable cost (dollars per sweater)	Marginal cost (dollars per sweater)	Price (dollars per sweater)	Total revenue (dollars per day)	Marginal revenue (dollars per sweater)	Profit (+) or loss (−) (dollars per day)
6	25	103	128	17.17		16.99	101.94		−26.06
					16			16.99	
7	25	119	144	17.00		16.99	118.93		−25.07
					19			16.99	
8	25	138	163	17.25		16.99	135.92		−27.08

The shutdown point is reached when the price equals minimum average variable cost. At this price, Swanky is indifferent between producing the profit-maximizing output and producing nothing. If price falls below minimum average variable cost, it pays Swanky to produce nothing. Swanky's minimum average variable cost is $17 per sweater and occurs at an output of 7 sweaters per day. If the price is $17 per sweater and Swanky produces 7 sweaters per day, its loss equals its total fixed cost of $25 per day (part a). If the price falls to $16.99 per sweater, even if the firm produces the profit-maximizing output, it makes a loss that is bigger than its total fixed cost and so it pays to shut down (part b).

point of the average variable cost. Table 12.2 illustrates what happens at the shutdown point. The table has two parts. Part (a) shows a case in which it just pays the firm to keep producing, and part (b) shows one in which it just pays the firm to shut down. The table shows Swanky's fixed cost, variable cost, and total cost of producing 6, 7, and 8 sweaters. It also shows the average variable cost and marginal cost. The cost data are the same in parts (a) and (b) of the table.

Next let's look at Swanky's revenue. In part (a) of Table 12.2, the price of a sweater is $17. To find Swanky's total revenue, multiply the price by the quantity sold. We calculate the economic profit or loss (it is a loss in this case) by subtracting total cost from total revenue. For example, if Swanky sells 7 sweaters at $17 each, total revenue is $119. Total cost is $144, so the loss equals $144 minus $119, which is $25. We calculate the loss from producing 6 sweaters or 8 sweaters in a similar way.

The minimum economic loss occurs when 7 sweaters are produced. You can see that fact directly by looking at the profit or loss column. You can also check that the loss is minimized by looking at marginal cost and marginal revenue. Increasing output from 6 to 7 sweaters has a marginal cost of $16 but a marginal revenue of $17, so total revenue increases by more than total cost. Profit rises (loss falls). Increasing output still further, from 7 to 8 sweaters, has a marginal cost of $19. Since marginal cost exceeds marginal revenue, profit falls (the loss rises).

Swanky's loss when it produces 7 sweaters exactly equals its total fixed costs — $25. Alternately, if Swanky produces nothing, it also loses its $25 of fixed costs. So at a price of $17, Swanky is indifferent between producing and shutting down — either way, it makes an economic loss exactly equal to its total fixed cost.

In part (b) of Table 12.2 the price is $16.99 — a penny lower than in part (a). Costs are unchanged. We calculate total revenue and profit in the same way as before. The output that minimizes loss maximizes profit and is still 7 sweaters, but in this case the minimum possible loss is $25.07. Swanky loses 7 cents more than it would if it produced nothing at all. The firm will shut down. Its minimum average variable cost is $17. At a price of $17, it just pays to produce 7 sweaters, and at $16.99, it just pays to shut down. The minimum output that it pays Swanky to produce is 7 sweaters.

Real World Shutdowns Shutdowns occur in the real world either because of a fall in price or a rise in costs. In the raw-material-producing sectors, shutdowns occur most frequently as a result of fluctuating prices. For example, if the price of gold falls, gold mines temporarily stop producing. If the price of nickel falls, nickel mines shut down until the price goes up again. Shutdowns also occur in manufacturing industries, such as those producing automobiles and agricultural equipment, and in agriculture, forestry, and fisheries.

An important recent example of a shutdown has occurred in the fishery industry in Newfoundland. As reported in the press, the reason for this shutdown is a shortage of fish stock in the North Atlantic region. Translated into economic terms, what this means is that the cost of harvesting the fish is too high relative to the price that the fish can command on the market. Another important recent example of a shutdown is that of VIA rail, Canada's national rail passenger service. About one-half of all the routes have been shut down because the cost of operating them vastly exceeded the revenue they could earn.

R E V I E W

In perfect competition, a firm's marginal revenue equals its price. A firm maximizes profit by producing the output at which marginal cost equals marginal revenue (price). The smallest output a firm will produce is that at which average variable cost is a minimum. If price falls below the firm's minimum average variable cost, the best it can do is to stop producing and make a loss equal to its total fixed cost. Maximizing profit is not the same thing as making a profit. In the short run, a firm can make a profit, break even, or make a loss. The maximum loss that a firm will make is equal to its total fixed cost. ■

The Firm's Supply Curve

A **perfectly competitive firm's supply curve** shows how a firm's profit-maximizing output varies as the market price varies. We are now going to derive it. Actually, we have already calculated three points on Swanky's supply curve. We discovered that when the price is $25 a sweater, Swanky produces 9 sweaters a day; when the price is $20, Swanky produces 8 sweaters a day; and when the price is $17, Swanky is indifferent between producing 7 sweaters a day and shutting down. We are now going to derive Swanky's entire supply curve. Figure 12.5 illustrates the analysis. Part (a) shows Swanky's marginal cost and average variable cost curves, and part (b) shows Swanky's supply curve. There is a direct connection between the marginal cost and average variable cost curves and the supply curve. Let's see what that connection is.

The smallest quantity that Swanky will supply is at the shutdown point. If the price equals minimum average variable cost, the marginal revenue curve is MR_0 and the firm produces the output at its shutdown point — point *s* in the figure. If the price falls below minimum average variable cost, Swanky produces nothing. As the price rises above minimum average variable cost, Swanky's output rises. Since the firm maximizes profit by producing the output at which marginal cost equals price, we can determine from its marginal cost curve how much the firm produces at each price. At a price of $25, the marginal revenue curve is MR_1. Swanky maximizes profit by producing 9 sweaters. At a price of $31, the marginal revenue curve is MR_2 and Swanky produces 10 sweaters. The supply curve, shown in Fig. 12.5(b), has two separate parts. First, in the range of prices that exceed Swanky's minimum average variable cost, the supply curve is the same as the marginal cost curve. Second, at prices below minimum average variable cost, Swanky shuts down and produces nothing. Its supply curve runs along the vertical axis.

So far, we have studied a single firm in isolation. We have seen that the firm's profit-maximizing actions depend on the market price — which the firm takes as given. The higher the price, the larger is the quantity that the firm will choose to produce — the firm's supply curve is upward sloping. But how is the market price determined? To answer this question, we need to study not one firm in isolation but the market as a whole.

Figure 12.5 Swanky's Supply Curve

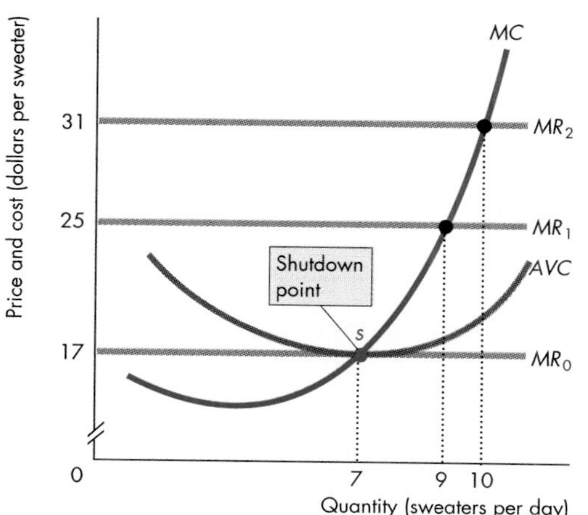

(a) Marginal cost and average variable cost

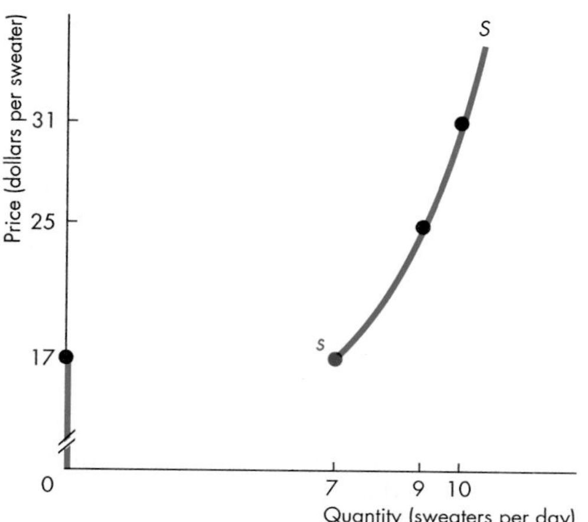

(b) Firm's supply curve

Part (a) shows Swanky's profit-maximizing output at each market price. At $25 per sweater, Swanky produces 9 sweaters. At $17 per sweater, Swanky produces 7 sweaters. At any price less than $17 per sweater, Swanky produces nothing. Swanky's shutdown point is *s*. Part (b) shows Swanky's supply curve — the number of sweaters Swanky produces at each different price. Swanky's supply curve is made up of its marginal cost curve (part a) at all points above the average variable cost curve and the vertical axis at all prices below minimum average variable cost.

Short-Run Equilibrium

Market price is determined by industry demand and industry supply. It is the price at which the quantity demanded equals the quantity supplied. But the quantity supplied depends on the supply decisions of all the individual firms in the industry. Those supply decisions, in turn, depend on the market price.

Short-run equilibrium prevails in a competitive market when each firm operates its plant to produce the profit-maximizing output level and when the total quantity produced by all the firms in the market equals the quantity demanded at that price. To find the short-run equilibrium, we first need to construct the short-run industry supply curve.

Short-Run Industry Supply Curve

The **short-run industry supply curve** shows how the total quantity supplied in the short run by all firms in an industry varies as the market price varies. The quantity supplied in the short run by the industry at a given price is the sum of the quantities supplied in the short run by all firms in the industry at that price. To construct the industry supply curve, we sum horizontally the supply curves of the individual firms. Let's see how we do that.

Suppose that the competitive sweater industry consists of 1,000 firms exactly like Swanky. The relationship between a firm's supply curve and the industry supply curve, for this case, is illustrated in Fig. 12.6. Each of the 1,000 firms in the industry has a supply schedule like Swanky's, which is set out in the table. At a price of less than $17, every firm in the industry shuts down production, so the industry supplies nothing. At $17, each firm is indifferent between shutting down and producing 7 sweaters. Some may decide to produce and others to shut down. Industry supply can be anything between 0 (all firms shut down) and 7,000 (all firms produce 7 sweaters a day each). Thus at $17, the industry supply curve is horizontal — it is perfectly elastic. As the price rises to more than $17, each firm increases its quantity supplied; the increase in the industry quantity supplied is 1,000 times that of each individual firm.

The supply schedules set out in the table are graphed in Fig. 12.6. Swanky and every other firm has the supply curve (S_F) shown in Fig. 12.6(a); the

Figure 12.6 Firm and Industry Supply Curves

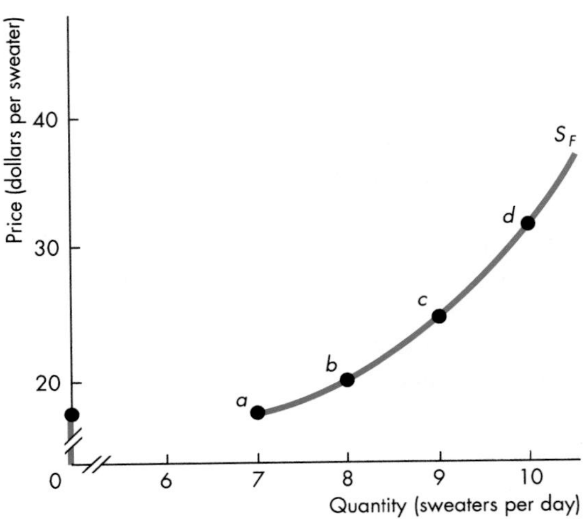

(a) Swanky Inc.

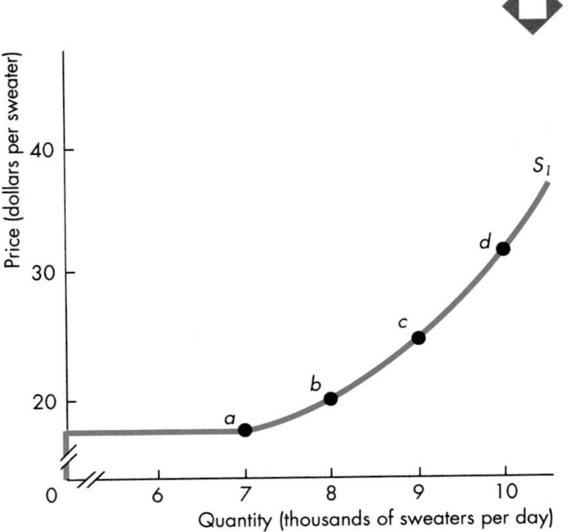

(b) Sweater industry

	Price (dollars per sweater)	Quantity supplied by Swanky Inc. (sweaters per day)	Quantity supplied by industry (sweaters per day)
a	17	0 or 7	0 to 7,000
b	20	8	8,000
c	25	9	9,000
d	31	10	10,000

The industry supply schedule is the sum of the supply schedules of all individual firms. An industry that consists of 1,000 identical firms has a supply schedule similar to that of the individual firm, but the quantity supplied by the industry is 1,000 times as large (see table). At the shutdown point, the firm produces either 0 or 7 sweaters per day. The short-run industry supply curve is perfectly elastic at the shutdown price. Part (a) shows Swanky's supply curve (S_F), and part (b), the sweater industry supply curve (S_I). Points *a*, *b*, *c*, and *d* correspond to the rows of the table. Note that the unit of measurement on the horizontal axis for the industry supply curve is 1,000 times the unit for Swanky.

industry supply curve (S_I) is shown in Fig. 12.6(b). Look carefully at the units on the horizontal axes of parts (a) and (b). In part (a) the units are individual sweaters, while in part (b), they are thousands of sweaters. The two graphs have two other important differences. First, at each price, the quantity supplied by the industry is 1,000 times the quantity supplied by a single firm. Second, at a price of $17, the firm supplies either 0 or 7 sweaters a day. There is no individual firm supply curve between those two numbers. But at that price, the whole industry may produce any quantity between 0 and 7,000, so the industry supply curve is perfectly elastic over that range.

Short-Run Competitive Equilibrium

Price and industry output are determined by industry demand and supply. Three different possible short-run competitive equilibrium positions are shown in Fig. 12.7. The supply curve *S* is the same as S_I, which we derived in Fig. 12.6. If demand is D_1, the equilibrium price is $25 and industry output is 9,000 sweaters a day. If demand is D_2, the price is $20 and industry output is 8,000 sweaters a day. If demand is D_3, the price is $17 and industry output is 7,000 sweaters a day.

To see what is happening to each individual firm and its profit in these three situations, check back to Fig. 12.4. If the demand curve is D_1, each firm produces 9 sweaters a day and makes a profit as shown in Fig. 12.4(a). If the demand curve is D_2, each firm produces 8 sweaters a day and makes a zero profit, as shown in Fig. 12.4(b). If the demand curve is D_3, each firm is indifferent between producing 7 sweaters a day and shutting down temporarily; in either event, it is making a loss, as shown in

Figure 12.7 Three Short-Run Equilibrium Positions for a Competitive Industry

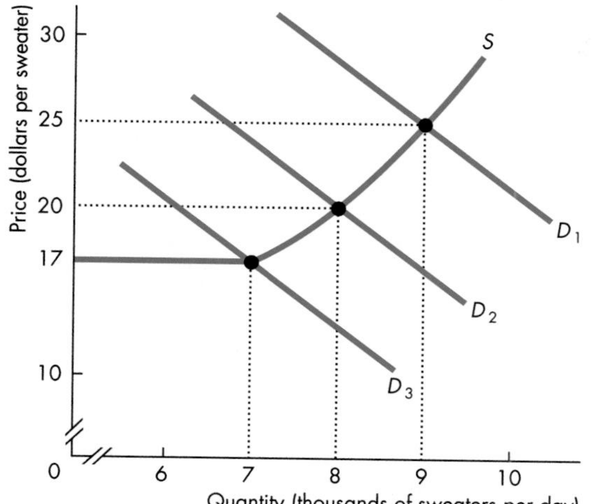

The competitive sweater industry's supply curve is *S*. If demand is D_1, the price of a sweater is $25 and the industry produces 9,000 sweaters. If demand is D_2, the price is $20 and industry output is 8,000 sweaters. If demand is D_3, the price is $17 and industry output is 7,000 sweaters. To see what is happening to the individual firms, look back at Fig. 12.4. When the price is $25, the firms make a profit; when the price is $20, they break even (make a zero profit), and when the price is $17, they incur a loss. Even when they make a loss, the firms are maximizing profit (minimizing loss).

Fig. 12.4(c). The loss equals total fixed cost. If the demand curve shifts farther to the left than D_3, the price will remain constant at $17 since the industry supply curve is horizontal at that price. Some firms will continue to produce 7 sweaters a day and others will shut down. Firms will be indifferent between these two activities; whichever they choose, they will make a loss equal to their fixed cost. The number of firms continuing to produce will just be enough to satisfy the market demand at a price of $17.

R E V I E W

Short-run equilibrium is described by three conditions:

- Price and the total quantity traded are determined at the point of intersection of the industry supply and demand curves.
- The industry has a fixed number of firms, and each firm has a given scale of plant.
- Firms maximize profit by producing the output at which marginal cost equals marginal revenue (equals price). ■

Long-Run Equilibrium

We have seen that in *short-run equilibrium* a firm may make a profit, a loss, or a zero profit. But only one of these three situations is a long-run equilibrium. To see why, we need to examine the dynamic forces at work in a competitive industry. An industry adjusts over time in two ways. First, the number of firms in the industry changes. Second, the existing firms change the scale of their plants, thereby shifting their short-run cost curves. Let's study the effects of these two dynamic forces in a competitive industry.

Entry and Exit

Entry is the act of setting up a new firm in an industry. **Exit** is the act of closing down a firm and leaving an industry. When will a new firm enter an industry or an existing one leave? How do entry and exit affect the market price, profit, and output in an industry? Let's first look at the causes of entry and exit.

Profits and Losses as Signals What triggers entry and exit? The prospect of profit triggers entry, and the prospect of continuing losses triggers exit. Temporary profits and temporary losses that are purely random, such as winnings and losings at a casino, do not trigger entry or exit, but the prospect of profits or losses for some foreseeable future period does. An industry making economic profits attracts new entrants; one making economic losses induces exits; and one in which neither economic losses nor economic profits are being made stimulates neither entry nor exit. Thus profits and losses are the signals to which firms respond in making entry and exit decisions.

What are the effects of entry and exit on price and profits?

Effects of Entry and Exit on Price and Profits The immediate effect of entry and exit is to shift the short-run industry supply curve. If more firms enter an industry, the short-run industry supply curve shifts to the

Figure 12.8 Entry and Exit

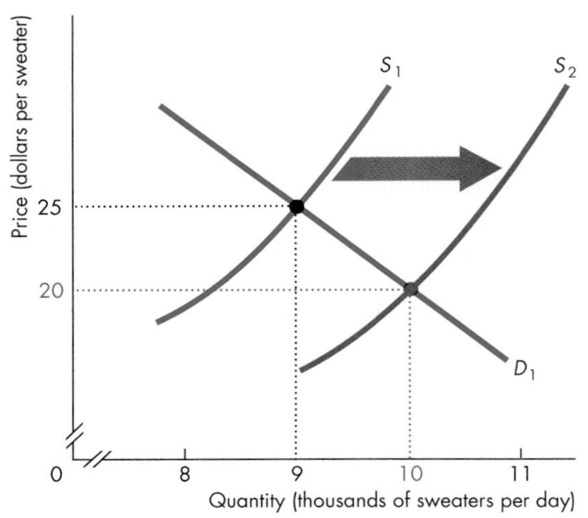

(a) Effect of entry

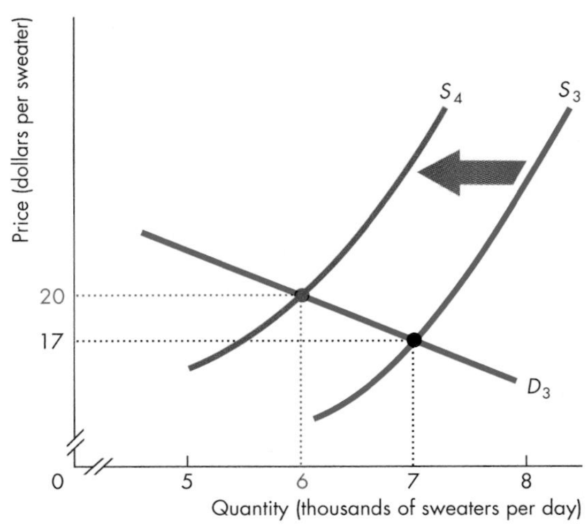

(b) Effect of exit

When new firms enter the sweater industry, the short-run industry supply curve shifts to the right, from S_1 to S_2 (part a). The equilibrium price falls from \$25 to \$20, and the quantity traded rises from 9,000 to 10,000 sweaters. When firms exit the sweater industry, the short-run industry supply curve shifts to the left, from S_3 to S_4 (part b). The equilibrium price rises from \$17 to \$20, and the quantity traded falls from 7,000 to 6,000 sweaters.

right: supply increases. If firms exit an industry, the short-run industry supply curve shifts to the left: supply falls. The effects of entry and exit on price and on the total quantity traded in the sweater industry are shown in Fig. 12.8.

Entry First, let's look at what happens when new firms enter an industry. Suppose that the demand curve for sweaters is D_1 and the short-run industry supply curve is S_1, so sweaters sell for \$25 and 9,000 sweaters are bought and sold. Now suppose that some new firms enter the industry. As they do so, the industry supply curve shifts to the right to become S_2. With the higher supply and unchanged demand, there is a fall in price from \$25 to \$20 a sweater and a rise in the quantity of sweaters traded from 9,000 to 10,000.

As the price falls, Swanky and the other firms in the industry will react by lowering their output. That is, for each existing firm in the industry the profit-maximizing output falls. Since the price falls and since each firm sells less, profit falls for each firm. You can see this reduction of profit by glancing back at Fig. 12.4. Initially, when the price is \$25, each firm makes a profit and is in the situation shown in Fig. 12.4(a). When the price falls to \$20, the firm's profit disappears, and it is in the situation shown in Fig. 12.4(b).

You have just discovered an important result:

As new firms enter an industry, the profit of each existing firm falls.

A good example of this process has occurred in the last few years in the personal computer industry. When IBM introduced its first personal computer in the early 1980s, the price of PCs gave IBM a big profit. Very quickly thereafter, new firms such as Compaq, Zenith, Leading Edge, and a host of others entered the industry with machines technologically identical to the IBM. (In fact, they were so similar that they came to be called "clones".) The massive wave of entry into the personal computer industry shifted the industry supply curve to the right and lowered the price and the profits for all firms.

Exit Let's see what happens when firms leave an industry. Again, the short-run industry supply curve shifts, but this time to the left. Figure 12.8(b) illustrates. Suppose that initially the demand curve is D_3

with a short-run industry supply curve S_3, so the market price is \$17 and 7,000 sweaters are sold. As firms leave the industry, the industry supply curve shifts to the left and becomes S_4. With the fall in supply, industry output falls from 7,000 to 6,000 sweaters and the price rises from \$17 to \$20.

To see what is happening to Swanky, go back again to Fig. 12.4. With the demand curve D_3 and a price of \$17, Swanky is in the situation illustrated in Fig. 12.4(c). Price is lower than average total cost and Swanky is making a loss. Some firms exit, but Swanky (and some others) hang in. As firms exit, the price rises from \$17 to \$20, so the firms that remain increase their output and their losses vanish. They are then back in the situation illustrated in Fig. 12.4(b).

You have just worked out the second important result:

As firms leave an industry, the price rises and so do the profits of the remaining firms.

An example of a firm that exited an industry is Massey-Ferguson, the farm equipment manufacturer whose main centre of operation was in Brantford, Ontario. Another farm equipment maker that exited the business was International Harvester. For decades, people associated the names of these two firms with tractors, combines, and other farm machines. But the industry became intensely competitive and several firms, including these two, began losing money. After several years of losses, they got out of the farm equipment business, leaving it to John Deere and a host of smaller firms such as AgriMetal, Butler, Houle, as well as Japanese and European companies. The exits of Massey-Ferguson and International Harvester lowered the industry supply of farm machinery and made it possible for the remaining firms in the industry to break even.

Equilibrium We've seen that the prospect of profit triggers entry and the prospect of continuing loss triggers exit. We have also seen that entry into an industry lowers the profits of the existing firms and that exit from an industry increases the profits of the remaining firms. Long-run equilibrium results from the interaction of profits and losses as signals to entry and exit and from the effects of entry and exit on profits and losses.

Long-run equilibrium occurs in a competitive industry when economic profits are zero. If an industry makes economic profits, firms enter and the industry supply curve shifts to the right. As a result, the market price falls and so do profits. Firms will continue to enter and profits continue to fall as long as the industry is earning positive economic profits.

In an industry with economic losses, some firms exit. As they leave, the industry supply curve shifts to the left and the market price rises. As the price rises, the industry's losses shrink. As long as losses continue, some firms will leave the industry. Only when losses have been eliminated and zero economic profits are being made will firms stop exiting.

Now let's examine the second way in which a competitive industry adjusts in the long run — existing firms change their plant size.

Changes in Plant Size

A firm will change its plant size whenever it can increase its profit by doing so. A situation in which a firm can profitably expand its output by increasing its plant is illustrated in Fig. 12.9. In that figure, price (and marginal revenue) is \$20. With its current plant, Swanky's marginal and average total cost — its short-run costs — are shown by the curves *SRMC* and *SRAC*. Swanky maximizes profit by producing 8 sweaters a day, but in doing so it makes zero economic profit.

Figure 12.9 Changes in Plant Size

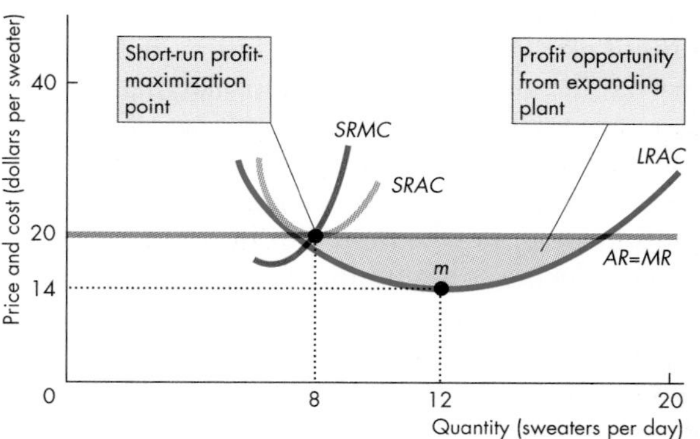

Swanky has a plant whose short-run cost curves are *SRMC* and *SRAC*. The price of a sweater is \$20, so average revenue and marginal revenue (*AR* = *MR*) are \$20. The profit-maximizing short-run output is 8 sweaters per day. Swanky's long-run costs are described by the long-run average cost curve (*LRAC*). The firm will want to move into the blue area, expanding its plant to take advantage of lower average costs and making a bigger profit. As firms expand, the industry supply increases and the price falls.

Swanky's long-run average cost curve is *LRAC*. By installing more knitting machines — increasing its plant size — Swanky can lower its costs and operate at a positive economic profit. For example, if Swanky increases its plant size so that it operates at point *m*, the minimum of its long-run average cost, it lowers its average cost from $20 to $14 and makes a profit of $6 a sweater. Since Swanky is a price taker, expanding output from 8 to 12 sweaters does not lower the market price and so would be a profitable thing to do. But changing the production plant takes time, so for a while the short-run equilibrium prevails. Nevertheless, over time, the firm will gradually expand its plant.

As Swanky and other firms expand their plants, the short-run industry supply curve starts to shift to the right. (Recall that the industry supply curve is the sum of the supply curves of all the individual firms.) With increases in industry supply and a given industry demand, the price gradually falls, and so do profits. Even though profits are falling as a consequence of increasing industry supply, it will pay each firm to expand as long as it can obtain further cost reductions from economies of scale. Only when no further reduction in average total cost is possible will a firm stick with its existing plant size. There is only one possible plant size consistent with long-run equilibrium in a competitive industry, and that is the one associated with the minimum long-run average cost (point *m*) in Fig. 12.9.

Figure 12.10 illustrates the firm's long-run competitive equilibrium. It occurs at a price of $14 and an output of 12 sweaters a day. Each firm in the industry has the plant size such that its marginal cost and average total cost curves are *SRMC* and *SRAC*. Each firm produces the output at which its marginal cost equals price. No firm can change its output in the short run and make more profit. Since each firm is producing at minimum long-run average cost (point *m* on *LRAC*), none of them has an incentive to expand or contract its production plant — a bigger plant or a smaller plant would lead to a higher average cost and an economic loss. Finally, no firm has an incentive to enter or exit the industry.

Figure 12.10 Long-Run Equilibrium of a Firm

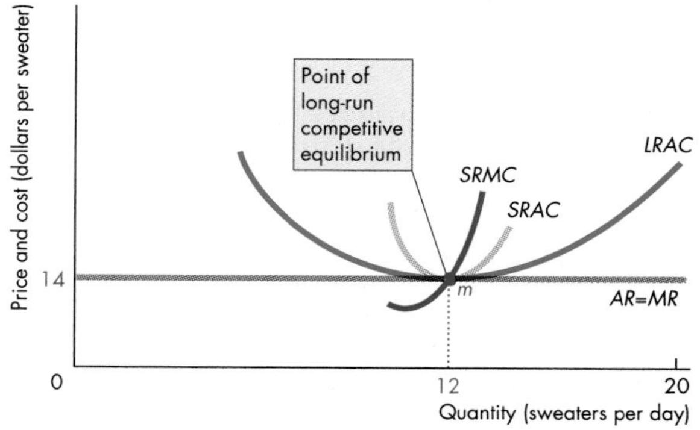

As firms expand their plants, industry supply increases and the price falls. Long-run equilibrium occurs when the price is $14 a sweater and each firm is producing at point *m*, its point of minimum long-run average cost.

R E V I E W

Long-run competitive equilibrium is described by three conditions:

- Firms maximize profit by producing the output at which marginal cost equals marginal revenue (price).
- Economic profit is zero so that no firm has an incentive to enter or to exit the industry.
- Long-run average cost is at a minimum so no firm has an incentive to expand or to contract its plant. ■

Predictions

Let's now use the theory of perfect competition to make some predictions.

A Permanent Decrease in Demand

The real world offers many examples of a permanent decrease in demand. Increased awareness of the health hazard of smoking has caused a decrease in the demand for tobacco and cigarettes. The development of inexpensive car and air transportation has caused a huge decrease in the demand for long-distance trains and buses. Solid-state electronics have caused a large decrease in the demand for TV and radio repair. The demand for North American cars has fallen as a result of high-quality alternatives from Japan and other

Figure 12.11 A Decrease in Demand

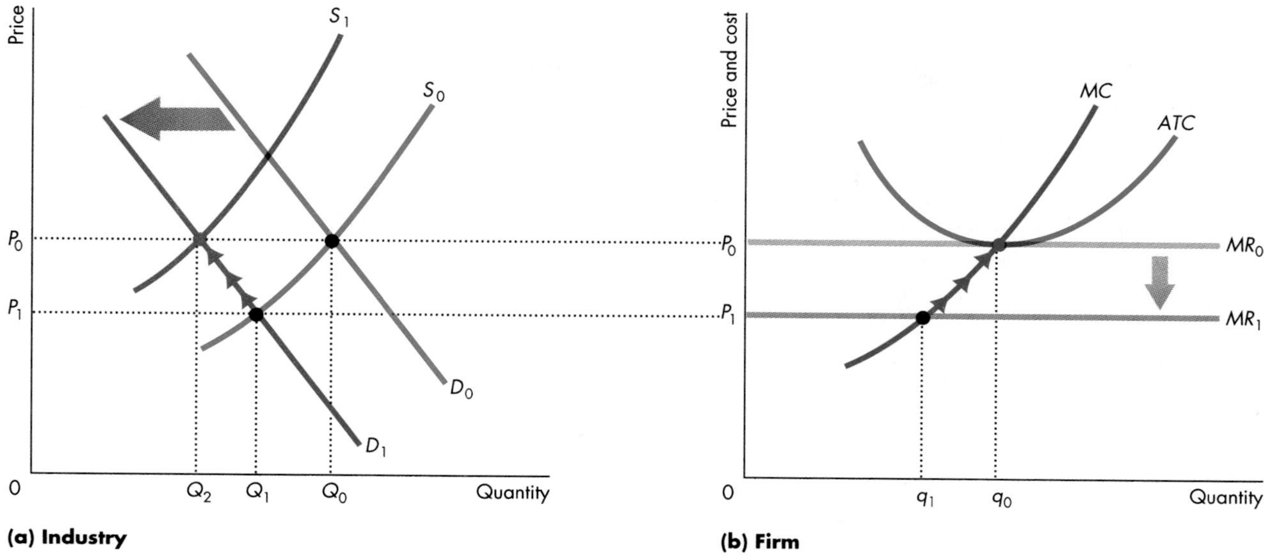

(a) Industry **(b) Firm**

An industry starts out in long-run competitive equilibrium. In part (a), the industry demand curve is D_0, the short-run industry supply curve S_0, the equilibrium quantity Q_0, and the market price P_0. Each firm (part b) sells at price P_0, so its marginal revenue curve is MR_0. Each firm produces q_0 and makes a zero profit. Then demand decreases from D_0 to D_1 (part a). The equilibrium price falls to P_1, each firm lowers its output to q_1 (part b), and industry output falls to Q_1. In this new situation, firms are making losses and some exit the industry. As they do so, the industry short-run supply curve gradually shifts to the left, from S_0 to S_1. This shift gradually raises the market price from P_1 back to P_0. Once the price has returned to P_0, each of the smaller number of firms whose supply curves add up to the industry short-run supply curve (S_1) is making a zero profit. There is no further incentive for any firm to exit the industry. Each firm produces q_0 and total industry output is Q_2.

countries. What happens in a competitive industry when there is a permanent decrease in demand?

Let's suppose that an industry starts out in the long-run competitive equilibrium shown in Fig. 12.11(a). The demand curve D_0 and the short-run supply curve S_0 represent the initial demand and supply in the market; the price is P_0 and the total industry output is Q_0. A single firm, shown in Fig. 12.11(b), initially produces the quantity q_0 and makes zero economic profit. The industry is in long-run equilibrium.

Now suppose that demand decreases to D_1, as shown in Fig 12.11 (a). This decrease in demand causes the price to drop to P_1. At the lower price, each firm produces a smaller output (q_1), and the quantity supplied by the industry decreases from Q_0 to Q_1 as the industry slides down its short-run supply curve (S_0). The industry is now in short-run equilibrium because it has a fixed number of firms, each with a fixed amount of capital, and each firm is maximizing profit. But it is not in long-run equilibrium because each firm is making an economic loss — its average total cost exceeds the price. Firms will have an incentive to exit the industry.

Some firms now leave the industry. As they do so, the short-run industry supply curve starts shifting to the left, the quantity supplied shrinks, and the price gradually rises. At each higher price, the profit-maximizing output is higher, so the firms remaining in the industry raise their output. Each firm slides up its supply curve (its marginal cost curve) in Fig. 12.11(b). Eventually, enough firms will have left the industry for the industry supply curve to have shifted to S_1 (part a). When that has happened, the price will have returned to its original level of P_0, and each firm remaining in the industry will produce q_0, the same amount as before the fall in demand. No firms will now want to leave the industry or enter it because each

Figure 12.12 An Increase in Demand

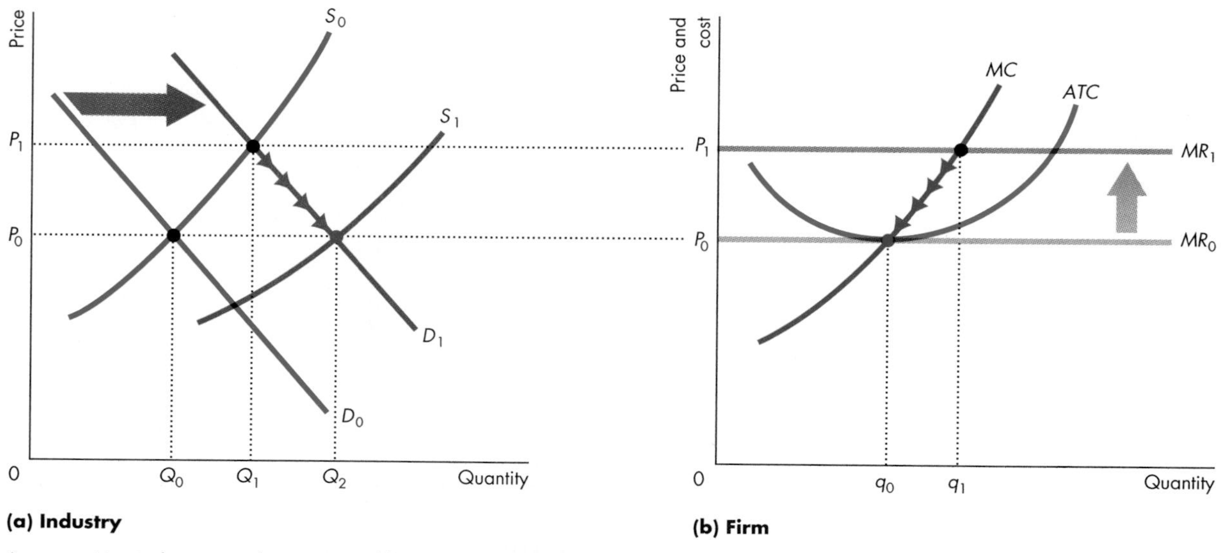

A competitive industry is in long-run equilibrium (part a). The demand curve is D_0 and the supply curve S_0. The equilibrium quantity is Q_0 and the market price is P_0. Each firm (part b) faces the marginal revenue curve MR_0 and maximizes profit by producing q_0. Then demand increases from D_0 to D_1. The price rises to P_1 and the quantity rises to Q_1. Each firm increases its output to q_1. In this situation, firms are making a profit (price is greater than average total cost). New firms enter the industry, and as they do so, the short-run industry supply curve shifts to the right. As it shifts, the price gradually falls and each individual firm gradually cuts its output from q_1 back to q_0. Since firms are entering the industry, total industry output rises even though each firm's output is cut back. The new equilibrium occurs when enough firms have entered the industry for the industry supply curve to have moved to S_1 with the price restored to its original level, P_0. Each firm is making a zero profit. At this point, industry output is Q_2. There is no further tendency for new firms to enter the industry, so the industry supply curve remains stationary at S_1.

firm in the industry is making zero economic profit. The industry supply curve settles down at S_1 and the total industry output is Q_2. The industry is again in long-run equilibrium.

The difference between the initial long-run equilibrium and the final long-run equilibrium is the number of firms in the industry. Fewer firms remain after the adjustment. Each remaining firm produces the same output in the new long-run equilibrium as it did initially. While the industry is moving from the original equilibrium to the new one, the firms that remain suffer losses. But they minimize their losses because they adjust their output to keep marginal cost equal to price.

A Permanent Increase in Demand

The most spectacular real-world examples of permanent increases in demand stem from technological change. For example, the development of the microwave oven has produced an enormous increase in demand for paper, glass, and plastic cooking utensils and for plastic wrap. The demand for almost all products is also steadily increasing as a result of increasing population and increasing incomes.

What happens in a competitive industry when the demand for its product increases? Again, let's begin the story in long-run equilibrium, as shown in Fig. 12.12(a). With demand curve D_0 and supply curve S_0, the market price is P_0 and quantity Q_0 is sold by the industry. Figure 12.12(b) shows that at the price P_0 each firm produces the output q_0 and makes zero economic profit. Now suppose that the demand for the industry's output increases from D_0 to D_1 (part a). The increased demand raises the price to P_1, and the quantity supplied by the industry rises from Q_0 to Q_1 as each firm increases its output from q_0 to q_1 (part b). At price P_1 and quantity Q_1, the industry is in short-run equilibrium but not long-run equilibrium. Firms in the industry are making positive economic profits, which will attract new firms to enter.

As new firms enter, the short-run industry supply curve starts shifting to the right, and as it does so, it intersects the demand curve at lower and lower prices and higher and higher quantities. Firms in the industry react to the falling price by cutting their output; that is, each firm slides back down its marginal cost curve in Fig. 12.12(b) in order to maximize profit at each successively lower price. Eventually, enough new firms will have entered for the industry supply curve to have shifted all the way to S_1. By that time, the market price will have fallen to P_0, the original price, and each firm will have cut its output back to its original level, q_0. Each firm will again be making zero economic profit, and no firm will enter or exit the industry. This new situation is a long-run equilibrium. During the adjustment process from the initial long-run equilibrium to the new one, all firms — both those that were in the industry originally and those that entered — made positive economic profits.

External Economies and Diseconomies One feature of the predictions that we have just generated seems odd: in the long-run, regardless of whether demand increases or decreases, the price returns to its original level. Is that outcome inevitable? In fact, it is not. It is possible for the long-run equilibrium price to rise, to fall, or to stay the same. Figure 12.13 illustrates these three cases. In part (a), the long-run supply curve (LS_A) is perfectly elastic; an increase in demand from D_0 to D_1 (or a decrease in demand from D_1 to D_0) results in a change in the quantity traded but an unchanged price. This is the case that we have just analysed. In part (b), the long-run supply curve (LS_B) slopes upward. In this case, when demand increases from D_0 to D_1, the price increases, and when demand decreases from D_1 to D_0, the price decreases. Finally, part (c) shows a long-run supply curve (LS_C) that slopes downward. In this case, an increase in demand from D_0 to D_1 results in a fall in the price, and a decrease in demand from D_1 to D_0 results in a higher price.

Whichever outcome occurs depends on external economies and external diseconomies. **External economies** are factors beyond the control of an individual firm that lower its costs as industry output rises. **External diseconomies** are factors outside the control of a firm that raise its costs as industry output rises.

There are many examples of external economies and diseconomies. The agricultural sector provides good illustrations of external economies. As farm output increased in the nineteenth and early twentieth centuries, the services available to farmers expanded and their costs fell. Farm machinery, fertilizers, transportation networks, storage, and marketing facilities all improved, lowering farm costs as farm output expanded. As a consequence, as the demand for farm products has increased, the quantity produced has increased but the price has fallen (as in Fig. 12.13c).

One of the best examples of external diseconomies is congestion. The airline industry provides a good illustration. As the airline industry continues to grow, there is greater congestion of both airports and airspace, resulting in longer delays and extra waiting time for passengers and airplanes. These external diseconomies mean that as the demand for air transportation continues to increase, eventually (in the absence of further technological change), prices will rise.

Technological Change

Industries are constantly discovering lower-cost techniques of production. Most cost-saving production techniques cannot be implemented, however, without investing in new plant and equipment. As a consequence, it takes time for a technological advance to spread through an industry. Those firms whose plants are on the verge of being replaced will be quick to adopt the new technology, while firms whose plants have recently been replaced will continue to operate with older technology until they can no longer cover their average variable cost. Once average variable cost cannot be covered, it pays a firm to scrap even a relatively new plant embodying the original technology in favour of a plant with the new technology.

Let's work out exactly what happens to the output and profit of each firm in an industry that is reshaped by a new technology. Figure 12.14(a) shows the industry demand curve (D), and initial short-run supply curve (S_0). The price is P_0 and the quantity Q_0. Each of the original-technology firms has a marginal cost curve MC_0 and an average total cost curve ATC_0. At the market price (P_0), each firm faces a marginal revenue curve MR_0, produces the output

Figure 12.13 Long-Run Price and Quantity Changes

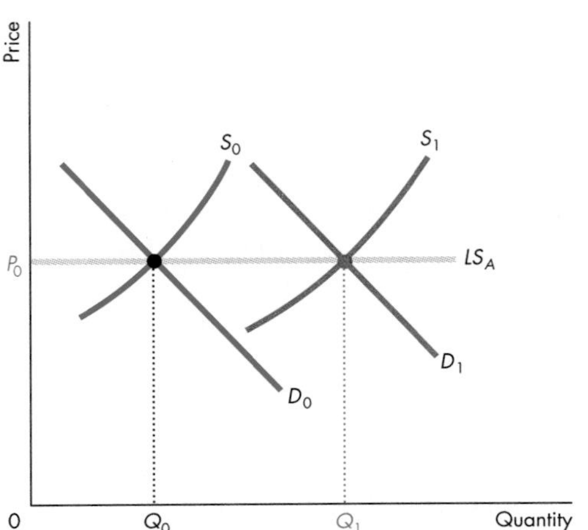

(a) Constant cost industry

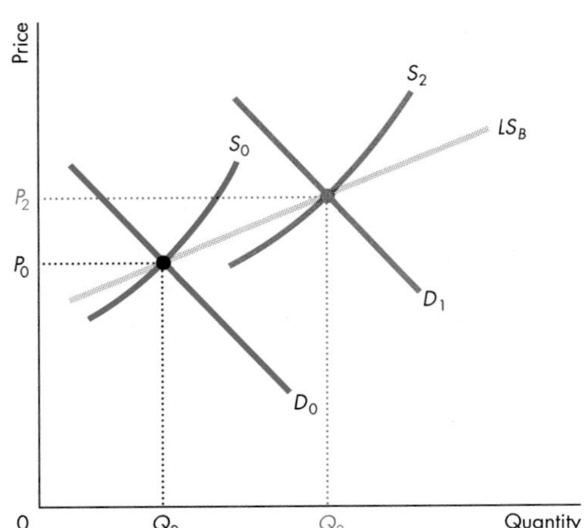

(b) Increasing cost industry

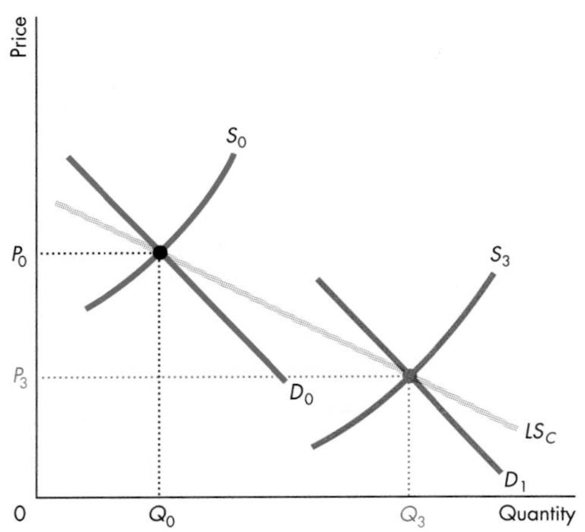

(c) Decreasing cost industry

The figure illustrates three possible long-run changes in price and quantity. When demand increases from D_0 to D_1, firms enter the industry and the short-run industry supply curve shifts from S_0 to S_1. In part (a), the long-run industry supply curve, which is LS_A, is horizontal; the quantity increases from Q_0 to Q_1 and the price remains constant at P_0. In part (b), the long-run industry supply curve is LS_B; the price increases to P_2, and the quantity increases to Q_2. This case occurs in industries with external diseconomies. In part (c), the long-run industry supply curve is LS_C; the price decreases to P_3, and the quantity increases to Q_3. This case occurs in industries with external economies.

q_0^O, and makes zero economic profit (part b). The industry is in long-run equilibrium.

New technology allows firms to produce at substantially lower cost than the existing technology. The cost curves of firms with the new technology are shown in Fig. 12.14(c). Suppose that one firm with the new technology enters the industry. Since the industry is competitive, this single firm is a negligible part of the total industry and hardly affects the industry supply; so the industry supply curve remains at S_0 and the price at P_0. However, the new-technology firm produces its profit-maximizing output q_0^N and makes a positive economic profit. Gradually, more new-technology firms enter the industry. After a period, enough have entered to shift the industry supply curve to become S_1. By this time, the market price has fallen to P_1 and the industry output has risen to Q_1. Each firm takes the price P_1 and maximizes its profit. Each new-technology firm maximizes profit by producing the output q_1^N and continues to

Figure 12.14 Technological Change in a Competitive Industry

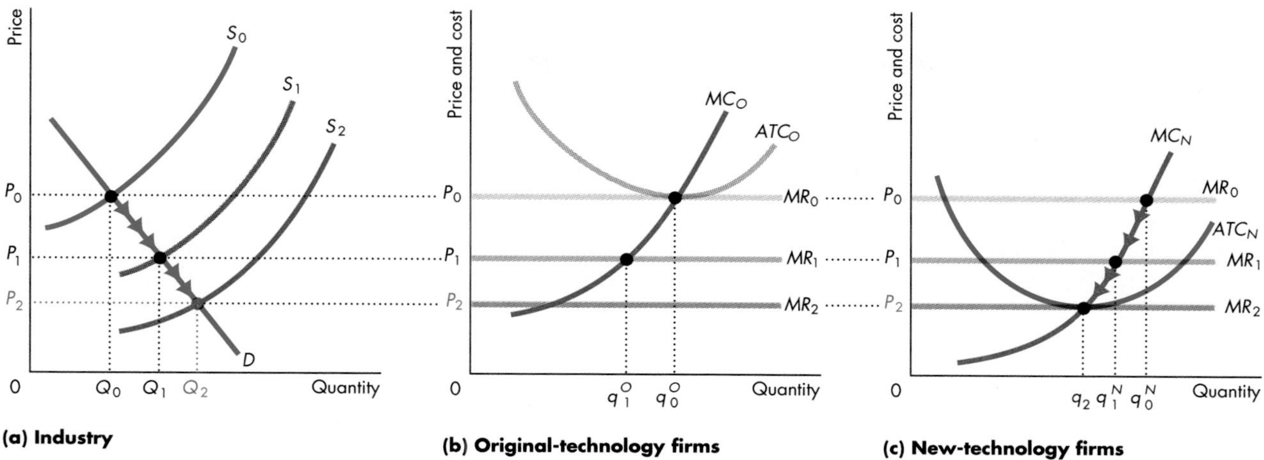

Initially, in part (a), the industry supply curve is S_0 and the demand curve is D, so the equilibrium price is P_0 and output is Q_0. Each firm, as shown in part (b), produces q_0^O and makes a zero profit. A new technology is developed. The costs for a firm using the new technology (ATC_N and MC_N) are lower than those for firms using the original technology (as shown in part c). A new-technology firm, faced with the price P_0, produces a profit-maximizing output of q_0^N and makes a profit. Since the new technology is profitable, more and more firms use it, and as they do so, the industry supply curve (part a) begins to shift to the right, from S_0 to S_1. Industry output rises to Q_1, but the price falls to P_1. As a result, new-technology firms cut their output from q_0^N to q_1^N, but they are still making a profit. Original-technology firms cut their output from q_0^O to q_1^O. They are making losses. As firms with the original technology begin to close down and more new-technology firms enter the industry, the supply curve continues to shift to the right, from S_1 to S_2. The price falls to P_2 and the industry output rises to Q_2. Each new-technology firm is now producing q_2 and making a zero profit; there are no firms using the original technology.

The effect of the introduction of the new technology has been to raise output and lower price. In the process, firms that adopted the new technology early made profits while those that stuck with the original technology too long incurred losses.

make an economic profit. Each original-technology firm minimizes its loss by producing the output q_1^O.

More new-technology firms continue to enter since the new technology is profitable. Original-technology firms begin to exit or to switch to the new technology because the original technology is unprofitable. Eventually, all the firms in the industry will be new-technology firms. By this time, the industry supply curve will have moved to S_2, which is based on the marginal cost curves of the new-technology firms. (The supply curve S_0 is based on the marginal cost curves of the original-technology firms, while S_1 is based on the marginal cost curves for both original-technology and new-technology firms.) With supply curve S_2, the market price is P_2 and the industry output Q_2. At price P_2, the new technology firms produce a profit-maximizing output of q_2, making a zero profit. The industry long-run equilibrium price is P_2.

The process that we have just analysed is one in which some firms experience economic profits and others economic losses. It is a period of dynamic change for an industry. Some firms do well and others do badly. An example is the dairy industry, which is undergoing a major technological change arising from the use of hormones. Often such a change has a geographical dimension. For example, the new-technology firms may be located in a new industrial region of a country while the original-technology firms are located in a traditional industrial region. Alternatively, the new-technology firms may be in a foreign country while the original-technology firms are in the domestic economy. The struggle of the Canadian textile industry to keep up with the fierce competition from Hong Kong and Taiwan is a good example of this phenomenon.

Although many sectors of the Canadian economy are highly competitive, one of the most competitive is agriculture. The model of perfect competition is especially useful for analysing this sector. Let's see how we can make sense of some of the important and, for farmers, distressing developments in this industry in the 1980s.

Farms in Distress

In 1981, there were approximately 320,000 farms in Canada. The average farm was about 210 hectares. The number of farms has been steadily declining over the years and the average farm size has been steadily rising. But in the five years from 1981 to 1986 there was an unusually rapid advance in this process. During that period, there was a nearly 10 percent decline in the number of farms and a similar percentage increase in the average farm size. Throughout the 1980s, there were many indications of financial distress in the farm sector. Many farmers were unable to cope with high interest rates and unable to meet their loan repayment schedules; they had borrowed up to their limits; they were leaving the business at a rapid rate; and some were in bankruptcy. Why have Canadian farms gone through a period of such tremendous financial distress? Why have so many farms gone out of business? Why, after such a shakeout, is the remaining farm larger, on the average?

The farm problem is a complex one. In fact, there is no single "farm problem" but many individual problems which arise due to regional differences, crop yields, and a host of other factors. But a single, common problem did affect all farmers to some degree during the early 1980s. It's on this problem that we'll focus.

Although some farmers are wealthy, many are not. They have to buy their land and farm buildings and equipment by borrowing from the bank. In the early 1980s, the cost of bank borrowing increased on an unprecedented scale. Bank loans that in the 1970s had cost an average of 7 or 8 percent a year were suddenly costing an average of 13 percent; interest rates climbed briefly to 20 percent a year in 1981, and they remained high at 15 percent through 1982. This massive increase in the cost of borrowing represented an increase in the fixed costs of a farm. Recall that fixed costs are those incurred independently of the volume of output. Even if a farm produces nothing, it has to pay the bank the interest on its loans.

We can analyse the effects of an increase in fixed costs in the farm sector by using the model of a perfectly competitive industry that we've just been studying. Figure 12.15 shows what happens. In part (a), a farm's average total cost curve (*ATC*), marginal cost curve (*MC*), and average and marginal revenue curves (*AR* = *MR*) are shown. The market price is P_0 and the farm's profit-maximizing output is q_0. Initially, there is long-run equilibrium with the farm making a zero economic profit when its average total cost curve is *ATC*.

An increase in fixed cost shifts the average total cost curve but does not change the marginal cost curve. (Recall that marginal cost is the cost of producing one additional unit of output. Since the increase in interest charges increases total fixed cost but not total variable cost, marginal cost is unchanged.) Suppose that the increased fixed cost shifts the average total cost curve to *ATC* ′ in Fig. 12.15(a). If the price remains P_0, the farm's profit-maximizing output remains at q_0. But the farm is now losing money. The loss is equal to the red rectangle.

The size of a farm's loss depends on its financial situation. Farms with large debts have the largest losses. Many farms have loans that approach the value of their land and buildings. It is these farms that incur the largest losses and begin to leave the industry. As farms go out of business, the supply curve of farm products starts to shift to the left and the price of farm products begins to increase. Figure 12.15(b) shows what happens in the long run. When enough farms leave the industry, the price increases from P_0 to P_1. At the higher price, farm output increases from q_0 to q_1 and farms are no longer losing money. Individual farm outputs are now bigger than before, which means that the average farm uses more inputs — more labour, more machines, and more land.

But the situation shown in Fig. 12.15(b) will take a long time to come about. The price does not rise quickly from P_0 to P_1. The main factor slowing the rise in price is the fact that Canadian farms, even with many having exited, represent but a small fraction of the world market for most agricultural products. As a consequence, farms will make losses for a prolonged period of time, during which the adjustment process is taking place.

Figure 12.15 The Effects of High Interest Rates on Farm Profits and Prices

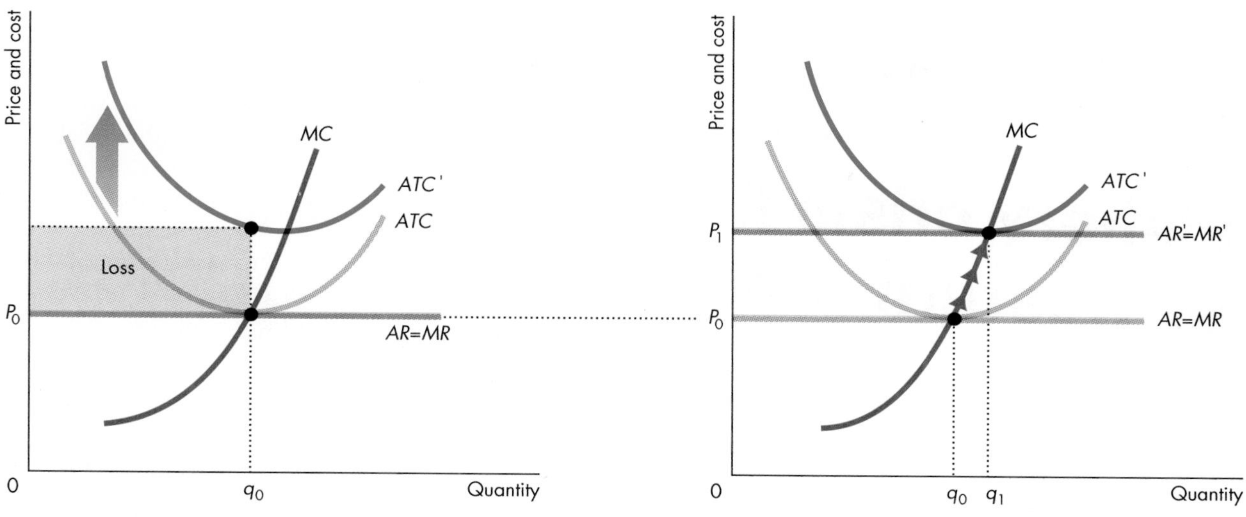

(a) High interest rates cause losses

(b) Exit raises prices—eventually

Initially, the individual farm's average total cost curve is ATC. At a price of P_0, its profit-maximizing output is q_0 (part a). Fixed costs increase, shifting the average total cost curve upward to ATC'. Marginal cost and price remain constant, and so does the profit-maximizing output. Farms now make a loss shown by the red rectangle. As some farms exit, the industry supply curve shifts to the left, the price begins to rise from P_0 to P_1, and the profit-maximizing output increases from q_0 to q_1 (part b). The process of adjustment is not instantaneous, and farms make losses for a prolonged period.

You've now studied how a competitive market works and have used the model of perfect competition to interpret and explain a variety of aspects of real world economic behaviour. Reading Between the Lines on pp. 306-307 gives a further application of the model of perfect competition. Our final topic in this chapter is the efficiency of competition.

Competition and Efficiency

In perfect competition, freedom of entry ensures that firms produce at the least possible cost. Also, because each firm is a price taker, it faces a perfectly elastic demand curve and, as a result, produces the quantity that makes marginal cost equal price. These features of a perfectly competitive market have important implications for the efficiency of such a market.

Allocative Efficiency

Allocative efficiency occurs when no resources are wasted — when no one can be made better off without making someone else worse off as judged by the standards of each individual's own preferences. If someone can be made better off without making someone else worse off, a more efficient allocation of resources can be achieved. Allocative efficiency requires satisfaction of three conditions:

- Economic efficiency
- Consumer efficiency
- Equality of marginal social cost and marginal social benefit

We defined economic efficiency in Chapter 9 as a situation in which the cost of producing a given output is minimized. Economic efficiency involves technological efficiency — producing the maximum possible output from given inputs — as

Perfect Competition in Action

Fishery crisis likened to western drought

Politicians and those lobbying for aid to the more than 3,000 fishery workers who face losing their jobs often compare the lack of fish in the sea with a drought in Western Canada.

Prime Minister Brian Mulroney has said the fishery workers will get the same attention from the federal government as Western Canadian farmers, who received more than $1-billion in aid after three recent droughts.

But those who study the Atlantic fishery say the two problems are about as similar as a trawler and a tractor.

While droughts are generally considered to be acts of God, the decline and fall of the Atlantic fishery is a human-made disaster, created by a decade of overfishing and mismanagement of fish stocks.

As well, a Western farmer hit by a drought plants a crop the next year if it rains. Scientists say the Atlantic fishery workers have to reduce their fish harvests for at least a decade or there will not be any fish left to harvest.

That scenario leaves the federal government with a tough choice—spend billions of dollars to keep fishing towns alive or send thousands of fishery workers, most of whom have little education or training for other jobs, to other provinces to find work....

National Sea Products Ltd. and Fishery Products International Ltd. have already announced layoffs of more than 3,000 workers after two years of reductions in the federally set allowable catch of northern cod....

But Leslie Harris, president of Memorial University in St. John's and the head of a federally appointed review panel on the northern cod stocks, said the reductions, which amount to about a 26 per cent cut in northern cod catches in the last two years, have not begun to address the problem of the slow-growing cod stocks.

Some federal scientists had recommended that the 1990 northern cod catch be cut to about half of the 1989 total of 235,000 tonnes....

Until last year, federal scientists believed northern cod stocks had been rebuilding since 1977, when Canada banned foreign fishing boats from areas closer than 200 miles from the Atlantic coastline.

But in February of last year, Newfoundlanders were stunned by the news from the federal Department of Fisheries and Oceans that cod numbers were not growing rapidly, and the fish being caught were often only half the size of those caught a decade ago...

The demand for fish resulted in the number of fish processing plants in Atlantic Canada increasing from 500 in 1977 to 876 in 1988.

Fishermen are angry that [the federal Department of] Fisheries and Oceans licenced those plants and allowed the fishermen to invest in the new techniques with no warning of the consequences...

The Globe and Mail,
January 15, 1990
By Kevin Cox

The Essence of the Story

- Growth in the demand for fish during the 1980s resulted in the number of fish processing plants in Atlantic Canada increasing from 500 in 1977 to 876 in 1988.
- By the late 1980s a depletion of the stock of fish (particularly northern cod) was imposing hardship on Atlantic fishermen that some likened to the hardship faced by farmers when there is a drought.
- But drought is a random and temporary phenomenon while the depletion of the fish stock could take decades to overcome.
- Quotas limiting the size of the catch were imposed in 1988 and more than 3,000 fishery workers faced the prospect of losing their jobs.
- The Prime Minister promised that fishery workers would get the same kind of federal government aid as Western Canadian farmers get when drought strikes.

Background and Analysis

- The Atlantic fishery industry is competitive. Fishermen there compete not only with each other but also with fishermen in the United States and other countries. As a result, each firm and the entire Atlantic Canada industry face a perfectly elastic demand curve.
- A long-run equilibrium in the Atlantic fishery industry is illustrated in Fig. (a). In part (i) the demand curve is perfectly elastic at the price P_W determined in the world market. The Atlantic supply curve is S_A and the total quantity produced is Q_A. An individual firm is shown in part (ii). It produces q_A, the quantity at which marginal cost equals marginal revenue and at which average total cost is a minimum. The firm makes zero economic profit.
- For this long-run equilibrium to persist, the fish stock must remain constant—the catch rate must equal the reproduction rate of the fish stock.
- Fish have been caught at a rate far higher than that at which the fish are reproducing. The fish stock has declined. Other things remaining unchanged, the declining fish stock would result in an upward shift in the firm's cost curves and in a leftward shift in the supply curve. But other things have not remained the same: advances in fishing technology have lowered costs and offset the effects of the declining fish stock.
- Eventually, the declining fish stock will lead to cost increases that cannot be offset by advances in fishing technology. When that happens, costs will rise, economic losses will be incurred, and firms will begin to leave the industry.
- To counter the declining fish stock, the federal government has imposed quotas on the fishermen, limiting the size of the total catch and the catch of each firm. The short-run effects of these quotas is shown in Fig. (b). Total Atlantic output is cut back to Q_Q (in part i), and each firm's output is cut back to q_Q (in part ii). At this output rate firms incur losses since average total cost exceeds price. But the firms remain in business until their plants wear out and need to be replaced. At that point, they will exit the industry.
- There is an immediate decrease in employment in the industry as each firm scales back its production to its allotted level. In the long-run, the decrease in employment increases as firms leave the industry.
- By making payments to fishermen similar to those made to drought-stricken farmers, the federal government can cover the fishery firms' losses and prevent them from leaving the industry. But even with government aid, job loss cannot be prevented since a cutback in production is essential if the fish stock is eventually to be stabilized.
- If firms leave the industry, job loss will be larger than if they do not, but the industry will operate at minimum average total cost.
- In deciding the scale of aid, the government will balance the cost of aid to the fish industry against the cost of large scale unemployment in Atlantic Canada.

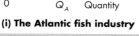

(a) No quota

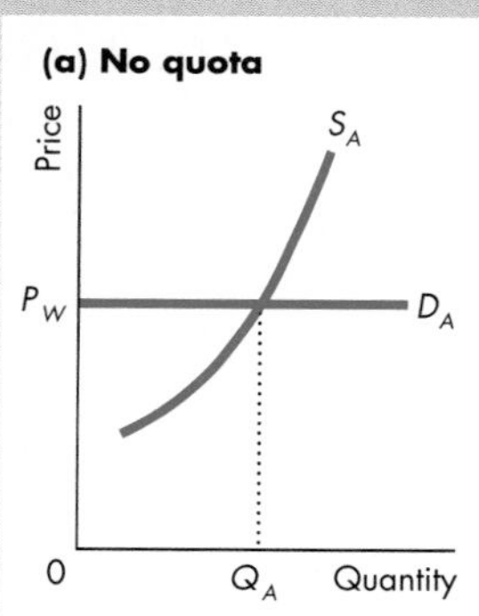

(i) The Atlantic fish industry

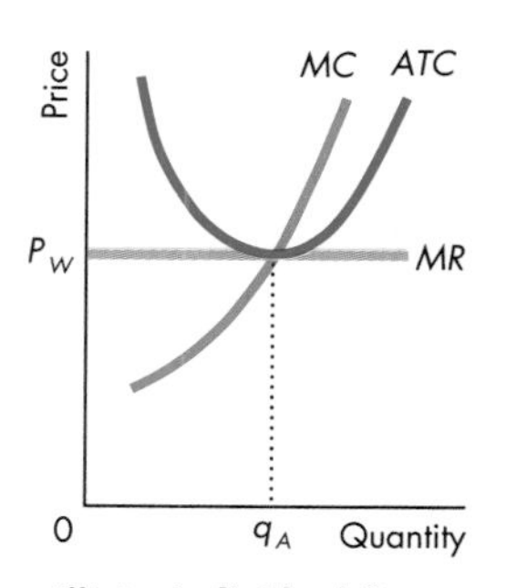

(ii) An individual firm

(b) With quota

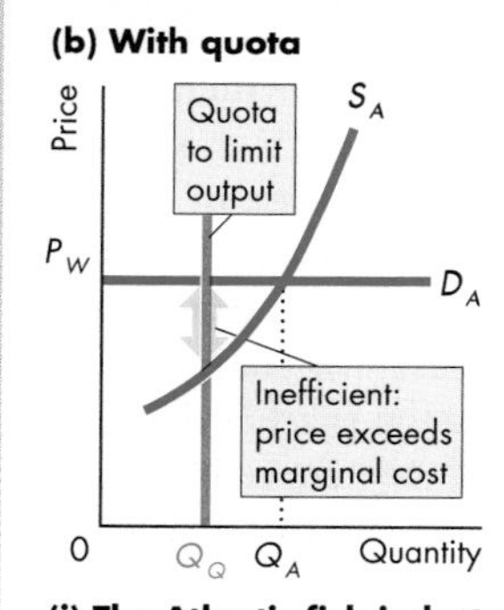

(i) The Atlantic fish industry

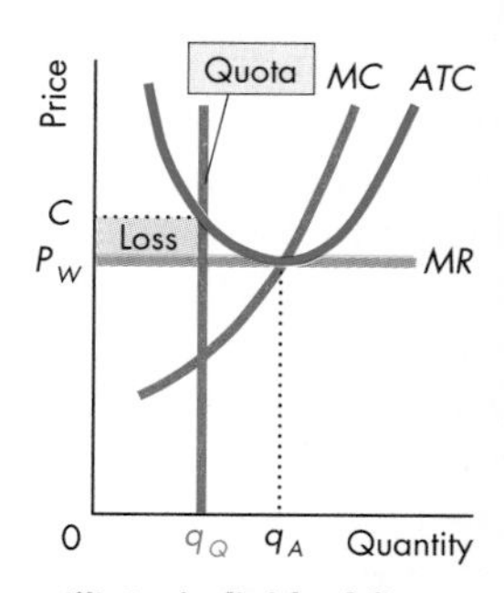

(ii) An individual firm

well as using inputs in their cost-minimizing proportions. Economic efficiency occurs whenever firms maximize profit. Since firms in perfect competition maximize profit, perfect competition is economically efficient.

Consumer efficiency occurs when consumers cannot make themselves better off by reallocating their budgets. A consumer's best possible budget allocation is summarized in the consumer's demand curves. That is, a demand curve tells us the quantity demanded at a given price when the consumer has made the best possible use of a given budget. Thus when the quantity bought at a given price is a point on the demand curve, the allocation satisfies consumer efficiency.

The third condition occurs in perfect competition if there are no external costs and benefits. **External costs** are those costs of a good borne by people other than its producer. Examples of such costs are the costs of pollution and congestion. **External benefits** are those benefits from a good accruing to people other than its buyer. Examples of such benefits are the pleasure people get from well-designed buildings and beautiful works of art. We don't have to buy these things to enjoy them, but someone does.

Marginal social cost is the cost of producing one additional unit of output, including external costs. **Marginal social benefit** is the dollar value of the benefit from one additional unit of consumption, including any external benefits. Allocative efficiency occurs when marginal social cost equals marginal social benefit. Figure 12.16 illustrates such a situation. The marginal social benefit curve is the blue curve labelled *MSB*, and the marginal social cost curve is the red curve labelled *MSC*. Allocative efficiency occurs at a quantity Q^* and price P^*. In this situation, there is no waste. No one can be made better off without making someone else worse off. If output is above Q^*, marginal social cost will exceed marginal social benefit; the cost of producing the last unit will exceed its benefit. If output is below Q^*, marginal social benefit will exceed marginal social cost; producing one more unit will bring more benefit than cost.

There are some circumstances in which perfect competition delivers allocative efficiency, as shown in Fig. 12.16. These circumstances are those in which there are no external costs and benefits. All the benefits accrue to the buyers of a good and the costs are borne by its producer. In that case, the marginal social benefit curve is the same as the market demand curve. Also, the marginal social cost curve is the market supply curve. With perfect competition, price and quantity are determined at the point of intersection of the demand and supply curves. Hence, a perfectly competitive market produces an output Q^* at a price P^*. Perfect competition delivers allocative efficiency.

To check that in this situation no resources are being wasted — no one can be made better off without someone being made worse off — consider what will happen if output is restricted to Q_0. Marginal social cost is C_0 but marginal social benefit is B_0. Everyone can be made better off by increasing output. Producers will willingly supply more of the good for a price higher than C_0. Consumers will willingly buy more of the good for a price lower than B_0. Everyone would like to trade more. But once output rises to Q^*, there are no further gains available from increasing the output of this good. The benefit to the consumer of the last unit produced exactly equals the cost to the producer of the last unit.

Figure 12.16 Allocative Efficiency

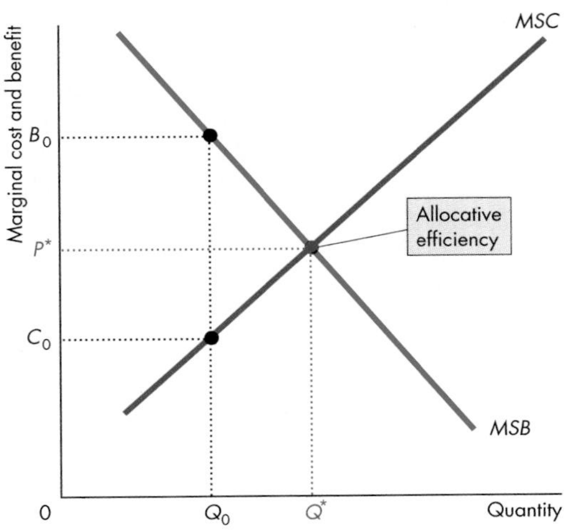

Allocative efficiency, which occurs when no resources are wasted, requires that marginal social cost (*MSC*) be equal to marginal social benefit (*MSB*). Allocative efficiency occurs at output Q^*. If output is Q_0, marginal social cost (C_0) is less than marginal social benefit (B_0). The benefit from one additional unit of output exceeds its cost. A perfectly competitive market delivers allocative efficiency when there are no external costs and benefits. In such a situation, the marginal social cost curve is the industry supply curve and the marginal social benefit curve is the industry demand curve; the price is P^* and the quantity traded is Q^*.

The Invisible Hand

The founder of economic science, Adam Smith, suggested that a competitive market acts like an invisible hand to guide buyers and sellers to achieve the best possible social outcome. Each participant in a competitive market is, according to Smith, "led by an invisible hand to promote an end which was no part of his intention." You can see the invisible hand at work in the cartoon on the right. Adam Smith was not able to work out his conclusion with the clarity and precision with which we are able to do so today. It is the work of Léon Walras, Vilfredo Pareto, and, more recently, Nobel-prize-winning economists Kenneth Arrow and Gérard Debreu that demonstrates the precise conditions under which perfect competition and maximum social welfare coincide.

Drawing by M. Twohy; © 1988 The New Yorker Magazine, Inc.

Obstacles to Efficiency

Allocative efficiency encounters two main obstacles:

- External costs and external benefits
- Monopoly

The existence of external costs and external benefits means that many goods cannot be efficiently produced, even in perfectly competitive markets. Such goods as national defence, the enforcement of law and order, the provision of clean drinking water, and the disposal of sewage and garbage are all examples of goods that have enormous external benefits. Left to competitive markets, the level of output of such goods will be too small. There are also many examples of goods that impose high external costs. The production of steel and chemicals generates air and water pollution. Perfect competition will result in an overproduction of such goods. One of the key functions of government is to modify the outcome of competitive markets in cases such as these. Government institutions (which we study in Chapters 19 to 21) arise, in part, because of external costs and benefits.

Another obstacle to allocative efficiency is the existence of monopoly. Monopoly, which we study in the next chapter, restricts output below its competitive level in order to increase price and make a larger profit.

■ We have now completed our study of perfect competition. We have seen how a firm in a perfectly competitive market chooses its profit-maximizing output. We have seen how the actions of all the firms in a market combine to determine the market supply curve and how the market supply and demand curves determine the price and quantity. We have seen how a competitive industry operates in the short run, and we have studied the dynamic forces that move such a market to a long-run equilibrium. We have used the model of perfect competition to understand several important features of real-world markets. Finally, we have seen that under some specific circumstances, perfect competition delivers an economically efficient allocation of resources.

Although many markets approximate the model of perfect competition, many do not. Our next task, in Chapters 13 and 14, is to study markets that depart from perfect competition. We begin, in the next chapter, by going to the opposite extreme of perfect competition — pure monopoly. Then in Chapter 14, we'll study the markets between perfect competition and pure monopoly — monopolistic competition and oligopoly (competition among a few producers). When we have completed this study, we'll have a toolkit of alternative models of markets that will enable us to study all the possible situations that arise in the real world.

SUMMARY

Perfect Competition

Perfect competition occurs in a market in which a large number of firms produce an identical good; there are many buyers; firms face competition from potential new entrants; and all firms and buyers are fully informed about the prices charged by each firm. In perfect competition, each firm sells its good for the same price, and no single firm can influence the market price. Even if one firm doubles its output, the industry output will change by a tiny percentage and the market price will hardly be affected. (pp. 283-285)

Firms' Choices in Perfect Competition

A competitive firm takes the market price as given and chooses how much to produce, when to shut down temporarily, and when to leave an industry permanently. The firm's choices are based on its desire to maximize profit. The firm maximizes profit by producing the output at which marginal cost equals marginal revenue (price).

A firm's maximum profit is not necessarily a positive profit. If price is above average total cost, the firm makes a positive economic profit. If price equals average total cost, the firm breaks even. If price is below average total cost, the firm makes an economic loss. If price is low enough, the firm maximizes profit by temporarily shutting down and laying off its workers. This occurs if price is below minimum average variable cost. When price equals minimum average variable cost, the firm makes a loss equal to its total fixed costs; if the firm shuts down production, it also makes a loss equal to its total fixed costs.

The firm's supply curve is the upward-sloping part of its marginal cost curve, at all points above the point of minimum average variable cost. (pp. 285-293)

Short-Run Equilibrium

The short-run industry supply curve shows how the total quantity supplied in the short run by all the firms in an industry varies as the market price varies.

The price at which the quantity supplied equals the quantity demanded is the market price. Each firm takes the market price as given and chooses the output that maximizes its profit. In short-run equilibrium, each firm can be making an economic profit, an economic loss, or a zero economic profit. (pp. 293-295)

Long-Run Equilibrium

If firms in an industry make positive economic profits, existing firms will expand and new firms will enter the industry. If firms in an industry make economic losses, some of them will leave the industry and the remaining firms will produce less. Entry and exit shift the short-run industry supply curve. As firms enter, the industry supply curve shifts to the right. As firms leave, the industry supply curve shifts to the left. Entry causes the profits of existing firms to fall, and exit causes those profits to rise (or losses to fall). In long-run equilibrium, all firms in the market make a zero economic profit. No firm wants to enter or leave the industry, and no firm wants to expand or contract its production plant. Long-run competitive equilibrium occurs when each firm maximizes its short-run profit; economic profit is zero, so no firms enter or exit; and each firm produces at the point of minimum long-run average cost, so it has no incentive to change its plant size. (pp. 295-298)

Predictions

In a perfectly competitive market, a permanent decrease in demand leads to a lower industry output and a smaller number of firms in the industry. A permanent increase in demand leads to a rise in industry output and an increase in the number of firms in the industry. If there are no external economies or diseconomies, a change in demand does not change the market price in the long run. If there are external economies, price falls as demand rises. If there are external diseconomies, price rises as demand rises.

New technology increases the short-run industry supply, and in the long run, the market price falls and the quantity produced rises. The number of firms in the industry falls. Firms that are slow to change to the new technology will make losses and eventually go out of business. Firms that are quick to adopt the new technology will make economic profit initially, but in the long run their economic profits will fall to zero.

The farm problem of the 1980s, although a complex one, has a central feature that can be understood using the model of perfect competition. A large increase in interest rates increased farms' fixed costs. As a result, their average total cost curves shifted upward. Increased average total cost brought losses. These losses, in turn, have forced many farms out of business. As the number of farms declines, the supply curve of farm products shifts to the left and prices increase. But this process takes time — time during which losses will persist in the farm sector. Eventually, after the adjustment process is complete, the market will comprise a smaller number of farms, which will break even. (pp. 298-305)

Competition and Efficiency

Allocative efficiency occurs when no one can be made better off without making someone else worse off. The three conditions for allocative efficiency — economic efficiency, consumer efficiency, and equality of marginal social cost and marginal social benefit — occur in perfect competition when there are no external costs and benefits. It is this situation that Adam Smith was describing when he said that the economy is led by an "invisible hand."

The achievement of allocative efficiency has two main obstacles — the existence of external costs and benefits and of monopoly. (pp. 305-310)

K E Y E L E M E N T S

Key Terms

Allocative efficiency, 305
Average revenue, 285
Break-even point, 287
Entry, 295
Exit, 295
External benefits, 308
External costs, 308
External diseconomies, 301
External economies, 301
Marginal revenue, 285
Marginal social benefit, 308
Marginal social cost, 308
Perfect competition, 283
Perfectly competitive firm's supply curve, 292
Price taker, 283
Short-run industry supply curve, 293
Shutdown point, 290

Key Figures 

Figure 12.2 Total Revenue, Total Cost, and Profit, 288
Figure 12.3 Marginal Revenue, Marginal Cost, and Profit-Maximizing Output, 289
Figure 12.5 Swanky's Supply Curve, 293
Figure 12.6 Firm and Industry Supply Curves, 294
Figure 12.13 Long-Run Price and Quantity Changes, 302
Figure 12.16 Allocative Efficiency, 308

REVIEW QUESTIONS

1 What are the main features of a perfectly competitive industry?

2 Why can't a perfectly competitive firm influence the industry price?

3 List the three key decisions that a firm in a perfectly competitive industry has to make in order to maximize profit.

4 Why is marginal revenue equal to price in a perfectly competitive industry?

5 When will a perfectly competitive firm temporarily stop producing?

6 What is the connection between the supply curve and the marginal cost curve of a perfectly competitive firm?

7 What is the relationship between a firm's supply curve and the short-run industry supply curve in a perfectly competitive industry?

8 When will firms enter an industry and when will they leave it?

9 What happens to the short-run industry supply curve when firms enter a competitive industry?

10 What is the effect of entry on the price and quantity produced?

11 What is the effect of entry on profit?

12 Trace the effects of a permanent increase in demand on price, quantity, number of firms in the industry, and profit.

13 Trace the effects of a permanent decrease in demand on price, quantity, number of firms in the industry, and profit.

14 Under what circumstances will a perfectly competitive industry have

a) A perfectly elastic long-run supply curve?

b) An upward-sloping long-run supply curve?

c) A downward-sloping long-run supply curve?

15 Use the model of a perfectly competitive industry to explain why such a large number of farms went out of business in the 1980s.

16 What is allocative efficiency, and under what circumstances does it arise?

PROBLEMS

1 Suppose that a firm produces one-thousandth of an industry's output. The industry's elasticity of demand is 3. What is the firm's elasticity of demand?

2 Pat's Pizza Kitchen is a price taker. It has the following hourly costs:

Output (pizzas per hour)	Total cost (dollars per hour)
0	10
1	12
2	16
3	22
4	30
5	40

a) If pizzas sell for $9, what is Pat's profit-maximizing output per hour?

b) What is Pat's shutdown point?

c) Derive Pat's supply curve.

d) What price will cause Pat to leave the pizza industry?

e) What price will cause other firms with costs identical to Pat's to enter the industry?

f) What is the long-run equilibrium price of pizzas?

3 Why have the prices of pocket calculators and VCRs fallen?

4 What has been the effect of a rise in world population on the wheat market and on the individual wheat farmer?

5 How has the diaper service industry been affected by the fall in the Canadian birth rate and the development of disposable diapers?

6 The market demand schedule for record albums is as follows:

Price (dollars per album)	Quantity demanded (albums per week)
0.75	440,000
1.75	430,000
2.75	420,000
3.75	410,000
4.75	400,000
5.75	390,000
6.75	380,000
7.75	370,000
8.75	360,000
9.75	350,000
10.75	340,000
11.75	330,000
12.75	320,000

The market is perfectly competitive, and each firm has the cost structure described by the following table:

Output (albums per week)	Marginal cost	Average variable cost	Average total cost
	(dollars per album)		
150	4.82	8.80	15.47
200	4.09	7.69	12.69
250	4.63	7.00	11.00
300	6.75	6.75	10.07
350	9.75	6.91	9.75
400	13.95	7.50	10.00
450	19.62	8.52	10.74
500	26.57	9.97	11.97

There are 1,000 firms in the industry.

a) What is the industry price?

b) What is the industry quantity traded?

c) What is the output of each firm?

d) What is the economic profit of each firm?

e) What is the shutdown point?

7 The same demand conditions as those in problem 6 prevail, but total fixed costs increase by $500.

a) What is the short-run profit-maximizing output for each firm?

b) Do firms enter or exit the industry?

c) What is the new long-run equilibrium price?

d) What is the new long-run equilibrium number of firms in the industry?

8 The same cost conditions as those in problem 6 prevail, but the falling price of compact discs decreases the demand for record albums and the demand schedule becomes as follows:

Price (dollars per album)	Quantity demanded (albums per week)
0.75	360,000
1.75	350,000
2.75	340,000
3.75	330,000
4.75	320,000
5.75	310,000
6.75	300,000
7.75	290,000
8.75	280,000
9.75	270,000
10.75	260,000
11.75	250,000
12.75	240,000

a) What is the short-run profit-maximizing output for each firm?

b) Do firms enter or exit the industry?

c) What is the new long-run equilibrium price?

d) What is the new long-run equilibrium number of firms in the industry?

CHAPTER 13

Monopoly

After studying this chapter, you will be able to:

- Define monopoly.
- Explain the conditions under which monopoly arises.
- Distinguish between legal monopoly and natural monopoly.
- Explain how a monopoly determines its price and output.
- Define price discrimination.
- Explain why price discrimination leads to a bigger profit.
- Compare the performance of a competitive and a monopolistic industry.
- Define rent seeking and explain why it arises.
- Explain the conditions under which monopoly is more efficient than competition.

The Profits of Generosity

YOU HAVE BEEN HEARING A LOT in this book about firms that want to maximize profit. But perhaps you've been looking at some of the places where you do business and wondering if they are really so intent on profit. After all, don't you get a student discount when you get a haircut? Don't museums and movie theatres give discounts to students, too? And what about the airline that gives a discount for buying a ticket in advance? Are your barber and movie theatre owner, as well as the museum and airline operators, simply generous folks to whom the model of profit-maximizing firms does not apply? Aren't they simply throwing profit away by cutting ticket prices and offering discounts? ■ When you want a phone line installed, you have only one choice: call the local phone company. If you want to buy cable TV service, you have one option: buy from the local cable company. Regardless of where you live, you have no choice about the supplier of your phone service, gas, electricity, or water. If you want to mail a letter, there is only one producer of letter-carrying services (aside from expensive couriers), Canada Post. These are all examples of a single producer of a good or service controlling its supply. Such firms are obviously not like firms in perfectly competitive industries. They don't face a market-determined price. They can choose their own price. How do they choose the quantity to produce and the price at which to sell it? Do they charge prices that are too high, damaging the interests of consumers? Do such firms bring any benefits?

■ This chapter studies markets in which individual firms can influence the quantity of goods supplied and, as a consequence, exert some influence on price. Whether the firm is the only producer in the economy, such as Canada Post, or the only producer in a particular location, such as a public utility, it does not take the market price for its output as given; rather, it chooses its price. We begin by studying conditions under which a single producer controls a market. Then we analyse the price and quantity decisions of such a firm when it sells its output for a single price to all its customers. After that, we study markets in which a firm can charge a higher price to some customers than others. Finally, we ask whether a market controlled by a single firm achieves allocative efficiency as does a perfectly competitive market.

How Monopoly Arises

A **monopoly** is an industry in which there is one supplier of a good, service, or resource that has no close substitutes and in which there is a barrier to the entry of new firms. The suppliers of phone service, gas, electricity, and water are examples of local monopolies — monopolies restricted to a given location. Canada Post is an example of a national monopoly — a sole supplier of letter-carrying services.

Barriers to Entry

The key feature of a monopoly is the existence of barriers preventing the entry of new firms. **Barriers to entry** are legal or natural impediments protecting a firm from competition from potential new entrants.

Legal Barriers to Entry Legal barriers to entry give rise to legal monopoly. **Legal monopoly** occurs when a law, licence, or patent restricts competition by preventing entry. There are several kinds of legal barriers to entry.

The first legal barrier to entry is a public franchise. A **public franchise** is an exclusive right granted to a firm to supply a good or service. An example of a public franchise is Canada Post, which has the exclusive right to carry first-class mail. Another common form of public franchise occurs on university and college campuses where particular firms are given exclusive rights to sell food and banking services.

The second kind of legal barrier is a government licence. A **government licence** controls entry into a particular occupation, profession, or industry. Government licensing in the professions is the most important example of this type of barrier to entry. For example, a licence is required to practise medicine, law, dentistry, school-teaching, architecture, and a variety of other professional services. Various kinds of firms must also obtain government licences. For example, a radio or TV station cannot broadcast without a licence from the Canadian Radio-television and Telecommunications Commission. Licensing does not create monopoly, but it does restrict competition.

A third legal restriction on entry is the use of patents. A **patent** is an exclusive right granted by the government to the inventor of a product or service; it is valid for a limited time period that varies from country to country. In Canada, patents issued before October 1, 1989 are valid for 17 years; those issued later are valid for 20 years. Patents are designed to protect inventors and thereby encourage invention by preventing others from copying a new idea until sufficient time has elapsed for its inventor to have reaped some rewards.

Natural Barriers to Entry Natural barriers to entry give rise to natural monopoly. **Natural monopoly** occurs when there is a unique source of supply of a raw material or when economies of scale enable one firm to supply the entire market at a lower price than two or more firms can. As the definition of natural monopoly implies, natural barriers to entry take two forms. First, a single firm may own and control the entire supply of a mineral or natural resource. This type of monopoly occurs in the production of, say, a mineral water for which there is a single source and in the production of some raw materials. De Beers, a South African company, for example, owns and controls four-fifths of the world's diamond mines. All the sources of chromium, also concentrated in southern Africa, are controlled by a small number of producers.

Second, natural monopoly can arise because of *economies of scale*. When a single producer can supply the entire market at an average total cost of production that is lower than what can be achieved by two or more firms, only a single firm can survive in the industry. Examples of natural monopoly arising from economies of scale are public utilities, such as the distribution of electricity, natural gas, and water.

In the real world, most monopolies, whether legal or natural, are regulated in some way by government or by government agencies. We will study the effects of such regulation in Chapter 21. Here we will consider an unregulated monopoly for two important reasons. First, we can better understand why governments regulate monopolies and the effects of regulation if we know how an unregulated monopoly would behave. Second, even in industries with more

Monopoly

Joan Robinson

What determines the price at which a monopolist sells its output? This question has puzzled generations of economists. Adam Smith (see Our Advancing Knowledge, pp. 20-21) said that "The price of a monopoly is upon every occasion the highest which can be got." You will discover, in this chapter, just why Adam Smith was wrong. The question was first answered correctly in the 1830s by Antoine-August Cournot (see Our Advancing Knowledge, pp. 84-85), but his answer was not appreciated until almost a century later.

The modern theory of monopoly was first worked out in the 1930s by Joan Robinson (1903-1983) of Cambridge University. At thirty, Joan Robinson published *The Economics of Imperfect Competition*, a brilliant book that challenged her teacher, Alfred Marshall (see Our Advancing Knowledge, pp. 84-85) and provided a new approach to the study of industrial economics. She coined the term *marginal revenue* and invented the modern diagram that shows the determination of monopoly price, output, and profit. That diagram is reproduced here. Notice its similarity with Fig. 13.3(c).

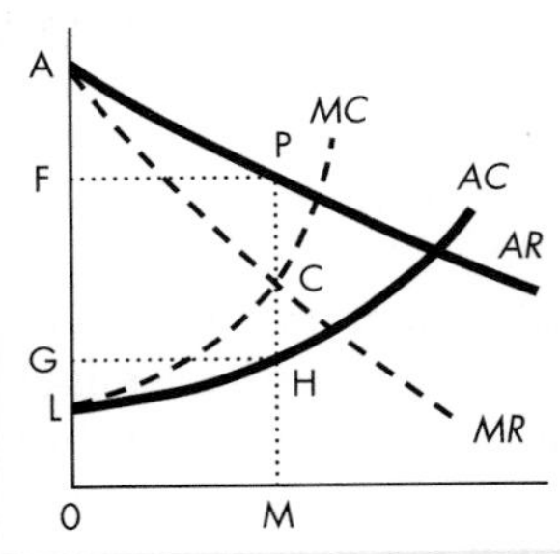

Here is a true story about Joan Robinson practising monopoly! In the spring of 1960, on her first visit to the United States, she presented a paper at the Massachusetts Institute of Technology (MIT) on the theory of capital that gave rise to a fierce and at times acrimonious dispute with the celebrated MIT economist Paul Samuelson. Anxious to make a point, Samuelson asked Robinson for the chalk (so that he could write some equations or draw a diagram on the blackboard). Monopolizing the chalk and the board, Robinson snarled at Samuelson, "Say it in words, young man."

This story illustrates both monopoly and Joan Robinson's approach to economics: Work out answers to economic problems using the most powerful methods of logic available, but then, "say it in words." Don't be satisfied with a formal argument if you don't *understand* it.

than one producer, each firm often has an element of monopoly power, arising from locational advantages or from important differences in product quality protected by patents. The theory of monopoly sheds important light on the behaviour of such firms and industries.

We'll begin by studying the behaviour of a single-price monopoly. A **single-price monopoly** is a monopoly that charges the same price for each and every unit of its output. How does a single-price monopoly determine the quantity to produce and the price to charge for its output?

Single-Price Monopoly

The starting point for understanding how a single-price monopoly chooses its price and output is to work out the relationship between the demand for the good produced by the monopoly and the monopoly's revenue.

Demand and Revenue

Since in a monopoly there is only one firm, the demand curve facing that firm is the industry demand curve. Let's look at an imaginary example: Bobbie's Barbershop, the sole supplier of haircuts in Trout River, Newfoundland. The demand schedule that Bobbie faces is set out in Table 13.1. At a price of $20, Bobbie sells no haircuts. The lower the price, the more haircuts per hour Bobbie is able to sell. For example, at a price of $12, consumers demand 4 haircuts per hour (row *e*), and at a price of $4, they demand 8 haircuts per hour (row *i*).

Total revenue (*TR*) is the price (*P*) multiplied by the quantity sold (*Q*). For example, in row *d*, Bobbie sells 3 haircuts an hour at $14 each, so total revenue is $42 an hour. Marginal revenue (*MR*) is the change in total revenue resulting from a one-unit rise in the quantity sold. For example, if the price falls from $18 (row *b*) to $16 (row *c*), the quantity sold rises from 1 to 2 haircuts an hour. Total revenue rises from $18 to $32, so the change in total revenue is $14. Since the quantity sold rises by 1 haircut an hour, the change in total revenue is marginal revenue of $14.

Figure 13.1 shows Bobbie's demand curve (*D*). Each row of Table 13.1 corresponds to a point on the demand curve. For example, row *d* in the table and point *d* on the demand curve tell us that at a price of $14, Bobbie sells 3 haircuts. The figure also shows Bobbie's marginal revenue curve (*MR*). Notice that the marginal revenue curve is below the demand curve; that is, at each level of output marginal revenue is less than price. Why is marginal revenue less than price? Lowering the price to sell one more unit has two opposing effects on total revenue. The lower price results in a revenue loss and the increased quantity sold results in a revenue gain. For example, at a

Table 13.1 Single-Price Monopoly's Revenue

	Price (*P*) (dollars per haircut)	Quantity demanded (*Q*) (haircuts per hour)	Total revenue ($TR = P \times Q$) (dollars per hour)	Marginal revenue ($MR = \Delta TR/\Delta Q$) (dollars per haircut)
a	20	0	0	
				18
b	18	1	18	
				14
c	16	2	32	
				10
d	14	3	42	
				6
e	12	4	48	
				2
f	10	5	50	
				−2
g	8	6	48	
				−6
h	6	7	42	
				−10
i	4	8	32	
				−14
j	2	9	18	
				−18
k	0	10	0	

The table shows Bobbie's demand schedule — the number of haircuts demanded per hour at each price. Total revenue (*TR*) is price multiplied by quantity sold. For example, row *c* shows that when the price is $16 per haircut, two haircuts are sold for a total revenue of $32. Marginal revenue (*MR*) is the change in total revenue resulting from a one-unit rise in the quantity sold. For example, when the price falls from $16 to $14 per haircut, the quantity sold increases from 2 to 3 haircuts and total revenue increases by $10. The marginal revenue of the third haircut is $10. Total revenue rises through row *f*, where 5 haircuts are sold for $10, and it falls thereafter. In the output range over which total revenue is increasing, marginal revenue is positive; in the output range over which total revenue is decreasing, marginal revenue is negative.

price of $16 Bobbie sells 2 haircuts (point *c*). If she reduces the price to $14, she sells 3 haircuts and has a total revenue gain of $14 on the third haircut. But she receives only $14 on the first two as well — $2 less than before — so her total revenue loss on the first 2 haircuts is $4. She has to deduct this loss from the total revenue gain of $14. Marginal revenue — the difference between the total revenue gain and the total revenue loss — is $10.

Figure 13.2 shows Bobbie's demand curve (*D*), marginal revenue curve (*MR*), and total revenue curve (*TR*) and illustrates the connections between them. Again, each row in Table 13.1 corresponds to a point on the curves in Fig. 13.2. For example, row *d* in the table and point d on the graphs tell us that when 3 haircuts are sold for $14 each (part a), total revenue is $42 (part b). Notice that as the quantity sold rises, total revenue rises to a peak of $50 (point *f*) and then declines. To understand the behaviour of total revenue, notice what happens to marginal revenue as the quantity sold increases. From 0 to 5 haircuts, marginal revenue is positive. When more than 5 haircuts are sold, marginal revenue becomes negative. The output range over which marginal revenue is positive is the same as that over which total revenue is rising. The output range over which marginal revenue is negative is the same as that over which total revenue declines. When marginal revenue is 0, total revenue is at a maximum.

Figure 13.1 Demand and Marginal Revenue for a Single-Price Monopoly

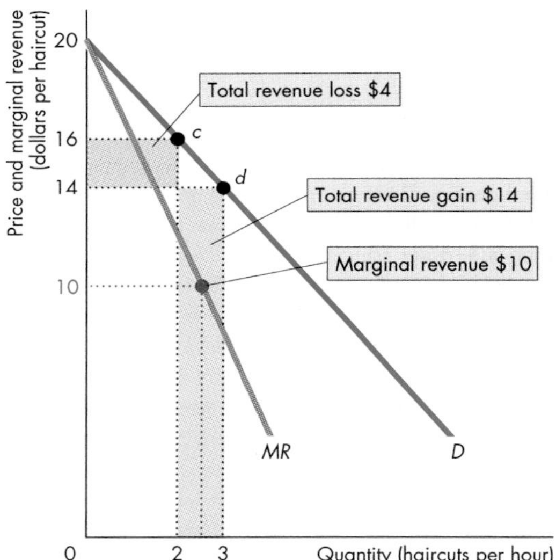

The monopoly demand curve *D* is based on the numbers in Table 13.1. At a price of $16 per haircut, Bobbie sells 2 haircuts per hour. If she lowers the price to $14, she sells 3 haircuts per hour. The sale of the third haircut brings a total revenue gain of $14 (the price charged for the third haircut). But there is a revenue loss of $4 ($2 per haircut) on the 2 haircuts that she could have sold for $16 each. The marginal revenue (extra total revenue) from the third haircut is the difference between the total revenue gain and the total revenue loss — $10. The marginal revenue curve (*MR*) shows the marginal revenue at each level of sales. Marginal revenue is lower than price.

Revenue and Elasticity

When we studied elasticity in Chapter 5, we discovered a connection between the elasticity of demand and the effect of a change in price on total expenditure or total revenue. Let's refresh our memories of that connection.

Recall that the elasticity of demand is the percentage change in the quantity demanded divided by the percentage change in price. If the elasticity of demand is greater than 1, a 1 percent decrease in price results in a greater than 1 percent increase in the quantity demanded. If the elasticity of demand is less than 1, a 1 percent decrease in price results in a less than 1 percent increase in the quantity demanded.

The responsiveness of the quantity demanded to a change in price also influences the change in total revenue. If a 1 percent decrease in price results in an increase in the quantity demanded of more than 1 percent, total revenue increases. But the output range over which total revenue increases when the price decreases is the same as that over which marginal revenue is positive. Thus the output range over which marginal revenue is positive is also the output range over which the elasticity of demand is greater than 1. The output range over which total revenue decreases when price decreases is the same as that over which marginal revenue is negative. Thus the output range over which marginal revenue is negative is also the output range over which the elasticity of demand is less than 1.

We've seen what happens to marginal revenue and total revenue when the elasticity of demand is greater than 1 and when it is less than 1. If the elasticity of demand is exactly 1, the percentage decrease in price equals the percentage increase in the quantity demanded. In this case, a price change results in no change in total revenue. Marginal revenue is zero. Thus when the elasticity of demand is 1, total revenue is at its maximum and marginal revenue is zero.

Figure 13.2 A Single-Price Monopoly's Revenue Curves

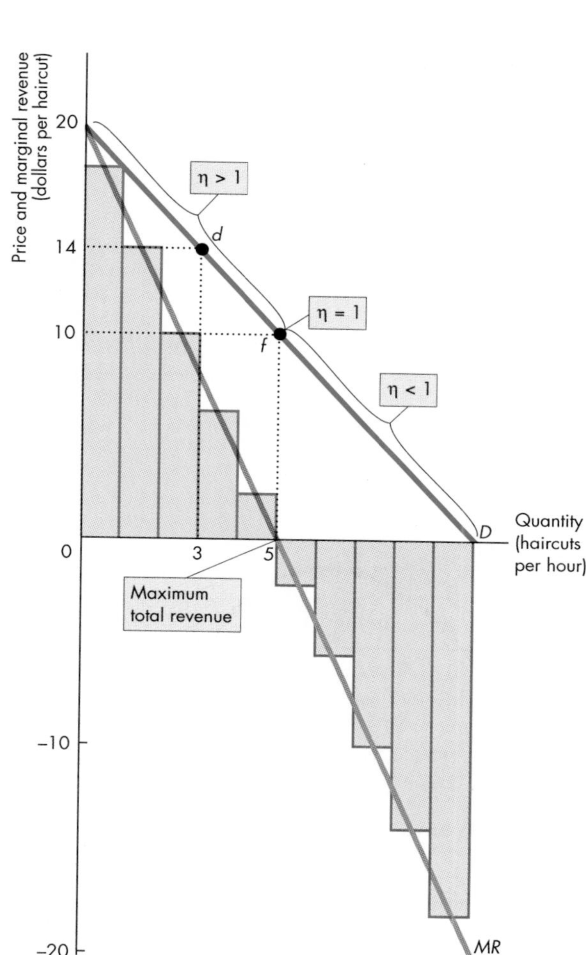

(a) Demand and marginal revenue curves

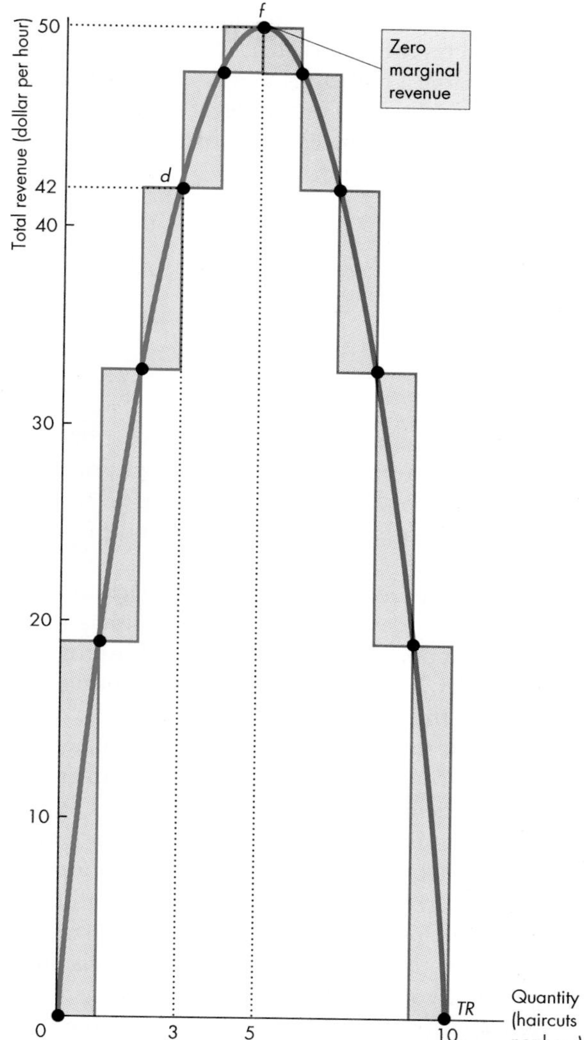

(b) Total revenue curve

Bobbie's demand curve (*D*) and marginal revenue curve (*MR*), shown in part (a), and her total revenue curve (*TR*), shown in part (b), are based on the numbers in Table 13.1. For example, at a price of $14, Bobbie sells 3 haircuts per hour (point *d* in part a) for a total revenue of $42 (point *d* in part b). Over the range 0 to 5 haircuts per hour, total revenue is increasing and marginal revenue is positive, as shown by the blue bars. Over the range 5 to 10 haircuts an hour, total revenue declines and marginal revenue is negative, as shown by the red bars. Over the output range for which marginal revenue is positive, the elasticity of demand is greater than 1 — demand is elastic. Over the output range for which marginal revenue is negative, the elasticity of demand is less than 1 — demand is inelastic. At the output at which marginal revenue is zero, total revenue is at a maximum and the elasticity of demand equals 1 — point *f*.

The relationship that you have just discovered has an interesting implication: a profit-maximizing monopoly will never produce an output in the inelastic range of its demand curve. If it does so, marginal revenue will be negative — each additional unit sold will lower total revenue. In such a situation, it will always pay to charge a higher price and sell a smaller quantity. But exactly what output level does the single-price monopoly produce? And what price does it charge?

Price and Output Decision

Profit is the difference between total revenue and total cost. To determine the output level and price that maximize a monopoly's profit, we need to study the behaviour of both revenue and cost as output varies.

A monopoly faces the same types of technology and cost constraints as a competitive firm. It has a production function that is subject to diminishing returns. It buys its inputs in competition with other firms, at prices that it cannot influence. The sole difference between the monopoly that we'll study here and a perfectly competitive firm lies in the market constraint for the output that each firm faces. The competitive firm is a price taker, whereas the monopoly supplies the entire market. Because the monopoly supplies the entire market, its output decision affects the price at which that output is sold. It is this fact that gives rise to the difference between the decisions faced by these two types of firm.

We have already looked at Bobbie's revenue in Table 13.1. Figure 13.3 repeats part of that information and also gives her costs and profit. Total cost rises as output rises, and so does total revenue. Profit equals total revenue minus total cost. As you can see in the table, the maximum profit ($12) occurs when Bobbie sells 3 haircuts for $14 each. If she sells 2 haircuts for $16 each or 4 haircuts for $12 each, her profit is only $8.

You can see why 3 haircuts is the profit-maximizing output by looking at the marginal revenue and marginal cost columns of the table in Fig. 13.3. When Bobbie raises output from 2 to 3 haircuts, she generates a marginal revenue of $10 and incurs a marginal cost of $6. Profit increases by the difference, $4. If Bobbie further increases output, from

Figure 13.3 A Single-Price Monopoly's Profit-Maximizing Output and Price

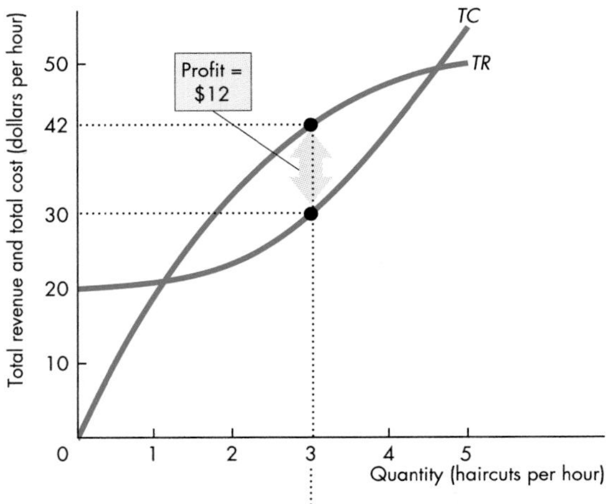

(a) Total revenue and total cost curves

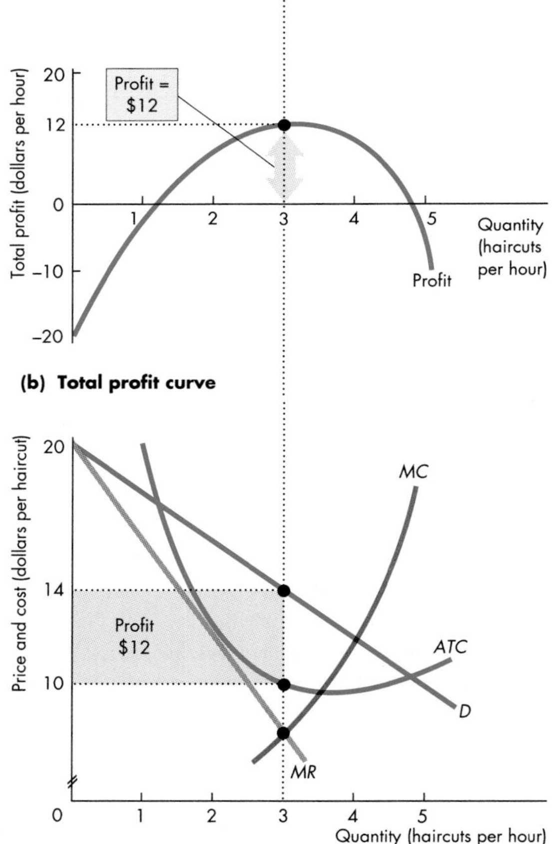

(b) Total profit curve

(c) Demand and marginal revenue and cost curves

Figure 13.3 Continued

Price (*P*) (dollars per haircut)	Quantity demanded (*Q*) (haircuts per hour)	Total revenue ($TR = P \times Q$) (dollars per hour)	Marginal revenue ($MR = \Delta TR/\Delta Q$) (dollars per haircut)	Total cost (*TC*) (dollars per hour)	Marginal cost ($MC = \Delta TC/\Delta Q$) (dollars per haircut)	Profit ($TR - TC$) (dollars per hour)
20	0	0		20		−20
			18		1	
18	1	18		21		−3
			14		3	
16	2	32		24		+8
			10		6	
14	3	42		30		+12
			6		10	
12	4	48		40		+8
			2		15	
10	5	50		55		−5

The table adds information about total cost (*TC*), marginal cost (*MC*), and profit (*TR* minus *TC*) to the information on demand and revenue in Table 13.1. For example, at a price of \$16, 2 haircuts will be sold for a total revenue of \$32. The total cost of producing 2 haircuts is \$24, so profit equals \$8 (\$32 minus \$24). Profit is at a maximum in the row highlighted in red.

The numbers in the table are graphed in the three parts of the figure. The total cost and total revenue curves appear in part (a). The vertical gap between total revenue (*TR*) and total cost (*TC*) equals total profit. Maximum profit occurs at 3 haircuts per hour. Part (b) shows the total profit curve, which reaches a maximum at 3 haircuts per hour. The total profit curve is at a maximum (in part b) when the vertical gap between the total revenue and total cost curves is also at a maximum (in part a). Where total revenue equals total cost (in part a), the total profit curve cuts the horizontal axis (in part b). Part (c) shows that at the profit-maximizing output of 3 haircuts, marginal cost (*MC*) equals marginal revenue (*MR*). The monopoly sells the output for the maximum possible price as determined by its demand curve; in this case, that price is \$14. The monopoly's profit is illustrated in part (c) by the blue rectangle. That profit is \$12 — the profit per haircut (\$4) multiplied by 3 haircuts.

3 to 4 haircuts, she generates a marginal revenue of \$6 and a marginal cost of \$10. In this case, marginal cost exceeds marginal revenue by \$4, so profit falls by \$4. It always pays to produce more if marginal revenue exceeds marginal cost and to produce less if marginal cost exceeds marginal revenue. It pays to produce neither more nor less when marginal cost and marginal revenue are equal to each other. Thus the profit-maximizing output occurs when marginal revenue equals marginal cost.

The information set out in the table is also shown graphically in Fig. 13.3. Part (a) shows Bobbie's total revenue curve (*TR*) and total cost curve (*TC*). Profit is the vertical gap between *TR* and *TC*. Bobbie maximizes her profit at 3 haircuts an hour — profit is \$42 minus \$30, or \$12. Part (b) shows how Bobbie's profit varies with the number of haircuts sold.

Figure 13.3(c) shows the demand curve (*D*) and the marginal revenue curve (*MR*) along with the marginal cost curve (*MC*) and the average total cost curve (*ATC*). The profit-maximizing output is 3 haircuts, the output at which marginal cost equals marginal revenue. The price charged is found by reading from the demand curve the price at which 3 haircuts can be sold. That price is \$14. When Bobbie produces 3 haircuts, average total cost is \$10 (read from the *ATC* curve). Her profit per haircut is \$4 (\$14 minus \$10). Bobbie's total profit is indicated by the blue rectangle, which equals the profit per haircut

Figure 13.4 Short-Run Profit, Costs, and Demand

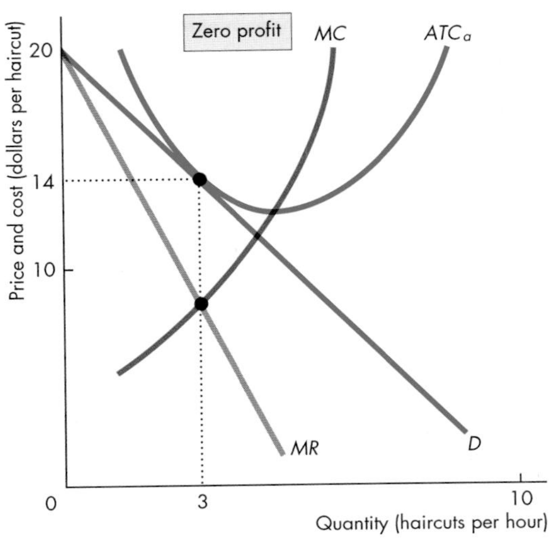

(a) Zero economic profit

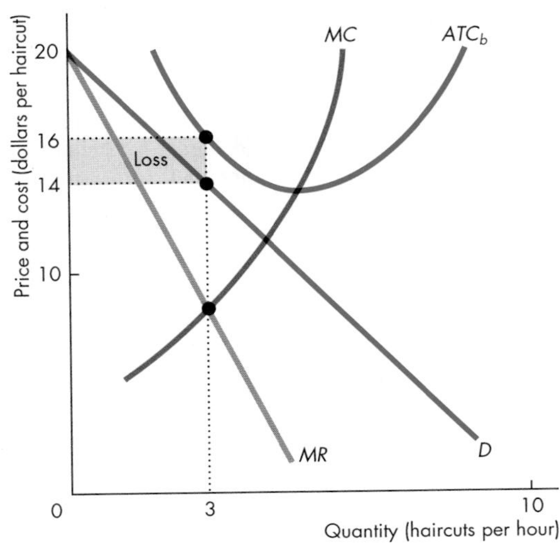

(b) Economic loss

In the short run, a monopoly can make a zero economic profit or even an economic loss. Part (a) shows a monopoly making a zero economic profit. At the profit-maximizing output — 3 haircuts per hour — average total cost and price are each $14. Part (b) shows a monopoly making a short-run economic loss. In this case, at the profit-maximizing output (again 3 haircuts per hour) average total cost is $16 and price is $14, so the firm incurs an economic loss of $6. The loss is represented by the red rectangle.

($4) multiplied by the number of haircuts (3), for a total profit of $12. Since price always *exceeds* marginal revenue and at the profit-maximizing output marginal revenue equals marginal cost, price always exceeds marginal cost.

Bobbie makes a positive profit. But there is nothing to guarantee that a monopoly will be able to make a profit. A monopoly can make a zero economic profit or even, in the short run, an economic loss. Figure 13.4 shows the conditions under which these other two outcomes will occur.

If Bobbie's average total cost is ATC_a, as shown in Fig. 13.4(a), the profit-maximizing output is 3 haircuts — the output at which marginal revenue equals marginal cost. At this output, average cost just equals price, so both the profit per haircut and total profit are zero. If Bobbie's average total cost curve is ATC_b, as shown in Fig. 13.4(b), marginal cost equals marginal revenue at 3 haircuts and average total cost is $16. But 3 haircuts can only be sold for $14 each, so Bobbie makes an economic loss of $2 a haircut. A monopoly that makes an economic loss will only do so in the short run. If the situation shown in Fig. 13.3(b) were permanent, Bobbie would go out of business.

When we studied a competitive firm, we checked to see whether price was higher or lower than average variable cost. With a price below average variable cost, it pays a firm to shut down temporarily and produce nothing, so as to minimize its loss. In such a situation, it makes a loss equal to total fixed cost. Like a competitive firm, Bobbie also needs to check her average variable cost to see whether it pays to shut down temporarily. No firm, whether a competitor or monopoly, will make an economic loss that exceeds total fixed cost.

When firms in a perfectly competitive industry are making a positive economic profit, new firms enter. That does not happen in a monopoly industry. Barriers to entry prevent new firms from entering. So a monopoly can make a positive economic profit and continue to do so indefinitely. Sometimes that profit is large, as in the cable TV industry (see Reading Between the Lines, pp. 326-327).

No Monopoly Supply Curve Unlike a perfectly competitive firm, a monopoly has no supply curve. Recall that a supply curve shows the quantity supplied at each different price. A change in demand in a competitive industry moves the industry along its supply curve and each firm along its marginal cost curve. A change in demand in a monopoly also produces a change in price and quantity, but the monopoly does not slide along a supply curve. Instead, the monopoly picks the new combination of output and price that maximizes profit, given its cost curves. As in competitive conditions, the monopoly chooses to sell the quantity that makes marginal revenue equal marginal cost. But the relationship between price and marginal revenue and, therefore, between price and profit-maximizing output depends on the shape of the demand curve. For a given profit-maximizing quantity, the less elastic the demand, the higher is the price at which that quantity is sold. It is for this reason that there is no unique relationship between the monopoly's profit-maximizing quantity and price and, therefore, no such thing as a monopoly supply curve.

R E V I E W

A single-price monopoly maximizes profit by producing an output at which marginal cost equals marginal revenue. At that output, the monopoly charges the highest price that consumers are willing to pay. Since a monopoly's price exceeds its marginal revenue, its price also exceeds its marginal cost. But there is no guarantee that a monopoly will make an economic profit in the short run. Depending on its cost curves and the demand for its output, the monopoly may make a positive economic profit, a zero economic profit, or an economic loss. But a monopoly can make a positive economic profit even in the long run since barriers prevent the entry of new firms. There is no unique relationship between the quantity that a monopoly produces and its price — there is no monopoly supply curve. ■

Price Discrimination

Price discrimination is the practice of charging some customers a higher price than others for an identical good or of charging an individual customer a higher price on a small purchase than on a large one. An example of price discrimination is the practice of charging children and students less than adults to see a movie. Another example is the common practice of discounts for senior citizens and students at the barber and hairdresser. Price discrimination can be practised in varying degrees. **Perfect price discrimination** occurs when a firm charges a different price for each unit sold and charges each consumer the maximum price that he or she is willing to pay for it. Perfect price discrimination does not happen in the real world, but the concept illustrates the limit to which price discrimination can be taken.

Not all price *differences* imply price *discrimination*. In many situations, goods that are similar but not identical have different costs and sell for different prices *because* they have different costs. For example, we saw in Chapter 12 that the marginal cost of producing electricity depends on the time of day. If a power company charges a higher price for consumption between 7:00 and 9:00 in the morning and between 4:00 and 7:00 in the evening than it does at other times of the day, this practice is not price discrimination. Rather, it reflects differences in the cost of production at peak and off-peak hours. In contrast, price discrimination is the practice of charging consumers varying prices, not because the costs of producing the good vary, but because different consumers have different demands for the good.

At first sight, it appears that price discrimination contradicts the assumption of profit maximization. Why would a movie operator allow children to see movies at half price? Why would a barber charge students and senior citizens less? Aren't these producers losing profit by being nice guys? Deeper investigation shows that far from losing profit, price discriminators actually make a bigger profit than they would otherwise. Thus a monopoly has an incentive to try to find ways of discriminating among groups of consumers and charging each group the highest possible price. Some people may pay less with price discrimination, but others pay more. How does price discrimination bring in more total revenue?

Price Discrimination and Total Revenue

The total revenue received by a single-price monopoly equals the quantity sold multiplied by the single price charged. That revenue is illustrated in Fig. 13.5(a). Suppose that Bobbie sells 4 haircuts for a single price

Monopoly in Action

Cable-TV firms seek to conquer rich new worlds

Canada's top 10 cable-TV operators

Company	'000's of subscribers	Main market
Rogers Cablesystems	1,500	Metro Toronto; Metro Vancouver
Vidéotron Ltée	927	Quebec
Maclean Hunter Cable†	440	Southern Ontario
Shaw Cablesystems	367	Alberta; Nova Scotia; B.C.
Cablecasting	298	Calgary; Toronto
CUC Broadcasting	276	Scarborough
CF Cable	195	Montreal
Cablenet	192	Saskatchewan; B.C.; Ontario
Cogeco Telecom††	149	Quebec
Winnipeg Videon	148	Winnipeg

†Maclean Hunter figures do not include the purchase of Ottawa Cablevision or Armstrong Communications which operates cable systems in southern Ontario. Both deals are pending CRTC approval.
††Cogeco bought Cablenet in July, pending CRTC approval. Source; Industry sources; Financial Post estimates

Canada's Cable-television companies are feverishly knocking on cabinet ministers' doors and digging up city streets to ensure they have room to grow in the 1990s and beyond.

Spearheaded by the two largest cable systems—**Rogers Communications Inc.** of Toronto and Montreal-based **Videotron Ltée.**—virtually all the big cable players are driving to acquire new technology, shoulder their way into the telecommunications business and seek growth opportunities in the U.S. and Europe.

Industry watchers say capital spending by cable companies may top $1 billion by 1995, with almost 50% of it coming from Rogers alone. But it is an outlay the industry must make if it is to fight off the threat of slower growth in its existing business.

Canadians embraced cable in its early days in the 1950s, initially because it brought them clear signals from the Big Three U.S. television networks.

But the plethora of new channels added since the late 1970s has speeded up what the industry calls the "penetration rate." Almost 80% of Canadian homes now receive cable-TV...

In pondering their future, the companies do have some powerful weapons at their disposal. The combination of a huge subscriber base and a monopoly in each area provide steady cash flow to Canada's...cable-TV providers....

Rogers, which has a commanding lead with almost 24% of the cable market, wants to use its network to transmit data for business, and aims to enter the long-distance market as a rival to Bell Canada...

The Financial Post,
September 16-18, 1989
By Jamie Hubbard

The Essence of the Story

- Cable-TV firms have local monopolies and make large profits.
- But almost 80 percent of Canadian homes receive cable-TV and further expansion in this market is limited.
- The biggest companies, such as Rogers and Videotron are investing in new technology and seeking to expand into the broader telecommunications market both in Canada and in other countries.
- In Canada, this expansion challenges the monopoly position in the telecommunications industry of Bell Canada.

Background and Analysis

- Until the late-1970s, the main programming available on cable-TV was provided by the three large U.S. networks, PBS, and a limited number of Canadian networks and local stations. The demand for cable services was low, as shown in the figure by demand curve D_{70}. The marginal revenue curve was MR_{70}.
- The marginal cost of adding homes to cable services is low (shown as *MC* in the figure) and in the mid-1970s average total cost was ATC_{70}.
- In the 1970s, profit was maximized by providing cable service to Q_{70} homes at a price of P_{70} a month. Profits were modest, as shown by the small blue-shaded rectangle in the figure.
- The development of satellite and computer technology in the 1980s made it profitable to establish a large number of new channels specializing in news, sport, movies, music, foreign languages and cultures, and other areas. These new, improved-quality television services, were available exclusively on cable. Consequently, the demand for cable service increased, and the demand curve shifted to D_{89}. The marginal revenue curve shifted to MR_{89}.
- The increased cost of providing the improved cable services shifted the average total cost curve to ATC_{89}, but the marginal cost of adding homes to cable service (probably) did not change, so the marginal cost curve remained at *MC*.
- The profit-maximizing situation in 1989 was for cable service to be sold to Q_{89} homes—the quantity that makes marginal cost and marginal revenue equal—at a price of P_{89} a month. Profits were high (large blue rectangle).
- By 1990, the scope for further profitable expansion of cable-TV was limited and, with large surpluses to invest, the cable companies were looking for other profit opportunities. Another monopoly, that in long-distance telecommunications, dominated by Bell Canada looked attractive to them.

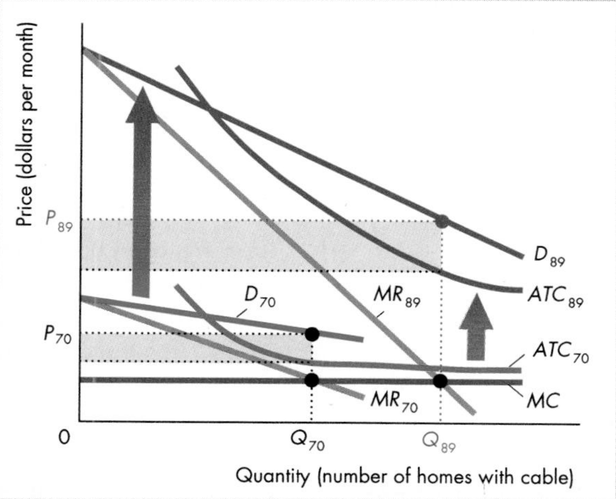

Figure 13.5 Total Revenue and Price Discrimination

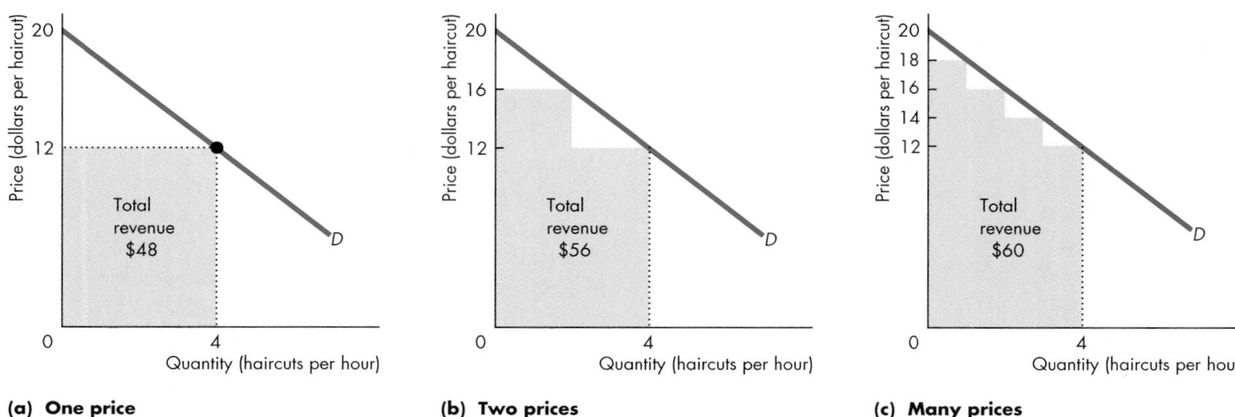

If Bobbie sells 4 haircuts for the same price — $12 each — her total revenue is $48, as shown by the blue rectangle in part (a). If she charges two prices — $16 each for the first 2 haircuts and $12 each for the next 2 — her total revenue will be $56, as shown by the blue area in part (b). If Bobbie charges four different prices — $18 for the first haircut, $16 for the second haircut, $14 for the third haircut, and $12 for the fourth haircut — her total revenue will be $60, as shown by the blue area in part (c). The more finely a monopoly can discriminate, the larger is its total revenue from a given level of sales.

of $12 each. Her total revenue, $48, is the area of the blue rectangle — the quantity sold (4 haircuts) multiplied by the price ($12). Now suppose that Bobbie can sell some haircuts for one price and some for another, higher price. Figure 13.5(b) illustrates this case. The first 2 haircuts are sold for $16 each, and then two more are sold for the original price, $12. In this case, Bobbie has greater total revenue than when she charges a single price. The extra revenue earned on the first 2 haircuts sold is now added to the original revenue. Total revenue, the blue area shown in part (b), is $56 (2 at $12 plus 2 at $16).

What happens if Bobbie can perfectly price discriminate? The answer is shown in Fig. 13.5(c). Each haircut is sold for the maximum possible price. The first haircut sells for $18, the next for $16, the third for $14, and the fourth for $12. Total revenue, the blue area in part (c), is $60.

Price Discrimination and Consumer Surplus

Demand curves slope downward because the value that an individual places on a good falls as the quantity consumed of that good rises. When all the units consumed can be bought for a single price, consumers make a surplus — *consumer surplus.* (If you need to refresh your understanding of consumer surplus, flip back to Chapter 7.) Price discrimination can be seen as an attempt by a monopoly to capture the consumer surplus (or as much of the surplus as possible) for itself.

There are three ways in which a monopoly might price discriminate:

- Discrimination based on the volume purchased by an individual buyer
- Discrimination based on the type of buyer but not on the volume purchased
- Discrimination based both on the volume purchased and the type of buyer

Discrimination Based on Volume Purchased The common practice of offering goods for sale on the same terms to each individual consumer but offering discounts for bulk buying is price discrimination based on the volume purchased. The larger the volume purchased, the larger is the discount and the lower is the price of each unit of the good.

This type of price discrimination works because

each individual's demand curve slopes downward. For example, suppose that Lisa is willing to pay $7 to see one movie a month, $6 a movie to see two, and $5 a movie to see three. If movies cost $5, she sees three and pays $15. The value to her of the first movie is $7, which is $2 more than she pays for it. The value to her of the second movie is $6, which is $1 more than she pays for it. Lisa's consumer surplus is $3.

Now imagine that a movie theatre makes a subscription offer. For $7, patrons can see one movie a month; for $13, they can see two; for $18, they can see three. Individual movies can also be seen for $7 each. If Lisa opts for the three-movie package, the theatre extracts her entire consumer surplus.

To extract every dollar of consumer surplus from *every buyer*, the monopolist would have to offer each individual customer a separate deal based on his or her own demand curve. Clearly, a firm cannot practise such fine price discrimination because it does not have sufficient information about each individual consumer's demand curve to be able to do the necessary calculations. But by making arrangements of the type just described, arrangements that extract most of the consumer surplus of a typical consumer, firms can move towards perfect price discrimination. They can get even closer by discriminating among individuals based on buyer type. Let's see how.

Discrimination Based on Type of Buyer Even when it is not possible to charge each individual a different price for each unit bought, it may still be possible to discriminate among individuals in groups. This possibility arises from the fact that some groups of individuals place a higher value on consuming one more unit of a good than do other individuals. By charging such individuals a higher price, the producer can obtain some of their consumer surplus.

An example of this type of price discrimination is that seen in the barbershop and the hairdressing salon. Charging a lower price to students and senior citizens than that charged to other customers takes advantage of the fact that a typical student or senior citizen places a lower value on one additional haircut per year than do other types of customers. Another example is airline companies' practice of offering a lower fare to travellers who make advance reservations and a higher fare to those who make their travel plans closer to the day of travel.

A monopoly can do even better by combining these two forms of price discrimination — discriminating by volume purchased *and* by type of customer.

Discrimination by Volume and Type of Buyer Discrimination by both volume and type of buyer enables a monopoly to get as close as possible to extracting all the consumer surplus available. But to practise this type of price discrimination requires some ingenuity. One example of such price discrimination again comes from air travel. We've just seen how airlines are able to discriminate between different types of customers. How do they discriminate on volume purchased? They do it with their frequent-flyer programs. The highest fare is paid by an infrequent traveller who is unable to take advantage of advanced purchase discounts or frequent-flyer discounts. The lowest fare is paid by a frequent traveller who plans ahead and is able to obtain both types of discounts. Lying between these two extremes are travellers who are able to take advantage of one type of discount but not the other.

We're going to work out how price discrimination enables a monopoly to make a larger profit. To do so, we return to the example of Bobbie's barbershop, and we'll deal with the case where the monopoly is able to discriminate between different types of buyers, but not able to discriminate on the basis of the volume purchased by an individual buyer. Let's look at this case a bit more closely.

Price and Output Decisions with Price Discrimination

Price discrimination often takes the form of discriminating between different groups of consumers on the basis of age, employment status, or other easily distinguished characteristics. Price discrimination works only if each group has a different price elasticity of demand for the product. If one group has a high elasticity and the other a low elasticity, then a firm can increase profit by charging a lower price to the group with the high elasticity and a higher price to the group with a low elasticity.

Bobbie suspects that the students and the elderly of Trout River have a higher elasticity of demand for haircuts than do other people — they do not seem to care as much about getting a bit shaggy as do other clients. Let's see how Bobbie exploits these differences in demand and raises her profit by price discriminating. Until now, Bobby has sold 3 haircuts an hour at $14 a haircut, for a total revenue of $42 an hour. With a total cost of $30 an hour, Bobbie makes an hourly profit of $12. Bobbie's costs, together with her revenues and profit, are shown in the table in Fig. 13.3.

Table 13.2 Profiting from Price Discrimination

Price (P) (dollars per haircut)	**Students and the elderly** Quantity demanded (Q) (haircuts per hour)	Total revenue (TR) (dollars per hour)	Marginal revenue (MR) (dollars per haircut)	**Others** Quantity demanded (Q) (haircuts per hour)	Total revenue (TR) (dollars per hour)	Marginal revenue (MR) (dollars per haircut)
20	0	0		0	0	
			0			18
18	0	0		1	18	
			0			14
16	0	0		2	32	
			14			–4
14	1	14		2	28	
			10			–4
12	2	24		2	24	
			6			–4
10	3	30		2	20	

Profit calculation

Profit = $TR - TC$

= (\$12 × 2) + (\$16 × 2) – \$40

= \$16

As a single-price monopoly, Bobbie sells 3 haircuts per hour for \$14 each and makes a maximum profit of \$12, as was shown in Fig. 13.3. By discriminating between two groups of customers — the first group consisting of students and the elderly and the second of all other clients — Bobbie is able to make a bigger profit. She raises the price for other clients to \$16 and lowers the price for students and the elderly to \$12. Her output rises to 4 haircuts per hour, and her profit rises to \$16.

Bobbie notices that students and elderly customers come in less frequently than other clients. In fact, of the three haircuts she does each hour, one is for an elderly customer or a student and two are for other customers. Bobbie suspects that she can get students and seniors to have their hair cut more frequently by offering them a lower price and that the other customers will turn up as frequently as they do now for an even higher price than the \$14 that she is charging. She decides to price discriminate between the two groups, but she has to figure out what price to charge each group to maximize her profit. Table 13.2 sets out her calculations. It shows Bobbie's estimates of the demand schedules for her two groups of customers, as well as the total revenue and marginal revenue calculations for the two separate groups. Bobbie's marginal costs are the same for both groups — hair is hair, whether it belongs to a student or another client. But marginal revenue differs between the two groups of customers. For example, when the price falls from \$18 to \$16, the marginal revenue from students and the elderly is zero, while from other clients it is \$14. When the price falls from \$16 to \$14, the marginal revenue from students and the elderly is \$14, while from others it is minus \$4.

Bobbie maximizes her profit by lowering the price and increasing output if marginal revenue exceeds marginal cost and by raising the price and decreasing output if marginal cost exceeds marginal revenue. In this example, Bobbie calculates her profit-maximizing output and prices in the following way. She knows that without price discrimination the marginal cost of the third haircut that she is producing is \$6. (To see this, look back at the table in Fig. 13.3.) If her output increases with price discrimination, the marginal cost of the fourth haircut is \$10. She looks at her marginal revenues and compares them with

Figure 13.6 Output and Profit with Perfect Price Discrimination

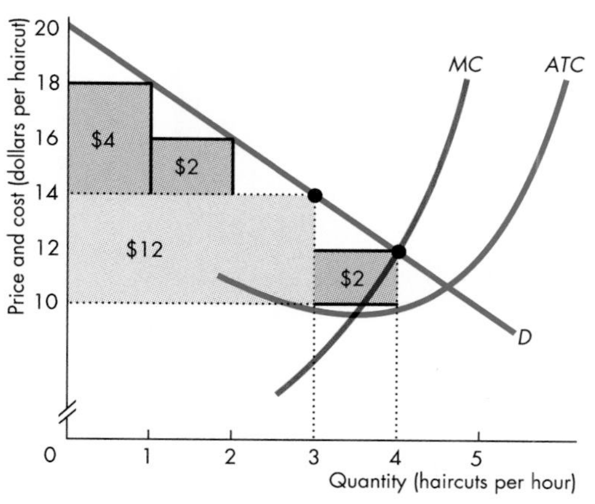

Bobbie's profit as a single-price monopoly, shown by the light blue area, is $12. With perfect price discrimination, Bobbie charges $18 for the first haircut, $16 for the second, $14 for the third, and $12 for the fourth. Marginal revenue equals price in each case because, with perfect price discrimination, the marginal revenue curve is the same as the demand curve. Profit is maximized when the demand curve intersects the marginal cost curve. It does not pay Bobbie to sell a fifth haircut because its marginal revenue (price) is less than its marginal cost. Bobbie's additional profit as a perfect price discriminator, shown by the darker blue areas, is $8. Her maximum total profit with perfect price discrimination is $20.

Maximum profit with single price:			$12	Quantity: 3 haircuts
add	extra profit from 1st haircut		$ 4	
add	extra profit from 2nd haircut		$ 2	
add	extra revenue from 4th haircut	+$12		
less	marginal cost of 4th haircut	– $10		
add	extra profit from 4th haircut		$ 2	
equals	maximum profit with price discrimination		$20	Quantity: 4 haircuts

this $10 marginal cost. She notices that by charging her other customers $16, this group buys 2 haircuts an hour for a marginal revenue of $14. By charging her elderly customers and students $12, that group buys 2 haircuts an hour and brings in a marginal revenue of $10. Thus when she sells a total of 4 haircuts (2 to students and elderly and 2 to other customers), the marginal revenue from the students and elderly ($10) just equals the marginal cost of the fourth haircut.

Bobbie can also see that if she lowers the price to either group, marginal revenue will fall short of marginal cost. If Bobbie lowers the price so that an extra haircut is sold to students and the elderly, marginal cost will climb to $15 and marginal revenue will fall to $6. Other customers have an inelastic demand curve and will not buy any more than 2 haircuts, so marginal revenue from lowering the price to that group is negative. Thus Bobbie cannot increase her profit by lowering the price to either group. She maximizes her profit by producing 4 haircuts an hour and charging students and the elderly $12 and other customers $16. The profit from such price discrimination is $16. (The calculation is set out at the bottom of Table 13.2.)

Perfect Price Discrimination

Suppose that Bobbie is able to devise a means of being a perfect price discriminator. How much profit can she make in this case? Bobbie's demand and cost curves are shown in Fig. 13.6. As a single-price monopoly, she produces 3 haircuts, sells them for $14 each, and makes a profit of $12 — the light blue rectangle. Refresh your memory if necessary by referring back to Fig. 13.3 (c). If Bobbie can get each of her customers to pay the maximum price that he or she is willing to pay for a haircut, then she can sell the first haircut for $18. She makes an extra profit of $4 ($18 minus $14) from that first haircut sold. She can sell the second haircut for $16, $2 more than before. She will still sell the third for $14, since that is the maximum price that the third customer is willing to pay. If Bobbie continues to produce 3 haircuts, her profit rises to $18, an increase of $6.

But Bobbie will not stop at 3 haircuts an hour. You can see from the table in Fig. 13.3 that she can sell a fourth haircut for $12, and its marginal cost is only $10. So by producing a fourth haircut and selling it for $12, Bobbie makes a further $2 profit. Bobbie maximizes her profit by selling 4 haircuts, each for the maximum price that the consumers are willing to pay. That profit is $20. It is illustrated in the figure as the sum of the light blue and the three darker blue rectangles. The table in Fig. 13.6 summarizes this calculation.

When a firm practises perfect price discrimination, its output exceeds that of a single-price monopoly — it produces the output at which the marginal cost curve cuts the demand curve. The less perfect the price discrimination, the smaller is the additional output produced.

REVIEW

Price discrimination increases a monopoly's profit by increasing its total revenue. By charging the highest price for each unit of the good that each person is willing to pay, a monopoly perfectly price discriminates and captures all of the consumer surplus. Much price discrimination takes the form of discriminating among different groups of customers, charging some a higher price and others a lower price. Such price discrimination increases total revenue and profit, but it is possible only if the two groups have different elasticities of demand. A price-discriminating monopoly produces a larger output than a single-price monopoly. ■

Discrimination Among Groups

You can now see why the sign in Bobbie's window — "Haircuts $16: special for students and seniors, only $12" — is no generous gesture. It is profit-maximizing behaviour. The model of price discrimination that you have just studied explains a wide variety of familiar pricing practices, even by firms that are not pure monopolies. For example, airlines offer lower fares for advance-purchase tickets than for those booked closer to the departure date. People who buy their tickets relatively late, often people travelling on business or family matters, usually have a low elasticity of demand, while vacation travellers, who can plan ahead, have a higher elasticity of demand. Retail stores of all kinds hold seasonal "sales" when they reduce their prices, often by substantial amounts. These sales are a form of price discrimination. Each season, the newest fashions carry a high price tag but retailers do not expect to sell their entire stock at such high prices. At the end of the season, they sell off what is left at a discount. Thus such stores discriminate between buyers who have an inelastic demand (for example, those who want to be fashionable instantly) and buyers who have an elastic demand (for example, those who pay less attention to up-to-the-minute fashion and more attention to price).

"Yoo-hoo! My husband gets the senior-citizen discount! Yoo-hoo, Officer, yoo-hoo!"

Drawing by Booth; © 1989 The New Yorker Magazine, Inc.

Limits to Price Discrimination

Since price discrimination is profitable, why don't more firms do it? Why don't we see senior citizen discounts for speeding tickets? What are the limits to price discrimination?

Profitable price discrimination can take place only under certain conditions. First, it is possible to price discriminate only if the good cannot be resold. If it could be resold, customers who get the good for the low price could resell it to someone willing to pay a higher price, and price discrimination would break down. For this reason, price discrimination usually occurs in markets for services rather than in markets for goods that can be stored. One major exception, price discrimination in the retailing of fashion clothes, works because when the clothes go on sale, the fashion plates are looking for next season's clothes. People buying on sale have no one to whom they can resell at a higher price.

Second, a price-discriminating monopoly must

be able to identify groups with different elasticities of demand. The characteristics used for discrimination must also be within the law. These requirements usually limit price discrimination to cases based on age, on employment status, or on the timing of the purchase.

Despite these limitations, firms find some ingenious criteria for discriminating. For example, Air Canada discriminates among five passenger groups on many of its flights. At one point in 1989, the economy-class alternatives between Toronto and Vancouver were:

- $1730 — no restrictions
- $821 — 14-day advance purchase
- $771 — 14-day advance purchase, midweek travel only
- $658 — 30-day advance purchase
- $608 — 30-day advance purchase, midweek travel only

These different prices discriminate between different groups of customers with different elasticities of demand.

We've now seen how a monopoly operates to maximize its profit. We've discovered that a single-price monopoly makes the largest possible profit by restricting output to the point at which marginal cost equals marginal revenue and by charging the highest single price at which that output level can be sold. A price-discriminating monopoly is able to make an even larger profit. Sometimes it does so by producing the same quantity as a single-price monopoly, but the more finely a monopoly can price discriminate, the larger is its output level. Thus the more finely a monopoly can price discriminate, the closer its output gets to that of a competitive firm. Does this fact mean that a perfectly discriminating monopoly achieves the same economic outcome as a competitive industry? Let's now turn to that question and to a series of related questions by comparing monopoly and competition.

Comparing Monopoly and Competition

We have now studied a variety of ways in which firms and households interact in markets for goods and services. In Chapter 12, we saw how perfectly competitive firms behave and discovered the price and output at which they operate. In this chapter, we have studied the price and output of a single-price monopoly and a monopoly that price discriminates. How do the quantities produced, prices, and profits of these different types of firms compare with each other?

To answer this question, let's imagine an industry made up of a large number of identical competitive firms. We will work out what the price charged and the quantity traded will be in that industry. Then we will imagine that a single firm buys out all the individual firms and creates a monopoly. We will then work out the price it charges and the quantity it produces, first when it charges a single price and second when it price discriminates.

Price and Output

We will conduct the analysis by using Fig. 13.7. The industry demand curve is *D* and the industry supply curve is *S*. In perfect competition, the market equilibrium occurs where the supply curve and the demand curve intersect. The quantity produced by the industry is *C* and the price is P_C.

Each firm takes the price P_C and maximizes its profit by producing the output at which its own marginal cost equals the price. Since each firm is a small part of the total industry, none has an incentive to try to manipulate the price by varying its output.

Now suppose that the industry is taken over by a single firm. No changes in production techniques occur, so the new combined firm has costs identical to those of the original separate firms. The new single firm recognizes that by varying output it can influence price. It also recognizes that its marginal revenue curve is *MR*. To maximize profit, the firm chooses an output at which marginal revenue equals marginal cost. But what is the monopoly's marginal cost curve? To answer this question, recall the relationship between the marginal cost curve and the supply curve of a competitive firm. The supply curve of an individual competitive firm is its marginal cost curve. The supply curve of a competitive industry is derived from the supply curves of all the individual firms. The industry supply curve tells us how the sum of the quantities supplied by each firm varies as the price varies. Thus the industry supply curve is also the industry's marginal cost curve. (The supply curve of a competitive industry in Fig. 13.7 has also been labelled *MC* to remind you of this fact.) Therefore when the industry is taken over by a single firm, that firm's marginal cost curve is the same as what used to be the competitive industry's supply curve.

Figure 13.7 Monopoly and Competition Compared

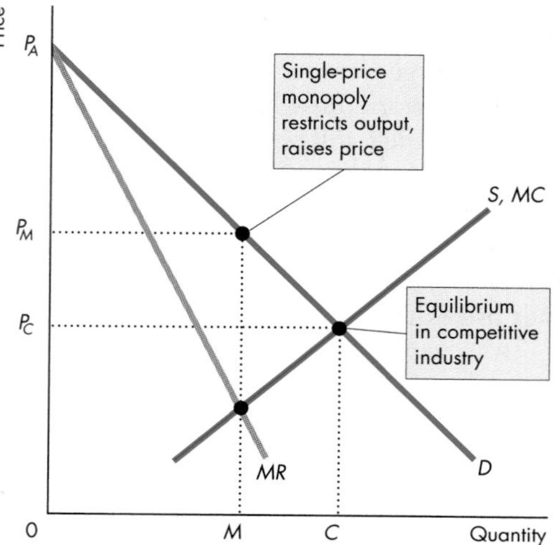

A competitive industry has a demand curve *D* and a supply curve *S*. Equilibrium occurs where the quantity demanded equals the quantity supplied, at quantity *C* and price P_C. If all the firms in the industry are taken over by a single producer who sells the profit-maximizing output for a single price, marginal revenue is *MR* and the supply curve of the competitive industry (*S*) becomes the monopoly's marginal cost curve (*MC*). The monopoly produces the output at which marginal revenue equals marginal cost. A single-price monopoly produces *M* and sells that output for the price P_M. A perfectly price-discriminating monopoly produces *C* and charges a different price for each unit sold. The prices charged range from P_A to P_C. Monopoly restricts output and raises the price. But the more perfectly it can price discriminate, the closer its output gets to the competitive output.

We have seen that a competitive industry always operates at the point of intersection of its supply and demand curves. In Fig. 13.7, this is the point at which price is P_C and the industry produces the quantity *C*. The single-price monopoly maximizes profit by restricting output to *M*, where marginal revenue equals marginal cost. Since the marginal revenue curve is below the demand curve, output *M* is always smaller than output *C*. The monopoly charges the highest price for which the output *M* can be sold, and that price is P_M.

If the monopoly can perfectly price discriminate, it will charge a different price for each unit sold and increase output to *C*. The highest price charged will be P_A and the lowest price P_C, the price in a competitive market. The price P_A is the highest that is charged because at yet higher prices nothing can be sold. The price P_C is the lowest charged because when a monopoly perfectly price discriminates, its marginal revenue curve is the same as the demand curve, and at prices below P_C marginal cost exceeds marginal revenue.

The key price and output differences between competition and monopoly are:

- Monopoly price exceeds competitive price.
- Monopoly output is less than competitive output.
- The more perfectly the monopoly can price discriminate, the closer its output gets to the competitive output.

Allocative Efficiency

Monopoly is less efficient than competition. It prevents achievement of some of the gains from trade. To see why, look at Fig. 13.8. The maximum price that consumers are willing to pay for each unit is shown by the demand curve. The difference between the maximum price that they are willing to pay for each unit bought and the price they do pay is *consumer surplus.* Under perfect competition (part a), consumers have to pay only P_C for each unit bought, and they obtain a consumer surplus represented by the green triangle.[1]

The single-price monopoly (part b) restricts output to *M* and sells that output for P_M. Consumer surplus is reduced to the smaller green triangle. Consumers lose partly by having to pay more for what is available and partly by getting less of the good. Is the consumers' loss equal to the monopoly's gain? Is there simply a redistribution of the gains from trade? A closer look at Fig. 13.8(b) will convince you that the gains from trade are actually reduced. It is true that some of the loss in consumer surplus does accrue to the monopoly — the monopoly gets the difference between P_M and P_C on the quantity sold (*M*). So the monopoly has taken the blue rectangle part of the consumer surplus.

What has become of the rest of the consumer surplus? The answer is that it is lost because output has been restricted. But more than that amount has

[1] In Fig. 7.3, Lisa's consumer surplus is less than the entire area between her demand curve for movies and the price paid because movies can be bought only in whole units. For a good that is divisible into arbitrarily small units, consumer surplus is the entire area between the demand curve and the price paid, as shown in Fig. 13.8(b).

Figure 13.8 The Allocative Inefficiency of Monopoly

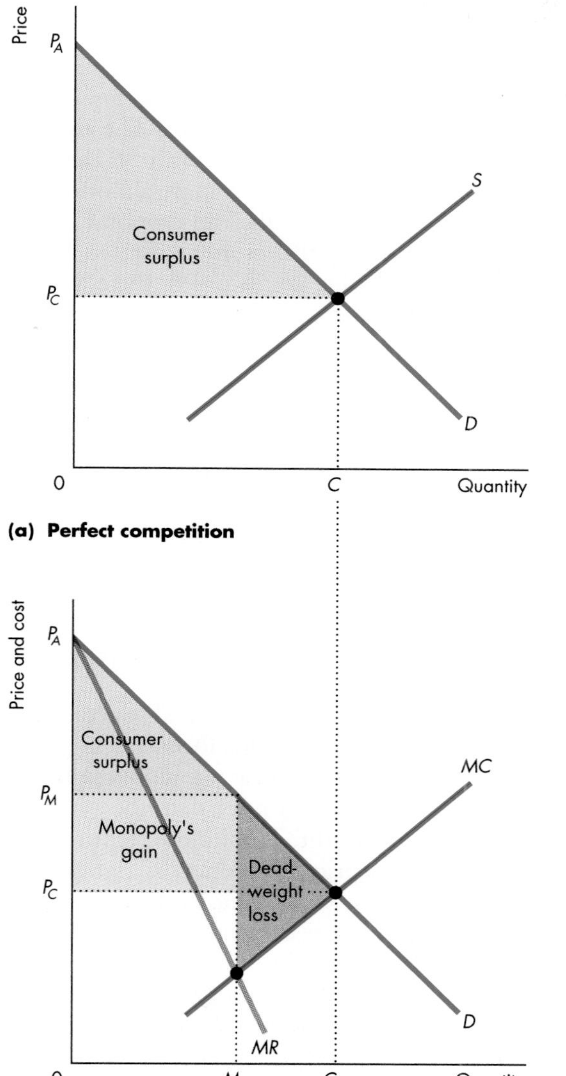

In perfect competition (part a), demand curve *D* intersects supply curve *S* at quantity *C* and price P_C. Consumer surplus is represented by the green triangle. With free entry, firms' profits in long-run equilibrium are zero. Consumer surplus is maximized. Under a single-price monopoly (part b), output is restricted to *M* and the price increases to P_M. Consumer surplus is reduced to the smaller green triangle. The monopoly takes the blue rectangle for itself, but the grey triangle is a deadweight loss. Part of the deadweight loss (the portion above P_C) is a loss of consumer surplus, and part (the portion below P_C) is a loss of producer surplus.

been lost. The total loss resulting from the lower monopoly output (*M*) is the grey triangle in Fig. 13.8(b). The part of the grey triangle above P_C is the loss of consumer surplus, and that part below P_C is a loss to the producer — a loss of producer surplus. **Producer surplus** is the difference between a producer's total revenue and the opportunity cost of production. It is calculated as the sum of the differences between price and the marginal cost of producing each unit of output. Under competitive conditions, the producer sells the output between *M* and *C* for a price of P_C. The marginal cost of producing each extra unit of output through that range is shown by the supply curve. Thus the vertical gap between the marginal cost curve and price represents a producer surplus. Part of the producer surplus is lost when a monopoly restricts output below its competitive level.

The grey triangle, which measures the total loss of both consumer and producer surplus, is called the deadweight loss. **Deadweight loss** measures allocative inefficiency as the reduction in consumer and producer surplus resulting from a restriction of output below its efficient level. Because monopoly reduces its output and charges a higher price for it, the monopoly captures some of the consumer surplus. But it also eliminates the producer surplus and consumer surplus on the output that a competitive industry would have produced but that the monopoly does not.

We have seen that a single-price monopoly creates a deadweight loss by restricting output. What is the deadweight loss if the monopoly practises perfect price discrimination? The answer is zero. A perfect price discriminator produces the same output as the competitive industry. The last item sold costs P_C, the same as its marginal cost. Thus from the point of view of allocative efficiency, a perfectly price-discriminating monopoly achieves the same result as perfect competition.

Redistribution

Under perfect competition, the consumer surplus is the green triangle in Fig. 13.8(a). With free entry, the long-run equilibrium economic profit of each perfectly competitive firm is zero. We've just seen that the creation of monopoly reduces consumer surplus. Further, in the case of a single-price monopoly, a deadweight loss arises. But what happens to the distribution of surpluses between producers and consumers? The answer is that the monopoly always wins. In the case of a single-price monopoly (Fig. 13.8b), the monopoly gains the blue rectangle at the expense of the consumer. That gain is somewhat offset by the firm's loss of producer surplus — its share of the deadweight loss. But there is always a net positive gain for the monopoly and a net loss for the consumer. We also know that because there is a deadweight loss, the consumer loses more than the monopoly gains.

In the case of a perfectly price-discriminating monopoly, there is no deadweight loss, but there is an even larger redistribution away from consumers to the monopoly. In this case, the monopoly captures the entire consumer surplus, the green triangle in Fig. 13.8(a).

R E V I E W

The creation of a monopoly results in a redistribution of economic gains away from consumers and to the monopoly producer. If the monopoly can perfectly price discriminate, it captures the entire consumer surplus. If the monopoly cannot perfectly price discriminate, it creates a deadweight loss by restricting output below its perfectly competitive level. The monopoly gains and the consumers lose, but the consumers' loss exceeds the monopoly's gain. In this case, monopoly is not as allocatively efficient as is perfect competition. ■

Rent Seeking

Operating a monopoly is more profitable than operating a firm in a perfectly competitive industry. Economic profit can be made in a competitive industry in the short run but not in the long run. Freedom of entry brings new firms into a profitable industry with the result that economic profit is competed away. Barriers to entry prevent this process in a monopoly industry, so a monopoly can enjoy economic profit even in the long run. Because monopoly is more profitable than perfect competition, there is an incentive to attempt to create monopoly. The activity of creating monopoly is called **rent seeking**. The term "rent seeking" arises from the fact that another name for consumer surplus and producer surplus is "rent." We've just seen that a monopoly makes its profit by diverting part of the consumer surplus to itself. Thus profit maximization for a monopoly is the same thing as diverting consumer surplus, or rent seeking.

Rent seeking is not a costless activity. To obtain a monopoly right, a producer has to use resources. Furthermore, everyone has an incentive to seek monopoly power, so there is competition for monopoly rights. People compete for monopoly rights in two ways — they buy an existing right or they create a new one. But existing monopoly rights had to be created at some time, so ultimately, competition for monopoly rights is a process that uses productive resources in order to establish a monopoly right. What is the value of the resources that a person or firm will use to obtain a monopoly right? The answer is any amount up to the monopoly's profit. If the value of resources spent trying to acquire a monopoly exceeds that profit, the net result is an economic loss. But as long as the value of the resources used to acquire a monopoly falls short of its profit, there is a profit to be earned. If there is no barrier to rent seeking, more and more resources will be used in rent seeking with the result that, in equilibrium, the resources used up in rent seeking equal the monopoly's profit.

Because of rent seeking, monopoly imposes costs that exceed the deadweight loss that we calculated earlier. To calculate the total cost, we must add to the deadweight loss the value of resources used in rent seeking. That amount equals the monopoly's entire profit since that is the value of the resources that it pays to use in rent seeking. Thus the cost of monopoly is the deadweight loss plus the monopoly's profit.

What exactly are the resources used in rent seeking? What do rent seekers do? One form of rent seeking is the searching out of existing monopoly rights that can be bought for a lower price than the monopoly's economic profit. This kind of rent seeking results in a market price for monopoly rights that is close to the monopoly's economic profit. Such rent-seeking activity has many real-world examples. A well-known one is the purchase of taxicab licences. Most cities regulate taxicabs, restricting both the fares and the number of cabs that are permitted to operate. Operating a taxicab is profitable — resulting in economic profit or rent being earned by the operator. A person or firm can buy the right to operate one from someone who already has that right. Competition for that right leads to a price sufficiently high to eliminate long-run economic profit. For example, in Metro Toronto, the price of a taxicab licence is \$80,000.[2]

[2]Even in Metro Toronto, taxicabs do not earn \$80,000 in a single year (if they did, there would be fewer economics professors and far more cabbies). Rather, the profits on a cab are expected to be earned over several future years. Thus the \$80,000 price tag on the right to operate a cab is the present value of the expected future profits — see Chapter 9.

Another example occurred in the airline industry. In 1986, United Airlines bought the rights to all the international air routes across the Pacific Ocean that had previously been owned and operated by Pan American Airlines. United paid Pan Am $500 million for the exclusive rights to these routes, which Pan Am had originated and on which other U.S. airlines were prohibited from competing by an international air transportation agreement. The price United had to pay to acquire those routes had to provide Pan Am with as much profit as it would have made by hanging onto the rights and operating the routes itself. The price paid by United was determined by competition among potential buyers. The routes went to the operator willing to offer the highest price for them. That operator was the one who believed it could operate the routes at the least cost.

Although a great deal of rent-seeking activity involves searching out existing monopoly rights for purchase, much of it is devoted to the creation of monopoly. This type of rent-seeking activity takes the form of lobbying and seeking to influence the political process. Sometimes firms make campaign contributions in the hope of legislative support. Sometimes they seek to influence political outcomes indirectly through publicity in the media or more directly through contacts with politicians and bureaucrats. (This type of rent seeking is discussed and explained more fully in Chapters 20 and 21.)

R E V I E W

When rent seeking is taken into account, there are no guaranteed economic profits in the long run, even from monopoly. Competition for monopoly rights results in the use of resources to acquire those rights, resources equal in value to the monopoly's potential profit. As a consequence, monopoly imposes costs equal to the deadweight loss plus the monopoly's economic profit. ■

Gains from Monopoly

In our comparison of monopoly and competition, monopoly comes out in a pretty bad light. If monopoly is so bad, why do we put up with it? Why don't we have laws that crack down on it so hard that it never rears its head? As we'll see in Chapter 21, we do indeed have laws that limit monopoly power. We also have laws that regulate those monopolies that exist. But monopoly is not all bad. Let's look at its potential advantages and some of the reasons for its existence.

The main reasons for the existence of monopoly are:

- Economies of scale and economies of scope
- Incentive to innovate

Economies of Scale and Scope You met *economies of scale* in Chapters 9 and 10, where we defined them as decreases in long run average total cost resulting from increasing a firm's scale. The scale of a firm increases when it increases all its inputs — capital, labour, and materials — in the same proportions. For example, if all inputs double, total cost also doubles. If output then more than doubles, average total cost declines or, equivalently, the firm has economies of scale.

Economies of scope are decreases in average total cost made possible by increasing the number of different goods produced. For example, McDonald's can produce both hamburgers and french fries at an average total cost that is lower than what it would cost two separate firms to produce the same goods. Economies of scope are important when highly skilled (and expensive) technical inputs can be shared by different goods. For example, computer programmers, designers, and marketing experts can apply their skills to producing a variety of goods, thereby spreading their costs and lowering the cost of production of each good.

Large-scale firms that have control over supply and can influence price — and that therefore behave like the monopoly firm we've been studying in this chapter — can reap these economies of scale and scope. Small, competitive firms cannot. As a consequence, there are situations in which the comparison of monopoly and competition that we made earlier in this chapter is not a valid one. Recall that we imagined the takeover of a large number of competitive firms by a single monopoly firm. We assumed that the monopoly would use exactly the same technology as the small firms and have the same costs. But if one large firm can reap economies of scale and scope, its marginal cost curve will lie below the supply curve of a competitive industry made up of thousands of small firms. It is possible for such economies of scale and scope to be so large as to result in a higher output and lower price under monopoly than a competitive industry would achieve.

Figure 13.9 illustrates such a situation. Here, the demand curve and the marginal revenue curve are the same regardless of whether the industry is a

Figure 13.9 When Economies of Scale and Scope Make Monopoly More Efficient

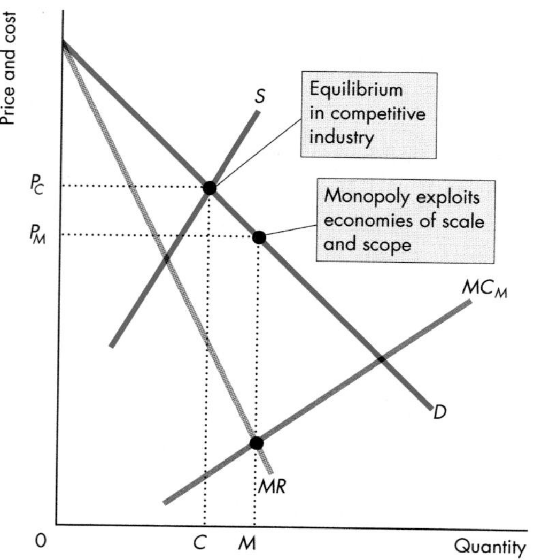

In some industries, economies of scale and economies of scope result in a marginal cost curve for a monopoly (MC_M) that lies below the competitive industry supply curve (S). In such a case, it is possible that the single-price monopoly output (M) exceeds the competitive output (C) and that the monopoly price (P_M) is below the competitive price (P_C).

competitive one or a monopoly. With a competitive industry, the supply curve is S, the quantity produced is C, and the price is P_C. With a monopoly that can reap economies of scale and scope, the marginal cost curve is MC_M. The monopoly maximizes profit by producing the output M at which marginal revenue equals marginal cost. The price that maximizes profit is P_M. By using a superior technology not available to each of the large number of small firms, the monopoly is able to achieve a higher output and lower price than the competitive industry.

There are many examples of industries in which economies of scale are so important that they lead to outcomes similar to that shown in Fig. 13.9. Public utilities, such as those providing gas, electric power, water, telephone service, and garbage collection, are all such cases. In many other cases, the combination of economies of scale and economies of scope is important. Examples are the brewing of beer, the manufacture of refrigerators and other household appliances, pharmaceuticals, and the refining of petroleum.

Innovation Innovation is the first-time application of new knowledge in the production process. Innovation may take the form of developing a new product or of finding a lower-cost way of making an existing product. Controversy rages among economists over whether large firms with monopoly power or small, competitive firms lacking such power are the most innovative. It is clear that some temporary monopoly power arises from innovation. A firm that develops a new product or process and patents it obtains exclusive right to that product or process for the term of the patent. But does the granting of a monopoly, even a temporary one, to an innovator increase the pace of innovation? One line of reasoning suggests that it does. With no protection, an innovator is not able to enjoy the profits from innovation for very long and thus the incentive to innovate is weakened; it is strengthened by the temporary monopoly granted by a patent. A contrary argument is that monopolies can afford to be lazy while competitive firms cannot. Competitive firms must strive to innovate and cut costs even though they know that they cannot hang on to the benefits of their innovation for long. That knowledge spurs them on to greater and faster innovation.

A question such as this one cannot be resolved by listing arguments and counterarguments. It requires a careful empirical investigation. Many such investigations have been conducted, but their evidence is mixed. They show that large firms do much more research and development than do small firms. They also show that large firms are significantly more prominent at the development end of the research and development process. But measuring research and development is measuring the volume of inputs to the process of innovation. What matters is not input but output. Two measures of the output of research and development are the number of patents granted and the rate of productivity growth. In these measures, there is no clear evidence that big is best.

What is clear is the pattern of diffusion of technological knowledge. After innovation, a new process or product spreads gradually through the industry. Whether an innovator is small or large, large firms jump on the bandwagon more quickly than do small ones. Thus large firms are important in speeding the process of diffusion of technological advances.

In determining public policy towards monopoly (a matter discussed in Chapter 21), laws and regulations are designed that balance these positive aspects of monopoly against the deadweight loss and redistribution that they also generate.

■ We've now studied two models of market structure — perfect competition and monopoly. We've discovered the conditions under which perfect competition achieves allocative efficiency, and we've compared the efficiency of competition with that of monopoly. We've also used these two models to make predictions about the effects on prices and quantities of changing cost and demand conditions.

Although there are examples of markets in the Canadian economy that are highly competitive or highly monopolistic, the markets for most goods and services lie somewhere between these two extremes. In the next chapter, we'll study this middle ground. We're going to discover that many of the lessons that we learned from these two extreme models are still relevant and useful in understanding behaviour in real world markets.

SUMMARY

How Monopoly Arises

Monopoly arises because of barriers to entry that prevent competition. The barriers to the entry of new firms may be legal or natural. Legal barriers take the form of public franchise, government licence, or patent. Natural barriers exist when a single firm possesses total control of a natural resource and when economies of scale are so large that a single firm can supply an entire market at a lower average total cost than can several firms. (pp. 317-319)

Single-Price Monopoly

A monopoly is an industry in which there is a single supplier of a good, service, or resource. A single-price monopoly is a firm that charges the same price for each unit of output. Its demand curve is the market demand curve for the good. For a single-price monopoly, marginal revenue is less than price. Total revenue rises at first, but above some output level it begins to decline. When total revenue is rising, marginal revenue is positive. When total revenue is falling, marginal revenue is negative. When marginal revenue is positive (total revenue is rising), the elasticity of demand is greater than 1. The elasticity of demand equals 1 when total revenue is at a maximum.

A monopoly's technology and costs behave in a way similar to those of any other type of firm. The monopoly maximizes profit by producing the output that makes marginal revenue equal to marginal cost and by charging the maximum price that consumers are willing to pay for that output. The price charged always exceeds marginal cost. A monopoly has no supply curve. (pp. 319-325)

Price Discrimination

Price discrimination is the practice of charging a higher price to some consumers than to others for an identical item or charging an individual customer a higher price on a small purchase than on a large one. Price discrimination is an attempt by the monopoly to convert consumer surplus into profit. Perfect price discrimination extracts all the consumer surplus. A monopoly practising perfect price discrimination charges a different price for each unit sold and obtains the maximum price that each consumer is willing to pay for each unit bought. With perfect price discrimination, the monopoly's marginal revenue curve is the same as its demand curve, and the monopoly produces the same output as would a perfectly competitive industry.

A monopoly can discriminate between different groups of customers on the basis of age, employment status, or other distinguishable characteristics. Such price discrimination increases the monopoly's profit if each group has a different elasticity of demand for the product. To maximize profit with price discrimination, the monopoly produces an output such that marginal cost equals marginal revenue, but then charges each group the maximum price that it is willing to pay.

Price discrimination can be practised only when it is impossible for a buyer to resell the good and when consumers with different elasticities can be identified. (pp. 325-333)

Comparing Monopoly and Competition

If a monopoly takes over all the firms in a perfectly

competitive industry and if the technology and input prices in the industry remain unchanged, the monopoly charges a higher price and produces a lower quantity than would prevail in a perfectly competitive industry. If the monopoly can perfectly price discriminate, it produces the competitive quantity and sells the last unit for the competitive price.

Monopoly is less efficient than competition because it prevents achievement of some of the gains from trade. A monopoly captures part of the consumer surplus, but to do so it has to restrict output so that when it maximizes profit it creates a deadweight loss. The more a monopoly is able to price discriminate, the smaller the deadweight loss but the larger the monopoly profit and the smaller the consumer surplus.

Monopoly always redistributes the gains from trade away from consumers towards the producer. The more perfectly a monopoly can price discriminate, the smaller the deadweight loss but the larger the reallocation of surpluses from consumers to the producer.

Monopoly imposes costs that equal its deadweight loss plus the cost of the resources devoted to rent seeking — to searching out profitable monopoly opportunities. It pays to use resources equal in value to the entire monopoly profit that might be attained. As a result, the cost of monopoly equals its deadweight loss plus the entire monopoly profit.

In some industries, a monopoly is more efficient than a large number of perfectly competitive firms. Such industries are those in which economies of scale and scope are so large that the monopoly's output is higher and its price lower than those that would arise if the industry had a large number of firms. There are also situations in which monopoly may be more innovative than competition, resulting in a faster pace of technological change. (pp. 333-339)

KEY ELEMENTS

Key Terms

Barriers to entry, 317
Deadweight loss, 335
Economies of scope, 337
Government licence, 317
Legal monopoly, 317
Monopoly, 317
Natural monopoly, 317
Patent, 317
Perfect price discrimination, 325
Price discrimination, 325
Producer surplus, 335
Public franchise, 317
Rent seeking, 336
Single-price monopoly, 319

Key Figures 

Figure 13.1 Demand and Marginal Revenue for a Single-Price Monopoly, 320
Figure 13.2 A Single-Price Monopoly's Revenue Curves, 321
Figure 13.3 A Single-Price Monopoly's Profit-Maximizing Output and Price, 322
Figure 13.7 Monopoly and Competition Compared, 334

REVIEW QUESTIONS

1 What is a monopoly? What are some examples of monopoly in your town?

2 How does monopoly arise?

3 Distinguish between a legal monopoly and a natural monopoly. Give examples of each type.

4 Explain why marginal revenue is always less than average revenue for a single-price monopoly.

5 Why does a monopoly's profit increase as output rises initially but eventually decrease when output gets too big?

6 Explain how a monopoly chooses its output and its price.

7 Does a monopoly operate on the inelastic part of its demand curve? Explain why or why not.

8 Explain why a monopoly produces a smaller output than an equivalent competitive industry.

9 Is monopoly as efficient as competition?

10 What is deadweight loss?

11 Can any monopoly price discriminate? Explain why or why not?

12 Show graphically the deadweight loss under perfect price discrimination.

13 As far as allocative efficiency is concerned, is single-price monopoly better or worse than perfect price discrimination? Why?

14 Explain why people indulge in rent-seeking activities.

15 When one takes account of the cost of rent seeking, what is the social cost of monopoly?

16 What are economies of scale and economies of scope? What effects, if any, do they have on the allocative efficiency of monopoly?

17 Monopoly redistributes consumer surplus. Explain why the consumer loses more under perfect price discrimination than under single-price monopoly.

PROBLEMS

1 Minnie's Mineral Springs, a single-price monopoly, faces the following demand schedule for bottled mineral water:

Price (dollars per bottle)	Quantity demanded (bottles)
5	0
4	1
3	2
2	3
1	4
0	5

a) Calculate Minnie's total revenue schedule.

b) Calculate its marginal revenue schedule.

c) At what price is the elasticity of demand equal to 1?

2 Minnie's has the following total cost:

Quantity produced (bottles)	Total cost (dollars)
0	1
1	2
2	4
3	7
4	11
5	16

What is Minnie's profit-maximizing

a) Output?

b) Price?

c) Marginal cost?

d) Marginal revenue?

e) Profit?

3 Suppose that Minnie's can perfectly price discriminate. What is its profit-maximizing

a) Output?

b) Total revenue?

c) Profit?

4 How much would someone be willing to pay Minnie's for a licence to operate its mineral spring?

5 Two demand schedules for round-trip flights between Ottawa and Halifax are set out below. The schedule for weekday travellers is for those making round trips on weekdays and returning within the same week. The schedule for weekend travellers is for those who stay through the weekend. (The former tend to be business travellers, and the latter vacation and pleasure travellers.)

Weekday travellers		Weekend travellers	
Price (dollars per round trip)	Quantity demanded (hundreds of round trips)	Price (dollars per round trip)	Quantity demanded (hundreds) of round trips)
1500	0	500	0
1000	10.0	250	10.0
500	20.0	125	10.0
250	25.0	0	20.0
125	27.5		
0	30.0		

The marginal cost of a round trip is $125. If a single-price monopoly airline controls the Ottawa-Halifax route, use a graph to find out

a) What price is charged?

b) How many passengers travel?

c) What is the consumer surplus?

6 If the airline in problem 5 discriminates between round trips within a week and round trips through the weekend,

a) What is the price for the round trip within the week?

b) What is the price of the airline ticket with a weekend stay?

c) What is the consumer surplus?

7 Barbara runs a truck stop on the Prairies. She has a monopoly and faces the following demand schedule for meals:

Price (dollars per meal)	Quantity demanded (meals per week)
1.00	160
1.50	140
2.00	120
2.50	100
3.00	80
3.50	60
4.00	40
4.50	35
5.00	30
5.50	25

Barbara's marginal cost and average total cost are a constant $1 a meal.

a) If Barbara charges all customers the same price for a meal, what is that price?

b) What is the consumer surplus of all the customers who buy a meal from Barbara?

c) What is the producer surplus?

d) What is the deadweight loss?

8 Barbara discovers that some of the people stopping for meals are truck drivers and some of them are tourists. She estimates that the demand schedules for the two groups are

Price (dollars per meal)	Quantity demanded (meals per week) Truck drivers	Tourists
1.00	70	90
1.50	65	75
2.00	60	60
2.50	55	45
3.00	50	30
3.50	45	15
4.00	40	0
4.50	35	0
5.00	30	0
5.50	25	0

If Barbara price discriminates between the two groups,

a) What price does she charge truck drivers?

b) What price does she charge tourists?

c) What is her output per week? Is it higher, lower, or the same as when she did not price discriminate?

d) What is her weekly profit? Is it higher, lower, or the same as when she did not price discriminate?

e) What is the consumer surplus? Is it higher, lower or the same as when she did not price discriminate?

CHAPTER 14

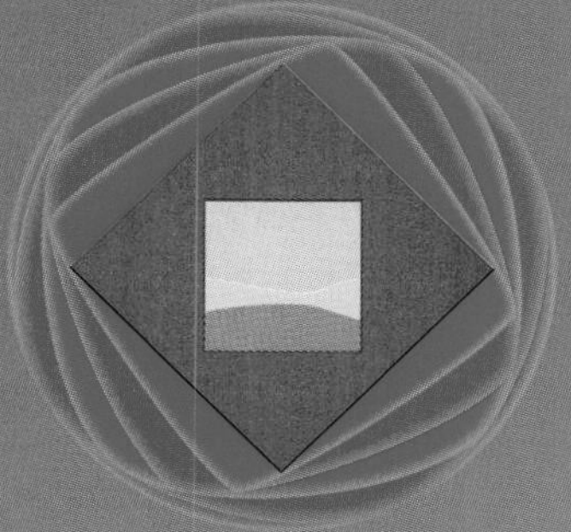

Monopolistic Competition and Oligopoly

After studying this chapter, you will be able to:

- Describe and distinguish among market structures that lie between perfect competition and monopoly.
- Define monopolistic competition.
- Explain how price and output are determined in a monopolistically competitive industry.
- Define oligopoly and duopoly.
- Explain what game theory is.
- Explain the prisoner's dilemma game.
- Explain duopoly and oligopoly as games that firms play.
- Predict the price and output behaviour of duopolists.
- Make predictions about price wars and competition among small numbers of firms.

Fliers and War Games

EVERY WEEK, WE RECEIVE a newspaper stuffed with supermarket fliers describing this week's "specials," providing coupons and other enticements, all designed to grab our attention and persuade us that A&P, Safeway, Zehr's, Loblaws, or Miracle Mart has the best deals in town. Supermarkets are not the only businesses that cut prices in order to attract customers. Every few months, clothing and furniture stores hold sales designed partly to clear space for the new season's inventory, but also partly to attract new customers. ■ Firms compete with each other not only on price but also on product quality. Millions of dollars are spent on TV and magazine advertising, all designed to enable us to pick the best brand and, having picked it, to keep buying it again and again, even if its price is slightly higher than that of some competing brands. ■ How do firms that are locked in fierce competition with other firms pick their products, set their prices, and choose the quantities to produce? How are the profits of such firms affected by the actions of other firms? ■ Suddenly, in 1973, the prices that people paid for gasoline, heating oil, and other petroleum products came to depend on the whims of the Organization of Petroleum Exporting Countries (OPEC). In that year, OPEC acted like a monopoly, restricting the production of oil and raising prices. For almost a decade, the price of oil kept rising until, in 1982, it stood at 11 times the price of a decade before. Horrified consumers speculated about the day when it would cost $50, $60, $70 a barrel. ■ Equally suddenly and to the surprise of millions of people, OPEC fell apart. Oil prices faltered for a bit, and then, in a matter of months, they fell by more than half. Headlines in early 1986 screamed, "The Price War Is Here," and "Frenzied Gas Wars Push Down Pump Prices." ■ Why did OPEC's stranglehold on oil prices, which had brought its members enormous riches, suddenly disappear? Not only did OPEC stop raising prices; it saw them fall dramatically. Why did prices suddenly break? Will OPEC ever control oil prices again? ■ Price-fixing arrangements such as those practised by OPEC are illegal in

Canada. This means that any conspiracies by firms to fix prices have to be undertaken in secrecy. As a result we get to know about such agreements only after they have been cracked by the judicial process. One of the most famous price-fixing arrangements occurred in the United States, where such practices are also illegal. This agreement involved almost 30 firms and was known as "the incredible electrical conspiracy."[1] For most of the 1950s, 30 producers of electrical equipment, including such giants as General Electric and Westinghouse, fixed prices "on items ranging from $2 insulators to huge turbine generators costing several million dollars."[2] Though the conspiracy operated throughout the 1950s, the particular firms conspiring often changed. In particular, General Electric sometimes participated in the price-fixing agreement and sometimes dropped out, undercutting the agreed price and dragging down the industry price and profit. ■ Why do firms start price wars and drag down the industry's profit? Do competitors always follow suit? When do price wars end?

The theories of perfect competition and monopoly, which we studied in Chapters 12 and 13, do not predict the kind of behaviour that we've just described. There are no fliers and coupons or price wars in perfect competition because each firm is a price taker. There are none in monopoly either because each monopoly firm has the entire market to itself and so never needs to fear the actions of a competitor. To understand fliers, coupons, discounts, sales, price-fixing agreements, and price wars, we need richer models of the behaviour of firms in markets than those of perfect competition and monopoly. This chapter presents such models. The industries that we're going to study lie between the two extremes of perfect competition and monopoly. We'll study two cases. In the first, there are many firms but each produces a slightly different product so that, although the firms compete with each other, each has a small element of monopoly power arising from the uniqueness of its own product. This model will enable us to understand markets such as those for food and clothing, soft drinks and plastics, and printing and book publishing. The second model applies to industries that contain only a few firms. These few firms are locked in an unusual game. Each one has to keep a wary eye on how its competitors are acting. And in choosing its own actions, each firm must work out what its competitors' response will be and what its own best response is to its competitors' actions. Our model of the competition that arises in this type of situation will enable us to understand industries such as oil and electrical equipment supply.

But first, before turning to these two additional models, we are going to describe the characteristics of different types of markets so that we can identify those to which each model applies.

[1]Richard A. Smith, "The Incredible Electrical Conspiracy," part 1 and part 2, *Fortune* April 1961, 132, and May 1961, 161.

[2]James V. Koch, *Industrial Organization and Prices*, 2nd ed. (Englewood Cliffs, N.J.: Prentice-Hall, 1980), 423.

Varieties of Market Structure

We have studied two types of market structure — perfect competition and monopoly. In perfect competition, a large number of firms produce identical goods and there are no barriers to the entry of new firms into the industry. In this situation, each firm is a price taker, and, in the long run, there is no economic profit. The opposite extreme, monopoly, is an industry in which there is one firm. That firm is protected by barriers preventing the entry of new firms. The firm sets its price to maximize profit, and the firm enjoys economic profit even in the long run.

Although there are some industries in the real world that have the characteristics of a perfectly competitive or a monopoly industry, most do not. Most industries lie somewhere between these two extreme cases. There are many situations in which firms are in fierce competition with a large number of other firms but they do have some power to set prices. There are other cases in which the industry consists of a very few firms, and each has considerable power in price determination. In order to tell how close to the competitive or monopolistic extreme an industry comes, economists have developed a measure of industrial concentration. This measure is designed to indicate the degree of control that a small number of firms have over a market. The most commonly used measure of concentration is called the four-firm concentration ratio. The **four-firm concentration ratio** is the percentage of the value of sales accounted for by the largest four firms in an industry. (Concentration ratios are also defined and measured for the largest 8, 20, and 50 firms in an industry.) Table 14.1 sets out two hypothetical concentration ratio calculations,

Table 14.1 Concentration Ratio Calculations (hypothetical)

Tiremakers		Printers	
Firm	**Sales (millions of dollars)**	**Firm**	**Sales (millions of dollars)**
Top Inc.	200	Fran's	2.5
ABC Inc.	250	Ned's	2.0
Big Inc.	150	Tom's	1.8
XYZ Inc.	100	Jill's	1.7
Top 4 firms	700	Top 4 firms	8.0
Other 10 firms	175	Other 1000 firms	1592.0
Industry sales	875	Industry sales	1600.0

Four-firm concentration ratios:			
Tiremakers:	700/875	=	80 %
Printers:	8/1600	=	0.5%

one for tires and one for printing. In this example, there are 14 firms in the tire industry. The biggest four have 80 percent of the sales of the industry, so the four-firm concentration ratio for that industry is 80 percent. In the printing industry, with 1004 firms, the top four firms account for only 0.5 percent of total industry sales. In that case, the four-firm concentration ratio is 0.5 percent.

Using data on each firm's sales, Statistics Canada calculates concentration ratios for a large number of industry groups. Some industries, such as commercial printing, plastic products, and soft drinks have low concentration ratios. These industries are highly competitive. At the other extreme are industries with a high concentration ratio, such as electric light bulbs, motor vehicles, and household refrigerators. These are industries in which there is competition but among a small number of firms, each of which has considerable control over its price. Medium concentration ratios exist in the newspaper, pharmaceutical preparation, and meatpacking industries.

The idea behind calculating concentration ratios is to provide information about the degree of competitiveness of a market: a low concentration ratio indicates a high degree of competition, and a high concentration ratio indicates an absence of competition. In the extreme case of monopoly, the concentration ratio is 100 — the largest (and only) firm makes the entire industry sales. But there are problems with concentration ratios as measures of competitiveness, and although the ratios themselves are useful, they have to be supplemented by other information. There are three key problems:

1. Geographical Scope of Market Concentration ratio data are based on a national view of the market. Many goods are indeed sold on a national market, but some are sold on a regional market and some on a global one. The newspaper industry is a good example of one in which the local market is more important than the national market. Although the concentration ratio for newspapers is not high, there is nevertheless a high degree of concentration in the newspaper industry in most cities. The automobile industry is an example of one for which there is a global market. Although the biggest four Canadian car producers account for almost 90 percent of all cars sold by Canadian producers, they account for a much smaller percentage of the total Canadian car market (which includes many imports) and an even smaller percentage of the global market for cars.

2. Barriers to Entry and Turnover Measures of concentration do not tell us how severe are the barriers to entry in an industry. Some industries, for example, are highly concentrated but have virtually free entry and experience an enormous amount of turnover of firms. A good example is the market in local restaurants. Many small towns have few restaurants. But there are no restrictions on entering the restaurant industry, and indeed firms do enter and exit with great regularity.

3. Market and Industry The classifications used to calculate concentration ratios allocate every firm in the Canadian economy to a particular industry. Markets for particular goods do not always correspond exactly to particular industries. For example, Labatt's produces beer and milk, among many other products. Thus this firm operates in several separate markets. Furthermore, the market or markets in which a firm operates depend on the profit opportunities that exist. There are many spectacular examples of firms that have built their initial organization on one product but then diversified into a wide variety of others.

Nevertheless, concentration ratios, combined with information about the geographical scope of the market, barriers to entry, and the extent to which large, multiproduct firms straddle a variety of markets, do provide a basis for classifying industries. The less concentrated an industry and the lower its barriers to entry, the more closely it approximates perfect competition. The more concentrated an industry and the higher the barriers to entry, the more it approximates monopoly.

Yet there is a great deal of space between perfect competition and monopoly. That space is occupied by two other market types: monopolistic competition and oligopoly.

Monopolistic competition is a market type in which a large number of firms compete with each other by making similar but slightly different products. Making a product slightly different from the product of a competing firm is called **product differentiation**. Because of product differentiation, a monopolistically competitive firm has an element of monopoly power. The firm is the sole producer of the particular version of the good in question. For example, in the market for microwave popcorn, only Nabisco makes Planters Premium Select. Only General Mills makes Pop Secret. And only American Popcorn makes Jolly Time. Each of these firms has a monopoly on a particular brand of microwave popcorn. Differentiated products are not necessarily different in an objective sense. For example, the various brands of microwave popcorn may actually be only different ways of packaging an identical commodity.

Table 14.2 Market Structure

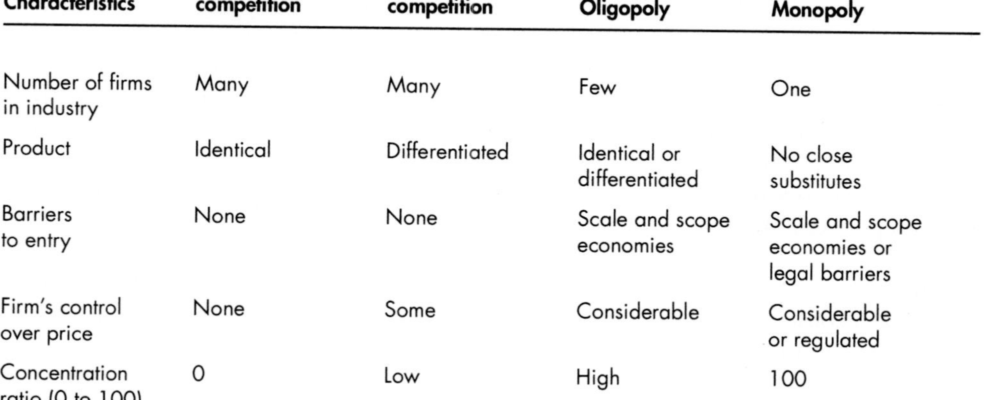

Characteristics	Perfect competition	Monopolistic competition	Oligopoly	Monopoly
Number of firms in industry	Many	Many	Few	One
Product	Identical	Differentiated	Identical or differentiated	No close substitutes
Barriers to entry	None	None	Scale and scope economies	Scale and scope economies or legal barriers
Firm's control over price	None	Some	Considerable	Considerable or regulated
Concentration ratio (0 to 100)	0	Low	High	100
Examples	Wheat, corn	Food, clothing	Automobiles, cereals	Phone service, electric and gas utilities

What matters is that consumers perceive products to be differentiated. In fact, there are claims that the various brands of microwave popcorn differ in ways other than their packaging — for example, in popability.

Oligopoly is a market type in which a small number of producers compete with each other. There are hundreds of examples of oligopolistic industries. Oil and gasoline production, the manufacture of electrical equipment, and international air transportation are but a few. In some oligopolistic industries, each firm produces an almost identical product, while in others products are differentiated. For example, oil and gasoline are essentially the same, whether they are made by Petrocan or Exxon. But Chrysler's Plymouth Reliant is a commodity differentiated from Chevrolet's Celebrity and Ford's Mercury Topaz.

Table 14.2 summarizes the characteristics of monopolistic competition and oligopoly, which we're going to study in this chapter, along with those of perfect competition and monopoly.

Monopolistic Competition

Three conditions define a monopolistically competitive industry:

- Each firm faces a downward-sloping demand curve.
- There is free entry.
- There are a large number of firms.

Because each firm faces a downward-sloping demand curve, it has to choose its price as well as its output. Also, the firm's marginal revenue curve differs from its demand curve. These features of monopolistic competition are also present in monopoly. The important difference between monopoly and monopolistic competition lies in free entry.

In monopoly, there is no entry. In monopolistic competition, there is free entry, and, as a consequence, economic profits cannot persist in the long run. When profits are available in the short run, new firms will enter the industry. Such entry will result in lower prices and lower profits. When losses are being incurred in the short run, firms will leave the industry. Such exit will increase prices and profits. In long-run equilibrium, firms will neither enter nor leave the industry, and firms will be making a zero economic profit.

Because a monopolistically competitive industry consists of a large number of firms, no one firm can effectively influence what the others will do. Each firm is such a small part of the total industry that if one changes its price, that action will have no effect on the actions of the other firms in the industry.

Price and Output in Monopolistic Competition

To see how price and output are determined by a firm in a monopolistically competitive industry, let's look at Fig. 14.1. Part (a) deals with the short run and part (b) with the long run. To keep things simple, we will suppose that the industry consists of a large number of firms with differentiated products and that all firms in the industry have identical demand and cost curves. Let's concentrate initially on the short run. The demand curve (D) is the demand curve for the firm's own variety of the product. It is, for example, the demand for Bayer Aspirin rather than for painkillers in general, or for McDonald's hamburgers rather than for hamburgers in general. The curve MR is the marginal revenue curve associated with the demand curve. The firm's average total cost (ATC) and marginal cost curve (MC) are also shown in the figure. A firm maximizes profit in the short run by producing output Q_S, where marginal revenue equals marginal cost, and charging the price P_S. The firm's average total cost is C_S, and the firm makes a short-run profit, which is shown by the blue rectangle.

So far, the monopolistically competitive firm looks just like a monopoly. It produces the quantity at which marginal revenue equals marginal cost and then charges the highest possible price for that quantity. The key difference between monopoly and monopolistic competition lies in what happens next. In monopolistic competition there is no restriction on entry so, with economic profit being earned in the short run, new firms enter the industry and take some of the market away from the existing firms. As they do so, the firm's demand curve starts to shift to the left. The marginal revenue curve also starts to shift to the left. At each point in time, the firm seeks to maximize its short-run profit. That is, it chooses its output so that marginal revenue equals marginal cost, and it charges the highest possible price for the good. But as the demand curve shifts to the left, the profit-maximizing quantity and price fall. In long-run equilibrium, shown in Fig. 14.1(b), the firm produces Q_L and sells it at a price of P_L. In this situation, the

Figure 14.1 Monopolistic Competition

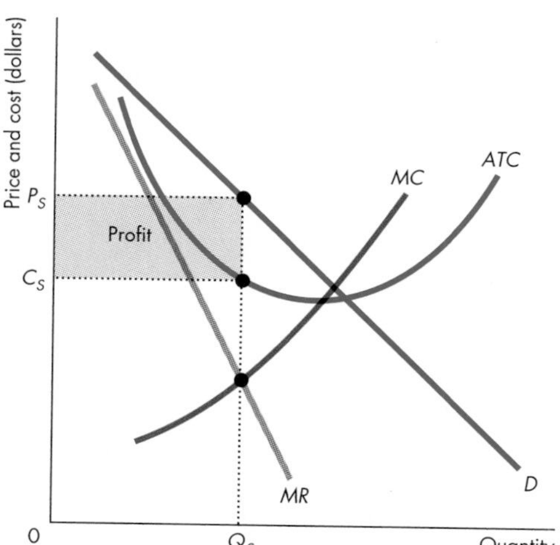

(a) Short run

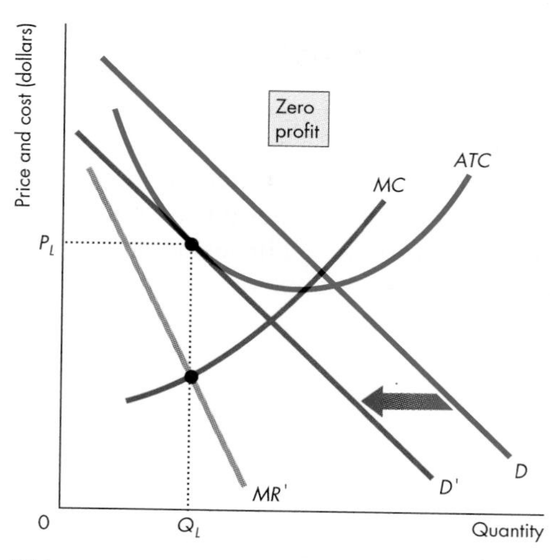

(b) Long run

Under monopolistic competition, a firm faces a downward-sloping demand curve and so has to choose its price and the quantity to produce. Profit is maximized at the output at which marginal revenue equals marginal cost. Part (a) shows a short-run profit-maximizing situation. The quantity produced is Q_S, the price is P_S, average total cost is C_S, and profit is represented by the blue rectangle.

Profit encourages new entrants, so the firm's demand curve begins to shift to the left, as shown in part (b). As the demand curve shifts, so does the firm's marginal revenue curve. When the demand curve has shifted all the way from D to D', the marginal revenue curve is MR' and the firm is in a long-run equilibrium. The output that maximizes profit is Q_L, and the price is P_L. Profit, in long-run equilibrium, is zero. There is no further entry into the industry.

firm is making a zero economic profit. Average total cost exactly equals price. There is no incentive for firms to enter or exit.

Excess Capacity Notice that in the long run the firm in monopolistic competition always has excess capacity in that its output is lower than that at which average total cost is at a minimum. This result arises from the fact that the firm faces a downward-sloping demand curve. Only if the demand curve facing the firm is perfectly elastic is the long-run equilibrium at the point of minimum average total cost. The demand curve slopes downward because of product differentiation. If each firm produced an identical product, each firm's output would be a perfect substitute for the outputs of all other firms and so the demand curve would be perfectly elastic. Thus it is product differentiation that produces excess capacity.

Efficiency of Monopolistic Competition

When we studied a perfectly competitive industry, we discovered that in some circumstances such an industry achieves allocative efficiency. A key feature of allocative efficiency is that price equals marginal cost. Recall that price measures the value placed on the last unit bought by the consumer and marginal cost measures the opportunity cost of producing the last unit. We also discovered that monopoly is allocatively inefficient because it restricts output below the level at which price equals marginal cost. As we have just discovered, monopolistic competition shares this feature with monopoly. Even though there is a zero profit in long-run equilibrium, the monopolistically competitive industry produces an output at which price equals average total cost and exceeds marginal cost.

Does this feature of monopolistic competition mean that this market structure, like monopoly, is allocatively inefficient? It does not. It is true that if the firms in a monopolistically competitive industry all produced identical products, products that were perfect substitutes, then each firm would face a perfectly elastic demand curve and would produce, in the long run, at the point of minimum average total cost and charge a price equal to marginal cost. But achieving that outcome itself would have a cost. That cost would be the absence of product differentiation. Consumers value variety, but it is achievable only if firms make differentiated products. The loss in allocative efficiency that occurs in monopolistic competition has to be weighed against the gain of greater product variety.

Product Innovation

Another source of gain from monopolistically competitive industries is product innovation. Monopolistically competitive firms are constantly seeking out new products that will provide them with a competitive edge, even if only temporarily. A firm that manages to introduce a new, differentiated variety will temporarily face a steeper demand curve than before and will thus be able to increase its price temporarily. The entry of new firms will eventually compete away the profit arising from this initial advantage.

Advertising

Monopolistically competitive firms seek to differentiate their products partly by designing and introducing products that actually are different from those of the other firms in the industry. They also attempt to differentiate the consumer's perception of the product, principally by advertising. But advertising increases the monopolistically competitive firm's costs above those of a competitive firm or a monopoly that does not advertise.

To the extent that advertising provides consumers with information about the precise nature of the differentiation of products, it serves a valuable purpose, enabling consumers to make a better product choice. But the opportunity cost of the additional information through advertising has to be weighed against the gain to the consumer from making a better choice.

The bottom line on the question of allocative efficiency of monopolistic competition is ambiguous. In some cases, the gains from extra product variety unquestionably outweigh the costs of advertising and excess capacity. The tremendous variety of books and magazines, clothing, food, and drink are examples of such gains. It is less easy to see the gains from being able to buy a brand name drug whose chemical composition is identical to that of a generic alternative. But some people willingly pay more for the brand name option.

R E V I E W

A firm in a monopolistically competitive industry faces a downward-sloping demand curve, so it has to choose its price as well as the quantity to produce. Such firms also compete on product variety and by advertising. A lack of barriers to entry into such an industry ensures that, in the long run, economic profit is competed away. In long-run equilibrium, firms make a zero economic profit, charging a price equal to average total cost. But price exceeds marginal cost and the quantity produced is below that which minimizes average total cost. The cost of monopolistic competition is excess capacity and high advertising expenditure; the gain is a wide product variety. ■

We can use the model of monopolistic competition to interpret and analyse many real world industries. One such industry is air transportation (see Reading Between the Lines, pp. 352-353). Although this industry has a small number of producers that dominate the market (it has a high concentration ratio), it does have differentiated products and there are no obvious restrictions on the entry of new firms. Thus it is an industry in which new firms may enter and compete away the economic profit in the long run. There are some industries, however, in which barriers to entry prevent such an outcome. In such industries, competition is restricted to a small number of firms, each of whose actions affects not only its own profits but those of the other firms in the industry. This is the case of oligopoly, to which we now turn.

Oligopoly

We have defined oligopoly as a market in which a small number of producers compete with each other. In such a market, the producers are interdependent. The sales of any one of them depend on its price and on the prices charged by the other producers. If one firm lowers its price, its own sales increase, but the sales of the other firms in the industry decrease. In such a situation, other firms will, most likely, lower their prices, too. Then the price cuts of the other firms will lower the profits of the first firm. So, before deciding to cut its price, each firm tries to predict how other firms will react and attempts to calculate the effects of those reactions on its own profit.

The situation faced by firms in an oligopolistic industry is not unlike that faced by military planners. For example, in deciding whether to build additional weapons or to dismantle existing ones, U.S. military planners have to take into account the effects of their actions on the behaviour of the Soviet Union. Similarly, in making its plans, the Soviet Union has to take into account the reactions of the United States. Neither side can assume that its rival's behaviour will be independent of its own actions.

Whether we're studying price wars or star wars, we need a method of analysing choices that takes into account the interactions between agents. Such a method has been developed. It is called game theory.

Game Theory

Game theory is a method of analysing strategic interaction. **Strategic interaction** is acting in a way that takes into account the expected behaviour of others and the mutual recognition of interdependence. Game theory was invented by John von Neumann in 1937 and further extended by von Neumann and Oskar Morgenstern in 1944 (see Our Advancing Knowledge, pp. 356-357). It is the topic of a massive amount of current research.

Game theory seeks to understand oligopoly as well as political and social rivalries by using a method of analysis specifically designed to understand games of all types, including the familiar games of everyday life. We will begin our study of game theory and its application to the behaviour of firms by considering those familiar games.

Familiar Games: What They Have in Common

What is a game? At first thought, the question seems silly. After all, there are many different games — ball games and parlour games, games of chance, and games of skill. What do games of such diversity and variety have in common? To answer this question, we will focus on only those features of games that are relevant and important for game theory and for analysing oligopoly as a game. All games have three things in common:

- Rules
- Strategies
- Payoffs

Let's see how these common features of ordinary games apply to oligopoly.

Rules of the Oligopoly Game

The rules of the oligopoly game have not been written down by the "National Oligopoly League." They arise from the economic, social, and political environment in which the oligopolists operate.

One rule of the oligopoly game is the number of players — the number of firms in the market. Another rule is the method of calculating the score. This rule states that the score of each player is the player's economic profit or loss. The goal of each player is to make the largest possible profit. The remaining rules of the oligopoly game are determined by the framework of laws within which the oligopolists are operating. Oligopolists' actions are restricted only by the legal code.

Strategies in the Oligopoly Game

In game theory as in ordinary games, **strategies** are all the possible actions of each player. A comprehensive list of strategies in the oligopoly game would be very long, but it would include, for each player, such actions as

- Raise price, lower price, hold price constant.
- Raise output, lower output, hold output constant.
- Increase advertising, cut advertising, hold advertising constant.
- Enhance features of product, simplify product, leave product unchanged.

Payoffs in the Oligopoly Game

In game theory, the score of each player is called the **payoff**. In the oligopoly game, the payoffs are the profits and losses of the players. These payoffs are determined by the oligopolists' strategies and by the

Monopolistic Competition in Action

Airlines worried over jump in price of fuel

Canadian air carriers are reeling from a 20% jump in fuel prices so far this year that is expected to erode most of the meagre profits they were expecting.

But they are reluctant to increase fares because of a deteriorating market.

"That is a problem for us as the market is not strong and costs are increasing," said **Air Canada** spokesman Denis Coutre.

The number of passengers travelling has shown little growth in the past six months. Most airlines expect only a 2% increase for the entire year, with most of it coming in the traditionally strong summer season.

But fuel prices have increased 50% from a year ago. The full impact of the jump will not be felt immediately as the airlines made bulk purchases at the lower prices. As these reserves are drawn down, the airline will have to buy more expensive fuel.

As a result, Calgary-based **Canadian Airlines International Ltd.** is expecting a fuel bill of about $450 million this year, compared with $350 million last year, said Canadian spokesman Mike Dukelow...

Air Canada, whose fuel accounts for 15% of its expenses, spent $450 million on fuel last year...

***The Financial Post,* February 5, 1990**
By Cecil Foster

The Essence of the Story

- The price of aircraft fuel increased by 20 percent in January 1990, and had increased by 50 percent from one year earlier.
- Fuel costs for Air Canada are 15 percent of total cost.
- Despite higher fuel costs, airlines were reluctant to increase prices because demand was weak and growing slowly.
- Also, airlines had large inventories of fuel bought at lower prices so the full impact of the fuel price increase would not be felt until those inventories were replaced at the higher price.

Background and Analysis

- Although there are only two major Canadian international airlines, these firms compete on all their international routes with U.S. and other foreign carriers.
- On the most densely traveled routes, the airline industry is monopolistically competitive.
- Figure (a) shows the marginal cost curve (MC_0), average total cost curve (ATC_0), demand curve (D), and marginal revenue curve (MR), of a typical firm in the airline industry.
- The airline maximizes profit by producing an output level, Q_0, at which marginal cost is equal to marginal revenue. The price charged is P_0. In this example, the airline firm makes zero economic profit—the industry is in long-run equilibrium*.
- When the price of aircraft fuel increases, the costs faced by an airline increase. The news article is wrong in its suggestion that an airline's costs increase only when it has to *buy* new fuel at the higher price. Its *opportunity cost* increases as soon as it *uses* existing fuel stocks, since depleted stocks must be replaced at the higher price.
- Higher fuel costs shift the marginal cost curve and the average total cost curve upward to MC_1 and ATC_1, as illustrated in Fig. (b).
- Despite the higher costs, the airlines do not increase their prices, in the short run, by an amount sufficient to cover the increased costs. Figure (b) shows why.
- The demand for air travel is increasing only slowly according to the news story. Assume that there is no change in demand when the fuel price increases.
- The airline maximizes profit by cutting back its output to Q_1 so that marginal cost and marginal revenue remain equal.
- Average total cost increases to C, but the price increases only to P_1, and an economic loss is incurred**.
- It is the slope of the demand curve that limits the extent to which an increase in fuel costs increases price in the short run, not the fact that airlines carry inventories that delay the impact of fuel cost increases.
- In the long run, some airlines will stop competing on routes where losses are incurred. As they do so, the demand curve facing an airline that continues to operate the route will shift to the right. So will its marginal revenue curve. Through such a process, the price will gradually increase and so will the quantity produced by each of the airlines still operating the route. Eventually this process will lead to a price increase that matches the cost increase and profit will return to its original level.

---

*Although we are starting out at a zero economic profit, we would reach the same conclusions about price and output changes if we started out with a positive economic profit.

**If the airline starts out with a positive economic profit, its profit will decrease, but it may continue to make a positive economic profit.

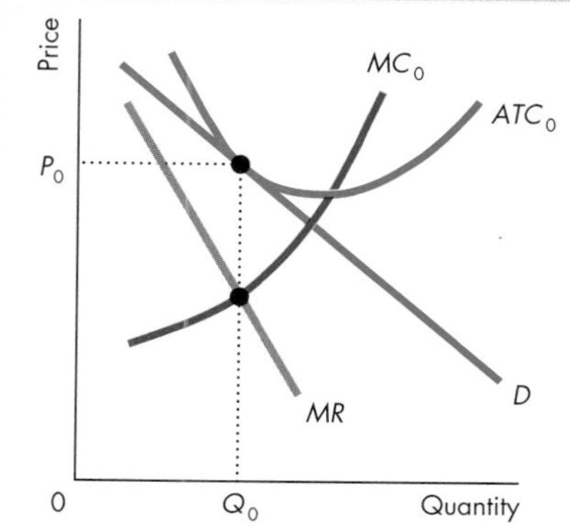

(a) Initial equilibrium

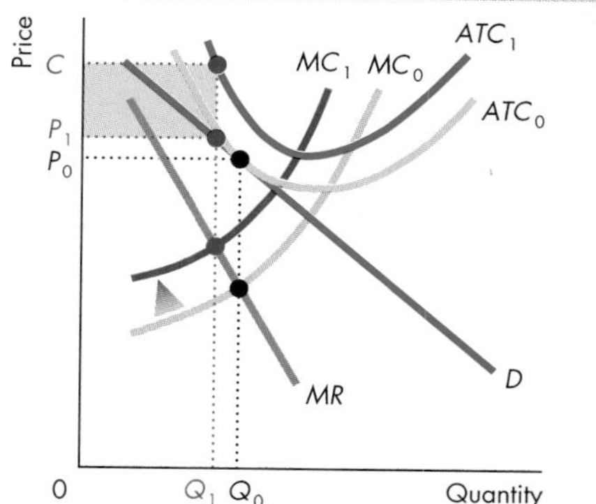

(b) Short-run effect of higher fuel price

constraints that they face. Constraints come from customers who determine the demand curve for the product of the oligopoly industry, from the technology available, and from the prices of the resources used by the oligopolists.

To understand how an oligopoly works, it is revealing to study a special case of oligopoly called duopoly. **Duopoly** is a market structure in which there are two producers of a commodity competing with each other. Duopoly appears only occasionally on a national and international scale, but local duopolies are more common — for example, some communities have two suppliers of milk, two local newspapers, two taxi companies, two car rental firms. The main reason for studying duopoly is not its realism, however, but the fact that it captures all the essential features of oligopoly and yet is more manageable to analyse and understand. Furthermore, there is a well-known game, called the prisoner's dilemma, that captures some of the essential features of duopoly and that provides a good illustration of how game theory works and how it leads to predictions about the behaviour of the players. Let's turn our attention to studying a duopoly game, beginning with the prisoner's dilemma.

The Prisoner's Dilemma

Alf and Bob have been caught red-handed stealing a car. Facing airtight cases, they will receive a sentence of two years each for their crime. During interviews with the two prisoners, the Crown attorney begins to suspect that he has stumbled on the two people who were responsible for a multimillion-dollar bank robbery some months earlier. The Crown attorney also knows, however, that this is just a suspicion. He has no evidence on which he can convict them of the greater crime unless he can get each of them to confess. The Crown attorney comes up with the following idea.

He places the prisoners in separate rooms so that they cannot communicate with each other. Each prisoner is told that he is suspected of having carried out the bank robbery and that if he and his accomplice both confess to that crime, each will receive a sentence of three years. Each is also told that if he confesses and his accomplice does not, he will receive an even shorter sentence of one year while his accomplice will receive a ten-year sentence. The prisoners know that if neither of them confesses, they will be tried for and convicted of only the lesser offence of car theft, which carries a two-year prison term. How do the prisoners respond to the Crown attorney?

First, notice that the prisoner's dilemma is a game with two players. Each player has two strategies: to confess to the bank robbery or to deny the charge. Because there are two players, each with two strategies, there are four possible outcomes:

1 Neither player confesses.

2 Both players confess.

3 Alf confesses, but Bob does not.

4 Bob confesses, but Alf does not.

Each prisoner can work out exactly what will happen to him — his payoff — in each of these four situations. We can tabulate the four possible payoffs for each of the prisoners.

The Payoff Matrix

A **payoff matrix** is a table that shows the payoffs for every possible action by each player for every possible action by each other player. Table 14.3 shows a payoff matrix for Alf and Bob. Each square shows the payoffs for each prisoner — *A* for Alf and *B* for Bob. If both prisoners confess (top left), they each get a prison term of 3 years. If Bob confesses but Alf denies (top right), Alf gets a 10-year sentence and Bob gets a 1-year sentence. If Alf confesses and Bob denies (bottom left), Alf gets a 1-year sentence and Bob gets a 10-year sentence. Finally, if both of them deny (bottom right), neither can be convicted of the bank robbery charge but both are sentenced for the car theft — a 2-year sentence.

The Dilemma The dilemma can be seen by considering the consequences of confessing and of not confessing. Each prisoner knows that if he and his accomplice remain silent about the bank robbery, they will be sentenced to only 2 years for stealing the car. Neither prisoner, however, has any way of knowing that his accomplice will remain silent and refuse to confess. Each knows that if the other confesses and he denies, the other will receive only a 1-year sentence while the one denying will receive a 10-year sentence. Each poses the following questions: should I deny and rely on my accomplice to deny so that we may both get only 2 years? Or should I confess in the hope of getting just 1 year (providing my accomplice denies), knowing that if my accomplice does

Table 14.3 Prisoner's Dilemma Payoff Matrix

		Alf's strategies: Confess	Alf's strategies: Deny
Bob's strategies	Confess	*A* 3 years *B* 3 years	*A* 10 years *B* 1 year
	Deny	*A* 1 year *B* 10 years	*A* 2 years *B* 2 years

Each square shows the payoffs for the two players, *A* for Alf and *B* for Bob, for each possible pair of actions. For example, if both confess, the payoffs are in the top left square. Alf reasons as follows. If Bob confesses, it pays me to confess because then I get 3 years rather than 10. If Bob denies, it pays me to confess because then I get 1 year rather than 2. Regardless of what Bob does, it pays me to confess. Alf's dominant strategy is to confess. Bob reasons similarly. If Alf confesses, it pays me to confess and get 3 years rather than 10. If Alf denies, it pays me to confess and get 1 year rather than 2. Bob's dominant strategy is to confess. Since each player's dominant strategy is to confess, the equilibrium of the game is for both players to confess and get 3-year sentences.

confess we will each get 3 years in prison? Resolving the dilemma involves finding the equilibrium for the game.

Equilibrium

The equilibrium of this type of game is called a Nash equilibrium. It is so named because it was first proposed by John Nash (see Our Advancing Knowledge, pp. 356-357). A **Nash equilibrium** occurs when *A* takes the best possible action given the action of *B* and *B* takes the best possible action given the action of *A*. In the case of the prisoner's dilemma, the equilibrium occurs when Alf makes his best choice given Bob's choice and Bob makes his best choice given Alf's choice.

The prisoner's dilemma is a game that has a special kind of Nash equilibrium called a dominant strategy equilibrium. A **dominant strategy** is a strategy that is the same regardless of the action taken by the other player. In other words, there is a unique best action regardless of what the other player does. A **dominant strategy equilibrium** occurs when there is a dominant strategy for each player. In the prisoner's dilemma, no matter what Bob does, Alf's best strategy is to confess, and no matter what Alf does, Bob's best strategy is to confess. Thus the equilibrium of the prisoner's dilemma is that each player confesses.

If each prisoner plays the prisoner's dilemma game in his own individual best interest, the outcome of the game will be that each confesses. To see why, let's consider again their strategies and the payoffs from the alternative courses of action.

Strategies and Payoffs

Look at the situation from Alf's point of view. He realizes that his outcome depends on the action Bob takes. If Bob confesses, it pays Alf to confess also, for in that case he will be sentenced to 3 years rather than 10 years. But if Bob does not confess, it still pays Alf to confess, for in that case he will receive 1 year rather than 2 years. Regardless of Bob's action, Alf's own best action is to confess.

The dilemma from Bob's point of view is identical to Alf's. Bob knows that if Alf confesses, he will receive 10 years if he does not confess or 3 years if he does. Therefore if Alf confesses, it pays Bob to confess. Similarly, if Alf does not confess, Bob will receive 2 years if he does not confess and 1 year if he does. Again, it pays Bob to confess. Bob's best action, regardless of Alf's, is to confess.

Each prisoner sees that, regardless of what the other prisoner does, his own best action is to confess. Therefore each will confess, each will get a 3-year prison term, and the Crown attorney will have solved the bank robbery. This is the equilibrium of the game.

A Bad Outcome

For the prisoners, the equilibrium of the game, with each confessing, is not the best outcome. If neither of them confesses, each will get only 2 years for the lesser crime. Isn't there some way in which this better outcome can be achieved? It seems that there is not, because the players cannot communicate with each other. Each player can put himself in the other player's place, and so each player can figure out that there is a dominant strategy for each of them. The prisoners are indeed in a dilemma. Each knows that

Models of Oligopoly

John von Neumann

Economists have studied oligopoly and duopoly since the time of Cournot (see Our Advancing Knowledge, pp. 84-85). The earliest models were based on assumptions about each firm's beliefs concerning the reactions of another firm (or firms) to its own actions. A particularly influential model was proposed in the 1930s by Paul M. Sweezy, editor of the *Monthly Review* for the past 40 years.

Sweezy's concern was to explain why prices did not fall more quickly during the years of the Great Depression. He proposed a theory based on the following propositions about the beliefs held by firms:

- If we increase our price, we will be on our own—others will not follow us.
- If we decrease our price, so will everyone else.

The figure illustrates what happens if these beliefs are correct. A firm faces a demand curve for its product that has a kink occurring at the current price (P). At prices greater than P, the demand curve is relatively flat, reflecting the belief that if the firm increases its price, it will be out of line with all of the other firms and so will experience a large fall in the quantity demanded. At prices less than P, the demand curve is relatively steep, reflecting the belief that since all other firms are matching the price cut, the increase in the quantity demanded will not be as large as the decrease in the quantity demanded resulting from a price rise.

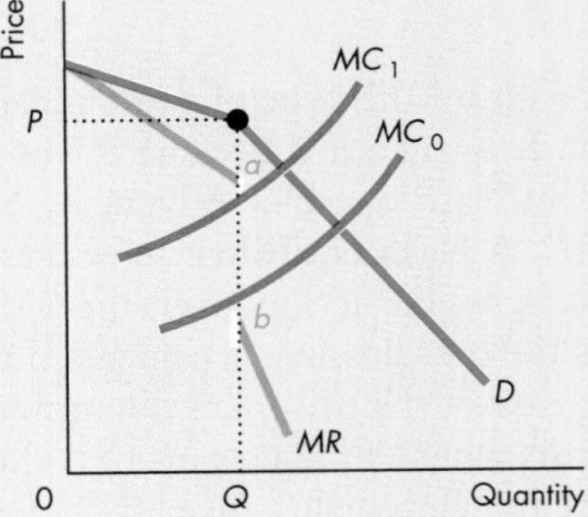

The kink in the demand curve (D) results in a break in the marginal revenue curve (MR). Profit-maximizing output (Q) is at the point where the marginal cost curve passes through the discontinuity in the marginal revenue curve — the gap *ab*. If marginal cost fluctuates between *a* and *b*, an example of which is shown in the figure with the marginal cost curves MC_0 and MC_1, the firm will change neither its price nor its quantity of output. Only if marginal cost fluctuates outside the range *ab* will the firm change its price and quantity produced.

Sweezy's model has two problems:

- It does not tell us how the price (P) is determined.
- It does not tell us what happens if firms discover that their belief about the demand curve is incorrect.

Suppose, for example, that marginal cost increases by enough to cause the firm to increase its price and that all firms experience the marginal cost increase. In such a case, all firms will increase their prices together — the belief that other firms will not match the price increase is incorrect. The firm's beliefs are inconsistent with reality, and the demand and marginal revenue curves, which summarize those beliefs, are not the correct ones for the purpose of calculating the new profit-maximizing price and output.

A widespread dissatisfaction with the state of the theory of oligopoly was a main source of impetus to the development of game theory, which was invented in 1928 by John von Neumann. A brilliant mathematician and physicist and a pioneer in mathematical economics, von Neumann established the logical basis for the computer and built the first modern computing machine. He also worked on the Manhattan Project, which developed the atomic bomb in Los Alamos, New Mexico.

Born in Budapest, Hungary, in 1903, von Neumann studied in Budapest and Zurich and from 1931 worked at the Institute for Advanced Study at Princeton University. His mathematical brilliance was recognized at an early age, and his first mathematical publication, which grew out of lessons with his tutor, appeared when he was only 18. But it was at the age of 25, in 1928, that von Neumann published an article that started a flood of research in game theory. In that article, von Neumann studied a game with two players in which the sum of the payoffs is zero — what one player gains, the other player loses. (Bargaining for shares of a fixed pie is an example.) Such a game is called a zero-sum game, a phrase that has entered common English usage. He proved that in a zero-sum game, there exists a best strategy for each player. In 1944, von Neumann and his collaborator Oskar Morgenstern published *Theory of Games and Economic Behavior*, a book in which they extended von Neumann's earlier results to games involving any number of players and to cases in which the payoffs added up to more than zero.

Von Neumann strongly believed that the social sciences would progress by applying mathematical tools, but he also believed that they required tools completely different from the mathematics used by the physical sciences.

The next major step in the development of game theory was taken in 1951 by John F. Nash, Jr., a mathematician at the Massachusetts Institute of Technology (MIT), who developed the equilibrium concept that now bears his name and that you have learned about in this chapter.

Today there is an enormous volume of research being done on game theory, and a large number of brilliant economists and mathematicians are at work on the subject. Among these is John Harsanyi, who teaches decision science — the mathematical analysis of economic decisions — at the University of California at Berkeley. Harsanyi has studied games in which the players are not fully informed, and each knows some things that the others do not know.

Another interesting contribution is by Eric Maskin of Harvard and Jean Tirole of MIT, who have recently shown that even the kinked demand curve theory of Sweezy can be viewed as the outcome of a game. The particular game is one in which firms take turns at determining the market price and all other firms accept the price that has been set. The model proposed by Maskin and Tirole overcomes all the problems of the original Sweezy theory: firms' beliefs, on the average, are correct, and the model even predicts where the kink in the demand curve will occur — at the monopoly profit-maximizing price and quantity point.

Game theory has now firmly established itself as one of the main tools of analysis in mathematical economics.

he can serve 2 years only if he can trust the other not to confess. Each prisoner also knows, however, that it is not in the best interest of the other not to confess. Thus each prisoner knows that he has to confess, thereby delivering a bad outcome for both.

Let us now see how we can use the ideas that we have just developed to understand price fixing, price wars, and the behaviour of duopolists.

A Duopoly Game

To study a duopoly game, we're going to build a model of a duopoly industry. The model is inspired by "the incredible electrical conspiracy." But don't lose sight of the fact that what follows is a model. It is not a description of a real historical episode.

Suppose that only two firms make a particular kind of electric switchgear. We will call the firms Trick and Gear. Our goal is to make predictions about the price charged and the output produced by each of the two firms. We can pursue that goal by constructing a duopoly game that the two firms play.

To set out the game, we need to specify the strategies of the players and the payoff matrix. Suppose that the two firms enter into a collusive agreement. A **collusive agreement** is an agreement between two (or more) producers to restrict output in order to raise prices and profits. Such an agreement is illegal and is undertaken in secret. A group of firms that has entered into a collusive agreement to restrict output and increase prices and profits is called a **cartel**.

Firms in a cartel can pursue one of two strategies:

- Comply
- Cheat

Complying simply means sticking to the terms of the agreement. Cheating means breaking the agreement in a manner designed to benefit the cheating firm and harm the other firm.

Since each firm has two strategies, there are four possible combinations of actions:

- Both firms comply.
- Both firms cheat.
- Trick complies and Gear cheats.
- Gear complies and Trick cheats.

We need to work out the payoff to each firm from each of the four possible sets of actions. To do that we need to explore the costs and demand conditions in the industry.

Costs and Demand

The cost of producing switchgear is the same for both Trick and Gear. The average total cost curve (ATC) and the marginal cost curve (MC) for each firm are shown in Fig. 14.2(a). The market demand curve for switchgears (D) is shown in Fig. 14.2(b). The two firms produce identical products, so one's switchgear is a perfect substitute for the other's. The market price of each firm's product is, therefore, identical. The quantity demanded depends on that price — the higher the price, the lower is the quantity demanded.

Notice that in this industry, there is room for only two firms. For each firm the *minimum efficient scale* of production is 3,000 switchgear units a week. When the price equals the average total cost of production at this scale, total industry demand is 6,000 switchgear units a week. Thus there is no room for three firms in this industry. If there were only one firm in the industry, it would make an enormous profit and invite competition. If there were three firms, at least one of them would make a loss. The number of firms that an industry can sustain depends on the relationship between cost and the industry's demand conditions. In our model industry, we've assumed particular cost and demand conditions to generate an industry in which two firms can survive in the long run. In real-world oligopoly and duopoly, barriers to entry may arise from economies of scale of the type featured in our model industry, but other barriers are possible as well, as discussed in Chapter 13.

Colluding to Maximize Profits

Let's begin by working out the payoffs to the two firms if they collude to make the maximum industry profit — the profit that would be made by a single monopoly. The calculations that the two firms perform are exactly the same calculations that a monopoly performs. (You have already studied such calculations in the previous chapter.) The only additional thing that the colluding duopolists have to do is to agree how much of the total output each of them will produce.

The price and quantity that maximizes industry profit for the duopolists is shown in Fig. 14.3.

Part (a) shows the situation for each firm, and part (b) for the industry as a whole. The curve labelled *MR* is the industry's marginal revenue curve. The curve labelled MC_I is the industry's marginal cost curve if each firm produces the same level of output. That curve is constructed by adding together the outputs of the two firms at each level of marginal cost. That is, at each level of marginal cost, industry output is twice as much as the output of each individual firm. Thus MC_I in part (b) is twice as far to the right as *MC* in part (a).

To maximize industry profit, the duopolists agree to restrict output to the rate that makes the industry marginal cost and marginal revenue equal. That output rate, as shown in part (b), is 4,000 switchgear units a week. The highest price for which the 4,000 units can be sold is $9,000 each. Let's suppose that Trick and Gear agree to split the market equally so that each firm produces 2,000 units a week. The average total cost (*ATC*) of 2,000 units a week is $8,000, so the profit per unit is $1,000 and the total profit for each firm is $2 million (2,000 units × $1,000). The profit of each firm is represented by the blue rectangle in Fig. 14.3(a).

We have just described one possible outcome for the duopoly game: the two firms collude to produce the monopoly profit-maximizing output and divide that output equally between themselves. From the industry point of view, a duopoly that operates in this way is indistinguishable from a monopoly. The profit that is made by a monopoly is the maximum profit that can be made by colluding duopolists.

Cheating on a Collusive Agreement

Under a collusive agreement, the colluding firms restrict output to make the industry's marginal revenue equal to its marginal cost. They set the highest price for which the quantity produced can be sold — a price higher than marginal cost. In such a situation, each firm recognizes that if it cheats on the agreement and raises its output, the price will fall but more will be added to total revenue than to total cost, so its own profit will increase. Since each firm recognizes this fact, each has a temptation to cheat.

Figure 14.2 Costs and Demand

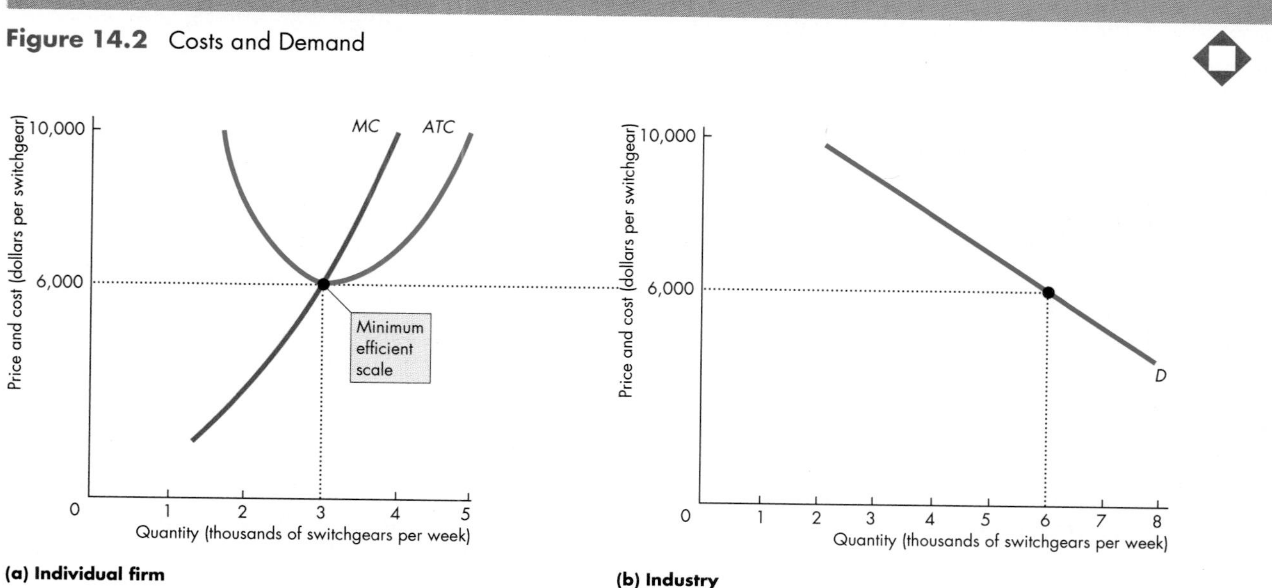

Part (a) shows the costs facing Trick and Gear, duopolists who make switchgear. Each firm faces identical costs. The average total cost curve for each firm is *ATC* and the marginal cost curve is *MC*. For each firm, the minimum efficient scale of production is 3,000 units per week, and the average total cost of producing that output is $6,000 per unit. Part (b) shows the industry demand curve. At a price of $6,000, the quantity demanded is 6,000 units per week. This industry has room for only two firms.

Figure 14.3 Colluding to Make Monopoly Profits

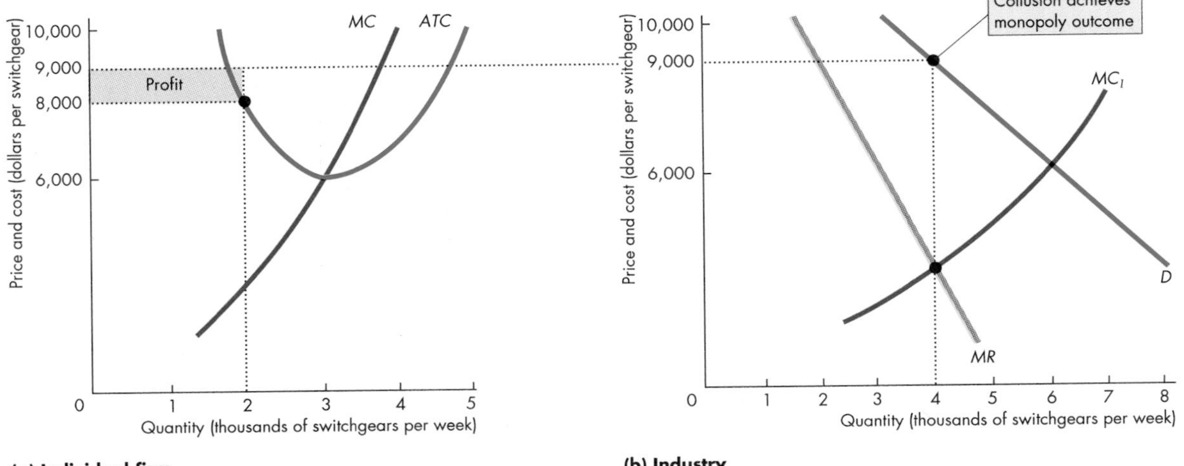

If Trick and Gear come to a collusive agreement, they can act as a single monopolist and maximize profit. Part (a) shows the consequences of reaching such an agreement for each firm, and part (b) shows the situation in the industry as a whole.

To maximize profit, the firms first calculate the industry's marginal cost curve (MC_I in part b) — the horizontal sum of the two firms' marginal cost curves (*MC* in part a). Next they calculate the industry's marginal revenue (*MR* in part b). They then choose the output rate that makes marginal revenue equal to marginal cost (4,000 units per week). They agree to sell that output for a price of $9,000 per unit, the price at which 4,000 switchgear units are demanded.

The costs and profit of each firm are seen in part (a). Each firm produces half the total output — 2,000 units per week. Average total cost is $8,000 per unit, so each firm makes a profit of $2 million (blue rectangle) — 2,000 units multiplied by $1,000.

There are two possible cheating situations: one in which one firm cheats and one in which both firms cheat.

One Firm Cheats What happens if one firm cheats on a collusive agreement? How much extra profit does it make? What happens to the profit of the firm that sticks to the agreement? Let's work out the answers to these questions.

A firm can cheat in many different ways. We will work out just one possibility. Suppose that Trick convinces Gear that the industry demand has fallen and that it cannot sell its share of the output at the agreed price. It tells Gear that it plans to cut its price in order to sell the agreed 2,000 switchgear units each week. Since the two firms produce a virtually identical product, Gear has no alternative but to match Trick's price cut. In fact, there has been no fall in demand, and Trick has calculated the lower price to be exactly the price needed to sell the additional output that it plans to produce. Gear, though lowering its price in line with that of Trick, restricts its output to the previously agreed level.

Figure 14.4 illustrates the consequences of Trick's decision to cheat in this way: part (a) shows what happens to Gear (the complier); part (b) shows what happens to Trick (the cheat); and part (c) shows what happens in the industry as a whole.

Suppose that Trick decides to raise output from 2,000 to 3,000 units a week. It recognizes that if Gear sticks to the agreement to produce only 2,000 units a week, total output will be 5,000 a week and, given the demand shown in part (c), the price will have to be cut to $7,500 a unit. Gear continues to produce 2,000 units a week at a cost of $8,000 a unit and so incurs a loss of $500 a unit or $1 million a

Figure 14.4 Cheating on a Collusive Agreement

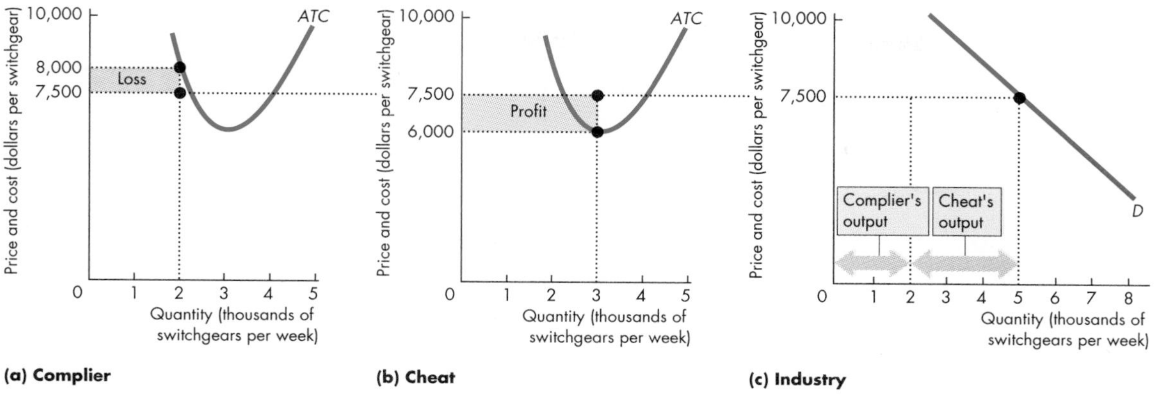

In part (a), one firm complies with the agreement. In part (b), the other firm cheats by increasing output, above the agreed limit, to 3,000 switchgears per week. (Either firm can be the complier and the other the cheat.) In part (c), the effect on the industry price of the actions of the cheat are shown. Industry output rises to 5,000 units per week, and the market price falls to $7,500 — the price at which 5,000 units can be sold.

Part (a) describes the complier's situation. Output remains at 2,000 units, and average total cost remains at $8,000 per unit. The firm loses $500 per switchgear and makes a total loss of $1 million (red rectangle). Part (b) describes the cheat's situation. Average total cost is $6,000 per unit, and profit per switchgear is $1,500, so the cheat's total profit is $4.5 million (blue rectangle).

week. This loss is represented by the red rectangle in part (a). Trick produces 3,000 units a week at an average total cost of $6,000 each. With a price of $7,500, Trick makes a profit of $1,500 a unit or a total profit of $4.5 million a week. This profit is the blue rectangle in part (b).

We have now described a second possible outcome for the duopoly game — one of the firms cheats on the collusive agreement. In this case, the industry output is larger than the monopoly output and the industry price is lower than the monopoly price. The total profit made by the industry is also smaller than the monopoly's profit. Trick (the cheat) makes a profit of $4.5 million and Gear (the complier) incurs a loss of $1 million, so the industry profit is $3.5 million — $0.5 million less than it would be with the monopoly outcome. But that profit is distributed unevenly. Trick makes an even bigger profit than it would under the collusive agreement, while Gear makes a loss.

We have just worked out what happens if Trick cheats and Gear complies with the collusive agreement. However, if Gear cheats and Trick complies with the agreement, the outcome is similar. The industry profit and price are the same, but in this case Gear (the cheat) makes a profit of $4.5 million and Trick (the complier) incurs a loss of $1 million.

Both Firms Cheat Suppose that both firms cheat on the collusive agreement. In particular, suppose that each firm behaves in exactly the same way as the cheating firm that we have just analysed. Each firm tells the other that it is unable to sell its output at the going price and that it plans to cut its price. Since both firms are cheating, each will propose a successively lower price. They will stop lowering the price only when it has reached $6,000, the price that equals minimum average total cost. At a price of less than $6,000, each firm would make a loss. At a price of $6,000, each firm will want to produce 3,000 units a week, so the industry weekly output will be 6,000 units. Given the demand conditions, 6,000 units can be sold at a price of $6,000 each. So each firm will cover all its costs and make a zero economic profit.

Figure 14.5 Both Firms Cheat

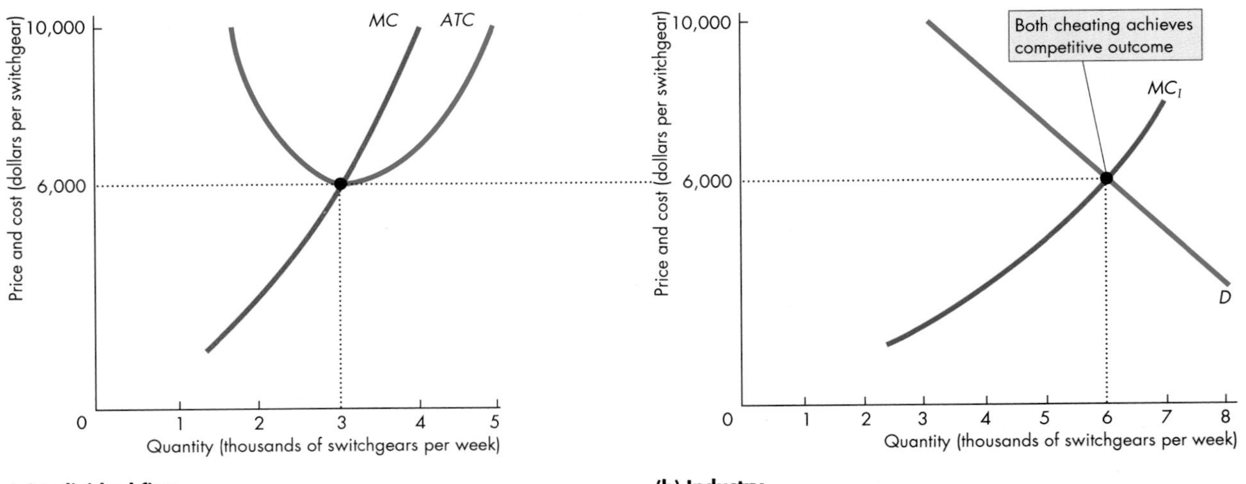

(a) Individual firm

(b) Industry

If both firms cheat by raising their output and lowering the price, the collusive agreement completely breaks down. The limit to the breakdown of the agreement is the competitive equilibrium. Neither firm will want to cut the price below $6,000 (minimum average total cost), for to do so will result in losses. Part (a) shows the situation facing each firm. At a price of $6,000, the firm's profit-maximizing output is 3,000 units per week. At that output rate, price equals marginal cost, and it also equals average total cost. Economic profit is zero. Part (b) describes the situation in the industry as a whole. The industry marginal cost curve (MC_I) — the horizontal sum of the individual firms' marginal cost curves (MC) — intersects the demand curve at 6,000 switchgear units per week and at a price of $6,000. This output and price are those that would prevail in a competitive industry.

The situation just described is illustrated in Fig. 14.5. Each firm, shown in part (a), is producing 3,000 units a week, and this output level occurs at the point of minimum average total cost ($6,000 a unit). The market as a whole, shown in part (b), operates at the point at which the demand curve (D) intersects the industry's marginal cost curve. This marginal cost curve is constructed as the horizontal sum of the marginal cost curves of the two firms. Each firm has lowered its price and increased its output in order to try to gain an advantage over the other, and both have pushed the process as far as they can without incurring losses.

We have now described a third possible outcome of this duopoly game — both firms cheat. If both firms cheat on the collusive agreement, the output of each firm is 3,000 units a week and the price is $6,000. Each firm makes a zero profit.

The Payoff Matrix and Equilibrium

Now that we have described the strategies and payoffs in the duopoly game, let's summarize the strategies and the payoffs in a payoff matrix and then calculate the equilibrium.

Table 14.4 sets out the payoff matrix for this game. It is constructed in exactly the same way as the payoff matrix for the prisoner's dilemma in Table 14.3. The squares show the payoffs for the two firms — Gear and Trick. In this case, the payoffs are profits.

The table shows that if both firms cheat (top left), they achieve the perfectly competitive outcome — each firm makes a zero economic profit. If both firms comply (bottom right), the industry makes the monopoly profit and each firm earns a profit of $2 million. The top right and bottom left squares show what happens if one firm cheats while the other complies. The firm that cheats collects a profit of $4.5 million and the one that complies makes a loss of $1 million.

This duopoly game is, in fact, the same as the prisoner's dilemma that we examined earlier in this chapter; it is a duopolist's dilemma. You will see this point once you have determined the equilibrium of this game.

To find the equilibrium, let's look at things from the point of view of Gear. Gear reasons as follows. Suppose that Trick cheats. If we comply with the agreement, we make a loss of $1 million. If we also cheat, we make a zero profit. A zero profit is better than a $1 million loss, so it will pay us to cheat. But suppose Trick complies with the agreement. If we cheat, we will make a profit of $4.5 million, and if we comply, we will make a profit of $2 million. A $4.5 million profit is better than a $2 million profit, so it will again pay us to cheat. Thus regardless of whether Trick cheats or complies, it pays us to cheat. Gear's dominant strategy is to cheat.

Trick comes to the same conclusion as Gear. Therefore both firms will cheat. The equilibrium of this game then is that both firms cheat on the agreement. Although the industry has only two firms, price and quantity are the same as in a competitive industry.

Although we have done this analysis for only two firms, it would not make any difference (other than to increase the amount of arithmetic) if three, four, or more firms played the game. In other words, the game theory approach can also be used to analyse oligopoly. The analysis of duopoly is much easier, but the essential ideas that we have learned apply to oligopoly.

Table 14.4 Duopoly Payoff Matrix

		Gear's strategies	
		Cheat	Comply
Trick's strategies	Cheat	Gear $0 Trick $0	Gear –$1.0m Trick +$4.5m
	Comply	Gear +$4.5m Trick –$1.0m	Gear +$2.0m Trick +$2.0m

Each square shows the payoffs from a pair of actions. For example, if both firms comply with the collusive agreement, the payoffs are those in the square at the bottom right corner of the table. Gear reasons as follows. If Trick cheats, it pays us to cheat and make a zero economic profit rather than a $1 million loss. If Trick complies, it pays us to cheat and make a $4.5 million profit rather than a $2 million profit. Cheating is Gear's dominant strategy. Trick reasons similarly. If Gear cheats, it pays us to cheat and make a zero profit rather than a $1 million loss. If Gear complies, it pays us to cheat and make a $4.5 million profit rather than a $2 million profit. The equilibrium is a Nash equilibrium in which both firms cheat.

Repeated Games

The first game that we studied, the prisoner's dilemma, was played just once. The prisoners did not have an opportunity to observe the outcome of the game and then play it again. The duopolist game just described was also played only once. But real world duopolists get opportunities to play repeatedly against each other. This fact suggests that real-world duopolists might find some way of learning to cooperate so that their efforts to collude are more effective.

If a game is played repeatedly, one player always has the opportunity to penalize the other player for previous "bad" behaviour. If Trick refuses to cooperate this week, then Gear can refuse to cooperate next week (and vice versa). If Gear cheats this week, won't Trick cheat next week? Before Gear decides to cheat this week, shouldn't it take account of the possibility of Trick's cheating next week?

What is the equilibrium of this more complicated prisoner's dilemma game when it is repeated indefinitely? Actually, there is more than one possibility. One is the Nash equilibrium that we have just analysed. Both players cheat, and each makes a zero profit forever. In such a situation, it will never pay one of the players to start complying unilaterally, for to do so would result in a loss for that player and a profit for the other. The price and quantity will remain at the competitive levels forever.

But another equilibrium is possible — one in which the players make and share the monopoly profit. How might this equilibrium come about? Why wouldn't it always pay each firm to try to get away with cheating? The key to answering this question is the fact that when a prisoner's dilemma game is played repeatedly, the players have an increased array of strategies. Each player can punish the other player for previous actions. There are two extremes of punishment. The smallest penalty that one player can impose on the other involves what is called "tit-for-tat." A **tit-for-tat strategy** is one in which a player cooperates in the current period if the other player cooperated in the previous period, but cheats in the current period if the other player cheated in the previous period. The most severe form of punishment that one player can impose on the other arises in what is called a trigger strategy. A **trigger strategy** is one in which a player cooperates if the other player cooperates, but plays the Nash equilibrium strategy forever thereafter if the other player cheats. A tit-for-tat strategy and a trigger strategy are the extremes of punishment — the most mild and most severe. There are also intermediate degrees of punishment. For example, if one player cheats on the agreement, the other player could punish by refusing to cooperate for a certain number of periods. In the duopoly game between Gear and Trick, it turns out that a tit-for-tat strategy keeps both players cooperating and earning monopoly profits. Let's see why.

Table 14.5 sets out the profits that each firm will make in each period of play if they cooperate and if cheating is responded to with a tit-for-tat strategy. As long as both firms stick to the collusive agreement, each makes the monopoly profit, $2 million a period. Suppose that Trick contemplates cheating in period 2. The cheating would produce a quick $4.5 million profit and inflict a $1 million loss on Gear. But in the next period Gear would hit Trick with its tit-for-tat response and cheat. If Trick then reverted to cooperating (to induce Gear to cooperate in period 4), Gear would make a profit of $4.5 million and Trick a loss of $1 million. Adding up the profits for two periods of play, Trick would come out ahead by cheating ($6.5 million compared with $4 million). But if we run the game forward for four periods, Trick would be better off having cooperated throughout. In that case, it would have made $8 million in profit compared with $7.5 million

Table 14.5 A Repeated Duopoly Game

	Collude		Cheat with tit-for-tat strategy	
Period of play	**Trick** (profit in millions of dollars)	**Gear**	**Trick** (profit in millions of dollars)	**Gear**
1	2	2	2.0	2.0
2	2	2	4.5	– 1.0
3	2	2	– 1.0	4.5
4	2	2	2.0	2.0
.	.	.	.	.
.	.	.	.	.
.	.	.	.	.

If duopolists repeatedly play the game using the cooperative strategy, they each make $2 million in each period. If one player cheats in one period, the other player cheats in the following period — tit for tat. The profit from cheating can be made only for a single period. In the following period, the other player cheats and the first player must cooperate if the cooperative agreement is to be restored in period 4. The profit from cheating, calculated over 4 periods of play, is lower than that from colluding. Under collusion, each player makes $8 million; with a single cheat responded to with a tit-for-tat, each makes a profit of $7.5 million. It pays each player to cooperate, so cooperation is an equilibrium.

from cheating and generating Gear's tit-for-tat response.[3]

If we turn the tables and see what happens if Gear cheats in period 2, we come up with the same conclusion — it pays Gear to collude. Since it pays both firms to stick with the collusive agreement, both will do so, and the monopoly price, quantity, and profit will prevail in the industry. This equilibrium is called a **cooperative equilibrium** — an equilibrium that results when each player responds rationally to the other player's credible threat to inflict heavy damage if the agreement is broken. But for this strategy to work, the threat must be credible: that is, each player must recognize that it is in the interest of the other player to respond with a tit for tat. The tit-for-tat strategy is credible because if one player cheats, it clearly does not pay the other player to continue complying. So the threat of cheating next period is credible and sufficient to support the monopoly equilibrium outcome.

Uncertainty

In reality, random fluctuations in demand and in costs make it impossible for one firm to detect whether the other firm is cheating. For example, the industry price may drop because of a fall in demand or because one firm has increased its output. If a firm observes only that the industry price has fallen, it cannot tell which of these forces caused it. If it knows that the price has fallen because of a fall in demand, its profit-maximizing action is to continue cooperating with the other firm to maintain the monopoly agreement. But if the price fall resulted from the other firm's cheating and increasing its output, the profit-maximizing response is to hit the other firm with a tit-for-tat in the next period. Yet by observing only the price fall, neither firm can tell whether the other has cheated. What can the firms do in such a situation?

If each firm always *assumes* that whenever the price falls it is because the other firm has cheated, the monopoly agreement will break down repeatedly and the potentially available monopoly profits will not be realized. Yet if one firm assumes that the other is always cooperating and that any price falls have resulted from market forces beyond the control of either, that other firm will have an incentive to cheat. (Recall that with one firm cheating and the other cooperating, the cheat makes even bigger profits than when they both cooperate.) To remove that incentive to cheat, each firm will assume that the other is cooperating provided the price does not fall more than a certain amount. If the price does fall below that predetermined amount, each firm will react as if the other firm had cheated. When market forces take the price back up above the critical level, the firms will cooperate again.

[3] In calculating Trick's profits from colluding compared with cheating, we've ignored the fact that future profits have a smaller present value than current profits (see Chapter 9). However, provided that the interest rate at which future profits are discounted is not too high, it will still pay Trick to cooperate rather than cheat.

Other Oligopoly Models

The oligopoly model based on the prisoner's dilemma game is only one of several models that have been suggested for understanding this important type of market. But it is the approach that dominates recent and current research in the area. Earlier attempts to understand oligopoly are briefly explained and reviewed in Our Advancing Knowledge, pp. 356-357.

Games and Price Wars

Let's see whether the theory of price and output determination under duopoly can help us understand real-world behaviour — in particular, price wars. Suppose that two (or more) producers reach a collusive agreement and set their prices at the monopoly profit-maximizing level, and that the agreement is enforced because each firm pursues a strategy of cooperating in the agreement unless the price falls below a certain critical level, as described above. Fluctuations in demand lead to fluctuations in the industry price and output. Most of the time, these fluctuations are small, and the price does not fall far enough to make either firm depart from the agreement. Occasionally, however, a large decrease in demand brings about a large decrease in price. When the price falls below the critical level, each firm responds by abandoning the agreement. What happens looks exactly like a price war. It is extremely unlikely that each firm abandons the agreement and lowers its price at exactly the same moment. But it appears as if one firm abandons the agreement and then the other abandons it in retaliation. But what is actually happening is that each firm is reacting to the large price fall in a manner that maintains the credibility of the threat to the other firm and that preserves the monopoly cooperative equilibrium in normal demand conditions. When demand increases again and market forces increase the price, the firms revert to their cooperative behaviour, reaping the monopoly profit.

Thus there will be cycles of price wars and the restoration of collusive agreements. The behaviour of prices and outputs in the oil industry (see Reading Between the Lines, pp. 368-369) can be explained by the type of game that you have just studied.

Preserving Secrecy

Because collusion is illegal, a problem that colluding firms face is preserving the secrecy of what they are doing. The real-world case of "the incredible electrical conspiracy" provides a fascinating view of one way in which the problem of hiding collusion has been solved. The particular device used in this conspiracy was called the "phases of the moon" pricing formula.

> [These pricing formulas were listed on] sheets of paper, each containing a half dozen columns of figures. . . . One group of columns established the bidding order of the seven switchgear manufacturers — a different company, each with its own code number, phasing into the priority position every two weeks (hence "phases of the moon"). A second group of columns, keyed into the company code numbers, established how much each company was to knock off the agreed-upon book price. For example, if it were No. 1's (G.E.'s) turn to be low bidder at a certain number of dollars off book, then all Westinghouse (No. 2), or Allis-Chalmers (No. 3) had to do was look for their code number in the second group of columns to find how many dollars they were to bid above No. 1. These bids would then be fuzzed up by having a little added to them or taken away by companies 2, 3, etc. Thus, there was not even a hint that the winning bid had been collusively arrived at.[4]

Before stumbling on the "phases of the moon" papers, the U.S. Justice Department was having a very hard time proving conspiracy but, with the formula in hand, it was able to put the conspiracy under the spotlight and end it.

[4]Richard A. Smith, "The Incredible Electrical Conspiracy," part 2, *Fortune* May 1961, 210.

Other Strategic Variables

We have focused here on firms that play a simple game and consider only two possible strategies — complying and cheating — concerning price and quantity produced. The same approach can be extended to a much wider range of the choices facing firms. A firm has to decide whether to enter or leave an industry, whether to mount an expensive advertising campaign, whether to modify its product, how reliable to make its product (the more reliable a product, usually the more expensive it is to produce), whether to price discriminate and if so, among which groups of customers and to what degree, or whether to undertake a large research and development (R&D) effort aimed at lowering production costs. The basic method of analysis that you have studied can be applied to these choices by working out the payoff for each of the alternative strategies and then finding the equilibrium of the game. Let's look at an example — based on an important, real-world case — of an R&D game.

An R&D Game in the Disposable Diaper Industry

Since the 1960s, the two market leaders in the disposable diaper industry have been Procter & Gamble (makers of Pampers) and Kimberly-Clark (makers of Huggies). Procter & Gamble has 60 to 70 percent of the total market while Kimberly-Clark has 25 percent. When the product was first introduced in the 1960s, it had to be cost-effective in competition against reusable, cloth diapers. A massive research and development effort resulted in the development of machines that could make disposable diapers at a low enough cost to achieve that initial competitive edge. The diaper industry is fiercely competitive. As it has matured, a large number of firms have tried to get into the industry and take market share away from the two leaders, and the leaders themselves have battled each other to maintain or increase their own market share.

The disposable diaper industry is one in which technological advances that result in small decreases in the average total cost of production can provide an individual firm with an enormous competitive advantage. For example, the current machines can produce disposable diapers at a rate of 3,000 an hour — ten times the output rate of just a decade ago. The firm that develops and uses the least-cost technology gains a competitive edge, undercutting the rest of the market, increasing its market share, and increasing its profit. But the R&D effort that has to be undertaken to achieve even small cost reductions is itself very costly. Its cost has to be deducted from the profit resulting from the increased market share that lower costs achieve.

Thus each firm in the disposable diaper industry is in a research and development dilemma. If no firm does R&D, every firm can be better off, but if one firm initiates such activity, all must do so. Table 14.6 illustrates the dilemma (with hypothetical numbers) for the R&D game that Kimberly-Clark and Procter & Gamble are playing. Each firm has two strategies: to spend $25 million a year on R&D or to spend nothing on R&D. If neither spends on R&D, the two firms make a total profit of $100 million: $30 million for Kimberly-Clark and $70 million for Procter & Gamble (bottom right square of the payoff matrix). If each firm conducts R&D, both maintain their market shares but the profit of each firm is lower by the amount spent on R&D (top left square of the payoff matrix). If Kimberly-Clark pays for R&D but Procter & Gamble does not, Kimberly-Clark gains a large part of Procter & Gamble's market; Kimberly-Clark profits and Procter & Gamble loses (top right square of the payoff matrix). Finally, if Procter & Gamble invests in R&D and Kimberly-Clark does not, Procter & Gamble increases its profit by gaining market share from Kimberly-Clark, which makes a loss (bottom left square of the payoff matrix).

Confronted with the payoff matrix in Table 14.6, the two firms calculate their best strategies. Kimberly-Clark reasons as follows. If Procter & Gamble does not undertake R&D, we will make $85 million if we do and $30 million if we do not. Therefore it pays us to conduct R&D. If Procter & Gamble conducts R&D, we will lose $10 million if we don't and make $5 million if we do. Again, R&D pays off. Thus conducting R&D is a dominant strategy for Kimberly-Clark. Doing it pays regardless of Procter & Gamble's decision.

Procter & Gamble reasons similarly. If Kimberly-Clark does not undertake R&D, we will make $70 million if we follow suit and $85 million if we conduct R&D. It therefore pays to conduct R&D. If Kimberly-Clark does undertake R&D, we will make $45 million by doing the same and lose $10 million by not doing so. Again, it pays to conduct R&D. So for Procter & Gamble, R&D is also a dominant strategy.

Table 14.6 Pampers Versus Huggies: An R&D Game

		Proctor & Gamble's strategies: R&D	Proctor & Gamble's strategies: No R&D
Kimberly-Clark's strategies	R&D	P&G $45m K-C $ 5m	P&G – $10m K-C $85m
	No R&D	P&G $85m K-C – $10m	P&G $70m K-C $30m

If both firms undertake R&D, their payoffs are those shown in the top left square. If neither firm undertakes R&D, their payoffs are those in the bottom right square. If one firm undertakes R&D and the other does not, their payoffs are those in the top right and bottom left squares. The dominant strategy equilibrium for this game is for both firms to undertake R&D. The structure of this game is the same as that of the prisoner's dilemma.

Since R&D is a dominant strategy for both players, the game has a Nash equilibrium. The outcome is that both firms conduct R&D. They make lower profits than they would if they could collude to achieve the cooperative outcome of no R&D.

The real-world situation actually has more players than Kimberly-Clark and Procter & Gamble. There are a large number of other firms sharing a small portion of the market, all of them ready to eat into the share of the two industry leaders. So, the R&D efforts by these two firms not only serve the purpose of maintaining shares in their own battle, but also helps to keep the barriers to entry high enough to preserve their joint market share.

■ We have now studied the four main market types — perfect competition, monopolistic competition, oligopoly, and monopoly — and discovered how prices and outputs, revenue, cost, and profit are determined in these industries. We have used the various models to make predictions about behaviour and to assess the efficiency of alternative market structures. A key element in our analysis of the markets for goods and services is the behaviour of costs. Costs are determined partly by technology and partly by the prices of factors of production. We have treated those factor prices as given. We're now going to see how

Oligopoly in Action

The price war is here

Saudi Arabia's Oil-production Binge May Cost Its Competitors Dearly

When petroleum prices were doubling and redoubling during the 1970s, oil buyers wondered whether the increases would ever hit a ceiling. Last week the problem was reversed: as global prices continued to plummet, traders despaired about the lack of a firm floor. "The market is in a careening tailspin," said one oil-futures analyst. Warned another: "Put on your hard hat. The sky is falling." The price for next month's delivery of West Texas Intermediate, a major U.S. crude, plunged $3.39 on Monday and Tuesday to $15.44 per bbl., its lowest point since 1979 and a nearly 50% decline from just three months ago. Only toward the end of the week did the markets calm down a bit, and the price recovered part of its losses, to finish at $17.68.

The steep slide early in the week occurred when members of the Organization of Petroleum Exporting Countries confirmed that the group has in effect abandoned any effort to curb its production, thus ensuring a worsening global glut. Meeting in Vienna under dark snow clouds, a committee of oil ministers from five OPEC nations—Venezuela, Indonesia, Iraq, Kuwait and the United Arab Emirates—declined to propose any new output limit for the 13-member group. Their decision goes along with the strategy being pursued by Saudi Arabia, Kuwait and other wealthy oil producers, who are flooding the market with excess petroleum....

How did OPEC go from a strategy of one-for-all to a free-for-all? The cartel's disintegration began in 1981, when prices started sliding because of worldwide overproduction, partly caused by consumption cutbacks in many oil-dependent nations. To sop up the surplus, OPEC imposed output limits on its members. But that only provided a chance for such new producers as Mexico and Britain to steal business from OPEC countries, whose market share consequently dropped from 63% in 1979 to 38% currently.

Saudi Arabia tried for years to set an example of self-restraint in OPEC. The country slashed its production from a peak 10.3 million bbl. a day in 1981 to a low of 2 million bbl. a day last June. But gradually the Saudis began to feel that they were being played for a sucker by other OPEC members like Colonel Muammar Gaddafi's Libya, which has exceeded its quotas, and by some non-OPEC countries, which were producing at peak capacity. Finally fed up, the Saudis quietly began opening their spigots last autumn, when a seasonal in-crease in demand temporarily camouflaged the additional supply. By now the kingdom has more than doubled its output, to nearly 4.5 million bbl. a day.

Time,
February 17, 1986
By Stephen Koepp

The Essence of the Story

- In the 1970s, oil prices rose sharply.
- In 1986, OPEC abandoned its efforts to curtail production and oil prices fell quickly.
- OPEC's cartel came under pressure in 1981, but Saudi Arabia kept total production limited and maintained high prices by cutting its own output from 10.3 million barrels a day in 1981 to 2 million barrels a day in 1985.
- Other OPEC members produced more than their agreed output, and by 1985 Saudi Arabia decided to abandon its efforts to single-handedly restrain OPEC production.

Background and Analysis

- OPEC is made up of 13 countries (Algeria, Ecuador, Gabon, Indonesia, Iran, Iraq, Kuwait, Libya, Nigeria, Qatar, Saudi Arabia, the United Arab Emirates, and Venezuela) and seeks to achieve the best available returns for its members' exports of crude oil and petroleum products.
- The world oil industry is an oligopoly.
- In 1973, the OPEC producers controlled two-thirds of the world's oil supply. In that year, they entered into a collusive agreement to restrict world oil production and raise its price.
- The OPEC producers stuck to their agreement from the early 1970s until 1982.
- Faced with a fall in demand and lower profits, individual OPEC members began to abandon the collusive agreement. By 1985, all members except Saudi Arabia were cheating. In 1985, Saudi Arabia also abandoned the agreement.
- The events just summarized can be understood in terms of the game that we have analysed in this chapter. The OPEC members are playing an oligopoly game similar to the duopoly game that we have studied.
- They began by colluding, and they stuck to the agreement for a remarkable length of time. Eventually, responding to falling profits, the smaller producers abandoned the agreement. Ultimately the big producer, Saudi Arabia, abandoned its production limits in order to punish its partners who had previously abandoned their own part of the agreement.
- Although at this writing it has not happened, OPEC has a strong incentive to try to restore its collusive agreement and again restrict output and raise the world price of oil.

factor prices are themselves determined. Factor prices interact with the goods market that we have just studied in two ways. First, they determine the firm's production costs. Second, they determine household incomes and, therefore, influence the demand for goods and services. Factor prices also have an important effect on the distribution of income. The firms that we've been studying in the past five chapters decide how to produce; the interactions of households and firms in the markets for goods and services decide what will be produced. And the factor prices determined in the markets for factors of production determine for whom the various goods and services are produced.

SUMMARY

Varieties of Market Structure

Most industries in the real world lie between the extremes of perfect competition and monopoly. The degree of competition is sometimes measured by the concentration ratio. The four-firm concentration ratio measures the percentage of the value of the sales of an industry accounted for by its four largest firms. A high concentration ratio indicates a relatively low degree of competition and vice versa, with some important qualifications. There are three key problems related to concentration ratios: (1) concentration ratios refer to the national market, but some industries are local and others are international; (2) concentration ratios do not tell us about the degree of turnover of firms and the ease of entry; and (3) some firms classified in one industry operate in several others.

There are two models of industries that lie between monopoly and perfect competition: monopolistic competition and oligopoly. Monopolistic competition is a market type in which a large number of firms compete, each making a product slightly differentiated from the others, and by competing on price, quality, and advertising. Oligopoly is a market type in which a small number of firms compete with each other and in which the actions of any one firm have an important impact on the profit of the others. (pp. 345-348)

Monopolistic Competition

Monopolistic competition occurs when a large number of firms compete with each other by making slightly different products. Under monopolistic competition, each firm faces a downward-sloping demand curve and so has to choose its price as well as its output level. Because there is free entry, a zero economic profit is earned in long-run equilibrium. When profit is maximized, with marginal cost equal to marginal revenue, average cost also equals price in the long run. But average cost is not at its minimum point. That is, firms in monopolistic competition operate with excess capacity. (pp. 348-350)

Oligopoly

Oligopoly is a situation in which a small number of producers compete with each other. The key feature of oligopoly is that the firms interact strategically. Each has to take into account the effects of its own actions on the behaviour of the other and the effects of the others' actions on its own profit.

Game theory is a method of analysing strategic interaction. Game theory focuses on three aspects of a game: rules, strategies, and payoffs. The rules of the oligopoly game specify the permissible actions by the players. In oligopoly, these actions, which are limited only by the legal code, involve such things as raising or lowering prices, raising or lowering output, raising or lowering advertising effort, and enhancing or not enhancing the product. The strategies in the oligopoly game are all the possible actions that each player can take given the action of the other player. The payoff is the player's profit or loss; it depends on the actions of both the players and on the constraints imposed by the market, technology, and input costs. (pp. 350-354)

The Prisoner's Dilemma

Duopoly, which is a special case of oligopoly, is a market structure in which there are two producers of a good competing against each other. The duopoly game is similar to the prisoner's dilemma game. Two prisoners are faced with the problem of deciding whether or not to confess to a crime. If neither confesses, they are tried for a lesser crime and receive a light penalty. If both confess, they receive a higher penalty. If one confesses and the other does not, the one confessing receives the lightest of all penalties and the one not confessing receives a very heavy penalty.

The prisoner's dilemma has a dominant strategy Nash equilibrium; that is, regardless of the action of the other player, each player has a unique best action to confess. (pp. 354-358)

A Duopoly Game

A duopoly game can be constructed in which two firms contemplate the consequences of colluding to achieve a monopoly profit or of cheating on the collusive agreement to make a bigger profit at the expense of the other firm. Such a game is identical to the prisoner's dilemma. The equilibrium of the game is that both firms cheat on the agreement. In this case, the industry output is the same as if the industry was perfectly competitive. The industry price is the competitive price, and the firms make a zero economic profit. If, however, the firms are able to enforce the collusive agreement, the industry looks exactly like a monopoly industry; price, output, and profit are the same as in a monopoly.

If a game is repeated indefinitely, there is an opportunity for one player to punish another for previous "bad" behaviour. In such a long-running duopoly game, a tit-for-tat strategy can produce an equilibrium in which both firms stick to the agreement. A tit-for-tat strategy is one in which the players begin by colluding; if one player cheats, the other responds at the next play by also cheating. Since each knows that it pays the other to respond in this manner, no one cheats. This equilibrium is a cooperative equilibrium — one in which each player cooperates because such behaviour is a rational response to the other's credible threat to inflict damage if the agreement is broken. Uncertainty makes it possible for such an equilibrium to break down from time to time. (pp. 358-365)

Games and Price Wars

Price wars can be interpreted as the outcome of a repeated duopoly game. The competing firms comply with the agreement unless market forces bring about a sufficiently large fall in price; at that point, each firm responds as if the price fall had resulted from the other firm's cheating. Only by responding in this manner can each firm maintain as credible the threat that it will punish a cheat and thereby ensure that the ever-present temptation to cheat is held in check and the monopoly agreement maintained. When market conditions bring about an increase in price, the firms revert to their cooperative behaviour. Industries will go through cycles, starting with a monopoly price and output and occasionally, when demand falls enough, temporarily pursuing noncooperative actions. At these times, the industry price and output will be the competitive ones. (p. 365-366)

Other Strategic Variables

A firm in an oligopolistic industry has to make a large range of decisions: whether to enter or leave the industry, how much to spend on advertising, whether to modify its product, whether to price discriminate, whether to undertake research and development. All these choices result in payoffs for the firm and the other firms in the industry. A game can be constructed to predict the outcome of such choices.

An interesting real-world example is the research and development game played between producers of disposable diapers. The equilibrium of that game results in the undertaking of a large amount of R&D and in lower profits than would emerge if the firms could collude somehow to keep out new entrants and undertake less R&D. Thus the game is similar to the prisoner's dilemma. (pp. 366-370)

K E Y E L E M E N T S

Key Terms

Cartel, 358
Collusive agreement, 358
Cooperative equilibrium, 365
Dominant strategy, 355
Dominant strategy equilibrium, 355
Duopoly, 354
Four-firm concentration ratio, 345
Game theory, 351
Monopolistic competition, 347
Nash equilibrium, 355
Oligopoly, 348

Key Figures and Tables 

REVIEW QUESTIONS

1 What are the main varieties of market structure? What are the main characteristics of each of those market structures?

2 What is a four-firm concentration ratio? What does it mean to say that an industry's four-firm concentration ratio is 90 percent?

3 Give examples of Canadian industries that have high concentration ratios and of some that have low concentration ratios.

4 What are barriers to entry? Give some examples of barriers to entry that exist in the Canadian economy.

5 Explain how a firm can differentiate its product.

6 What is the difference between monopolistic competition and perfect competition?

7 Is monopolistic competition more efficient or less efficient than perfect competition?

8 What is the difference between duopoly and oligopoly?

9 What is the essential feature of both duopoly and oligopoly?

10 List the key features that all games have in common.

11 What are the features of duopoly that allow us to treat it as a game between two firms?

12 What is the prisoner's dilemma?

13 What is a dominant strategy equilibrium?

14 What is meant by a repeated game?

15 Explain a tit-for-tat strategy.

16 What is a price war? What is the effect of a price war on the profit of the firms in the industry and on the profitability of the industry itself?

PROBLEMS

1 A monopolistically competitive industry is in long-run equilibrium, as illustrated in Fig. 14.1(b). An increase in demand for the industry's product shifts the demand curves of each firm to the right. Using diagrams similar to those in Fig. 14.1, analyse the short-run and long-run effects on price, output, and profit of this change in demand.

2 Another monopolistically competitive industry is in long-run equilibrium, as illustrated in Fig. 14.1(b), when a large increase in wages raises the costs of all the firms. Using diagrams similar to those in Fig. 14.1, analyse the short-run and long-run effects on price, output, and profit of this change in costs.

3 Describe the game known as the prisoner's dilemma. In doing so,

a) Make up a story that motivates the game.

b) Work out a payoff matrix.

c) Describe how the equilibrium of the game is arrived at.

4 Consider the following game. Each of two players is asked a question. They can answer the question honestly or they can lie. If they both answer honestly, they each receive $100. If one answers honestly and the other lies, the liar receives $500 and the honest player gets nothing. If they both lie, each receives $50.

a) Describe this game in terms of its players, strategies, and payoffs.

b) Construct the payoff matrix.

c) What is the equilibrium for this game?

5 Explain the behaviour of oil prices by using a repeated prisoner's dilemma game.

6 Two firms, Soapy Inc. and Sudsies Inc., are the only producers of washing powder. They collude and agree to share the market equally. If neither firm cheats on the agreement, they can each make $1 million profit. If either firm cheats, the cheater can increase its profit to $1.5 million, while the firm that abides by the agreement makes a loss of $0.5 million. Neither firm has any way of policing the actions of the other.

a) Describe the best strategy for each firm in a game that is played just once.

b) What is the payoff matrix and equilibrium in a game that is played just once?

c) If the buyers of washing powder lobby successfully for government regulation of the washing powder industry, explain what happens to the price of washing powder and the profits made by the washing powder industry.

d) If this duopolist game can be played many times, describe some of the strategies that each firm may adopt.

7 Explain the behaviour of world oil prices since 1973 by using a repeated prisoner's dilemma game. Describe the types of strategies that individual countries that belong to OPEC have adopted.

8 Use the model of oligopoly to explain why, in the disposable diaper industry, Proctor & Gamble and Kimberly-Clark spend so much on R&D.

PART 6

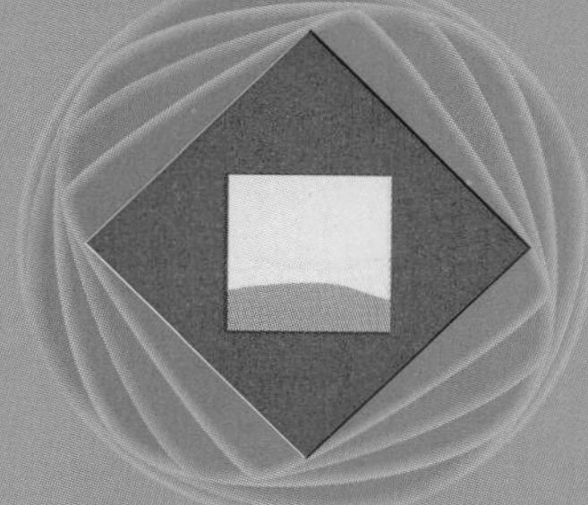

Markets for Factors of Production

TALKING WITH MORLEY GUNDERSON

Morley Gunderson received a BA from Queen's University, an MA (in industrial relations), and a PhD (in economics) from the University of Wisconsin. Now both a professor in the Department of Economics and director of the Centre for Industrial Relations at the University of Toronto, he has held visiting appointments at the National Bureau of Economic Research at Stanford University and at the International Institute of Labour Studies in Geneva, Switzerland. His work has covered various features of the labour market, but he has concentrated on gender discrimination—the

"To me, the appeal of labour economics is the practical importance of many of the issues to everyday lives of people — their pay, employment, and job satisfaction."

facts about and the reasons for differences between the earnings of women and men. Michael Parkin talked with Morley Gunderson about labour economics and gender discrimination.

Professor Gunderson, what first attracted you to economics?

When I was in high school, I became obsessed with two big questions: (1) where is the end of the universe and what is beyond it? and (2) what causes unemployment? I naively thought that the second question was the easier to answer and hence started down the road of economics rather than physics. As an aside, I don't think I have a better answer to either question today than I did then.

What drew you to the study of labour markets?

To me, the appeal of labour economics is the practical importance of many of the issues to everyday lives of people — their pay, employment, and job satisfaction. Many of the key questions are interesting to and understandable by most people. What explains the dramatic increase in the labour force participation of women? the trend towards the reduced work week and earlier retirement? Do minimum wages and equal pay laws lead to employment reductions? What causes wage differentials between men and women? public and private sector workers? union and nonunion workers?

At graduate school, you studied industrial relations as well as labour economics, and today you hold appointments in both areas. What are the main differences between the two?

Labour economics is the application of microeconomcis and econometrics to the study of behaviour in labour markets. It takes as given the institutional features of the labour market (compensation arrangements, laws, unions, seniority rules, and so on) and rigorously analyses their effect on behaviour. In contrast, industrial relations tries to explain why these institutional features exist and why they change. It uses knowledge from a variety of disciplines — economics, history, law, psychology, and sociology — as well as concepts developed within the field itself.

Although the two fields differ, there is considerable overlap, which offers exciting areas of research. Cause and effect are interrelated in that the existence of the institutional features of labour markets depends in part on their effect. And understanding the effect of such features requires understanding why they arose in the first place.

You are Canada's foremost student of one of the most controversial issues in economics today — the magnitude of and reasons for differences in earnings between men and women. How do you view gender differences in earnings?

Conventional economic theory does not seem to explain the persistence of some male-female wage differentials. In theory, if women are paid less than men of equal productivity, profit-maximizing firms in competitive markets should replace "more expensive" males with "less expensive" females, and the resultant increase in the demand for females would increase their wages until the wage differential disappears. Nevertheless, the empirical evidence strongly suggests that at least some portion of the overall male-female wage gap reflects discriminatory pay differences for men and women of equal productivity. Analysts give various plausible explanations: noncompetitive market forces, pressures from customers and co-workers, the cost of replacing more expensive male workers with less expensive females, the use of legislative and regulatory intervention to protect the privileged positions of male-dominated jobs, and even social pressures.

Would competitive economic forces, left to their own devices, eliminate discrimination, within any reasonable period of time?

Certainly, there is a lively debate as to whether the market is part of the solution or part of the problem. My perception is that we cannot rely on market forces alone but that policy interventions should try to harness market forces, rather than work against them. Market forces can often undo the potentially beneficial effects of well-intended policy interventions.

What are the main trends in gender differentials?

There is remarkably little hard information on this important question. The limited data that exists suggest that in Canada the *overall* earnings gap has narrowed slightly and very slowly: for full-time workers who work full-year, the ratio of female to male earnings increased from 0.58 in 1967 to 0.65 in 1988. Those are averages, however. The types of workers involved may be changing over time. For example, the rapid increase in the labour force participation of women means that the female work force may be increasingly composed of recent entrants; having relatively little experience, they pull down the average wage and thus sustain the gap. However, women are also staying in the labour force longer and hence accumulating more experience.

What solid, research-based knowledge do we have about the causes of gender differences in earnings?

The research results indicate that some portion of the male-female earnings gap reflects differences in productivity-related factors and some portion reflects labour market discrimination. The relative contribution of these two components is the subject of considerable controversy. Also, many of the productivity-related differences between male and female workers arise from inequality of opportunities, from constraints arising outside the labour market (especially differences in household responsibilities). In other words, the problem manifest in differential

"Many of the productivity-related differences between male and female workers arise from inequality of opportunities, from constraints arising outside the labour market."

"Economics . . . is about how decisions are made in a world of uncertainty and limited information, subject to a variety of constraints."

earnings reflects a complex interaction of forces arising not only from the labour market but also from the household, educational institutions, the legal system, and social norms in general. That makes the issue, and the appropriate policy responses, more complex but also more interesting.

What are the main unresolved issues concerning earnings differences between men and women?

They include: the extent to which changes in the overall earnings gap reflect changes in the composition of the male and female work forces (as opposed to changes in the earnings of otherwise similar male or female workers); the effect on the earnings gap of differences in work experience and its continuity; the effect of legislative initiatives, especially equal pay for work of equal value and affirmative action; and the effect of such factors as free trade, public and private pension plans, unions, and public sector retrenchment.

How can these outstanding issues be resolved?

We need more work on all fronts: better data, better application of econometric techniques, better theoretical work to interpret the underlying causal relationships and hence to understand the appropriate policy response, and better understanding of the policy alternatives. These can be done by different people—after all, we should practice the principle of comparative advantage that we preach. However, there is also need for people to specialize in interrelating the theory, evidence, and policy and to translate the academic research to policymakers and the policy questions to academic researchers.

What principles of economics that you learned as an undergraduate have repeatedly proved indispensable in your research career?

Most decisions involve tradeoffs; economics can help to articulate those tradeoffs and show how they are affected by such factors as scarce resources, scarce time, and political and institutional constraints. Economics can be very useful in showing us how individuals and groups respond to changes in the constraints they face. Economics is not really about money or profits or banks—the sorts of images people often conjure up when you say the word. Rather it is about how decisions are made in a world of uncertainty and limited information, subject to a variety of constraints. This is true of labour economics as it is of all applied economics.

CHAPTER 15

Pricing and Allocating Factors of Production

After studying this chapter, you will be able to:

- Explain how firms choose the quantities of labour, capital, and land to employ in their production activities.
- Explain how households choose the quantities of labour, capital, and land to supply.
- Explain how wages, interest, and rent are determined in competitive factor markets.
- Explain the concept of economic rent.
- Distinguish between economic rent and transfer earnings.

Many Happy Returns

IT MAY NOT BE YOUR BIRTHDAY, and even if it is, chances are that you are spending most of the day working. But at the end of the week or month (or, if you're devoting all your time to school, when you graduate), you will receive the *returns* from your labour. ■ Of course, those returns vary a lot from one person to another and from one kind of job to another. An average person in full-time employment in Canada in 1987 earned $21,000 — about $12 an hour. Most of us are clustered around that average. Ed Jones is such a person. Ed spends his day in a small container, suspended by cables attached to the top of Toronto's Bank of Montreal tower. With the wind whipping off Lake Ontario chilling his toes, fingers, and ears, Ed cleans the hectares of glass that form the windows of that skyscraper. Ed works hard for his $12 an hour, but when those happy returns come in at the end of the week, it all seems worthwhile. ■ For some workers, the returns are very happy indeed. Dan Rather is one such worker. Dan collects a cool $3.6 million a year for that 30-minute news show he puts on each weekday evening. And he's not alone on those dizzy heights of happy paycheques. Barbara Walters, Tom Brokaw, Bryant Gumbel, and Diane Sawyer are all up there with him in the million-dollar-plus annual pay range. ■ At the other extreme are people working for the minimum wage and, in some cases, for even less than the minimum wage. Student help at McDonald's and farm workers in the fields of the Niagara Peninsula labour away for just a few dollars an hour. But even for those workers, the returns are worthwhile. Sure they'd like more, but they prefer working for low wages than not working at all and having no income. ■ What determines the wages that people are paid? What determines the kinds of jobs they do? How does our economy allocate its labour resources to the many thousands of different tasks that must be performed? ■ Most of us have little trouble spending our pay. But most of us manage to save some of what we earn. Some of our savings are put on deposit at a bank or trust company. Some go to buying bonds and shares. The returns that we get on our savings depend on which of these various things we do with them. If we put the money in the bank or a trust company or use it to buy bonds, we earn interest on it. If we buy shares, we're paid a dividend and enjoy stock price increases — or suffer decreases. The size of our return on a share depends on the company whose stock we've bought. We may be lucky and get a huge return, or we may be unlucky and get little or nothing at all. Fluctuations in Robert Campeau's financial fortunes are a good example of the range of returns on financial investments. For many years, Campeau operated as a real estate developer, accumulating a fortune for himself and those who bought shares in the Campeau Corporation. Then, in the late 1980s, Campeau began to diversify, buying famous retail stores such as Bloomingdale's in New York City. Campeau's ability to put together a good deal in property development did not translate into an ability to make profitable decisions in retailing. His retail interests failed, and the value of Campeau Corporation stocks plummeted. ■ What determines the amount of saving that people do and the returns they make on that saving? How do the returns on saving influence the allocation of savings across the many industries and activities that use our capital resources? ■ Savings can also be used to buy land. That use of a person's savings generates a return in the form of rent. The amount of rent earned varies enormously with the location and quality of land. For example, if you buy a hectare of farmland in Manitoba, you can rent it out for something approaching $2,000 a year. If you buy a block in Toronto's Yorkville, you can collect several million dollars a year in rent income. ■ What determines the rent that people are willing to pay for different blocks of land? Why are rents so enormously high in big cities and so relatively low in the great farming regions of the nation? ■ It is not only land rents that are much higher in cities than in other parts of the country. Many of the things we buy are more expensive in a city than in a small town. For example, a cup of coffee that costs a quarter in your university cafeteria costs 50 cents in a downtown snack bar, $1.25 in Vancouver, and $2 in Tokyo. Why? Obvious, you answer. High rent leads to high cost, so coffee shops in high-rent areas have to charge high prices for their coffee. But wait! Is it high rents that lead to high prices of coffee in big cities, or is it that a high demand for coffee leads to high prices that, in turn, lead to high rents?

■ In this and the following three chapters, we deal with the kinds of questions that have just been posed. We'll study markets for factors of production — for labour, capital, and land — and learn how the prices of these factors of production are determined. This first chapter provides an overview of all three types of factor markets and also introduces you to the important concept of economic rent. It begins by introducing you to the terminology of factor markets and setting out the link between factor prices and incomes.

Factor Prices and Incomes

Factors of production are divided into three broad categories: labour, capital, and land. (We defined these factors of production in Chapter 1.) The owners of factors of production receive an income from the firms that use those factors as inputs for their production activities. These incomes are *wages* paid for labour, *interest* paid for capital, and *rent* paid for land. Wages include all labour income including salaries, commissions, and any other supplementary forms of income paid in compensation for labour. Interest includes all forms of capital income, including dividends paid by firms. Rent is the income paid for the use of land and natural resources. (Apartment rents include an element of rent and also an element of interest — a payment for the use of capital.)

Labour is the most important factor of production and generates almost 60 percent of all income. Of the capital owned by households, by far the most important element is the houses in which they live.

In the rest of this chapter, we're going to build a model of a factor market. We'll use that model to determine factor prices, the quantities of factors traded, and the incomes that factors of production earn.

An Overview

Factor prices are determined in factor markets, and we can understand those prices by using the model of demand and supply. The quantity of a factor of production demanded depends on the factor's price. That is, the quantity of labour demanded depends

Figure 15.1 Demand and Supply in a Factor Market

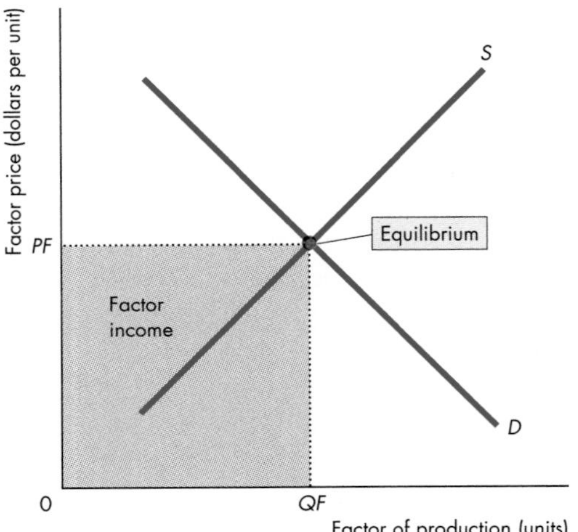

The demand curve for a factor of production (*D*) slopes downward and the supply curve (*S*) slopes upward. Where the demand and supply curves intersect, the factor price (*PF*) and the quantity of a factor traded (*QF*) are determined. The factor income is the product of the factor price and the quantity of the factor, as represented by the blue shaded area.

on the wage rate, the quantity of capital demanded depends on the interest rate, and the quantity of land demanded depends on the rent. The law of demand applies to factors of production just as it applies to all other economic entities. Thus as the price of a factor of production decreases, the quantity of the factor demanded increases. Figure 15.1 shows the demand curve for a factor of production as the curve labelled *D*.

The quantity supplied of a factor of production depends on its price. With some exceptions that we'll identify later in this chapter, the law of supply applies to factors of production, so as the price of a factor increases, the quantity supplied increases. Figure 15.1 shows the supply of a factor of production as the curve labelled *S*.

The equilibrium factor price is determined at the point of intersection of the factor demand and factor supply curves. Figure 15.1 shows such an equilibrium — *QF* is the quantity of the factor of production traded and *PF* is the factor price.

The income earned by a factor of production is its price multiplied by the quantity traded. In Fig. 15.1, the price is measured by the distance from the origin to *PF*, and the quantity traded is measured by the distance from the origin to *QF*. The factor income is the product of these two distances and it is equivalent to the blue shaded area in the figure.

All the influences on the quantity of a factor bought, other than its price, result in a shift in the factor demand curve. We'll study what those influences are in the next section. For now, let's simply work out the effects of a change in the demand for a factor of production. An increase in demand, as illustrated in Fig. 15.2(a), shifts the demand curve to the right, leading to an increase in the quantity of the factor traded and an increase in its price. Thus when the demand curve shifts from D_0 to D_1, the quantity traded increases from QF_0 to QF_1 and the price increases from PF_0 to PF_1. An increase in the demand for a factor of production increases that factor's income. The dark blue area in Fig. 15.2(a) illustrates the increase in income.

When the demand for a factor of production decreases, its demand curve shifts to the left. Figure 15.2(b) illustrates the effects of a decrease in demand: the demand curve shifts to the left from D_0 to D_2; the quantity traded decreases from QF_0 to QF_2; and the price decreases from PF_0 to PF_2. When the demand for a factor of production decreases, the income of that factor also decreases. The light blue area in Fig. 15.2(b) illustrates the decrease in income.

The extent to which a change in the demand for a factor of production changes the factor price and the quantity traded depends on the elasticity of supply. If the supply curve is very flat (supply is elastic), the change in the quantity traded is large and the change in price is small. If the supply curve is very steep (supply is inelastic), the change in the price is large and the change in the quantity traded is small.

A change in the supply of a factor of production changes the price and quantity traded as well as the income earned by those supplying the factor. An increase in supply results in an increase in the quantity traded and a decrease in the factor price. A decrease in supply results in a decrease in the quantity traded and an increase in the factor price. But whether a change in supply increases or decreases income depends on the elasticity of demand for the factor.

Suppose initially that 3 units of the factor of production are traded at \$10 a unit, as illustrated in Fig. 15.3. Now suppose that the quantity supplied

Figure 15.2 Changes in Demand

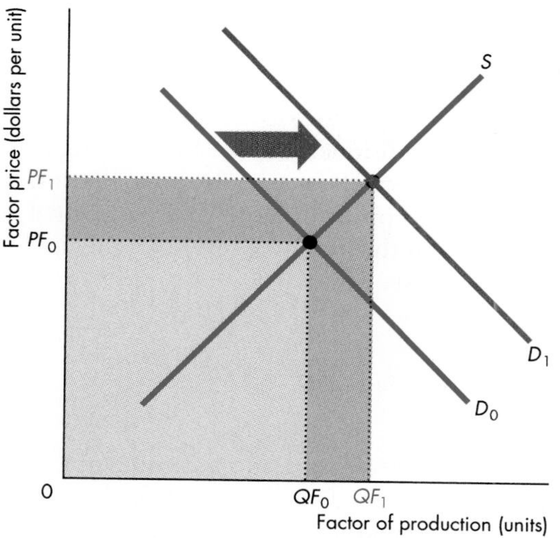

(a) An increase in demand

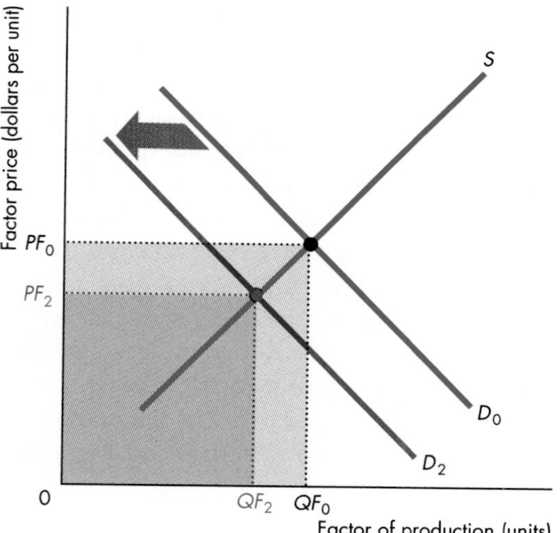

(b) A decrease in demand

An increase in the demand for a factor of production (part a) shifts its demand curve to the right — from D_0 to D_1. The quantity traded increases from QF_0 to QF_1 and the price increases from PF_0 to PF_1. The factor income increases; that increase is shown by the dark blue area. A decrease in the demand for a factor of production from D_0 to D_2 results in a decrease in the quantity traded from QF_0 to QF_2 and a decrease in the factor price, from PF_0 to PF_2. The decrease in demand results in a decrease in the factor income; that decrease is illustrated by the light blue area.

Figure 15.3 Factor Income and Demand Elasticity

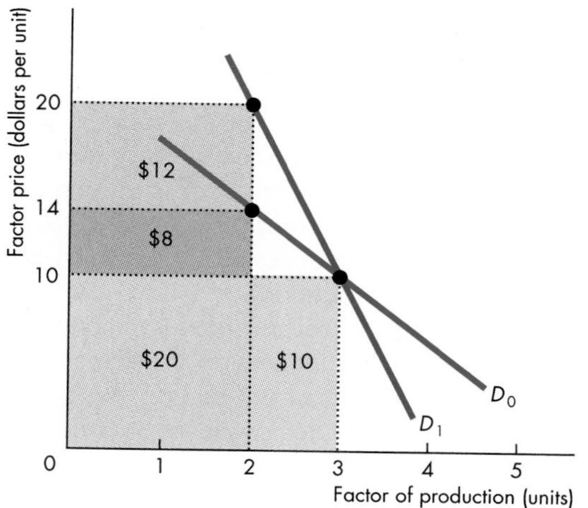

Initially, 3 units of the factor are traded at $10 per unit. A decrease in the quantity traded of a factor of production may result in a decrease or an increase in the factor's income. If the demand curve is D_0 (an elastic demand curve over the relevant range), a decrease in the quantity traded from 3 to 2 results in a decrease in the factor income from $30 to $28. If the demand curve is D_1 (an inelastic demand curve over the relevant range), a decrease in the quantity traded from 3 to 2 results in an increase in the factor's income from $30 to $40.

decreases from 3 units to 2 units. If the demand curve is D_0, the decrease in supply results in an increase in the price of the factor but a decrease in the income of those supplying this factor of production. You can see that income decreases by multiplying the factor price by the quantity traded. Initially, when 3 units are traded at a price of $10 each, the income earned by the suppliers is $30 (the $20 light blue area plus the $10 red area). When the quantity traded decreases to 2 units and the price increases to $14, income decreases by $10 (the red area) *and* increases by $8 (the dark blue area) for a net decrease of $2. Over the range of the price of change that we've just considered, the demand curve D_0 is elastic — its elasticity is greater than 1.

Now suppose that the demand curve is D_1. In this case, when the quantity traded decreases to 2 units, the price increases to $20 a unit. Income increases to $40. The smaller quantity traded lowers income by $10 (the red area), but the higher factor price increases it by $20 (the dark blue plus the green area). Over the range of the price change that we've just considered, the demand curve D_1 is inelastic — its elasticity is less than 1.

The markets for factors of production determine factor prices in much the same way as goods markets determine the prices of goods and services. These markets also determine factor incomes. Factor income is the factor price multiplied by the quantity of the factor traded. Thus to work out the influences on incomes we have to pay attention simultaneously to the determination of the prices and the quantities traded of the factors of production.

We're going to spend the rest of this chapter exploring more closely the influences on the demand for and the supply of factors of production. We're also going to discover what determines the elasticities of supply and demand for factors. These elasticities are important because of their effects on factor prices and the incomes earned. Let's begin by studying the demand for inputs.

Demand for Factors

The demand for any factor of production is a derived demand. A **derived demand** is a demand for an input not for its own sake but in order to use it in the production of goods and services. A firm's derived demand for inputs depends on the constraints the firm faces — its technology constraint and its market constraint — as well as on the firm's objective. The objective of the model firms that we have studied is to maximize profit. We'll continue to study the behaviour of such firms.

A firm's demand for factors stems from its profit-maximization decision. *What* to produce and *how* to produce it are the questions that the firm must answer in order to make maximum profit. Those choices have implications for the firm's demand for inputs, which we'll now investigate.

Profit Maximization

A firm's inputs fall into two categories: fixed and variable. In most industries, the fixed inputs are capital (plant, machinery, and buildings) and land, and the variable input is labour. A firm meets permanent changes in output by changing the scale of its inputs of capital and land. It meets short-run variations in output by varying its input of labour.

Profit-maximizing firms produce the output at which marginal cost equals marginal revenue. This principle holds true whether the firm is in a perfectly competitive industry, monopolistic competition, oligopoly, or a monopoly. If one more unit of output adds less to total cost than it adds to total revenue, the firm can increase its profit by producing more. It maximizes profit by producing the output at which the additional cost of producing one more unit of output equals the additional revenue from selling it. If we shift our perspective, we can also state the condition for maximum profit in terms of the marginal cost of an input and the marginal revenue generated by that input. Let's see how.

Marginal Revenue Product and Factor Price

The change in total revenue resulting from employing one more unit of any factor is called the factor's **marginal revenue product**. The concept of marginal revenue product sounds a bit like the concept of marginal revenue that you have met before. These concepts are indeed related, but there is an important distinction between the two. *Marginal revenue product* is the extra total revenue generated as a result of employing one extra unit of a factor of production; *marginal revenue* is the extra total revenue generated as a result of selling one additional unit of output.

A profit-maximizing firm hires the quantity of a factor that makes the marginal revenue product of the factor equal to the marginal cost of the factor. For a firm that buys its factors of production in competitive factor markets, the marginal cost of a factor is the factor's price. That is, in a competitive factor market, each firm is such a small demander of the factor that it has no influence on its price. The firm simply has to pay the going factor price — the market wage rate for labour, the interest rate for capital, and the rent for land.

Factor Price as Opportunity Cost You may be wondering why the interest rate is the factor price for capital. It looks different from the other two factor prices. Why isn't the factor price for capital the price of a piece of machinery — the price of a knitting machine for Swanky's sweater factory, the price of a computer for a tax consulting firm, or the price of an automobile assembly line for GM? The answer is that these prices do not represent the opportunity cost of using capital equipment. They are the prices at which a piece of capital can be traded. A firm can buy or sell a piece of capital equipment at its going market

Table 15.1 Marginal Revenue Product and Average Revenue Product at Max's Wash 'n' Wax

	Quantity of labour (L) (workers)	Output (Q) (cars washed per hour)	Marginal product of labour ($MP = \Delta Q/\Delta L$) (washes per worker)	Total revenue ($TR = P \times Q$) (dollars per hour)	Marginal revenue product ($MRP = \Delta TR/\Delta L$) (dollars per worker)	Average revenue product ($ARP = TR/L$) (dollars per worker)
a	0	0		0		
			5		20	
b	1	5		20		20
			4		16	
c	2	9		36		18
			3		12	
d	3	12		48		16
			2		8	
e	4	14		56		14
			1		4	
f	5	15		60		12

The marginal revenue product of labour is the change in total revenue that results from a one-unit increase in labour input. To calculate marginal revenue product, first work out total revenue. If Max hires 1 worker (row *b*), output is 5 washes per hour, and total revenue, at \$4 per wash, is \$20 per hour. If he hires 2 workers (row *c*), output is 9 washes per hour, and total revenue is \$36 per hour. By hiring the second worker, total revenue rises by \$16 — the marginal revenue product of labour is \$16. The average revenue product of labour is total revenue per unit of labour employed. For example, when Max employs 2 workers, total revenue is \$36, and average revenue product is \$18 (\$36 ÷ 2).

price. The opportunity cost of *using* the equipment is the interest rate that has to be paid on the funds tied up in its purchase. These funds may be borrowed, in which case there is an explicit payment of interest to a bank or other lender. Or the funds used may be owned by the firm, in which case there is an implicit interest cost — the interest that could have been earned by using those funds in some other way.

Quantity of Factor Demanded We have defined the additional revenue resulting from employing one more unit of a factor as the factor's marginal revenue product. We have seen that in competitive factor markets the marginal cost of a factor equals its price. Therefore a profit-maximizing firm — a firm that makes the marginal revenue product equal to the marginal cost of each input — hires each factor up to the point at which its marginal revenue product equals its price. As the price of a factor varies, the quantity demanded of it also varies. The lower the price of a factor, the larger is the quantity demanded of that factor. Let's illustrate this proposition by working through an example — that of labour.[1]

The Firm's Demand for Labour

Labour is a variable input. Thus a firm can change the quantity of labour it employs in both the short run and the long run. We'll focus first on a firm's short-run demand for labour.

A firm's short-run technology constraint is described by its *short-run production function.* Table 15.1 sets out the production function for a car wash

[1] The principles governing the demand for factors of production are the same for all factors — labour, capital, and land. There are some interesting special features concerning the demand for capital, however, that are explained in greater detail in Chapter 17. This part of Chapter 17 is relatively self-contained and may be studied at the same time as the material that you are now studying in this chapter.

Table 15.2 Compact Glossary of Factor Market Terms

Factors of production	Labour, capital, and land
Factor prices	Wages — price of labour; interest — price of capital; rent — price of land
Marginal product	The extra output produced by one additional unit of input hired; for example, the marginal product of labour is additional output produced by employing one more person
Average product	Output per unit of input; for example, the average product of labour is output divided by labour input
Marginal revenue	The extra total revenue resulting from selling one additional unit of output
Marginal revenue product	The extra total revenue resulting from hiring one additional unit of a factor of production; for example, marginal revenue product of labour is the extra total revenue resulting from selling the output produced by employing one more person
Average revenue product	Total revenue per unit of input; calculated as total revenue divided by labour input

operated by Max's Wash 'n' Wax. (This production function is similar to the one that we studied in Chapter 10, Fig. 10.1.) The numbers in the first two columns of the table tell us how the maximum number of car washes each hour varies as the amount of labour employed varies. The third column shows the *marginal product of labour* — the change in output resulting from a one-unit increase in labour input.

Max's market constraint is the demand curve for his product. If, in the goods market, a firm is a monopoly or engaged in monopolistic competition or oligopoly, the firm faces a downward-sloping demand curve for its product. If a firm is perfectly competitive, it faces a fixed price for its product regardless of its output level and, therefore, faces a horizontal demand curve for its product. We will assume that Max operates his car wash in a perfectly competitive market and can sell as many washes as he chooses at a constant price of $4 a wash. Given this information, we can calculate Max's total revenue (fourth column) by multiplying the number of cars washed per hour by $4. For example, if 9 cars are washed each hour (row *c*), total revenue is $36 an hour.

The fifth column shows the calculation of marginal revenue product of labour — the change in total revenue per unit change in labour input. For example, if Max hires a second worker (row *c*), total revenue increases from $20 to $36, so marginal revenue product is $16. An alternative way of calculating the marginal revenue product of labour is to multiply marginal product by marginal revenue. To see that this method gives the same answer, multiply the marginal product of hiring a second worker — 4 cars — by marginal revenue — $4 a car — and notice that the answer is the same ($16).

Total revenue divided by the quantity of the factor hired is called the **average revenue product** of the factor. Thus average revenue product is the average contribution of each unit of an input to the firm's total revenue. The last column of Table 15.1 shows the average revenue product of labour at Max's Wash 'n' Wax. For example, when Max employs 3 workers (row *d*), total revenue is $48. Thus the average revenue product of labour is $48 divided by 3 workers, which is $16 per worker.

Notice that as the quantity of labour rises, the marginal revenue product of labour falls. When Max hires the first worker, the marginal revenue product of labour is $20. For the second worker, it is $16, and it continues to decline as Max hires more workers.

Marginal revenue product diminishes as Max hires more workers because of the principle of diminishing returns that we first studied in Chapter 10. With each additional worker hired, the marginal product of labour falls and so brings in a smaller marginal revenue product. Because Max's Wash 'n' Wax is a perfectly competitive firm, the price of each additional car wash is the same and brings in the same marginal revenue. Alternatively, if Max's has a monopoly, it will have to lower its price to sell more washes. In such a case, the marginal revenue product of labour diminishes even more quickly than in perfectly competitive conditions. Marginal revenue product diminishes because of diminishing marginal product of labour and also because of diminishing

Figure 15.4 Marginal Revenue Product and the Demand for Labour at Max's Wash 'n' Wax

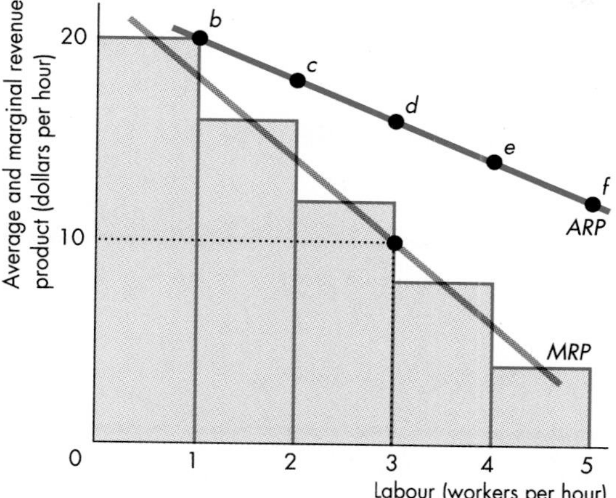

(a) Average and marginal revenue product

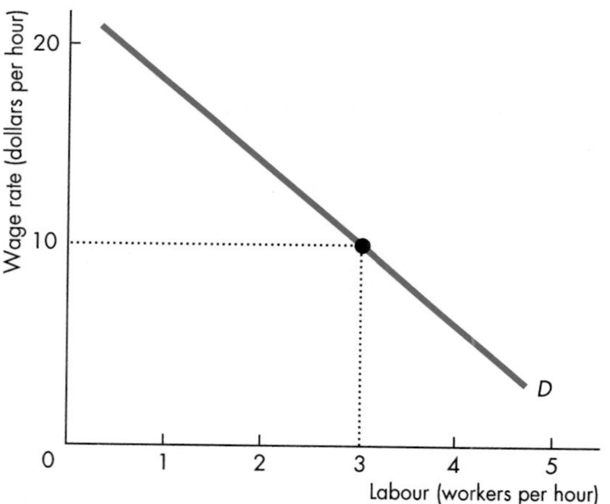

(b) Demand for labour

Part (a) shows the average and marginal revenue product curves for Max's Wash 'n' Wax. Points *b* through *f* on the average revenue product curve correspond to the rows of Table 15.1. The blue bars representing marginal revenue product are also based on the numbers in that table. (Each point is plotted midway between the labour inputs used in its calculation.) Average revenue product and marginal revenue product decline, and the marginal revenue product curve is always below the average revenue product curve.

Part (b) shows Max's demand for labour curve. It is identical to his marginal revenue product curve. Max demands labour up to the point at which the wage rate (the worker's marginal cost) equals marginal revenue product.

marginal revenue. Table 15.2 provides a compact glossary of factor market terms.

We can illustrate average revenue product and marginal revenue product of labour by using the average revenue product and marginal revenue product curves. The **average revenue product curve** shows the average revenue product of a factor at each quantity of that factor hired. The **marginal revenue product curve** shows the marginal revenue product of a factor at each quantity of that factor hired.

Figure 15.4(a) shows the marginal revenue product and average revenue product curves for workers employed by Max. The horizontal axis measures the number of workers per hour that Max hires and the vertical axis measures the marginal and average revenue product of labour. The curve labelled *ARP* is the average revenue product curve and is based on the numbers in Table 15.1. For example, point *d* on the *ARP* curve represents row *d* in the table. Max employs 3 workers, and the average revenue product of labour is $16 a worker. The blue bars show the marginal revenue product of labour as Max employs more workers. These bars correspond to the numbers in Table 15.1. The curve labelled *MRP* is the marginal revenue product curve.

The firm's demand for labour curve is based on its marginal revenue product curve. You can see Max's demand for labour curve (*D*) in Fig. 15.4(b). The horizontal axis measures the number of workers hired, just as in part (a). The vertical axis measures the wage rate in dollars per hour. The demand for labour curve is exactly the same as the firm's marginal revenue product curve. For example, when Max employs 3 workers an hour, his marginal revenue product is $10 an hour, as in Fig. 15.4(a); at a wage rate of $10 an hour, Max hires 3 workers an hour, as in Fig. 15.4(b).

Why is the demand for labour curve identical to the marginal revenue product curve? Because the firm hires the profit-maximizing quantity of labour. If the cost of hiring one more worker is less than the additional total revenue that worker will bring in — the wage rate is less than the marginal revenue product of labour — then it pays the firm to employ one more worker. Conversely, if the cost of hiring one more worker is greater than the additional total revenue that worker will bring in — the wage rate exceeds the marginal revenue product — then it does not pay the firm to employ one more worker. When the cost of the last worker hired equals the revenue brought in by that worker, the firm is making the maximum possible profit. Such a situation occurs when the wage rate equals the marginal revenue product. Thus the quantity of labour demanded by the firm is such that the wage rate equals the marginal revenue product of labour.

R E V I E W

A firm chooses the quantity of labour to hire so that its profit is maximized. The additional total revenue generated by hiring one additional worker is called the marginal revenue product of labour; it is the change in total revenue generated by a one-unit change in labour input. In a competitive industry, the marginal cost of labour is the wage rate. Profit is maximized when the marginal revenue product of labour equals the wage rate. The marginal revenue product of labour curve is the firm's demand for labour curve. The lower the wage rate, the higher is the quantity of labour demanded. ■

Two Conditions for Profit Maximization When we studied firms' output decisions, we discovered that a condition for maximum profit is that marginal revenue equal marginal cost. We've now discovered another condition for maximum profit — that marginal revenue product equal the factor price. How can there be two conditions for a maximum profit? There are two conditions because they are equivalent to each other. That marginal revenue equals marginal cost is the condition that tells us the quantity of goods a firm produces, and that marginal revenue product equals the factor price is the condition that tells us the quantity of a factor that a firm hires to produce its profit-maximizing output. The equivalence of the two conditions is set out in Table 15.3.

Table 15.3 Two Conditions for Maximum Profit

Symbols

Marginal revenue	*MR*
Marginal cost	*MC*
Marginal revenue product	*MRP*
Price of factor	*PF*

Two conditions for maximum profit

1. $MR = MC$
2. $MRP = PF$

Equivalence of conditions

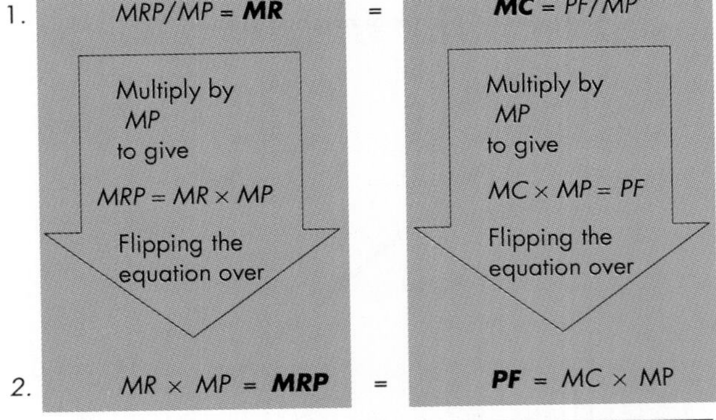

Marginal revenue product (*MR*) equals marginal cost (*MC*), and marginal revenue product (*MRP*) equals the price of the factor (*PF*). The two conditions for maximum profit are equivalent because marginal revenue product (*MRP*) equals marginal revenue (*MR*) multiplied by marginal product (*MP*), and the factor price (*PF*) equals marginal cost (*MC*) multiplied by marginal product (*MP*).

We have just derived the law of demand as it applies to the labour market. Let's now turn to the influences that result in a change in the demand for labour and, therefore, in a shift in the demand for labour curve.

Shifts in the Firm's Demand for Labour Curve The position of the demand for labour curve is influenced by

- The price of the firm's output.
- The prices of other inputs.
- Technology.

The higher the price of a firm's output, the greater is the quantity of labour demanded by the firm, other things being equal. The price of the output affects the demand for labour through its influence on marginal revenue product. A higher price for the firm's output increases marginal revenue, increasing, in turn, the marginal revenue product of labour. A change in the price of a firm's output leads to a shift in the firm's demand for labour curve. If the output price increases, the demand for labour increases.

The other two influences on the demand for labour have their main effects not in the short run but in the long run. The **short-run demand for labour** is the relationship between the wage rate and the quantity of labour demanded when the firm's capital is fixed and labour is the only variable input. The **long-run demand for labour** is the relationship between the wage rate and the quantity of labour demanded when all inputs can be varied. A change in the relative price of an input — such as the relative price of labour in terms of capital — leads to a substitution away from the input whose relative price has increased and towards the input whose relative price has decreased. Thus if the price of using capital decreases relative to that of using labour, the firm substitutes capital for labour, increasing the quantity of capital demanded and decreasing its demand for labour.

Finally, a technological change that affects the marginal product of labour also affects the demand for labour. Again, this effect is felt in the long run, as the firm takes the opportunity to adjust all its inputs and incorporate the new technology into its production process. A technological change that decreases the marginal product of labour results in a decrease in the demand for labour, and one that increases the marginal product of labour results in an increase in the demand for labour. Table 15.4 summarizes the influences on a firm's demand for labour.

As we saw earlier, Fig. 15.2 illustrates the effects of a change in the demand for a factor. If that factor is labour, the figure shows how a change in the demand for labour affects the wage rate and the quantity of labour hired. But we can now say why the demand for labour curve shifts. For example, an increase in the price of the firm's output, an increase in the price of capital, or a technological change that increases the marginal product of labour shifts the demand for labour curve from D_0 to D_1 in Fig. 15.2(a). Conversely, a decrease in the price of the firm's output, a decrease in the price of capital, or a technological change that lowers the marginal product of labour shifts the demand curve for labour from D_0 to D_2 in Fig. 15.2(b).

Table 15.4 A Firm's Demand for Labour

The law of demand

The quantity of labour demanded by a firm

Decreases if	*Increases if*
• The wage rate increases	• The wage rate decreases

Changes in demand

A firm's demand for labour

Decreases if	*Increases if*
• The firm's output price decreases	• The firm's output price increases
• The prices of other inputs decrease	• The prices of other inputs increase
• A technological change decreases the marginal product of labour	• A technological change increases the marginal product of labour

Market Demand

So far, we've studied only an individual firm's demand for labour. Let's now look at the market demand. The market demand for a factor of production is the total demand for that factor by all firms. The market demand curve for a given factor is obtained by adding up the quantities demanded of that factor by each firm at each given factor price. Thus the concept of the market demand for labour curve is exactly like the concept of the market demand curve for a good or service. The market demand curve for a good is obtained by adding together the quantities demanded of that good by all households at each price; the market demand curve for labour is obtained by adding together the quantities of labour demanded by all firms at each wage rate.

Elasticity of Demand for Labour

The elasticity of demand for labour measures the responsiveness of the quantity of labour demanded to a change in the wage rate. We calculate this elasticity in the same way that we calculate a price elasticity: elasticity of demand for labour is the percentage change in the quantity of labour demanded divided by the percentage change in the wage rate. The elasticity of demand for labour depends on the elasticity of demand for the good that the firm is producing and on the properties of the firm's production function. There is, however, a slight difference in the things that affect the elasticity of demand for labour in the short run and in the long run.

Short-Run Elasticity The **short-run elasticity of demand for labour** is the percentage change in the quantity of labour demanded divided by the percentage change in the wage rate when labour is the only variable input. Since the quantity of labour demanded always falls when the wage rate rises, there is no need to attach a negative sign. The elasticity of demand for labour, in positive numbers, tells us the responsiveness of a quantity *fall* to a wage rate *rise.* A higher elasticity means a more responsive demand.

The short-run elasticity of demand for labour depends on three things:

1. **The short-run elasticity of demand for the product** If the demand for the good that labour produces is elastic, a small change in the price of the good creates a large change in the quantity demanded of it. One thing that can change the price of a good is a change in costs, and costs change in the short run if the wage rate changes. For a given wage rate change, the larger the elasticity of demand for the good, the larger is the change in the quantity of the good demanded and, therefore, the larger is the change in the labour input used to produce that good. Other things being equal, the larger the elasticity of demand for the product, the larger is the elasticity of demand for labour.
2. **Labour intensity** The proportion of labour in the production of a good — the labour intensity of the production process — also affects the elasticity of demand for labour. Suppose that the cost of labour is 90 percent of the total cost of producing a good. In such a situation, a 10 percent change in the cost of labour generates a 9 percent change in total cost. But if the cost of labour is only 10 percent of the total cost, a 10 percent change in the cost of labour produces only a 1 percent change in total cost. The larger the percentage change in total cost, the larger is the percentage change in price and, for a given elasticity of demand for the product, the larger is the percentage change in output. The larger the change in output, the larger is the change in labour input. So, the larger the proportion of total cost coming from labour (labour intensity), the more elastic is the demand for labour, other things being equal.
3. **The slope of the marginal product of labour curve** The slope of the marginal product of labour curve depends on the production technology used. In some processes, marginal product diminishes quickly; in others, it remains fairly constant as a firm hires more workers. The steeper the slope of the marginal product curve, the more responsive is the marginal revenue product to a change in labour input. When the revenue brought in by an extra worker diminishes quickly, a firm will not hire many new workers to produce more of its product. Therefore the steeper the marginal product curve, the less elastic is the firm's demand for labour.

Long-Run Elasticity The **long-run elasticity of demand for labour** is the percentage change in the quantity of labour demanded divided by the percentage change in the wage rate when all inputs are varied. Long-run elasticity, like short-run elasticity, depends on the elasticity of demand for the product in the long run rather than in the short run and on *labour intensity.* In addition, the long-run elasticity depends on the *substitutability of capital for labour.* The more easily capital can be substituted for labour in production, the larger is the long-run elasticity of demand for labour. For example, it is fairly easy to substitute robots for assembly line workers in car factories and automatic picking machines for labour in vineyards and orchards. At the other extreme, it is difficult (though not impossible) to substitute robots for newspaper reporters, bank loan officers, and stockbrokers. The more readily capital can be substituted for labour, the more elastic is the firm's demand for labour.

R E V I E W

The short-run elasticity of demand for labour depends on three factors:

- The short-run elasticity of demand for the product
- The labour intensity of the production process
- The slope of the marginal product of labour curve

The long-run elasticity of demand for labour also depends on three factors:

- The long-run elasticity of demand for the product
- The labour intensity of the production process
- The substitutability of capital for labour in the production process ■

Supply of Factors

The supply of factors is determined by the decisions of households. They allocate the factors of production that they own to their most rewarding uses. The quantity supplied of any factor of production depends on its price. Usually, the higher the price of a factor of production, the larger is the quantity supplied. An important possible exception to this general law of supply concerns the supply of labour. It arises from the fact that labour is the single most important factor of production and the source of the largest portion of household income.

Let's examine household factor supply decisions, beginning with the supply of labour.

Supply of Labour

A household chooses how much labour to supply as part of its time allocation decision. Households allocate their time between two broad activities:

- Market activity
- Nonmarket activity

Market activity is the same thing as supplying labour. **Nonmarket activity** consists of leisure and nonmarket production activities including education and training. Market activities bring the household an immediate return in the form of income. Nonmarket activities generate a return in the form of goods and services produced in the home, in the form of a higher future income, or in the form of leisure, which is valued for its own sake and which economists classify as a good.

In deciding how to allocate its time between market activity and nonmarket activity, a household weighs the returns that it can get from the different activities. Here we are interested in the effects of the wage rate on the household's allocation of its time and on how much labour it supplies.

Wages and Quantity of Labour Supplied To induce a household to supply labour, it must be offered a high enough wage rate. Households value nonmarket activities either because they use the time in some productive activity or because they attach value to leisure. For a household to find it worthwhile to supply labour, it has to be offered a wage rate that is at least equal to the value it places on the last hour it spends in nonmarket activities. This wage rate — the lowest one for which a household will supply labour to the market — is called its **reservation wage**. At wage rates below the reservation wage, the household supplies no labour. Once the wage rate reaches the reservation wage, the household begins to supply labour. As the wage rate rises above the reservation wage, the household varies the quantity of labour that it supplies. But a higher wage rate has two offsetting effects on the quantity of labour supplied — a *substitution effect* and an *income effect.*

1. Substitution Effect Other things being equal, the higher the wage rate, the more people will economize on their nonmarket activities and increase the time they spend working. As the wage rate rises, the household will discontinue any nonmarket activity that yields a return that is less than the wage rate and will switch to market activity. For example, a household may use some of its time to cook meals and do laundry — nonmarket activities — that can, alternatively, be bought for $10 an hour. If the wage rate available to the household is less than $10 an hour, the household will cook and wash for itself. If the household's wage rate rises above $10 an hour, the household may find it worthwhile to work more hours and use part of its income to buy laundry services and to eat out. The higher wage rate induces a switch of time from nonmarket activity to market activity.

2. Income Effect The higher the household's wage rate, the higher is its income. A higher income, other things being equal, induces a rise in demand for most goods. Leisure, a component of nonmarket activity, is one of those goods. Since an increase in income creates an increase in the demand for leisure, it also creates a decrease in the amount of time allocated to market activities and, therefore, a fall in the quantity of labour supplied.

Backward-Bending Household Supply of Labour Curve

For the labour market, the substitution effect and the income effect work in opposite directions. The higher the wage rate, the higher is the quantity of labour supplied via the substitution effect, but the lower is the quantity of labour supplied via the income effect. At low wage rates, the substitution effect is larger than the income effect; as the wage rate rises, the household supplies more labour. But as the wage rate continues to rise, there comes a point at which the substitution effect and the income effect just offset each other. At that point, a change in the wage rate has no effect on the quantity of labour supplied. If the wage rate continues to rise, the income effect

Figure 15.5 The Supply of Labour

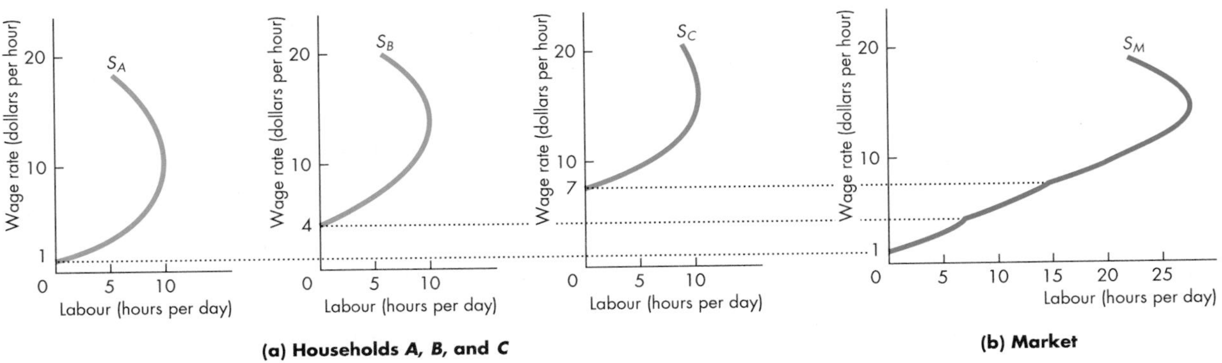

Part (a) shows the labour supply curves of three households (S_A, S_B, and S_C). Each household has a reservation wage below which it will supply no labour. As the wage rises above the reservation wage, the quantity of labour supplied rises to a maximum. If the wage continues to rise, the quantity of labour supplied begins to decline. Each household's supply curve eventually bends backward. When the quantity of labour supplied increases as the wage increases, the substitution effect dominates the income effect. When the quantity of labour supplied begins to fall as the wage rate increases, the income effect (which leads people to demand more leisure) dominates the substitution effect.

Part (b) shows that by adding together the quantities of labour supplied by the individual households at each wage rate, we derive the market supply curve of labour (S_M). The market supply curve also eventually bends backward. In the real world, this would happen at higher wage rates than those currently experienced. The upward-sloping part of the labour supply curve, before it bends backward, is the part along which the market operates.

begins to dominate the substitution effect and the quantity of labour supplied declines. Thus the household's supply of labour curve does not slope upward throughout its entire length; rather, at some wage rate, it begins to bend back on itself. It is called a backward-bending supply curve.

Three individual household labour supply curves are shown in Fig. 15.5(a). Each household has a different reservation wage. Household *A* has a reservation wage of $1 an hour, household *B* of $4 an hour, and household *C* of $7 an hour. Each household's labour supply curve is backward bending.

Market Supply The quantity of labour supplied to the entire market is the aggregate quantity supplied by all households. The market supply of labour curve is the sum of the supply curves of all the individual households. Figure 15.5(b) shows the market supply curve (S_M) derived from the supply curves of the three households (S_A, S_B, and S_C) in Fig. 15.5(a). At wage rates of less than $1 an hour, the three households do laundry and cook, but they do not supply any market labour. Household *A*, the one most eager to supply market labour, has a reservation wage of $1 an hour; as the wage rate rises to $4 an hour, it increases the quantity of labour that it supplies. The reservation wage of household *B* is $4 an hour, so as the wage rate rises above $4 an hour, the quantity of labour supplied in the market is the sum of the labour supplied by households *A* and *B*. When the wage rate reaches $7 an hour, household *C* begins to supply some labour to the market. At wage rates above $7 an hour, the quantity supplied in the market is equal to the sum of the quantities supplied by the three households.

Notice that the market supply curve (S_M), like the individual household supply curves, eventually bends backward. But the market supply curve has a long upward-sloping section. The reason it slopes up for such a long stretch is that the reservation wages of individual households are not equal; at higher wage rates, additional households are able to earn a wage that equals or exceeds their reservation wage and so begin to supply labour.

Though the market supply curve eventually bends backward, no real-world economy has reached a wage rate so high that it operates on the backward-bending portion of its labour supply curves. Many individual households are on the backward-bending portion of their own labour supply curves. Thus as wage rates rise, some people work fewer hours. But higher wage rates induce both those workers who are on the upward-sloping parts of their labour supply curves to supply more hours and additional workers to enter the work force. The response of these workers to higher wage rates dominates that of those whose work hours decline as wage rates rise. Therefore for the economy as a whole, the labour supply curve slopes upward. For this reason, we will restrict our attention to the upward-sloping part of the labour supply curve in Fig. 15.5.

Supply to Individual Firms We've studied the labour supply decisions of individual households and seen how those decisions add up to the market supply. But how is the supply of labour to each individual firm determined? The answer to this question depends on the degree of competitiveness in the labour market.

In a perfectly competitive labour market, each firm faces a perfectly elastic supply of labour curve. This situation arises because the individual firm is such a small part of the total labour market that it has no influence on the wage rate.

Some labour markets are noncompetitive in the sense that firms can and do influence the price of the labour that they hire. In these cases, firms face an upward-sloping supply of labour curve. The more labour they wish to employ, the higher is the wage rate they have to offer. We will examine how this type of labour market operates in Chapter 16. Here, we deal only with the case of perfectly competitive factor markets.

R E V I E W

As part of its time allocation decision, a household chooses the quantity of labour to supply. If the wage rate is below the household's reservation wage, the household supplies no labour and uses all its time for nonmarket activities. At wage rates above the household's reservation wage, the household supplies some labour. A rising wage has two opposite effects on the quantity of labour that the household supplies: a substitution effect and an income effect. Other things being equal, the higher wage rate induces the household to economize on leisure and other nonmarket time and to work more hours — the substitution effect. The higher wage rate also raises the household's income, which increases its demand for most goods including leisure. More time taken for leisure means less labour is supplied. That is, other things being equal, the higher wage rate induces the household to spend more time on leisure and to work fewer hours — the income effect.

The market supply of labour is the aggregate quantity of labour supplied by all households. The market supply curve, like a household's supply curve, bends backward above a certain wage rate. Actual economies operate on the upward-sloping part of the market supply of labour curve. The labour supply curve faced by each individual firm depends on the degree of competitiveness of the labour market. In a perfectly competitive labour market, each firm faces a perfectly elastic supply curve. ■

Next, let's examine the supply of capital.

Supply of Capital

Households supply capital to firms by consuming less than their income — that is, they save. Thus the scale on which a household supplies capital depends on how much of its income it saves.

The most important factors determining a household's saving are:

- Its current income in relation to its expected future income
- The interest rate

Current and Future Income A household with a current income that is low compared with its expected future income saves little and may even have negative saving — that is, it goes into debt. A household with a current income that is high compared with its expected future income saves a great deal in the present in order to be able to consume more in the future. The main factor influencing whether current income is high or low compared with expected future income is the household's stage in its life cycle. The current income of young households is typically low compared with their expected future income; in contrast, older households have a high current income relative to their expected future income. The consequence of this pattern over the life cycle is that young people have negative saving and older people have positive saving. Thus the young incur debts (such as mortgages and consumer credit) to acquire durable goods and to consume more than their income, while older people save and accumulate assets (often in the form of pension and life insurance arrangements) to provide for their retirement years.

The Interest Rate and Capital Supply A household's supply of capital is the stock of capital that it has accumulated as a result of its past saving. The household's supply curve of capital shows the relationship between the quantity of capital supplied and the interest rate. Other things being equal, a higher interest rate encourages people to economize on current consumption in order to take advantage of the higher return available from saving. Thus the higher the interest rate, the greater is the quantity of capital supplied.

The market, or aggregate, quantity of capital supplied is the sum of the supplies of all the individual households. The market supply of capital curve shows how the aggregate quantity of capital supplied varies as the interest rate varies. The market supply of capital is highly elastic. Such a market supply curve is the curve labelled *LS* in Fig. 15.6. At interest rates above *R*, enough households are willing to save so that the total stock of capital supplied increases. At interest rates below *R*, a sufficient number of households plan to consume more than their income, and the total quantity of saving decreases so that the total stock of capital supplied decreases.

Figure 15.6 The Short-Run and Long-Run Supply of Capital

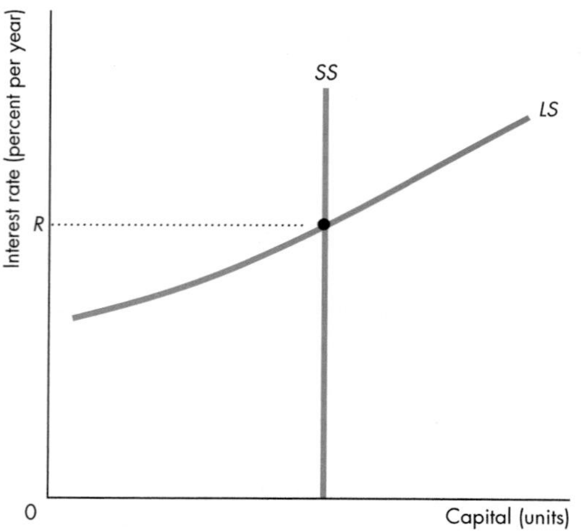

The long-run supply of capital (*LS*) is highly elastic. If the interest rate is above *R*, households increase their saving and increase the total amount of capital supplied. If the interest rate is below *R*, households decrease their saving and reduce the amount of capital supplied. The short-run supply of capital (*SS*) is highly inelastic (perfectly inelastic in the figure). For the economy as a whole and for individual firms in the short run, once capital is put in place, it is difficult to vary its quantity easily and quickly. Thus no matter what the interest rate, there is a given amount of capital supplied at a given point in time.

Supply to Individual Firms When studying the supply of capital to an individual firm, it is important to distinguish between the short-run and long-run supply of capital. Recall the distinction between the short run and the long run. The short run is a period during which a firm can vary its labour input but not its capital input. Thus in the short run, the firm's capital input is fixed. The long run is a period during which a firm can vary all its inputs. Thus in the long run, the firm can vary its capital as well as its labour inputs. In the long run, a firm operating in a competitive capital market can obtain any amount of capital at the going market interest rate. It faces a perfectly elastic supply of capital. In the short run, however, the firm has acquired a specific set of assets. For example, an auto producer has acquired a production assembly line; a laundromat operator has acquired a number of washing machines and driers; the campus print shop has acquired a number of photocopying and other printing machines. In the short run, the supply of capital facing an individual firm can be highly inelastic. Specific pieces of machinery and equipment have been bought and bolted in place. They cannot be quickly disposed of or added to. In the extreme case, the short-run supply of capital is perfectly inelastic. Such a case is illustrated as the vertical line (*SS*) in Fig. 15.6.

The fact that the short-run supply of capital is inelastic and the long-run supply of capital is elastic has important implications for the returns obtained from different types of capital. We'll explore those implications later in this chapter when we study equilibrium in the capital market. But before that, let's complete our analysis of the supply of factors of production by examining the supply of land.

Supply of Land

Land is the surface area of the earth and the stock of natural resources that it contains. Here we'll focus on land in its more common sense — blocks of land. We'll study natural resources in Chapter 17.

Figure 15.7 The Supply of Land

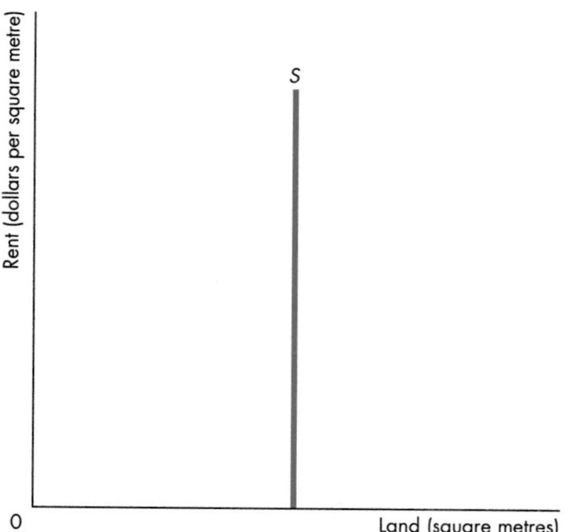

The supply of a given piece of land is perfectly inelastic. No matter what the rent, no more land than exists can be supplied.

The aggregate quantity of land supplied is fixed and cannot be changed by individual decisions. Individual households can vary the amount of land they own, but whatever land is acquired by one household is sold by another so the aggregate quantity supplied of land of a particular type and in a particular location is fixed, regardless of the decisions of any individual household. This fact means that the supply of each particular piece of land is perfectly inelastic. Figure 15.7 illustrates such a supply. Regardless of the rent available, the quantity of land supplied in Toronto's Yorkville, the city's trendiest business district, is a fixed number of square metres. Nothing can increase or decrease the amount of land that is there.

Expensive land can be, and is, used more intensively than inexpensive land — for example, the construction of highrise buildings. For more intensive use, however, land has to be combined with another factor of production — capital. But increasing the amount of capital per block of land does nothing to change the supply of land itself.

Although the supply of each type of land is fixed and its supply is inelastic, each individual firm, operating in competitive land markets, faces an elastic supply of land. That is, each firm can acquire the land that it demands at the going rent, as determined in the marketplace. Thus provided land markets are highly competitive, firms are price takers in these markets, just as they are in the markets for other factors of production.

R E V I E W

The supply of capital is determined by households' saving decisions. Other things being equal, the higher the interest rate, the greater is the amount of capital supplied. The supply of capital to individual firms is highly inelastic in the short run but elastic in the long run.

Individual households can vary the amount of land that they supply, but the aggregate supply of land is determined by the fact that there is a fixed quantity of it available. Thus the supply of each particular piece of land is perfectly inelastic. However, in a competitive land market, each firm faces an elastic supply of land at the going rent. ■

Let's now see how factor prices and quantities are determined.

Competitive Equilibrium

The price of a factor of production and the quantity of it traded are determined by the interaction of the demand for the factor and its supply. We'll illustrate competitive equilibrium by looking at the markets for labour, capital, and land and by considering two examples of each.

Labour Market Equilibrium

Figure 15.8 shows two labour markets. The one in part (a) is the labour market for network news anchors. Such people have a very high marginal revenue product, which is reflected in the demand curve for their services (D_N). The supply of individuals with the required talents for this kind of job is low, as reflected in the supply curve (S_N). Equilibrium occurs at a high hourly wage rate ($500 in this example) and a low quantity traded (Q_N).

Figure 15.8(b) shows the market for fast-food servers. Although people value the output of fast-food servers, the marginal revenue product of these servers is low, a fact reflected in the demand curve (D_S). There are many households, typically those

Figure 15.8 Labour Market Equilibrium

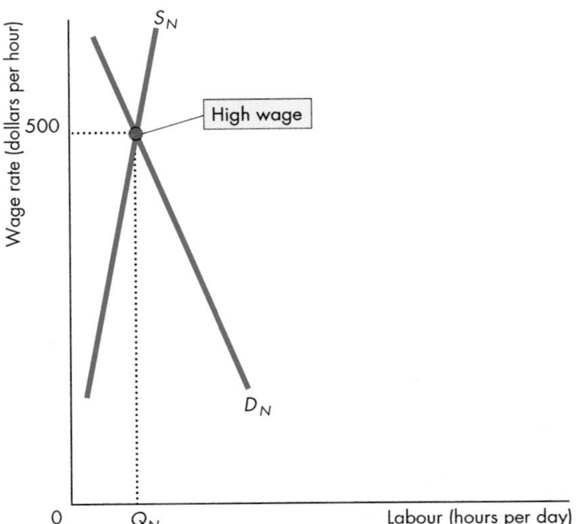

(a) News anchors

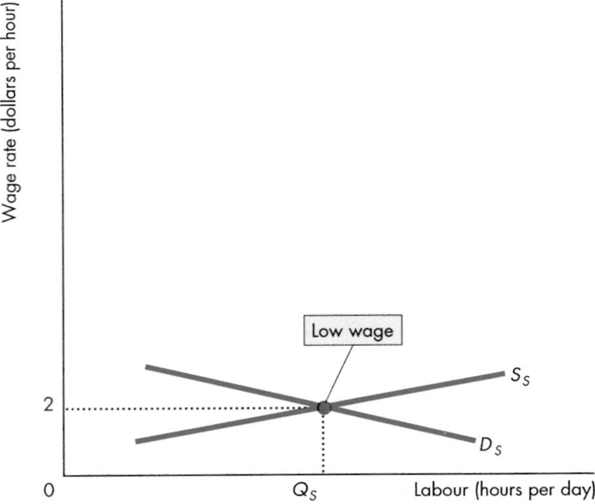

(b) Fast-food servers

News anchors (part a) have a high marginal revenue product, which is reflected in the high demand for their services — curve D_N. The number of people with the talents required for this job is few and the supply curve is S_N. Equilibrium occurs at a high hourly wage rate of $500 and a low quantity traded, Q_N. The marginal revenue product of fast-food servers (part b) is low, so the demand curve is D_S. There is a huge supply of fast-food servers, and the supply curve is S_S. Equilibrium occurs in this market at a low wage rate of $2 per hour and a high quantity traded, Q_S.

with high school students, willing to supply these services, as reflected in the supply curve (S_S). This market achieves an equilibrium at a low wage rate ($2 an hour in this example) and at a relatively high quantity traded (Q_S).

If there is an increase in the demand for news anchors, D_N in Fig. 15.8(a) shifts to the right, increasing their wage rate and increasing the quantity traded. The higher wage rate will induce more households to offer their services in this activity. If there is an increase in demand for food servers, D_S in Fig. 15.8(b) shifts to the right, increasing their wage rate and increasing the quantity traded. Again, a higher wage rate will induce an increase in the quantity supplied. Movements in wage rates occur to achieve a balance between the quantities demanded and supplied in each individual labour market. Changes in demand result in changes in the wage rate that achieve a reallocation of the labour force.

Capital Market Equilibrium

Figure 15.9 shows capital market equilibrium. Part (a) illustrates that part of the capital market in the steel industry — the market for steel mills. The long-run supply of capital to the steel industry is shown as the perfectly elastic supply curve *LS*. But the actual quantity of steel mills in place is Q_1, and the short-run supply curve is SS_1. The demand curve for steel mills, determined by their marginal revenue product, is D_1. The interest rate earned by the owners of steel mills — the shareholders of Stelco and similar firms — is R_1.

Figure 15.9(b) shows the capital market in the computer industry. Again, the long-run supply curve is *LS*, the same curve as in the steel industry; that is, in the long run, capital is supplied to each of these industries at the same interest rate — *R*. But the amount of computer-producing capital in place is Q_3, and the short-run supply curve is SS_3. The interest rate earned by the owners of computer production equipment — the shareholders of IBM and similar firms — is R_2.

You can see that the interest rate paid to owners of capital in the steel industry is lower than that in the computer industry. This inequality of interest rates on capital sets up an interesting dynamic adjustment process that gradually lowers the stock of capital in the steel industry and increases the stock of capital in the computer industry. With a low interest rate on capital in the steel industry and a high interest rate on capital in the computer industry, it pays

Figure 15.9 Capital Market Equilibrium

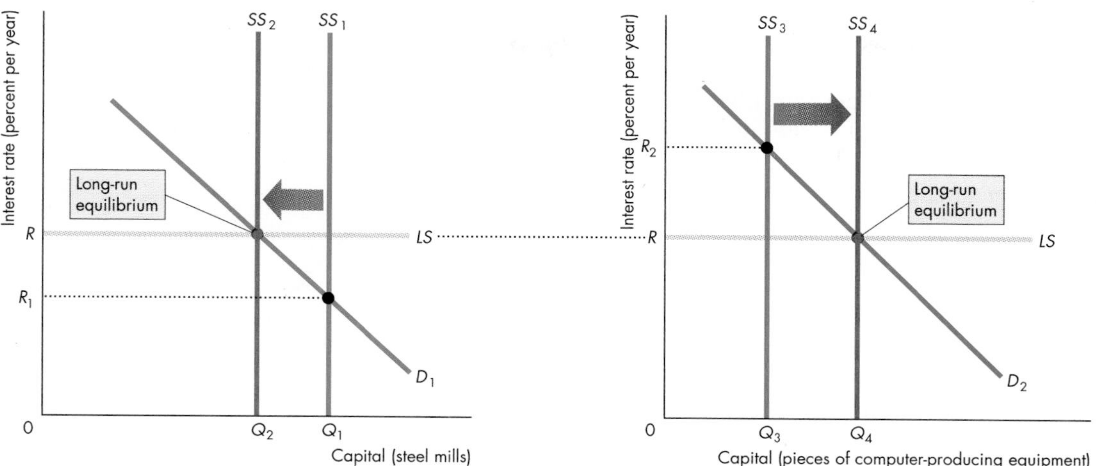

(a) Steel industry

(b) Computer industry

The long-run supply curve of capital (*LS*) in the steel industry (part a) and the computer industry (part b) is perfectly elastic. The number of steel mills in place is fixed at Q_1, so the short-run supply curve in the steel industry is SS_1. The demand curve for steel mills is D_1. The interest rate on capital invested in the steel industry is R_1. The amount of computer-producing equipment in place is fixed at Q_3, so the short-run supply curve in the computer industry is SS_3. The demand curve for computer-producing equipment is D_2. The interest rate in the computer industry is R_2. With the higher interest rate in the computer industry, capital leaves the steel industry and goes into the computer industry. The short-run supply curves shift. In the steel industry, it shifts to the left to SS_2, and the interest rate rises. In the computer industry it shifts to the right to SS_4, and the interest rate falls. In long-run equilibrium, interest rates are the same in both industries.

people to take their investments out of the steel industry and put them into the computer industry. But physical plants and equipment have been put in place in the steel industry, and they cannot be readily transformed into computer-making equipment. An individual steel producer could sell off its unwanted capital or operate it until it has worn out. Even if it does sell off the equipment, the firm that buys it will be willing to pay only a low price for it and that firm also will not replace the equipment when it finally wears out. Whether the equipment is operated by its present owner or a new owner that buys it for a low price, the equipment continues to be operated. But it gradually depreciates and is not replaced, so the capital stock in the steel industry declines. The short-run supply curve shifts to the left, to SS_2. Conversely, as capital is freed up and additional saving is made, it is directed towards the computer industry, so its short-run supply curve shifts to the right, to SS_4. During this process, interest rates adjust in the two industries, increasing in the steel industry and decreasing in the computer industry. Eventually, in long-run equilibrium, the interest rate on capital in the two industries will have equalized at *R*.

The Stock Market In the story of a contracting steel industry and expanding computer industry that we have just worked through, you may be wondering why people are willing to own shares in the steel industry when the interest rate being earned in that industry is less than what can be earned in the computer industry. The answer is that the stock market will react by lowering the value of steel shares relative to computer shares. The fall in the price of steel shares raises the expected rate of interest that can be earned on steel shares to equal that on computer shares. That is, during the period in which the steel industry is declining and its capital stock is decreasing, the stock market instantly lowers the value of the steel industry to equalize the expected returns on shares in that industry and in all other industries.

Next, let's see how rents are determined in the market for land.

Land Market Equilibrium

Equilibrium in the land market occurs at rents that allocate the fixed amounts of land available to their highest value uses. Figure 15.10 illustrates two land markets. Part (a) shows the market for land in Toronto's Yorkville. Its marginal revenue product gives rise to the demand curve D_Y. There are a fixed number of square metres of land (Q_Y) so the supply is inelastic, as shown by S_Y. Equilibrium occurs at an annual rent of $1,000 per square metre.

Figure 15.10(b) illustrates the market for farmland in Manitoba. Here, the marginal revenue product produces the demand curve D_M. There is a vast amount of land available but again only a fixed quantity — in this case, Q_M. Thus the supply curve lies a long way to the right, but it is vertical — perfectly inelastic — at S_M. Here the equilibrium rent occurs at an annual rent of $500 per hectare.

Now that we've studied the markets for the three factors of production and seen how wages, interest, and rent are determined, we can turn to our final task in this chapter — defining and distinguishing between economic rent and transfer earnings.

Economic Rent and Transfer Earnings

The total income of a factor of production is made up of its economic rent and its transfer earnings. **Economic rent** is an income received by the owner of a factor over and above the amount required to induce that owner to offer the factor for use. The income required to induce the supply of a factor of production is called **transfer earnings**. It is important to distinguish between *economic rent* and *rent*. Rent is the price paid to the owner of the factor of production, land. Economic rent is a component of the income received by every factor of production.

The concepts of economic rent and transfer earnings are illustrated in Fig. 15.11, which shows the market for a factor of production — it could be *any* factor of production — labour, capital, or land. The demand curve for the factor of production is D and its supply curve is S. The factor price is P_F and the quantity traded Q_F. The income of the factor is the sum of the yellow and green areas. The yellow area below the supply curve measures transfer earnings, and the green area below the factor price but above the supply curve measures economic rent.

Figure 15.10 Land Market Equilibrium

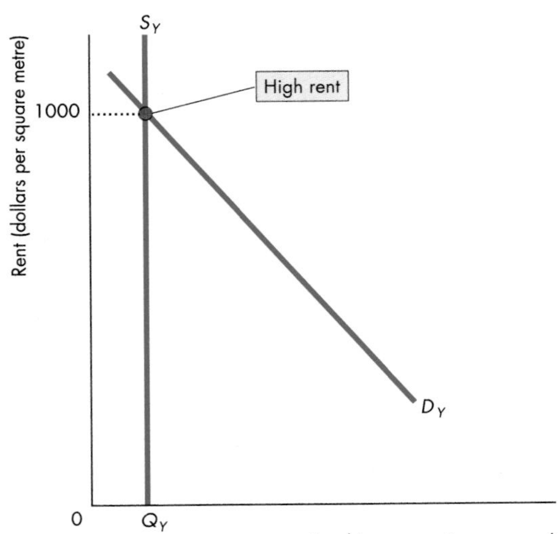

(a) Yorkville

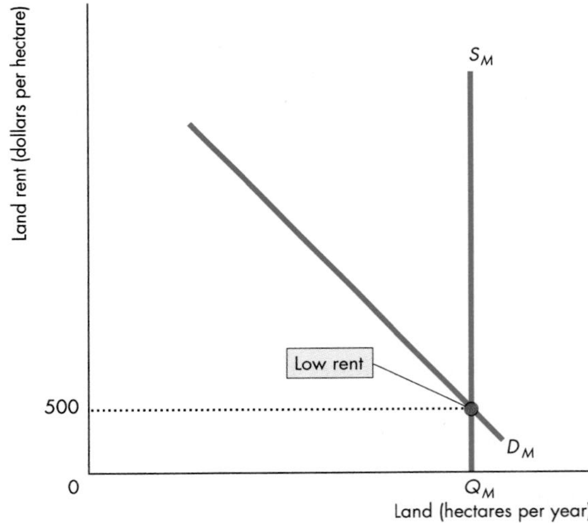

(b) Manitoba farmland

The marginal revenue product of land in Toronto's Yorkville district gives rise to the demand curve D_Y (part a). The quantity of land in Yorkville is fixed at Q_Y, so the supply curve is S_Y. Equilibrium occurs at an annual rent of $1,000 per square metre. The marginal revenue product of farmland in Manitoba (part b) gives rise to a demand curve D_M. The quantity of farmland in Manitoba is fixed at Q_M and the supply curve is S_M. Equilibrium occurs at an annual rent of $500 per hectare.

To see why the area above the supply curve measures economic rent, recall that a supply curve can be interpreted in two different ways. The standard interpretation is that it indicates the quantity supplied at a given price. The alternative interpretation is that it shows the minimum price at which a given quantity is willingly supplied. If suppliers receive only the minimum amount required to induce them to supply each unit of the factor of production, they will be paid a different price for each unit; those prices will trace the supply curve and the income received will be entirely transfer earnings — the yellow area in Fig. 15.11.

The concept of economic rent is similar to the concept of consumer surplus that you studied in Chapter 7. Consumer surplus, recall, is the difference between the price the household pays for a good and the maximum price it would be willing to pay, as indicated by the demand curve. In a parallel sense, economic rent is the difference between the factor price a household actually receives and the minimum factor price at which it would be willing to supply a given amount of a factor of production.

Figure 15.11 Economic Rent and Transfer Earnings

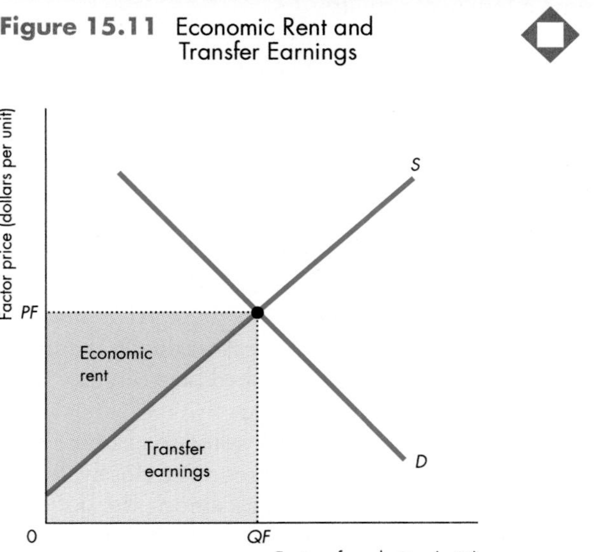

The total income of a factor of production is made up of its economic rent and its transfer earnings. Transfer earnings are measured by the yellow area under the supply curve, and economic rent is the green area above the supply curve and below the factor price.

The portion of the income of a factor of production that consists of economic rent depends on the elasticity of its supply. When a factor's supply is inelastic, its entire income is economic rent. When its supply is perfectly elastic, none of its income is economic rent. In general, when the supply curve is neither perfectly elastic nor perfectly inelastic (like that illustrated in Fig. 15.11), some part of the factor income is economic rent and the other part is transfer earnings.

Figure 15.12 illustrates the three possibilities. Part (a) shows the market for a particular parcel of land in Vancouver. The land is fixed in size at *L* square metres. Therefore the supply curve of the land is vertical — perfectly inelastic. No matter what the rent on the land is, there is no way of increasing the quantity that can be supplied.

The demand for that block of land is determined by its marginal revenue product, which, in turn, depends on the uses to which the land can be put. In a central business district of Vancouver, the marginal revenue product is high because a large number of people are concentrated in that area, making it a prime place for conducting valuable business. Suppose that the marginal revenue product of this block of land is shown by the demand curve in Fig. 15.12(a). Then it commands a rent of *R*. The entire income accruing to the owner of the land is the green area in the figure. This income is *economic rent.* The rent charged for this piece of land depends entirely on its marginal revenue product — on the demand curve. If the demand curve shifts to the right, the rent rises. If the demand curve shifts to the left, the rent falls. The quantity of land supplied remains constant at *L*.

Our conclusion about how the rent on a block of land is determined answers one of the questions posed at the beginning of this chapter: is coffee expensive in Vancouver because rents are high or are rents high because people are willing to pay a high price for coffee in Vancouver? We've seen that the rent on land is determined entirely by the demand for it, and that the demand, in turn, is determined by marginal revenue product. Land has a high marginal revenue product only if people are willing to pay a high price to use it. Of course, restaurateurs feel that they have to charge a high price for coffee in downtown Vancouver because of the high rent they pay there. But the rent wouldn't be high if they (and other potential users) did not have a high marginal revenue product "attached" to that land, making them willing to pay those high rents.

Figure 15.12 Economic Rent and Supply Elasticity

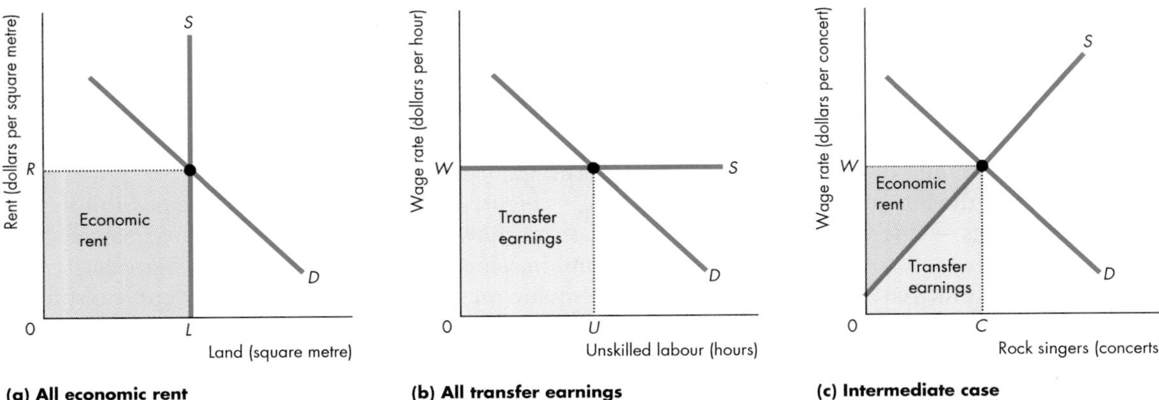

When the supply of a factor is perfectly inelastic (the supply curve is vertical) as in part (a), the entire factor income is economic rent. When the supply of the factor of production is perfectly elastic, as in part (b), the factor's entire income is transfer earnings. When a factor supply curve slopes upward, as in part (c), part of the factor income is economic rent and part is transfer earnings.

Figure 15.12(b) shows the market for a factor of production that is in perfectly elastic supply — say, unskilled labour in a poor country, such as Bangladesh, where large numbers of people flock to the cities and are available for work at the going wage rate (in this case, *W*). In such a situation, the supply of labour is almost perfectly elastic. The entire income earned by these workers is transfer earnings. They receive no economic rent.

Figure 15.12(c) shows the market for rock singers. To induce a rock singer to sing at a larger number of concerts, producers have to offer a higher income; thus the rock singer's supply curve is upward-sloping. The demand curve — measuring the marginal revenue product of the rock singer — is that labelled *D* in the figure. Equilibrium occurs where the rock singer receives a wage of *W* and sings in *C* concerts. The green area above the rock singer's supply curve is economic rent and the yellow area below the supply curve is the rock singer's transfer earnings. If the rock singer is not offered at least the amount of the transfer earnings, he or she will withdraw from the rock concert market and perform some alternative activity.

■ We've now studied the market for the three factors of production — labour, capital, and land — and we've seen how the returns to these factors of production — wages, interest, and rent — are determined. We've seen the crucial role that a factor's marginal revenue product plays in determining the demand for it. We've seen how the interaction of demand and supply determines factor prices and factor incomes. We've also seen how changes in these prices and incomes come about from changes in demand and supply. Finally, we've distinguished between economic rent and transfer earnings.

In the next chapter, we're going to examine some details of the labour market more closely, explaining differences in wage rates among the skilled and the unskilled, males and females, and racial and ethnic minorities.

SUMMARY

Factor Prices and Incomes

The factors of production — labour, capital, and land — earn a return — wages, interest, and rent. Labour is the most important source of income. Factor prices are determined by the demand for and supply of factors of production. Incomes are determined by the prices of factors of production and the quantities traded. An increase in the demand for a factor of production increases the factor's price and income; a decrease in the demand decreases its price and income. An increase in supply increases the quantity traded of a factor of production but decreases its price. A decrease in supply decreases the quantity traded but increases its price. Whether an increase in supply leads to an increase or a decrease in the income of a factor of production depends on the elasticity of demand of the factor. If the elasticity of demand is greater than 1, an increase in supply leads to an increase in the factor's income. If the elasticity of demand for a factor is less than 1, an increase in supply leads to a decrease in the factor's income. (pp. 381-384)

Demand for Factors

A firm's demand for a factor stems from its desire to maximize profit. The extra revenue generated by hiring one more unit of a factor is called the marginal revenue product of the factor. A firm's demand for a factor is derived from that factor's marginal revenue product. A firm demands an input up to the point at which the marginal revenue product of the factor equals the factor's price.

A firm's labour input is variable in both the short run and the long run. The firm's capital input can be varied only in the long run. The elasticity of the demand for labour in the short run depends on the short-run elasticity of demand for the firm's product, on the labour intensity of the production process, and on the slope of the marginal product of labour curve. The long-run elasticity of a firm's demand for labour depends on the long-run elasticity of demand for the product, on the labour intensity of the production process, and on the ease with which capital can be substituted for labour.

The market demand for labour is the sum of the demands by each individual firm. (pp. 384-390)

Supply of Factors

The supply of factors is determined by households' decisions on the allocation of their time and the division of their income between consumption and saving. In choosing how much time to allocate to market activities, each household compares the wage rate it can earn with the value of its time in nonmarket activities. The household will supply no market labour at wage rates below its reservation wage. At wage rates above the household's reservation wage, the quantity of labour supplied rises as long as the substitution effect of the higher wage rate is larger than the income effect. As the wage rate continues to rise, the income effect, which leads to more time taken for leisure, becomes larger than the substitution effect, and the quantity of labour supplied by the household falls.

The market supply curve of labour is the sum of the supply curves of all households. Like the household's labour supply curve, the market supply of labour curve eventually bends backward. However, the response to higher wage rates of those on the upward-sloping part of the labour supply curve dominates the response of those on the backward-bending part, so the market supply curve slopes upward over the range of wage rates that we experience.

Households supply capital by saving. Saving increases as the interest rate increases. The supply of capital to an individual firm is highly inelastic in the short run but highly elastic in the long run.

The supply of land is fixed and independent of its rent. (pp. 391-395)

Competitive Equilibrium

In a competitive factor market, the factor price and quantity traded are determined at the point of intersection of the demand and supply curves. High factor prices occur for factors of production that have a high marginal revenue product and a low supply. Low factor prices occur for factors of production with a low marginal revenue product and a high supply. (pp. 395-398)

Economic Rent and Transfer Earnings

Economic rent is that part of the income received by a factor owner over and above the amount needed to induce that owner to supply the factor for use. The rest of a factor's income is transfer earnings. When the supply of a factor is perfectly inelastic, its entire income is made up of economic rent. Factors that have a perfectly elastic supply receive only transfer earnings. In general, the supply curve of a factor is upward sloping; part of its income (the part below the supply curve) is transfer earnings, and part (the part above the supply curve but below the factor price) is economic rent. (pp. 398-400)

KEY ELEMENTS

Key Terms

Key Figures and Tables 

REVIEW QUESTIONS

1 Explain what happens to the price of a factor of production and its income if the following occurs:
   a) Demand for the factor increases
   b) Supply of a factor increases
   c) Demand for the factor decreases
   d) Supply of the factor decreases

2 Explain why the effect of a change in supply of a factor on its income depends on the elasticity of demand for that factor.

3 Define marginal revenue product, and distinguish between marginal revenue product and marginal revenue.

4 Why does marginal revenue product decline as the quantity of a factor employed increases?

5 What is the relationship between the demand curve for a factor of production and its marginal revenue product curve? Why?

6 Show that the condition for maximum profit in the product market — marginal cost equals marginal revenue — is equivalent to the condition for maximum profit in the factor market — marginal revenue product equals the marginal cost of the factor (equals factor price in a competitive factor market).

7 Review the main influences on the demand for a factor of production — the influences that shift its demand curve.

8 What determines the short-run and the long-run elasticity of demand for labour?

9 What determines the supply of labour?

10 Why might the supply of labour curve bend backward at a high enough wage rate?

11 What determines the supply of capital?

12 Define economic rent and transfer earnings, and distinguish between these two components of income.

13 Suppose that a factor of production is in perfectly inelastic supply. If the marginal revenue product of the factor decreases, what happens to its price, the quantity traded, its income, its transfer earnings, and its rent?

PROBLEMS

1 Wendy owns an apple orchard and she employs students to pick the apples. In an hour they can pick the following amounts:

Number of students	Quantity of apples (kilograms)
1	20
2	50
3	90
4	120
5	145
6	165
7	180
8	190

a) Draw the average and marginal product curves of these students.

b) If Wendy can sell her apples for 50 cents a kilogram, draw the average and marginal revenue product curves.

c) Draw Wendy's demand for labour curve.

d) If all apple growers in Wendy's neighbourhood pay their pickers $7.50 an hour, how many students will Wendy hire?

2 The price of apples falls to 33.33 cents a kilogram, and apple pickers' wages remain at $7.50 an hour.

a) What happens to Wendy's average and marginal product curves?

b) What happens to her average and marginal revenue product curves?

c) What happens to her demand for labour curve?

d) What happens to the number of students that she hires?

3 Apple pickers' wages increase to $10 an hour, but the price of apples remains at 50 cents a kilogram.

a) What happens to the average and marginal revenue product curves?

b) What happens to Wendy's demand curve?

c) How many pickers does Wendy hire?

4 Using the information provided in problem 1, calculate Wendy's marginal revenue, marginal cost, marginal revenue product, and marginal cost of labour. Show that when Wendy is making maximum profit, marginal cost equals marginal revenue and marginal revenue product equals the marginal cost of labour.

5 You are given the following information about the labour market in an isolated town in northern Quebec. Everyone works for logging companies, but there are many logging companies in the area. The market for logging workers is perfectly competitive. The local labour supply is given as follows:

Wage rate (dollars per hour)	Quantity of labour supplied (hours)
2	120
3	160
4	200
5	240
6	280
7	320
8	360

The market demand for labour from all the logging firms in the area is as follows:

Wage rate (dollars per hour)	Quantity of labour demanded (hours)
2	400
3	360
4	320
5	280
6	240
7	200
8	160

a) What is the competitive equilibrium wage rate?

b) What is the quantity of labour employed?

c) What is the total labour income?

d) How much of that labour income is economic rent and how much is transfer earnings? (You may find it easier to answer this question by drawing graphs of the demand and supply curves and then finding the economic rent and transfer earnings as areas on the graph in a manner similar to what was done in Fig. 15.11.)

6 A steel company in Hamilton experiences a *permanent* decrease in the demand for its product. Explain what happens to the following:

a) The price of a share of its stock

b) The dividends it pays to its stockholders

c) The amount of capital that it employs
   i) in the short-run
   ii) in the long-run

d) The quantity of labour that it employs
   i) in the sort-run
   ii) in the long-run

7 Suppose that the decrease in the demand for the product of the Hamilton steel producer in problem 6 was *temporary*. Demand decreases for a few months but then returns to its previous level. What happens to the following:

a) The price of a share of its stock

b) The dividends it pays to its stockholders

c) The amount of capital that it employs
   i) in the short-run
   ii) in the long-run

d) The quantity of labour that it employs
   i) in the short-run
   ii) in the long-run

8 Suppose there is a huge increase in the demand for Big Macs and the McDonald's are able to double their prices with no decrease in sales. What happens to the rents that McDonald's have to pay for the land on which their restaurants are located?

CHAPTER 16

Labour Markets

After studying this chapter, you will be able to:

- Explain why university graduates earn more, on the average, than high school graduates.
- Explain why skilled workers earn more, on the average, than unskilled workers.
- Explain why union workers earn higher wages than nonunion workers.
- Explain why men earn more, on the average, than women.
- Predict the effects of pay equity legislation.
- Explain why some people are paid by the hour and others by formulas based on performance.
- Explain how performance-related compensation rules induce greater effort and higher profit.

The Sweat of Our Brows

AS YOU WELL KNOW, school is not all fun. Those exams, quizzes, tests, and problem sets require a lot of hard work. Are they worth all the effort that goes into them? What is the payoff? Part of the payoff is a higher income. At age 22, university graduates earn 30 percent more, on the average, than high school graduates. When they reach middle age, their earnings are more than 50 percent higher than high school graduates and three times the level of those who attended elementary school only. Have you ever wondered why? After all, an accountant or a lawyer or even an economist doesn't sweat as hard as a person who works as a labourer. Why do they earn more? ■ Suppose that you do earn more after you get your degree. Ignoring the many cultural and social benefits of schooling and focusing only on money, let's ask a simple question: how much more income will you have to earn after graduation to make up for your years of paying tuition, room, and board, as well as your lost wages? (You could, after all, be washing dishes now instead of slogging through this economics course.) ■ Many workers, both blue collar and white collar, belong to labour unions. Usually, union workers earn a higher wage than nonunion workers in comparable jobs. Why? How are unions able to get wages for their members that are higher than the wages that nonunion workers are paid? ■ Among the most visible and persistent differences in earnings are those between men and women. Men, on the average, earn incomes that are one-third higher than the incomes earned by women. Certainly a lot of individuals defy the averages. But why do women so consistently earn less than men? Is it because of discrimination and exploitation? Could it be because of economic factors? Or is it a combination of the two? ■ Pay equity legislation has resulted in programs that try to ensure that jobs of equivalent value receive the same pay regardless of the pay set by the market. Can such programs bring economic help to women and minorities? ■ Most people work for an hourly wage rate. The total they earn depends on the total hours they work. But not everyone is paid in this way. For example, some doctors get paid by the number of X-rays they analyse or appendectomies they perform. Garment workers receive an income based on the number of shirts they make. Salespeople receive a percentage of the value of their sales. Senior managers often get to share in their company's profits. Tennis players and boxers are compensated by prize money. Managers and production workers sometimes receive bonuses for achieving target profits or output levels. Why is there such variety in the ways in which people are compensated for their work? Why don't we all get an hourly wage rate?

■ In this chapter, we answer questions such as these by studying the way labour markets work. We begin by using a model of a competitive labour market, such as that developed in Chapter 15, to analyse the effects on wages of differences in education and training. We then extend the model to explain differences in union and nonunion wages and in pay among men and women and to analyse the effects of pay equity laws. Finally, we study compensation arrangements based not on hours of work but on performance. We explain how such schemes lead to greater effort and higher profits. We'll even discover that chief executives and tennis stars get paid in a similar way.

Skill Differentials

Differences in earnings among workers with varying levels of education and training can be explained using a model of competitive labour markets. There are many levels and varieties of education and training in the real world. To keep our analysis as clear as possible, we'll study a model economy in which there are just two levels of education and training that result in two types of labour, which we will call skilled labour and unskilled labour. We'll study the demand for and supply of these two types of workers and see why there is a difference in their wages and what determines that difference. Let's begin by looking at the demand for the two types of labour.

The Demand for Skilled and Unskilled Labour

Skilled workers can perform a wide variety of tasks that unskilled workers would perform badly or perhaps could not even perform at all. Imagine an untrained, inexperienced person performing surgery or piloting an airplane. Because skilled workers perform complex tasks, they have a higher marginal revenue product than unskilled workers. As we learned in Chapter 15, the demand for labour curve is derived from the marginal revenue product curve. The larger the marginal revenue product of labour, the greater is the demand for labour.

Figure 16.1(a) shows the demand curves for skilled and unskilled labour. At the same level of employment of skilled and unskilled workers, firms are willing to pay a higher wage to a skilled worker than to an unskilled worker. The gap between these two wages is the difference between the marginal revenue products of a given number of skilled and unskilled workers. This difference is the marginal revenue product of skill. For example, at an employment level of 2,000 hours a day, firms are willing to pay $12.50 an hour for a skilled worker and only $5 an hour for an unskilled worker. The difference in the two marginal revenue products is $7.50 an hour. Thus the marginal revenue product of skill is $7.50 an hour.

The Supply of Skilled and Unskilled Labour

Skills are costly to acquire. Furthermore, a worker pays the cost of acquiring a skill *before* benefiting from a higher wage. For example, attending college or university usually leads to a higher income, but that income is not earned until after graduation. These facts make the acquisition of skills similar to investment. To emphasize the investment nature of acquiring a skill, we call that activity an investment in human capital. **Human capital** is the accumulated skill and knowledge of human beings. The value of a person's human capital is the present value of the extra earnings that will be received as a result of acquiring skill and knowledge. (The concept of present value is explained in Chapter 9.) It is equivalent to a sum of money that, if invested today at the average interest rate, will yield a stream of income equivalent to the extra earnings resulting from a person's acquired knowledge and skills.

Figure 16.1 Skill Differentials

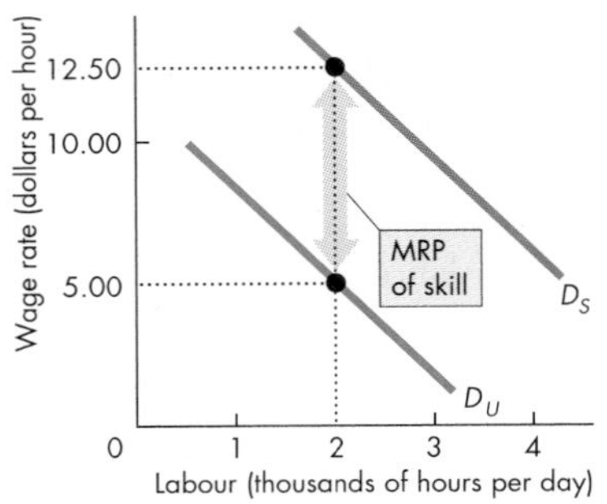

(a) Demand for skilled and unskilled labour

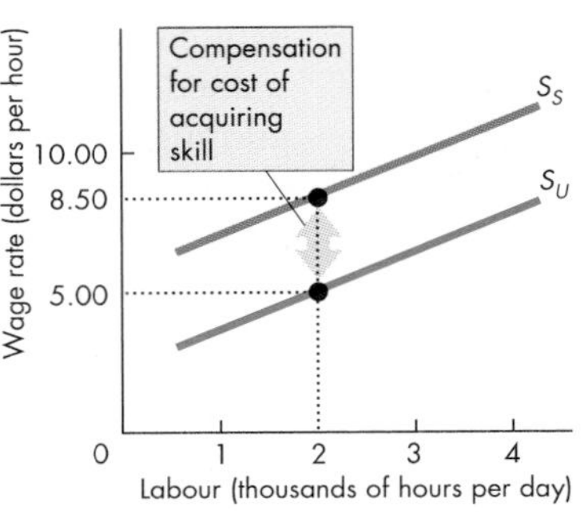

(b) Supply of skilled and unskilled labour

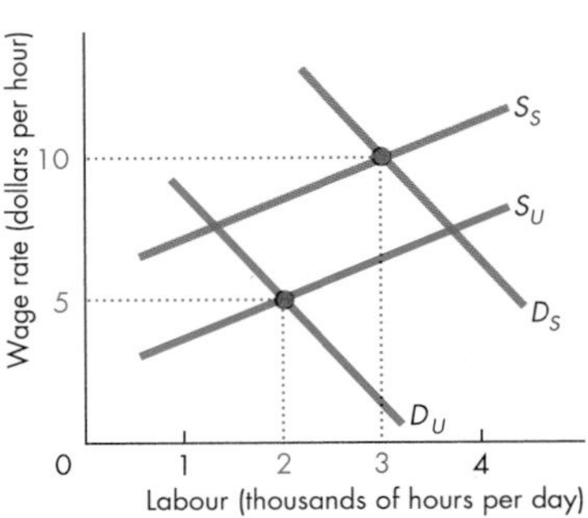

(c) Markets for skilled and unskilled labour

Part (a) illustrates the marginal revenue product of skill. Unskilled workers have a marginal revenue product that gives rise to the demand curve marked D_U. Skilled workers have a higher marginal revenue product; therefore the demand curve for skilled workers (D_S) lies to the right of D_U. The vertical gap between these two curves is the marginal revenue product of the skill.

Part (b) shows the effects of the cost of acquiring skills on the supply curves of labour. The supply curve for unskilled workers is S_U. Skilled workers have to incur costs in order to acquire their skills; therefore they will supply labour services only at a wage rate that exceeds that of unskilled labour. The supply curve for skilled workers is S_S. The vertical gap between these two curves is the compensation required for the cost of acquiring a skill.

Part (c) shows the determination of the equilibrium levels of employment and the wage differential between skilled and unskilled labour. In equilibrium, the quantities of each type of labour demanded and supplied are equal. Unskilled workers earn \$5 per hour and are hired for 2,000 hours per day. Skilled workers earn \$10 per hour and are hired for 3,000 hours per day. Wages for skilled workers are always greater than those for unskilled workers.

The cost of acquiring a skill includes actual expenditure on such things as tuition, books, and room and board and also costs in the form of lost or reduced earnings while the skill is being acquired. When a person goes to school full time, that cost is the total earnings foregone. Some people acquire skills through on-the-job training. Usually a worker undergoing on-the-job training is paid a lower wage than one doing a comparable job but not undergoing training. In such a case, the cost of acquiring the skill is the difference between the wage paid to a person not being trained and that paid to a person being trained.

Supply Curves of Skilled and Unskilled Labour The position of the supply curve of skilled workers reflects the cost of acquiring the skill. Figure 16.1(b) shows two supply curves, one for skilled workers (S_S) and the other for unskilled workers (S_U).

The skilled worker's supply curve lies above the unskilled worker's supply curve. The vertical gap between the two supply curves is the compensation for the cost of acquiring the skill (the difference is the amount that has a present value equal to the cost of acquiring the skill.) For example, suppose that the quantity of unskilled labour supplied is 2,000 hours a day at a wage rate of \$5 an hour. This wage rate compensates the unskilled workers purely for their time on the job. To induce 2,000 hours of skilled labour to be supplied, firms have to pay a wage rate of \$8.50 an hour. This wage rate for skilled labour is higher than that for unskilled labour since skilled workers must be compensated not only for the time on the job but also for the time and other costs of acquiring the skill.

Wage Rates of Skilled and Unskilled Labour

To work out the wage rates of skilled and unskilled labour, we bring together the effects of skill on the demand and supply of labour. Figure 16.1(c) shows the demand curves and the supply curves for skilled and unskilled labour — plotted in parts (a) and (b). Equilibrium occurs in the market for unskilled labour where the supply and demand curves for unskilled labour intersect. The equilibrium wage rate is $5 an hour and the quantity of unskilled labour employed is 2,000 hours. Equilibrium in the market for skilled workers occurs where the supply and demand curves for skilled workers intersect. The equilibrium wage rate is $10 an hour and the quantity of skilled labour employed is 3,000 hours.

As you can see in Fig. 16.1(c), the equilibrium wage rate of skilled labour is higher than that of unskilled labour. This difference occurs for two reasons: first, skilled labour has a higher marginal revenue product than unskilled labour; second, skills are costly to acquire. The wage differential (in this case, $5 an hour) depends on both the marginal revenue product of the skill and the cost of acquiring it. The larger the marginal revenue product of the skill, the larger is the vertical gap between the demand curves for skilled and unskilled labour. The more costly it is to acquire a skill, the larger is the vertical gap between the supplies of skilled and unskilled labour. The larger the marginal revenue product of the skill and the more costly it is to acquire, the larger is the wage differential between skilled and unskilled workers.

Figure 16.2 Education and Earnings

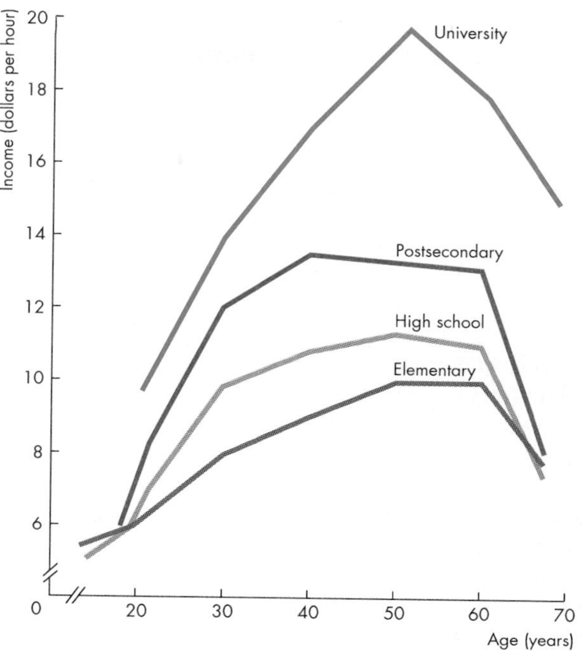

The figure shows the average earnings of employees at various ages and with varying levels of schooling. Earnings increase with the length of education. They also increase with age but only up to the mid-40s. Beyond that age earnings decrease. These differences show the importance of education and experience in influencing skill differentials.

Source: Statistics Canada, *Labour Market Activity Survey*, 1986. *
* This analysis is based on Statistics Canada microdata tape, *Labour Market Activity Survey*, 1986 which contains anonymized data collected in the 1986 Labour Market Activity Survey. All computations on these microdata were prepared by Chris Robinson, University of Western Ontario and the responsibility for the use and interpretation of these data is entirely that of the authors.

Do Education and Training Pay?

There are large and persistent differences in earnings based on the degree of education and training. An indication of those differences can be seen in Fig. 16.2. This figure highlights two important sources of earnings differences. The first is the degree of education itself. The higher the level of education, the higher are a person's earnings, other things being equal. The second source of earnings differences apparent in Fig. 16.2 is age. Age is strongly correlated with experience and the degree of on-the-job training a person has had. Thus as a person gets older, up to middle age, earnings increase.

We can see from Fig. 16.2, that going through high school and postsecondary education leads to a higher income. But does it pay in the sense of yielding enough income to compensate for the cost of education and for the delay in the start of earnings? For most people, postsecondary education does indeed pay. Rates of return have been calculated suggesting that a postsecondary degree is a better investment than almost any other a person can undertake. Rates of return as high as 15 percent, after allowing for inflation, are not uncommon.

Differences in education and training are an important source of differences in earnings. But they are not the only source. Another is the activities of labour unions. Let's see how unions affect wages and why, on the average, union wages exceed nonunion wages.

Union-Nonunion Wage Differentials

A **labour union** is a group of workers organized for the purpose of increasing wages and influencing other job conditions. A labour union acts in the labour market like a monopolist in the product market. The union seeks to restrict competition and, as a result, raises the price at which labour is traded. A compact glossary of labour terms can be found in Table 16.1.

There are two main types of union: craft unions and industrial unions. A **craft union** is a group of workers who have a similar range of skills but work for many different firms in many different industries and perhaps regions. An example of a craft union is the carpenters' union. An **industrial union** is a group of workers who have a variety of skills and job types but work for the same firm or industry. The Canadian Auto Workers (CAW) is an example of an industrial union.

The most important national organization representing three-fifths of Canadian union members is the Canadian Labour Congress (CLC). The CLC was created in 1956 when two labour organizations combined: the Labour Council of Canada (TLC), founded in 1883 to organize craft unions, and the Canadian Congress of Labour (CCL), founded in 1940 to organize industrial unions. The CLC often acts as the national voice of organized labour in the media and in politics.

Unions vary enormously in size. Craft unions are the smallest and industrial unions are the largest. The largest unions in Canada — measured by number of members — are shown in Fig. 16.3. Union strength peaked in 1983 when 40 percent of the work force belonged to unions. That percentage has fallen slightly since then. Changes in union membership, however, have been uneven in the past several decades. Some unions have declined dramatically while others, especially those in the public sector, have increased in strength.

In some firms or plants where a union operates, all the workers employed are required to be members of the union. Such a situation is known as a closed shop. A **closed shop** is a plant or firm in which all the employees are required to belong to the labour union. There are other firms and plants in which the terms and conditions of employment are negotiated by a union but in which workers are not required to join the union. Nevertheless, in such situations, an arrangement called the Rand formula applies. The **Rand formula** is a rule (set out by Mr. Justice Ivan Rand in 1945) making it compulsory for all workers to contribute to the union whether or not they belong to the union.

Unions negotiate with employers (or their representatives) in a process called **collective bargaining**.

Table 16.1 A Compact Glossary on Unions

Labour union	A group of workers organized for the purpose of increasing wages and improving other conditions of employment.
CLC	A federation of unions formed in 1956 by a merger of the Labour Council of Canada (TLC) and the Canadian Congress of Labour (CCL). It acts as the voice of organized labour in media and political arenas.
Craft union	A union in which workers have a similar range of skills but work for many firms and in many different industries
Industrial union	A union in which workers have a variety of skills and job types but work in the same industry.
Closed shop	A plant or firm in which all the employees are required to join the labour union.
Rand formula	A rule (set out by Mr. Justice Ivan Rand in 1945) making it compulsory for all workers in a unionized plant to contribute to the union whether or not they belong to the union.
Collective bargaining	The process of negotiation between employers (or their representatives) and a union on wages and other employment conditions.
Strike	A group decision to refuse to work under prevailing conditions.
Lockout	A firm's refusal to operate its plant and employ its workers.
Binding arbitration	Determination of wages and other employment conditions by a third party (an arbitrator) acceptable to both parties.

Figure 16.3 Unions with Largest Membership

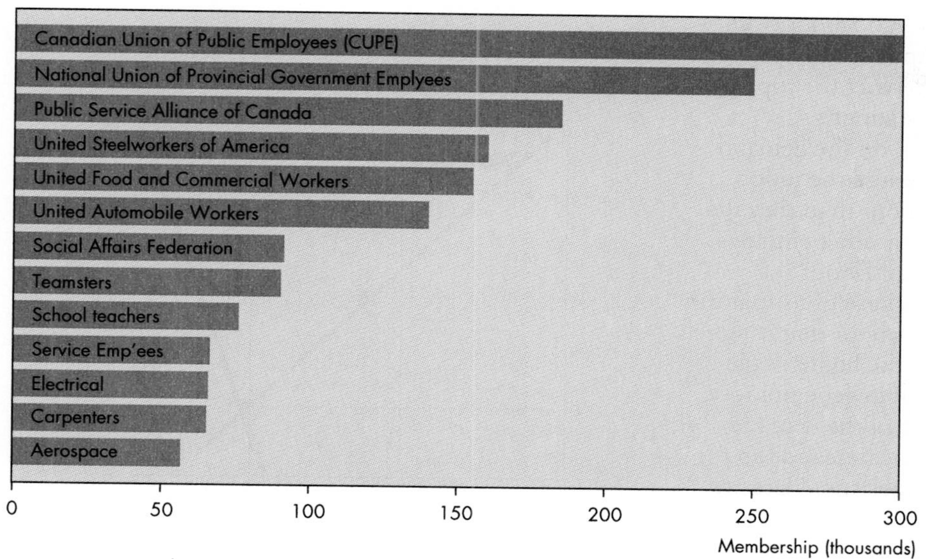

The unions with the largest memberships in Canada are the three big public service workers' unions. Together they have more than a million members. The next ten largest unions each have more than 50,000 members.

Source: Statistics Canada, *Canada Yearbook*, 1988, 5-9.

The main weapons available to the union and the employer in collective bargaining are the strike and the lockout. A **strike** is a group decision to refuse to work under prevailing conditions. A **lockout** is a firm's refusal to operate its plant and employ its workers. Each party uses the threat of a strike or a lockout to try to get an agreement in its own favour. Sometimes when the two parties in the collective bargaining process cannot agree on wages and other conditions of employment, they agree to put their disagreement to binding arbitration. **Binding arbitration** is a process in which a third party — an arbitrator — determines wages and other employment conditions on behalf of the negotiating parties.

Though not labour unions in a legal sense, professional associations act, in many ways, like labour unions. A **professional association** is an organized group of professional workers, such as lawyers, dentists, or doctors, that seeks to influence the compensation and other labour market conditions affecting its members. An example of a professional association is the Ontario Medical Association (OMA).

Unions' Objectives and Constraints

Unions have three broad objectives:

- Improving compensation
- Improving working conditions
- Improving employment prospects

Each of these objectives contains a series of more detailed goals. For example, in seeking to improve members' compensation, unions operate on a variety of fronts: wages, fringe benefits, retirement pay, and such things as vacation allowances. In seeking to improve working conditions, unions are concerned with occupational health and safety as well as the environmental quality of the workplace. In seeking to improve employment prospects, unions try to obtain greater job security for existing union members and to expand their job opportunities.

A union's ability to pursue its objectives is restricted by constraints on both the supply and demand sides of the labour market. On the supply side, the union's activities are limited by how well it can restrict nonunion workers from offering their labour. The larger the fraction of the work force controlled by the union, the more effective the union can be. For example, unions in the construction industry are extremely effective in the pursuit of their goals because they can influence the number of people obtaining skills as electricians, plasterers, and carpenters. Those best able to restrict supply are the professional associations who control the number of qualified workers by controlling the examinations that new entrants must pass. At the other extreme, there are several limits on the effectiveness of unions in markets such as that for unskilled farm labour in southern California, where unions are unable to control the flow of nonunion (and illegal) labour from Mexico. Also because of their abundant supply, it would be difficult for a union to restrict the supply of high school help at fast-food restaurants.

The constraint facing a union on the demand side of the labour market arises because the union cannot force firms to hire more labour than they demand. Anything that raises wages or other employment costs will lower the quantity of labour demanded. Unless the union can take actions that increase the demand for the kind of labour that it represents, it has to accept the fact that the higher wage can be obtained only at the price of lower employment. Recognizing the importance of the demand for labour, unions try to increase the demand for their labour and to make it more inelastic. Here are some of the methods that they employ

- Encouraging import restrictions
- Supporting minimum wage laws
- Supporting immigration restrictions
- Increasing product demand
- Increasing the marginal product of union members

One of the best examples of the encouragement of import restrictions is the garment workers' support for import restrictions on foreign textiles. Unions support minimum wage laws in order to increase the wages of unskilled labour, which has the effect of increasing the cost of unskilled labour, a substitute for skilled union labour. Also, supporting restrictive immigration laws leads indirectly to an increase in the wages of unskilled workers (through the decrease in their supply) and again increases the cost of labour that might otherwise be substituted for the higher cost union labour. Increasing product demand increases producers' profits and indirectly increases the demand for labour. The best examples of attempts by unions in this activity are in the textile and auto industries. Garment workers are encouraged to buy union-made clothes and auto workers to buy only Canadian-produced cars. Increasing the marginal product of union members directly shifts the demand curve for their services. Unions use apprenticeship, training, and professional certification to increase the marginal product of their members, which increases their marginal revenue product and thus the demand for this type of labour.

Figure 16.4 A Union in a Competitive Labour Market

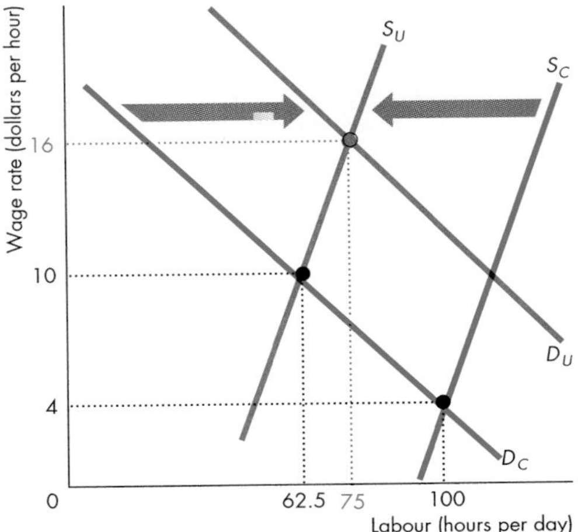

In a competitive labour market, the demand curve is D_C and the supply curve S_C. Competitive equilibrium occurs at a wage rate of \$4 per hour with 100 hours of labour employed. By restricting employment below its competitive level, the union shifts the supply of labour to S_U. If the union can do no more than that, the wage rate will rise to \$10 per hour but employment will fall to 62.5 hours per day. If the union can also increase the demand for labour (by increasing the demand for the good produced by the union members or by raising the price of substitute labour) and shift the demand curve to D_U, then it can raise the wage rate still higher, to \$16 per hour, and achieve employment of 75 hours per day.

Unions in a Competitive Labour Market

When a union operates in an otherwise competitive labour market, it seeks to raise wages and other compensation and to limit employment reductions by increasing demand for the labour of its members.

Figure 16.4 illustrates a labour market. The demand curve is D_C and the supply curve is S_C. If the market is a competitive one with no union, the equilibrium wage rate is \$4 an hour and 100 hours of labour will be employed. Suppose now that a union is formed to organize the workers in this market and that it gains sufficient control over the supply of labour to be able to artificially restrict that supply below its competitive level — to S_U. If that is all the union does, employment will fall to 62.5 hours of labour and the wage rate will rise to \$10 an hour. If the union can also take steps that increase the demand for labour to D_U, it can achieve an even bigger rise in the wage rate with a smaller fall in employment. By maintaining the restricted labour supply at S_U, the union raises the wage rate to $16 an hour and achieves an employment level of 75 hours of labour.

A recent attempt to unionize the labour force in a competitive industry is examined in Reading Between the lines pp. 414-415.

Next we examine the case of monopsony.

Monopsony

A **monopsony** is a market structure in which there is just a single buyer. With the growth of large-scale production over the past century, large plants, such as coal mines, steel and textile mills, and pulp and paper companies, have become the major employers of labour in some regions, and in some places a single firm employs almost all the labour. Such a firm is a monopsonist in the local labour market. Monopsony also arises when there is only one employer of a particular kind of labour in a town or region. For example, a city school board is a monopsonist in the local market for teachers.

A monopsonist can make a bigger profit than a group of firms that have to compete with each other for their labour. Figure 16.5 illustrates how a monopsonist operates. The monopsonist's marginal revenue product curve labelled *MRP* tells us the extra total revenue from selling the output produced by the last hour of labour hired. The curve labelled *S* is the supply curve of labour, which tells us how many hours are supplied at each wage rate and, conversely, the minimum wage that is acceptable at each level of labour supplied.

The monopsonist recognizes that to hire more labour it must pay a higher wage and, equivalently, that by hiring less labour it can get away with paying a lower wage. The monopsonist takes account of this fact when calculating its marginal cost of labour, which is shown in Fig. 16.5 by the curve *MCL*.

The relationship between the marginal cost of labour curve and the supply curve is similar to the relationship between the marginal cost and average total cost curves that you studied in Chapter 10. The supply curve is like the average total cost of labour curve. For example, the firm in Fig. 16.5 can hire 50 hours of labour at $5 an hour, so its average total cost is $5 an hour. The total cost of labour is $250 ($5 an hour × 50 hours). But suppose that the firm hires slightly less than 50 hours of labour, say, 49. The wage rate at which 49 hours of labour can be hired is $4.90 an hour. The firm's total labour cost is now $240.10 (49 × $4.90). Hiring the fiftieth hour of labour raises the total cost of labour from $240.10 to $250, which is an increase of almost $10. The curve *MCL* shows the $10 marginal cost of hiring the fiftieth hour of labour.

Figure 16.5 A Monopsony Labour Market

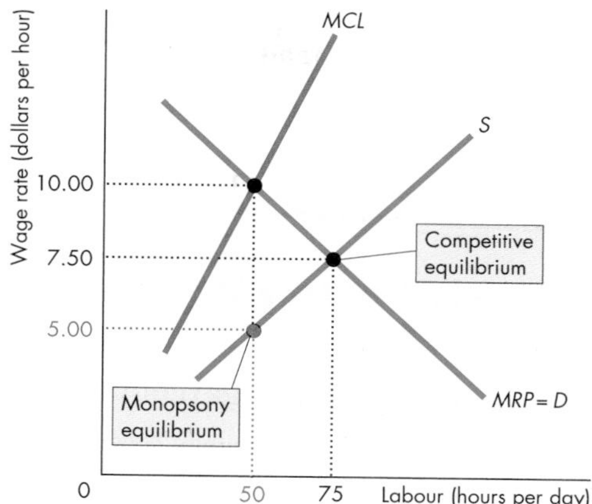

A monopsony is a market structure in which there is a single buyer. A monopsonist whose marginal revenue product curve is *MRP* faces a labour curve *S* and has a marginal cost of labour curve *MCL*. Profit is maximized by making the marginal cost of labour equal to marginal revenue product. The monopsonist hires 50 hours of labour and pays the lowest wage for which that labour will work, $5 per hour.

To calculate the profit-maximizing quantity of labour to hire, the firm sets the marginal cost of labour equal to the marginal revenue product of labour. That is, the firm wants the cost of the last worker hired to equal the extra total revenue that worker brings in. In Fig. 16.5, this outcome occurs when the monopsony employs 50 hours of labour. To hire 50 hours of labour, the firm has to pay $5 an hour. The marginal revenue product of labour, however, is $10 an hour, which means that the firm makes an economic profit of $5 on the last hour of labour that it hires. Each worker gets paid $5, and marginal revenue product is $10. So the firm gets an extra $5 of economic profit from the last hour of labour hired.

The ability of a monopsonist to make an economic profit depends on the elasticity of labour supply. The more elastic the supply of labour, the less opportunity a monopsonist has to make an economic profit. If the labour market in Fig. 16.5 were

To Unionize or Not?

Oil rig workers may form union

Groundswell of unrest gathering momentum, union leader says

Fed up with meagre wages, skimpy benefits and poor prospects for steady employment, Alberta's oil rig workers are talking about forming a union.

It's a surprise development in an industry renowned for the fierce independence of its "roughneck" workers.

In fact, rig workers have grown so angry, says Rolf Nielsen, Edmonton-based western co-ordinator of the Energy & Chemical Workers Union, that the impetus toward unionization may prove irreversible...

Employer groups, while acknowledging that wages for rig workers have deteriorated for a variety of reasons, maintain the unionization drive is unnecessary.

"I'm not sure what unionization can offer to the industry or to its workers that couldn't be better addressed through negotiations between contractors and producers," says Don Herring, Managing Director of the Canadian Association of Oilwell Drilling Contractors [CAODC], which represents the companies that employ roughnecks...

But Nielsen feels rig workers have been offered too little too late. The recent round of negotiations between contractors and producers has done nothing to address a number of labor concerns, such as the lack of steady work, he says. The CAODC estimates the average driller worked only 73 days last year for total pay of $11,826. In 1980, he worked 193 days for $19,460.

"We met rig hands and tool pushers that weren't making enough to live on, and in many cases weren't working enough to qualify for unemployment benefits," Nielsen says. "Last year, lots [of rig workers] were only working for one month."...

But the union faces a formidable task if it's serious about unionizing the drilling industry: drilling contractors employ a largely transient labor force, spread among a number of temporary locations, usually in remote terrain...

Whether rig workers eventually form a union, it's all but certain that rising labor costs will soon force drilling costs up for Canadian oil and gas producers.

Petroleum Services Association of Canada Chairman Bud Bell says rig workers are finding steadier and better-paid employment in Alberta's booming construction sector and provincially subsidized pulp and paper projects. He predicts the oilfield service industry's biggest headaches in the coming decade will be caused by labor shortages. In particular, drilling and oilfield service companies will have difficulty retaining experienced employees, he says.

***The Financial Post,* March 5, 1990**
By Tamsin Carlisle

The Essence of the Story

- It is estimated that the average driller on an Alberta oil rig worked 73 days in 1989 and was paid $11,826. In 1980, he worked 193 days for $19,460.
- Angered by this situation, the workers are considering forming a union.
- Employer groups do not believe that unionization will improve the workers' situation.
- Unionizing the drilling industry will be a difficult task because the labor force is a transient one, spread among temporary and remote locations.
- Even without a union, it is predicted that rig workers' wages will increase because rig workers are finding alternative, steadier, and better-paid employment.

Background and Analysis

- The market for oil rig workers is illustrated in the figure.
- In 1980, the demand for oil rig workers was D_{1980} and the supply of oil rig workers was S_{1980}.
- The market for oil rig workers is a competitive one and the equilibrium wage rate in 1980 was $100 a day with L_{1980} hours of labor employed.
- During the 1980s, two major factors influenced the market for oil rig workers:
  - Wage rates in other industries increased.
  - The price of oil decreased.

  These two factors shifted the supply and demand curves for oil rig workers as shown in the figure.
- By 1989, the quantity of oil rig workers employed had decreased to L_{1989} hours and the wage rate had increased to $167 a day.
- The percentage decrease in hours worked by a typical worker was much larger than the percentage increase in the wage rate. Weekly incomes declined.
- Although the daily wage rate increased between 1980 and 1989, prices also increased and by a similar percentage amount as the increase in the daily wage rate. Thus by 1989 oil rig workers were suffering a severe cut in their living standards.
- Forming a union can do little to increase the wages of the oil rig workers unless a union can limit entry into that type of work.
- Even if a union could limit the number of oil rig workers it could achieve an increase in their wages only by preventing some workers from having access to those higher wages.
- A continuation of rising wages in other industries will lead to a continued upward movement of the supply curve of oil rig workers and, if there is no further decrease in the demand for those workers, their wage rate will increase—and employment level decrease—even in the absence of a union.

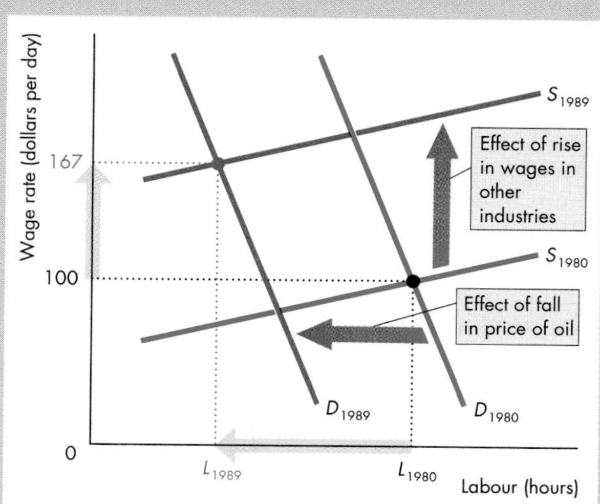

competitive, the wage rate would be $7.50 and the level of employment 75 hours. Employment and the wage rate are lower under monopsony than in a competitive labour market.

Monopsony Tendencies With today's low costs of transportation, it is unlikely that many pure monopsonists remain. Workers can easily commute long distances to a job, so most people do not have just one potential employer. Nevertheless, many firms still face an upward-sloping supply of labour curve. Though they are not pure monopsonists, there is a monopsony tendency in their market in the sense that they have to offer higher wages to attract more workers. A firm's monopsony element may come from its location — it is more conveniently reached by some workers than others. Firms compete with each other for labour by offering wages that not only compensate their workers for time on the job but also for commuting time. The more workers a firm hires, the longer the commute for the marginal worker and, therefore, the higher the wage that the firm has to pay to attract that worker. How strong such a monopsony tendency is depends on the size and density of the area in which the labour market is situated.

Next, let's see the effects of minimum wage laws and unions in a monopsonistic labour market.

Figure 16.6 Minimum Wage in Monopsony

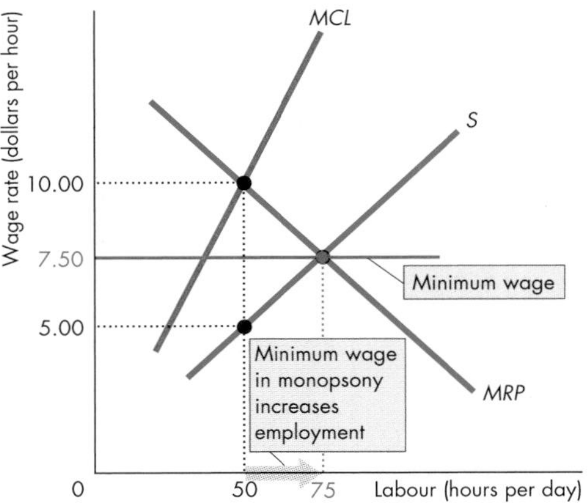

The wage rate is $5 per hour in a monopsony labour market. If a minimum wage law is introduced that raises the wage rate to $7.50 per hour, employment rises to 75 hours per day. Equivalently, if a union enters the market, it will attempt to increase the wage rate to more than $5 per hour. If the union is all powerful, the highest wage it can achieve is $10 per hour. If the union and the firm are equally powerful, they will bargain and agree to a wage rate of $7.50 per hour — the wage rate that splits the difference between the marginal revenue product and the lowest wage for which labour will work.

Monopsony, Minimum Wage, and Unions

In Chapter 6, we saw that a minimum wage usually decreases employment. In a situation where a firm is a monopsonist, however, minimum wage regulations can actually raise both the wage rate and employment. A union can also raise the wage rate and employment. Let's see how.

Minimum Wages and Monopsony Suppose that the labour market is that shown in Fig. 16.6 and that the wage rate is $5 an hour with 50 hours of labour being employed. The government now passes a minimum wage law that prohibits anyone from hiring labour for less than $7.50 an hour. Firms can hire labour for more than $7.50 an hour but not for less. The monopsonist in Fig. 16.6 now faces a perfectly elastic supply of labour at $7.50 an hour up to 75 hours a day. To increase the quantity of hours supplied to more than 75 hours a day, a higher wage than $7.50 an hour has to be offered. Since the wage rate is a fixed $7.50 an hour up to 75 hours a day, the marginal cost of labour is also constant at $7.50 up to 75 hours. Beyond 75 hours, however, the marginal cost of labour rises to more than $7.50 an hour. To maximize profit, the monopsonist sets the marginal cost of labour equal to its marginal revenue product. That is, it hires 75 hours of labour at $7.50 an hour. The minimum wage law has made the supply of labour perfectly elastic and has made the marginal cost of labour the same as the wage rate up to 75 hours. The law has not affected the supply of labour curve or the marginal cost of labour at employment levels of more than 75 hours. The minimum wage law has succeeded in raising the wage rate by $2.50 an hour and raising the amount of labour employed by 25 hours a day.

Monopsony and Unions When we studied monopoly in Chapter 13, we discovered that a single seller in a market is able to determine the price in that market. We have just studied monopsony — a market with a single buyer — and discovered that in such a market the buyer is able to determine the price. Suppose that a union starts to operate in a monopsony labour market. A union is like a monopoly. It controls the supply of labour and acts like a single seller of labour. If the union (monopoly seller) faces a monopsony buyer, the situation is one of **bilateral monopoly**. In bilateral monopoly, the wage rate is determined by bargaining between the two traders. Let's study the bargaining process.

Recall that if the monopsony in Fig. 16.5 is free to determine the wage rate and the level of employment, it will hire 50 hours of labour for a wage rate of $5 an hour. If a union that represents the workers can maintain employment at 50 hours but charge the highest wage rate acceptable to the employer, the wage rate will be $10 an hour. That is, the wage rate will equal the marginal revenue product of labour. If the monopsonist and the union bargain over the wage rate, the result will be a wage rate between $10 an hour (the maximum that the union can achieve) and $5 an hour (the minimum that the firm can achieve).

The actual outcome of the bargaining depends on the costs that each party can inflict on the other as a result of a failure to agree on the wage rate. The firm can shut down the plant and lock out its workers, and the workers can shut down the plant by striking. Each party knows the strength of the other. It also knows what it itself stands to lose if it does not agree to the demands of the other. If the two parties are equally strong — and they realize it — they will split the difference and agree to a wage rate of $7.50 an hour. If one party is stronger than the other — and both parties know that — the agreed wage will favour the stronger party. Usually, an agreement is reached without a strike or lockout. The threat — the knowledge that such an event can occur — is usually enough to bring the bargaining parties to an agreement. When strikes or lockouts do occur, it is because one party has misjudged the situation.

The Scale of Union-Nonunion Wage Differentials

We have seen that unions can influence the wages of their members partly by restricting the supply of labour and partly by manipulating the demand for labour. How much of a difference to wage rates do unions make in practice?

The answer to this question is not known with certainty. But many studies have been undertaken, and the answer can be put in a range — between 15 and 35 percent.[1]

Assessing the effects of unions is difficult because so many factors must be taken into account simultaneously to determine the source of a differential in earnings. For example, in some industries, union wages are higher than nonunion wages because union members do jobs that involve greater skill. Even without a union, those who perform such tasks receive a higher wage.

To calculate the effects of unions, the analyst has to examine the wages of unionized and nonunionized workers who do nearly identical work. The evidence suggests that after allowing for the effects of skill differentials and other factors, the union-nonunion wage differential is between 10 and 35 percent.

Wage Differentials Between the Sexes

Earnings differences between the sexes persist. Figure 16.7 provides a snapshot of these differences in the mid-1980s for a number of office occupations. (We chose these occupations because they offer the best possible opportunity for comparing the wages of women and men who do virtually identical work.) Ignoring occupational differences, women in Canada earn about 65 percent of the earnings of men. A large part of that difference arises from the fact that women do more of the lower-paid jobs than men. But, as Fig. 16.7 shows, women do earn less than men, on the average, for identical jobs.

Why do these differentials exist, and why do they persist? Do they arise because there is discrimination against women or is there some other explanation? This controversial question generates an enormous amount of passion. It is not our intention to make you angry, though that may happen as an unintended consequence of this discussion. The objective of this section is to show you how to use economic analysis to address controversial and emotionally charged issues.

[1] Chris Robinson, "The Joint Determination of Union Status and Union Wage Effects: Some Tests of Alternative Models," *Journal of Political Economy* 97, 3, (June 1989): 639-67.

Figure 16.7 Sex Differentials

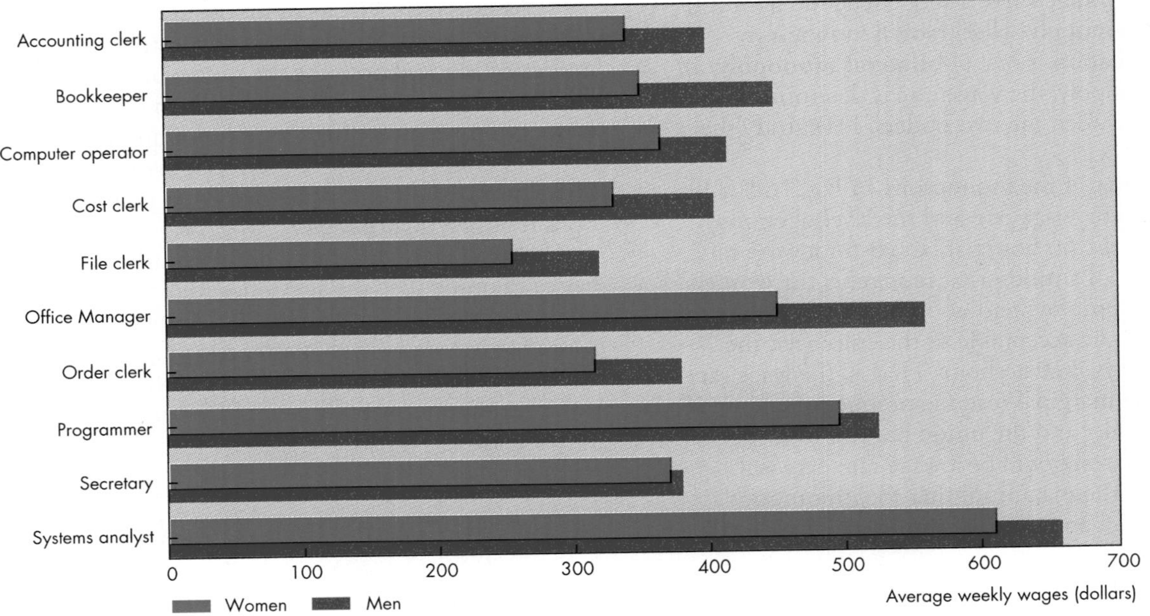

Women, on the average, earn about 65 percent of the amount earned by men. Much of this difference is accounted for by the fact that women predominate in lower-paid jobs. The figure compares the wages of women and men in similarly described occupations. Here the differences range from close to nothing (secretary) to about 20 percent (office manager).

Source: Statistics Canada, *Women in the Workforce*, 1988, 47.

We are going to examine three possible explanations for these earnings differences:

- Discrimination
- Differences in human capital
- Differences in degree of specialization

Discrimination

To see how discrimination can affect earnings, let's look at an example — the market for investment advisors. Suppose that there are two groups of investment advisors — women and men — who are identical in terms of picking good investments. Figure 16.8 shows the supply curve of women (S_W) in part (a) and the supply curve of men (S_M) in part (b). These supply curves are identical. The marginal revenue product of investment advisors is identical whether they are women or men. These are shown by the two curves labelled *MRP* in parts (a) and (b). (The revenues received by investment advisors are the fees their customers pay for advice.)

Suppose that everyone in this society is free of prejudice about sex. The market for female investment advisors determines a wage rate of $40,000 a year, and there are 2,000 female investment advisors. The market for male investment advisors also determines a wage rate of $40,000 a year, and there are 2,000 male investment advisors.

In contrast to the previous situation, suppose that the customers of investment banks are prejudiced against women. As before, the two types of advisors are equally able, but the prejudice is so strong that the customers are not willing to pay as much for investment advice given by a woman as they will pay for such advice from a man. Because of the differences in the amounts that people are willing to pay,

Figure 16.8 Discrimination

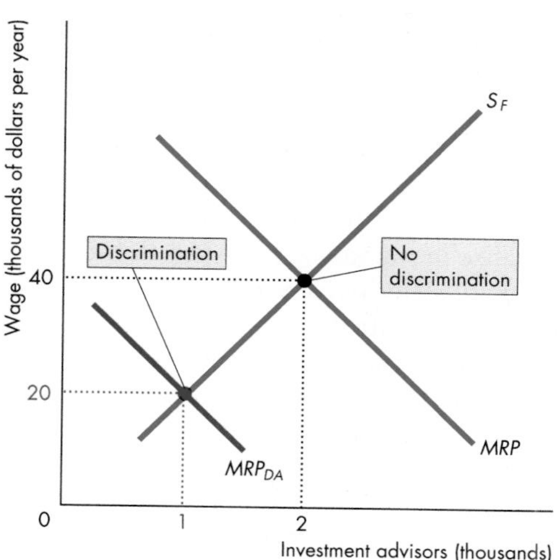

(a) Women

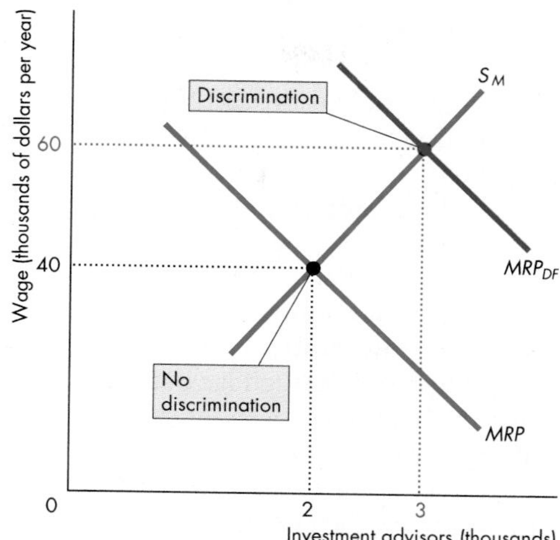

(b) Men

The supply curve for female investment advisors is S_F (part a), and the supply curve for male investment advisors is S_M (part b). If the marginal revenue product of both groups of investment advisors is *MRP* (the same curve in each part), the equilibrium wage rate for each group is \$40,000 per year and 2,000 of each type of advisor are employed. If there is discrimination against women, the marginal revenue product curve of the female advisors is to the left of the original curve. It is the curve labelled MRP_{DA} — *DA* standing for "discriminated against." There is discrimination in favour of males, so their marginal revenue product curve is MRP_{DF} — *DF* standing for "discriminated in favour of." The wage rate for women falls to \$20,000 per year and only 1,000 are employed. The wage rate for men rises to \$60,000 per year and 3,000 are employed.

based purely on their prejudices, the marginal revenue products of the two groups are different. The abilities of the two groups are the same, but the values that prejudiced consumers place on their output are not the same. Suppose that the marginal revenue product of the women, when discriminated against, is the line labelled MRP_{DA} — *DA* standing for "discriminated against." Suppose that the marginal revenue product for men is MRP_{DF} — *DF* standing for "discriminated in favour of." Given these marginal revenue product curves, the markets for the two groups of investment advisors now determine very different wages and employment levels. Women earn \$20,000 a year and only 1,000 will work as investment advisors. Men earn \$60,000 a year, and 3,000 of them will work as investment advisors. Thus purely on the basis of the prejudice of the demanders of investment advice, women will earn one-third the wages of men. Three-quarters of all investment advisors will be men, and only one-quarter will be women.

The case that we have just examined is a hypothetical example of how prejudice can produce differences in earnings. Does prejudice actually cause wage differentials? Economists disagree for a simple reason but one that is difficult to overcome: you can recognize prejudice when you see it, but you cannot easily measure it. Our model shows that sex differentials may come from prejudice. But without a way of measuring prejudice in the real world, we cannot easily test that model to see if it is true.

Let's now turn to a second possible source of earnings differences — differences in human capital.

Human Capital Differences

As we saw earlier in this chapter, wages are compensation, in part for time spent on the job and in part for the cost incurred in acquiring skill — in acquiring human capital. The more human capital a person supplies, the more that person earns, other things being equal. Measuring human capital with any precision is difficult, but there are some rough indicators. One such indicator is the number of years of schooling that a person has had. The most recent figures indicate that the median time in school is almost equal for both sexes at about 12 years.

A second possible indicator of human capital is the number of job interruptions. Interruptions to a career disrupt and reduce the effectiveness of job experience and slow down the accumulation of human capital. Also, during a job interruption, it is possible that human capital depreciates through lack of use. Traditionally, women's careers have been interrupted more frequently than men's, usually for bearing and rearing children. This factor is a possible reason why women earn lower wages, on the average. Just as education differences have virtually disappeared, so career interruptions for women are becoming less severe. Maternity leave and day-care facilities are providing an increasing number of women with uninterrupted employment that makes their human capital accumulation indistinguishable from that of men.

Thus it is possible that human capital differences can account for earnings differentials among the sexes in the past and for some of the differentials that still remain. The trends, however, suggest that wage differentials from this source will eventually disappear.

Degrees of Specialization

People undertake two kinds of production activities: they supply labour services to the market (market activity) and they undertake household production (nonmarket activity). **Household production** creates goods and services to be consumed within the household, rather than to be supplied to the market. Such activities include cooking, cleaning, minor repair work, education, and organizational services such as arranging vacations and other leisure activities. Bearing and rearing children is another important nonmarket activity.

In Chapter 3, we discovered that people can gain from specializing in activities and trading their output with each other. Specialization and the gains from trade do not operate exclusively in the marketplace. They also occur within the household. It is not uncommon for one member of a household to specialize in shopping, another in cleaning, another in laundry, and so on. Specialization in bearing children is a biological necessity, although rearing them is not.

Consider, for example, a household that has two members — Bob and Sue. They have to decide how they will allocate their time between market activity and various nonmarket household production activities. One solution is for Bob to specialize in market activity and Sue to specialize in nonmarket activity. Another solution is to reverse the roles and have Sue specialize in market activity and Bob in nonmarket activity. Alternatively, one or both of them can become diversified, doing some market and some nonmarket activity. A completely egalitarian allocation will have the two share the nonmarket tasks equally and each devote the same amount of time and energy to market activity. But unequal allocations of time are also possible, with one of the household members specializing in market activity and the other being diversified.

In deciding which of the many alternative time allocations to choose, Bob and Sue will take into consideration their future plans for having children. The particular allocation chosen by Bob and Sue will depend on their preferences and on their market earning potential. An increasing number of households are choosing the egalitarian allocation with each person diversified between nonmarket household production and market activity. Most households, however, still choose an allocation that would have Bob almost fully specialized in market activity and Sue covering a diversity of tasks in both the job market and the household. What are the effects of this more common assignment of market and nonmarket tasks? Though there will always be exceptions, it seems likely, on the average, that if Bob specializes in market production and Sue diversifies between market and nonmarket production, Bob will have higher earning potential in the marketplace than Sue. If Sue devotes a great deal of productive effort to ensuring Bob's mental and physical well-being, the quality of Bob's market labour will be higher than if he were undertaking his household production tasks on his own. If the roles were reversed, Sue would be able to supply market labour capable of earning more than Bob.

Economists have attempted to test whether differences in the degree of specialization of women and men can account for differences in their earnings. To do so, they have examined the wages of men and women where, as far as possible, the degree of specialization is the same for both sexes. To make the degree of specialization as similar as possible, two groups have been chosen for analysis. They are "never-married" men and "never-married" women who live alone. The idea is that if the degree of specialization is an important factor influencing a person's wage, then men and women of identical ages and identical backgrounds in identical occupations will be paid different wages depending on whether they are single, married to a spouse who specializes in household production, or married to a spouse who works outside the home. Single men and women who live alone, who are equally specialized in household and market production, who have the same amounts of human capital, and who do similar jobs will be paid a similar wage. The available evidence suggests that, on the average, when "never-married" men and "never-married" women have the same amount of human capital — measured by years of schooling, work experience, and career interruptions — the wages of the two groups are not identical, but they are much closer than the difference between average wages for men and women. With allowance made for degree of specialization and human capital, the wage differential between women and men lies between 5 and 10 percent, by some estimates. Some economists suspect the remaining discrepancy stems from discrimination against women, although the difficulty of measuring it makes this hypothesis hard to test.

Most of the difference in men's and women's wages arises from the fact that men and women do different jobs, and for the most part, men's jobs are better paid than women's jobs. There are, however, an increasing number of women entering areas that have traditionally been the preserve of men. This trend is particularly clear in professions such as architecture, medicine, economics, law, accounting, and pharmacology. The enrolment of women as a percentage of total enrolments in university courses in these subjects has increased from less than 15 percent in 1975 to near, and in some cases more than, 50 percent today.

Figure 16.9 The Problem of Equal Pay for Work of Equal Value

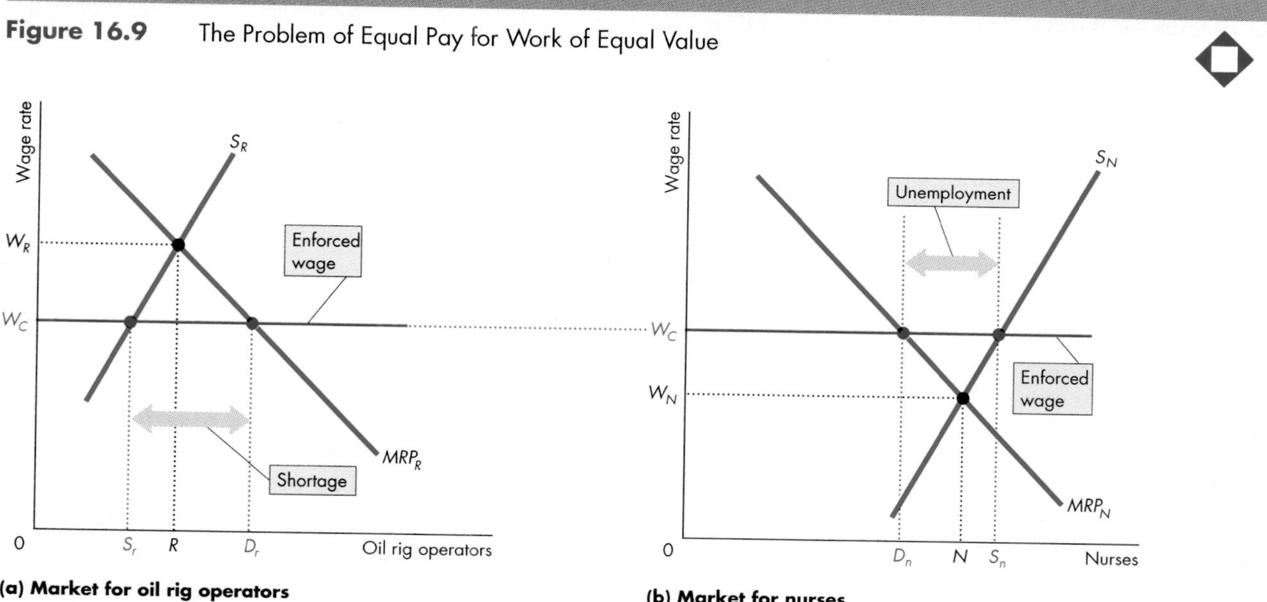

(a) Market for oil rig operators

(b) Market for nurses

The marginal revenue product and supply curves of oil rig operators (MRP_R and S_R) are shown in part (a) and for nurses (MRP_N and S_N) in part (b). The competitive equilibrium wage rate for oil rig operators is W_R and for nurses is W_N. If an evaluation of the two jobs finds that they are of equal value and rules that the same wage rate (W_C) be paid to both types of workers, there will be an excess demand for oil rig operators and an excess supply of nurses. There will be a shortage of $D_r - S_r$ oil-rig operators and $S_n - D_n$ nurses unemployed. Oil producers will have to find other ways of producing oil (ways that are more expensive) and nurses will have to find other jobs (jobs that are less desirable to them and less well paid).

Pay Equity Laws

The federal government and all the provincial governments have passed laws that require "equal pay for equal work without discrimination on the basis of sex."[2] Increasingly, attempts are being made to find ways of comparing jobs that are essentially different but require, on some criteria, similar degrees of skill. Such comparisons lead to a broader concept than "equal pay for equal work"; they call for equal pay for comparable work. Paying the same wage for different jobs that are judged to be comparable is called **equal pay for work of equal value**.

Advocates of pay equity legislation argue that wages should be determined by analysing the characteristics of jobs and determining their worth on objective grounds. However, such a method of determining wage rates does not achieve the objectives sought by supporters of wage equality. Let's see why.

Figure 16.9 shows two markets: that for oil rig operators in part (a) and that for nurses in part (b). The marginal revenue product curves (MRP_R and MRP_N) and the supply curves (S_R and S_N) are shown for each type of labour. Competitive equilibrium generates a wage rate W_R for oil rig operators and W_N for nurses.

Suppose that the knowledge and skills required in those two occupations — the mental and physical demands, the responsibilities, and the working conditions — result in a judgement that these two jobs are of equal value. Suppose that the wage rate that is judged to apply to each of them is W_C. Now suppose that W_C is enforced as part of a pay equity ruling. What will happen? First, there will be a shortage of oil rig operators. Oil rig companies will be able to hire only S_r workers at the wage rate W_C. They will have to cut back their production or build more expensive labour-saving oil rigs. There will also be a fall in nursing employment. But this fall occurs because hospitals will demand fewer nurses. At the higher wage W_C, hospitals will demand only D_n nurses. The quantity of nurses supplied will be S_n. The difference between S_n and D_n will be the number of unemployed nurses looking for jobs.

Thus legislating equal pay for work of equal value may have serious and costly unintended consequences.

[2]Agarwal, N., and Harish, Jain, "Pay Discrimination Against Women in Canada," *International Labour Review*" 117 (March-April 1978): 169-178.

R E V I E W

Differences in earnings based on skill or education level arise because skilled labour has a higher marginal revenue product than unskilled labour and because skills are costly to acquire. Union workers have higher wages than nonunion workers because unions are able to control the supply of labour and indirectly influence the marginal revenue product of their members. Wage differences between the sexes are harder to explain. They may arise from discrimination and from differences in human capital. Sex differentials may also arise in part from differences in the degree of specialization between women (less specialized) and men (more specialized). Pay equity laws cannot, on their own, eliminate wage differentials. Differentials will be reduced only if differences in marginal revenue product are reduced. The process of equalization of human capital and of the degree of specialization will lead to lower differentials and may possibly eliminate them. ■

So far, we have studied labour markets in which workers are compensated for the amount of *time* that they work. Let's now turn our attention to compensation arrangements based on *performance*.

Alternative Compensation Rules

A **compensation rule** is a formula for calculating a person's income. There are four commonly used compensation rules:

- Time-related payments
- Performance-related payments
- Payments based on the performance of a team or group
- Payments based on the performance of one person compared with that of another

Let's consider each of these in turn.

Time-Related Compensation Rules

A compensation rule based on time — the number of hours an individual works — is called a **time rate**; it is expressed in dollars per unit of time — for example, dollars per hour. Many occupations are compensated on a time basis, and almost all production line jobs are rewarded in this way.

Performance-Related Compensation Rules

There are three common measures of output on which performance-related compensation rules are based:

- Physical production (piece rates)
- Value of sales (commissions and royalties)
- Profit (profit-sharing)

Piece Rates A compensation rule based on the amount of output a worker produces is called a **piece rate**. Workers are paid a dollar amount for each piece they produce. The piece may be a very simple item, such as a shirt sleeve, or a more complicated service, such as performing an appendectomy or writing a will. In all these cases, the worker gets paid for the number of units of output produced, not for the number of hours he or she works.

Commissions and Royalties Common among salespersons, realtors, stockbrokers, pop singers, and authors, **commissions and royalties** are forms of compensation based on the value of sales. In all these cases, the person buying the output does not observe the amount of time that the individual works or the amount of effort exerted.

Profit-Sharing A compensation rule that allocates a certain fraction of a firm's profit to its employees is called **profit-sharing**. Such compensation schemes are not as common as the others that we have just considered, and they are usually reserved for senior executives of corporations. Each year, newspapers and magazines publish lists of the top money-making executives of the year. Usually most of their multi-million dollar income is not from salary but from profit-sharing. The compensation of Canada's highest paid executives is examined in Reading Between the Lines on pp. 424-425.

Team Performance

In some production situations that involve teams of workers, the output of the entire team decides the compensation of each of its members. This method of compensation is used, for example, in some team sports — a win results in higher pay for each member of the team. It is also used in team production — a bonus is paid if the team achieves a particular target output level.

Team performance compensation rules can also involve penalties for failure. For example, a buyer and a seller may agree on a price provided delivery takes place by a certain time. Failure to meet the deadline results in a penalty paid by the supplier. Such penalty clauses are not common in labour contracts, but they are often found in transactions between firms.

Comparative Performance

Compensation rules based on comparative performance are a major form of compensation in professional sports. The winner of a tennis tournament typically is paid twice as much as the runner-up, who in turn receives twice as much as the defeated semifinalists, and so on. As we'll see below, the compensation of senior executives in firms can also be interpreted as having a "prize element" for winning.

Our goal is to work out why firms use compensation schemes based on performance. To achieve that understanding, we study what is known as the principal-agent model.

Principals and Agents

A **principal** is an employer — individual, firm, or government — that sets a compensation rule to motivate an agent to choose activities advantageous to the principal. An **agent** is a person hired by a principal to perform various activities, some of which are not observable by the principal. A principal may hire just one or many agents.

The compensation rule chosen by the principal will contain appropriate incentives. An **incentive** is an inducement to an agent to behave in a particular way. The word "incentive" is derived from Latin and means "setting the tune." Thus an incentive can be thought of as a "tune" that induces an agent to "sing the appropriate song."

The observation of an agent's actions by a principal is called **monitoring**. A principal cannot monitor an agent without incurring costs. We call these costs **monitoring costs**. In some situations, monitoring costs are modest; in others, they are high. There are even situations in which, no matter how much is spent on monitoring, the relevant actions of an agent cannot be observed. An example of low monitoring costs occurs in quality-control work. A quality-control worker's effort can be checked by observing how many defective items are missed. An example of a situation in which expensive monitoring costs would

High Pay Executives

Top paycheques feel pinch

The corporate million-dollar club

1989

J.G. Garbutt, American Barrick	$2.1
D.J. Philips, Inco	$1.9
R.M. Smith, American Barrick	$1.9
Edgar Bronfman, Seagram	$1.8
Peter Steen, Corona Corp	$1.7
Paul Stern, Northern Tel	$1.4
E.B Fitzgerald, Northern Tel	$1.3
David Sacks, Seagram	$1.2
J.V.R Cyr, BCE	$1.2
A.R. Haynes Imperial Oil	$1.2
Frank Stronach, Magna	$1.2
W.R. Holland, Amca	$1.1

1988

Peter Munk, American Barrick	$4.6
G. Drabinsky, Cineplex	$3.9
John Walton, Placer Dome	$2.2
R.G. Welty, Gulf Cda	$2.1
D.J. Philips, Inco	$2.0
Edgar Bronfman, Seagram	$1.9
David Sacks, Seagram	$1.8
William James, Falconbridge	$1.7
D.M. Culver, Alcan	$1.5
S.R. Blair, Nova	$1.4
Frank Stronach, Magna	$1.4
M.I. Gottlieb, Cineplex	$1.3
J.H. Butler, Nova	$1.2
J.V.R. Cyr, BCE	$1.1
A.R Haynes, Imperial Oil	$1.1
V.A. Rice, Varity	$1.0
W.G. Wilson, Nova	$1.0
W.E. Stinson, Canadian Pacific	$1.0

Executives expecting lucrative salary increases this year may have their hopes dashed by directors worried about the sluggish economy and dwindling profits.

The Post's annual executive compensation survey shows that although the million-dollar club shrank in 1989, base salary levels for most executives climbed despite a 13% drop in corporate earnings. That has compensation committees of some big companies demanding to know why rising performance-based compensation packages are out of line with corporate profits...

The heady years of stellar earnings growth and soaring stock prices are gone, at least for the near term...

Scott MacCrimmon, a principal at management consultants Peat Marwick Stevenson & Kellogg in Toronto...expects compensation packages will continue to increase in value despite the sluggish economy and an anticipated 6% drop in corporate profits this year.

MacCrimmon's firm, which tracks corporate pay scales, is forecasting a 6% annual rise in the base salaries for Canadian corporate executives...

Peat Marwick studies show the average Canadian corporate executive earns between $125,000 and $261,000 a year. For an executive earning about $200,000, a typical incentive package would provide a $60,000 payment, or a 30% bonus, at yearend...

MacCrimmon says the new trend in executive incentive programs is toward plans designed to be flexible and address specific corporate operations.

"The plans should be designed to award people for pushing the company in the direction it wants to move," he says. "It makes sense to reward sales growth in high-margin products...but offer no bonus for low-margin sales."...

The Financial Post,
April 7-9, 1990
By Heather D. Whyte

The Essence of the Story

- A study by the Toronto management consultants Peat Marwick Stevenson & Kellogg shows that the average Canadian corporate executive earns between $125,000 and $261,000 a year —70 percent of which is base salary and 30 percent of which is bonus.
- The Financial Post's annual executive compensation survey shows that the number of executives with earnings in excess of $1,000,000 decreased in 1989. The table in the news item gives some details and shows that most top earners took a pay cut in 1989.
- The survey also shows that base salary levels for most executives increased.
- Scott MacCrimmon, a principal at Peat Marwick Stevenson & Kellogg says the trend in executive incentive programs is towards "plans designed to award people for pushing the company in the direction it wants to move."

Background and Analysis

- The compensation packages of top executives have two components: a guaranteed minimum income called *base salary* and a *bonus*, the total scale of which depends partly on the effort of the executive and partly on market forces outside the executive's control.
- To hire the services of a top executive, a firm must offer a total compensation package that is at least as good (evaluated by the executive) as that offered by some competing firm. Other things being equal, the quantity of work effort supplied by an executive is larger, the greater the total compensation offered. This is illustrated by the curve *S* in the figure.
- The demand for an executive is determined by his or her marginal revenue product. Just as in the case of any other worker, an executive's marginal revenue product diminishes as the executive's work effort increases. One extra hour of work generates a smaller extra amount of revenue for the firm than the previous hour.
- But the marginal revenue product of an executive cannot be forecasted with accuracy. It depends partly on the quality of the executive, partly on the executive's work effort, and partly on market forces outside the executive's control. Nevertheless, the worst case and most likely marginal revenue products can be assessed. The figure illustrates the worst case as the curve MRP_{min} and the most likely as the curve MRP_{ave}. The actual but unforcastable marginal revenue is the curve *MRP*.
- If the executive is offered a package that includes a base salary equal to the worst case marginal revenue product and a bonus based on actual marginal revenue product, the executive will supply an effort of *E* and expect to receive a total compensation of *CE*. The actual bonus, in the example in the figure, is larger than the expected bonus and total compensation is *CA*.
- Steadily rising prices and steadily advancing technology result in a steady upward movement in three of the curves in the figure: *S*, MRP_{min}, and MRP_{ave}. These forces result in a steady upward movement in base salaries over time.
- Actual marginal revenue product, *MRP*, fluctuates and results in fluctuating bonuses. In 1989, bonuses paid in some industries declined substantially. The cause of this decline was a slowdown in the growth of demand for goods and services and, thus, in the marginal revenue product of executives.

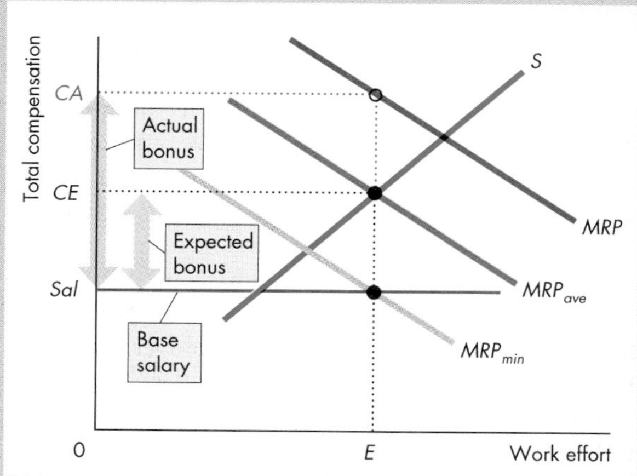

occur is if an auto manufacturer hired a second worker to monitor every assembly line worker. (We don't observe such expensive monitoring on car assembly lines, but if it did occur, the auto manufacturer would probably go broke.) An example of a situation in which monitoring is impossible is in the work of designers, film makers, and other creative artists.

Where monitoring is impossible, a principal has no choice but to use a compensation rule based on those parts of the agent's actions that can be observed. Where monitoring is possible but costly, the principal may be able to avoid monitoring costs by using a compensation rule based on only those aspects of an agent's behaviour that can be observed at low cost. Let's look more closely at the monitoring of an agent's actions. There are many situations in which getting a job done presents problems of monitoring either the output of the worker or the effort that the worker is exerting. Often it is fairly easy to observe output but virtually impossible to measure effort.

Observing Output

Some of the best examples in which we can observe output but not effort are those of professional services. Doctors, dentists, lawyers, and accountants provide services that in many cases are easily observed by their clients. Performing an appendectomy, crowning a tooth, drawing up a will, or preparing an income tax return are all reasonably well-defined activities that can be monitored and observed by the client. The client cannot, however, observe how much effort the doctor, dentist, lawyer, or accountant exerts to produce the service. In all cases, the quantity and quality of the product are known to the buyer, but the time and effort needed to produce it are known only to the supplier — the worker.

Other examples concern the efforts of people who work in a different geographical location from their employer. Salespersons, for example, are hired to sell as much as they can. The employer can readily observe their output, measured in sales, but not the time and energy they put into their job. It is easy for a salesperson to take off a day or two or to mix pleasure with business to the point at which no business is being done. Provided the salesperson's output, measured in terms of sales, is large, the employer will never discover the low volume of effort. In other cases, it is possible to observe effort but hard or impossible to observe output.

Observing Effort

When people work together as a team, it is often easy to observe effort but impossible to observe an individual's output. The team effort produces the output. No one individual can produce the output alone, and the contribution of any one individual to the final output cannot be determined.

Individual effort can be observed, however, when there are precise standards by which to judge it. These standards are present when the output is controlled by some objective circumstance, such as the speed at which a production line is running. In such a case, an individual worker has no choice but to put in the effort required to keep up with the production line. Examples of jobs in which effort can be observed are car assembly lines and steel-rolling mills.

In some cases, neither the output nor the effort of an individual can be observed. Let's now consider these.

Observing Neither Output nor Effort

The best examples of cases in which it is difficult or impossible to observe either the effort being exerted or the output achieved by a single individual are in the area of sports. The effort exerted by a tennis player, a boxer, a football player, and so on is known only to the individual player. The output is a sports event whose quality depends on the joint efforts and interactions of all the players. Each individual player's contribution to the output is virtually impossible to assess. And it is also not possible to calculate each player's contribution to the commercial success of the event — the revenue from selling tickets and broadcast rights.

Although sporting examples are the most obvious ones, there are many other cases in which neither individual effort nor output can be easily monitored. The effort exerted in the board rooms and executive suites of large corporations by chief executives is virtually impossible for their employers (the shareholders of the company) to monitor. The value of the executive's output, the extent to which his or her effort increases the profitability of the corporation, cannot be calculated directly.

When it is not possible to observe effort and output, how can people be compensated so that they do nevertheless supply the right amount of effort and a high-quality output? In a nutshell, how can a principal devise a compensation rule that spurs an agent to take an action that is not observed but brings maximum attainable benefit to the principal?

Efficient Compensation Rules

An efficient compensation rule has two characteristics. The first is that it delivers a maximum expected profit for the principal. A compensation rule that does not maximize the principal's expected profit (net of monitoring costs) can be improved on. Profit-maximizing principals constantly seek out an efficient compensation rule in each situation.

A second characteristic of an efficient compensation rule is that it is acceptable to the agent. That is, whatever rule the principal proposes, it delivers a compensation package that the agent is willing to accept. In a competitive environment, an agent has alternative job possibilities. An efficient compensation rule makes the agent at least as well off as the best available alternative job.

Let's consider an example. Jenny has invented a revolutionary new vacuum cleaner — the Dustbeater — and she is going to hire a salesperson to go on the road and sell her product. She knows that a salesperson can put in a great deal of effort or take a lot of leisure on the job. The salesperson who takes leisure on the job is not going to encounter many potential customers and sales will be low. The salesperson who works hard may have bad luck and do no better than the lazy salesperson but may also have good luck and find a lot of customers with filthy rugs and worn-out vacuum cleaners. But Jenny does not have the time to follow the salesperson around checking on the amount of effort being expended. How is she to tell the difference between a hard-working salesperson who has bad luck and a lazy one?

She structures the compensation package for the salesperson in such a way as to induce him to exert an effort that maximizes her expected income. In figuring out the appropriate contract, she begins by working out the effects of his effort on her income.

Income, Effort, and Luck

Suppose that the total income of Jenny and the salesperson depends on two things: the effort of the salesperson and luck. Let's also suppose that there are two levels of effort — "work" and — "shirk" — and that

Table 16.2 Compensation Schemes for Dustbeater Salespersons

Total incomes, effort, and luck

		Effort: Work	Effort: Shirk
Luck	Good	$140	$60
	Bad	$60	$60

There is an equal (50 percent) chance of good luck or bad luck.

Agent's preferences and alternative employment

Value of time spent working is $20 per day.
Income from alternative employment is $70 per day.
Value of work is $70 minus $20, which is $50 per day.

Compensation rules and outcomes

Rule 1: Principal pays $50.

Value to agent

If the agent works: $50 – $20 = $30
If the agent shirks: $50 – $0 = $50

Outcome: Agent's choice is to shirk.

Total income	=	principal's income	+	agent's income
$60	=	$10	+	$50

Rule 2: Principal pays agent $20 plus 51 percent of value of output.

Value to agent

If the agent works: $\$20 + 0.51\left(\frac{\$140}{2} + \frac{\$60}{2}\right) - \$20 = \$51.00$

If the agent shirks: $\$20 + 0.51(\$60) - \$0 = \$50.60$

Outcome: Agent's choice is to work.

Total income	=	principal's income	+	agent's income
$100	=	$29	+	$71

there are two levels of luck — "good" and "bad." Income depends on the combination of effort and luck. The incomes arising from each of these considerations are set out in Table 16.2. If the agent shirks, total income is $60 regardless of whether there is good or bad luck. If the agent works, total income is $140 if there is good luck and $60 if there is bad luck. The probability (or chance) of good luck is 50 percent, or one-half.

Jenny, the principal, can figure out the four possible outcomes shown in Table 16.2, but she cannot observe the effort of the agent nor tell whether he had good or bad luck. The agent — the salesperson — knows whether or not he is shirking but has no incentive to tell Jenny.

Jenny's problem is to figure out how to compensate the salesperson given the possible outcomes shown in the table. Her next step is to figure out what the salesperson's next best alternative employment prospect is.

Agent's Preferences and Alternatives The agent has alternative employment prospects (selling encyclopaedias or brushes) and also has preferences that Jenny has to take into account in designing the compensation rule. Let's suppose that the agent places a $20 value on shirking. That is, he prefers shirking to working, but a day of shirking and a day of working compensated by $20 are equally acceptable to him.

The agent does not have to sell vacuum cleaners. Let's suppose that selling encyclopaedias would yield him an income of $70 a day but that $20 worth of work would have to be expended to earn it. The net gain to the agent would be $50 a day. Thus to attract the agent, the principal has to offer compensation worth at least $50.

Jenny can now compare two compensation rules: rule 1, which is a daily wage, and rule 2, which is a commission. Under rule 1, Jenny pays the agent $50 a day. The agent calculates the value of working and shirking. Working yields a value of $30 — the $50 paid by Jenny minus the $20 worth of work effort. Shirking yields a value of $50; nothing has to be subtracted from the wage for work effort. In this situation, the agent chooses to shirk. Table 16.2 shows the outcome. The total income generated is $60. According to the compensation rule, Jenny gets $10 and the salesperson $50. Tough luck for Jenny.

Under rule 2, Jenny pays the salesperson $20 a day plus 51 percent of the total income generated. If the agent shirks, regardless of his luck, he generates a total income for Jenny and himself of $60. He is paid 51 percent of that income — $30.60 — plus the fixed payment of $20. Thus his income from shirking is $50.60. If the agent works, his income depends on whether he has good or bad luck. So he calculates his expected or average income. With good luck, total income is $140; with bad luck, it is $60. Since there is an equal chance of good luck and bad luck, total income on the average is $100 (that is, $140 + $60 ÷ 2). The agent gets 51 percent of this amount, or $51. Over and above this amount, Jenny pays $20 a day, but this payment is offset by the value of the effort the agent expends in working. Thus the expected net value of work under this compensation scheme is $51.

The agent compares the outcome from working, $71, with that from shirking, $50.60, and concludes that work yields an income sufficiently higher than shirking to induce him to work. Since expected total income is $100, and the salesperson is paid an average income of $71, Jenny has an average income of $29.

Let's compare rule 1 with rule 2 from both Jenny and the salesperson's viewpoints. Under rule 1, the salesperson has an income of $50. Under rule 2, the salesperson has an income of $71 on the average, but because he has to work, its value is only $51. Even taking into account the distaste for work, the salesperson has $1 more under rule 2 than under rule 1. Jenny has an average income under rule 1 of $10 and under rule 2 of $29. She is better off under rule 2 by $19. Since both Jenny and the salesperson gain by using rule 2, that is the compensation rule that Jenny offers.

This example illustrates why most salespersons are compensated for their work by a commission rather than a fixed daily wage rate. It also explains why piece rates are used to compensate textile workers and royalties to compensate authors. All of these cases are examples in which output can be measured but the effort of the individual worker in producing that output cannot.

Compensation Rules and Teams

The compensation scheme that we have just considered arises in a situation in which the principal can observe the agent's output but not the agent's effort. In other situations, neither individual effort nor individual output can be directly observed. These situations occur when the production process involves a team whose combined efforts determine how much is produced and at what cost. In such cases, a performance-related compensation rule can be used, but it has to be based on the total output of the team rather than on the effort of any individual. The most comprehensive team compensation rule is profit-sharing.

Profit-Sharing The objective of any firm is to maximize profit. Since that is the objective, why is it that not *all* compensation schemes are related to profit? Why aren't all agents compensated by an agreed share of the firm's profit? The main answer to this question is that many situations do not provide a precise enough connection between profit and the output of an individual agent. Profit is the consequence of the joint output of all the firm's inputs.

Profit does, however, give a good indication of the effectiveness of senior managers. It is their job to coordinate the other inputs to achieve maximum profit. That is why profit-sharing arrangements are usually seen in compensation rules for senior managers.

Compensation Rules Based on Rank

Compensation rules that are based on rank deliver a payment related not to the *absolute* output performance of an agent but on the performance of one agent *relative* to another. This type of compensation rule is also common in sports; for that reason, such a rule is usually referred to as a rank-tournament compensation rule. A **rank-tournament compensation rule** is one in which the payment to the agent depends on the agent's rank in the tournament.

Let's see how rank-tournament compensation rules work. Table 16.3 contains an example that we'll use in our exploration. Suppose that there are ten agents, each of whom generates a value of output based on effort and luck in the same way as the agent in Table 16.2. Each agent has the same preferences as before and has the opportunity, from alternative employment, to generate a net return of \$50. Compensation rule 1 simply has the principal paying each agent \$50. The agents accept this compensation rule, but they shirk. Total income is \$600 (10 × \$60); the principal pays the agents \$500 and makes \$100 of income.

Now consider rule 2. The principal pays a prize of \$260 to the agent with the highest output — the agent who comes first in rank — and pays \$50 each to all the other agents. (If two or more agents tie in producing the highest output, the prize is shared.) How do the agents respond to this compensation rule? The answer is worked out in the final part of Table 16.3.

Table 16.3 Rank-Tournament Compensation Scheme

Value of output of each agent

		Effort	
		Work	Shirk
Luck	Good	\$140	\$60
	Bad	\$60	\$60

There is an equal (50 percent) chance of good luck or bad luck. There are 10 agents and the output of each agent is observable.

Compensation rules and outcomes

Rule 1: Principal pays each agent \$50.

Outcome: Each agent's choice is to shirk.

Total income = principal's income + agent's income
\$600 = \$100 + \$500

Rule 2: Principal pays a prize of \$260 to the agent with highest output and \$50 to each other agent (a tie results in sharing the prize).

Value to each agent

If the agent works: (1⁄10) (\$260) + (9⁄10) (\$50) – \$20 = \$51
If the agent shirks: = \$50

Outcome: Each agent's choice is to work.

Total income = principal's income + agent's income
\$1000 = \$290 + \$710

Each agent figures that by working he or she has a one in ten chance of winning the prize and nine in ten chances of not winning the prize. Therefore the agent who works can expect an income of \$71 (1⁄10 × \$260 + 9⁄10 × \$50). The cost of working as opposed to shirking is \$20. Subtracting that amount from the expected income leaves the working agent with an expected dollar value of work effort of \$51. If the agent shirks, there is no chance of winning the prize, so income is $50. In this situation, each agent will choose to work. Since they all work, they will all share the prize and each will receive an income of $71 (the sum of $50, the income for coming in second, plus 1⁄10 of $210, the excess of the prize income over the normal income).

The total value of the work done by the agents — and therefore the principal's income — depends on whether good or bad luck occurs. On the average, the value of the output of a single agent is $100 (the average of $140 and $60). The total income generated by the 10 agents is, on the average, $1,000 ($100 × 10). The agents receive $710 and the principal receives $290.

Comparing the outcomes of the two rules, it is clear that both the principal and the agents gain by operating under rule 2 rather than rule 1.

In practice, rank tournaments usually involve one outright winner rather than a tie, but such compensation rules work for exactly the same reason that this example works. When an agent is given an incentive to try for the prize, he or she finds it advantageous to work, thereby raising the income of the principal as well as that of the agent.

Professional tennis illustrates this type of compensation rule very well. If Martina Navratilova and Steffi Graff were paid by the hour, it would be in their interest to play a match in which the length of the game was such that the cost to each of them of the last hour played equalled the hourly wage rate. If the wage rate was fairly high, they would play a long and boring game. If the wage rate was low, the game would be short (and probably equally boring). It wouldn't matter to either of them who won — they could even agree on the winner before the game began. Compensating such people with a prize for the best player induces each to try to be the best and produces a greater total output — a higher-quality and more exciting game of tennis that people are willing to pay more to watch.

Similar situations can be found in network newsrooms. Newscasters such as Tom Brokaw, Peter Jennings, and Dan Rather receive compensation packages well in excess of $1 million a year. They are talented broadcasters. But there are dozens of other talented broadcasters working with them in their newsrooms and news-gathering organizations around the world. It is hard to monitor the activities of reporters, but the quality of the job that they do influences such things as the total audience size and thus the total revenue that can be generated from advertising during the newscasts. In such a situation, the news-gathering and reporting business can be treated like a tennis match, though the rules for scoring and winning are less precise and more complicated. Those who perform best win the prize of being promoted to the most prestigious position in the news organization. The top prize, anchor on the nightly network news, has to be worth enough to keep the people below that position working hard and competing for it.

The same considerations apply to the executive suites and boardrooms of large corporations. Having large differences in compensation between the chief executive officer and the people on the next rung below that level and so on down the executive ladder creates a competitive environment similar to that of tennis and other sports tournaments. The result is an average level of effort that, though not observed and monitored by anyone, is higher than it would be otherwise. Paying the chief executive twice as much as everybody else makes everybody work harder!

Many individuals are compensated by a combination of the schemes that we have just reviewed. For example, some senior executives are rewarded with a prize for winning a tournament, with a profit share, and with an hourly wage.

We have now seen how simple compensation rules based on observable characteristics of performance can spur agents to work hard for the principal, even when much of their effort cannot be observed. If it is impossible to observe the agent's actions, the principal has no choice but to use such compensation rules. In some other situations, the principal can monitor the agent, making sure that behaviour is in the principal's interest. But monitoring always has costs. With appropriate compensation rules, however, principals can sometimes avoid monitoring costs.

Avoiding Monitoring Costs

To see how a principal can avoid monitoring costs, let's go back to the example of Jenny's vacuum cleaner summarized in Table 16.2. Suppose that by spending $1, Jenny can monitor the salesperson's effort. If a principal can monitor an agent's effort, then it is possible to base the agent's compensation on that effort. Suppose that Jenny incurs the cost of $1 to monitor the salesperson and offers the following compensation rule: if you work, I will pay you $71; if you shirk, I will pay you $50. The salesperson knows that Jenny can monitor his actions and therefore computes the value of working and shirking in the following way:

- If I work, I receive an income of $71 but incur a cost of working of $20. So the net value of my effort is $51.
- If I shirk, I receive an income of $50 but avoid the cost of working. So the net value I receive is $50.
- It pays me to work.

The salesperson works and receives an income of $71. Jenny receives an average income of $28, calculated in the following way. The average income generated by the agent who works is $100 (the average of $140 for good luck and $60 for bad luck). Jenny pays $71 to the salesperson and incurs a $1 monitoring cost. Subtracting these costs from the average total income of $100 leaves her with an average income of $28.

Compare the results we have just worked through with the example in Table 16.2 if rule 2 is employed. Under that rule, Jenny pays the salesperson $20 plus 51 percent of the value of the output. The salesperson works and receives an income, on the average, of $71. Jenny receives an average income of $29. The only difference between monitoring and not monitoring is Jenny's income, which falls by the cost of monitoring. The salesperson earns the same income in both situations. This example shows that a compensation rule can encourage an agent to work hard for a principal, enabling the principal to avoid incurring the cost of monitoring the agent's efforts.

Labour Market Equilibrium

You may be wondering, in light of this discussion of performance-related compensation, what has become of the idea that wages and employment are determined by equilibrium in the labour market. We have simply added a more detailed account of the labour market, one that requires a more detailed notion of labour market equilibrium. Workers supply their time and effort in whatever way makes them best off. They have a variety of choices concerning not only the type of job to take and the number of hours to work but also the type of compensation scheme to accept. On the demand side of the market, firms decide not only how much of each type of labour to hire but also which available compensation scheme to choose for paying those workers. An equilibrium in the labour market consists of wage rates for different types of jobs, employment quantities in different jobs and industries, and a list of compensation rules that are actually used in each different type of employment. In labour market equilibrium, no individual worker (agent) can switch from one job to another or from one compensation rule to another and become better off. Moreover, no firm (principal) can offer a different compensation rule that will raise profit.

This description of equilibrium does not mean that clever principals cannot devise new, previously unthought of compensation rules that work better than the existing ones. There is technical progress in devising compensation rules, just as there is technical progress in devising ways of getting cows to produce milk and tomato plants to produce fruit. But at any particular point in time, given the alternative rules that have been invented, the best available compensation rule for each situation is being used. That is the compensation rule that provides the agent with at least as good a deal as the next best alternative employment and that maximizes the principal's profit.

■ In this chapter, we have extended the factor markets model and applied it to an understanding of a wide variety of phenomena in labour markets, such as wage differentials and alternative compensation schemes. In the next chapter, we apply and extend the factor markets model to deal with markets for capital and for natural resources.

S U M M A R Y

Skill Differentials

Skill differentials arise partly because skilled labour has a higher marginal product than unskilled labour and partly because skills are costly to acquire. The higher marginal product of skilled workers results in a higher marginal revenue product. Since the demand for labour curve is derived from the marginal revenue product curve, the higher the marginal revenue product of skilled labour, the greater is the demand for skilled labour.

Skills are costly to acquire because households have to invest in human capital to become skilled.

Investment sometimes means making direct payments, such as tuition and other training fees, and sometimes means working for a lower wage during on-the-job training. Because skills are costly to acquire, households supply skilled labour on terms that compensate them for both the time spent on the job and the costs of acquiring the skills. Thus the supply curve of skilled labour lies above the supply curve of unskilled labour.

The wage rates of skilled and unskilled labour are determined by demand and supply in the two labour markets. The equilibrium wage rate for skilled labour exceeds that for unskilled labour. The wage differential reflects the higher marginal product of skill and the cost to acquire skill. (pp. 407-409)

Union-Nonunion Wage Differentials

Labour unions influence wages by controlling the supply of labour. In competitive labour markets, unions obtain higher wages only at the expense of lower employment. Even so, unions can increase the total wage bill by forcing firms to hire at the point on their marginal revenue product curve at which the demand for labour is less elastic. Unions in competitive industries also influence the marginal revenue product of their members by restricting imports, raising minimum wages, supporting immigration restrictions, increasing demand for their product, and increasing the marginal product of their members.

In a monopsony — a market in which there is a single buyer — unions increase wages without sacrificing employment. Bilateral monopoly occurs when the union is a monopoly seller of labour, the firm is a monopsony buyer of labour, and the wage rate is determined by bargaining between the two parties.

In practice, union workers earn an estimated 15 to 35 percent more than comparable nonunion workers. (pp. 410-417)

Wage Differentials Between the Sexes

There are persistent differentials in earnings between women and men. Three possible explanations are discrimination, differences in human capital, and differences in degree of specialization.

Discrimination results in lower wage rates and lower employment for those discriminated against and higher wage rates and higher employment levels for those discriminated in favour of. Human capital differences result from differences in schooling and work experience. Differentials based on schooling have been falling and are almost eliminated. Differentials based on work experience have kept women's pay below men's because women's careers have traditionally been interrupted more frequently than those of men, resulting, on the average, in a smaller accumulation of human capital. This difference is less important today than in the past. Differentials arising from different degrees of specialization are probably important and may persist. Men have traditionally been more specialized in market activity than women. Women have traditionally undertaken both nonmarket (household production) activities and market activities. Attempts to test for the importance of the degree of specialization suggest that it is an important source of the earnings difference between men and women. (pp. 417-421)

Pay Equity Laws

Pay equity laws determine wages by assessing the value of different types of jobs on objective characteristics rather than on what the market will pay. Determining wages through the principle of equal pay for work of equal value will result in a cut in the number of people employed in jobs in which the market places a lower value and shortages of those workers whom the market values more highly. Thus the attempt to achieve equal wages for work of equal value has costly, unintended consequences. (pp. 422)

Alternative Compensation Rules

There are four commonly used compensation rules:

- Time-related payments
- Performance-related payments
- Payments based on the performance of a team or group
- Rank-related payments (pp. 422-423)

Principals and Agents

Compensation rules are studied by using a principal-agent model. A principal is a person who specifies the compensation rule and the agent is a person who works for a principal and receives an income determined by the compensation rule. The principal's goal is to devise a compensation rule that will spur the agent to maximize the principal's profit.

In many production situations, observing or

monitoring a worker's effort or output is either expensive or impossible. In some situations, output is easily observed but effort is not. In other situations, effort is easily observed but output is not. In some cases, neither output nor effort is readily observable. For situations in which effort, output, or both are unobservable, principals have to devise compensation rules that induce agents to work in a profit-maximizing way. (pp. 423-427)

Efficient Compensation Rules

Compensation rules have two characteristics: acceptability to the agent and profit maximization for the principal. When an individual agent's effort can be easily monitored but output is harder to observe, principals commonly use time rates of pay. When effort is not easily measured but output is, a compensation rule based on the agent's output can result in maximum profit for the principal. By paying an agent an amount that varies with output or that is some fraction of the value of the agent's output, the principal can induce the agent to work harder and produce more.

Even when the principal can monitor the agent at some expense, it may still be possible to use a compensation rule that enables the principal to make maximum profit while avoiding the monitoring costs.

In labour market equilibrium, no individual worker or firm can become better off by adopting a different compensation rule. On the supply side, workers determine how much time and effort to supply, but they also decide which compensation scheme to accept. On the demand side, firms decide not only how much labour to hire but also what compensation schemes to offer. Labour market equilibrium consists of wage rates for different types of labour, the amount of employment in different jobs and industries, and a list of compensation rules for each different type of job. (pp. 427-431)

K E Y E L E M E N T S

Key Terms

Agent, 423
Bilateral monopoly, 417
Binding arbitration, 411
Closed shop, 410
Collective bargaining, 411
Commissions and royalties, 423
Compensation rule, 422
Craft union, 410
Equal pay for work of equal value, 422
Household production, 420
Human capital, 407
Incentive, 423
Industrial union, 410
Labour union, 410
Lockout, 411
Monitoring, 423
Monitoring costs, 423
Monopsony, 413
Piece rate, 423
Principal, 423
Professional association, 411
Profit-sharing, 423
Rand formula, 410
Rank-tournament compensation rule, 429
Strike, 411
Time rate, 422

Key Figures and Table 

REVIEW QUESTIONS

1 Explain why skilled workers are paid more than unskilled workers.

2 What are the main types of labour unions?

3 How does a labour union try to influence wages?

4 What can a union do in a competitive labour market?

5 How might a union increase the demand for its members' labour?

6 Under what circumstances would a minimum wage increase employment?

7 How big are the union-nonunion wage differentials in Canada today?

8 What are the three main reasons why earnings differentials exist between men and women?

9 How do pay equity laws work? What are their predicted effects?

10 What are the main alternative compensation schemes?

11 Define and distinguish between a principal and an agent.

12 What are monitoring costs?

13 Why are student helpers at McDonald's paid by the hour rather than by the number of hamburgers they sell?

14 Why does Dan Rather make a higher wage than the cameraman filming the war-torn streets of Beirut for the evening news?

PROBLEMS

1 Wendy owns an apple orchard. She employs students to pick the apples. Students can pick the following amounts of apples in an hour:

Number of students	Quantity of apples (kilograms)
1	20
2	50
3	90
4	120
5	145
6	165
7	180
8	190

The price of apples is 50 cents a pound and the competitive wage rate is $7.50 an hour. The fruit pickers become unionized and the union forces an increase in the wage rate to $10 an hour.

a) How many unionized pickers will Wendy hire?

b) How many students who worked as pickers before the union was established lose their jobs?

c) What do you predict will happen to the wage rates of students doing nonunion jobs in Wendy's town?

d) What could the union do to protect the jobs of fruit pickers?

e) What could the union do to prevent wages in the nonunion sector from falling?

2 In a small isolated town in the Rocky Mountains the only firm hiring workers is a logging company. The firm's demand for labour and the town's supply of labour are given by:

Wage rate (dollars per hour)	Quantity supplied (hours per day)	Quantity demanded (hours per day)
2	120	400
3	160	360
4	200	320
5	240	280
6	280	240
7	320	200
8	360	160

The townspeople form a union that is more powerful than the logging company.

a) What is the wage rate that the union establishes?

b) How many people does the logging company employ?

c) How many people who had a job with the logging company before the union was formed, lose their jobs?

d) Does the total wage bill of the logging company increase, decrease, or remain the same after the formation of the union?

e) What can the union do to prevent the loss of jobs in the town's logging industry?

f) What can the unemployed logging workers do to undermine the union and obtain work?

3 The value of the output of labour in a particular production process depends on how many potential snags it has and how hard the firm's agents work. An agent may work hard, give average effort, or shirk, and the production process may have lots of snags, average snags, or no snags. Depending on which combination of these situations prevail, the marginal revenue product of a worker will be one of the numbers set out in the table:

	Work hard	Average effort	Shirk
Lots of snags	$100	$70	$70
Average snags	140	100	70
No snags	180	140	100

From a worker's point of view, shirking has no cost. Supplying an average effort has a cost of $10 and working hard has a cost of $20. The worker has to be offered a compensation arrangement that is worth at least $50.

Devise a compensation scheme that will make the maximum possible profit for the principal.

4 Suppose there were three national football leagues: the Time League, the Goal Difference League, and the Bonus for Win League. The teams are of approximately equal quality, but the players in each league are paid differently. In the first league, they are paid by the hour for time spent practising and time spent playing. In the second league, they are paid an amount that depends on the number of points that the team scores minus the number of points scored against it. In the third league, the players are paid one wage for a loss, a higher wage for a tie, and the highest wage of all for a win.

Briefly describe the predicted differences in the quality of the games played by each of these leagues. Which league will be the most attractive to players and generate the biggest profits?

CHAPTER 17

Capital and Natural Resource Markets

After studying this chapter, you will be able to:

- Define and distinguish among financial and real assets, capital, and investment.
- Define and distinguish between saving and portfolio choice.
- Describe the structure of capital markets in Canada today.
- Explain how interest rates and stock prices are determined and why the stock market fluctuates.
- Define natural resources and explain how their prices are determined.
- Explain how markets regulate the pace at which we use exhaustible resources such as oil.

Boom and Bust

On Monday, October 19, 1987, an air of panic filled the cavernous stock exchanges of Montreal and Toronto, New York, and Tokyo. It had taken five years, from August 1982, for the average price of a common stock to climb 200 percent. But on that single day, stock prices fell an unheard-of 11.3 percent in Toronto and 22.6 percent in New York — knocking billions of dollars off the value of people's investments. The crash touched off other stock market plunges around the world. Why did the stock market boom for five years and then crash so suddenly and so spectacularly? ■ If you had bought $1,000 worth of the stock of Circuit City Stores in August 1982, five years later your $1,000 would have grown in value to an impressive $3,337,300. In contrast, if in 1981 you had bought $1,000 worth of the stock of Mitel Corporation, a maker of office telephone equipment based in Kanata, Ontario, by February 1989, you would have had only $53 left. Why do shares of some companies' stocks boom and others slump? What determines the prices of individual companies' stocks? ■ The Toronto Stock Exchange, large as it is, is only a part of the enormous capital market of North America. And the capital market of North America is just a part of an even more enormous worldwide capital market. Every year, billions of dollars are saved and flow into the nation's and the world's capital markets. Savings flow through various channels — banks, insurance companies, and stock exchanges — and end up financing the purchases of machinery, factory and office buildings, cars, homes, and a host of other capital goods. How does a dollar saved and placed on deposit in a bank help a firm to finance the purchase of a shiny new machine? How does your purchase of life insurance enable Labatts to buy a new beer-bottling plant? ■ Giant firms, such as the Hudson's Bay Company, and household names, such as Wardair and Holiday Inns, have been taken over by other companies in recent years. Other firms, such as Molson Breweries and an Australian company, Elders IXL, have merged to pool their strength in an attempt to capture a larger share of the North American beer market. Takeovers and mergers affect the jobs of hundreds of thousands of people and change the competitive balance in entire industries. Why do firms merge or get taken over?

■ Many of our natural resources are exhaustible, and yet we are using up these resources at an alarming rate. Every year we burn billions of cubic metres of natural gas and petroleum. We burn millions of tonnes of coal, we extract bauxite to make aluminium and iron ore and other minerals to make steel. Aren't we one day going to run out of natural gas, oil, coal, bauxite, iron ore, and other natural resources? How do markets allocate these exhaustible resources? How are their prices determined? And do their prices adjust to encourage us to conserve such resources, or does the market need help to ensure that we do not pillage the exhaustible endowments of nature?

■ In this chapter, we're going to study capital and natural resource markets. We'll find out why people save as much or as little as they do and why firms buy the amount of new capital equipment that they do. We will find out how interest rates and stock values are determined. In our study of natural resource markets, we'll discover that these markets obey some of the same economic laws as capital markets. We'll pay special attention to markets for exhaustible resources and discover how market forces act to encourage conservation.

Capital, Investment, and Saving

Let's begin with some capital market vocabulary and define three key terms:

- Asset
- Liability
- Balance sheet

An **asset** is anything of value that a household, firm, or government *owns*. A **liability** is a debt — something that a household, firm, or government *owes*. A **balance sheet** is a list of assets and liabilities.

Table 17.1 shows an example of a balance sheet — that for Rocky's Mountain Bikes. It lists three assets: cash in the bank, an inventory of bikes, and fixtures and fittings — that add up to $243,000. The balance sheet contains two liabilities: a bank loan of $120,000 and the amount the firm owes to Rocky — Rocky's equity in the firm — which is $123,000.

Financial Assets and Real Assets

Assets fall into two broad classes: financial and real. A **financial asset** is a claim against another household, firm, or government. It is a type of IOU. When you hold an IOU, it means that somebody else owes you money. Similarly, if you own a financial asset, someone else has a financial liability — owes you money. For example, the savings deposit that you own (your asset) is a liability of your bank. The difference between financial assets and financial liabilities is called **net financial assets.** Net financial assets are the net value of the paper claims that one household, firm, or government has against everyone else.

Real assets are physical things such as buildings, plant, and equipment, inventories, and consumer durable goods. Real assets are also called capital. **Capital** is the real assets owned by a household, firm, or government.

Table 17.2 illustrates the distinction between financial assets and real assets by again presenting the information contained in the balance sheet of

Table 17.1 Balance Sheet of Rocky's Mountain Bikes as at January 1, 1991

Assets		Liabilities	
Cash in bank	$ 18,000	Bank loan	$120,000
Inventory of bikes	15,000	Rocky's equity	123,000
Fixtures and fittings	210,000	Total liabilities	$243,000
Total assets	$243,000		

Table 17.2 Financial Assets, Financial Liabilities, and Real Assets of Rocky's Mountain Bikes as at January 1, 1991

Financial assets (+) and financial liabilities (–)	
Cash in bank	$ 18,000
Bank loan	– 120,000
Rocky's equity	– 123,000
Net financial assets	–$225,000
Real assets	
Inventory of bikes	$ 15,000
Fixtures and fittings	210,000
Capital	$225,000

Rocky's Mountain Bikes. But this time the information is sorted into financial and real items. The financial items in the balance sheet are the cash in bank (an asset) and the bank loan (a liability). To calculate net financial assets, we have to subtract financial liabilities from financial assets, so the bank loan and Rocky's equity appear with negative signs. The net financial assets of Rocky's Mountain Bikes are $225,000. The real assets are the inventory of bikes and the fixtures and fittings — the firm's capital — which add up to $225,000.

Capital and Investment

All the assets and liabilities recorded in a balance sheet are stocks. A **stock** is a quantity measured at a point in time. An example of a stock is the amount of water in Lake Ontario at a given moment. Capital is a stock because it is the quantity of buildings, plant, and machinery in existence at a given point in time.

A concept related to the stock of capital is the flow of investment. A **flow** measures a quantity per unit of time. An example of a flow is the number of litres of water per hour passing from Lake Erie over the Niagara Falls into Lake Ontario. It is a flow that adds to the stock of water in Lake Ontario. **Investment** is the amount of new capital equipment purchased in a given time period. It is a flow that adds to the stock of capital.

There is another flow that reduces the stock of capital — like the water flowing out of Lake Ontario into the St. Lawrence River. That flow is called depreciation. **Depreciation** is the fall in the value of capital resulting from its use and from the passage of time. Investment adds to the capital stock; depreciation lowers the capital stock. The net change in the capital stock is the difference between investment and depreciation. To emphasize this fact, we distinguish between **gross investment**, the value of all the new capital purchased in a given time period, and **net investment**, which equals gross investment minus depreciation.

Saving and Portfolio Choice

The quantity of capital supplied results from people's saving decisions. **Saving** is income minus consumption. The sum of a household's past saving, together with any inheritances it has received, is the household's **wealth**. Wealth is allocated across a variety of financial and real assets in a manner described by the household's balance sheet. A household's choice regarding how much to hold in various assets and how much to owe in various liabilities is called a **portfolio choice**. For example, if a household decides to borrow $100,000 from a bank and to use that $100,000 to buy shares of stock in a corporation, the household is making a portfolio choice. It is choosing the amount of an asset (the equity in a corporation) and the amount of a liability (the bank loan).

In everyday language, we often refer to the purchase of stocks or bonds as investment. That everyday use of the word "investment" can cause confusion in economic analysis. It is to avoid that confusion that we use the term *portfolio choice* to refer to the choices that households make in allocating their wealth across the various assets available to them. We reserve the word *investment* to refer to the purchases of new real assets by firms and households.

We can see examples of the concepts of saving, wealth, and portfolio choice by looking at Rocky's *personal* situation — at Rocky's household balance sheet. On January 1, 1991, Rocky has wealth of $150,000 (see Table 17.3). During 1991, Rocky earns an income of $58,000, consumes $50,000, and saves $8,000. His wealth rises to $158,000 on January 1, 1992.

How has Rocky allocated his wealth among the various assets and liabilities? Table 17.4 separates Rocky's financial assets and liabilities from his real

Table 17.3 Rocky's Income, Consumption, Saving, and Wealth

	Income	Consumption	Saving	Wealth
Net worth on January 1, 1991				$150,000
Flows during 1991	$58,000	$50,000	$8,000	
Net worth on January 1, 1992				$158,000

assets. His financial assets include, first of all, his equity in Rocky's Mountain Bikes. Second, Rocky has some cash in the bank; this is his own personal bank account and is completely separate from the cash in the bike business. Third, Rocky has a mortgage on his home of $140,000 and a bank loan of $10,000 secured by the value of his car. Rocky's personal net financial assets are -$17,000. Note the minus sign. It tells us that Rocky *owes* $17,000 more than he *owns* — his net financial assets are negative.

Rocky's real assets are his house (valued at $160,000), and his car (valued at $15,000), so his capital stock is $175,000. Rocky's wealth is the sum of his capital stock and his net financial assets. Since Rocky's net financial assets are negative (he owes more than he owns), his wealth is his capital stock minus what he owes — $158,000.

With exactly the same saving, investment, and wealth, Rocky could have chosen a different portfolio allocation. For example, he could have used his bank deposit to pay off his car loan or part of his mortgage. Alternatively, he could have taken a bigger mortgage and a smaller car loan. Saving and investment decisions determine how much wealth a person has. Portfolio decisions determine how that wealth is held and financed.

Table 17.4 Rocky's Financial Assets and Real Assets at January 1, 1992.

Financial assets (+) and financial liabilities (–)	
Equity in Rocky's Mountain Bikes	$123,000
Cash in bank	10,000
Mortgage	–140,000
Car loan	– 10,000
Net financial assets	–$17,000
Real assets	
House	$160,000
Car	15,000
Capital	$175,000
Wealth	$158,000

R E V I E W

There are two kinds of assets, financial and real. Financial assets are the paper claims that lenders have on borrowers. One person's financial asset is another person's financial liability. Real assets are buildings, plant and equipment, and inventories. Physical capital is the stock of real assets in existence at a point in time. Additions to the stock of capital are called investment. Capital wears out over time. This process is called depreciation. The quantity of capital supplied results from people's saving decisions. Saving is income minus consumption. The accumulated sum of past saving is wealth. The allocation of wealth among different assets is called portfolio choice. ■

Capital Markets in Canada Today

Capital markets are the channel whereby savings are translated into investment — into the accumulation of capital. Investment takes place in three broad ways:

- Households buy capital.
- Firms buy capital and finance it by selling stocks and bonds to households.
- Firms buy capital and finance it by obtaining loans from financial intermediaries, who in turn take in households' savings.

Figure 17.1 illustrates the structure of capital markets and the financing of investment. The arrows in the figure show that households can employ their savings (allocate their portfolios of wealth) in the three ways just listed:

- They can own firms directly (proprietorships and partnerships).
- They can buy stocks or bonds issued by firms.
- They can place deposits with financial intermediaries.

A **financial intermediary** is a firm whose principal business is taking deposits, making loans, and buying securities. The best known type of financial intermediary is a chartered bank. A **chartered bank** is a financial intermediary that takes deposits and makes loans.

Other important types of financial intermediaries are insurance companies and trust companies. An **insurance company** takes in the savings of households and provides life insurance and pensions. It lends the money received from households to firms by buying equity or bonds. A **trust company** takes in savings from households and makes loans, mainly back to households in the form of mortgages. A **mortgage** is a loan secured by the value of land and buildings.

Coordinating the actions of households, firms, and financial intermediaries are the markets for stocks and bonds. The **stock market** is a market in which the equities of firms are traded. The **bond market** is a market in which the bonds issued by firms and governments are traded. (Governments are not shown in the figure, but they are important participants in the bond market). The distinction between equity and bonds was made in Chapter 9. Firms sell stocks and bonds in exchange for money to finance their investment. Governments also sell bonds to finance their budget deficits. Households

Figure 17.1 Capital Market Flows

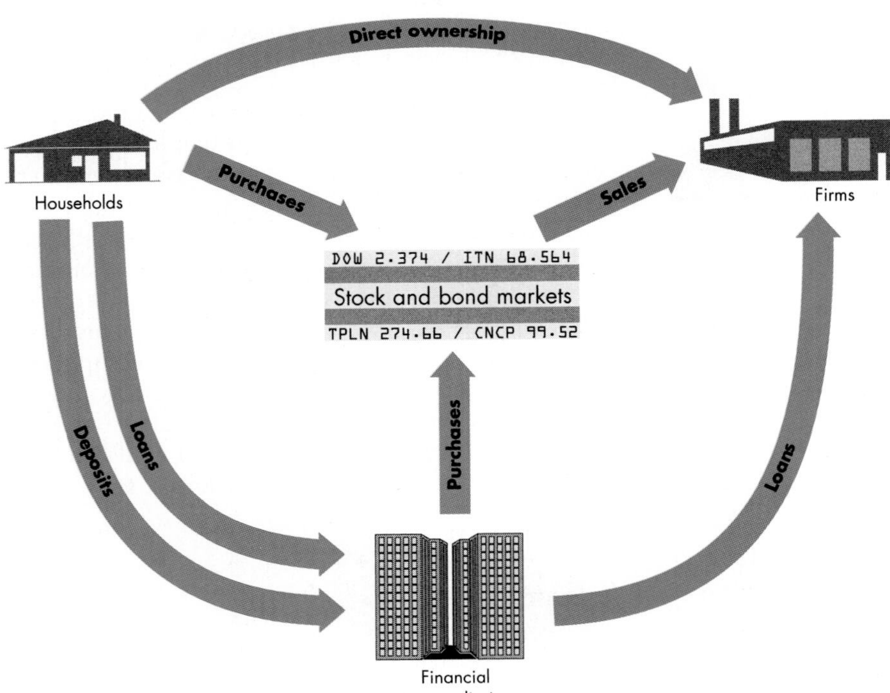

Households, firms, and financial intermediaries have extensive interactions in capital markets. These three institutions have direct transactions with each other and indirect transactions through the stock and bond markets. The flows of funds among these institutions are shown by the green arrows.

and financial intermediaries buy new stocks and bonds and also buy and sell existing ones.

Bearing Risk

The direct ownership of capital is the riskiest portfolio choice for a household. It is placing all one's eggs in a single basket. For instance, if Rocky's bike firm fails, his household loses its wealth. If the bike firm succeeds, Rocky can earn an enormous return. Buying stocks, such as shares in Stelco or bonds in Seagram's, is the second most risky way of allocating one's wealth. By holding a diverse collection of stocks, a household can spread its risk and avoid the extremes that can occur from lending to a single firm or a single project. Even so, there is still some risk because stock prices fluctuate. When stock prices fall, a household loses some of its wealth. Nevertheless, buying stocks is a much safer portfolio choice than putting everything into a single firm or project.

Bonds are less risky than stocks, but their prices fluctuate so they are not a completely safe portfolio choice.

The safest place to put one's wealth is on deposit with a financial intermediary. The risk associated with this portfolio choice is that a financial intermediary may make bad loans and be unable to repay its depositors. Although financial intermediaries fail on occasion, such failures are rare. Furthermore, deposit insurance provides guarantees in the event of a failure.

The Nation's Balance Sheet

How large are the Canadian capital markets? How big a role do the various elements play? The borrowing and lending pictured in Fig. 17.1 can be measured in the nation's balance sheet. This balance sheet lists the assets and liabilities of each of the economy's major groups of agents — households, financial intermediaries, firms, and governments. Figure 17.2 provides a picture of those balance sheets. The data, in billions of dollars, are for December 31, 1988, the most recent available. (To enable us to focus on the major patterns in the national balance sheet, the items have been rounded to the nearest $50 billion.) Financial assets are shown in blue, real assets in orange, and liabilities in red. The green arrows show the direction of the flow of funds.

First, look at the households. They had financial assets in the form of deposits with financial intermediaries, savings in pension funds and life insurance, a stake in the equity of the firms whose shares they own, and bonds. The total of these items at the end of 1988 was $1,550 billion. Households had financial liabilities in the form of mortgages and consumer credit, which at the end of 1988 totalled $300 billion. The total financial assets of households exceeded their liabilities by $1,250 billion ($1,550 billion –$300 billion). Households owned real assets in the form of houses, consumer durable goods, and land which was valued at the end of 1988 at a total of $850 billion ($450 billion houses + $200 billion consumer durables + $200 billion land). Total household wealth, the sum of net financial and real assets, was $2,100 billion.

Next look at the financial intermediaries. Their liabilities are the deposits and pension funds and life insurance that we have just seen as the assets of households. They are liabilities of financial intermediaries because the financial intermediaries "owe" them to households. These institutions are ultimately owned by the households who have bought shares in their stock — equity. The assets of financial intermediaries represent loans by these institutions to households, firms, and governments. Financial intermediaries make loans to households in the form of mortgages and consumer credit. They also make mortgage loans to firms. They make additional loans to firms and to governments by purchasing the bonds issued by these institutions. These bond sales and mortgage loans provide firms and governments with funds to buy real assets. At the end of 1988, the financial assets and liabilities of financial intermediaries were each $750 billion.

The financial liabilities of firms — bonds ($250 billion), mortgages ($50 billion), and equity ($700 billion) — totalled $1,000 billion. This amount was matched by their capital — buildings ($500 billion), plant and equipment ($250 billion), land ($150 billion), and inventories ($100 billion).

Government financial liabilities (bonds) generate funds to finance the purchase of buildings and land.

The numbers in Fig. 17.2 give you an idea of the scale of the operations of the various elements in the capital markets. But they do not provide a sense of the huge volume of transactions that take place — the flow of activity each day — or of the dynamic change over time in the scale of capital market transactions. The daily turnover in the ownership of stocks and bonds is enormous. On an average day in 1987, 23 million individual stocks changed hands on

Figure 17.2 The Nation's Balance Sheet

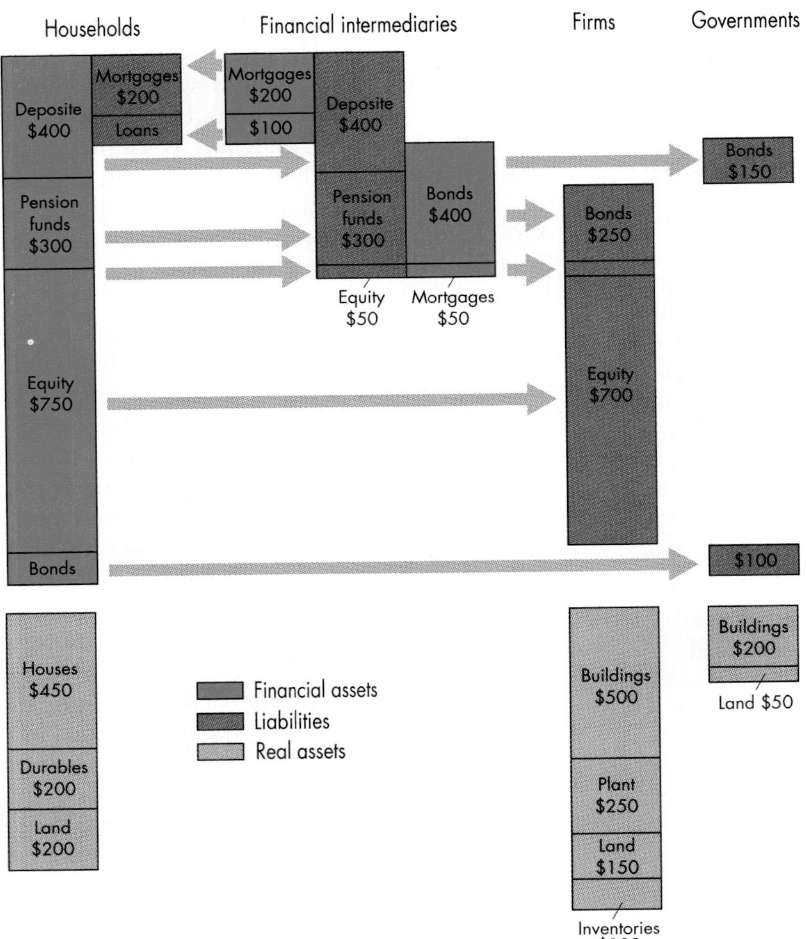

The nation's balance sheet records the indebtedness between the sectors of the economy — households, firms, financial intermediaries, and governments. The financial assets (blue) and liabilities (red) are shown in the top part of the figure, and capital or real assets (orange) appear in the bottom part. All numbers are billions of dollars (rounded to the nearest $50 billion).

Households' financial assets are deposits with financial intermediaries, life insurance and pension funds, equity, and bonds. These assets are the liabilities of financial intermediaries, firms, and governments. Financial intermediaries take deposits and life insurance and pension fund contributions from households. Then they lend some of these funds back to households as mortgages and consumer credit; the remainder are lent to firms and governments in the form of bonds and mortgages. Both firms and governments borrow from financial intermediaries and households. Capital (real assets) consists of houses and consumer durables owned by households and of plant and equipment and buildings owned by firms and governments.

Source: Statistics Canada, *National Balance Sheet Accounts Matrix*, (Ottawa, 1989).

the Toronto Stock Exchange. On what has come to be called Black Monday — October 19, 1987 — a record 64 million shares were traded.

The Demand for Capital

The demand for capital, like the demand for any other input, stems from firms' profit-maximizing choices. As a firm increases the quantity of capital employed, other things being equal, the marginal revenue product of capital diminishes. To maximize profit, a firm uses additional amounts of capital until the marginal revenue product of capital equals the opportunity cost of a unit of capital. That is, the firm increases its capital stock until the additional total revenue generated by one extra unit of capital equals the opportunity cost of one unit of capital.

Sometimes a firm rents capital equipment and sometimes it buys it. When a firm rents capital equipment, its calculations are identical to those it makes in choosing its labour input. The firm faces an hourly rate for renting a machine. This is the machine's opportunity cost. To decide whether or not to rent a unit of capital for one more hour, the firm calculates the marginal revenue product of the machine per hour and compares that number with the hourly rental rate. So long as the marginal revenue product per hour exceeds the rental rate per hour, the firm increases the number of units of capital hired each hour. Many machines are, in fact, rented — for example, earth-moving equipment, cars, and airplanes — so these calculations are relevant in such cases.

But most capital is not rented. Firms *buy* buildings, plant, and equipment and operate them for several years. To decide how much capital equipment to buy, the firm has to compare the price of the equipment to be paid here and now with the return — the marginal revenue product — that the equipment will generate over its entire life. To see how a firm decides how much capital to buy, we need to convert the future stream of marginal revenue products into its present value so that it can be compared directly with the price of buying a new piece of capital equipment. You have already met the concept of present value in Chapter 9, and you may want to flip back to it to refresh your memory before moving on.

Net Present Value of Investment

Let's calculate the present value of the marginal revenue product of a capital input and see how we can use the result to make an investment decision. Table 17.5 summarizes the data that we'll use.

Table 17.5 Net Present Value of an Investment — Taxfile Inc.

(a) Data

Price of computer	$10,000
Life of computer	2 years
Marginal revenue product	$5,900 at end of each year
Interest rate	4% per year

(b) Present value of the flow of marginal revenue product

$$PV = \frac{MRP}{1+r} + \frac{MRP}{(1+r)^2}$$

$$= \frac{\$5{,}900}{1.04} + \frac{\$5{,}900}{(1.04)^2}$$

$$= \$5{,}673 + \$5{,}455$$

$$= \$11{,}128$$

(c) Net present value of investment

$$NPV = PV \text{ of marginal revenue product} - \text{cost of computer}$$

$$= \$11{,}128 - \$10{,}000$$

$$= \$1{,}128$$

Tina runs a firm called Taxfile Inc. The firm sells advice to taxpayers designed to minimize the taxes that they have to pay. Tina is considering buying a new computer that will cost $10,000. The computer has a life of two years, after which it will be worthless. Although Tina works hard all year studying tax law and writing sophisticated computer programs that will enable her to corner a good share of the market, she generates an income only once each year — at tax filing time. If she buys the computer that she is now evaluating, Tina expects to be able to sell tax advice in each of the next two years that will bring in $5,900 at the end of each year. The interest rate that she has to pay is 4 percent a year.

We can calculate the present value of the marginal revenue product of Taxfile's computer by using a formula similar to the one that you met in Chapter 9. The formula is set out in Table 17.5(b). The present value (*PV*) of $5,900 one year in the future is $5,900 divided by 1.04 (one plus the interest rate expressed as a proportion — 4 percent as a proportion is 0.04). The present value of $5,900 two years in the future is \$5,900 divided by $(1.04)^2$. Working out those two present values and then adding them gives the present value of the flow of marginal revenue product from the machine as \$11,128.

To decide whether or not to buy the computer, Tina compares the present value of its stream of marginal revenue product with its price. She makes this comparison by calculating the net present value (*NPV*) of the investment. The **net present value of an investment** is the present value of the stream of marginal revenue product generated by the investment minus the cost of the investment. If the net present value of an investment is positive, it pays to buy the item. If the net present value of an investment is negative, it does not pay to buy this item. Part (c) of Table 17.5 shows the calculation of the net present value of Tina's investment in a computer. It is

Table 17.6 Taxfile's Investment Decision

(a) Data

Price of computer	\$10,000
Life of computer	2 years
Marginal revenue product:	
Using 1 computer	\$5,900 a year
Using 2 computers	\$5,600 a year
Using 3 computers	\$5,300 a year

(b) Present value of the stream of marginal revenue product

If $r = 0.04$ (4% a year):

Using 1 computer: $PV = \frac{\$5,900}{1.04} + \frac{\$5,900}{(104)^2} = \$11,128$

Using 2 computers: $PV = \frac{\$5,600}{1.04} + \frac{\$5,600}{(1.04)^2} = \$10,562$

Using 3 computers: $PV = \frac{\$5,300}{1.04} + \frac{\$5,300}{(1.04)^2} = \$\ 9,996$

If $r = 0.08$ (8% a year):

Using 1 computer $PV = \frac{\$5,900}{1.08} + \frac{\$5,900}{(108)^2} = \$10,521$

Using 2 computers $PV = \frac{\$5,600}{1.08} + \frac{\$5,600}{(1.08)^2} = \$\ 9,986$

If $r = 0.12$ (12% a year):

Using 1 computer $PV = \frac{\$5,900}{1.12} + \frac{\$5,900}{(1.12)^2} = \$\ 9,971$

\$1,128 — a positive number. Therefore the investment is worth undertaking. Tina buys the computer.

Like all other inputs, capital is subject to diminishing marginal returns. The more capital is added, the lower is its marginal product and the lower is its marginal revenue product. We have seen in the above example that it pays the firm to buy one machine because that investment yields a positive net present value. Should Tina invest in two computers or three? To answer this question, she must do more calculations similar to those summarized in Table 17.5.

Suppose, in particular, that Taxfile's investment opportunities are as set out in Table 17.6. Tina can buy any number of computers. They each cost \$10,000 and have a life of two years. The marginal revenue product generated by each computer depends on how many computers Taxfile operates. If it operates just one computer, it has a marginal revenue product of \$5,900 a year (the case just reviewed). If Taxfile uses a second computer, marginal revenue product falls to \$5,600 a year, and in the case of a third computer, to \$5,300 a year. Table 17.6(b) calculates the present value of the marginal revenue product of each of these three levels of investment in computers.

We have seen that if the interest rate is 4 percent, it pays to invest in the first computer — the net present value of that computer is positive. It also pays to invest in a second computer. The present value of the marginal revenue product resulting from using two computers, \$10,562, exceeds the cost of the second machine by \$562. You can also see that it does not pay to invest in a third computer. The present value of the marginal revenue product resulting from using three computers is \$9,996. But the computer costs \$10,000, so the net present value of the third computer is –\$4. Tina buys a second computer but not a third one.

We have just discovered that at an interest rate of 4 percent a year it pays Tina to buy two computers but not three. Suppose that the interest rate is higher — say, 8 percent a year. In this case, the present value of one machine (see the calculations in Table 17.6b) is \$10,521. Therefore it still pays to buy the first machine. But its net present value is smaller when the interest rate is 8 percent than at the lower 4 percent interest rate. At an 8 percent interest rate, the net present value resulting from using two machines is negative. The present value of the marginal revenue product, \$9,986, is less than the \$10,000 that the second computer costs. Therefore at an interest rate of 8 percent it pays Tina to buy one computer but not two.

Suppose that the interest rate is even higher — say, 12 percent a year. In this case the present value of the marginal revenue product of one computer is $9,971 (see Table 17.6b). At this interest rate, it does not pay to buy even one computer.

The calculations that you have just reviewed trace out Taxfile's demand schedule for capital. It shows the number of computers demanded by Taxfile at each interest rate. As the interest rate falls, the quantity of capital demanded increases. At an interest rate of 12 percent a year, the firm demands no computers. At an interest rate of 8 percent a year, one computer is demanded; at 4 percent a year, the quantity demanded is two; and at an interest rate of less than 4 percent a year, the quantity demanded is three. (Although we have stopped our calculations at three computers, at lower interest rates Tina would buy yet more machines.)

Figure 17.3 A Firm's Demand for Capital

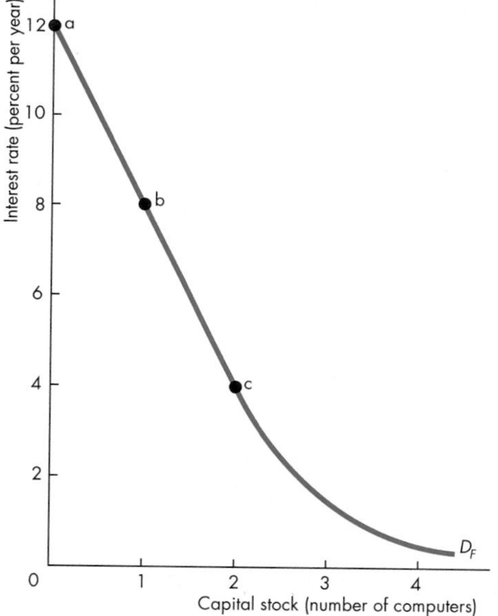

The quantity of computers demanded by Taxfile Inc. is such that the present value of the stream of marginal revenue products of a computer equals its price. The present value depends on the interest rate. The lower the interest rate, the larger the number of computers demanded. At an interest rate of 12 percent a year, Taxfile demands no computers (point *a*). At an interest rate of 8 percent, the firm demands 1 computer (point *b*). At an interest rate of 4 percent, the firm demands 2 computers (point *c*). If computers of different types (fractions of a $10,000 computer) can be bought, a demand curve that passes through points *a*, *b*, and *c* is generated.

The Demand Curve for Capital

A firm's demand curve for capital relates the quantity of capital demanded to the interest rate. Figure 17.3 illustrates the demand for computers (D_F) by Tina's firm. The horizontal axis measures the number of computers that Taxfile owns and the vertical axis measures the interest rate. Points *a*, *b*, and *c* correspond to the example that we have just worked through. At an interest rate of 12 percent a year, it does not pay Tina to buy any computers — point *a*. At an interest rate of 8 percent, it pays to buy 1 computer — point *b*. At an interest rate of 4 percent, it pays to buy 2 computers — point *c*.

In our example, we've only considered a single type of computer — one that costs exactly $10,000. In practice, Tina could consider buying a different type of computer whose power could be expressed as a multiple or fraction of one of the $10,000 computers that we've been considering here. For example, there may be a $5,000 computer that has half the power of a $10,000 machine, and a bigger machine costing $12,500 that has one and a quarter times the power of a $10,000 machine. If we consider all the different types of computers that Tina can buy, we will generate not just points *a*, *b*, and *c* but an entire demand curve, such as the one shown in Fig. 17.3.

The market demand curve for capital is obtained by adding all the individual firms' demand curves. Since different firms demand different types of machines (and since even the same firm demands different types of machines), we have to use common units of measurement to calculate the market demand curve for capital. The dollar value is a convenient unit. The market demand curve is shown in Fig. 17.4. It measures the total quantity of capital demanded in trillions of dollars on the horizontal axis and the interest rate on the vertical axis. On that curve, at an interest rate of 6 percent per year, the quantity of capital demanded is $2 trillion. Like the firm's demand curve, the market demand curve slopes downward.

Figure 17.4 The Market Demand for Capital

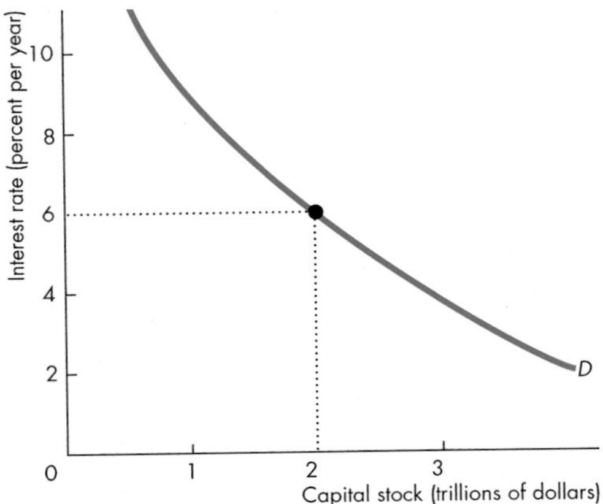

The market demand curve for capital is obtained by adding together the demand curves for capital of all the firms in the economy. An example of a market demand curve is *D*. On this curve, the quantity of capital demanded is $2 trillion when the interest rate is 6 percent per year, and the quantity of capital falls as the interest rate rises, other things being equal.

Changes in the Demand for Capital

The demand for capital is constantly changing, and the demand curve for capital is constantly shifting. Also, the composition of the demand for capital is constantly changing: the demand for some types of capital increases, while the demand for other types decreases. Technological change is the main force generating these changes in the demand for capital. For example, the development of diesel engines for railway transportation resulted in a decrease in demand for steam engines, an increase in demand for diesel engines, and not much change in the overall demand for capital in the railway industry. Developments in road and air transportation technology have led to a massive increase in the demand for highways, automobiles, airports, airplanes, and air traffic control systems and a decline in the demand for railway transportation equipment. In recent years, the development of desktop computers has led to a large increase in demand for office and research computing equipment.

The general trend resulting from the development of new technology and its exploitation through innovation is for the demand for capital to increase steadily over time with a steady rightward shift of the demand curve for capital.

R E V I E W

The demand for capital is determined by firms' profit-maximizing choices. The marginal product of capital declines as the amount of capital used rises. As a consequence, the marginal revenue product of capital declines as more capital is used. Capital is demanded up to the point at which the present value of its stream of marginal revenue products equals its price. The interest rate is an important factor in the present value calculation. The higher the interest rate, the lower is the present value of the stream of marginal revenue products.

The demand curve for capital is the relationship between the quantity of capital demanded and the interest rate. The higher the interest rate, the lower is the present value of the stream of marginal products and the smaller is the quantity of capital demanded by a firm. The demand curve for capital slopes downward. The demand for capital changes as a result of technological change. There is a general tendency for the demand for capital to increase over time with the demand curve for capital shifting to the right. ■

The Supply of Capital

The quantity of capital supplied results from the saving decisions of households. The most important factors determining a household's savings are:

- The household's current income in relation to its expected future income
- The interest rate

The stage in the household's life cycle is the major factor influencing whether its current income is high or low compared with its expected future income. Households smooth their consumption over the life cycle. As we saw in Chapter 15, young households typically have low current income compared with their expected future income, and older households have high income relative to expected future income; young people incur debts, while older people save and accumulate assets. A household's savings depends on how much it smooths its consumption over the life cycle.

Interest Rate

The interest rate has two distinct effects on the level of savings:

- A substitution effect
- An income effect

Substitution Effect A higher interest rate increases the future payoff from today's saving. It therefore increases the opportunity cost of current consumption. Thus a higher interest rate encourages people to economize on current consumption and to take advantage of the higher interest rate available on savings. As the interest rate rises, people substitute higher future consumption for current consumption, and savings increase.

Income Effect A change in the interest rate changes people's incomes. Other things being equal, the higher a person's income, the higher is the level of current consumption and the higher are the levels of future consumption and saving.

If the interest changes, the effect on income and, therefore, on saving depends on whether a person is a borrower or a lender. For a lender — a person with positive net financial assets — an increase in interest rates increases income, so the income effect is positive. The income effect reinforces the substitution effect, and a higher interest rate results in higher saving.

For a borrower — a person with negative net financial assets — an increase in interest rates decreases the income available for consumption. In this case, the income effect is negative — higher interest rates lower consumption and saving. The income effect works in a direction opposite to that of the substitution effect. Thus a higher interest rate may result in lower savings.

Figure 17.5 The Supply of Capital

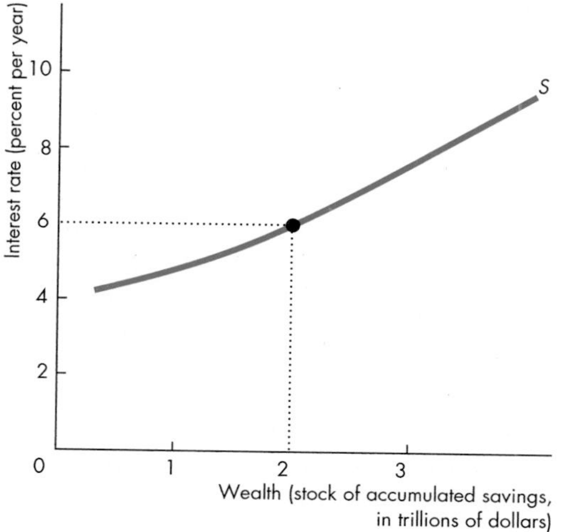

The higher the interest rate, the greater is the quantity of capital that households supply — the supply curve of capital slopes upward. At an interest rate of 6 percent per year, the quantity of capital supplied is $2 trillion.

The Supply Curve of Capital

The supply of capital is the total stock of households' accumulated savings. The supply curve of capital shows the relationship between the quantity of capital supplied and the interest rate. We've seen that this relationship depends on the relative strength of the income effect and the substitution effect. For an individual household, the relationship may be either positive or negative. For the economy as a whole, however, the substitution effect is stronger than the income effect, so a higher interest rate encourages saving and the supply curve of capital is upward sloping. Figure 17.5 illustrates the supply curve of capital. On that curve, at an interest rate of 6 percent a year, the quantity of capital supplied is $2 trillion.

Changes in the Supply of Capital

The supply of capital changes constantly. The main influences on the supply of capital are demographic. As the population and its age distribution change, so does the supply of capital. A population with a larger proportion of young people has a smaller supply of capital than a population with a larger proportion of middle-aged people. The age distribution of the population affects the supply of capital as a result of the life-cycle consumption smoothing described above.

Another influence on the supply of capital is the average income level. The higher the level of income, the larger is the supply of capital. A growing population and steadily rising income result in a gradual shift to the right of the supply of capital curve.

Portfolio Choices

Households have to choose not only how much to save (the total quantity of capital to supply) but also how to allocate their savings across various financial assets — that is, which financial assets to hold.

In making portfolio choices, households take account of two primary factors:

- Relative interest rates
- Relative degrees of risk

Relative Interest Rates A relative interest rate is the interest rate on a particular asset relative to the average level of interest rates. Other things being equal, the higher the relative interest rate on a particular asset, the more of that asset and the less of other assets households will choose to hold. For example, if the interest rate on bonds is 10 percent a year and on equities 5 percent a year, households will want to switch their portfolios away from holding equities into holding bonds. If the gap widens even further so that bonds are yielding 12 percent a year and equities 3 percent a year, households will want to switch out of equities and hold even more bonds.

If the interest rates on equities and bonds are identical and if all other things are equal, households will be indifferent between putting their wealth into bonds or equities.

Relative Degrees of Riskiness In general, comparing two securities means taking into account more things than their interest rates. The certainty with which those interest rates are available is also an important consideration. To see this point clearly, suppose that you have two choices:

1 Put your money in the bank for a guaranteed interest rate of 5 percent a year.

2 Lend your money to a friend who has an exciting business idea. If his business succeeds, he will pay you back with interest at a rate of 150 percent. If his business fails, not only will he pay you no interest, but he will not even give you your original money back.

The first option has no risk. For every dollar you put in the bank, you will have $1.05 one year from now for sure. The second option has a great deal of risk. To compare this second risky project with the first safe project, you need to calculate the expected interest rate that you would make and also to make some assessment of the degree of risk. Suppose your friend has been involved in several other business ventures and you know that half of them succeeded and the other half failed. Let's also suppose that you have no reason to expect this project to be any different from the others. If you put your savings into a large number of your friend's projects, half of the time you'd lose your savings and the other half of the time you'd receive $2.50 on every dollar. So on the average, you would receive $1.25 on each dollar you put in. Thus you can expect an interest rate of 25 percent on your financial stake in your friend's projects. Whether an interest rate of 25 percent with a lot of risk is better or worse than an interest rate of 5 percent with no risk is something that only you can decide. It depends on your attitude towards risk. Some people feel that the risk is worth taking. Others would rather sleep well at night. In general, the wealthier people are and the larger the number of projects they can put their savings into, the more willing they are to take risks on any individual project. But one thing is clear: the higher the degree of risk, the higher is the interest rate required to make a project worthwhile.

R E V I E W

The quantity of capital supplied is determined by households' saving decisions. Saving depends on the amount of consumption smoothing the household undertakes over its life cycle and on the interest rate. The more the household smooths its consumption and the higher the interest rate, the larger is the amount people save. The supply curve of capital is the relationship between the interest rate and the quantity of capital supplied. It slopes upward — the higher the interest rate, the larger the quantity of capital supplied, other things being equal. The supply of capital changes as a result of changes in the population and its age composition and in the level of income. Increasing population and increasing income result in a steady increase in the supply of capital — with the supply curve shifting steadily to the right.

People allocate their savings to different types of assets depending on relative interest rates and relative degrees of risk. Other things being equal, the higher the interest rate and the lower the riskiness of a particular asset, the larger the amount of savings people will allocate to that asset. ■

Now that we have studied the demand for and supply of capital, we can bring these two sides of the capital market together and study the determination of interest rates and asset prices. We'll then be able to answer some of the questions posed at the beginning of this chapter about the stock market and understand the forces that produce stock market booms and crashes.

Interest Rates and Asset Prices

Households' saving plans and firms' investment plans are coordinated through capital markets. Asset prices and interest rates adjust to make these plans compatible. We are now going to study the way in which these market forces work. And we are going to discover what determines the stock market value of a firm.

Two Sides of the Same Coin

Interest rates and asset prices can be viewed as two sides of the same coin. We'll look first at interest rates, then at asset prices, and finally at the connection between them.

Some assets, such as bank deposits, earn a guaranteed interest rate. Others, such as bonds and shares in the stocks of firms, do not. The interest rates on these assets are usually called bond yields and stock yields. A **bond yield** is the interest on a bond expressed as a percentage of the price of the bond. A **stock yield** is the income from a share in the stock of a firm expressed as a percentage of the price of the share — the stock market price. A bond earns a guaranteed dollar income, but its market price fluctuates and hence its yield fluctuates. A share in the stock of a firm earns a dividend based on the profitability of the firm. The stock market value of the share also fluctuates. Thus a stock yield fluctuates for two reasons — fluctuations in the dividend and fluctuations in the stock market price.

Let's now look at the two sides of the same coin — the price of an asset and its yield or interest rate. To calculate a bond yield or stock yield, we divide the income from an asset by the price paid for it. For example, if Taxfile, Inc. pays a dividend of $5 a share and if a share can be bought for $50, the stock yield is 10 percent ($5 ÷ $50, expressed as a percentage). It follows from this calculation that for a given amount of income, the higher the price of an asset, the lower is its yield. For example, if the price of a share in Taxfile, Inc. increases to $100 but its dividend remains constant at $5, its yield falls to 5 percent. This connection between the price of an asset and its yield or interest rate means that we can study the market forces in capital markets as simultaneously determining asset yields (interest rates) and asset prices. We will first look at capital market equilibrium in terms of interest rate (or yield) determination and then in terms of the stock market value of a particular firm.

Equilibrium Interest Rate

Figure 17.6 brings together the relevant parts of the previous analysis of the demand for and supply of capital. The diagram shows the entire capital market. The horizontal axis measures the total quantity of capital. Notice that the axis is labelled "capital stock and wealth." This label emphasizes the fact that the values of capital stock and of wealth are equivalent. The vertical axis measures the interest rate. The demand curve (D) is the market demand for capital that you met in Fig. 17.4. The supply curve (S) is the market supply of capital shown in Fig. 17.5.

Capital market equilibrium occurs where the quantity of capital supplied equals the quantity of capital demanded. In Fig. 17.6, this equilibrium occurs at an interest rate of 6 percent a year with $2 trillion of capital supplied and demanded. The market forces that bring about the equilibrium are exactly

Figure 17.6 Capital Market Equilibrium

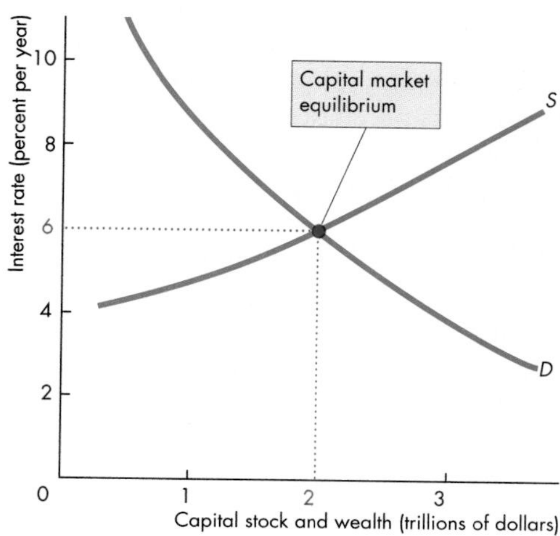

Capital market equilibrium occurs when the interest rate is such that the quantity of capital demanded equals the quantity of capital supplied. Here the demand curve is D and the supply curve is S. These curves intersect at an interest rate of 6 percent per year and a capital stock of $2 trillion.

the same as those that we discussed for the markets for goods and services. In the case of the capital market, there are organized institutions — banks, insurance companies, and specialized dealers — that constantly trade, thus maintaining equality between the quantity of capital demanded and quantity supplied.

The interest rate determined in Fig. 17.6 is the *average* interest rate. Interest rates on individual assets are distributed around that average, based on their relative degree of riskiness. An asset with a high degree of risk earns an interest rate that exceeds the average, and a very safe asset earns an interest rate that is less than the average. For example, if the average interest rate is 6 percent a year, as shown in Fig. 17.6, the interest rate on a bank deposit (a safer asset) might be 4 percent a year and that on equities (riskier assets) 8 percent a year.

We've now seen how asset yields or interest rates are determined. Let's look at the other side of the coin — asset prices. To determine asset prices, we will change our focus and look not at the capital market in aggregate but at the stock market value of an individual firm.

Stock Market Value of a Firm

We've seen that there is a connection between an asset's yield (or interest rate) and that asset's price. The yield is the earnings on the asset divided by its price (expressed as a percentage). Let's use this fact to work out the stock market value of a firm. Suppose that a firm finances its purchases of capital by selling shares of its stock. What determines the price of a share? What determines the total value of all the shares sold?

The value of a share depends on the total value of the firm and on the number of shares sold. The value of one share is equal to the value of the firm divided by the number of shares sold; equivalently, the value of the firm is equal to the value of one share multiplied by the number of shares sold. So for a firm with a given number of shares, asking what determines the price of a share is the same as asking what determines the value of the firm.

When a person buys a share in the stock of a firm, that person becomes entitled to receive a dividend each year. The price of a share depends on the expected future dividend to be paid out by the firm. As we discovered in Chapter 9 when we looked at the value of a share in Royal Trustco Limited, the price of a share is the present value of its expected future dividend. If a firm is expected to pay out no dividend at all in the future, its shares are worthless. If it is expected to pay out $10 a year on a share and the interest rate is 10 percent a year, its shares are worth $100 each. If it is expected to pay out $20 a year on a share and the interest rate is 10 percent, its shares are worth $200 each.

The price of a share is determined by current expectations of the future profitability of a firm. Shareholders must, therefore, form expectations about future profit. How do they go about that task?

Rational Expectations

We defined a *rational expectation* in Chapter 6 as the best forecast that can be made on the basis of all the available and relevant information. To form a rational expectation about future profit, it is necessary to make a forecast of the future profitability of a firm.

Shareholders calculate the profitability of a firm

Figure 17.7 Price-Earnings Ratios

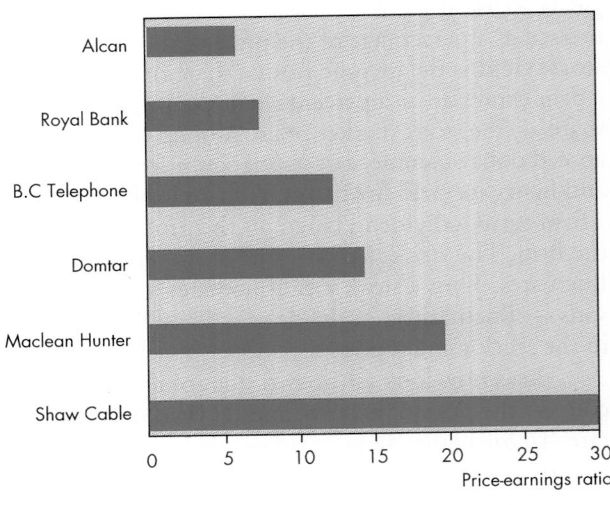

Price-earnings ratios vary from one company to another. For companies whose expected future earnings growth is strong, such as Maclean Hunter and Shaw Cable, the price-earnings ratio is high. For companies whose future profit prospects do not look strong, such as Alcan, the price-earnings ratio is low. For companies whose expected future profit is similar to their current profit, such as B.C. Telephone, the price-earnings ratio is intermediate.

by making forecasts of conditions in its output and input markets and the technological developments that will influence the firm. For example, forecasts are made of the demand for a firm's product, the degree of competition that it faces, new cost-saving technologies that might become available to it, and the prices of the inputs that it employs to produce a good. Armed with forecasts of all these things, shareholders forecast the future profit of a firm by discounting the forecasted future profit. Thus they can calculate the price that it is worth paying today for a share of the stock of a firm.

The effects of expectations on the price of individual shares and the market average is illustrated and discussed in Reading Between the Lines on pp. 454-455.

Price-Earnings Ratio

A commonly used measure to describe the performance of a firm's stock is its price-earnings ratio. A **price-earnings ratio** is the current price of a share in a firm's stock divided by the most recent year's profit per share. In March 1982, the average price-earnings ratio of the stocks that formed the TSE 300 was 7.6. By July 1987, the price-earnings ratio had risen to 21.6, but that was a peak month. The ratio then fell off and, in October 1989, stood at about 12.7. Figure 17.7 shows price-earnings ratios in October 1989 for some firms that are household names. What determines a price-earnings ratio? Why, in October 1989, was Alcan's price-earnings ratio only 5.3 while Shaw Cable's was 30?

We have seen that the price of a share of stock is determined by the present value of the expected future profit of a firm. The higher the *expected future* profit, the higher is *today's* price. Thus the price-earnings ratio of a firm depends on its current profit in relation to its expected future profit. When expected future profit is high relative to current profit, the price-earnings ratio is high. When expected future profit is low relative to current profit, the price-earnings ratio is low. Fluctuations in the price-earnings ratio arise from fluctuations in expected future profit relative to current profit.

Stock Market Volume and Prices

Sometimes the prices quoted on the stock market rise or fall with little trading taking place. At other times, stock market prices rise or fall with an enormous volume of trading. On yet other occasions, there is little change in the stock prices but there is a huge volume of trading. Why do stock prices rise or fall and what determines the volume of trading on the stock market?

Stock prices rise and fall because of changes in expectations of future profit. Consider the firm whose profit per share is $1. Suppose that the interest rate on assets that are as risky as a share of this firm's stock is 8 percent a year. Further suppose that the firm's future profit in each future year is expected to be exactly the same as this year's. The price of the firm's stock will adjust until a share can be bought for the price that makes the stock yield equal to 8 percent a year. That price is $12.50. People will buy shares in this company for $12.50 and expect, on the average, to make $1 a share each year — or a stock yield of 8 percent ($1 is 8 percent of $12.50). The price-earnings ratio will be 12.5 — today's price ($12.50) divided by last year's profit ($1 per share).

Suppose that market conditions change and people now expect the firm's profit to double to $2 a share starting next year. With an expected profit of $2 a share the stock market price jumps to $25. It's true that at $25 a share this year's profit ($1 a share) represents only a 4 percent stock yield ($1 is 4 percent of $25), but with profit expected to be $2 a share next year and every year thereafter, the expected yield is 8 percent a year — the interest rate available on other assets of similar risk. This price jump to $25 occurs with no change in the current year's profitability of the firm. It occurs entirely because people observe some event today that leads them to expect higher profit in the future.

Suppose that the change in market conditions leading to expected higher future profit is so obvious that everyone can see it and everyone agrees that this firm's earnings are indeed going to double next year. In such a situation, the market value of the firm's shares rises to $25 but no one buys or sells shares. Shareholders are happy with the shares that they already hold. If the price does not rise to $25, everyone will want to buy some shares. If the price rises to more than $25, everyone will want to sell some shares. If the price rises to exactly $25, everyone will be indifferent between hanging on to those shares or buying some other shares that are currently yielding 8 percent a year.

On the other hand, suppose that the event that changed expectations about this firm's profitability is difficult to interpret. Some people think it will lead

The Economy and the Stock Market

Disappointing economic figures and profits depress stock markets

Wall and Bay streets took another bruising yesterday, jarred by some disappointing economic numbers and more bad news about corporate profits...

In **New York**, the Dow Jones industrial average charted a roller-coaster course, rising to session highs in midday after an early decline, only to succumb to widespread selling later in the session. It plunged 33.49 points at the closing bell to finish the day at 2659.13.

Analysts said the market had to confront a formidable array of unsettling news, including a further erosion on the influential Tokyo stock market, unimpressive earnings reports from blue chip heavyweights International Business Machines and Aluminum Co. of America, and a U.S. Commerce Department report that the trade deficit for November had widened to a discouraging $10.5-billion (U.S.), up from a revised $10.25-billion in October...

The 300-stock composite index on the Toronto Stock Exchange, which closed at its low for the day with a slump of 27.71 points to 3872.27, was also hurt when one of its front-runners fell into disfavor. Laidlaw...stock plummeted $2... to $25... after company chairman Michael DeGroote told analysts that the purchase of Tricil Ltd. will not contribute as much as had been anticipated to Laidlaw's war chest this year.

The decline in Laidlaw helped wipe 4.77 per cent from the transportation sector, which led 11 of the TSE's 14 stock groups on a whirlwind tour into negative territory. Among other big losers, the metals index lost 2.60 per cent, consumer products 1.24 per cent, and communications and media 0.95 per cent....

The Globe and Mail,
January 18, 1990
By Gail Lem

The Essence of the Story

- On January 17,1990, the Dow Jones Industrial Average (DJIA) declined by 33.49 points.
- The decline was attributed to:
  - A decline in the Tokyo share market
  - Reports of low profits by International Business Machines (IBM) and Aluminum Company of America (ALCOA)
  - News that the U.S. trade deficit for November had widened
- The 300-stock composite index on the Toronto Stock Exchange declined by 27.71 points to 3872.27.
- The sector that declined most was transportation, but metals, consumer products, and communications and media shares also declined.
- One of the hardest hit companies was Laidlaw whose share price declined by $2 to $25, attributed to news that Laidlaw's purchase of Tricil Ltd. would not add as much as had been anticipated to Laidlaw's profits.

Background and Analysis

What are the indexes of stock market performance?

- The Dow Jones Industrial Average (DJIA) is the average price of 30 industrial shares traded on the New York stock exchange.
- The Toronto 300-stock composite index is, as its name implies, an index of the average price of 300 shares traded on the Toronto stock exchange. The index includes shares from all sectors of the economy and is divided into 14 separate sector indexes.

How large were those price declines on January 17, 1990?

- The news story tells us the number of points by which the two indexes declined and the number of dollars by which Laidlaw's share price declined. To assess and compare these price changes we must express them in common terms. Percentages are a convenient way of doing this. The percentage changes were:
  - DJIA −1.2 percent
  - TSE 300 −0.7 percent
  - Laidlaw −7.4 percent

Why do the prices of different stocks tend to move together and why do the different stock markets tend to move together?

- The price of a firm's share is determined by *current* expectations of the firm's *future* profitability.
- Some news items affect current expectations of the future profitability of *all* firms. Examples are:
  - A U.S. trade deficit with the rest of the world creates an expectation that the U.S. government may take measures to cut spending on imports leading other governments to take retaliatory measures to cut their imports from the United States. Such actions would cause world recession and lower profits for most firms.
  - A decline in the stock market of another major country, such as Japan, implies that firms in that country are expecting weak profit performances and creates an expectation that future exports, and therefore future profits may decline.
- Some news items affect current expectations of the future profitability of the firms in a particular industry. Examples are:
  - A low profit report by IBM creates an expectation that the profits of other computer producers may be down.
  - A low profit report by ALCOA creates an expectation that the profits of other aluminum producers may be down.

Why does the share price of an individual firm (such as Laidlaw) experience a larger decline than the average?

- Some news items affect only a single firm. For example, when Laidlaw bought Tricil Ltd. there was a widely held expectation that the profitability of the larger company would increase considerably. This expectation led to the rise in Laidlaw's share price. When Laidlaw's chairman reported that those expectations were false ones, the share price declined, falling into line with the new expectations about future profitability.
- Sometimes the news affecting a single firm points in the same direction as the news affecting the market as a whole, such as occurred in the case of Laidlaw on January 17, 1990. Other times a single firm's profit prospects move against the average of the market. Hence, individual share prices fluctuate much more than the averages summarized by the share price indexes.

to a rise in the firm's profit, and others think it will have no effect on profit. Let's call the first group optimists and the second group pessimists. The optimists will want to buy shares of that stock and will be willing to do so as long as the price is less than $25. The pessimists will sell their shares as long as the price is more than $12.50. In such a situation, the pessimists will sell out and the optimists will buy in. The price will not necessarily change, but there will be a large volume of trading activity. What causes the trading activity is the disagreement, not the event that triggered the change in expected profitability. Large price changes with a low volume of trading imply a great deal of agreement that something fundamental has changed. A large volume of trading with hardly any price change means that the underlying changes are difficult to interpret: some people predict that things will move in one direction while others predict the opposite.

Takeovers and Mergers

The theory of capital markets that you've now studied can be used to explain why takeovers and mergers occur. A **takeover** is the purchase of the stock of one firm by another firm. A takeover occurs when the stock market value of a firm is lower than the present value of the expected future profits from operating that firm. For example, suppose that Taxfile, Inc. has a stock market value of $120,000. But suppose also that the present value of the future profit of the firm is $150,000. It will pay for someone to try to take over the firm. Takeover activity affects the price of a firm; often the threat of a takeover drives the price to the point at which the takeover is no longer profitable.

There are other takeover situations in which the expected future profit of a firm depends on the firm that takes it over. A recent example illustrates this point very well. The Atari Computer Company was having difficulty breaking into the retail computer market on the scale that it desired. To overcome its problems, Atari searched out a retail chain that was losing money. The present value of a firm that is making a loss is less than the value of its plant and equipment. So Atari was able to buy retail outlets for a lower price from the current owners than it could have done by starting afresh. Atari believed that by buying the firm and using the retail stores to sell Atari computers, it could convert the other firm's loss into a profit.

A **merger** is the combining of the assets of two (or more) firms to form a single new firm. Mergers take place when two firms perceive that by combining their assets, they can increase their combined stock market values. For example, the merger of Molson and the Australian company Elders IXL Ltd. in 1989 enabled these two firms to form a more effective marketing organization to compete in the U.S. beer market against such giants as Miller and Budweiser.

R E V I E W

Saving plans and investment plans are coordinated through capital markets. Adjustments in asset prices and interest rates make the saving plans and investment plans compatible. Interest rates and asset prices are two sides of the same coin. The interest rate on an asset is the income from the asset divided by its price. The average interest rate makes the quantity of capital demanded equal to the quantity of savings supplied.

The value of a share of a firm's stock is determined by the firm's current and expected future profit. Expected future profit is based on rational expectations of future prices, costs, and technologies that the firm will face. The stock market value of a firm is often expressed as a ratio of the firm's current profit per share — the price-earnings ratio; it depends on expected profit growth.

Stock market prices sometimes move dramatically, and the volume of trading on the stock market is sometimes high and sometimes low. Prices change quickly when there are changes in expectations of future profitability. The volume of stock market trading rises when people disagree strongly about what the future holds.

Mergers and takeovers occur when the stock market value of a firm is lower than the present value of the future profit stream that another firm believes it could generate with the first firm's assets. ■

The lessons that we've just learned about capital markets have wider application than explaining fluctuations in the stock market. They also enable us to understand how natural resource markets operate. These lessons are particularly important and interesting in the case of exhaustible natural resources — resources that we are using up and will eventually use up completely. Let's now turn to this important range of issues.

Natural Resource Markets

Natural resources are the nonproduced factors of production with which we are endowed. They fall into two categories: exhaustible and nonexhaustible. **Exhaustible natural resources** are natural resources that can be used only once and that cannot be replaced once used. Examples of exhaustible natural resources are coal, natural gas, and oil — the hydrocarbon fuels. **Nonexhaustible natural resources** are natural resources that can be used repeatedly without depleting what's available for future use. Examples of nonexhaustible natural resources are land, sea, rivers and lakes, rain, and sunshine. Plants and animals are also examples of nonexhaustible natural resources. With careful cultivation and husbandry, more of these natural resources can be produced to replace those used up in production and consumption activities.

Natural resources have two important economic dimensions — a stock dimension and a flow dimension. The stock of each natural resource is determined by nature and by the previous rate of use. The flow of a natural resource is the rate at which it is being used. Human choices determine this flow and thus whether a given stock of natural resources is used up quickly, slowly, or not at all. In studying the operation of natural resource markets, we'll begin by considering the stock dimension of a natural resource.

Supply and Demand in a Natural Resource Market

The stock of a natural resource supplied is the amount of that resource in existence. For an exhaustible natural resource, that amount is not influenced by the resource's price. In such a case, the supply of the stock of the natural resource is perfectly inelastic. Its position depends on the amount of the resource available initially and on the rate at which it has been used up in the past. The smaller the initial stock and the faster the rate of use, the smaller is the stock available.

The demand for a stock of a natural resource is one aspect of portfolio choice. People own stocks of natural resources as an alternative to owning equities in corporations, other financial assets such as bonds, and other real assets, such as plant, equipment, and buildings.

The demand for a stock of a natural resource is determined in the same way as the demand for any other asset — by the income that it is expected to earn, expressed as an interest rate or yield. If the expected yield — or interest rate — on a stock of a natural resource exceeds that on other assets (with comparable risk), people will allocate more of their net worth to owning some of it and less to other assets. Conversely, if the expected interest rate on a natural resource falls short of that on other assets (with comparable risk), portfolios will be reallocated by selling the stock of a natural resource and buying other assets. When the yield from owning a stock of a natural resource equals the yield on other comparably risky assets, there will be no tendency for people to either buy or sell stocks of that resource or of other assets. Everyone will be satisfied with his or her existing portfolio allocation and with the quantity of the stock of the natural resource that he or she is holding.

Equilibrium occurs in the market for a stock of a natural resource when the price of the natural resource is *expected* to rise over time at a rate equal to the interest rate. This proposition is known as the **Hotelling Principle.**[1] Why is the price of a natural resource expected to grow at a rate equal to the interest rate? It is to make the expected yield on the natural resource equal to the yield available on other comparably risky assets. But the yield on a stock of a natural resource is the rate of change in the price of that resource. If you buy a stock of a natural resource, you buy it at today's price. If you sell that stock a year later, you sell it at the price prevailing at that time. The percentage change in the price of the resource over the year is your yield or interest rate. Thus the more rapid the increase in the price of a natural resource, other things being equal, the larger is the yield on that natural resource.

There is only one yield that is consistent with an equilibrium portfolio allocation. That yield is the same as the interest rate or yield on other comparably risky assets. Thus the equilibrium yield on a stock of a natural resource occurs when the price of that resource rises at a rate equal to the interest rate. Of course, when people make portfolio allocation decisions, future prices are not known, so those decisions are based on expectations. Thus when the price of a natural resource is expected to rise at a rate equal to the interest rate, the portfolio allocation is in equilibrium.

The supply and demand for the stock of a natural resource determine the yield or interest rate from

[1]Harold Hotelling discovered this principle and first described it in "Economics of Exhaustible Resources," *Journal of Political Economy* 39, (April 1931): 137-175.

owning that stock. That yield is determined by the expected rate of increase in the price of the natural resource. But the supply and demand for the stock of the resource do not determine the current *level* of the price — only its future expected rate of change. To determine the level of the price of a natural resource, we have to consider not only the supply and demand for the stock of the resource but also the demand for its flow.

The Price of a Natural Resource

To determine the price of a natural resource, we first consider the influences on the demand for the flow of the natural resource and then we study the equilibrium that emerges from the interaction of the demand for the flow and the available stock.

Demand for a Flow The demand for the flow of a natural resource is determined in the same way as the demand for any other input. It arises from firms' profit-maximizing decisions. A firm maximizes profit when the marginal revenue product of an input equals the marginal cost of the input. In a perfectly competitive market, the marginal cost of an input equals the factor price. The quantity demanded of a flow of a natural resource is the amount that makes the marginal revenue product of that flow equal to the price of the resource. As is the case for all other inputs, the marginal revenue product of a natural resource diminishes as the quantity used increases. Thus the lower the price of a resource, the greater is the quantity demanded of the flow of the natural resource. Figure 17.8 illustrates the demand for a flow of oil.

The demand for a flow of a natural resource has one special feature. For any resource, there is a high price at which it does not pay anyone to use the resource. The price at which it no longer pays to use a natural resource is called the **choke price**. Figure 17.8 shows the choke price of a barrel of oil (P_C). Everything has substitutes, and at a high enough price, a substitute is used. For example, we do not have to use oil as fuel for cars; we could use alcohol or electricity instead. We do not have to use gas and electric power to heat our homes; we could use solar energy instead. We do not have to use aluminium or steel to make cans for soft drinks; we could use plastic instead. The natural resources that we *do* use are the least expensive resources available. They cost us less than the next best alternative would.

Figure 17.8 Demand for a Flow of Natural Resources

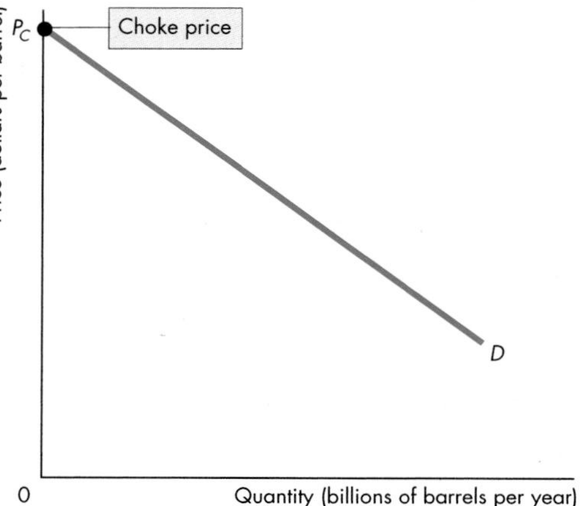

Natural resources have substitutes. If the price of a natural resource is too high, a substitute will be used. The figure shows the market for oil. At a price below P_C, the quantity of oil demanded is positive, and the lower the price, the larger is the quantity of oil demanded. The price P_C is called the choke price. At P_C, no oil is demanded and a substitute will be used.

Equilibrium Stock and Flow The price and the flow of a natural resource depend on three things:

- The interest rate
- The demand for the flow
- The stock of the resource remaining

Figure 17.9 shows how these three factors combine to determine the price of a barrel of oil, the expected path of that price, the rate at which oil is used up, and the stock of oil remaining. Let's take one part of the figure at a time.

Part (a) shows the expected path of the price of oil. This path is determined by the interest rate r. The line with a slope of $1 + r$ shows the relationship between the price in the current year and the price next year if the price rises at a rate equal to the interest rate. Suppose that initially the price is P_0. Next year, the price will rise to P_1, the price that is r percent higher than P_0. You can see the rise in price by following the steps between the 45° line and the line with a slope of $1 + r$. Each step represents a price increase. The height of each step is a constant percentage of the previous year's price, so the steps themselves become progressively larger. Since the price keeps rising, it eventually reaches the choke price, identified as P_C in the figure.

Next, consider Fig. 17.9(b), which shows the rate at which the resource is used up. The demand for the flow, based on the marginal revenue product of the natural resource, is illustrated by the curve D. In the initial year, at a price of P_0, the quantity Q_0 is used. In the following year, we know from part (a) that the price increases to P_1. At this price, the quantity used up is Q_1. Each year, as the price increases, the quantity used decreases.

Figure 17.9(c) shows the initial stock and the stock remaining after each year. For example, the stock after one year is the initial stock minus Q_0, the amount used up in the first year. In this example, there is no stock left after six years. The price increases from P_0 to the choke price P_C, and the quantity used in each year declines until, in the final year, it becomes zero — the quantity of the flow of oil demanded at the choke price.

How do we know that P_0 is the current price? It is because it is the price that achieves an equilibrium between the remaining stock and the current year's flow and the future years' expected flows. That is, it is the only current price that leads to a sequence of future prices (growing at the interest rate) that generate a sequence of flows such that the stock is exhausted in the same year that the choke price is

Figure 17.9 An Exhaustible Natural Resource Market

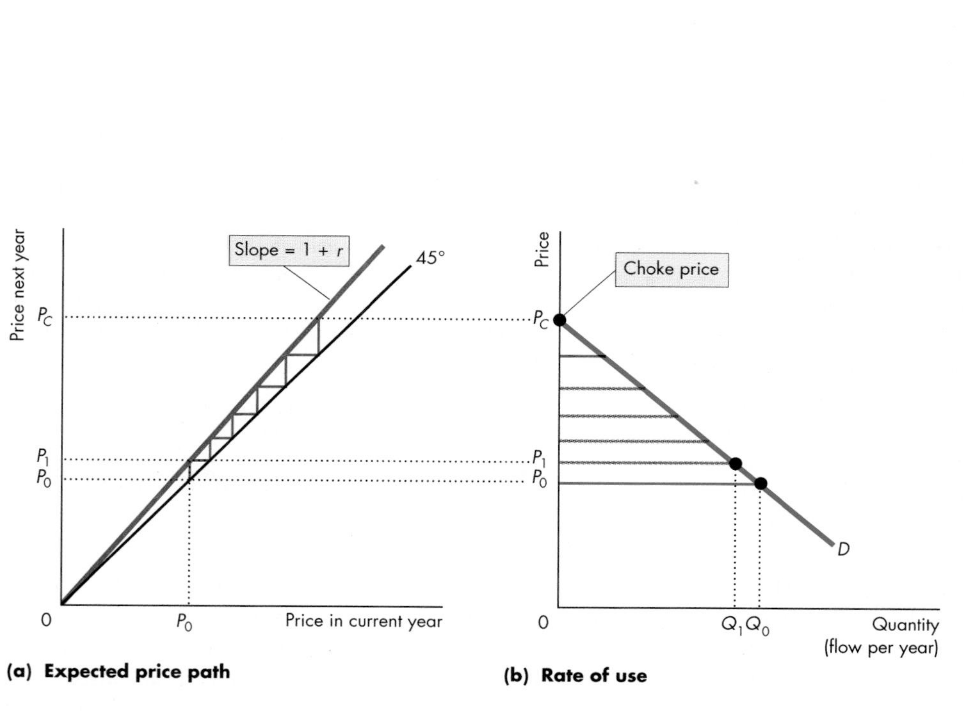

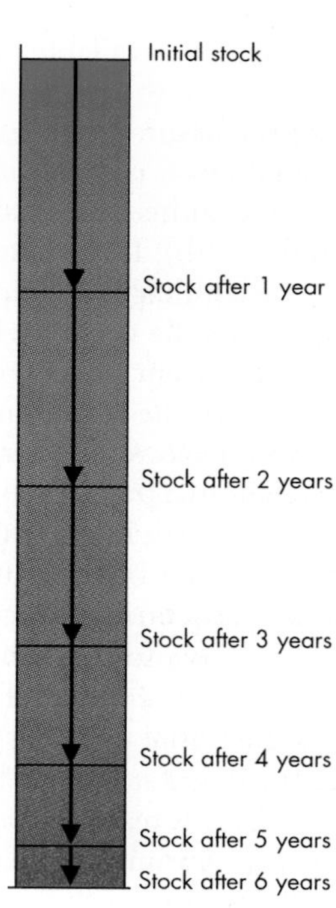

The expected rate of increase in the price of a natural resource equals the interest rate. The figure illustrates the oil market. Starting at P_0, in part (a), the price of oil increases first to P_1 and eventually to P_C. The price path follows the steps shown, with each step bigger than the previous one. Part (b) shows the rate at which oil is used up. Its demand curve (D) determines the quantity demanded for use (a flow) at each price. Initially, when the price is P_0, that flow is Q_0. As the price increases, the flow decreases. When the price reaches the choke price (P_C) the flow is zero. Part (c) illustrates the stock that remains after each year. The initial stock is used up in decreasing amounts until, after six years, all the stock is exhausted. The price P_0 is the equilibrium price of oil because it achieves equality between the initial stock and the sum of the flows in each year.

reached. If the current price is more than P_0 and future prices are expected to rise at the interest rate, the choke price will be reached before the stock is exhausted. If the current price is less than P_0 and future prices are expected to rise at the interest rate, the stock will be exhausted before the choke price is reached.

We can now see how the current price is determined by the three factors identified above. First, the higher the interest rate, the lower is the current price of a natural resource. The higher interest rate means that the price is going to increase more quickly, and thus, starting from the same initial price, the choke price will be reached sooner. But if the choke price is reached sooner, the stock available will not be used up at that point in time. Thus the initial price has to be lower when the interest rate is higher to ensure that by the time the price does reach the choke price, the total stock available has been used.

Second, the higher the marginal revenue product of the natural resource — the higher the demand for the flow — the higher is the current price. You can see why this relationship exists by looking again at Fig. 17.9(b). If the demand for the flow of oil were higher than that shown in this figure, the demand curve would lie to the right of the one shown. In this case, the current price would be higher than P_0.

Third, the larger the initial stock of the natural resource, the lower the current price. You can see why this relationship holds by considering Fig. 17.9(c). If the initial stock is larger than that shown in the figure, P_0 cannot be the equilibrium price since it will lead to a sequence of prices that will generate a sequence of quantities demanded that will not exhaust the stock by the time the choke price is reached. Thus the initial price has to be less than P_0 to ensure that the larger stock is exhausted by the time the choke price is reached.

Equilibrium in the market for a natural resource determines the current price of the natural resource and the expected path of future prices. But the price path actually followed is rarely the same as its expected path. For example, in 1984, expectations about the future price of oil were that it would rise at a rate equal to the interest rate. Opinions differed about the long-term average interest rate, so projections ranged from a low growth rate of 1.8 percent a year to a high growth rate of 7.1 percent a year. As events turned out, the price of oil fell after 1984 (see Fig. 17.10).

Why do natural resource prices change unexpectedly, sometimes even falling rather than following their expected path?

Figure 17.10 Unfulfilled Expectations

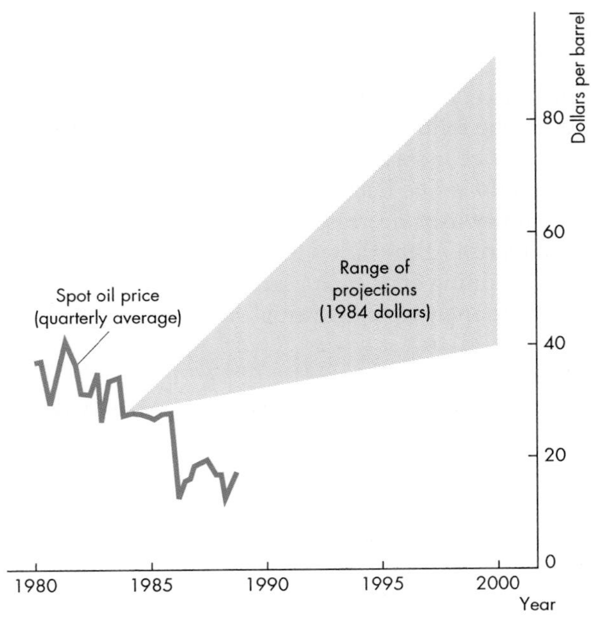

In 1984, the price of oil was expected to increase at a rate equal to the interest rate. There were different views of the future interest rate, so there was a range of expected price increases. Then the events of the 1980s unfolded in a way that was different from what had been expected in 1984. Higher interest rates, the discovery of new reserves, and new energy-saving technologies all contributed to a falling price of oil. The breakup of the OPEC cartel also had significant effect.

Source: "Future Imperfect," *The Economist,* February 4, 1989, 67.

Unexpected Price Changes

The price of a natural resource depends on expectations about future events — about the interest rate, the future demand for the flow of the resource, and the size of the remaining stock. Natural resource markets are constantly being bombarded by new information that leads to new expectations. For example, new information about the stock of a resource or the technologies available for its use can lead to sudden and perhaps quite large changes in its price.

All these forces have been at work in many of the markets for exhaustible natural resources in recent years. The market for oil illustrates these effects very well. Increased interest rates and the discovery of new supply sources have taken place in recent years;

at the same time the price of oil, far from rising at a rate equal to the interest rate, has actually fallen. Changes in the marginal revenue product of an input are harder to document, but, for example, the development of energy-efficient automobile and airplane engines represents a technological change that increased the marginal revenue product of capital — engines — and decreased the marginal revenue product of the exhaustible resource — oil — that those engines burn.

An additional force leading to price changes in natural resource markets in general and in the oil market in particular is the degree of competitiveness in the market. The model of the oil market that we have been studying is a perfectly competitive one. But the real world market for oil has oligopolistic elements (some of which we analysed in Chapter 14). Oligopolistic influences on price can produce price fluctuations over and above those arising from the forces at work in a competitive market. Furthermore, to forecast the future price of a natural resource correctly, it is necessary to forecast future changes in market structure. Adding this complication to an already complex forecasting problem makes it clear that the fluctuations in prices of natural resources such as oil cannot, for the most part, be forecast accurately.

Conservation and Doomsday

The analysis that you have just reviewed has important implications for the popular debate about natural resources and their use. Many people fear that we are using the earth's exhaustible natural resources at such a rapid pace that we shall eventually (perhaps in the not very distant future) run out of important sources of energy and of other crucial raw materials. Such people urge slowing the rate of use of exhaustible natural resources so that the limited stocks available will last longer.

This topic is an emotional one and generates passionate debate. It is also a matter that involves economic issues that can be understood using the economic model of a depletable natural resource that you have just studied.

The economic analysis of an exhaustible natural resource market predicts that doomsday — the using up of the entire stock of a natural resource — will eventually arise if our use of natural resources is organized in competitive markets. But it also implies that a competitive market will provide an automatic conservation program, arising from a steadily rising price. As a natural resource gets closer and closer to being depleted, its price will get closer to the choke price — the price at which no one wants to use that resource any more. Each year, as the price rises, the quantity demanded of the flow declines.

What if the resource does get completely used up? Won't we have a real problem then? We will have the problem of scarcity but in no more acute a form than we had it before. The resource that will then be no longer available will have been used because doing so was more efficient than using some alternative. Once that resource is completely used up, then and only then will it pay to turn to a more expensive substitute. In other words, the market economy handles the depleting stocks of natural resources by persistently forcing up their prices. Higher prices cause people to ration their use and eventually drive the flow quantity demanded to zero when the stock quantity supplied disappears.

An important economic issue is whether or not a competitive market leads us to use our scarce exhaustible natural resources at an efficient rate. Recall that we have studied the allocative efficiency of a perfectly competitive market in Chapter 12. There we discovered that perfectly competitive markets achieve allocative efficiency if there are no external costs and benefits. The same conclusion applies to markets for natural resources. If no external costs or benefits impinge on these markets, the rate of use determined in a perfectly competitive market is the allocatively efficient one. But if there are external costs associated with the use of the natural resource, allocative efficiency will result from a slowdown in the rate of use of the resource compared with that arising in the competitive market. For example, if burning hydrocarbon fuels increases the carbon dioxide in the atmosphere and a warming of the earth's atmosphere results — called the greenhouse effect — the costs associated with this atmospheric change have to be added to the costs of using oil and coal as fuels. When these costs are taken into account, the allocatively efficient rate of using these fuels is lower than that resulting from a perfectly competitive market. We will examine ways in which government intervention can achieve allocative efficiency in such a situation in Chapter 19.

■ We have now studied the way in which factor markets allocate scarce productive resources — labour, capital, and land — and the determination of factor prices and factor incomes. The outcome of the operation of the factor markets is the determination of the distribution of income among individuals and families — the determination of *for whom* goods and services are produced. We are now going to examine that distribution and discover the main features and sources of income and wealth inequality in our economy.

SUMMARY

Capital, Investment, and Saving

There are two kinds of assets: financial and real. Financial assets are all the paper claims of one economic agent against others. Real assets, or capital, are the stock of all the productive assets owned by households and firms. Investment is the flow of additions to the stock of capital. Depreciation is the flow reduction in the stock of capital through use or the passage of time.

The quantity of capital supplied results from people's saving decisions. Saving equals income minus consumption. People allocate their savings to a variety of alternative financial and real assets. (pp. 439-441)

Capital Markets in Canada Today

Capital markets provide the link between the savings decisions of households and the investment decisions of firms and governments. Households finance firms' investments by buying equity and bonds and by making deposits with financial intermediaries that, in turn, make loans to firms. Households also make loans to governments by buying bonds and indirectly through deposits with financial intermediaries. (pp. 441-445)

The Demand for Capital

The demand for capital is determined — like the demand for any factor — by firms' profit-maximizing choices. The quantity of capital demanded by a firm is such that the marginal revenue product of capital equals its opportunity cost. A firm can make the comparison between marginal revenue product and cost by calculating the present value of marginal revenue product and comparing the present value with the price of a new piece of capital.

The quantity of capital demanded by a firm depends on the interest rate. The higher the interest rate, the lower is the present value of the future stream of marginal revenue products, and the smaller is the quantity of capital equipment a firm buys. The lower the interest rate, the greater is the quantity of capital demanded — the demand curve for capital is downward sloping. The demand curve for capital shifts steadily to the right as a result of technological change and the general tendency to exploit innovations over time. (pp. 445-448)

The Supply of Capital

The quantity of capital supplied results from the saving decisions of households. Savings depend on how much households smooth their consumption over the life cycle and on the interest rate. People's portfolio allocations depend on the relative rates of return on assets. Relative rates of return, in turn, reflect differing degrees of riskiness. The supply curve for capital is upward sloping — as interest rates rise, the quantity of capital supplied increases. The supply curve of capital shifts over time as a result of changes in the population and its age composition and in the level of income. (pp. 448-451)

Interest Rates and Asset Prices

Interest rates and asset prices can be viewed as two sides of the same coin. They adjust to achieve equality between the quantity of capital demanded and the quantity supplied. Interest rates on particular assets are distributed around the average rate according to the degree of riskiness of different types of assets.

The stock market value of a firm depends on its current profit and expectations of its future profit. The higher the expected growth rate of a firm's profit, the higher is the price of a share of its stock. The price-earnings ratio is the ratio of the current price of a share in a firm's stock to its current profit per share. That ratio depends on the expected growth rate of profit.

The volume of trading on the stock market is determined by the extent of the divergence of expectations of the future. When everyone agrees about the future, the volume of trading is low. When there is widespread disagreement, the volume of trading is high. There can be large changes in prices with a low or high volume of trading. Price changes occur when there is a change in expectations about profit growth.

Mergers and takeovers occur as part of the process of maximizing profit. If a firm's stock market value is lower than the value of its assets when used by another firm, it will pay that other firm to take over the first one. Mergers occur when there is a mutually agreed benefit from combining the assets of two (or more) firms. (pp. 451-456)

Natural Resource Markets

Natural resources are the nonproduced factors of production with which we are endowed. The price of a natural resource is determined by the interest rate, its marginal revenue product (which determines the demand for its flow), and the stock of the natural resource (which determines the supply of its stock). The price of a natural resource is such that its future price is expected to rise at a rate equal to the interest rate and to reach the choke price at the time at which the resource is exhausted. The actual price changes constantly to take account of new information. Even though the future price is expected to increase, the actual price often decreases as a result of new information leading to an increase in the estimate of the remaining stock or to a decrease in the demand for the flow of the resource. (pp. 457-462)

KEY ELEMENTS

Key Terms

Key Figures and Tables 

REVIEW QUESTIONS

1 Why does the quantity of capital demanded by a firm rise as the interest rate falls?

2 Set out the key reasons for differences in interest rates on different types of assets.

3 What is the relationship between interest rates and asset prices?

4 Explain how the stock market value of a firm is determined.

5 Define the price-earnings ratio and explain how it is determined.

6 Why are there some occasions on which stock market prices change a lot with little trading and others when prices are stable but trading volumes are high?

7 Why do mergers and takeovers occur?

8 Distinguish between the stock and the flow of an exhaustible natural resource.

9 Explain why the price of an exhaustible natural resource is expected to rise at a rate equal to the interest rate.

10 What determines the price of a natural resource?

11 Why is it impossible to forecast most of the fluctuations in the price of a natural resource?

PROBLEMS

1 At the end of 1989, a firm had a production plant worth $1,000,000. During 1990, its plant depreciated by 10 percent. During the same year, the firm bought new capital equipment for $250,000. What is the value of the firm's stock of capital at the end of 1990? What was the firm's gross investment during 1990? What was the firm's net investment during 1990?

2 You earn $10,000 a year for three years, and you spend $8,000 each year. How much do you save each year? What happens to your wealth during this three-year period?

3 What are the ways in which a holder of wealth can channel capital into firms?

4 How can a holder of wealth lower the risk of supplying capital to firms?

5 Why is a deposit in a financial intermediary less risky than buying equity or bonds?

6 A firm is considering buying a new machine. It is estimated that the marginal revenue product of the machine will be $1,000 a year for five years. The machine will have a scrap value at the end of five years of $1,000. The interest rate is 10 percent a year.

a) What is the maximum price that the firm will pay for the machine?

b) If the machine costs $4,000, would the firm buy the machine? What is the highest interest rate at which the firm would buy the machine?

CHAPTER 18

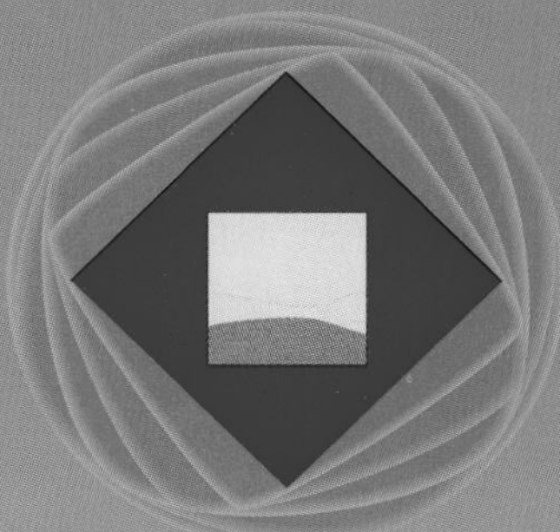

The Distribution of Income and Wealth

After studying this chapter, you will be able to:

- Describe the distribution of income and wealth in Canada today.
- Explain why the data on wealth distribution show greater inequality than the data on income distribution.
- Explain how the distribution of income arises from the prices of productive resources and the distribution of endowments.
- Explain how the distribution of income and wealth is affected by individual choices.
- Explain the different views about fairness in the distribution of income and wealth.
- Explain the effects of redistribution policies on the distribution of income and wealth.

Riches and Rags

ROY THOMSON BEGAN to build a newspaper organization in the 1930s. It has grown into a multinational empire, half of which is in the news business and the other half of which is in such diverse activities as retailing (the Hudson's Bay Company), North Sea oil, travel, and publishing. Today, the International Thomson Organization Limited is managed and operated by Ken Thomson, whose family fortune, estimated as Canada's largest, is more than $6 billion. In the same league as Ken Thomson are Albert, Paul, and Ralph Reichmann, owners of Olympia and York Development Limited, a company with worldwide operations, and of such companies as Hiram Walker and Gulf Canada. The Reichmann family is also reputed to be worth more than $6 billion. Other billionaire Canadians are Charles Bronfman, owner of the Seagram Company, and Derek A. Price, owner of Starlaw Holdings, a massive Montreal firm supplying investment and financial services. These families and individuals are, of course, exceptionally wealthy. But, according to Statistics Canada, each of the top 1 percent of Canadian families has an income that exceeds $200,000 a year. And they have been getting richer and are likely to continue to do so. ■ The opposite end of Canada's income distribution can be seen any evening on the park benches of our major cities and in the hostels operated by such organizations as the Salvation Army. Here are men and women who have no visible wealth at all other than their meagre clothes and a few possessions. Although many Canadians are much wealthier than these, the poorest citizens, Statistics Canada estimates that one in five households has an income of less than $20,000 a year for a family of four and less than $10,000 a year for a single person. These poorest households spend close to half their income on rent and, in contrast to the richest of households, are apparently becoming relatively poorer. ■ What determines the distribution of wealth and income? Why are some people exceedingly rich while others earn very little and own almost nothing? Are there any trends in the distribution of income? Is the distribution becoming more equal or more unequal? Is it fair that some people should be so incredibly rich while others live in miserable poverty? And what do we mean by fairness?

■ In this chapter, we will study the sources of income and wealth inequality. We'll see how factor prices and the quantities of factors hired, as determined in factor markets, result in unequal incomes. We'll study the connection between income and wealth and discover why the distribution of wealth is much more uneven than that of income. We'll also see how inequality results in part from the choices that people make.

Most of the chapter deals with positive issues — with trying to understand the world as it is — and not normative matters — commenting on or making judgements about what is desirable. Nevertheless, in the final section of the chapter we will review some of the key contributions to the perennial search for a widely acceptable concept of fairness.

Let's begin by looking at some facts about the distribution of income and wealth.

Distribution of Income and Wealth in Canada Today

The incomes earned by the factors of production are the wages (including salaries and other forms of compensation) paid to labour, the interest (and dividend) income paid to the owners of capital, and the rental incomes received by the owners of land and minerals. Labour earns the largest share of total income, and that share has increased slightly over the years.

The distribution of income among individuals and families depends on the amount of labour, capital, and land that they supply and on the wage rates, interest and dividend rates, and rental rates they receive.

The one resource that everyone has in identical amounts is time. But the price at which a person can sell his or her time, the wage rate, depends on the individual's marginal product. That marginal product, in turn, depends partly on natural ability, partly on luck or chance, and partly on the amount of human capital that the individual has built up. The income from working is a mixture of a return on human capital as well as a compensation for forgoing leisure.

Ownership of the other factors of production — capital and land — is distributed with a great deal of inequality. And the interest rates and rental rates earned per unit of capital and land supplied also vary enormously.

Income is distributed unequally because of unequal wage rates, unequal ownership of capital and land, and unequal interest rates and rental rates. Let's look at some facts about the distribution of income in Canada. In 1989, the median Canadian household income was around $40,000. The median household is located in the middle of the income distribution — 50 percent of households have higher incomes and 50 percent have lower incomes than the median income. About one-third of all households had incomes of $55,000 or more. One-fifth of all households had incomes of less than $20,000.

Figure 18.1 illustrates the distribution of income in Canada. It shows the percentage of total income received by each of five equal-sized groups, from the poorest 20 percent to the richest 20 percent of families. The 20 percent of families with the lowest incomes received only 5 percent of total income. The second lowest 20 percent received 10 percent of total income. You can continue reading the figure from top to bottom to see the percentages of income received by families that are increasingly better off. The 20 percent of families with the highest incomes received 43 percent of total income.

Although the data on the distribution of income display considerable inequality, a picture of even greater inequality emerges from the data on the distribution of wealth. Wealth and income are linked in a way that we will examine shortly, but it's important to remember the distinction: income is what you earn, wealth is what you own. Data on the wealth distribution measure the value of individual and family holdings of real estate and financial assets. These data are expensive to collect, so they are updated infrequently. The most comprehensive data available measure the wealth of families in 1980. In that year, the average family owned net assets of $47,000. The range about that average was enormous. The poorest 40 percent of families owned only 0.8 percent of the total wealth. The richest 10 percent owned almost 57 percent of total wealth.

Figure 18.2 provides a picture of the distribution of wealth in Canada. The figure is arranged

Figure 18.1 Family Income Shares

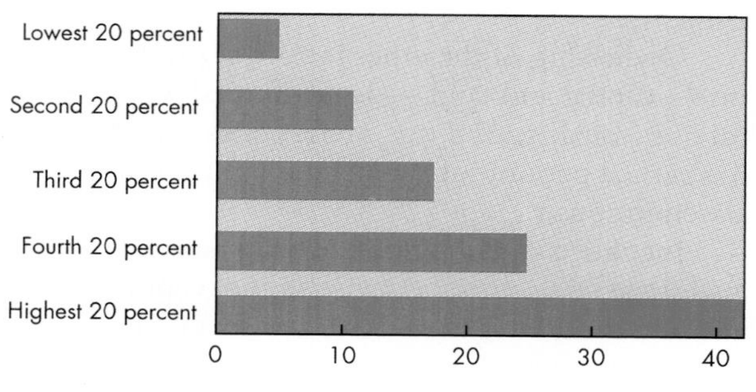

One way of measuring income inequality is to calculate the percentage of total income earned by a given percentage of families, starting with the poorest. The figure shows us that the poorest 20 percent of families earn only 5 percent of the income, while the richest 20 percent earn 43 percent of the income. The richest 20 percent are, on the average, almost nine times as well off as the poorest 20 percent.

Source: Statistics Canada, *Canada Year Book 1988*, 5-41.

to let you compare the distribution of wealth with the distribution of income. As in the case of the distribution of income, there is considerable inequality in the distribution of wealth. But there is even more inequality of wealth than of income. For example, the poorest 80 percent of families own 27 percent of the wealth but earn 57 percent of total income. The richest 20 percent own 73 percent of the wealth and earn 43 percent of total income.

The amount of inequality in the distribution of wealth is even greater if we break down the richest group. The richest 1 percent of all families own 19 percent of total wealth, the next 4 percent own 24 percent of the wealth, and the next 5 percent own 14 percent of the wealth.

Lorenz Curves for Income and Wealth

Another way of describing the distribution of income and wealth is presented in Fig. 18.3. The table records the cumulative percentages of income and wealth of various cumulative percentages of families. For example, row *a* of the table shows the percentages of income and wealth of the lowest 20 percent of families, row b shows the data for the lowest 40 percent of families, and so on. These data can be illustrated with what is called a Lorenz curve. A **Lorenz curve** shows the cumulative percentage of income or wealth of any given cumulative percentage of families. The Lorenz curve derives its name from its founder, Konrad Lorenz, who devised this type of figure in 1905.

The horizontal axis of the figure measures the cumulative percentages of families, ranked from the poorest to the richest. For example, the point marked 40 on the horizontal axis represents the 40 percent of families with the lowest income and wealth. The vertical axis measures the cumulative percentages of income and wealth. For example, the point marked 40 indicates 40 percent of total income or total wealth.

If each family had the same amount of income and wealth, the cumulative percentages of income received and wealth owned by the cumulative percentages of families would fall along the straight line labelled "Line of equality." The actual distribution of income and wealth are shown by the curves labelled "Income" and "Wealth." The points on the income distribution curve labelled *a* through *e* correspond to the family income shares shown in the table. The points on the wealth distribution curve labelled *a′*

Figure 18.2 Income and Wealth Distribution

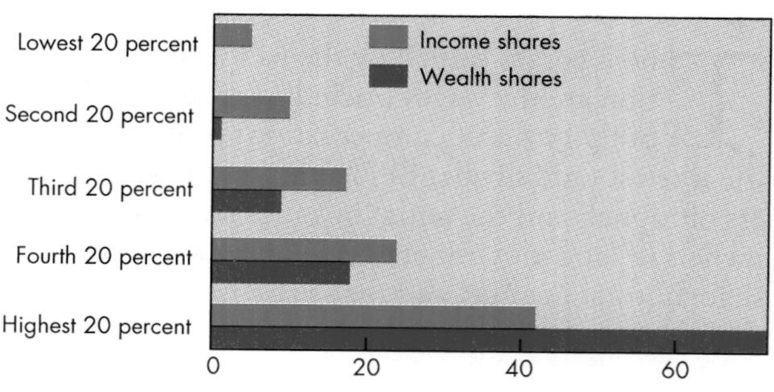

Wealth is distributed even more unequally than income. The poorest 40 percent of the population own less than 1 percent of the wealth in the economy. The richest 20 percent own more than 70 percent of total wealth. Even the middle 20 percent of the population own only 8 percent of total wealth.

Sources: Statistics Canada, *Canada Yearbook 1988*, 5-41, and Lars Osberg, *Economic Inequality in Canada* (Toronto: Butterworths, 1981), 37.

Figure 18.3 Lorenz Curves for Income and Wealth

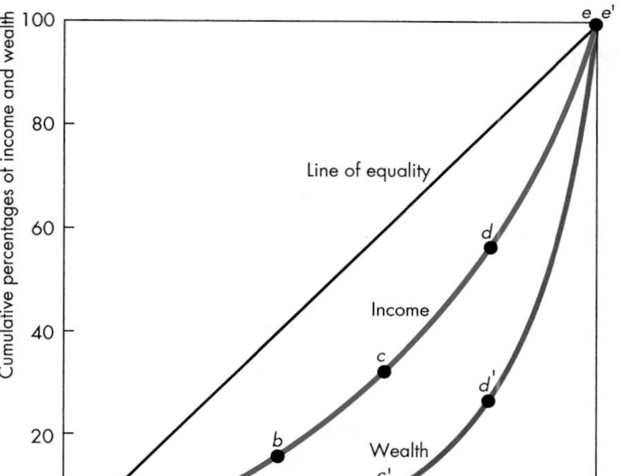

The cumulative percentages of income and wealth are graphed against the cumulative percentage of families. If income and wealth were distributed equally, each 20 percent of families would have 20 percent of the income and wealth — the line of equality. Points *a* through *e* on the Lorenz curve for income correspond to the rows of the table showing family income, and points *a′ through e′* on the Lorenz curve for wealth correspond to the rows of the table showing family wealth. Wealth is distributed more unequally than income.

Sources: See Figure 18.2.

	Cumulative percentage of families	Cumulative percentage of income	Cumulative percentage of wealth	
a	Lowest 20	4.7	0	*a′*
b	40	15.1	0.8	*b′*
c	60	32.1	9.0	*c′*
d	80	57.0	26.7	*d′*
e	100	100.0	100.0	*e′*

through *e′* correspond to the family wealth shares shown in the table.

The advantage of using Lorenz curves to describe the distribution of income and wealth is that they provide a graphic illustration of the degree of inequality. The closer the Lorenz curve is to the line of equality, the more equal the distribution. As you can see from the two Lorenz curves in Fig. 18.3, the distribution of wealth is much more unequal than the distribution of income. That is, the Lorenz curve for the wealth distribution is much farther away from the line of equality.

The numbers in the table tell the same story. For example, the poorest 60 percent of all families own only 9 percent of total wealth but earn 32 percent of total income. The poorest 80 percent of all families own only 27 percent of the wealth but earn 57 percent of the income.

Lorenz curves and the data from which they are drawn are useful not only for comparing two different distributions, such as those of income and wealth, but also for comparing distributions at different points in time. Such comparisons reveal whether the distribution of income has become more or less equal over time.

Let's take a look at the distribution in Canada about 40 years earlier than the time that we have just been studying. Table 18.1 provides a comparison. It shows the cumulative percentage of income shares in 1951 as well as those in 1985. As you can see from

Table 18.1, there was remarkably little change in the distribution of income between 1951 and 1985.

We have seen that there is a great deal of inequality in income and wealth. But *who* are the rich and *who* are the poor? What are the key characteristics of rich and poor families?

Who Are the Rich and the Poor?

To answer these questions, we can use data compiled by Statistics Canada that show how the incidence of low income is related to other family characteristics. The **incidence of low income** is measured as the percentage of households whose income falls below a low-income cutoff. A **low-income cutoff** is an income level, determined separately for different types of families (for example, single persons, couples, one parent), that is selected so that families with incomes below that limit normally spend 58.5 percent or more of their income on food, shelter, and clothing. The low-income cutoffs currently used by Statistics Canada are based on family expenditure data for 1978.

Based on Statistics Canada's measure of the incidence of low income, the poorest family in Canada today is likely one in which there is a single-parent mother, less than 25 years old, who has no job and lives in Québec. The highest-income family is one in which a married couple both have jobs, are between 45 and 54 years old, and live in Ontario. These snapshot profiles are the extremes in Fig. 18.4. That figure illustrates the importance of age of householder, marital status, and other household characteristics and region of residence in influencing the size of a family's income.

Table 18.1 A Comparison of the Distribution of Income in 1951 and in 1985

Cumulative percentage of families	Cumulative percentage of income 1951	1985
Lowest 20	4	5
40	15	15
60	33	32
80	56	57
100	100	100

The distributions of income in 1951 and 1985 were remarkably similar — at the low end, almost identical. The 1985 distribution had a slightly lower degree of inequality than the 1951 distribution; the richest 20 percent of families had 44 percent of the income in 1951 but only 43 percent by 1985.

Source: The 1951 figures are from Osberg 1981 (see Fig. 18.2), whose original source is J.R. Podoluk, *Incomes of Canadians* (Ottawa: Dominion Bureau of Statistics, 1968), 294; those for 1985 are from Fig. 18.1.

Income Redistribution

Because poverty is so dreadful for those experiencing it and so fearful for everyone else, there is almost universal agreement that the government should play the role of a kind of giant insurance company — a sort of institutionalized Robin Hood, taking from the rich and giving to the poor. Governments in Canada today use two main ways of redistributing income:

- Income taxes
- Social security benefits

Income Taxes The amount and nature of the redistribution achieved through income taxes depend on the form that those taxes take. Income taxes can be progressive, regressive, or proportional. A **progressive income tax** is one that taxes income at a marginal rate that rises with the level of income. The term "marginal" applied to income tax rates refers to the fraction of the last dollar earned that is paid in taxes. A **regressive income tax** is one that taxes income at a marginal rate that falls with the level of income. A **proportional income tax** is one that taxes income at a constant rate regardless of the level of income.

The income tax rates that apply in Canada are composed of two parts: federal and provincial. There is variety in the detailed tax arrangements in the individual provinces, but the tax system, at both the federal and provincial levels, is progressive. The most heavily taxed Canadians are those who live in Québec, with those in Manitoba not far behind. Albertans and Ontarians bear the lightest taxes. The marginal tax rates that applied to earned income (wages and salaries) in those provinces in 1989 are illustrated in Fig. 18.5. Rates in the other provinces fell in between. Most Canadians earned between $10,000 and $30,000 a year, so, except for those living in Québec, they paid taxes at around 25 percent on their marginal dollar of earnings. In Québec, for the

Figure 18.4 The Incidence of Low Income by Selected Family Characteristics

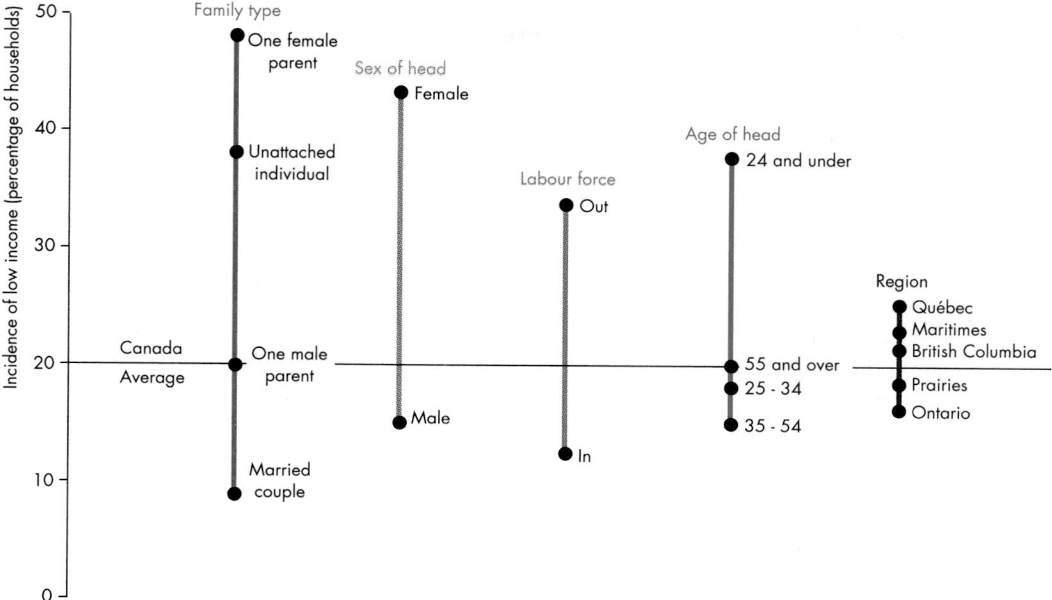

The vertical axis shows the incidence of low income — the percentage of households whose income falls below a low-income cutoff (the income level such that almost 60 percent of income is spent on food, shelter, and clothing). For Canada, on the average, 20 percent of families have incomes below the low-income cutoff. But that percentage varies depending on family type, sex of household head, labour force status, age of household head, and region of residence in the manner indicated in the figure. Family type is by far the single most important factor influencing incidence of low income.

Source: Statistics Canada, *Canada Year Book*, 1989, 5-41, 5-42.

same income range, marginal tax rates ranged from percentages in the low 30s to almost 40. Canadians with incomes between $30,000 and $60,000 a year paid between 40 and 45 percent of their marginal dollar in taxes and those with incomes of more than $60,000 paid taxes of 45 to 50 percent at the margin. Obviously, an income tax structure such as the one we have in Canada makes the distribution of after-tax income much less unequal than the distribution of before-tax income. But the tax system is not the only way in which inequality is reduced. Social security also has important effects.

Social Security Benefits All levels of government in Canada administer social security programs that benefit a wide variety of groups. The major programs operated by the federal government are:

- Senior citizens' benefits
- Family allowances
- Child tax credits
- Unemployment insurance
- Benefits for special groups, such as veterans, the blind, and native peoples

The main provincial programs are:

- Social assistance
- Tax credits (to assist renters and the elderly)
- Income supplements

Local governments administer general welfare programs for those Canadians who fall through the gaps in the federal and provincial nets.

Social security benefit programs in Canada have such variety, diversity, and complexity that it

Figure 18.5 Marginal Income Tax Rates

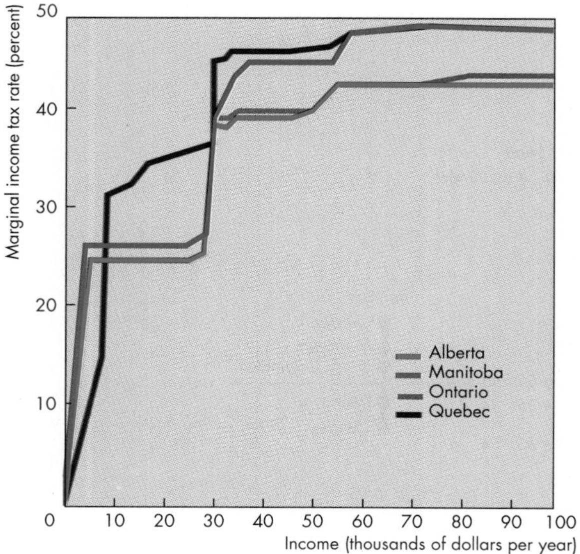

One method of redistributing income is through progressive income taxes. Such taxes take a larger fraction of the last dollar earned the larger a person's income. Marginal tax rates are highest in Québec and Manitoba and lowest in Alberta and Ontario. In all provinces, they range between the mid-40s and 50 percent on incomes greater than $60,000 per year. In Québec, marginal tax rates climb even through the income range experienced by most households.

Source: Thorne, Ernst, & Whinney, reported in *The Financial Post 1990 Investor's Guide*, fall 1989, 63-4.

would be impossible to describe them here in any detail. By way of an example, however, Table 18.2 lists the maximum benefits available under the main programs for senior citizens, families, and the unemployed in Ontario in 1989.

The main feature of all social security benefits is that benefits are at their highest for families with no other income; as other sources of income increase, benefits are gradually withdrawn. In effect, benefits are "taxed." For example, the Guaranteed Income Supplement is "taxed" at a rate of 50 percent. That is, for each $2 of earnings in excess of a specified minimum ($9,624 for a single person in Ontario in 1989), the Guaranteed Income Supplement benefit is reduced by $1. As a matter of fact, some of the highest *marginal* rates of tax are paid by benefit recipients.

Figure 18.6 shows how the combination of benefit and tax programs affects single Canadians over the age of 65. The figure shows that those with an income of less than $22,000 receive net benefits and those with an income above that level pay net taxes. The scale of the benefits received and taxes paid varies with income. The highest benefits are received by those who otherwise would have no income. The highest taxes are paid by those with the highest income. With a benefit and tax program, such as that illustrated in Fig. 18.6, in place, the degree of inequality of income after benefits and taxes is smaller than it is before benefits and taxes. We'll see below just how much redistribution takes place in aggregate. But first, let's look at other policies that redistribute income.

Other Policies That Redistribute Income In addition to income taxes and social security programs, governments undertake other measures that have the effect of redistributing income even though that is not their primary aim. The most important of these measures are the provision of public education and of subsidized health care. Because of such programs, the poor are better educated and healthier than they otherwise would be. As a consequence, they have more human capital and so are able to increase their earnings.

Table 18.2 Selected Benefit Rates in 1989, Ontario

Program	Maximum benefit	
Old Age Security (OAS)	$337.04	per month
Guaranteed Income Supplement (GIS)	$400.53	per month, single person
	$521.76	per month, married couple
Spouse Allowance (SPA)	$260.88	per month, single person
Child Allowance	$ 32.74	per month, per child
Unemployment Insurance	$363.00	per week, or 60% of gross weekly earnings

There are five major ways in which low income families receive benefits in Ontario. Old Age Security and Guaranteed Income Supplement support retired persons; Spouse Allowance and Child Allowance give help to families with a single parent or a large number of children; Unemployment Insurance provides a temporary safety net for those persons temporarily without a job.

Source: Health and Welfare Canada.

Figure 18.6 Net Benefits and Taxes

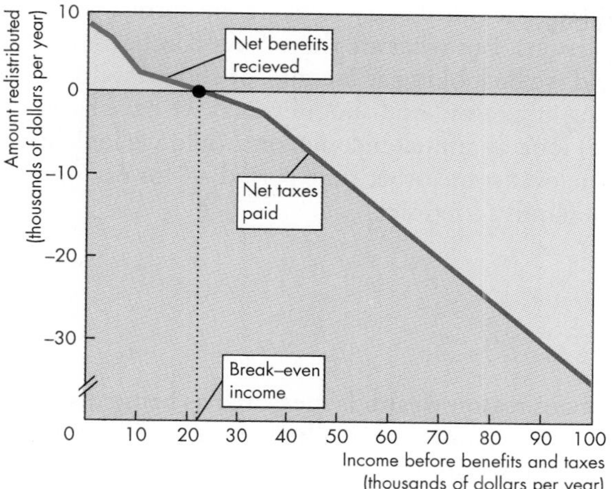

Net benefits and taxes are shown for typical senior citizens. Benefits in the form of OAS and GIS provide a maximum income of $8,850 per year. The higher the individual's income befôre benefits and taxes, the lower the rate of benefits. At an income level of around $23,000 per year, net benefits are zero. At income levels above that rate, taxes paid exceed benefits received.

Note: Our calculations are based on Revenue Canada and Health and Welfare Canada schedules and programs prevailing in Ontario in October 1989.

The Scale of Income Redistribution The distribution of income that would prevail in the absence of government policies is called the **market distribution**. The income distribution that takes account of government policies is called the **distribution after taxes and transfers**. Calculating the effects of all the many tax and transfer arrangements in place is a complicated matter; the most recent year for which we have a thorough analysis is 1976. Figure 18.7(a) illustrates the scale of redistribution in Canada. The amount of redistribution that takes place among the five income groups is 12.6 percent of total income. The amount taken from the richest group is 4.9 percent and from the second-richest group, 1.4 percent. The poorest group receives 3.3 percent, and the second-poorest group receives 2.4 percent. The middle group receives 0.6 percent. The effects of redistribution policies can also be seen by comparing the Lorenz curves for the market distribution of income and the distribution after taxes and transfers. Figure 18.7(b) shows these Lorenz curves. As you can see, there is a considerable amount of redistri-

Figure 18.7 The Effect of Taxes and Transfers on the Distribution of Income

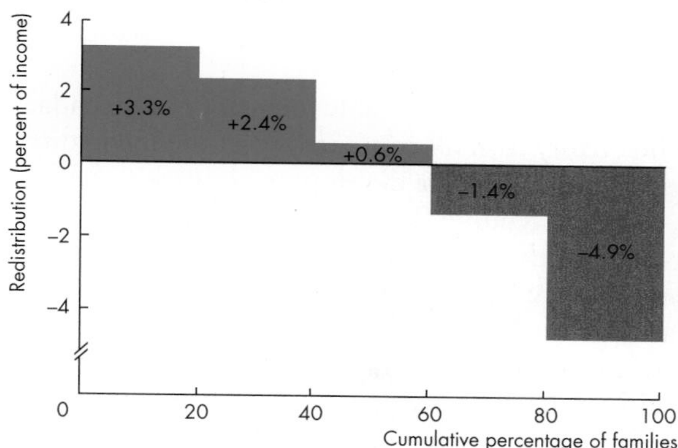

(a) Redistribution of income

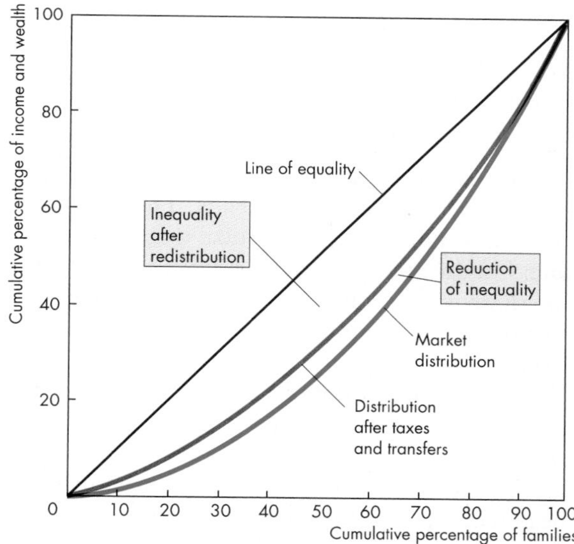

(b) Lorenz curves before and after redistribution

Taxes and transfers reduce the degree of inequality that the market generates. Part (a) shows that 4.9 percent of income is taken from the richest fifth of the population and 1.4 percent from the second-richest fifth and redistributed to the poorest two-fifths. The poorest fifth receives 3.3 percent and the second-poorest fifth, 2.4 percent. The middle income group receives almost 0.6 percent. Part (b) shows the effects of this redistribution on the Lorenz curve for income.

Source: Osberg, 1981 (see Fig. 18.2), whose original source is W.I. Gillespie, "Taxes Expenditures and the Redistribution of Income in Canada, 1951-1977," *Reflections on Canadian Incomes* (Ottawa: Economic Council of Canada, 1980), 27-50.

bution, especially to boost the incomes of the very poor, but a great deal of inequality remains after redistribution.

World inequality and Redistribution

Although there is considerable inequality in Canada, that inequality is small compared with the inequality across countries. In the developing countries of Africa, Asia, the Middle East, and Central America, four-fifths of the world's population live on average incomes that are substantially below 50 per cent of the average income in Canada. Some international redistribution of income takes place as a result of foreign aid but its scale is tiny compared with the scale of redistribution within a country. For example, Canada, one of the world's most generous providers of foreign aid (in per capita terms) gives only about one per cent of its total income to poorer countries.

R E V I E W

There is considerable inequality in the distribution of income and wealth in Canada. The distribution of wealth is much more unequal than that of income. On the average, the poorest families in Canada are those with a young, single-parent mother. The highest-income families are middle-aged married couples, both of whom have jobs. Government policies redistribute income by taxing incomes at progressively higher rates and by paying a variety of social security benefits to those who otherwise would have little or no means of support. Even after income has been redistributed through taxes and transfers, a considerable amount of inequality of income remains. ■

We've now examined some facts about the distribution of income and wealth in Canada. But what is the reason for the enormous inequality that exists? And why is the distribution of wealth so much more unequal than that of income? Which of these two distributions paints the more accurate picture concerning the degree of inequality? In the next section, we will examine the reasons for the *differences* in the degree of inequality as measured by wealth and by income. After that, we will study some of the reasons for inequality itself.

Comparing Like with Like

In order to determine just how much inequality there is, it is necessary to make the correct comparisons. But what are the correct comparisons? Should we be looking at income, or should we be looking at wealth? And should we (as we have been doing) look at annual income, or should we look at income over some other time period — for example, over a family's lifetime?

Wealth Versus Income

The main reason wealth is measured as being distributed so much more unequally than income is that the data on wealth and income measure different things. The wealth data refer only to nonhuman capital — tangible assets that are traded on capital markets (such as those items analysed in Chapter 17). The income data refer to income from all sources, not only from nonhuman capital but also from human capital. We can explore the sources of these differences a bit more closely by looking at an example. Let's begin by recalling the distinction between income and wealth.

Income and Wealth: Flow and Stock Income and wealth can be considered different ways of looking at precisely the same thing. *Wealth* is the *stock* of assets owned by an individual. *Income* is the *flow* of earnings received by an individual. *Income* is the *flow of earnings* that results from the *stock of wealth.* It is easiest to see the relationship between income and wealth by considering an example. Suppose that Lee owns assets worth $1 million. Thus Lee's wealth is $1 million. If the rate of return on assets is 5 percent a year, then Lee will receive an income of $50,000 a year from his assets of $1 million. We can describe Lee's economic condition by saying that he has either wealth of $1 million or an income of $50,000. If the rate of return is 5 percent, these two statements are equivalent to each other.

Now let's consider another individual, Peter, who has assets of $500,000. Peter and Lee have the same investment opportunities, and they invest their assets at the same rate of return — 5 percent a year. Thus Peter has an income of $25,000 (5 percent of $500,000).

We can now talk about the distribution of wealth and income between Peter and Lee. Lee has wealth of $1 million compared with Peter's wealth of $500,000. Thus Lee has twice as much wealth as Peter. Lee has an income of $50,000 and Peter has an income of $25,000. Again, Lee's income is twice as much as Peter's. Regardless of whether we compare Peter and Lee on the basis of their wealth or their income, we reach the same conclusion: Lee is twice as rich as Peter.

Human Capital

So far, we have discussed only the earnings that Peter and Lee receive from their nonhuman wealth. We sometimes refer to physical and financial assets as *tangible assets* or, to contrast them with human capital, as *nonhuman capital.* What about Peter's and Lee's work effort? The earnings received from work are partly a compensation for giving up leisure time and partly a return on *human capital.* Although human capital represents intangible things such as skills, we can put a value on it. We value human capital by looking at the earnings that a person can make from working, over and above what would be earned by someone who has had no education or training. The extra earnings are the income from human capital. The value of human capital is the amount of money that a person would have to be given today so that, if invested today, it would generate an interest income equal to the income from that individual's human capital.

Consider Peter and Lee again. But suppose now that each of them has no assets other than their productive skills. Lee earns $50,000 a year. Thus if the interest rate is 5 percent a year, Lee has $1 million of human capital. (A million dollars invested at an interest rate of 5 percent a year will earn $50,000 a year.) Peter earns $25,000 a year, so, again if the interest rate is 5 percent a year, he has human capital of $500,000. Lee earns twice as much income as does Peter and has twice as much human capital.

Human and Nonhuman Capital

We have now considered the distribution of income and wealth in two extreme cases. In the first one, Lee and Peter own no human capital so their entire income is generated by their financial and real assets. In the second case, Lee and Peter have only human capital — their productive skills. Most people have both nonhuman and human capital. Wealth, correctly measured, includes both these types of capital.

No matter what the source of income — human capital or nonhuman capital — the distribution of wealth and income is the same as long as we count both human and nonhuman capital. In both the cases that we have just examined, Lee has twice the wealth and twice the income of Peter. So the distribution of wealth between Lee and Peter is identical to the distribution of income between them.

Finally, let's examine the case in which Peter and Lee have both human capital and nonhuman capital. For a reason that will become apparent shortly, let's suppose that Peter has much more human capital than Lee and that Lee has more nonhuman capital than Peter. Table 18.3 sets out some hypothetical numbers to illustrate this case. As before, Lee has twice the total wealth and twice the total income of Peter. Lee's human capital is only $200,000, so his labour income is just $10,000. But Lee has nonhuman capital of $800,000, which generates an income of $40,000. In contrast, Peter's wealth is almost exclusively human capital. Peter earns $24,950 of income from $499,000 worth of human capital. Peter has only $1,000 worth of tangible assets (nonhuman capital), which generates an annual income of $50.

Suppose that a national wealth and income surveyor is examining this economy comprised of Peter and Lee and observes their incomes of $25,000 and $50,000 respectively. The surveyor concludes that, on the basis of income, Lee is twice as rich as Peter. The surveyor then measures their assets. Remember — the only assets that are measured are tangible assets. The surveyor observes that Lee owns $800,000 worth of such assets and Peter has $1,000 worth. The national surveyor concludes that, in terms of assets, Lee is 800 times as wealthy as Peter. The survey concludes that wealth is much more unevenly distributed than income.

As you can see, the national survey techniques measure the distribution of wealth in a way that does not include human capital. The distribution of income takes into account human capital, so it is the correct measure of the distribution of economic resources. Measured wealth distribution that ignores the distribution of human capital overstate the inequality among individuals.

Table 18.3 Capital, Wealth, and Income

	Lee		Peter	
	Wealth	Income	Wealth	Income
Human capital	$ 200,000	$10,000	$499,000	$24,950
Nonhuman capital	800,000	40,000	1,000	50
Total	$1,000,000	$50,000	$500,000	$25,000

When wealth is measured so as to include the value of human capital as well as nonhuman capital, the distribution of income and the distribution of wealth display the same degree of inequality.

Annual or Lifetime Income and Wealth?

The income distributions that we examined earlier in this chapter were based on annual incomes and the wealth distributions were based on measurements of family wealth in a given year. These kinds of measures are standard. Yet many sources of inequality in annual income and in wealth in a given year do not imply inequality over a family's entire lifetime. For example, young people earn less, on the average, than middle-aged people. Thus in a given year a typical young family has a lower income than a middle-aged family. But when the young family itself becomes middle-aged, its income will not differ, on the average, from that of the current middle-aged family. Thus the inequality in annual incomes does not reflect an inequality across families over their entire lifetimes.

The case of wealth is more extreme. Most young families have few assets and often have debts that exceed those assets. Families with people between middle age and retirement age are at a stage in life when they're building up their assets to provide for a retirement income. Again, the middle-aged family looks wealthier than the younger family, but by the time the younger family reaches that later stage in the life cycle, it will have accumulated assets similar in scale to those of the current older family.

In order to compare the income and wealth situation of one family with another, it is important to take into account the family's stage in the life cycle so as to avoid being misled by differences arising purely from that factor. To illustrate the importance of this source of inequality, we'll work through an example.

Figure 18.8 shows a family's income, consumption, and wealth over its entire life cycle. The horizontal axis in both parts measures the age of the head of the household. The vertical axis measures thousands of dollars of income and consumption in part (a) and of wealth in part (b).

Figure 18.8(a) shows the family's pattern of income and consumption. It consumes at a steady rate of $20,000 a year throughout its life. The family's income from employment starts out at $18,000 a year. It gradually rises until, just before retirement, the family is earning $30,000 a year. After retirement, the family's income from work is zero, but it continues to receive an income in the form of interest on the capital that it has accumulated in the years before retirement. Fig. 18.8(b) shows the family's nonhuman wealth. Early in its life cycle, the family has to borrow to sustain its consumption level. As it does so, it incurs debt (and has to pay interest on the debt). The family is at its deepest point of debt when the household head is age 35. After that, the family gradually gets out of debt, and after age 45, starts accumulating a great deal of nonhuman wealth. After retirement, that nonhuman wealth is spent on postretirement consumption.

Now consider two families who are identical to the one we've looked at here, but who are at different

Figure 18.8 Life-Cycle Income, Consumption, and Wealth

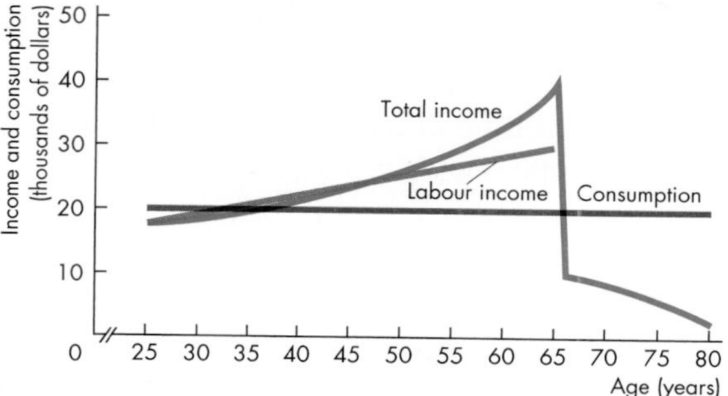

(a) Income and consumption

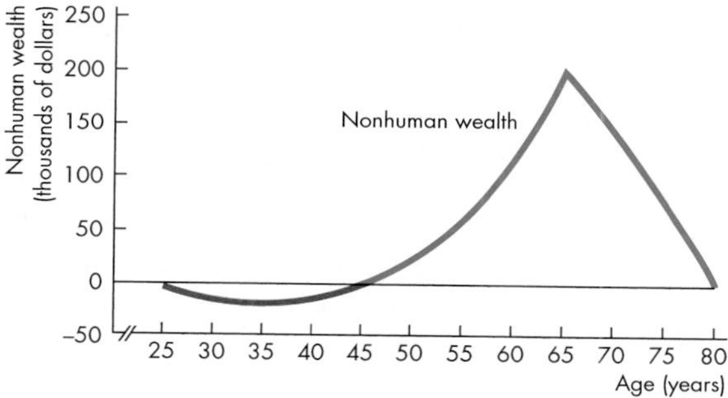

(b) Nonhuman wealth

Part (a) of the figure shows the consumption and income of a household. Consumption is constant at $20,000 per year throughout its lifetime. Labour income is $18,000 when the family head is 25 years old and gradually increases to $30,000 at retirement. After retirement, the household has no labour income. Total income is labour income plus interest on capital (nonhuman wealth). Part (b) shows the household's nonhuman wealth. In its early years, the household consumes more than its income and goes in debt, which reaches its maximum when the household head is age 35. From age 45 to 65, the household gradually gets out of debt and begins to accumulate nonhuman wealth. After retirement age, the household spends its nonhuman wealth throughout the rest of its life. An economy that is populated by households like this one but with each household at a different stage in its life cycle will have highly unequal distributions of *annual* income and wealth. The small fraction of the population close to retirement (both before and after) will own almost all the economy's nonhuman wealth.

stages of the life cycle. One of these families is 25 years old and the other is 66. If all we look at is income, we will conclude that the 25-year-old family is almost twice as well off as the 66-year-old family. If all we look at is nonhuman wealth, we will conclude that the 66-year-old family, which has accumulated assets worth $200,000, is much better off than the 25-year-old family. Yet from the point of view of consumption, these two families are identical.

If the entire population of this imaginary economy is made up of families that are identical except for their stage of the life cycle and if there are an equal number of families of each age, we can discover some startling facts about the distribution of wealth and annual income. First, let's look at the distribution of nonhuman wealth, which is illustrated in Fig. 18.9. In comparison, the wealth distribution in Canada is also shown. As you can see, the Lorenz curve for the imaginary economy's wealth distribution lies inside that for the actual Canadian economy, so wealth in Canada is more unequally distributed than wealth in the imaginary economy. This means that although the wealth inequality arising from measuring different families at different points in the life cycle accounts for some of the wealth inequality in the real world, it does not account for all of it.

Second, let's consider the distribution of annual income. Figure 18.9 also shows the Lorenz curves for the imaginary economy and for the Canadian economy. As you can see, there is more income inequality in Canada than in the imaginary economy, but the difference is smaller than it appears when we do not take account of the differences in the stage of the life cycle.

R E V I E W

The measured distribution of wealth is more unequal than that of income because it ignores human wealth. Income and wealth are different aspects of the same thing. Wealth is the stock of assets owned by an individual, and income is the flow of earnings that results from that stock of wealth. Properly measured, the degree of inequality in wealth is identical to that in income. Measures of inequality focus on inequality of annual income and wealth at a point in time. Much of this inequality arises from variations in income and wealth over an individual's lifetime. Inequality in lifetime income and wealth is much less than that in annual income and wealth, though important inequalities persist even when measured on a lifetime basis. ■

Figure 18.9 Lorenz Curves for Imaginary and Actual Economies

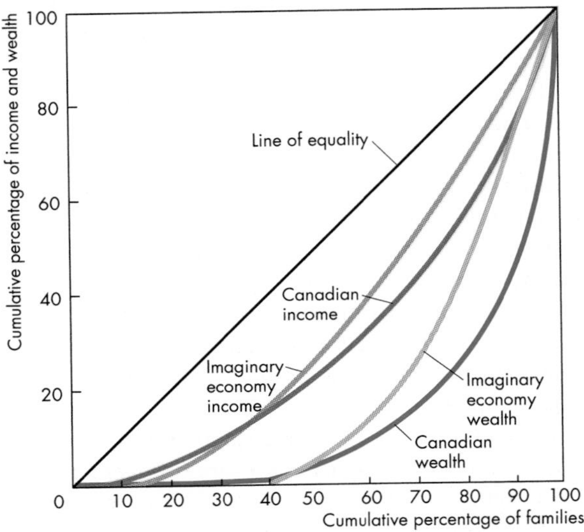

The Lorenz curves for income and wealth in the Canadian economy are shown alongside those for an imaginary economy in which everyone has the same lifetime income and consumption. The Lorenz curves for the imaginary economy show a considerable amount of inequality in *annual* income and in *nonhuman wealth*. Yet there is complete equality in *lifetime income* and *total wealth* in the imaginary economy. The amount of inequality in annual income and nonhuman wealth in the Canadian economy is similar to that in the imaginary economy. Thus the degree of lifetime inequality is exaggerated by looking only at the distribution of annual income and nonhuman wealth.

The example that we have just worked through shows that some of the measured inequality in income and wealth arises purely from the fact that different families are at different stages in the life cycle. It also shows, however, that there are important remaining inequalities in income and wealth in Canada today. In the next two sections, we're going to explore the sources of those inequalities.

Factor Prices and Endowments

Each individual owns factors of production and sells the services of those factors to provide an income. A person's income is the total of the prices paid for the use of each factor multiplied by the quantities supplied. Factor prices are determined by the forces that we analysed in Chapters 15 through 17. The amount of each factor service that an individual supplies depends partly on his or her endowment of that factor and partly on the choices that he or she makes. Let's now examine the extent to which differences in income arise from differences in factor prices and from differences in the quantity of factors that people supply.

Labour Market and Wages

We've seen that the biggest single source of income is labour. To what extent do variations in wage rates account for the unequal distribution of income? Table 18.4 helps to answer this question. It sets out the average hourly earnings of private sector employees in seven occupations in 1985 along with the average hourly earnings in all industrial occupations. There is a large spread around the average of $10.52, ranging from the minimum wage in Alberta (the province with the lowest minimum wage) up to $18.86 for a skilled plumber (also in Alberta). We can measure the spread between the highest- and lowest-paid workers in these employment categories by calculating the wage differential, which is the ratio of one wage to another. Taking the highest wage ($18.86) and dividing it by the lowest wage ($3.85) gives a wage differential of 4.9. That is, the highest-paid worker in the list in Table 18.4 earns 4.9 times the wage of the lowest-paid worker in that list.

One of the factors reflected in this wage differential is the difference in skill, or human capital, of the various workers. For example, a skilled plumber has had much more training and has a great deal more work experience than an unskilled gas station attendant.

The distribution of income is generated not only by differences in wage rates but also by differences in the endowments or abilities of individuals. Let us now consider this source of difference.

Distribution of Endowments

Ability Although people are endowed with equal amounts of time, they are not endowed with equal abilities. Physical and mental differences (some inherited, some learned) are such an obvious feature of human life that they hardly need mentioning. But

Table 18.4 Average Hourly Earnings in 1985

Occupation/location	Wage (dollars per hour)
Gas station attendant in Edmonton	3.85
Security guard in Halifax	5.31
Heavy-duty cleaner in Halifax	7.61
Word-processing operator in Vancouver	11.43
Welder in Toronto	13.00
Heavy-truck driver in Vancouver	15.29
Plumber in Edmonton	18.86
Average, all industrial occupations	10.52

Average hourly earnings show considerable inequality across occupations. But the range of inequality is much lower than the inequality of income. For example, the highest-paid worker in this list, a plumber in Edmonton, earns almost 5 times the income of the lowest-paid worker, the gas station attendant, who earns the Alberta minimum wage of $3.85 per hour.

Source: Statistics Canada, *Canada Yearbook*, 1988, 5-5, 5-31, 5-32.

these differences produce differences in earnings and, therefore, differences in income and wealth.

It is impossible to know for sure how such an intangible as "earnings potential based on ability" is distributed among the population. People do, however, have many measurable characteristics that probably influence their earnings. For example, physical attributes such as height, weight, strength, and endurance can all be measured objectively.

All these measurable attributes appear to have what is called a normal distribution in the population. For example, Fig. 18.10 shows the distribution of heights of male students. The horizontal axis measures those heights; the average height is 180 centimetres. The vertical axis measures the number of students of each height. The curve that traces the percentage of students at each height is a bell-shaped curve. That is, the distribution is symmetric. For each person above the average height, there is another person who is below the average by the same amount. So the two halves of the curve are like a mirror image of each other. There are more people clustered around the average than there are at the two extremes.

The range of individual ability is a major source of differences in income and wealth. But it is not the only source. If it were, the distribution of income and wealth would look like the bell-shaped curve that describes the distribution of height in Fig. 18.10. In fact, the distribution of income looks like Fig. 18.11. That figure shows different levels of income on the horizontal axis and the percentage of households on the vertical axis. By definition, the median income is the income level that separates households into two equal groups. Fifty percent of households have an income above the median, and 50 percent have an income below the median. In this example, the median income is $30,000 a year. Incomes below the median range between zero and $30,000 a year and incomes above the median range upward from $30,000 to more than $100,000 a year. As a consequence, the average income is higher than the median income and is about $35,000 a year. But the most common income is below the median — and is $20,000 a year. The asymmetric shape of the distribution of income and wealth has to be explained by something more than the distribution of individual abilities.

Figure 18.10 A Normal Distribution

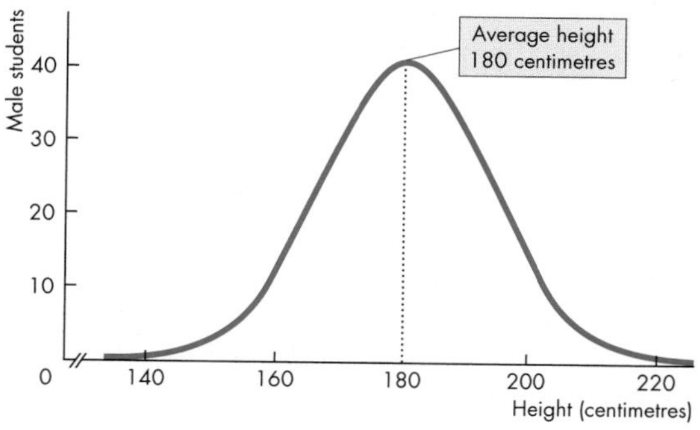

A normal distribution is shaped like a bell and is symmetric around the average. The distribution shown here is the height of a group of male students. The average is 180 centimetres. For every person whose height falls above 180 centimetres, there is a mirror-image person whose height falls an equal distance below 180 centimetres. A symmetric, bell-shaped distribution describes a large number of human characteristics.

Figure 18.11 The Distribution of Income

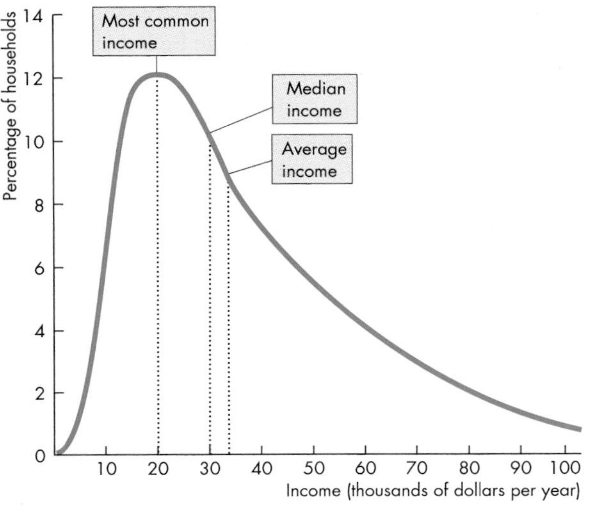

The distribution of income is unequal and is not symmetric around the average. There are many more people with incomes below the average than above the average. Also, the distribution has a thin upper tail representing a small proportion of people earning very large incomes.

Choices and the Distribution of Income and Wealth

A person's income and wealth depend partly on the prices of those factors of production — labour services, capital, and land — that the person supplies, and partly on the quantities of those factors of production that the person chooses to supply. In most cases, people can't influence factor prices. In contrast, people can and do choose how much of each factor to supply. They also choose whether to babysit or to work in a bank, whether to put their savings in the bank or in stocks. So the distribution of income depends not only on factor prices but also on people's choices about supplying factors.

The choices that people make exaggerate the differences among individuals. Their choices make the distribution of income more unequal than the distribution of abilities. They also skew the distribution of income. A skewed distribution is one in which there are a larger number of people on one side of the average than on the other. In the case of income distribution, there are more people below the average than above the average.

Let's go on to see why people's choices lead to an unequal and skewed income distribution.

Wages and the Supply of Labour

A family's labour supply curve shows the relationship between the quantity of labour the household supplies and the wage rate. Suppose that a family has a labour supply curve like the one shown in Fig. 18.12. At a wage rate at or below $1 an hour, the household supplies no labour. As the wage rate increases, the quantity of labour supplied increases, and at a wage rate of $9 an hour, 40 hours a week of labour are supplied. The fact that the quantity of labour supplied increases as the wage rate increases results in a distribution of income that is more unequal than the distribution of hourly wages. It also results in a skewing of the distribution of income even if the distribution of wages is symmetric.

To see why these features of the income distribution occur, let's imagine a population of 1,000 people, each one of whom has a labour supply curve like the one shown in Fig. 18.12. Although everyone has the same labour supply curve, suppose that each person has a different marginal revenue product of labour and so is paid a different wage rate (see Chapter 15). Figure 18.13 illustrates this economy. Part (a) shows the distribution of marginal revenue products and hourly wage rates for the 1,000 people. This distribution is a normal curve (bell-shaped) like the distribution of students' heights. The wage rate ranges from $1 to $9 an hour, with an average of $5 an hour.

Figure 18.13(b) shows the distribution of weekly income. Since people who earn a higher hourly wage work longer hours, their weekly income is disproportionately larger than that of people with low hourly wages who work shorter hours. As you can see from Fig. 18.13(b), the most common income is $100 a week, but the average income is $128 a week. Those who earn $2 an hour work only 5 hours a week for a weekly wage of $10. Those who earn $9 an hour work 40 hours a week for a weekly wage of $360. Thus the highest income earned is 36 times the lowest. In contrast, the wage rate of the highest paid person is only 4.5 times that of the lowest paid.

Choices also skew the distribution of income. You can see this by looking again at Fig. 18.13(b). A larger proportion of the population has an income below the average than above the average.

The example that we have just worked through is, of course, artificial. But the point that it illustrates applies in the real world. Other things being equal, the higher the wage rate, the more labour a person will supply; therefore the distribution of income is more unequal than the underlying distribution of abilities. Even if the distribution of abilities is symmetric, the distribution of income is skewed. More people have incomes below the average than above the average.

Another choice that makes for unequal distribution in income and wealth is savings and bequests. Let's look at this source of inequality.

Savings and Bequests

A **bequest** is a gift from one generation to the next. The wealthier the family, the more it tends to save and bequeath to later generations. By making a bequest, a family can spread good and bad luck across the generations.

Savings and bequests are not inevitably a source of increased inequality. Savings that merely redistribute uneven income over the life cycle to enable consumption to be constant have no effect on inequality. A generation that is lucky may make a bequest to a generation that is unlucky; in that case, the bequest is

Figure 18.12 The Supply of Labour

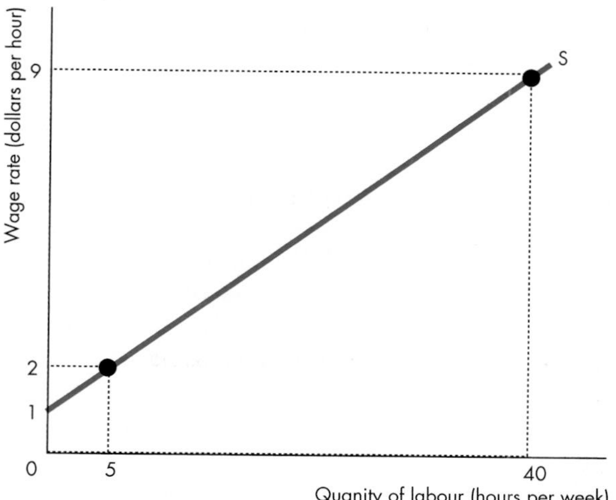

As the wage rate increases, so does the quantity of labour supplied. A person facing a wage rate of $2 per hour works 5 hours a week and so earns $10 per week. A person facing a wage rate of $9 per hour works 40 hours per week and so earns $360 per week. The wage rate of the second person is 4.5 times that of the first, but the second person's income is 36 times larger.

Figure 18.13 The Distribution of Wages, Hours, and Income

(a) Distribution of wage rates

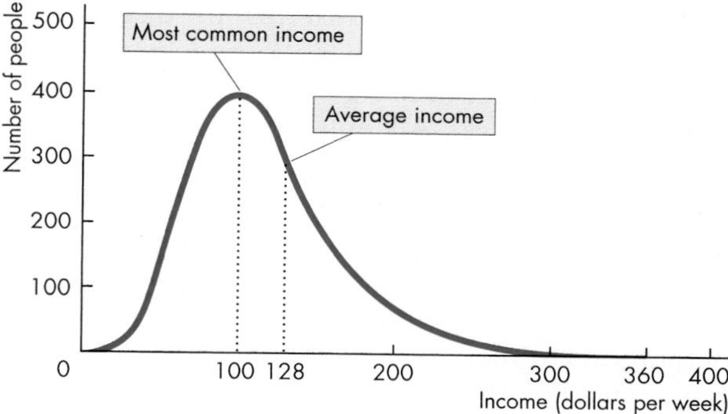

(b) Distribution of weekly incomes

Economic choices create a skewed income distribution. Part (a) graphs the distribution of wages. It is symmetric around the average wage rate of $5 per hour. Part (b) graphs the distribution of weekly income. A majority of the people earn less than the average income. The higher the wage rate, the more labour a person will supply; therefore the distribution of income is more unequal and not symmetric around the average. The range of inequality in wage rates — $1 to $9 — is accentuated in the inequality of weekly income — $0 to $360.

a source of equality, not inequality. But there are two important features of bequests that do make intergenerational transfers of wealth a source of increased inequality:

- Debts cannot be bequeathed.
- Mating is assortative.

Debts Cannot be Bequeathed Though a person may die with debts in excess of assets, those debts cannot be bequeathed — that is, they cannot be forced onto the remaining members of the family. Thus a zero inheritance is the smallest inheritance that anyone can receive. Therefore savings and bequests can only add to future generations' wealth and income potential.

The vast majority of people inherit nothing or a very small amount from the previous generation. A tiny number of people inherit enormous fortunes. As a result of bequests, the distribution of income and wealth is not only more unequal than the distribution of ability and job skills but also more persistent. A family that is poor in one generation is more likely to be poor in the next. A family that is enormously wealthy in one generation is more likely to be enormously wealthy in the next. Yet there is a tendency for income and wealth to converge, across the generations, to the average. Although there can be long runs of good luck or bad luck or good judgement or bad judgement, they are uncommon across the generations. An additional feature of human behaviour does, however, slow convergence to the average and make wealth and income inequalities persist. It is called **assortative mating**.

Assortative Mating People tend to marry within their own socioeconomic class, a phenomenon called **assortative mating**. In the vernacular, "like attracts like." Although there is a good deal of folklore that "opposites attract," perhaps Cinderella tales appeal to us because they are so rare in reality. Marriage partners tend to have similar socioeconomic characteristics. Wealthy individuals seek wealthy partners. The consequence of assortative mating is that inherited wealth becomes more unequally distributed.

R E V I E W

Economic inequality arises from inequality of endowments of factors of production and inequality of the prices for which those factors of production can be sold. Individual choices in the face of unequal opportunities accentuate inequality in the distributions of both income and wealth. Other things being equal, the higher the wage rate, the larger is the quantity of labour supplied so the resulting inequality of income reflects inequality both in the wage opportunity and in the amount of hours worked. Inequality is transmitted across the generations as a result of savings and bequests and assortative mating. ■

We've now completed our positive analysis of inequality in the distribution of income and wealth. We've described the extent of inequality and have identified some of the reasons that it exists. But we have not attempted to make any assessment about fairness or justice. Is it fair that some people can be so incredibly rich and others so abjectly poor? In the final section of this chapter, we will examine the way in which economists and philosophers have tried to wrestle with this type of question.

Ideas About Fairness

We all have views about fairness and what constitutes a "fair" distribution of income and wealth. These views are diverse, and they are a source of political and philosophical debate. Throughout the ages, moral philosophers have tried to find a satisfactory theory of distributive justice. A **theory of distributive justice** is a set of principles against which people can test whether a particular distribution of economic well-being is fair.

The theories of distributive justice fall into two broad classes: end-state theories and process theories. An **end-state theory of distributive justice** focuses on the justice or fairness of the *outcomes* or *ends* of economic activity. A **process theory of distributive justice** focuses on the justice or fairness of the *mechanisms* or *means* whereby the ends are achieved. For example, the belief that each person should have exactly the same income and wealth is an end-state theory. Equality of income and wealth requires an equality of outcomes or ends. That is, when the process is over, everyone has to have the same income and wealth. In contrast, the belief that everyone should have the same opportunity to earn and accumulate wealth is a process theory. Requiring that people have equal opportunities does not imply that they will have equal income and wealth because people will use their opportunities in different ways. Depending on how they use their opportunities and on a variety of chance events (good and bad luck), unequal income and wealth will emerge.

End-State Theories

The two leading end-state theories of distributive justice are the utilitarian and Rawlsian theories. The **utilitarian theory** is that the fairest outcome is the one that makes the sum of the utilities of all the individuals in a society as large as possible. If Rob gets less utility than does Ian from the last dollar spent, fairness, in this theory, requires that a dollar be taken from Rob and given to Ian. The reduction in Rob's utility is less than the gain in Ian's utility, so society is better off. Redistribution should take place until the marginal utility of the last dollar spent by each individual is the same. Utilitarian theories of fairness were developed in the eighteenth and nineteenth centuries by such economists as David Hume, Adam Smith, Jeremy Bentham, and John Stuart Mill.

The **Rawlsian theory of fairness** is that the fairest distribution is the one that gives the least well-off member of society the biggest income possible. In the Rawlsian view, if the poorest person can be made better off by taking income from any other person, justice requires that such redistribution take place. The Rawlsian theory of fairness was developed in the 1960s by John Rawls, a philosopher at Harvard University, and published in his classic work, *A Theory of Justice*, in 1971.[1]

As you can see, the two end-state theories of justice differ in what they regard as the desirable end-state or outcome. For the utilitarian, it is the average or sum of all the individuals that counts; for Rawls, it is the least well-off individual or individuals that count.

How Much Inequality is Consistent with End-State Theories?

It used to be thought that an end-state theory of justice implied that complete equality in the distribution of income was the best outcome. This conclusion was reached by reasoning along the following lines. First, people are much alike in their capacity for enjoyment (in the technical language of economics, they have the same marginal utility of income schedule). Second, marginal utility declines with income. Therefore by taking a dollar from a rich person and giving it to a poorer person, the marginal utility lost by the rich person is less than the marginal utility gained by the poorer person. Thus taking from the rich and giving to the poor increases total utility. Maximum utility occurs when each individual has the same marginal utility, a point that is reached only when incomes — after redistribution — are equal. When incomes have been equalized, the total utility of the society has been maximized and "fair shares" have been achieved.

The Big Tradeoff

Although it used to be thought that justice implied complete equality, it is now recognized that there exists what has been called the "big tradeoff" between fairness and economic efficiency. (The term comes from the title of a 1975 book[2] by Arthur Okun, a famous American economist.)

The big tradeoff is based on the following idea. Greater equality can be achieved only by taxing productive activities. Taxing people's income from their work and savings lowers the after-tax income they receive. This lower income makes them work and save less. In economic terms, lower after-tax factor prices result in reduced factor supplies. Lower factor supplies result in smaller output, and the smaller output results in less consumption not only for the rich but also possibly for the poor. According to this line of reasoning, the correct amount of redistribution to undertake balances greater equality against lower average consumption.

It also must be recognized that taking resources from the rich to give to the poor cannot be achieved without using resources to administer the redistribution. Tax-collecting agencies, such as Revenue Canada, as well as all the tax accountants, auditors, lawyers, and welfare-administering agencies use massive quantities of skilled labour and capital equipment, such as computers, to do their work. Thus a dollar collected from a rich person does not translate into a dollar received by a poor person. The bigger the scale of redistribution, the greater are the costs of administering the process.

When these aspects of redistribution are taken into account, it is not obvious that taking a dollar from a rich person to give to a poor person increases

[1]John Rawls, *A Theory of Justice* (Cambridge: Harvard University Press, 1971).

[2]Arthur Okun, *Equality and Efficiency: The Big Tradeoff* (Washington, D.C.: Brookings Institution, 1975).

the welfare of the poor person. The wealth available for redistribution could be reduced to the point at which everyone was worse off. Taking account of the disincentive effects of redistribution and the resource costs of administering the redistribution is what produces the "big tradeoff." A more equally shared pie results in a smaller pie.

The Process View of Justice

The process view of distributive justice was given its most recent statement by Harvard philosopher Robert Nozick in his 1974 book *Anarchy, State, and Utopia*[3]. Nozick argues that no end-state theory of justice can be valid and that a theory of justice must be based on the justice of the mechanisms through which the distribution of income and wealth arises. Nozick argues for a system based on private property rights, one in which private property can be acquired and transferred only through voluntary exchange.

Nozick's reasoning can be illustrated with the following story. Start out with a distribution that you personally regard as the best possible. Now suppose that your favourite rock singer enters into a contract with a recording company and a rock concert organizer. The deal is that she will get 5 cents on every record sold and 50 cents for every ticket sold to her rock concerts. In a given year, she sells 5 million records and 500,000 people attend her concerts. Her total income is $500,000. This income is much larger than the average and much larger than what she had under the original distribution.

Is she entitled to this income? Is the new distribution fair? Nozick believes that she is entitled to the income and that the new distribution is fair. These conclusions follow from Nozick's process view of justice. It is legitimate for you and your friends to attend rock concerts and to buy records. If the consequence of the choices that you and your friends make is that someone becomes extremely wealthy, that outcome is legitimate and the new distribution of income and wealth is fair.

[3]Robert Nozick, *Anarchy, State, and Utopia* (New York: Basic Books, 1974).

Those who subscribe to an end-state theory of justice, of course, do not agree. If the original distribution of income was fair, then the new one cannot be fair. The successful rock singer must be taxed and the proceeds of the tax redistributed to those who buy records and attend concerts, in order to restore a fair distribution.

The philosophical debate continues and perhaps will never be settled. This state of affairs is no deterrent to those in the practical world of politics. While moral philosophers continue to disagree about fairness, politicians are creating and implementing policies designed to chop off the extremes of the distribution of income and achieve a greater measure of equality.

■ We have examined the distribution of income and wealth in Canada and seen that there is a large amount of inequality across families and individuals. Some of that inequality arises from comparing families at different stages in the life cycle. Yet even if one takes a lifetime view, a great deal of inequality remains. Some of that inequality arises from differences in rates of pay. And economic choices accentuate those differences. Also, savings and bequests result in the growth of huge wealth concentrations over the generations.

The topic that we have examined in this chapter is highly political, and, as we've seen, governments attempt to redistribute income to alleviate the worst aspects of poverty. In the next three chapters, we're going to undertake a systematic study of a broad range of political economic issues and of the economic behaviour of government. We'll return to questions concerning the distribution of income and wealth as part of that broader study.

SUMMARY

Distribution of Income and Wealth in Canada Today

Labour is the factor of production with the largest share of income, and that share has grown slightly over the years. The distribution of wealth and income among individuals is uneven. The richest 1 percent of Canadians own almost one-fifth of the total wealth in the country. The poorest 40 percent own less than 1 percent of the total wealth. Income is distributed less unevenly than wealth. The income distribution has changed only slightly over time and in the direction of a lower degree of inequality. The poorest families in Canada are most likely to be those with young, single, out-of-work mothers living in Québec. The richest families are most likely to live in Ontario and to be middle-aged with husband and wife living together. Income tax and social security programs result in a redistribution of income, transferring some income from the rich to the poor and, to some degree, alleviating poverty. (pp. 467-474)

Comparing Like with Like

In order to judge the extent of inequality, it is important that we make the valid comparisons. The measured distribution of wealth exaggerates the degree of inequality because it fails to take into account the distribution of human capital. The distributions of annual income and wealth exaggerate the degree of lifetime inequality because they do not take into account the household's stage in its life cycle. (pp. 474-478)

Factor Prices and Endowments

Differences in income and wealth arise partly from differences in individual endowments and partly from differences in factor prices. Wage rates vary considerably with skill and other factors. But these differences, on their own, are not enough to account for differences in the distribution of income and wealth. Those differences are exaggerated by the economic choices that people make. (pp. 478-480)

Choices and the Distribution of Income and Wealth

The economic choices that people make have an important influence on income and wealth. Attitudes towards work vary. As a result, some people take a larger amount of leisure than others, earn a smaller income, and consume a smaller amount of goods. Also, savings and bequests affect wealth across the generations. Because of assortative mating — the tendency for people to marry within their own socioeconomic group and thus for wealthy individuals to seek wealthy partners — bequests accentuate inequality. (pp. 480-482)

Ideas About Fairness

People disagree about what constitutes a fair distribution of income. Moral philosophers have tried to resolve the issue by finding principles on which we can all agree, but agreement still has not been reached. They have developed two broad groups of theories: end-state theories, which assert that it is the outcome that matters, and process theories, which assert that it is equality of opportunity that matters. (pp. 482-484)

KEY ELEMENTS

Key Terms

Assortative mating, 482
Bequest, 481
Distribution after taxes and transfers, 473
End-state theory of distributive justice, 482
Incidence of low income, 470
Lorenz curve, 468
Low-income cutoff, 470
Market distribution, 473
Process theory of distributive justice, 482
Progressive income tax, 470
Proportional income tax, 470
Rawlsian theory of fairness, 483
Regressive income tax, 470
Theory of distributive justice, 482
Utilitarian theory, 483

Key Figures

Figure 18.3 Lorenz Curves for Income and Wealth, 469
Figure 18.4 The Incidence of Low Income by Selected Family Characteristics, 471
Figure 18.13 The Distribution of Wages, Hours, and Income, 481

REVIEW QUESTIONS

1 Which of the following describe the distributions of personal income and wealth in Canada today?

a) The distribution of income and wealth is best represented by normal or bell-shaped curves.

b) The richest people are more than 800 times as wealthy as the poorest people, but the same percentage of people are at each level of wealth.

c) More than 50 percent of the population have an income above the average.

d) More than 50 percent of the population have an income below the average.

2 Which is more unequally distributed, income or wealth? In answering this question, pay careful attention both to the way in which "income" and "wealth" are measured by official statistics and to the fundamental concepts of the terms.

3 What is wrong with the way in which official surveys measure the distribution of wealth?

4 Explain why the work/leisure choices made by individuals can result in a distribution of income and consumption that is more unequal than the distribution of ability. If ability is distributed normally (a bell-shaped curve), will the resulting distribution of income also be a bell-shaped curve?

5 Explain how the distribution of income and wealth is influenced by bequests and assortative mating.

6 What is a Lorenz curve? How does a Lorenz curve illustrate inequality? How do the Lorenz curves for the distributions of income and wealth in the Canadian economy differ?

PROBLEMS

1 Imagine an economy in which there are five people who are identical in all respects. Each lives for 70 years. For the first 14 of those years, they earn no income. For the next 35 years, they work and earn $30,000 a year from their work. During their remaining years, they are retired and have no income from labour. To make the arithmetic easy, suppose that the interest rate in this economy is zero, and that the individuals consume all their income during their lifetime and at a constant annual rate. What is the distribution of income and wealth in this economy if the individuals have the following ages:

a) All are 45.

b) 25, 35, 45, 55, and 65.

Is the inequality in case (a) greater than in case (b)?

2 You are given the following information about income and wealth shares:

	Income shares (percent)	Wealth shares (percent)
Lowest 20%	5	0
Second 20%	11	1
Third 20%	17	3
Fourth 20%	24	11
Highest 20%	43	85

Draw the Lorenz curves for income and wealth for this economy. Explain which of the two variables — income or wealth — is more unequally distributed.

3 An economy consists of 10 people, each of whom has the following labour supply schedule:

Wage rate (dollars per hour)	Hours worked per day
1	0
2	1
3	2
4	3
5	4

The people differ in ability and earn different wage rates. The distribution of wage rates is:

Wage rate (dollars per hour)	Number of people
1	1
2	2
3	4
4	2
5	1

a) Calculate the average wage rate.

b) Calculate the ratio of the highest wage rate to the lowest.

c) Calculate the average daily income.

d) Calculate the ratio of the highest daily income to the lowest.

e) Graph the distribution of hourly wage rates.

f) Graph the distribution of daily incomes.

g) What is the median daily income?

h) What important lesson is illustrated by this problem?

PART 7

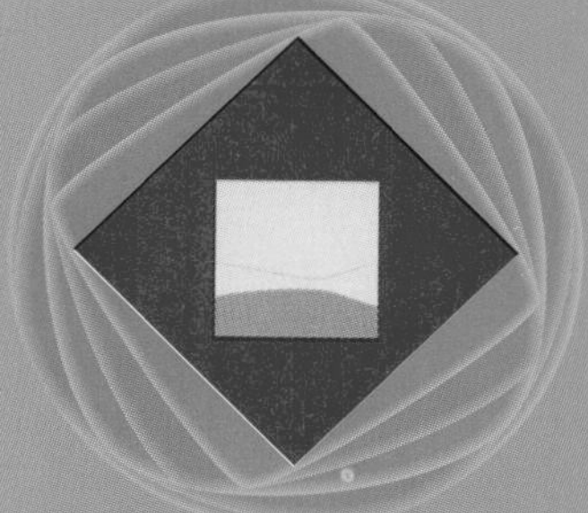

Markets and Government

TALKING WITH PETER LOUGHEED

The Honourable Peter Lougheed, QC, received BA and LLB degrees from the University of Alberta and an MBA from Harvard University. He was premier of Alberta from 1971 to 1985. For part of this time, the province's economy experienced unprecedented prosperity as energy prices increased. It received a severe blow in the recession of 1982, but expanded again during the rest of the 1980s. Michael Parkin talked with Peter Lougheed about his experiences as premier of Alberta and his views on economic policy in Canada.

"The whole period of the OPEC crises was a fascinating example of politics' relationship to economics."

Mr. Lougheed, you had been premier of Alberta for about two years when the first OPEC oil price hike came in 1973. Did it take you by surprise?

Oh yes. We were battling with the industry at that time. The major oil companies controlled the reserves and they purposely kept down the price because they wanted to make their money as integrated companies, not in the upstream but the downstream. I was determined—and just about ready to make a move—that the price be increased by 20 cents a barrel from, I think, $2.85. And then along came OPEC. Overnight it reversed the historical price pattern, and that caused the dramatic surge in prices.

What do you think of the way the federal government handled national energy policy in the 1970s?

To use a strong word, it was a rape of Western Canada. After the OPEC-led price rises, the federal government was worried about fiscal disparities—in essence, it was afraid Alberta would be like oil-rich Kuwait in the middle of Canada. So Ottawa basically ignored the constitution on provincial control of resources and used its control of interprovincial and international trade to control the wellhead price of oil and natural gas. From 1973 until the Western Energy Accord of 1985, we were involved in a constant battle. But it came out, I think, where it should have come out. There was a recognition that neither jurisdiction is paramount. The province controls supply and the federal government controls interprovincial and international trade. So if there isn't settlement in the market (which is what we wanted), there has to be settlement by agreement. The whole period of the OPEC crises was a fascinating example of politics' relationship to economics.

You believe in provinces that are strong vis-a-vis the federal government.

Yes, because we have a federal system. I mean, we decided not to have a unitary system, we decided on a federal one. That's where Prime Minister Pierre Trudeau and I had the greatest philosphical conflict, because he wanted a unitary country run from the centre. But as a country with a small population spread over a wide area with very diverse resources, Canada just wouldn't function other than as a federal system. We've got a certain deck of cards: we have to play with what we have. As we did when I was premier, the provinces have to work hard to develop ways to balance the federal power. They have to make sure that the decisions are made in Québec City and Edmonton, not in Ottawa. Inherent in this country is a never-ending process of conflict between provincal powers and federal powers. The levels of conflict and the degrees of intensity change, but the process is never-ending.

One of the economic links between Ottawa and the provinces is fiscal transfers. What do you think of the scale and direction of those transfers—and of the strings on them?

I think we've generally struggled our way along. There's give and take in the process of fiscal sharing. For example, Alberta fought and lost the issue of imposing hospital user fees on people with incomes above a certain level. Because of the requirement of universality, the federal government (under the Liberals and the Conservatives) used its control of health care transfer money to prevent the introduction of user fees. I thought Alberta should have been able to do it, since the jurisdiction in health care is provincial. But I also recognize that one of the great strengths of Canada is its social services. We lost on the user-fee issue, but we won on some others.

Why has Canada's regional economics developed the way it has? Why isn't the rest of the country as economically diversified and resilient as central Canada?

I think it's a matter of history and geography. The population centres developed where transportation was easiest, which, of course, was along the Saint Lawrence and the Great Lakes. Then there were political inputs, which always came out of representation by population. An additional geographic factor is accessibility to the population centres of the United States. Western Canada is rich in resources, but it's a long distance from markets. So if economic policy is distorted by tarriffs or taxation, or other elements, the resource-based provinces are running uphill when they are ready to diversify and improve their positions.

What has to be done to strengthen the economies of those provinces?

I worked very hard for the Canada-United States Free Trade Agreement because most of the market for what we produce is to the south. That agreement is very important to us. But within one year of the signing, we've had three major federal government actions take the edge off what it can give us. The first is the Bank of Canada's monetary policy; you couldn't have had a worse year to have a high Canada-U.S. exchange rate and high interest rates than in the first year of the agreement. The second is the use of environmental laws to constrain resource production in Western Canada. The third is the prospect of having the National Energy Board use its regulatory authority to force expansion of the sale of natural gas. It's a never-ending battle.

How are environmental laws being used?

One way is through federal control of navigable waters and migratory birds. Recent court rulings—the Rafferty Dam case in Saskatchewan and the Oldman River Dam case in Alberta—are giving the federal government a significant degree of jurisdiction over the environment through the use of environmental impact assessment. (Applying the term "navigable waters" to the Oldman River Dam is interesting. In the summertime, you can cross it on foot without having water above your ankles.) Another way is the use of taxes. Suppose the federal government imposes a

"Western Canada is rich in resources, but it's a long distance from markets. So . . . economic policy is distorted by tarriffs or taxation, or other elements."

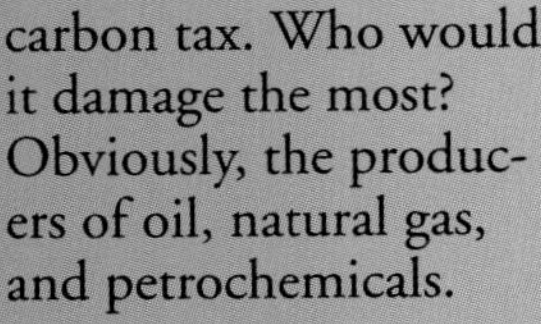

carbon tax. Who would it damage the most? Obviously, the producers of oil, natural gas, and petrochemicals.

"balance your formal education with whatever practical experience you can obtain."

What do you think of the goods and services tax? Do you see it as fair, or do you think it has regional bias?

I differ from my successor. I believe we need a consumption tax if we're going to maintain social services without building too large a deficit in our country. I don't think the federal government has gotten enough credit for the fact that they will eliminating the manufacturer's sales tax, a ridiculous tax for an exporting country, since it penalized our exporters. The problem with the GST is political. Similar taxes have been a hard sell when introduced in many countries, and it hasn't been well communicated. I'd like to see the federal government overcome public resistance by, say, committing by statute, 50 percent of GST revenue to deficit reduction. As a pure economist, you might say that wouldn't be very intelligent, but I think something like that may be politically necessary to get public support.

What economic lesson has proved really valuable to you in your work?

I suppose the most important one is that with a commodity you're very seldom in a pure economic environment. There's theory about particular economic commodities but it's dramatically affected by government policy—trade policy, taxation policy, resource policy. There's the interplay of economic reality and business realities together with the nature of business itself and differences between large and small corporations. You have to be aware of what all these factors are, how they work, how they might change, how they might affect pricing and markets and opportunities.

What advice would you give a student interested in pursuing a career that includes an element of political life?

Give a high priority to studying economics, but balance your formal education with whatever practical experience you can obtain. Join a political party and get involved at the constituency level. Sit in the legislatures and the House of Commons, not just once but often enough to get a feel for what is involved and a sense of the process. Don't be shy about talking to people. Lots of young people ask me questions and I welcome that. I meet so many people who would like to go into politics but become afraid of it for the wrong reasons. I hope more will reconsider and do it.

CHAPTER 19

Market Failure

After studying this chapter, you will be able to:

- Describe the range of economic actions governments undertake.
- Outline the structure of the government sector of the Canadian economy.
- Distinguish between a normative and a positive analysis of government economic behaviour.
- Define market failure and explain how it might be overcome by government action.
- Distinguish between private goods and public goods.
- Explain the free-rider problem.
- Explain how government provision of public goods avoids the free-rider problem.
- Explain how property rights and taxes and subsidies may be used to achieve a more efficient allocation of resources when externalities are present.

Government — The Solution or the Problem?

GOVERNMENT IS BIG BUSINESS — one of the biggest. In 1989, there were more than a quarter of a million public service employees in Canada, and the federal, provincial, and local governments together spent just about 33 cents for every dollar earned by every Canadian. What do all these public servants and dollars do for us? Is the government sector of our economy doing more than it should? Is it simply too big? Is government, as the Fraser Institute has often suggested, the problem? Or, despite its enormous size, is government doing less than it should? Is government too small? Are more government activity and intervention the solution to many outstanding problems? ■ Governments provide an enormous array of goods and services. Some are intangibles, such as laws and their enforcement; others are tangibles, such as schools and highways. Why does government supply some goods and not others? You've probably seen a Brinks security truck delivering cash to your local bank. Why does Brinks, a private company, supply security services to banks while the local police department provides similar services to residential neighbourhoods? What is so special about highways, national defence, and judicial services that results in their always being provided by government and never by private firms? ■ We've been hearing a lot recently about our endangered planet. The massive quantities in which we burn fossil fuels — coal, natural gas, and oil — have some obvious and immediate effects on the atmosphere that result in acid rain. And there are harder to measure, but potentially more serious, effects on the chemical balance of the earth's atmosphere, increasing the proportion of carbon dioxide and reducing the proportion of other elements. It is also predicted that the continuation of this process will result in a gradual warming of the planet — called the "greenhouse effect." Yet further, it is predicted that the persistent and large-scale use of chlorofluorocarbons (CFCs) will cause irreparable damage to the earth's ozone layer, thereby exposing us to an increased amount of radiation. These environmental issues are simultaneously everybody's problem and nobody's problem. Everyone is put at risk by the continued damage to our atmosphere, and yet no one individual can take the action necessary to protect the environment. What, if anything, might government do to protect our environment? How can government help us to take account of the damage that we cause others every time we turn on our heating or air conditioning systems? ■ We have spent a great deal of time studying the economic choices of households and firms. We have seen how households make choices governing the allocation of the factors of production that they own and how those choices determine their incomes. We've also seen how they choose their spending and saving. We've seen how firms choose the quantities of goods and services to produce and the techniques with which to produce them. We've seen how households and firms interact in markets for goods and services and for factors of production. ■ We've also seen that households and firms do not make their choices in a political vacuum. Their choices are influenced by actions taken by government. For example, rent controls and minimum wage laws influence the way competitive markets operate. We've also seen that many markets are not competitive. They have monopoly elements, and those elements often arise from legal restrictions on competition.

■ In this chapter and the next two, we turn our attention to the economic choices that governments make and to the effects of those choices on the economy. Our main concern in this chapter is to describe the government sector and explain how the market economy, in the absence of a government, would fail to achieve an efficient allocation of resources. The chapter also provides an outline of the economic theory of government behaviour; this outline will be elaborated and applied in the subsequent two chapters on this broad and important topic.

The Government Sector

We'll begin by describing the anatomy of the government sector.

The Structure and Scale of Government

The government sector of the Canadian economy consists of more than 4,000 separate organizations, some tiny, such as rural municipalities, and some enormous, such as the government of Canada and the governments of the larger provinces.

There are three levels of government in Canada:

- Federal
- Provincial
- Local

In terms of expenditure and employment, the federal government is by far the largest, accounting for about half of the government sector. Together, the provincial governments account for about 40 percent, and municipalities and other local government units account for the rest.

The Scale and Growth of Government

The scale of government in relation to the economy has changed dramatically over the years. In 1940, for example, government sector expenditure accounted for less than 20 percent of the economy's total expenditure. By 1990, it had reached 33 percent. But the growth of expenditure over the past 50 years probably understates the growth of the importance of government in economic life. That importance stems partly from its spending and partly from the extent of the laws and regulations that affect the economic actions of individual households and firms. We'll look at this aspect of government in Chapter 21, where we study regulation and anti-combine legislation.

Our main task in this chapter is not to describe the anatomy of government and the pace at which it has grown but to analyse the failure of markets to achieve *allocative efficiency* and to explore the role of government in coping with market failure. Before we embark on that main task, we're going to take an overview of the alternative approaches that economists use to study the economic behaviour of government.

Positive and Normative Analysis

We all have opinions on political matters and some of those opinions are strongly held. As students of economics, our task is to understand, explain, and predict the economic choices that the government sector makes. Although we cannot suppress our political views, it is important, if we are to make progress in studying political behaviour, to remind ourselves continually of the important distinction between positive and normative analysis. We first explored that distinction in Chapter 1, and it's been mentioned since, including in the last chapter. But because the distinction is so important for the economic study of political behaviour, let's recall what that distinction is.

An economic analysis of government choices may be either *positive* or *normative.* A positive analysis of government seeks to explain the reasons for and the effects of government economic choices. A normative analysis seeks to evaluate the desirability of a government action and argues for or against some particular proposal. Positive analysis seeks to understand what *is;* normative analysis tries to conclude what *ought* to be. The economic analysis used in both of these activities is similar, but the use to which that analysis is put differs.

In this chapter, we undertake a positive study of government action; that is, we seek to understand the reasons for and the effects of the actions that we see being undertaken by governments in Canada today.

Economic Theory of Government

All government economic action stems from two aspects of economic life:

- Market failure
- Redistribution of income and wealth

Let's examine each in turn.

Market failure One explanation for government intervention in the economy is market failure. **Market failure** is the inability of an unregulated market to achieve, in all circumstances, allocative efficiency. Market failure arises for three main reasons:

- Some of the goods and services that people in a group consume are necessarily consumed in common with everyone else in that group.
- In the production of some goods and services, *external costs* or *external benefits* are present.
- In the production of some goods and services, output is restricted by monopolies and cartels.

In all three cases, the unregulated market produces waste in the sense that a different allocation would result in producing more of some goods without producing less of others and could make someone better off without making anyone worse off. It is important not to take this last statement as being normative. The presence or absence of waste is a positive matter. It is a statement about what *is.* A prediction that government action *will* (or will not) occur to eliminate such waste is also a positive statement. The proposition that government *ought* (or ought not) to intervene to eliminate waste is normative. In dealing with market failure, it is its positive aspects that are our concern.

Redistribution of Income and Wealth Another explanation for government intervention in the economy is that it seeks to redistribute income and wealth. Such redistribution is usually justified on the basis of notions of equity or distributive justice, which we discussed in Chapter 18. But not all redistribution is explained in this way. The creation of monopoly and government protection of cartels also results in the redistribution of income and wealth. And the *rent-seeking* activities that we described in Chapter 13 have an important political dimension.

Again, it is important to keep clear the distinction between positive and normative aspects of the redistributive role of government. The proposition that most people believe that the market distributions of income and wealth are unfair is positive. The proposition that government intervention can redistribute income from the rich to the poor is also positive. The proposition that the government *ought* to redistribute income and wealth is normative. We described the scale of income redistribution in Chapter 18, and we will study it further in Chapter 20. When we do so, our focus will be entirely on its positive aspect.

Public Interest and Public Choice

Positive economic theories of government behaviour fall in two broad classes:

- Public interest theories
- Public choice theories

A **public interest theory** of government behaviour predicts that government action will take place to eliminate waste and achieve an efficient allocation of resources. A **public choice theory** predicts that the behaviour of the government sector is the outcome of individual choices made by voters, politicians, and bureaucrats interacting with each other in a political marketplace. According to the public interest theory of government, whenever there is market failure, government action can be designed to eliminate the consequences of that failure and to achieve allocative efficiency. According to the public choice theory, matters are not that simple. Not only is there the possibility of market failure (arising in the situations that we outlined above); there is also the possibility of "government failure." That is, it is possible that when voters, politicians, and bureaucrats each pursue their own best interests and interact in the political "marketplace," the resulting "public choice" no more achieves the elimination of waste and the attainment of allocative efficiency than does an unregulated market. (Understanding why not is the main topic of Chapter 20.)

In the next section, we're going to explain more fully the economic role of the government arising from two of the sources of market failure — the provision of goods and services that people consume in common, and the production of goods and services when external costs or external benefits are present. The other source of market failure — the existence of monopolies and cartels — and the resulting government regulation of such industries is dealt with in Chapter 21.

Public Goods

Why does the government provide certain goods and services such as a legal system, national defence, schools and highways, and public health services? Why don't we simply leave the provision of these goods and services in the hands of private firms that sell their output in markets? How much national defence would we have if a private firm, North Pole Protection Inc., had to compete for our dollars in the marketplace in the same way that McDonald's and Coca-Cola do?

Most of the answers to these questions lie in the distinction between private goods and public goods.

Private Goods and Public Goods

A **private good** is a good or service each unit of which is consumed by only one individual. An example of a private good is a can of pop. A private good has two important features. The first is called *rivalry.* One person's consumption can take place only at the expense of another person's. If you increase your consumption of pop by one can, other things being equal, someone else has to consume one can less. The second feature of a private good is called *excludability.* Once you have bought a can of pop, it is yours to do with as you choose. You can exclude others from using it.

A **public good** is a good or service each unit of which is consumed by everyone and from which no one can be excluded. An example is the national defence system. A public good has two important features that parallel the features that we identified for a private good. The first is called *nonrivalry.* One person's consumption of a public good does not reduce the amount available for someone else. For example, your consumption of the security provided by the national defence system does not decrease the security of anyone else. The second feature is called *nonexcludability.* No one can be excluded from the additional security that every citizen enjoys from the national defence system.

Many goods lie in between a public good and a private good. Such goods are called **mixed goods**. An example is a highway. Until it becomes congested, a highway is like a public good. One more car or truck on a highway with plenty of space on it does not reduce anyone else's consumption of highway services. But once the highway reaches the congestion point, the addition of one more user lowers the quality of the service available for everyone else — it becomes like a private good.

Public goods and mixed goods with a large public element give rise to what is called the free-rider problem.

Free Riding

A **free rider** is someone who consumes a good without paying for it. The **free-rider problem** is the tendency for the scale of provision of a public good to be too small if it is produced and sold privately. The free-rider problem arises because a person has no incentive to pay for a good if the payment makes no difference to the quantity of the good that he or she is able to consume. Public goods are such goods. To see why, let's look at an example.

Imagine that an effective method of controlling sulfur dioxide emissions has been developed, one that makes it possible to eliminate acid rain. Imagine also that this method is costly to operate, that firms have to be monitored by a specially designed satellite system to observe violations, and that firms polluting the atmosphere are fined an amount sufficient to deter them. Let's call one of these satellites an "acid-rain check." One satellite can observe only about a fifth of the potential polluters, and the larger the number of acid-rain checks put in place, the larger the number of polluters that can be detected and the smaller the amount of pollution that actually takes place. But the new acid-rain check satellites are expensive. To build them, resources have to be diverted from other productive activities. As a result, the larger the number of acid-rain checks installed, the greater is their marginal cost.

Our task is to work out the scale on which to install this new acid-rain check system to achieve allocative efficiency. We'll then examine whether private provision could achieve allocative efficiency. We'll discover that it could not — that there is a free-rider problem.

Benefits and Costs

The benefits provided by the acid-rain control system are based on the preferences of the consumers of the services of that system. The costs are based on technology and the prices of the factors of production used to produce the system. When studying private goods, we observed that the value of a good to an individual is the maximum amount that that person is willing to pay for one more unit of the good. We worked out this value from the individual's demand curve. That is, the demand curve tells us the quantity demanded at a given price or, for a given quantity, the maximum price that is willingly paid for the last unit bought. We can work out the value a person places on a public good in a similar manner. That is, the value that a person places on a public good is the maximum amount he or she is willing to pay for one additional unit of the good.

To calculate that amount, we first need to establish that person's total benefit schedule. **Total benefit** is the total dollar value that a person places on a given level of provision of a public good. The greater the scale of provision, the larger is the total benefit. The table in Fig. 19.1 sets out the total benefits to Lisa and Max of different scales of provision of the proposed acid-rain control system. The more acid-rain check satellites in place, the greater is the reduction in acid rain — but up to a maximum level. Each additional satellite provides less additional protection than the previous one. The increase in total benefit resulting from a unit increase in the scale of provision of a public good is called its **marginal benefit**. The marginal benefits to Lisa and Max are calculated in the table in Fig. 19.1. As you can see, the greater the scale of provision, the smaller is the marginal benefit. By the time 4 satellites are deployed, Lisa perceives no additional benefits, and Max perceives only $10 worth. Lisa's and Max's marginal benefits are graphed as MB_L and MB_M respectively in Fig. 19.1 (a) and (b).

The marginal benefit of a public good is the maximum amount that a person is willing to pay for one more unit of the good. This amount varies with the quantity of the good consumed. The greater the quantity, the smaller is the maximum amount that will be paid for one more unit.

Figure 19.1(c) shows the marginal benefit curve (*MB*) of the whole economy (which has only two people, Lisa and Max). The marginal benefit curve of a public good for an individual is similar to the demand curve for a private good. But there is an important difference between the economy's marginal benefit curve for a public good and the market demand curve for a private good. To obtain the market demand curve for a private good, we add up the quantities demanded by each individual at each price. In other words, we sum the individual demand curves horizontally (see Chapter 7, Fig. 7.1). In contrast, to find the economy's marginal benefit curve of a public good, we add up the marginal benefits to each individual at each quantity of provision. That is, we sum the individual marginal benefit curves *vertically*. The resulting marginal benefit for the economy comprised of just Lisa and Max is calculated in the table, and the economy's marginal benefit curve is graphed in Fig. 19.1(c) as the curve labelled *MB*.

An economy with just two people would not buy any acid-rain check satellites — their total benefits fall far short of their cost. But an economy with 25 million people might. To determine the efficient scale of provision, consider the example set out in the table in Fig. 19.2. The first two columns of that table show the total and marginal benefits to the entire economy (which consists of 25 million people). The next two columns show the total and marginal costs of producing acid-rain check satellites. These costs are opportunity costs, which are derived in exactly the same way as the costs associated with the production of sweaters that we studied in Chapter 10. The final column of the table shows net benefit. **Net benefit** is total benefit minus total cost. The efficient scale of provision is the one that maximizes net benefit.

Total benefit and total cost are graphed in Fig. 19.2(a) as the total benefit curve (*TB*) and total cost curve (*TC*). Net benefit is also visible in that part of the figure as the vertical distance between the two curves. Net benefit is maximized when that distance

Figure 19.1 Benefits of a Public Good

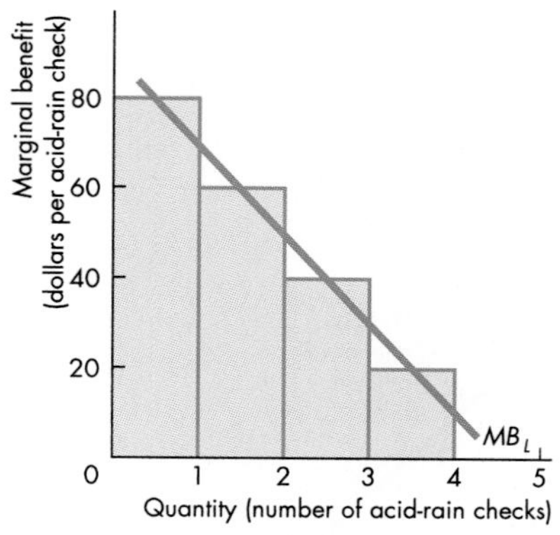

(a) Lisa's marginal benefit curve

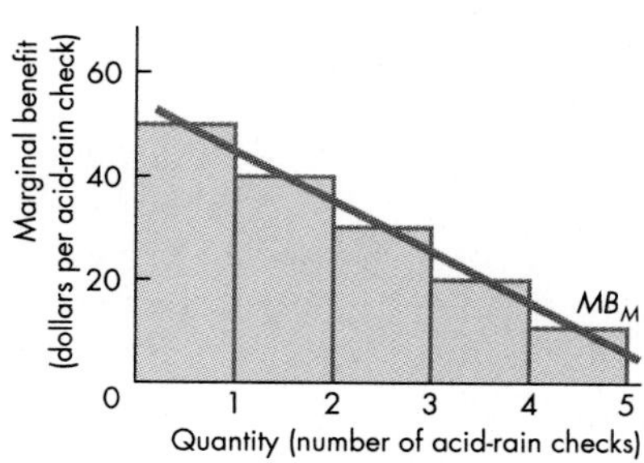

(b) Max's marginal benefit curve

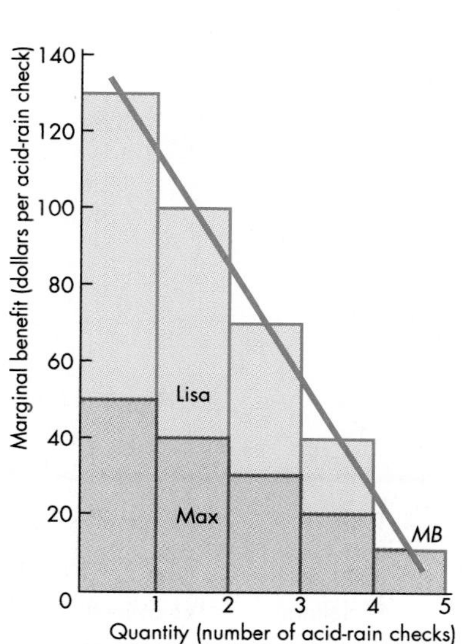

(c) Economy's marginal benefit curve

The table shows various scales of provision of an acid-rain control system. It also lists the total benefits accruing to Lisa, Max, and the economy (comprised of only Lisa and Max) from those scales of provision. The table also calculates the marginal benefit — the change in the total benefit resulting from a unit increase in the scale of provision to Lisa, Max, and the economy. The marginal benefits are graphed in the figure. For Lisa, the marginal benefit curve is MB_L in part (a), and for Max, the marginal benefit curve is MB_M in part (b). The marginal benefit curve for the whole economy is the sum of the marginal benefits to each individual at each level of provision and is shown in part (c) as the curve *MB*.

	Lisa		**Max**		**Economy**	
Quantity (number of acid-rain checks)	**Total benefit (dollars)**	**Marginal benefit (dollar per unit)**	**Total benefit (dollars)**	**Marginal benefit (dollar per unit)**	**Total benefit (dollars)**	**Marginal benefit (dollar per unit)**
0	0		0		0	
		80		50		130
1	80		50		130	
		60		40		100
2	140		90		230	
		40		30		70
3	180		120		300	
		20		20		40
4	200		140		340	
		0		10		10
5	200		150		350	

is at its largest, a situation that occurs at a scale of provision of 2 satellites. This is the efficient scale of provision.

Another way of describing the efficient scale of provision is in terms of marginal benefit and marginal cost. The marginal benefit and marginal cost of acid-rain checks are graphed as the marginal benefit curve (*MB*) and marginal cost curve (*MC*) in

Figure 19.2 The Efficient Scale of Provision of a Public Good

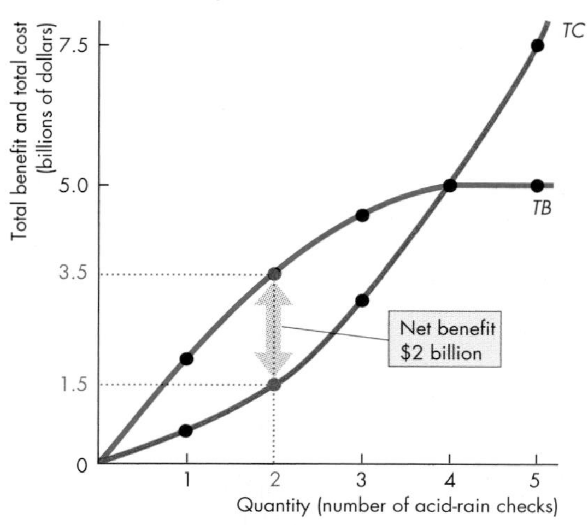

(a) Total benefit and total cost curves

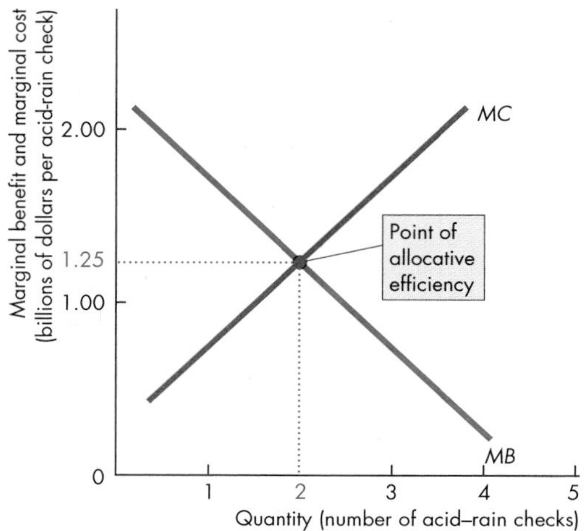

(b) Marginal benefit and marginal cost curves

Quantity (number of acid-rain checks)	Total benefit (billions of dollars)	Marginal benefit (billions of dollars)	Total cost (billions of dollars)	Marginal cost (billions of dollars)	Net benefit (billions of dollars)
0	0		0		0
		2.0		0.5	
1	2.0		0.5		1.5
		1.5		1.0	
2	3.5		1.5		2.0
		1.0		1.5	
3	4.5		3.0		1.5
		0.5		2.0	
4	5.0		5.0		0
		0		2.5	
5	5.0		7.5		–2.5

The table shows the total benefit and marginal benefit to the entire economy of various scales of provision of an acid-rain control system. It also shows the total cost and marginal cost of the various scales of provision. Total benefit and total cost are graphed in part (a) as the total benefit curve (*TB*) and the total cost curve (*TC*). Net benefit is visible as the vertical distance between these two curves; it is maximized when 2 satellites are installed. Part (b) shows the marginal benefit curve (*MB*) and marginal cost curve (*MC*). When marginal cost equals marginal benefit, net benefit is maximized and allocative efficiency is achieved.

Fig. 19.2(b). When marginal benefit exceeds marginal cost, net benefit increases if the quantity produced increases. When marginal cost exceeds marginal benefit, net benefit increases if the quantity produced decreases. When marginal benefit equals marginal cost, net benefit cannot be increased — it is at its maximum possible level. Thus when marginal benefit equals marginal cost, net benefit has been maximized and allocative efficiency has been achieved.

Now that we have worked out the efficient scale of provision of a public good, let's go on to see how much of such a good can be provided by a private producer.

Private Provision

Can a private firm — call it Acid-Rain Watch Inc. — provide acid-rain checks on a scale that maximizes net benefit and achieves allocative efficiency? It cannot. To do so, it would have to cover its costs by collecting \$1.5 billion — or \$60 from each of the 25 million people in the economy. But no one would have any incentive to buy his or her "share" of the satellite system. Each person would reason as follows. The number of acid-rain check satellites Acid-Rain Watch provides is not going to be affected by my \$60. But my own private consumption will be affected by whether or not I pay. If I do not pay, I will enjoy the same level of protection from the satellites and more of other goods. Therefore it pays me to keep my \$60 and spend it on other goods. In other words, it pays me to free ride on the public good and buy private goods.

Since everyone reasons in the same manner, Acid-Rain Watch has zero revenue and zero production.

Public Provision

Suppose that the people in this economy have instituted a government that makes the following proposition: the government will collect \$60 from each person and spend the resulting \$1.5 billion to provide 2 acid-rain check satellites. Will the people vote for this proposition? Clearly they will. If there is no acid-rain control system (the output of Acid-Rain Watch), the marginal benefit of installing one satellite greatly exceeds its marginal cost. By proposing to provide 2 satellites, the government is offering each voter a level of protection that maximizes net benefit. The voters obtain a benefit of \$3.5 billion — \$140 each — for a total cost of \$1.5 billion — \$60 each. Since the voters recognize this as an improvement over the zero provision by Acid-Rain Watch, they will vote for it.

Whether or not actual governments produce public goods on a scale that maximizes net benefit is something that we will examine in Chapter 20. But we have established a key proposition: a government is able to provide any public good on a scale larger than that provided by a private producer.

R E V I E W

If people make their own decisions about the provision of public goods and buy those goods in private markets, there is a free-rider problem. It is in everyone's individual interest to free ride, with the result that the scale of provision of the goods is smaller than that required for allocative efficiency. A government that balances marginal cost and marginal benefit will provide the public good on a scale that achieves allocative efficiency. ■

Let's now turn to the second source of market failure, externalities.

Externalities

An **externality** is a cost or a benefit arising from an economic transaction that falls on a third party and that is not taken into account by those who undertake the transaction. For example, when a chemical factory dumps its waste products into a river, killing the fish, it imposes an externality — in this case, an external cost — on the fisherman who lives downstream. Since the chemical factory does not bear these costs, it does not take them into account in deciding whether to dump waste into the river and if so, how much. When a person in Montreal drives a car that burns leaded gasoline and does not have a catalytic converter, an externality — again, an external cost — is imposed on everyone who tries to breathe the polluted air. When a homeowner fills her garden with beautiful spring bulbs, she generates an externality — in this case, an external benefit — for all the joggers and walkers who pass by. But, in deciding how much to spend on this lavish display, she takes into account only the benefits accruing to herself.

Two particularly dramatic externalities have received a lot of attention in recent years. The first arises from the use of chlorofluorocarbons (CFCs). These chemicals are used in a wide variety of products, from coolants in refrigerators and air conditioners to plastic phones to cleaning solvents for computer circuits. Though the precise chemistry of the process is not understood and is the subject of dispute, many physicists believe that the consumption of CFCs damages the atmosphere's protective ozone layer. Discoveries of depleted ozone over Antarctica have heightened fears of ozone depletion. The National Academy of Sciences has estimated that a 1 percent drop in ozone levels might cause a 2 percent rise in the incidence of skin cancer. Diminished ozone is also believed to be a possible cause of cataracts.

Another much-discussed externality arises from burning fossil fuels that add carbon dioxide and other gases to the atmosphere. These gases collect and prevent infrared radiation from escaping, resulting in what has been called the "greenhouse effect." If the greenhouse scenario turns out to be correct, it is predicted that parts of the Prairies and much of the midwest of the United States will become a dustbowl and that many parts of North America's eastern seaboard, especially the Gulf Coast regions of the United States, will disappear under an expanded Atlantic Ocean (see Reading Between the Lines, pp. 504-506).

When you take a cold drink from the refrigerator or switch on the air conditioner on a steamy August evening, you do not take into account the consequences of your actions on global atmospheric matters. You contemplate the private benefits to yourself of drinking the cold can of pop or having a comfortable night's sleep with the costs that *you* incur. You do not count the costs of an increase in the incidence of skin cancer as part of the price that has to be paid for cold pop or a comfortable night.

Externalities are not always negative — external costs. Many activities bring external benefits. Education is a good example. Not only do more highly educated people derive benefits for themselves in the form of higher incomes and the enjoyment of a wider range of artistic and cultural activities, but they also bring benefits to others through social interaction. But in deciding how much schooling to undertake, people make this calculation on the basis of the costs they themselves bear and the benefits accruing to them as individuals. They do not take into account the extra benefits that they're creating for others.

Public health services also create external benefits. The pursuit of good public health and personal hygiene reduces the risk that people will be infected by transmitted diseases. Yet in making economic choices about the scale of resources to devote to public health and hygiene, people take account only of the costs and benefits to themselves, not the greater benefits that these choices bring to others.

Government Action in the Face of Externalities

There are two main types of action that governments can take to achieve a more efficient allocation of resources in the face of externalities:

- Establish and enforce private property rights.
- Tax activities that produce external costs and subsidize those that bring external benefits.

First, let's briefly consider the use of private property rights for dealing with externalities.

Private Property Rights and Externalities

In some cases, externalities arise because of an absence of private property rights. A **private property right** is a legally established title to the sole ownership of a scarce resource that is enforceable in the courts. The creation of externalities in the absence of private property rights is well illustrated by the example of a chemical factory and a private fishing club. Members of the club use a particular stretch of a stream that is well stocked with excellent fish. A chemical factory opens upstream from the fishing club. It has to make a decision about how it will dispose of some of its waste products.

Consider two different legal situations. In the first, no one owns the stream. If the factory dumps its waste products in the stream, its cost of waste disposal is almost zero. But the waste kills the fish, and the fishing club goes out of business.

In the second situation, property rights to the stream have been established. The fishing club owns its stretch of the stream and the fish that swim in it. The chemical factory might still dump its waste into the stream, but if it does so and kills the fish, the fishing club will sue it successfully for damages. The damages paid to the fishing club will be the cost to the chemical company of disposing of the chemical waste by dumping it in the stream. If the firm has available some other method of waste disposal that has a lower cost, it will choose that alternative. Whenever externalities arise from the lack of property rights that could easily be established and enforced, this method of dealing with externalities is a natural one for governments to contemplate. But there are many situations in which private property rights simply cannot be established and enforced. In these cases, governments resort to an alternative method of coping with externalities — using taxes and subsidies. Let's see how these government tools work.

Taxes and External Costs

As noted earlier, every time you burn fossil fuel, you

release CO_2 into the atmosphere and impose unintended costs on others. Let's see how the government might modify your choices and encourage you to take account of the potential costs that you're imposing on others.

One activity that creates CO_2 is driving a gasoline-fuelled vehicle. To study the demand for this activity, let's examine the market for transportation services. Figure 19.3 illustrates this market. The demand curve is also the marginal benefit curve ($D = MB$). It tells us how much consumers value each different level output. Curve *MPC* measures the marginal private cost of producing transportation services. **Marginal private cost** is the marginal cost directly incurred by the producer of a good. Thus the *MPC* curve shows the marginal cost directly incurred by the producers of transportation services. But there are externalities in transportation. It involves burning fossil fuels, which creates atmospheric pollution and contributes to the greenhouse effect. It also causes more immediate health problems. Furthermore, one person's decision to use a highway imposes congestion costs on others. All these costs are external costs. Adding all the external costs to the private cost yields the marginal social cost of transportation services. **Marginal social cost** is the marginal cost incurred by the producer of a good together with the marginal cost imposed as an externality on others. Marginal social cost is illustrated by the curve *MSC* in Fig. 19.3.

Suppose that the transportation market is competitive and unregulated. People balance the marginal private cost against the marginal benefit and travel Q_0 million kilometres at a price of P_0 per kilometre. This scale of travel generates a large amount of external cost. The marginal social cost is SC_0. The difference between P_0 and SC_0 represents the marginal cost imposed on others — the external marginal cost.

Now suppose that the government taxes transportation and that it sets the tax equal to the external marginal cost. By imposing such a tax, the government raises the marginal private cost — the original marginal private cost *plus* the tax — to equal the marginal social cost. The *MSC* curve is now the relevant marginal cost curve for each person's decision since each now faces a marginal cost of transportation equal to its marginal social cost. The market supply curve shifts upward to become the *MSC* curve. The price rises to P_1, and the amount of travel falls to Q_1. The marginal cost of the resources used in producing Q_1 million kilometres of travel is C_1, but the

Figure 19.3 Taxing and Regulating an Externality

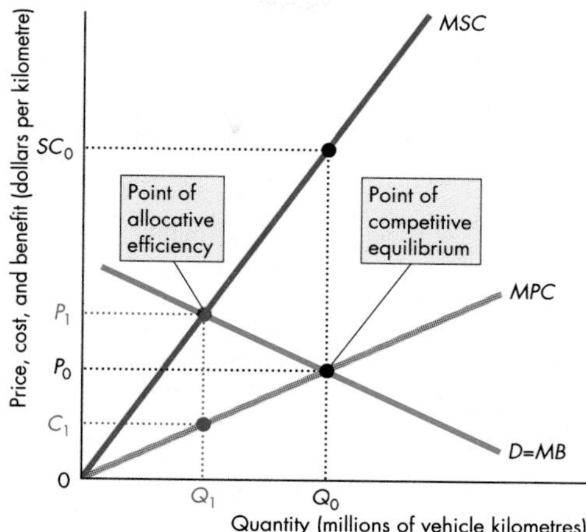

The demand curve for transportation services is also the marginal benefit curve ($D = MB$). The marginal private cost curve is *MPC*. Because of congestion and environmental pollution, the marginal cost of providing transportation services exceeds the marginal private cost. The marginal social cost is shown by the curve *MSC*. If the market is competitive, output is Q_0 and the price is P_0. Marginal social cost is SC_0. If a tax is imposed to confront producers of transportation services with its full marginal social cost, the *MSC* curve becomes the relevant marginal cost curve for suppliers' decisions. The price increases to P_1 and the quantity decreases to Q_1. Allocative efficiency is achieved.

marginal external cost generated is P_1 minus C_1. That external marginal cost is paid by the consumer through the tax.

The situation depicted at the price P_1 and the quantity Q_1 is allocatively efficient. At an output rate of more than Q_1, social marginal cost exceeds the marginal benefit; at an output of less than Q_1, social marginal cost is less than the marginal benefit. In the first situation, producing less reduces costs by more than it reduces benefits and increases the net benefit. Only at Q_1 is it impossible to increase net benefit.

Subsidies and External Benefits

Some goods bring external benefits — benefits to people who do not directly consume the good. The government sometimes induces additional consumption of

The Greenhouse Effect

Feeling the heat

For more than a decade, many scientists have warned that cars and factories are spewing enough gases into the atmosphere to heat up the earth in a greenhouse effect that could eventually produce disastrous climatic changes. ...Unfortunately, scientists cannot agree on how much global warming has occurred, how much more is on the way and what the climatic consequences will be.... But no one disputes the fact that the amount of CO_2 in the atmosphere has risen and continues to increase rapidly.

Recent research has confirmed that [the CO_2 buildup] is more than just theory. By drilling deep into Antarctic and Arctic ice, scientists have been able to measure the amount of CO_2 in air bubbles trapped in ancient layers of snow. They have also looked at fossilized plant tissues for clues as to how warm the air was during the same period. The conclusion: CO_2 levels and global temperatures have risen and fallen together, over tens of thousands of years. And there is evidence from space: Mars, which has little CO_2 in its atmosphere, has a surface temperature that reaches –24°F at best, while Venus, with lots of CO_2, is a hellish 850°F....

Carbon dioxide is released in large quantities when wood and such fossil fuels as coal, oil and natural gas are burned. By the late 1800s atmospheric CO_2 had risen to between 280 and 290 parts per million. Today it stands at 350 p.p.m., and by 2050 it could reach 500 to 700 p.p.m., higher than it has been in millions of years.

By far the most efficient and effective way to spur conservation is to raise the cost of fossil fuels. Current prices fail to reflect the very real environmental costs of pumping carbon dioxide into the air. The answer is a tax on CO_2 emissions—or a CO_2 user fee.... The fee need not raise a country's overall tax burden; it could be offset by reductions in income taxes or other levies.

Imposing a CO_2 fee would not be as difficult as it sounds. It is easy to quantify how much CO_2 comes from burning a gallon of gasoline, a ton of coal or a cubic yard of natural gas. Most countries already have gasoline taxes; similar fees, set according to the amount of CO_2 produced, could be put on all fossil-fuel sources. At the same time, companies could be given credits against their CO_2 taxes if they planted trees to take some of the CO_2 out of the air.

A user fee would have benefits beyond forcing a cutback in CO_2 emissions. The fuels that generate carbon dioxide also generate other pollutants, like soot, along with nitrogen oxides and sulfur dioxide, the primary causes of acid rain. The CO_2 tax would be a powerful incentive for consumers to switch from high-CO_2 fuels, such as coal and oil, to power sources that produce less CO_2, notably natural gas....

Ultimately, though, the world must move away from fossil fuels for most of its energy needs. Said Berrien Moore, director of the Institute for the Study of the Earth, Oceans and Space: "Even if you cut emissions of CO_2 in half, the atmospheric concentration will keep going up. You're still adding CO_2 faster than you're withdrawing it, so the balance keeps rising."

Of all the known nonfossil energy sources, only two are far enough along in their development to be counted on: solar and nuclear, neither of which generates any greenhouse gases at all. Solar power is especially attractive. It produces no waste, and it is inexhaustible. Not all solar power comes directly from the sun: both wind and hydroelectric power are solar, since wind is created by the sun's uneven warming of the atmosphere and since the water that collects behind dams was originally rain, which in turn was water vapor evaporated by solar heating.

But wind and hydroelectric power can be generated at only a relatively few sites, and so governments should redouble financing for research to develop efficient, low-cost photovoltaic power. Photovoltaic cells produce electric current when bathed in sunlight. If their capital costs were to drop to $1, a peak watt solar power will become competitive.

Time,
January 2, 1989
By Michael D. Lemonick

The Essence of the Story

- The amount of carbon dioxide (CO_2) in the earth's atmosphere has been increasing and continues to do so.
- During the late 1800s, atmospheric CO_2 was between 280 and 290 p.p.m.; during the late 1900s, it has been 350 p.p.m.; by 2050, it could reach 500 to 700 p.p.m.
- Although there is disagreement among scientists, many predict that these increasing concentrations of CO_2 are leading, and will continue to lead, to an increase in the earth's average temperature.
- The relationship between CO_2 and temperature is suggested by evidence from CO_2 air bubbles in ancient snow layers and fossilized plant tissue. Evidence is also provided by the relationship between the CO_2 content of the atmosphere and the surface temperature on the neighbouring planets of Mars and Venus.
- There are two ways the government can intervene to control the greenhouse effect:
  - Impose a tax on CO_2 emission.
  - Subsidize the development of solar enegy.

Background and Analysis

- The marginal private cost of generating electricity by using fossil fuels is the curve *MPC* in each figure. The marginal cost of generating electricity using solar power is the curve *MC*.
- The power generated by solar energy has no externalities.
- The power generated by using fossil fuel creates a carbon dioxide buildup with a possible greenhouse effect.
- The greenhouse effect imposes potentially large social costs. By changing weather patterns and land use patterns, it will increase the cost of food production; by melting the polar ice caps, it will raise the ocean levels, reducing the amount of usable land.
- The marginal social cost of generating electricity using fossil fuels, including the external costs of the greenhouse effect, is the curve *MSC*.
- The market demand for electricity is *D*.
- With no intervention (Fig. a), the market supply curve is *S*; this curve is made from the *MPC* curve for fossil fuels and the *MC* curve for solar power.
- Equilibrium occurs at price P_0 and quantity Q_0. The marginal social cost is MSC_0, which exceeds the price. There is an allocative inefficiency—too much electricity is generated.
- If a CO_2 tax is imposed (Fig. b) equal to the external costs, fossil-fuel producers of electricity face costs shown by the curve $MPC + tax = MSC$.

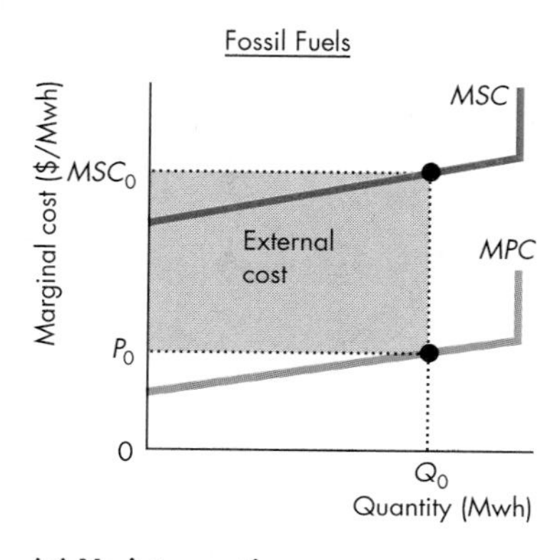

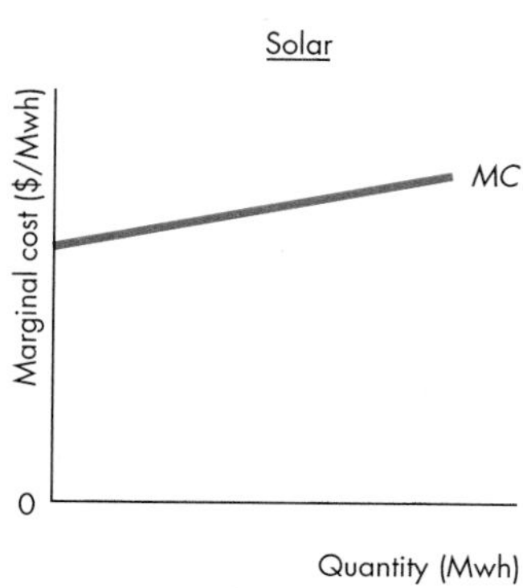

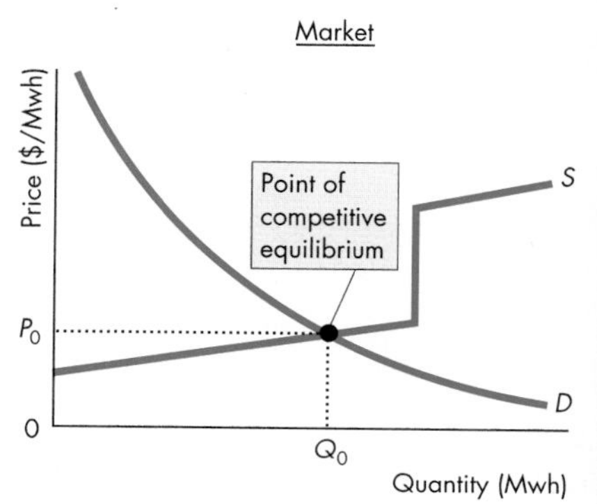

(a) No intervention

Conclusion

- The market supply curve becomes the curve $S + tax$.
- Equilibrium occurs at price P_1 and quantity Q_1; Q_{1F} is produced by fossil fuels and Q_{1S} by solar energy; marginal social cost is MSC_1 which equals the price P_1; allocative efficiency is achieved.
- If the development of solar energy is subsidized and fossil fuels are not taxed (Fig. c), fossil-fuel producers of electricity face the marginal cost curve *MPC* and solar producers face the marginal cost curve *MC - subsidy*.
- The market supply curve is *S - subsidy*.
- Equilibrium occurs at price P_2 and quantity Q_2; Q_{2F} is produced using fossil fuels and Q_{2S} using solar enegy.
- Marginal social cost is MSC_2, which exceeds price P_2, and an allocative inefficiency remains; too much electric power is generated.
- A similar, analysis can be applied to CFCs and other atmospheric pollutants.
- To achieve allocative efficiency in the face of an externality, the externality has to be identified and its magnitude assessed.
- If a tax is imposed equal to the external marginal cost, allocative efficiency is achieved.
- Subsidizing a substitute activity that does not have external costs is not equivalent to taxing an activity that does have an external cost. Such a policy does not achieve allocative efficiency.

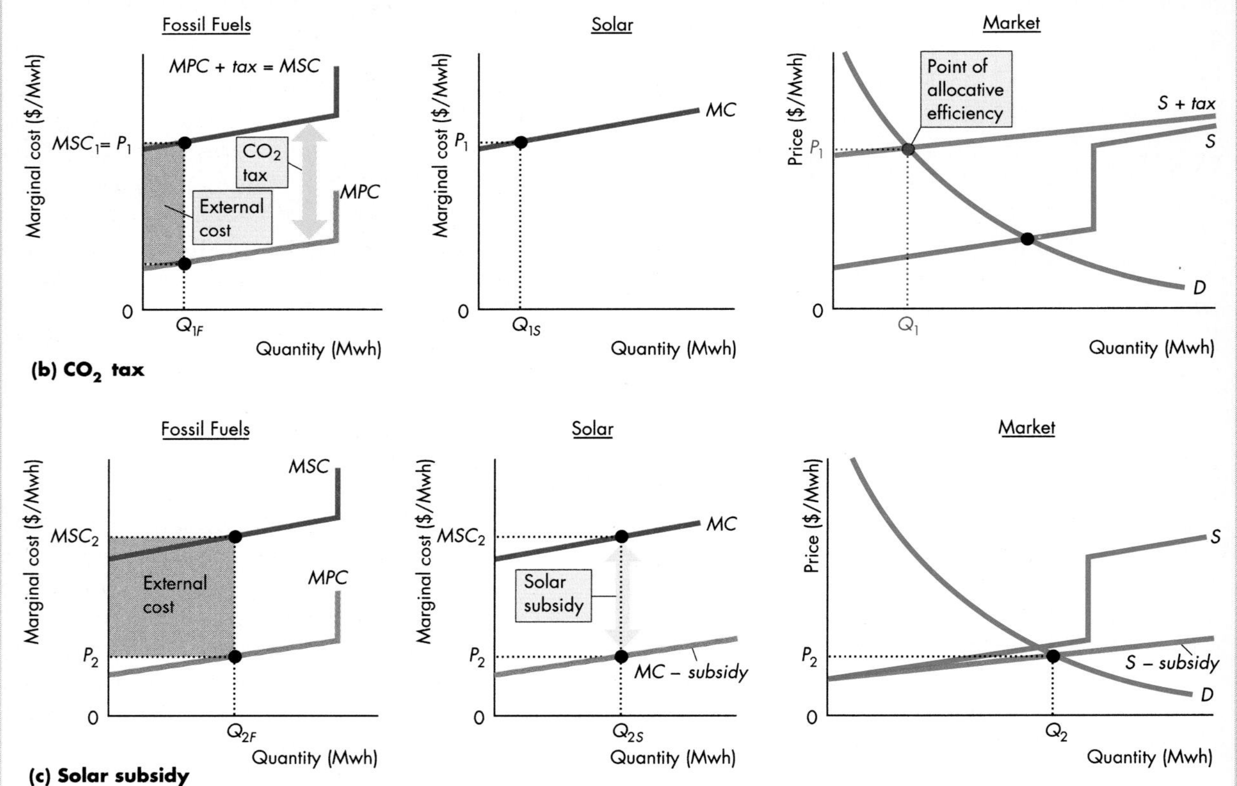

Figure 19.4 Subsidizing an External Benefit

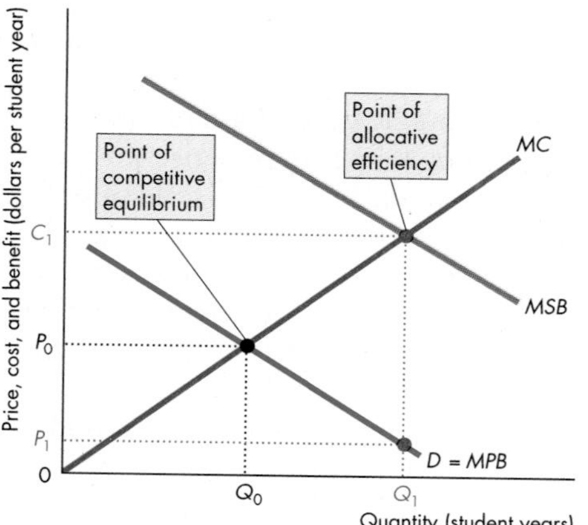

The demand curve for education also measures the marginal private benefit — *MPB* — to education. The marginal cost of education is shown by the curve *MC*. If education is provided in a competitive market with no government intervention, the price of education is P_0 and the quantity bought Q_0. But education produces a social benefit, and the marginal social benefit is shown by the curve *MSB*. Allocative efficiency is achieved if the government provides education services on a scale so that marginal social cost equals marginal social benefit. This scale of provision is Q_1, which is achieved if the government subsidizes education, making it available for a price of P_1. The quantity demanded at price P_1 is Q_1. At that quantity, marginal cost equals marginal social benefit at a level of C_1.

such goods by subsidizing them. A **subsidy** is a payment made by the government to producers that depends on the level or value of output. Figure 19.4 shows how subsidizing education increases the amount consumed and can achieve allocative efficiency. Suppose that there is no difference between marginal private cost and marginal social cost and that the marginal cost of producing education is shown by the curve *MC*. The demand curve for education (D) tells us the quantity of education demanded at each price when people are free to choose the amount of education that they undertake and have to pay for it themselves. It measures the marginal private benefit — the benefit perceived by the individuals undertaking education — so it is labelled $D = MPB$. A private competitive education market will produce an output of Q_0 at a price of P_0.

Suppose that the external benefit — the benefit derived by people other than those undertaking education — results in marginal social benefits described by the curve *MSB*. Allocative efficiency occurs at the point at which marginal cost equals marginal social benefit — C_1, at output Q_1. By providing the quantity of education Q_1 and by making it available at price P_1, the government can achieve allocative efficiency in the education sector. In other words, by producing education at a low price, the government is able to encourage people to undertake the amount of education that makes its marginal social benefit equal to its marginal cost, rather than having the marginal private benefit equal to marginal cost.

We've now looked at two examples of the way in which government action can achieve an economic outcome different from that of a private unregulated market by helping market participants take account of the external costs and benefits deriving from their actions. We've also illustrated government interventions that achieve allocative efficiency where the unregulated market fails to do so — where there is market failure.

R E V I E W

When externalities are present, the market allocation is not efficient. Sometimes an efficient allocation can be achieved by establishing private property rights. But in many cases, private property rights simply cannot be established and enforced. In such cases, if the government confronts people with a tax equivalent to the external marginal cost or a subsidy equivalent to the external marginal benefit, it induces people to produce goods on a scale that achieves allocative efficiency, even in the face of externalities. ■

■ We've seen that markets do not always achieve allocative efficiency. When the market fails, we can describe an allocation that is efficient. But showing an efficient allocation is not the same thing as designing institutions to achieve one. Do governments in fact achieve allocative efficiency? Or are there economic problems arising from the functioning of a political system that leads to "government failure" and prevents the attainment of an efficient allocation of resources? These questions will be dealt with in the next chapter.

SUMMARY

The Government Sector

The government sector of the Canadian economy consists of more than 4,000 separate organizations employing a quarter of a million public servants and spending a third of all the income generated in Canada. The government share of the economy has grown over the years.

When economists study political behaviour, they are careful to maintain the distinction between positive and normative analysis. Their main focus is on positive matters — on what *is* and how the political system works, rather than on what *ought* to be and how the political system *ought* to function.

All government economic actions stem from either market failure or the redistribution of income and wealth. Market failure arises from the provision of public goods and services, from externalities, and from monopolies and cartels. The redistribution of income and wealth arises partly from notions of equity and justice and partly from rent-seeking activities.

There are two broad approaches to the economic analysis of government: public interest theories and public choice theories. Public interest theories emphasize the idea of government as an institution able to eliminate waste and achieve allocative efficiency — an agent that operates on behalf of the public interest. Public choice theories emphasize the idea that government operates in a political marketplace in which politicians, bureaucrats, and voters interact with each other. According to the public choice view, government failure to achieve allocative efficiency is as real a possibility as failure of the market. (pp. 495-497)

Public Goods

Public goods have two distinctive features: nonrivalry and nonexcludability. One person's consumption does not reduce the amount available for someone else (nonrivalry), and no one can be kept from sharing the consumption of such a good (nonexcludability). An example of a pure public good is the national defence system.

The existence of public goods (and of mixed goods with a large public element) gives rises to the free-rider problem: the tendency for the scale of provision of a public good to be too small if it is produced and sold privately. The free-rider problem arises because an individual has insufficient incentive to pay for a good if that payment has no effect on the quantity of the good he or she consumes. Since it pays everyone to free ride, no revenue can be raised from the sale of a public good that is privately provided. In such a situation, no public goods will be produced. In contrast, the government can produce a public good, paying for it out of taxation. People will vote for the necessary taxes if the net benefit is positive. The government is able to provide any public good on a scale larger than that provided by a private producer, but it does not necessarily produce an allocatively efficient amount of a public good. (pp. 497-501)

Externalities

An externality is a cost or a benefit arising from an economic transaction that falls on a third party and that is not taken into account by those undertaking the transaction. When external costs are present, allocative efficiency requires a reduction in the scale of output to less than what the market will produce. When external benefits are present, allocative efficiency requires an increase in output. Government can deal with externalities in two main ways: by establishing and enforcing private property rights, or by using taxes and subsidies. If the government uses taxes and subsidies, it imposes taxes where there are external costs and gives subsidies where there are external benefits. (pp. 501-507)

KEY ELEMENTS

Key Terms

Externality, 501
Free rider, 497
Free-rider problem, 497
Marginal benefit, 498
Marginal private cost, 503
Marginal social cost, 503
Market failure, 496

Key Figures 

REVIEW QUESTIONS

1 How big is the government sector of the Canadian economy today?

2 What is market failure?

3 What are the sources of market failure that result in government action?

4 What is a public good?

5 Name examples of three goods: a public good, a private good, and a mixed good.

6 What is the free-rider problem? How does government help overcome it?

7 What is an externality?

8 Give three examples of externalities.

9 Describe the two main methods used by government in the face of externalities.

10 Explain, with an example, how the establishment and enforcement of private property rights can achieve allocative efficiency when externalities would otherwise prevent an efficient use of resources.

11 Explain, with examples, how taxes and subsidies can correct market failure resulting from externalities.

PROBLEMS

1 You are given the following information about a sewage disposal system that a city of 1 million people is considering installing:

Capacity (thousands of litres a day)	Marginal private benefit to one person (dollars)	Total cost (milllions of dollars a day)
0		0
	 50	
1		5
	 40	
2		15
	 30	
3		30
	 20	
4		50
	 10	
5		75

a) What is the capacity that achieves maximum net benefit?

b) How much will each person have to pay in taxes in order to pay for the efficient capacity level?

c) What are the total and net benefits?

2 A chemical factory dumps waste in a river. Damage is done to the local fish stock and membership fees at a nearby fishing club are lowered by the following amounts:

Output of chemical plant (litres per hour)	Lost fees to fishing club (dollars)
0	0
100	10
200	30
300	70
400	210

a) The local government plans to tax the chemical factory. Devise a tax that will achieve allocative efficiency.

b) How might private property rights be used in this situation?

3 You are given the following information about a mobile library that is planned for a city of 1 million people:

Price of a subscription	Number of subscribers (dollars)	Marginal external benefit per subscriber (dollars)	Marginal cost of one subscription (dollars)
10	180,000	20	90
15	160,000	30	75
20	140,000	40	60
25	120,000	50	45
30	100,000	60	30
25	80,000	70	15

a) Explain why a mobile library would generate an external benefit to a community.

b) Derive and sketch the demand curve for the mobile library.

c) Derive the marginal social benefit curve for the mobile library.

d) Find the competitive equilibrium price of a subscription and the number of subscribers.

e) Calculate the marginal social benefit of the mobile library to the community when there is a competitive equilibrium.

f) Determine the number of subscribers that achieves allocative efficiency and the price of a subscription that ensures this outcome.

g) Calculate the marginal social benefit of the mobile library to the community when allocative efficiency is achieved.

4 Explain why your provincial government subsidizes colleges and universities, permitting students to attend for tuition fees below the full cost of the education provided.

CHAPTER 20

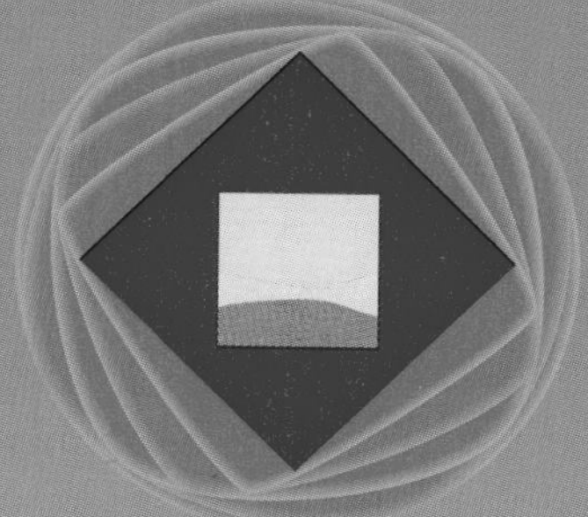

Public Choice

After studying this chapter, you will be able to:

- Describe the components of the political marketplace.
- Define a political equilibrium.
- Explain how the main political parties choose their economic policy platforms.
- Explain how government bureaucracy interacts with politicians to determine the scale of provision of public goods and services.
- Explain why we vote for redistributions of income and wealth.
- Explain why we tax some goods at much higher rates than others.
- Predict the effects of taxes on prices, quantities produced, and profits.
- Explain why we subsidize the producers of some goods.
- Predict the effects of subsidies on prices, quantities produced, and profits.

Rhetoric and Reality

POLITICIANS LOVE TO ENGAGE in verbal combat. No matter what the topic — the Canada – United States Free Trade Agreement, the Meech Lake Accord, women's rights, the right to life, national defence, protection of the environment, restoration of the ecological balance of the great lakes — the verbal combat of our politicians, their rhetoric, reflects the diversity and variety of opinion in the country at large. Yet, in contrast to the tremendously different positions taken by politicians, the policies actually enacted by them are remarkably similar. We do not see, for example, Progressive Conservative governments slashing taxes and cutting spending or Liberal governments raising taxes and spending at a faster pace than Conservatives do. It is true that governments of different parties have differences in policies reflecting different political attitudes, but these differences do not match the differences in rhetoric. Why do politicians exaggerate their differences on the campaign trail and pursue relatively similar policies in office? ■ One dominant fact of political life over the past 40 or so years has been the relentless and steady growth in the scale of government. Government has grown under both Conservatives and Liberals at the federal level and under a wide variety of political philosophies at the provincial level. What determines the scale of government? What are the forces that generate the level of provision of public goods and services, and why has government grown over the years to command an increasing fraction of the economy's resources? ■ Government pervades many aspects of our lives. It is present at our birth, supporting the hospitals in which we are born and training the doctors and nurses who deliver us. It is present throughout our education, supporting schools, colleges, and universities, and training our teachers. It is present throughout our working lives, taxing our incomes, regulating our work environment, and paying us benefits when we are unemployed. It is present throughout our retirement, paying us a small income, and when we die, taxing our estates. But the government does not make all our economic choices. We decide for ourselves what work to do, how much to save, and what to spend our income on. Why does the government intervene in some aspects of our lives but not others? Why doesn't the government provide more of our housing services? Why doesn't it provide less of our education and health services? ■ There are many situations in which it is obvious why the government intervenes. Attempting to stem the flow of dangerous drugs is an example. But there are other areas in which the government does not intervene although many people believe it should. One such area is the protection of the quality of our air. Why doesn't the government do more to protect air quality? ■ Almost everyone grumbles about government bureaucracy. The poor single mother complains about the treatment that she receives from bureaucrats who administer the social welfare programs that she uses; the wealthy taxpayer complains about her treatment by the bureaucrats at Revenue Canada; and even the prime minister, premiers, and members of the legislatures complain that the bureaucracy is too big, too slow, and inefficient. Why is the bureaucracy so unpopular and the target of so much scorn? How do government bureaus operate to deliver the many public services for which they are responsible? ■ Government taxes almost all the goods and services that we buy. Some of these taxes are very high — for example, those on gasoline, alcohol, and tobacco products. A few items that we buy are not taxed and their producers are even subsidized by the government. An example is milk. Why does government impose heavy taxes on some goods and subsidize others? What are the effects of taxes on prices, on the quantities bought and sold, and on the amount of revenue raised by the government?

■ In this chapter, we study the economic interactions of voters, politicians, and bureaucrats and discover how the scale and variety of government economic activity are determined. Our focus here is on providing public goods and services, raising taxes to pay for those services, controlling externalities, and redistributing income. In Chapter 21, we apply the same basic theory of government economic behaviour to the regulation and control of monopolies and cartels.

The Political Marketplace

Government is not a huge computer that grinds out solutions to resource allocation problems plagued with free riders and externalities. It does not simply calculate and balance marginal social costs and benefits, automatically achieving allocative efficiency. Rather, it is a complex organization made up of thousands of individuals. These individuals have their *own* economic objectives, and government policy choices are the outcome of the choices made by these individuals. To analyse these choices, economists have developed a theory of the political marketplace that parallels theories of ordinary markets — *public choice theory.* There are three types of actors in the political marketplace:

- Voters
- Politicians
- Bureaucrats

Voters are the consumers of the outcome of the political process. In ordinary markets for goods and services, people express their demands by their willingness to pay. In the political marketplace, voters express their demands in three principal ways. First, they express them by a willingness to vote, either in an election or on a referendum issue. Second and less formally, they express their demands through campaign contributions. Third, they express their demands by lobbying. **Lobbying** is the activity of bringing pressure to bear on government agencies or institutions through a variety of informal mechanisms. The pro-life and pro-choice lobbies are two of the most prominent examples of such organizations in Canada today.

Politicians are the elected officials in federal, provincial, and local government — from the chief executives (the prime minister, premier, and mayor) to the members of each legislature. Politicians are chosen by voters.

Bureaucrats are the appointed officials who work at various levels in the many government departments, again at the federal, provincial, and local levels. The most senior bureaucrats are appointed by politicians. Junior bureaucrats are appointed by senior ones.

Voters, politicians, and bureaucrats make their economic choices in a way that best furthers their own objectives, but they each face two types of constraints. First, each group is constrained by the preferences of the others: bureaucrats are constrained by the preferences of politicians; politicians are constrained by the preferences of bureaucrats and voters; and voters are constrained by the preferences of bureaucrats and politicians. Second, voters, bureaucrats, and politicians cannot ignore technological constraints. They can do only things that are technologically feasible. We are going to examine the objectives of voters, politicians, and bureaucrats and the constraints they face when making their choices. We're also going to study the interactions among the three types of actors. In so doing, we are going to discover how the political system actually works.

The predictions of an economic model of voter, politician, and bureaucrat behaviour are the equilibrium of the political process — the political equilibrium. A **political equilibrium** is a situation in which the choices of voters, politicians, and bureaucrats are all compatible and in which no one group of these agents can become better off by making a different choice. Thus a political equilibrium has the same characteristics as an equilibrium in the market for goods and services or factors of production.

The theory of public choice that we are about to study is a relatively new branch of economics that has grown rapidly in the past 30 years. It was recently recognized by the awarding of the Nobel Prize for economics to one of its principal architects, James Buchanan (see Our Advancing Knowledge, pp. 516-517).

Let's begin our study of public choice theory by looking at the behaviour of politicians.

The Behaviour of Politicians and Voters

All kinds of people go into politics. Some have noble ideals and want to make a lasting contribution to improving the conditions of their fellow citizens. Others are single-minded in pursuit of their own self-interest and profit. Most politicians, no doubt, blend these two extremes. Economic models of public choice are based on the assumption that in a democratic political system politicians' central objective is to get enough votes to be elected and to keep enough support to remain in office. Votes to a politician are like dollars to a private firm. In order to obtain enough votes, politicians form coalitions with each other; we call these coalitions political parties. A political party is a collection of politicians who have banded together for the purpose of achieving and maintaining office. A political party attempts to develop policies that appeal to a majority of the voters.

Public choice theory assumes that voters support policies that they believe make them better off and oppose policies that they believe make them worse off. They neither oppose nor support — they are indifferent toward's — policies that they believe have no effect on them. Voters' *perceptions*, rather than reality, are what guide their choices.

To obtain the support of voters, a politician (or political party) must offer a package of policies that voters believe will make them better off than the policies proposed by the opposing political parties. A political program can seek to make a voter better off in two ways. One way is to implement policies that make *everyone* better off. Providing national defence and protecting the environment are examples of such policies. Another way is to implement policies that make some voters worse off but at least 50 percent of the voters better off. Redistributing income in such a way that at least half of the electorate reaps net benefits is one example. Supporting or opposing abortion is another, and supporting or opposing the Canada – United States Free Trade Agreement yet another.

Political programs that make everyone better off feature in the platforms of all parties. Policies that favour one group against another differ from party to party and depend on which segment of the population or particular interest groups a political party wants to appeal to. Let's see how politicians and voters interact and how the policy platforms of political parties emerge by examining how the political process handles the provision of public goods and external costs and benefits.

Public Goods In Chapter 19, we compared the scale of provision of public goods that achieves allocative efficiency with the scale that would be provided through the private marketplace. Now we want to work out the scale of provision of public goods that a political system will actually deliver.

For the moment, let's ignore differences among individual voters and suppose that people have identical views about the benefits of public goods and externalities. We'll consider what happens when people disagree and have different preferences shortly. To be concrete, let's stick with the example of acid-rain control that we studied in Chapter 19.

Suppose that the total costs and total benefits of monitoring and preventing sulfur dioxide emissions that cause acid rain are the ones shown in Fig. 20.1. (These are the same costs and benefits that we used in Chapter 19.) Suppose also that there are two political parties. Let's call one the Greens

Figure 20.1 Provision of a Public Good in a Political System

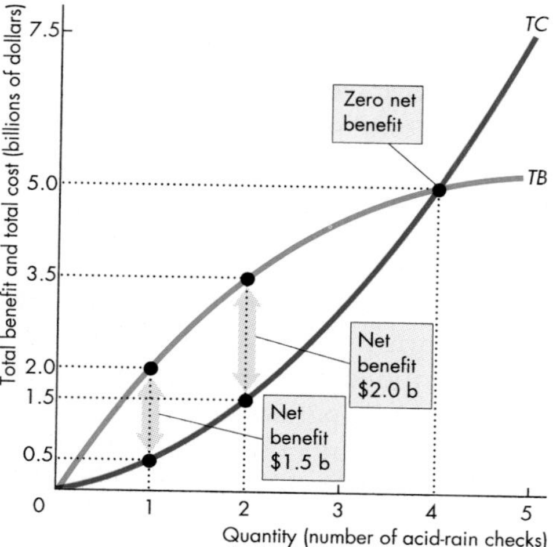

The total benefit curve for an acid-rain check system is *TB*, and the total cost curve is *TC*. Net benefit is maximized if 2 acid-rain check units are installed, with a total benefit of $3.5 billion and a total cost of $1.5 billion. There are two political parties: the Smokes and the Greens. Their platforms are identical on all matters except the environment. The Smokes propose installing 1 acid-rain check unit and the Greens 4 units. In an election, the Smokes would win since their proposal generates a larger net benefit than the Greens' proposal. But if the Greens proposed installing 2 units, they would beat the Smokes since the net benefit resulting from 2 units exceeds that from 1 unit. To get even, the Smokes would have to match the Greens. If voters are well informed and in general agreement about the value of a public good, competition between political parties for their votes can achieve an efficient scale of provision.

and the other the Smokes. Suppose that the Greens and the Smokes propose policy platforms that are exactly the same in all respects except for acid-rain control. The Greens offer a high level of protection. They propose providing 4 acid-rain check satellites at a cost of $5 billion, with benefits of $5 billion and a net benefit of zero ($5 billion – $5 billion). The Smokes propose providing just 1 satellite at a cost of $0.5 billion, with a benefit of $2 billion and a net benefit of $1.5 billion ($2 billion – $0.5 billion).

In an election in which voters are presented with the two platforms just described, the Smokes will win. Recall that we assumed that both parties are offering programs identical in every respect except for acid-rain control. The acid-rain control program of the Smokes provides the voters with a net benefit of $1.5 billion over and above the taxes that they are asked to pay, while the Greens are offering no net benefit, so the Smokes will get all the votes.

Now suppose that the Greens, contemplating the election outcome that we have just described, realize that their party is offering too high a level of acid-rain control — that it is too green — to get elected. They figure that they have to offer net benefits in excess of $1.5 billion if they are to beat the Smokes. They therefore scale back their plans and propose building 2 acid-rain check units. At this level of provision, the total cost is $1.5 billion and total benefit is $3.5 billion, so net benefit is $2 billion ($3.5 billion – $1.5 billion). The Greens are now offering a package that the voters prefer to the one offered by the Smokes. Now in an election, the Greens will win.

The Smokes, contemplating this outcome, realize that the best they can do is to match the Greens. They too propose providing 2 acid-rain check satellites on exactly the same terms as the Greens. The voters are now indifferent between the proposals of the two parties and are indifferent about which one to vote for.

Competition for votes among political parties, even when there are only two of them, produces a political platform that maximizes the perceived net benefit accruing to the voters. For this outcome to occur, however, it is necessary that the voters be able to evaluate the alternatives. We'll see below that this condition may not be satisfied.

Externalities

The example that we have just worked through deals with a situation in which the voters are in agreement about the goal and can calculate the benefits arising from different proposals. The same line of reasoning applies to policies concerning the control of externalities. Provided the voters are in agreement about the benefits and can evaluate them, the political party that offers the level of control of externalities that maximizes net benefits will be the one that wins an election. The political party that proposes a total ban on the production of chlorofluorocarbons (CFCs) or sulfur dioxide emissions will lose an election to a party that proposes more limited controls. A party that proposes a free-for-all on CFCs and sulfur dioxide emissions will lose an election to one that

OUR ADVANCING KNOWLEDGE

Public Choice

Kenneth Arrow

James Buchanan

The past 30 years have seen an enormous growth in the study of the economic choices of government and of the interactions of politicians, bureaucrats, and voters. The result of this work is a well-recognized discipline within economics called *public choice theory.*

The father of modern public choice theory is Duncan Black. Born in Motherwell, Scotland, in 1908, Black first studied mathematics and physics and then economics and politics at the University of Glasgow (where, 150 years earlier, Adam Smith had worked). Black's work was monumental. His vision was to develop a science of politics — having the same degree of rigour as economics — based on a theory of committees. In Black's model, consumers' preferences are replaced by the preferences of committee members; goods and services are replaced by motions or propositions before a committee. Black's work of the 1940s and 1950s was summarized in his book *The Theory of Committees and Elections* (Cambridge University Press, 1958).

One of Black's discoveries is the possibility of *cyclical voting.* An example is illustrated in the accompanying table.

Cycles in Voting

	Possible income distribution		
	1	2	3
Ann	150	50	100
Ben	100	150	50
Con	50	100	150

The table shows three people and three possible income distributions. If the distribution is 1, then Ben and Con will vote for distribution 2. Ann will oppose distribution 2, but in a majority vote she will lose. If the distribution is 2, Ann and Con will vote for distribution 3. Ben will vote against that distribution, but if the majority decides the day, he will lose. But if the distribution is 3, Ann and Ben will vote for distribution 1 while Con will oppose that distribution. Again, majority vote will result in a win for distribution 1. We are now back where we started. Ben and Con can now vote that distribution down, and so the whole cycle begins again.

The possibility of voting cycles is just one potential flaw in democracy. Another was suggested by Kenneth Arrow. Arrow, a Nobel Prize winner in economic science in 1972, was born in New York City in 1921. He now teaches at Stanford University, where he currently holds two positions—professor of economics and of operations research. Arrow's contributions to economics span an amazing range (as his dual professorship signifies), but in the public choice area his book *Social Choice and Individual Values* (John Wiley & Sons, 1951) has been of substantial influence. In it, Arrow demonstrates what has come to be called the "Arrow impossibility theorem." In simplified terms, the theorem states that it is not possible to aggregate the preferences of individuals to arrive at social preferences that can be used to guide government choice.

One of the major contributors to modern public choice theory is James Buchanan, whose work was recognized by his being awarded the Nobel prize in economic science in 1986. Born in Tennessee in 1919, Buchanan has devoted his working life to understanding political decision-making by using the same tools of analysis that economists use to understand all economic choices. Buchanan's ideas are given their most extensive development in *The Calculus of Consent: Logical Foundation of Constitutional Democracy* (University of Michigan Press, 1962), which he wrote with his colleague, Gordon Tullock. In this book, Buchanan and Tullock analyse the effects of different voting systems: for example, simple majority versus qualified majority (a qualified majority being a two-thirds majority or unanimity) and the effects of having two legislative chambers, such as the House of Commons and the Senate. The authors also examine the economics and ethics of pressure groups, special interests, and the constitution.

Two other scholars who have made important contributions to the subject that we have been studying in this chapter are Anthony Downs and William Niskanen. Downs, born near Chicago in 1930, received his Ph.D. from Stanford University in 1956. His doctoral thesis turned into what has become a great classic: *An Economic Theory of Democracy* (Harper and Row, 1957). In that book, Downs first set out the "median voter theorem." He also pointed out what has come to be called the "paradox of voting." It centres on a question: why do we bother to vote? From a purely economic point of view, voting seems silly. If the political parties offer the policies that best benefit the median voter, no individual's vote is going to make any difference to the outcome of an election. Since voting takes time and effort, the individually rational thing to do is to stay home and give the election a miss. The fact that most of us do vote implies either that the economic theory of voting is overlooking an important aspect of economic behaviour or that voting is not to be understood purely and narrowly in economic terms.

Niskanen, born in Oregon in 1933, has had an interesting and highly varied career: he has worked as an economist in the U.S. Department of Defense and in the American armed forces and has been a professor at the University of California at Berkeley and Los Angeles. He also served as head of the economic division of the Ford Motor Company and as a member of the Council of Economic Advisors to U.S. President Ronald Reagan. With this rich variety of experience, Niskanen has made significant advances in the theory of bureaucracy. His classic book *Bureaucracy and Representative Government* (Aldine-Atherton) was published in 1971. It is in this work that Niskanen proposes the theory of budget maximization that we have studied in this chapter.

proposes restraint in the production of goods that generate these external costs. Competition for votes will force each party to find the degree of control that maximizes net benefit.

In the examples of public goods and externalities that we have just worked out, we have ignored differences of opinion among the voters. We'll now go on to consider cases in which the preferences of voters differ and in which these differences are crucial in determining the outcome of the political process.

Interest Groups and Redistribution

Most matters decided in the political arena are ones on which people have different opinions. Some people favour a large national scientific research program while others urge leaving such a matter to private enterprise; some favour a large scale of income redistribution while others urge tax cuts; some want massive government intervention to protect the environment while others want more limited environmental controls; some want government to provide day care while others believe that day care is a private good that should be paid for by its users.

Faced with this diversity of opinion, no political party can propose a platform that pleases everyone. It must propose a platform that benefits some individuals while imposing costs on others — a platform that *redistributes* economic benefits. But to attain office, a party must put together a package that attracts a majority of the votes. To do so, each party has to deliver a package that makes a majority of the voters better off (as the voters perceive it) than they would be under the policies proposed by the opposing party or parties. The outcome of this search for a majority is that each political party offers policies very close to the policies of the others. This tendency toward similar policies is known as the principle of minimum differentiation.

The Principle of Minimum Differentiation The tendency for competitors to make themselves almost identical in order to appeal to the maximum number of clients or voters is called the **principle of minimum differentiation**. Let's study the principle of minimum differentiation by looking at a problem that is more familiar and concrete than that faced by political parties.

There are two ice cream vendors on a beach. The beach, one kilometre long, is illustrated in Fig. 20.2 as the distance from *A* to *B*. Sunbathers lounge at equal intervals over the entire kilometre. One of the ice cream vendors comes along and sets up a stand. Where will she locate? The answer is at position *C* — exactly halfway between *A* and *B*. With the stand in this position, the farthest that anyone has to walk to buy an ice cream is a kilometre (half a kilometre to the ice cream stand and half a kilometre back to the beach towel).

Now suppose that a second ice cream vendor comes along. Where will he place his stand? The answer is right next to the original one at point *C*. To understand why, imagine that the second vendor locates his stand at point *D* — halfway between *C* and *B*. How many customers will he attract and how many will go to the stand at *C*? The stand at *D* will pick up all the customers on the beach between *B* and *D* because it is closer for them. It will also pick up all the customers between *D* and *E* (the point halfway between *C* and *D*) because they too will have a shorter trip by going to *D* than by going to *C*. But

Figure 20.2 Principle of Minimum Differentiation

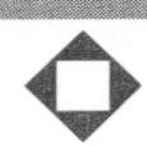

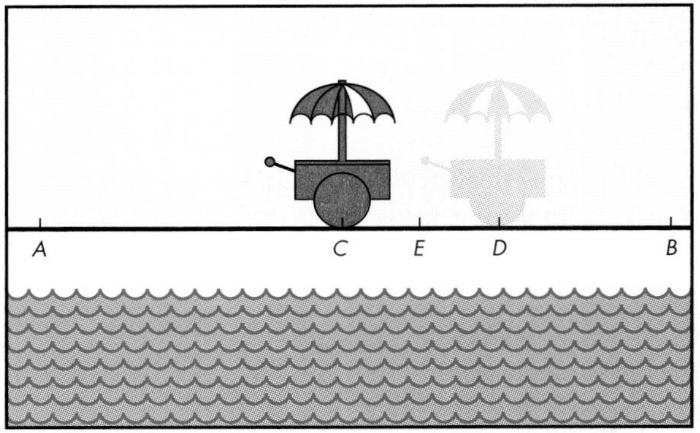

A beach stretches from *A* to *B*, and sunbathers are distributed at even intervals along the whole length. An ice cream vendor sets up a stand at point *C*. The distance that people have to walk for ice cream is the same no matter which side of the stand they have put their beach towels on. If a second ice cream vendor sets up a stand, it will pay to place it exactly next to *C* in the middle of the beach. If the second stand is placed at *D*, only the customers on the beach between *E* and *B* will buy ice cream there. Those between *A* and *E* will go to *C*. By moving as close to *C* as possible, the second ice cream vendor picks up half the customers.

all the people between *A* and *C* and all those between *C* and *E* will go to the ice cream stand located at *C*. So it will get all the people on the beach between *A* and *E* and the stand located at *D* will get all the people located between *E* and *B*.

Now suppose that the vendor with a stand at *D* moves to *C*. There are now two stands at *C*. Half the customers will go to the first vendor and the other half to the second. Only if each locates in the centre of the beach can each draw half the customers. If either of them moves slightly away from the centre, then that vendor will get less than half the customers and the one remaining at the centre will draw a majority of them.

This example illustrates the principle of minimum differentiation. By having no differentiation in location, both ice cream vendors do as well as they can and share the market evenly.

The principle of minimum differentiation has been applied to explain a wide variety of choices. It explains how supermarkets choose their location, how the makers of automobiles and microwave popcorn design their products, and how political parties choose their platforms.

The principle of minimum differentiation predicts that political parties will be similar to each other. But it does not tell us which policies they will favour — only that they will favour similar ones. In the case of the ice cream vendor, the location is determined by technological considerations — minimizing the distance that the bathers have to walk. But what determines a political party's choice of platform? Let's now address this question.

Figure 20.3 The Median Voter Theorem

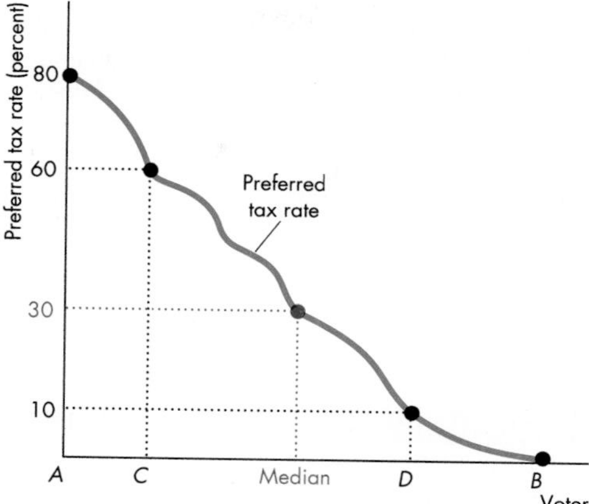

A political party can win an election by proposing policies that appeal to the median voter and to all the other voters on one side of the median. If the median mildly favours a policy, that policy will be proposed. In the figure, voters have different preferences concerning the rate at which to tax an externality. They are ranked from *A* to *B* in descending order of their preferred tax rate. There are two political parties. If one proposes a 61 percent tax and the other a 59 percent tax, the lower tax party will win the election — voters between *A* and *C* will vote for the high tax rate and those between *C* and *B* for the low tax rate. If both parties propose low tax rates — 11 percent and 9 percent — the party proposing the higher rate will win. It will pick up the votes between *A* and *D*, leaving only the votes between *D* and *B* for the party proposing the lower tax rate. Each party will have an incentive to move towards the tax rate preferred by the median voter. At that point, each party picks up half of the votes and neither can improve its share.

The Median Voter Theorem An interesting proposition about a political party's choice of platform is provided by the median voter theorem. The **median voter theorem** states that political parties will pursue policies that maximize the net benefit of the median voter. (The median of a distribution of, say, student heights is the height of the student in the middle. One-half of the students are taller and one-half of the students are shorter than the median.) Let's see how the median voter theorem applies to the question of how large a tax to impose on sulfur dioxide emissions that cause acid rain.

Imagine arranging all the voters along a line running from *A* to *B*, as shown in Fig. 20.3. The voter who wants the highest tax rate is at *A*, and the one who wants no tax is at *B*; all the other voters are arranged along the line according to the level of the tax rate that they favour. The curve in the figure shows the tax rate favoured by each voter between *A* and *B*. As shown in the graph, the median voter favours a tax rate of 30 percent.

Suppose that two political parties propose similar but not quite identical taxes on emissions of sulfur dioxide. One party proposes a tax of 61 percent and the other of 59 percent. All the voters lying between *A* and *C* prefer the higher tax and will vote for it. All the voters lying between *C* and *B* prefer the lower tax and will vote for it. The lower-tax party wins the election.

Alternatively, suppose that the two political parties offer a low tax — again, at slightly different rates. One party offers a rate of 11 percent and the other of

Table 20.1 Voting for Income Redistribution: A Tie

Number of voters	Income before redistribution (thousands of dollars)	Income after redistribution (thousands of dollars)	Gain (+) or loss (−) (thousands of dollars)
25	10	15	+ 5
25	20	23	+ 3
25	40	37	− 3
25	90	85	− 5
Total 100	Average 40	40	0

9 percent. The voters between A and D will vote for the higher tax rate and those between D and B for the lower one. This time, the higher-tax party will win.

In each of these situations, each party will see that it can win the election by moving closer to the tax rate preferred by the median voter. Once both parties are offering that tax rate, however, neither will be able to increase its share of the vote by changing its proposal. One party will get the votes between A and the median, and the other the votes between the median and B. All the voters except the median voter will be dissatisfied — for those between A and the median the tax rate is too low, and for those between B and the median the tax is too high. But no political party can propose a tax other than 30 percent and expect to win the election.

The principle of minimum differentiation and the median voter theorem seem to imply that all political parties will be identical in all respects. If that is so, it is too bad for the principle and the theorem. The world that we live in has political parties that certainly do differ. Many of us are heated in our support for and opposition to particular parties and policy proposals. One of the major differences among political parties is their approach to redistribution of income and wealth. Let's use the principle of minimum differentiation and the median voter theorem to see if we can understand why all political parties favour some redistribution but differ in the policies that they propose.

Voting for Income Redistribution

The first model of redistribution that we'll consider is one that results in voting cycles. Imagine a society with 100 voters divided into four income groups as set out in Table 20.1. Twenty-five of the voters earn \$10,000 a year, another 25 earn \$20,000 a year, another 25 earn \$40,000 a year, and the richest 25 earn \$90,000 a year. The average income in this community is \$40,000 a year.

Suppose that a political party proposes taxing the richest quarter of the people \$5,000 and the second richest \$3,000. It proposes to use the funds to make transfers of \$5,000 to the poorest quarter of the people and \$3,000 to the next poorest quarter. The incomes resulting from the tax and transfers in this proposal are set out in the third column of Table 20.1. The average income is still \$40,000. The final column of the table shows the gains and losses to each income group. The poor half of the voters gain and the rich half lose.

Suppose that a second political party in this society opposes the redistribution scheme just described. Which party will win the election? The answer is that it will be a tie. The party proposing the redistribution scheme will pick up 50 percent of the votes — those of the poor half of the electorate. The party opposing the redistribution scheme will pick up the other half of the votes — those at the wealthier end of the income distribution.

Now suppose that one of the parties offers the modified scheme set out in Table 20.2. The proposal is to tax the richest quarter of the people not \$5,000 but \$8,000 and not to tax the second richest quarter at all. Under this scheme, the two poorest groups of people will receive benefits of \$5,000 and \$3,000 respectively. One party supports these measures, and the other opposes them and proposes no redistribution at all. Which party will win? The answer is the

Table 20.2 Voting for Income Redistribution: The Rich Lose

Number of voters	Income before redistribution (thousands of dollars)	Income after redistribution (thousands of dollars)	Gain(+) or loss (−) (thousands of dollars)
25	10	15	+5
25	20	23	+3
25	40	40	0
25	90	82	−8
Total 100	Average 40	40	0

party supporting redistribution. All the people with original incomes of $10,000 and $20,000 will vote for the scheme. Those with incomes of $30,000 will be indifferent between the two parties, so we can suppose that half will vote for one party and half for the other. The party opposing the redistribution scheme will collect the votes of the richest quarter of the people plus half of those in the second richest group.

This example shows one particular redistribution proposal that could gain the support of the majority of voters. But there will be many other proposals that could also gain majority support (with different groups of people making up the majority in each case). There is no end to the different proposals that could win a majority. As these various schemes are proposed, there are cycles in the voting similar to those described in Our Advancing Knowledge, pp. 516-517.

Why do we not observe voting cycles in reality? Why do we see a tendency for redistribution policies to remain in place for very long periods of time? The answer is suggested by a second model of redistribution — a median voter model. A key feature of this model is what has been called the "big trade-off" (see Chapter 18). The greater the amount of income redistributed, the smaller is the incentive to work and the lower is the average level of income. As a consequence, redistributive taxes have two effects on the median voter: they raise the median voter's income by taking from those above the median and redistributing to those at and below the median; they also lower the median voter's income by reducing the incentive to work, which lowers average income. Which of these two opposing effects is stronger depends on the scale of redistribution. At low tax rates, the disincentive effects are small, so an increase in taxes makes the median voter better off. The higher income resulting from the transfers from the rich is more than enough to offset the lower income resulting from disincentive effects. If tax rates are set too high, however, a cut in taxes will make the median voter better off. In this case, the lower income resulting from smaller transfers from the rich is more than made up for by the higher average income resulting from improved incentives. But there is a level of taxes and an amount of redistribution that is exactly right from the point of view of the median voter. This scale of redistribution is the one that balances these two considerations and maximizes the median voter's income. This amount of redistribution is a possible political equilibrium.

Model and Reality

We've now looked at two models of equilibrium redistribution — a voting cycles model and a median voter model. In the voting cycles model, there is a never-ending sequence of different majorities for different directions of redistribution. In the median voter model, there is a unique equilibrium that maximizes the net benefit to the median voter.

Which of these models best fits the facts about income redistribution? The median voter model comes closest. Its strength lies in its prediction that the political parties will differ in their rhetoric but be very close to each other in the actual redistribution measures for which they vote. This prediction accords well with reality. In contrast, the voting cycles model predicts a sequence of different majorities for different directions of redistribution that we do not observe in reality.

R E V I E W

Politicians seek to obtain enough votes to achieve and maintain power. They do this by appealing to slightly more than half of the electorate. The key voter is the median voter. To appeal to the median voter, political parties offer programs that favour a majority of the electorate. Each party tries to outdo the other by appealing to the median voter. In part, that appeal results from the political parties' proposing income-increasing policies. It also, in part, results from the redistribution of income to the point at which no one can invent a way of raising the income of the median voter.

We have analysed the behaviour of politicians but not that of the bureaucrats who translate the choices of the politicians into programs. Let's now turn to an examination of the economic choices of bureaucrats. ■

The Behaviour of Bureaucrats

An interesting model of the behaviour of bureaucrats has been suggested by William Niskanen (see Our Advancing Knowledge, pp. 516-517). In that model, each bureaucrat aims to maximize the budget of the agency, ministry, or department in which he or she works. The bigger the budget of the agency, the greater is the prestige of the agency chief and the larger is the opportunity for promotion for people further down the bureaucratic ladder. Thus all the members of an agency have an interest in maximizing its budget. In seeking to obtain the largest budget it can, each government agency marshals the best arguments for why it should have more funds to spend. Since each agency does its best to obtain more funds, the net result is upward pressure for expenditure on all publicly provided goods and services.

The constraints on maximizing the budget of a government agency, ministry, or department are the taxes that the politicians have to levy and the implications of those taxes for the politicians' own ability to win votes. But government agencies recognize and appreciate the interplay between their own objectives and those of the politicians and so do their best to help the politicians appreciate the vote-winning consequences of spending more on that particular agency. Thus budget maximization, to some degree, translates itself into political campaigns designed to explain to voters why they need more health services, more environmental protection, and so on.

Let's examine the consequences of bureaucratic budget maximization for the provision of public goods and their cost by looking again at the example of acid-rain control. We've studied this example twice before. The first time (in Chapter 19), our concern was to establish that a government could overcome the free-rider problem and produce a larger quantity of a public good than would be produced by the private market. Earlier in this chapter, we examined the way in which political parties' competing for votes determines the scale of provision of a public good in a situation in which the voters agree about the benefits of the public good and are able to assess the costs and benefits of different scales of provision. In that example, no bureaucrats intervened in the process.

But the creation and operation of acid-rain control systems requires the establishment of a large and complex government bureaucracy. How does the environmental protection bureaucracy influence the scale and cost of the anti-acid-rain program? Let's answer this question by returning to the example of the installation of our futuristic acid-rain check.

Take a look at Fig. 20.4. You will recognize that it is similar to Fig. 20.1. The horizontal axis shows the number of acid-rain check units and the vertical axis their total benefit and total cost. The curve labelled *TB* shows the total benefit as perceived by all the individuals in the economy and the curve labelled *TC* shows the total cost.

We saw earlier that the level of provision that maximizes net benefit is 2 units. This level of provision costs $1.5 billion, and it yields a total benefit of $3.5 billion and a net benefit of $2 billion. A political party that proposes installing 2 units will win an election because there is no higher net benefit possible. But will the Ministry of the Environment press Parliament to vote for 2 acid-rain check satellites? According to Niskanen's model of bureaucracy, it will not. The bureaucracy will push to expand the scale of provision, and thus the budget for environmental protection, to the largest possible level. If it is able to increase the number of acid-rain checks to 4, for example, it can increase the budget to $5 billion. In this situation, total benefit will equal total cost and

Figure 20.4 Bureaucratic Overprovision

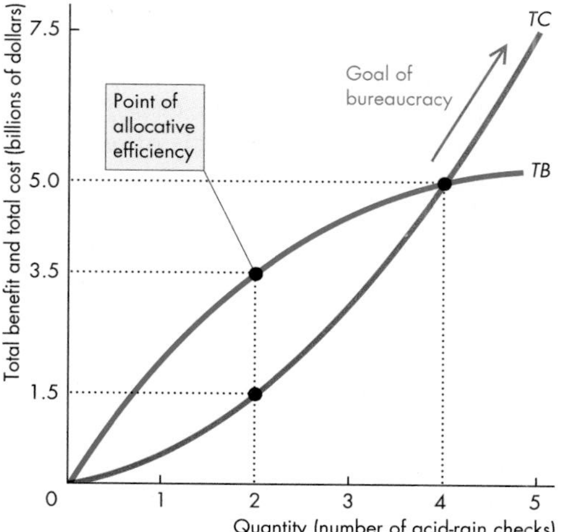

A bureau that maximizes its budget will seek to expand output and expenditure as far as possible. For example, the Ministry of the Environment prefers 4 acid-rain checks at a cost of $5 billion to the allocatively efficient number — 2 at a cost of $1.5 billion. The goal of the bureau is to move as far up the total cost curve as possible, as shown in the figure. If voters are well informed, politicians will not be able to deliver the taxes that enable the bureau to get beyond the point of allocative efficiency. But if some voters are rationally ignorant while others are well informed, the bureau may be able to raise its budget above the allocatively efficient level. In general, the bureau will produce a higher quantity than the one that maximizes net benefit.

net benefit will be zero. If the bureaucracy is able to increase its budget yet further, net benefit will be negative.

Is it really possible for the Ministry of the Environment to get away with pressing the politicians for a scale of spending greater than the one that will maximize net benefit? Won't it always pay the politicians to take control of the bureaucrats and cut back the scale of spending? We've already seen that when two political parties compete for votes, the party that gets closest to maximizing net benefit is the one that picks up the most votes. Don't these forces of competition for votes dominate the wishes of the bureaucrats and ensure that the maximum budget allowed them is the one that maximizes net benefit?

If voters are well informed and if their perception of their self-interest is correct, the political party that will win the election is the one that will hold the Ministry of the Environment budget to the efficient level of protection. But there is another possible equilibrium. It is one based on the principle of voter ignorance and well-informed interest groups.

Voter Ignorance and Well-Informed Interest Groups

One of the major propositions of public choice theory is that it does not pay voters to be well-informed about the issues on which they are voting unless those issues have an immediate and direct consequence for their own income. In other words, being rationally ignorant pays voters. **Rational ignorance** is the decision *not* to acquire information because the cost of doing so is greater than the benefit to be derived from having it. For example, each voter knows that he or she can make virtually no difference to the environment policy actually pursued by the government. Each voter also knows that it takes an enormous amount of time and effort to become even moderately well informed about alternative technologies and the most effective ways of achieving various levels of protection from acid rain. As a result, voters see it as being in their best interests to remain relatively uninformed about the technicalities of environmental protection issues. (Though we are using environmental protection as an example, the same applies to all aspects of government economic activity).

All voters are consumers of a clean environment, but not all voters produce it. Only a small number are in the latter category. Those voters who produce a clean environment, whether they work for firms that produce pollution control and monitoring equipment, or for government agencies charged with developing an environment policy, have a direct personal interest in the environment because it affects their incomes. These voters, in collaboration with the bureaucracies that deliver environmental protection, will exert a larger influence through the voting process than the relatively uninformed general voters who only consume this public good.

If the rationality of the uninformed voter and the rationality of the informed special interest group are taken into account, a political equilibrium emerges in which the size of government bureaus and the scale of provision of public goods exceed those that would maximize net benefit. This prediction of the economic model of bureaucracy applies to all public goods, including such items as national defence and public health, as well as environmental protection.

Before we leave this set of issues, you may be wondering why, if government tends to overproduce public goods, we have so much of a problem with acid rain and other atmosphere pollutants. There are two types of answer. First, most environmental pollution problems transcend national boundaries. To deal effectively with acid rain requires agreement between governments in Canada and the United States (as well as, more generally, with governments throughout the industrialized world). In just the same way as each individual stands to gain by being a free rider, so countries can also gain by free riding where global public goods are concerned. It is politically unpopular to propose policies to U.S. voters that impose costs on them that exceed the benefits accruing to them. Most of the benefits from controlling sulfur dioxide emission in the United States accrue to Canadian, not U.S., voters.

A second reason acid rain remains such a problem is technological. In the example that we worked with above, we imagined a technology that is not available. If such a technology did become available at relatively low cost, the predictions of the economic model of bureaucracy would become relevant and would imply a huge Ministry of Environment to rival that of the Ministry of National Defence today. But because the technologies for controlling acid rain are costly, they have only been adopted on a limited scale.

R E V I E W

Politicians implement their policies through ministries, departments, and agencies staffed by bureaucrats. In the economic model of bureaucracy, bureaucrats pursue the objective of budget maximization. Each agency tries to persuade politicians that its own budget should be increased. The politician has to balance the need for a bigger bureau budget against the cost of losing votes through higher taxes. If voters are well informed about the costs and benefits of the activities of a bureau, the maximum budget permitted it will be the one that maximizes net benefit. If voters are rationally ignorant, the best-informed voters will be those who both produce and consume a public good. Voters who only consume a public good will be relatively uninformed. The well-informed voters, in collaboration with the bureaucracies that produce public goods, will exert a larger influence than the uninformed voters who only consume the public goods, and so the scale of provision of public goods will exceed the one that maximizes net benefit. ■

We've now seen how voters, politicians, and bureaucrats interact to determine the scale of provision of public goods and services and the scale of redistribution and how they deal with external costs and benefits. But public goods and services have to be paid for with taxes. How does the political marketplace determine the scale and variety of taxes that we pay? And why is it that some goods are not only untaxed but are actually subsidized by the government? We've already seen one partial answer to some of these questions — taxes and subsidies may be used as a part of the government's attempt to deal with externalities. But that is not the entire story, as we'll now see.

Taxes and Subsidies

The largest portion of government revenue in Canada comes from income taxes, but sales taxes and the recently introduced goods and services tax (GST) are also important. In fact, the highest rates of tax in Canada are those on such goods as gasoline, alcoholic beverages, tobacco products, and some imported goods. Taxes on these types of items along with general sales taxes account for more than one-sixth of the revenue of the federal and provincial governments. Why are some goods taxed very highly and others hardly at all? Why are some goods even subsidized? What are the effects of taxes and subsidies on prices and on the quantities of the goods bought and sold? And who winds up paying the tax? Does the consumer pay, does the producer pay, or do they somehow share the tax between them?

Excise Taxes

An **excise tax** is a tax on the sale of a particular commodity. The tax may be set as a fixed dollar amount per unit of the commodity, in which case it is called a *specific tax*. Alternatively, the tax may be set as a fixed percentage of the value of the commodity, in which case it is called an *ad valorem tax*. The taxes on gasoline, alcoholic beverages, and tobacco products are all examples of excise taxes.

Figure 20.5 An Excise Tax

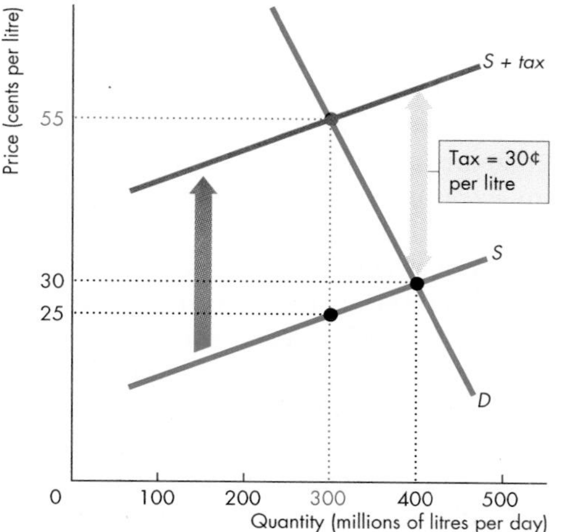

The demand curve for gasoline is *D* and the supply curve is *S*. In the absence of any taxes, the price of gasoline will be 30 cents per litre and 400 million litres a day will be bought and sold. When a tax of 30 cents per litre is imposed, the supply curve shifts upward to the curve labelled *S + tax*. The new equilibrium price is 55 cents per litre and 300 million litres a day are traded. The tax is shared between the consumer, who pays 25 cents, and the producer, who pays 10 cents.

Let's study the effects of an excise tax by considering the tax on gasoline. We'll assume that the market for gasoline is competitive. (The presence of monopolistic elements does affect the answer to the question that we're now examining, and we'll consider what that effect is when we've worked through the competitive case.)

Figure 20.5 illustrates the market for gasoline. The quantity of gasoline (measured in millions of litres a day) is shown on the horizontal axis and the price of gasoline (measured in cents per litre) is on the vertical axis. The demand curve for gasoline is *D* and the supply curve is *S*. If there is no tax on gasoline, its price is 30 cents a litre and 400 million litres of gasoline a day are bought and sold.

Let's suppose that a tax is imposed on gasoline at the rate of 30 cents a litre. If producers are willing to supply 400 million litres a day for 30 cents when there is no tax, they will be willing to supply that same quantity in the face of a 30 cent tax only if the price increases to 60 cents a litre. That is, they will want to get the 30 cents a litre they received before, plus the additional 30 cents that they now have to hand over to the government in the form of a gasoline tax. As a result of the tax, the supply curve shifts upward by the amount of the tax and becomes the red curve labelled *S + tax*. The new supply curve intersects the demand curve at a quantity of 300 million litres a day and at a price of 55 cents a litre. This situation is the equilibrium after the imposition of the tax. Why doesn't the equilibrium occur at 60 cents — the original price plus the tax?

Who Pays the Tax? When a tax of 30 cents a litre is imposed on gasoline, Fig. 20.5 illustrates that the price of gasoline increases, but only by 25 cents, to 55 cents. Thus the price paid by gasoline consumers increases by less than the tax. The government collects 30 cents a litre in tax, but the consumer pays only an extra 25 cents a litre for gasoline. Who pays the other 5 cents? The answer must be the producer. You can see that the producer does, in fact, pay the missing 5 cents because the net receipts fall from 30 cents a litre to 25 cents a litre when the quantity traded falls to 300 million litres a day.

The way the tax payment is divided between the increase in the price paid by the consumer and the fall in the price received by the producer depends on the elasticity of demand and supply. If supply is perfectly elastic — the supply curve is horizontal — the rise in price will be equal to the tax. If supply is perfectly inelastic — the supply curve is vertical — there will be no change in either the price or the quantity traded and the producer will pay the entire amount of the tax.

If demand is perfectly elastic, the tax will leave the price unchanged, so the entire burden will fall on the producers. They will decrease the quantity supplied until marginal cost is below the price by the amount of the tax. The more inelastic the demand, the larger is the rise in price and the smaller is the fall in the quantity traded that results from the imposition of a tax. Furthermore, the more inelastic the demand, the larger is the fraction of the tax paid by the consumer and the smaller is the fraction borne by the producers.

Although we have just examined the effects of an excise tax on gasoline, the same basic analysis has widespread application. Taxes on alcohol and tobacco, sales taxes, and even taxes imposed in the labour market — for example personal income taxes and health and social insurance levies (taxes) — can be analysed in the same manner. The imposition of a tax shifts the supply curve upward by the amount of the tax. The new equilibrium is determined at a higher price and a lower quantity traded. The division of the burden of the tax between a rise in the price of the good being traded and a fall in the receipts of its producer depends on the elasticities of demand and supply.

Monopoly Markets The imposition of a sales tax or excise tax on a monopoly works in a manner similar to the way it works in a competitive industry. However, a monopoly industry starts with a higher price and smaller quantity traded than the same industry would have in competitive conditions. The monopoly determines its profit-maximizing price by making marginal revenue and marginal cost equal. The tax represents an increase in the marginal cost. The monopoly's marginal cost curve shifts upward by the amount of the tax. Monopoly profit is maximized by producing the output at which marginal cost plus the tax equals marginal revenue. Thus the imposition of a sales tax or an excise tax on a monopoly industry has the effect of raising the price and lowering output in the same way that it does in a competitive industry.

Why Do Tax Rates Vary?

Why is the structure of taxes the way it is? Why do we tax alcohol, tobacco, and gasoline at a very high rate and some goods not at all? There are two main reasons. First, the consumption of some goods, as we saw in Chapter 19, imposes external costs. By taxing the purchase and consumption of such goods, the government can make people take into account the external costs they are imposing on others when they make their own consumption choices. Second, taxes create *deadweight losses*, and by levying taxes on different commodities at different rates, the deadweight loss arising from raising a given amount of revenue can be minimized. Let's look at these two explanations for different tax rates a bit more closely.

External Costs Many goods that are taxed at a high rate have external costs. For example, the high tax on gasoline in part enables road users to be confronted with the marginal social cost of the congestion that they impose on others. The high taxes on alcohol and tobacco products in part serve to confront drinkers and smokers with the external costs that their consumption habits impose on others. The impairment of long-term health that results from using these products and the subsequent health care costs may lead to costs that are borne by others. These costs are not taken into account when a person is deciding whether or not to drink or smoke.

Some goods that have high external costs associated with their consumption are not taxed. Instead, they are made illegal. Marijuana and cocaine are important examples of such goods. Large amounts of these goods are consumed every day in Canada, and the illegal markets in which they are traded generate large external costs. An alternative way of organizing these markets would be to make these drugs legal but to impose heavy taxes on them. Sufficiently high taxes would leave the quantities consumed similar to (perhaps even smaller than) what they are now, and would confront the users with the marginal social cost of their actions. Such taxes would also result in a source of revenue (perhaps a large one) for the government. (Of course, matters relating to drugs have dimensions that go beyond a narrow economic calculation. Some people believe that the consumption of these drugs is so immoral that it would be equally immoral for the government or anyone else to profit legally from their production and consumption. These considerations, important though they are, go beyond the scope of economics.)

Let's now look at the deadweight loss that arises from taxes and the way in which this loss can be minimized.

Minimizing the Deadweight Loss of Taxes It's easy to see that taxes create deadweight loss by returning to the example of the gasoline tax that you studied in Fig. 20.5. The deadweight loss associated with the gasoline tax is illustrated in Fig. 20.6. Without a tax, 400 million litres of gasoline a day are consumed at a price of 30 cent a litre. With a 30-cent tax, the price paid by the consumer rises to 55 cents a litre and the quantity consumed declines to 300 million litres a day. There is a loss of consumer surplus arising from this price increase and quantity decrease. There is also a loss of producer surplus. Producers now receive

Figure 20.6 The Deadweight Loss from an Excise Tax

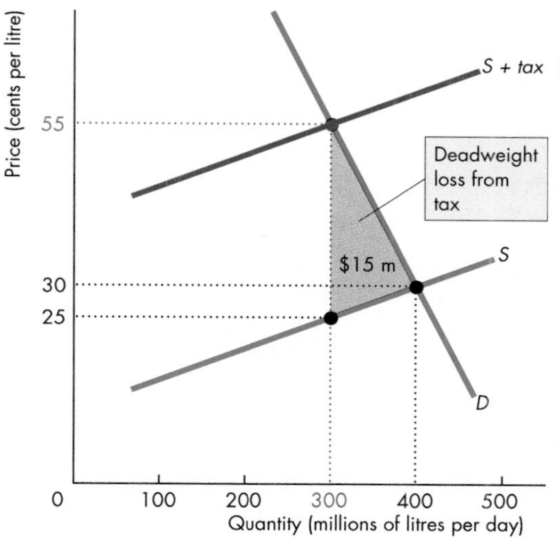

An excise tax creates a deadweight loss represented by the grey triangle. The tax revenue collected is 30 cents per litre on 300 million litres, $90 million per day. The deadweight loss from the tax is $15 million per day. That is, raising a tax revenue of $90 million per day creates a deadweight loss of $15 million per day.

25 cents a litre for 300 million litres, compared with 30 cents a litre for 400 million litres in the absence of taxes. The deadweight loss — the sum of the loss of consumer surplus and producer surplus — is indicated by the grey triangle in Fig. 20.6. The value of that triangle is $15 million a day.[1] But how much revenue is raised by this tax? Since 300 million litres of gasoline are sold each day and since the tax is 30 cents a litre, total revenue from the tax is $90 million a day (300 million litres × $0.30). Thus raising revenue of $90 million a day by using the gasoline tax creates a deadweight loss of $15 million a day — one-sixth of the tax revenue.

[1]You can calculate the area of the triangle by using the following formula:

$$\frac{\text{base} \times \text{height}}{2}.$$

If you turn the triangle on its side, its base is 30 cents, the size of the tax. Its height then becomes the reduction in the quantity sold — 100 million litres a day.

$$\frac{\$0.30 \times 100 \text{ million}}{2} = \$15 \text{ million}$$

One of the main influences on the deadweight loss arising from a tax is the elasticity of demand for the product. The demand for gasoline is fairly inelastic. As a consequence, when a tax is imposed, the quantity demanded falls by a smaller percentage than the percentage rise in price. In the example that we've just studied, the quantity demanded falls by 25 percent, but the price increases by 83.33 percent. To see the importance of the elasticity of demand, let's consider a different commodity — apple juice. So that we can make a quick and direct comparison, let's assume that the apple juice market is exactly as big as the market for gasoline. Figure 20.7 illustrates this market. The demand curve for apple juice is *D* and the supply curve is *S*. Apple juice is not taxed, and so

Figure 20.7 Why We Don't Tax Apple Juice

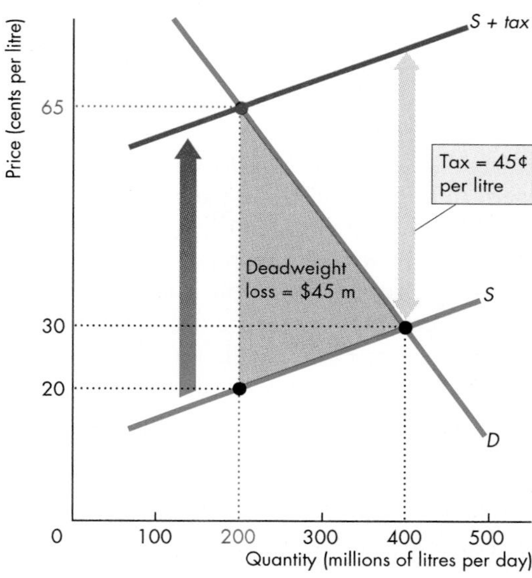

The demand curve for apple juice is *D* and the supply curve is *S*. The equilibrium price is 30 cents per litre and 400 million litres of juice are traded per day. To raise $90 million of tax revenue, a tax of 45 cents per litre will have to be imposed. The introduction of this tax shifts the supply curve to the one labelled *S + tax*. The price rises to 65 cents per litre and the quantity traded falls to 200 million litres a day. The deadweight loss is represented by the grey triangle and equals $45 million per day. The deadweight loss from taxing apple juice is much larger than that from taxing gasoline (Fig. 20.6) because the demand for apple juice is more elastic than the demand for gasoline. Items that have a low elasticity of demand are taxed more heavily than items that have a high elasticity of demand.

the price is 30 cents a litre — where the supply curve and the demand curve intersect — and the quantity of apple juice traded is 400 million litres a day.

Now suppose that the government contemplates abolishing the gasoline tax and taxing apple juice instead. The demand for apple juice is more elastic than the demand for gasoline because apple juice has many good substitutes in the form of other fruit juices. The government wants to raise $90 million a day so that its total revenue is not affected by this tax change. The government's economists, armed with their statistical estimates of the demand and supply curves for apple juice that appear in Fig. 20.7, calculate that a tax of 45 cents a litre will do the job. With such a tax, the supply curve will shift upward to the curve labelled *S + tax*. This new supply curve intersects the demand curve at a price of 65 cents a litre and at a quantity of 200 million litres a day. The price at which suppliers are willing to produce 200 million litres a day is 20 cents a litre. The government collects a tax of 45 cents a litre on 200 million litres a day, so it collects a total revenue of $90 million a day — exactly the amount that it requires.

But what is the deadweight loss in this case? The answer can be seen by looking at the grey triangle in Fig. 20.7. The magnitude of that deadweight loss is $45 million.[2] Notice how much bigger the deadweight loss is from taxing apple juice than from taxing gasoline. For apple juice, the deadweight loss is one-half the revenue raised, while for gasoline it is only one-sixth. Yet the two supply curves are identical, and the examples were set up to ensure that the initial no-tax prices and quantities were identical. The difference between the two cases is the elasticity of demand. For gasoline, the quantity demanded falls by only 25 percent when the price almost doubles, but for apple juice, the quantity demanded falls by 50 percent when the price slightly more than doubles.

You can now see why taxing apple juice is not on the political agenda of any of the major parties.

Vote-seeking politicians seek out taxes that benefit the median voter. Other things being equal, they thus try to minimize the deadweight loss of raising a given amount of revenue. Equivalently, they tax items with inelastic demand more heavily than items with elastic demand.

The Goods and Services Tax

The goods and services tax (GST) that was introduced in Canada in 1991 can be analysed using the same type of economic model that we have just used to study the effects of excise taxes. In introducing the GST, the federal government has replaced the old federal sales tax on *manufactured* goods with a tax on a broader range of goods and services. The old sales tax was levied at a higher rate than the new tax but on a narrower range of activities. By lowering the tax rate on manufactures, the government is reducing the deadweight loss that results from its tax collection on those goods. By imposing a tax on previously untaxed services, the government is increasing the deadweight loss of its tax collection on those activities. Whether the deadweight loss of raising a given amount of tax will increase or decrease as a result of the introduction of the GST depends on the elasticity of demand for services relative to the elasticity of demand for manufactures. But even if services and manufactures have the same elasticity of demand, on the average, the broader-based GST will lower the deadweight loss compared with that incurred from the sales tax on manufactures. The reason is that the deadweight loss arising from a tax increases more quickly than in proportion to the scale of the tax itself. If the demand for services is less elastic than the demand for manufactures, then the deadweight loss from the GST will be smaller, compared with that from the sales tax on manufactures. Most economists estimate that the GST will have a smaller deadweight loss per dollar of revenue raised than the tax that it replaced.

Let's now leave our study of taxes and turn to an examination of subsidies.

Subsidies

In the aggregate, subsidies do not constitute a large fraction of government expenditure at either the federal or the provincial level. Nevertheless, subsidies constitute an important component of income in one industry — agriculture. Let's study subsidies by examining the market for wheat.

Suppose that the wheat market is as illustrated

---

[2]This deadweight loss is calculated in exactly the same way as the deadweight loss from the gasoline tax (note 1 on p. 527). Turning the deadweight loss triangle on its side, the base is 90 cents and the height is 200 million litres. Using the formula for the area of the triangle — the base multiplied by the height divided by 2 — you can calculate the daily deadweight loss as:

$$\frac{\$0.45 \times 200 \text{ million}}{2} = \$45 \text{ million}$$

Figure 20.8 Subsidies

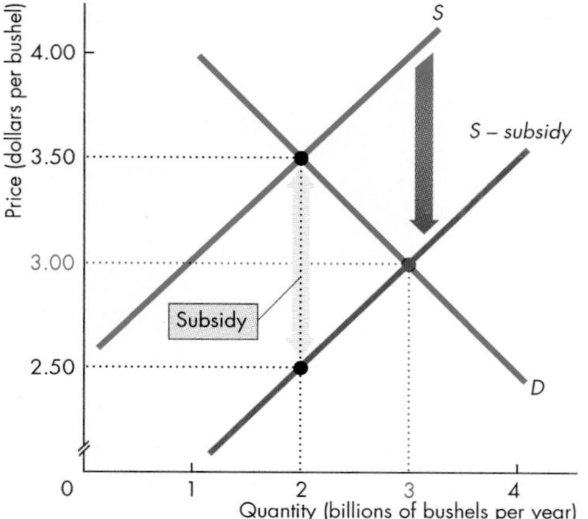

The demand curve for wheat is *D* and the supply curve is *S*. A competitive market with no taxes or subsidies produces 2 billion bushels of wheat per year at a price of $3.50 per bushel. If the government subsidizes wheat production by $1 per bushel, the supply curve shifts downward to the curve labelled *S – subsidy*. The price of wheat falls to $3 per bushel and the quantity produced increases to 3 billion bushels per year. Along with the subsidy, wheat growers receive just enough revenue from the market to cover their costs.

in Fig. 20.8. The demand curve is *D* and the supply curve is *S*. Two billion bushels a year are produced at a price of $3.50 a bushel. Now suppose that the government offers wheat growers a subsidy of $1 a bushel. If suppliers are willing to supply 2 billion bushels a year for $3.50 without a subsidy, they will be willing to supply that same quantity for $2.50 with a $1 subsidy. The supply curve for wheat, therefore, shifts downward by the amount of the subsidy and becomes the curve labelled *S – subsidy*. The new supply curve intersects the demand curve at a price of $3 a bushel and a quantity of 3 billion bushels a year. This price and quantity is the new equilibrium. The price of wheat falls by 50 cents a bushel. Consumers pay 50 cents a bushel less and producers' costs rise by 50 cents a bushel. The 50-cent increase in costs and the 50-cent cut in the price are made up by the subsidy to the producer.

The effect of subsidies in agriculture, and of the taxes that pay those subsidies, are examined in Reading Between the Lines, pp. 530-531.

Subsidies with Quotas

In Canada, farmers not only receive subsidies on production but also have quotas imposed on their sales. A **quota** is a limit to the quantity that a firm is permitted to sell. When a group of producers can enforce quotas, it is possible to restrict output and thereby obtain monopoly profit. We can see the effects of quotas and subsidies in Fig. 20.9. Suppose that the wheat marketing board establishes and enforces quotas for each producer that result in total output of 2 billion bushels a year (shown by the vertical line marked "Quota" in the figure). At this output level, consumers are willing to pay $3.50 a bushel for the wheat, so that will be its market price. Producers also get a subsidy of $1 on every bushel they produce, so the supply curve becomes the one labelled *S – subsidy*. With the subsidy and a market price of $3.50, producers would like to supply

Figure 20.9 Subsidies with Quotas

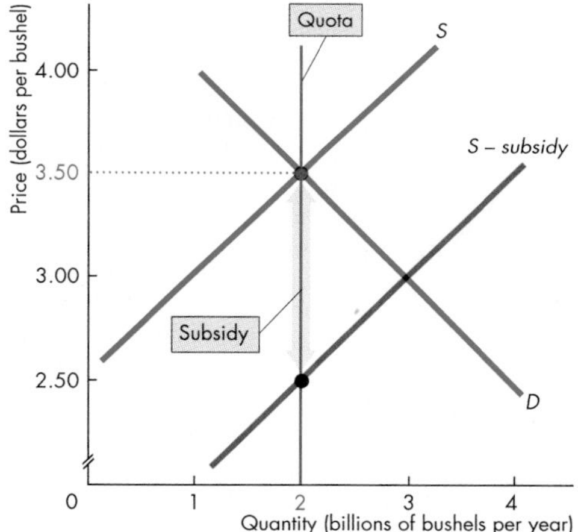

A competitive wheat market with no taxes or subsidies produces 2 billion bushels per year at a price of $3.50 per bushel — the point of intersection of the curves *D* and *S*. A subsidy of $1 per bushel shifts the supply curve to *S – subsidy*. But if a quota is introduced at the same time as the subsidy, the output of each producer is restricted so that total output stays at 2 billion bushels per year, and the price remains $3.50 per bushel. With the quota, producers receive $3.50 from the market plus $1 from the government. Producers gain from the quota. The revenue from the market covers costs, so the subsidy is like a monopoly profit.

Farm Subsidies

Costly business

Big subsidies for agriculture

A study by the Organization for Economic Co-operation & Development [OECD] gives further evidence of the high cost of agricultural subsidies.

The report provides a multi-country comparison of subsidies, price supports and tariff protection for agriculture. Not surprisingly, Japan's farming community is found to be the most heavily subsidized and New Zealand's, the least.

Canada fares worse than anticipated. Measures including import controls for supply-managed milk, eggs, poultry and turkey producers, more than $700 million in grain-transport subsidies and billions in income support for Prairie grain farmers provide protection for Canadian farmers to levels almost as high as farmers in the European Community. In terms of each farm job saved, the cost is US $100,000 for Canada, compared with $13,000-$20,000 in the U.S., Japan and the EC.

Agricultural subsidies cost OECD countries an estimated $72 billion in lost and forgone income. Elimination of subsidies would lead to overall standard of living increases for all countries. The Australian and New Zealand agricultural communities would be major beneficiaries. The study estimates Canada's agricultural production would go down by 16.7%, compared with an average decline of 13.6% for all OECD countries. However, nonfarm output in Canada would rise by 0.9% and real household income would increase by 1.3%.

Canada is part of the Cairns group of 14 agricultural exporting countries calling for the elimination of all farm protection. At the latest meeting of the Uruguay Round of General Agreement on Tariffs & Trade negotiations on agriculture, Canada gave mixed signals, pushing for freer trade in grains but seeking maintenance and clarification of supply-management provisions under Article 11 of GATT.

Clearly, the overnight elimination of subsidies would create havoc. But that's not what is contemplated in the GATT negotiations. The principle adopted by the negotiating countries is that agricultural policies should be more market-oriented with respect to trade, and agricultural support and protection programs should be substantially and progressively reduced over an agreed-on period of time. This permits each country to work out measures to help the agricultural community adjust to less protection.

As the OECD study confirms, that principle remains sound.

***The Financial Post,* April 9, 1990**

The Essence of the Story

- An Organization for Economic Cooperation & Development (OECD) study shows that Japan's farmers are the most heavily subsidized and New Zealand's, the least.
- Canadian farm subsidies are high and almost as high as those in the European Community.
- Each farm job saved in Canada costs US $100,000. The comparable figure for the United States, Japan, and the European Community is $13,000-$20,000.
- Eliminating subsidies would increase agricultural production in Australia and New Zealand and decrease it in Canada and in the OECD countries in total. But nonfarm output in Canada would rise by 0.9% and real household income would increase by 1.3%. The standard of living would increase for all countries.
- The sudden elimination of subsidies would cause hardship but their gradual elimination would bring benefits and enable each country to help its farmers adjust to less protection.

Background and Analysis

- Canada's farm sector is subsidized and its nonfarm industrial and service sectors are taxed to pay for the farm subsidies.
- Figure (a) illustrates these subsidies and taxes and their effects on prices and output levels.
- Farm subsidies (part i) shift the supply curve of farm products downward leading to a lower price for consumers and a higher quantity of farm products.
- Taxes levied on the rest of the economy (part ii) shift the supply curve of nonfarm products upward leading to a higher price for consumers and a lower quantity of nonfarm products.
- The existing high level of subsidies and taxes is a political equilibrium that balances the interests of a strong agricultural lobby against the interests of less organized consumers.
- Figure (b) shows the effect of removing farm subsidies and the taxes that pay them: the prices of farm products increase and Canadian farm output decreases; the prices of nonfarm products decrease and nonfarm output increases.
- In fact, the prices of farm products would increase very little because there is an abundant supply of farm products from the rest of the world at prices close to those now prevailing.
- There is a net gain to consumers because the benefits of lower priced nonfarm products more than compensates them for the slightly higher priced farm products.
- There is net loss to Canadian farmers and many of them have to leave the farm sector and find their next highest value employment in the nonfarm sector.
- International initiatives such as the Cairns group and the Uruguay Round of the General Agreement on Tariffs & Trade are attempts to change the balance of power between farmers and consumers and to change the political equilibrium.

(a) Prices and outputs with subsidies and taxes

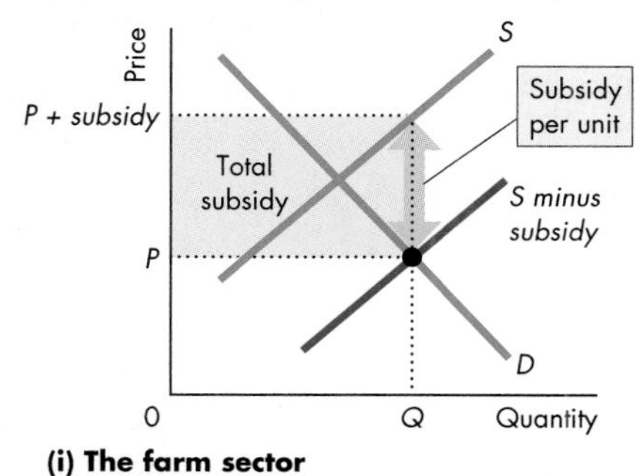

(i) The farm sector

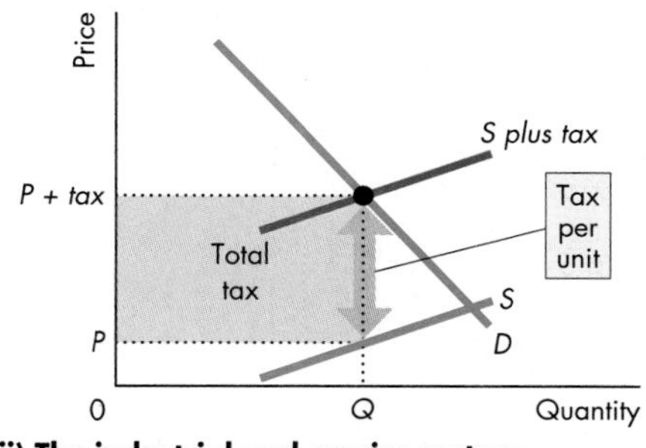

(ii) The industrial and service sectors

(b) Prices and outputs with subsidies and taxes eliminated

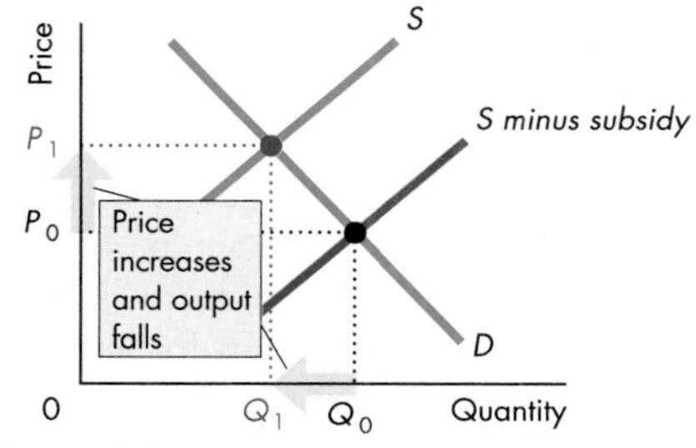

(i) The farm sector

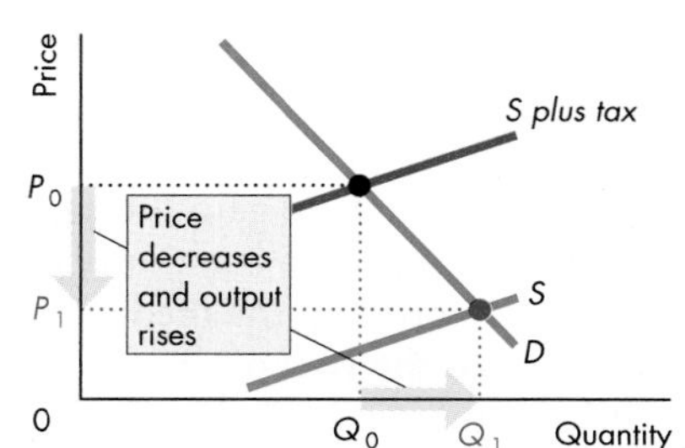

(ii) The industrial and service sectors

4 billion bushels a year — the quantity read off from the new (red) supply curve at the price of $3.50. But they're prevented from doing so by the quota.

With output restricted to 2 billion bushels of wheat, producers' costs are $3.50 a bushel. They also sell their wheat for $3.50 a bushel. In addition, they receive $1 a bushel in subsidies from the government. The subsidy is like a monopoly profit.

It is interesting to contrast this situation with the one in which there is a subsidy but no quota. Without a quota, output is 3 billion bushels and marginal cost is $4 a bushel. The market price is $3 a bushel so the subsidy of $1 a bushel makes up the difference between the market price and marginal cost. Without a quota, the price plus the subsidy just cover marginal cost. With a quota, price covers marginal cost and the subsidy is a surplus for the producer — an excess revenue over cost.

From the point of view of producers, subsidies with quotas are clearly a good thing. But they are a bad thing from the point of view of consumers. To pay a subsidy, the government has to raise taxes that create deadweight loss. So why do we have subsidies with quotas?

Why Subsidies and Quotas? The existence of quotas and subsidies is explained by the fact that the people who stand to gain from such a system are a relatively well-defined group and easily organized into a political force. Those who stand to lose are highly diffused and much more difficult and costly to organize. As a result, the political equilibrium that prevails is one in which a relatively small number of people gain a significant amount per person while a relatively large number of people each lose a small — perhaps unnoticeable — amount.

■ We have now reviewed the structure of the government sector, market failure, and the theory of public choice that explains how politicians, bureaucrats, and voters interact to determine the scale of provision of public goods, the extent to which taxes and subsidies are used to cope with externalities, the amount of income redistribution, and the levels of taxes and subsidies.

We have seen that a political equilibrium emerges in which no individual can improve his or her own situation by proposing or implementing a different policy. Each political party devises a program that appeals as closely as possible to half the electorate. The parties differ in their rhetoric because of differences in the particular half of the electorate to which they appeal, but the actions of each are similar to those of the others. Bureaus grow to such a size that the benefit from increasing their budgets still further offsets, in the eyes of politicians, the perceived cost of higher taxes and their consequences for lost votes. Voters are as well informed as it pays them to be — they are rationally ignorant.

In the next chapter, we're going to study a further range of government actions — interventions in markets for goods and services in which there are monopoly and cartel elements.

SUMMARY

The Political Marketplace

The political marketplace has three types of actors: voters, politicians, and bureaucrats. Voters are the consumers of the outcome of the political process. They express their demands through votes, campaign contributions, and lobbying. Public choices are made by politicians and implemented by bureaucrats. The objective of politicians is to win enough votes to be elected and then to remain in office. They do so by offering policies that are likely to gain the support of a majority of voters. To appeal to a majority of voters, politicians have to appeal to the median voter. Since politicians aim for the vote of the median voter, their policies will resemble each others' — they will be minimally differentiated. For example, in designing income redistribution policies, politicians will transfer from the rich not only to the poor but to all those with incomes at or below the median. Redistribution will be aimed at making the median voter as rich as possible.

Bureaucrats, in pursuing their own objectives, seek to maximize the budgets of their own bureaus. If voters are well informed, politicians will not be able to collect taxes to enable bureaucrats to achieve budgets in excess of those that maximize net benefit. But if voters are rationally ignorant, producer interests may result in voters' support for taxes that, in turn, support a level of provision of public goods exceeding the one that maximizes net benefit. (pp. 513-524)

Taxes and Subsidies

The imposition of a tax on a good shifts the supply curve upward, raises the price of the good, and lowers the quantity traded. A tax is shared between the consumer and the producer. A tax creates a deadweight loss whose size depends on the elasticity of demand. Taxing goods that have a low elasticity of demand minimizes the deadweight loss from taxation. Thus the highest tax rates are applied to goods with a low elasticity of demand.

Subsidizing a good shifts the supply curve downward, lowers the price of the good, and increases the quantity traded. Subsidies combined with quotas generate additional income for producers at the expense of consumers. (pp. 524-532)

KEY ELEMENTS

Key Terms

Bureaucrats, 513
Excise tax, 524
Lobbying, 513
Median voter theorem, 519
Political equilibrium, 514
Politicians, 513
Principle of minimum differentiation, 518
Quota, 529
Rational ignorance, 523
Voters, 513

Key Figures

Figure 20.1 Provision of a Public Good in a Political System, 515
Figure 20.2 The Principle of Minimum Differentiation, 518
Figure 20.3 The Median Voter Theorem, 519
Figure 20.4 Bureaucratic Overprovision, 523
Figure 20.5 An Excise Tax, 525
Figure 20.8 Subsidies, 529
Figure 20.9 Subsidies with Quotas, 529

REVIEW QUESTIONS

1 What are the three types of actors in the political marketplace?

2 Describe the economic functions of voters, and explain how they make their economic choices.

3 Describe the economic functions of politicians, and explain how they make their economic choices.

4 What is meant by "political equilibrium"?

5 What is the principle of minimum differentiation?

6 How does the principle of minimum differentiation explain political parties' policy platforms?

7 What is the median voter theorem?

8 What features of political choices does the median voter theorem explain?

9 What are the economic functions of bureaucrats, and how do they make their economic choices?

10 Why is it rational for voters to be ignorant?

11 Explain why it is likely that the scale of provision of public goods will exceed the allocatively efficient scale.

PROBLEMS

1 Your local city council is contemplating upgrading its system for controlling traffic signals. By installing a sophisticated computer with sensing mechanisms at all the major intersections, the council believes that it can better adjust the timing of the signal changes and improve the speed of the traffic flow. The bigger the computer it buys, the better job it can do, and the more sensors installed, the more intersections it can monitor and the faster the overall traffic flow that will result. The mayor and the other elected officials who are working on the proposal want to determine the scale and sophistication of the system that will win them the most votes. The bureaucrats in the city traffic department want to maximize the budget. Suppose that you are an economist observing this public choice. Your job is to calculate the scale of provision of this public good that maximizes net benefit — that achieves allocative efficiency.

a) What data would you need in order to reach your own conclusions?

b) What does the public choice theory predict will be the scale of provision chosen?

c) How could you, as an informed voter, attempt to influence the choice?

2 Three people — Joe, Jim, and Jon — have incomes of $1,000, $500, and $250 respectively. Set up a proposed redistribution of income between these three people that will achieve majority support.

Now assume that your proposal is implemented. Set up another scheme that will also command a majority support. Show that you can find a voting cycle.

3 A community of 9 people, identified by letters A through I, have strong but differing views about a local factory that is polluting the atmosphere. Some of them work at the factory and don't want the government to take any action against it, while others want to see the imposition of a huge tax based on the scale of pollution. The preferences of each person concerning the scale of the tax that should be imposed are as follows:

Person	Tax rate (percent of firm's profit)
A	100
B	90
C	80
D	70
E	60
F	0
G	0
H	0
I	0

Suppose there are two political parties competing for office in this community. What tax rate would the parties propose?

4 You are give the following information about a perfectly competitive market for cookies:

Price (dollars per kilogram)	Quantity demanded (kilograms per month)	Quantity supplied (kilograms per month)
30	0	12
24	1	10
18	2	8
12	3	6
6	4	4
0	5	0

a) What are the competitive equilibrium price and quantity traded?

b) Suppose that a 10 percent tax is imposed on cookies.

(i) What is the new price of cookies?

(ii) What is the new quantity traded?

(iii) What is the total amount of tax revenue raised by the government?

(iv) What is the deadweight loss?

c) Now suppose that cookies are not taxed but are instead subsidized by 10 percent.

(i) What happens to the price of cookies?

(ii) What happens to the quantity traded?

(iii) How much is the subsidy paid out by the government?

(iv) Suppose that along with the subsidy a quota is imposed on cookie producers. What is the scale of the quota that will maximize profit for the producer?

5 A city of 1 million people has established a permanent Department of Library Services, staffed by public servants and experts in library science. The department decides to establish a mobile library service. The benefits and costs of the mobile library are set out in the following table:

Price of one subscription (dollars)	Number of subscribers	Marginal external benefit per subscriber (dollars)	Marginal cost of one subscription (dollars)
10	180,000	20	90
15	160,000	30	75
20	140,000	40	60
25	120,000	50	45
30	100,000	60	30
35	80,000	70	15

a) What is the objective of the head of the Department of Library Services?

b) Suppose that the City Council limits the budget of the department to the maximum budget that covers total social benefit.

i) What is the size of the budget for the mobile library?

ii) How many subscribers does the mobile library attract?

c) Compare the budget and number of subscribers of the mobile library with the levels that would achieve allocative efficiency.

d) Compare the budget and number of subscribers of the mobile library with the levels that would prevail in a competitive equilibrium.

CHAPTER 21

Competition Policy

After studying this chapter, you will be able to:

- Define regulation.
- Describe the main trends in regulation and deregulation.
- Explain what a Crown corporation is.
- Describe the main elements of Canada's anti-combine law.
- Explain how anti-combine law has evolved in Canada.
- Distinguish between the public interest and capture theories of government intervention in the marketplace.
- Explain how the regulation of natural monopolies affects prices, outputs, profits, and the distribution of the gains from trade between consumers and producers.
- Explain how Crown corporations' outputs, costs, and prices are determined and how these corporations distribute the gains from trade between consumers and producers.
- Explain how anti-combine laws affect prices, outputs, profits, and the distribution of the gains from trade between consumers and producers.

Public Interest or Special Interests?

SOME OF THE MOST important goods and services that you consume are bought from regulated natural monopolies. Water, gas, and cable TV are examples. Why are the industries that produce these goods and services regulated? How are they regulated? And do the regulations work in the interests of consumers — the public interest — or do they serve the interests of the producer — a special interest? ■ Regulation extends beyond natural monopoly to cartels. For example, until 1984, the price of all air transport in Canada and the routes that airlines could fly were regulated by the Canadian Transport Commission. But in 1984, a process of domestic air travel deregulation began. The government still regulates the airline industry to ensure safety standards, but airlines have become less restricted in their choice of routes and fares. Crude oil, domestic gas, and the financial sector — banking and insurance and other financial services — were regulated in the past but in recent years have begun to be deregulated. Why do we sometimes regulate an industry and at other times deregulate that same industry? Whose interest is served by regulation and deregulation — the consumer or the producer? ■ Many vital consumer goods and services are bought from publicly owned natural monopolies — federal and provincial Crown corporations. Among the more important federal Crown corporations are Canada Post, the Canadian Broadcasting Corporation (CBC), Canadian National Railways, and VIA Rail. The biggest provincial Crown corporations are the hydro companies such as B.C. Hydro. Just as there has been a retreat from regulation of natural monopoly, there has also been a tendency to reduce government influence in the ownership of natural monopoly — a process called privatization. For example, in recent years, such national Crown corporations as Air Canada have been sold to private owners. Provincial Crown corporations, such as the Potash Corporation of Saskatchewan, have also been privatized. Why do Crown corporations operate some industries while others are left in private hands? And how do

Crown corporations operate? Are they more efficient or less efficient than private corporations? ■ Regulation and public ownership represent just two ways in which government actions influence the market economy. A third is the enactment of laws known in Canada as anti-combine laws. Anti-combine laws can be used to block mergers between large competing companies, to break up large combines, and to prevent combines and collusive agreements to restrict competition. For example, until 1980, if you wanted to buy telephone equipment to hook onto your Bell Canada wires, you had no choice but to buy from Northern Telecom. Northern Telecom happened to be a wholly owned subsidiary of Bell Canada. In 1980, after an investigation by the Restrictive Trade Practices Commission (part of Consumer and Corporate Affairs Canada), Bell was ordered to permit its customers to buy equipment from any supplier. The result was dramatic. A proliferation of the variety of equipment, in terms of both quality and features, resulted in a huge gain for consumers, and competition among the many suppliers kept prices far below the levels that had prevailed before 1980. What exactly are Canada's anti-combine laws? How have they evolved over the years? How are they used today? And do our anti-combine laws always serve consumer interests — the public interest — or do they sometimes serve the interests of producer groups — special interests?

■ This chapter[1] studies government intervention in the marketplace — the actions taken by government to regulate, control, and influence trading in markets for goods and services. It begins by describing the various ways in which government intervenes in monopolistic and oligopolistic markets. The chapter draws on your earlier study of how these markets work and on your knowledge of the gains from trade — of consumer surplus and producer surplus. It shows how consumers and producers might redistribute those gains and identifies who stands to gain and who stands to lose from various types of government intervention. And since such intervention is supplied by politicians and bureaucrats, the chapter also looks at the economic behaviour of these groups, expanding on what you learned in the previous chapter about public choice and the political "marketplace."

[1]The chapter has benefitted enormously from the work of Christopher Green. See Christopher Green, *Canadian Industrial Organization and Policy*, 3rd ed. (Toronto: McGraw Hill Ryerson, 1990).

Market Intervention

There are three main ways in which the government intervenes in the marketplace to influence *what, how,* and *for whom* various goods and services are produced:

- Regulation
- Nationalization
- Legislation

Regulation

Regulation consists of rules administered by a government agency to restrict economic activity by determining prices, product standards and types, and the conditions under which new firms may enter an industry. In order to implement its regulations, the government establishes agencies to oversee the rules and ensure their enforcement. The first such economic regulation in Canada was the Railway Act of 1888, which regulated railway rates. Since that time, regulation has spread to such industries as banking and financial services, telecommunications, trucking, airlines and buses, and dozens of agricultural products. Since the early 1980s, there has been a tendency to deregulate the Canadian economy. **Deregulation** is the process of removing restrictions on prices, product standards and types, and entry conditions. In recent years, deregulation has occurred in domestic air transport, crude oil and natural gas, and banking and financial services.

Nationalization

Nationalization is the act of placing a corporation under public ownership. In Canada, nationalized corporations are called **Crown corporations**. The most important Crown corporations, aside from Canada Post, the CBC, CN, and VIA Rail, are Atomic Energy of Canada Ltd. and Petro-Canada. There are many provincial Crown corporations, the most important of which are the provincial hydro companies. Just as there has been a tendency to deregulate the Canadian economy in recent years, there has also been a tendency to privatize it. **Privatization** is the process of selling a publicly owned corporation to private shareholders.

Legislation

Legislation to influence market behaviour takes the form of laws defining illegal conduct. These laws are then enforced through the courts. In Canada, we call a law that regulates market behaviour an **anti-combine law**. The main thrust of our anti-combine law is the prohibition of monopoly practices and of restricting output in order to achieve higher prices and profits.

To understand why the government intervenes in the market economy and to work out the effects of its interventions, we need to identify the gains and losses that government actions can create. These gains and losses are the consumer surplus and producer surplus associated with different output levels and prices. These concepts were explained in some detail in Chapters 7 and 13. This chapter, therefore, gives a more streamlined overview of these concepts and of the way in which their magnitudes are affected by the price at which a good is sold and the quantity traded.

Surpluses and Their Distribution

Consumer surplus is the difference between the maximum amount that consumers are willing to pay and the amount that they actually do pay for a given quantity of a good. It is the gain from trade accruing to consumers. *Producer surplus* is the difference between the producer's revenue and the opportunity cost of production. It is the gain from trade accruing to producers. **Total surplus** is the sum of consumer surplus and producer surplus.

The lower the price and the larger the quantity traded, the larger is consumer surplus. The closer the price and quantity traded to the monopoly profit maximizing levels, the larger is producer surplus. Total surplus is maximized (in the absence of external costs and benefits) when marginal cost equals price. In this situation, allocative efficiency is achieved.

There is a conflict between maximizing producer surplus and maximizing total surplus. Monopoly firms have an incentive to restrict output below the competitive level, increasing producer surplus but reducing consumer surplus and creating deadweight loss. Thus there is a tension between the public interest of maximizing total surplus and the producer's interest of maximizing monopoly profit and producer surplus. This tension is of central importance in the economic theory of regulation. Let's now examine that theory.

Economic Theory of Intervention

The economic theory of intervention is part of the broader theory of public choice. You have already met that theory in Chapter 20 and seen the main components of a public choice model. We're going to re-examine the main features of such a model but with an emphasis on the regulatory aspects of government behaviour. We'll examine the demand for government actions, the supply of those actions, and the political equilibrium — the balancing of demands and supplies.

The Demand for Intervention

The demand for intervention is expressed through political institutions. Both consumers and producers vote, lobby, and campaign for interventions that best further their own interests. None of these activities is costless. Voters incur costs in order to acquire information to use in deciding their votes. Lobbying and campaigning cost time, effort, and contributions to the campaign funds of political parties. Individual consumers and producers demand political action only if the benefit that they receive individually from such action exceeds the costs they incur in obtaining it. There are four main factors that affect the demand for intervention:

- Consumer surplus per buyer
- Number of buyers
- Producer surplus per firm
- Number of firms

The larger the consumer surplus per buyer resulting from intervention, the greater is the demand for intervention by buyers. Also, as the number of buyers increases, so does the demand for intervention. But numbers alone do not necessarily translate into an effective political force. The larger the number of buyers, the greater is the cost of organizing them, so the demand for intervention does not increase proportionately with the number of buyers.

The larger the producer surplus per firm arising from a particular intervention, the larger is the demand for that intervention by firms. Also, as the number of firms that might benefit from some intervention increases, so does the demand for that intervention. But as in the case of consumers, large numbers do not necessarily mean an effective political force. The larger the number of firms, the greater is the cost of organizing them.

For a given surplus, consumer or producer, the smaller the number of households or firms who share it, the larger is the demand for the intervention that creates it.

The Supply of Intervention

Intervention is supplied by politicians and bureaucrats. As we saw in the previous chapter, politicians choose policies that appeal to a majority of voters, thereby enabling themselves to achieve and maintain office, and bureaucrats support policies that maximize their budgets. Given these objectives of politicians and bureaucrats, the supply of intervention depends on

- Consumer surplus per buyer.
- Producer surplus per firm.
- The number of persons affected.

The larger the consumer surplus per buyer or producer surplus per firm generated and the larger the number of persons affected by an intervention, the greater is the tendency for politicians to supply that intervention. If intervention benefits a large number of people significantly enough for it to be noticed and if the recipients know who is the source of the benefits, that intervention appeals to politicians and it is supplied. If intervention affects markets that benefit a large number of people but by a small amount per person and if such benefits do not attract notice, that intervention does not appeal to politicians and it is not supplied. Intervention that bestows clear and large benefits on a small number of people may be attractive to politicians provided some of those benefits flow back and thus enable the politicians to fight more effective election campaigns.

Equilibrium

In equilibrium, the interventions that exist are such that no interest group feels it is worthwhile to use additional resources to press for changes and no group of politicians feels it is worthwhile to offer different interventions. A political equilibrium is not the same thing as a situation in which everyone is in agreement. It is a situation in which some lobby groups devote resources to trying to change interventions that are already in place and others groups devote resources to maintaining the existing interventions. But no one feels it is worthwhile *increasing* the resources he or she is devoting to such activities. Also, in a political equilibrium, the political parties do not agree with each other. Some support the existing interventions, and others propose different interventions. But in equilibrium, no one wants to change the proposals that they are making.

What does a political equilibrium look like? There are two theories of political equilibrium: one is called the public interest theory, and the other the capture theory. Let's look at these two theories.

Public Interest Theory The **public interest theory of intervention** states that intervention is supplied to satisfy the demand of consumers and producers for the maximization of total surplus — or the attainment of allocative efficiency. Public interest theory predicts that the political process will relentlessly seek out deadweight loss and introduce interventions that eliminate it. For example, where monopoly or monopolistic practices by collusive oligopoly exist, the political process will introduce price regulation to ensure that output and price are close to their competitive levels.

Capture Theory The **capture theory of intervention** states that the intervention that exists is that which maximizes producer surplus. The key idea of capture theory is that the cost of intervention is high so that only intervention that increases the surplus of groups that are small and easily identified and that have low organization costs will be supplied by the political process. Such intervention will be supplied even if it imposes costs on others, provided those costs are spread so thinly and widely that they do not have negative effects on votes.

The predictions of the capture theory of intervention are less precise than the predictions of the public interest theory. According to the capture theory, intervention benefits cohesive interest groups by large and visible amounts and imposes on everyone else costs so small, in per capita terms, that no one feels it is worthwhile to incur the cost of organizing an interest group to try to avoid them. To make these predictions concrete enough to be useful, the capture theory needs a model of the costs of political organization.

Whichever theory of intervention is correct, the political system delivers an amount and type of intervention that best furthers the electoral success of politicians. Since we have seen that producer-oriented intervention and consumer-oriented intervention are in direct conflict with each other, it is clear that the political process cannot satisfy both groups in any particular industry. Only one group can win. This makes the intervention of government a bit like a unique product — for example, a painting by A. Y. Jackson. There is only one original, and it will be sold to just one buyer. Normally, a unique commodity is sold through an auction: the highest bidder takes the prize. Equilibrium in government intervention can be thought of in much the same way: the suppliers of intervention will satisfy the demands of the higher bidder. If the producer demand offers a bigger return to the politicians, either directly through votes or indirectly through campaign contributions, the producers' interests will be served. If the consumer demand translates into a larger number of votes, the consumers' interests will be served by intervention.

We have now completed our study of the theory of intervention in the marketplace. Let's turn our attention to an examination of the intervention that exists in our economy today.

Regulation and Deregulation

The past decade has seen dramatic changes in the way in which the Canadian economy is regulated by government. We're going to examine some of the more important of those changes. To begin, we'll look at what is regulated and also at the scope of regulation. Then we'll turn to the regulatory process itself and examine how regulators control prices and other aspects of market behaviour. Finally, we'll tackle the more difficult and controversial questions: why do we regulate some things but not others? Who benefits from the regulation that we have?

The Scope of Regulation

Regulations touch a wide range of economic activity in Canada. The major federal regulatory agencies, together with a brief statement of their responsibilities, are set out in Table 21.1. As you can see by inspecting that table, the predominant sectors subject to regulation are agriculture, energy, transport, and telecommunications.

Table 21.1 Federal Regulatory Agencies

Agency	Responsibility
Atomic Energy Control Board	Administers the Atomic Energy Control Act governing all uses of radioactive material.
Canadian Dairy Commission	Administers national dairy policy and "aims to provide efficient milk and cream producers with the opportunity of obtaining a fair return ... and consumers with ... adequate supply of high-quality products."*
Canadian Radio-television and Telecommunications Commission	Regulates all aspects of radio, television, and telecommunications.
Canadian Transport Commission	Regulates transport under federal jurisdiction including rail, air, water, and pipeline and some interprovincial commercial motor transport.
Canadian Wheat Board	Regulates exports of wheat, oats, and barley and domestic sales for human consumption.
National Energy Board	Regulates oil, gas, and electrical industries "in the public interest."*
National Farm Products	Advises government on the establishment and operation of national agricultural marketing agencies and works with those agencies and provincial governments to promote marketing of farm products. Chicken, egg, and turkey agencies have been established under its aegis.

*Statistics Canada, *Canada Year Book, 1989*.

Provincial and municipal governments also establish regulations covering a wide range of economic activity. Some of these — for example, municipal regulation of the taxicab industry — have important direct effects on the marketplace. Our analysis of the regulatory process and the effects of regulation applies with equal force to price, output, and profit regulation at these other governmental levels.

Regulatory agencies have many varied responsibilities and activities. Our focus here is on only one aspect of their work — the regulation of prices and the implications of that regulation for the output, efficiency, and profitability of the industries that they regulate. How do agencies regulate prices, and what are their effects?

The Regulatory Process

Although regulatory agencies vary in size and scope and in the detailed aspects of economic life that they control, they have certain common features that are relevant to their regulation of prices, outputs, and profits.

First, the senior bureaucrats, who are the key decision makers in a regulatory agency, are appointed by the government. In addition, all agencies have a permanent bureaucracy made up of experts in the industry being regulated, who are often recruited from the regulated firms. Agencies have financial resources, voted by Parliament (or a provincial legislature), to cover the costs of their operations.

Second, each agency adopts a set of practices or operating rules for controlling prices and other aspects of economic performance. These rules are based on well-defined physical and financial accounting procedures that are relatively easy to administer and to monitor.

In a regulated industry, individual firms are free to determine the technology that they will use in production. But they are not free to determine the prices at which they will sell their output, the quantities that they will sell, or the markets that they will serve. The regulatory agency grants certification to a company to serve a particular market with a particular line of products, and that agency determines the level and structure of prices that will be charged. In some cases, the agency also determines the scale of output permitted.

To analyse the way in which regulation works, it is convenient to distinguish between the regulation of natural monopoly and the regulation of cartels. Let's begin with natural monopoly.

Natural Monopoly

Natural monopoly is defined in Chapter 13 as an industry in which one firm can supply the entire market at a lower price than two or more firms can. As a consequence, a natural monopoly experiences economies of scale no matter how high an output rate it produces. Examples of natural monopolies include gas and electric utilities and railway services. It is much more expensive to have two or more competing sets of pipes, wires, and train lines serving every neighbourhood than it is to have a single set.

Let's consider the example of a train service. The demand for train service and the railway

Figure 21.1 Natural Monopoly: Marginal Cost Pricing

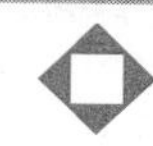

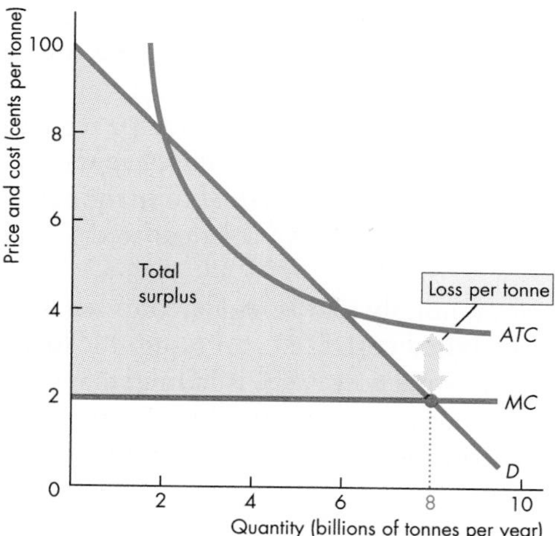

A natural monopoly is an industry in which average total cost is falling even when the entire market demand is satisfied. The natural monopoly in railway transport here has a demand curve *D*. Marginal costs are constant at 2 cents per tonne, as shown by the curve *MC*. Fixed costs are heavy, and the average total cost curve, which includes average fixed cost, is shown as *ATC*. A marginal cost pricing rule that maximizes total surplus sets the price of a tonne at 2 cents, with 8 billion tonnes per year being sold. The resulting consumer surplus is shown as the green area. The producer makes a loss on each tonne indicated by the red arrow. In order to remain in business, the producer must either price discriminate or receive a subsidy.

company's cost curves are illustrated in Fig. 21.1. The demand curve is *D*. The marginal cost curve is *MC*. Notice that the marginal cost curve is horizontal at 2 cents a tonne — that is, the cost of each additional tonne carried is a constant 2 cents. The railway company has a heavy investment in track, trains, and control equipment, and so it has high fixed costs. These fixed costs feature in the company's average total cost curve, shown as *ATC*. The average total cost curve slopes downward because as the number of tonnes carried increases, the fixed cost is spread over a larger number of tonnes. (If you need to refresh your memory on how the average total cost curve is calculated, take a quick look back at Chapter 10).

Regulation in the Public Interest How will this railway monopoly be regulated according to the public interest theory? Recall that in that theory, regulation maximizes total surplus — it achieves allocative efficiency. Allocative efficiency occurs when marginal cost equals price. Equivalently, it occurs when total surplus is maximized — when the area above the marginal cost curve and below the demand curve is at a maximum. As you can see in the example in Fig. 21.1, that outcome occurs if the price is regulated at 2 cents a tonne if 8 billion tonnes are produced. Such a regulation is called a marginal cost pricing rule. A **marginal cost pricing rule** sets price equal to marginal cost. It maximizes total surplus in the regulated industry.

A natural monopoly that is regulated to set price equal to marginal cost makes an economic loss. Because its average total cost curve is falling, marginal cost is below average total cost. Because price equals marginal cost, price is below average total cost. The difference between price and average total cost is the loss per unit produced. It's pretty obvious that a private railway — such as Canadian Pacific — that is required to use a marginal cost pricing rule will not stay in business for long. How can a company cover its costs and, at the same time, obey a marginal cost pricing rule?

One possibility is price discrimination. Some natural monopolies can price discriminate fairly easily. For example, local phone companies can charge consumers a monthly fee for being connected to the telephone system and then charge a low price (perhaps even zero) for each local call. A railway company can price discriminate by offering volume discounts.

But a natural monopoly cannot always price discriminate. When a natural monopoly cannot price discriminate, it can cover its total cost and follow a marginal cost pricing rule only if it receives a subsidy from the government. The government has to raise the revenue for such a subsidy by taxing some other activity. But as we saw in Chapter 20, taxes themselves generate deadweight loss. Thus the deadweight loss resulting from additional taxes has to be offset against the allocative efficiency gained by forcing the natural monopoly to adopt a marginal cost pricing rule. It is possible that deadweight loss will be minimized, not by taxing some other sector of the economy in order to subsidize the natural monopoly, but by permitting the natural monopoly to charge a price higher than marginal cost. Such a pricing arrangement is called an average cost pricing rule. An **average cost pricing rule** sets price equal to average total cost. The average cost pricing solution is shown in Fig. 21.2. The railway company charges 4 cents for each tonne carried and sells 6 billion tonnes of service a year. Deadweight loss arises as represented by the grey triangle in the figure. This situation may be allocatively efficient even though there is a

Figure 21.2 Natural Monopoly: Average Cost Pricing

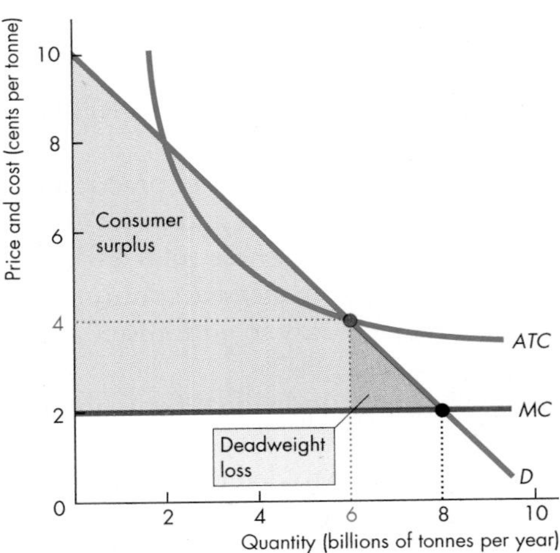

Average cost pricing sets price equal to average total cost. The railway company charges 4 cents per tonne and sells 6 billion tonnes per year. In this situation, the railway company will break even — average total cost equals price. Deadweight loss, shown by the grey triangle, is generated. Consumer surplus is reduced to the green area.

deadweight loss. Recall that the railway company goes out of business if it doesn't cover its costs. If a subsidy is required to cover costs and if the subsidy requires a tax that has a deadweight loss larger than the one shown in the figure, then the average cost pricing rule is the best one available.

Capturing the Regulator What does the capture theory predict about the regulation of this railway? Recall that according to the capture theory, regulation serves the interests of the producer. The producer captures the regulator and sets the regulatory process to work in a manner that leads to the maximum possible profit. To work out the price that achieves profit maximization, we need to look at the relationship between marginal revenue and marginal cost. As you know, a monopoly maximizes profit by producing the output at which marginal revenue equals marginal cost. The monopoly's marginal revenue curve in Fig. 21.3 is the curve *MR*. Marginal revenue equals marginal cost when output is 4 billion tonnes a year and the price is 6 cents a tonne. Thus a regulation that best serves the interest of the producer will set the price at 6 cents a tonne.

Figure 21.3 Natural Monopoly: Profit Maximization

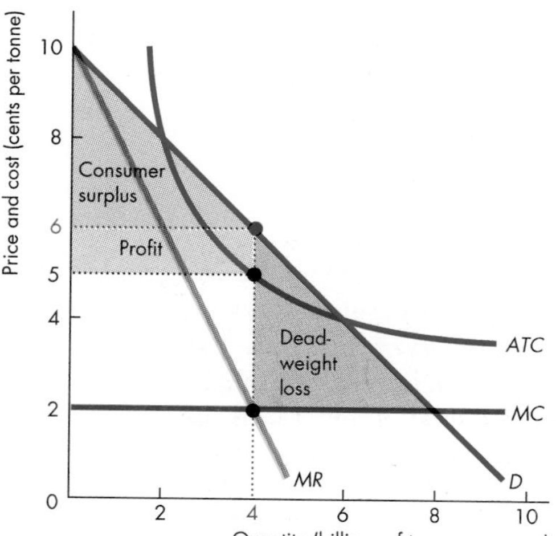

The railway company would like to maximize profit. To do so, marginal revenue (*MR*) is made equal to marginal cost. At a price of 6 cents per tonne, 4 billion tonnes per year are sold. Consumer surplus is reduced to the green triangle. The deadweight loss increases to the grey triangle. The monopoly makes the profit shown by the blue rectangle. If the producer can capture the regulator, the outcome will be the situation shown here.

But how can a producer go about obtaining regulation that results in this monopoly profit-maximizing outcome? To answer this question, we need to look at the way in which agencies determine the level at which to set a regulated price. The key method used is called rate of return regulation.

Rate of Return Regulation A regulated price determined by **rate of return regulation** enables a regulated firm to earn a specified target rate of return on its capital. The target rate of return is determined with reference to what is normal in competitive industries. This rate of return is part of the opportunity cost of the natural monopolist and is included in the firm's average total cost. By examining the firm's total cost, including the normal rate of return on capital, the regulator attempts to determine the price at which average total cost is covered. Thus rate of return regulation is equivalent to average cost pricing.

In the example that we have just been examining — in Fig. 21.2 — average cost pricing results at a regulated price of 4 cents a tonne with 6 billion tonnes a year being sold. Thus rate of return regulation, based on a correct assessment of the producer's average total cost curve, results in a price and quantity that favours the consumer and does not enable the producer to maximize monopoly profit. The special interest group of the producer has failed to capture the regulator, and the outcome will be closer to that predicted by the public interest theory of regulation.

But there is an important feature of many real world situations that the above analysis does not take into account — the ability of the monopoly firm to mislead the regulator about its true costs.

Padding Costs The senior managers of the railway company may be able to pad the firm's costs by spending part of the firm's revenue on inputs that are not strictly required for the production of the good. By this device, the firm's apparent cost curves exceed the true cost curves. On-the-job luxury in the form of sumptuous office suites, limousines, free hockey tickets (disguised as public relations expenses), company jets, lavish international travel and entertainment, or just hiring more and more people so that they are in charge of a bigger "empire" are ways in which managers can pad costs.

If the railway company manages to pad its costs and persuade the regulatory agency that its true cost curve is that shown as *ATC* (padded) in Fig. 21.4, then the regulator, applying the normal rate of return

Figure 21.4 Natural Monopoly: Padding Costs

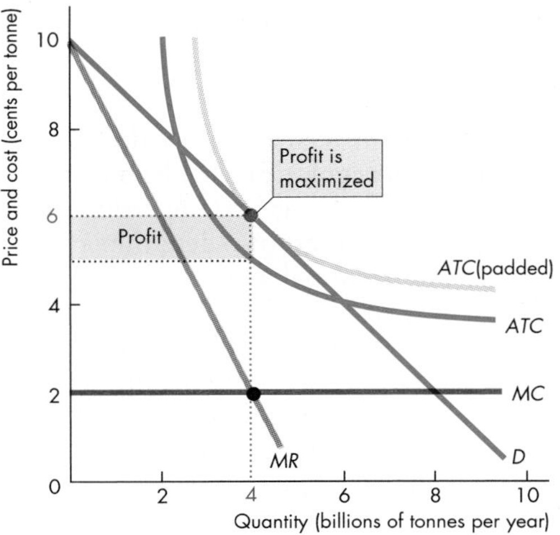

If the railway company is able to inflate its costs to *ATC* (padded) and persuade the regulator that these are genuine minimum costs of production, rate of return regulation will result in a price of 6 cents per tonne — the profit-maximizing price. To the extent that the producer can inflate costs above average total cost, price will rise, output will fall, and deadweight loss will increase.

principle, will set the price at 6 cents a tonne. In this example, the price and quantity will be the same as those under unregulated monopoly. Although it may be impossible for a real world firm to pad its costs as much as shown in the figure, to the extent that costs can be padded, the apparent average total cost curve will lie somewhere between the true *ATC* curve and *ATC* (padded). The greater the ability of the firm to pad its costs, the closer its profit (measured in economic terms) approaches the maximum possible. The shareholders of this firm don't receive this economic profit. It gets used up by the managers of the firm on the self-serving activities that they have used to pad the company's costs.

Public Interest or Capture?

It is not clear whether actual regulation produces prices and quantities that correspond more closely with the predictions of capture theory or with those of public interest theory. One thing is clear, however. Price regulation does not require natural monopolies to use the marginal cost pricing rule. If it did, most natural monopolies would make losses and receive hefty government subsidies to enable them to remain in business. There are even exceptions to this conclusion. For example, many local telephone companies do appear to use marginal cost pricing for local phone calls. They cover their total cost by charging a flat fee each month for connection to their telephone system and then permit each call to be made at its marginal cost — zero or something very close to it.

A test of whether natural monopoly regulation is in the public interest or the interest of the producer is to examine the rates of return earned by regulated natural monopolies. If those rates of return are significantly higher than those in the rest of the economy, then, to some degree, the regulators may have been captured by the producers. If the rates of return in the regulated monopoly industries are similar to those in the rest of the economy, then we cannot tell for sure whether or not the regulators have been captured for we cannot know the extent to which the managers of the regulated firms have padded costs. We do not know of any definitive studies that address this issue directly. There is plenty of casual, empirical evidence, however, suggesting that many natural monopolies in Canada do earn higher rates of return than the economy average. One recent striking example is cable television service; telephone service is another.

We've now examined the regulation of natural monopoly. Let's next turn to regulation in oligopolistic industries — to the regulation of cartels.

Cartel Regulation

A *cartel* is a collusive agreement among a number of firms designed to restrict output and achieve a higher profit for the members of the cartel. Cartels arise naturally in oligopolistic industries. An *oligopoly* is an industry in which a small number of firms compete with each other. We studied oligopoly (and duopoly — two firms competing for a market) — in Chapter 14. There we saw that if firms manage to collude and behave like a monopoly, they can set the same price and sell the same total quantity as a monopoly firm would. But we also discovered that in such a situation, each firm will be tempted to "cheat," increasing its own output and profit at the expense of the other firms. The result of such cheating on the collusive agreement is the unravelling of the monopoly equilibrium and the emergence of a competitive outcome with zero profit for the producers. Such an outcome will benefit consumers at the expense of producers.

How is oligopoly regulated? Does regulation prevent or encourage monopoly practices?

According to the public interest theory, oligopoly is regulated to ensure a competitive outcome. Consider, for example, the market for trucking tomatoes from the fields of southwestern Ontario to the ketchup factory at Leamington, as illustrated in Fig. 21.5. The demand curve for trips is *D*. The industry marginal cost curve — and the competitive supply curve — *MC*. Public interest regulation will set the price of a trip at $20, and there will be 300 trips a week.

How would this industry be regulated according to the capture theory? Regulation that is in the producer's interest will set the price at $30 a trip and, to ensure that that price is maintained, will restrict the number of trips to 200 a week. Each producer will make a maximum profit, and the industry marginal revenue will be equal to the industry marginal cost. If there are 10 trucking companies, this outcome can be achieved by issuing a production quota to each restricting it to 20 trips a week, so that the total number of trips in a week is 200. Penalties can be imposed to ensure that no single producer violates its quota.

Figure 21.5 Collusive Oligopoly

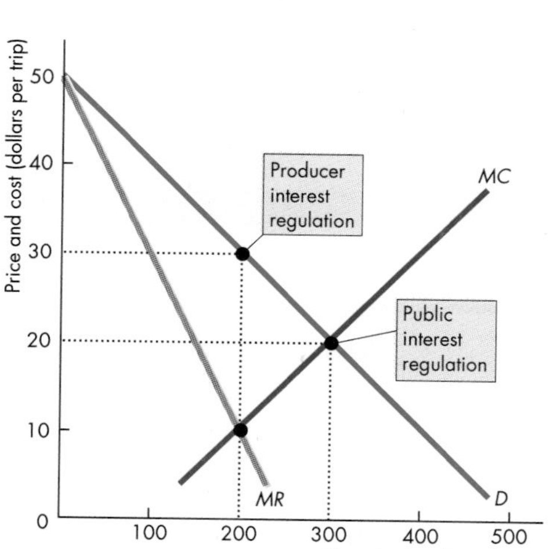

Ten trucking firms transport tomatoes from Essex County to Leamington. The demand curve is *D*, and the industry marginal cost curve is *MC*. Under competition, the *MC* curve is the industry supply curve. If the industry is competitive, the price of a trip will be $20, and 300 trips will be made each week. Producers will demand regulation that restricts entry and holds the output of producers to 200 trips per week. This regulation will raise the price to $30 per trip with the result that each producer makes maximum profit — as if it was a monopoly. The industry marginal revenue will be equal to industry marginal cost.

What does regulation of oligopoly do in practice? Though there is disagreement about the matter, the consensus view is that regulation tends to favour the producer. Trucking and airlines (regulated by the Canadian Transport Commission) and taxicabs (regulated by cities) are examples of industries for which it has been calculated that increased profits have accrued to producers as a result of regulation. But the most dramatic examples of regulation favouring the producer are in agriculture. An Economic Council of Canada study, based on the situation prevailing in the early 1980s, estimated that regulation of the egg-producing and broiler chicken industries alone transferred more than $100 million a year to just 4,600 individual producers.[2]

Further evidence on cartel and oligopoly regulation can be obtained from the performance of prices and profit following deregulation. If, after deregulation, prices and profit fall, then, to some degree, the regulation must have been serving the interest of the producer. In contrast, if, after deregulation, prices and profits remain constant or increase, then the regulation may be presumed to have been serving the public interest.

Since there has been a substantial amount of deregulation in North America in recent years, we can try to see which of the two theories of oligopoly regulation better fits the facts by looking at prices and profits after deregulation. The evidence is mixed, but there are many cases both in Canada and in the United States in which deregulation has been accompanied by falling prices. Airlines, trucking, railways, long-distance telephone service, and banking and financial services are all industries in which deregulation was, initially at least, associated with more competition, lower prices, and a large increase in the volume of transactions. Interpreting the deregulation evidence is, however, made difficult by the possibility that firms in oligopoly industries will find other ways of restricting competition in a deregulated environment. There is evidence, for example, that the U.S. airlines managed to do this in the 1980s by monopalizing terminal gates and restricting information in computerized reservation systems.

[2]J.D. Forbes, R.D. Hughes, and T. K. Warley, *Economic Intervention and Regulation in Canadian Agriculture* (Ottawa: Department of Supply and Services, 1982).

Making Predictions

Most industries have a few producers and many consumers. In these cases, public choice theory predicts that regulation will protect producer interests because a small number of people stand to gain a large amount — a situation that makes them fairly easy to organize as a cohesive lobby. Under such circumstances, politicians will be rewarded with campaign contributions, rather than votes. But there are situations in which the consumer interest is strong and well organized and thus able to prevail. There are also cases in which the balance switches from producer to consumer, as seen in the deregulation process that began in the late 1970s.

Deregulation raises one of the hardest questions for economists seeking to understand and make predictions about regulation. Why has the transportation sector been deregulated? If the producers gained from regulation and if the producer lobby was strong enough to achieve regulation, what happened in the 1980s to change the equilibrium to one in which the consumer interest prevailed? We do not have a good answer to this question at the present time. One possibility — though it is an after-the-fact rationalization — is that regulation had become so costly to consumers and the potential benefits to them from deregulation so great that the cost of organizing the consumer voice became one worth paying. Furthermore, as communication technology improves and the cost of communication falls, it is probable that the cost of organizing larger groups of individuals will also fall. If this line of reasoning is correct, we should expect to see more consumer-oriented regulation in the future. In practice, more consumer-oriented regulation means deregulation — removing the regulations that are already in place to serve the interests of producer groups.

There is another puzzling feature of the deregulation movement. In the United States, although the movement was begun by a Democratic administration, its major impetus in the 1980s came not from the Ralph Nader consumer movement but from the Republican party and the business interests that it is perceived to support. In Canada, too, business and those on the conservative end of the political spectrum have been the leaders. If the regulators really have been captured and serve the interests of producers, why are producers the ones pressing hardest for deregulation? This is another question to which we do not know the answer.

REVIEW

Natural monopolies are regulated in Canada by federal, provincial, and municipal governments. Regulation in the public interest would ensure that the goods and services produced by natural monopolists would be sold at a price equal to their marginal cost. Producers would make a loss and receive a subsidy. Regulation in the interest of the producer would result in restricting output to the level at which marginal revenue equals marginal cost with the price of the good or service equal to that charged by an unregulated monopoly. In practice, regulation uses rate-of-return regulation, which, if producers are able to pad their costs, results in the situation intermediate between unregulated profit maximization and public interest regulation.

Cartels (collusive agreements among a number of the firms) are also regulated in Canada. Regulation in these industries has tended to favour producers. In recent years, a change in the political equilibrium has resulted in a wave of deregulation that appears to be advancing the interests of consumers. ■

Let's now leave regulation and turn to the second main method of intervention in markets — public ownership.

Table 21.2 Crown Corporations

Sector	Federal	Provincial	Total
Transport	5	6	11
Telecommunications and broadcasting	4	4	8
Energy	0	9	9
Energy development	1	8	9
Industrial	7	17	24
Financial	6	10	16
Marketing	6	4	10
Development corporations	1	7	8
Housing	0	13	13
Informational	5	0	5
Alcoholic beverages	0	12	12
	35	90	125

Source: Statistics Canada, *Canada Year Book, 1988.*

Public Ownership

Canada has 125 publicly owned corporations — federal and provincial Crown corporations — operating in many sectors of the economy (see Table 21.2). Public ownership provides another way in which the government can influence the behaviour of natural monopoly. What are the effects of this method of natural monopoly control? How does a publicly owned corporation operate? Let's explore some alternative patterns of behaviour for such corporations.

An Efficient Crown Corporation

One possibility is that a Crown corporation is operated in a manner that results in economic efficiency — maximization of total surplus. Figure 21.6(a) illustrates such a case. (The figure continues to use the example of a railway that we analysed in Figs. 21.1 through 21.4.) To be efficient, a Crown corporation obeys the rule:

> Produce an output such that price equals marginal cost

In this example, that output level is 8 billion tonnes a year at a price — and marginal cost — of 2 cents a tonne. To be able to operate in this manner, a nationalized industry has to be subsidized; the subsidy on each unit of output must equal the difference between average total cost and marginal cost. Somehow that subsidy has to be collected other than through the price of the good or service produced — in other words, by taxation. If the government taxes each household a fixed amount regardless of its consumption of the output of the railway, the consumer surplus will shrink to the amount shown in Fig. 21.6(a), but it will be at its maximum possible level.

The situation depicted in Fig. 21.6(a) is the one that maximizes consumer surplus — that achieves economic efficiency. But it is not an outcome that is necessarily compatible with the interests of the managers of the Crown corporation. One model of the behaviour of managers is that suggested by the economic theory of bureaucracy. What does that alternative model predict about Crown corporation behaviour?

A Bureaucracy Model of Public Enterprise

The basic assumption of the economic theory of bureaucracy is that bureaucrats aim to maximize the budget of their bureau. The equivalent assumption for the managers of a Crown corporation is that they seek to maximize the budget of their corporation. To work out what the pursuit of this objective implies for the behaviour of a Crown corporation, we need to know the constraints under which its managers are operating. We will consider two alternatives: 1) make price equal to marginal cost; and 2) make the service available at zero cost to the consumer.

Budget Maximization with Marginal Cost Pricing If the bureau maximizes its budget but obeys the marginal cost pricing rule, it will operate in a manner illustrated in Fig. 21.6(b). Its output will remain at the economically efficient level — 8 billion tonnes a year — and it will sell the output for 2 cents a tonne. But the corporation will operate in a manner that does not minimize production cost. It will become inefficient in the sense that its costs will be padded. It will hire more workers than the number strictly required to produce the output, and its internal control mechanisms, which would ensure internal efficiency in a private profit-maximizing firm will be weak. As a result, the average total cost of the corporation will rise to ATC_1 (padded).

What determines the limit on the extent to which the corporation can pad its costs? The answer is the maximum amount that the users of the output can be made to pay through taxation. That maximum is the total consumer surplus. That maximum consumer surplus is the area beneath the demand curve and above the marginal cost curve. You can work out how big it is by using the usual formula for the area of the triangle. The height of this triangle is 8 cents and its base is 8 billion tonnes a year, so the consumer surplus is $320 million. This will be the upper limit that any government — in a political democracy — can extract from the taxpayer-consumers of the product of this corporation. Spread over 8 billion tonnes, $320 million gives a subsidy of 4 cents a tonne, the amount shown in the figure.

Budget Maximization at Zero Price What happens if a government bureau provides its goods or service free? Of course, it is improbable that a nationalized railway would be able to persuade politicians and taxpayers that its activities should be expanded to the point of providing its services free, but there are several examples of publicly provided goods that are indeed free. Primary and secondary education and health care are the two outstanding examples. For the sake of comparison, we'll continue with our railway, improbable though the case is.

Figure 21.6(c) illustrates the analysis. Here the bureau increases output to the point at which the price that consumers are willing to pay for the last unit produced is zero. In this example, output rises to 10 billion tonnes a year. A deadweight loss is created because the marginal cost of production, 2 cents, is higher than the marginal benefit or willingness to pay. The deadweight loss is illustrated in the figure as the grey area between the marginal cost curve and the demand curve. The bureau will pad its costs and be inefficient in its internal operations and will have an average total cost curve given by *ATC* (padded). That curve is the highest possible *ATC* curve, assuming that people cannot be made to pay more than their consumer surplus and would vote to shut down this Crown corporation if they were required to pay more than their consumer surplus to subsidize it. The subsidy will be 5 cents a tonne.

Figure 21.6 Public Enterprise

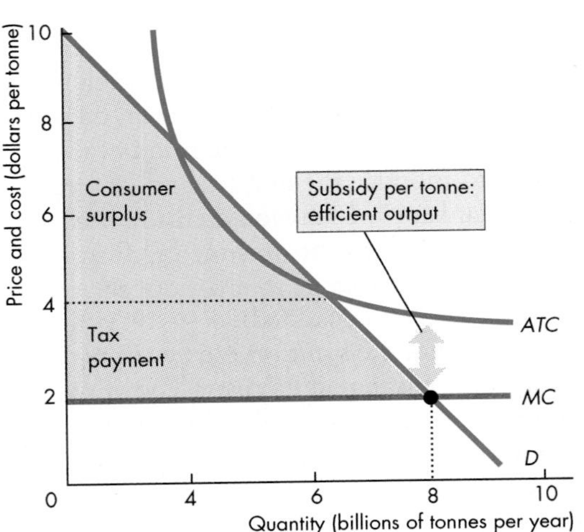

(a) Allocative Efficiency

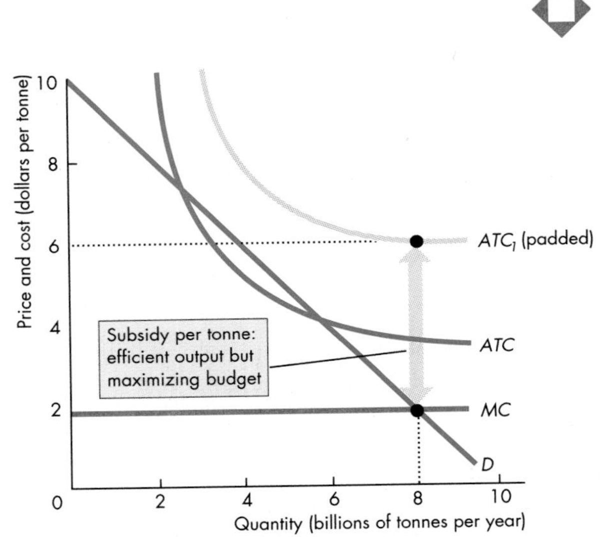

(b) Budget Maximization

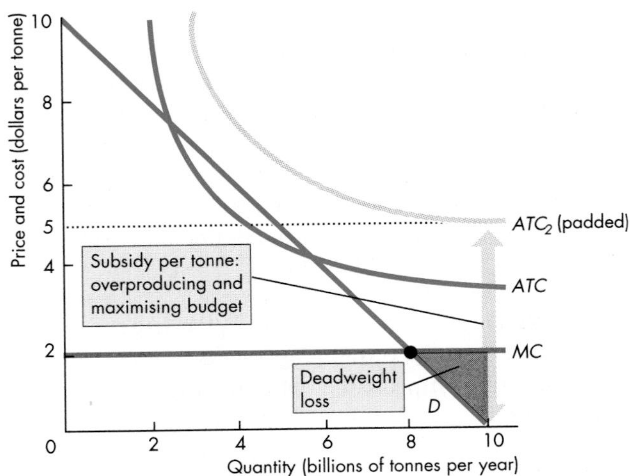

(c) Budget Maximization at zero price

A railway operated by a Crown corporation that achieves allocative efficiency is shown in part (a). Output is such that price equals marginal cost (8 billion tonnes per year) and price equals marginal cost (2 cents per tonne). The enterprise receives a subsidy that enables it to cover its average total cost and that cost is the minimum possible cost of providing the service. If the managers of the enterprise pursue their own interest, maximizing their budget, costs are padded and the maximum possible cost rises to *ATC* (padded) in part (b). If the corporation is constrained to keep price equal to marginal cost, it continues to produce an output that achieves allocative efficiency, but the managers of the bureau divert the entire consumer surplus to themselves.

If the bureau is able to increase output all the way to the point at which its services are provided free of charge (part c), output rises (to 10 billion tonnes per year), and a deadweight loss is created. The bureau will pad its costs. The subsidy rises still higher. The maximum subsidy is 5 cents — the subsidy that requires the government to raise taxes that equal the consumer surplus to pay for it.

Compromise Outcomes

The three situations that we have just examined are extreme ones. The first (Fig. 21.6a) is efficient and maximizes consumer surplus. The second (Fig. 21.6b) is efficient but maximizes the benefit of the producer. The third (Fig. 21.6c) is inefficient, results in overproduction, and maximizes the benefit of the producer. In the second and third cases, consumer surplus is squeezed all the way down to zero.

In general, to achieve any particular distribution — or redistribution — of the gains from trade, agents must incur costs. To achieve the outcome of Fig. 21.6(a), political parties and voters must incur costs of organization in order to press for and secure maximum consumer benefits. In the other two cases, producers (and those with an interest in them) must organize and influence the political process in order to achieve their best interests. When the costs of political organization and the efficient degree of voter ignorance are taken into account, the actual outcome for the behaviour of a public enterprise is likely to lie somewhere between the extremes that we've considered. There will be a tendency for the enterprise to overproduce as in Fig. 21.6(c), but not by as much as in that figure. There will be a tendency for the corporation to pad its budget, but not to the extent shown in Figs. 21.6(b) and 21.6(c). There will be a tendency for consumer interest to have some effect, but not to the degree shown in Fig. 21.6(a). The basic prediction concerning the behaviour of a Crown corporation, then, is that it will overproduce, and in the sense that its costs will be padded, it will be less efficient than the profit-maximizing private firm.

Crown Corporations in Reality

So far, we've only considered model Crown corporations that pursue either the consumer or the producer interest or some compromise of the two. How do actual Crown corporations behave? Several studies have been directed to answering this question. One of the most fruitful ways of approaching the question is to compare public and private enterprises in which, as far as possible, other things are equal. There are two well-known and well-studied cases for which other things do seem to be fairly equal. One such comparison is of Canada's public and private railways — Canadian National (CN) and Canadian Pacific (CP). The other is from Australia, which has two domestic airlines, one private and the other public, that fly almost identical routes at almost identical times every day. Economists have studied the costs of these similar enterprises and concluded that each of the publicly owned enterprises operate with a cost structure that is significantly higher than that of the corresponding private firm. In the case of CN and CP, the estimated difference was 14 percent.[3]

One crown corporation, Via Rail, not only provides a transportation service but is seen by many Canadians as part of the nation's fabric. It became the subject of a great deal of public debate and controversy in 1989 when the federal government decided to cut back its services and the scale of its subsidy. An economic analysis of the consequences of that decision is presented in Reading Between the Lines on pp. 552-553.

Privatization

Largely because of an increasing understanding of how bureaucracies work and of the inefficiency of publicly operated enterprises, there has been a move, in Canada and around the world, to sell off publicly owned corporations. During the second half of the 1980s, the federal government sold a dozen companies, including Air Canada. Companies that were too unprofitable to sell, such as CN, were savagely cut back. As this process has taken place, we have witnessed a gradual change in the political equilibrium, with the interest of the consumer having a larger weight placed on it and that of the producer a smaller weight. Economists are only beginning their study of this kind of process, and at this stage, they cannot predict whether recent privatization moves constitute a fundamental change or a temporary departure from the previous trend towards greater government involvement and ownership in markets dominated by natural monopoly.

Opinions among economists are sharply divided on the question of whether privatization has gone too far or not far enough to achieve allocative efficiency. Some, such as Christopher Green (see Talking with Christopher Green, pp. 203-206), believe that privatization is not necessary if a public corporation is operating in competition with private enterprises. Others believe that the tendency for bureaucracies to pad costs is so strong that even more privatization is needed.

Let's now leave public enterprises and turn to the third method of intervention in markets — anti-combine law.

---

[3]W.S.W. Caves, and Laurits Christensen, "The Relative Efficiency of Public *v.* Private Firms in a Competitive Environment: the Case of Canada's Railroads," *Journal of Political Economy* 88, 5 (September-October 1980): 958-76.

The Via Rail Cut Back

Via Rail can't be judged as a private business, Crown corporation says

Critics who judge Via Rail by applying the yardstick of private business are on the wrong track, the company says.

The Crown-owned Via Rail Canada Inc. says candidly that it not only lost money, but it also could not cover its expenses through revenue. Yet it does not believe that such numbers tell the whole story.

For critics such as Julius Lukasiewicz, the story of Via Rail is straightforward. In an interview, the professor of mechanical engineering at Carleton University in Ottawa described it as "increasing cost and decreasing output."

But for Paul Raynor, a Via spokesman, the logic goes differently. "Via takes a beating because, under standard business practice, how can you run a business and lose half a billion dollars a year?"

Instead, Mr. Raynor argues, one must view Via as a Crown corporation providing a subsidized service and then determine how well it "manages the government subsidy," which was about $636.6-million in 1988...

"No, we don't cover our costs," Mr. Raynor said. "The revenue-to-cost ratio is about 32 per cent. But then railway accounting is different. Greyhound wouldn't be in business if it had to build and maintain its highways. Air Canada wouldn't be in business if it had to build airports and provide air traffic control."

With the 50 per cent cut in service announced by Via Rail, this ratio should rise because costs have been decreased, Mr. Raynor said.

He said it should not be forgotten that certain services, such as the remote service to northern areas, will have to be provided as part of Via Rail's public mandate.

This week's cuts include the elimination of about 2,700 jobs. Although the cuts will save money—the federal subsidy will fall to $350-million in the 1992-93 fiscal year—Via faces a $140-million severance bill over the next five years.

Prof. Lukasiewicz has developed his own figures based on Via annual reports that show the ratio of government subsidy to passenger revenue averaged about 3 to 1 from Via's inception. This means that the subsidy was usually about three times what Via made from ticket sales.

The total federal subsidies from 1977 (when Via was established) until the end of the 1988 fiscal year totalled about $5.21-billion. They are expected to reach $5.75-billion when the 1989 subsidy of $541-million is added.

VIA facts and figures

	1981	1988
Passengers carried	8 million	6.4 million
Total passenger miles (calculated from tickets sold)	1.94 billion	1.4 billion
Average length of trips	389 km	359 km
Passenger revenue	$159.8-million	$220.4-million
Contract revenue (from fed. govt.)	$422.3-million	$509.2-million
Total revenue	$585.3-million	$788.2-million
Profit (loss)	($873,000)	($1.9-million)
Expenses	$619.3-million	$790.11million
Component of expenses paid CN/CP for tracks, etc.	$392.5-million	$105-million
Annual fed. subsidy	$414.7-million	$636.6-million

Source: *VIA Rail Canada Inc.*

***The Globe and Mail,* January 19, 1990**
By Zuhair Kashmeri

The Essence of the Story

- Via Rail, a Crown Corporation established in 1977, has received a subsidy from the federal government of more than $500 million in 1989 and $5.75 billion between 1977 and 1989—three times its revenue from ticket sales.
- Paul Raynor, a Via Rail spokesman, says:
  - Via should be judged by how well it manages its government subsidy, not by whether it can cover its costs.
  - Via pays the full cost of its operation while other transporters do not: Greyhound does not pay for highways and Air Canada does not pay for airports and air traffic control services.
  - Via is required to provide services to remote northern areas that do not cover their costs.
- With a 50 per cent cut in Via Rail service, 2,700 jobs will be eliminated and Via's subsidy will be reduced to $350 million in 1992-93.

Background and Analysis

- Via Rail produces services that have both private and external benefits.
- The demand curve for Via Rail's services tells us the value placed on those services by its customers—it tells us how much they are willing to pay for the last unit of Via output bought. (See Fig. a).
- The external benefits of Via Rail's services include:
  - Less congested highways
  - Less congested air routes and airports
  - Accessibility to remote areas
- By adding the value of the external benefits per unit of output to the price that its customers are willing to pay we obtain Via Rail's marginal social benefit* curve, *MSB*. (Fig. a).
- The marginal social benefit curve tells us the value placed on the last unit of Via's output to its users and to those who obtain external benefits. The vertical distance between the demand and marginal social benefit curves is the value of the external benefit of the last unit of Via service produced.

Via with too big a subsidy

- Figure (b) shows Via Rail producing too large a level of output and receiving too large a subsidy, a situation which its critics and the federal government say existed before the cuts.
- Via's average total cost curve is *ATC*, and its marginal cost curve is *MC*. The demand curve *D* and the marginal social benefit curve *MSB* are the same curves as in Fig. (a).
- Via produces an output of 1.4 billion passenger miles a year which it sells for a price of 15 cents per passenger mile. It receives a total revenue shown by the shaded blue rectangle. The difference between its total cost and total revenue is the federal government subsidy shown by the shaded red rectangle.
- You can tell that Via is producing too large an output because its marginal cost, *MC*, exceeds its marginal social benefit, *MSB*. To achieve allocative efficiency, Via must cut back its scale of operation.

An efficient Via

- Figure (c) shows Via operating to achieve allocative efficiency. Routes are closed down and fixed costs reduced so the average total cost curve shifts downward to ATC_1. There is no change in the demand curve, the marginal social benefits curve, or the marginal cost curve. Output is cut back to 0.9 billion passenger miles per year, the level at which marginal cost equals marginal social benefit. Price is increased slightly.
- But Via continues to need a subsidy to cover its total cost. There are two reasons for this: 1) Via is a natural monopoly whose average total cost curve is downward sloping and above its marginal cost curve; 2) Via produces services that create external benefits so that marginal social benefit exceeds the price that its customers are willing to pay.
- When Via operates at an efficient level its subsidy continues, but at a reduced level.

---

* Marginal social benefit is explained in Chapter 12

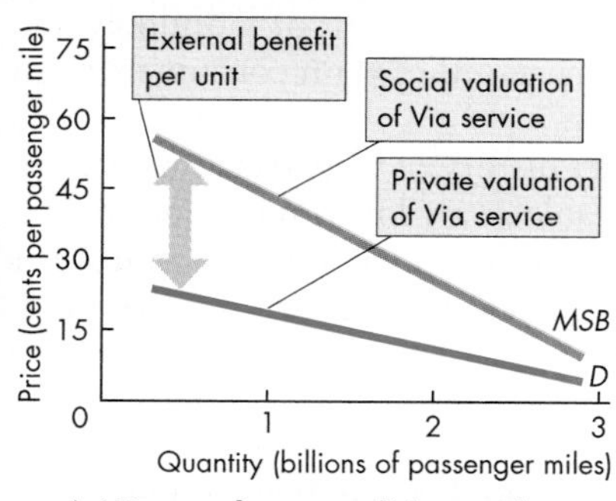

(a) Demand, externalities, and marginal social benefit

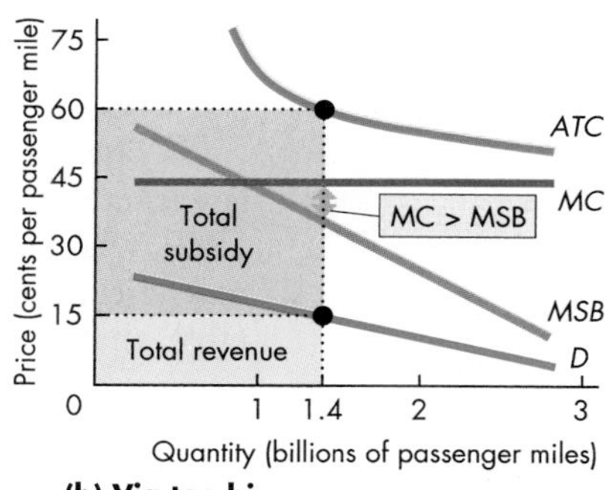

(b) Via too big

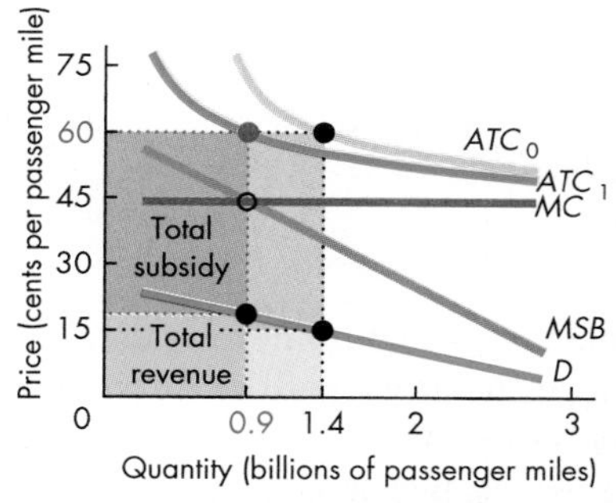

(c) Via operates efficiently

Table 21.3 Canada's Anti-Combine Law: A Compact History

Original Law: 1889, 1892

An Act for the Prevention and Suppression of Combinations in Restraint of Trade, 1889. Became section 520 of the Criminal Code in 1892. It read:

> Every one is guilty of an indictable offence . . . who conspires, combines, agrees or arranges with any other person, or with any railway, steamship, steamboat or transportation company, *unlawfully* —
>
> a) to unduly limit the facilities for transporting, producing, manufacturing, supplying, storing or dealing in any article or commodity which may be a subject of trade or commerce; or —
>
> b) to restrain or injure trade or commerce in relation to any such article or commodity; or —
>
> c) to unduly prevent, limit, or lessen the manufacture or production of any such article or commodity, or to unreasonably enhance the price thereof; or —
>
> d) to unduly prevent or lessen competition in the production, manufacture, purchase, barter, sale, transportation or supply of any such article or commodity, or in the price of insurance upon person or property.

Amendment: 1900

Deleted the word "unlawfully" (our italics above) from the original law.

Combines Act: 1910

Permitted any six persons to apply to a judge for an order directing an investigation into an alleged combine — defined as a trust, monopoly, merger, or agreement "against the interest of the public."

Combines and Fair Prices Act: 1915

Established a board to regulate prices and prevent the hoarding of necessities to profit from higher prices. The act was declared unconstitutional (beyond the power given to the government of Canada under the British North America Act) in 1922.

Combines Investigation Act: 1923

Established new (and constitutional) investigative machinery.

Combines Investigation Act: 1960 Amendment

Brought the Criminal Code section containing the original law of 1889, with amendments, into the Combines Investigation Act.

Competition Act: 1986

Radical reform of Canadian law on monopoly and mergers. Placed responsibility for enforcement with a quasi-judicial tribunal operating under detailed and lengthy rules for determining "abuse of dominant position" and whether a merger "prevents or substantially lessens competition."

Anti-Combine Law

First, we'll describe Canada's anti-combine laws and then we'll examine some of the landmark anti-combine cases that have given substance to the law.

Canada's Anti-Combine Laws

Canada's anti-combine laws date back to the last decade of the nineteenth century. In the mid-1880s, monopoly had become a major political issue. For industries as diverse as sugar and groceries, biscuits and confectionery, coal, binder twine, agricultural implements, stoves, coffins, eggs, and fire insurance, concerns were raised about the extent of monopoly power and the damage inflicted on consumers from a lack of competition.

The compact history of Canada's anti-combine law is set out in Table 21.3. The original law, of 1889, was rendered almost ineffective by an unfortunate circularity in its wording. It declared (see the table) that

> Every one is guilty of an indictable offence . . . who conspires . . . *unlawfully* to . . . restrain or injure

Table 21.4 Canada's Anti-Combine Law: the Law Today

Competition Act, 1986

Abuse of Dominant Position

79(1)Where on application by the Director, the Tribunal finds that:

a) one or more persons substantially or completely control, throughout Canada or any area thereof, a class or species of business,

b) that person or those persons have engaged in or are engaging in a practice of anti-competitive acts, and

c) the practice has had, is having or is likely to have the effect of preventing or lessening competition substantially in a market,

the Tribunal may make an order prohibiting all or any of those persons from engaging in that practice.

Mergers

92(1)Where on application by the Director, the Tribunal finds that a merger or proposed merger prevents or lessens, or is likely to prevent or lessen, competition substantially . . . the Tribunal may . . . [,] in the case of a completed merger, order any party to the merger

i) to dissolve the merger . . .

ii) to dispose of assets and shares . . .

[or] in the case of a proposed merger, make an order directed against any party to the proposed merger

i) ordering the person . . . not to proceed with the merger. . . .

iii) ordering the person not to proceed with part of the merger.

Remark

In reaching its conclusion, the Tribunal is directed by the Competition Act with highly detailed and lengthy guidelines.*

*For a detailed description of the more important of these, consult Christopher Green, *Canadian Industrial Organization and Policy*, 3rd ed. (Toronto: McGraw-Hill Ryerson, 1990), 362-71.

trade, . . . unreasonably enhance price . . . or lessen competition.

The act did not say what it meant by the word "unlawfully," and as a consequence, the act was totally without force. In 1900, however, the unfortunate word was deleted from the act, and in the early years of this century, cases started to come before the courts.

The law, as it stands today, is summarized in Table 21.4. That law is the result of almost two decades of economic research and analysis and political debate and discussion. The process leading to the current law began with an Economic Council of Canada report published in 1969 and titled *Interim Report on Competition Policy.* Following many attempts to introduce and enact a new law, the Progressive Conservative government of Prime Minister Brian Mulroney finally achieved this goal in the summer of 1986. The most important features of Canada's current anti-combine law are its placing of responsibility for its enforcement with a quasi-judicial tribunal, rather than with the criminal or even civil courts, and the provision of highly detailed criteria under which the tribunal must reach its conclusions. How the new law will operate in practice will depend on how the tribunal interprets its mandate and on the economic and political climate in which it operates. Let's now turn to an examination of how anti-combine law has been applied in practice.

Landmark Anti-Combine Cases

Although the original anti-combine laws themselves are brief and easily summarized, the case law that has been built on them is extensive and has been the subject of a large number of specialist studies. The real force of any law rests not in the words written down by the Parliament but in the interpretation placed upon them by the courts. Table 21.5 gives a brief summary of the landmark anti-combine cases that have been before the courts of Canada.

Table 21.5 Landmark Anti-Combine Cases

Case	Year	Charge, verdict, precedent/importance
(a) Collusive agreements		
Weidman v. Schragge	1912	Two Winnipeg junk dealers had an agreement to fix prices and controlled 95 percent of the market. Agreement illegal and nonenforceable. First case to reach the Supreme Court of Canada.
R. v. Container Materials	1942	Shipping container companies had price fixing agreements and quotas. Guilty. Established principle that "the public is entitled to the benefits of competition."*
R. v. Howard Smith Paper Mills Limited et al.	1947	Seven Canadian manufacturers and 21 wholesalers of writing paper and (the "fine papers" case) printers' paper, all of whom belonged to the Canadian Pulp and Paper Association, engaged in price fixing over 19 years (1933-1952). Guilty. Defined "unduly" in terms of proportion of market controlled — agreement must leave participants "*virtually unaffected* by . . . competition."
R. v. Abitibi	1960	Seventeen paper companies, accounting for 75 percent of the domestic market, had an agreement to limit the maximum price they would pay for pulp. Guilty. Defined "unduly" more broadly than in the "fine paper" case.
R. v. Canadian Apron and Supply Ltd. et al.	1967	Twenty-two Montreal Island companies, accounting for 90 percent of the market supplying and laundering towels and uniforms for restaurants, organized the Montreal League of Linen Suppliers, which fixed prices. Guilty. Virtual monopoly sufficient (though not necessary) to indicate "undue restraint."
(b) Monopolies		
R. v. Eddy Match Co.	1952	Eddy Match Co. attempted to maintain a monopoly in the wooden match industry. Guilty Classic case of monopoly.
R. v. Electric Reduction Company	1970	ERCO attempted to monopolize the market for industrial phosphates (an important ingredient in soap) by clever price discrimination; three large U.S.-owned buyers, who could easily have entered the industry as suppliers, were charged a low — competitive — price, and the rest of the market was charged a high — monopoly — price. Guilty. Established strong powers for government to prohibit attempts to deter new entry.
R. v. Allied Chemicals Ltd. and Cominco Ltd.	1975	Allied Chemical and Cominco combined to operate a monopoly in the supply of sulfuric acid in western British Columbia. *Not* guilty. Competition stiff in rest of B.C., and competition between Allied and Cominco would have eliminated one of them.
(c) Mergers		
R. v. Canadian Breweries Ltd.	1960	By 1958, as a result of 30 years of takeovers, Canadian Breweries Ltd. controlled 60 percent of the beer market in Ontario and 52 percent in Quebec. Not guilty. Tough competition remained (notably from Molson and Labatt).
R. v. B.C. Sugar Refining Co. Ltd.	1961	B.C. Sugar acquired its only competitor in western Canada, Manitoba Sugar Refining Co. After the acquisition, B. C. Sugar had the following market shares: British Columbia, 100 percent; Alberta, 100 percent; Saskatchewan, 100 percent; and Manitoba, 70 percent. Not guilty. Effective competition from eastern suppliers prevented B.C. Sugar from operating in detriment to public interest.

*Christopher Green, *Canadian Industrial Organization and Policy*, 3rd ed. (Toronto: McGraw-Hill Ryerson, 1990), 170.

The first case to reach the Supreme Court of Canada under Canada's anti-combine laws was that of *Weidman v. Schragge*, a collusive agreement case. It came to the Supreme Court not because of a prosecution by the Crown but as the result of a civil suit between the two parties. Weidman and Schragge, two

Winnipeg junk dealers, had agreed to fix prices and together controlled 95 percent of the market. A dispute between the two arose, and Weidman attempted to sue Schragge for breaking their price--fixing agreement. The Supreme Court of Canada ruled that the agreement was illegal and non-enforceable.

The major importance of the other collusive agreement cases set out in Table 21.5 arises from the light they shed on the way in which the court interpreted another crucial word in the law — *unduly.* As you can see from Table 21.3, the offence was that of "unduly" limiting, restraining, or preventing competition or enhancing price. The act did not define "unduly," so its meaning had to be determined by the courts. The first interpretation offered came in a statement made in 1947 by Justice Cartwright, who interpreted "unduly" as meaning, in effect, a total monopoly or total absence of competition. In the Abitibi case in 1960, however, "unduly" was given a broader interpretation.

The monopoly cases that have been successfully prosecuted seem to have been fairly straightforward. The Eddy Match Company was a clear and classic monopoly. The Electric Reduction Company case was a little different. Here, a company that controlled virtually the whole market for industrial phosphates could easily have been subject to competitive pressure from the entry of new, (U.S.-owned) suppliers, but by cleverly price discriminating, it kept those suppliers out. Nevertheless, the company was found guilty and ordered to stop its attempts at deterring new entrants. An important case in which the defendants were found not guilty was that of Allied Chemical and Cominco in 1975. The company had a complete monopoly in a particular region (a large and important one), but potential competition from the rest of the country prevented high prices and monopoly profit.

There have been no merger cases in which the defendants were found guilty. The two cases briefly described in Table 21.5 indicate why. Mergers rarely result in a firm that has an effective monopoly of the entire industry. In the brewery case, even though Canadian brewers controlled 60 percent of the market for beer in Ontario and 52 percent in Québec, the court found that there was enough competition from other major brewers to prevent monopoly profits. The B.C. Sugar case was similar. The underlying economics had some parallels with those of Allied Chemicals and Cominco. B.C. Sugar certainly had a regional monopoly, but according to the court, it faced severe competition from eastern suppliers and, therefore, was not able to restrain trade or act in a manner detrimental to the public interest.

Public or Special Interest?

It is clear from the historical contexts in which anti-combine law has evolved that its intent has been to protect and pursue the public interest and restrain the profit-seeking and anti-competitive actions of producers. But it is also clear from our brief history of anti-combine legislation and cases that, from time to time, the interest of the producer has had an influence on the way in which the law has been interpreted and applied. Nevertheless, the overall thrust of anti-combine law appears to have been directed towards achieving allocative efficiency and, therefore, towards serving the public interest.

It is interesting to note that there is an important difference between the way in which the original anti-combine law and regulation and the new anti-combine law are administered. Regulation and the new law are administered by a bureaucracy. The old anti-combine law was interpreted and enforced by the legal process — the courts. Economists are now beginning to extend theories of public choice to include an economic analysis of the law and the way the courts interpret the law. It is interesting to speculate that the legal institutions that administer anti-combine law are more sensitive to the public interest than the political and bureaucratic institutions that deal with regulation and the new anti-combine laws.

The breakup of the American Telphone and Telegraph Company (AT&T) monopoly in the United States is a strikingly good example of the consumer interest and the public interest emerging and dominating that of the producer. Before the breakup, AT&T had a monopoly on all long-distance telephone service. Following the breakup, suppliers such as US Sprint and MCI compete with AT&T for long-distance business. Consumers are free to choose their long-distance carrier. Pay phones even have special buttons permitting callers to select their carriers. The effects of the breakup and deregulation of long-distance telecommunications, although controversial, appear to have brought some visible benefits to consumers. These benefits are so large that some Canadian consumers are now using private lines (of controversial legality) to access the U.S. long-distance carriers, thereby cutting the costs of their long-distance calls between, for example, Windsor and Vancouver.

Another example is that of Safeway Canada and its bid to acquire Woodward Stores Limited, a food-retailing company operating in 17 cities in British Columbia and Alberta. Safeway is a major retailer of food in those cities, and the director of the Competition Tribunal opposed Safeway's proposal on the grounds that it would severely limit competition. Safeway eventually agreed to sell 12 stores in six of the markets in which the director believed competition would be substantially reduced. In return for this divestiture, the director agreed that Safeway could go ahead and acquire Woodward.

It is difficult to reach a firm conclusion on how the new anti-combine law is working and whose interests are most effectively being served. Between June 1986 and March 1989, the Bureau of Competition Policy examined 369 mergers. Almost all of these were allowed to proceed as planned and only in 19 cases were the proposals opposed. We cannot, of course, conclude on the basis of these numbers that the new law is being loosely enforced. Before any conclusion can be reached, it will be necessary to study the way in which the newly merged firms operate.

International Competition Policy

An additional important factor influencing competition policy is policy towards international competition and international trade. Over the postwar years, international competition has become more severe and tariffs have gradually been lowered. Canada took a decisive step in this regard with the passage of the Canada – United States Free Trade Agreement, which, by the end of this century, will provide for almost completely open competition between Canada and the United States. International competition is perhaps the most effective form of competition and, therefore, tariff reduction is one of the most effective methods of implementing competition policy.

■ In this chapter, we've seen how the government intervenes in markets, when there is monopoly or oligopoly, to affect prices, quantities, the gains from trade, and the division of those gains between consumers and producers. We've seen that there is a conflict between the pursuit of the public interest — achieving allocative efficiency — and the pursuit of the special interests of producers — maximizing monopoly profit. The political and legal arenas are the places in which these conflicts are resolved. We've reviewed the two theories — public interest and capture — concerning the type and scope of government intervention.

SUMMARY

Market Intervention

The government can intervene to regulate monopolistic and oligopolistic markets in three ways: regulation, nationalization, and legislation. All of these methods are used in Canada.

Government action can influence consumer surplus, producer surplus, and total surplus. Consumer surplus is the difference between what consumers are willing to pay for a given consumption level and what they actually pay. Producer surplus is the difference between a producer's revenue from its sales and the opportunity cost of production. Total surplus is the sum of consumer surplus and producer surplus. Total surplus is maximized under competition. Under monopoly, producer surplus is increased and consumer surplus decreased, and a deadweight loss is created. (pp. 539-540)

Economic Theory of Intervention

Consumers and producers use voting, lobbying, and making campaign contributions to express their demand for the intervention that influences their surpluses. The larger the surplus that can be generated by a particular intervention and the smaller the number of people affected, the larger is the demand for the intervention. A small number of people are easier than a large number to organize into an effective political lobby. Intervention is supplied by politicians, who pursue their own best interest. The larger the surplus per head generated and the larger the number of people affected by it, the larger is the supply of intervention. In equilibrium, the intervention that exists is such that no interest group feels it worthwhile to use additional resources to press for changes. There are two theories of political equilibrium: public interest theory and capture theory. Public interest theory predicts that total surplus will be maximized; capture theory predicts that producer surplus will be maximized. (pp. 540-542)

Regulation and Deregulation

Regulation began in Canada with the Railway Act of 1888. Regulation expanded and experienced steady growth until the mid-1970s. Since the early 1980s, a deregulation process has been under way in transport, oil and gas, and financial services.

Regulation is conducted by regulatory agencies controlled by politically appointed bureaucrats and staffed by a permanent bureaucracy of experts. Regulated firms are required to comply with rules about price, product quality, and output levels. The two kinds of industries that are regulated are natural monopolies and cartels. In both cases, regulation has enabled firms in the industries affected to achieve profit levels equal to or greater than those attained on the average in the rest of the economy. This outcome is closer to the predictions of the capture theory of regulation than to the predictions of the public interest theory. (pp. 542-548)

Public Ownership

There are more than 100 federal and provincial Crown corporations in Canada. They produce some of the most important goods and services that we consume, such as rail transport, hydroelectric power, and telecommunications. The economic model of public enterprise is the same as that of bureaucracy. The managers of a public enterprise aim to maximize their budget. The political process places constraints on that aim. The outcome is a tendency for public enterprises to be inefficient in two respects: they overproduce, and their costs are higher than the minimum possible ones.

Studies of public and private enterprises operating in similar circumstances indicate that public enterprises are significantly less efficient than their private enterprise counterparts. In recent years, there has been a tendency for the consumer interest to be more assertive, and a process of privatization or cutbacks in the scale of public enterprises has occurred. (pp. 549-551)

Anti-Combine Law

Anti-combine law provides an alternative way for government to control monopoly and monopolistic practices. The original law itself was brief, and its interpretation tended to favour the consumer. The overall thrust of the law was directed towards serving the public interest. The Competition Act of 1986 radically reforms the anti-combine law, placing responsibility for the enforcement of the law with a quasi-judicial tribunal, and providing a highly detailed criteria under which the tribunal must reach its conclusion. In recent years, increased international competition has reduced monopoly power. (pp. 555-558)

KEY ELEMENTS

Key Terms

Anti-combine law, 540
Average cost pricing rule, 544
Capture theory of intervention, 541
Crown corporation, 539
Deregulation, 539
Marginal cost pricing rule, 544
Nationalization, 539
Privatization, 539
Public interest theory of intervention, 541
Rate of return regulation, 545
Regulation, 539
Total surplus, 540

Key Figures and Tables 

REVIEW QUESTIONS

1 What are the two main ways in which the government can intervene in the marketplace?

2 What is consumer surplus? How is it calculated? How is it represented in a diagram?

3 What is producer surplus? How is it calculated? How is it represented in a diagram?

4 What is total surplus? How is it calculated? How is it represented in a diagram?

5 Why do consumers demand intervention? In what kinds of industries are their demands for intervention greatest?

6 Why do producers demand intervention? In what kinds of industries are their demands for intervention greatest?

7 Explain the public interest and capture theories of intervention. What does each theory imply about the behaviour of politicians?

8 How is oligopoly regulated in Canada? In whose interest is it regulated?

9 How do publicly owned corporations behave:

a) As predicted by the economic theory of bureaucracy?

b) In the real world?

10 What was the original anti-combine law in Canada?

11 What is the main anti-combine law in Canada today? How does it differ from the original law?

PROBLEMS

1 Cascade Springs Inc., is a natural monopoly that bottles water from a spring high in the Rocky Mountains. The total fixed cost it incurs is $80,000, and its marginal cost is 10 cents a bottle. The demand for bottled water from Cascade Springs is:

Price (cents per bottle)	Quantity demanded (thousands of bottles per year)
100	0
90	100
80	200
70	300
60	400
50	500
40	600
30	700
20	800
10	900
0	1,000

What is the price of a bottle of water, and how many bottles does Cascade Springs sell?

2 Does Cascade Springs maximize total surplus or producer surplus?

3 If the government regulates Cascade Springs by imposing a marginal cost pricing rule, what is the price of a bottle of water? How many bottles does Cascade Springs sell?

4 Is the regulation in problem 3 in the public interest or in the private interest?

5 If the government regulates Cascade Springs by imposing an average cost pricing rule, what is the price of a bottle of water? How many bottles does Cascade Springs sell?

6 Is the regulation in problem 5 in the public interest or in the private interest?

7 Cascade Springs is taken over by the B.C. government and captured by its bureaucrats. They obey the rule "price equals marginal cost," but they maximize their budget and persuade the B.C. government to subsidize them by an amount equal to the consumer surplus on their bottled water.

a) What is their output rate?

b) At what price do they sell?

c) How big is their subsidy?

d) What is the amount of consumer surplus retained by the consumers?

PART 8

Introduction to Macroeconomics

TALKING WITH JAMES TOBIN

James Tobin has had a long and distinguished career in macroeconomics, extending the model suggested by Keynes, paying special attention to the demand for money, consumption and saving, fiscal and monetary policy, and economic growth. For most of his career, he has been at Yale University. He was a member of President John F. Kennedy's Council of Economic Advisers. For his many contributions, James Tobin received the Nobel Prize in economic science in 1981. Michael Parkin spoke with Professor Tobin about the challenges that face the economy.

"Today, if I have to be labeled — and considering the alternatives — I'm proud to be a Keynesian."

Professor Tobin, you were a young boy during the Great Depression. Do you remember that period as a time of great hardship?

Not of personal hardship, although my grandfather lost his job and his entire fortune when the bank of which he was president went under, and my father suffered serious losses when creditors took over the office building he had constructed in 1929. My father was a journalist at the University of Illinois. In 1932, my mother became head of the local Family Service agency. Her job kept us aware of the ravages of the Depression. Our hometown, Champaign, Illinois, was on the main rail line. Many poor people from the South, hoping for jobs and better lives in the North, got off the train in Champaign.

When did you first study economics?

As a Harvard sophomore in 1936. We met weekly with a tutor and discussed what we were reading or writing. My tutor was also my introductory economics teacher. He had just come back from a year in England, where he had heard a lot about a new book by John Maynard Keynes. He suggested that we read it. I was too green to understand that it was absurd for a sophomore to tackle *The General Theory of Employment, Interest, and Money*. So I plunged into it and got very excited about the book and about economics.

People usually refer to you as a Keynesian macroeconomist. Do you agree with that term?

I don't like labelling. I tried to contribute to economics, especially to macroeconomics. I tried to strengthen what we now call the microfoundations of macroeconomics. In the 1950s and 1960s we hoped that the Keynesian-Neoclassical controversy would soon be behind us, superseded by a synthesis of the two strands. Beginning with my first published article in 1940, which disagreed with Keynes about the relation between wages and employment, I wrote many pieces critical of *The General Theory*. Unfortunately, the old debates have been revived and magnified over the past two decades and we are far from a new synthesis. Today, if I have to be labelled—and considering the alternatives—I'm proud to be a Keynesian.

How would you characterize the controversy in macroeconomics? Has it stayed the same over the years, or is it different today?

The original controversy in the 1930s and 1940s was whether a capitalist market economy possesses reliable automatic mechanisms of adjustment, which would restore equilibrium between jobs and workers and between output and capacity whenever some shock to demand pushes the economy from full employment. Orthodox economists—Keynes called them Classical—said yes. Keynes said no. Today's New Classical macroeconomists are more extreme than their old Classical predecessors. They assert that the economy is *always* in full employment equilibrium. That the economy as a whole operates like a rational maximizing individual. Keynesians believe the economy can fall out of equilibrium and that government interventions can speed up recoveries.

Given that macroeconomists still have important disagreements, can they use any of the same approaches? Might a Keynesian, for instance, use the idea of rational expectations, which is identified with the New Classical school?

Thoughtful economists of all sorts have long incorporated rational expectations in their models, to a limited degree. They would not postulate a stable, repetitive equilibrium that depended on expectations at odds with the actual values of variables. For example, if the interest rate is 2 percent year after year, people would surely learn not to act on the expectation that it will become 4 percent. But I think it stretches credibility to assume that ordinary business people and consumers can learn to form rational expectations in volatile economic enviroments whose structures even econometricians cannot discern.

I think rational expectations of quantities like output and employment could have a place in Keynesian models. Those are important variables once the New Classical assumption that markets are always clearing is abandoned.

Many economists regard the macroeconomic performance of the early 1960s as a very successful period of moderate inflation, low unemployment, and strong growth in real output. Was that the high point of macroeconomic management from which we've been sliding ever since?

Yes. I suppose I have a vested interest in believing that to be true—I helped to inaugurate the policy in 1961. And it was a pleasant period, when economists and policymakers were not as divided and combative as they are now. At the beginning of the Kennedy administration, unemployment was 7 percent, considered unacceptably high in those days. Inflation was only 1 or 2 percent, thanks in good part to the two recent Eisenhower recessions. We economists pushed for stimulative fiscal policy. We got some, but it took some time to bring President Kennedy and Congress to accept a major initiative. We were lucky, when what looked like a hesitation in the recovery before our policies were firmly in place, turned out to be temporary. The administration pursued a wage-price guidepost policy, seeking to get management and labour to agree to noninflationary wage settlements and price decisions. By 1966 unemployment was down to 4 percent and inflation was still around 2 percent.

Were all the breaks good ones? Was there any bad luck?

The bad luck was the Vietnam War. Despite the advice of his Keynesian economists, President Johnson would not ask for a tax increase to finance his escalation of the war in 1966. His budget overheated the economy in the late 1960s. Unemployment fell to 3 percent and inflation rose to 4 or 5 percent. At the time, 5 percent inflation was considered very serious, bad enough to induce President Nixon to introduce price controls. Today 5 percent is accepted as "zero" inflation, a reminder that attitudes are relative.

"It was a pleasant period, when economists and policymakers were not as divided as they are now."

"Students who understand the macro identities know more than most politicians and journalists."

What have we learned from the events of the 1970s?

Maybe what we should have learned is that those events were exceptional. There were two enormous shocks in oil and energy prices. A major increase in an important price raises the price index, but OPEC price shocks don't happen every year and shouldn't be incorporated into projections of overall inflation. What it was proper to worry about was the inflation potential of wage increases seeking to catch up with the increases in energy prices. The 1980s indicate that under normal circumstances, we experience less severe inflation.

We've just experienced seven years of economic recovery. How did economic policy contribute?

I give the Federal Reserve high marks for monetary policy since 1982. From October 1979 until 1982, the Fed was very monetarist. The overriding priority was to rid the economy of the temporary double-digit inflation that accompanied the second oil shock. Restrictive monetary policy and recession did bring it down to about 5 percent. The strategy worked faster than I had expected—though not so fast as the optimists were sugessting. By 1982, unemployment reached its highest level since the Depression.

In 1982, Paul Volcker, the chairman of the Fed, turned both his policy and the economy around. Monetarism was displaced by concern for macroeconomic performance. The Fed fine-tuned the recovery, reducing the unemployment as long as no new inflation threatened. By 1989 unemployment was down to 5 percent, lower than the Fed, and most economists thought "inflation-safe" 10 years earlier.

Fiscal policy in the 1980s has been a radical departure from that of any previous federal administration in peacetime. The tremendous reduction in taxes in 1981 along with the expansion of defence spending generated a series of deficits that raised federal public debt from 25 to 43 percent of GDP over the eight years of the Reagan presidency.

Regan's fiscal policy was a massive demand stimulus. The Fed had to worry about whether it would overheat the economy. It was like having two drivers in the same car. The fiscal driver had a heavy foot on the gas pedal. The monetary driver had to keep a foot on the brake. As I said, the Fed fine-tuned the brake quite well. But the by-products of this combination of policies have been disastrous—high interest rates, low capital investment, enormous trade deficits, threatening the living standards of future Americans.

What economic principles would you share with students?

First, opportunity cost—a simple, fruitful concept. Students can learn it; most people innocent of economics don't understand it. Second, fungibility—"money mingles," a friend of mine liked to say. You can give people money, ostensibly for your own purpose, but the recipients will generally find a way to accommodate their own priorities.

Third, economics students who understand the macro identities—for example, $Y = C + I + G + NX$—know more than most politicians and journalists.

CHAPTER 22

Inflation, Unemployment, Cycles, and Deficits

After studying this chapter, you will be able to:

- Define inflation and explain its effects.
- Define unemployment and explain its benefits and costs.
- Define gross domestic product (GDP).
- Distinguish between nominal GDP and real GDP.
- Explain the importance of growth and fluctuations in real GDP.
- Define the business cycle.
- Describe how unemployment, stock prices, and inflation fluctuate over the business cycle.
- Define the government budget deficit and the country's current account deficit.

Shopping Cart Blues

A SHOPPING CART of groceries that today costs $100 cost less than $60 in 1980, $27 in 1970, and $17 in 1950. In fact, in the past 50 years, there has only been one year in which prices have not increased. The same is true of wages. An average hour of work earned $1.04 in 1950. The same average hour earned $3.01 in 1970 and $7.17 in 1980. Today it earns more than $13. This persistent increase in prices and wages means that firms need more dollars to pay us and we need more dollars to buy the goods and services that we consume. Does this increase matter? What are the effects of persistently rising prices and wages? ■ In 1983, for every 8 people with jobs, one other was unemployed — that is, looking for work but not able to find any. Another unknown number of people had become discouraged about their chances of finding jobs and had stopped looking. Although unemployment was unusually high through most of the 1980s, its rate then was modest compared with the 1930s — the years of the Great Depression. In the depression's worst year, 1933, one-fifth of the labour force was unemployed. Unemployment fluctuates but it never disappears. At its lowest levels, during World War II, unemployment fell to just less than 2 percent of the labour force. And yet we talk about "full employment." How can there be "full employment" when there are people looking for work? Why is there always some unemployment? What is the cost of unemployment? And does it bring any benefits? ■ In the depths of the Great Depression, the value of all the goods and services produced in Canada was $3.5 billion. By 1989, 56 years later, the value of Canadian output approached $650 billion (a 185-fold increase over its 1933 level). From 1970 to 1989, the nation's output increased sevenfold in value. How much of the growth in the value of our output is real and how much of it is an illusion created by inflation? ■ Our economy does not follow a smooth and predictable course. From 1983 to 1987, the economy was on a course of sustained expansion: production grew, unemployment fell, stock prices rose, and inflation was modest. Then, in October 1987, the stock market crashed. Overnight, thousands of people found themselves poorer by millions of dollars. But the economy kept on expanding. Production continued to grow and unemployment held steady. Expansions as strong and prolonged as that of the 1980s are unusual. Periods of expansion are usually punctuated by periods of contraction, sometimes severe ones like that of 1981-1982. In those years, production sagged and unemployment climbed. We call these waves of expansion and contraction business cycles. Which features of business cycles are similar from one cycle to another and which are different? Does the economy normally keep booming when the stock market crashes as it did in 1987? Or do stock market crashes sometimes signal an upcoming contraction? ■ We hear a lot these days about deficits. One of these deficits is the government's. Every year since 1975, the government of Canada has spent more than it has collected in taxes. To make up the difference, the government borrows. Some of that borrowing is domestic and some international. Just how big is the government's deficit? Has it been getting bigger? And is it unusual for the government to have a deficit? ■ The other deficit that we hear a lot about is our international deficit — the difference between the value of the goods and services Canada sells to the rest of the world and the value of our own purchases. In the three years 1986 through 1988, that deficit averaged $10 billion a year — $100 for every adult Canadian or 2 cents on every dollar we earned. What happens when we buy more from the rest of the world than we sell to it? How do we make up the difference? And what are the consequences?

■ The questions that we have just posed are the subject matter of macroeconomics — the branch of economics that seeks to understand the problems of rising prices, high unemployment, fluctuating output, and government and international deficits. It also studies the government's attempts to cope with these problems. ■ The macroeconomic events through which we are now living are as exciting and tumultuous as any in history. Governments here and around the world face a daily challenge to find policies that will give all of us a smoother macroeconomic ride. With what you learn in these chapters, you will be better able to understand these macroeconomic policy challenges and the political debate that surrounds them. We begin our study of macroeconomics by looking at inflation.

Inflation

Inflation is an upward movement in the average level of prices. Its opposite is **deflation**, a downward movement in the average level of prices. The boundary between inflation and deflation is price stability. **Price stability** occurs when the average level of prices is moving neither up nor down. The average level of prices is called the **price level**. It is measured by a price index. A **price index** measures the average level of prices in one period as a percentage of their average level in an earlier period called the **base period**.

Price indexes in Canada go all the way back to Confederation, and the story they tell is shown in Fig. 22.1. Over the 122-year period shown in that figure, prices have risen seventeenfold — an average annual rate of increase of 2.34 percent. But prices have not moved upward at a constant and steady pace. During some periods, such as the years of World War I and those between 1974 and 1982, the increase was sharp and pronounced — at times exceeding 10 percent per year. At the opposite extreme are years in which prices have fallen. The last occasion on which this occurred in a sustained way was during the Great Depression years of the 1930s. Prices also fell in the early 1920s, following World War I. There were also some periods of price decline during the nineteenth century.

Perhaps the most striking fact revealed by Fig. 22.1 is the recent origin of high and persistent inflation. For the first 45 years of Canada's history, prices were almost constant. They increased sharply during World War I but then fluctuated around a more or less constant level again until World War II. Since the end of World War II (with one minor exception in the early 1950s), prices have increased each and every year.

Inflation Rate and the Price Level

The **inflation rate** is the percentage change in the price level. The formula for the annual inflation rate is:

Figure 22.1 The Price Level, 1867–1989

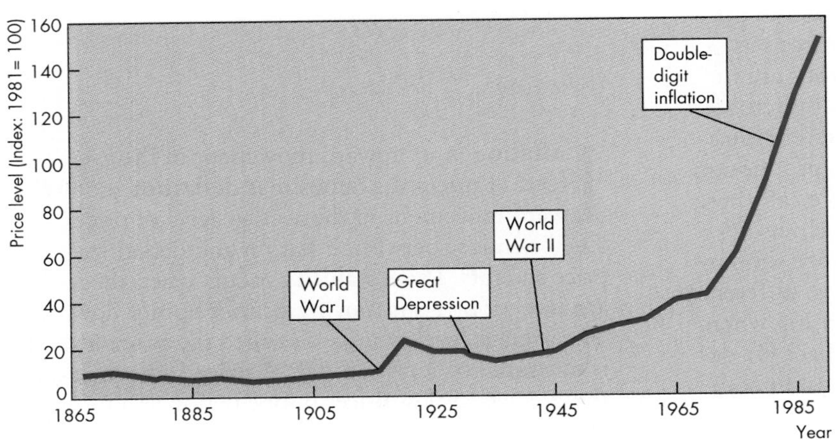

Prices, on the average, have increased seventeenfold between 1867 and 1989. In some periods, such as the years of World War I and the 1970s and early 1980s, price increases were rapid. In other periods, such as the 1950s, increases were more moderate. At yet other times prices fell, such as in the 1870s, the years following World War I, the early 1920s, and the Great Depression years of the 1930s.

Sources: 1867–1912: F. H. Leacy, ed., *Historical Statistics of Canada*, 2nd ed. General Wholesale Price Index, Series K–33. (Ottawa, Statistics Canada and the Social Science Federation of Canada, 1983). 1913–1975: *Historical Statistics*, Consumer Price Index for Canada, Series K–8. 1976–1989: Consumer Price Index, CANSIM series D484000. The raw data were converted to an index number with a base of 1981 = 100; excessive fluctuations in the Wholesale Price Index (used for 1867 to 1912) were smoothed out using the average relationship between wholesale and retail prices between 1913 and 1975.

$$\text{Inflation rate} = \frac{\text{Current year's price level} - \text{Last year's price level}}{\text{Last year's price level}} \times 100$$

A common price index (one we'll learn more about in Chapter 23) is called the Consumer Price Index or simply the CPI. We can illustrate the calculation of the annual inflation rate by using this index and the above formula. In December 1987, the CPI was 140.5, and in December 1988, it was 146.1. The inflation rate for 1988 was:

$$\text{Inflation rate} = \frac{146.1 - 140.5}{140.5} \times 100$$

$$= 4.0 \text{ percent}$$

The Recent Inflation Record

Recent Canadian economic history has seen some dramatic changes in the rate of inflation. The inflation rate between 1960 and 1989, as measured by the CPI, is shown in Fig. 22.2.

As you can see, the inflation rate in the early 1960s was low and steady, lying between 1 and 2 percent a year. The inflation rate has been more or less steady since 1984, but at a higher level than that of the early 1960s. It was the nearly 20-year period between the middle 1960s and middle 1980s that saw the most dramatic changes in inflation. At its peak, in 1981, the inflation rate reached 13 percent a year. Between 1960 and 1980, inflation increased strongly. The figure also shows distinct cycles in the inflation rate with peaks in 1969, 1974, and 1981 and troughs in 1971, 1976, and 1985.

Although the inflation rate has gone up and down over the years, since 1953 the price level has never fallen. The inflation rate has fallen from time to time, but the price level (see Fig. 22.1) has increased relentlessly, year after year. The price level falls only when the inflation rate is negative. There has not been such a year in the period since 1953. Thus even in a year, such as 1960, when the inflation rate was low, the price level was rising.

Inflation and the Value of Money

When inflation is present, money is losing value. The **value of money** is the amount of goods and services

Figure 22.2 Inflation, 1960–1989

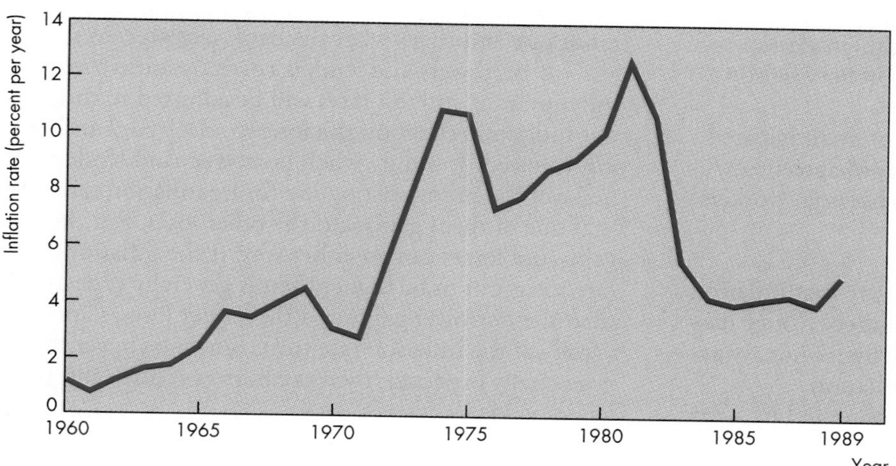

Inflation is a persistent feature of modern economic life in Canada. The inflation rate was low in the first half of the 1960s, but then moved upward until it peaked in 1981. After 1981, it fell dramatically. Inflation has followed a series of cycles, with peaks in 1969, 1974, and 1981 and troughs in 1971, 1976, and 1985.

Source: See Fig. 22.1.

that can be bought with a given amount of money. When an economy experiences inflation, the value of money falls. In other words, you cannot buy as many groceries with $50 this year as you could last year. The rate at which the value of money falls is equal to the inflation rate. When the inflation rate is high, as it was in 1981, money loses its value at a rapid pace. When inflation is low, as it was in 1961, the value of money falls slowly.

Inflation is a phenomenon experienced in all countries. But inflation *rates* vary from one country to another. When inflation rates differ by a lot over a prolonged period of time, the result is a change in the foreign exchange value of money. A **foreign exchange rate** is the rate at which one country's money exchanges for another's. For example, in mid-1989 one Canadian dollar exchanged for 122 Japanese yen. A decade earlier, in mid-1979, one Canadian dollar exchanged for 186 Japanese yen. Thus, since 1979, the value of the dollar has fallen in terms of the Japanese yen. This performance reflects the fact that the value of money in Canada has been falling more quickly than the value of money in Japan. We'll learn more about exchange rates and how they are influenced by inflation in Chapter 29.

Is Inflation a Problem?

Is it a problem if money loses its value and at a rate that varies from one year to another? It is, indeed, a problem, but to understand why, we need to distinguish between anticipated and unanticipated inflation. When prices are moving upward, most people are aware of that fact. They also have some notion about the rate at which they are rising. The rate at which people (on the average) believe that the price level will rise is called the **expected inflation rate**. But expectations may be right or wrong. If they turn out to be right, the actual inflation rate equals the expected inflation rate and inflation is said to be anticipated. That is, an **anticipated inflation** is an inflation rate that has been correctly forecast (on the average). To the extent that the inflation rate is misforecast, it is said to be unanticipated. That is, **unanticipated inflation** is the part of the inflation rate that has caught people by surprise.

The problems arising from inflation differ depending on whether its rate is anticipated or unanticipated. Let's begin by looking at the problems arising from unanticipated inflation.

The Problem of Unanticipated Inflation

Unanticipated inflation is a problem because it produces unanticipated changes in the value of money. Money is used as a measurement of value in the transactions that we undertake. Borrowers and lenders and workers and their employers all make contracts in terms of money. If the value of money varies unexpectedly over time, then the amounts *really* paid and received differ from those that people intended to pay and receive when they signed contracts. Measuring value with a rod whose units vary is a bit like trying to measure a piece of cloth with an elastic ruler. The size of the cloth depends on how tightly the ruler is stretched.

Let's take a look at the effects of unanticipated inflation by looking at what happens to agreements between borrowers and lenders and between workers and employers.

Borrowers and Lenders People often say that inflation is good for borrowers and bad for lenders. To see how they reach that conclusion — and why it's not always correct — consider the following situation.

Sue borrows $5,000 from the bank to buy a car and agrees to repay the loan with interest one year later. The agreed interest rate is 10 percent a year. Sue repays the bank $5,500 after one year. Suppose there is no inflation. The goods and services that can be bought with $5,000 are the same after one year as they are when Sue borrows the money. In this situation, to pay the bank $500 in interest, Sue has to forego the consumption of $500 worth of goods and services. Now, in contrast, suppose that the economy is experiencing inflation at a rate of 10 percent a year. In this case, when the bank receives $5,500, the quantity of goods and services that it can buy with that money is exactly what it could have bought with $5,000 a year earlier. (With a 10 percent inflation rate, the price of a car, for example, will have risen from $5,000 to $5,500.) As far as Sue is concerned, although she pays the bank $500 in interest, that payment does not impose an opportunity cost on her. Over the year, the value of money has fallen. The $5,000 that she borrowed is now worth only $4,500 in terms of goods and services. This fall in the value of money cancels out the interest payment and leaves her having *really* paid no interest at all. Sue, the borrower, gains at the expense of the bank, the lender.

But the borrower does not always gain and the lender lose when there is inflation. Suppose that both Sue and the bank anticipate a 10 percent inflation rate. They can act to offset the decreasing value of money by adjusting the interest rate they agree upon. If they agree that 10 percent is the appropriate interest rate with no inflation, they will agree to a 20 percent interest rate when they expect a 10 percent inflation rate. Let's see what happens in this case. Sue repays the bank $6,000 at the end of the year. Of this, $5,000 is the amount borrowed and $1,000 is the interest payment (20 percent of $5,000). Of the additional $1,000 that Sue pays the bank, $500 is interest and the other $500 is compensation for the loss in the value of money. Sue *really* pays a 10 percent interest rate and that's what the bank *really* receives.

If borrowers and lenders correctly anticipate the inflation rate, interest rates will be adjusted to cancel out inflation's effect on the interest *really* paid and *really* received. It is only when borrowers and lenders make errors in forecasting the future inflation rate that one of them gains and the other loses. But those gains and losses can go either way. If the inflation rate turns out to be higher than is generally expected, then the borrower gains and the lender loses. Conversely, if the inflation rate turns out to be lower than is generally expected, then the borrower loses and the lender gains.

Thus it is not inflation itself that produces gains and losses for borrowers and lenders. It is an *unanticipated increase* in the inflation rate that *benefits borrowers* and hurts lenders and an *unanticipated decrease* in the inflation rate that *benefits lenders* and hurts borrowers.

In Canada in the late 1960s and 1970s, the inflation rate kept rising and to some degree the rise was unanticipated, so borrowers tended to gain. In the 1980s, the fall in the inflation rate was also, at least initially, unanticipated and lenders gained. On the international scene, many developing countries, such as Mexico and Brazil, borrowed large amounts of money in the late 1970s and early 1980s at high interest rates, anticipating that an inflation rate of more than 10 percent a year would persist. These countries are now stuck with paying the interest on these loans without the extra revenue that they expected to receive from the higher prices of their exports.

Workers and Employers Another common belief is that inflation redistributes income between workers and their employers. Some people believe that workers gain at the expense of employers, and others believe the contrary.

The previous discussion concerning borrowers and lenders applies to workers and their employers as well. If inflation increases unexpectedly, then wages will not have been set high enough. Profits will be higher than expected and wages will buy fewer goods than expected. Employers gain at the expense of workers. Conversely, if the anticipated inflation rate is higher than the actual inflation rate turns out to be, wages will have been set too high and profits will be squeezed. Workers will be able to buy more with their income than was originally anticipated. In this case workers gain at the expense of employers.

In recent Canadian experience, unanticipated changes in the inflation rate have produced fluctuations in the buying power of earnings — the value of pay cheques in terms of the goods they buy. For example, in 1974, when the inflation rate climbed to more than 10 percent a year, the buying power of earnings continued to increase but at a substantially slower pace than normal. When the inflation rate came down sharply in 1976, wage growth outpaced inflation and real wages grew at an unusually quick pace. The rebound of inflation in 1978 and 1979 was, to a large degree, unanticipated and wages did not keep up with inflation, so the buying power of earnings actually declined.

We've now seen the problems that unanticipated inflation can cause. Let's now examine the problems arising from anticipated inflation.

The Problem of Anticipated Inflation

Anticipated inflation can be a problem for two reasons. First, it imposes an opportunity cost on holding money. Second, it encourages a wasteful increase in the volume and frequency of transactions that people undertake. Let's explore these two propositions more closely.

Opportunity Cost of Holding Money Whether you hold money in the form of notes and coins in your purse or in the form of a deposit at the bank, the opportunity cost of holding money equals the inflation rate. To make this idea clearer, compare two situations in which you have $100 in the bank. In the first, inflation is 10 percent a year. At the end of the year, you still have $100 in the bank, but it now buys goods that were worth only $90 at the beginning of the year. In the second situation, there is no inflation. At the end of the year, the bank charges you $10 (a 10 percent fee) on bank deposits. Now you have $90, and so again you can buy only $90 worth of goods.

From your point of view, the two situations just described are identical. Either way you wind up at the end of the year being able to buy only $90 worth of goods. An inflation rate of 10 percent a year reduces the value of your money by the same amount as does a 10-percent fee on money holdings. The inflation rate is the opportunity cost of holding money. The higher the inflation rate, the greater is the opportunity cost of holding money.

Volume and Frequency of Transactions Since the inflation rate is the opportunity cost of holding money, anticipated inflation is the anticipated opportunity cost of holding money. People can avoid an anticipated cost of holding money only by economizing on the amount of money that they hold. For example, if the inflation rate is 10 percent a year and if, on the average, you keep $100 in your purse, then the opportunity cost of holding that money is $10 a year. With the same 10 percent inflation rate, if you hold only $10 on the average, the opportunity cost is $1 a year.

But it's not easy to vary the amount of money that you hold. To do so, you have to vary the frequency with which you are paid. For example, suppose that you have a job that pays $100 a week. If you are paid once a week and you spend all your income pretty evenly over the week, the amount of money that you hold, on the average, is $50. (You have $100 at the beginning of the week and nothing at the end of the week, averaging out at $50.) If you are paid once a month, you have $400 on payday, nothing just before the next payday, and $200 on the average. If you are paid every day of a five-day week, you are paid $20 a day and, on the average, you have $10 in your pocket.

Transacting at a high frequency is much less convenient and more costly than transacting at a lower frequency. But the higher the anticipated inflation, the higher is the frequency with which transactions are undertaken. This aspect of the problem of anticipated inflation is not very serious for the inflation rates experienced in Canada. But it can be serious if the inflation rate is sufficiently high. For example, during hyperinflations (situations in which prices are rising faster than 50 percent per month), the opportunity cost of holding money is enormous. To avoid holding money that is losing its value at a rapid pace, people transact with incredibly high frequency. Firms pay out wages twice a day, and as soon as people have been paid, they go off and spend their wages before they lose too much value. To buy a handful of groceries, you need a shopping cart of bank notes. Such situations are rare but they are not unknown. In Germany, Poland, and Hungary in the 1920s, the picture just painted was a reality. People who lingered too long in the coffee shop found that the price of their cup of coffee had increased between the time they placed their order and the time the bill was presented.

Indexing

It is sometimes suggested that the costs of inflation can be avoided by indexing. **Indexing** is a technique that links payments made under a contract to the price level. With indexing, Sue in our example above would not agree to pay back the car loan in terms of a set number of dollars; instead, she would agree to an indexing formula for calculating the number of dollars to pay. For example, the interest rate under an indexed loan contract might be specified to be 3 percent a year plus the annual inflation rate. Similarly, an indexed employment contract does not specify the number of dollars that will be paid to workers; instead, it specifies an indexing formula for calculating the number of dollars. For example, the wage rate under an indexed employment contract might be specified to be $10 an hour for the first year and increasing by the same percentage amount as the annual inflation rate in subsequent years.

The amount of interest to be paid on bank deposits can also be linked to the inflation rate in order to avoid the opportunity cost of holding such deposits. Indexing is thought likely to be most important in preserving the buying power of pensions. Indexing is also used to limit the effects of inflation on the long-term loans that people take to buy homes.

Adopting indexing to cope with changes in the value of money is not a simple matter, however, for, as we will see in Chapter 23, there isn't a unique measure of the price level and, therefore, of the inflation rate. If borrowers and lenders and workers and employers are to index their contracts, they have to agree on the price index to be used to measure the inflation rate. Such agreements are hard to reach and increase the cost of engaging in transactions.

Though indexing can be helpful in some situations, it is not a universal solution to the problem of fluctuations in the value of money. Only by somehow holding the price level constant can the costs of inflation be avoided.

Unemployment

At many times in Canada's history, unemployment has been a severe problem. For example, in the winter of 1982-83, almost 2 million people were seeking jobs. What exactly is unemployment? How is it measured? How has its rate fluctuated? Does it have any benefits? What are its costs?

What Is Unemployment?

Employment is measured as the number of adult workers (aged 16 and over) who have jobs. **Unemployment** is the number of adult workers who are not employed and who are seeking jobs. To be classified as unemployed, a person must be able and willing to work, be actively seeking work, and be without a job. Everyone who fits this description is unemployed. The **labour force** is the total number of employed and unemployed workers. The **unemployment rate** is unemployment expressed as a percentage of the labour force.

Measuring Unemployment

Unemployment is measured in Canada every month by the Canadian Labour Force Survey. The results of the survey appear in a publication called *The Labour Force*. This survey is used as the basis for the unemployment figures reported monthly in the news media.

To be counted as unemployed by the Labour Force Survey, a person must be available for work and be in one of the following three categories:

1. Without work but have made specific efforts to find a job within the previous 4 weeks
2. Waiting to be called back to a job from which he or she has been laid off for 26 weeks or less
3. Waiting to start a new job within the next 4 weeks

Anyone surveyed who satisfies one of these three criteria is counted as unemployed. Part-time workers are counted as employed.

There are three reasons why the unemployment level as measured by the Labour Force Survey may be misleading. Let's examine these.

Unrealistic Wage Expectations If someone is willing to work but only for a much higher wage than what is available, it does not make sense to count that person as unemployed. For example, suppose that a jobless high school graduate has applied for work as a checkout clerk in a local supermarket. He is offered such a job at a wage rate of $4 an hour. He doesn't like the pay, so he rejects the offer and keeps looking for a job that pays more. Such a person is available for work but not available at the wage offered. Nevertheless, he is counted as unemployed.

Correcting the unemployment data to take account of wage and job expectations would result in a lower measured unemployment rate. But we do not know how much lower.

Discouraged Workers Many people who fail to find a suitable job after prolonged and extensive search effort come to believe that there is no work available for them. They become discouraged and stop looking for work. Such people are called discouraged workers. **Discouraged workers** are people who do not have jobs and would like work, but have stopped seeking work. Discouraged workers are not counted as unemployed by the Labour Force Survey because they have not actively sought work within the previous 4 weeks. If discouraged workers were added to the unemployment count, the unemployment rate would be higher than the one currently measured.

Part-Time Workers As we have noted, part-time workers are counted as employed. But many part-time workers are available for, and seek, full-time work. The measured unemployment rate does not capture this element of part-time unemployment. This source of unemployment is a potentially important one.

The Unemployment Record

The Canadian unemployment record from 1926 to 1989 is set out in Fig. 22.3. The dominant feature of that record is the Great Depression of the early 1930s. During that period of our history, almost 20 percent of the labour force was unemployed. Although we have not experienced anything as devastating as the Great Depression in recent years, we have experienced some high unemployment rates. One such period is highlighted in the figure — the worldwide recession of the early 1980s. There have also been periods of low unemployment. The most extreme such period was during World War II — also highlighted in the figure. The average unemployment rate over the whole 63-year period was 6.6 percent.

The Benefits and Costs of Unemployment

Unemployment is a highly charged topic. We chart the course of the unemployment rate as a measure of Canada's economic health with the intensity that a physician keeps track of a patient's temperature. What does the unemployment rate tell us about the economic health of the nation? Is a high unemployment rate a sign of economic ill health, or is there

Figure 22.3 Unemployment, 1926–1989

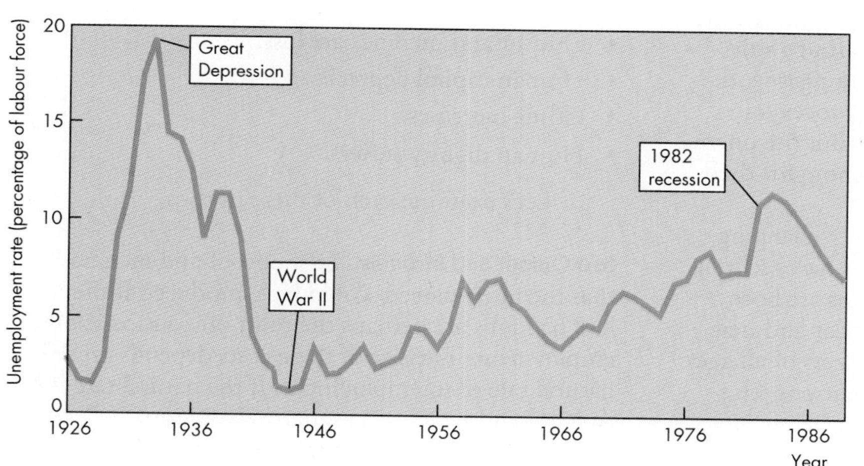

Unemployment is a persistent feature of economic life, but its rate varies considerably. At its worst — during the Great Depression — close to 20 percent of the labour force was unemployed. Even in the most recent recession, the unemployment rate climbed toward 13 percent. Since the end of World War II, there has been a general tendency for the unemployment rate to increase.

Sources: 1926–1952: *Historical Statistics* (see Fig. 22.1), Series D–132 expressed as a percentage of Series D–127. 1953–1965: CANSIM series D755041. 1966–1989: CANSIM series D767611.

such a thing as too low an unemployment rate? Let's address these questions by first examining what is gained from unemployment.

The Benefits of Unemployment Try to imagine a world in which there is no unemployment. In such a world, no one would be looking for a job. Everyone who wanted a job would have one and everyone who didn't have a job would have no regrets and no intention of seeking one. When people finished school and joined the labour force, they would take the first job that came along, no matter how bad it was or how ill suited they were to it. If a steel plant in Hamilton closed down and laid off its workers, they would immediately snap up any kind of employment available.

The world that we've just described would not be a nice place in which to live and work. Workers and jobs would be badly mismatched, productivity would probably not be very high, and there would be a good deal of unhappiness and lack of job satisfaction. The world that we live in differs from this fictional world in many respects. We'll focus on two of them.

First, in the real world, people don't usually take the first job that comes their way. Instead, they spend time searching out what they believe will be the best job available for them. By doing so, they can match their own skills and interests with the available jobs and find a satisfying job and income. This benefit from unemployment results in substantial age differences in the incidence of unemployment. Young people (aged 16 to 19) who have recently entered the labour market take much more time to find a suitable job than do older workers. Also, younger workers change jobs more frequently in the process of trying to find the best available match. But the unemployed are not only young people searching for their first or second jobs.

The real world is dynamic and ever-changing. Production and consumption change as new technologies are developed and employed. Firms are born and die. In this process, old jobs disappear and new jobs are created. As a consequence, workers of all ages constantly face the risk of losing their current job and the prospect of finding a potentially better one. Unemployment arising from this source has been particularly important in Canada in recent years. The rapid expansion of jobs in the high-tech computer-oriented sectors and the loss of jobs in traditional sectors, such as automobiles and steelmaking, have resulted in a high labour turnover rate. Many workers have moved not only from one sector of the economy to another but from one region of the country to another.

Unemployment associated with people who are seeking their first jobs and with labour turnover arising from technological change is called **frictional unemployment**. When the only unemployment is frictional unemployment, the economy is said to be at **full employment**. When the economy is at full employment — and the only unemployment is frictional — the unemployment rate is called the **natural rate of unemployment**.

Measuring frictional unemployment and the natural unemployment rate and distinguishing frictional from other types of unemployment is controversial. Some economists believe that the natural rate of unemployment in Canada is approximately constant, lying between 5 and 6 percent of the labour force. Some believe that the natural rate of unemployment varies and that most of the fluctuations in the actual unemployment rate represent fluctuations in its natural rate. Yet others believe that neither of these extreme views is correct. They believe that the natural rate of unemployment does change gradually over time, but that the actual unemployment rate fluctuates about the natural rate. We will examine some of the reasons for these differences of opinion in Chapter 31.

Next, let's examine the costs of unemployment.

The Cost of Unemployment High unemployment is costly for four reasons:

- Output and incomes are lost.
- Human capital depreciates.
- Crime increases.
- Human dignity suffers.

Let's examine each of these in turn.

Lost Output and Incomes Lost output and incomes that the unemployed would have produced if they had had jobs are perhaps the most obvious costs of unemployment. The size of these costs depends on the natural rate of unemployment. If the natural rate is between 5 and 6 percent, as many economists believe, the lost output from unemployment is enormous.

Arthur Okun, a well-known U.S. economist who was President Lyndon Johnson's economic advisor, studied the relationship between unemployment and aggregate output and formulated what has come to be known as Okun's Law (see Our Advancing

Knowledge, Chapter 31). Okun's Law, applied to Canadian data, can be stated as follows:

Other things being equal, for every 1 percentage point increase in the unemployment rate, the nation's output of goods and services falls by 2.5 percentage points.

One percent of aggregate output in Canada was approximately $6.5 billion in 1989. Thus the fall in the unemployment rate from 10 percent (where it stood at the beginning of 1987) to 7 percent (where it stood in the middle of 1989) — a decrease of 3 percentage points — increased the value of Canadian output by 7.5 percent, or almost $50 billion. With an increase in output of this magnitude, every Canadian could buy, on the average, close to an extra $2,000 worth of goods and services each year. You can now see why those economists who believe that the natural rate of unemployment is constant also believe that the value of output lost in periods of high unemployment is very large.

Those economists who believe that the natural rate of unemployment itself varies, think that the lost-output cost of unemployment is small. If the unemployment rate is temporarily high because a lot of technical change calls for a higher than normal amount of labour turnover, then lowering the unemployment rate would prevent the necessary reallocation of labour. To reap the full advantage of the new technologies, people need to change jobs. If they do not, both output and income will be lower than the new technologies could otherwise have achieved.

Human Capital A second and important cost of unemployment is the permanent damage that can be done to an unemployed worker by hindering his or her career development and acquisition of human capital. **Human capital** is the value of a person's education and acquired skills. It is measured as the amount of money that, invested at the average interest rate, would yield the same income as that produced by the person's acquired skills. These skills include the mechanical and mental skills we acquire in school as well as those we develop on the job. They also include our work habits and our ability to concentrate. Prolonged unemployment seriously lowers the value of a person's human capital. When unemployment is prolonged, human capital depreciates or deteriorates — skills lose their value.

Crime A rise in the unemployment rate usually causes an increase in the amount of crime. When people cannot earn an income from legitimate work, they sometimes turn to crime. A high crime rate is also one of the costs of high unemployment.

Human Dignity A final cost of unemployment is the loss of self-esteem that afflicts many who suffer prolonged periods of unemployment. This cost is difficult to measure, but it is probably the aspect of unemployment that makes it so highly charged with political and social significance.

Unemployment is not the only indicator of the state of the nation's economic health. Another is its gross domestic product. Let's now examine that.

Gross Domestic Product

The value of all the *final* goods and services produced in the economy in a year is called **gross domestic product** or GDP. **Final goods and services** are goods and services that are not used as inputs in the production of other goods and services, but are bought by their final user. Examples of final goods are cans of pop and cars. Examples of final services are automobile insurance and haircuts.

Not all goods and services are final. Some are intermediate goods and services. **Intermediate goods and services** are those used as inputs into the production process of another good or service. Examples of intermediate goods are the windshields, batteries, and gearboxes used by car producers and the paper and ink used by newspaper manufacturers. Examples of intermediate services are the banking and insurance services bought by car producers and news printers. Whether a good or service is intermediate or final depends on who buys it and for what purpose. For example, electric power purchased by a car producer or a printer is an intermediate good. Electric power bought by a household is a final good.

When we measure gross domestic product, we do not include the value of intermediate goods and services produced. If we did, we would be counting the same thing more than once. When someone buys a new car from the local Chrysler dealer, it is a final transaction and the value of the car is counted as part of GDP. So we must not also count as part of GDP the amount the dealer paid Chrysler for the car or the amounts Chrysler paid all its suppliers for the car's various parts.

If we want to measure GDP, we somehow have to add together all the *final* goods and services produced. Obviously, we can't achieve a useful measure by simply adding together the number of cars, newspapers, kilowatts of electric power, haircuts, and automobile insurance policies. To determine GDP, we first calculate the dollar *value* of the output of each final good or service. This calculation just involves multiplying the quantity produced of each final good or service by its price. That is, we measure the output of each good and service in the common unit of dollars. We then add up the dollar values of the outputs of the different goods to arrive at their total value, which is GDP.

We measure GDP in dollars, but it is a mixture of real quantities — the numbers of final goods and services produced — and dollar quantities — the prices of the goods and services. Therefore a change in GDP contains a mixture of the effects of changes in prices and changes in the quantities of final goods and services. For many purposes, it is important to distinguish price changes from quantity changes. To do so, we use the concepts of nominal GDP and real GDP. Let's examine these two concepts.

Nominal GDP and Real GDP

Nominal GDP measures the value of the output of final goods and services using *current* prices. It is sometimes called *current dollar GDP*. **Real GDP** measures the value of the output of final goods and services using the prices that prevailed in some base period. An alternative name for real GDP is *constant dollar GDP*. Each measure refers to a specific time period, usually a year.

Comparing real GDP from one year to another enables us to say whether the economy has produced more or fewer goods and services. Comparing nominal GDP from one year to another does not permit us to compare the quantities of goods and services produced in those two years. Nominal GDP may be higher in 1990 than 1989, but that might reflect only higher prices, not more production.

The importance of the distinction between real GDP and nominal GDP is illustrated in Fig. 22.4. Real GDP is shown by the red area and nominal GDP is shown by the sum of the red and the green areas. The green area shows the inflation component of nominal GDP. In 1970, nominal GDP was $89 billion. By 1989, it had grown to $643 billion. But only part of that increase represents an increase in goods and services available — an increase in real GDP. Notice that nominal GDP increased every year, but that on one occasion — in 1982 — the real component of GDP declined.

Real GDP — the Record

Estimates of real GDP in Canada go back to 1926. Figure 22.5 illustrates the record. Two facts stand

Figure 22.4 Gross Domestic Product, 1970–1989

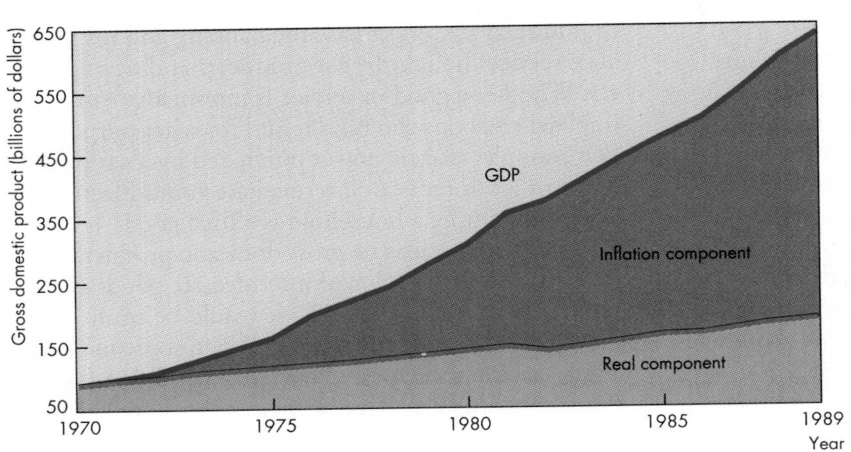

Gross domestic product increased more than sevenfold between 1970 and 1989. But much of that increase was the result of inflation. The increase in real GDP, which is the increase in nominal GDP attributable to the increase in the volume of goods and services produced, also increased but at a more modest pace. The figure shows how the real and the inflation components of nominal GDP have evolved. Nominal GDP increased in every year, but real GDP fell in 1982.

Source: Nominal GDP: CANSIM series D20000. Real GDP: CANSIM series D20031.

Figure 22.5 Real GDP, 1926–1989

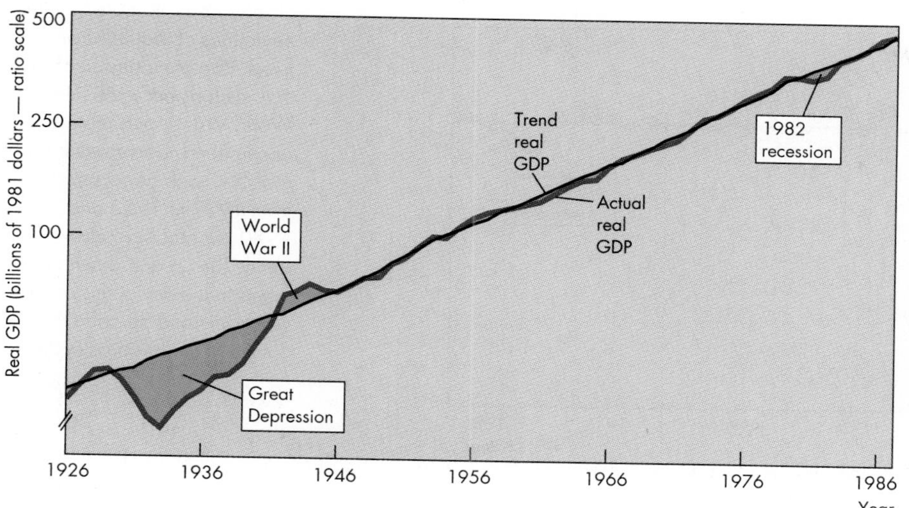

Real GDP grew at an average rate of 4.2 percent per year between 1926 and 1989. This general tendency of real GDP to increase is illustrated by trend real GDP. But GDP has not grown at the same rate each year. In some periods, such as the years during World War II, real GDP expanded quickly and moved above trend (blue areas). In other periods, such as the Great Depression and the 1982 recession, real GDP declined and fell below trend (red areas).

Sources: Historical Statistics (see Fig. 22.1), Series F–55; and CANSIM series D20031. (The historical series measures gross national expenditure.)

out. First, there has been a general tendency for real GDP to increase. Second, the rate of upward movement has not been uniform, and sometimes real GDP has actually declined. The most precipitous decline occurred in the early 1930s during the Great Depression. More recently, a decline occurred during the 1982 recession. There have also been periods in which real GDP grew extremely quickly — for example, during the years of World War II.

In order to obtain a clearer picture of the changes in real GDP, we'll consider separately the two general tendencies we identified above:

- Trend real GDP
- Fluctuations in real GDP

Trend Real GDP **Trend real GDP** is a measure of the general upward tendency or drift of real GDP that ignores its fluctuations. Trend real GDP rises for three reasons:

- Growing population
- Growing stock of capital equipment
- Advancing technology

These forces have produced the general upward tendency that you can see in Fig. 22.4. Trend real GDP is illustrated in Fig. 22.5 as a thin black line passing through the middle of the path actually followed by real GDP in its meanderings above trend (blue areas) and below trend (red areas).

Fluctuations in Real GDP Fluctuations in real GDP are measured by the deviations of actual real GDP from trend real GDP. These deviations from trend appear again in Fig. 22.6. As you can see there are distinct cycles in economic activity, the most pronounced of which are the Great Depression, the 1982 recession, and the output boom during the years of World War II.

The Importance of Real GDP

The upward trend in real GDP is the major source of improvements in living standards. The pace of this upward movement has a powerful effect on the standard of living of one generation compared with its predecessor. For example, if real GDP trends upward at 1 percent a year, it takes 70 years for real GDP to double. But with a trend of 10 percent a year, real GDP doubles in just seven years. Over the 63-year period between 1926 and 1989, Canada

Figure 22.6 Real GDP — Deviations from Trend, 1926–1989

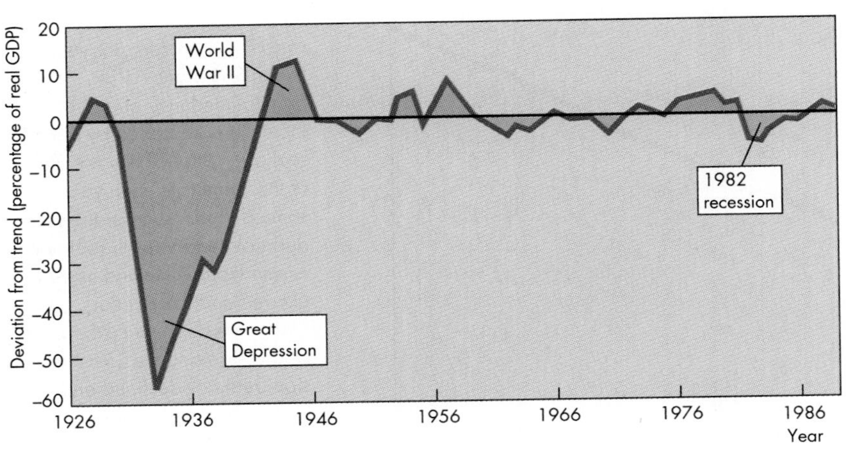

The uneven pace of increase of real GDP is illustrated by the deviations of real GDP from trend. Rapid expansion of real GDP, such as occurred during World War II, puts real GDP above trend. Decreases in real GDP, such as occurred from 1929 to 1933 and in 1980 put real GDP below trend. The up and down movements in the deviations of real GDP from trend describe the course of the business cycle.

Source: See Fig. 22.5.

achieved an average growth rate of real GDP of 4.2 percent a year, which means real GDP doubled approximately every 16 years.

But an upward trend in real GDP has its costs. The more quickly we increase real GDP, the faster exhaustible resources, such as oil and natural gas, are depleted and the more severe our environmental and atmospheric pollution problems become. Furthermore, the more quickly real GDP increases, the more we have to accept change, both in what we consume and in the jobs that we do. But increases in real GDP also bring benefits in the form of a greater volume and variety of consumption goods. These benefits have to be balanced against the costs. The choices that people make to balance these benefits and costs, acting individually and through government institutions, determine the actual pace at which real GDP increases.

As we have seen, real GDP does not increase at an even pace. In some years the economy booms and in other years it busts. Are the fluctuations in real GDP important? This question is a hard one to answer and one on which economists disagree. Some economists believe that fluctuations are costly: when real GDP is below trend GDP, output is lost, and when real GDP is above trend GDP, bottlenecks and shortages arise. With output below trend, unemployment is above its natural rate and the economy's stock of capital equipment is underused. If a downturn in real GDP can be avoided, average income and consumption levels can be increased. If large fluctuations above trend GDP can be controlled, shortages and bottlenecks can be avoided and inflation better kept in check.

An alternative view is that most of the fluctuations in real GDP represent the best possible response to the uneven pace of technological change. When technological progress is rapid, capital accumulation is also rapid, so total production increases as more new-technology capital is produced. Once a boom driven by the exploitation of new technologies has run its course, the economy temporarily drops into low gear, ready to accelerate with the next burst of technological progress and innovation. Since we are not able to order the pace of new technology to be smooth, all we can do is smooth the pace of economic growth by delaying the implementation of new technologies. Such delays would result in never-to-be-recovered waste.

Regardless of which position economists take, they all agree that depressions as deep and long as that of the early 1930s result in extraordinary waste and human suffering. The disagreements concern the more common and gentler ebbs and flows of economic activity that have occurred in the years since World War II.

Let's now take a more systematic look at the ebbs and flows of economic activity.

The Business Cycle

The **business cycle** is the periodic but irregular up and down movement in economic activity, measured by fluctuations in real GDP and other macroeconomic variables. As we've just seen, real GDP can be divided into two components:

- Trend real GDP
- Deviations of real GDP from trend

To identify the business cycle, we focus our attention on the deviations of real GDP from trend since this variable gives a direct measure of the uneven pace of economic activity, separate from its underlying trend growth path. A business cycle is not a regular, predictable, or repeating phenomenon like the swings of the pendulum of a clock. Its timing is random and, to a large degree, unpredictable.

A business cycle is identified as a sequence of four phases:

- Contraction
- Trough
- Expansion
- Peak

These four phases are shown in Fig. 22.7. This figure, which is an enlargement of part of Fig. 22.6, shows the deviation of real GDP from trend for 1975 to 1989.

Notice the four phases of the cycle. A **contraction** is a slowdown in the pace of economic activity, such as occurred between 1979 and 1983. An **expansion** is a speedup in the pace of economic activity, such as occurred between 1983 and 1988. A **trough** is the lower turning point of a business cycle, where a contraction turns into an expansion. A trough occurred in 1983. A **peak** is the upper turning point of a business cycle, where an expansion turns into a contraction. A peak occurred in 1979.

A recession occurs if a contraction is severe enough. A **recession** is a downturn in the level of economic activity in which real GDP declines in two successive quarters. A deep trough is called a slump or a **depression**.

Unemployment and the Business Cycle

Real GDP is not the only variable that fluctuates over the course of the business cycle. Its fluctuations are matched by related fluctuations in a wide range of other economic variables. One of the most important of these is unemployment. In the contraction phase of a business cycle, the unemployment gap increases; in the expansion phase, the unemployment gap decreases; at the peak, the unemployment gap is at its lowest; at the trough, the unemployment gap is at its highest. This relationship between the unemployment

Figure 22.7 The Business Cycle, 1975–1989

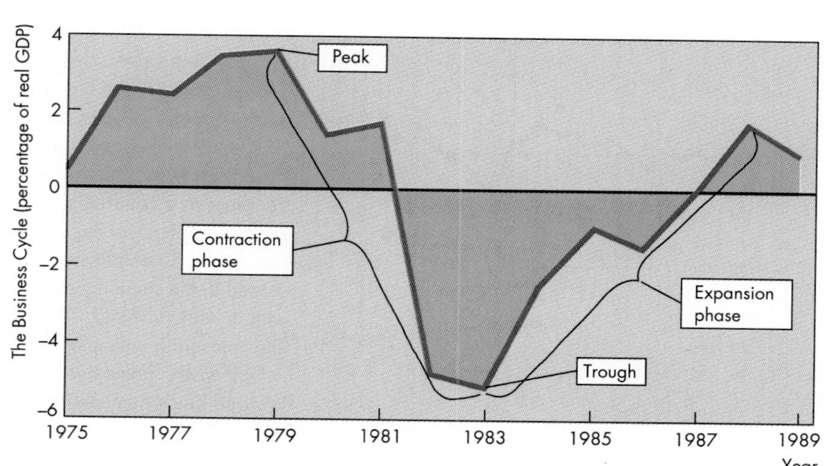

The business cycle has four phases: contraction, trough, expansion, and peak. Our most recent experience is used to illustrate these phases. There was a contraction from 1979 through 1983. In 1983, the trough was reached and an expansion began. That expansion reached a peak in 1988.

Source: See Fig. 22.5.

gap and the phases of the business cycle is illustrated in Fig. 22.8.

That figure shows deviations of real GDP from trend and unemployment in Canada from 1926 to 1989. The Great Depression, World War II, and the 1982 recession are highlighted in the figure. The figure also shows the unemployment rate. So that we can see how unemployment lines up with deviations of real GDP from trend, the unemployment rate has been measured with its scale inverted. That is, as we move down the vertical axis on the right-hand side, the unemployment rate increases. As you can see, fluctuations in unemployment closely follow those in the deviation of real GDP from trend.

The Stock Market and the Business Cycle

We have defined the business cycle as the ebb and flow of economic activity and have measured these movements by the deviation of real GDP from trend. We have seen that unemployment fluctuations mirror the business cycle very closely. Another indicator of the state of the economy, and perhaps the most visible of all such indicators, is provided by the stock market. Every weekday evening, newscasts tell us of the day's events on the Toronto, Montreal, New York, and Tokyo stock exchanges. Movements in share prices attract attention partly for their own sake and also partly for what they may foretell about our *future* economic fortunes.

Do stock prices move in sympathy with fluctuations in real GDP and unemployment? Is a stock price downturn a predictor of economic contraction? Is a stock price boom a predictor of economic expansion? To answer these questions, let's take a look at the behaviour of stock prices and see how they relate to the expansions and contractions of economic activity.

Figure 22.9 tracks the course of stock prices from 1914 to 1989. The prices plotted in this figure are inflation adjusted. Actual stock prices increased much more than indicated here because of inflation, but the purely inflationary parts of the price increases have been removed so that we can see what has *really* been happening to stock prices — that is, the path of *real* stock prices. The most striking feature of stock prices is their extreme volatility and lack of obvious cyclical patterns. Two stock price crashes are highlighted in the figure: those of 1929 and 1987. The 1929 crash was a sharp one, and it was followed by two successive years of massive stock price decline. The 1987 crash was much smaller and the decline in prices short-lived. There have also been periods of rapid increases in stock price, the most dramatic being that which preceded the 1929 crash. There were also strong increases in stock prices before the 1987 mini-crash.

Figure 22.8 Unemployment and the Business Cycle, 1926–1989

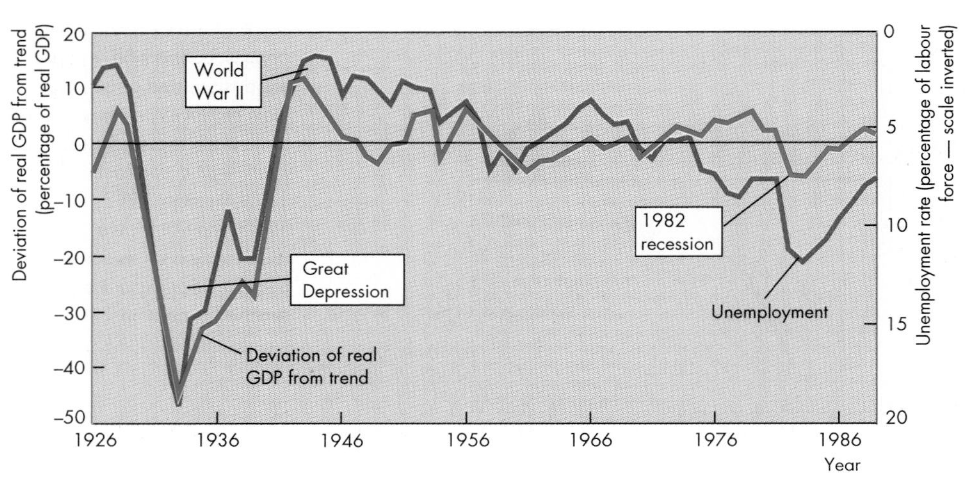

The figure shows the relationship between unemployment and the phase of the business cycle. The deviation of real GDP from trend tells us when the economy is at a peak or trough or in a contraction or expansion phase of the business cycle. Unemployment is plotted in the same figure but with its scale inverted. The line measuring unemployment is high when unemployment is low and low when unemployment is high. As you can see, the cycles in real GDP are closely matched by the cycles in unemployment.

Source: See Figs. 22.3 and 22.6.

Figure 22.9 Stock Prices, 1914–1989

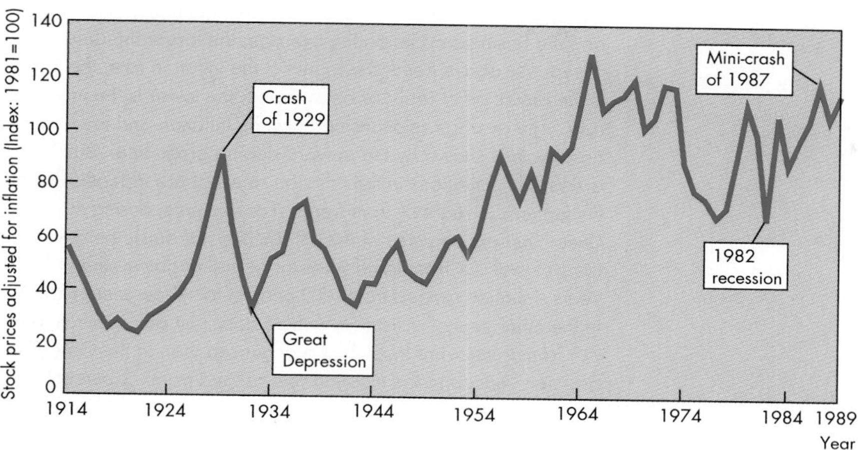

Stock prices are among the most volatile elements of our economy. Real stock prices (actual prices adjusted to take out the effects of changes in the value of money) climbed strongly in the late 1920s. Then, in 1929, came the crash that preceded the Great Depression. Stock prices began a new climb after World War II, reaching a peak in 1965. They gradually fell to a trough in 1977, rebounded for two years, and returned to their trough level again in 1982. They then climbed to a new peak in 1987 before the October crash of that year.

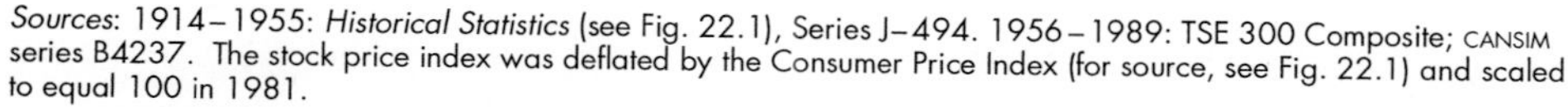

Sources: 1914–1955: *Historical Statistics* (see Fig. 22.1), Series J–494. 1956–1989: TSE 300 Composite; CANSIM series B4237. The stock price index was deflated by the Consumer Price Index (for source, see Fig. 22.1) and scaled to equal 100 in 1981.

How do fluctuations in stock prices correspond with the business cycle? The movements in stock prices through the Great Depression and the recovery from it suggest that the stock market provides information about where the economy is heading. The stock market moved in sympathy with, but slightly ahead of, the contraction and expansion of real GDP and the rise and fall in the unemployment rate.

But do turning points in the stock market always reliably predict the turning points in the economy? The answer is no. In some periods the stock market and real GDP move together, but in others the movements oppose each other. For example, the mini-crash of 1987 occurred at a time when the economy, both in Canada and in the rest of the world, was expanding strongly.

When stock prices collapsed in October 1987, many people drew parallels between that episode and the 1929 stock price crash. In 1930, the economy collapsed. In 1988, the economy continued to grow. Why were the two episodes so different? The key answer — and the key reason for the lack of a strong connection between stock price fluctuations and the business cycle — is our inability to forecast the business cycle. Stock prices are determined by people's expectations about future profitability of firms. Future profitability, in turn, depends on the state of the economy. Hence, stock prices are determined by expectations about the future state of the economy. But those expectations turn out to be wrong about as often as they turn out to be right. Thus the movement in stock prices is not an entirely reliable predictor of the state of the economy.

Inflation and the Business Cycle

We've looked at fluctuations in real variables: real GDP, the unemployment rate, and real stock prices. We've seen that there is a systematic relationship between fluctuations in real GDP and in the unemployment rate. We've also seen that there is sometimes a systematic relationship between real stock prices and the business cycle and at other times there isn't. How does inflation behave over the business cycle? Are fluctuations in its rate closely connected with the business cycle or does the inflation rate vary independently of the business cycle?

To answer these questions, look at Fig. 22.10. That figure contains a scatter diagram of the inflation rate plotted against the deviation of real GDP from trend. Each point in the figure represents a year. The pattern made by the points tells us how the inflation rate relates to the deviation of real GDP from trend — a measure of the business cycle. Two clear features of this relationship are visible in the figure.

Figure 22.10 Inflation and the Business Cycle

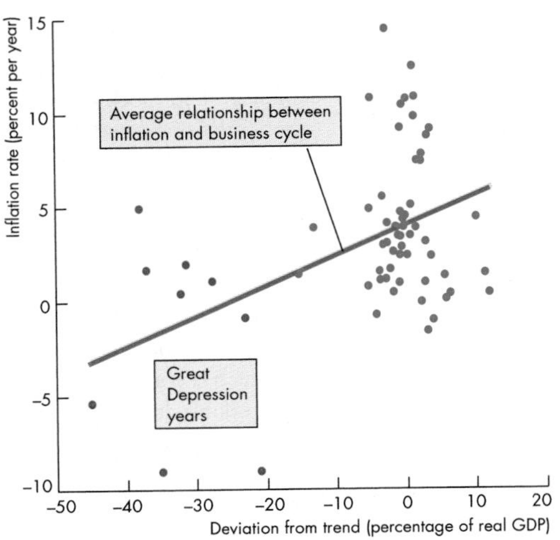

Source: See Figs. 22.1 and 22.5.

There is a loose positive relationship between the inflation rate and the business cycle: on the average, the larger the deviation of real GDP above trend, the higher is the inflation rate; the larger is the deviation of real GDP below trend, the lower is the inflation rate. The average relationship between inflation and the business cycle is shown by the upward-sloping green line. But there are large fluctuations in the inflation rate that are independent of fluctuations in real GDP from trend. For example, during the Great Depression years of the 1930s (the red dots), the deviations of real GDP from trend were large and negative and in those years, inflation ranged from −10 percent to +4 percent per year. In the other years illustrated (the blue dots), the deviations of real GDP from trend were much less pronounced than in the Great Depression years and the inflation rate ranged from −2 percent to +14 percent per year. In these years, there is no visible relationship between inflation and the deviation of real GDP from trend.

They are:

- A general tendency for the inflation rate to be higher, the larger is the deviation of real GDP above trend and lower, the larger is the deviation of real GDP below trend
- A considerable amount of independence between the inflation rate and the deviation of real GDP from trend

The average relationship between inflation and the business cycle is illustrated by the green line in the figure. The slope of this line tells us the degree to which the inflation rate responds to the state of the business cycle, on the average. That response is a small one.

The relationship between inflation and the business cycle is also a loose one in the sense that there is a large amount of variation in the inflation rate, which is unassociated with the phase of the business cycle. For example, when real GDP is close to its trend value (when the deviation from trend is small) the inflation rate has varied between −2 percent and +14 percent a year. These years are illustrated by the blue dots in the figure. The Great Depression years of the 1930s, identified by the red dots in the figure, were years in which there were large negative deviations of real GDP from trend. They were also years of highly variable inflation ranging from a 10 percent per year fall in prices to a 4 percent a year rise.

These two features of the relationship between inflation and the business cycle, illustrated in Fig. 22.10, raise two questions. First, why is there a general tendency for inflation to move in sympathy with the business cycle? Second, why is that relationship such an imprecise one — that is, why are there large variations in the inflation rate independent of the business cycle phase through which the economy is passing? We'll address these questions in Chapter 24 and give more thorough answers in Chapters 27 and 32.

Now that we've examined inflation, unemployment, real GDP fluctuations, and business cycles, let's turn to our final topic, deficits.

Government Deficit and International Deficit

If you spend more than you earn, you have a deficit. To cover your deficit, you have to borrow or sell off some of the things that you own. Just as individuals can have deficits, so can governments and entire nations. These deficits — the government deficit and the international deficit — have attracted a lot of attention recently.

Government Deficit

The **government deficit** is the total expenditure of the government sector less the total revenue of that sector. The government sector of the economy is composed of the federal government and the provincial and local governments. These governments spend on a variety of public and social programs and obtain their revenue from taxes. Sometimes the government sector is in surplus, and at other times it is in deficit. Occasionally, the deficit is a very large one, as it was, for example, in 1975. Deficits and surpluses have alternated. However, since 1975, the government sector has had a persistent deficit, averaging more than 5 percent of gross domestic product. To some degree, the balance of the government budget is related to the business cycle. When the economy is in the expansion phase of the business cycle, tax receipts rise quickly and the government's spending on unemployment benefits decreases. Through this phase of the business cycle, the government usually runs a surplus. When the economy is in a contraction phase, tax receipts decline and unemployment benefits increase and the government budget goes into deficit. What is interesting about Canada's budget deficit is that it has persisted despite the fact that the economy has experienced strong and prolonged expansion since 1983.

We'll study the government deficit more closely and at greater length in Chapter 35. In that chapter, we'll discuss its sources and consequences.

International Deficit

The difference between the value of all the goods and services that Canada sells to other countries (exports) and the value of all the goods and services that Canadians buy from foreigners (imports) is called the **current account balance.** If we sell more to the rest of the world than we buy from it, Canada has a current account surplus. If we buy more from the rest of the world than we sell to it, Canada has a current account deficit. Most of the time since 1950 Canada has had a small current account surplus. But in recent years, a large current account deficit has emerged.

When a country has a current account deficit, it has to borrow from the rest of the world to pay for the goods and services that it is buying in excess of the value of those that it is selling. One country's current account deficit and borrowing from the rest of the world is mirrored by a current account surplus and lending to the rest of the world in some other countries. The most notable country on the opposite side of Canada's balance sheet is Japan, which has had a current account surplus — in recent years, an increasing one.

The causes of these international surpluses and deficits and their consequences will be discussed at greater length in Chapter 37.

■ In our study of macroeconomics, we're going to find out what we currently know about the causes of inflation and of variations in its rate; we're also going to discover what we know about the causes of unemployment and the phases of the business cycle. We're going to discover why there are times when the stock market is a good predictor of the state of the economy and others when it is not. We're also going to discover why inflation and the business cycle sometimes move in sympathy with each other and sometimes follow separate courses. Finally, we're going to learn more about deficits — the government deficit and the international deficit — their causes, their importance, and their consequences.

The next step in our study of macroeconomics is to learn more about macroeconomic measurement — about how we measure gross domestic product, the price level, and inflation.

SUMMARY

Inflation

Inflation is an upward movement in the average level of prices. To measure the average level of prices, we calculate a price index. The inflation rate is the percentage change in the value of a price index.

Inflation is a persistent feature of Canadian economic life, but the rate of inflation fluctuates. In the early 1960s, inflation was between 1 and 2 percent a year. By 1981, it hit 13 percent a year. Inflation increased through the 1960s and 1970s, but since 1981 it has fallen.

Inflation is a problem because it brings a fall in the value of money at an unpredictable rate. The more unpredictable the inflation rate, the less useful money is as a measuring rod for conducting transactions. Inflation makes money especially unsuitable for transactions that are spread out over time, such as borrowing and lending or working for an agreed wage rate. The inflation rate is the opportunity cost of holding money. (pp. 567-572)

Unemployment

Unemployment is the number of adult workers (aged 16 and over) who are not employed and who are actively seeking jobs. Employment is the number of adult workers holding jobs. The labour force is the sum of those employed and those unemployed. The unemployment rate is the percentage of the labour force unemployed. Unemployment is measured each month by a survey of households.

Unemployment was a major problem in Canada during the Great Depression years of the 1930s and became a serious problem again in the early 1980s. The unemployment rate has increased on the average, since the end of World War II. Over the past 63 years the average unemployment rate has been 6.6 percent.

Unemployment has some benefits. It provides an individual with the time and opportunity to search out the job that best matches his or her own skills and temperament. It also permits an ongoing response to the ever-changing technologies in our economy.

The major costs of unemployment are the lost output and earnings that could have been generated if the unemployed had been working. Other major costs include the deterioration of human capital and when unemployment is prolonged, increased crime and severe social and psychological problems for unemployed workers and their families. (pp. 572-575)

Gross Domestic Product

Canada's total output is measured by its gross domestic product (GDP). Gross domestic product is the dollar value of all final goods and services produced in Canada in a given time period. Changes in gross domestic product reflect both changes in prices and changes in the quantity of goods and services available. To separate the effects of prices from real quantities, we distinguish between nominal GDP and real GDP. Nominal GDP is measured using current prices. Real GDP is measured using prices for some base year.

Real GDP grows, on average, every year. This general upward tendency is called trend real GDP. But real GDP does not increase at a constant rate. Its rate of expansion fluctuates so that real GDP fluctuates around trend GDP. Increases in real GDP bring a rise in living standards but not without costs. The main costs of fast economic growth are resource depletion, environmental pollution, and the need to face rapid and often costly changes in job type and location. The benefits of higher consumption levels have to be balanced against such costs. (pp. 575-578)

The Business Cycle

The business cycle is the periodic but irregular up and down movement in economic activity. The cycle has four phases: contraction, trough, expansion, and peak. Deep troughs are called slumps or depressions. The deviation of real GDP from trend measures the ebbs and flows in economic activity — the business cycle.

Unemployment fluctuates with the business cycle. When real GDP is above trend, the unemployment rate is low; when real GDP is below trend, the unemployment rate is high. Real stock prices often fluctuate in sympathy with the business cycle; sometimes a stock market crash precedes a recession, but it does not always do so.

There is no simple relationship between the inflation rate and the business cycle. On the average, the inflation rate is high when real GDP is above trend and low when real GDP is below trend. But there are times when the inflation rate moves independently of the business cycle. Thus there are two types of forces at work generating inflation — those that are related to the business cycle and those that are not. (pp. 579-582)

Government Deficit and International Deficit

The government deficit is the total expenditure of the government sector less the total revenue of that sector. To some degree the government deficit fluctuates over the course of the business cycle. But since 1975, the government sector has persistently operated with a deficit that has often exceeded 5 percent of GDP.

A country's current account balance is the difference between the value of the goods and services that it sells to other countries and the value of the goods and services that it buys from the rest of the world. Canada normally has had a current account surplus, but in recent years, a deficit has emerged and it has grown in magnitude. Mirroring Canada's current account deficit is a current account surplus in some other countries. Japan is one of the countries that has had a large surplus in recent years. (pp. 582-583)

KEY ELEMENTS

Key Terms

Anticipated inflation, 569
Base period, 567
Business cycle, 579
Contraction, 579
Current account balance, 583
Deflation, 567
Depression, 579
Discouraged workers, 573
Employment, 572
Expansion, 579
Expected inflation rate, 569
Final goods and services, 575
Foreign exchange rate, 569
Frictional unemployment, 574
Full employment, 574
Government deficit, 582
Gross domestic product, 575
Human capital, 575
Indexing, 572
Inflation, 567
Inflation rate, 567
Intermediate goods and services, 575
Labour force, 572
Natural rate of unemployment, 574
Nominal GDP, 576
Peak, 579
Price index, 567
Price level, 567
Price stability, 567
Real GDP, 576
Recession, 579
Trend real GDP, 577
Trough, 579
Unanticipated inflation, 569
Unemployment, 572
Unemployment rate, 572
Value of money, 568

Key Figures 

REVIEW QUESTIONS

1 What is inflation?

2 What are some of the costs of inflation?

3 What, if any, are the benefits from inflation? If there are none, explain why.

4 Why doesn't inflation always benefit borrowers at the expense of lenders?

5 Explain why the opportunity cost of holding money is higher, the higher the inflation rate.

6 Define unemployment.

7 How is the unemployment rate measured in Canada?

8 Why may the measured unemployment rate understate or overstate the true unemployment rate? What are the main costs of unemployment? Are there any benefits arising from unemployment? If so, what are they?

9 What is a business cycle? Describe the four phases of a business cycle. What was the phase of the Canadian business cycle in 1977? In 1982? In 1985?

10 When the economy is in a recovery phase, what is happening to the unemployment rate? The stock market?

11 How does the inflation rate fluctuate over the business cycle?

12 Compare the fluctuations in Canadian inflation and unemployment since 1930.

PROBLEMS

1 At the end of 1989 the price index was 105. At the end of 1990 the price index was 110. Calculate the inflation rate in 1990.

2 In a noninflationary world, Joe and Mary are willing to borrow and lend at 2 percent a year. Joe expects that inflation next year will be 4 percent and Mary expects that it will be 8 percent. Would Joe and Mary be willing to sign a contract in which one of them borrows from the other? Explain why or why not.

3 Lucy operates the Cone-Heads Ice Cream Parlour. She expects that inflation next year will be 4 percent. The students who work at Cone-Heads expect inflation to be only 2 percent. Will Lucy and the students be able to agree now on a wage rate for next summer? Explain your answer.

4 Obtain data on unemployment in your home province. If the library that you use has Statistics Canada's publication, *The Labour Force*, you can get the data from there. Otherwise, you may have to call the business desk of your local newspaper. Compare the behaviour of unemployment in your home province with that in Canada as a whole. Why do you think your province has a higher or lower unemployment rate than the Canadian average?

CHAPTER 23

Measuring Output and the Price Level

After studying this chapter, you will be able to:

- Describe the circular flow of expenditure and income.
- Explain why aggregate expenditure, aggregate income, and value of output are equal to each other.
- Explain the three ways in which gross domestic product (GDP) is measured—the expenditure approach, the income approach, and the output approach.
- Explain how *real* GDP is measured.
- Explain how the cost of living is measured by the Consumer Price Index (CPI).
- Distinguish between two measures of the price level—the CPI and the GDP deflator.
- Distinguish between inflation and changes in relative prices.

Reading the Tea Leaves

EVERY THREE MONTHS, Statistics Canada publishes the latest quarterly estimates of the gross domestic product, or GDP — a barometer of our nation's economy. As soon as it is published, analysts pore over the data, trying, like tea readers, to understand the past and divine the future. But how do government accountants add up all the blooming, buzzing economic activity of the country to arrive at the number called GDP? And what exactly is GDP? ■ We saw in the last chapter that the pace of expansion of GDP fluctuates and is occasionally interrupted by a period of contraction. We described these ebbs and flows of economic activity as the business cycle. But to reveal the business cycle, we have to measure the extent to which GDP has expanded because production has increased and the extent to which it has expanded because prices have risen. In other words, we have to distinguish between real GDP and nominal GDP. How do we go about measuring the real component of GDP and separating out the inflation component? ■ Most economic activity results in transactions taking place in markets for goods and services and factors of production. But not all economic activity results in such transactions. Some people make a living from crime. Others, although undertaking work that is legal, try to hide the payments they receive in order to evade taxes or other regulations. And finally, some people undertake economic activity that does not take place in the marketplace at all. Fixing meals, laundering shirts, mowing the lawn, and washing the car are all examples of production activities that take place within the household. Are these activities taken into account when we measure GDP? If they are not, how important are they? And does it matter if they aren't accounted for in GDP? ■ From economists to homemakers, inflation watchers of all types pay close attention to the monthly publication of the Consumer Price Index, the CPI. The government publishes new figures each month, and analysts in newspapers and on TV quickly leap to conclusions. How does the government determine the CPI?

How well does it measure the consumer's living costs? If oranges go up in price by 40 percent and haircuts go up by only 4 percent, are rising orange prices causing inflation?

■ In this chapter, we're going to learn more about the macroeconomic concepts of GDP and the price level. We'll see how GDP is measured. We'll also see how the real and inflationary components of GDP are separately measured and identified. Finally we'll learn how to calculate and interpret the CPI. We're going to begin by describing the circular flow of expenditure and income.

The Circular Flow of Expenditure and Income

The circular flow of expenditure and income provides the conceptual basis for measuring aggregate expenditure, aggregate income, and the value of output (GDP). We'll see some of the key ideas and relationships more clearly if we begin with a model economy that is simpler than the one in which we live. We'll then add some features to make our model economy correspond more closely to the real economy.

Circular Flows in a Model Economy

Our model economy has just two kinds of economic institutions: households and firms. Households

- Receive incomes in exchange for the supply of factors of production to firms.
- Make expenditures on consumption goods and services bought from firms.
- Save some of their incomes.

Firms

- Pay incomes to households for the factors of production hired (these payments include wages paid for labour, interest paid for capital, rent paid for land, and profits).
- Receive revenue from the sale of consumption goods and services to households.
- Receive revenue from the sale of capital goods to other firms.
- Borrow to finance purchases of capital goods from other firms.

The economy has three types of markets:

- Goods (and services) markets
- Factors markets
- Financial markets

Two kinds of flows occur between households and firms in this economy. First, real objects are supplied by households to firms and by firms to households. Second, money passes between households and firms in exchange for these real objects.

The real flows from households to firms are the services of factors of production. That is, households supply factors of production — labour, capital, and land — to firms. The real flows from firms to households are consumption goods and services. That is, firms produce popcorn and pop, movies and chocolate bars, microwave ovens and dry cleaning services and sell them to households.

Moving in the opposite direction to the real flows are money flows. These money flows represent the payments made in exchange for the real flows that have just been described. First, there is a flow of factor income payments made by firms to households. They include wages paid to households for their labour services, interest for the use of their capital, rents for the use of their land, and profits to the owners of the firms. The payments that firms make to households in exchange for factor services are the households' income. **Income** is the amount received by households in payment for the services of factors of production.

Second, there are flows of expenditures on goods and services. One of these is expenditure by households on consumption goods and services. Examples of these are households' purchases of popcorn and pop, movies and chocolate bars, microwave ovens and dry cleaning services. The total expenditure by households on consumption goods and services is called **consumption expenditure**.

Firms do not sell all their output to households. First, some output may be added to inventory. For example, if General Motors produces 1,000 cars and sells 950 of them to households, 50 cars will still remain unsold and GM's inventory of cars will increase by 50. Second, some output is new capital

Figure 23.1 The Circular Flow of Expenditure and Income Between Households and Firms

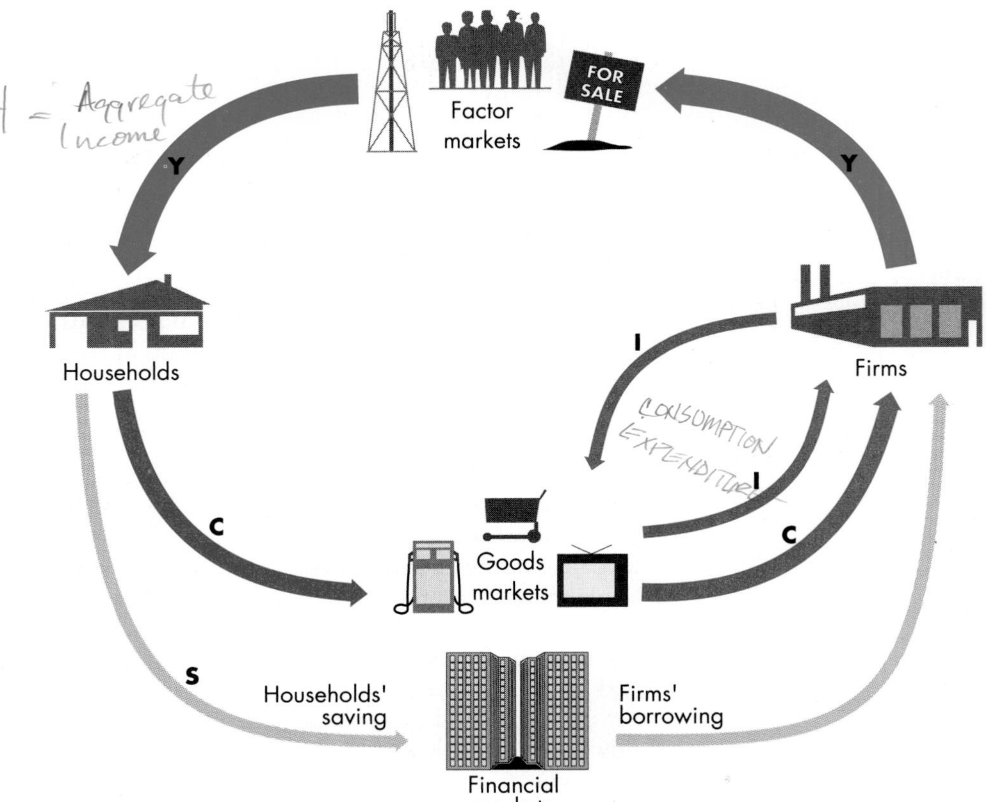

Three types of money flows are illustrated: payments for factors of production (blue), payments for final goods and services (red), and borrowing and lending (green). Households receive factor incomes from firms in exchange for factor services supplied. Households purchase consumer goods and services from firms and firms purchase capital goods from other firms (and inventories from themselves). Households save part of their income and firms borrow to finance their purchases of capital goods and inventory holdings. Firms' receipts from the sale of goods and services are paid out to households as wages, interest, rent, or profit. Aggregate expenditure (consumption expenditure plus investment) equals aggregate income. The value of output is also equal to aggregate income and aggregate expenditure.

equipment that is sold to other firms. For example, IBM sells a mainframe computer to GM. The purchase of new plant, equipment, and building and additions to inventories are called **investment**.

The money flows that we have just described are illustrated in Fig. 23.1. To help you keep track of the different types of flows, they have been colour-coded. The blue flow represents aggregate income — that is, total income received by all households in exchange for the services of factors of production. We denote aggregate income by *Y*.

The red flows represent expenditure on goods and services. The flow of consumption expenditure from households to firms is denoted by *C*. Investment — additions to inventory and purchases of new capital goods — is denoted by *I*. Notice that investment expenditure is illustrated in the figure as a flow from firms through the goods markets and back to firms. It is illustrated in this way because some firms produce capital goods and other firms buy them. When a firm adds unsold output to inventory, we can think of the firm as buying goods from itself.

There are two additional flows in the figure shown in green. These flows do not represent payments made in exchange for the services of factors of production or for the purchases of goods and services. They are payments made in exchange for future commitments — they are loans. Households do not spend all their income — they save some of it. In this model economy, saving is the difference between household income and consumption expenditure. Saving (*S*) gets channelled through financial markets. Firms borrow the funds required to finance their purchases of new capital, equipment, and inventory holdings in financial markets.

The flows illustrated in Fig. 23.1 give a complete description of all the money flows that occur in the model economy that we're studying. For present purposes, however, the most important of these flows are the payments for the services of factors of production (the blue flow) and the payments made in exchange for goods and services (the red flows). We're going to discover that the blue flow and the two red flows in aggregate are equal — that is, aggregate income and aggregate expenditure are equal. Let's see why.

Equality of Income and Expenditure To see the equality of aggregate income and aggregate expenditure, let's focus on firms. Notice first that there are two red arrows indicating flows of revenue to firms. They are consumption expenditure (C) and investment (I). The sum of these two flows is aggregate expenditure on final goods and services (more briefly, aggregate expenditure). Everything that a firm receives from the sale of its output it also pays out for the services of the factors of production that it hires. To see why, recall that payments for factors of production include not only wages, interest and rent paid for the services of labour, capital, and land, but also profits. Any difference between the amount received by a firm for the sale of its output and the amount paid to its suppliers of labour, capital, and land is a profit (or loss) for the owner of the firm. The owner of the firm is a household and the owner receives the firm's profit (or makes good the firm's loss). Thus the total income each firm pays out to households equals its revenue from the sale of final goods and services.

Since the above reasoning applies to each and every firm, for the economy as a whole, then

Aggregate income = Aggregate expenditure.

Equality of Expenditure, Income, and Value of Output The value of output is the value of all the goods and services produced by firms. We can value the goods and services produced by firms in two ways. One is to value them on the basis of the cost of the factors of production used to produce them. The other is to value them on the basis of what the buyers have paid for them. But we've just discovered that aggregate expenditure equals aggregate income. That is, the total amount spent on the goods and services produced equals the total amount paid for the factors of production used to produce them. Thus the value of output equals aggregate income, which in turn equals aggregate expenditure. That is,

$$\text{Aggregate income} = \text{Aggregate expenditure} = \text{Value of output (GDP)}.$$

Government and Foreign Sectors In the model economy that we've just examined, we focused exclusively on the behaviour of households and firms. In real world economies, there are two other important institutions that add additional flows to the circular flow of expenditure and income: the government and the rest of the world. These institutions do not change the fundamental results that we've just obtained. Aggregate income is equal to aggregate expenditure and to the value of output, no matter how many sectors we consider and how complicated a range of flows we consider between them. Nevertheless, it is important to add the government and the rest of the world to our model so that we can see the additional expenditure and income flows they generate. Let's now add these two sectors to our model economy.

The government

- Receives tax revenue from, and pays benefits and subsidies to, households and firms.
- Makes expenditures on goods and services bought from firms.
- Borrows to finance the difference between its revenue and spending.

The rest of the world

- Makes expenditures on goods and services bought from domestic firms and receives revenue from the sale of goods and services to domestic firms.
- Lends to (or borrows from) households and firms in the domestic economy.

The additional flows arising from the transactions between the government, the rest of the world, and households and firms, along with the original flows that we've already considered, are illustrated in Fig. 23.2.

Let's first focus on the flows involving the government. Net taxes are the net flows of money from households to the government.[1] These net flows are the difference between the taxes paid and benefits received. The flows of money from the government to households in the form of social benefits are called **transfer payments**. It is important not to confuse government transfer payments with government purchases of goods and services. The term "transfer payments" is designed to remind us that these items

[1]The diagram does not show firms paying any taxes. You can think of taxes paid by firms as being paid on behalf of the households that own the firms. For example, a tax on a firm's profit means that the households owning the firm receive less income. It is as if the households receive all the profit and then pay the tax on the profit. This way of looking at taxes simplifies Fig. 23.2, but does not change any conclusions.

Figure 23.2 The Circular Flow Including Government and the Rest of the World

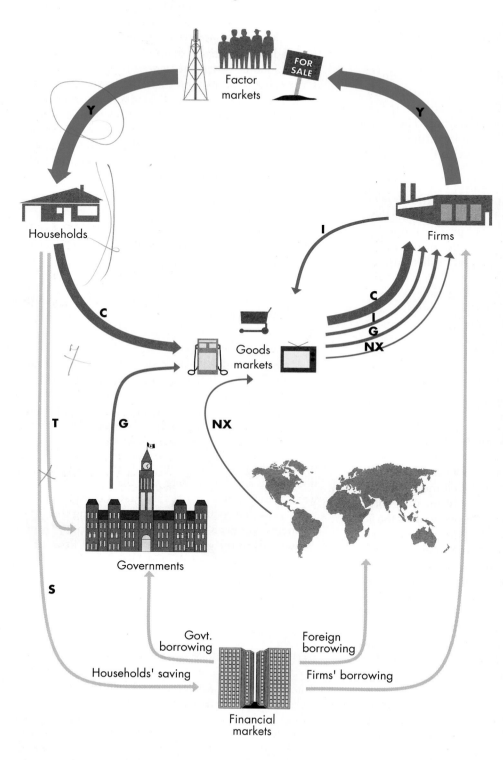

Three types of money flows between firms, households, government, and the rest of the world are illustrated: payments for factors of production (blue), expenditures on final goods and services (red), and borrowing, lending, and taxes (green). Firms hire factors of production and make income payments to households in exchange (Y). Households make consumption expenditures (C), firms undertake investment — purchase new capital goods from other firms and accumulate inventories — (I), government purchases goods and services from firms (G), and purchases of goods and services by the rest of the world minus purchases of goods and services from the rest of the world result in net exports (NX). The sum of consumption expenditure, investment, government purchases of goods and services, and net exports is equal to aggregate expenditure, which also equals aggregate income. The green flows illustrate household saving and tax payments, government borrowing, and borrowing by firms and the rest of the world.

are simply transfers of money and, as such, are a bit like taxes except that they flow in the opposite direction — they flow from government to households. Net taxes are illustrated in the figure as a green flow to remind you that this flow does not represent a payment in exchange for goods and services or a factor income. It is simply a transfer of financial resources from households to the government.

Government purchases of goods and services from firms are shown as the flow *G*. This flow is shown in red to indicate that it represents a money flow in exchange for goods and services. It is expenditure by government and revenue for firms.

The difference between government expenditure on goods and services and the net taxes received by government is the government's budget deficit. Government covers its deficit by borrowing in financial markets. Such borrowing is illustrated by the green flow in the figure.

Next, look at transactions with the rest of the world. The red flow labelled NX is net exports. **Net exports** are the difference between exports of goods and services to the rest of the world and imports of goods and services from the rest of the world. This flow represents the money that flows from the rest of the world to domestic firms in exchange for goods and services produced by domestic firms. It is a net flow in the sense that it represents the difference between the value of the goods sold by domestic firms to the rest of the world (exports) and the value of goods purchased by domestic firms from the rest of the world (imports). If exports exceed imports, net exports are positive. There is a net flow into the domestic economy. To finance that net inflow, the rest of the world has to borrow from the domestic economy. This flow is illustrated by the green flow labelled foreign borrowing. (If imports exceed exports, net exports are negative and there is a flow from domestic firms to the rest of the world. In this case, the domestic economy borrows from the rest of the world. That is, the rest of the world lends to the domestic economy through the financial markets. This case is not illustrated in the figure. To illustrate it, we simply would reverse the directions of the flows of net exports and foreign borrowing.)

Now that we have introduced more elements of the real world into our model economy, let's check that aggregate expenditure still equals aggregate income.

Expenditure Equals Income Again Aggregate expenditure equals aggregate income in this more complicated economy just as it does in the economy that has only households and firms. To see this equality, focus on the expenditures on goods and services (the red flows) received by firms and on firms' payments for factor services (the blue flow). We now have four flows representing firms' revenues from the sale of goods and services — consumption expenditure (C), investment (I), government purchases of goods and services (G), and net exports (NX). The sum of these four flows is equal to aggregate expenditure on final goods and services. As before, everything that a firm receives from the sale of its output is paid out as income to the owners of the factors of production that it employs and to the households that have a claim on its profits. The blue factor income flow, therefore, equals the sum of the red expenditure flows. That is,

$$Y = C + I + G + NX.$$

Thus as we discovered in the case of the simpler model economy, aggregate income equals aggregate expenditure.

The value of output (GDP) also equals aggregate expenditure or aggregate income. This equality occurs because we can measure the value of output either as the sum of the incomes paid to the factors of production or as the expenditure on that output.

Households Next let's look at households in Fig. 23.2. There is one flow into households and three flows out. The flow in is income (Y). The flows out are consumption expenditure (C), saving (S), and net taxes (T). The difference between income and net taxes is called disposable income. Recall that net taxes are equal to total taxes paid minus transfer payments received. Thus **disposable income** is income plus transfer payments from the government minus taxes. **Saving** is disposable income minus consumption expenditure. With this definition of saving, it is clear that income equals consumption expenditure plus saving plus net taxes. That is,

$$Y = C + S + T.$$

Income and Expenditure Accounts

We can record the transactions shown in the circular flow diagram in a set of accounts, one for firms and one for households. Table 23.1(a) shows the firm's revenue and expenditure account. The first two sources of revenue are the sale of consumption goods and services to households (C) and the sale of capital goods to other firms (I). In addition, firms receive revenue from the sale of goods and services to the

Table 23.1 Firms' and Households' Accounts

(a) Firms

Revenue		**Expenditure**	
Sale of consumption goods and services	C	Payments to factors of production	Y
Sale of capital goods	I		
Sale of goods and services to government	G		
Sale of goods and services to rest of world *less* purchases of goods and services from rest of world	NX		
Total	Y		Y

(b) Households

Income		**Expenditure**	
Payments for supplies of factors of production	Y	Purchases of consumption goods and services	C
		Taxes paid *less* transfer payments received	T
		Saving	S
Total	Y		Y

Firms, shown in part (a), receive income from the sale of consumption goods and services to households (C), capital goods to other firms (I), goods and services to government (G), and net exports (NX) or the difference between the value of their sales to the rest of the world and their purchases of goods and services from the rest of the world. Firms make payments for the services of factors of production (Y). The total income firms pay equals their total revenue: $Y = C + I + G + NX$. Households, shown in part (b), receive an income for factors of production supplied (Y). They buy consumer goods and services from firms (C) and pay net taxes (taxes minus transfer payments) to the government (T). The part of households' income that is not spent on consumption goods or paid in net taxes is saved (S). Consumption expenditure plus net taxes plus saving is equal to income: $Y = C + T + S$.

government (G) and from their sale of goods and services (net of purchases) to the rest of the world (NX). The sum of all their sources of revenue $(C + I + G + NX)$ equals the payments made to the owners of factors of production (Y).

The households' income and expenditure account is shown in Table 23.1(b). Households receive income (Y) in payment for the factors of production supplied and spend that income on consumption goods (C). They also pay net taxes (T) and, as before, the balancing item is household saving (S).

Injections and Leakages The flow of income from firms to households and of consumption expenditure from households to firms is the circular flow of income and expenditure. Investment, government purchases of goods and services, and exports are called **injections** into the circular flow of expenditure and income. Net taxes, saving, and imports are called **leakages** from the circular flow of expenditure and income. Let's take a closer look at these leakages and injections.

We have seen from the firms' account that

$$Y = C + I + G + NX.$$

Let's break net exports into its two components, exports of goods and services (EX) and imports of goods and services (IM). That is,

$$NX = EX - IM.$$

Combining this equation with the previous one, you can see that

$$Y = C + I + G + EX - IM.$$

We have also seen from the households' account that

$$Y = C + S + T.$$

Since the left-hand sides of these two equations are the same, it follows that

$$I + G + EX - IM = S + T.$$

If we add IM to both sides of this equation, we get

$$I + G + EX = S + T + IM.$$

The left-hand side here shows the injections into the circular flow of expenditure and income and the right-hand side shows the leakages from the circular flow. *The injections into the circular flow equal the leakages from the circular flow.* The circular flow of income and expenditure and the income and expenditure accounts of firms and households are our tools for measuring GDP.

Let's now see how the accountants at Statistics Canada use these concepts to measure Canada's GDP.

Table 23.2 GDP: The Expenditure Approach

Item	Symbol	Amount in 1988 (billions of dollars)	Percentage of GDP
Consumption expenditure	C	350	58
Investment	I	119	20
Government purchases of goods and services	G	126	21
Net exports	NX	4	1
Statistical discrepancy	—	3	—
Gross domestic product	Y	602	100

The expenditure approach measures GDP by adding together consumption expenditure, investment, government purchases of goods and services, and net exports. In 1988, GDP measured by the expenditure approach was $602 billion. The largest component of aggregate expenditure was expenditure on consumption goods and services — 58 percent of GDP.

Source: Statistics Canada, *National Income and Expenditure Accounts*

Canada's Income and Expenditure Accounts

Statistics Canada uses the concepts that we have just studied to measure Canada's Gross Domestic Product. In doing so, it uses three alternative, but related approaches. They are:

- Expenditure approach
- Factor incomes approach
- Output approach

Let's look at what is involved in using each.

The Expenditure Approach

The **expenditure approach** measures GDP by adding together consumption expenditure (C), investment (I), government purchases of goods and services (G), and net exports (NX). This approach is illustrated in Table 23.2, where the numbers refer to 1988. To measure GDP using the expenditure approach, we add together consumption expenditures (C), investment (I), government purchases of goods and services (G), and net exports of goods and services (NX). There is a statistical discrepancy that we'll explain shortly.

Consumption expenditure is the aggregate expenditure on goods and services produced by firms and sold to households. It includes goods such as pop, records, books and magazines as well as services such as insurance, banking, and legal advice. It does not include the purchase of new residential houses, which is counted as part of investment.

Investment is expenditure on capital equipment by firms and expenditure on new residential houses by households. It also includes the change in firms' inventories. **Inventories** are the stocks of raw materials, semifinished products, and unsold final products held by firms. Inventories are an essential input into the production process. If a firm does not hold inventories of raw materials, its production process can operate only as quickly as it can get new raw materials delivered. Similarly, if a firm does not have inventories of semifinished goods, breakdowns or accidents associated with their production may lead to disruption of processes at later stages of production. Finally, by holding inventories of finished goods, firms can respond to fluctuations in sales, standing ready to meet an exceptional surge in demand. The stock of plant, equipment, and buildings (including residential housing) is called the **capital stock**. Additions to the capital stock are investment.

Government purchases of goods and services is the expenditure on goods and services by all levels of government — from Ottawa to the local town hall. This item of expenditure includes the costs of providing national defence, law and order, street lighting, and garbage collection. It does not include *transfer payments.* As we have seen, such payments do not represent a purchase of goods and services but rather a transfer of money from government to households.

Net exports of goods and services are the difference between the value of exports and imports. When Northern Telecom sells telephone equipment to Volkswagen, the German car producer, the value of that equipment is part of Canada's exports. When you buy a new Mazda RX7, your expenditure is part of Canada's imports. The difference between what the country earns by selling goods and services to the rest of the world and what it pays for goods and services bought from the rest of the world is the value of net exports.

Table 23.2 shows the relative importance of the four items of aggregate expenditure. As you can see, consumption expenditure is by far the largest component of the expenditures that add up to GDP.

Statistical discrepancy is the difference between GDP as measured by the expenditure approach and GDP as measured by the factor incomes approach (described below). Although these two approaches rarely give the same numerical estimate of GDP, the discrepancy is usually small relative to the aggregates being measured. In 1988 it was $3 billion, or 0.5 percent of GDP.

The Factor Incomes Approach

The **factor incomes approach** measures GDP by adding together all the incomes paid by firms to households for the services of the factors of production they hire — wages for labour, interest for capital, rent for land, and profits. But this addition, on its own, does not give GDP. Some further adjustments have to be made. Let's see what these adjustments are, and how the factor incomes approach works.

The *National Income and Expenditure Accounts* divide factor incomes into five components:

- Wages, salaries, and supplementary labour income
- Corporate profits
- Interest and miscellaneous investment income
- Farmers' income
- Income of non-farm unincorporated businesses

Wages, salaries, and supplementary labour income is total payments by firms for labour services. This item includes the net wages and salaries (called take-home pay) that workers receive each week or month, plus taxes withheld on earnings, plus all fringe benefits, such as unemployment insurance and pension fund contributions.

Corporate profits are the total profits made by corporations. Some of these profits are paid out to households in the form of dividends and some are retained by corporations as undistributed profits.

Interest and miscellaneous investment income are the total interest payments received by households on loans made by them minus the interest payments made by households on their own borrowing. In other words, interest is a net item in the sense that households' interest payments are netted out from their interest receipts. This item includes, on the plus side, payments of interest by firms to households on bonds and on the minus side, households' interest payments on the outstanding balances on their credit cards.

Farmers' income and the *income of non-farm, unincorporated businesses* can be added together and called proprietors' income. These items are a mixture of the elements that we have just studied. The proprietor of an owner-operated business supplies labour, capital, and perhaps land and buildings to the business. National income accountants find it difficult to split up the income earned by an owner-operator into its component parts — compensation for labour, payment for the use of capital, rent payments for the use of land or buildings, and profit. As a consequence, the national income accounts lump all these separate factor incomes earned by proprietorships into a single category. Rental income — the payment for the use of land and other rented inputs — is also included in this category. It is the payments for rented housing and imputed rent for owner-occupied housing. (Imputed rent is an estimate of what homeowners would pay to rent the housing they own. By including this item in the national income accounts, we measure the total value of housing services, whether they are owned or rented.)

Net domestic income at factor cost is the sum of all factor incomes. Thus by adding together the items that we have just reviewed, we arrive at this measure of aggregate income. To measure GDP using the factor incomes approach, we have to make two adjustments to net domestic income at factor cost. Let's see what these adjustments are.

Market Price and Factor Cost To calculate GDP using the expenditure approach, we add together expenditures on *final goods and services.* These expenditures are valued at the prices people pay for various goods and services. The price that people pay for a good or service is called the **market price**.

Another way of valuing a good is factor cost. **Factor cost** is the value of a good measured by adding together the costs of all the factors of production used to produce it. If the only economic transactions that take place were between households and firms — if there were no government — the market price and factor cost methods of measuring value would be identical. But transactions involving the government can drive a wedge between these two methods of valuation. The source of that wedge is indirect taxes and subsidies.

An **indirect tax** is a tax on the production or sale of a good or service. Indirect taxes are included in the price paid for a good or service by its final purchaser. Examples of indirect taxes are the goods and services tax (GST), provincial sales taxes, and taxes on alcohol, gasoline, and tobacco products. Indirect taxes result in the consumer paying more than the producer receives for a good. For example, when you buy a chocolate bar, the price that you pay for it includes a 7 percent goods and services tax, together with the provincial sales tax. If the rate of provincial sales tax in the province in which you live is also 7 percent, you pay a 14 percent rate of indirect tax. Thus if you buy a chocolate bar which, in the absence of taxes, would sell for $1, you wind up paying $1.14. Seven cents go to the federal government, 7 cents to the provincial government, and $1 to the maker of the chocolate bar. The market value of the chocolate bar is $1.14. The costs of all the inputs used to produce the chocolate bar, including the profit of the firm producing it, is $1. Thus the factor cost value of the chocolate bar is $1.

A **subsidy** is a payment made by government to producers. Examples are subsidies paid to grain growers and dairy farmers. Like an indirect tax, a subsidy also drives a wedge between the market price value and the factor cost value but in the opposite direction. A subsidy lowers the market price below the factor cost — consumers pay less for the good than it costs the producer to make the good.

To use the factor incomes approach to measure gross domestic product, we need to add indirect taxes to total factor incomes and to subtract subsidies. Making this adjustment still does not quite get us to GDP. One further adjustment is needed.

Net Domestic Product and Gross Domestic Product If we sum all the factor incomes and add indirect taxes less subsidies to that total, we arrive at net domestic product at market prices. **Net domestic product at market prices** equals the sum of all factor incomes plus indirect taxes minus subsidies. What do the words "gross" and "net" mean? What is the distinction between "net domestic product" and "gross domestic product"?

The difference between these two terms is accounted for by the depreciation of capital. **Depreciation** is the reduction in the value of the capital stock that results from wear and tear and the passage of time. We've seen that investment is the purchase of new capital equipment. Depreciation is the opposite — the wearing out or destruction of capital equipment. Part of investment represents the purchase of capital equipment to replace equipment that has worn out. That investment does not add to the stock of capital; it simply maintains the capital stock. The other part of investment represents additions to the capital stock — the purchase of additional plant, equipment, and inventories. Total investment is called gross investment. **Gross investment** is the amount spent on replacing depreciated capital and on making net additions to the capital stock. The difference between gross investment and depreciation is called net investment. **Net investment** is the net addition to the capital stock. Let's illustrate these ideas with an example.

On January 1, 1989, Swanky Inc. had a capital stock consisting of three knitting machines that had a market value of $7,500. In 1989, Swanky bought a new machine for $3,000. But during the same year the machines owned by Swanky depreciated by a total of $1,000. By December 31, 1989, Swanky's stock of knitting machines was worth $9,500. Swanky's purchase of a new machine for $3,000 was the firm's gross investment. The firm's net investment — the difference between gross investment ($3,000) and depreciation ($1,000) — was $2,000. These transactions and the relationship among gross investment, net investment, and depreciation are summarized in Table 23.3.

Gross domestic product equals net domestic product plus depreciation. (Depreciation is called "capital consumption" by the national income accountants of Statistics Canada.) Total expenditure *includes* depreciation because it includes gross investment. In contrast, total factor incomes plus indirect taxes less subsidies excludes depreciation. When firms calculate their profit they make an allowance for depreciation and so subtract from their gross profit their estimate of the decrease in the value of their capital stock. As a result, adding up factor incomes gives a measure of domestic product net of the depreciation of the capital stock. To reconcile the factor incomes and expenditure approaches, we must add depreciation (capital consumption) to net domestic product.

Table 23.3 Capital Stock, Investment, and Depreciation for Swanky Inc., 1989

Capital stock on January 1, 1989 (value of knitting machines owned at beginning of year)		$7,500
Gross investment (value of new knitting machine bought in 1989)	$3,000	
less Depreciation (fall in value of knitting machines during 1989)	$1,000	
equals Net investment in 1989		$2,000
Capital stock on December 31, 1989 (value of knitting machines owned at end of year)		$9,500

Swanky's capital stock at the end of 1989 equals its capital stock at the beginning of the year plus net investment. Net investment is equal to gross investment less depreciation. Gross investment is the value of new machines bought during the year, and depreciation is the fall in the value of Swanky's knitting machines over the year.

Table 23.4 summarizes these calculations and shows how the factor incomes approach leads to the same estimate of GDP as the expenditure approach. The table also shows the relative importance of the various factor incomes. As you can see, wages, salaries, and supplementary labour income (compensation of employees) is by far the most important factor income.

The Output Approach

The **output approach** measures GDP by summing the value added of each firm in the economy. **Value added** is the value of a firm's output minus the value of inputs bought from other firms. Let's illustrate value added by looking at the production of a chocolate bar.

Table 23.5 takes you through the brief but sweet life of a chocolate bar. It starts with the producers of the raw materials that go into the chocolate bar. Milk, sugar, cocoa beans, and electric power are produced by farmers and an electric utility company. Let's suppose (just for the purpose of this story) that these producers buy no inputs other than factor services — labour, capital, and land. When the chocolate producer buys milk, sugar, cocoa beans, and electric power, it pays for the value added by firms in those other sectors of the economy. The chocolate producer combines the milk, sugar, and cocoa, using equipment driven by the electric power that it purchases and operated by the labour that it hires to make the chocolate bars. The payment made by the chocolate producer to the labour that it hires is part of the value added in the chocolate sector of the economy.

When the chocolate producer sells the chocolate bar to a wholesaler, more value is added in the chocolate sector — the profit of the chocolate producer. That profit is obviously not the entire 72 cents received from the wholesaler. Rather, it is the difference between the 72 cents and all the previous expenditures. If you add up those expenditures, you will see that they total 60 cents, which means that the chocolate producer's profit is 12 cents (72 cents – 60 cents). The value added in the chocolate sector is 40 cents — the workers' wages of 28 cents and the producer's profit of 12 cents. When the wholesaler sells the chocolate bar to the retailer, more value is added. That value added is 8 cents, and it represents the wholesaler's profit and the payments it made for

Table 23.4 GDP: The Factor Incomes Approach 

Item	Amount in 1988 (billions of dollars)	Percentage of GDP
Wages, salaries, and supplementary labour income	326	54
Interest and miscellaneous investment income	46	8
Corporate profits	58	10
Farmers' income	5	1
Income of nonfarm unincorporated businesses	34	5
Indirect taxes less subsidies	65	11
Depreciation (capital consumption)	68	11
Gross domestic product	602	100

The sum of all factor incomes equals net domestic income at factor cost. Gross domestic product equals net domestic income at factor cost plus indirect taxes minus subsidies plus capital consumption (depreciation). In 1988, GDP measured by the factor incomes approach was $602 billion. The compensation of employees — labour income — was by far the largest part of total factor incomes.

Source: Statistics Canada, *National Income and Expenditure Accounts*

Table 23.5 Value Added in the Life of a Chocolate Bar

Transaction	Total amount paid/received (dollars)	Value added (dollars)	Sector in which value is added
Chocolate producer buys milk	0.04	0.04	Dairy
Chocolate producer buys sugar	0.08	0.08	Sugar
Chocolate producer buys cocoa beans	0.08	0.08	Cocoa
Chocolate producer buys electric power	0.12	0.12	Electric power
Chocolate producer pays labour	0.28	0.28	Chocolate
Chocolate producer sells to wholesaler	0.72	0.12	Chocolate
Wholesaler sells to retailer	0.80	0.08	Wholesale
Retailer sells to you	1.00	0.20	Retail
Total	3.12	1.00	

To produce a $1 chocolate bar, a chocolate producer buys milk, sugar, cocoa beans, and electric power from other producers. The value of these inputs into the chocolate bar are part of the output — the value added — of the dairy, sugar, cocoa, and electric power sectors of the economy. The chocolate producer buys labour services and sells the chocolate bar to the wholesaler at a profit. Its labour cost and profit are part of the value added in the chocolate sector. The wholesaler sells to the retailer, providing a service and adding further value to the chocolate bar. Finally, the retailer sells to you, the customer, adding further value in the form of retail services. The sum of all the amounts paid and received — $3.12 — is a mixture of expenditure on intermediate goods and services and expenditure on the final good; it has no economic meaning. The sum of the value added in each sector equals final expenditure on the chocolate bar.

labour and other factors of production hired. Finally, when the retailer sells the chocolate bar to you, yet further value is added — 20 cents — which represents the retailer's profit and factor costs.

If we add up all the value added in the dairy, sugar, cocoa, electric power, chocolate, wholesale, and retail sectors, we see that they come to $1, the price you pay for the chocolate bar. If we add up all the amounts received and paid, they total $3.12. That total has no economic meaning — it is a mixture of expenditure on intermediate goods and services and expenditure on the final good.

Final Goods and Intermediate Goods The story of the life of a chocolate bar illustrates an important distinction between expenditure on final goods and expenditure on intermediate goods.

In valuing output, we count only expenditure on *final goods.* The only thing that's been produced and consumed in our example is a $1 chocolate bar. All the other transactions involved the purchase and sale of *intermediate goods.* To count the expenditure on intermediate goods and services as well as the expenditure on the final good would involve counting the same thing twice (or more than twice when there are several intermediate stages, as there are in this example). Counting expenditure on both final goods and intermediate goods is known as **double counting**.

Milk, sugar, cocoa, and electric power are all intermediate goods in the production of a chocolate bar — the final good. But the milk, sugar, cocoa, and electric power that you consume directly yourself are final goods. Thus whether a good is intermediate or final depends not on what it is but on what it is used for.

Table 23.6 shows the output approach to measuring GDP in Canada. This approach adds together the values added in all sectors of the economy. This sum is gross domestic product at factor cost. Then GDP is calculated by adding indirect taxes less subsidies to gross domestic product at factor cost.

Table 23.6 GDP: The Output Approach

Sector	Value added in 1988 (billions of dollars)
Agriculture, fishing, and trapping	12
Logging and forestry	4
Mines, quarries, and oil wells	31
Construction	40
Manufacturing	10
Transportation, storage, and communications	43
Other utilities	16
Trade (wholesale and retail)	67
Finance, insurance, and real estate	78
Community, business, and personal services	55
Nonbusiness sector	87
Gross domestic product at factor cost	443
Indirect taxes less subsidies	65
Gross domestic product at market prices	508

The output approach adds together the value added in each sector of the economy, which is gross domestic product at factor cost. To measure GDP, indirect taxes less subsidies is added to gross domestic product at factor cost. In 1988, GDP measured by the output approach was $602 billion.

Source: Statistics Canada, *National Income and Expenditure Accounts*

Figure 23.3 Aggregate Expenditure, Output, and Income

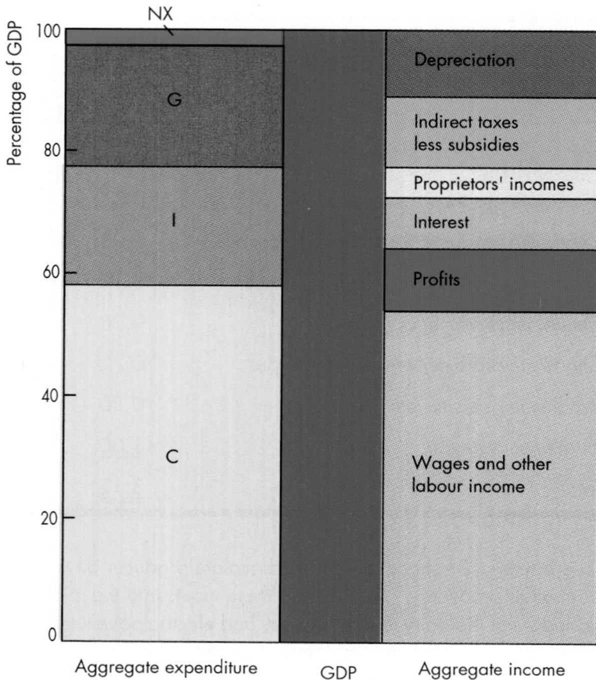

This figure emphasizes the equality between aggregate expenditure, the value of output (GDP), and aggregate income. It also illustrates the relative magnitudes of the main components of each of these aggregate concepts.

Aggregate Expenditure, Output, and Income

We've now studied the concepts of aggregate expenditure, aggregate income, and the value of output as well as the measurement of these concepts by Statistics Canada. The relationship among the three concepts and the relative importance of the components of each is illustrated in Fig. 23.3. This figure provides a snapshot summary of the entire preceding description of the national accounting concepts that you've studied in this chapter. It also provides a further reminder of the relative magnitudes — on the average — of the components of aggregate expenditure and aggregate income.

Now that we know what GDP is and how it is measured, let's examine its usefulness as a measure of the aggregate value of economic activity.

Measured and Actual Gross Domestic Product

Gross domestic product aims to measure the total value of economic activity taking place in the nation. But some productive activities are not measured as part of GDP. Let's review the more important of them.

Crime

Some people make a living by "working" in activities that are illegal. In today's economy, various forms of illegal gambling, prostitution, and drug trading are an important, omitted component of economic activity.

It is impossible to measure the scale of illegal

activities, but guesses range between 1 and 2 percent of GDP (between $6 billion and $12 billion).

The Underground Economy

All economic activity that is legal but unreported comprises the **underground economy**. Though much of the economic activity that takes place in the underground economy is legal, the participants withhold information about it to evade taxes or regulations. For example, avoiding safety regulations, minimum wage laws, and the GST are motives for operating in the underground economy. Attempts have been made to estimate the scale of the underground economy and guesses range between 5 and 15 percent of GDP ($30 billion to $90 billion).

Nonmarket Activities

An enormous amount of economic activity that is perfectly legal and that no one is obliged to report takes place every day in our own homes. Changing a light bulb, cutting the grass, washing the car, laundering a shirt, painting a door, and teaching a child to catch a ball are all examples of productive activities that do not involve market transactions and that are excluded from GDP.

Is Measurement Error a Problem?

Whether the activities left out of GDP are important depends on the questions being asked. Measures of GDP are used for three main purposes:

- To assess which phase of the business cycle the economy is in
- To compare standards of living in different countries
- To compare standards of living at different points in time

For business cycle questions, errors in measuring domestic income are probably not important at all. The ups and downs of measured economic activity are probably mirrored fairly closely by fluctuations in most of the unmeasured components. But for the other two uses of GDP, measurement errors can be important. For example, in developing countries the nonmarket activities and the underground economies involve a much larger fraction of economic activity than they do in developed countries. This fact makes comparisons of GDP between countries such as Canada and Nigeria, for example, unreliable measures of comparative living standards, unless the GDP data are supplemented with other information.

Using GDP data to gauge changes in living standards over time is unreliable. Living standards depend only partly on the value of output. They also depend on the composition of output, the amount of leisure time available, the quality of the environment, the security of jobs and homes, the safety of city streets, and so on. It is possible to construct broader measures that combine the many factors that contribute to human happiness. GDP will be one element in that measure, but it will be by no means the whole of it.

The Price Level and Inflation

To measure the price level, we use a *price index.* The value of a price index in the current year is the ratio of the value of a basket of goods in the current year to the value of that same basket of goods in an earlier year, called the *base period,* multiplied by 100. For example, suppose that Tom buys the basket of goods listed in Table 23.7. That is, he buys 4 movies and 2 six-packs of pop. In 1990, the base period, the price of a movie was $6 and the price of pop was $3 a six-pack. The value of Tom's basket in the base period was $30. In 1991, the current period, a movie costs $6.75 and pop costs $4.20 a six-pack. The current value of Tom's basket is $35.40. The current value of the price index of Tom's basket is

$$\frac{\$35.40}{\$30.00} \times 100 = 118\ .$$

Notice that if the current period and the base period were the same, the value of the price index would be 100.

In Canada today, there are two main price indexes used to measure the price level: the Consumer Price Index and the GDP deflator. The **Consumer Price Index** (CPI) measures the average level of the prices of the basket of goods and services typically consumed by an urban Canadian family. The **GDP deflator** measures the average level of the prices of all the goods and services that are included in GDP. We are now going to study the method used for determining these price indexes. In calculating the actual indexes, Statistics Canada processes millions of pieces of information. But we can learn the principles involved in its calculations by working through some simple examples.

Table 23.7 Calculating a Price Index

Good	Base period (1990)			Current period (1991)	
	Quantity in basket	Price	Expenditure	Price	Expenditure
Movies	4	$6 each	$24	$6.75 each	$27.00
Six-packs of pop	2	$3 each	$ 6	$4.20 each	$ 8.40
			$30		$35.40

Price index for 1991 = $\frac{\$35.40}{\$30.00} \times 100 = 118$

A price index for 1991 is calculated in two steps. The first step is to value the basket of goods at the prices prevailing in both 1990 and 1991. The second step is to divide the value of those goods in 1991 by their value in the base period 1990 and to multiply the result by 100.

Consumer Price Index

The Consumer Price Index measures the average level of prices of the goods and services typically consumed by an urban Canadian family. Statistics Canada calculates and publishes the CPI every month.

To construct this price index, Statistics Canada first selects a base period. Currently the base period is 1981. It then selects a basket of goods — the quantities of approximately 490 different goods and services that were typically consumed by urban households in the base period.

Every month a team of observers descends on 64 urban centres across Canada to record the prices for these 490 items. When all the data are collected, the CPI is calculated by valuing the base-period basket of goods at the current month's prices. That value is expressed as a percentage of the value of the same basket in the base period.

To see more precisely how the CPI is calculated, let's work through an example. Table 23.8 summarizes the calculations.

Let's suppose that there are only three goods in the typical consumer's basket: oranges, haircuts, and bus rides. The quantities bought by the typical consumer in the base period are shown in the table — 5 bags of oranges, 6 haircuts and 200 bus rides. The prices prevailing and total expenditure in the base period are also shown: the typical consumer buys 200 bus rides at 70 cents each and so spends $140 on bus rides. Expenditure on oranges and haircuts is worked out in the same way. Total expenditure is the sum of the expenditures on the three goods, which is $210.

To calculate the price index for the current period, we need to discover the prices of the goods in the current period. (We do not need to know the quantities bought in the current period.) Let's suppose that the prices are those set out in the table under "current period." We can now calculate the current period's value of the basket of goods by using the current period's prices. For example, the current price of oranges is $1.20 per bag, so the current period's value of the base-period quantity (5 bags) is 5 multiplied by $1.20, which is $6. The base-period quantities of haircuts and bus rides are valued at this period's prices in a similar way. The total value in the current period of the base-period basket is $231.

We can now calculate the CPI — the ratio of this period's value of the goods to the base period's value, multiplied by 100. In this example, the CPI for the current period is 110. The CPI for the base period is, by definition, 100.

GDP Deflator

The GDP deflator measures the average level of the prices of all the goods and services that make up GDP. It is calculated by dividing nominal GDP by real

Table 23.8 The Consumer Price Index: (A Simplified Calculation)

Items in the basket	Base period			Current period	
	Quantity	Price	Expenditure	Price	Expenditure
Oranges	5 bags	$ 0.80/bag	$4	$1.20/bag	$6
Haircuts	6	$11.00 each	$66	$12.50 each	$75
Bus Rides	200	$ 0.70 each	$140	$ 0.75 each	$150
Total Expenditure			$210		$231

$$\text{CPI} = \frac{210}{210} \times 100 = 100 \qquad \text{CPI} = \frac{231}{210} \times 100 = 110$$

A fixed basket of goods — 5 bags of oranges, 6 haircuts, and 200 bus rides — is valued in the base period at $210. Prices change and that same basket is valued at $231 in the current period. The CPI is equal to the current-period value of the basket divided by the base-period value of the basket multiplied by 100. In the base period the CPI is 100, and in the current period it is 110.

GDP and multiplying the result by 100. We use the term "nominal GDP" because it measures the money value of output. Real GDP is a measure of the physical volume of output arrived at by valuing the current period output at prices that prevailed in the base period. Currently, the base period for calculating real GDP is 1981. We refer to the units in which real GDP is measured as "1981 dollars."

Table 23.9 shows nominal GDP, real GDP, and the GDP deflator for selected years since 1969. As you can see, nominal GDP increased by a much larger proportion than real GDP. In fact, nominal GDP in 1988 was 7 times what it was in 1969, while real GDP was only twice its 1969 value. The GDP deflator was 3.5 times as high in 1988 as it was in 1969.

We are going to learn how to calculate the GDP deflator by studying an imaginary economy. We will calculate nominal GDP and real GDP as well as the GDP deflator. To make our calculations simple, let's imagine an economy that has just three final goods: the consumption good is oranges; the capital good is computers; and the government good is red tape. (Net exports are zero in this example.) Table 23.10 summarizes the calculations.

Let's focus first on calculating nominal GDP. We'll use the expenditure approach. The table shows the quantities of the final goods produced and their prices in the current period. To calculate nominal

Table 23.9 Nominal GDP, Real GDP, and the GDP Deflator

Year	Nominal GDP (billions of dollars)	Real GDP (billions of 1981 dollars)	GDP deflator (1981 = 100)
1969	83	214	38.8
1975	172	283	60.8
1981	356	356	100.0
1988	602	448	134.4

Nominal GDP measures the *money* value of output. Real GDP measures the *physical volume* of output. Nominal GDP values output in the prices that prevailed in the period in question. Real GDP values output in the prices of the base period. In the table, goods and services produced between 1969 and 1988 are valued in the prices that prevailed in 1981. The GDP deflator is equal to nominal GDP divided by real GDP, multiplied by 100. In 1981, the *base period*, the GDP deflator is 100. Nominal GDP in 1988 is 7 times what it was in 1969, real GDP is twice as high, and the GDP deflator is 3.5 times as high.

Source: Statistics Canada, *National Income and Expenditure Accounts*

Table 23.10 Nominal GDP, Real GDP, and the GDP Deflator: Simplified Calculations

	Current period			Base period	
Item	**Quantity**	**Price**	**Expenditure**	**Price**	**Expenditure**
Oranges	4,240 bags	$1.05/bag	$ 4,452	$1/bag	$ 4,240
Computers	5	$2,100 each	$10,500	$2000 each	$10,000
Red tape	1,060 metres	$1/metre	$ 1,060	$1/metre	$ 1,060
		Nominal GDP	$16,012	Real GDP	$15,300

Deflators for current period

GDP deflator	$= \frac{\$16,012}{\$15,300} \times 100 = 104.7$
Consumption expenditure deflator	$= \frac{\$\ 4,452}{\$\ 4,240} \times 100 = 105.0$
Investment deflator	$= \frac{\$10,500}{\$10,000} \times 100 = 105.0$
Government purchases of goods and services deflator	$= \frac{\$\ 1,060}{\$\ 1,060} \times 100 = 100.0$

An imaginary economy produces only oranges, computers, and red tape. In the current period, nominal GDP is $16,012. If the current-period quantities are valued at base-period prices, we obtain a measure of real GDP, which is $15,300. The GDP deflator in the current period — which is calculated by dividing nominal GDP by real GDP in that period and multiplying the result by 100 — is 104.7. Deflators for the components of GDP are calculated in a similar manner.

GDP, we work out the expenditure on each good in the current period and then add the three expenditures. Consumption expenditure (oranges) is $4,452, investment (computers) is $10,500, government purchases (red tape) are $1,060, so nominal GDP is $16,012.

Next, let's calculate real GDP. To do this we value the current-period quantities at the base-period prices. The table shows the prices for the base period. Real expenditure on oranges for the current period is 4,240 bags of oranges valued at $1 per bag, which is $4,240. If we perform the same types of calculations for computers and red tape and add up the real expenditures, we arrive at a real GDP of $15,300.

To calculate the GDP deflator for the current period, we divide nominal GDP ($16,012) by real GDP ($15,300) and multiply the result by 100. The GDP deflator that we obtain is 104.7. If the current period is also the base period, nominal GDP equals real GDP and the GDP deflator is 100. Thus the GDP deflator in the base period is 100, just as it is for the CPI.

The national income accountants also calculate deflators for consumption expenditure, investment, and government purchases of goods and services (as well as other more detailed components of GDP). We can calculate deflators for consumption expenditure, investment, and government purchases of goods and services for our imaginary economy. These deflators are calculated in a manner similar to the GDP deflator. For example, the consumption expenditure deflator is calculated by dividing the current period's consumption expenditure by the real consumption expenditure and multiplying the result by 100. A similar calculation is performed for the other two components of GDP. In our example, the consumption expenditure deflator and the investment deflator are each 105, while the government purchases of goods and services deflator is 100. These deflators make sense when you compare them with the price changes. Oranges and computers have each increased in price by 5 percent and their deflators have moved from 100 to 105. The price of red tape has remained constant at $1 a metre and its deflator has remained constant at 100.

Inflation and Relative Price Changes

The inflation rate is calculated as the percentage increase in the price index. For example, in the case we studied in Table 23.8, the CPI rose by 10 percent from the base period to the current period. Underlying that change in the price index are the individual changes in the prices of oranges, haircuts, and bus rides. No individual price rose by 10 percent. The price of oranges rose by 50 percent, the price of haircuts by 13.6 percent, and the price of bus rides by 7.1 percent. This example captures a common feature of the world in which we live: it is rare for all prices to change by the same percentage. When the prices of goods rise by different percentages, there is a change in relative prices. The **relative price** is the ratio of the price of one good to the price of another good. For example, if the price of a bag of oranges is $0.80 and the price of a haircut is $11, the relative price of a haircut is 13 ¾ bags of oranges. It costs 13 ¾ bags of oranges to buy one haircut.

Many people are confused by the difference between the inflation rate and relative price changes. Inflation and relative price changes are completely separate and independent phenomena. To see why this is true, we'll work through an example showing that, for the same relative price changes, we can have two entirely different inflation rates.

We will first learn how to calculate a change in relative prices. We can calculate the percentage change in a relative price as the difference between the percentage change in the price minus the inflation rate. Let's again use the calculations that we worked through in Table 23.8, now presented in Table 23.11(a). For example, the price of a bag of oranges rose from 80 cents to $1.20, or by 50 percent. We have already calculated that prices on the average

Table 23.11 Relative Price Changes With and Without Inflation

(a) 10 percent inflation

Item	Base-period price	New price	Percentage change in price	Percentage change in relative price
Oranges	$ 0.80	$ 1.20	+50.0	+40.0
Haircuts	$11.00	$12.50	+13.6	+ 3.6
Bus rides	$ 0.70	$ 0.75	+ 7.1	– 2.9

(b) No inflation

Item	Base-period price	New price	Percentage change in price	Percentage change in relative price
Oranges	$ 0.80	$ 1.12	+40.0	+40.0
Haircuts	$11.00	$11.40	+ 3.6	+ 3.6
Bus rides	$ 0.70	$ 0.68	– 2.9	– 2.9

A relative price is the price of one good divided by the price of another good. Relative prices change whenever the price of one good changes by a percentage different from that of some other good. Relative price changes do not cause inflation. They can occur with or without inflation. In part (a), the price index rises by 10 percent. In part (b), the price index remains constant. In both parts, the relative price of oranges increases by 40 percent and that of haircuts by 3.6 percent, and the relative price of bus rides falls by 2.9 percent. The rise in the price of oranges cannot be regarded as the cause of the rise in the price index in part (a) because that same rise in the price of oranges occurs with no change in the price index in part (b).

Inflation and Relative Prices

Food and energy costs blamed for CPI rise

Canada's inflation rate dipped slightly in February to 5.4% from January's 5.5%.

But the consumer price index was up 0.6% from January, and is not expected to ease significantly for several months.

The increase in the CPI—the price of a basket of goods and services—was spread across all its components in February, with food and energy prices showing the most significant jumps.

Excluding food and energy, the CPI was up 5.2% from February 1989, the lowest yearly pace of growth since last April.

John Clinkard, senior economist at Canadian Imperial Bank of Commerce, expects this "core" rate of inflation to continue to ease. "Inflation could be down below 5% by May or June—if we don't get any shocks," he said.

The shocks could come from provincial budgets, all due in the next couple of months. Prince Edward Island has already announced it will push up taxes on tobacco, gasoline and hotel accommodation. If repeated by other provinces, such tax increases could scuttle any easing of inflation in early summer.

Last year, the CPI shot up from 4.6% in April to 5.4% by June, mostly the result of provincial and federal sales tax increases.

Clinkard said he doesn't expect to see tax hikes in the Ontario or British Columbia budgets, because those governments are getting close to elections. Newfoundland has also brought down its budget without major sales tax hikes.

Much of the jump in the CPI during February was because of price increases for fresh produce. Frost damage to southern U.S. crops during December sent fruit and vegetable prices soaring in January.

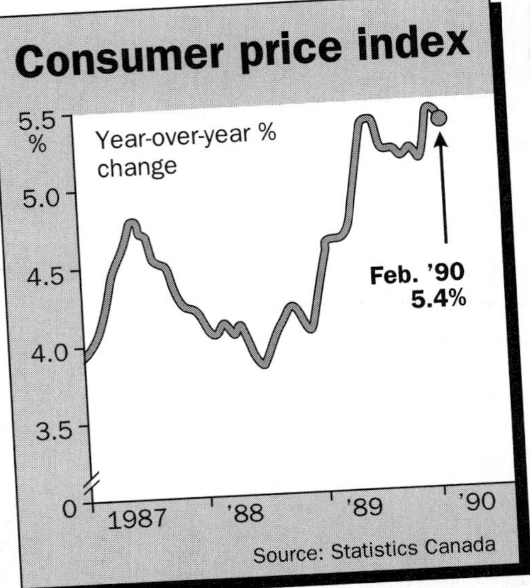

The resulting shortages affected February prices as well.

However, Harv Bradley, economist at Wood Gundy Ltd., said shortages should be alleviated in the coming months as new crops are harvested.

But he warned the prices for other components of the CPI, such as clothing, housing and services, could remain high until May or June. The end of post-Christmas sales and promotional pricing pulled up clothing prices by 1.3% in the month.

Transportation prices were up to 0.5%, mainly because of higher gas prices, the cancellation of a gas tax rebate in Saskatchewan, and higher peak-season air fares to southern holiday destinations.

The Financial Post,
March 19, 1990
By Jill Vardy

The Essence of the Story

- In February 1990, Canada's Consumer Price Index (CPI) was 0.6 per cent above its January 1990 level and 5.4 per cent above its February 1981 level.
- Excluding food and energy prices, the CPI was 5.2 per cent above its February 1989 level.
- The CPI increased during February 1990 because:
  - Frost damage to southern U.S. crops during December resulted in shortages that were still having effects on prices of fresh fruit and vegetables.
  - The end of post-Christmas sales and discounts increased clothing prices.
  - Higher gas prices, the cancellation of a gas tax rebate in Saskatchewan, and higher peak-season air fares to southern holiday destinations increased transportation prices.
- In 1989 inflation increased from 4.6% in April to 5.4% in June because of provincial and federal sales tax increases.

Background and Analysis

- This news article does not distinguish between inflation and relative price changes. It claims that inflation in February 1990 resulted from such factors as crop failures, the end of post-Christmas sales and gas price increases.
- The story is really about two independent sets of events:
  - Relative price changes
  - Inflation

Relative price changes

- In February 1990, the *relative prices* of fruits and vegetables, clothing, and gas increased and the *relative prices* of most other goods decreased.

Inflation rate

- In February 1990, the inflation rate as measured by the CPI fell slightly from its January 1989 level.
- As you know from your study of the distinction between inflation and relative price changes (see Table 23.11), any inflation rate is possible in combination with any pattern of relative price changes. We cannot look at relative price changes, and from those numbers, work out why the inflation rate performed in the way that it did.
- A common way of reporting inflation is to examine the change in the inflation rate and then to look at those items in the price index that changed most in the direction of the change in the inflation rate.
- Suppose that the inflation rate had slowed down dramatically in February. Also suppose that relative price changes were exactly the same as those reported for February. How would the story on the consumer price increase have been written? The conclusion would have been that inflation had decreased because of a decrease in car prices, house prices, and entertainment costs.

Conclusion

- The change in the CPI is an *average* of the changes in the prices of *all* goods. Since relative prices are always changing, some goods will have the fastest price rise and some the slowest price rise (or fastest fall). It is correct to describe the change in the CPI as being made up of individual price changes. It is incorrect to attribute cause and effect.

rose by 10 percent. To calculate the percentage change in the relative price of a good, subtract the inflation rate from the percentage change in its price. The price of oranges increased relative to the average price of all goods by 50 percent minus 10 percent, which is 40 percent. Bus rides fell in price relative to goods on the average by 2.9 percent. The change in relative prices on the average is zero by definition. That is, for every good whose relative price increases by *x* percent there must be other goods whose relative prices fall by an average of *x* percent.

In Table 23.11(b), we see that relative prices can change without inflation. In fact, part (b) illustrates the same changes in relative prices that occurred in part (a) but with no inflation. In this case, the price of oranges increases by 40 percent to $1.12 a bag, the price of haircuts increases by 3.6 percent to $11.40 a haircut, and the price of bus rides falls by 2.9 percent to 68 cents a ride. If you calculate the current and base-period values of the basket in part (b), you will find that consumers spend exactly the same at the new prices as they do at the base-period prices. There is no inflation, even though relative prices have changed.

We've now looked at two cases in which the relative price of oranges increases by 40 percent. In one, inflation is 10 percent; in the other, there is no inflation. Clearly, inflation has not been *caused* by the change in the price of oranges. In the first case, the price of each good increases by 10 percent more than it does in the second case. Singling out the good whose relative price has increased most does not help us explain why all prices are rising by 10 percent more in the first case than in the second.

Any inflation rate can occur with any behaviour of relative prices. Relative prices are determined by supply and demand in the markets for the individual goods and services. The price level and the inflation rate are determined independently of *relative* prices. To explain an increase (or decrease) in the inflation rate, we have to explain why all prices are inflating at a different rate, not why some prices are increasing faster than others. This is an important distinction (see Reading Between the Lines, pp. 606-607).

The Consumer Price Index and the Cost of Living

Does the Consumer Price Index measure the cost of living? Does a 5 percent increase in the CPI mean that the cost of living has increased by 5 percent?

A change in the CPI measures the percentage change in the price of a *fixed* basket of goods and services. The actual basket of goods and services bought depends on relative prices and on consumers' preferences. Changes in relative prices will lead consumers to economize on goods that have become relatively expensive and to buy more of those goods whose relative prices have fallen. If chicken doubles in price but the price of beef increases by only 5 percent, people will substitute the now relatively less expensive beef for the relatively more expensive chicken. Because consumers make such substitutions, a price index based on a fixed basket will overstate the effects of a given price change on the consumer's cost of living.

Discrepancies between the CPI and the cost of living also arise from the disappearance of some commodities and the emergence of new ones. For example, suppose that you want to compare the cost of living in 1990 with that in 1890. Using a price index that has horse feed in it will not work. Though that price was important in people's transportation costs in 1890, it plays no role today. Similarly, a price index with gasoline in it will be of little use since gasoline, while relevant today, did not feature in people's spending in 1890. Even comparisons between 1990 and 1980 suffer from this same problem. The compact discs and microwave popcorn that are part of our budgets in 1990 were not available in 1980.

Substitution effects and the arrival of new goods make the connection between the CPI and the cost of living imprecise. To reduce the problems that arise from this source, Statistics Canada updates the weights used for calculating the CPI from time to time. Even so, the CPI is of limited value for making comparisons of the cost of living over long periods of time. But for the purpose for which it was devised — calculating month-to-month and year-to-year rates of inflation — the CPI does a pretty good job.

■ In Chapter 22, we examined Canada's macroeconomic performance in recent years and over a longer period of history. In this chapter, we studied the methods used for measuring the macroeconomy, in particular, the average level of prices and the overall level of real economic activity. In the following chapters, we're going to study some macroeconomic models — models designed to explain and predict the behaviour of real GDP, the price level, employment and unemployment, the stock market, and other related phenomena. We start this process in the next chapter by examining a macroeconomic model of demand and supply — a model of *aggregate* demand and *aggregate* supply.

SUMMARY

The Circular Flow of Expenditure and Income

All economic agents — households, firms, government, and the rest of the world — interact in the circular flow of income and expenditure. Households supply factors of production to firms and buy consumption goods and services from firms. Firms hire factors of production from households and pay incomes to households in exchange for factor services. Firms sell consumption goods and services to households and capital goods to other firms. Government collects taxes from households and firms, pays benefits under various social programs to households, and buys goods and services from firms. Foreigners buy goods from domestic firms and sell goods to them.

The flow of expenditure on final goods and services winds up as somebody's income. Therefore,

Aggregate income = Aggregate expenditure.

Furthermore, expenditure on final goods and services is a method of valuing the output of the economy. Therefore,

$$\text{Aggregate income} = \text{Aggregate expenditure} = \text{Value of output (GDP)}.$$

From the firm's accounts we know that

$$Y = C + I + G + EX - IM,$$

and from the household's accounts we know that

$$Y = C + S + T.$$

Combining these two equations we obtain

$$I + G + EX = S + T + IM.$$

This equation tells us that injections into the circular flow (left-hand side) equal the leakages from the circular flow (right-hand side). (pp. 589-594)

Canada's Income and Expenditure Accounts

Because aggregate expenditure, aggregate income, and the value of output are equal, national income accountants can measure GDP using one of three approaches: expenditure, factor incomes, and output.

The expenditure approach adds together consumption expenditure, investment, government purchases of goods and services, and net exports to arrive at an estimate of GDP.

The factor incomes approach adds together the incomes paid to the various factors of production plus profit paid to the owners of firms. It is then necessary to adjust the factor cost value of GDP to the market price value by adding indirect taxes and subtracting subsidies. It is also necessary to add capital consumption (depreciation) in order to arrive at GDP.

The output approach sums the value added by each firm in the economy. In using the output approach, it is necessary to be careful to avoid double counting, to measure only value added rather than total sales in each sector of the economy.

Actual GDP does not measure all the economic activity in the nation. It excludes crime, the underground economy, and nonmarket activities. (pp. 595-601)

The Price Level and Inflation

There are two major price indexes that measure the price level and inflation: the Consumer Price Index and the GDP deflator.

The CPI measures the average level of prices of goods and services typically consumed by an urban family in Canada. The CPI is the ratio of the value of a base-period basket of commodities at current-period prices to the same basket valued at base-period prices, multiplied by 100.

The GDP deflator is nominal GDP divided by real GDP, multiplied by 100. Nominal GDP is calculated by valuing the current-period quantities produced at current-period prices. Real GDP is calculated by valuing the current-period quantities produced at base-period prices.

In interpreting changes in prices, we need to distinguish between inflation and relative price changes. A relative price is the ratio of the price of one good to the price of another good. Relative prices are constantly changing. We cannot tell anything about the sources of inflation by studying which relative prices have changed most. Any relative price changes can occur with any inflation rate.

Because relative prices are constantly changing, causing consumers to substitute less expensive items for more expensive items, and because of the disappearance of some goods and the arrival of new goods, the CPI is an imperfect measure of the cost of living, especially for making comparisons across a long time span. (pp. 601-609)

KEY ELEMENTS

Key Terms

Capital stock, 595
Consumer Price Index, 601
Consumption expenditure, 589
Depreciation, 597
Disposable income, 593
Double counting, 599
Expenditure approach, 595
Factor cost, 597
Factor incomes approach, 596
GDP deflator, 601
Gross investment, 597
Indirect tax, 597
Injections, 594
Inventories, 595
Investment, 590
Leakages, 594
Market price, 597
Net domestic income at factor cost, 596
Net domestic product at market prices, 597
Net exports, 593
Net investment, 597
Output approach, 598
Relative price, 605
Saving, 593
Subsidy, 597
Transfer payments, 591
Underground economy, 600
Value added, 598

Key Figures and Tables 

Figure 23.1 The Circular Flow of Expenditure and Income Between Households and Firms, 590
Figure 23.2 The Circular Flow Including Government and the Rest of the World, 592
Table 23.2 GDP: The Expenditure Approach, 595
Table 23.4 GDP: The Factor Incomes Approach, 598
Table 23.6 GDP: The Output Approach, 600

REVIEW QUESTIONS

1 What are the components of aggregate expenditure?

2 What are the components of aggregate income?

3 Why does aggregate income equal aggregate expenditure?

4 Why does the value of output (or GDP) equal aggregate income?

5 Distinguish between government purchases of goods and services and transfer payments.

6 What are injections into the circular flow of expenditure and income?

7 What are leakages from the circular flow of expenditure and income?

8 What are the three methods used by Statistics Canada to measure GDP?

9 Describe how the expenditure approach is used to measure GDP.

10 Describe how the factor incomes approach is used to measure GDP.

11 Describe how the output approach is used to measure GDP.

12 What is the distinction between expenditure on

final goods and expenditure on intermediate goods?

13 What are the main omissions from measured GDP?

14 What are the two main price indexes used to measure the price level and inflation?

15 How is the Consumer Price Index calculated?

16 How is the GDP deflator calculated?

17 Explain what a relative price change is.

18 How can relative price changes be identified in periods when the inflation rates are different?

PROBLEMS

1 The following flows of money took place in an imaginary economy last year:

Item	Millions of dollars
Wages paid to labour	800,000
Consumption expenditure	650,000
Taxes paid on wages	200,000
Government payments to support the unemployed, sick, and aged	50,000
Firms' profits	200,000
Investment	250,000
Taxes paid on profits	50,000
Government purchases of goods and services	200,000
Export earnings	250,000
Saving	200,000
Import payments	300,000

a) Calculate the GDP for this economy.

b) Did you use the expenditure approach, factor incomes approach, or output approach to make this calculation?

c) Does your answer to part (a) value output in terms of market prices or factor cost? Why?

d) Calculate the value added last year.

e) What extra information do you need in order to calculate net domestic product?

2 People in an imaginary island economy consume only apples, bananas, and cloth. The base period is year 1. Prices in the base period are $2 per bag for apples, $3 per kilogram for bananas, and $5 per metre for cloth. The typical family spends $40 on apples, $45 on bananas, and $25 on cloth. In year 2, apples cost $3 per bag, bananas cost $3 per kilogram, and cloth costs $8 per metre. Calculate the economy's Consumer Price Index for year 2 and the inflation rate between year 1 and year 2.

3 A newspaper in the economy in problem 2, commenting on the inflation figures that you have just calculated, runs the headline "Steeply Rising Clothing Prices Cause Inflation." Write a letter to the editor pointing out the weakness in the economic reasoning of the headline-writer.

4 An economy has the following real GDP and nominal GDP in 1989 and 1990:

Year	Real GDP	Nominal GDP
1989	$1,000 billion	$1,200 billion
1990	$1,050 billion	$1,386 billion

a) What is the GDP deflator for 1989?

b) What is the GDP deflator for 1990?

c) What is the inflation rate as measured by the GDP deflator between 1989 and 1990?

CHAPTER 24

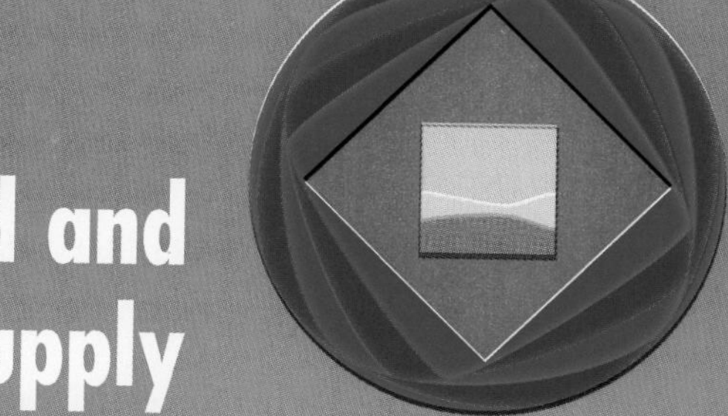

Aggregate Demand and Aggregate Supply

After studying this chapter, you will be able to:

- Define aggregate demand and explain what determines it.
- Explain the sources of growth and fluctuations in aggregate demand.
- Define aggregate supply and explain what determines it.
- Explain the sources of growth and fluctuations in aggregate supply.
- Define macroeconomic equilibrium.
- Predict the effect of changes in aggregate demand and aggregate supply on real GDP and the price level.
- Explain why real GDP grows.
- Explain why we have inflation and why its rate varies, sometimes exploding as it did in the 1970s.
- Explain the recession of 1982 and the recovery of the 1980s.

What Makes Our Garden Grow?

IN THE 16 YEARS FROM 1972 to 1988, Canadian real gross domestic product almost doubled. In fact, a near doubling of Canada's real GDP every 16 years has been routine. What forces drive our economy to grow? ■ At the same time as real GDP has been growing, our dollar has been falling in value — we've experienced persistent inflation. Today, you need $303 to buy what $100 would have bought in 1972. Most of this fall in the value of the dollar occurred in the 1970s when the price level more than doubled. What causes inflation? Why does it persist over many decades, and why did it explode in the 1970s? ■ The Canadian economy doesn't grow in a smooth, unperturbed expansion. Instead, it ebbs and flows over the business cycle. What makes real GDP grow unevenly, sometimes speeding up and sometimes slowing down or even shrinking? ■ Recent years have shown great turbulence in the economy. In 1983, the unemployment rate shot up to its highest level since the Great Depression. It then fell. In the same decade, real GDP went from shrinking in 1982 to extremely rapid growth in 1984 and then to more moderate but sustained growth in the subsequent five years. Can we make sense of such rapid economic change? ■ Sometimes our economy is hit with a big disturbance — for example, the worldwide recession and Bank of Canada's interest rate hike of 1981; the radical reform of our international trading arrangements with the passage of the Canada-United States Free Trade Act in 1989; and the introduction of new taxes such as the goods and services tax (GST) in 1991. How do developments such as these affect prices and production?

■ To answer questions like these, we need a model — a macroeconomic model. Our first task in this chapter is to build such a model. It is a model based on the general principles that we discussed in Chapter 1. The particular macroeconomic model that we'll study in this chapter contains three key concepts: aggregate demand, aggregate supply, and macroeconomic equilibrium. Our second task is to use this model to answer the following questions. What makes our economy grow? Why do we have inflation? Why do we have business cycles? What are the effects of the Bank of Canada's interest rate hikes? Why did we have a deep recession in 1982? And why did the economy grow so strongly and persistently through the mid-1980s?

Aggregate Demand

The aggregate quantity of goods and services produced is measured as real GDP — GDP valued in constant dollars. The average price of all these goods and services is measured by the GDP deflator. We are going to build a model that determines the values of real GDP and the GDP deflator. The model that we will build is based on the same concepts of demand, supply, and equilibrium that we studied in Chapter 4. But here the good is not tapes — it is real GDP —and the price is not the price of tapes — it is the GDP deflator.

The **aggregate quantity of goods and services demanded** is the sum of the quantities of consumption goods and services demanded by households, of investment goods demanded by firms, of goods and services demanded by governments, and of net exports demanded by foreigners. Thus the aggregate quantity of goods and services demanded depends on decisions made by households, firms, governments, and foreigners. When we studied the demand for tapes in Chapter 4, we summarized the buying plans of households in a demand schedule and a demand curve. Similarly, when we study the forces influencing aggregate buying plans, we summarize the decisions of households, firms, governments, and foreigners by using an aggregate demand schedule and an aggregate demand curve.

An **aggregate demand schedule** lists the quantity of real GDP demanded at each price level, holding all other influences on buying plans constant. The **aggregate demand curve** plots the quantity of real GDP demanded against the price level. **Aggregate demand** refers to the entire relationship between the quantity of real GDP demanded and the price level.

Figure 24.1 shows an aggregate demand schedule and aggregate demand curve. Each row of the table corresponds to a point in the figure. For example, row *c* of the aggregate demand schedule tells us that if the GDP deflator is 150, the level of real GDP demanded is 500 billion 1981 dollars. This row is plotted as point *c* on the aggregate demand curve.

Figure 24.1 The Aggregate Demand Schedule and Aggregate Demand Curve

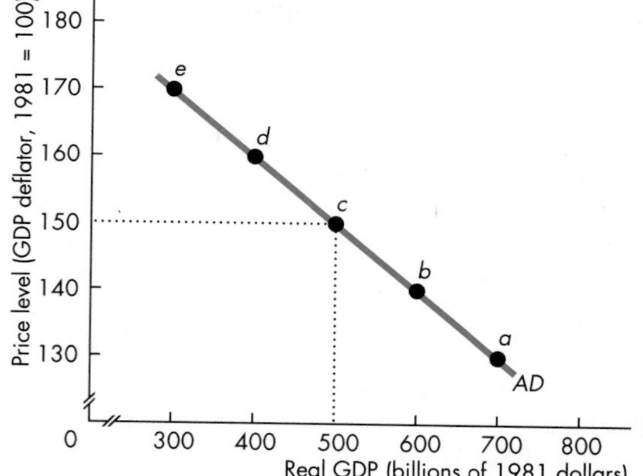

	Price level (GDP deflator)	Real GDP (billions of 1981 dollars)
a	130	700
b	140	600
c	150	500
d	160	400
e	170	300

The aggregate demand curve (*AD*) traces the quantity of real GDP demanded as the price level varies, holding everything else constant. The aggregate demand curve is derived from the schedule in the table. Points *a* through *e* on the curve correspond to the rows in the table identified by these letters. Thus when the price level is 150, the quantity of real GDP demanded is 500 billion 1981 dollars, illustrated by point *c* in the figure.

In constructing the aggregate demand schedule and aggregate demand curve, we hold constant all the influences on the quantity of real GDP demanded other than the price level. The effect of a change in the price level is shown as a movement along the aggregate demand curve. A change in any of the other influences on the quantity of real GDP demanded results in a new aggregate demand schedule and a shift in the aggregate demand curve. First, let's concentrate on the effects of a change in the price level on the quantity of real GDP demanded.

You can see from the downward slope of the aggregate demand curve and from the numbers that describe the aggregate demand schedule that the higher the price level, the smaller is the quantity of real GDP demanded. Why does the aggregate demand curve slope downward?

Why the Aggregate Demand Curve Slopes Downward

It's easy to understand why the demand curve for a single good slopes downward. If the price of Coca-Cola rises, the quantity of Coca-Cola demanded falls because people switch to drinking Pepsi-Cola and other substitutes. It's also easy to understand why the demand curve for a whole class of goods and services slopes downward. If the prices of Coca-Cola, Pepsi-Cola, and all other pops rise, the quantity of pop demanded falls because people switch from drinking pop to other substitute drinks and other goods. But it's less easy to see why the demand curve for *all* goods and services slopes downward. If the price of all goods increases and people demand a smaller quantity of *all* goods, what do they demand a larger quantity of? What do they substitute for goods and services?

There are three types of substitutes for the goods and services that make up real GDP. They are:

- Money and financial assets
- Goods and services in the future
- Goods and services produced in other countries

People may plan to buy a smaller quantity of the goods and services that make up real GDP and to hold a larger quantity of money or other financial assets. They may plan to buy a smaller quantity of goods and services today but a larger quantity at some future time. Also, people may decide to buy a smaller quantity of the goods and services made in Canada and buy a larger quantity of goods and services made in other countries. These decisions are influenced by the price level and as a result of those influences the aggregate demand curve slopes downward.

We can identify three separate effects of the price level on the quantity of real GDP demanded. They are:

- Real balance effect
- Intertemporal substitution effect
- International substitution effect

Money and the Real Balance Effect The influence of a change in the quantity of real money on the quantity of real GDP demanded is called the **real balance effect**. The **quantity of money** is the quantity of currency, deposits at banks and other financial institutions (such as trust companies) that are held by households and firms. **Real money** is a measure of money based on the quantity of goods that it will buy. Real money is measured as dollars divided by the price level. For example, suppose that you have $20 in notes and coins in your pocket and $480 in the bank. The quantity of money that you are holding is $500. Suppose that you continue to hold $500 and that the price level increases by 25 percent. Then your real money holdings decrease by 25 percent. That is, the $500 of money that you are holding will now buy what $375 would have bought before the price level increase.

The real balance effect is the proposition that the higher the quantity of real money, the larger is the quantity of goods and services demanded — of real GDP demanded. To understand the real balance effect, let's think about how your spending plans are influenced by your real money holdings. We'll continue with the above example.

You have $20 in your pocket and $480 in the bank. You also own a Walkman and some tapes worth $200. Your total assets are $700. Furthermore, you have decided that you don't want to change the way you are holding your assets. You don't want to have less money and more tapes or a better Walkman, and you don't want to trade in your Walkman for an inferior product or sell some tapes in order to have more money. Given that your total assets are $700, you are as happy as you can imagine with $500 in money and $200 worth of music equipment.

Now suppose that the prices of most goods and services and the average price level fall. Suppose that among the prices that fall are those of tapes and Walkmans. The money that you are now holding buys more goods than it would before. You've got more real money. But your music-making equipment is now worth less than before. This change in the price level has increased your holdings of real money and decreased the value of your holdings of music-making equipment. Since you were happy before about the proportions in which you owned money and music-making equipment, you will now, in general, want to make a change. You'll want more music-making equipment and less money. You use some of your extra real money to buy a better Walkman and a bigger stock of tapes. But Walkmans and tapes are two of the goods that make up real GDP. Thus your decision to use some of your extra real money to buy more music-making equipment results in an increase in the quantity of goods and services demanded, an increase in real GDP demanded. Of course, if you are the only person who behaves in this manner, there will not be a very large effect on real GDP demanded. The real balance effect will be tiny. But if everyone else behaves like you, the aggregate quantity of goods and services demanded will be higher than before. This increase in the quantity of goods and services demanded results from a fall in the price level.

The real balance effect is the first reason the aggregate demand curve slopes downward. A decrease in the price level increases the quantity of real money. The larger the quantity of real money, the larger is the quantity of goods and services demanded.

Intertemporal Substitution Effect The substitution of goods now for goods later or of goods later for goods now is **intertemporal substitution**. An example of intertemporal substitution is your decision to buy a new Walkman today instead of waiting until the end of the month. Another example is IBM's decision to speed up its installation of a new computer production plant. Yet another example is your decision to postpone that long-hoped-for vacation.

An important influence on intertemporal substitution is the level of interest rates. Low interest rates encourage people to borrow and to change the timing of their spending on capital goods — plant and equipment, houses, and consumer durable goods — shifting some of that spending from the future to the present. High interest rates discourage people from borrowing and shift some of their spending on capital goods from the present to the future.

Interest rates, in turn, are influenced by the quantity of real money. We have just seen that the quantity of real money increases if the price level falls. We've also seen that the more real money people have, the larger is the quantity of goods and services that they demand. But people do not necessarily use all their additional real money to buy other goods. They may lend some of it to others or use some of it to decrease their own borrowing. That is, with more real money, people increase their supply of loans and decrease their demand for loans. An increase in the supply of loans and a decrease in the demand for them results in a fall in interest rates. And lower interest rates lead to an intertemporal substitution effect — shifting spending plans from the future to the present and increasing the quantity of goods and services demanded.

In contrast, an increase in the price level decreases the real money supply and has the opposite effect on spending plans. With a decrease in the quantity of real money, people, to some degree, decrease their spending plans (real balance effect) and, to some degree, decrease their supply of loans or increase their demand for loans. As a consequence, interest rates increase and spending is shifted from the present to the future (intertemporal substitution effect).

The intertemporal substitution effect is the second reason the aggregate demand curve slopes downward. A lower price level

- Increases the quantity of real money.
- Increases the supply of loans.
- Decreases the demand for loans.
- Lowers interest rates.
- Shifts spending from the future to the present and increases the quantity of goods and services demanded.

Let's now look at the third reason the aggregate demand curve slopes downward.

International Substitution Effect The substitution of domestic goods for foreign goods or of foreign goods for domestic goods is **international substitution**. An example of international substitution is your decision to buy a General Motors car made in Windsor instead of a Toyota made in Japan. Another example of international substitution is the British government's decision to equip its armed forces with U.S.-produced weapons rather than weapons made in Great Britain. Yet another example is your decision to take a skiing vacation in Wyoming instead of Banff.

If the Canadian price level falls, holding everything else constant, Canadian-made goods become cheaper and, therefore, more attractive relative to goods made in other countries. Canadians will plan to buy more domestically produced goods and fewer imports; foreigners will plan to buy more Canadian-made goods and fewer of their own domestically produced goods. Thus at a lower Canadian price level, people and firms will demand a larger quantity of Canadian-produced goods and services. International substitution gives us the third reason for the downward slope of the aggregate demand curve.

R E V I E W

The aggregate demand curve traces the effects of a change in the price level — the GDP deflator — on the aggregate quantity of goods and services demanded — real GDP demanded. The effect of a change in the price level is shown as a movement along the aggregate demand curve. Other things being equal, the higher the price level, the smaller is the quantity of real GDP demanded — the aggregate demand curve slopes downward.

The aggregate demand curve slopes downward for three reasons: money and goods are substitutes (real balance effect); goods today and goods in the future are substitutes (intertemporal substitution effect); and domestic goods and foreign goods are substitutes (international substitution effect).

For a decrease in the price level, these effects work in the following ways:

- Real balance effect — money increases in real value so people hold a smaller quantity of money and buy a larger quantity of goods and services.
- Intertemporal substitution effect — the supply of loans increases, the demand for loans decreases, interest rates fall, and people buy a larger quantity of goods and services.
- International substitution effect — domestically produced goods become cheap relative to foreign-produced goods, so people buy smaller amounts from abroad and a larger quantity of domestically produced goods and services. ■

Table 24.1 Aggregate Demand 

Aggregate demand

Increases if	*Decreases if*
• Interest rates decrease	• Interest rates increase
• The expected inflation rate increases	• The expected inflation rate decreases
• The foreign exchange rate falls	• The foreign exchange rate rises
• Expected future profit increases	• Expected future profit decreases
• The quantity of money increases	• The quantity of money decreases
• Aggregate wealth increases	• Aggregate wealth decreases
• Government spending on goods and services increases	• Government spending on goods and services decreases
• Taxes decrease or transfer payments increase	• Taxes increase or transfer payments decrease
• Foreign income increases	• Foreign income decreases
• Population increases	• Population decreases

All of these influences on aggregate demand are spread out over time and are not completely predictable.

Changes in Aggregate Demand

We've just seen that real GDP demanded varies when the price level varies. The effects of a change in the price level on real GDP demanded are shown as a movement along an aggregate demand curve. But an aggregate demand schedule and aggregate demand curve describe aggregate demand at a point in time, and aggregate demand does not remain constant. There are many factors that lead to changes in aggregate demand. When any one of these factors changes, the aggregate demand curve shifts. Let's review the most important of these factors. They are summarized in Table 24.1.

1. Interest Rates An increase in interest rates, other things being equal, leads to a decrease in aggregate demand. We've just seen that a change in the price level, through its effect on the quantity of real money, influences the level of interest rates. A change in interest rates induced by a change in the price level changes the aggregate quantity of goods and services demanded. But, as we saw above, this change is represented as a movement along an aggregate demand curve, not as a change in aggregate demand.

However, interest rates can and do change for many other reasons. Whatever the reason for a change in interest rates, their level influences aggregate demand. Whenever interest rates change independently of changes in the price level, the aggregate demand curve shifts. For example, in recent years, there has been an enormous increase in the government of Canada's demand for loans to cover its deficit. Such an increase in the demand for loans, other things being equal, increases interest rates and has a depressing effect on the spending plans of households and firms. But in recent years, there has also been a large increase in the supply of loans from the rest of the world, especially from Japan and Western Europe. These increases in the supply of loans have kept interest rates moderate and prevented aggregate demand from falling.

2. Expected Inflation An increase in the expected inflation rate, other things being equal, leads to an increase in aggregate demand. The higher the expected inflation rate, the higher is the expected price of goods and services in the future and the lower is the expected real value of money and other assets in the future. As a consequence, when people expect a higher inflation rate, they plan to buy more goods and services in the present and hold smaller quantities of money and other financial assets.

Inflation expectations changed during the 1980s. At the beginning of the decade, people expected inflation to persist at close to 10 percent a year. But the severe recession in 1982 reduced those inflation expectations. Other things being equal, the effect of this decrease in inflation expectations was to decrease aggregate demand.

3. The Foreign Exchange Rate We've seen that a change in the Canadian price level, other things being equal, leads to a change in the prices of our goods and services relative to the prices of goods and services produced in other countries. Another important influence on the price of our goods and services relative to those produced abroad is the *foreign exchange rate.* The foreign exchange rate affects aggregate demand because it affects the prices that foreigners have to pay for Canadian-produced goods and the prices that we have to pay for foreign-produced goods.

Suppose that the dollar is worth 125 Japanese yen. Then you can buy a Fujitsu cellular telephone, made in Japan, that costs 125,000 yen for $1,000. What if you can buy a Canadian-made Northern Telecom cellular phone that is just as good as the Fujitsu for $900? In such a case, you will buy the Canadian-made telephone.

But which phone will you buy if the value of the Canadian dollar rises to 150 yen and everything else remains the same? Let's work out the answer. At 150 yen per dollar, you pay only $833.33 to buy the 125,000 yen needed to buy the Fujitsu phone. Since the Northern Telecom phone costs $900, the Fujitsu is now cheaper and you will substitute the Fujitsu for the Northern Telecom. The demand for Canadian-made phones falls as the foreign exchange value of the dollar rises. So as the foreign exchange value of the dollar rises, everything else held constant, aggregate demand decreases.

There have been huge swings in the foreign exchange value of the dollar through the 1980s, leading to large swings in aggregate demand.

4. Expected Future Profit A change in expected future profit changes firms' demands for new capital equipment. For example, suppose that a recent wave of technological change has increased productivity. Firms will expect that by installing new equipment that uses the latest technology, their future profit will rise. This expectation leads to an increase in demand for new plant and equipment and so to an increase in aggregate demand.

Profit expectations were pessimistic in 1981 and led to a decrease in aggregate demand. Expectations were optimistic through the rest of the 1980s, leading to sustained increases in aggregate demand.

5. The Quantity of Money A change in the quantity of money has two effects on agregate demand:

- Real balance effect
- Interest rate effect

The Real Balance Effect The quantity of *real money* in the economy depends on the quantity of money and the price level. Thus the quantity of real money can change because either the quantity of money changes or the price level changes. In each case there is a real balance effect. We've already described that effect when there is a change in the price level. In that case, there is a change in the aggregate quantity of goods and services demanded — a movement along the aggregate demand curve. When real money changes because of a change in the quantity of money, there is a change in aggregate demand — the aggregate demand curve shifts.

An easy way to see why there is a real balance effect on aggregate demand is to imagine what would happen if the government loaded all the Canadian Armed Forces' helicopters with millions of dollars worth of new $10 bills and sprinkled then like confetti across the nation. We would all stop whatever we were doing and rush out to pick up our share of the newly available money. We wouldn't, though, just put all the money that we picked up in the bank. We would spend some of it, so our demand for goods and services would increase. In practice, changes in the quantity of money arise from the operations of the Bank of Canada (operations that we'll study in Chapter 28), not the Canadian Armed Forces helicopter squadrons! Nevertheless, the above story does illustrate that an increase in the quantity of money increases aggregate demand.

The Interest Rate Effect The interest rate effect of a change in the quantity of money on aggregate demand can also be illustrated by the helicopter drop story. When people pick up their share of the new $10 bills they spend some of them — the real balance effect. But most of what is not spent is taken to banks or trust companies and put into savings accounts. The banks want to make a profit by lending these new deposits so the supply of loans increases. As a consequence interest rates fall. With lower interest rates people borrow and spend more. Investment and purchases of consumer durables increase.

Fluctuations in the quantity of money and in interest rates induced by those fluctuations have been some of the most important sources of changes in aggregate demand. Throughout the 1970s, sustained increases in the quantity of money increased aggregate demand, contributing to the inflation of those years; decreases in the growth rate of the quantity of money slowed aggregate demand growth, contributing to the 1982 recession.

6. Aggregate Wealth Wealthy people consume larger quantities of goods and services than do poor people. If everyone's wealth increases, aggregate wealth also increases and so does aggregate demand. This source of changes in aggregate demand exerts a steady upward influence as wealth gradually accumulates.

7. Government Demand for Goods and Services The scale of government demand for goods and services has a direct effect on aggregate demand. If taxes are held constant, the more highways, weapons, schools, colleges, and universities the government demands, the higher is government demand and so the higher is aggregate demand.

8. Taxes and Transfer Payments A decrease in taxes increases aggregate demand. An increase in transfer payments — for example, unemployment benefits, family allowances, and old age pensions — also increases aggregate demand. Both of these influences operate by increasing households' *disposable* income. The higher the level of disposable income, the greater is the demand for goods and services. Since lower taxes and higher transfer payments increase disposable income, they also increase aggregate demand.

This source of changes in aggregate demand has been an important one in recent years. Through the late 1960s, a large increase in government payments under various social programs led to a sustained increase in aggregate demand.

9. Foreign Income The income of foreigners affects the aggregate demand for domestically produced goods and services. For example, an increase in income in the United States, Japan, and Germany increases the demand by U.S., Japanese, and German consumers and producers for Canadian-made consumption goods and capital goods. These sources of change in aggregate demand have been important ones in the postwar period. The rapid economic growth of Japan and Western Europe and of some of the newly industrializing countries of the Pacific Rim, such as Korea and Singapore, has led to a sustained increase in demand for Canadian-made goods and services.

10. Population An increase in population increases aggregate demand. The more people there are, the greater is the demand for housing, clothing, food, and the many other goods and services that people buy. Our population grows at about 1 percent a year, exerting a steady increase in aggregate demand.

Time Lags The effects of all the influences on aggregate demand that we have just considered do not occur in an instant or in a predictable manner. A change in any of the influences on aggregate demand affects aggregate demand for many months following the initial change. For example, if the Bank of Canada increases the quantity of money, there may first be no effect on aggregate demand at all. A little later, as people reallocate their wealth, there is an increase in the supply of loans and a tendency for interest rates to fall. Later yet, some households and firms, confronted with lower interest rates, change their buying plans for consumer durables and capital goods. As more time passes, more and more households and firms change their plans and aggregate demand gradually increases. The total effect of the initial change in the quantity of money is spread out over many months. But the next time the Bank of Canada takes exactly the same action, there is no guarantee that its effects will take place with exactly the same timing as before. The lags in the effects of influences on aggregate demand are varied and, to a degree, unpredictable.

Now that we've reviewed the factors that influence aggregate demand, let's summarize their effects on the aggregate demand curve.

Shifts in the Aggregate Demand Curve

We illustrate a change in aggregate demand as a shift

Figure 24.2 Changes in Aggregate Demand

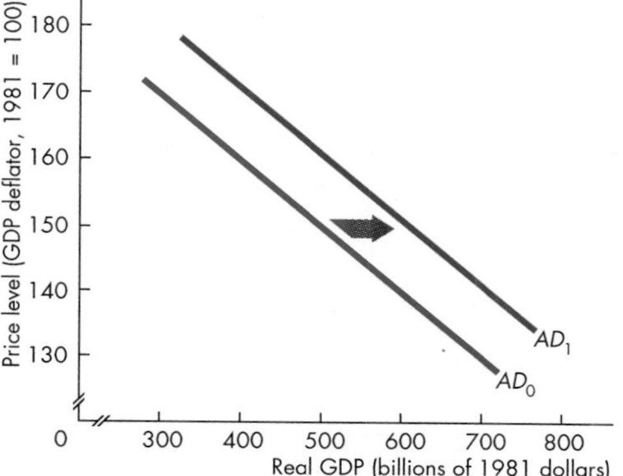

(a) An increase in aggregate demand

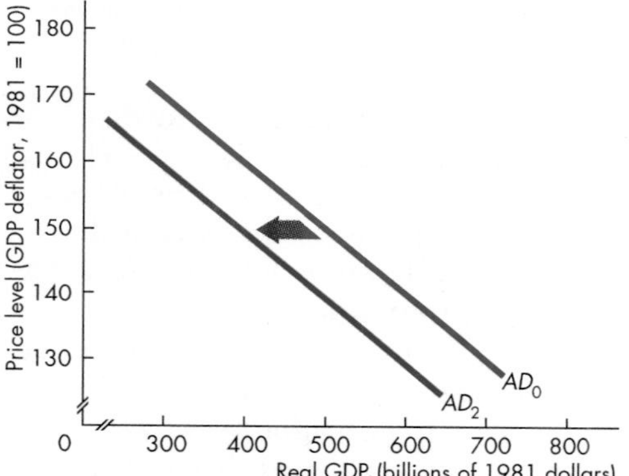

(b) A decrease in aggregate demand

The factors that increase aggregate demand (listed in Table 24.1) shift the aggregate demand curve to the right. Such a shift is illustrated by the movement from AD_0 to AD_1 in part (a). The factors that decrease aggregate demand (also listed in Table 24.1) shift the aggregate demand curve to the left. Such a shift is illustrated by the movement from AD_0 to AD_2 in part (b).

in the aggregate demand curve. Figure 24.2 illustrates two changes in aggregate demand. Aggregate demand is initially AD_0 (the same as in Fig. 24.1). In part (a) there is an increase in aggregate demand and in part (b) a decrease in aggregate demand.

The aggregate demand curve shifts to the right, from AD_0 to AD_1, as shown in part (a), if there is an increase in expected future profit, the expected inflation rate, the quantity of money, aggregate wealth, government spending on goods and services, transfer payments, foreign income, or population. A decrease in interest rates, the foreign exchange rate, or taxes also cause the aggregate demand curve to shift to the right.

The aggregate demand curve shifts to the left, from AD_0 to AD_2 as shown in Fig. 24.2(b), if there is a decrease in expected future profit, the expected inflation rate, the quantity of money, aggregate wealth, government spending on goods and services, transfer payments, foreign income, or population. An increase in interest rates, the foreign exchange rate, or taxes also cause the aggregate demand curve to shift to the left.

R E V I E W

A change in the price level leads to a change in the aggregate quantity of goods and services demanded. That change is shown as a movement along the aggregate demand curve. A change in any other factor that influences aggregate demand shifts the aggregate demand curve. Some of these other factors are:

- Interest rates
- The expected inflation rate
- The foreign exchange rate
- Expected future profit
- The quantity of money
- Aggregate wealth
- Government spending on goods and services
- Taxes and transfer payments
- Foreign income
- Population ■

Aggregate Supply

The **aggregate quantity of goods and services supplied** is the sum of the quantities of all the final goods and services produced by all the firms in the economy. It is measured as real gross domestic product. When we studied the supply of tapes in Chapter 4, we summarized the selling plans of firms in a supply schedule and a supply curve. Similarly, when we study the forces influencing aggregate selling plans, we summarize the decisions of firms by using an aggregate supply schedule and an aggregate supply curve. But in studying aggregate supply, we distinguish between two time frames: the long run and the short run.

Long-run Aggregate Supply

Long-run aggregate supply is the relationship between the aggregate quantity of final goods and services (real GDP) supplied and the price level (GDP deflator) when all factor prices have adjusted in step with changes in the price level so that *real* factor prices are unchanged. *Factor prices* are the wage rates paid to labour, the rental rates paid for the use of capital equipment and land, and the prices of raw material inputs. Long-run aggregate supply is represented by the long-run aggregate supply curve. The **long-run aggregate supply curve** plots the relationship between the quantity of real GDP supplied and the price level when all factor prices have changed by the same percentage as the change in the price level so that *real* factor prices are unchanged. The long-run aggregate supply curve is vertical and is illustrated in Fig. 24.3 as the curve labelled *LAS*.

As the economy moves along its long-run aggregate supply curve

- Each firm is producing its capacity output.
- There is full employment.

Figure 24.3 The Long-run Aggregate Supply Curve

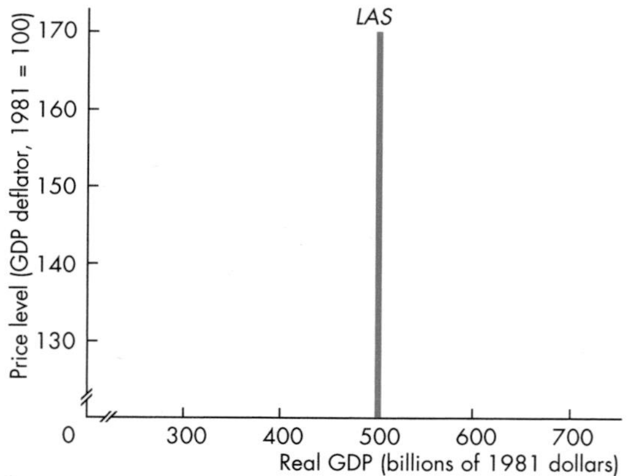

The long-run aggregate supply curve (*LAS*) shows the full-employment level of real GDP — it is independent of the price level. There is uncertainty about the position of the long-run aggregate supply curve because we are not able to measure accurately the economy's capacity output and its natural rate of unemployment, two factors on which long-run aggregate supply depends.

Capacity Output A firm's **capacity output** is the output at which its cost per unit produced is minimized. Each firm has a unique capacity output. The concept of capacity output can be illustrated by an automobile production line. For example, if General Motors' output is below capacity, the enormous fixed costs of its production line are spread over a smaller output and the cost of each car produced is higher than it might otherwise be. Conversely, if GM operates its production line above its capacity output, the fixed costs are now spread over a larger output, the plant is being operated closer to its limits and machinery breakdowns and maintenance problems add to the cost of producing a car. There is a particular output that balances the gains from spreading fixed costs over a larger output against the costs of bottlenecks and increased plant breakdowns. That output is the firm's capacity output.

Suppose that a firm is making the largest possible profit and that its output is equal to its capacity output. Let's work out what happens to the firm's output if there is an increase in the price at which it can sell its output. Will the firm increase its output? The answer depends on whether there are any changes in the prices of the firm's inputs — in the prices of the factors of production that it employs. If factor prices do not change, the firm will be able to make a bigger profit by increasing its output, so output will increase. But if factor prices increase by the same percentage as the increase in the price of the firm's output, the firm will not be able to make a bigger profit by changing its output. Output will remain at its capacity level. The firm is able to sell its output at a higher price but it must pay higher factor prices and so it is in the same *real* situation as before.

With all firms in the economy behaving like this firm, as the price level rises output will remain constant, if factor prices, on the average, rise by the same percentage as the increase in the price level. The economy moves along its long-run aggregate supply curve.

Full Employment As the economy moves along its long-run aggregate supply curve, there is full employment. Full employment occurs when there is a balance between the quantity of labour demanded and the quantity of labour supplied. In this situation the only unemployment is frictional unemployment, arising from job search by new labour market entrants and from job turnover that results from technological change. At full employment, unemployment is at its natural rate.

Let's see why there is full employment along the long-run aggregate supply curve. Suppose that the economy is operating at full employment and the price level rises. What happens to the level of unemployment?

The answer depends on what happens to wages. If the price level increases and wages do not increase, *real* wages fall. With lower real wages, firms will want to hire more labour and produce a larger output. If they manage to hire more labour, unemployment declines. But if the price level and wages move in step with each other, *real* wages remain constant. In this case nothing happens to the level of unemployment: it remains at its natural rate. Thus when wages change in step with changes in the price level the economy moves along its long-run aggregate supply curve.

Measuring Long-run Aggregate Supply Real GDP is a measure of the actual quantity of final goods and services produced. It is not a measure of long-run aggregate supply. At the present time, we do not have a sure method for calculating long-run aggregate supply. We can estimate it, using one of two approaches, but neither of them gives a completely reliable answer. The two methods are the

- Trend approach.
- Production function approach.

Trend Approach The trend approach to estimating long-run aggregate supply calculates a smooth trend line through the actual path of real GDP. Such a trend line was used in Chapter 22 to calculate the deviations from trend that form the business cycle. However, we can calculate many different trend lines — and each gives rise to a different estimate of long-run aggregate supply. For example, if long-run aggregate supply is based on a trend line with a *constant* growth rate from 1926 through 1988, actual real GDP has been below long-run aggregate supply for most of the 1970s and 1980s. But if we use the trend calculations of Chapter 22, real GDP fluctuated around long-run aggregate supply during the 1970s and 1980s, falling below long-run aggregate supply in 1982 but rising above long-run aggregate supply in the 1980s expansion.

Production Function Approach The production function approach to estimating long-run aggregate supply uses the fact that long-run aggregate supply depends on the stock of capital equipment and full employment of the labour force. To estimate long-run aggregate supply by this method, we need an estimate of the natural rate of unemployment. But we do not yet have a reliable way of making that estimate. As a consequence, this method produces different estimates of long-run aggregate supply based on different views of the natural rate of unemployment.

Thus, because of the imprecision of current methods of measuring long-run aggregate supply, there is uncertainty about the position of the long-run aggregate supply curve. We know that the long-run aggregate supply curve is vertical, but we do not know its exact position. This uncertainty is a source of some of the disagreements among economists and policymakers about how to conduct macroeconomic policy. We'll briefly meet some of that controversy later in this chapter and in Chapters 31 and 34.

Let's now turn to an examination of short-run aggregate supply.

Short-Run Aggregate Supply

Short-run aggregate supply is the relationship between the aggregate quantity of final goods and services (real GDP) supplied and the price level (the GDP deflator), holding constant the prices of the factors of production — in particular, holding money wage rates constant. We can represent short-run aggregate supply as either a short-run aggregate supply schedule or a short-run aggregate supply curve.

The **short-run aggregate supply schedule** lists quantities of real GDP supplied at each price level, holding everything else constant. The **short-run aggregate supply curve** plots the relationship between the quantity of real GDP supplied and the price level, holding everything else constant.

Figure 24.4 shows a short-run aggregate supply schedule and the corresponding short-run aggregate supply curve (labelled *SAS*). Each row of the table corresponds to a point in the figure. For example, row c' of the short-run aggregate supply schedule and point c' on the curve tell us that if the price level is 150 (the GDP deflator is 150) the quantity of real GDP supplied is 500 billion 1981 dollars. In constructing the short-run aggregate supply schedule and the short-run aggregate supply curve, we hold constant *all* the influences on the quantity of real GDP supplied other than the price level.

The short-run aggregate supply schedule and the short-run aggregate supply curve in Fig. 24.4 tell us that the higher the price level, the larger is the aggregate quantity of goods and services supplied, up to some maximum. Why does the short-run aggregate supply curve slope upward? Why does it become vertical at some output level?

Figure 24.4 The Aggregate Supply Schedule and Aggregate Supply Curve

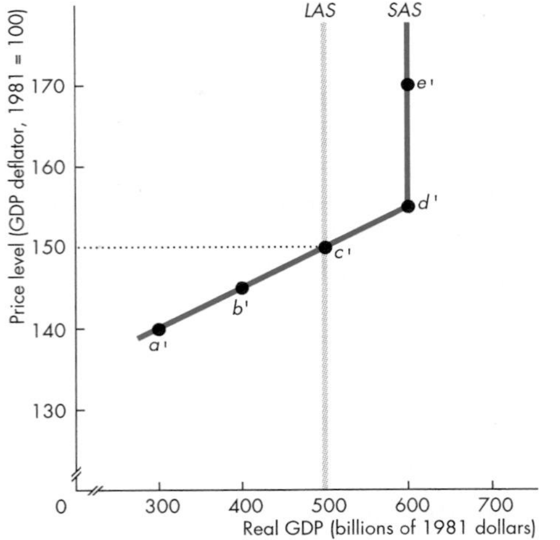

	Price level (GDP deflator)	Real GDP (billions of 1981 dollars)
a'	140	300
b'	145	400
c'	150	500
d'	155	600
e'	170	600

The long-run aggregate supply curve (*LAS*) is the same as the curve in Fig. 24.3. The short-run aggregate supply curve (*SAS*) traces the quantity of real GDP supplied as the price level varies, holding everything else constant. The short-run aggregate supply curve in this figure is derived from the schedule in the table. Points *a'* through *e'* correspond to the rows in the table identified by those letters. Thus when the price level is 150, real GDP supplied is 500 billion 1981 dollars (point *c'*).

The easiest way to understand why the short-run aggregate supply curve slopes upward is to consider how an individual firm responds to an increase in the price of its output, while the prices of its inputs remain constant. Suppose, for example, that car prices increase and that auto workers' wage rates and the prices of auto parts remain constant. In this situation, General Motors will increase its output and offer more cars for sale. It will also hire more workers and increase the work hours of its existing work force. Conversely, if auto prices fall while auto workers' wage rates and parts prices remain constant, GM will decrease its output and offer fewer cars for sale. It will lay off workers and cut back on its parts orders.

Thus changes in the price level, with input prices held constant, lead to a change in the aggregate quantity of goods and services supplied and to changes in the level of employment and unemployment. The higher the price level, the higher is the aggregate quantity of goods and services supplied, the higher is the level of employment, and the lower is the level of unemployment.

Why does the short-run aggregate supply curve eventually become vertical? It is because there is a physical limit to the output capacity of the economy. When the economy is on its long-run aggregate supply curve, unemployment is at its natural rate and each firm produces its capacity output — the output that minimizes the cost per unit produced. If output prices increase while input prices stay constant, each firm increases its output above its capacity level. It does so by working its labour overtime, hiring more labour, and working its plant and equipment at a faster pace. But there is a limit to the extent to which workers will accept overtime, and there is a limit to which the unemployment rate can be pushed below its natural rate. There is also a limit beyond which firms will not operate their plant and equipment. Once these limits have been reached, no more output is produced no matter how high prices become, relative to costs. At that point, the short-run aggregate supply curve becomes vertical.

R E V I E W

The long-run aggregate supply curve shows the relationship between real GDP supplied and the price level when all factor prices change along with changes in the price level keeping *real* factor prices constant. Along the long-run aggregate supply curve each firm is producing its capacity output and there is full employment. This level of real GDP is independent of the price level. The long-run aggregate supply curve is vertical. Its position tells us the level of real GDP when the economy is at full employment. The short-run aggregate supply curve shows the relationship between real GDP supplied and the price level, holding everything else constant. With constant input prices, an increase in the price level results in an increase in real GDP supplied. The short-run aggregate supply curve is upward sloping. ■

A change in the price level with everything else held constant results in a movement along the short-run aggregate supply curve. A change in the price level results in a movement along the long-run aggregate supply curve if there is an accompanying change in input prices that keeps each firm producing its capacity output and keeps unemployment at its natural rate. But there are many other influences on real GDP supplied. These influences result in changes in aggregate supply and in shifts in the aggregate supply curves.

Some factors change both long-run aggregate supply and short-run aggregate supply; others affect short-run aggregate supply but leave long-run aggregate supply unchanged. Let's examine these influences on aggregate supply starting with those that affect *both* long-run aggregate supply and short-run aggregate supply.

Changes in Both Long-Run and Short-Run Aggregate Supply

Table 24.2 sets out the important factors that influence long-run and short-run aggregate supply. Let's examine each of them.

1. The Labour Force The larger the labour force, the larger is the quantity of goods and services that will be produced.

2. The Capital Stock The larger the stock of productive plant and equipment, the more productive the labour force will be and thus the greater is the output that it will be able to produce.

3. Human Capital The value of the skills that people acquire in school and through on-the-job training has an important influence on the level of aggregate supply. The more highly trained and experienced the labour force, the more human capital it has, and the greater is its output.

4. Raw Materials The availability of raw materials has an important effect on output. The discovery of new, easily accessed deposits of raw materials lowers their cost and increases output. The depletion of raw materials has the reverse effect, lowering output.

5. Climate The climate has an obvious effect on output, especially in the agricultural sector. Ideal amounts of rainfall and sunshine and ideal temperatures can produce an increase in output while extreme climatic conditions restrict output.

6. Technology The state of technology obviously has an important effect on aggregate supply. Inventing new and better ways of doing things enables firms to produce more from any given amount of inputs. So, even with a constant population and constant capital stock, improvements in technology increase production and increase aggregate supply.

7. Changing Composition of Real GDP When the different sectors and regions of the economy grow at a similar pace, the composition of GDP remains stable. But if some sectors expand very rapidly and others decline, then the composition of GDP changes quickly. An example of a rapid change in the composition of GDP was the explosive growth in banking and financial services and the relative decline in manufacturing in Canada in the 1980s. Other things being equal, the more rapidly the economy changes the composition of

Table 24.2 Aggregate Supply

Short-run aggregate supply and long-run aggregate supply curves	
Shift to right if	*Shift to the left if*
• The labour force increases	• The labour force decreases
• The capital stock increases	• The capital stock decreases
• Human capital increases	• Human capital decreases
• New raw material sources are discovered	• Raw materials are depleted
• Climatic conditions improve	• Climatic conditions deteriorate
• Technology advances	
• Composition of GDP changes slowly	• Composition of GDP changes quickly
• Incentives are strengthened	• Incentives are weakened
Short-run aggregate supply curve also	
Shifts down if	*Shifts up if*
• Wages decrease	• Wages increase
• Raw material prices decrease	• Raw material prices increase

its output, the larger is the rate of turnover of its labour force. Job search activity increases and the natural rate of unemployment rises. Such a process leads to a decrease in aggregate supply.

8. Incentives Aggregate supply can be influenced by the incentives people face. For example, high taxes may discourage people from working and also discourage saving and the accumulation of capital. Aggregate supply falls as disincentives from high taxes rise. Another incentive influencing aggregate supply is the regulatory environment: safety and environmental protection regulations that raise costs lower the quantity of goods and services produced and reduce aggregate supply.

These are the major influences on long-run aggregate supply and short-run aggregate supply. But there are two other important influences on short-run aggregate supply that do not affect long-run aggregate supply.

Changes in Short-Run Aggregate Supply

The factors that change short-run aggregate supply but not long-run aggregate supply are wages and the prices of other factors of production.

1. Wages Wages affect short-run aggregate supply through their influence on a firm's costs. The higher the level of wages, the higher are a firm's costs and the lower the quantity of output the firm will want to supply at each price level. Thus an increase in wages decreases short-run aggregate supply.

2. Other Factor Prices The prices of other factors of production affect short-run aggregate supply in the same way that wages do. An increase in the price of any other factor of production, such as capital, increases a firm's costs and decreases the output supplied at each price level.

Why do factor prices affect short-run aggregate supply but not long-run aggregate supply? The answer lies in the definition of long-run aggregate supply. Recall that long-run aggregate supply refers to the quantity of real GDP supplied when each firm is producing its capacity output and when there is full employment. When the economy is producing its long-run aggregate supply, any changes in factor prices are matched by an equivalent change in the price level.

Let's now summarize the factors that influence aggregate supply by examining how they lead to shifts in the long-run and the short-run aggregate supply curves.

Shifts in the Aggregate Supply Curves

If any of the events listed in Table 24.2 that increase long-run aggregate supply occur, the long-run aggregate supply curve and the short-run aggregate supply curve shift to the right. Both curves shift by the same amount. Figure 24.5 illustrates these shifts. Initially, the long-run aggregate supply curve is LAS_0 and the short-run aggregate supply curve is SAS_0. These curves intersect at a price level of 150 where real GDP is 500 billion 1981 dollars. An increase in the productive capacity of the economy that increases full-employment real GDP to 700 billion 1981 dollars shifts both the long-run aggregate supply curve to LAS_1 and the short-run aggregate supply curve to SAS_1. Long-run aggregate supply is now 700 billion 1981 dollars.

Notice that the price level at which the long-run and the short-run aggregate supply curves intersect

Figure 24.5 Changes in Aggregate Supply

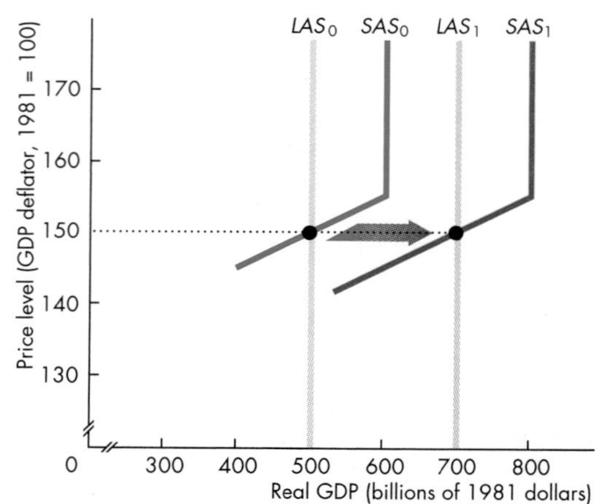

Any of the factors that increase long-run aggregate supply and short-run aggregate supply (listed in Table 24.2) shift both supply curves to the right by the same amount. Such a shift is illustrated by the change from LAS_0 and SAS_0 to LAS_1 and SAS_1. The size of the horizontal shift in the short-run aggregate supply curve is the same as that in the long-run aggregate supply curve. As a result, SAS_1 intersects LAS_1 at the same price level (150) that SAS_0 intersects LAS_0.

remains at 150. The short-run aggregate supply curve shifts to the right by exactly the same amount as the long-run aggregate supply curve.

Next, let's look at the effect of a change in factor prices. Figure 24.6 illustrates this case. Long-run aggregate supply is *LAS* and initially the short-run aggregate supply curve is SAS_0. These curves intersect at the price level 150. Now suppose that factor prices rise by 20 percent. Since firms are willing to supply, in total, $500 billion worth of output at a price level of 150, they will supply that same level of output when input prices are 20 percent higher only if they can get 20 percent higher prices. Thus the short-run aggregate supply curve shifts upward. The new short-run aggregate supply curve is SAS_1. This supply curve intersects *LAS* at a price level of 180 — 20 percent above 150. The curve SAS_1 is located 20 percent above SAS_0 at every output level.

The direction in which we measure the distance between two short-run aggregate supply curves depends on the source of the shift. If short-run aggregate supply changes because of changes in the economy's productive capacity, the *horizontal* distance between the two short-run aggregate supply curves is the same as the horizontal distance between the two long-run aggregate supply curves; it is the amount by which the economy's full-employment output has changed. If short-run aggregate supply changes because of a change in input prices, the *vertical* distance between the initial and the new short-run aggregate supply curves is equal to the percentage change in factor prices.

Figure 24.6 A Change in Aggregate Supply: A Change in Input Prices

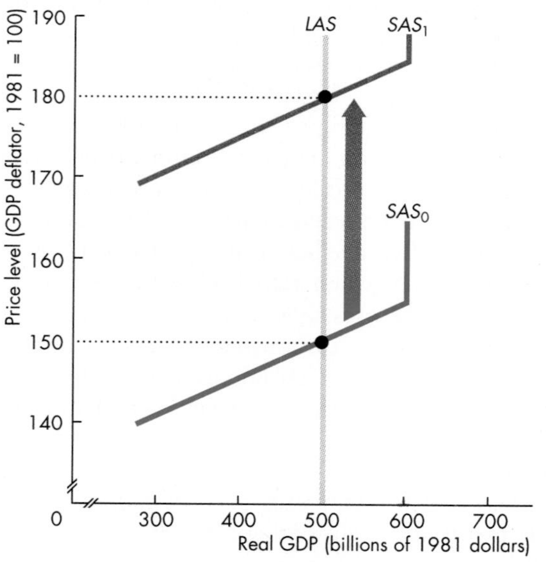

A change in input prices shifts the short-run aggregate supply curve but leaves the long-run aggregate supply curve unaffected. If all input prices increase by 20 percent, the short-run aggregate supply curve shifts upward by 20 percent. If the original short-run aggregate supply curve is SAS_0, the new short-run aggregate supply curve is SAS_1, 20 percent above SAS_0. (Note that the price level of 180 is 20 percent higher than the price level of 150.)

R E V I E W

When firms are producing their capacity output and there is full employment, the economy is on its long-run aggregate supply curve. The long-run aggregate supply curve is vertical. When there is a change in the price level and everything else (including input prices) is held constant, the economy slides up or down its short-run aggregate supply curve. A movement along a short-run aggregate supply curve is referred to as a change in the aggregate quantity of goods and services supplied. The short-run aggregate supply curve is upward sloping. Everything that shifts the long-run aggregate supply curve also shifts the short-run aggregate supply curve. A change in factor prices shifts the short-run aggregate supply curve but leaves the long-run aggregate supply curve unchanged. ■

Next, we'll study macroeconomic equilibrium.

Macroeconomic Equilibrium

Our purpose in building a model of aggregate demand and aggregate supply is to determine and predict changes in real GDP and the price level. To make predictions about real GDP and the price level, we need to combine aggregate demand and aggregate supply and determine macroeconomic equilibrium. **Macroeconomic equilibrium** occurs when the quantity of real GDP demanded equals the quantity of real GDP supplied. Let's see how macroeconomic equilibrium is determined.

Determination of Real GDP and the Price Level

We have seen that the aggregate demand curve tells us the quantity of real GDP demanded at each price level and the short-run aggregate supply curve tells us the quantity of real GDP supplied at each price level. There is one and only one price level at which the quantity demanded equals the quantity supplied. Macroeconomic equilibrium occurs at that price level. Figure 24.7 illustrates such an equilibrium at a price level of 150 and real GDP of 500 billion 1981 dollars (point *c* and *c*′).

To see why this position is an equilibrium, let's work out what happens if the price level is something other than 150. Suppose, for example, that the price level is 170. In that case, the quantity of real GDP demanded is $300 billion (point *e*) but the quantity of real GDP supplied is $600 billion (point *e*′). There is an excess of the quantity supplied over the quantity demanded, a surplus of goods and services. Unable to sell all their output, firms willingly accept lower prices. Prices are cut until the surplus is eliminated — at a price level of 150.

Next consider what happens if the price level is 140. In this case, the quantity of real GDP that firms supply is $300 billion worth of goods and services (point *a*′) and the quantity of real GDP demanded is $600 billion (point *b*). The quantity demanded exceeds the quantity supplied. Aware of shortages, firms push their prices upward and continue to do so until the quantities demanded and supplied are in balance — again at a price level of 150.

Figure 24.7 Macroeconomic Equilibrium

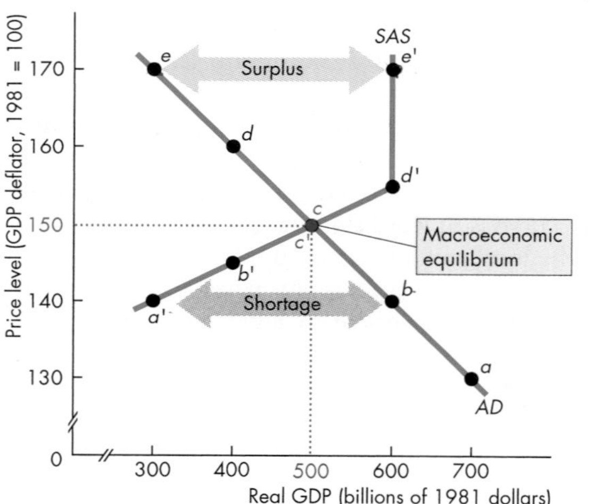

Macroeconomic equilibrium occurs when real GDP demanded equals real GDP supplied. Such an equilibrium is at the intersection of the aggregate demand curve (*AD*) and the short-run aggregate supply curve (*SAS*) — points *c* and *c*′. At price levels of more than 150, (for example, 170) there is an excess of the quantity of goods and services supplied over the quantity demanded — a surplus — and prices fall. At price levels of less than 150 (for example, 140), there is an excess of the quantity of goods and services demanded over the quantity supplied — a shortage — and prices rise. Only when the price level is 150 is the quantity of goods and services demanded equal to the quantity supplied. This is the equilibrium price level. The quantity of goods and services traded at this price level is the equilibrium level of real GDP — 500 billion 1981 dollars.

Macroeconomic Equilibrium and Full Employment

Macroeconomic equilibrium occurs at the intersection of the short-run aggregate supply curve and the aggregate demand curve — at the price level where the aggregate quantity of goods and services demanded equals the aggregate quantity of goods and services supplied. But macroeconomic equilibrium does not necessarily occur at full employment. It can occur at, below, or above full employment. We can see the three possible types of macroeconomic equilibrium by considering Fig. 24.8.

In part (a) of the figure the fluctuations of real GDP are shown for an imaginary economy over a five year period. In year 2, real GDP falls below its capacity level and there is a recessionary gap. A **recessionary gap** is the difference between capacity real GDP and actual real GDP when actual is less than capacity. In year 4, real GDP rises above capacity and there is an inflationary gap. An **inflationary gap** is the difference between actual real GDP and capacity real GDP when actual exceeds capacity. In year 3 actual and capacity real GDP are equal and the economy is at full employment.

These situations are illustrated in parts (b), (c), and (d) as three different types of macroeconomic equilibrium. In part (b) there is an unemployment equilibrium. An **unemployment equilibrium** is a situation in which macroeconomic equilibrium occurs at a level of real GDP below capacity real GDP and there is a recessionary gap. The unemployment equilibrium illustrated in Fig. 24.8(b) occurs where the aggregate demand curve AD_0 intersects the short-run aggregate supply curve SAS_0 at a real GDP of 400 billion 1981 dollars and a price level of 150. There is a recessionary gap of 100 billion 1981 dollars. The

Figure 24.8 Three Types of Macroeconomic Equilibrium

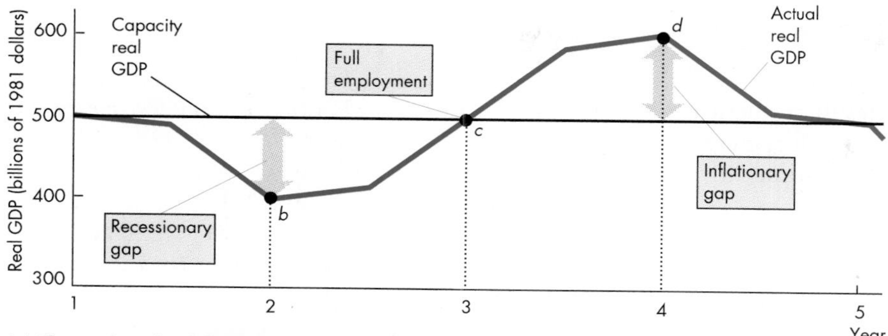

(a) Fluctuations in real GDP

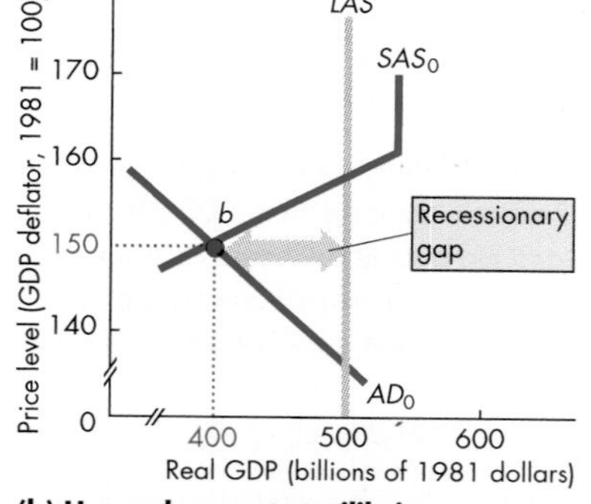

(b) Unemployment equilibrium

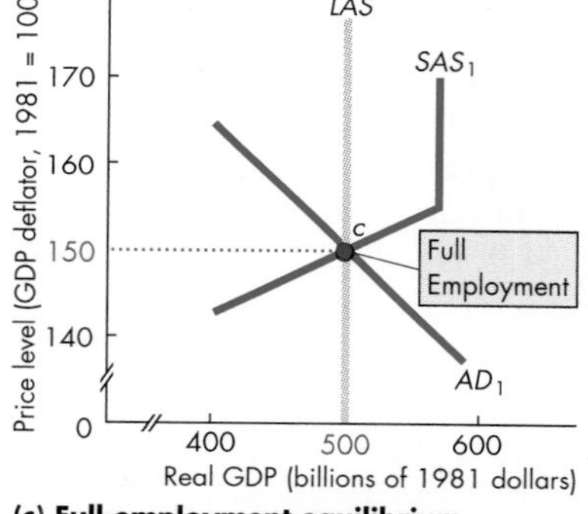

(c) Full-employment equilibrium

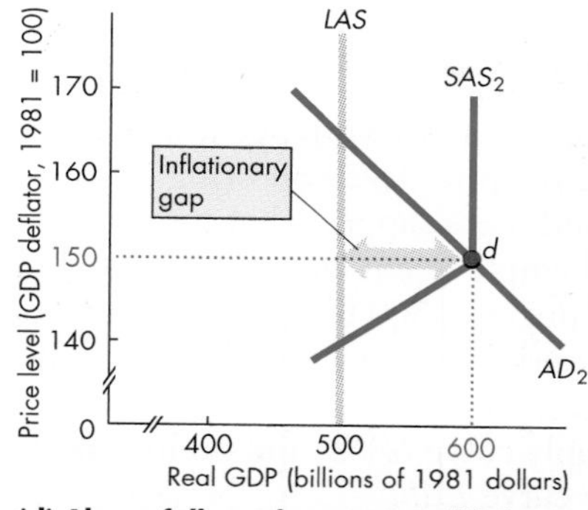

(d) Above full-employment equilibrium

In part (a) real GDP in an imaginary economy fluctuates around its capacity level. When actual real GDP is below capacity, there is a recessionary gap (as in year 2). When real GDP is above capacity, there is an inflationary gap (as in year 4). When real GDP is equal to capacity real GDP, there is full employment (as in year 3). The situation in year 2 is illustrated in part (b) where the aggregate demand curve (AD_0) intersects the short-run aggregate supply curve (SAS_0). The gap between that point of intersection and the long-run aggregate supply curve (*LAS*) is the recessionary gap. The situation in year 3 is illustrated in part (c) where the aggregate demand curve (AD_1) intersects the short-run aggregate supply curve (SAS_1) on the long run aggregate supply curve (*LAS*). The situation in year 4 is illustrated in part (d) where the aggregate demand curve (AD_2) intersects the short-run aggregate supply currve (SAS_2). The gap between that intersection point and long-run aggregate supply curve (*LAS*) is the inflationary gap.

Canadian economy was in a situation such as that shown in Fig 24.8(b) in 1982.

Figure 24.8(c) illustrates a full-employment equilibrium. **Full-employment equilibrium** is a macroeconomic equilibrium in which actual real GDP equals capacity real GDP. In this example, the equilibrium occurs where the aggregate demand curve AD_1 intersects the short-run aggregate supply curve SAS_1 at an actual and capacity real GDP of 500 billion 1981 dollars. The Canadian economy was in a situation such as that shown if Fig 24.8(c) in the mid-1980s.

Finally, Fig. 24.8(d) illustrates an above full-employment equilibrium. An **above full-employment equilibrium** is a situation in which macroeconomic equilibrium occurs at a level of real GDP above capacity real GDP and there is an inflationary gap. The above full-employment equilibrium illustrated in Fig. 24.8(d) occurs where the aggregate demand curve

AD_2 intersects the short-run aggregate supply curve SAS_2 at a real GDP of 600 billion 1981 dollars and a price level of 150. There is an inflationary gap of 100 billion 1981 dollars. The Canadian economy was in a situation such as that shown in Fig. 24.8(d) in 1989-90.

The economy moves between the three types of equilibrium shown in Fig. 24.8 as a result of fluctuations in aggregate demand and in short-run aggregate supply. These fluctuations produce fluctuations in real GDP and the price level.

Let's see how these fluctuations arise, first by looking at the effects of imaginary changes in aggregate demand and aggregate supply. We'll then use the theory of aggregate demand and aggregate supply to interpret some recent events in the Canadian economy.

Figure 24.9 The Effect of a Change in Aggregate Demand

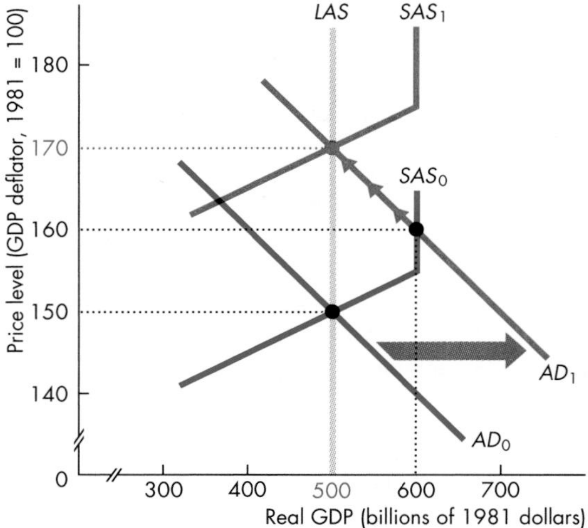

An increase in aggregate demand shifts the aggregate demand curve from AD_0 to AD_1. Real GDP increases from 500 billion to 600 billion 1981 dollars and the price level increases from 150 to 160. A higher price level induces higher wages and other factor prices, which, in turn, cause the short-run aggregate supply curve to move upward. As the *SAS* curve moves upward from SAS_0 to SAS_1, it intersects the aggregate demand curve AD_1 at higher price levels and lower real GDP levels. Eventually, the price level increases to 170 and real GDP falls back to 500 billion 1981 dollars — its full-employment level.

The Effects of a Change in Aggregate Demand

We're going to work out what happens to real GDP and the price level following a change in aggregate demand. Let's suppose that the economy starts out at full employment and, as illustrated in Fig. 24.9, is producing $500 billion worth of goods and services at a price level of 150. The economy is on the aggregate demand curve AD_0, on the short-run aggregate supply curve SAS_0, and on its long-run aggregate supply curve *LAS*.

Now suppose that the Bank of Canada takes steps to increase the quantity of money. With more money in the economy, people increase their demand for goods and services — the aggregate demand curve shifts to the right. Suppose that the aggregate demand curve shifts from AD_0 to AD_1 in Fig. 24.9. A new equilibrium occurs, where the aggregate demand curve AD_1 intersects the short-run aggregate supply curve SAS_0. Output rises to 600 billion 1981 dollars and the price level rises to 160. The economy is now at an above full-employment equilibrium. Real GDP is above its capacity level and there is an inflationary gap.

The increase in aggregate demand has increased the prices of all goods and services. Faced with higher prices, firms have increased their output rates. At this stage, prices of goods and services have increased but factor prices, such as wage rates, have not changed. (Recall that as the economy moves along a short-run aggregate supply curve, factor prices are constant.)

The economy cannot stay above its long-run aggregate supply and full-employment levels forever. Why not? What are the forces at work bringing real GDP back to its capacity level and restoring full employment? First, if the price level has increased but wages have remained constant, workers have experienced a fall in the purchasing power of their wages. Furthermore, firms have experienced a fall in the real cost of labour. In these circumstances, workers demand higher wages, and firms, anxious to maintain their employment and output levels, meet those demands. If firms do not raise wages, they either lose workers or have to hire less productive ones. Second, the owners of other factors of production, facing higher prices for the things that they buy, have also experienced a fall in the purchasing power of their income. They demand higher prices for their factors of production.

As factor prices rise, the short-run aggregate supply curve begins to shift. It moves upward from SAS_0 towards SAS_1. The rise in factor prices and the shift in the *SAS* curve produce a sequence of new equilibrium positions. At each point on the adjustment path, output falls and the price level rises. Eventually, factor prices will have risen by so much that

Figure 24.10 The Effects of a Change in Short-run Aggregate Supply

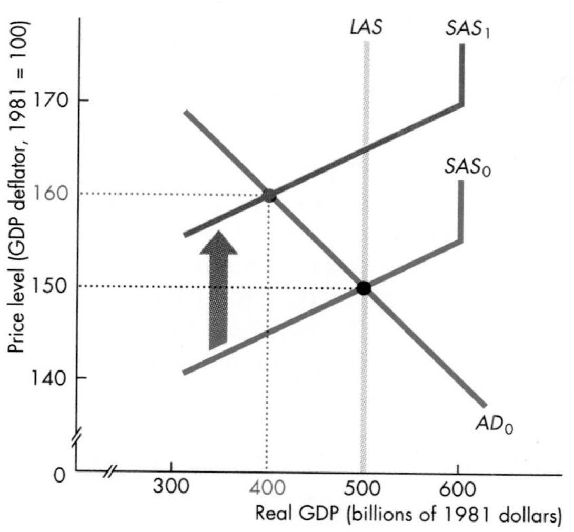

(a) No change in aggregate demand

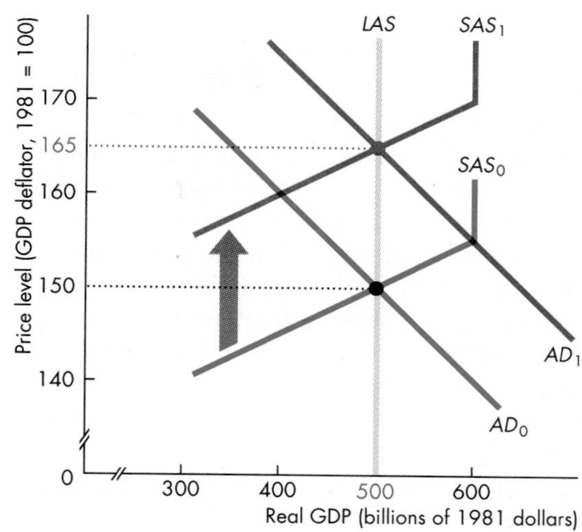

(b) An increase in aggregate demand

An increase in the price of a factor — say, oil — shifts the short-run aggregate supply curve upward. Such a shift is illustrated as the movement from SAS_0 to SAS_1 in part (a). Real GDP falls from 500 billion to 400 billion 1981 dollars and the price level increases from 150 to 160. In the absence of any changes in aggregate demand, factor prices gradually fall, returning the economy to its initial position with a price level of 150 and real GDP of 500 billion 1981 dollars. But factor prices may take a long time to fall; in the meantime unemployment remains above its natural rate. To restore full employment, an increase in aggregate demand from AD_0 to AD_1 can be undertaken as shown in part (b). This change in aggregate demand returns real GDP to 500 billion 1981 dollars (its full-employment level) but increases the price level to 165.

the *SAS* curve is SAS_1, by which time the aggregate demand curve AD_1 intersects SAS_1 at a full-employment equilibrium. The price level has risen to 170, and output is back where it started, at its capacity level. Unemployment is again at its natural rate.

Throughout the adjustment process, higher input prices raise firms' costs and, with rising costs, firms offer a smaller quantity of goods and services for sale at any given price level. By the time the adjustment is over, firms are producing exactly the same amount as they produced initially, but at higher prices and higher costs. The level of costs relative to prices will be the same as it was initially.

We've just worked out the effects of an increase in aggregate demand. A decrease in aggregate demand has similar but opposite effects to those that we've just studied. That is, when aggregate demand falls, real GDP falls below its capacity level and unemployment rises above its natural rate and there is a recessionary gap. The lower price level increases the purchasing power of wages and other factor incomes and increases firms' costs relative to their output prices. Eventually, as the slack economy leads to falling wages and other factor prices, the short-run aggregate supply curve shifts downward and, gradually, full employment is restored.

The Effects of a Change in Short-Run Aggregate Supply

Let's now work out the effects of a change in short-run aggregate supply on real GDP and the price level. Figure 24.10 illustrates the analysis. Suppose that, as shown in part (a), the economy is initially at full-employment equilibrium. The aggregate demand curve is AD_0 and the short-run aggregate supply curve is SAS_0. The long-run aggregate supply curve is *LAS*. Output is 500 billion 1981 dollars and the price level is 150.

Now suppose that there is an increase in the price of a factor of production. For example, a rise in the price of oil, such as that imposed by OPEC in 1973. The oil price rise shifts the short-run aggregate supply curve to SAS_1. As a result of this change in short-run aggregate supply, the economy moves to a new equilibrium where SAS_1 intersects AD_0. The price level rises to 160 and real GDP falls to 400 billion 1981 dollars. The economy is now in a recession: real GDP is below its capacity level and unemployment is above its natural rate. What happens next?

One possibility is that the economy remains in a prolonged recession. With excessive unemployment, wages and raw material prices may eventually fall. If they do, the short-run aggregate supply curve shifts downward again to SAS_0 and full employment is eventually restored. But such a process may take a long time.

A second possibility is that the government might intervene and cut taxes on oil to lower its price back to the original level. In this case the short-run aggregate supply curve returns to SAS_0 and full employment is maintained. This was the initial policy pursued in Canada in 1973-1974 when the OPEC oil price hike occurred.

A third possibility is that the government may stimulate aggregate demand. The effect of this policy is shown in Fig. 24.10(b). Faced with a deep recession, either the government or the Bank of Canada decides to stimulate aggregate demand. The government may cut taxes or increase its purchases of goods and services; the Bank of Canada may increase the money supply. If aggregate demand is stimulated so that the aggregate demand curve shifts to AD_1, full employment is restored at a real GDP level of 500 billion 1981 dollars. But the price level also increases yet further — to 165 in this example. This policy was pursued in many other countries and by the mid-1970s became Canada's response to ever rising oil prices.

We've now studied aggregate demand, aggregate supply, and macroeconomic equilibrium. We've worked out the effects of changes in aggregate demand and aggregate supply on real GDP and the price level. The story of the evolution of this aggregate demand-aggregate supply model is told in Our Advancing Knowledge on pp. 634-635. Let's now put our new knowledge to work and see how it helps us understand Canada's macroeconomic performance.

Trends and Cycles in the Canadian Economy

We're now going to use our new tools of aggregate demand and aggregate supply to interpret some recent trends and cycles in the Canadian economy. We'll begin by looking at the state of the Canadian economy in 1989.

The Economy in 1989

Canadian real GDP in 1989 was $458 billion (measured in 1981 dollars). The price level was 141. We can illustrate this state of the Canadian economy by using the aggregate demand and aggregate supply model. Figure 24.11 shows the state of the economy in 1989. The aggregate demand curve (AD_{89}) cuts the short-run aggregate supply curve (SAS_{89}) at a price level of 141 and at a real GDP of $458 billion.

We do not know with certainty where the long-run aggregate supply curve was in 1989, for, as discussed above, there is no single method for determining long-run aggregate supply. In Fig. 24.11 the long-run aggregate supply curve (LAS_{89}) is based on the *assumption* that long-run aggregate supply in 1989 was $450 billion. Thus actual real GDP was above capacity real GDP, and unemployment was below its natural rate.

In 1989 and early 1990 there was a widely held expectation that the economy was not going to stay at this high level of activity. Fears of inflation and of a slowdown were widespread. You can see why these fears of inflation and an economic slowdown existed by comparing Fig. 24.11 with Fig. 24.9. In the earlier figure, we analysed what happens when aggregate

Figure 24.11 The Canadian Economy in 1989

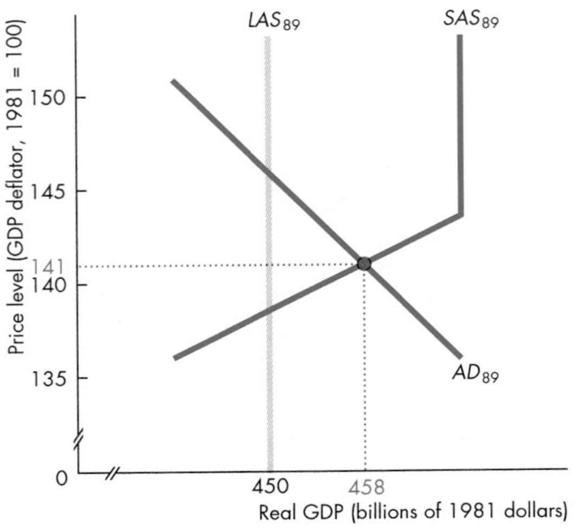

In 1989, the Canadian economy was on the aggregate demand curve AD_{89} and the aggregate supply curve SAS_{89}. The price level was 141 and real GDP was 458 billion 1981 dollars. The long-run aggregate supply curve (LAS_{89}) and full-employment real GDP were at 450 billion 1981 dollars.

demand increases so as to put real GDP above its capacity level. By returning to Fig. 24.9, you can see that, in such a situation, there is a tendency for wages to increase and, as they do so, for the short-run aggregate supply curve to shift upward. In the absence of any change in aggregate demand or in long-run aggregate supply, we can predict, using Fig. 24.11, that wage increases and increases in other input prices will shift the *SAS* curve upward above the SAS_{89} curve, raising the price level and lowering output.

Of course, other things are unlikely to remain constant. Several of the factors that we identified and discussed above would be shifting the long-run aggregate supply curve and the short-run aggregate supply curve to the right and other factors would be increasing aggregate demand. However, if the forces that we have just analysed operate, output would probably not fall but its pace of expansion would slow down.

Not everyone agreed, at the beginning of 1990, that a recession and increased inflation were just around the corner. Some took a more optimistic view. They believed that the long-run aggregate supply curve would shift to the right quickly enough to avoid recession and rising inflation. If the accumulation of capital and the advance of technology was sufficiently strong, long-run aggregate supply increases could prevent the type of inflationary recession that we described in Fig. 24.9 and that would follow from the conditions described in Fig. 24.11.

Figure 24.12 Aggregate Demand and Aggregate Supply, 1970–1989

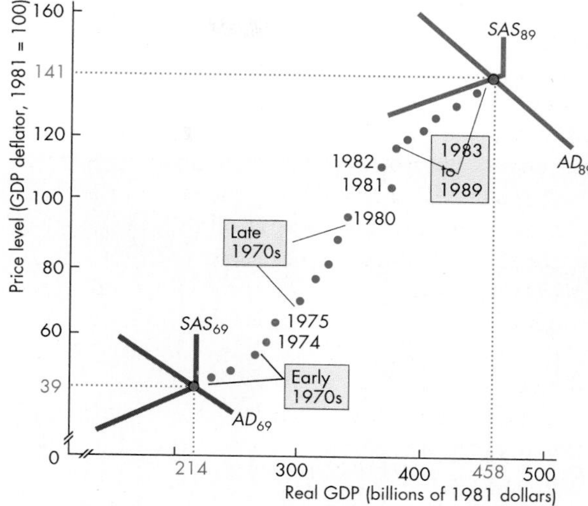

Each dot indicates the value of the GDP deflator and real GDP in a given year. In 1969, these variables were determined at the intersection of the aggregate demand curve AD_{69} and the short-run aggregate supply curves SAS_{69}. Each dot is generated by the gradual shifts of the *AD* and *SAS* curves. By 1989, the curves were AD_{89} and SAS_{89}. Real GDP had grown and the price level had increased. But growth and inflation did not proceed smoothly. Real GDP grew quickly and inflation was moderate in the early 1970s; real GDP growth sagged in 1974 and 1975. The 1975 slowdown was caused by an unusually sharp increase in prices (oil prices). In the late 1970s, real GDP again grew quickly but with high inflation. From 1980 to 1982 inflation remained high and real GDP growth sagged, turning negative in 1982. The recession was caused by a slowdown in the growth of aggregate demand resulting from a slowdown in income growth in the rest of the world and the Bank of Canada's monetary policy. The period from 1982 to 1989 was one of strong, persistent recovery. Inflation was rapid during the 1970s but moderated after the 1982 recession.

Growth, Inflation, and Cycles

The economy is continually changing. If you imagine the economy as a video, then Fig. 24.12 is a freeze-frame. We're going to run the video again — an instant replay — but keep our finger on the freeze-frame button, looking at some important parts of the previous action. Let's run the video from 1969.

Figure 24.12 shows the state of the economy in 1969 at the point of intersection of the aggregate demand curve AD_{69} and the short-run aggregate supply curve SAS_{69}. Real GDP was $214 billion and the GDP deflator was 39.

By 1989, the economy had reached the point marked by the intersection of aggregate demand curve AD_{89} and short-run aggregate supply curve SAS_{89}. Real GDP was $458 billion and the GDP deflator was 141.

The dots trace out the path followed by the economy. It has three important features:

- Growth
- Inflation
- Cycles

To see growth, inflation, and cycles in this figure you need to compare each year (each dot) with the one year (dot) that preceded it. The bigger the move from left to right, the faster is the growth of real GDP. The bigger the move upward (vertically) the faster is the pace of inflation. Let's examine the three features of the economy's path shown in Fig. 24.12.

OUR ADVANCING • KNOWLEDGE •

The Evolution of Modern Macroeconomics

Jean-Baptiste Say

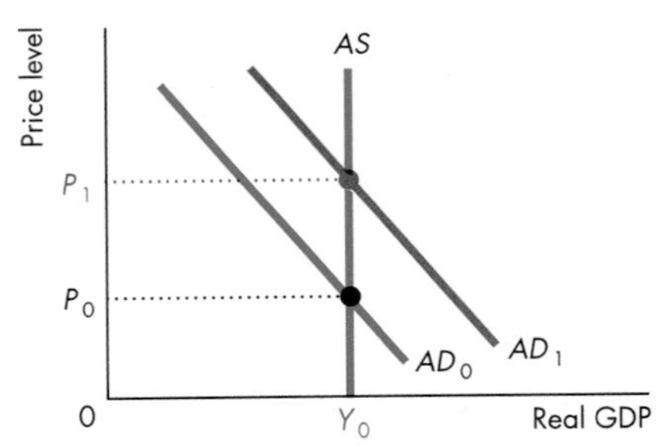

(a) The classical model

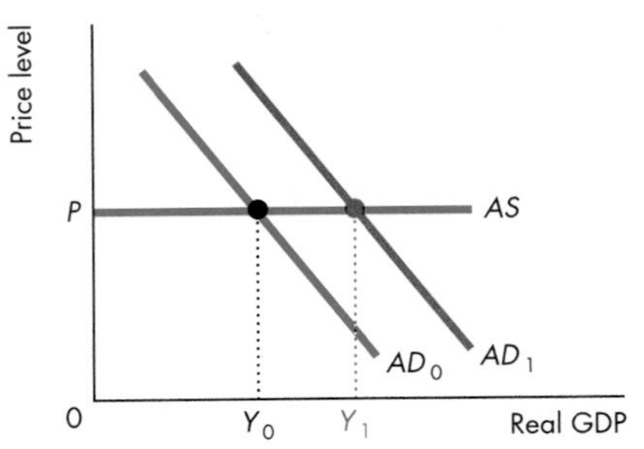

(b) The Keynesian model

Macroeconomics has been around for more than 200 years and one of the earliest macroeconomists was Jean-Baptiste Say. Born in Lyons, France, in 1767, Say worked as a journalist, a businessman manufacturing cotton, and a professor of economics in Paris. His major book, *Traité d'économie politique* (*A Treatise on Political Economy*), published in 1803, was a brilliant, more systematic and yet more compact presentation of Adam Smith's economics than Smith himself was able to write. By the early nineteenth century, Say was one of the most famous economists in both Europe and America and his *Traité* was used as a university textbook on both sides of the Atlantic.[1]

Say's most lasting contribution to macroeconomics was what came to be called Say's Law. **Say's Law** is the proposition that supply creates its own demand.

In the years following the Industrial Revolution in England and on the European continent, there was controversy as to whether the economy could continue expanding indefinitely or whether it would reach a limit beyond which there would not be sufficient demand to buy the goods and services that could be produced.

Say explained that the production of goods and services creates an income that is sufficient to purchase those goods and services — supply creates its own demand. Say's Law became the cornerpiece of what came to be called classical macroeconomics.

Classical Macroeconomics

Classical macroeconomics, building on the work of Adam Smith and Jean-Baptiste Say, gradually evolved until it was replaced by Keynesian macroeconomics in the 1930s. The classical system has five key elements. They are:

- The demand for labour and the supply of labour interact to determine the level of wages and employment.
- Given the level of employment and the economy's capital resources and technology, there is a unique aggregate quantity of real GDP supplied.

- The demand for and supply of loans determines interest rates and the levels of consumption, saving, and investment.
- The aggregate quantity of goods and services supplied creates a large enough income to enable those goods and services to be bought and adjustments in interest rates ensure that total spending equals total income.
- Aggregate demand determines only the price level. It has no effect on real GDP.

The classical macroeconomic system can be summarized in an aggregate demand-aggregate supply diagram with a vertical aggregate supply curve (see Fig. a). The aggregate supply curve, *AS*, is vertical and its position is determined by the economy's resources and technology. The aggregate demand curve slopes downward and its position is determined by the quantity of money. If the aggregate demand curve is AD_0, the price level is P_0. If aggregate demand increases so that the aggregate demand curve shifts to AD_1, the price level increases to P_2, but real GDP remains constant at Y_0. In 1936, classical macroeconomics was delivered a serious blow, the onset of the Keynesian revolution.

Keynesian Macroeconomics

Keynesian macroeconomics was founded by John Maynard Keynes (see Our Advancing Knowledge, pp. 662-664). The centrepiece of Keynes's macroeconomic system is the **principle of effective demand**— the opposite of Say's Law and the proposition that the level of real GDP is determined by aggregate demand. Keynes argued that Say's Law was wrong and that there were impediments to the self-regulation of the economy that did not guarantee that supply would create its own demand. Instead, the quantity of goods and services supplied is determined by the demand for goods, not the supply. Keynes developed an economic model in which:

- Wages do not adjust to determine employment. The dollar value of wages is rigid and a large and persistent gap can emerge between the quantity of labour demanded and the quantity supplied.
- Interest rates do not adjust to ensure equality between saving and investment. If saving exceeds investment, spending falls short of income and income declines.

The Keynesian system can be described by an aggregate demand-aggregate supply model in which the aggregate supply curve is horizontal, such as that shown in Fig. (b). Here, because wages do not adjust to keep the quantities of labour demanded and supplied equal, the quantity of goods produced is free to vary and is not determined by labour market conditions and technology. Any quantity of goods and services (up to some maximum) can be produced. Thus the aggregate supply curve is horizontal over this range. In this situation, if aggregate demand increases from AD_0 to AD_1, there is an increase in real GDP from Y_0 to Y_1 and no change in the price level.

Neo-classical Synthesis and Modern Macroeconomics

Modern macroeconomics can be seen as a mixture of classical and Keynesian macroeconomics and has been called the **neo-classical synthesis**. In the neo-classical synthesis, classical macroeconomics describes the long-run situation — the situation that prevails after a sufficient time lag for all factor prices to have adjusted in step with the prices of final goods and services. Keynesian macroeconomics is seen as being relevant for short-run adjustments over a time interval during which factor prices remain constant. In this case, however the aggregate supply curve is not horizontal as in the extreme Keynesian model shown in Fig. (b), but is upward-sloping as shown in Fig. 24.4 in this chapter.

Modern macroeconomics pays careful attention to the distinction between aggregate demand and aggregate supply as schedules and the quantities of real GDP demanded and supplied as points on schedules. It also pays careful attention to the factors that make the short-run and long-run aggregate supply curves and aggregate demand curve shift and to the processes of adjustment of wages, prices, and output.

The macroeconomics that you will study in the following chapters spells out these developments.

---

[1]Thomas Sowell, entry on Say in *The New Palgrave , A Dictionary of Economics* , edited by John Eatwell, Murray Milgate, and Peter Newman (Stockton Press: New York, 1987), vol. 4, p. 249.

Growth Over the years, real GDP grows. This growth results from population growth, the accumulation of capital — both physical plant and equipment and human capital — the discovery of new resources, and the advance of technology. All of these forces gradually shift the long-run and short-run aggregate supply to the right.

Inflation The steady and persistent increase in prices results from a persistent increase in aggregate demand. Of all the factors that can shift the aggregate demand curve, the quantity of money is the single most important one leading to persistent increases in aggregate demand.

Cycles The pace of economic growth and inflation is uneven. The unevenness arises because neither the growth of aggregate supply nor the growth of aggregate demand proceeds at a steady pace.

The Record Since 1969 Let's examine the growth, inflation, and cycles in the period since 1969 (Fig. 24.12) by considering five time periods. First, you can see that in the early 1970s, there was a strong increase in real GDP with only small increases in prices. This was a period of steady increases in long-run aggregate supply and of moderate increases in aggregate demand.

Second, look at 1974 and 1975. In 1973 and 1974, a series of massive oil price increases put the Canadian — and world — economy into a slowdown. Real GDP continued to increase but its growth rate was sharply reduced, especially in 1975, and the inflation rate increased to more than 10 percent. The growth slowdown and increased inflation occurred because the increase in oil and other factor prices shifted the short-run aggregate supply curve upward at a faster pace than the increase in aggregate demand. The result was a contraction with rising prices. Real GDP fell below its long-run aggregate supply level.

Third, look at the late 1970s. This was a period of renewed strength in real GDP growth but with continued high inflation.

Fourth, look at 1980 to 1982. In these years inflation remained high and real GDP growth slowed, eventually turning negative in 1982. These years of continued inflation and slowing real GDP growth were the result of a battle between OPEC on the one hand and the Bank of Canada and the Federal Reserve (the Fed) — the manager of U.S. monetary policy — on the other. OPEC jacked up the price of oil, and an inflationary recession ensued. Eventually, the Bank of Canada and the Fed gave way and increased the money supply to bring the Canadian and U.S. economies back to full employment. Then OPEC played a similar hand again, raising up the price of oil still further. The Bank of Canada and the Fed were faced with a dilemma. Should they inject more money and bring their economies back to full employment, notching up the inflation rate yet further or should they keep the growth of aggregate demand in check? The answer, delivered by the Bank of Canada governor Gerald Bouey and Fed chairman Paul Volcker, was to keep aggregate demand growth in check.

You can see the effects of the central bankers' actions in the figure. Aggregate demand increased but too slowly to keep up with the upward movement of the short-run aggregate supply curve resulting from wage and other factor price increases. As a consequence, by 1982 the upward movement of the short-run aggregate supply curve was so strong relative to the growth of aggregate demand that the economy went into a further deep recession.

Fifth, look at the years 1983 to 1989. In this period, moderate wage growth slowed the pace of the upward movement in the short-run aggregate supply curve, and sustained but steady growth in aggregate demand and in long-run aggregate supply kept the economy expanding and held inflation relatively steady. The economy moved from a recession with output well below its long-run aggregate supply level to full employment and perhaps beyond.

The Canada-United States Free Trade Agreement

On January 1, 1989, a free trade agreement came into effect between Canada and the United States. The purpose of this agreement is to reduce trade barriers between the two countries. The idea is that with no restrictions on international trade, Canadian consumers will be able to buy U.S. goods at lower prices and Canadian firms will be given greater access to U.S. markets. Studying the effects of the free trade agreement on the Canadian economy is a major undertaking, and most of that task is pursued in Chapter 36. But what are the effects of the free trade agreement on those aspects of Canada's macroeconomic performance that we are considering in this chapter? That is, how will the free trade agreement affect aggregate output and the price level? No one knows the answer to this question. Some economists point to the fact that Canada's net exports declined sharply in 1989 and attribute this decline to the initial effects of the free trade agreement. Other economists believe that the decline in net exports was the consequence of a slowdown in the U.S. economy and was not caused by the free trade agreement.

Although economists are not able, at the present time, to say which of these two views is correct, it is possible to work out the consequences of each view for aggregate output and the price level. If the free trade agreement has indeed resulted in a decrease in net exports, then it has resulted in a decrease in aggregate demand — a shift to the left in the aggregate demand curve. Earlier in this chapter, we worked out the effects of a decrease in aggregate demand on real GDP and the price level. When aggregate demand decreases, with constant factor prices, the economy slides down its short-run aggregate supply curve. Real GDP decreases and the price level falls. In an economy experiencing ongoing inflation, the price level does not actually decline but the inflation rate slows down. These are the possible initial effects of the free trade agreement on output and the price level *if* those who believe that net exports declined because of the free trade agreement are correct. If the alternative view, that net exports declined for reasons other than the free trade agreement, is correct, then the agreement had no perceptible effect on aggregate output and the price level in 1989.

What about future, longer-term effects of the free trade agreement? A free trade agreement such as that entered into between Canada and the United States will, in the long run, increase the volume of international trade between the two countries. That is, it will increase U.S. imports from Canada and Canadian imports from the United States. There is no presumption, however, as to the direction of the change in net exports resulting from such an agreement. Indeed, the most likely outcome is that exports and imports will increase by roughly the same amounts so that the free trade agreement will leave the balance of trade between the two nations unaffected. This being the case, the free trade agreement's long-run effects on aggregate demand are predicted to be negligible.

But the agreement will, in the long run, affect aggregate supply. By encouraging a rationalization of economic activity and increased efficiency in the use of resources in both Canada and the United States, the free trade agreement will, in the long run, lead to a higher level of aggregate supply than would otherwise have been achieved. It is important to recognize that this is a long-run effect, not necessarily a short-run one. In the early stages of implementation of the agreement, it is possible that aggregate supply will decrease: some Canadian firms will go out of business in the face of tough U.S. competition, and other Canadian firms will not yet have undergone the reorganization and expansion that will result from their enhanced access to U.S. markets. Thus the introduction of the free trade agreement may decrease aggregate supply in Canada for some years — perhaps for a relatively prolonged period. In the longer run, however, the agreement is predicted to increase aggregate supply.

Bringing together the future effects of the free trade agreement on both aggregate demand and aggregate supply, we predict an initial slowdown in Canada's growth rate of real GDP and an increase in Canada's inflation rate. In the longer run, these effects will be reversed, with the growth rate of real GDP increasing and the inflation rate moderating.

It is important to recognize that the effects that we have just analysed are based on the assumption of other things being equal. Changes in the Bank of Canada's monetary policy can influence aggregate demand and the price level in a much more dramatic way than can the free trade agreement. Such changes can result in an inflation rate that is completely dominated by the Bank's actions rather than by the consequences of the free trade agreement itself.

The Goods and Services Tax

Another major policy development in Canada in 1991 was the introduction of the goods and services tax. The **goods and services tax** (GST) is a tax on the value added to almost all goods and services in all sectors of the economy. (The exceptions are health and dental services, day-care services, most educational and financial services, and long-term residential rents.) What will be the effects of that tax on real GDP and the price level? The answer depends on the extent to which the introduction of the GST increases the total tax receipts of the federal government. Though the GST is a new tax, it replaces an old tax that has been abolished — the federal sales tax. The federal sales tax was a tax levied at a rate of 11 percent on manufactured goods. Manufactured goods comprise less than one-half of all the goods and services produced. In contrast the GST is a tax on all goods and services and at a rate lower than that of the federal sales tax. The GST rate is 7 percent on all goods and services except exports, agricultural and fish products, some groceries, and prescription drugs and medical devices. (These goods are "zero-rated"

Forecasting the Economy

Forecast bleak for economy

The next two years will probably be dreary for Canada's economy, with interest rates remaining high and unemployment climbing.

The Post's quarterly economic forecast predicts a yearend prime rate of 12%, down from the current 14 1/4% but still high in real (after-inflation) terms—about 7%, given inflation of about 5%.

That is likely to bring economic growth down to about 1% from last year's 2.9% and push the jobless rate up to 8.5% by yearend.

It doesn't look much brighter for 1991. Interest rates will come down a little further but not until late in the year. Unemployment will remain at about 8.5% as the economy stays in low gear.

This dreary picture is unavoidable, given the move to the goods and services tax Jan. 1, 1991. That will boost inflation, forcing the Bank of Canada to keep interest rates high so the higher inflation does not become embedded in the economy through compensating wage gains.

The Post forecasts average wage gains of 5% in 1991, down from 6% this year and 7.2% in 1989, assuming the jobless rate remains at 8.5%. If unemployment shows signs of declining sharply, the Bank of Canada will probably jack up interest rates.

With luck, 1992 will be a better year. Provided wage gains and inflation are contained, the stage will be set for good growth, shrinking unemployment and falling interest rates.

A major assumption in the forecast is that the C$ will drop to about US80¢ by yearend, stemming the deterioration in Canadian companies' profitability and trade performance that has resulted from a high exchange rate.

Economic fundamentals—the deteriorating trade picture and Ottawa's continued inability to reduce its deficit significantly—point to a lower C$. It is only the very large short-term Canada-U.S. interest rate spread that is keeping the C$ so high.

The spread will probably narrow by mid-year when the Bank of Canada is forced to lower interest rates to keep the economy out of recession.

Canada in 1989 and 1990

				PERCENTAGE CHANGES		
					Forecast	
	1989	1990	1991	1989	1990	1991
Gross Domestic Product ($ billion)	648.5	687.8	740.2	+7.8%	+6.1%	+7.6%
GDP on 1981$ ($ billion)	460.6	465.2	474.5	+2.9%	+1%	+2%
Domestic demand ($ billion)	459.9	466.8	471.5	+4.5%	+1½ %	+1%
GDP price index (1981=100)	140.8	147.8	156.0	+4.8%	+5%	+5½ %
Consumer price index (1981=100)	151.0	158.6	160.0	+5.0%	+5%	+6%
Labor force (million)	13.50	13.71	13.91	+1.7%	+1½ %	+1½ %
Employment (million)	12.49	12.57	12.73	+2.0%	+¾ %	+1¼ %
Unemployment ('000)	1,017	1,140	1,180	–1%	+12%	+4%
Unemployment rate (%)	7.5	8¼%	8¼			
Misery index*	12.5	13¼	14¼			
Housing starts ('000)	215	180	170	–3%	–16%	–6%
Goods trade balance ($ billion)	+4.7	+7.0	+10.0			
Services & transfers balance ($ billion)	–24.3	–24.0	–25.0			
Current account balance ($ billion)	–19.7	–17.0	–15.0			
Wages and salaries per employee ($)	28,528	30,250	31,750	+7.2%	+6%	+5%
After-tax corp. profits ($ billion)	37.3	35.4	37.2	–15.1%	–5%	+5%
Banks prime lending rate (%) yearend	13½	12	11			
C$ (in US¢) yearend	86.3	80	80			

* Sum of unemployed rate and increase in consumer price index

Source: Financial Post Economics Unit

The Financial Post,
24-26 March, 1990
By Catherine Harris

The Essence of the Story

- The *Financial Post* forecasts for the Canadian economy in 1990 and 1991 are:

Table 1	1990	1991
Real GDP growth rate	+1%	+2%
Inflation rate	+5%	+5.5%
Unemployment rate	8.25%	8.5%
Wage rate change	+6%	+5%
Dollar (cents per $US)	80	80
Banks prime lending rate	12%	11%

- The *Financial Post* says:
  - The introduction of the goods and services tax on January 1, 1991 will boost inflation and cause the Bank of Canada to keep interest rates high.
  - A deteriorating foreign trade balance and a continued federal government deficit will force the dollar down from its 84 U.S. cents level in March 1990 to 80 U.S. cents by end 1990.
  - The Bank of Canada will eventually be forced to lower interest rates to avoid a recession.

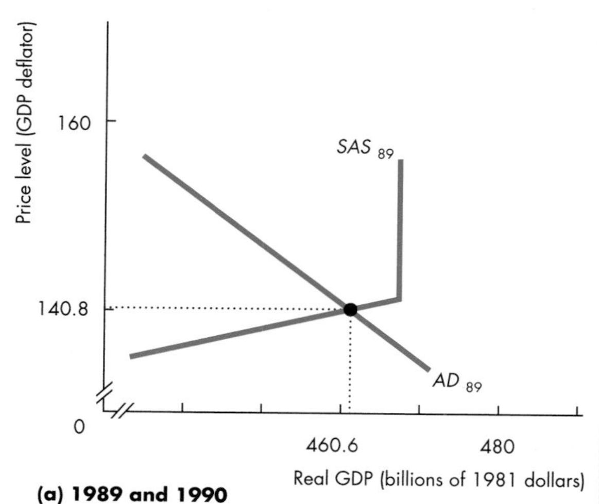

(a) 1989 and 1990

Background and Analysis

- The *Financial Post* is forecasting slow real GDP growth and steady inflation for Canada during 1990 and 1991.
- To make its forecasts the *Financial Post* uses a computer based model of the economy. The model is based on the aggregate demand-aggregate supply model that you have studied in this chapter. We can interpret the *Financial Post* forecasts using that model.
- The economy in 1989 is shown in Fig. (a). The aggregate demand curve is AD_{89} and the short-run aggregate supply curve is SAS_{89}. Real GDP ($460.6 billion) and the price level (140.8) are determined at the point of intersection of these curves.
- The forecasts for 1990 and 1991 are shown in Figs. (b) and (c). Aggregate demand changes and the aggregate demand curve shifts for the reasons listed in Table 24.1. Short-run aggregate supply changes and the short-run aggregate supply supply curve shifts for the reasons listed in Table 24.2.
- The most important factors expected to affect aggregate demand in 1990 and 1991 are:

Table 2	1990	1991
Increase in quantity of money	*	*
Increase in aggregate wealth	*	*
Increase in foreign income	*	*
Increase in population	*	*
Decrease in foreign exchange value of dollar	*	*

- The most important factors expected to affect short-run aggregate supply in 1990 and 1991 are:

Table 3	1990	1991
Increase in wages	*	*
Decrease in foreign exchange value of dollar	*	*
Goods and services tax	*	*
Increase in labour force	*	*
Increase in capital stock	*	*
Technological advances	*	*

- The predicted effects of these factors on the aggregate demand and short-run aggregate supply curves, and the resulting effects on real GDP and the price level are shown in Figs. (b) and (c).

- The forecasts of other variables such as unemployment, wages, the value of the dollar, and interest rates, the aggregate demand-aggregate supply model is extended and elaborated to include markets for labour, foreign exchange, money and loans.
- The factors influencing demand and supply in these other markets are assessed and forecasts are made of the positions of their demand and supply curves. From such an excercise, forecasts are made of the prices—wage rate, foreign exchange rate, and interest rates—in these markets.
- One of the key ingredients in the forecast of unemployment is the relationship between unemployment and deviations of real GDP from trend shown in Fig. 22.8 (p. 580). Since real GDP is expected to grow slowly in 1990 and 1991, the unemployment rate is expected to increase slightly.
- There were two reasons for suspecting, on the basis of information available in March 1990 when the forecasts were made, that the Financial Post's prediction of inflation for 1991 could turn out to be too high:
  - The goods and services tax (GST) is not a net additional tax but a replacement for the federal sales tax. Therefore some prices will fall and some will rise but the net impact on the price level may be modest.
  - The Bank of Canada was pursuing a policy of slowing the growth rate of the quantity of money and, by 1991, it is possible that this policy will result in a smaller rightward shift in the aggregate demand curve than that shown in Fig. (b).
- The first of the above factors would make real GDP grow faster than the Financial Post forecast and the second factor would make real GDP grow slower than forecast.
- Other events that occurred after March 1990 point to modifications of the Financial Post's forecast:
  - The Iraqi invasion of Kuwait in August 1990 produced a large increase in world oil prices. This shock lead to a sharp shift in the short-run aggregate supply curve, reinforcing the shift shown in Fig. (b). Other things being equal, this shock will lead to faster inflation and slower real GDP growth.
  - The Bank of Canada continued through the summer of 1990 to pursue a tight monetary policy. Other things being equal, this policy would lead to lower inflation and slower real GDP growth
- Viewed from September 1990, the above factors point to a high probability of recession in Canada—to two quarters of *falling* real GDP—in late 1990 or early 1991.

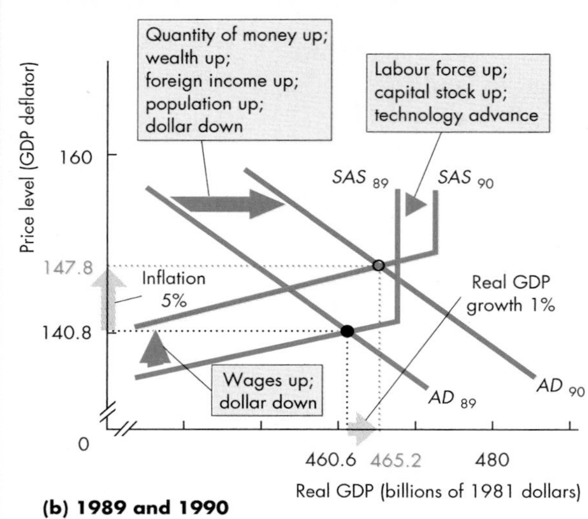

(b) 1989 and 1990

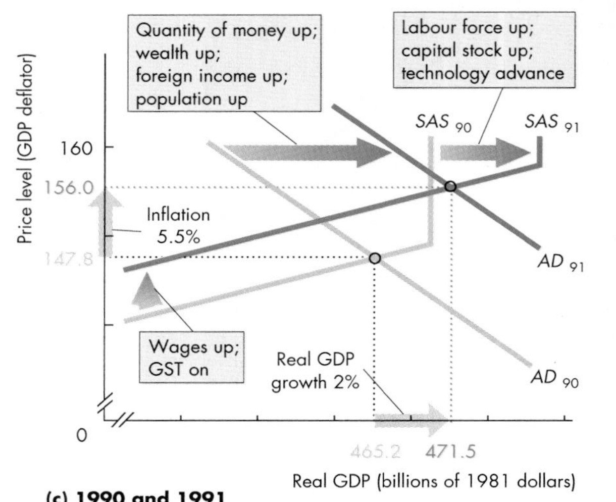

(c) 1990 and 1991

goods — goods on which the tax rate is zero.) Although the federal government can work out fairly precisely how much tax revenue it will lose from removing the federal sales tax, it cannot predict with confidence how much revenue the GST will raise. If the GST brings in exactly the same amount of revenue as the displaced federal sales tax, then the GST will have no effect on aggregate demand. If the GST raises more tax revenue than the old federal sales tax, aggregate demand will decrease — the aggregate demand curve will shift to the left. This is the most likely outcome.

To work out the effects of the GST on real GDP and the price level, we also need to predict its effects on aggregate supply. The popular discussions of GST suggest that its introduction will be inflationary. This conclusion is based on the observation that imposing a tax on goods that are not now taxed will result in a rise in their prices. But this conclusion ignores the effects of removing the federal sales tax. Replacing it with the GST will result in a decrease in taxes on manufactured goods and their prices will fall. Thus there will be a decrease in the prices of manufactured goods and an increase in the prices of goods not previously taxed but now falling under the goods and services tax. As a consequence, *relative prices* will change. Advocates of the GST argue that the replacement of the federal sales tax — a tax on a narrow range of goods at a high rate — by the GST —a tax on a wider range of goods at a lower rate — will lead to increased economic efficiency and an increase in overall production of goods and services. If this prediction is correct, the GST will result in an increase in aggregate supply — a rightward shift of the aggregate supply curves. These effects are likely to be small and gradual. Nevertheless, to the extent that they occur, the GST will result, other things being equal, in an increase in real GDP and a decrease in the price level. That is, its effects on inflation will be exactly the opposite of those predicted in popular discussions of this subject. Reading Between the Lines, on pp. 638-640 deals with this topic in the broader context of forecasting Canada's future inflation and real GDP growth.

What the ultimate actual effects of the GST will be on our economy will be known only after some years of its operation. But the tools of analysis that will be used to assess its effects are the ones that we have just been working with in our attempt to predict its effects.

■ This chapter has provided a model of real GDP and the GDP deflator that can be used to understand the growth, inflation, and cycles that our economy experiences. The model is a useful one because it enables us to keep our eye on the big picture — on the broad trends and cycles in inflation and output. But the model lacks detail. It does not tell us as much as we need to know about the components of aggregate demand — consumption, investment, government purchases of goods and services, and exports and imports. It doesn't tell us what determines interest rates or wages. It doesn't even tell us directly what determines employment and unemployment. In the following chapters, we're going to start to fill in that detail.

In some ways, the study of macroeconomics is like doing a large jigsaw puzzle. The aggregate demand and aggregate supply model provides the entire edge of the picture. We know its general shape and size, but we haven't completed the picture. One block of the jigsaw contains the story of aggregate demand. Another contains the story of aggregate supply. When we put the two together, we place them in the frame of the model developed in this chapter, and the picture is complete.

SUMMARY

Aggregate Demand

Aggregate demand is the relationship between the aggregate quantity of goods and services demanded — real GDP demanded — and the price level — the GDP deflator. The aggregate demand curve slopes downward. A rise in the price level produces a movement along the aggregate demand curve, reducing the quantity of real GDP demanded. Factors that change aggregate demand shift the aggregate demand curve. (pp. 615-621)

Aggregate Supply

Aggregate supply is studied in two time frames: the long run and the short run.

Long-run aggregate supply is the relationship between the aggregate quantity of final goods and services (real GDP) supplied and the price level (the GDP deflator) when factor prices change in step with changes in the price level, each firm is producing its capacity output, and there is full employment. The long-run aggregate supply curve is vertical — long-run aggregate supply is independent of the price level.

Short-run aggregate supply is the relationship between the aggregate quantity of final goods and services (real GDP) supplied and the price level (the GDP deflator) with money wages and other factor prices held constant. The short-run aggregate supply curve slopes upward. Other things being equal, the higher the price level, the more output firms plan to sell.

The factors that change short-run aggregate supply shift the short-run aggregate supply curve. Anything that shifts the long-run aggregate supply curve also shifts the short-run aggregate supply curve. Changes in the prices of factors of production shift the short-run aggregate supply curve but leave the long-run aggregate supply curve unaffected. (pp. 621-627)

Macroeconomic Equilibrium

Macroeconomic equilibrium occurs when the quantity of real GDP demanded equals the quantity of real GDP supplied. Macroeconomic equilibrium occurs at the intersection of the aggregate demand curve and the short-run aggregate supply curve. The price level that achieves that equality is the equilibrium price level and the output level is equilibrium real GDP.

Macroeconomic equilibrium does not always occur at full employment — at a point on the long-run aggregate supply curve. Unemployment equilibrium occurs when equilibrium real GDP is less than its long-run aggregate supply level. Above full-employment equilibrium occurs when equilibrium real GDP is above its long-run level.

An increase in aggregate demand shifts the aggregate demand curve to the right and increases both real GDP and the price level. If real GDP increases above its long-run level, input prices begin to increase, and as they do so, the short-run aggregate supply curve shifts upward. The upward shift of the short-run aggregate supply curve results in an even higher price level but lower real GDP. Eventually, real GDP returns to its long-run level.

An increase in input prices shifts the short-run aggregate supply curve upward and results in a fall in real GDP and a rise in the price level. If there is no subsequent change in aggregate demand, the economy stays in a recession until input prices have fallen back to their original levels. If aggregate demand is increased to restore full employment, then the price level rises still higher. (pp. 627-632)

Trends and Cycles in the Canadian Economy

Long-term growth in the Canadian economy results from population growth, capital accumulation, and technological change. Inflation persists in Canada because of steady increases in aggregate demand brought about by increases in the quantity of money. The Canadian economy experiences cycles because the short-run aggregate supply and aggregate demand curves shift at an uneven pace.

A large hike in the price of oil in 1973 resulted in an inflationary slowdown in the mid-1970s. A replay in 1979 intensified the inflationary situation. Restraint in aggregate demand growth in 1980 and 1981 resulted in a severe recession in 1982. This recession resulted in lower output and a lower inflation rate. Moderate increases in factor prices and steady technological advance and capital accumulation resulted in a sustained expansion through the rest of the 1980s.

The Canada-United States Free Trade Agreement may affect real GDP and the price level through its effects on aggregate demand and aggregate supply. The long-run effects on aggregate demand are likely to be negligible. In the short run, the agreement may decrease aggregate supply, but in the long run, it is predicted to increase aggregate supply. Thus in the short run, real GDP growth may slow and the inflation rate may increase, but in the long run, these tendencies will be reversed, other things being equal.

The effects of the goods and services tax on real GDP and the price level will depend on its effects on aggregate demand and aggregate supply. If the tax increases government revenue, it will decrease aggregate demand. If the replacement of the federal sales tax with the GST increases economic efficiency, it will result in an increase in aggregate supply. The combined consequences of these effects will be an increase in real GDP growth and a slowdown in inflation — the opposite of the conclusion reached in popular discussions. (pp. 632-640)

KEY ELEMENTS

Key Terms

Above full-employment equilibrium, 629
Aggregate demand, 615
Aggregate demand curve, 615
Aggregate demand schedule, 615
Aggregate quantity of goods and services demanded, 615
Aggregate quantity of goods and services supplied, 621
Capacity output, 622
Full-employment equilibrium, 629
Goods and services tax, 637
Inflationary gap, 628
International substitution, 617
Intertemporal substitution, 617
Long-run aggregate supply, 622
Long-run aggregate supply curve, 622
Macroeconomic equilibrium, 627
Quantity of money, 616
Real balance effect, 616
Real money, 616
Recessionary gap, 628
Short-run aggregate supply, 623
Short-run aggregate supply curve, 623
Short-run aggregate supply schedule, 623
Unemployment equilibrium, 628

Key Figures and Tables 

REVIEW QUESTIONS

1 What is aggregate demand?

2 What is the difference between aggregate demand and the aggregate quantity of goods and services demanded?

3 List the main factors that affect aggregate demand. Separate them into those that make aggregate demand rise and those that make it fall.

4 Which of the following do not affect aggregate demand:

a) Quantity of money?

b) Interest rates?

c) Technological change?

d) Human capital?

5 What is short-run aggregate supply?

6 What is the difference between short-run aggregate supply and the aggregate quantity of goods and services supplied?

7 Distinguish between short-run aggregate supply and long-run aggregate supply.

8 Consider the following events:

a) The labour force increases.

b) Technology improves.

c) The money wage rate increases.

d) The quantity of money increases.

e) Foreign incomes increase.

f) The foreign exchange value of the dollar increases.

Sort these events into the following four categories:

A: Those that affect the long-run aggregate supply curve but not the short-run aggregate supply curve;
B: Those that affect the short-run aggregate supply curve but not the long-run aggregate supply curve;
C: Those that affect both the short-run aggregate supply curve and the long-run aggregate supply curve;
D: Those that have no effect on the short-run aggregate supply curve or on the long-run aggregate supply curve

9 Define macroeconomic equilibrium.

10 Distinguish between macroeconomic equilibrium and full-employment equilibrium.

11 Explain what is meant by an unemployment equilibrium and an above full-employment equilibrium.

12 Explain what a recessionary gap and an inflationary gap are. What conditions will give rise to each of these?

13 Work out the effect of a rise in the quantity of money on the price level and on real GDP.

14 Work out the effect of a rise in the price of oil on the price level and on real GDP.

15 What are the main factors generating growth of long-run aggregate supply in the Canadian economy?

16 What are the main factors generating persistent inflation in the Canadian economy?

17 Why does the Canadian economy experience cycles in aggregate economic activity?

PROBLEMS

1 You are the prime minister's economic advisor and you are trying to determine where the Canadian economy is headed next year. You have the following forecasts for the *AD*, *SAS*, and *LAS* curves:

Price level	Real GDP demanded	Real GDP supplied in the short-run	Long-run aggregate supply
	(billions of 1981 dollars)		
140	550	250	460
150	500	350	460
160	450	450	460
170	400	475	460

This year, real GDP is $460 billion and the price level is 150.
The prime minister wants answers to the following questions:

a) What is your forecast of next year's real GDP?

b) What is your forecast of next year's price level?

c) What is your forecast of the inflation rate?

d) Will unemployment be above or below its natural rate?

e) Will real GDP be above or below trend? By how much?

2 Draw some figures similar to those in this chapter and use the information in problem 1 to explain:

a) What has to be done to aggregate demand to achieve full employment?

b) What is the inflation rate if aggregate demand is manipulated to achieve full employment?

PART 9

Aggregate Product Markets

TALKING WITH
PAUL VOLCKER

Paul Volcker served as chairman of the board of governors of the Federal Reserve System from 1979 to 1987, a time when double-digit inflation was gripping the U.S. economy. Michael Parkin spoke with Mr. Volcker about his experience as chairman of the Fed and about his vision and concerns for the future of the economy.

"Economics does teach you that the immediate effects of some action may not be the full story."

Mr. Volcker, what originally attracted you to economics?

I was an undergraduate immediately after the Second World War. I think a lot of people at the time got interested in economics because of the experience of the Depression and the war years. They thought things must be able to work better than they had during the Depression, and they were filled with a zeal for doing better. That was part of my thinking, but just as important, economics seemed to me, of all the social sciences, to have a little more precision. I thought I could combine this practical logical structure with an instinct for public service. In retrospect, I'm sure I overestimated the logic and coherence!

What are the economic principles that you learned in school that have proved useful in your professional life?

Some economic principles are eternally useful. All that business about "no free lunch" remains a valid observation—although we in the public sector sometimes wonder! Economics does teach you the discipline of understanding that the direct immediate effects of some action may not be the full story—that without close analysis and study you may have unintended and unanticipated effects later on. Those later "side effects" may be greater than the immediate effects. Finally, the concept of looking at the margin—at incremental effects—is very important in terms of actual policy.

Is a background in economics, familiarity with economic principles, mandatory for a chairman of the Federal Reserve?

I haven't been able to detect any correlation in performance between chairmen that were economists and those who were not. The chairman doesn't have to be a trained economist if he or she has a staff of very good economists. Without that, you'd really be in trouble.

There must be as many opinions about what the Fed should be doing as there are economists. How do these controversies among macroeconomists affect the Fed's job? Are they relevant for the conduct of monetary policy?

Oh, I think they're relevant. The internal technical debate doesn't make that much difference. But to the extent that economists' positions on public policy influence public opinion and differ widely, you lack a consensus against which to conduct policy. In a political context, some of these different points of view become politicized. That's part of the environment in which the Fed must operate.

The one advantage when you're the chairman of the Federal Reserve Board is that you can sometimes influence—or can lead yourself and everyone else into thinking that you can influence—the nature of the consensus about economic policy, as it is actually reflected in public opinion.

There has certainly not been consensus about the consequences of the Fed's policy in fighting inflation during the late 1970s and early 1980s, while you were chairman. When you embarked on you war against inflation, did you expect to be presiding over the longest peacetime recovery in U.S. history?

I thought then, and think now, that inflation is the enemy of sustained expansion. But dealing with these things always turns out to be more difficult, more complicated, and to take longer than you expect. I guess I did misjudge how long we could put up with internal government deficits and external trade imbalances.

What were you missing?

In part I think there is a much more fluid international capital market than we had recognized. I would not have guessed that the United States could borrow, or that the Japanese would be willing to lend, so much money year after year without more uncertainty about the dollar. I would not have guessed that the value of the dollar could come down from its high level as much as it has without more disturbance in interest rates and inflation. We've been very fortunate in being able to manage that big a decline in the value of the dollar with as little inflation as we've had.

Did your war on inflation cost more in human terms than you had thought?

Probably—stopping inflation is never easy. What I object to is that people said that the Federal Reserve caused the recession in the early 1980s and all its pain and suffering. But, in my view, we were going to have the pain anyway. It was just a question of when and how. We thought it would be less if we dealt with the inflation earlier rather than later.

One of my predecessors, Bill Martin, once described the Fed's job as taking away the punch bowl just when the party's getting good. You avoid the hangover that way, or reduce it anyway.

Do you bring the punch bowl back if the party starts to fade?

My critique of Federal Reserve history is not that it was always too harsh and brought all these expansions to an end when they could have gone forever. But sometimes the Fed was overeager to get the party started. Once you get in a recession, the pressures on the Fed are very strong. Even after you come out of the recession, the temptation is to overstimulate. But policy only works with a lag and the lags catch up with you. You're off to another jolly party again. We tried to avoid this last time, I think with some success.

We've talked a bit about the government's budget deficit. Did the government's need to finance its budget deficit affect your job as chairman of the Fed?

I do not believe that the Federal Reserve was forced into inflationary

"Inflation is the enemy of sustained expansion."

"A major policy challenge is to find a way of cutting the growth of consumption."

financing. In retrospect, the government's budget deficit position did not in fact appear to impair our ability to achieve a record expansion. But if you look at whether the expansion can be carried on for another seven years, you have to get concerned about our relatively low level of investment, our low productivity, and our dependence of foreign lending and investment. None of these can be dealt with by monetary policy alone. Fiscal policy gives you an expansionay thrust, which then has to be countered by tighter monetary policy—by higher interest rates. This leaves you with a vulnerable economy, increasingly dependent on money borrowed from overseas.

The United States' economic relationship with other countries also includes the exchange of good and services. In recent years it has experienced a substantial decline in net exports. What do you see as the principal cause of the external trade deficit?

It's an internal inbalance between our ability to produce and our propensity to spend. Our spending is mostly consumption—personal and public. Investment is, at best, just so-so for a period of expansion. So a major policy challenge is to find a way of cutting consumption. On the other hand, there are inbalances in the opposite direction in other economies. The Japanese are doing a good job in beginning to deal with this problem. But it is true that there is a bias in the trading world towards less openness. If you took a snapshot of the world trading scene, you'd have to agree that the United States is by far the most open market of all, and our trading partners are more closed. How do you deal with that complaint? You can't ignore how these imbalances are aggravated by our own internal economic policies—our own consumption.

What will improve the situation?

We've got to contain domestic spending and we've got to see foreign markets open up so that foreign expenditure on our goods increases. Of course, just opening foreign markets wouldn't induce any change in our own spending by itself. Moreover, changing our spending pattern can't be done just by monetary policy, by high interest rates. Monetary policy won't move spending from consumption into investment. That means you've got to bring fiscal policy to bear. More taxes or less spending, or both. But now you've got a lot of political choices. You'll have to make some political bargains in order to get expenditure cuts.

When a student seeks your advice on the choice of a career, what do you suggest?

I'd strongly encourage him or her to consider a career in public service. There are so many important jobs for people in the government. Who do we look to for the solution of problems like AIDS? The government. Who's going to solve the drug problem, if anyone can? The government. We need young people who recognize the challenge and excitement and satisfaction of service to the public. Without their contributions, we will have a serious problem in this country.

CHAPTER 25

Expenditure Decisions

After studying this chapter, you will be able to:

- Describe the importance and degree of fluctuation in the components of aggregate expenditure—consumption expenditure, investment, government purchase of goods and services, and net exports.
- Explain how people make their consumption and saving decisions.
- Explain how consumption and saving are influenced by income and wealth.
- Define and calculate the average and marginal propensities to consume and save.
- Explain the relationship between consumption expenditure and GDP.
- Explain how firms make their investment decisions.
- Explain why there are large fluctuations in investment.
- Explain how export and import decisions are made and how net exports are determined.

Fear and Trembling in the Shopping Aisles

"DESPITE MARKET PLUNGE, It's Business as Usual for Consumers." With this headline, and an almost audible sigh of relief, the *Montreal Gazette* reported the early response of retail sales to the stock market crash of October 1987. "Even the popularity of luxury goods," the article said, "which many predicted would be the first to suffer as nervous shoppers put off discretionary spending, doesn't seem to have dropped severely in the wake of Meltdown Monday."[1] However, by December 1987, the headlines spoke fearfully of weak holiday season sales and of retailers' cutting prices to attract shoppers. ■ Why all the fear and trembling over what happens in the shopping aisles? Besides a few manufacturers and stores, who really cares whether people buy a lot of gifts for the holidays or whether they continue to buy cars and VCRs after a stock market crash? How does this affect the rest of us? What makes people decide to spend less and save more? ■ It's not only consumer spending that stirs up hope and fear in the economy. "Big Spending by Business Seen as Driving Economy," trumpeted a *Montreal Gazette* story in May 1988. It went on to say, "Most of Canada's economic forecasters say booming business spending on everything from computers to delivery trucks will be the driving force behind the country's economic growth this year."[2] Another headline, in the *Calgary Herald,* read "Exporters Feel Stronger Dollar's Pinch," and the news story reported, "While a stronger dollar is a boon to travellers, importers, consumers, and companies with debts in U.S. funds, it's pinched the pocketbooks of exporters — 80 percent of whose goods go to American markets."[3] How do business investment and exports affect us? How much of the country's spending do they make up, compared with consumer spending? Are fluctuations in these components of aggregate expenditure sources of fluctuations in our job

[1] *Montreal Gazette,* October 31, 1982.
[2] *Montreal Gazette,* May 25, 1988.
[3] *Calgary Herald,* April 19, 1987.

prospects and living standards? ■ What about the government's spending on goods and services? How large a component of aggregate expenditure is the spending by the government sector of our economy? Has government spending been increasing or decreasing in importance? Is the government a source of instability in the economy, with fluctuations in its spending reinforcing fluctuations in spending by the private sector; or do fluctuations in government spending counteract those of the private sector so that, as a result of the government's actions, aggregate expenditure is more stable than it otherwise would be?

■ We discovered in Chapter 24 how the interaction of aggregate demand and aggregate supply determines the price level and real GDP. In this chapter and the four that follow, we are going to take a closer look at the aggregate demand side of the economy. In Chapter 24, we learned some propositions about the aggregate demand curve and what makes that curve shift. That is, we catalogued the influences on aggregate demand, including the influences of taxes and government purchases and of the Bank of Canada's monetary policy. We're now going to learn more about those influences on aggregate demand, discovering why they operate in the way they do and also how aggregate demand might be influenced by policy to smooth out fluctuations. Our first step in this process is to study people's spending decisions more closely.
■ We discovered in our study of the national income accounts in Chapter 23 that when one person spends a dollar, it shows up as a dollar of income spread out among a lot of other people. The spending that people do in shopping aisles spreads out in waves across the economy, affecting millions of people. In this chapter, we study the composition of those waves and see why consumption has a big effect outside the stores. We also study the other components of aggregate expenditure — investment, government purchases of goods and services, and net exports.
■ Our concern in this chapter is to study each of these components of aggregate expenditure in isolation. Then, in Chapter 26, we'll bring the separate elements together and see how they interact with each other to determine the levels of aggregate expenditure and GDP. When we have completed our study of these two chapters, we'll have a clearer and deeper understanding of how aggregate demand is determined and why it fluctuates.
■ Let's begin by looking at the components of aggregate expenditure.

The Components of Aggregate Expenditure

The components of aggregate expenditure are:

- Consumption expenditure
- Investment
- Government purchases of goods and services
- Net exports (exports minus imports)

Relative Importance

What are the relative magnitudes of the components of aggregate expenditure? Which is the largest component? Figure 25.1 answers these questions for the years 1969 to 1989. By far the biggest portion of aggregate expenditure is consumption expenditure, which ranges between 54 and 57 percent of GDP and averages 55 percent. The smallest portion is net exports, which averages 3 percent. Investment ranges from 17 to 25 percent of GDP and averages 20 percent. Government purchases of goods and services is slightly larger than investment. It ranges from 20 to 25 percent of GDP and averages 23 percent.

Growing Importance of International Transactions Although net exports is the smallest component of aggregate expenditure, the two seperate components of net exports, exports and imports of goods and services, are important and of growing importance in our economy. In 1969, each of these items represented about 22 percent of GDP. By 1989 they had grown to more than 35 percent of GDP.

Next, let's examine the relative volatility of the components of aggregate expenditure.

Relative Volatility

Which of the components of aggregate expenditure fluctuate the most — which are the most volatile? Figure 25.2 gives the answer. And that answer is investment and net exports. Consumption expenditure and government purchases of goods and services fluctuate much less than these two items.

In studying this figure, notice that the vertical axis measures the extent to which the four components of aggregate expenditure deviate from their own average values (as percentages of GDP). The

Figure 25.1 The Components of Aggregate Expenditure, 1969–1989

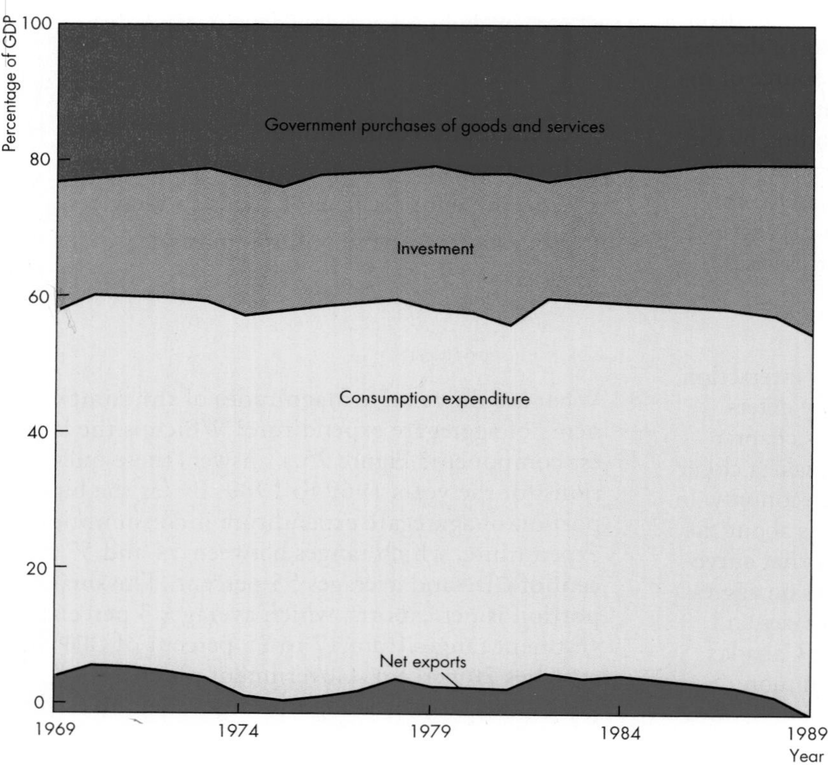

The biggest component of aggregate expenditure is consumption expenditure. It ranges from 54 to 57 percent of GDP and averages 55 percent. Investment fluctuates between 17 and 25 percent of GDP and averages 20 percent. Government purchases of goods and services ranges from 20 to 25 percent of GDP and averages 23 percent. Net exports is the smallest item and averages approximately 3 percent of GDP.

Source: Statistics Canada, *National Income and Expenditure Accounts*

scales on which each of the four variables are measured are identical, so the up and down movements in the lines give a precise indication of the relative volatility of the four components. Note that although the fluctuations in consumption expenditure have a much smaller range than those in investment, the two series move in sympathy with each other. Note also that the biggest decline in investment — in 1982 — occurred at precisely the time that the economy was at the trough of its most severe postwar recession (a recession that we studied in Chapter 22 and 24). Government purchases of goods and services shows a general tendency to decline (as a percentage of GDP). Net exports are especially volatile and to some degree represent a mirror image of investment.

Does Government Stabilize?

You can already begin to see the answer to one of the questions about government spending that was posed at the beginning of this chapter. You can see, in Fig. 25.2, how fluctuations in government purchases of goods and services align with fluctuations in investment, the most volatile component of aggregate expenditure, to determine whether the government is a stabilizing or destabilizing influence on aggregate expenditure. There is a distinct tendency for fluctuations in government purchases to counteract those in investment to some degree. Notice, in particular, the years 1970 and 1981. These were years in which investment was below average. They were also years in which government purchases were above average. Although the fluctuations in government purchases do go in the opposite direction to those in investment, the amplitude of those fluctuations is smaller than those in investment. Thus fluctuations in government purchases only partly offset the fluctuations in investment.

Government purchases of goods and services are the *public* components of aggregate expenditure and are determined by decisions made by governments in their interactions with voters. Consumption expenditure, investment, and net exports are the

Figure 25.2 Fluctuations in the Components of Aggregate Expenditure, 1969–1989

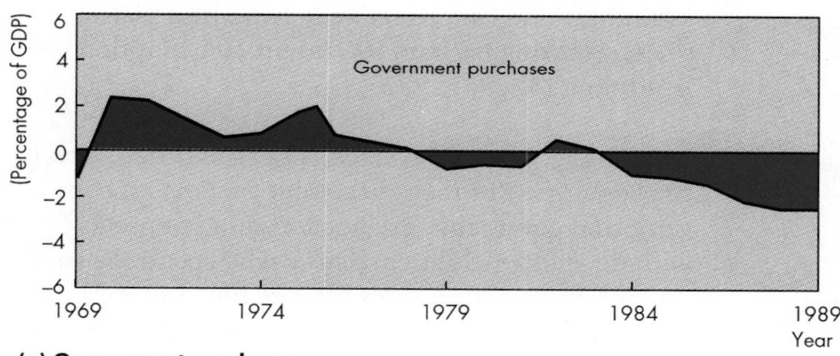

(a) Government purchases

Percentage of GDP

Investment

1969 1974 1979 1984 1989

Year

(b) Investment

Percentage of GDP

Consumpion expenditure

1969 1974 1979 1984 1989

Year

(c) Consumption expenditure

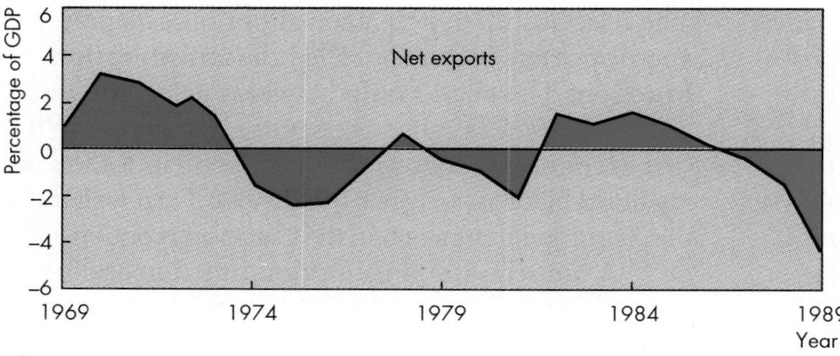

(d) Net exports

Fluctuations in the components of aggregate expenditure are shown as deviations from averages expressed as percentages of GDP. Although consumption expenditure is the biggest component of aggregate expenditure, it is the one that fluctuates least in percentage terms. Investment and net exports fluctuate most. Government purchases of goods and services steadily declined during the 20 years shown here.

Source: Statistics Canada, *National Income and Expenditure Accounts private* components of aggregate expenditure, determined by decisions of households and firms. In the material that follows, we're going to study the choices that determine the private components of aggregate expenditure. Let's begin with the largest component —consumption expenditure.

Consumption Expenditure and Saving

Consumption expenditure is the value of the consumption goods and services bought by households. There are five main factors that influence a household's consumption expenditure. They are:

- Disposable income
- Expected future income
- Stage in life
- Degree of patience
- Interest rate

Disposable Income *Disposable income* is the total income that households receive in exchange for supplying the services of factors of production, plus transfers from the government minus taxes. A household can do only two things with its disposable income: spend it on consumption goods and services or save it.

As a household's disposable income increases, so does its expenditure on food and beverages, clothing, housing, transportation, medical care, and most other goods and services. That is, a household's consumption expenditure increases as its disposable income increases.

Expected Future Income Other things being equal, the higher a household's expected future income, the greater is its current consumption expenditure. That is, of two households that each have the same disposable income in the current year, the household with the larger expected future income will spend a larger portion of current disposable income on consumption goods and services. Consider, for example, two households whose principal income earner is a senior executive in a large corporation. One executive has just been told of an important promotion that will increase the household's income by 50 percent in the following years. The other has just been told that the firm has been taken over and there will be no employment beyond the end of the year. The first household buys a new car and takes an expensive foreign vacation, thereby increasing its current consumption expenditure. The second household sells the family's second car and cancels its winter vacation plans, thereby cutting back on its current consumption expenditure.

Stage in Life On the average, households that spend the largest part of their disposable income on consumption goods and services are young households with dependent children. Those who spend the smallest part of their disposable income on consumption goods and services are the elderly and retired.

Degree of Patience The degree of patience varies from one person to another and from one household to another. Some, impatient to consume, do not worry if they run into debt. Others prefer to save, thereby deferring consumption. These personal characteristics influence the level of a household's consumption expenditure. The more impatient the household, the larger is its consumption expenditure, other things being equal.

Interest Rates The higher the interest rate, the lower is the level of consumption expenditure. High interest rates discourage consumption by making consumer loans more expensive or by making it more attractive for a household to save, lending part of its income to others.

Of the five influences on consumption expenditure, the most important is the level of disposable income. Let's look at the relationship between consumption expenditure and disposable income more closely.

The Consumption Function and the Saving Function

The relationship between consumption expenditure and disposable income is called the **consumption function**. The relationship between saving and disposable income is called the **saving function**. We'll first examine the consumption function and the saving function for an imaginary household. Then we'll study the consumption function in the Canadian economy.

A household's consumption function and its saving function are a statement about its consumption expenditure and saving plan at each possible level of disposable income. Figure 25.3 sets out the consumption function and the saving function for the Polonius household. Notice two important things. First, even if the Polonius household has no disposable income, it still consumes. It does so by having a negative level of saving. Negative saving is called **dissaving**. Households that consume more than their disposable income do so either by living off assets or by borrowing, a situation that cannot, of course, last forever.

Second, as the Polonius household's disposable income increases, so does the amount that it plans to spend on consumption and the amount that it plans to save. Since a household can only consume or save its disposable income, these two items always add up to disposable income. That is, consumption and saving plans are consistent with disposable income.

The Consumption Function The Polonius household's consumption function is plotted in Fig. 25.3(a). The horizontal axis measures disposable income and the vertical axis measures consumption expenditure. The points labelled *a* through *f* in the figure correspond with the rows having the same letters in the table. For example, point *c* indicates a disposable income of $20,000 and consumption expenditure of $18,000.

The 45° Line Figure 25.3(a) also contains a line labelled "45° line." It is a line drawn from the origin, at an angle of 45° to the horizontal axis. This line connects the points at which consumption expenditure,

Figure 25.3 The Polonius Household's Consumption Function and Saving Function

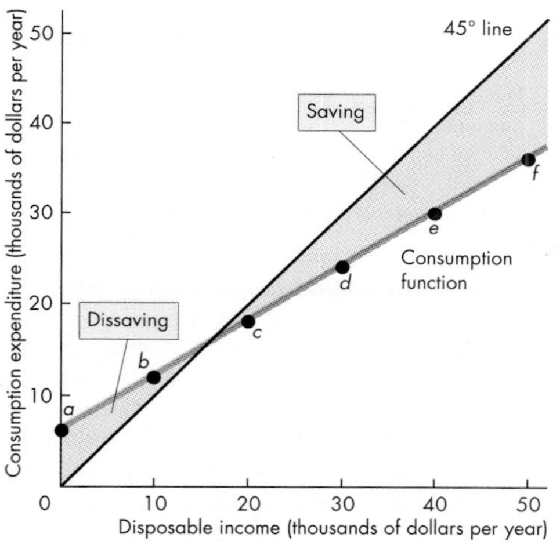

(a) Consumption function

(b) Saving function

	Disposable income	Consumption expenditure	Saving
		(thousands of dollars per year)	
a	0	6	−6
b	10	12	−2
c	20	18	2
d	30	24	6
e	40	30	10
f	50	36	14

The table sets out the consumption and saving plan of the Polonius household at various levels of disposable income.

Part (a) of the figure shows the relationship between consumption expenditure and disposable income (the consumption function).

Part (b) shows the relationship between saving and disposable income (the saving function). Points *a* through *f* on the consumption and saving functions correspond to the rows in the table. The 45° line in part (a) is the line of equality between consumption expenditure and disposable income. The Polonius household's consumption expenditure and saving equals its disposable income. When the consumption function is above the 45° line, saving is negative (dissaving occurs) and the saving function is below the horizontal axis. When the consumption function is below the 45° line, saving is positive and the saving function is above the horizontal axis. At the point, where the consumption function intersects the 45° line, all disposable income is consumed, saving is zero, and the saving function intersects the horizontal axis.

measured on the vertical axis, equals disposable income, measured on the horizontal axis. When the consumption function is above the 45° line, consumption expenditure exceeds disposable income; when the consumption function is below the 45° line, consumption expenditure is less than disposable income; and at the point where the consumption function intersects the 45° line, consumption expenditure and disposable income are equal.

The Saving Function The saving function is graphed in Fig. 25.3(b). The horizontal axis is exactly the same as that in part (a). The vertical axis measures saving. Again, the points marked *a* through *f* correspond to the rows of the table.

There is a relationship between the consumption function and the saving function. We can see this relationship by looking at the two parts of the figure. When the saving function is below the horizontal axis, saving is negative (dissaving) and the consumption function is above the 45° line. When the saving function is above the horizontal axis, saving is positive and the consumption function is below the 45° line. When saving is zero, the saving function cuts the horizontal axis and when consumption equals disposable income, the consumption function cuts the 45° line. The level of disposable income at which the saving function cuts the horizontal axis is the same as that at which the consumption function cuts the 45° line.

The Average Propensities to Consume and to Save

The **average propensity to consume** (APC) is consumption expenditure divided by disposable income. Table 25.1(a) shows you how to calculate the average propensity to consume. Let's do a sample calculation. At a disposable income of $20,000, the Polonius household consumes $18,000. Its average propensity to consume is $18,000 divided by $20,000, which equals 0.9.

As you can see from the numbers in the table, the average propensity to consume declines as disposable income rises. At a disposable income of $10,000, the household consumes more than its income, so its average propensity to consume is greater than 1. But at a disposable income of $50,000, the household consumes only $36,000, so its average propensity to consume is $36,000 divided by $50,000, which equals 0.72.

The **average propensity to save** (APS) is saving divided by disposable income. It too is calculated in Table 25.1(a). For example, when disposable income is $20,000 the Polonius household saves $2,000. The average propensity to save is $2,000 divided by $20,000, which equals 0.1. When saving is negative, the average propensity to save is negative. As disposable income increases, the average propensity to save increases.

Table 25.1 Average and Marginal Propensities to Consume and to Save

(a) Calculating average propensities to consume and to save

Disposable income (*YD*)	Consumption expenditure (*C*)	Saving (*S*)	APC (C/YD)	APS (S/YD)
(dollars per year)				
0	6,000	−6,000	—	—
10,000	12,000	−2,000	1.20	−0.20
20,000	18,000	2,000	0.90	0.10
30,000	24,000	6,000	0.80	0.20
40,000	30,000	10,000	0.75	0.25
50,000	36,000	14,000	0.72	0.28

(b) Calculating marginal propensities to consume and to save

Change in disposable income	$\Delta YD = 10{,}000$
Change in consumption	$\Delta C = 6{,}000$
Change in saving	$\Delta S = 4{,}000$
Marginal propensity to consume	$MPC = \Delta C/\Delta YD = 0.6$
Marginal propensity to save	$MPS = \Delta S/\Delta YD = 0.4$

Consumption and saving depend on disposable income. At zero disposable income, some consumption is undertaken and saving is negative (dissaving occurs). As disposable income increases, so do both consumption and saving. The average propensities to consume and to save are calculated in part (a). The average propensity to consume — the ratio of consumption to disposable income — declines as disposable income increases; the average propensity to save — the ratio of saving to disposable income — increases as disposable income increases. These two average propensities sum to 1. Each additional — *marginal* — dollar of disposable income is either consumed or saved.

Part (b) calculates the marginal propensities to consume and to save. The marginal propensity to consume is the change in consumption that results from a $1 change in disposable income. The marginal propensity to save is the change in saving that results from a $1 change in disposable income. The marginal propensities to consume and to save sum to 1.

As disposable income increases, the average propensity to consume falls and the average propensity to save rises. Equivalently, as disposable income increases, the fraction of income saved increases and the fraction of income consumed decreases. These patterns in the average propensities to consume and to save reflect the fact that people with very low disposable incomes are so poor that their incomes are not even sufficient to meet their consumption expenditure. Consumption expenditure exceeds disposable income. As people become richer, with higher incomes, they are able to meet their consumption requirements with a smaller and smaller fraction of their disposable income.

The sum of the average propensity to consume and the average propensity to save equals 1. These two average propensities add up to 1 because consumption and saving exhaust disposable income. Each dollar of disposable income is either consumed or saved.

You can see that the two average propensities add up to 1 by using the following equation:

$$C + S = YD$$

Divide both sides of the equation by disposable income to obtain:

$$C / YD + S / YD = 1$$

C / YD is the *average propensity to consume* and S / YD is *average propensity to save.* Thus:

$$\text{APC} + \text{APS} = 1$$

The Marginal Propensities to Consume and to Save

The last dollar of disposable income received is called the marginal dollar. Part of that marginal dollar is consumed and part of it is saved. The division of the marginal dollar between consumption expenditure and saving is determined by the marginal propensities to consume and to save.

The **marginal propensity to consume** (MPC) is the fraction of the last dollar of disposable income that is spent on consumption goods and services. It is calculated as the change in consumption expenditure divided by the change in disposable income. The **marginal propensity to save** (MPS) is the fraction of the last dollar of disposable income saved. The marginal propensity to save is calculated as the change in saving divided by the change in disposable income.

Table 25.1 calculates the Polonius household's marginal propensities to consume and to save. Looking back at part (a) of the table, you can see that the Polonius household's disposable income increases by $10,000 as we move from one row to the next — $10,000 is the change in disposable income. You can also see from part (a) that when disposable income increases by $10,000, consumption increases by $6,000. The marginal propensity to consume — the change in consumption divided by the change in disposable income — is therefore $6,000 divided by $10,000, which equals 0.6. The Polonius household's marginal propensity to consume is constant. It is the same at each level of disposable income. Out of the household's marginal dollar of disposable income, 60 cents is spent on consumption goods and services.

Table 25.1 calculates the marginal propensity to save. You can see from part (a) that when the Polonius household's disposable income increases by $10,000, saving increases by $4,000. The marginal propensity to save — the change in saving divided by the change in disposable income — is therefore, $4,000 divided by $10,000, which equals 0.4. The Polonius household's marginal propensity to save is constant. It is the same at each level of disposable income. Out of the last dollar of disposable income, 40 cents is saved.

The marginal propensity to consume plus the marginal propensity to save equals 1. Each additional dollar must be either spent or saved. In this example, when disposable income increases by $1, 60 cents more is spent and 40 cents more is saved.

Marginal-Average Relations In the calculations we have just done, the marginal propensity to consume is less than the average propensity to consume, and as disposable income increases, the average propensity to consume falls.

This relationship between the marginal propensity to consume and the average propensity to consume is a feature of all marginal and average relations. You may appreciate the relationship more clearly if you think of a baseball batting average. Suppose that George Bell comes up to the plate with a batting average of .300. All his previous at bats contributed to this average. His current at bat is going to produce his marginal score. If he gets a hit, his marginal score is better than his average and his average rises. If he strikes out, his marginal score is worse than his average and his average falls.

The marginal-average relationship also holds in the case of saving. The marginal propensity to save is larger than the average propensity to save.

Consequently, as disposable income increases, so does the average propensity to save.

Saving is like a batter getting a hit: the marginal propensity to save exceeds the average propensity to save, so the average propensity increases as disposable income increases — the score from the marginal innings exceeds the average, so the average increases as the number of times at bat increases. The marginal and average propensities to consume are like making an out. The marginal propensity to consume is less than the average propensity, and the average propensity to consume decreases as disposable income increases — the marginal score is less than the average score so the average declines as the number of times at bat increases.

Marginal Propensities and Slopes The marginal propensity to consume is equal to the slope of the consumption function. You can see this equality by looking back at Fig. 25.3. In that figure, the consumption function has a constant slope that can be measured as the change in consumption divided by the change in income. For example, when income increases from $20,000 to $30,000 — an increase of $10,000 — consumption increases from $18,000 to $24,000 — an increase of $6,000. The slope of the consumption function is $6,000 divided by $10,000, which equals 0.6 — the same value as the marginal propensity to consume that we calculated in Table 25.1.

The marginal propensity to save is equal to the slope of the saving function. You can see this equality by again looking back at Fig. 25.3. When income increases by $10,000, saving increases by $4,000. The slope of the saving function is $4,000 divided by $10,000, which equals 0.4 — the same value as the marginal propensity to save that we calculated in Table 25.1.

We've studied the consumption and saving choices of a representative household. Let's now look at the consumption expenditure of actual households in Canada and see how that expenditure varies as disposable income varies.

Table 25.2 Disposable Income and Consumption Expenditure in Canada

Income group	Disposable income (dollars per year)	Consumption expenditure (dollars per year)	Average propensity to consume	Marginal propensity to consume
a	6,754	7,454	1.10	
				0.84
b	13,844	13,424	0.97	
				0.75
c	21,446	19,095	0.89	
				0.69
d	28,717	24,139	0.84	
				0.61
e	36,206	28,742	0.79	
				0.51
f	52,230	36,840	0.71	

The rows record average disposable income and average consumption expenditure for Canadian income groups, ranging from the lowest to the highest. These data are used to calculate the average and marginal propensities to consume. The average propensity to consume — consumption expenditure divided by disposable income — declines as income increases. The marginal propensity to consume — the change in consumption divided by the change in disposable income — also declines as income increases. The marginal propensity to consume is less than the average propensity to consume.

Source: Statistics Canada, *Family Expenditure in Canada*, Family Expenditure Survey for 1982.

The Canadian Consumption Function

Data for the Canadian consumption function in 1982 are shown in Table 25.2. Each row represents disposable income and consumption expenditure averaged over a group of households. There are six such rows, arranged from the lowest to the highest income.

Consumption expenditure in Canada increases as disposable income increases. We can calculate the average and marginal propensities to consume using these data. First, let's calculate the average propensity to consume — consumption expenditure divided by disposable income. As you can see, the lowest income group consumes more than its disposable income — its average propensity to consume is greater than 1. But the average propensity to consume declines as income increases, and the group of households with the highest income has an average propensity to consume of 0.71.

Next, we'll calculate the marginal propensity to consume — the change in consumption expenditure divided by the change in disposable income. As disposable income increases between the lowest and second lowest income group, the marginal propensity to consume is 0.84. As income increases through the higher income groups, the marginal propensity to consume declines to only 0.51 for the highest income group. Thus low-income Canadians spend more than 90 cents of each additional dollar of disposable income received, while high-income Canadians spend barely more than 50 cents of each additional dollar's worth of disposable income.

We saw in the case of the Polonius household (and in the case of the baseball batting scores) that when the marginal exceeds the average, the average increases; when the marginal is below the average, the average decreases. You can see the same relationship between the marginal and average propensities here. The marginal propensity to consume is below the average propensity to consume, and as disposable income increases the average propensity to consume declines.

Figure 25.4 plots the data given in Table 25.2. Each point (*a* through *f*) represents a row in the table. The line passing through these points is the Canadian consumption function. It describes the average relationship between consumption expenditure and disposable income across these income groups. Notice the similarity between the Canadian consumption function in Fig. 25.4 and the Polonius household's consumption function in Fig. 25.3(a).

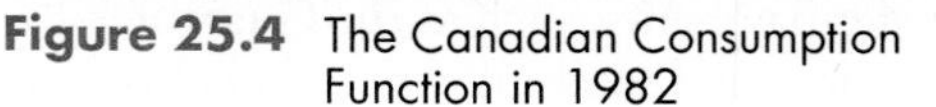

Figure 25.4 The Canadian Consumption Function in 1982

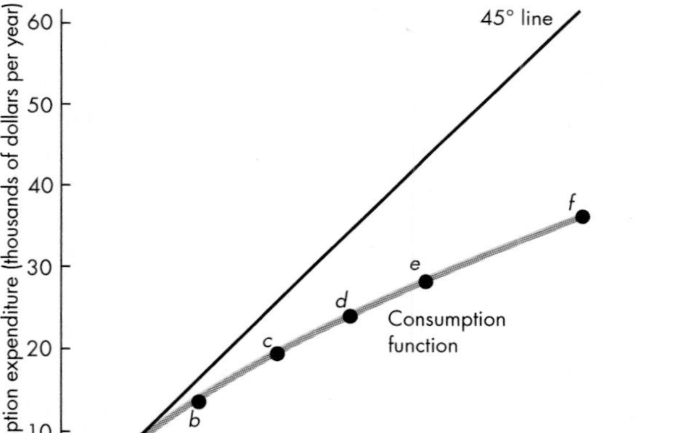

To graph the consumption function, we plot household consumption expenditure on the vertical axis against household disposable income on the horizontal axis. The Canadian consumption function shown here is based on disposable income and consumption expenditure data for six income groups in 1982, as shown in Table 25.2. Points *a* through *f* on the consumption function correspond to the rows in the table. For example, the highest income households had an average income of $52,230 in 1982 and a consumption expenditure of $36,840. This consumption expenditure and disposable income is shown as point *f* on the consumption function.

Shifts in the Consumption Function

We have noted that there are five main factors that influence a household's consumption expenditure. Its disposable income is only one of them. The other four factors — expected future income, stage in life, degree of patience, and interest rates — influence consumption expenditure and are represented by shifts in the consumption function. For example, an increase in expected future income shifts the consumption function upward; a decrease in expected future income shifts it downward. The consumption function shifts upward as a result of a decrease in interest rates. As a family progresses through its life cycle, its consumption function shifts upward as the number of children in the household increases and as the children get older. The consumption function then shifts downward when the children leave home and as the adults in the family approach retirement age.

These factors that shift the consumption function may be very important for individual households, but on the average they do not have large effects. The average consumption function, measured across all households, is a remarkably stable economic relationship.

The Aggregate Consumption Function

Our purpose in developing a theory of the consumption function is to explain the determination of aggregate expenditure and real GDP. So far, we have studied the relationship between consumption expenditure and disposable income for a typical household, and we have described the average consumption function across households in Canada. We're now going to turn our attention away from individual households and households at different income levels and examine the aggregate consumption function.

The **aggregate consumption function** is the relationship between real consumption expenditure and real GDP. To obtain the aggregate consumption function, we first calculate the relationship between real consumption expenditure and real disposable income. This relationship is shown in Fig. 25.5(a). The vertical axis measures real consumption expenditure (in 1981 dollars) and the horizontal axis measures real disposable income (also in 1981 dollars). Each point identified by a blue dot represents real consumption expenditure and real disposable income for a particular year between 1969 and 1989. The line passing through these points is the time-series consumption function. The **time-series consumption function** is the relationship between real consumption expenditure and real disposable income over time. The slope of this consumption function, and hence the marginal propensity to consume, is 0.9.

It is important to understand why this time-series consumption function looks different from the consumption function for individual households that we examined in Fig. 25.4. The individual household consumption function tells us how consumption expenditure varies with disposable income across households in a given year. The time-series consumption function tells us how aggregate consumption expenditure varies with aggregate disposable income from one year to another. Equivalently, it tells us about the relationship between average consumption expenditure and average disposable income over time. Averaging over families with low incomes and high incomes, consumption expenditure represents 90 cents in every dollar of disposable income. But there is a large amount of variation around this average, and that variation is illustrated in the consumption function for individual households.

Figure 25.5(b) shows the aggregate consumption function — real consumption expenditure plotted against real GDP. To express consumption expenditure as a function of GDP, we need to establish the link between disposable income and GDP. That link is implicit in the definition of disposable income. Recall that we have defined disposable income as the difference between aggregate income and net taxes (net taxes are taxes minus transfer payments). Aggregate income is GDP. To work out the relationship between consumption and GDP, we need to know what happens to net taxes as GDP changes.

Net taxes increase as GDP increases. Almost all the taxes that we pay — personal taxes, corporate taxes, and Canada Pension Plan and unemployment insurance contributions — increase as our incomes increase. Transfer payments, such as the Guaranteed Income Supplement and unemployment benefits, decrease as incomes increase. Since taxes increase and transfers decrease, net taxes clearly increase as incomes increase. It turns out that there is a tendency for net taxes to be a fairly stable percentage of GDP — about 40 percent. If 40 percent of GDP is paid in net taxes, 60 percent of GDP is available as disposable income.

The table in Fig. 25.5 sets out the relationship between real GDP, disposable income, and consumption expenditure. It incorporates the 60 percent relationship between GDP and disposable income. For example, if real GDP is $300 billion, disposable income is 60 percent of that amount, which is $180 billion. The table also shows us the amount of consumption expenditure at various levels of disposable income. We have seen that the marginal propensity to consume out of disposable income is 0.9. That is, out of each additional dollar of disposable income, 90 cents is consumed and 10 cents is saved. Thus if disposable income is $180 billion, consumption expenditure is nine-tenths of that amount, which is $162 billion.

Consumption as a function of real GDP — the aggregate consumption function — is shown in Fig. 25.5(b) as the straight line passing through the dots that represent actual real consumption expenditure and real GDP for the years 1969 to 1989.

The position of the aggregate consumption function depends both on the propensity to consume out of disposable income and on the relationship between disposable income and GDP.

Figure 25.5 The Aggregate Consumption Function

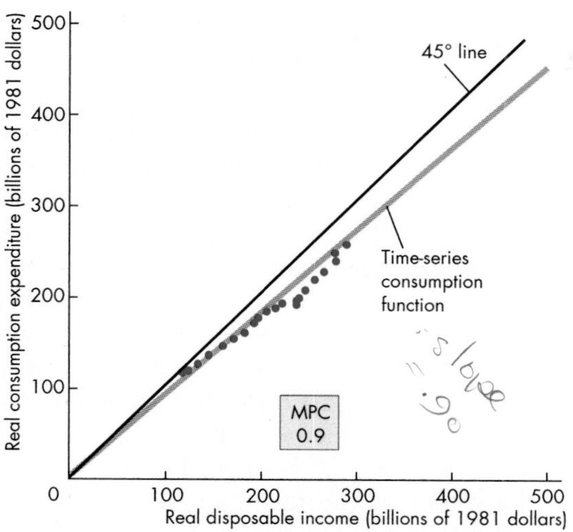

(a) Consumption as a function of disposable income

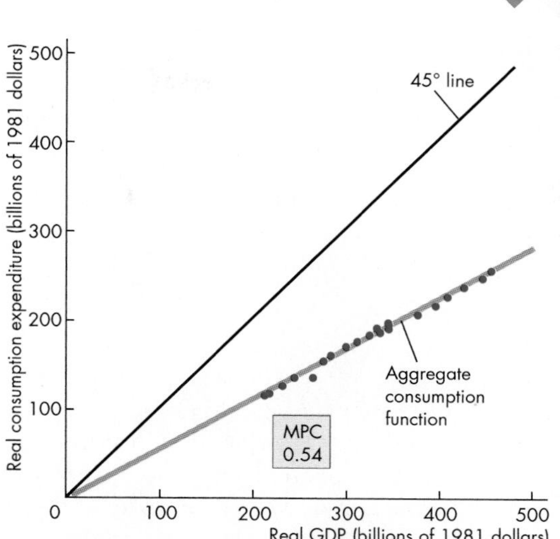

(b) Consumption as a function of real GDP

Real GDP (Y)	Disposable income ($YD = 0.6Y$)	Consumption expenditure ($C = 0.9YD = 0.54Y$)
	(billions of 1981 dollars)	
100	60	54
200	120	108
300	180	162
400	240	216
500	300	270
600	360	324

Part (a) shows the Canadian time-series consumption function — the relationship between real consumption expenditure and real disposable income — for each year from 1969 to 1989. Each dot in the figure represents real consumption expenditure and real disposable income for a particular year. The marginal propensity to consume out of disposable income is approximately 0.9.

Part (b) shows the Canadian aggregate consumption function — the relationship between real consumption expenditure and real GDP. This consumption function takes into account the fact that as real GDP increases, so do net taxes. The marginal propensity to consume out of real GDP is approximately 0.54. The connection between the time-series consumption function and the aggregate consumption function is shown in the table. The tax rate is 40 percent, so that disposable income is 0.6 times real GDP. The marginal propensity to consume out of disposable income is 0.9. Combining a tax rate of 40 percent with a marginal propensity to consume out of disposable income of 0.9 gives a marginal propensity to consume out of real GDP of 0.54.

Since nine-tenths (0.9) of disposable income is consumed and since six-tenths (0.6) of GDP is available as disposable income, the fraction of GDP consumed is 0.54 ($0.9 \times 0.6 = 0.54$). The vertical gap between the 45° line and the aggregate consumption function reflects the amount of saving and the level of net taxes. The higher are net taxes, the greater is that gap, and the lower is the aggregate consumption function.

The story of the development of the theory of consumption and saving is told in Our Advancing Knowledge pp. 662-664.

R E V I E W

Consumption is a function of disposable income. Disposable income is a stable percentage of GDP. Thus consumption is also a function of GDP. In Canada today, each additional dollar of real GDP generates, on the average, an additional 54 cents of real consumption expenditure. ■

Let's now turn to the other main private component of aggregate expenditure, investment.

OUR ADVANCING KNOWLEDGE

Consumption and Saving

Irving Fisher

John Maynard Keynes

By 1930, a consensus had emerged among economists concerning the determination of consumption and saving. That consensus was crystallized by Irving Fisher of Yale University in his classic work, *The Theory of Interest*, published in 1930.[1] The accepted view was that consumption and saving depend primarily on the real interest rate. A high real interest rate causes a decrease in consumption and an increase in saving. Fisher assumed that people have to be induced to decrease their spending with the reward of a high rate of return. The higher the reward, the greater is the tendency to put off consumption and to save.

This consensus received a revolutionary challenge from John Maynard Keynes of Cambridge, England, in his book, *The General Theory of Employment, Interest, and Money*, published in 1936. Keynes' idea was that consumption and saving do not depend on the interest rate but on the level of disposable income:

"The propensity to consume is a fairly stable function so that, as a rule, the amount of aggregate consumption mainly depends on the amount of aggregate income,... changes in the propensity itself being... a secondary influence.... The fundamental psychological law, upon which we are entitled to depend with confidence both a priori from our knowledge of human nature and from the detailed facts of experience, is that men are disposed, as a rule and on the average, to increase their consumption as their income increases, but not by as much as the increase in their income. That is to say, if ΔC is the amount of consumption and ΔY is income, C has the same sign as Y but is smaller in amount, i.e. $\Delta C / \Delta Y$ is positive and less than unity." [2]

A little earlier than the time that Keynes was writing, Colin Clark, working in England, and Simon Kuznets, at the University of Chicago, were beginning to compile national income data. These data fitted Keynes's theory remarkably closely.

During the 1940s and 1950s, a large amount of additional data was being collected — but this time by government bureaus. Official national income accounts were providing additional observations of consumption and income each year and, after 1947, each quarter-year. Cross-section data — that is, data on the consumption and income of individual groups of people classified by age, race, and location — were also being collected. These new data revealed shortcomings in Keynes' theory. Even as early as the late 1940s, the Keynesian theory of the consumption function began to make important forecasting errors. Also, the cross-section data showed that the fraction of income consumed varied systematically depending on whether people were young or old, black or white, or from urban or rural areas.

The anomalies and puzzles in the data brought forth two related new theories and advances in our understanding. The first of these was the *life-cycle hypothesis* proposed by Franco Modigliani of The Massachusetts Institute of Technology (MIT); the second was the *permanent income hypothesis* proposed by Milton Friedman, then at the University of Chicago. Modigliani's work, done jointly with a young English economist, Richard Brumberg, was published in 1954.[3] Friedman's work was published three years later, in 1957, in a book entitled *A Theory of the Consumption Function*.[4]

Each of these scholars suggested that consumption is determined not by income but by wealth. Other things being equal, the wealthier an individual, the more that individual will consume. Income and wealth are related to each other, but not directly on a year-by-year basis. A wealthy person might have a low income in a particular year. A poor person might have a big income (a windfall) in a particular year. Random fluctuations in income not associated with fluctuations in wealth will produce small or even no fluctuations in consumption.

Modigliani's main contribution was to emphasize the connection between an individual's stage of life and the relationship between income and wealth. Young people with secure jobs may have a small income but be wealthy in the sense that their future incomes will grow. Such people therefore tend to consume a large fraction of their current income. People in mid-life have an income that is high relative to their wealth. They consume a small fraction of their income.

Friedman's main contribution was to emphasize the distinction between permanent and transitory changes in income. Permanent changes in income have a large effect on consumption while transitory changes have a small effect. The ideas of Modigliani and Friedman resolved most of the paradoxes of both the cross-section and time-series data. Each scholar received a Nobel Prize in economics, partly for his contributions in this area.

Another revolution in economics — the rational expectations revolution — began in the 1960s and gathered momentum in the 1970s. This revolution forced economists to change their views about Modigliani's and Friedman's theories of the consumption function. An important contribution to this reformulation was made by Robert Hall of Stanford University in 1978.[5]

The rational expectations theory of the consumption function as proposed by Hall starts from the same point as Modigliani and Friedman: consumption depends on wealth. Wealth can be thought of as depending on all future income. The more income a person is going to earn in the future, whether in wages or in interest, the wealthier that person is. People do not know how much they are going to

Franco Modigliani

OUR ADVANCING • KNOWLEDGE •

Milton Friedman

earn in the future, but to make consumption decisions today, they have to form an expectation of what that future income will be. In forming their expectations, people will use all the information that is available. Having made a best estimate of their wealth, people will make consumption plans that achieve the best (in their assessment) allocation of consumption over time.

Expectations will change only as a result of "news" — of new information not previously known. News arrives at random. As a consequence, people's estimates of how wealthy they are also change in a random fashion. Since consumption plans depend on wealth, these plans will also vary in a random fashion.

Changes in consumption from one period to another will reflect both the working out of a consumption plan, as Modigliani and Friedman sketched, and changes in plans because of new information. As a result, changes in consumption from one year to another will be random. The average value will reflect average long-run consumption plans, but their change from year to year will reflect changes in information and expectations about future wealth. No variable, other than current consumption, should be of any value for predicting future consumption.

Robert Hall's contribution is, for the time being, the most recent milestone in the path of our evolving understanding of consumption and saving. It is by no means the last word, though. Every month new contributions on this topic, some of which will turn out to be milestones when viewed in a longer perspective, are being published in the economics journals.

---

[1] Irving Fisher, *The Theory of Interest* (New York: the Macmillian Company, 1930).

[2] John Maynard Keynes, *The General Theory of Employment, Interest, and Money* (London: Macmillan, 1936), 96.

[3] Franco Modigliani and Richard Brumberg, "Utility Analysis of the Consumption Function: An Interpretation of Cross-Section Data," in *Post-Keynesian Economics*, ed. K. Kurihara (New Brunswick: Rutgers University Press, 1954).

[4] Milton Friedman, *A Theory of the Consumption Function* (Princeton: Princeton University Press, 1957).

[5] Robert E. Hall "Stochastic Implications of the Life-Cycle Permanent Income Hypothesis: Theory and Evidence," *Journal of Political Economy* 86 (December 1978): 971-88.

Investment

Investment is the purchase of new plant, equipment, and buildings and additions to inventories. As we saw in Fig. 25.2, this component of aggregate demand is a volatile one. What determines the level of investment and why does it fluctuate so much? For example, how does Olympia and York — the Reichmann multinational empire — decide how much to spend on a new urban redevelopment program? What determines IBM's outlays on new computer designs? How does Bell Canada choose what it will spend on fibre optic communications systems? And why are there times when firms invest at a high rate and other times when they invest at a low rate?

What Determines Investment?

Obviously, Olympia and York, IBM, and Bell Canada take thousands of factors into account when they make their investment choices. But the four principal factors are:

- Interest rates
- Expected inflation
- Expected profit
- Depreciation

Interest Rates The lower the level of interest rates, the greater is the amount of investment. Firms sometimes pay for capital goods with money that they have borrowed, and sometimes they use their own funds — called retained earnings. Regardless of the method of financing an investment project, the interest rate is part of its *opportunity cost.* The interest paid on borrowing is a direct cost. But retained earnings could be lent to another firm at the going interest rate so the interest foregone is the opportunity cost of using those retained earnings to finance an investment project. The lower the interest rate, the lower is the opportunity cost of any given investment project. Some projects that would not be profitable at a high interest rate become profitable at a low interest rate. The lower the interest rate, the larger is the number of investment projects that are profitable and, therefore, the greater is the level of investment.

For example, suppose that Chrysler is contemplating building a new automobile assembly line in Windsor, Ontario, at a cost of $100 million. The assembly line is expected to produce cars for three years; then it will be scrapped completely and re-

Table 25.3 Investment in Automobile Assembly Line

Cost of assembly line		$100,000,000
Expected net revenue:	year 1	40,000,000
	year 2	50,000,000
	year 3	20,000,000

An automobile assembly line costs $100 million to build and is expected to generate net revenue of $40 million in the first year, $50 million in the second year, and $20 million in the third year. The line will then be scrapped and replaced by a new one.

placed with a new line that produces an entirely new range of models. The expected net revenue in each of the three years is the amount shown in Table 25.3. Net revenue is the difference between the total revenue from car sales and the costs of producing those cars. In calculating net revenue, we do not include the initial cost of the assembly line or the interest that has to be paid on it. We take separate account of these costs. To build the assembly line, Chrysler plans to borrow the initial $100 million; at the end of each year, it plans to pay the interest on the amount outstanding and to use its net revenue to pay off as much of the loan as it can each year. Does it pay Chrysler to invest $100 million in this car assembly line? The answer depends on the interest rate.

Part (a) of Table 25.4 shows what happens if the interest rate is 10 percent per year. Chrysler borrows $100 million and at the end of the first year has to pay $10 million in interest. It has a net revenue of $40 million and so can reduce the amount of its borrowing to $70 million. At the end of the second year, it pays $7 million in interest (10 percent of the $70 million loan outstanding) and uses the $50 million of net revenue to reduce the outstanding loan to $27 million. At the end of the third year, Chrysler owes $2.7 million in interest payments plus the $27 million worth of outstanding loan. It therefore has to pay $29.7 million. But net revenue in the third year is only $20 million, so Chrysler makes a loss of $9.7 million on this project. That is, by the end of the third year, Chrysler has to find an extra $9.7 million, compared with what would have been the case if the assembly line had not been purchased and operated.

Part (b) shows what happens if the interest rate

Table 25.4 Investment in Automobile Assembly Line

(a) Interest rate is 10 percent per year

	Loan outstanding	Interest payment	Amount repaid
Initially	$100,000,000	—	—
End of year 1	70,000,000	$10,000,000	$40,000,000
End of year 2	27,000,000	7,000,000	50,000,000
End of year 3	—	2,700,000	29,700,000

Loss: $9,700,000

(b) Interest rate is 5 percent per year

	Loan outstanding	Interest payment	Amount repaid
Initially	$100,000,000	—	—
End of year 1	65,000,000	$5,000,000	$40,000,000
End of year 2	18,250,000	3,250,000	50,000,000
End of year 3	—	912,500	19,162,500

Profit: $837,500

In part (a), the interest rate is 10 percent a year. The expected net revenue stream is too low to cover the total expense and the project is not worth undertaking. In part (b), the interest rate is 5 percent a year. The expected net revenue stream is sufficient to repay the initial amount borrowed, pay all the interest, and still leave a small profit. In this case, the project is worthwhile and is undertaken. The lower the interest rate, the larger is the number of projects that are profitable.

is 5 percent per year. In this case, Chrysler pays only $5 million in interest at the end of the first year and so can reduce its outstanding borrowing to $65 million. In the second year, the interest payment on the loan is $3.25 million. In this year, the loan outstanding is reduced to $18.25 million. In the third and final year of the project, the outstanding loan plus the interest on it amounts to $19.1625 million, which Chrysler repays. But the project brings in $20 million in that year, so Chrysler has $837,500 in pocket at the end of this project.

You can see that at an interest rate of 10 percent a year, it does not pay Chrysler to invest in this car assembly plant. At a 5 percent interest rate, it does pay. The lower the interest rate, the larger is the number of projects, such as the one considered here, that yield a positive net profit. Thus the lower the interest rate, the larger is the scale of investment.

Expected Inflation The higher the expected inflation rate, the greater is the amount of investment. Higher expected inflation brings higher expected future net revenue. And the larger the expected future net revenue relative to the initial cost of an investment project, the larger is the return on the project.

In the Chrysler example above, the new car assembly plant costs $100 million to build in the current year regardless of the inflation rate. But the higher the inflation rate, the faster car prices rise. Wages and other production costs rise faster as well. The gap between car prices and wages and other production costs rises at the same rate as the inflation rate. Thus higher inflation leads to higher net revenue and, at a given level of interest rates, more investment projects are profitable.

The effect of expected inflation on investment is opposite to that of the interest rate. There is an important consequence of these opposing effects on a firm's investment decision. It is that investment depends on the real interest rate. The **real interest rate** is the interest rate minus the expected inflation rate. That is, the real interest rate is the actual interest rate paid adjusted for the percentage change in the value of money arising from the expected inflation. You can see why it is the real interest rate that influences investment by considering again Chrysler's decision whether to build a $100 million automobile assembly line.

We saw that with a 10 percent interest rate, it does not pay to build the assembly line; with a 5 percent interest rate, it does. Suppose that the interest rate is 10 percent (as in Table 25.4a). But also suppose that prices are expected to rise by 5 percent a year. With rising prices, expected net revenue will also rise by 5 percent a year. With the extra expected net revenue, Chrysler will be able to repay more of the loan each year and cut its interest payments on the outstanding loan. The combined effect of a 10 percent interest rate and a 5 percent expected inflation rate is almost the same as the combined effect of a 5 percent interest rate and no expected inflation. That is, when the interest rate is 10 percent and the expected inflation rate is 5 percent, the profit after three years is approximately the same as in the case in which the interest rate is 5 percent and the expected inflation rate is zero.[4]

Thus, although investment is affected positively by lower interest rates and by higher expected inflation, we can combine these two influences into a single determinant of investment — the real interest rate. The lower the real interest rate, the higher is the level of investment.

Expected Profit The higher the expected profitability of new capital equipment, the greater is the amount of investment. To see why, consider Chrysler's assembly line once again. In deciding whether or not to build the assembly line, Chrysler has to work out its expected net revenue. To perform that calculation, it has to work out the expected total revenue from car sales, which in turn, is affected by its expectations of car prices and the share of the market that it can attain. Chrysler also has to figure out its expected operating costs, which include the wages of its assembly workers and the costs of the products that it buys from other producers. The larger the net revenue that it anticipates, the more profitable is the investment project that generates those net revenues, and the more likely is it that the project will be undertaken.

Depreciation *Depreciation* is the wearing out of existing capital equipment. The larger the stock of capital equipment and the older that stock, the larger is the amount of capital that wears out. Worn out capital is often, but not always, replaced. The larger the amount of capital that is depreciating, the larger the volume of investment to replace that worn out capital. Investment on new additions to plant and machinery and inventories plus replacement investment (investment that replaces worn-out or depreciated capital) is called *gross investment.* Additions to the capital stock — that is, gross investment minus depreciation — is called *net investment.*

Investment Demand

Investment demand is the relationship between the level of investment and the real interest rate, holding all other influences on the level of investment constant. The **investment demand schedule** is a list of the quantities of planned investment at each real interest rate, holding all other influences on investment constant. The **investment demand curve** graphs the relationship between the real interest rate and the level of planned investment, holding everything else constant. Some examples of investment demand schedules and investment demand curves appear in Fig. 25.6. The investment demand schedule and the position of the investment demand curve depend on the other influences on investment — expected profit and depreciation.

To calculate its expected profit on an investment, a firm has to do its best to foresee future events. The firm has to forecast the scale of demand for its output so that it can make a forecast of its revenue from sales. It has to forecast future technological developments and future prices of its inputs so that it can forecast its costs. Sometimes the firm will be pessimistic about the future. At other times it will be optimistic. Pessimistic expectations arise when a firm foresees poor general business conditions or when it expects rapid technological change that will make current technology obsolete. Expectations are optimistic when the firm foresees booming business conditions or when a new technology has become available that is not expected to be surpassed for a reasonable period of time. At yet other times, firms will be neither optimistic nor pessimistic. In such periods, profit expectations are average.

Fluctuations in firms' profit expectations are the main source of fluctuations in investment demand. The three investment demand schedules in the table in Fig. 25.6 give examples of investment demand under the three types of expectations. One example is with average profit expectations. In this case, if the real interest rate is 4 percent a year, investment is $100 billion. If the real interest rate decreases to 2 percent a year, investment increases to $120 billion. If the real interest rate increases to 6 percent a year, investment decreases to $80 billion. The second example is with optimistic profit expectations. In this case, investment is higher at each interest rate than it is when expectations are average. The third case is with pessimistic profit expectations. In this case, investment is lower at each interest rate than with average expectations.

The investment demand curve is shown in Fig. 25.6. In part (a), the investment demand curve (*ID*) is that for average expected profit. Each point (*a* through *c*) corresponds to a row in the table. A change in the real interest rate causes a movement along the investment demand curve. Thus if the real interest rate is 4 percent a year, planned investment is

[4] This proposition is demonstrated in the appendix to this chapter.

Figure 25.6 The Investment Demand Schedule and Investment Demand Curve

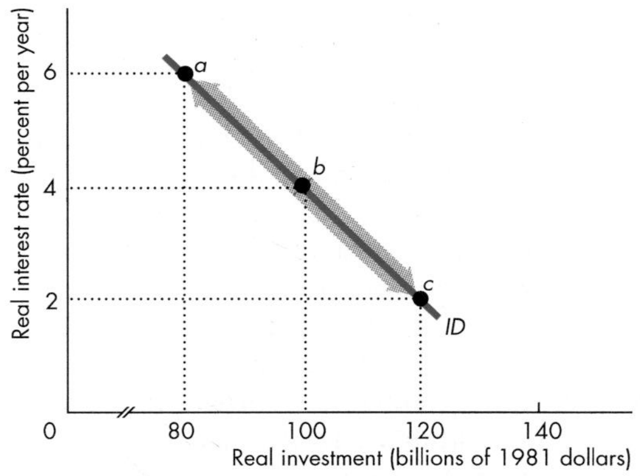

(a) The effect of a change in real interest rate

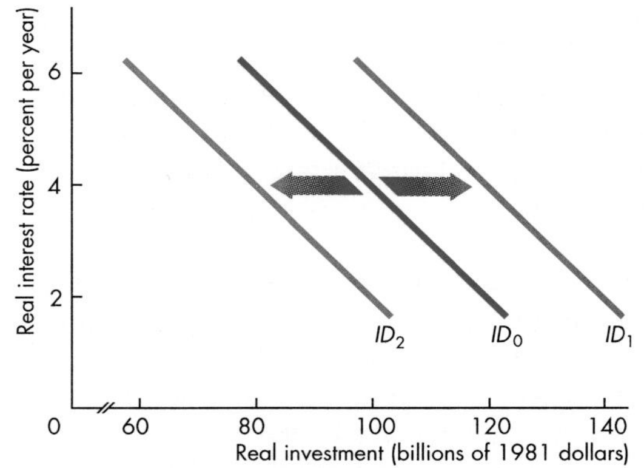

(b) The effect of a change in profit expectations

	Real interest rate (percent per year)	Real investment (billions of 1981 dollars)		
		Pessimistic	**Average**	**Optimistic**
a	6	60	80	100
b	4	80	100	120
c	2	100	120	140

The investment demand schedule lists the quantities of aggregate planned investment at each real interest rate. The table shows three investment demand schedules. As the real interest rate decreases from 6 percent a year to 2 percent a year, planned investment increases from \$80 billion to \$120 billion. The investment demand curve graphs the investment demand schedule in part (a). As the real interest rate rises from 2 percent to 6 percent, there is a movement along the investment demand curve from *c* to *a*. Investment plans are affected by the state of expectations of future profit. When profit expectations are average, the investment demand curve is ID_0. Swings in expectations about future profit lead to shifts in the investment demand curve. If there is optimism about future profit, planned investment increases at each real interest rate and the investment demand curve shifts to the right to ID_1. If there is pessimism about future profit, planned investment decreases at each real interest rate and the investment demand curve shifts to the left to ID_2.

\$100 billion. If the interest rate rises to 6 percent a year, there is a movement up the investment demand curve (see the blue arrow) and investment decreases to \$80 billion. If the interest rate falls to 2 percent a year, there is a movement down the investment demand curve (see the blue arrow), and investment increases to \$120 billion.

The effects of profit expectations are shown in Fig. 25.6 (b). A change in profit expectations shifts the investment demand curve. The demand curve ID_0 represents average expected profit. When profit expectations become optimistic, the investment demand curve shifts to the right, from ID_0 to ID_1. When profit expectations become pessimistic, the investment demand curve shifts to the left, from ID_0 to ID_2.

The investment demand curve also shifts when there is a change in the amount of investment to replace depreciated capital. This influence leads to a steady rightward shift in the *ID* curve.

There is a special theory of shifts in the investment demand curve called the acceleration principle. Let's see what that principle is.

The Acceleration Principle

The **acceleration principle** states that the investment demand curve shifts in response to *changes* in the level of real GDP. When the growth rate of real GDP increases, the investment demand curve shifts to the right. When the growth rate of real GDP decreases, the investment demand curve shifts to the left. This mechanism is called the accelerator. You can perhaps see the reason for the name "accelerator." When the growth rate of real GDP *speeds up*, the investment demand curve shifts to the right. When the growth rate of real GDP *slows down*, the investment demand curve shifts to the left. There are two possible explanations for the acceleration principle. They are:

- Capital stock adjustment
- Profit expectations and the business cycle

The explanation for the acceleration principle based on capital stock adjustment arises from the idea that there is a stable relationship between the *level* of real GDP and the *stock* of capital. Investment is the *change* in the *stock* of capital. A change in the *level* changes the desired *stock* of capital. To change the capital stock, investment takes place. The larger the change in real GDP, the greater is the desired change in the capital stock and, therefore, the greater is the level of investment.

The second explanation for the acceleration principle is the influence of the business cycle on profit expectations. We've already seen that profit expectations are an important factor influencing the level of investment demand. We identified three cases of profit expectations: optimistic, pessimistic, and average. Optimistic expectations are likely to occur when real GDP is rising rapidly. In such circumstances, expectations for profit in the near future are high. With the economy booming, sales are expected to rise, and with rising sales, profit is also expected to rise. Thus rapidly expanding real GDP brings optimism about future profit and higher investment demand. When real GDP is rising slowly or when it is falling as in a recession, expectations for profit in the immediate future are pessimistic. With pessimistic profit expectations, the investment demand declines. Swings in the pace of change of real GDP that generate swings in profit expectations produce fluctuations in investment demand.

R E V I E W

Investment depends on the real interest rate, profit expectations, and the scale of replacement of depreciated capital. Other things held constant, the lower the real interest rate, the higher is the level of investment. With optimistic profit expectations, the investment demand curve shifts to the right; with pessimistic profit expectations, it shifts to the left. Profit expectations are influenced by the business cycle. When the economy is expanding quickly, profit expectations are optimistic and investment demand is high. When the economy is expanding slowly or contracting, profit expectations are pessimistic and investment demand is low. Investment to replace depreciated capital grows steady over time. ■

We've just studied the theory of investment demand. Let's now see how that theory helps us to understand the fluctuations in investment that occur in the Canadian economy.

Investment Demand in Canada

As we saw in Fig. 25.2, investment is one of the most volatile components of aggregate expenditure. In some years, investment is as much as 25 percent of GDP and in others as little as 17 percent. Let's see how we can interpret these fluctuations in investment using the theory of investment demand that we have just been studying.

We'll begin by looking at Fig. 25.7(a). It shows investment (in billions of 1981 dollars) between 1969 and 1989. It also shows the way in which gross investment is divided between net investment and depreciation (the replacement of depreciated capital). As you can see, both depreciation and gross investment increase steadily over time. Depreciation follows a very smooth path, reflecting the fact that the capital stock grows steadily and smoothly. Net investment is the component of investment that fluctuates. You can see that fluctuation as the blue area between gross investment and depreciation.

Figure 25.7 Investment and the Real Interest Rate in Canada

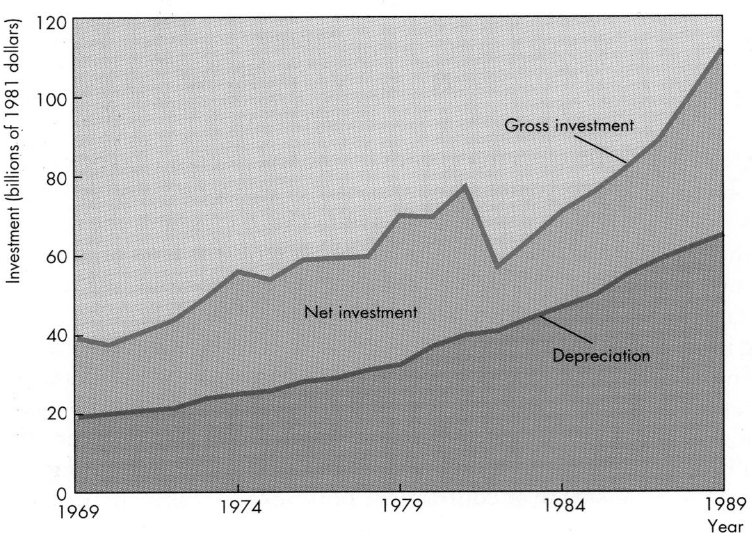

(a) Gross and net investment

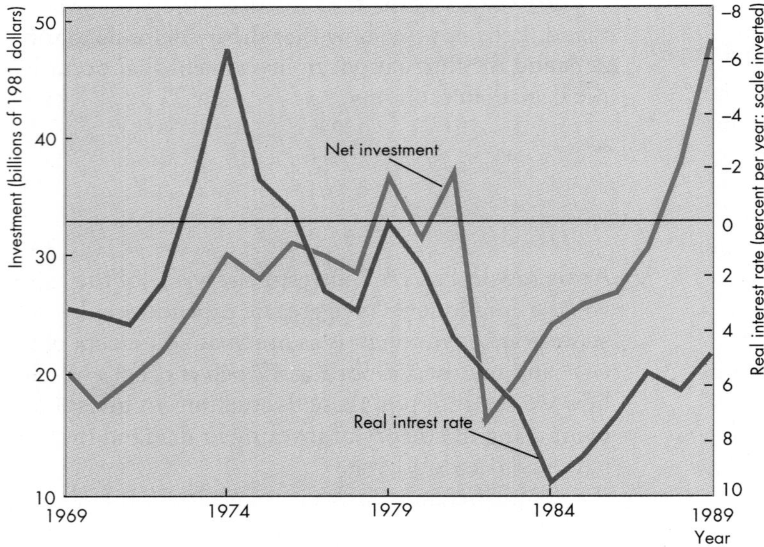

(b) Net investment and the real interest rate

In part (a), gross investment is separated into two parts — the replacement of depreciated capital, which grows steadily, and net investment, which fluctuates.

In part (b), net investment fluctuates in sympathy with the real interest rate. When the real interest rate is high (as measured on the inverted scale on the right-hand vertical axis), net investment is low.

The theory that we have been studying predicts that fluctuations in investment result from fluctuations in the real interest rate and in expectations of future profit. What is the relative importance of these two factors? Figure 25.7(b) partly answers this question. It leaves out of the picture the steady increase in investment arising from depreciation and focuses on net investment and the real interest rate. The real interest rate, which is measured on the right-hand scale, is inverted. That is, the interest rate increases as we move down the right-hand scale. Thus when the real interest rate line is close to the bottom of the figure, real interest rates are high and when the line is close to the top of the figure, real interest rates are low.

There is a visible relationship between net investment and the real interest rate, as predicted by the theory. But there are also some important changes in net investment that are independent of changes in the real interest rate. These are caused by fluctuations in profit expectations. We can see these fluctuations more directly by looking at Fig. 25.8. Each point in the figure represents a value of the real interest rate and net investment for a given year. The two investment demand curves describe the relationship between net investment and the real interest rate for different profit expectations. The curve labelled ID_{opt} is the investment demand curve when expectations are optimistic, and the curve labelled ID_{pes} represents the relationship when profit expectations are pessimistic. As you can see, most of the points lie reasonably close to one of these two curves.

Figure 25.8 The Canadian Investment Demand Curve

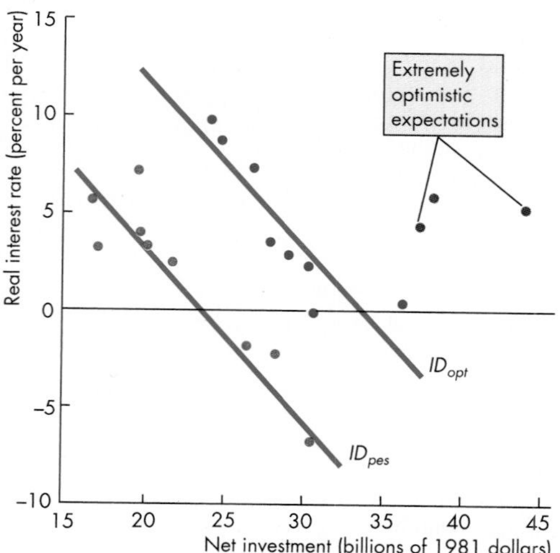

Each dot in the figure represents the level of net investment and the real interest rate in a given year. With pessimistic profit expectations, the Canadian investment demand curve is ID_{pes}. With optimistic profit expectations, the Canadian investment demand curve is ID_{opt}. When profit expectations are extremely optimistic, as they were in the late 1980s, the investment demand curve lies further to the right than ID_{opt}. For given profit expectations, a change in the real interest rate leads to a movement along the investment demand curve. As profit expectations change, the investment demand curve shifts.

The Booming Eighties The late 1980s were years of extremely optimistic profit expectations. They were years in which both investment and the real interest rate were high and in which the investment demand curve was further to the right than those shown. Why was investment demand so strong during the late 1980s? The answer probably lies in the dramatic technological advances that occurred in the electronic sector. The development of the low cost microchip opened up an amazing array of applications for computer technology in manufacturing, transportation and communication, and in consumer products which were developed and marketed during the second half of the 1980s resulting in a prolonged investment boom comparable to that of 200 years earlier when steam power was first harnessed. The optimistic expectations of the 1980s seem to have persisted into 1990 (see Reading Between the Lines, pp. 672-673).

Thus, as predicted by the theory, investment is high, on the average, when real interest rates are low. The investment demand curve slopes downward. But large fluctuations in investment occur independently of changes in the real interest rate. The investment demand curve shifts. It shifts to the right (to pass through the green and purple points) in years of optimism about future profits, and it shifts to the left (to pass through the red points) in years of pessimism.

Fluctuations in the level of investment have important effects on the economy, regardless of whether they are generated by shifts in the investment demand curve or movements along it. We'll find out what some of those effects are in Chapter 26. Before doing that, we need to look at the last private component of aggregate expenditure — net exports.

Net Exports

Net exports is the expenditure by foreigners on Canadian-produced goods and services minus the expenditure by Canadian residents on foreign-produced goods and services. That is, net exports is the value of Canadian exports minus the value of imports. *Exports* are the sales of goods and

Investment Demand

Business investment plans show economy strong: Wilson

Finance Minister Michael Wilson says stronger-than-expected investment intentions by business back up his contention that the economy is not on the brink of a recession.

The investment intentions, published in a survey by Statistics Canada yesterday, show business and government plan to increase investment spending by an average of 7.4 per cent in 1990, compared with 1989.

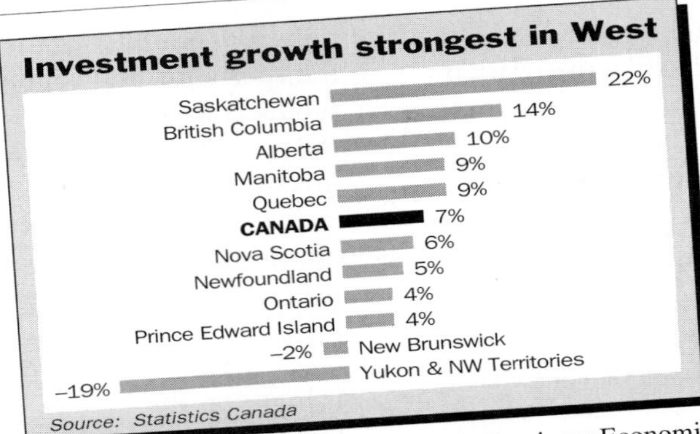

A further breakdown shows spending on machinery and equipment is estimated to rise by 10 per cent, spending on non-residential construction is expected to increase 7.5 per cent and spending on housing to rise 5.9 per cent.

"I guess it indicates what I've been saying all along that this economy still has some steam in it and those people who talk about recession are not noticing what's happening in the economy," Mr. Wilson said yesterday.

He acknowledged that the investment intentions expressed in the survey, which was conducted between November and early February, were higher than those contained in his Feb. 20 budget.

The budget forecast called for an increase of only 3.9 per cent in non-residential construction by business, a rise of 4.3 per cent in purchases of machinery and equipment and a drop of 3 per cent in housing construction.

The budget forecast overall economic growth in Canada would average 1.3 per cent this year and 3 per cent in 1991. In 1989, the Canadian economy expanded by 2.9 per cent.

"Everyone is going to be going away and recalculating their numbers now," said Fred Morley, an economist with the Atlantic Provinces Economic Council.

Mr. Morley said many forecasters thought that in 1990 both business investment and consumer spending would be weak and export growth would be the main driving force in the economy. However, yesterday's figures, if they are not revised later this year, seem to indicate that business investment will remain strong.

Phillip Cross, chief of current analysis at Statscan [Statistics Canada], says continued investment by business is an international phenomenon that is occurring in most industrialized countries despite rising interest rates.

***The Globe and Mail*, March 8, 1990**

By Madelaine Drohan

The Essence of the Story

- Statistics Canada's investment intentions survey published in March 1990 showed the following increases for planned investment spending by business and government in 1990 compared with 1989:
  - Machinery and equipment, 10 per cent
  - Non-residential construction, 7.5 per cent
  - Housing, 5.9 per cent
  - Average, 7.4 per cent
- The finance minister said that these stronger-than-expected investment intentions by business showed the economy to be strong and not on the brink of a recession.
- Fred Morley, an economist with the Atlantic Provinces Economic Council, said many forecasters had previously thought that business investment spending would be weak in 1990 and would now have to revise their forecasts.
- Phillip Cross, chief of current analysis at Statscan, said strong business investment is occurring in most industrialized countries despite rising interest rates.

Background and Analysis

- The real interest rates paid by corporations on the long-term loans used to finance their investment expenditure in 1989 and 1990 were the following:

	1989	1990
Corporate long-term bond rate	10.5	11.5
Forcasted inflation rate	5.0	5.0
Real interest rate	5.5	6.5

- The Statistics Canada investment survey gives information about *gross investment* intentions measured in *current dollars.*

- The following table gives our estimates of the implications of the Statscan survey both for gross investment and *net investment* in *constant 1981 dollars*:

	1989	1990
	(millions of dollars)	
Gross investment, current dollars	134	144
Gross investment, constant dollars	114	120
Net investment, constant dollars	49	51

- The figure shows the relationship between the *real interest rate* and *real net investment* between 1969 and 1989, and between the *real interest rate* and *planned investment* for 1990.

- The years shown as red dots are those of pessimistic expectations and a low level of investment demand. The years shown as blue dots are those of average expectations and an average level of investment demand. The years shown as green dots are those of optimistic expectations and of high investment demand.

- The figure also shows investment demand curves for 1989 and 1990, years of high investment demand. Compared with the years 1969 to 1988, investment was high in 1989 and is forecasted to be even higher in 1990. The investment demand curve was unusually far to the right in 1989 and shifted even further to the right in 1990.

- Possible explanations for the high and increasing level of investment are that firms are taking advantage of new opportunities arising from
  - The Canada-United States Free Trade Agreement.
  - The economic unification of Western Europe.
  - The opening up of markets in the USSR and Eastern Europe.
  - Continuing rapid cost saving advances in technology.
  - Continued strong economic expansion in Germany, Japan, and other Pacific Rim countries.

All of these factors could explain why investment demand remains strong, not only in Canada but also around the world.

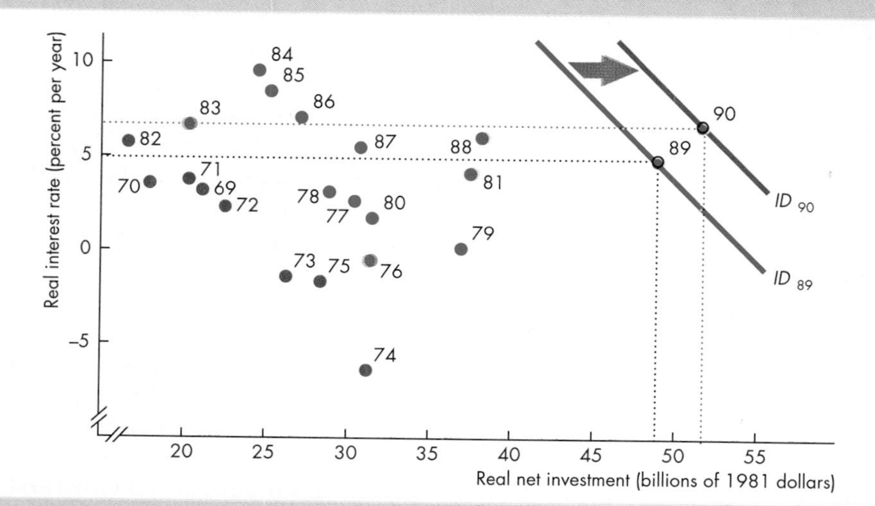

services produced in Canada to the rest of the world. *Imports* are the purchase of goods produced in the rest of the world by firms and households in Canada.

Exports

Exports are determined by decisions made in the rest of the world. They are influenced by four main factors:

- GDP in the rest of the world
- The degree of international specialization
- Prices of Canadian-made goods relative to the prices of similar goods made in other countries
- Foreign exchange rates

Other things being equal, the higher the level of real GDP in the rest of the world, the greater is the demand by foreigners for Canadian-made goods and services. For example, an economic boom in Japan increases that country's demand for B.C. lumber, Alberta wheat, and Ontario machine tools and thus increases Canada's exports. A recession in Japan cuts its demand for those goods and thus decreases Canada's exports.

Also, the greater the degree of specialization in the world economy, the larger is the volume of exports, other things being equal. Over time, international specialization has been increasing. For example, Canada has become a dominant producer of lumber, pulp, paper, wheat, and high-technology machine tools. The world aircraft industry is now heavily concentrated in the United States and Western Europe. Many goods and services, notably in the consumer electronics industry, that were once made in North America in large quantities are now made almost exclusively in Japan, Hong Kong, and other countries on the Asian rim of the Pacific Ocean.

Next, other things being equal, the lower the price of Canadian-made goods relative to the prices of similar goods made in other countries, the greater is the quantity of Canadian exports.

Finally, and again other things being equal, the lower the value of the Canadian dollar, the larger is the quantity of Canadian exports. For example, as the Canadian dollar fell in value against the German mark and the Japanese yen in 1987, the demand for Canadian-made goods by those two countries increased sharply.

Imports

Imports are determined by four main factors:

- Canada's real GDP
- The degree of international specialization
- Prices of foreign-made goods relative to the prices of similar goods made in Canada
- Foreign exchange rates

Other things being equal, the higher the level of Canada's real GDP, the larger is the quantity of Canadian imports. For example, the long period of sustained income growth in Canada between 1983 and 1987 brought a huge increase in Canadian imports.

Also, the higher the degree of international specialization, the larger is the volume of Canadian imports, other things being equal. For example, there is a high degree of international specialization in the production of VCRs. As a consequence, all the VCRs sold in Canada are now produced in other countries — mainly Japan and Korea.

Finally, and again other things being equal, the higher the prices of Canadian-made goods and services relative to the prices of similar foreign-made goods and services and the higher the value of the Canadian dollar, the larger is the quantity of Canadian imports. Although high real GDP growth in Canada in 1985 and 1986 produced an increase in imports, that increase was less severe than it otherwise would have been because of the fall in the value of the Canadian dollar. The falling dollar made foreign-made goods more expensive and so slowed down, to some degree, the growth of Canadian imports.

Net Export Function

The **net export function** is the relationship between net exports and Canadian real GDP, holding constant real GDP in the rest of the world, prices, and the exchange rate. The net export function can also be described by a net export schedule, which lists the level of net exports at each level of real GDP with everything else held constant. The table in Fig. 25.9 gives an example of a net export schedule.

In the table, exports are a constant $152 billion regardless of the level of real GDP. Imports increase by $0.34 billion for each $1 billion increase in real GDP. Net exports, the difference between exports and imports, is shown in the final column of the table. When real GDP is $100 billion, net exports are $118 billion. Net exports decline as real GDP rises. At a real GDP of $447 billion, net exports are zero, and at real GDP levels higher than that, net exports become increasingly negative (imports exceed exports).

Exports and imports are graphed in Fig. 25.9(a)

Figure 25.9 Net Export Schedule and Net Export Function

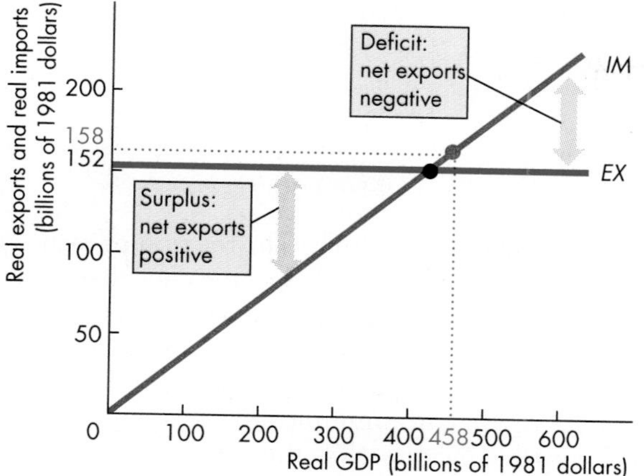

(a) Real exports and real imports

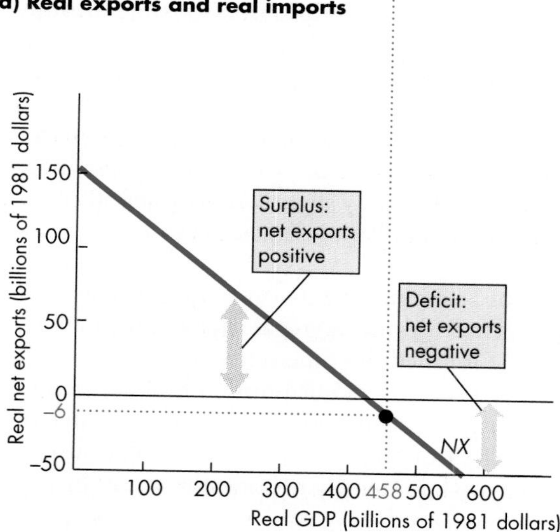

(b) Real net exports

Real GDP (*Y*)	Real exports (*EX*)	Real imports (*IM*)	Real net exports (*EX – IM*)
	(billions of 1981 dollars)		
0	152	0	152
100	152	34	118
200	152	68	84
300	152	102	50
400	152	136	16
500	152	170	−18
600	152	204	−52

The net export schedule in the table shows the relationship between real net exports and real GDP. Real net exports is equal to real exports (*EX*) minus real imports (*IM*). Exports are independent of real GDP, but imports rise as real GDP rises. In the table, imports are 34 percent of real GDP. Net exports fall as GDP rises. Part (a) graphs the export and import schedules. Since exports are independent of real GDP, they are graphed as a horizontal line. Since imports rise as real GDP rises, they appear as an upward-sloping line. The vertical gap between the export curve and the import curve represents net exports. When exports exceed imports, net exports are positive. When imports exceed exports net exports are negative. Net exports are graphed in part (b) of the figure. The net export function is downward sloping because the import curve is upward sloping. The real GDP level at which the net export function intersects the horizontal axis in part (b) is the same as that at which the import curve intersects the export curve in part (a). That level of real GDP is $447 billion. Below that level of real GDP there is a surplus (net exports are positive) and above it there is a deficit (net exports are negative). In 1988, when real GDP was $458 billion, imports exceeded exports and net exports were –$6 billion.

and the net exports function is graphed in Fig. 25(b). By comparing part (a) and part (b) you can see that when exports exceed imports, net exports are positive (there is a surplus) and when imports exceed exports, net exports are negative (there is a deficit). When real GDP is $447 billion, there is a balance between exports and imports.

The data in Fig. 25.9 are based on the Canadian economy in 1989. In that year, real GDP was $458 billion, exports were $152 billion, imports were $158 billion, and net exports were –$6 billion, as highlighted in the figure.

The position of the net export function depends on real GDP in the rest of the world, on the degree of international specialization, and on prices in Canada compared with those in the rest of the world. If real GDP in the rest of the world increases, the net export function shifts upward. If Canadian goods become cheap relative to goods in the rest of the world, the net export function also shifts upward. A change in the degree of international specialization has an ambiguous effect on the position of the net export function. If Canada becomes more specialized in goods for which there is an increase in world demand, the net export function shifts upward.

If Canadian demand increases for goods in which the rest of the world specializes, the net export function shifts downward.

- In this chapter, we've studied the factors that influence private expenditure decisions, looking at each item of aggregate expenditure in isolation from the others. In the next chapter, we'll study the interactions between the components of aggregate expenditure.

SUMMARY

The Components of Aggregate Expenditure

The components of aggregate expenditure are:

- Consumption expenditure
- Investment
- Government purchases of goods and services
- Net exports

The main component of aggregate expenditure is consumption expenditure. On the average, 55 percent of GDP comes from consumption expenditure, 20 percent from investment, and 23 percent from government purchases of goods and services. Net exports average 3 percent of GDP.

The components of aggregate expenditure that fluctuate most are investment and net exports. (pp. 651-654)

Consumption Expenditure and Saving

Consumption expenditure is influenced by five factors:

- Disposable income
- Expected future income
- Stage in life
- Degree of patience
- Interest rates

The most important influence on consumption expenditure is disposable income. As disposable income increases, so does consumption expenditure. The relationship between consumption expenditure and disposable income is called the consumption function. As disposable income increases, so does saving. The relationship between saving and disposable income is called the saving function. At low levels of disposable income, consumption expenditure exceeds disposable income, which means that saving is negative (dissaving occurs). As disposable income increases, consumption increases but by less than the increase in disposable income. The fraction of each additional dollar of disposable income consumed is called the marginal propensity to consume. The fraction of each additional dollar of disposable income saved is called the marginal propensity to save. All the influences on consumption and saving, other than disposable income, shift the consumption and saving functions.

If we look at variations in disposable income and consumption expenditure across families, we see that low-income families spend 84 cents of each additional dollar of disposable income on consumption goods and services. As incomes increase, the marginal propensity to consume decreases; the highest-income families consume only slightly more than 50 cents of each additional dollar of disposable income, on the average.

The relationship between aggregate consumption expenditure and aggregate disposable income over time is called the time-series consumption function. The time-series consumption function shows how aggregate consumption varies as disposable income varies from one year to the next. The average and marginal propensity to consume out of disposable income, on the average, is 0.9. But there is a large variation around that average across individual families.

The relationship between real consumption expenditure and real GDP is called the aggregate consumption function. To calculate the aggregate consumption function, we take into account the difference between real disposable income and real GDP. Disposable income equals GDP plus transfer payments minus taxes. Transfer payments minus taxes are a fairly stable percentage of GDP. As a result, since consumption is a fairly stable percentage of disposable income, it is also a fairly stable percentage of GDP. Taxes net of transfers payments are approximately 40 percent of GDP. Equivalently, disposable income is approximately 60 percent of GDP. Since the marginal propensity to consume out of disposable income is 0.9 and since disposable income is

60 percent of GDP, the marginal propensity to consume out of GDP is 54 percent, on the average. (pp. 654-665)

Investment

The level of investment depends on

- Interest rates.
- Expected inflation.
- Expected profit.
- Depreciation.

The lower the interest rate, the higher is the level of investment; the higher the expected inflation rate, the greater is the level of investment. The higher the expected profit, the greater is the volume of investment. Interest rates and expected inflation have equal and opposite effects on investment. As a consequence, the two effects can be combined into a real interest rate effect. The higher the real interest rate, the lower is the volume of investment.

The main influence on investment demand is fluctuations in profit expectations. Sometimes expectations are optimistic, and at other times they are pessimistic. Swings in the degree of optimism and pessimism lead to shifts in the investment demand curve. Swings in profit expectations are closely associated with business cycle fluctuations. When the economy is in an expansion phase, profit expectations are optimistic and investment is high. When the economy is in a contraction phase, profit expectations are pessimistic and investment is low. (pp. 665-671)

Net Exports

Net exports are the difference between exports and imports. Exports are determined by decisions made in the rest of the world and are influenced by GDP in the rest of the world, the degree of international specialization, Canadian prices relative to prices of similar goods made in other countries, and the foreign exchange rate. Imports are determined by Canadian real GDP, the degree of international specialization, Canadian prices relative to prices of similar goods made in other countries, and the foreign exchange rate.

The net export function shows the relationship between net exports and Canadian real GDP, holding constant all the other influences on exports and imports. (pp. 671-676)

KEY ELEMENTS

Key Terms

Acceleration principle, 669
Aggregate consumption function, 660
Average propensity to consume, 656
Average propensity to save, 656
Consumption function, 654
Dissaving, 655
Investment demand, 667
Investment demand curve, 667
Investment demand schedule, 667
Marginal propensity to consume, 657
Marginal propensity to save, 657
Net export function, 674
Real interest rate, 666
Saving function, 654
Time-series consumption function, 660

Key Figures and Tables 

REVIEW QUESTIONS

1 What are the components of aggregate expenditure?

2 Which component of aggregate expenditure is the largest?

3 Which components of aggregate expenditure fluctuate the most?

4 What is the consumption function?

5 What is the fundamental determinant of consumption?

6 What is the difference between disposable income and GDP?

7 What does the term "marginal propensity to consume" mean? Why is it less than 1?

8 What is the saving function? What is the relationship between the saving function and the consumption function?

9 What determines investment? Why does investment increase as the real interest rate falls?

10 What is the effect of the following on Canadian net exports:

a) An increase in Canadian GDP?

b) An increase in Japanese GDP?

c) A rise in the price of Japanese-made cars with no change in the price of Canadian-made cars?

PROBLEMS

1 You are given the following information about the Batman family (Batman and Robin):

Disposable income (dollars per year)	Consumption expenditure (dollars per year)
0	10,000
10,000	15,000
20,000	20,000
30,000	25,000
40,000	30,000

a) Calculate Batman and Robin's marginal propensity to consume.

b) Calculate the average propensity to consume at each level of disposable income.

c) Calculate how much the Batman family saves at each level of disposable income.

d) Calculate their marginal propensity to save.

e) Calculate their average propensity to save at each level of disposable income.

2 A car assembly plant can be built for $10 million. It will have a life of five years and, at the end of that time, a scrap value of $1 million. The firm will have to hire labour at a cost of $1 million a year and buy parts and fuel costing another $1 million. If the firm builds the plant, it will be able to produce cars that will sell for $5 million each year. Will it pay the firm to invest in this new production line at the following interest rates:

a) 2 percent a year?

b) 5 percent a year?

c) 10 percent a year?

3 You are given the following information about a hypothetical economy. The marginal propensity to consume out of disposable income is 0.8, and taxes net of transfer payments are one-quarter of national income. What is the marginal propensity to consume out of GDP in this economy?

Appendix to Chapter 25

Net Present Value and Investment

To decide whether or not to undertake an investment project, we may calculate the project's net present value.

Calculating Net Present Value

Net present value is the sum of the present value of the stream of payments and revenue generated by an investment project. The *present value* of a future sum of money is the sum that, if invested in the present, will accumulate to the future sum if it earns compound interest at a given rate. If the net present value of an investment project is positive, it pays to undertake the investment. If the net present value is negative, it does not pay to undertake the investment. Let's calculate a net present value.

An investment of \$2,775 is expected to yield the future stream of earnings of \$1,000 a year for three years. Thus an initial payment of \$2,775 dollars results in a future revenue of \$1,000 in each of three years. Obviously, more comes back than is paid out. But the returns come later. To decide whether enough flows in later, we calculate the project's net present value. To calculate that net present value, we use the following formula, where r is the interest rate:

$$NPV = \frac{\$1,000}{(1+r)} + \frac{\$1,000}{(1+r)^2} + \frac{\$1,000}{(1+r)^3} - \$2,775$$

The higher the interest rate, the lower is the net present value. Table A25.1 sets out some calculations for three different interest rates. Part (a), uses an interest rate of 4 percent a year. In this case, the net present value is zero. Let's see how that present value is calculated by using the formula. The initial cost of the project (\$2,775) is paid out today, so its present value is exactly the same as the amount spent. The first \$1,000 of revenue from the project is received one year in the future. Its present value is \$961. That is, if \$961 is invested today at an interest rate of 4 percent a year, it accumulates to \$1,000 one year from today. The next \$1,000 is received two years hence. Its present value is \$925. That is, if \$925 is invested today for a two-year period at an interest rate of 4 percent a year, it accumulates to \$1,000 by the end of that period. Finally, the last \$1,000 is received three years hence and has a present value of \$889. If \$889 is invested today at an interest rate of 4 percent a year, it accumulates to \$1,000 after three years. Adding these present values together and subtracting the present value of the initial cost of the project gives the overall net present value for the project, which, at an interest rate of 4 percent a year, is zero.

Part (b) calculates the net present value at a lower interest rate — 2 percent a year. In this case, the net present value of the project is positive at \$108. Part (c) calculates the net present value at an

Table A25.1 Net Present Value of an Investment Project

	Dollars paid	Dollars received	Present value (dollars)
(a) Interest rate: 4 percent per year			
Initial cost of project	2,775		–2,775
Revenue 1 year in the future		1,000	961
Revenue 2 years in the future		1,000	925
Revenue 3 years in the furture		1,000	889
Net present value:			0
(b) Interest rate: 2 percent per year			
Initial cost of project	2,775		–2,775
Revenue 1 year in the future		1,000	980
Revenue 2 years in the future		1,000	961
Revenue 3 years in the future		1,000	942
Net present value:			108
(c) Interest rate: 6 percent per year			
Initial cost of project	2,775		–2,775
Revenue 1 year in the future		1,000	943
Revenue 2 years in the future		1,000	890
Revenue 3 years in the future		1,000	840
Net present value:			–102

interest rate of 6 percent a year. This net present value is –$102.

At any interest rate lower than 4 percent a year, it pays to undertake this investment project. But at an interest rate highter than 4 percent a year, it does not pay to invest in the project.

Investment projects differ in their initial capital costs and in the revenue streams that they generate. To decide which projects to undertake, a firm calculates the net present value of each project using the current interest rate at which it can borrow. All those projects that have a positive net present value are undertaken and all those that have a negative net present value are rejected. The lower the interest rate at which the firm can borrow, the larger is the number of projects that have a positive net present value and so the larger is the number of projects undertaken and the larger is the firm's investment.

Expected Inflation and Real Interest Rate

The real interest rate is the interest rate that people expect to earn after taking into account changes in the value of money. If you lend a dollar at an annual interest rate of r, you will have $1 + r$ dollars at the end of the year. If prices are expected to rise at an annual rate of π, you will need $1 + \pi$ dollars at the end of the year to buy what one dollar buys today. Your $1 + r$ dollars will only really be worth $(1 + r)/(1 + \pi)$ dollars. The interest that you have really earned is the amount that your money is really worth — $(1 + r)/(1 + \pi)$ — minus the dollar that you lent. That is:

$$\text{Real interest rate} = \frac{(1+r)}{(1+\pi)} - 1$$

In this formula, r is the interest rate (sometimes called the nominal interest rate) and π is the expected inflation rate. You can interpret this formula most easily by considering the case in which the interest rate and the expected inflation rate are the same. Suppose that the interest rate and the expected inflation rate are each 6 percent a year. Then the formula tells us that

$$\text{Real interest rate} = \frac{1.06}{1.06} - 1$$

$$= 0$$

That is, the interest that is paid when the interest rate is 6 percent a year is enough to compensate for only the expected fall in the value of money, which means that no "real" interest is paid.

Let's do one more calculation. If the interest rate is 6 percent a year and the expected inflation rate is 1.92 percent a year, the real interest rate is 4 percent a year. To see this, put the numbers for interest rate and the expected inflation rate into the formula. We obtain:

$$\text{Real interest rate} = \frac{1.06}{1.0192} - 1$$

$$= 0.04 \text{ (or 4 percent)}$$

Let's work out the net present value when the interest rate is 6 percent a year and the expected inflation rate is 1.92 percent a year, so that the real interest rate is 4 percent a year. Table A25.2 summarizes the calculations. As before, the project costs $2,775. The expected revenue at the end of the first year is now higher because of inflation. With inflation expected to be running at 1.92 percent a year, revenue is expected to be $1,019. The present value of $1,019 at a 6 percent interest rate is $961. That is, if $961 is invested today at an interest rate of 6 percent a year, it accumulates to $1,019 after one year. At the end of the second year, the firm expects to receive $1,039. That is, over a two-year period, prices are expected to increase by 3.9 percent. The present value of $1,039 two years hence is $925. That is, if $925 is invested today at an interest rate of 6 percent a year, it accumulates to $1,039 after two years. With inflation expected to continue into the third year at the same rate, revenue is expected to increase to $1,059. The present value of $1,059 received three years in the future at an interest rate of 6 percent is $889. That is, if $889 is invested today at an interest rate of 6 percent a year, it accumulates to $1,059 three years in the future.

Table A25.2 Present Value, Inflation, and the Real Interest Rate

Interest rate: 6 percent per year

Expected inflation rate: 1.92 percent per year

Real interest rate: 4 percent per year

	Current dollars	Real dollars	Present value (dollars)
Initial cost of project	–2,775	–2,775	–2,775
Expected revenue 1 year in the future	1,019	1,000	961
Expected revenue 2 years in the future	1,039	1,000	925
Expected revenue 3 years in the future	1,059	1,000	889
Net present value:			0

Adding the present value of the income stream and subtracting the present value of the cost of the project gives the net present value of the project. That net present value is zero. Notice that when the interest rate is 6 percent a year and expected inflation is 1.92 percent a year, we obtain exactly the same net present value as we did in Table A25.1 with no inflation and an interest rate of 4 percent a year. But notice also that the real interest rate in Table A25.2 is 4 percent a year. Comparing the numbers in Tables A25.1 and A25.2, you can see that the net present value of an investment project depends on the real interest rate. That is, the project that we are considering here has a net present value of zero when the real interest rate is 4 percent a year. It makes no difference whether that real interest rate arises from an actual interest rate of 4 percent a year and no inflation or an actual interest rate of 6 percent a year and 1.92 percent inflation. Either way, the net present value of the project is zero. The lower the real interest rate, the larger is the number of projects that have a positive net present value and that are undertaken.

Investment Demand

The investment demand schedule of the firm is obtained by calculating the total cost of all the projects that have a positive net present value at each interest rate. As the interest rate falls, the number of projects that are undertaken increases and the total amount of investment undertaken increases. Thus the firm's investment demand schedule shows an increase in the amount of investment as the real interest rate falls. Adding up all the investment projects of all the firms in the economy produces the aggregate investment demand schedule.

The net present value calculation of an investment project depends on the firm's best forecast of the future stream of revenue generated by the project. If firms have optimistic expectations, a larger number of projects will have positive net present values at each interest rate. If firms have pessimistic expectations about future revenue, a smaller number of projects will have positive net present values. Thus the number of projects that are undertaken at each interest rate depends on the degree of optimism or pessimism embodied in firms' forecasts of future revenue streams. Changes in the degree of optimism and pessimism lead to shifts in investment demand schedules.

CHAPTER 26

Expenditure and Income

After studying this chapter, you will be able to:

- Derive the aggregate expenditure function.
- Distinguish between autonomous expenditure and induced expenditure.
- Explain how the level of aggregate expenditure is determined.
- Define and calculate the multiplier.
- Explain why changes in investment and exports lead to changes in consumption expenditure and have multiplier effects on aggregate expenditure.
- Explain how the government can stabilize aggregate expenditure and how taxes and transfer payments act as automatic stabilizers.
- Explain the relationship between the aggregate expenditure curve and the aggregate demand curve.

Economic Amplifier or Shock Absorber?

MICK JAGGER BREATHES into a microphone at a barely audible whisper. The electronic signal picked up by the sensitive instrument travels along wires to a huge bank of amplifiers and then through high-fidelity speakers to the ears of 50,000 fans spread out across the Skydome in Toronto. Moving to a louder passage, Jagger increases the volume of his voice and now, through the magic of electronic amplification, it booms across the stadium, drowning out every other sound. ■ Gary Filmon, the premier of Manitoba, is being driven to a business meeting along one of Winnipeg's less well-repaired highways. (Winnipeg has some highways that are pretty badly pot-holed, especially after the thaw.) He is dictating notes to a secretary who is taking down the words in impeccable shorthand. The car's wheels are bouncing and vibrating over some of the worst highway in the nation, but its passengers are completely undisturbed, and the shorthand notes are written without a ripple, thanks to the car's efficient shock absorbers. ■ Investment and exports fluctuate like the volume of Mick Jagger's voice and the uneven surface of a Winnipeg highway. How does the economy react to those fluctuations? Does it react like Gary Filmon's limousine, absorbing the shocks and providing a smooth ride for the economy's passengers? Or does it behave like Mick Jagger's amplifier, blowing up the fluctuations and spreading them out to affect the many millions of participants in an economic rock concert? ■ And is the economic machine built to a design that we simply have to live with, or can we modify it, changing its amplification and shock-absorbing powers? ■ We are now going to explore these questions. We are going to discover that the economy contains an important amplification unit that tends to magnify the effects of fluctuations in investment and exports, resulting in a larger change in aggregate expenditure than the change in investment or exports that initiated it. But we are also going to discover that taxes act as a kind of shock absorber. They don't provide the smooth ride of a Lincoln Continental, but they do a better job than the springs of a stagecoach.

■ In Chapter 25, we studied the factors that determine the components of aggregate expenditure. We discovered that the largest component, consumption expenditure, is a remarkably stable proportion of gross domestic product. But we also saw that consumption expenditure can be influenced by the distance between disposable income and GDP. We also discovered that the most volatile components of aggregate expenditure are investment and exports. Our goal in this chapter is to work out how fluctuations in investment and exports, and in government purchases of goods and services and taxes influence consumption and aggregate expenditure. That is, in contrast to Chapter 25, where we studied each component of aggregate expenditure in isolation from the other, this chapter examines how the components of aggregate expenditure interact to determine aggregate expenditure. We begin by studying the relationship between aggregate expenditure and GDP.

Aggregate Expenditure and Real GDP

There is a relationship between aggregate planned real expenditure and real GDP. **Planned expenditure** is the expenditure that economic agents (households, firms, governments, and foreigners) plan to undertake in given cirumstances. Planned expenditure is not necessarily equal to actual expenditure. We'll see how these two expenditure concepts — planned and actual — differ from each other later in this chapter.

The relationship between aggregate planned real expenditure and real GDP can be described by either an aggregate expenditure schedule or an aggregate expenditure curve. The **aggregate expenditure schedule** lists the level of aggregate planned expenditure at each level of real GDP. The **aggregate expenditure curve** is a graph of the aggregate expenditure schedule.

Aggregate Expenditure Schedule

An aggregate expenditure schedule is set out in the table of Fig. 26.1. (The data in this table and figure are examples and do not refer to the real world. Later in the chapter we'll look at data for the Canadian economy.) The table shows not only aggregate planned expenditure but also its components — consumption expenditure (C), investment (I), government purchases of goods and services (G), and net exports (NX). To work out the level of aggregate planned expenditure, we add the various components together. The first column of the table shows real GDP and the second column shows the consumption expenditure that is planned at each level of real GDP. When real GDP is \$1 billion, so is planned consumption expenditure. A \$1 billion increase in real GDP generates an \$0.65 billion increase in planned consumption expenditure.

The next two columns show planned investment and planned government purchases of goods and services. Recall that investment plans depend on the real interest rate and the state of profit expectations. Suppose that those factors are constant and that at a given point in time, they generate a level of planned investment of \$0.5 billion. This planned investment level is independent of the level of real GDP. It is influenced solely by the real interest rate and expectations of profit that we are holding constant.

Government purchases of goods and services is determined by decisions made by the federal cabinet and Parliament, by the provincial governments and legislatures, and by local governments. These expenditure plans vary from year to year, but at any given point in time, their level has been determined by past decisions. Thus we'll suppose that this item is also fixed. That is, like investment plans, planned government purchases of goods and services are fixed at any given point in time and do not vary as real GDP varies. Here their value is \$0.7 billion.

The next three columns show exports, imports, and net exports. Exports are influenced by events in the rest of the world and by Canadian prices compared with prices in other countries, as well as the foreign exchange value of the Canadian dollar. They are not directly affected by the level of real GDP. In the table, planned exports appear as a constant \$0.45 billion. But planned imports do increase as real GDP increases. In the table, a \$1 billion increase in real GDP results in \$0.15 billion increase in planned imports. Thus net exports — the difference between exports and imports — also varies as real GDP varies. It decreases by \$0.15 billion for each \$1 billion increase in real GDP.

The final column of the table shows aggregate planned expenditure. This amount is the sum of planned consumption expenditure, investment, government purchases of goods and services, and net exports.

Figure 26.1 The Aggregate Expenditure Schedule and Aggregate Expenditure Curve

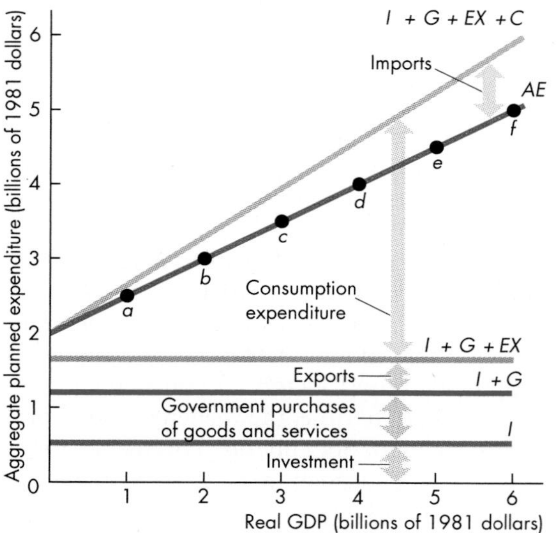

The aggregate expenditure function shows how aggregate planned expenditure varies as real GDP varies. The aggregate expenditure function may be described by an aggregate expenditure schedule (as shown in the table) or an aggregate expenditure curve (as shown in the diagram). Aggregate planned expenditure is calculated as the sum of planned consumption expenditure, investment, government purchases of goods and services, and net exports. For example, in row *a* of the table, if real GDP is $1 billion, aggregate planned consumption is $1 billion, planned investment is $0.5 billion, planned government purchases of goods and services is $0.7 billion, and planned net exports are $0.3 billion. Thus when real GDP is $1 billion, aggregate planned expenditure is $2.5 billion ($1 + $0.5 + $0.7 + $0.3). The expenditure plans are graphed as the aggregate expenditure curve *AE* in the figure, the line *af*.

		Planned expenditure						
	Real GDP (*Y*)	**Consumption expenditure (*C*)**	**Investment (*I*)**	**Government purchases (*G*)**	**Exports (*EX*)**	**Imports (*IM*)**	**Net exports (*NX* = *EX* − *IM*)**	**Aggregate planned expenditure (*AE* = *C* + *I* + *G* + *NX*)**
				(billions of 1981 dollars)				
a	1.0	1.00	0.5	0.7	0.45	0.15	0.30	2.5
b	2.0	1.65	0.5	0.7	0.45	0.30	0.15	3.0
c	3.0	2.30	0.5	0.7	0.45	0.45	0	3.5
d	4.0	2.95	0.5	0.7	0.45	0.60	−0.15	4.0
e	5.0	3.60	0.5	0.7	0.45	0.75	−0.30	4.5
f	6.0	4.25	0.5	0.7	0.45	0.90	−0.45	5.0

Aggregate Expenditure Curve

The aggregate expenditure curve appears in the diagram in Fig. 26.1. Real GDP is shown on the horizontal axis and aggregate planned expenditure on the vertical axis. The aggregate expenditure curve is the red line labelled *AE*. Points *a* through *f* on that curve correspond to the rows in the table in Fig. 26.1. The *AE* curve is a graph of the last column, aggregate planned expenditure, plotted against real GDP.

The figure also shows the components of aggregate planned expenditure. The constant components — investment, government purchases of goods and services, and exports — are indicated by the horizontal lines in the figure. Consumption expenditure is the vertical distance between the line labelled *I* + *G* + *EX* + *C* and that labelled *I* + *G* + *EX*.

To calculate the *AE* curve, we subtract imports from the *I* + *G* + *EX* + *C* line. Imports are subtracted because they are not expenditure on *domestic* output. The purchase of a new car is part of consumption expenditure, but if that car is a BMW, made in Germany, expenditure on it has to be subtracted from consumption expenditure to find out how much is spent on goods produced in Canada — on Canadian GDP. Money paid to BMW for car imports from Germany does not add to aggregate expenditure on Canadian-produced output.

Autonomous and Induced Expenditure

The components of aggregate planned expenditure that we've just considered can be divided into two broad groups:

- Autonomous expenditure
- Induced expenditure

Autonomous expenditure is the sum of those components of aggregate planned expenditure that are not influenced by real GDP. These autonomous components of aggregate planned expenditure are investment, government purchases of goods and services, exports, and that part of consumption expenditure that does not vary with real GDP. In the example in Fig. 26.1, there is $0.35 billion of consumption expenditure even if real GDP is zero. This component of consumption expenditure is part of autonomous expenditure.

Induced expenditure is the sum of those components of aggregate planned expenditure that vary as real GDP varies. The induced components of aggregate planned expenditure are the part of consumption expenditure that varies with real GDP and imports. In the example in Fig. 26.1, each $1 billion increase in real GDP induces an additional $0.65 billion of consumption expenditure. This is the induced part of consumption expenditure. Imports are also part of induced expenditure since they increase as real GDP increases. But recall that imports have to be *subtracted* from total spending to arrive at aggregate expenditure on real GDP.

Autonomous expenditure and induced expenditure are shown in Fig. 26.2. Autonomous expenditure is made up of investment ($0.5 billion), government purchases of goods and services ($0.7 billion), exports ($0.45 billion), and the autonomous component of consumption expenditure ($0.35 billion). The sum of these items is $2 billion. Induced expenditure increases by 50 cents for each $1 increase in real GDP. This increase is made up of 65 cents of consumption expenditure minus 15 cents of imports. For example, when real GDP is $4 billion, aggregate expenditure is also $4 billion, (point *d* on the *AE* curve), which is made up of $2 billion of autonomous expenditure and $2 billion of induced expenditure. Autonomous expenditure remains at $2 billion regardless of the level of real GDP, but the induced component of aggregate expenditure increases from zero when real GDP is zero to $3 billion when real GDP is $6 billion.

Figure 26.2 Autonomous and Induced Expenditure

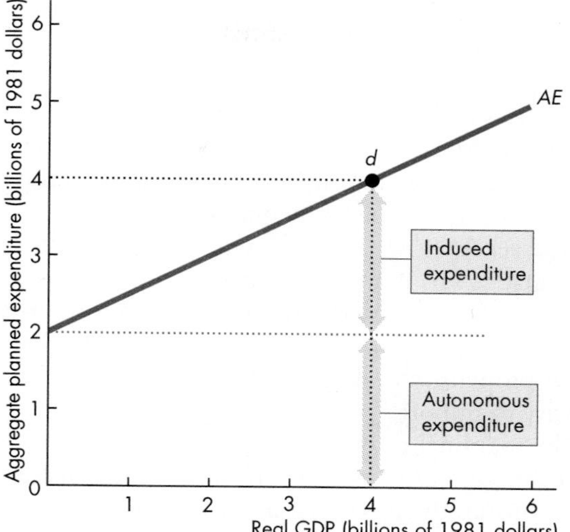

Planned autonomous expenditure, shown at the bottom of the figure, consists of planned investment, government purchases of goods and services, exports, and the autonomous component of consumption expenditure. Planned induced expenditure consists of the remainder of planned consumption expenditure minus imports. The sum of autonomous and induced expenditure is aggregate expenditure. For example, at point *d*, aggregate expenditure is $4 billion — $2 billion of autonomous expenditure and $2 billion of induced expenditure.

Slope of the Aggregate Expenditure Curve

What determines the slope of the aggregate expenditure curve? The answer is the extent to which planned expenditure is induced by an increase in real GDP. As we've just seen, an increase in real GDP of $1 increases planned consumption expenditure by 65 cents and planned imports by 15 cents. The difference between these two, 50 cents, is the increase in induced expenditure.

Recall that the fraction of the last dollar of real GDP consumed is called the *marginal propensity to consume.* In Fig. 26.1, the marginal propensity to consume is 0.65. The fraction of the last dollar of real GDP spent on imports is called the **marginal propensity to import.** In this case, the marginal propensity to import is 0.15. The difference between these two marginal propensities is the marginal propensity to spend on domestic goods and services.

The **marginal propensity to spend on domestic goods and services,** which we'll call the **marginal propensity to spend**, is the fraction of the last dollar of real GDP spent on domestic goods and services. In Fig. 26.2, a $1 increase in real GDP induces an increase in aggregate expenditure of 50 cents, so the marginal propensity to spend is 0.5.

Notice the distinction between the marginal propensity to consume and the marginal propensity to spend. The marginal propensity to consume is the fraction of the last dollar of income spent on all goods and services, regardless of where in the world they are made. The marginal propensity to spend is the fraction of the last dollar of income spent on domestically produced goods and services. It equals the marginal propensity to consume minus the marginal propensity to import.

The marginal propensity to spend equals the slope of the aggregate expenditure curve. You can see this relationship by looking again at Fig. 26.2. If real GDP increases from $1 billion to $2 billion, an increase of $1 billion, aggregate planned expenditure increases from $2.5 billion to $3 billion, an increase of $0.5 billion. The slope of the aggregate expenditure curve equals the increase in aggregate planned expenditure divided by the increase in real GDP — $0.5 billion ÷ $1 billion = 0.5.

R E V I E W

Aggregate planned expenditure is the sum of consumption expenditure, investment, government purchases of goods and services, and net exports. Aggregate planned expenditure is classified into two components: autonomous expenditure and induced expenditure. Investment, government purchases of goods and services, exports, and part of consumption expenditure are autonomous. The other part of consumption expenditure minus imports is induced expenditure. Autonomous expenditure is independent of real GDP; induced expenditure varies as real GDP varies. The higher the level of autonomous expenditure, the greater is the level of aggregate expenditure. The fraction of the last dollar of income spent on domestic goods and services is called the marginal propensity to spend. The marginal propensity to spend equals the marginal propensity to consume minus the marginal propensity to import. The larger the marginal propensity to spend, the steeper is the slope of the aggregate expenditure curve. ■

We've now seen how to calculate the aggregate expenditure schedule and aggregate expenditure curve. We've seen that aggregate planned expenditure increases as real GDP increases. But what determines the point on the aggregate expenditure curve at which the economy operates?

Equilibrium Expenditure

When aggregate planned expenditure equals real GDP **equilibrium expenditure** occurs. At levels of real GDP below equilibrium, planned expenditure exceeds real GDP; at levels of real GDP above equilibrium, planned expenditure falls short of real GDP.

To see how equilibrium expenditure is determined, we need to distinguish between actual expenditure and planned expenditure and understand how actual expenditure, planned expenditure, and income are related.

Actual Expenditure, Planned Expenditure, and Income

Actual aggregate expenditure is always equal to actual aggregate income. One person's expenditure is another person's income. Therefore aggregate expenditure on final goods and services is equal to the aggregate income of the factors of production that produced those final goods and services. Aggregate expenditure on final goods and services and aggregate income are not only equal to each other but are equal to the value of output — to real GDP. Thus actual aggregate expenditure is always equal to real GDP.

We've seen, in the preceding section of this chapter, that the level of real GDP influences the level of aggregate *planned* expenditure. However, planned expenditure is not necessarily equal to actual expenditure and, therefore, is not necessarily equal to actual real GDP. How can actual expenditure and planned expenditure differ from each other? Why don't people implement their plans? In the real world, expenditure plans may not be carried out for many reasons. In the model economy that we are studying, there is just one reason: firms may end up with unwanted excess inventories or with an unwanted shortage of inventories. People carry out their consumption expenditure plans, the government implements its planned purchases of goods and services, and net exports are as planned. Firms carry out their plans to invest in buildings, plant, and equipment. One component of investment, however, is the change in firms' inventories of goods that have not yet been sold. Inventories change when aggregate planned expenditure differs from aggregate output. If output exceeds expenditure, inventories rise, and if output is smaller than expenditure, inventories fall. When inventories change as a result of an unplanned difference between output and sales (equivalently, between output and expenditure), aggregate planned expenditure differs from aggregate actual expenditure.

When aggregate planned expenditure is equal to aggregate actual expenditure and equal to real GDP, the economy is in an expenditure equilibrium. When aggregate planned expenditure and aggregate actual expenditure are unequal, a process of convergence towards an equilibrium expenditure occurs. Let's examine equilibrium expenditure and the process that brings it about.

When Planned Expenditure Equals Real GDP

The table in Fig. 26.3 shows different levels of real GDP in our model economy. Against each level of real GDP, the second column shows aggregate planned expenditure. Only when real GDP equals $4 billion is aggregate planned expenditure equal to real GDP. This level of expenditure is equilibrium expenditure.

The equilibrium is illustrated in Fig. 26.3(a). The aggregate expenditure curve is *AE*. Since aggregate planned expenditure on the vertical axis and real GDP on the horizontal axis are measured in the same units and on the same scale, a 45° line drawn in Fig. 26.3 shows all the points at which aggregate planned expenditure equals real GDP. Such a line appears in the figure and is labelled "45° line." Equilibrium expenditure is determined at point *d* where the aggregate expenditure curve intersects the 45° line.

Convergence to Equilibrium

You will get a better idea of why point *d* is the equilibrium if you consider what is happening when the economy is not at point *d*. Suppose that real GDP is $2 billion. You can see from Fig. 26.3(a) that in this situation aggregate planned expenditure is $3 billion (point *b*). Thus aggregate planned expenditure is larger than real GDP. If aggregate expenditure is actually $3 billion as planned, then real GDP would also be $3 billion, since every dollar spent by one person is a dollar of income for someone else. But real GDP is $2 billion. How can real GDP be $2 billion if people *plan* to spend $3 billion? The answer is that *actual* spending is less than *planned* spending. If real GDP is $2 billion, the value of output is also $2 billion. The only way that people can buy goods and services worth $3 billion when the value of output is $2 billion is if firms' inventories fall by $1 billion (point *b* in Fig. 26.3b). Since changes in inventories are part of investment, actual investment is less than planned investment.

But this is not the end of the story. Firms have target levels for inventories, and when inventories fall below those targets, they increase output to restore inventories to their target levels. To restore their inventories, firms hire additional labour and increase output. Suppose that they increase output in the next period by enough to replenish their inventories. Aggregate output rises by $1 billion to $3 billion. But again, aggregate planned expenditure exceeds real GDP. When real GDP is $3 billion, aggregate planned expenditure is $3.5 billion (point *c* in Fig. 26.3a). Again, inventories fall, but this time by less than before. With an output of $3 billion and planned expenditure of $3.5 billion, inventories fall by only $0.5 billion (point *c* in Fig. 26.3b). Again, firms hire additional labour, and output increases; real GDP increases yet further.

The process that we have just described — planned expenditure exceeds income, inventories fall, and output rises to restore the unplanned inventory reduction — ends when real GDP has reached $4 billion. At this level of real GDP, there is an equilibrium. There are no unplanned inventory changes and firms do not change their output.

Next, let's perform a similar experiment to that above but one starting with a level of real GDP greater than the equilibrium. Suppose that real GDP is $6 billion. At this income level, aggregate planned expenditure is $5 billion (point *f* in Fig. 26.3a), $1 billion less than real GDP. With aggregate planned expenditure less than real GDP, inventories rise by $1 billion (point *f* in Fig. 26.3b) — there is unplanned investment. With unsold inventories on their hands, firms cut back on production. They lay off workers and reduce the amount that they pay out in wages; real GDP falls. If they cut back

Figure 26.3 Equilibrium Expenditure and Real GDP

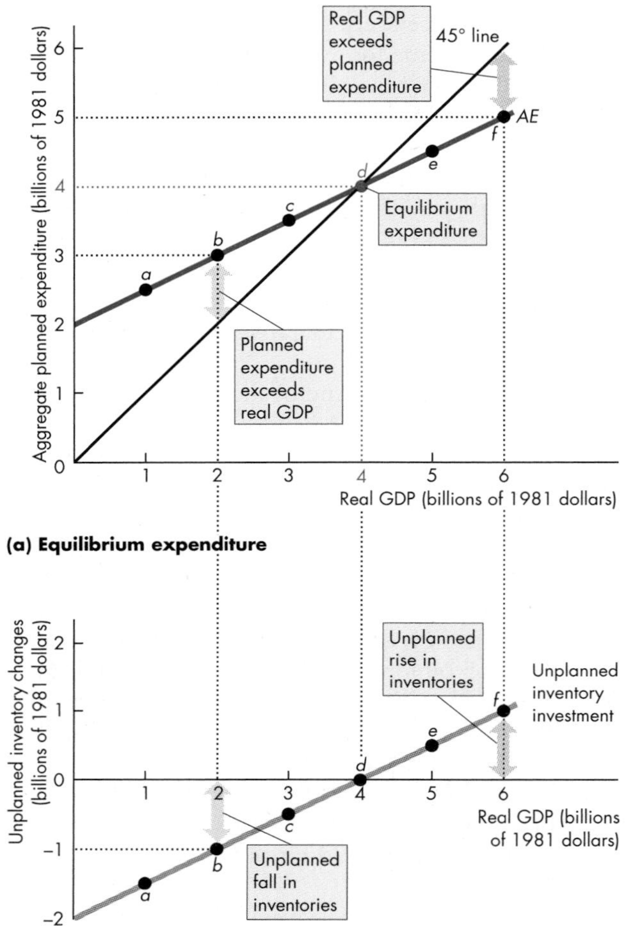

	Real GDP (*Y*)	Aggregate planned expenditure (*AE*)	Unplanned inventory changes (*Y* – *AE*)
	(billions of 1981 dollars)		
a	1.0	2.5	–1.5
b	2.0	3.0	–1.0
c	3.0	3.5	–0.5
d	4.0	4.0	0
e	5.0	4.5	0.5
f	6.0	5.0	1.0

The table shows the aggregate expenditure schedule. When real GDP is $4 billion, aggregate planned expenditure equals real GDP. At real GDP levels less than $4 billion, aggregate planned expenditure exceeds real GDP. At real GDP levels more than $4 billion, aggregate planned expenditure is less than real GDP. The diagram illustrates equilibrium expenditure. The 45° line shows those points at which aggregate planned expenditure equals real GDP. The aggregate expenditure curve is *AE* and actual aggregate expenditure equals real GDP. Equilibrium expenditure and real GDP are $4 billion. That GDP level generates planned expenditure that equals real GDP — $4 billion. At real GDP levels less than $4 billion, aggregate planned expenditure exceeds real GDP and inventories fall — for example, at point *b* in both parts of the figure. In such cases, firms increase output to restore their inventories and real GDP rises. At real GDP levels greater than $4 billion, aggregate planned expenditure is less than real GDP and inventories rise — for example, at point *d* in both parts of the figure. In such a situation, firms decrease output to work off excess inventories and real GDP falls. Only where the aggregate planned expenditure curve cuts the 45° line is planned expenditure equal to real GDP. This position is equilibrium expenditure. There are no unplanned inventory changes and output remains constant.

production by the amount of the unplanned increase in inventories, real GDP falls by $1 billion to $5 billion. At that level of real GDP, aggregate planned expenditure is $4.5 billion (point *e* in Fig. 26.3a). Again, there is an unplanned increase in inventories, but it is only one-half the previous increase (point *e* in Fig. 26.3b). Again, firms will cut back production and lay off yet more workers, reducing real GDP still further. Real GDP continues to fall whenever unplanned inventories increase. As before, real GDP keeps on changing until it reaches its equilibrium level of $4 billion.

You can see, then, that if real GDP is below equilibrium, aggregate planned expenditure exceeds real GDP, inventories fall, firms increase output to restore their inventories, and real GDP rises. If real GDP is above equilibrium, aggregate planned expenditure is less than real GDP, unsold inventories prompt firms to cut back on production, and real GDP falls.

Only if real GDP equals aggregate planned expenditure are there no unplanned inventory changes and no changes in firms' output plans. In this situation, real GDP remains constant.

REVIEW

Equilibrium expenditure occurs when aggregate planned expenditure equals real GDP. If aggregate planned expenditure exceeds real GDP, inventories fall and firms increase output to replenish inventory levels. Real GDP increases and so does planned expenditure. If aggregate planned expenditure is less than real GDP, inventories accumulate and firms cut output to lower inventory levels. Real GDP and aggregate planned expenditure decline. Only when aggregate planned expenditure equals real GDP are there no unplanned changes in inventories and no changes in output. Real GDP remains constant. ■

We have now discovered how the equilibrium levels of real GDP and aggregate expenditure are determined. Our next task is to study the sources of *changes* in the equilibrium.

Fluctuations in Expenditure and in Real GDP

We've seen that equilibrium expenditure occurs where aggregate planned expenditure equals real GDP. For a given *AE* curve, there is only one such equilibrium. When the *AE* curve shifts, equilibrium expenditure changes. What are the factors that shift the *AE* curve?

Anything that changes autonomous expenditure shifts the *AE* curve but leaves its slope unchanged. Anything that affects the marginal propensity to spend changes induced expenditure and changes the slope of the *AE* curve. Any such changes — either a change in autonomous expenditure or a change in the marginal propensity to spend — shift the *AE* curve and bring about a new equilibrium expenditure. Let's look at these changes, starting with a change in autonomous expenditure.

A Change in Autonomous Expenditure

There are many possible sources of a change in autonomous expenditure. A fall in the real interest rate might induce firms to increase their planned investment. Booming business conditions may increase firms' optimism about future profits, adding yet more to their planned investment. Stiff competition in the auto industry from Japanese and European imports might force GM, Ford, and Chrysler to increase their investment in robotic assembly lines. An economic boom in Western Europe and Japan might lead to a large increase in expenditure in those countries on Canadian-produced goods — on Canadian exports. An increase in the number of working mothers might lead the Canadian government to increase its expenditure on day-care facilities — an increase in government purchases of goods and services. Decreased thriftiness may lead households to cut their saving and increase consumption expenditure. These are all examples of increases in autonomous expenditure. What are the effects of such increases on aggregate planned expenditure and real GDP? Let's answer this question.

Aggregate planned expenditure is set out in the table and illustrated in the diagram in Fig. 26.4. Autonomous expenditure initially is $2 billion. The marginal propensity to spend out of real GDP is 0.5. Thus for each $1 billion increase in real GDP, induced expenditure increases by $0.5 billion. Adding induced expenditure and autonomous expenditure together gives aggregate planned expenditure. Initially, equilibrium occurs when real GDP is $4 billion. This equilibrium can be seen in row *d* of the table, and in the figure at the point marked *d*, where the aggregate planned expenditure AE_0 cuts the 45° line .

Now suppose that planned investment, government purchases, and exports increase by an aggregate amount of $0.5 billion, so that autonomous expenditure becomes $2.5 billion. What is the new equilibrium? The answer is worked out in the final two columns of the table and illustrated in the diagram. When the new level of autonomous expenditure is added to induced expenditure, aggregate planned expenditure increases by $0.5 billion at each level of real GDP. The aggregate expenditure curve shifts upward to AE_1 — a parallel shift. That is, the vertical distance between AE_1 and AE_0 is $0.5 billion at all levels of real GDP. The new equilibrium, highlighted in the table (row e′) occurs where AE_1 intersects the 45° line; it is at $5 billion (point e′) . At this income level, aggregate planned expenditure equals real GDP. Autonomous expenditure is $2.5 billion and induced expenditure is also $2.5 billion.

Notice that equilibrium expenditure has increased by more than the increase in autonomous expenditure. Increased autonomous expenditure increases real GDP and the increase in real GDP produces an increase in induced expenditure. Aggregate

Figure 26.4 An Increase in Autonomous Expenditure

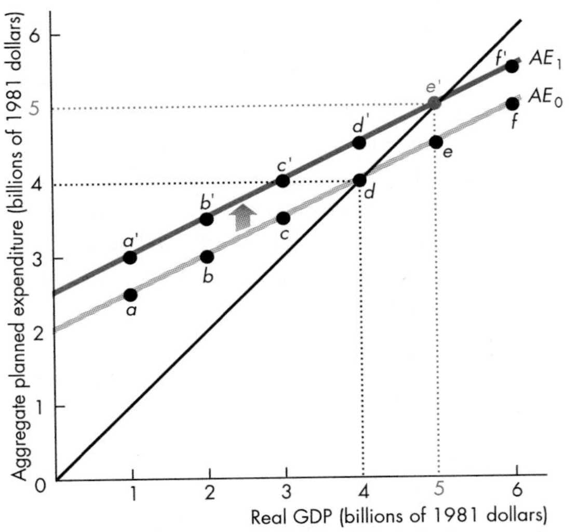

If autonomous expenditure increases from \$2 billion to \$2.5 billion, aggregate planned expenditure at each level of real GDP also increases by \$0.5 billion. As shown in the table, the initial equilibrium expenditure of \$4 billion is no longer the equilibrium. At that level of real GDP, aggregate planned expenditure is now \$4.5 billion. The new expenditure equilibrium is \$5 billion, the amount at which aggregate planned expenditure equals real GDP. The increase in real GDP is larger than the increase in autonomous expenditure. The figure illustrates the effect of the increase in autonomous expenditure. At each level of real GDP, aggregate planned expenditure is \$0.5 billion more than before. The aggregate planned expenditure curve shifts upward from AE_0 to AE_1 — a parallel shift. The new AE curve intersects the 45° line at e' where real GDP is \$5 billion — the new equilibrium point.

			Original			New	
Real GDP (Y)	Induced expenditure (N)		Autonomous expenditure (A_0)	Aggregate expenditure (AE_0)		Autonomous expenditure (A_1)	Aggregate expenditure (AE_1)
			(billions of 1981 dollars)				
1.0	0.5	*a*	2.0	2.5	*a′*	2.5	3.0
2.0	1.0	*b*	2.0	3.0	*b′*	2.5	3.5
3.0	1.5	*c*	2.0	3.5	*c′*	2.5	4.0
4.0	2.0	*d*	2.0	4.0	*d′*	2.5	4.5
5.0	2.5	*e*	2.0	4.5	*e′*	2.5	5.0
6.0	3.0	*f*	2.0	5.0	*f′*	2.5	5.5

expenditure increases by the sum of the initial increase in autonomous expenditure and the increase in induced expenditure.

The Paradox of Thrift

Thrift is another word for saving. The thriftier a household, the more it saves. Also, the thriftier a household, the wealthier it becomes. By consuming less than its income, a household increases its income. It lends what it saves and earns interest on it.

What happens if we all become thriftier? Does aggregate income increase? We can work out one answer to this question by using the analysis that we've just performed, but doing it in reverse.

Suppose that initially, the aggregate expenditure curve is AE_1 in Fig. 26.4. Real GDP is \$5 billion. Now suppose that there is an increase in thriftiness. As a result, autonomous expenditure decreases by \$0.5 billion, and consequently, the aggregate expenditure curve shifts downward from AE_1 to AE_0. Equilibrium GDP and expenditure fall to \$4 billion.

An increase in thriftiness has reduced real GDP. The fall in real GDP caused by an increase in saving is called the **paradox of thrift**. It is a paradox because an increase in thriftiness leads to an increase in income for an individual but to a decrease in income for the economy as a whole. The paradox arises in this model because an increase in saving is *not* associated with an increase in investment. Although people save more, no one buys additional capital goods.

If at the same time that saving increased, there was also an increase in investment, there would be no fall in income. An increase in saving shifts the *AE* curve downward but an increase in investment shifts it upward. If saving and investment each change by the same amount, the *AE* curve does not shift. The result is no change in real GDP. Thus the paradox of thrift is not so paradoxical after all. It is a consequence of increased saving with unchanged investment.

A Change in the Marginal Propensity to Spend

There are three main influences on the marginal propensity to spend. They are:

- The marginal propensity to consume
- The marginal propensity to import
- The marginal tax rate

The Marginal Propensity to Consume Some changes in households' consumption plans may change the marginal propensity to consume. We saw in the previous chapter that income has two important influences on consumption expenditure. First, an increase in current disposable income leads to an increase in consumption expenditure. Second, an increase in expected future income also leads to an increase in consumption expenditure. Sometimes an increase in current income is expected to be permanent. In such a case, both current income and expected future income increase together. But sometimes an increase in current income is expected to be only temporary. In this case, current income increases but expected future income does not. The effect on consumption of an increase in income that is expected to be permanent is larger than the effect of an increase that is expected to be temporary. For this reason, the fraction of the last dollar of income spent on consumption goods and services varies. And it varies in a way that is connected with the business cycle.

When the economy begins a period of expansion from recession, at first most people perceive the increases in income as permanent. Consumption increases and a large fraction of the increased income is spent on consumption goods and services — the marginal propensity to consume is high. As the expansion continues, however, more people start to suspect that a halt to expansion, or even a contraction, is going to occur soon — they perceive the current income increase as temporary. In this situation, the fraction of additional income consumed falls — the marginal propensity to consume falls. Then, when the economy actually goes into a recession and income falls, the decrease in income is regarded as temporary. Consumption does not fall by as large a percentage as the fall in income. In this situation, the marginal propensity to consume is low — a $1 decrease in disposable income leads to a small decrease in consumption expenditure.

Fluctuations in the marginal propensity to consume — some of them related to the business cycle — lead to changes in the slope of the aggregate expenditure curve. The higher the marginal propensity to consume, the higher is the marginal propensity to spend and the steeper is the *AE* curve.

The Marginal Propensity to Import We discovered in Chapter 25 that imports as a percentage of GDP have increased steadily over the past 20 years. This fact does not necessarily mean that the marginal propensity to import has increased. It could be that the import curve has shifted upward over time with no change in the marginal propensity to import — that is, with no change in the slope of the import curve. It is possible, however, that the marginal propensity to import has itself increased over the years. The steady increase in imports, relative to GDP, has resulted partly from changes in international relative prices — many goods and services are produced abroad at a lower cost than we can produce them in Canada. The increase has also resulted from a steady increase in the degree of international specialization in the production of goods and services. That is, we have become more specialized, increasing our exports, and other countries have also become more specialized, increasing their exports to us. All of these factors have increased imports relative to GDP.

To the extent that these factors have increased the marginal propensity to import — increased the slope of the import curve — they have decreased the marginal propensity to spend, making the *AE* curve flatter.

The Marginal Tax Rate The **marginal tax rate** is the fraction of the last dollar of income paid to the government in taxes. For individuals, some variation in the marginal tax rate depends on income level. People with very low incomes pay no taxes (and

Figure 26.5 An Increase in the Marginal Propensity to Spend

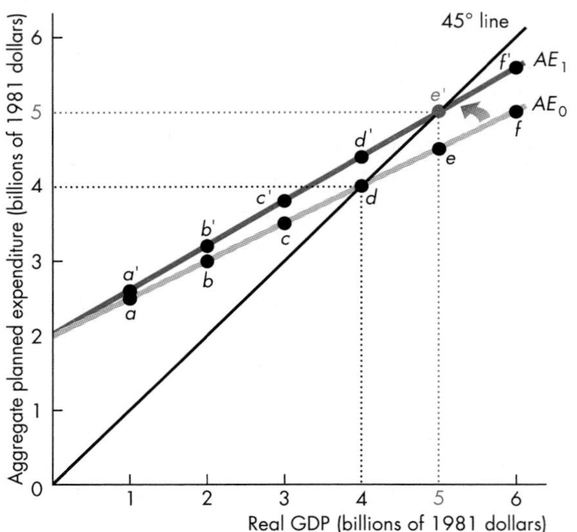

A tax cut increases the marginal propensity to spend from 0.5 to 0.6. Autonomous expenditure remains constant at $2 billion, but induced expenditure increases. For example, when real GDP is $2.0 billion (row *b* of the table), induced expenditure increases from $1 billion to $1.2 billion. In the figure, the aggregate expenditure curve shifts from AE_0 to AE_1. The aggregate expenditure curve becomes steeper because the marginal propensity to spend has increased. The new equilibrium occurs where aggregate planned expenditure equals real GDP — row *e'* in the table. In the diagram, the intersection of AE_1 and the 45° line determines equilibrium expenditure — $5 billion (point *e'*). Alternatively, an increase in saving would shift the aggregate expenditure curve down, say from AE_1 to AE_0, resulting in a fall in real GDP and lower equilibrium expenditure.

Real GDP (Y)	Autonomous expenditure (A)		Original: Induced expenditure (N_0)	Original: Aggregate expenditure (AE_0)		New: Induced expenditure (N_1)	New: Aggregate expenditure (AE_1)
			(billions of 1981 dollars)				
1.0	2.0	*a*	0.5	2.5	*a'*	0.6	2.6
2.0	2.0	*b*	1.0	3.0	*b'*	1.2	3.2
3.0	2.0	*c*	1.5	3.5	*c'*	1.8	3.8
4.0	2.0	*d*	2.0	4.0	*d'*	2.4	4.4
5.0	2.0	*e*	2.5	4.5	*e'*	3.0	5.0
6.0	2.0	*f*	3.0	5.0	*f'*	3.6	5.6

even receive net benefits from the government). As individual income increases, the marginal tax rate increases. For the economy, on the average, the marginal tax rate is calculated as the change in tax receipts of the government sector divided by the change in GDP. Other things being equal, the higher the marginal tax rate, the lower is disposable income. Thus for a given increase in GDP, the higher the marginal tax rate, the less disposable income increases. Thus a cut in marginal tax rates increases the marginal propensity to spend and makes the *AE* curve steeper.

We can analyse the effects of changes in the marginal propensity to consume, the marginal propensity to import, and the marginal tax rate by working out their effects on the marginal propensity to spend. We can then work out the effect of a change in the marginal propensity to spend, with a given level of autonomous expenditure, on equilibrium expenditure and on real GDP.

The Effects of a Change in the Marginal Propensity to Spend

What are the predicted effects of a cut in marginal tax rates on equilibrium expenditure and real GDP?

Suppose that a cut in marginal tax rates results in an increase in the marginal propensity to spend, from 0.5 to 0.6. The table in Fig. 26.5 lists the effects of this change on induced expenditure and on aggregate planned expenditure at each level of real GDP. Notice that the new induced expenditure (N_1) equals 0.6 times real GDP, whereas the original induced expenditure (N_0) equals 0.5 times real GDP. Aggregate planned expenditure equals induced expenditure plus the constant $2 billion of autonomous expenditure.

The aggregate expenditure curve associated with the higher marginal propensity to spend is shown as AE_1 in the diagram in Fig. 26.5. Since autonomous expenditure has not changed, the aggregate planned expenditure curve intersects the vertical axis at the same point as the original curve, AE_0, but the *AE* curve rotates upward. It does not shift in a parallel fashion; it becomes steeper because at higher levels of real GDP the increase in induced expenditure is greater.

The original equilibrium real GDP is $4 billion and the new equilibrium is $5 billion. At the original real GDP of $4 billion, the higher marginal propensity to spend increases aggregate expenditure to $4.4 billion (see row *d'* of the table). But now aggregate expenditure exceeds real GDP, so real GDP increases (by the process described in Fig. 26.3). Real GDP continues to increase until a new equilibrium is established. In the process, induced expenditure increases further. Only when real GDP is $5 billion has aggregate planned expenditure adjusted to the level required to attain a new expenditure equilibrium. You can verify this fact by noticing that at this level of real GDP, aggregate planned expenditure also equals $5 billion. That is, induced expenditure is $3 billion (real GDP of $5 billion multiplied by 0.6), and when this amount is added to autonomous expenditure of $2 billion, aggregate planned expenditure equals real GDP at $5 billion.

We have now discovered that changes in autonomous expenditure and changes in the marginal propensity to spend shift the aggregate expenditure curve and change equilibrium real GDP. But how big are the changes? What determines the magnitude of the change in equilibrium expenditure brought about by a change in autonomous expenditure?

The Multiplier

Suppose that the economy appears to be heading for a recession. Profit prospects look bleak and firms are cutting investment. The federal government, anxious to avoid the recession, wants to take steps to prevent the level of aggregate expenditure from falling. It knows that by cutting interest rates, it can encourage firms to invest more. It also knows that by cutting taxes or increasing its own purchases of goods and services, it can encourage a higher level of aggregate expenditure. But for effective economic management, the government needs to know more than the direction in which to change interest rates, taxes, or its own purchases of goods and services. It needs to answer a quantitative question: by how much must spending increase to avoid a recession? This is a hard question to answer but in order to answer it we must work out the connection between a change in autonomous expenditure and the change in equilibrium aggregate expenditure. We've already seen that when autonomous expenditure changes, equilibrium expenditure and real GDP change by a larger amount. But what is the quantitative relationship between the change in autonomous expenditure and the change in equilibrium real GDP?

The **autonomous expenditure multiplier** (often abbreviated to simply the **multiplier**) is the amount by which a change in autonomous expenditure is multiplied to calculate the change in equilibrium expenditure and real GDP that it generates. To calculate the multiplier, we divide the change in equilibrium real GDP by the change in autonomous expenditure that brought about that change. Let's calculate the multiplier for the example in Fig. 26.4. Autonomous expenditure increases from $2 to $2.5 billion and equilibrium real GDP increases from $4 billion to $5 billion, an increase of $1 billion. That is,

- Autonomous expenditure increases by $0.5 billion.
- Real GDP increases by $1 billion.

The multiplier is calculated as follows:

$$\text{Multiplier} = \frac{\text{Change in real GDP}}{\text{Change in autonomous expenditure}}$$

$$= \frac{\$1.0 \text{ billion}}{\$0.5 \text{ billion}}$$

$$= 2$$

Thus a change in autonomous expenditure of $0.5 billion produces a change in equilibrium real GDP of $1 billion, a change that is twice as big as the initial change in autonomous expenditure. That is,

Table 26.1 Calculating the Multiplier

	Symbols and Formulas	Numbers
1. Definitions		
Change in real GDP	ΔY	
Change in autonomous expenditure	ΔA	500
Marginal propensity to spend	ε	$2/3$
Change in induced expenditure	$\Delta N = \varepsilon \Delta Y$	$\Delta N = (2/3)\Delta Y$
Change in aggregate planned expenditure	$\Delta AE = \Delta A + \Delta N$	
The multiplier (autonomous expenditure multiplier)	$k = \Delta Y / \Delta A$	
The multiplier effect	$\Delta Y = k\Delta A$	
2. Calculations		
Aggregate planned expenditure	$AE = A + \varepsilon Y$	
Change in aggregate planned expenditure	$\Delta AE = \Delta A + \varepsilon \Delta Y$	$\Delta AE = 500 + (2/3)\Delta Y$
Change in equilibrium expenditure	$\Delta AE = \Delta Y$	
Replacing ΔAE with ΔY	$\Delta Y = \Delta A + \varepsilon \Delta Y$	$\Delta Y = 500 + (2/3)\Delta Y$
Subtracting $\varepsilon \Delta Y$ or $(2/3)\Delta Y$	$\Delta Y - \varepsilon \Delta Y = \Delta A$	$\Delta Y - (2/3)\Delta Y = 500$
Factoring ΔY	$\Delta Y(1 - \varepsilon) = \Delta A$	$\Delta Y(1 - 2/3) = 500$
Dividing both sides by $(1 - \varepsilon)$ or $(1 - 2/3)$	$\Delta Y = \frac{1}{1-\varepsilon} \Delta A$	$\Delta Y = \frac{1}{1-2/3} 500$ or $\Delta Y = \frac{1}{1/3} 500$ or $\Delta Y = 1500$
Dividing both sides by ΔA or 500 gives the multiplier	$\frac{\Delta Y}{\Delta A} = \frac{1}{1-\varepsilon}$	$\frac{\Delta Y}{\Delta A} = \frac{1500}{500} = 3$

The autonomous expenditure multiplier, or multiplier, is the ratio of the change in real GDP to a change in real autonomous expenditure. The multiplier effect is the change in real GDP brought about by a given change in autonomous expenditure — the change in autonomous expenditure multiplied by k. The table shows how to calculate the multiplier. The multiplier formula that results is

$$\frac{\Delta Y}{\Delta A} = \frac{1}{1-\varepsilon}.$$

the change in autonomous expenditure leads, like Mick Jagger's music-making equipment, to an amplified change in equilibrium expenditure and real GDP.

There is an interesting relationship between the value of the multiplier and the marginal propensity to spend. Let's see what that relationship is.

Figure 26.6 The Multiplier and the Marginal Propensity to Spend

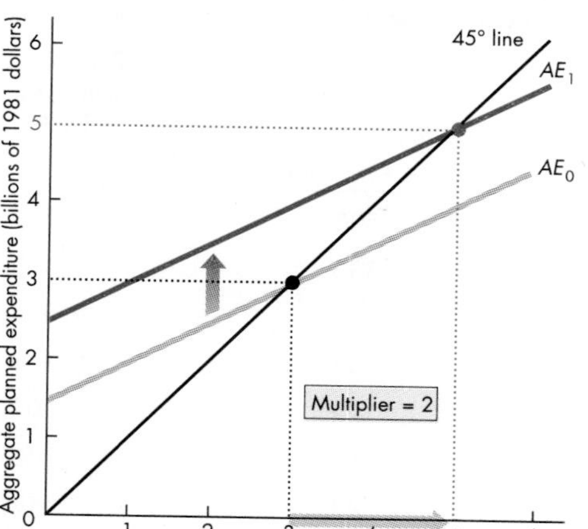

(a) Multiplier is 2

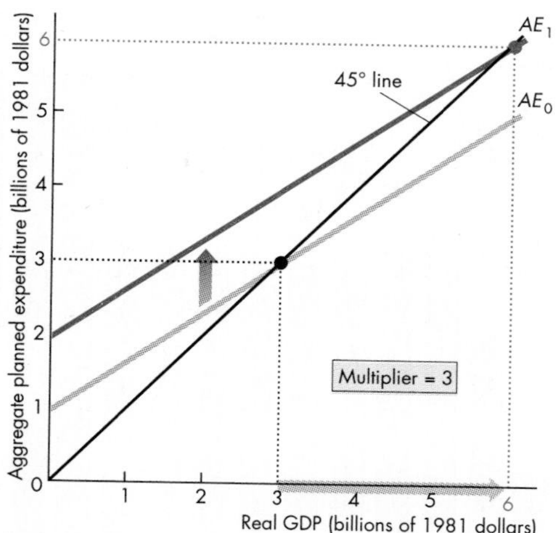

(b) Multiplier is 3

The size of the multiplier depends on the marginal propensity to spend. The multiplier formula, $k = 1/(1 - \varepsilon)$, tells us the relationship. If the marginal propensity to spend (ε) is ½, the multiplier is 2. In this case, an increase of autonomous expenditure of $1 billion shifts the *AE* curve upward from AE_0 to AE_1 in part (a). Real GDP increases from $3 billion to $5 billion. If ε equals ⅔, the multiplier is 3. In this case, a $1 billion increase in autonomous expenditure shifts the aggregate expenditure curve upward from AE_0 to AE_1 in part (b). Real GDP increases from $3 billion to $6 billion — by three times the size of the increase in autonomous expenditure.

The Multiplier and the Marginal Propensity to Spend

Table 26.1 shows how to calculate the value of the multiplier. The multiplier (k) is defined as

$$k = \frac{\Delta Y}{\Delta A},$$

and its value is

$$k = \frac{1}{(1 - \varepsilon)}.$$

The letter ε stands for the marginal propensity to spend. The marginal propensity to spend is a fraction — lying between 0 and 1 — so, $1/(1 - \varepsilon)$ is greater than 1. The larger the marginal propensity to spend, the larger is the multiplier.

If the marginal propensity to spend is 0 (if $\varepsilon = 0$), there is no induced expenditure. In such a case, the multiplier is 1. It is easy to see why. A $1 change in autonomous expenditure changes real GDP by $1 and, with no induced expenditure changes, that is the end of the matter.

If the marginal propensity to spend (ε) is ½, $1 of additional income induces 50 cents of additional expenditure. The multiplier is 2. This case is illustrated in Fig. 26.6(a). A $1 billion increase in autonomous expenditure shifts the *AE* curve upward from AE_0 to AE_1 and increases equilibrium real GDP from $3 billion to $5 billion. An autonomous expenditure increase of $1 billion increases equilibrium real GDP by $2 billion, so the multiplier is 2.

If the marginal propensity to spend (ε) is ⅔, the multiplier is 3. Figure 26.6(b) illustrates this case. Here a $1 billion increase in autonomous expenditure shifts the *AE* curve upward from AE_0 to AE_1 and increases equilibrium real GDP from $3 billion to $6 billion.

Figure 26.7 The Multiplier Process

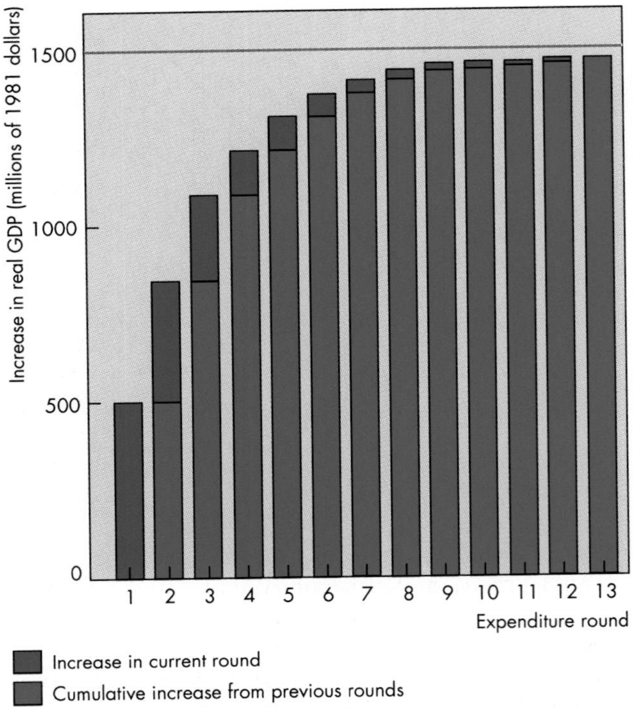

Expenditure round	Increase in expenditure	Cumulative increase in real GDP
	(millions of dollars)	
1	500	500
2	333	833
3	222	1,055
4	148	1,203
5	99	1,302
6	66	1,368
7	44	1,412
8	29	1,441
9	20	1,461
10	13	1,474
.	.	.
.	.	.
.	.	.
All others	26	1,500

Autonomous expenditure increases in round 1 by $500 million. Real GDP also increases by the same amount. In round 2, the round 1 increase in real GDP induces an increase in expenditure of $333 million. At the end of round 2, real GDP has increased by $833 million. The extra $333 million of real GDP in round 2 induces a further increase in expenditure of $222 million in round 3. Real GDP increases yet further to $1,055 million. This process continues until real GDP has eventually increased by $1,500 million. (The table stops counting after round 10 since the extra amounts become so small. Perhaps you would like to run the process further on your pocket calculator. As a matter of interest, after 19 rounds you will be within $1 of the $1,500 million total, and after 30 rounds within 1 penny of that total!) The diagram shows you how quickly the multiplier effect builds up. The multiplier in this case is 3 because the marginal propensity to spend is ⅔ (see Table 26.1). The larger the marginal propensity to spend, the larger is the multiplier.

Why Is the Multiplier Greater than 1?

The multiplier is greater than 1 because of induced expenditure — an increase in autonomous expenditure induces an increase in consumption expenditure. If GM spends $10 million on a new car assembly line, aggregate expenditure and real GDP immediately increase by $10 million. But that is not the end of the story. Engineers and construction workers now have more income and they spend part of the extra income on cars, microwave ovens, vacations, and a host of other goods and services. Real GDP now rises by the initial $10 million plus the extra consumption expenditure induced by the $10 million increase in income. The producers of cars, microwave ovens, vacations, and other goods now have increased incomes, and they, in turn, also spend part of their increase in income on consumption goods and services. Additional income induces additional expenditure, which creates additional income.

This multiplier process is illustrated in Fig. 26.7. In this example, the marginal propensity to spend (ε)

is ⅔ as in Fig. 26.6(b). In round 1, there is an increase in autonomous expenditure of $500 million. At that stage, there is no change in induced expenditure, so total expenditure increases by $500 million. In round 2, the higher income induces higher consumption expenditure. Since the marginal propensity to spend (ε) is ⅔, an increase in income of $500 million induces a further increase in expenditure of $333 million. This change in induced expenditure, when added to the initial change in autonomous expenditure, results in an increase in total expenditure of $833 million. The round 2 increase in income induces a round 3 increase in expenditure. The process repeats through successive rounds recorded in the table. Each increase in income is two-thirds the size of the previous increase. The cumulative increase in income gradually approaches $1,500 million. After 10 rounds it has almost reached that level.

As the multiplier process depicted in Fig. 26.7 is working itself out, inventories and output are being adjusted in the manner described in Fig. 26.3. But you should not think of each expenditure round depicted in Fig. 26.7 as taking place in a fixed amount of calendar time. This multiplier process can take place in a single day or even a single instant. The amount of time that it takes is important. But what is more important is that the multiplier process is a description of the forces that keep the economy at equilibrium.

It appears, then, that the economy does not operate like the shock absorbers on Gary Filmon's car. The economy's potholes are changes in autonomous expenditure, mainly brought about by changes in investment and exports. These economic bumps are not smoothed out but instead are amplified.

R E V I E W

Changes in autonomous expenditure or changes in the marginal propensity to spend change equilibrium expenditure and real GDP. The magnitude of the effect of a change in autonomous expenditure on equilibrium expenditure is determined by the multiplier. The multiplier, in turn, is determined by the value of the marginal propensity to spend. The higher the marginal propensity to spend, the larger is the multiplier. The multiplier acts like an amplifier. Fluctuations in autonomous expenditure — such as fluctuations in investment or exports — change real GDP, inducing a change in consumption expenditure and having amplified effects on equilibrium aggregate expenditure. ■

But the economic amplifier does not increase only fluctuations in investment and exports. It also amplifies fluctuations in government purchases of goods and services. Because of this fact, the government can take advantage of the multiplier in order to attempt to smooth out fluctuations in aggregate expenditure. Let's see how.

Fiscal Policy Multipliers

Fiscal policy is the attempt by government to smooth the fluctuations in aggregate expenditure by varying its purchases of goods and services, transfer payments, and taxes. If the government foresees a decline in investment or exports, it may attempt to offset the effects of the decline on autonomous expenditure by increasing its own purchase of goods and services, increasing transfer payments, or cutting taxes. But the government must figure out the size of the increase in purchases or transfers, or the size of the tax cut needed to achieve its goal. To make this calculation, the government needs to know the size of the multiplier effects of its own actions. Let's study the multiplier effects of changes in government purchases, transfer payments, and taxes.

Government Purchases Multiplier

The **government purchases multiplier** is the amount by which a change in government purchases of goods and services is multiplied to determine the change in equilibrium expenditure that it generates. Government purchases of goods and services are one of the components of autonomous expenditure. A change in government purchases has the same effect on aggregate expenditure as a change in any of the other components of autonomous expenditure. It sets up a multiplier effect exactly like the multiplier effect of investment or exports. That is,

$$\text{Government purchases multiplier} = \frac{1}{(1-\varepsilon)}.$$

By varying government purchases to offset changes in exports or investment, the government can attempt to keep total autonomous expenditure constant (or growing at a steady rate). Because the government purchases multiplier is the same size as the investment and exports multipliers, stabilization of autonomous expenditure would be achieved by increasing government purchases by \$1 for each \$1 decrease in those other items of autonomous expenditure.

In practice, using variations in government purchases to stabilize aggregate expenditure is not possible because the political decision process that produces changes in government purchases of goods and services operates with a long time lag. As a consequence, it is not possible to forecast the changes in private expenditure as far ahead as would be required to make this an effective instrument of macroeconomic stabilization policy.

A second way in which the government may seek to stabilize aggregate expenditure is by varying transfer payments. Let's see how this type of policy works.

Transfer Payments Multiplier

The **transfer payments multiplier** is the amount by which a change in transfer payments is multiplied to determine the change in equilibrium expenditure that it generates. A change in transfer payments influences aggregate expenditure by changing disposable income, which leads to a change in consumption expenditure and imports. The amount by which aggregate expenditure changes depends on the marginal propensity to spend on domestic goods and services (ε). That is, a \$1 increase in transfer payments increases consumption expenditure by an amount determined by the marginal propensity to spend. It increases aggregate expenditure on domestic goods and services by \$$\varepsilon$. For example, if the marginal propensity to spend is 0.5, a \$1 increase in transfer payments leads to a 50-cent increase in autonomous expenditure. This initial increase in expenditure gives rise to a multiplier process exactly like the one that we studied earlier in this chapter. But the initial injection of spending resulting from a \$1 increase in transfer payments is \$$\varepsilon$ — or 50 cents in the example. Therefore

$$\text{Transfer payments multiplier} = \frac{\varepsilon}{(1-\varepsilon)}.$$

Because the marginal propensity to spend is a fraction, the transfer payments multiplier is smaller than the government purchases multiplier. As a consequence, to achieve a particular change in aggregate expenditure, a larger change in transfer payments is required than in government purchases of goods and services. The use of variations in transfer payments to stabilize the economy has the same problems as the use of variations in government purchases of goods and services. The political process does not operate on the time scale required for timely changes in transfer payments to offset fluctuations in other components of autonomous expenditure.

Tax Multiplier

A third type of fiscal stabilization policy is to vary taxes. The effects of a change in taxes depend on whether the taxes are autonomous or induced. **Autonomous taxes** are taxes that do not vary directly with real GDP. Examples of such taxes are contributions for social insurance and property taxes. **Induced taxes** are taxes that vary directly with real GDP. Examples of induced taxes are personal income tax and sales taxes. The scale of induced taxes determines the marginal tax rate. That is, the marginal tax rate is the change in induced taxes divided by the change in real GDP. We'll study the effects of induced taxes later in the chapter. For now let's concentrate on changes in autonomous taxes and the autonomous tax multiplier.

The Autonomous Tax Multiplier The **autonomous tax multiplier** is the amount by which a change in autonomous taxes is multiplied to determine the change in equilibrium expenditure that it generates. Changes in taxes work like changes in autonomous expenditure but in the opposite direction. A *decrease* in taxes produces an *increase* in expenditure. It does so by increasing disposable income. Because a tax *increase* leads to a *decrease* in expenditure, the tax multiplier is *negative.* As in the case of a change in transfer payments, a tax change works by changing disposable income. But a \$1 increase in disposable income does not increase expenditure by \$1. Instead it increases expenditure by \$1 multiplied by the marginal propensity to spend on domestic goods and services. For example, if the marginal propensity to spend is 0.5, a \$1 increase in disposable income increases autonomous expenditure by 50 cents. The autonomous tax multiplier equals the negative of the transfer payments multiplier. That is,

$$\text{Autonomous tax multiplier} = \frac{-\varepsilon}{(1-\varepsilon)}$$

Balanced Budget Multiplier

The **balanced budget multiplier** is the amount by which changes in government purchases of goods and services and taxes of equal amounts is multiplied to determine the change in equilibrium expenditure that they generate. What is the multiplier effect of this fiscal policy action?

To answer we must combine the two multipliers that we have just worked out. We've seen that those two separate multipliers are:

$$\text{Government purchases multiplier} = \frac{1}{(1-\varepsilon)}$$

$$\text{Autonomous tax multiplier} = \frac{-\varepsilon}{(1-\varepsilon)}.$$

Adding these two multipliers together gives the balanced budget multiplier which is:

$$\text{Balanced budget multiplier} = \frac{(1-\varepsilon)}{(1-\varepsilon)} = 1.$$

Thus, even if the government increases both purchases of goods and services (an expenditure increasing move) and increases taxes (an expenditure decreasing move) the net effect of its actions is to increase aggregate autonomous expenditure. This balanced budget multiplier result is an important one because it means that the government does not have to run a deficit to stimulate aggregate expenditure. But because the balanced budget multiplier is smaller than the multipliers for government purchases and autonomous taxes, the magnitude of the balanced budget changes would have to be larger to achieve a given effect on aggregate expenditure.

A common drawback to all the fiscal policy actions that we have considered is that they take a long time in the legislative process and, as a consequence, they are of limited value for stabilizing the economy. However, one feature of the tax and transfer payments system does help stabilize the economy and acts as a automatic stabilizer.

Automatic Stabilizers

Taxes and transfer payments act as automatic stabilizers. An **automatic stabilizer** is a mechanism that decreases the fluctuations in *aggregate* expenditure resulting from fluctuations in some *component* of aggregate expenditure. The automatic stabilizing effects of taxes and transfer payments means that they act like an economic shock absorber, making the aggregate effects of fluctuations in investment and exports smaller than they otherwise would be.

To see how taxes and transfer payments act as an economic shock absorber, let's see how a change in investment or exports affects equilibrium expenditure in two model economies: in the first there are no induced taxes and transfer payments.

An economy with no induced taxes and transfer payments. In an economy with no induced taxes and transfer payments, the gap between GDP and disposable income is constant — it does not depend on the level of GDP. If the marginal propensity to consume out of disposable income is 0.9, the marginal propensity to consume out of GDP is also 0.9. That is, each extra dollar of GDP is an extra dollar of disposable income and induces an extra 90 cents of consumption expenditure. Suppose that there are no imports so that not only is the marginal propensity to consume 0.9, but so is the marginal propensity to spend.

What is the size of the multiplier if the marginal propensity to spend is 0.9? You can answer this question by using the formula

$$k = \frac{1}{(1-\varepsilon)}.$$

Substituting 0.9 for ε, the value of the multiplier is 10. In this economy, a $1 million change in autonomous expenditure produces a $10 million change in equilibrium expenditure. This economy has a very strong amplifier.

Let's now contrast the economy that we have just described with one that has induced taxes and transfer payments.

An Economy with Induced Taxes and Transfer Payments. To make our calculations easy, let's consider a model economy with the following structure of taxes and transfer payments.

First, for each dollar of income above a given amount, people pay a tax at a constant marginal tax rate of 0.3. That is, each extra dollar earned above a given amount generates a tax for the government of 30 cents and a disposable income of 70 cents. Second, for each dollar that a person's income falls below that same level, the government makes a transfer payment of 30 cents. Each additional dollar of real GDP creates 70 cents of disposable income.

If the marginal propensity to consume is 0.9, (the same as in the previous example) a $1 increase in

GDP increases disposable income by 70 cents and increases consumption by 63 cents (0.9 of 0.7 equals 0.63). In this economy, the marginal propensity to spend is 0.63. Substituting 0.63 for ε in the multiplier formula, the value of the multiplier is 2.7. The economy still amplifies shocks from changes in exports and investment but on a much smaller scale than the economy with no induced taxes and transfer payments. Thus to some degree, induced taxes and transfer payments absorb the shocks of fluctuating autonomous expenditure. The higher the marginal tax (and transfer payment) rate, the greater the extent to which autonomous expenditure shocks are absorbed by taxes (and transfer payments).

The existence of taxes and transfer payments that vary with income help the shock-absorbing capacities of the economy. They don't produce the economic equivalent of the suspension of a Lincoln Continental but they do produce the economic equivalent of something better than the springs of a stagecoach. As the economy fluctuates, the government's budget fluctuates absorbing some of the shocks, changing taxes and transfer payments, and smoothing the fluctuations in disposable income and expenditure.

R E V I E W

The government purchases multiplier is equal to the autonomous expenditure multiplier. By varying its purchases of goods and services, the government can try to offset fluctuations in investment and exports. In practice, such actions are difficult to arrange because of the time lags in the legislative process.

The transfer payments multiplier is equal to the marginal propensity to spend multiplied by the government purchases multiplier. A change in transfer payments works through a change in disposable income. Part of the change in disposable income is spent on domestic goods and services and part is saved. Only the part that is spent, which is determined by the marginal propensity to spend, has a multiplier effect.

The autonomous tax multiplier is negative — a tax increase leads to a decrease in equilibrium expenditure — but has the same magnitude as the transfer payments multiplier. The presence of taxes and transfer payments that vary directly with GDP results in an automatic stabilizer. Such taxes and transfer payments lower the value of the multiplier by lowering the marginal propensity to spend. The higher the marginal tax (and transfer payments) rate, the smaller is the change in disposable income that results from a \$1 change in GDP, and the smaller, therefore, is the change in induced expenditure and the greater is the degree of automatic stabilization. ■

We've now seen what determines the value of the autonomous expenditure multiplier, how the multiplier can be used by the government to influence aggregate planned expenditure by changing government purchases, transfer payments, or taxes, and how, by its choice of the marginal rate of taxes (and transfer payment), the government can influence the magnitude of the autonomous expenditure multiplier. But so far we have studied model economies with hypothetical numbers. Let's now turn to the real world. What is the size of the marginal propensity to spend in Canada? How big is the multiplier in the Canadian economy?

The Multiplier in Canada

The model economy that we studied earlier in this chapter (illustrated in Figs. 26.1 through 26.4) has a marginal propensity to spend of 0.5 — each additional dollar of income induces 50 cents of additional expenditure. The multiplier is 2.

The marginal propensity to spend in Canada, and the resulting multiplier, are smaller than those in the model economy but the precise value of the marginal propensity to spend is not known: there is a range of estimates. Let's look at some alternative estimates.

The Canadian Multiplier in 1990

In 1990, the marginal propensity to spend out of disposable income in Canada was approximately nine-tenths (0.9). In that year, each additional dollar of GDP generated approximately 60 cents of disposable income — six-tenths (0.6) of GDP. Putting these two pieces of information together, we can calculate that the marginal propensity to consume out of GDP was 0.54 (that is $0.6 \times 0.9 = 0.54$). Imports were 34 percent of GDP. Using this percentage as an estimate of the marginal propensity to import gives a value of 0.34. Each additional dollar of GDP induces 34 cents of imports. Subtracting the marginal propensity to import from the marginal propensity to consume gives the marginal propensity to spend on domestic goods and services, of 0.2 (that is, 0.54 – 0.34 = 0.2). With a marginal propensity to spend of 0.2, the multiplier is 1.25. That is,

$$k = \frac{1}{1 - 0.2} = \frac{1}{0.8} = 1.25\,.$$

Thus on the basis of these estimates, the Canadian multiplier in 1990 was a little more than 1.

Econometric Models and the Multiplier

An **econometric model** is a model economy with the numerical values for the marginal propensities to consume and import (and for other economic parameters) which are derived from data for an actual economy by using statistical methods of estimation that take account of all the possible influences on consumption expenditure and imports. There are, today, many such models in operation, attempting to forecast the future course of the economy. Most of these models are commercial tools used to produce forecasts that are sold by economic consultants. But the prototypes from which the commercial models were developed were created by research economists working in the universities, the Bank of Canada, and the Economic Council of Canada. There are four main models and their names, together with their estimates of the Canadian multiplier are set out in Table 26.2.

Table 26.2 Four Econometric Models' Estimates of the Multiplier in Canada

Model	Multiplier
CANDIDE — Economic Council of Canada	1.70
QFM — University of Toronto Quarterley Forcasting Model	1.37
RDX2 — Bank of Canada	0.96
TRACE — University of Toronto Institute for Policy Analysis	1.87

Four econometric models estimate that the Canadian multiplier lies between 0.96 and 1.87. Differences arise mainly because different models contain different assumptions about the structure of the economy.

Source: John F. Helliwell, T. Maxwell, and H.E.L. Waslander, "Comparing the Dynamics of Canadian Macro Models" *Canadian Journal of Economics*, XII, 2, May, 1979, pp.181-194.

As you can see the four models tell widely divergent stories about the magnitude of the Canadian multiplier. The largest estimate is that of TRACE at 1.87 and the smallest estimate is that of RDX2 at 0.96. The estimates that we obtained in the previous section lie between these values. The reason for different estimates of the multiplier is that the models incorporate different assumptions about the various influences on consumption and the other components of aggregate expenditure. What one model assumes is a movement along the consumption function, another model assumes is a shift in the consumption function. As a consequence, the models arrive at different estimates of the marginal propensity to consume and, therefore, different estimates of the multiplier. Rounding the various estimates, they lie between 1 and 2.

The Multiplier in Recession and Recovery

We've seen that the value of the multiplier in the Canadian economy lies between 1 and 2 and that in 1990, it was around 1.25. Is the multiplier a stable number — a constant — on which we can rely? Does the multiplier, although uncertain in value, nevertheless take on the same value when the economy is going into a recession as when it is recovering from a recession? Or does its value vary, and if so, in some systematic way? Answers to questions such as these are important for the design to policies to keep aggregate expenditure steady. How big an increase in government purchases or cut in taxes is needed to avoid a recession? How big a cut in government purchases or tax hike is needed to prevent the economy from overheating?

You can see part of the answers to these questions in Fig. 26.8, which shows estimates of the value of the multiplier in Canada for each year between 1970 and 1989. The estimates of the multiplier shown in the figure were calculated by dividing the change in real GDP by the change in autonomous expenditure. In these calculations, the change in autonomous expenditure was measured as the change in the sum of investment, government purchases of goods and services, and exports. The change in induced expenditure was measured as the change in consumption minus the change in imports.

As you can see from the figure the multiplier has been remarkably stable over the 20-year period shown. It has declined steadily, fluctuating along its

Figure 26.8 The Multiplier in Canada

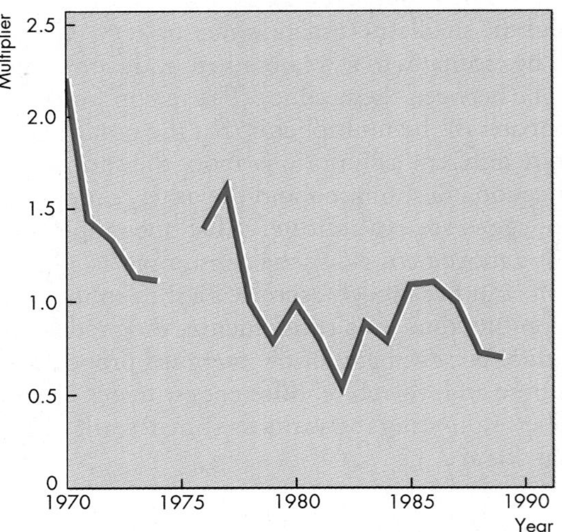

The Canadian multiplier, shown in this figure, is the change in real GDP divided by the change in the sum of investment, government purchaases on goods and services, and exports. The multiplier has declined gradually over the years, fluctuating gently around its falling trend.*

Source: See Fig. 25.1.

*No multiplier is shown for 1975. That was the year in which the world economy went into a deep recession following the OPEC oil price increase. In that year investment, government purchases of goods and services and exports decreased by $2 billion dollars but real GDP increased by $7 billion. Consumption expenditure increased, and imports decreased and their difference increased by $9 billion. These unusual circumstances make it impossible to use the method of calculation employed here to reveal a useful estimate of the mulitiplier for 1975.

declining trend, but the trend has been gentle and the fluctuations mild.

There is, however, a feature of the size of the multiplier that is important. The multiplier tends to be larger in a period of economic expansion than it is in a period of contraction. For example, the recession year of 1982 had a smaller multiplier than the expansion years of 1983 through 1986. Why is the multiplier smaller when the economy goes into recession than when it is in a recovery? The answer is that there are cycles in the marginal propensity to consume. At the start of a recovery, income gains are expected to be permanent and the marginal propensity to consume is high. When a cycle peak is approached and during recessions, income changes are viewed as temporary and the marginal propensity to consume is low. When income almost stopped growing in 1974–1975 and again in 1981–1982 as the economy went into recession, households regarded the income loss that they experienced as temporary. They did not cut their consumption expenditure. Instead consumption expenditure increased, but by less than it would have done in the absence of the recession. The increase in consumption expenditure was a rational reaction to events interpreted as a temporary halt to an otherwise ongoing period of economic growth and expansion. Because consumption expenditure did not decline, the recessions were less severe than they otherwise would have been. The multiplier was less than 1 and consumption expenditure acted, to some degree, like a shock absorber.

When a recovery gets under way and incomes increase, people regard a large part of those increased incomes as permanent. As a consequence, consumption expenditure increases to reinforce the increase in autonomous expenditure and the multiplier is larger than 1.

The Declining Canadian Multiplier

Although the multiplier in recovery is larger than that in recession, you can see from Fig. 26.8 that in the recovery years 1983–1987 the multiplier was still relatively small — and in some years less than 1. What kept the multiplier small in the 1980s? The answer is the behaviour of imports. Imports into Canada increased between 1983 and 1987 by $42 billion. In that same period, GDP increased by $69 billion. Thus the marginal propensity to import, over this period, was 0.61. For every extra dollar of GDP, our imports increased by 61 cents. This incredibly high marginal propensity to import was probably temporary, but it was sufficient over the recovery period to keep the multiplier low. Extra income spent on goods made abroad is a leakage from the circular flow of income and so lowers the multiplier effect of a change in autonomous expenditure.

R E V I E W

Econometric estimates of the multiplier in Canada range from 1 to 2. The multiplier is larger in recovery from recession than it is when the economy is going into a recession. Because our imports have increased steadily over the years, the Canadian multiplier has gradually declined in value. ■

In this chapter, we have studied the aggregate expenditure curve and the determination of equilibrium aggregate expenditure and real GDP. In Chapter 24, we studied the aggregate demand curve and the determination of macroeconomic equilibrium. What is the connection between the aggregate expenditure curve and the aggregate demand curve? And what is the connection between equilibrium expenditure and macroeconomic equilibrium?

Aggregate Expenditure and Aggregate Demand

The aggregate demand curve is the relation ship between the aggregate quantity of goods and services demanded and the price level. That is, the aggregate demand curve shows the quantity of real GDP demanded at each different price level. The aggregate expenditure curve tells us how aggregate planned expenditure varies as real GDP varies. The quantity of goods and services demanded is related to aggregate planned expenditure. Also, there is a connection between equilibrium expenditure and the aggregate demand curve. Let's explore the links between these concepts.

Aggregate Planned Expenditure and the Price Level

In studying aggregate planned expenditure, we have distinguished between autonomous expenditure and induced expenditure. Induced expenditure varies with real GDP. Autonomous expenditure does not vary with real GDP. But autonomous expenditure is not necessarily constant. In fact, we analysed the effects of changes in autonomous expenditure earlier in this chapter. Also, autonomous expenditure is not independent of other economic magnitudes. For example, a change in interest rates leads to a change in the investment component of autonomous expenditure. A change in the foreign exchange rate leads to a change in the export component of autonomous expenditure. Autonomous expenditure is also influenced by the price level.

At a given price level, there is a given level of autonomous expenditure and a given level of aggregate planned expenditure. But if the price level changes, so does autonomous expenditure. An increase in the price level decreases autonomous expenditure through the three effects described in Chapter 24 — the real balance effect, the intertemporal substitution effect, and the international substitution effect.

Figure 26.9 illustrates the effects of the price level on aggregate planned expenditure and the relation between equilibrium expenditure and the aggregate demand curve. (In this figure and in the rest of this section, we return to the example economy that we studied at the beginning of the chapter.) When the price level is 100, the aggregate expenditure curve is AE_0 in part (a). AE_0 intersects the 45° line at point *b*, where equilibrium expenditure is $4 billion. We have thus generated one point on the aggregate demand curve: at a price level of 100, the aggregate quantity of goods and services demanded is $4 billion — point *b* on the aggregate demand curve (*AD*) in part (b).

Now suppose that the price level increases to 150. As a result, the aggregate planned expenditure curve shifts downward. Suppose that the aggregate expenditure curve shifts to AE_1 in Fig. 26.9(a). The curve AE_1 intersects the 45° line at point *a*, and equilibrium expenditure is $2 billion. Thus the aggregate quantity of goods and services demanded at a price level of 150 is $2 billion, which is point *a* on the aggregate demand curve in Fig 26.9(b). A higher price level results in a downward shift in the *AE* curve and generates another point on the aggregate demand curve in part (b).

Next suppose that the price level falls to 50. A lower price level results in higher aggregate planned expenditure. Suppose that the aggregate expenditure curve shifts to AE_2. The curve AE_2 intersects the 45° line at point *c*, and equilibrium expenditure is $6 billion. Thus the aggregate quantity of goods and services demanded when the price level is 50 is $6 billion, which is point *c* on the aggregate demand curve in Fig. 26.9(b). The lower price level results in an upward shift in the *AE* curve, which generates another point on the *AD* curve. Joining points *a*, *b*, and *c*, we trace out the aggregate demand curve.

We can summarize the connection between the equilibrium expenditure at each price level and the *AD* curve in the following way: a rise in the price level causes the *AE* curve to shift downward, which lowers equilibrium expenditure and produces a movement along the aggregate demand curve.

Figure 26.9 Aggregate Planned Expenditure and Aggregate Demand

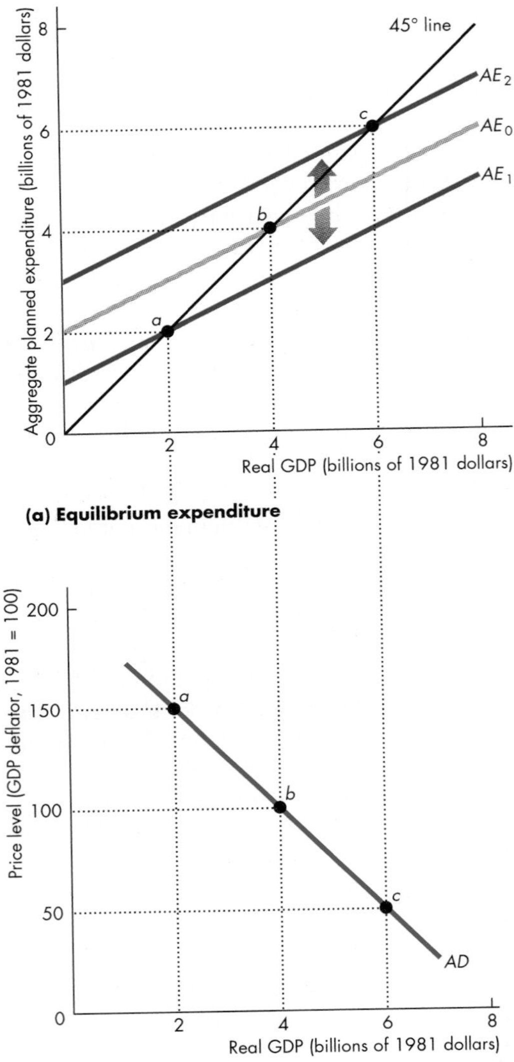

The position of the aggregate expenditure curve depends on the price level. An increase in the price level shifts the *AE* curve downward through the real balance effect, the intertemporal effect, and the international substitution effect. Suppose that when the price level is 100, the aggregate expenditure curve is AE_0, as shown in part (a). Equilibrium occurs where AE_0 intersects the 45° line, at point *b*. The level of real GDP demanded is $4 billion. In part (b) point *b* is a point on the aggregate demand curve — at a price level of 100, the aggregate quantity of goods and services demanded is $4 billion. Suppose that when the price level increases to 150, the aggregate expenditure curve shifts downward to AE_1. Equilibrium occurs at point *a* (in part a), where the aggregate quantity of goods and services demanded is $2 billion. Thus at a price level of 150 and an aggregate quantity of goods and services demanded of $2 billion, point *a* is a point on the aggregate demand curve (in part b). If the price level falls to 50 and the *AE* curve shifts upward to AE_2, the equilibrium quantity of goods and services demanded occurs at point *c* where AE_2 intersects the 45° line. Point *c* in part (b) is another point on the aggregate demand curve. A change in the price level leads to a shift in the aggregate expenditure curve and to a movement along the aggregate demand curve.

The Aggregate Demand Curve and Autonomous Expenditure

The aggregate expenditure curve shifts when the price level changes. It also shifts for a thousand other reasons. We studied these other sources of shift earlier in this chapter — for example, a change in profit expectations that shifts the investment demand curve or a change in real GDP in Japan that increases that country's demand for Canadian exports. Any factor other than the price level that shifts the aggregate expenditure curve also shifts the aggregate demand curve. Figure 26.10 illustrates these shifts.

Initially the aggregate planned expenditure curve is AE_0 in part (a) and the aggregate demand curve is AD_0 in part (b). The price level is 100. Now suppose that an increase in profit expectations leads to a rise in investment. Autonomous expenditure increases. If the price level remains at 100, the

Figure 26.10 Changes in Autonomous Expenditure and Aggregate Demand

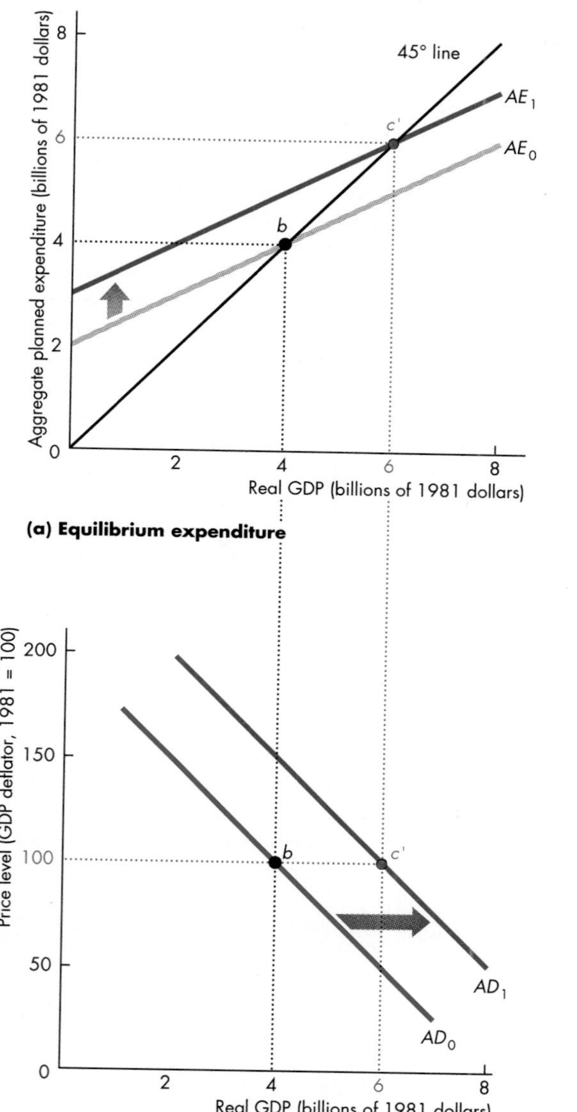

The price level is 100. When the aggregate expenditure curve is AE_0 (part a), the aggregate demand curve is AD_0 (part b). An increase in autonomous expenditure shifts the aggregate expenditure upward to AE_1. The new equilibrium occurs where AE_1 intersects the 45° line at a real GDP of $6 billion. The aggregate demand curve shifts to the right to AD_1. The magnitude of the rightward shift of the aggregate demand curve is determined by the change in autonomous expenditure and the size of the multiplier.

aggregate expenditure curve shifts upward to AE_1. This new higher *AE* curve intersects the 45° line at an equilibrium expenditure of $6 billion. This amount is the aggregate quantity of goods and services demanded at a price level of 100, as shown by point *c′* in part (a). Point *c′* also lies on a new aggregate demand curve. The aggregate demand curve has shifted to the right to AD_1.

The distance by which the aggregate demand curve shifts to the right is determined by the multiplier. The larger the multiplier, the larger is the shift in the *AD* curve resulting from a given change in autonomous expenditure. In this example, a $1 billion increase in autonomous expenditure produces a $2 billion increase in the aggregate quantity of goods and services demanded at each price level. The multiplier is 2. That is, a $1 billion increase in autonomous expenditure shifts the aggregate demand curve to the right by $2 billion.

A decrease in autonomous expenditure shifts the *AE* curve downward and shifts the aggregate demand curve to the left. You can see this effect by supposing that the economy initially is on aggregate expenditure curve AE_1 and aggregate demand curve AD_1. Then there is a decrease in autonomous expenditure, and the aggregate planned expenditure curve falls to AE_0. The aggregate quantity of goods and services demanded falls to $4 billion, and the aggregate demand curve shifts to the left to AD_0.

We can summarize what we have just discovered in the following way: an increase in autonomous expenditure arising from some source other than a change in the price level shifts the *AE* curve upward and shifts the *AD* curve to the right. The size of the shift of the *AD* curve is determined by the change in autonomous expenditure and the size of the multiplier.

Equilibrium GDP and the Price Level

In Chapter 24, we learned how to determine the equilibrium levels of real GDP and the price level as the intersection point of the aggregate demand curve and the short-run aggregate supply curve. In this chapter, we have put aggregate demand under a more powerful microscope and studied the factors that determine it and that make the aggregate demand curve shift. We have discovered that the aggregate demand curve shifts when there is a change in autonomous expenditure and that the magnitude of the shift depends on the size of the multiplier. Whether that

Figure 26.11 Changes in Autonomous Expenditure, Aggregate Demand, and the Price Level

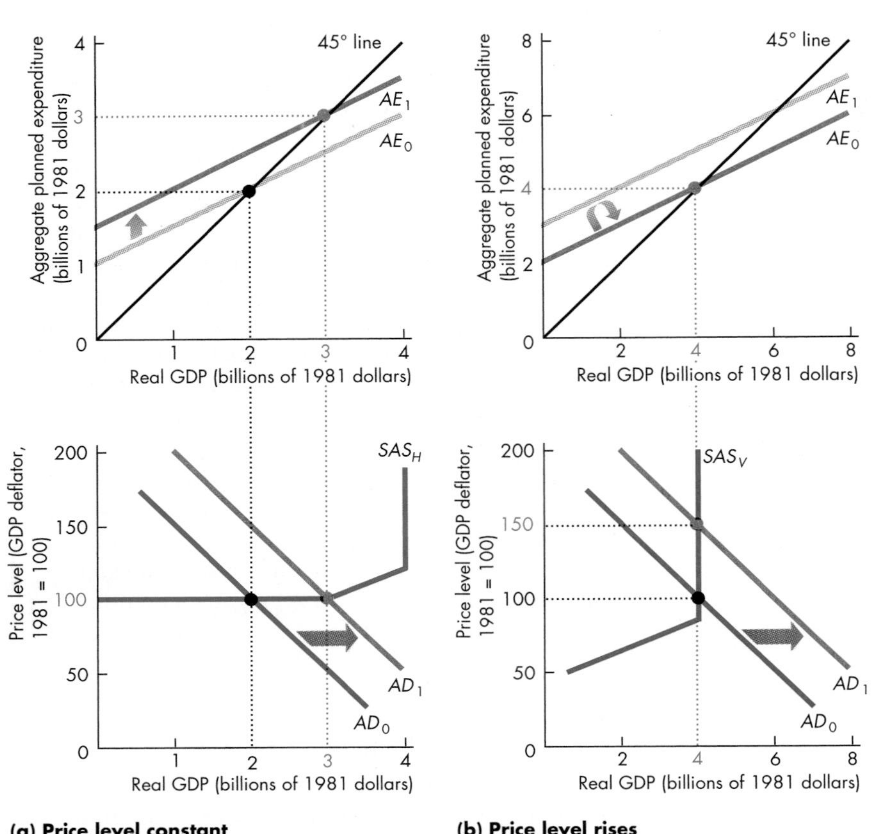

An increase in autonomous expenditure shifts the aggregate expenditure curve upward from AE_0 to AE_1 and shifts the aggregate demand curve from AD_0 to AD_1. Whether this increase in autonomous expenditure leads to an increase in real GDP, an increase in the price level, or a combination of the two, depends on the slope of the short-run aggregate supply curve at the equilibrium point. If that curve is horizontal, such as SAS_H in part (a), real GDP increases and the price level remains constant. If the short-run aggregate supply curve is vertical, such as SAS_V in part (b), the price level increases and real GDP remains constant. In this case, the increase in the price level leads to a decrease in planned expenditure that shifts the aggregate expenditure curve back to AE_0. In general, the short-run aggregate supply curve is neither horizontal nor vertical but upward sloping. As a consequence, when an increase in autonomous expenditure shifts the aggregate demand curve to AD_1, the price level rises to some extent, and the higher price level causes the AE curve to shift back down towards AE_0 but not by as much as the initial upward shift.

change in autonomous expenditure results ultimately in a change in real GDP or in a change in the price level, or in some combination of the two, depends on the slope of the short-run aggregate supply curve. That is, everything that we learned in Chapter 24 about how the intersection of the aggregate demand and aggregate supply curves determines real GDP remains valid. We simply have a richer understanding of aggregate demand than we had in Chapter 24.

You can see the importance of aggregate supply for determining real GDP and the price level by considering two extreme cases — one in which the short-run aggregate supply curve is horizontal at the equilibrium point and the other in which it is vertical. First, suppose that the short-run aggregate supply curve is horizontal at a price level of 100. This case, which may be relevant for an economy in deep recession, such as the Canadian economy was in the early 1930s, is illustrated in Fig. 26.11(a). The aggregate supply curve is SAS_H. A \$0.5 billion increase in autonomous expenditure shifts the aggregate expenditure curve upward from AE_0 to AE_1. The increase in autonomous expenditure also shifts the aggregate demand curve from AD_0 to AD_1. Real GDP increases from \$2 billion to \$3 billion, leaving the price level constant at 100.

Now suppose that \$4 billion is the capacity limit of the economy and that no more output can be produced. The aggregate supply curve is vertical at \$4 billion of real GDP. Suppose also that initially AD_0 intersects the short-run aggregate supply curve along its vertical part. This case, which is relevant for the Canadian economy at times of above full-employment, is illustrated in Figure 26.11(b). The aggregate supply curve is SAS_V. Suppose that autonomous expenditure increases by $1 billion. The increase in autonomous expenditure shifts the aggregate expenditure curve upward to AE_1 and shifts the aggregate demand curve to AD_1. But the shift in the aggregate demand curve increases the price level from 100 to 150 and leaves real GDP unchanged. The higher price level lowers aggregate planned expenditure and shifts the *AE* curve back to AE_0. The initial change in autonomous expenditure has been offset by a change in the opposite direction induced by the higher price level. With no change in autonomous expenditure, there is no change in the aggregate expenditure curve and no change in the equilibrium quantity of goods and services demanded. The *AD* curve has shifted, and there has also been a movement along the new *AD* curve; the combined effect is a higher price level and no change in real GDP.

The two cases that we have examined are the extremes of what is possible. In general, an increase in autonomous expenditure shifts the *AE* curve upward to AE_1 and shifts the demand curve to AD_1. The short-run aggregate supply curve is upward sloping — neither horizontal nor vertical — so there is an increase in the price level and an increase in real GDP. The higher price level shifts the *AE* curve downward from AE_1 but not as far as AE_0. The new *AE* curve intersects the 45° line at the same level of real GDP as that at which the aggregate demand curve AD_1 intersects the short-run aggregate supply curve.

■ We have now studied the forces that influence the components of aggregate expenditure and have analysed the way the components interact with each other to determine aggregate expenditure and the position of the aggregate demand curve. Fluctuations in the aggregate expenditure curve and in the aggregate demand curve are caused by fluctuations in autonomous expenditure. An important element of autonomous expenditure is investment, which, in turn, is determined by the level of interest rates (among other things). But how are interest rates determined? That is the question we turn to in the next chapter.

SUMMARY

Aggregate Expenditure and Real GDP

Aggregate planned expenditure is the sum of planned consumption expenditure, planned investment, planned government purchases of goods and services, and planned net exports. The relationship between aggregate planned expenditure and real GDP can be represented by the aggregate expenditure schedule and the aggregate expenditure curve. Aggregate expenditure is divided into two components: autonomous expenditure and induced expenditure. Autonomous expenditure is the part of consumption expenditure that does not vary as real GDP varies plus investment, government purchases of goods and services, and exports. Induced expenditure is that part of consumption expenditure that varies as real GDP varies minus imports.

The fraction of the last dollar of real GDP spent on domestic goods and services is called the marginal propensity to spend. Equivalently, the marginal propensity to spend is equal to the marginal propensity to consume minus the marginal propensity to import. The marginal propensity to spend determines the slope of the aggregate expenditure curve. (pp. 685-688)

Equilibrium Expenditure

Equilibrium expenditure occurs when aggregate planned expenditure equals real GDP. At real GDP levels larger than equilibrium expenditure, aggregate planned expenditure is less than real GDP; in such a situation, real GDP falls. At levels of real GDP smaller than equilibrium expenditure, aggregate planned expenditure exceeds real GDP, and real GDP rises. Only when real GDP equals aggregate planned expenditure is real GDP constant and in equilibrium. The main influence bringing real GDP and aggregate planned expenditure into equality is the behaviour of inventories. When aggregate planned expenditure exceeds real GDP, inventories fall. To restore their inventories, firms increase output, and this action increases real GDP. When planned expenditure is smaller than real GDP, inventories accumulate and firms cut back their output. This action lowers the level of real GDP. Only when there are no unplanned inventory changes do firms keep output constant and real GDP remains constant. (pp. 688-691)

Fluctuations in Expenditure and in Real GDP

Equilibrium expenditure is determined by autonomous expenditure and the marginal propensity to spend. Anything that increases autonomous expenditure — an increase in investment, government purchases, or exports — increases autonomous expenditure and increases equilibrium expenditure. Equilibrium expenditure and real GDP increase by more than the increase in autonomous expenditure. An increase in saving decreases expenditure and results in lower real GDP; this effect is called the paradox of thrift.

Anything that increases the marginal propensity to spend also increases equilibrium expenditure. The marginal propensity to spend is affected by the marginal propensity to consume, the marginal propensity to import, and the marginal tax rate. An increase in the marginal propensity to consume, a decrease in the marginal propensity to import, or a decrease in the marginal tax rate increases the marginal propensity to spend. (pp. 691-695)

The Multiplier

The autonomous multiplier is the amount by which a change in autonomous expenditure is multiplied to calculate the change in equilibrium expenditure. The size of the multiplier depends on the marginal propensity to spend: the larger the marginal propensity to spend, the larger is the multiplier. (pp. 695-699)

Fiscal Policy Multipliers

Fiscal policy is the government's attempt to smooth out fluctuations in aggregate expenditure by varying its own purchases of goods and services, transfer payments, and taxes. The government purchases multiplier is equal to the autonomous expenditure multiplier. The transfer payments multiplier is equal the marginal propensity to spend multiplied by the autonomous expenditure multiplier. The autonomous tax multiplier is equal in magnitude to the transfer payments multiplier but opposite in sign — it is negative. The balanced budget multiplier is 1.

Taxes and transfer payments act as automatic stabilizers. By weakening the link between GDP and disposable income, they reduce the fluctuations in consumption expenditure and therefore in aggregate expenditure resulting from a given change in autonomous expenditure. (pp. 699-702)

The Multiplier in Canada

Econometric estimates of the multipier in Canada place its value between 1 and 2. Its magnitude fluctuates over the business cycle and, because of gradually increasing imports, it has fallen over time. In 1990 it was about 1.25. (pp. 702-705)

Aggregate Expenditure and Aggregate Demand

The aggregate demand curve is the relationship between the aggregate quantity of goods and services demanded and the price level. The aggregate expenditure curve is the relationship between aggregate planned expenditure and real GDP. At a given price level, there is a given level of aggregate planned expenditure and a given aggregate expenditure curve. A change in the price level changes autonomous expenditure and shifts the aggregate expenditure curve. Thus a movement along the aggregate demand curve is associated with a shift in the aggregate expenditure curve.

A change in autonomous expenditure that is not caused by a change in the price level shifts the aggregate expenditure curve and also shifts the aggregate demand curve. The magnitude of the shift in the aggregate demand curve depends on the size of the multiplier and on the change in autonomous expenditure.

Real GDP and the price level are determined by both aggregate demand and aggregate supply. If, at the equilibrium point, the short-run aggregate supply curve is horizontal, as it might be in a deep business-cycle trough, an increase in autonomous expenditure that shifts the aggregate expenditure and aggregate demand curves increases real GDP; the price level remains constant. But if, at the equilibrium point, the short-run aggregate supply curve is vertical, as it might be at a business-cycle peak, an increase in autonomous expenditure shifts the aggregate expenditure curve upward and shifts the aggregate demand curve; the price level rises, and real GDP stays constant. The higher price level reduces autonomous expenditure and shifts the aggregate expenditure curve back down to its original position. (pp. 705-709)

KEY ELEMENTS

Key Terms

Aggregate expenditure curve, 685
Aggregate expenditure schedule, 685
Automatic stabilizer, 701
Autonomous expenditure, 687
Autonomous expenditure multiplier or multiplier, 695
Autonomous tax multiplier, 700
Autonomous taxes, 700
Balanced budget multiplier, 701
Econometric model, 703
Equilibrium expenditure, 688
Fiscal policy, 699
Government purchases multiplier, 699
Induced expenditure, 687
Induced taxes, 700
Marginal propensity to import, 687
Marginal propensity to spend on domestic goods and services or marginal propensity to spend, 688
Marginal tax rate, 693
Paradox of thrift, 692
Planned expenditure, 685
Transfer payments multiplier, 700

Key Figures and Tables 

REVIEW QUESTIONS

1 What is the aggregate expenditure function?

2 Distinguish between autonomous expenditure and induced expenditure.

3 Define the marginal propensity to spend.

4 What is the slope of the aggregate expenditure curve?

5 How is equilibrium expenditure determined? What happens if aggregate planned expenditure exceeds real GDP?

6 What is the multiplier?

7 What is the relationship between the multiplier and the marginal propensity to spend?

8 Why is the multiplier greater than 1?

9 What is the government purchases multiplier?

10 How does the government purchases multiplier compare with the autonomous expenditure multiplier?

11 What is the autonomous tax multiplier?

12 How does the autonomous tax multiplier compare with the autonomous expenditure multiplier?

13 What is the size of the transfer payments multiplier and how does it compare with the autonomous tax multiplier?

14 What is the size of the balanced budget multiplier?

15 Explain how induced taxes and transfer payments act as automatic stabilizers — automatic shock absorbers.

16 What was the size of the multiplier in Canada in 1990?

17 What is the relationship between the aggregate expenditure curve and the aggregate demand curve?

18 If the price level changes and everything else is held constant, what happens to the aggregate demand curve and the aggregate expenditure curve?

19 If there is a change in autonomous expenditure not produced by a change in the price level, what happens to the aggregate expenditure curve and the aggregate demand curve?

PROBLEMS

1 You are given the following information about a model economy. The autonomous part of consumption is \$100 million. The marginal propensity to consume out of disposable income is 0.8. Investment is \$460 million; government purchases of goods and services are \$400 million; taxes are a constant \$400 million and do not vary as income varies. Both imports and exports are zero.

a) Calculate the equilibrium levels of GDP and consumption.

b) If government expenditure is cut to \$300 million, what is the change in GDP and the change in consumption?

c) What is the size of the government purchases multiplier?

2 Suppose that the economy in problem 1 changes its tax laws. Instead of taxes being a constant \$400 million, taxes become one-eighth of GDP.

a) If nothing else is changed, calculate the equilibrium levels of GDP and consumption.

b) If government purchases are cut to \$300 million, what is the change in GDP and the change in consumption?

c) What is the size of the multiplier?

3 Suppose that the economy described in problem 1 has an absolute limit to its output of \$3,200 million. At that output level its aggregate supply curve is vertical.

a) If the government increases its purchases of goods and services, what happens to the economy's aggregate demand curve and aggregate expenditure curve?

b) What happens to the price level?

4 You are given the following information about the multiplier in an economy. Its average value is 2; in year A it is ½, and in year B it is 3½.

a) Make an educated guess about the state of this economy in year A and year B.

b) Was year A a recovery year or a recession year? Why?

c) Was year B a recovery year or a recession year? Why?

PART 10

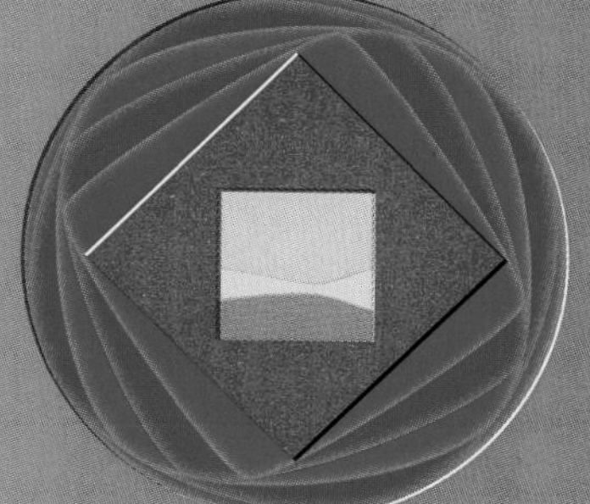

Money, Interest, and the Dollar

TALKING WITH GERALD BOUEY

Gerald Bouey earned his ba from Queen's University in 1948 and was awarded the medal in Economics. He was Governor of the Bank of Canada from 1973 to 1987, a period during which the world abandoned fixed exchange rates, the opec cartel repeatedly forced up world energy prices, and Canada became locked in the grip of double-digit inflation. Michael Parkin talked with Gerald Bouey about his work at the Bank of Canada and the role the Bank can play in stabilizing the Canadian economy.

"What I keep coming back to are the laws of supply and demand."

Mr. Bouey, how did you get into economics and central banking?

I grew up in southern Saskatchewan, in the 1930's, a time when young people didn't expect to get anything more than short-term jobs. I didn't know anybody who went to university; it was a long way off in Saskatoon. I was fortunate to get a job in a bank, although when I applied for the job it was the first time I'd ever been in a bank! Then the war came. When I was in the Air Force, most of my companions were young men who hadn't been able to get a job before the war. I developed some feeling of resentment about this situation and at the same time an interest in how the economic system worked. After graduating from Queens, I joined the research department at the Bank of Canada. That's where I really learned economics.

What are the economic principles and ideas that you have found most useful throughout your career?

What I keep coming back to are the basic laws of supply and demand. If you put too much demand pressure on the economy you're going to be in trouble. You can't expect to avoid inflation if you allow the money supply to grow too fast.

Another lesson I've found useful is one I learned when I first joined the Bank's research department. I remember the chief of the department saying to me: "You'll have to learn how to do economic analysis. But first of all, make sure you've got all the facts. Once you've got all the facts, quite often you don't need any analysis." So I would put a great emphasis on the empirical side of economics.

One of the facts is that since the mid-1970s there has been a large and persistent federal government deficit. How has this deficit affected the work of the Bank of Canada?

It has left the job of controlling inflation to monetary policy. As a result, we've had serious distortions from higher interest rates, and, in recent years, from a higher exchange rate, and a larger current account deficit than we would have had if fiscal policy had played a stronger role. It's true that inflation has been controlled, and that was essential, but we have been storing up trouble.

What do you think has to be done about the deficit? Do we have to bite the bullet and increase taxes?

My own view is that that is going to have to be part of the answer, mainly because of the size of the interest rate transfer. I think there's a limit to what you can do in cutting expenditures to offset this ever-increasing interest burden. Also, there are some expenditures we ought to be making that we are not. Look at the transportation system, health care, education, even the judicial system with people waiting two years for a trial. We are a pretty affluent society and should be able to do better.

What were the influences shaping your own attitudes towards monetary policy? Do they stem from the Depression?

Oh yes, I would say so. I think I always knew that an economy wouldn't work well under inflationary conditions. But I was always very concerned about unemployment. Central bankers are, although they may not always sound that way. There is nothing more distressing than seeing a lot of people unemployed. So when we began to see the inflation problem in the 1970s I was very much in favour of dealing with it in a gradual way to see if we couldn't bring inflation down without causing a real crunch on the unemployment side. It was my view when I became governor, that we should be able to get along with no more than 5 percent unemployment. Well, we never got it that low and I would say through most of the 1970s we didn't fully realize the importance of some of the changes affecting unemployment that were taking place—changes resulting from demographic factors and from unemployment insurance. And I don't think the government did either because when the unemployment rate would go up a little, fiscal policy would be eased. After the experience of the 1970s my approach did change. I now believe it is important to deal with inflation as early as you can. Everyone will be better off in the long run.

Does this change of approach explain why the Bank of Canada embraced monetary targeting in the 1970s and then abandon it in the early 1980s?

Well, we were right the second time! But there's a case for both. A central bank governor would like nothing better than a monetary aggregate that has a systematic, reliable relationship with gross domestic product. None of the measures was really satisfactory, but we chose M1 which seemed to us to be the most reliable. M1 was pretty much the transaction balances part of the money supply at that time and that seemed to us to be worth targetting, but with a pretty wide range for the target growth rate. Well, by the late 1970s, with the high interest rates and the computerization of cash management, the relationship between gross domestic product and M1 broke down.

Was the severe recession of 1982 a price worth paying for the reduction of inflation from its double-digit level?

I don't agree with people who talk about the costs of the disinflation; I regard these as the costs of inflation, because somehow or other you've got to bring it under control.

What do you think of the relationship between the Bank of Canada and the federal government? Is that relationship about right?

Yes it is. I was involved in that relationship for 14 years, with seven different ministers of finance, and I thought it worked well. The relationship was worked out in the 1960s, and embodied in the Bank of Canada Act of 1967. The Act requires regular consultation between the governor and the minister of finance. It also requires that if a serious difference of view develops, the government, after further consultation, has the right to direct the Bank in the policy it should follow. That arrangement has the advantage that, as long as the directive power is not used, the public is entitled to hold the Bank of Canada responsible for monetary policy. At the same time, it can also hold the government respon-

"I don't agree with talk about the costs of disinflation. I regard them as the costs of inflation."

sible, because it could issue a directive if it disagreed with the governor.

There's never been a directive. Why is that?

The chances of a directive being necessary seem very slim. There's a great deal of contact between the Bank and the government. In addition to meetings between the governor and the minister, there's contact between the Bank and department of finance staff at many levels. Everybody's looking at the same basic information and doing similar kinds of economic analysis.

Why, then, does the Bank need to be independent?

I think without that much independence, there might be a danger of monetary policy operating a bit more like fiscal policy with some of the decisions being influenced more by politics than economic considerations, especially when an election is imminent. In that connection, the great fear that people used to have about the lack of central bank independence was that governments would insist that the central bank print money to cover their deficit. I haven't seen any evidence of that. What has bothered me has been the willingness of governments, not only here but in other countries as well, to pay whatever interest rate it takes to go on with their expenditure programs for a long period before facing the need to cut back.

"The great fear that people used to have about the lack of central bank independence was that governments would insist that the central bank print money to cover their deficit."

Since people don't like high interest rates, why can't the Bank of Canada just create more money, lower interest rates, and let the dollar go down?

Well, it could try, but in a period of strong expectations of inflation how would financial markets react? For a short period a sharp increase in the money supply would be accompanied by a fall in short-term interest rates. The Canadian dollar would drop sharply, putting additional upward pressure on the price level, and these developments would cause financial markets to lose confidence that inflation would be controlled so that longer-term interest rates would tend to rise, not fall. If the central bank persisted in this policy inflation would become much more serious and in time interest rates would have to be much higher. However, in quite different circumstances, that is, when inflationary pressures have weakened, an increase in the money supply can in fact be accompanied by a general decline in interest rates and a moderate reduction in the value of the Canadian dollar.

What would you say to a student today who wants to work as an economist in the financial sector?

I think the main thing is to get a good education—a better one than I had. (I don't suppose I'd get into the Bank of Canada now with my academic qualifications.) If you really want to be an economist go all the way and get a Ph.D if you possibly can. The only other thing I'd say is that you need a certain amount of patience. You have to be realistic. Since the world is so unpredictable expect periods of frustration from time to time.

CHAPTER 27

Money, Banking, and Prices

After studying this chapter, you will be able to:

- Define money and describe its different forms.
- Describe the balance sheets of the main financial intermediaries.
- Explain the economic functions of chartered banks and other financial intermediaries.
- Explain how banks create money.
- Explain why the quantity of money is an important economic magnitude.
- Explain the quantity theory of money.
- Describe the historical and international evidence on the relationship between the quantity of money and the price level.

Money Makes The World Go Round

MONEY, LIKE FIRE and the wheel, has been around for a very long time. No one knows for sure how long or what its origins are. An incredible array of items have served as money — wampum (beads made from shells) were used by North American Indians; muskrat pelts were used in Upper Canada in the eighteenth and early nineteenth centuries; cowries (brightly coloured shells) were used in India; whales' teeth were used in Fiji; tobacco was used by early American colonists; large stone disks were used in the Pacific island of Yap; cigarettes and liquor have been used in more modern times; even cakes of salt have served as money in Ethiopia, Africa, and Tibet. The Roman army was paid in salt — an allowance called "salarium" (which is the origin of the word "salary"). What exactly is money? Why has this rich variety of commodities served as money? ■ Today, when you want to buy something, you can use coins or bills, or you can write a cheque or present a credit card. Are all these things money? ■ When you deposit some coloured paper in a bank or trust company, is that still money? And what happens when the bank or the trust company lends the money in your deposit accounts to other people? How can you get your money back if it's been lent out? Does lending by banks and trust companies create money — out of thin air? ■ The 1980s saw dramatic changes in the types of accounts that banks and other financial institutions offer. In the 1970s, you had either a savings account or a chequing account. The savings account earned interest and the chequing account didn't. Today, there are a wide variety of new accounts that provide the convenience of a chequing account and the income of a savings account. Why have these new kinds of bank accounts been developed? ■ The biggest transaction that most people ever undertake is the purchase of a house. Few are wealthy enough to buy a house with their own funds. Instead, they have to borrow. The main source of funds to buy a house is a bank or a trust company. Banks and trust companies obtain their funds from thousands of depositors, any one of whom can withdraw his or her deposit at a moment's notice

But these companies lend money on a long-term basis — from 1 year to 5 years and longer. When a lender is committed to long-term loans at a low interest rate and interest rates on deposits increase, these institutions get into trouble. Such was the situation in Alberta in 1986 when Canadian Commercial and Northland banks collapsed. A similar and more serious situation arose in the United States in 1989 when the savings and loan associations (the U.S. equivalent of our trust and mortgage companies) found themselves incurring huge losses. The U.S. government came to their rescue with the largest bailout in American history. Before the bailout, many feared that these institutions, which had been the source of finance for house purchases for the past 60 years, were on the edge of extinction. If mortgage companies were to disappear, did that mean that some depositors' money would disappear with them? ■ At certain times in Canadian history, the quantity of money in existence has increased quickly. In other countries — such as China in the late 1940s, Israel in the early 1980s, and some Latin American countries today — the quantity of money has increased at an extremely rapid pace. Does the rate of increase in the quantity of money matter? What are the effects of an increasing quantity of money on our economy?

■ In this chapter, we'll study that useful invention, money. We'll look at the functions of money, the different forms that money takes, and the way money is defined and measured in Canada today. We'll also study chartered banks and other financial institutions and learn how banks create money. Finally, we'll discover an important connection between the growth rate of the amount of money in the economy and the pace at which prices rise — the inflation rate. Whether we look at Canada's own historical experience or at the contemporary experience of the other major countries of the world, we see a clear and strong connection between the growth rate of the quantity of money and the inflation rate.

What is Money?

We've already had a brief encounter with money in Chapters 3 and 24. Let's begin by recalling the definition of money.

The Definition of Money

Money is a medium of exchange. A **medium of exchange** is anything that is generally acceptable in exchange for goods and services. Without a medium of exchange, it would be necessary to exchange goods directly for other goods — an exchange known as barter. **Barter** is the direct exchange of goods for goods. For example, if you wanted to buy a hamburger, you would offer in exchange the used paperback novel that you've just finished reading or half an hour of your labour in the kitchen. Barter can take place only when there is a double coincidence of wants. A **double coincidence of wants** is a situation that occurs when person A wants to buy what person B is selling and person B wants to buy what person A is selling. That is, to get your hamburger, you'd have to find someone who's selling hamburgers and who wants a paperback novel or your work in the kitchen. The occurrence of a double coincidence of wants is rare, so rare that barter exchange leaves most potential gains from specialization and exchange unrealized. The evolution of monetary exchange is a consequence of our economizing activity — of getting the most possible out of limited resources. We're going to study the institutions of monetary exchange that have evolved in the Canadian economy. But first we'll look at the functions of money.

The Functions of Money

Money has four functions. It serves as a

- Medium of exchange.
- Unit of account.
- Standard of deferred payment.
- Store of value.

Medium of Exchange Any commodity or asset that serves as a generally acceptable medium of exchange is money. Money guarantees that there will always be a double coincidence of wants. People with something to sell will always accept money in exchange for it, and people who want to buy will always offer money in exchange. Money acts as a lubricant that smooths the mechanism of exchange.

Unit of Account An agreed measure for stating the prices of goods and services is a **unit of account.** To get the most out of your budget you have to figure out, among other things, whether seeing one more movie is worth the price you have to pay, not in

Table 27.1 The Unit of Account Function of Money Simplifies Price Comparisons

Good	Price in money units	Price in units of another good
Movie	$6.00 each	2 submarines
Submarines	$3.00 each	2 ice-cream cones
Ice cream	$1.50 per cone	3 packs of jelly beans
Jelly beans	$0.50 per pack	2 cups of coffee
Coffee	$0.25 a cup	1 local phone call

Money as a unit of account
One movie costs $6 and coffee costs 25 cents, so one movie costs 24 cups of coffee ($6.00 ÷ $0.25 = 24).

No unit of account
You go to a movie theatre and learn that the price of a movie is 2 submarines. You go to a candy store and learn that a pack of jelly beans costs 2 cups of coffee. But how many cups of coffee does seeing a movie cost you? To answer that question, you go to the sub shop and find that a submarine costs 2 ice-cream cones. Now you head for the ice-cream store where an ice cream costs 3 packs of jelly beans. Now you get out your pocket calculator: 1 movie costs 2 submarines or 4 ice-cream cones or 12 packs of jelly beans, or 24 cups of coffee!

dollars and cents, but in terms of the number of ice creams, submarines, and coffees that you have to give up. It's not hard to do such calculations when all these goods have prices in terms of dollars and cents (see Table 27.1). If a movie costs $6 and a submarine costs $3, you know right away that seeing one more movie costs you 2 submarines. If jelly beans are 50 cents a pack, one more movie costs 12 packs of jelly beans. You need only one calculation to figure out the opportunity cost of any pair of goods and services.

But imagine how troublesome it would be if your local movie theatre posted its price as 2 submarines, the sub shop posted the price of a submarine as 2 ice-cream cones, the ice-cream shop posted the price of a cone as 3 packs of jelly beans, and the candy store priced jelly beans as 2 cups of coffee! Now how much running around and calculating do you have to do to figure out how much a movie is going to cost you in terms of the submarine, ice cream, jelly beans, or coffee that you must give up to see it? You get the answer for submarines right away from the sign posted on the movie theatre, but for all the other goods you're going to have to visit many different stores to establish the price of each commodity in terms of another and calculate prices in units that are relevant for your own decision. Cover up the column labelled "Price in money units" in Table 27.1 and see how hard it is to figure out the number of local phone calls it costs to see one movie. It's enough to make a person swear off movies! How much simpler it is for everyone to express their prices in terms of dollars and cents.

Standard of Deferred Payment An agreed measure that enables contracts to be written for future receipts and payments is called a **standard of deferred payment**. If you borrow money to finance your college education, your future commitment will be agreed to in dollars and cents. Money is used as the standard for a deferred payment. Imagine the complexity of a world that did not use money as a standard of deferred payment. Instead of guaranteeing to repay your student loan in money, you and the lender must agree on a standard. You might agree to repay your loan in an agreed quantity of grade A beef. Both you and the lender now bear a risk arising from uncertainty about the future price of beef. If beef rises in price relative to other goods, you will have struck a bad deal and the lender will have gained. If the price of beef falls relative to other goods, you will have gained and the lender will have lost. Since the prices of individual commodities fluctuate a great deal and cannot be predicted accurately, at least not a long way ahead, both borrowers and lenders would face much more risk than if money were used as the standard of deferred payment. Using money as a standard of deferred payment is not entirely without risk for, as we saw in Chapter 22, inflation leads to unpredictable changes in the value of money. But to the extent that borrowers and lenders anticipate inflation, its rate is reflected in the interest rates paid and received. Lenders, in effect, protect themselves by charging a higher interest rate, and borrowers, anticipating inflation, willingly pay the higher rate.

Store of Value Any commodity that can be held and exchanged later for some other commodity or service is a **store of value**. Most physical objects are stores of value. All financial assets, paper securities such as treasury bills, and bank accounts are also stores of value. Services are not stores of value. Once a service has been performed, that is the end of the matter.

There are no stores of value that are completely safe and predictable. The value of a physical object, such as a house, a car, or a work of art, as well as the value of a paper security and even of money itself fluctuates over time. The more stable and the more predictable the value of a commodity, the better can it act as a store of value. Thus the higher and the more unpredictable the inflation rate, the less useful is money as a store of value. It is essential that money be a store of value. Otherwise, it would not be acceptable as a medium of exchange.

The Different Forms of Money

Money can take four different forms:

- Commodity money
- Convertible paper money
- Fiat money
- Private debt money

Commodity Money **Commodity money** is a physical commodity valued in its own right and also used as a medium of exchange. An amazing array of items have served as commodity money at different times and places, several of which were described in the chapter opener. But the most common commodity money has been coins made from metals such as gold, silver, and copper. The first known coins were made in Lydia, a Greek city-state, at the beginning of the seventh century B.C. These coins were made of electrum, a natural mixture of gold and silver.

The earliest money used in pre-Confederation Canada was commodity money. Some of this money was gold coin of British, French, Spanish, or Mexican origin. More exotic forms of commodity money including muskrat pelts were also used.

Commodity money has considerable advantages but some drawbacks. Let's look at both.

Advantages of Commodity Money The main advantage of commodity money is that the commodity is valued for its own sake and can be used in ways other than as a medium of exchange. This fact provides a guarantee of the value of the money. For example, gold can be used to fill teeth and make rings; silver can be used to make tableware; cigarettes can be smoked; beads can be worn. The commodities that are most advantageous as money are the precious metals, such as gold and silver. Historically, these commodities were ideal because they were in constant demand by those wealthy enough to use them for ornaments and jewellery. Their quality was easily verified, and they were easily divisible into units small enough to facilitate exchange.

Disadvantages of Commodity Money Commodity money has two main disadvantages. First, there is a constant temptation to cheat on the value of the money. Two commonly used methods of cheating — are clipping and debasement. *Clipping* is reducing the size of coins by an imperceptible amount, thereby lowering their metallic content. *Debasement* is creating a coin with a lower-than-standard silver or gold content (the balance being made up of some cheaper metal).

This temptation to lower the value of money led to a phenomenon known as Gresham's Law named for the sixteenth-century English financial expert Sir Thomas Gresham. **Gresham's Law** is the tendency for bad money to drive out good money. Bad money is debased money; good money is money that has not been debased. It's easy to see why Gresham's Law works. Suppose that a person is paid with two coins, one debased and the other not. Each coin has the same value if used as money in exchange for goods. But one of the coins — the one that's not debased — is more valuable as a commodity than it is as a coin. It will not, therefore, be used as money. Only the debased coin will be used as money. It is in this way that bad money drives good money out of circulation.

A second major disadvantage of commodity money is that the commodity, valued for its own sake, could be used in ways other than as a medium of exchange if it was not being used as money — using the commodity as money has an opportunity cost. This cost creates incentives to find alternatives to the commodity for use in the exchange process. One such alternative is a paper claim to commodity money.

Convertible Paper Money A paper claim to a commodity that circulates as a medium of exchange is called **convertible paper money**. The first known example of paper money occurred in China during the Ming dynasty (1368 – 1399 A.D.). This form of money was also used extensively throughout Europe in the Middle Ages.

It was the inventiveness of goldsmiths and their clients that led to the widespread use of convertible paper money. Because gold was valuable, goldsmiths had well-guarded safes in which to keep their own gold. They also rented space to artisans and others who wanted to put their gold in safekeeping. The goldsmiths issued a receipt entitling the owner of the gold to reclaim his or her "deposit" on demand. These receipts were much like the cloak-check tokens that you get at a theatre or museum.

Suppose that Isabella had a gold receipt indicating that she had 100 ounces of gold deposited with Samuel Goldsmith. Then she decided to buy from Henry a piece of land valued at 100 ounces of gold. There were two ways that Isabella might undertake the transaction. The first way was to go to Samuel, hand over her receipt and collect her gold, transport the gold to Henry, and take title to the land. Henry now went back to Samuel with the gold and deposited it there for safekeeping, leaving with his own receipt. The second way of doing this transaction was for Isabella simply to hand over her gold receipt to Henry, completing the transaction by using the gold receipt as money. Obviously, it was much more convenient to complete the transaction in the second way (provided Henry could trust Samuel).

The gold receipt circulating as a medium of exchange was money. The paper money was *backed* by the gold held by Goldsmith. Also the paper money was *convertible* into commodity money.

Fractional Backing Once the convertible paper money system was operating and people were using their gold receipts rather than gold itself as the medium of exchange, goldsmiths noticed that their vaults were storing a large amount of gold that was never withdrawn. This gave them a brilliant idea. Why not lend people gold receipts? The goldsmith could charge interest on the loan, and the loan could be created just by writing on a piece of paper. As long as the number of such receipts created was not too large in relation to the stock of gold in the goldsmith's safe, the goldsmith was in no danger of not being able to honour his promise to convert receipts into gold on demand. By this device, *fractionally backed* convertible paper money was invented.

Fractional Backing in Canada There are important examples of the use of fractionally backed convertible paper money in Canada's early colonial history, as well as in the post-Confederation era. The earliest was the use of fractionally backed playing cards as money in New France in the late seventeenth century. Playing cards were declared to be money, different cards being denominated as different values. Playing cards circulated alongside gold coins and could be redeemed in Québec when gold arrived from France.

The first fractionally backed bank notes issued in Canada began to circulate in 1817 when the Bank of Montreal was permitted to issue notes backed by gold, silver, or government bonds up to three times the value of its capital. As more banks were chartered during the nineteenth century, the volume of private bank notes issued expanded steadily. In 1870, the Dominion Bank Note Act was passed. This act permitted the government to issue bank notes. Government bank notes grew at a more rapid pace than chartered bank notes and, by the beginning of this century, were the dominant form of currency in circulation in Canada.

Fractionally backed convertible paper money continued to be used in Canada until 1914. The Finance Act of that year, however, removed Canada from the gold standard. Chartered banks were no longer required to redeem their notes in gold on demand, although there was a temporary resumption of gold redemption between 1926 and 1929.

It is no accident that Canada (along with most other countries) eventually abandoned fractionally backed paper money. Even though paper money can be issued vastly in excess of the volume of commodities that back it, the exchange process still ties up valuable commodities that could be used for other productive activities. There remains an incentive to find a yet more efficient way of facilitating exchange and of freeing up the commodities used to back the paper money. This alternative is fiat money.

Fiat Money **Fiat money** is an intrinsically worthless or almost worthless commodity that serves the functions of money. The term "fiat" means "let it be done" or "by order of the authority." Some of the earliest fiat money in North America were the continental currency issued during the American Revolution and the "greenbacks" issued during the American Civil War. Greenbacks circulated until the restoration of the gold standard in 1879. Another early fiat money was that of the assignats issued during the French Revolution.

These early experiments with fiat money ended in rapid inflation because the amount of fiat money created was allowed to increase at a rapid pace, causing the money to lose value. However, provided the quantity of fiat money is not allowed to grow too rapidly, it has a reasonably steady value in terms of the goods and services that it will buy. People are willing to accept fiat money in exchange for the goods and services they sell only because they know it will be honoured when they go to buy goods and services.

Fiat Money in Canada The bank notes and coins that we use in Canada today — collectively known as **currency** — are examples of fiat money. Because of the creation of fiat money, people are willing to accept a piece of paper that has a special watermark, is printed in coloured ink, and is worth no more than a few cents as a commodity in exchange for $20 worth of goods and services. The small metal-alloy disk that we call a quarter is worth almost nothing as a piece of metal, but it pays for a local phone call and many other small commodities. The replacement of commodity money by fiat money enables the commodities themselves to be used productively. But the tokens that we use as fiat money do have an opportunity cost, and important decisions have to be made in designing our bills and coins (see Reading Between the Lines on pp. 724-725).

Fiat money in Canada has its origins in the 1914 Finance Act. That act not only freed the chartered banks from the obligation to redeem their notes in gold on demand, but also empowered the minister of finance to issue Dominion notes to the banks. The banks could exchange securities for Dominion notes and then use those notes as backing for their own notes. In other words, it permitted a chartered bank to make a loan to a private Canadian company and then to exchange the claim to that loan for Dominion notes against which it could issue more of its own notes. Canada's fiat money system was made more formal by the establishment of the Bank of Canada in 1935. With the passage of the Bank of Canada Act in that year, the note-issuing powers of the chartered banks were repealed and the Bank of Canada became the sole issuer of bank notes. These notes were backed by nothing other than the Bank of Canada's holdings of government debt and a small amount of gold and foreign currency.

Private Debt Money In the modern world, there is a fourth important type of money — private debt money. **Private debt money** is a loan that the borrower promises to repay in currency on demand. By transferring the entitlement to be repaid from one person to another, such a loan can be used as money. For example, you give me an IOU for $10; I give the IOU to a bookseller to buy a biography of Adam Smith; you pay the holder of the IOU $10 — only now it's the bookseller holding the IOU.

The most important example of private debt money is chequable deposits at chartered banks and other financial institutions. A **chequable deposit** is a loan by a depositor to a bank, the ownership being transferable from one person to another by writing an instruction to the bank — a cheque — asking the bank to alter its records. We'll have more to say about this type of money shortly. Before doing so, let's look at the different forms of money and their relative importance in Canada today.

Money in Canada Today

There are four official measures of money in current use: **M1**, **M2**, **M3**, and **M2+**. They are defined in Table 27.2 and the terms used to describe the components of the three measures are set out in the compact glossary in Table 27.3.

Are All the Measures of Money Really Money? We have defined money as a medium of exchange. The items that make up M1 fit that definition fairly closely. Currency (both coins and dollars bills of various denominations) is universally acceptable in exchange for goods and services. So are chequable deposits at chartered banks. But other important assets that serve as a medium of exchange are not included in M1. For example, personal savings deposits at chartered banks on which a cheque can be written also act as a

Table 27.2 The Four Official Definitions of Money

M1
- Currency held outside banks
- Privately held demand deposits at chartered banks

M2
- M1
- Personal savings deposits at chartered banks
- Nonpersonal notice deposits at chartered banks

M3
- M2
- Nonpersonal fixed-term deposits of residents booked in Canada

M2+
- M2
- Deposits at trust and mortgage loan companies
- Deposits and shares at caisses populaires (Québec savings banks) and credit unions

Economical Money

Loose change

A [U.S.] dollar bill buys hardly more than a quarter did two decades ago. Yet while other nations have adapted their currencies to the reality of inflation (see table), Americans cling to their devalued money, pulling out wads of notes for virtually all purchases larger than a newspaper. America's dearest commonly used coin, the quarter, is worth one seventh of Britain's, the pound; the dollar bill is worth barely one-ninth of a "fiver", now Britain's smallest-denomination note.

Two [U.S.] congressmen have re-introduced legislation calling for yet another attempt to introduce a dollar coin and to phase out the production of one-dollar bills. A similar proposal in 1987 got nowhere. Despite periodic attempts since the first silver dollar was introduced in 1794, the dollar coin has never captured the public's imagination. The [U.S.] Treasury's most recent effort was the Susan B. Anthony dollar (featuring that famous suffragette), which was introduced in 1979 and almost immediately dropped out of circulation. People complained that its size and shape made it too easy to confuse with a quarter. At last count there were 456m Anthony dollars stored in mints and Federal Reserve banks across the country.

In Britain, by contrast, the government's introduction in 1983 of the pound coin to replace the pound note succeeded despite similar grumbling about the new coin's similarity to a 5p piece.

Dollar-coin advocates claim the U.S. Treasury would save $125m a year because coins, although more expensive to produce, last for decades whereas paper money wears out after a couple of years. Businesses that use coin machines to sell items such as food and tickets are also enthusiastic. As ever-fewer things cost less than a dollar, they are driven to installing bill changers at $2,400 each.

Even the blind would benefit. "The visually handicapped would be able to make small purchases without fear of accidentally parting with a large bill or of being cheated when receiving change," says Mr James Benfield, an energetic Washington lobbyist who has made the dollar coin his personal crusade. The blind, and the merely careless, are inconvenienced by the fact that American notes of different values are all the same size and colour—a defect no one is proposing to remedy.

Defenders of America's existing coins point out that at least their bulk is as modest as their value, so does not tear holes in pockets. Some of Britain's least valuable coins are as unwieldy as electric plugs. In fact, the correlation between weight and worth is poor in both countries.

Tossed salad: Currencies great and small

	Highest coin (U.S. $ value)	Lowest note (U.S. $ value)
Australia	A$2 ($1.76)	A$5 ($4.40)
Britain	£1 ($1.77)	£5 ($8.85)
Canada	C$1 ($0.85)	C$2 ($1.70)
Germany	DM5 ($2.70)	DM10 ($5.41)
Japan	¥500 ($3.92)	¥1,000 ($7.80)
U.S.*	quarter ($0.25)	$1 ($1.00)

*The American mint still produces the 50-cent coin, although in small numbers. In fiscal 1988, for example, the mint produced 20m half-dollars, compared to 843m quarters.

	U.S. 25¢	U.S. 5¢	Britain £1.00	Britain 20p
Size and weight				
Size—square centimetre*	4.62	3.53	3.98	3.60
Value per square centimetre (Cents)	5.41	1.42	44.48	9.84
Weight—grammes*	5.67	5.00	9.50	5.00
Value per gramme (Cents)	4.41	1.00	18.64	7.08

*Approximate
Source: U.S. Treasury; Royal Mint.

***The Economist*, February 25, 1989**

The Essence of the Story

- A one-dollar bill buys about the same quantity of goods and services that a quarter did 20 years ago.
- Two U.S. congressmen want to replace the one-dollar bill with a one-dollar coin.
- The first U.S. one-dollar coin was introduced in 1794.
- The most recent one-dollar coin is the Susan B. Anthony dollar, introduced in 1979.
- Americans prefer the one-dollar bill and most of the one-dollar coins do not circulate as currency.
- In Britain, the one-pound note was replaced by a one-pound coin, but the move was unpopular.
- It is claimed by advocates of the one-dollar coin that it has the following advantages over the one-dollar bill: it lasts longer; it is easier to use in coin machines (bill-changing machines are expensive); it is easier for the blind.
- Existing U.S. coins are small and easier to use than those of some other countries—notably Britain.

Background and Analysis

- To buy goods and services that cost $1 in 1989, the following amounts were needed in earlier years:

1979	59 cents
1969	30 cents
1959	24 cents
1949	19 cents

- Coins are more expensive than notes to manufacture. If it is to be economical to use coins, their life has to be much longer than the life of a bill.
- The life of a bill is highly correlated with the frequency with which it changes hands.
- Bills that spend most of their lives in a wallet last a long time.
- Bills that change hands many times a day have a very short life.
- The smaller the denomination of a bill or coin, the more frequently it changes hands because it is used as change.
- One-dollar bills change hands with high frequency and have a life of less than two years.
- If it was economical to use a coin rather than a bill for a 25 cent transaction in 1959, then it is efficient to use a coin for a $1 transaction today.
- Many countries have adopted a coin even for denominations larger than $1 (see table).
- U.S. coins are among the smallest and most convenient to use in the world.
- Opponents of a $1 coin emphasize the inconvenience of carrying a larger number of coins that are heavier and bigger than a quarter.
- One solution, not discussed in the article, is to withdraw the penny from circulation and introduce a dollar coin the size of a penny but perhaps gold-like or silver-like in appearance.
- Eliminating the penny makes sense for the same reasons that eliminating the one-dollar bill does.
- To buy the goods and services that cost a penny in 1989, a coin worth one quarter of a penny would have been needed in 1959. We managed without such a coin in 1959 and so, presumably, we can manage without a penny today.
- The savings from eliminating pennies would likely pay for the dollar coin.

Conclusion

- Fiat money is more efficient than commodity money, but the design of the tokens that we use in our fiat money system has an important influence on the costs, benefits, and convenience of that system.

Table 27.3 Compact Glossary of the Components of Money

Currency	Notes issued by the Bank of Canada and coins made at the Royal Canadian Mint in Winnipeg and issued by the government of Canada
Demand deposit	A deposit at a chartered bank that may be withdrawn on demand
Notice deposit	A deposit at a chartered bank, trust company, mortgage loan company, or credit union that may be withdrawn after giving notice (in practice, most notice deposits are withdrawable on demand)
Term deposit	A deposit at a chartered bank, trust company, mortgage loan company or credit union that may be withdrawn on a fixed date
Chequable deposit	A deposit that may be withdrawn by writing a cheque
Nonchequable deposit	A deposit that may not be withdrawn by writing a cheque
Privately held demand deposit at a chartered bank	A chequable demand deposit held by a household, firm, or other financial institution at a chartered bank
Personal savings deposit at a chartered bank	A notice deposit or term deposit held by a household at a chartered bank that may be chequable or nonchequable
Nonpersonal notice deposit at a chartered bank	A notice deposit by a firm or other institution at a chartered bank
Nonpersonal fixed-term deposits of a resident booked in Canada	A term deposit held in a chartered bank in Canada of a resident, regardless of the currency of denomination
Deposit at trust and mortgage loan companies	Any type of deposit (demand, notice, or term) at a trust or mortgage loan company
Deposit or share at caisse populaire or credit union	Any type of deposit (demand, notice, or term) at or share in a caisse populaire or credit union

medium of exchange. These are included in the M2 definition of money. Not all the components of M2, however, act as a medium of exchange. For example, nonpersonal notice deposits and nonchequable personal savings deposits are not medium-of-exchange assets. There are other medium- of-exchange assets that are not included in either M1 or M2. These are the chequable deposits at trust and mortgage loan companies, caisses populaires (Québec savings banks), and credit unions. They are included in M2+. But not all M2+ deposits constitute a medium of exchange. For example, term deposits and nonchequable notice deposits in trust and mortgage loan companies, caisses populaires, and credit unions are not medium-of-exchange assets.

There is also a large volume of deposits included in M3 that are not part of the Canadian dollar money supply. These are U.S. dollar deposits and other foreign currency deposits. Some of these deposits are part of the money that is used for conducting international transactions but not (usually) for domestic transactions.

The official measures of the money supply in Canada are based on institutions rather than economics. The economic function of a deposit is the same regardless of whether it is in a chartered bank or a trust company. This fact is recognized in the M2+ definition of the money supply. But M2+ contains a large number of items that are not medium-of-exchange assets at all, such as term deposits — deposits that may not be withdrawn until a pre-agreed future date.

To measure the money supply in an economically relevant way we must distinguish among the three types of bank deposits:

- Demand deposits
- Notice deposits
- Term deposits

These different types of deposits are defined in Table 27.3. Currency, together with demand deposits, constitute the medium of exchange and means of payment. They are money.

Notice deposits and term deposits that are included in the broader definitions of money are not money, but they do have a high degree of liquidity. **Liquidity** is the degree to which an asset is instantly convertible into a medium of exchange at a known price. Assets vary in their degree of liquidity. Some are not very liquid because some minimum amount of notice has to be given before they can be converted into a medium of exchange. Others lack liquidity because they are traded on markets and their prices fluctuate, making uncertain the amount of the medium of exchange into which they can be converted. But the savings deposits and other notice and term deposits that make up M2, M3 and M2+ are easily converted into a medium of exchange. They are highly liquid — or almost money.

Because the official definitions of money in Canada are based on artificial institutional distinctions rather than on economic distinctions, we need to reclassify the various deposits at banks and other financial institutions to obtain an economic measure of money in its various forms. Table 27.4 contains three (unofficial) economic definitions of money. The magnitudes of the various items listed in Table 27.4 are shown in Fig. 27.1. As you can see from that figure, currency constitutes a small part of our money supply. The most important part is deposits at chartered banks, but deposits at other financial institutions have also become large in recent years.

In defining the money supply, we have included, along with currency, chequable deposits at banks and other financial institutions. We have not included the cheques that people actually write as part of the money supply. It is important to understand why deposits are money and the cheques that people write when they make a payment are not.

Table 27.4 Three Economic Definitions of Money

$M1_E$
- Currency held outside banks
- Privately held demand deposits at chartered banks and all other financial institutions

$M2_E$
- $M1_E$
- Personal and nonpersonal chequable notice deposits at chartered banks and all other financial institutions

$M3_E$
- $M2_E$
- Personal and nonpersonal term deposits at chartered banks and all other financial institutions

Chequable Deposits Are Money but Cheques Are Not

The best way to see why chequable deposits are money but cheques are not is to consider what happens when someone pays for goods by writing a cheque. Let's suppose that Barb buys a bike for $200 from Rocky's Mountain Bikes. When Barb goes to Rocky's bike shop on June 11, she has $500 in her demand deposit account at the Laser Bank. Rocky has $1,000 in his demand deposit — at the same bank, as it happens. The demand deposits of these two people total $1,500. When Barb buys the bike, she writes a cheque for $200. Rocky takes the cheque to the Laser Bank right away and deposits it. Rocky's bank balance rises from $1,000 to $1,200. But the bank does not only credit Rocky's account with $200. It also debits Barb's account $200, Barb's balance falls from $500 to $300. Notice that the total demand deposits of Barb and Rocky are still the same, $1,500. Rocky now has $200 more and Barb $200 less than before. These transactions are summarized in Table 27.5.

This transaction has not changed the quantity of money in existence. It has simply transferred money from one person to another. The cheque itself was never money. That is, there wasn't an extra $200 worth of money while the cheque was in circulation. The cheque simply served as a written instruction to the bank to transfer the money from Barb to Rocky.

In our example, Barb and Rocky use the same bank. Essentially, the same story — with some additional steps — describes what happens if Barb and Rocky use different banks. Rocky's bank will credit the cheque to Rocky's account and then take the

Figure 27.1 Three Economic Measures of Money (billions of dollars)

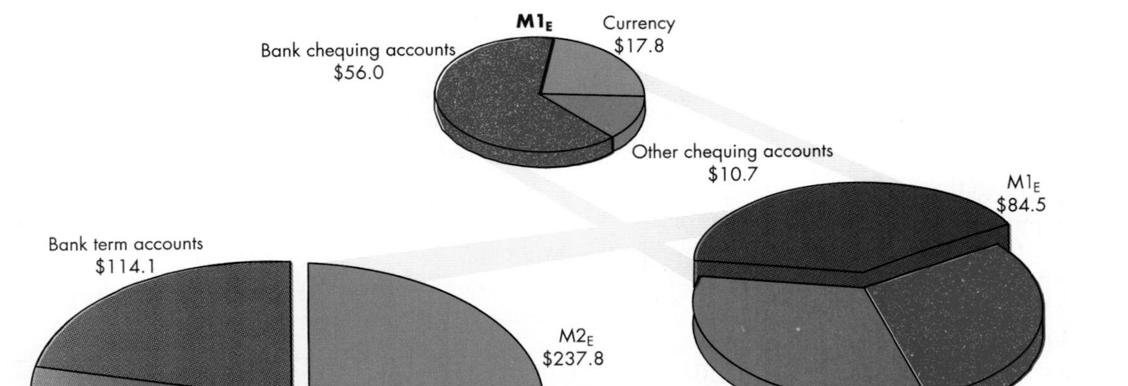

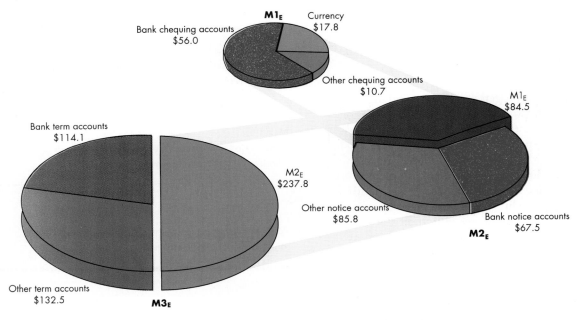

$M1_E$ consists of currency in circulation and chequable deposits at banks and other financial institutions. $M2_E$ consists of $M1_E$ plus notice deposits at banks and other financial institutions. $M3_E$ consists of $M2_E$ plus fixed-term deposits at banks and other financial institutions.

Source: Bank of Canada Review, February 1989, Tables C4, D1, D3, and E1.

cheque to the cheque-clearing centre. Barb's bank will pay Rocky's bank $200 and then debit Barb's account $200. This process can take a few days, but the principles are the same as when two people use the same bank.

So cheques are not money. But what about credit cards? Isn't having a credit card in your wallet and presenting the card to pay for a bike the same as using money? Why aren't credit cards somehow valued and counted as part of the quantity of money?

Credit Cards Are Not Money When you pay by cheque, you are frequently asked to prove your identity by showing your driver's licence. It would never occur to you to think of your driver's licence as money. Your driver's licence is just an ID.

A credit card is also an ID card — one that enables you to borrow money at the instant a purchase is made on the promise of repaying later. When you make a purchase, you sign a credit-card sales slip that creates a debt in your name. You are saying, in effect, "I agree to pay for these goods when the credit card company bills me." Once you get your statement from the credit card company, you have to make the minimum payment due. To make that payment, you need money — you need to have funds in your chequable deposit so that you can write a cheque to pay the credit card company.

R E V I E W

Money has four functions: medium of exchange, unit of account, standard of deferred payment, and a store of value. Any durable commodity can serve as money, but modern societies use fiat money and private debt money rather than commodity money. The most important component of money in Canada today is chequable deposits at banks and other financial institutions. Neither cheques nor credit cards are money. A cheque is an instruction to a

Table 27.5 Paying by Cheque

LASER BANK

142 Northern Street • Moose Jaw, Sask S6H 2P3 • (306) 555-3215

Date	Item	Debit	Credit	Balance
June 1	Opening balance			$500.00(CR)
June 11	Rocky's Mountain Bikes	$200.00		$300.00(CR)

Barb's Demand Deposit Account

LASER BANK

142 Northern Street • Moose Jaw, Sask S6H 2P3 • (306) 555-3215

Date	Item	Debit	Credit	Balance
June 1	Opening balance			$1,000.00(CR)
June 11	Barb buys bike		$200.00	$1,200.00(CR)

Rocky's Mountain Bikes Demand Deposit Account

*CR means "credit": the bank owes the depositor.

bank to transfer money from one account to another. Money is the balance in the account itself. A credit card is an ID card that enables a person to borrow at the instant a purchase is made on the promise of repaying later. When repayment is made, money (currency or a chequable deposit) is used for the payment. ■

We've seen that the most important component of money in Canada is deposits at banks and other financial institutions. Let's take a look at the banking and financial system a bit more closely.

Financial Intermediaries

We are going to study the banking and financial system of Canada first by describing the variety of financial intermediaries that operate in Canada today. Then we'll examine the operations of banks and of other financial institutions. After describing the main features of financial intermediaries, we'll examine their economic functions, looking at what they produce and how they make a profit. Finally, we'll explain how money gets created.

A **financial intermediary** is a firm that takes deposits from households and firms and makes loans to other households and firms. There are three types of financial intermediaries whose deposits are components of the nation's money:

- Chartered banks
- Trust and mortgage loan companies
- Local credit unions and caisses populaires

Table 27.6 provides a compact glossary on these financial intermediaries and an indication of their relative importance.

Let's begin by examining chartered banks.

Chartered Banks

A **chartered bank** is a private firm, chartered under the Bank Act to receive deposits and make loans. There were, in 1986, ten Canadian-owned banks chartered by Parliament and 55 foreign-owned banks. These banks operated more than 7,000 banking offices in Canada, 168 of which were offices of foreign banks. The scale and scope of the operations of chartered banks can be seen by examining the balance sheet of all the chartered banks added together.

Table 27.6 A Compact Glossary of Financial Intermediaries

Financial intermediary	Total assets (billions of dollars)	Main function
Chartered bank	531	A private company chartered under the Bank Act (1980) to receive deposits and make loans
Trust and mortgage loan company	118	A private company operating under the Loan Companies Act (1970) and Trust Companies Act (1970) (or corresponding provincial laws) that undertakes business almost identical to that of a chartered bank and that acts as a trustee for pension and other funds and for estates.
Credit union or caisse populaire	63	A co-operative organization, operating under provincial law, that receives deposits and makes loans.

A **balance sheet** is a statement that lists a firm's assets and liabilities. **Assets** are the things of value that a firm owns. **Liabilities** are the things that a firm owes to households and other firms. Such a balance sheet — that for all chartered banks in June 1989 — is set out in Table 27.7. The left-hand side — the assets — lists the items *owned* by the banks. The right-hand side — the liabilities — lists the items that the banks *owe* to others.

The first thing to notice about the chartered banks' balance sheet is that its assets and liabilities are divided into two broad groups — those denominated in Canadian dollars and those denominated in foreign currency. Foreign currency assets are loans or securities denominated in such currencies. Foreign currency liabilities are deposits made and repayable in the foreign currency. Partly because of Canada's proximity to the broader North American money and financial markets and partly because of the enormous volume of international trade undertaken by Canadians, a large amount of banking business is done in U.S. dollars and other foreign currencies. As you can see from Table 27.7, almost one-third of the assets and the liabilities of the chartered banks are in foreign currencies.

Business conducted in Canadian dollars constitutes the bulk of the work of the chartered banks and their Canadian dollar liabilities in June 1989 were $350.8 billion. By far the most important component of these liabilities is the deposits. Your deposit at a bank is an asset to you but a liability for your bank. The bank has to repay you your deposit (and sometimes interest on it too) whenever you decide to take your money out of the bank.

You have met the various types of banks' deposit liabilities before in the various definitions of money. They are the personal savings deposits (chequable, nonchequable, and fixed term), nonpersonal term and notice deposits, and demand deposits. The only other deposit liability shown in the table is a small item representing the government of Canada's deposits with the chartered banks.

Why does a bank obligate itself to pay you your money back with interest? Because it wants to use your deposit to make a profit for itself. The asset side of the balance sheet tells us what the banks did with their $531 billion worth of borrowed resources in June 1989.

First, the banks kept some of their assets in the form of cash in their vaults and of deposits at the Bank of Canada. The cash in a bank's vault plus its deposits at the Bank of Canada are called its **reserves**. You can think of a chartered bank's deposit at the

Table 27.7 The Balance Sheet of All Chartered Banks, June 1989

Assets (billions of dollars)		Liabilities (billions of dollars)		
Canadian dollar assets		***Canadian dollar liabilities***		
Bank of Canada deposits and notes	5.2	Personal savings deposits:		
Liquid assets	22.7	Chequable	32.3	
Securities	16.6	Nonchequable	66.2	
Loans	255.0	Fixed term	72.8	
Other assets	62.2			171.3
		Nonpersonal term and notice deposits		60.9
		Demand deposits		23.7
		Government of Canada deposits		1.1
		Total deposits		257.0
		Other liabilities		93.8
Total Canadian dollar assets	361.7	Total Canadian dollar liabilities		350.8
Foreign currency assets	169.6	***Foreign currency liabilities***		180.5
Total assets	**531.3**	**Total liabilities**		**531.3**

Source: *Bank of Canada Review*, December 1989, Table C3.

Bank of Canada as being similar to your deposit at your own bank. Chartered banks use these deposits in the same way that you use your bank account. A chartered bank deposits cash into or draws cash out of its account at the Bank of Canada and writes cheques on that account to settle debts with other banks. (We'll study the Bank of Canada in Chapter 28.)

If the banks kept all their assets in the form of cash and deposits at the Bank of Canada, they wouldn't make any profit. But if they didn't keep *some* of their assets in those forms, they wouldn't be able to meet the demands for cash that their customers place on them. Nor would they be able to keep that automatic teller replenished every time you, your friends, and all their other customers have raided it for cash for a midnight pizza.

The bulk of a bank's borrowed resources are put to work by making loans. Some of these loans are instantly convertible into cash and have virtually no risk. These are called liquid assets. **Liquid assets**, which take their name from the concept of liquidity, are those assets that are instantly convertible into a medium of exchange with virtually no uncertainty about the price at which they can be converted. An example of a liquid asset is a treasury bill, which can be sold at a moment's notice for an almost guaranteed price.

The bank's assets also include securities. A **security** is a marketable financial asset that a bank can sell but at a price that fluctuates. An example of a security is a government of Canada long-term bond. Such bonds can be sold instantly, but their prices fluctuate on the bond market. Banks earn a higher interest rate on their securities than they do on liquid assets, but securities involve higher risk.

Most of the banks' assets are the loans that they have made. A **loan** is a commitment of a fixed amount of money for an agreed period of time. Most of the loans made by banks are to corporations and are used to finance the purchase of capital equipment and inventories. But banks also make loans to households — personal loans. Such loans are used to buy consumer durable goods such as cars and boats. The outstanding balances on credit card accounts are also bank loans.

Banks make a profit by earning interest on loans, investment securities, and liquid assets in excess of the interest they pay on deposits and other liabilities. Also, banks receive revenue by charging fees for managing accounts.

A large part of the money supply is made up of the various liabilities of the banks. Personal savings deposits and demand deposits are the most important component of the M2 measure of money. And chartered bank deposits are an important component of M3. But the deposit liabilities of banks are not the only components of the nation's money supply. Other financial institutions also take deposits that form part — an increasing part — of the nation's money. Let's now examine those financial institutions.

Other Financial Intermediaries

Canada has always made a sharp legal distinction between banks and other deposit-taking financial institutions, such as trust and mortage loan companies, credit unions, and caisses populaires. But the economic functions of other financial intermediaries have grown increasingly similar to those of banks (a fact being recognized in new legislation is expected to be passed in 1990), and today, their liabilities that serve as money approach the same magnitude as those of the chartered banks. For example, the M2+ definition of money includes the deposit liabilities of the other deposit-taking financial intermediaries. These deposits amounted to 31 percent of M2+ in 1970 but they are more than 40 percent today.

Let's consider the economic functions of financial intermediaries.

The Economic Functions of Financial Intermediaries

All financial intermediaries make a profit from the spread between the interest rate they pay on deposits and the interest rate at which they lend. Why can financial intermediaries borrow at a low interest rate and lend at a higher one? What services do they perform that make their depositors willing to put up with a low interest rate and their borrowers willing to pay a higher one?

Financial intermediaries provide four main services:

- Minimizing the cost of obtaining funds
- Minimizing the cost of monitoring borrowers
- Pooling risk
- Creating liquidity

Minimizing the Cost of Obtaining Funds Finding someone from whom to borrow can be a costly business. Imagine how troublesome it would be if there were no financial intermediaries. A firm that was looking for $1 million to buy a new production plant would probably have to hunt around for several dozen people from whom to borrow in order to acquire enough funds for its capital project. Financial intermediaries lower those costs. The firm needing $1 million can go to a single financial institution to obtain those funds. The financial institution has to borrow from a large number of people, but it's not doing that just for this one firm and the $1 million it wants to borrow. The financial institution can establish an organization that spreads the cost of raising money from a large number of depositors.

Minimizing the Cost of Monitoring Borrowers Lending money is a risky business. There's always a danger that the borrower may not repay. Most of the money lent gets used by firms to invest in projects that they hope will return a profit. But sometimes those hopes are not fulfilled. Checking up on the activities of a borrower and ensuring that the best possible decisions are being made for making a profit and avoiding a loss is a costly and specialized activity. Imagine how costly it would be if each and every household that lent money to a firm had to incur the costs of monitoring that firm directly. By depositing funds with a financial intermediary, a household avoids those costs. The financial intermediary performs the monitoring activity much more economically — at much lower cost — than households could.

Pooling Risk As we just noted above, lending money is risky. There is always a chance of not being repaid — of default. The risk of default can be reduced by lending to a large number of different individuals. In such a situation, if one person defaults on a loan, it is a nuisance but not a disaster. In contrast, if only one person borrows and that person defaults, the entire loan is a write-off. Financial intermediaries enable people to pool risk in an efficient way. Thousands of people lend money to any one financial intermediary, and it, in turn, re-lends the money to hundreds, perhaps thousands, of individual firms. If any one firm defaults on its loan, that default is spread across all the depositors with the intermediary and no individual depositor is left exposed to a high degree of risk.

Creating Liquidity Financial intermediaries create liquidity. We defined liquidity earlier as the ease and certainty with which an asset can be converted into a medium of exchange. The liabilities of some financial intermediaries are themselves a medium of exchange. Others are easily convertible into a medium of exchange and so are highly liquid.

Financial intermediaries create liquidity by borrowing short and lending long. Borrowing short means taking deposits but standing ready to repay them on short notice (even no notice in the case of demand deposits). Lending long means making loan commitments for a prearranged and often quite long period of time. For example, when a person makes a deposit with a mortgage loan company, that deposit can be withdrawn immediately. The mortgage company, however, makes a lending commitment for perhaps 10 years to someone buying a new house.

Financial Innovation

In their pursuit of a profit, financial intermediaries are constantly seeking better ways of delivering their product — of lowering the costs of obtaining funds and monitoring borrowers, pooling risk, and of creating liquidity. They also are inventive in seeking ways of avoiding the costs imposed on them by financial regulation. The development of new financial products and methods of borrowing and lending is called **financial innovation**.

The pace of financial innovation has been remarkable in the 1980s. Some of the innovation has been aimed at reducing risk. An important example is the development of variable interest rate mortgages. Traditionally, house purchases have been financed on mortgage loans at a guaranteed interest rate. Rising interest rates brought higher borrowing costs for banks and trust companies, and since they were committed to fixed interest rates on their mortgages, the industry incurred severe losses. The creation of variable interest rate mortgages takes some of the risk out of long-term lending for house purchases.

Other financial innovations resulted from technological change, most notably that associated with the increased use of computers and the decreased cost of long distance communication. The spread of the use of credit cards and the development of international financial markets — for example, the increased importance of Eurodollars — are consequences of technological changes.

R E V I E W

Most of the nation's money is made up of deposits in financial intermediaries such as chartered banks, trust and mortgage loan companies, local credit unions, and caisses populaires. In the 1970s and 1980s, the deposit liabilities of financial institutions other than the chartered banks became increasingly important.

By minimizing the cost of obtaining funds, minimizing the cost of monitoring borrowers, pooling risk, and creating liquidity, financial intermediaries seek new ways of making a profit and of avoiding the adverse effects of regulations on their activities. ■

Because banks and other financial intermediaries are able to create liquidity and to create assets that are a medium of exchange — money — they occupy a unique place in our economy and influence the quantity of money in existence. Let's see how money gets created.

How Banks Create Money

Money is created by the activities of all those institutions whose deposits circulate as a medium of exchange. In this section, we'll use the term "banks" to refer to all these depository institutions.

As we saw in Table 27.7, banks don't have $100 in bills for every $100 that people have deposited with them. In fact, a typical bank today has about $1 in currency or on deposit at the Bank of Canada for every $100 deposited in it. No need for panic. Banks have learned from experience that these reserve levels are adequate for ordinary business needs. The fraction of a bank's total deposits that are held in reserves is called the **reserve ratio**. The value of the reserve ratio is influenced by the actions of a bank's depositors. If a depositor withdraws currency from a bank, the reserve ratio falls. If a depositor puts currency into a bank, the reserve ratio increases.

All banks have a desired reserve ratio. The **desired reserve ratio** is the ratio of reserves to deposits that banks regard as necessary in order to be able to conduct their business. The desired reserve ratio is determined partly by regulation (discussed in Chapter 28) and partly by what the banks regard as the minimum safety level for their reserve holdings. The difference between actual reserves and desired reserves is **excess reserves**.

Whenever banks have excess reserves, they are able to create money. When we say that banks create money, we don't mean that they have smoke-filled back rooms in which counterfeiters are busily working. Remember, most money is deposits, not currency. What the banks create is deposits, and they do so by making loans. To see how banks create money, we are going to look at a model of the banking system.

Let's suppose that the banks have a desired reserve ratio of 25 percent. That is, for each dollar deposited, they want to keep 25 cents in the form of reserves. Al, a customer of the Golden Nugget Bank, decides to reduce his holding of currency and puts $100 in his deposit account at the bank. Suddenly, the Golden Nugget Bank has $100 of new deposits and $100 of additional reserves. But the Golden Nugget Bank doesn't want to hold onto $100 of additional reserves. It has excess reserves. Its desired reserve ratio is 25 percent, so it plans to lend $75 of the additional $100 to another customer. Amy, a customer at the same bank, borrows $75. At this point, the Golden Nugget Bank has new deposits of $100, new loans of $75, and new reserves of $25.

No money has been created. Al has reduced his holding of currency by $100 and increased his bank deposit by $100, but the total amount of money has remained constant. As far as Golden Nugget is concerned, that is the end of the matter. But this is not the end of the story for the entire banking system. What happens next?

Amy uses the $75 loan to buy a jacket from Barb. To undertake this transaction, she writes a cheque on her account with the Golden Nugget and Barb deposits the cheque in the Laser Bank. The Laser Bank now has new deposits of $75 and an additional $75 of reserves. The total amount of money is now $75 higher than before.

The Laser Bank doesn't need to hang on to the entire $75 that it has just received in reserves: it needs only a quarter of that amount — $18.75. The Laser Bank lends the additional amount, $56.25, to Bob who buys some used stereo equipment from Carl. Bob writes a cheque on his account at the Laser Bank, which Carl deposits in his account at the Apollo Bank. The Apollo Bank now has new deposits of $56.25, so the amount of money has increased by a total of $131.25 (the $75 lent to Amy and paid to Barb plus the $56.25 lent to Bob and paid to Carl).

The transactions that we've just described are summarized in Table 27.8. You can see there that the story is still incomplete. The process continues through the remaining banks and their depositors and borrowers, all the way down the list in that table. The new deposits at each stage are listed in the first column of numbers in the table. By the time we get down to the Pirates Bank, Ken has paid Len $5.63 for a box of computer discs and so the Pirates Bank has new deposits of $5.63 and additional reserves of that same amount. Since it needs only $1.41 of additional reserves, it makes a loan of $4.22 to Lee, who in turn spends the money. By this time, the total amount of money has increased by $283.11.

This process continues but with amounts that are now getting so tiny that we do not bother to keep track of them here. All the remaining stages in the process taken together add up to the numbers in the second last row of the table. The final tallies appear as totals in the row at the bottom of the table. Deposits have increased by $400, loans by $300, and reserves by $100. The banks have created money by making loans. The quantity of money created is $300 — the same amount as the additional loans made. It's true that deposits have increased by $400, but $100 of that increase is Al's original deposit. The currency that Al deposited was already money so it does not increase the quantity of money. Only the new deposits created by the lending activity of the banks increases the quantity of money in existence.

The ability of banks to create money does not mean that they can create an indefinite amount of money. The amount that they can create depends on the size of their reserves and on the desired reserve ratio. In this example the desired reserve ratio is 25 percent, and bank deposits have increased by four times the new reserves. There is an important relationship between the change in reserves and the change in deposits.

The Simple Money Multiplier

The **simple money multiplier** is the amount by which an increase in bank reserves is multiplied to calculate the effect of the increase in reserves on total bank deposits. The simple money multiplier is given by

$$\text{Simple money multiplier} = \frac{\text{Change in deposits}}{\text{Change in reserves}}.$$

In the example that we've just worked through, the simple money multiplier is 4 — a $100 increase in reserves created the $400 increase in deposits.

Table 27.8 Creating Money by Making Loans: Many Banks

Bank	Depositor	Borrower	New deposits	New loans	New reserves	Increase in money	Cumulative increase in money
Golden Nugget	Al	Amy	100.00	75.00	25.00	0	0
Laser	Barb	Bob	75.00	56.25	18.75	75.00	75.00
Apollo	Carl	Con	56.25	42.19	14.06	56.25	131.25
Monty Python	Di	Dan	42.19	31.64	10.55	42.19	173.44
Plato	Ed	Eve	31.64	23.73	7.91	31.64	205.08
Mustang	Fran	Fred	23.73	17.80	5.93	23.73	228.81
Lancer	Gus	Gail	17.80	13.35	4.45	17.80	246.61
Stampede	Holly	Hal	13.35	10.01	3.34	13.35	259.96
Olympia	Jim	Jan	10.01	7.51	2.50	10.01	269.97
Expo	Kym	Ken	7.51	5.63	1.88	7.51	277.48
Pirates	Len	Lee	5.63	4.22	1.41	5.63	283.11
			.	.	.	.	.
			.	.	.	.	.
			.	.	.	.	.
All others			16.89	12.67	4.22	16.89	.
Total banking system			400.00	300.00	100.00	300.00	300.00

The simple money multiplier is related to the desired reserve ratio. In our example, that ratio is 25 percent (or ¼). That is,

$$\text{Desired reserves} = (1/4)\ \text{Deposits}\ .$$

Whenever desired reserves exceed actual reserves (a situation of negative excess reserves), the banks decrease their loans. When desired reserves are below actual reserves (a situation of positive excess reserves), the banks make additional loans. By adjusting their loans, the banks bring their actual reserves into line with their desired reserves, eliminating excess reserves. Thus when banks have changed their loans and reserves to make actual reserves equal desired reserves,

$$\text{Actual reserves} = (1/4)\text{Deposits}\ .$$

If we divide both sides of this equation by ¼ we obtain

$$\text{Deposits} = [1/(1/4)]\ \text{Actual reserves}\ .$$

If there is a change in reserves when desired reserves and actual reserves are equal, bank deposits change in order to satisfy the above equation. That is,

$$\text{Change in deposits} = [1/(1/4)]\ \text{Change in reserves}\ .$$

But $1/(1/4)$ is the simple money multiplier. It is the amount by which the change in reserves is multiplied to calculate the change in deposits. In our example, this multiplier equals 4. The relationship between the simple money multiplier and the desired reserve ratio is

$$\text{Simple money multiplier} = \frac{1}{\text{Desired reserve ratio}}\ .$$

Real World Money Multipliers

The money multiplier in the real world differs from the simple money multiplier that we have just calculated for two reasons. First, the desired reserve ratio of real world banks is much smaller than the 25 percent that we have used here. Second, in the real world, not all the loans made by banks return to them in the form of reserves. Some of the loans remain outside the banks in the form of currency in circulation. This tendency for some of the loans to leave the banking system is called the **currency drain**. These two differences between the real world money multiplier and the simple money multiplier work in opposing directions to each other. The smaller desired reserve ratio of real world banks makes the real world multiplier larger than the above numerical example. The cash drain makes the real world multiplier smaller. We will study the actual values of real world money multipliers in the next chapter.

Bank Panic and Failure

Because banks lend most of their customers' deposits, they cannot pay out all their deposits on demand if they are required to do so. Most of the time, if one bank finds itself short of reserves, it can easily remedy the situation by borrowing from another bank. But suppose that the whole banking system is short of reserves. In such a situation, the banks are not able to pay their depositors' demands. Depositors, in turn, become nervous about the security of their bank deposits and so try to get even more of their money out of the bank. When the amount of currency the depositors are trying to withdraw from banks exceeds the amount that the banks have, there is a banking panic and banks fail.

The last time widespread bank panic and failure occurred was in the United States during the Great Depression in the 1930s. Before that, bank panic and failure had been routine in the United States at roughly 10-year intervals. In contrast, bank failure in Canada has been extremely rare. Why have U.S. banks failed more frequently than Canadian banks?

Branch Banking Versus Unit Banking The Canadian banking system differs from that in the United States in many ways, but one is particularly important for its effects on bank solvency. Banking regulations in the United States prevent the emergence of large multibranch banks spanning the entire nation. In contrast, the Canadian law permits banks to have a large number of branches and to operate in all parts of the country. Because of this difference in the structure of the two banking systems, Canadian banks can diversify their risks much more effectively than U.S. banks. Losses on investments in one part of the country can be offset against profits in another part; unusually heavy drains of cash in one region can be offset by a deposit influx in another region.

Another important factor in reducing the likelihood of a failure of the financial system is deposit insurance. Bank deposits are insured by the Canadian Federal Deposit Insurance Corporation, established in 1967. Because deposits are insured, even if depositors believe that banks and other financial institutions might fail, the danger of personal loss is reduced. So a herdlike move to withdraw currency from the banks and the financial institutions is much less likely to occur.

But the most important source of stability and security for the Canadian financial system arises from the existence of the Bank of Canada, an institution that monitors and regulates the banking and financial industry and seeks to maintain relatively stable and predictable conditions in markets for money and financial assets. We will study this aspect of the financial system in Chapter 28.

Our next task in this chapter is to examine the effects of money on the economy and, in particular, the relationship between the quantity of money and the price level.

Money and the Price Level

We now know what money is. We also know that in a modern economy, such as that of Canada today, most money is made up of deposits at banks and other financial institutions. We've seen that these institutions can actually create money — by making loans. Does the quantity of money created by the banking and financial system matter? What effects does it have? Does it matter whether the quantity increases quickly or slowly?

We're going to address these questions first by refreshing our understanding of the aggregate demand-aggregate supply (*AD-AS*) model and recalling the role played by money in influencing real GDP and the price level. Then we're going to consider a special theory of money and prices — the quantity theory of money. Finally, we'll look at some historical and international evidence on the relationship between money and prices.

Money in the *AD-AS* Model

In Chapter 24, we developed a model of aggregate demand and aggregate supply in which money plays an important role in influencing the aggregate demand curve. Figure 27.2 illustrates the model. The long-run aggregate supply curve is *LAS*. Initially, the aggregate demand curve is AD_0 and the short-run aggregate supply curve is SAS_0. Equilibrium occurs where the aggregate demand curve AD_0 intersects the short-run aggregate supply curve SAS_0. The price level is 120 and real GDP is $4.5 billion. The economy is also on its long-run aggregate supply curve and is in full-employment equilibrium.

Now suppose that there is an increase in the quantity of money. For the reasons discussed in Chapter 24, this increase in the quantity of money results in an increase in aggregate demand. The aggregate demand curve shifts to the right to become AD_1. The new equilibrium is at the intersection point of AD_1 and SAS_0. The price level rises to 132 and real GDP increases to $5 billion. But this is the short-run effect of an increase in the quantity of money. Over time, the prices of factors of production increase and, as they do so, the short-run aggregate supply curve shifts upward. The upward movement of the short-run aggregate supply curve leads to an ever-higher price level and a lower real GDP. The long-run effect of an increase in the quantity of money occurs when the short-run aggregate supply curve has shifted upward to SAS_1, which intersects the aggregate demand curve AD_1 on the long-run aggregate supply curve (*LAS*). This equilibrium is at a price level of 144 with real GDP back at its original level of $4.5 billion.

The effects of this increase in the quantity of money have been, first, to increase both real GDP and the price level and, second, to increase the price level yet further, while returning real GDP to its original — full-employment — level. That is, the short-run effect of an increase in the quantity of money is to increase both real GDP and the price level, but the long-run effect of an increase in the quantity of money is to increase the price level only, leaving real GDP at its original level.

It is the long-run relationship between the money supply and the price level that gives rise to the quantity theory of money.

Figure 27.2 Aggregate Demand, Aggregate Supply, and the Quantity of Money

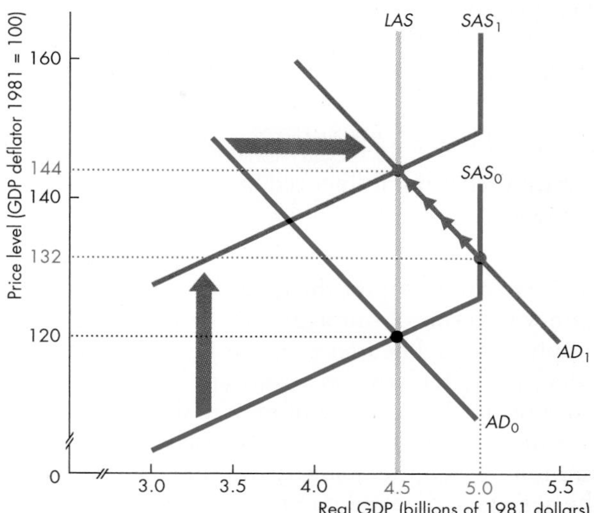

An economy's long-run aggregate supply curve is *LAS*. Initially, its short-run aggregate supply curve is SAS_0, and its aggregate demand curve is AD_0. The price level is 120 and real GDP is $4.5 billion. An increase in the quantity of money shifts the aggregate demand curve to AD_1. The price level increases to 132 and real GDP increases to $5.0 billion. The economy is at an above full-employment equilibrium. Wages and other input prices begin to rise, and the short-run aggregate supply curve shifts upward towards SAS_1. As it does so, real GDP falls back to its initial level and the price level increases to 144.

The Quantity Theory of Money

The **quantity theory of money** is the proposition that an increase in the quantity of money leads to an equal percentage increase in the price level. The original basis of the quantity theory of money is not the aggregate demand-aggregate supply model but the equation of exchange. The **equation of exchange** states:

$$\text{Quantity of money} \times \text{Velocity of circulation} = \text{Price level} \times \text{Real GDP}.$$

To understand the equation of exchange, let's start on the right-hand side — with the price level multiplied by real GDP. You will recognize this value as nominal GDP. That is, it is simply the total amount of expenditure on final goods and services valued in current dollars. The left-hand side of the equation of exchange can be thought of as defining the velocity of circulation. The **velocity of circulation** is the average number of times a dollar is used annually to buy the goods and services that make up GDP.

The equation of exchange is true by definition. That is, there is no independent way of going out and measuring the velocity of circulation to check whether the equation is true. Rather, the velocity of circulation is whatever number it has to be to make the equation true.

The equation of exchange becomes the quantity theory of money by making two propositions:

- The velocity of circulation is a constant.
- Real GDP is not influenced by the quantity of money.

We can interpret the quantity theory of money in terms of our aggregate demand-aggregate supply model. The first proposition — that the velocity of circulation is a constant — implies that a change in the quantity of money shifts the aggregate demand curve by a very precisely stated amount. When the quantity of money increases, the aggregate demand curve shifts, and the shift can be measured vertically by the percentage change in the quantity of money. For example, in Fig. 27.2, the aggregate demand curve shifts from AD_0 to AD_1. That shift, measured by the vertical distance between the two demand curves, is 20 percent. According to the quantity theory of money, a 20 percent increase in the quantity of money shifts the aggregate demand curve upward by 20 percent.

The second proposition of the quantity theory of money — that real GDP is not affected by the money supply — can be interpreted as a statement about full-employment equilibrium. As you can see in Fig. 27.2, if a 20 percent increase in the quantity of money increases aggregate demand from AD_0 to AD_1, in *full-employment equilibrium* the price level also increases by 20 percent (a rise from 120 to 144 being a 20 percent increase).

There are important factors influencing the velocity of circulation that result in its not being a constant. We will discuss these factors in the next chapter. Also, because a change in the money supply has a short-run effect that differs from its long-run effect, the relationship between the quantity of money and the price level is not going to be as precise as that predicted by the quantity theory of money. Nevertheless, it is interesting to ask to what extent the quantity theory of money correctly predicts the relationship between the quantity of money and the price level. Let's look at that relationship, both historically and internationally.

Historical Evidence on the Quantity Theory of Money

The quantity theory of money can be tested on the historical data in Canada by looking at the relationship between the growth rate of the quantity of money and the inflation rate. Figure 27.3 shows this relationship for the 76 years between 1913 and 1989.

The figure reveals four important features of the relationship between money supply growth and inflation. They are:

1 On the average, the money supply growth exceeds the inflation rate.

2 Variations in the growth rate of the money supply are correlated with variations in the inflation rate.

3 During World War II and its aftermath, there was a break in the relationship between money supply growth and inflation.

4 During the years since 1950, inflation has been less volatile than money supply growth.

1. Average Money Supply Growth and Inflation. You can see that the money supply growth rate is larger than the inflation rate, on the average, by looking at the two vertical axis scales in the figure. The money supply growth rate, measured on the left-hand scale, is 5 percentage points higher than the corresponding value of the inflation rate, measured on the right-hand scale. The difference in the averages is accounted for by the fact that, on the average, the economy has been expanding with real GDP growing. Money supply growth that matches real GDP growth does not cause inflation.

2. Correlation Between Money Supply Growth and Inflation. The correlation between money supply growth and inflation is most evident in the data for the years between 1913 and 1940. For example, the massive build up of inflation in the 1920s was accompanied by a huge increase in the growth rate of the quantity of money, and the falling prices of the Great Depression were associated with a decrease in the quantity of money. Although displaying a less strong relationship in the post World War II years, you can see that the steadily increasing money supply growth through the 1960s and 1970s brought steadily rising inflation through those decades.

Figure 27.3 Money Growth and Inflation in Canada

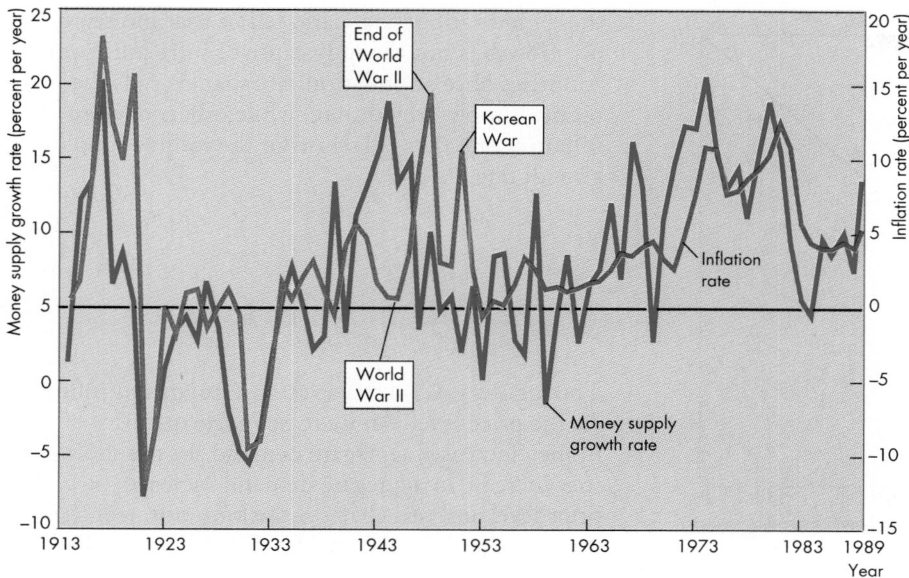

The growth rate of the money supply (measured on the left-hand scale) is plotted along with the inflation rate (measured on the right-hand scale) for year-to-year changes in the two variables from 1913 to 1989. The figure shows that: (1) on the average, the money supply growth exceeds the inflation rate; (2) variations in the growth rate of the money supply are correlated with variations in the inflation rate; (3) during World War II and its aftermath, there was a break in the relationship between money supply growth and inflation; and (4) during the years since 1950, inflation has been less volatile than money supply growth.

Sources: 1913 – 1945: F. H. Leacy, ed., *Historical Statistics of Canada*, 2nd ed. (Ottawa: Statistics Canada and Social Science Federation of Canada, 1983) Series J9. 1946 – 1969: *Historical Statistics*, Series J26. 1970 – 1988: *Bank of Canada Review*, (various issues), CANSIM series B2031, M2.

3. The Effects of Wars. During World War II, there was a large increase in the growth of the money supply but no corresponding increase in the inflation rate. Inflation was suppressed during World War II by a massive programme of price controls and rationing. When these emergency measures were lifted at the end of the war, inflation temporarily exploded even though the money supply growth rate was moderate by then. There was a further burst of inflation not directly triggered by more rapid money growth during the Korean War in the early 1950s.

4. Relative Volatility of Money Supply Growth and Inflation. In looking at historical data, we have to remember that the quantity theory of money is a proposition about long-run effects — about how money growth affects inflation in the long-run. We don't see (at least without some effort) long-run relationships in year-to-year data; we see a sequence of short-run effects. In the short-run, the relationship between inflation and money supply growth is broken by variations in the velocity of circulation and in the growth rate of real GDP. But in the long-run, it is the inflation rate, not the velocity of circulation or real GDP growth that is influenced by money growth. The importance of these short-run effects is especially apparent in the years since 1950. But the long-run relationship is also visible in the data.

What does the international evidence tell us?

International Evidence on the Quantity Theory of Money

The international evidence on the quantity theory of money is summarized in Figure 27.4, which shows the inflation rate and the money growth rate for

Figure 27.4 Money Growth and Inflation in the World Economy

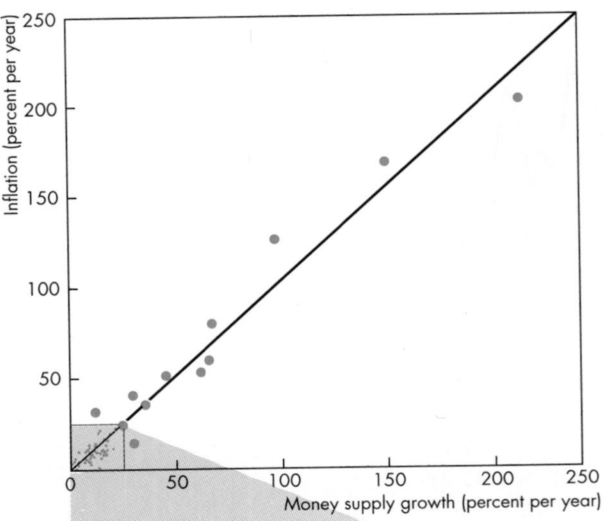

(a) All countries

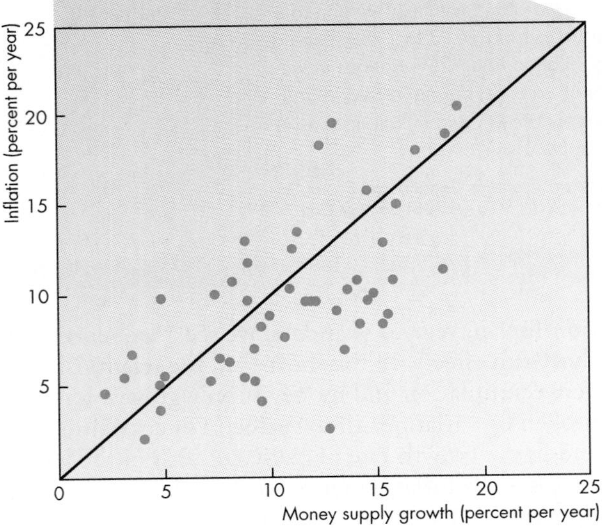

(b) Low-inflation countries

Inflation and money growth in 60 countries (in part a) and low-inflation countries (in part b) show that money growth is one of the most important influences, though not the only influence, on inflation.

Source: Federal Reserve Bank of St. Louis, *Review*, May/June 1988, 15.

60 countries. There is an unmistakable tendency for high money growth to be associated with high inflation.

But like the historical evidence in Canada, these international data also tell us that money supply growth is not the only cause of inflation. Some countries have an inflation rate that exceeds the money supply growth rate, while others have an inflation rate that falls short of the money supply growth rate.

REVIEW

The quantity of money exerts an important influence on the price level. An increase in the quantity of money increases aggregate demand. In the short run, that increase in aggregate demand increases both the price level and real GDP. In the long run, real GDP moves towards its original level and the price level continues to increase. The quantity theory of money predicts that an increase in the quantity of money will produce an equivalent percentage increase in the price level. The historical and international evidence on the relationship between the quantity of money and the price level provides broad support for the quantity theory of money, but the data also reveal important changes in the price level that occur independently of changes in the quantity of money. ■

■ In this chapter, we have studied the institutions that make up our banking and financial system. We've seen how the deposit liabilities of chartered banks and other financial institutions comprise our medium of exchange — our money. Banks and other financial institutions create money by making loans. The quantity of money in existence has important effects on the economy and, in particular, on the price level.

In the next chapter, we're going to see how the quantity of money is regulated and influenced by the actions of the Bank of Canada. We're also going to discover how the Bank of Canada, by its influence on the money supply, is able to influence interest rates, thereby affecting the level of aggregate demand. It is through its effects on the money supply and interest rates and their wider ramifications that the Bank of Canada is able to help steer the course of the economy.

SUMMARY

What is Money?

Money has four functions: it is a medium of exchange, a unit of account, a standard of deferred payment, and a store of value. The earliest forms of money were commodities. In the modern world, we use a fiat money system. The biggest component of money is private debt.

There are four official measures of money in Canada today: M1, M2, M3, and M2+. M1, M2, and M3 include currency and deposits at chartered banks. M2+ includes deposits at other financial institutions, such as trust companies, mortgage loan companies, caisses populaires, and credit unions. None of the official definitions of money exactly corresponds to the assets that function as money in Canada today. Money, the medium of exchange and means of payment, consists of currency and chequing deposits at chartered banks (official M1) plus chequing accounts at nonbank financial institutions. The deposits that are included in M2, M3, and M2+ are highly liquid but must be converted into currency or chequable deposits to be used directly as a medium of exchange and the means of payment. Demand deposits are money but cheques and credit cards are not. (pp. 719-729)

Financial Intermediaries

The main financial intermediaries whose liabilities serve as money are chartered banks, trust and mortgage loan companies, local credit unions, and caisses populaires. All of these institutions take in deposits, hold cash reserves to ensure that they can meet their depositors' demands for currency, hold securities, and make loans. Financial intermediaries make a profit by borrowing at a lower interest rate than that at which they lend. All financial intermediaries provide four main economic services: they minimize the cost of obtaining funds, minimize the cost of monitoring borrowers, pool risks, and create liquidity. The continual search for profitable financial opportunities leads to financial innovation — to the creation of new financial products such as new types of deposits and loans. (pp. 729-733)

How Banks Create Money

Banks and other financial institutions create money by making loans. When a loan is made to one person and the amount lent is spent, much of it ends up as someone else's deposit. The ratio of the total increase in deposits that can be supported by a given increase in reserves (the simple money multiplier) is equal to 1 divided by the desired reserve ratio. (pp. 733-736)

Money and the Price Level

The quantity of money affects aggregate demand. An increase in the quantity of money increases aggregate demand. In the short run, this increase in aggregate demand increases the price level and real GDP. In the long run, the price level continues to increase but real GDP returns to its original level. The quantity theory of money predicts that an increase in the money supply will increase the price level by the same percentage amount. Both historical and international evidence suggest that the quantity theory of money is correct only in a broad average sense. The quantity of money does exert an important influence on the price level. But there are other important influences too. Nevertheless, other things being equal, the higher the growth rate of the quantity of money, the higher is the inflation rate. (pp. 736-740)

KEY ELEMENTS

Key Terms

Assets, 730
Balance sheet, 730
Barter, 719
Chartered bank, 730
Chequable deposit, 723
Commodity money, 721
Convertible paper money, 721
Currency, 722
Currency drain, 736
Desired reserve ratio, 733
Double coincidence of wants, 719

Key Figures and Tables 

REVIEW QUESTIONS

1 What is money?

2 What are the functions of money?

3 What are the four official measures of money in Canada today? How closely do these official definitions correspond to the economic definition of money?

4 Are cheques and credit cards money? Explain your answer?

5 What is a chartered bank? How does it make a profit?

6 What are the main items in the balance sheet of a chartered bank?

7 What are the main deposit-taking institutions other than chartered banks?

8 How do banks create money?

9 Define the simple money multiplier.

10 What does the aggregate demand-aggregate supply model predict about the effects of a change in the quantity of money on the price level and real GDP?

11 What is the quantity theory of money?

12 What does the quantity theory of money predict about the relationship between the price level and the quantity of money?

13 What is the historical evidence on the quantity theory of money?

14 What is the international evidence on the quantity theory of money?

PROBLEMS

1 You are given the following information about a hypothetical economy. The chartered banks have deposit liabilities of $300 billion. Their reserves are $15 billion.

a) Using Table 27.7 as a guide, set out the balance sheet of the chartered banks. Supply any missing numbers using your knowledge of the fact that total assets equal total liabilities.

b) How much money is there in this economy if households and firms hold 10 times as much in their deposits as they do in cash?

c) What is the simple money multiplier for this economy?

2 An immigrant arrives in New Acadia with \$1,000. The \$1,000 is put into a bank deposit. All the banks in New Acadia have a desired reserve ratio of 10 percent.

a) What is the initial increase in the quantity of money of New Acadia?

b) What is the initial increase in the quantity of bank deposits?

c) How much does the immigrant's bank lend out?

d) Using a format similar to that in Table 27.8, calculate the amount lent and the amount of deposits created at each round, assuming that all the funds lent are returned to the banking system in the form of deposits.

e) By how much has the quantity of money increased after 20 rounds of lending?

f) What is the ultimate increase in the quantity of money, in bank loans, and in bank deposits?

3 An economy has a quantity of money of \$1,000 and GDP is \$4,000. What is the velocity of circulation in this economy?

4 You are given the following data on the money supply and the price level in Quantitheoria, an economist's tropical haven:

Year	Money supply (millions of marginals)	Price level (Index number, 1980 = 100)
1990	550,000	150
1991	605,000	165
1992	678,000	185
1993	678,000	192
1994	732,000	200
1995	805,000	210
1996	886,000	220
1997	930,000	220
1998	977,000	220

a) Calculate the inflation rate and the growth rate of the money supply in Quantitheoria for each year in the 1990s shown in the above table.

b) Does the quantity theory of money describe the relationship between the money supply and the price level in Quantitheoria?

c) Are there some years in which the quantity theory holds and others in which it does not? If so, in which years does the quantity theory hold and in which does it fail?

d) What do you predict about the growth rate of real GDP in Quantitheoria?

e) What factors other than changes in the money supply do you think might be at work in Quantitheoria influencing its price level?

CHAPTER 28

The Bank of Canada, Money, and Interest Rates

After studying this chapter, you will be able to:

- Describe the role of the Bank of Canada.
- Describe the tools used by the Bank of Canada to influence the money supply and interest rates.
- Explain what an open market operation is.
- Explain how an open market operation works.
- Explain how an open market operation changes the money supply.
- Distinguish between the nominal money supply and the real money supply.
- Explain what determines the demand for money.
- Explain the effects of financial innovations on the demand for money in the 1980s.
- Explain how interest rates are determined.
- Explain how the Bank of Canada influences interest rates.

Fiddling with the Knobs

A YOUNG COUPLE, PLANNING to buy a first home, have found the perfect place. They're in luck — the year is 1960 and mortgages are plentiful at interest rates of less than 6 percent a year. Twenty-two years later, that same couple's daughter is looking for her first home. She too finds the perfect place, but mortgage rates have now reached 20 percent a year. Amid much gnashing of teeth, she puts off her purchase until interest rates decline again, making a mortgage affordable. Why do interest rates rise and fall? What determines interest rates? Are they determined by forces of nature? Or is somebody "fiddling with the knobs" somewhere? ■ You suspect that someone is indeed fiddling with the knobs. For you've just read in your newspaper, "The Bank of Canada is prepared to continue nudging interest rates higher in order to head off the threat of inflation." And a few months earlier, you read, "The Bank of Canada doesn't plan to push interest rates lower unless it sees further weakness in the economy." What is "the Bank of Canada"? Why would the Bank of Canada want to change interest rates? And how can it influence them? ■ There is enough currency — coins and Bank of Canada bills — circulating in Canada for every single individual to have a wallet stuffed with $690. There are enough chequing deposits in banks and other financial institutions for everyone to have $2600 in these accounts. There are enough savings accounts for everyone to have a further $6000. Of course, not many people hold as much currency, chequable deposits, and savings deposits as these averages. But these *are* the averages. Therefore, if most people don't hold this much, some people must be holding a great deal more. What determines the quantity of money that people hold? And what determines the composition of their holdings? ■ The 1980s saw a revolution in our banking and financial sector. At the beginning of that decade, most banks and other financial institutions offered just two kinds of deposit arrangements: a demand deposit or a savings deposit. Cheques could be written on demand deposits but those deposits earned no interest; savings deposits earned interest but cheques couldn't be written on those accounts. Today, we are confronted with a rich variety of deposit arrangements: chequing accounts earn interest at a rate that depends on such things as average daily balances. How has the development of these new kinds of deposits influenced the amount of money that we hold? ■ Credit cards have been around for a long time (Diners' Club introduced the first card just after World War II). But there has been a virtual explosion in their use during the 1980s. Some people never use cash to buy gasoline, a restaurant meal, or many other commonly purchased items. But you can't buy everything with a credit card. For example, you feel like a midnight snack, but your favourite spot doesn't accept credit cards and you're out of cash. No problem! You head straight for the automatic teller and withdraw what you need tonight — and the next few days as well. As you leave, you wonder: how much cash would I need to hold if I didn't have quick access to an automatic teller machine? How did people get cash for midnight pizza before such machines existed? How have credit cards and computers affected the amount of money that we hold?

■ In the last chapter, we discovered that money is the currency (bills and coins) in circulation plus deposits at banks and other financial institutions. We also discovered that banks and other financial intermediaries create money by making loans. Finally, we discovered that the quantity of money has an important effect on the price level: increases in the quantity of money bring increasing prices. But we also saw that there is no precise relationship between the quantity of money and the price level — only a general tendency for the two to be correlated. ■ An important reason why the quantity of money and the price level do not have a precise relationship with each other is that the *velocity of circulation* of money fluctuates. In this chapter, we are going to discover what determines the velocity of circulation. We are going to discover that the velocity of circulation is determined by the demand for money. We are also going to discover that interest rates are determined in the market for money by the interaction of the demand for money and the supply of money. ■ But first we are going to study the Bank of Canada and learn how it influences the quantity of money in its attempts to influence interest rates and, more generally, the overall level of aggregate demand and inflation. At the end of the chapter, we will return to the Bank of Canada and see how its operations in the late 1970s and early 1980s generated huge swings in interest rates but eventually, with help from the Federal Reserve Bank in the United States, brought inflation under control.

The Bank of Canada

The **Bank of Canada** is Canada's central bank. A **central bank** is a public authority charged with regulating and controlling a country's monetary and financial institutions and markets. The Bank of Canada is also responsible for the nation's monetary policy. **Monetary policy** is the attempt to control inflation and the foreign exchange value of our currency and to moderate the business cycle by changing the quantity of money in circulation and adjusting interest rates. We are going to study the tools available to the Bank of Canada in its conduct of monetary policy and also work out the effects of the Bank's actions on interest rates later in this chapter. But first we'll examine its origins and structure.

The Origins of the Bank of Canada

The Bank of Canada was created by the Bank of Canada Act of 1935. Before then — for the first 68 years of our history — Canada had no formal, central bank. The major bank during that period was the Bank of Montreal, which acted as the government's bank. But the Bank of Montreal did not act as a modern central bank does. In effect, the federal minister of finance conducted Canada's monetary policy. But that monetary policy was crude and ill suited to the conditions of the age. None of the sophisticated tools of monetary policy that we're going to learn about in this chapter was employed in Canada prior to the creation of the Bank of Canada.

By the time that the Bank of Canada was created, most other countries already had a central bank. The United States had created its Federal Reserve System in 1913. The first central banks had been established in Sweden and England as long ago as the seventeenth century. But the origins of those earliest central banks were very different from that of the Bank of Canada. They were set up as private banks designed to solve the financial problems of monarchs. These banks gradually evolved into modern central banks, eventually becoming publicly owned corporations.

The Structure of the Bank of Canada

The Bank of Canada has three key structural components. They are:

- The governor
- The board of directors
- The senior staff

The Governor The governor of the Bank of Canada is appointed by the government of Canada for a term of seven years. There have been five governors of the bank:

- 1935–1954, Graham Towers
- 1955–1961, James Coyne
- 1961–1973, Louis Rasminsky
- 1973–1987, Gerald Bouey
- 1987– , John Crow

The governor of the Bank of Canada, with the advice of the Bank's senior staff, formulates and oversees the implementation of the nation's monetary policy. In these activities, the governor consults closely with the minister of finance and the Bank's board of directors, as well as the senior staff of the Bank.

The Board of Directors The Bank's board of directors consists of the governor, the senior deputy-governor, the deputy minister of finance, together with 11 men and women from all regions of Canada representing a variety of commercial, legal, and financial interests. The board meets approximately every month. The minutes of those meetings are summarized and reported in the Bank of Canada's monthly *Review*. The Bank's board meetings take the form of a dialogue between the governor and the board members. The governor reviews the state of the economy and describes and explains the Bank's recent and current policy positions. The board members comment on the Bank's policy from the perspective of the wide variety of interests that they represent.

Senior Staff The senior staff members of the Bank of Canada are key players in the formulation of the bank's monetary policy. They are economists and central bankers with considerable national and international experience in monetary and financial affairs. These are the people who monitor the Canadian and world economies on a day-by-day and even hour-by-hour basis. They record the ebbs and flows of economic activity, the rising and falling patterns of interest rates, exchange rates, inflation, unemployment, and gross domestic product (GDP). Using macroeconomic models similar to those you are studying in this book, they prepare forecasts of the Canadian economy and of the other major economies of the world and analyse the effects of alternative policy measures that the Bank might take — both those that it ultimately does take and other possible policies that have to be contemplated in the process of arriving at policy decisions.

The Bank of Canada and the Federal Government

There are two different models for the relationship between a country's central bank and its central government:

- Independence
- Subservience

An Independent Central Bank An independent central bank is one that has complete autonomy in determining the nation's monetary policy. Government public servants and elected officials may comment on monetary policy, but the governor of the central bank is under no obligation to take into account the views of anyone other than his own staff and board of directors.

The argument for an independent central bank is that it enables monetary policy to be formulated with a long-term view of maintaining stable prices and prevents monetary policy from being used for short-term political advantage. Countries that have independent central banks today are West Germany, the United States, and Switzerland.

When the Bank of Canada was founded in 1935, it too was established as an independent central bank. Governors Towers and Coyne enjoyed almost complete autonomy from the government of Canada in the formulation and pursuit of their monetary policies. In 1961, however, James Coyne, the governor of the Bank, who was pursuing tight, disinflationary monetary policies, had a severe clash with Prime Minister John Diefenbaker concerning who was in charge of the nation's monetary policy. As a consequence of this clash, Coyne resigned as governor. For a period, it was not clear whether the Bank of Canada was indeed independent, as the act that established it proclaimed, or whether it was under the direct control of the government as the outcome of the Coyne-Diefenbaker affair seemed to imply. The matter was resolved in clear-cut terms, however, when a revision of the Bank of Canada Act in 1967 redefined the relationship between the Bank of Canada and the government, making the government ultimately responsible for monetary policy (see Talking with Gerald Bouey, pp. 713-716).

Subservient Central Bank Most central banks are subservient to their governments. In the event of a difference of opinion between the central bank and government, the government carries the day and the central bank governor must resign if he is unwilling to implement the policies dictated by the government. The Bank of Canada has been in such a position since 1967.

Those advocating subservience of the central bank take the view that monetary policy is essentially political in its effects. Therefore, like fiscal policy and indeed all other government policies, monetary policy must ultimately be subject to democratic control.

In Canada, although the minister of finance is ultimately responsible for monetary policy, this fact does not reduce the governor of the Bank of Canada to a position of impotence. Because of his expertise and authority in the field and because of the quality of the advice that he receives from the Bank's staff of senior economists and advisors, the governor of the Bank has considerable power in both private and public discussions of monetary policy. Opinions would have to be sharply divided on a range of crucial matters before a government would be willing to run the risk of seeing the governor resign on a dispute over policy. Also, there are times when a government wants to pursue unpopular monetary policies; at such times, it is very convenient for democratically elected officials to hide behind the authority of a relatively independent monetary agency such as the Bank of Canada.

The Bank of Canada is also in a strong position vis-à-vis the government of Canada because the Bank is the government's main banker and financial agent. When the government is running a deficit, the Bank of Canada has the responsibility of helping to find a way of covering that deficit. One way of covering a deficit is simply to print more money. Another is to handle the sale of government securities. By taking a firm stand and being unwilling to print new money to cover a government's deficit, the Bank can force the government to face the higher interest rates that it brings upon itself by spending in excess of its tax receipts.

International Constraints on the Bank of Canada

The Canadian economy in general and its monetary and financial system in particular are closely integrated with the rest of the world. Economic integration was a fact of Canadian life long before Confederation. The sheer size and importance of the money and financial markets in New York have made it essential for Canadian financial institutions to seek profitable business not only in Canada but beyond its borders.

Faced with a giant for a neighbour, some countries seek to erect large barriers to limit the giant's access to the national economy and restrict the international activities of its citizens. Canada is not such a country. Just as we have civil freedom of travel between Canada and the United States, so also do we have considerable economic freedom. Neither the government of Canada nor the Bank of Canada imposes restrictions on the movement of goods (except illegal goods) or on borrowing and lending. Tariffs, duties, and taxes must, of course, be paid, where relevant, but there is free mobility of capital between Canada and the rest of the world. Foreigners are free to place deposits in Canadian banks, and Canadians are free to place deposits in foreign banks. Banks are free to make loans to foreigners or to Canadians. Furthermore, these loans and deposits may be denominated in Canadian dollars or in any other currency. As we saw in Chapter 27, a substantial portion of the deposits and loans of chartered banks is in the form of foreign currencies (much of it U.S. dollars).

These facts of financial life in Canada place some restrictions on the range of actions that the Bank of Canada might take. It cannot, for example, ignore interest rate pressures that stem from south of the border. Furthermore, the Bank must adopt some attitude towards the value of the Canadian dollar. That value is determined in a market — a worldwide market — for foreign exchange.

Exchange Rate Regimes One fundamental choice that the government of Canada and the Bank of Canada must make has far-reaching implications for the monetary policy that Canada can pursue. This is the choice among three possible foreign exchange regimes:

- Fixed exchange rate
- Flexible exchange rate
- Managed exchange rate

A **fixed exchange rate** is an exchange rate, the value of which is determined by the country's central bank. For example, the Bank of Canada could adopt a fixed exchange rate by defining the Canadian dollar to be worth, say, one U.S. dollar (or some other value). To make this exchange rate possible, the Bank of Canada would have to stand ready to buy U.S. dollars or sell Canadian dollars at this predetermined, fixed exchange rate and would have to hold sufficiently large reserves of U.S. dollars to enable it to do so.

A **flexible exchange rate** is an exchange rate, the value of which is determined by market forces in the absence of central bank intervention. A **managed exchange rate** is an exchange rate, the value of which is influenced by central bank intervention in the foreign exchange market. Under a managed exchange rate regime, the central bank's intervention does not seek to keep the exchange rate fixed at a pre-announced level, but it does try to smooth out wild fluctuations in the exchange rate.

Between 1962 and 1970, Canada had a fixed exchange rate. Before 1962 and in the period since 1970, the Canadian dollar has fluctuated in value against other currencies. When a country fixes its exchange rate, its central bank has virtually no freedom of manoeuvre for determining an independent, national monetary policy. To make a fixed exchange rate work, the central bank must be willing to supply as much, or as little, national currency as people want to hold. The central bank cannot control the nation's money supply.

A central bank is like a monopolist selling fresh mountain spring water. The monopolist can determine a price at which to sell the water, leaving the market to decide how much to buy at that price, or it can decide on a production rate, leaving the market to determine the price at which that quantity will be sold. The monopolist cannot choose both the price at which it will sell its output and the quantity that people will buy. The Bank of Canada is a monopolist in the supply of Canadian dollars. It can choose the quantity to supply but not the price at which it exchanges for other currencies (or for goods and services). Alternatively, the Bank of Canada can fix the price at which the Canadian dollar exchanges for some other currency (for example, the U.S. dollar), but in so doing, it abdicates control over the quantity of Canadian dollars outstanding.

By choosing to permit the foreign currency value of the Canadian dollar to fluctuate, the Bank of Canada retains control over Canadian monetary policy — over the Canadian money supply and interest rates. How the Bank exercises that control is the subject matter of the rest of this chapter. How the foreign exchange markets work to determine the value of the Canadian dollar and how the Bank's interest rate policies influence the dollar are the subject of Chapter 29. Our next task in studying the Bank of Canada's monetary policy is to examine the policy tools that the Bank has at its disposal.

Policy Tools

The Bank of Canada has many responsibilities, but we'll examine its single most important one — regulating the amount of money floating around in Canada and influencing the level of interest rates. How does the Bank of Canada control the money supply? It does so by adjusting the reserves of the banking system. It is also by adjusting those reserves of the banking system, and by standing ready to make loans to banks that the Bank of Canada is able to prevent banking panics and bank failures.

The Bank of Canada uses three main policy tools to achieve its objectives:

- Reserve requirements
- The bank rate
- Open market operations

Reserve Requirements All chartered banks in Canada (and other financial institutions) are required to hold reserves on a scale not less than that specified in the relevant laws. The minimum reserves that a bank is permitted to hold are called **required reserves**. Required reserves are specified as a minimum percentage of deposits of various classes. The reserve requirements on chartered banks in force in 1989 are set out in Table 28.1.

The Bank Rate The **bank rate** is the interest rate at which the Bank of Canada stands ready to lend reserves to the chartered banks. The bank rate is fixed every Thursday and is based on a formula that relates it to movements in the interest rate on three-month government of Canada treasury bills. The bank rate is usually about one-quarter of a percent above the treasury bill rate. In practice, chartered banks do not

Table 28.1 Chartered Banks' Required Reserves in 1989

Type of deposit	Minimum reserve required (percentage of deposits)
Very large chequing accounts	10
Notice and term deposits up to $500 million	2
Notice and term deposits in excess of $500 million	3
Foreign currency deposits	3

borrow very much from the Bank of Canada so the bank rate does not have any practical consequences for the chartered banks' profits. Instead, it acts as a type of barometer of the Bank of Canada's attitude towards short-term interest rates. An upward movement of the bank rate is a signal that the Bank of Canada is seeking to tighten monetary conditions. Other interest rates move with the bank rate in response to this general signal, rather than as a consequence of its making borrowed reserves more costly for the banks.

The two instruments of monetary policy that we have just considered are minor ones compared with the third — open market operations.

Open Market Operations The purchase or sale of government of Canada securities — treasury bills and bonds — by the Bank of Canada are **open market operations**. When the Bank of Canada sells government securities, they are paid for with bank deposits and bank reserves, creating tighter monetary and credit conditions. With lower reserves, the banks cut their lending, and interest rates rise. When the Bank of Canada buys government securities, its payment for them puts additional reserves in the hands of the banks and loosens credit conditions. With extra reserves, the banks increase their lending, and interest rates fall. In order to understand the Bank of Canada's open market operations, we first need to examine the structure of the Bank of Canada's balance sheet.

The Bank of Canada's Balance Sheet

The balance sheet of the Bank of Canada for August 1989 is set out in Table 28.2. The assets on the left-hand side are what the Bank owns and the liabilities on the right-hand side are what it owes. Most of the Bank of Canada's assets are government of Canada securities. The most important aspect of the Bank's balance sheet is on the liabilities side.

The largest liability of the Bank of Canada is Bank of Canada notes in circulation. These are the bank notes that we use in our daily transactions. Some of these bank notes are in pockets and wallets and cashdrawers of the public and others are in the tills and vaults of banks and other financial institutions.

You may be wondering why Bank of Canada notes are considered a liability of the Bank. Recall

Table 28.2 The Balance Sheet for the Bank of Canada, June 1989

Assets (billions of dollars)		Liabilities (billions of dollars)		
Government of Canada securities	22.0	Bank of Canada notes in circulation	20.2	
Other assets	1.7	Chartered banks' deposits	2.2	
		Monetary base liabilities		22.4
		Other liabilities		1.3
Total	23.7	Total		23.7

Source: *Bank of Canada Review*, December, 1989, Table B1.

from Chapter 27 that when notes were first used, they gave their owners a claim on the gold reserves of the issuing bank. Such notes were *convertible paper money* because they could be converted on demand into gold (or some other commodity such as silver) at a guaranteed price. Thus when a bank issued a note, it was holding itself liable to convert that note into a commodity. Modern bank notes are nonconvertible. A **nonconvertible note** is a bank note that is not convertible into any commodity and that obtains its value by government fiat — hence the term *fiat money*. Such bank notes are considered the legal liability of the bank that issues them. They are backed not by commodity reserves but by holdings of securities and loans. Bank of Canada notes are backed by the Bank of Canada's holdings of government of Canada securities.

The other important liability of the Bank of Canada is the deposits held there by chartered banks. Recall that we saw these deposits as an asset in the balance sheets of the banks in Chapter 27. The remaining liability of the Bank of Canada consists of items such as government of Canada deposits (government bank accounts at the Bank of Canada) and accounts held by foreign central banks (such as the Bank of England and the Federal Reserve System of the United States).

The two largest items on the liability side of the Bank of Canada's balance sheet make up most of the monetary base. The **monetary base** is the sum of Bank of Canada notes in circulation, chartered banks' deposits at the Bank, and coins in circulation. Coins are issued, not by the Bank of Canada, but by the government of Canada. They do not appear, therefore, as a liability of the Bank of Canada.

By buying or selling government securities, the Bank of Canada can directly determine the scale of its own liabilities and exert a considerable influence on the monetary base. Such purchases and sales of government securities are the Bank of Canada's open market operations. Let's see how open market operations work.

How Open Market Operations Work

When the Bank of Canada conducts an open market operation in which it buys government of Canada securities, it increases the reserves of the banking system. When it conducts an open market operation in which it sells government of Canada securities, it decreases the reserves of the banking system. Let's study the effects of an open market operation by working out what happens when the Bank of Canada buys $100 million of government of Canada securities. Open market operations affect the balance sheets of the Bank of Canada, the banks, and the rest of the economy. Table 28.3 keeps track of the changes in these balance sheets.

When the Bank of Canada buys securities, there are two possible sellers: the banks and other agents in the economy. Part (a) of the table works out what happens when banks sell the securities that the Bank of Canada buys. The Bank of Canada pays for these securities by crediting the banks' deposit accounts with itself. The changes in the Bank of Canada's balance sheet are that its assets increase by $100 million (the additional government of Canada securities bought) and its liabilities also increase by $100 million (the additional bank deposits). The banks' balance sheet also changes, but their total assets remain constant. Their deposits at the Bank of Canada increase by $100 million and their holdings of securities decrease by $100 million.

Part (b) of the table deals with the case in which the Bank of Canada buys securities from agents in the economy other than the banks. The Bank of Canada's holdings of government of Canada securities increase by $100 million and other agents' holdings of government of Canada securities decrease by $100 million. The Bank of Canada pays for the securities by giving cheques drawn on itself to the sellers. The sellers take the cheques to the banks and deposit them. Bank deposits increase by $100 million. The banks in turn present the cheques to the Bank of Canada, which credits the banks' accounts with the value of the cheques. Banks' deposits with the Bank of Canada — reserves — increase by $100 million.

Regardless of which of the two cases takes place, by conducting an open market purchase of securities, the Bank of Canada increases the banks' deposits with itself — increases the banks' reserves.

If the Bank of Canada conducts an open market *sale* of securities, the events that we have just traced occur in reverse. The Bank of Canada's assets and liabilities decrease in value and so do the reserves of the banks.

The effects of an open market operation on the balance sheets of the Bank of Canada and the banks that we've traced in Table 28.3 are not the end of the story — they are just the beginning. With an increase in their reserves, the banks are now able to make more loans — as the banks did in Chapter 27) when Al increased his deposit at the Golden Nugget Bank. That has a big effect on the quantity of money

Table 28.3 An Open Market Operation

(a) Banks sell securities

Effects on the balance sheet of the Bank of Canada

Change in assets (millions of dollars)		Change in liabilities (millions of dollars)	
Government of Canada securities	+100	Banks' deposits (reserves)	+ 100

Effects on the balance sheet of the banks

Change in assets (millions of dollars)		Change in liabilities (millions of dollars)	
Banks' deposits (reserves)	+100		
Government of Canada securities	−100		

(b) Banks do not sell securities

Effects on the balance sheet of the Bank of Canada

Change in assets (millions of dollars)		Change in liabilities (millions of dollars)	
Government of Canada securities	+100	Bank's deposits (reserves)	+100

Effects on the balance sheet of the banks

Change in assets (millions of dollars)		Change in liabilities (millions of dollars)	
Banks' deposits (reserves)	+100	Deposits	+100

Effects on the balance sheet of the other agents

Change in assets (millions of dollars)		Change in liabilities (millions of dollars)	
Deposits	+100		
Government of Canada securities	− 100		

for, as we saw in Chapter 27, by making loans the banks themselves create money. Let's see how this multiple expansion of money comes about.

The Multiplier Effect of an Open Market Operation

The **money multiplier** is the amount by which a change in the monetary base is multiplied to determine the resulting change in the quantity of money.[1] We'll work out the multiplier effect of an open market operation for an example in which the Bank of

[1] In Chapter 27 we worked with the *simple* money multiplier, defined as the amount by which a change in bank reserves is multiplied to determine the resulting change in deposits. The *money multiplier* and the *simple money multiplier* are related, but they are different concepts and must not be confused.

Canada buys securities from the banks. In this case, although the open market operation increases the banks' reserves, it has no immediate effect on the quantity of money. The banks simply hold additional reserves and fewer government of Canada securities. But now the banks have excess reserves. When the banks have excess reserves, the sequence of events shown in Fig. 28.1 takes place. These events are:

- Banks lend their excess reserves.
- New loans are used to make payments.
- Households and firms receive payments from new loans.
- Some of the receipts are held as currency — a *currency drain* occurs.
- Some of the receipts are deposited in banks.
- Bank reserves increase (by the same amount as the increase in deposits).
- Desired reserves increase (by a fraction — the desired reserve ratio — of the increase in deposits).
- Excess reserves decrease, but remain positive.
- The money supply increases by the amount of the currency drain and the increase in bank deposits.

The sequence just described is similar to that which we studied in Chapter 27 except that there we ignored the currency drain. The sequence repeats in a series of rounds but each begins with a smaller quantity of excess reserves than did the previous one. The process continues until excess reserves have finally been eliminated.

Table 28.4 keeps track of the magnitudes of new loans, the currency drain, the increase in deposits and reserves, the increase in desired reserves, and the change in excess reserves at each round of the multiplier process. The initial open market operation has increased the banks' reserves but, since deposits

Figure 28.1 A Round in the Multiplier Process Following an Open Market Operation

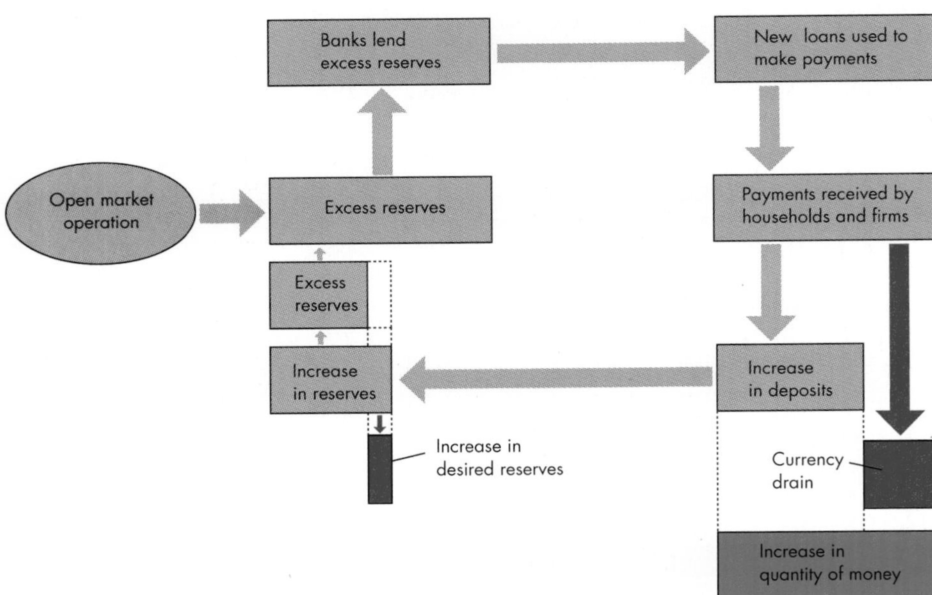

An open market purchase of government of Canada securities increases bank reserves and creates excess reserves. Banks lend their excess reserves, and the new loans are used to make payments. Households and firms receiving payments keep some of the receipts in the form of currency — a currency drain — and place the rest on deposit in banks. The increase in deposits increases banks' reserves but also increases their desired reserves. Desired reserves increase by less than actual reserves, so the banks still have some excess reserves, though less than before. The process repeats until the excess reserves have been eliminated. The increase in the quantity of money has two components: the currency drain and the increase in deposits.

have not changed, there is no change in desired reserves. The banks have excess reserves of 100. They lend those reserves. When the money borrowed from the banks is spent, some of it returns to the banks in the form of additional deposits and some of it drains off in the form of a currency drain. In the table, we're assuming that two-thirds of what the banks lend comes back to them in the form of deposits and one-third drains off and is held by households and firms in the form of currency. Thus when the banks lend the initial \$100 million of excess reserves, \$66.67 million comes back to them in the form of deposits and \$33.33 million drains off and is held outside the banks as currency. The quantity of money has now increased by \$100 million — the increase in deposits plus the increase in currency holdings.

The increased bank deposits now produce an increase in the bank's desired reserves. We're assuming that the desired reserve ratio is 3 percent. This means that an increase in deposits of \$66.7 million generates an increase in desired reserves of \$2 million. But actual reserves have increased by the same amount as the increase in deposits — \$66.7 million. Therefore, the banks now have excess reserves of \$64.67 million.

At this stage we have completed round 1. We have been around the loop shown in Fig. 28.1. The banks still have excess reserves, but the level has fallen from \$100 million at the beginning of the round to \$64.67 million at the end of the round. Round 2 now begins.

When the excess reserves of \$64.67 are lent and those loans spent, two-thirds of the amount — \$43.11 million — comes back to the banks in the form of deposits and one-third — \$21.56 million — drains off as currency. The quantity of money has now increased by a further \$64.67 million for a total increase of \$164.67 million. The process that we've just described keeps on repeating. Table 28.4 shows the first ten rounds in this process and collapses all the remaining ones into the second row of the table. At the end of the process, the quantity of money has increased by slightly more than \$283 million.

The accumulated increase in bank deposits,

Table 28.4 The Multiplier Effect of an Open Market Operation

Round	Excess reserves at start of round	New loans	Change in deposits	Currency drain	Change in reserves	Change in desired reserves	Excess reserves at end of round	Change in quantity of money
	(millions of dollars)							
1	100.00	100.00	66.67	33.33	66.67	2.00	64.67	100.00
2	64.67	64.67	43.11	21.56	43.11	1.29	41.82	64.67
3	41.82	41.82	27.88	13.94	27.88	0.84	27.04	41.82
4	27.04	27.04	18.03	9.01	18.03	0.54	17.49	27.04
5	17.49	17.49	11.66	5.83	11.66	0.35	11.31	17.49
6	11.31	11.31	7.54	3.77	7.54	0.23	7.31	11.31
7	7.31	7.31	4.87	2.44	4.87	0.15	4.72	7.31
8	4.72	4.72	3.15	1.57	3.15	0.09	3.06	4.72
9	3.06	3.06	2.04	1.02	2.04	0.06	1.98	3.06
10	1.98	1.98	1.32	0.66	1.32	0.04	1.28	1.98
	.	.	.	.	.	.	.	.
	.	.	.	.	.	.	.	.
	.	.	.	.	.	.	.	.
	.	.	.	.	.	.	.	.
All others		3.62	2.41	1.21		0.07		3.62
Total		283.02	188.68	94.34		5.66		283.02

Figure 28.2 The Multiplier Effect of an Open Market Operation

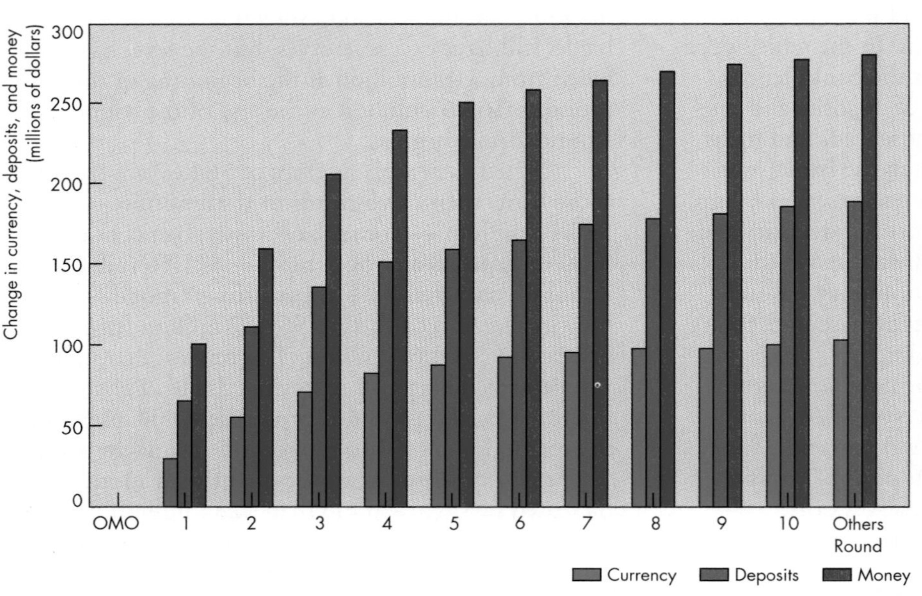

An open market operation (OMO) in which government securities are bought from the banks has no immediate effect on the money supply but it creates excess reserves in the banking system. When loans are made with these reserves and those loans are used to buy goods and services, bank deposits and currency holdings increase. Each time new loans are spent, part of them return to the banking system in the form of additional deposits and additional reserves. Banks continue to increase their lending until their excess reserves have been eliminated. The magnitude of the resulting increase in the money supply is determined by the money multiplier.

currency, and the quantity of money is illustrated in Fig. 28.2. As you can see, when the open market operation (labelled OMO in the figure) takes place, there is no initial change in either the quantity of money or its components. Then, after the first round of bank lending, the quantity of money increases by $100 million — the size of the open market operation. In successive rounds, the quantity of money and its components continue to increase but by successively smaller amounts. After 10 rounds, currency, deposits, and the quantity of money have almost reached the value to which they are ultimately heading.

What determines the size of the money multiplier and how big is the money multiplier in Canada?

The Canadian Money Multiplier

The money multiplier is calculated as the ratio of the quantity of money to the monetary base. That is,

Table 28.5 The Money Multiplier

Year	**Monetary base (*MB*)**	**(M1)**	**(M2)**	**(M3)**	**(M2+)**	**M1 money multiplier (M1/*MB*)**	**M2 money multiplier (M2/*MB*)**	**M3 money multiplier (M3/*MB*)**	**M2+ money multiplier (M2+/*MB*)**
1985	13.3	29.8	155.9	196.5	255.8	2.2	11.7	14.8	19.2
1986	14.3	30.9	160.0	206.0	279.9	2.2	11.2	14.4	19.6
1987	15.5	36.2	188.4	229.7	314.3	2.3	12.2	14.8	20.3
1988	16.7	37.4	200.0	245.2	340.0	2.2	12.0	14.7	20.4

Source: Bank of Canada Review, December 1988 and 1989, Tables B1 and E1.

Table 28.6 Calculating the Money Multiplier 

	In general	Numbers for M1
1. The variables		
Currency outside banks	C	
Banks' Reserves	R	
Monetary base	MB	
Deposits at banks	D	
Money supply	M	
Money multiplier	mm	
2. Definitions		
The monetary base (the sum of currency outside banks and banks' reserves)	$MB = C + R$	
The money supply (the sum of deposits and currency outside banks)	$M = D + C$	
The money multiplier (the ratio of the money supply to the monetary base)	$mm = M/MB$	
3. Ratios		
Currency to deposits	C/D	0.8
Reserves to deposits	R/D	0.1
4. Calculations		
Begin with the definition	$mm = M/MB$	
Use the definitions of M and MB to give	$mm = \frac{D + C}{C + R}$	
Divide top and bottom by D.	$mm = \frac{1 + C/D}{C/D + R/D}$	$\frac{1 + 0.8}{0.8 + 0.1}$
		$= \frac{1.8}{0.9}$
		$= 2.0$

$$\text{Money multiplier} = \frac{\text{Quantity of money}}{\text{Monetary base}}$$

The size of the money multiplier depends on which definition of money we're considering. The values of the M1, M2, M3, and M2+ multipliers in Canada between 1985 and 1988 are set out in Table 28.5. As you can see, the M1 multiplier ranges from 2.2 to 2.3, the M2 multiplier from 11.2 to 12.2, the M3 multiplier from 14.4 to 14.8, and the M2+ multiplier from 19.2 to 20.4. Multipliers of these magnitudes tell us that if the monetary base changes by \$1 million, M1 changes by about \$2.25 million, M2 changes by \$11 million to \$12 million, M3 changes by more than \$14 million, and M2+ changes by about \$20 million.

The monetary base is like the base of an inverted pyramid of money. The monetary base itself is divided into currency and reserves. Each dollar of currency creates a dollar of money. Each dollar of reserves supports a multiple of itself as money and the larger the multiple, the broader the definition of money. By changing the monetary base, the Bank of Canada changes reserves. The change in reserves has a multiplier or magnification effect on the quantity of money outstanding.

Why are the money multipliers so stable? They are stable because their values depend on two ratios that themselves do not vary much. These ratios are:

- Currency holdings of households and firms as a fraction of total deposits
- Reserve holdings of banks as a fraction of total deposits

Table 28.6 shows how the money multiplier depends on these two ratios. It also provides numbers that illustrate the M1 money multiplier. Currency holdings of households and firms are approximately 0.8 times the chequable deposits that make up M1. Equivalently, currency makes up 44 percent of M1 and deposits 56 percent. Reserve holdings are approximately 10 percent (0.1) of the deposits in M1. We used this value for the desired reserve ratio in the above calculation. Combining these ratios in the formula derived in the table shows that the M1 money multiplier is 2.

R E V I E W

The Bank of Canada is the nation's central bank. The Bank of Canada influences the quantity of money in circulation by changing the excess reserves of the banking system. It has three instruments at its disposal: reserve requirements, bank rate, and open market operations. The last of these is the most important and most frequently used. Open market operations change the excess reserves of the banking system and set in progress a multiplier effect. When excess reserves are lent, some of the loans drain out of the banking system, but others come back in the form of new deposits. The banks continue to lend until the currency drain and the increase in their desired reserves have eliminated excess reserves. The multiplier effect of an open market operation depends on the scale of the currency drain and the size of the banks' desired reserve ratio. ■

The Bank of Canada's objectives in undertaking open market operations or other actions that influence the quantity of money in circulation are not simply to affect the money supply for its own sake. Their objective is to influence the course of the economy — especially the level of output, employment, and prices. But these effects are indirect. The Bank of Canada's immediate objective is to move interest rates up or down. To see why the Bank of Canada's actions affect interest rates, we need to work out how and why interest rates change when the quantity of money changes. We'll begin by studying the demand for money.

The Demand for Money

The amount of money we *receive* each week in payment for our labour is income — a *flow.* The amount of money that we *hold* in our wallets or in deposit accounts at the bank is an inventory — a *stock.* There is no limit to how much income — or flow — we would like to receive each week. But there is a limit to how big an inventory of money each of us would like to hold, on the average.

The Motives for Holding Money

Why do people hold an inventory of money? Why do you carry coins and bills in your wallet, and keep money in a deposit account at your neighbourhood bank?

There are three main motives for holding money:

- Transactions motive
- Precautionary motive
- Speculative motive

Transactions Motive The main motive for holding money is to be able to undertake transactions and to minimize the cost of transactions. By carrying an inventory of currency, you are able to undertake small transactions such as buying your lunch at the college cafeteria. If you didn't carry an inventory of currency, you'd have to go to the bank every lunchtime and withdraw enough cash. The opportunity cost of these transactions, in terms of your own lost studying or leisure time, would be considerable. You avoid such transactions costs by keeping an inventory of currency large enough to make your normal purchases over some period, perhaps a week.

You also keep an inventory of money in the form of deposits at the bank to use for transactions such as paying the rent on your apartment or paying your college bookstore bill. Instead of having an inventory of bank deposits for these purposes, you could put all your assets into the stock or bond market — buying Labatt shares or government of Canada securities. But if you did that, you would have to call your broker and sell some stocks and bonds each time you needed to pay the landlord or the bookstore. Again, such transactions would have opportunity costs. By holding an inventory of bank deposits, you can avoid those costs.

Individual holdings of money for transactions purposes fluctuate during any week or month. But aggregate money balances held for transaction purposes do not fluctuate much because what one person is spending, someone else is receiving.

Firms' money holdings are at their peak just before the moment they pay their employees' wages. Households' money holdings are at a peak just after wages have been paid. As households spend their incomes, their money holdings decline and firms' money holdings increase. Firms' holdings of money are actually quite large — it is this fact that makes average money holdings so large. Households' average money holdings are much lower than the economy-wide averages presented in the chapter opener.

Precautionary Motive Money is also held as a precaution against unforeseen events that require unplanned purchases. For example, on an out-of-town trip you carry some extra money in case your car breaks down and has to be fixed. Or if you are headed for the January sales at the mall, you take with you more money than you plan to spend in case you come across a real bargain that you just can't pass up.

Speculative Motive The final motive for holding money is to avoid losses from holding stocks or bonds that are expected to fall in value. Suppose, for example, you had predicted the stock market crash of October 1987 a week before it happened. On the Friday afternoon before the markets closed, you would have sold all your stocks and put the proceeds into your bank deposit account for the weekend. You would have persisted in this temporary holding of money until stock prices had fallen to their lowest predicted level. Only then would you have reduced your bank deposit and bought stocks again.

The Influences on Money Holding

What determines the quantity of money that households and firms choose to hold? There are three important influences on this quantity:

- Prices
- Real expenditure
- The opportunity cost of holding money

The higher the level of prices, other things being equal, the larger is the quantity of money that people will want to hold. The higher the level of real expenditure, other things being equal, the larger is the quantity of money that people plan to hold. The higher the opportunity cost of holding money, the smaller is the quantity of money that people plan to hold.

These influences on individual decisions about money holding translate into three macroeconomic variables that influence the aggregate quantity of money demanded:

- The price level
- Real GDP
- Interest rate

Price Level and the Quantity of Money Demanded The quantity of money measured in current dollars is called the **nominal quantity of money**. The nominal quantity of money demanded is proportional to the price level. That is, other things being equal, if the price level (GDP deflator) increases by 10 percent, people will want to hold 10 percent more nominal money than before. What matters to people is not the number of dollars that they hold but the buying power of those dollars. Suppose, for example, that to undertake your weekly expenditure on movies and pop, you carry an average of $20 in your wallet. If your income and the prices of movies and pop increase by 10 percent you will increase your average cash holding by 10 percent to $22.

The quantity of money measured in constant dollars (for example, in 1981 dollars) is called *real money*. Real money is equal to nominal money divided by the price level. The quantity of real money demanded is independent of the price level. If the price level as measured by the GDP deflator is 200, people will want to hold, on the average, the same quantity of real money as they would if the GDP deflator were 100. Doubling the price level doubles the quantity of nominal money demanded but leaves the quantity of real money demanded unchanged.

Real GDP and the Quantity of Real Money Demanded An important determinant of the quantity of real money demanded is the level of real income — for the aggregate economy, real GDP. As you know, real GDP and real aggregate expenditure are the two sides of the same transaction. The amount of money that households and firms demand depends on the amount of spending that they want to do. The higher the expenditure — the higher the income — the larger is the quantity of money demanded. Again, suppose that you hold an average of $20 to finance your weekly purchases of movies and pop. Now imagine that the prices of these goods and of all other goods remain constant but that your income increases. As a consequence you now spend more, and you keep a larger amount of money on hand to finance your higher volume of expenditure.

The Interest Rate and the Quantity of Money Demanded The higher the level of interest rates, other things being equal, the lower is the quantity of real money demanded. Equivalently, the higher the level of interest rates, the higher is the velocity of circulation of money. The velocity of circulation is the ratio of real GDP to the quantity of real money demanded.[2] It

[2]In Chapter 27 we defined the velocity of circulation using the equation of exchange:

$$MV = PY,$$

where M is the quantity of nominal money, V is the velocity of circulation, P is the price level, and Y is real GDP.
Dividing this equation by P gives

$$(M/P)V = Y.$$

Then dividing by the real quantity of money (M/P) gives

$$V = Y/(M/P).$$

That is, the velocity of circulation is equal to the ratio of real GDP to the real money supply.

measures how much work a given amount of money does. A high velocity of circulation means that money is circulating quickly so each dollar coin and each dollar of chequable deposits is doing a lot of work. A low velocity of circulation means that currency and chequable deposits are circulating slowly.

Though there are physical limits to how quickly money can circulate, the velocity of circulation can vary greatly. For example, suppose that four people have just a single one-dollar coin between them. As the sun rises, Ann is holding the dollar coin and the other three people have no money at all. Ann uses the dollar coin at 9:00 a.m. to buy two cups of coffee from Bob. Bob uses the same dollar coin at lunchtime to buy a sandwich from Chuck. Chuck uses the dollar coin in the afternoon to buy an ice-cream cone from Debbie, who in turn uses it in the evening to rent a video from Ann. Ann holds the dollar coin overnight and the same transactions sequence repeats the next day.

In this example, a single one-dollar coin has produced $4 worth of transactions in a single day — involving coffee, a sandwich, ice cream, and a video. The dollar coin has circulated quickly. A small amount of money has produced many transactions with a high velocity of circulation.

These same transactions could have occurred with a low velocity of circulation and a larger quantity of money. For example, each of the four people could have started and ended the day with a dollar, buying and selling the same goods as before. In the first example, the velocity of circulation is 4 — $4 worth of expenditure is financed with a one-dollar coin. In the second example, the velocity of circulation is 1 — $4 worth of transactions are financed with $4 worth of money.

Does the velocity of circulation matter? Do people care how quickly they turn their money over? They do. There are both costs and benefits to having a high velocity of circulation.

The Costs of a High Velocity of Circulation The main cost of a high velocity of circulation is that people have to transact frequently. They also may have to transact at inconvenient times. For example, in the above story when there is only one dollar, only one person holds it at any one time, so none of the others can make a purchase until he or she has made a sale. Debbie can't rent her video until she has sold the ice cream. Chuck can't buy his ice cream until he has sold a sandwich, and so on. But if each person in the story starts and ends the day holding a dollar, any of the transactions can be undertaken at any time during the day. For example, it may be much more convenient for Debbie to rent the video on her way to work, before Ann has bought her breakfast, rather than having to run around to Ann's video rental shop in the late afternoon. It may be even more convenient for Debbie to rent three videos at a time and hang onto them for three days, thereby visiting the video store just twice a week rather than every day. However, to do so, Debbie needs at least as much money as the price of three videos. Economizing on transactions — transacting less frequently — always requires a larger quantity of money than transacting frequently. The increased costs of doing business are the main costs of a high velocity of circulation.

The Benefits of a High Velocity of Circulation What are the benefits of a high velocity of circulation of money? A high velocity of circulation means that a small quantity of money is being held relative to the amount of expenditure being undertaken. The lower the quantity of money held, the greater is the quantity of other assets that can be held. Cash in your pocket doesn't earn interest. Some bank deposits do earn interest but at lower rates than other assets such as bonds and stocks. By holding less money and more assets that earn a higher interest rate than do bank deposits, people can increase their incomes. A larger interest income is the main benefit of a high velocity of circulation.

Interest Rate and Opportunity Cost You already know the fundamental principle that as the opportunity cost of something rises, people try to find substitutes for it. Money is no exception to this principle. The opportunity cost of holding money is the interest that could be earned on other assets. The higher the interest rate, the higher is the opportunity cost of holding money and the more people will try to find substitutes for money and economize on their holdings of money. The main substitute for holding money is more frequent transactions. By transacting more frequently in smaller amounts, people can undertake a given amount of economic activity with a smaller amount of real money. The higher the opportunity cost of holding money, the lower is the quantity of money demanded and the higher is the frequency of transactions. In other words, the higher the interest rate, the higher is the velocity of circulation.

REVIEW

The quantity of money demanded depends on the price level, real GDP, and the interest rate. The quantity of nominal money demanded is proportional to the price level. Real money is the nominal quantity of money divided by the price level. The quantity of real money demanded increases as real GDP increases. The opportunity cost of holding money is the interest rate. The benefit from holding money is the avoidance of frequent transactions. The higher the opportunity cost of holding money (the higher the interest rate), the smaller is the quantity of real money demanded and the higher is the velocity of circulation. ■

The Demand for Real Money

The **demand for real money** is the relationship between the quantity of real money demanded and the interest rate, holding constant all other influences on the amount of money that people wish to hold. To make the demand for real money more concrete, let's consider an example. A person's demand for real money can be represented as a demand schedule. Such a schedule sets out the quantity of real money that a person wants to hold at a given level of real income for different levels of the interest rate.

Figure 28.3 sets out some numbers for the Polonius household. The household's real income is $20,000 a year. The price level is 1 (the GDP deflator is equal to 100), so the quantity of money is the same whether we measure it in nominal terms or real terms. The table tells us how the quantity of real money demanded by the Polonius household changes as the interest rate changes. For example, in row *a*, when the interest rate is 7 percent a year, the Polonius household holds $2,400 of money, on the average. When the interest rate is 5 percent a year, its real money holdings increase to $3,000, and when the interest rate falls to 3 percent a year, real money holdings increase to $4,000. The figure also graphs the Polonius household's demand curve for real money (*MD*).

The demand curve for real money slopes downward. The reason for this relationship between the amount of real money held and the interest rate is that the opportunity cost of holding money falls as the rate of interest falls. At an interest rate of 3 percent, the opportunity cost of holding money is small and the Polonius household holds a large average level of real money balances. But at an interest rate of 7 percent, the opportunity cost of holding money is high, so the Polonius household holds a smaller average level of real money.

Figure 28.3 The Polonius Household's Demand for Real Money

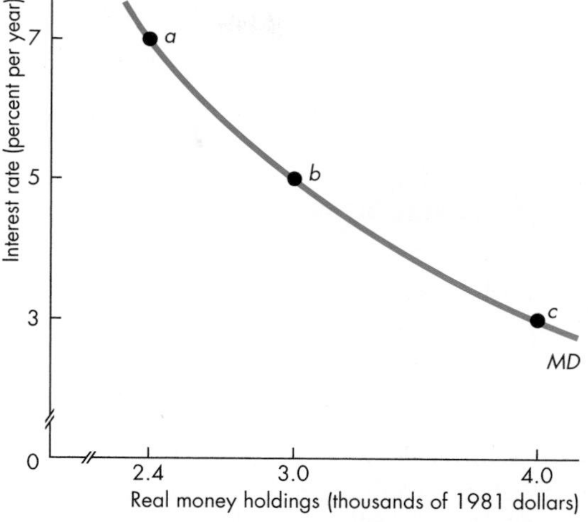

Polonius household's real income is $20,000; price level is 1

	Interest rate (percent per year)	Real money holdings (thousands of 1981 dollars)
a	7	2.4
b	5	3.0
c	3	4.0

The table shows the Polonius household's demand schedule for real money. The lower the interest rate, the larger is the quantity of real money that the household plans to hold. The graph shows the household's demand curve for real money (*MD*). Points *a*, *b*, and *c* on the curve correspond to the rows in the table. A change in the interest rate leads to a movement along the demand curve. The demand curve for real money slopes downward because the interest rate is the opportunity cost of holding money. The higher the interest rate, the larger is the interest foregone on holding another asset.

Shifts in the Demand Curve for Real Money

The demand curve for real money shifts when

- Real income changes.
- Financial innovation occurs.

Figure 28.4 Changes in the Polonius Household's Demand for Real Money

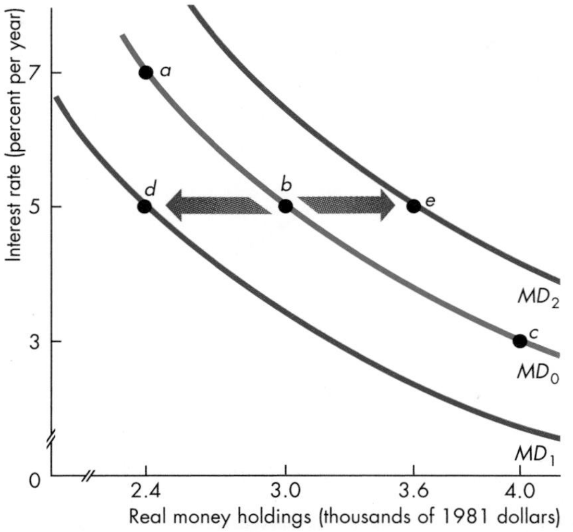

Interest rate is 5 percent; price level is 1

	Real income (thousands of 1981 dollars)	Real money holdings (thousands of 1981 dollars)
d	12	2.4
b	20	3.0
e	28	3.6

A change in real income leads to a change in the demand for real money. The table shows the quantity of real money held by the Polonius household at three different levels of real income when the interest rate is constant at 5 percent. The graph shows the effects of a change in real income on the demand curve for real money. When real income is $20,000 and the interest rate is 5 percent, the household is at point *b* on the demand curve for real money MD_0. When real income falls to $12,000, the demand curve is MD_1 and, at a 5 percent interest rate, the household is at point *d*. When real income rises to $28,000, the demand curve shifts to MD_2. With an interest rate of 5 percent, the household is at point *e*.

Changes in Real Income An increase in real income shifts the demand curve for real money to the right and a decrease shifts it to the left. The effect of real income on the demand curve for real money is shown in Fig. 28.4. The table in the figure shows the effects of a change in real income on the quantity of real money demanded when the interest rate is constant at 5 percent. Look first at row *b* of the table. It tells us that when the interest rate is 5 percent and real income is $20,000, the quantity of real money demanded by the Polonius household is $3,000. This row corresponds to point *b* on the demand curve for real money MD_0. If we continue to hold the interest rate constant, and real income falls to $12,000, the quantity of real money held falls to $2,400. Thus the demand curve for real money shifts from MD_0 to MD_1 in Fig. 28.4. If the Polonius household's real income increases to $28,000, the quantity of real money held by the household increases to $3,600. In this case, the demand curve shifts to the right from MD_0 to MD_2.

Financial Innovation Financial innovation also results in a change in the demand for real money and a shift in the demand curve for real money. The most important such innovation in recent years has been the development of daily interest chequing accounts with banks and other financial institutions. This innovation has been brought about mainly by the availability of low-cost computing power. Computers are an important part of the story of financial innovation because they have dramatically lowered the cost of keeping records and doing calculations. Doing the interest calculations on daily interest checking accounts by hand, although technologically feasible, would be prohibitively costly. Now that banks have access to a vast amount of extremely low-cost computing power, they can offer a wide variety of deposit arrangements that make it convenient to convert deposits that are not medium of exchange assets into those that are medium of exchange assets at extremely low cost. The development of these arrangements has led to a decrease in the demand for money.

The availability of low-cost computing power in the financial sector is also responsible, in large degree, for the widespread use of credit cards. Again, keeping the records and calculating the interest and outstanding debt required to operate a credit card system is feasible by hand but too costly to undertake on a wide scale. Few firms would find it worthwhile to use plastic cards, shuffle sales slips, and keep records if all the calculations had to be done by hand (or even by pre-electronic mechanical calculating machines). Thus the innovation of widespread use of credit cards — made possible by low-cost computing power — has also lowered the demand for money. By using a credit card to make purchases, it is possible to operate with a much lower inventory of money.

Instead of holding money for transactions purposes through the month, it is possible to charge purchases to a credit card, paying the credit card bill on or a day or two after payday with the consequence that the average holding of money throughout the month is much lower.

The financial innovations that we have just considered affect the demand for money. Other financial innovations have changed the composition of our money holdings but not its total amount. One such innovation is the automatic teller machine. On the average, we can now function efficiently with smaller currency holdings than before simply because we can easily obtain currency at almost any time or place. Although this innovation has decreased the demand for currency and increased the demand for deposits, it has probably not affected the overall demand for real money.

R E V I E W

We can represent the demand for money by a demand curve for real money. That demand curve for real money shows how the quantity of real money demanded varies as the interest rate varies. When the interest rate changes, there is a movement along the demand curve for real money. Equivalently, there is a change in the velocity of circulation of money. Other influences on the quantity of real money demanded shift the demand curve for real money. An increase in real income shifts the demand curve to the right; financial innovations that result in convenient methods of transacting and of holding wealth shift the demand curve to the left. ■

Now that we have studied the theory of the demand for real money, let's look at the facts about money holdings in Canada and see how they relate to real income and the interest rate.

The Demand for Money in Canada

We've just seen that the demand curve for real money, which shows how the quantity of real money demanded varies as the interest rate varies, shifts when real GDP changes or when a financial innovation influences money holding. Because these factors that shift the demand curve for real money are changing all the time in the real world, it is not easy to "see" the demand curve for real money for a real world economy.

We are interested in examining the demand curve for real money so that we can discover how that curve shifts as a result of changes in income and in the other factors that influence it. A good way of approaching this task is to study the demand for money measured not in dollars but as a percentage of GDP. We know that the demand for money changes when GDP changes. By measuring the amount of money held as a percentage of GDP, we can isolate the effects of interest rates, financial innovation, and other factors on the demand for money. Also, the amount of money held expressed as a percentage of GDP is related to the velocity of circulation of money. We've discovered that changes in the velocity of circulation are equivalent to movements along the demand curve for real money. When the velocity of circulation is high, the amount of money held as a percentage of GDP is low. One figure is the inverse of the other. By examining the amount of money held as a percentage of GDP and comparing that percentage with movements in the interest rate, we can check whether the theory of the demand for money provides a good description of variations in the quantity of money demanded in Canada.

Figure 28.5 shows the relationship between the interest rate and the quantities of M1 and M2 demanded (each expressed as a percentage of GDP). Part (a) deals with M1 and part (b) with M2. Each dot in the figure represents the combination of the interest rate and the amount of money held in a given year. As you can see from the two graphs, there is no single, simple demand curve for real money. Instead, that demand curve shifts.

In the case of M1 (part a), there was a fairly clear demand curve in the 1970s, as shown in the figure. As the interest rate increased, the quantity of M1 demanded (as a percentage of GDP) decreased. At the end of the 1970s, the demand curve for M1 shifted to the left. That is, the demand for M1 decreased. The negative relationship between the interest rate and the quantity of M1 demanded continued to prevail in the 1980s but at a lower level of money holdings than in the 1970s.

Part (b) deals with M2. Like the demand curve for M1, the demand curve for M2 also shifted between the 1970s and the 1980s. The M2 demand curve, however, shifted to the right. That is, there was an increase in the demand for M2. During the 1970s, as the interest rate increased, the quantity of

Figure 28.5 The Demand for Money in Canada

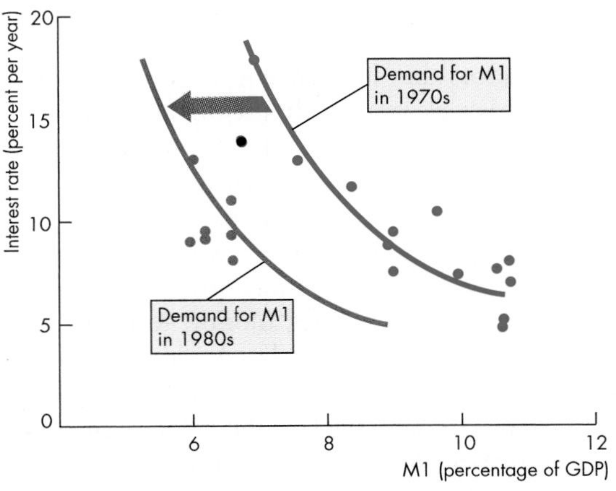

(a) Demand for M1

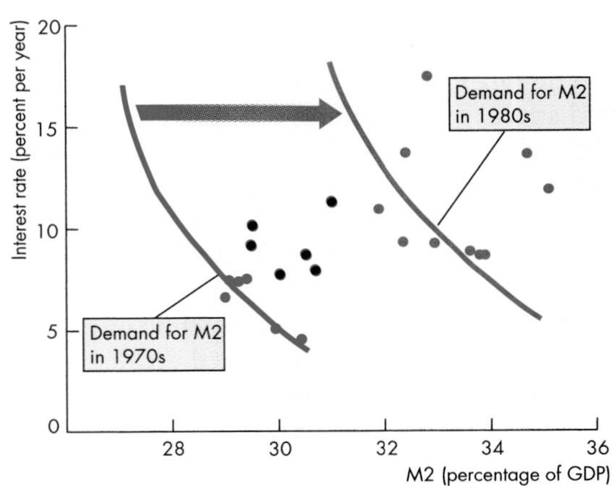

(b) Demand for M2

In part (a), the quantity of M1, expressed as a percentage of GDP, is graphed against the interest rate (the three-month treasury bill rate). In the 1970s, there was a clear negative relationship between these two variables. That relationship shifted to the left in the 1980s. That is, there was a decrease in the demand for M1. The decrease occurred because of financial innovation and increasingly attractive interest rates on chequable savings deposits.

Part (b) shows the demand for M2. The quantity of M2 money held (again, expressed as percentage of GDP) is plotted against the interest rate. The relationship between M2 holdings and the interest rate is less precise than the equivalent relationship for M1. Nevertheless, there is a tendency for the amount of M2 held to decline as the interest rate increases, other things held constant. During the 1980s, the demand curve for M2 shifted in the opposite direction to that for M1. M2 holdings increased at each interest rate. The main reason for this increase was the fact that savings deposits themselves earn interest and that interest rates became relatively more attractive during the 1980s.

Source: Interest rate (three-month treasury bill rate): CANSIM series B14007. M1: CANSIM series B1627. M2: CANSIM series B1630; *Bank of Canada Review*.

M2 demanded decreased. Then, during the late 1970s and early 1980s, interest rates and the quantity of M2 demanded increased together. There is a much less precise relationship between the quantity of M2 demanded and the interest rate than there is between the quantity of M1 demanded and the interest rate.

Why did the demand for M1 decrease and the demand for M2 increase in the 1980s? The main part of the answer to this question is that financial innovation and increasingly attractive interest rates on chequable and other forms of savings deposits encouraged people to substitute savings accounts (part of M2) for demand deposits (part of M1). These substitutions were pronounced during the middle of the 1980s when especially attractive interest rates were available on chequable savings accounts. In these years, the quantity of money held in the form of demand deposits actually declined, and the quantity held in chequable savings deposits increased at an extraordinary pace. It was these financial innovations that led to the shifts in the demand curves for M1 and M2 that you can see in Fig. 28.5.

There is another interesting way of looking at the facts summarized in Fig. 28.5. The interest rate, measured on the vertical axis, is the opportunity cost of holding money only in the case of monetary assets that do not themselves earn interest. Currency and non-interest-bearing demand deposits are in this category. Thus M1 is basically a non-interest-bearing form of money. Changes in the interest rate lead to a change in the opportunity cost of holding that type of money. The higher the interest rate, the greater is the incentive to economize on holdings of M1 money.

But all the other types of deposits that are included in M2 but not in M1 themselves earn interest. Variations in those interest rates lead to changes in the demand for M2 that are largely independent of the overall level of interest rates. In fact, if the difference between the interest rate on savings accounts and the interest rate on other assets were always constant, the opportunity cost of holding a savings account would be constant. In practice, the interest rate on savings accounts does fluctuate relative to other interest rates. So the opportunity cost of holding a savings account varies over time. When savings accounts are earning a relatively high interest rate, there is less incentive to switch funds out of them and into some other form of assets (for example, Canada savings bonds). At times when savings account interest rates are relatively low, the incentive to economize on savings account balances and transfer funds into other, higher-yielding forms of assets increases. Thus fluctuations in the interest rate on savings deposits lead to shifts in the demand curve for M2 money.

Changing interest rates on savings accounts also lead to shifts in the demand for M1. These shifts arise because chequing accounts and savings accounts are alternative ways of holding money — are substitutes. When the interest rate on a savings account (a substitute for a demand deposit) increases, the opportunity cost of holding the demand deposit increases; hence there is an increased incentive to cut back on the amount of money held in demand deposits and increase the amount held in savings deposits. Fluctuations in relative interest rates, then, lead to shifts in the demand curves for both M1 and M2.

We've now studied the factors that determine the demand for real money and have discovered that, other things held constant, the quantity of real money demanded decreases when the interest rate increases. We have also studied the way in which the Bank of Canada can influence the quantity of money supplied. We are now going to combine our models of the demand side and supply side of the money market and discover how the average level of interest rates is determined.

Interest Rate Determination

An interest rate is the percentage yield on a financial security such as a bond or a stock. There is an important relationship between the interest rate and the price of a financial asset. Let's spend a moment studying that relationship before analysing the forces that determine interest rates.

Interest Rates and Asset Prices

A bond is a promise to make a sequence of future payments. There are many different possible sequences but the simplest one for our purposes is that of a bond called a perpetuity. A **perpetuity** is a bond that promises to pay a certain fixed amount of money each year forever. The issuer of such a bond will never buy the bond back (redeem it); the bond will remain outstanding forever and will earn a fixed dollar payment each year. The fixed dollar payment is called the *coupon.* Since the coupon is a fixed dollar amount, the interest rate on the bond varies as the price of the bond varies. Table 28.7 illustrates this fact.

First, the table shows the formula for calculating the interest rate on a bond. The interest rate (r) is the coupon (c) divided by the price of the bond (p), all multiplied by 100 to convert the result into a percentage. Table 28.7 goes on to show some numerical

Table 28.7 Interest Rate and Price of a Bond 

Formula for interest rate

r = interest rate, c = coupon, p = price of bond

$$r = \frac{c}{p} \times 100$$

Examples

	Price of bond (dollars)	Coupon (dollars)	Interest rate (percent per year)
a	50	10	20
b	100	10	10
c	200	10	5

examples for a bond whose coupon is $10 a year. If the bond cost $100 (row *b*), the interest rate is 10 percent per year. That is, the holder of $100 worth of bonds receives $10 a year.

Rows *a* and *c* of Table 28.7 show two other cases. In row *a*, the price of the bond is $50. With the coupon at $10, this price produces an interest rate of 20 percent — $10 earned on a $50 bond is an interest rate of 20 percent. In row *c*, the bond costs $200 and produces an interest rate of 5 percent — $10 earned on a $200 bond is an interest rate of 5 percent.

Notice the inverse relationship between the price of a bond and the interest rate earned on the bond. As a bond price rises, the bond's interest rate declines. Understanding this relationship will make it easier for you to understand the process whereby the interest rate is determined. Let's now turn to studying that process.

Money Market Equilibrium

The interest rate is determined at each point in time by equilibrium in the markets for financial assets. We can study that equilibrium in the market for money. We've already examined the determination of the supply of money and the demand for money. We've seen that money is a stock. When the stock of money supplied equals the stock of money demanded, the money market is in equilibrium. *Stock equilibrium* in the money market contrasts with *flow equilibrium* in the markets for goods and services. A **stock equilibrium** is a situation in which all the available stock of an asset is willingly held. That is, regardless of what the available stock is, conditions are such that people actually want to hold precisely that stock, neither more nor less. A **flow equilibrium** is a situation in which the quantity of goods or services supplied per unit of time equals the quantity demanded per unit of time. The equilibrium expenditure that we studied in Chapter 26 is an example of a flow equilibrium. So is the equality of aggregate real GDP demanded and supplied. Let's study stock equilibrium and the market for money and see how it determines the level of interest rates.

The nominal quantity of money supplied is determined by the policy decisions of the Bank of Canada and by the lending actions of banks and other financial intermediaries. The real quantity of money supplied is equal to the nominal quantity supplied divided by the price level. At a given moment in time, there is a particular price level, so the quantity of real money supplied is a fixed amount.

The demand curve for real money depends on the level of real GDP. And on any given day, the level of real GDP can be treated as fixed. But the interest rate is not fixed. The interest rate adjusts to achieve stock equilibrium in the money market. If the interest rate is too high, people will try to hold less money than is available. If the interest rate is too low, people will try to hold more than the stock that is available. When the interest rate is such that people want to hold exactly the amount of money that is available, then a stock equilibrium prevails.

Figure 28.6 illustrates an equilibrium in the money market. The quantity of real money supplied is $3 billion. The table sets out the quantity of real money demanded at three different interest rates when real GDP is constant at $4 billion and the price level is constant at 1 (the price index equals 100).

At a 5 percent interest rate, the quantity of real money demanded is $3 billion, which equals the quantity of real money supplied. The equilibrium interest rate is 5 percent. If the interest rate is above 5 percent, people will want to hold less money than is available. At an interest rate below 5 percent, people will want to hold more money than is available. At a 5 percent interest rate, the amount of money available is willingly held.

How does money market equilibrium come about? To answer this question, let's perform a thought experiment. First, imagine that the interest rate is temporarily at 7 percent. In this situation, people will want to hold only $2 billion in real money even though $3 billion exists. But since $3 billion exists, people must be holding it. That is, people are holding more money than they want to. In such a situation, they will try to get rid of some of their money. Each individual will try to reorganize his or her affairs in order to lower the amount of money held and to take advantage of the 7 percent interest rate by buying more financial assets. But everybody will be trying to buy financial assets, and nobody will be trying to sell them. There is an excess demand for financial assets such as bonds. When there is an excess demand for anything, its price rises. So with an excess demand for financial assets, the prices of financial assets will rise. We saw earlier that there is an inverse relationship between the price of a financial asset and its interest rate. As the price of a financial asset rises, its interest rate falls.

As long as anyone is holding money in excess of the quantity demanded, that person will try to lower

Figure 28.6 Money Market Equilibrium

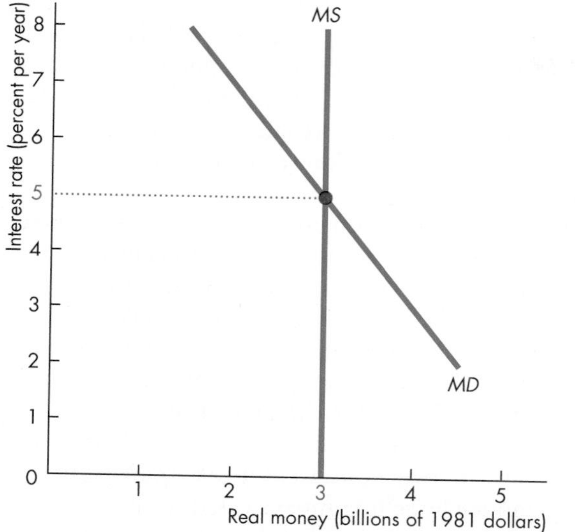

Real GDP is $4 billion; price level is 1

Interest rate (percentage per year)	Quantity of real money demanded (billions of 1981 dollars)	Quantity of real money supplied (billions of 1981 dollars)
7	2	3
5	3	3
3	4	3

Adjustments in the interest rate achieve money market equilibrium. If real GDP is $4 billion, the demand for real money is given by curve *MD*. If the supply of real money is $3 billion (curve *MS* in the figure), the equilibrium interest rate is 5 percent. At interest rates above 5 percent, the quantity of real money demanded is less than the quantity supplied, so interest rates will fall. At interest rates below 5 percent, the quantity of real money demanded exceeds the quantity supplied, so interest rates will rise. Only at an interest rate of 5 percent is the quantity of real money in existence willingly held.

his or her money holdings by buying additional financial assets. Financial asset prices will continue to rise and interest rates continue to fall. Only when the interest rate has moved down to 5 percent will the amount of money in existence be held willingly. That is, people's attempts to get rid of unwanted excess money do not result in reducing the amount of money held in aggregate. Instead, those efforts result in a change in the interest rate that makes the amount of money available willingly held.

The thought experiment that we have just conducted can be performed in reverse by supposing that the interest rate is 3 percent. In this situation, people want to hold $4 billion even though only $3 billion is available. To acquire more money, people will sell financial assets. There is be an excess supply of financial assets, so their prices will fall. As the prices of financial assets fall, the yield on them — the interest rate — rises. People will continue to sell financial assets and try to acquire money until the interest rate has risen to 5 percent, where the amount of money available is the amount that they want to hold.

The determination of the equilibrium interest rate is illustrated in the diagram in Fig. 28.6. The real money supply is the vertical curve *MS* at $3 billion. The demand curve for real money *MD* cuts the supply curve at an interest rate of 5 percent. At interest rates above 5 percent, there is an excess of the quantity of real money supplied over the quantity of real money demanded. At interest rates below 5 percent, there is an excess of the quantity of real money demanded over the quantity of real money supplied. The only interest rate that makes the quantity of real money available willingly held is 5 percent.

Changing the Interest Rate

Suppose that the economy is sagging and the Bank of Canada wants to encourage additional aggregate demand and spending. To do so, it wants to lower interest rates and encourage more borrowing and more investment. What does the Bank of Canada do? How does it fiddle the with knobs to achieve lower interest rates?

The Bank of Canada undertakes an open market operation, buying government securities from banks, households, and firms. As a consequence, the monetary base increases, and banks start making additional loans. The money supply increases.

Suppose that the Bank of Canada undertakes open market operations on a sufficiently large scale to increase the money supply from $3 billion to $4 billion. As a consequence the supply curve of real money, as shown in Fig. 28.7(a), shifts to the right from MS_0 to MS_1, and the thought experiment that we conducted earlier now becomes a real world event. The interest rate falls as individuals attempt to reduce their money holdings and buy additional financial assets. When the interest rate has fallen to

Figure 28.7 The Bank of Canada Changes the Interest Rate

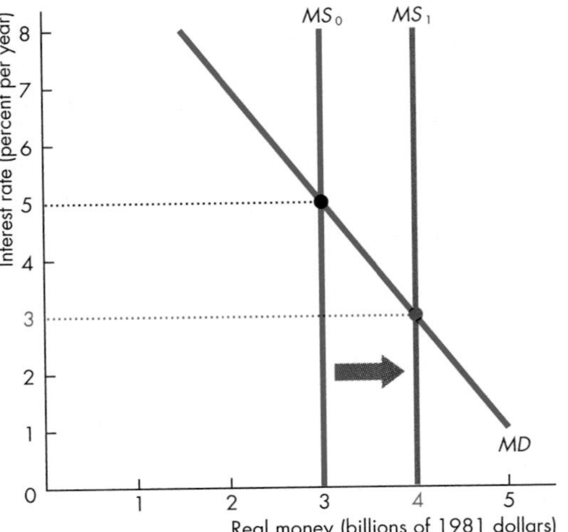

(a) An increase in the money supply

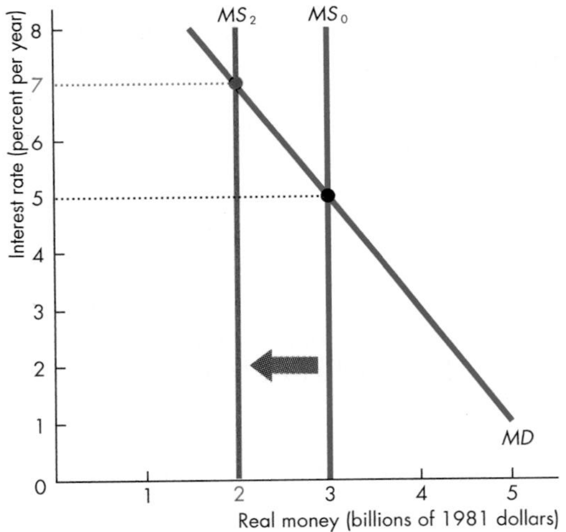

(b) A decrease in the money supply

In part (a), the Bank of Canada conducts an open market purchase of securities, increasing the money supply to $4 billion. The real money supply curve shifts to the right. The new equilibrium interest rate is 3 percent. In part (b), the Bank of Canada conducts an open market sale of securities, decreasing the real money supply to $2 billion. The money supply curve shifts to the left, and the interest rate rises to 7 percent. By changing the money supply, at a given real GDP and price level, the Bank of Canada can adjust interest rates daily or weekly.

3 percent, people are willingly holding the larger real money stock of $4 billion that the Bank of Canada and the banking system has now created.

Conversely, suppose that the economy is overheating and the Bank of Canada fears inflation. It decides to take action to slow down spending and cuts the money supply. In this case, the Bank of Canada undertakes an open market sale of securities. As it does so, it mops up bank reserves and induces the banks to cut down the scale of their lending. The banks make a smaller quantity of new loans each day until the stock of loans outstanding has fallen to a level consistent with the new lower level of reserves. Suppose that the Bank of Canada undertakes an open market sale of securities on a scale big enough to cut the real money supply to $2 billion. Now, as shown in Fig. 28.7(b), the supply of real money curve shifts to the left from MS_0 to MS_2. With less money available, people attempt to acquire additional money by selling interest-earning assets. As they do so, asset prices fall and interest rates rise. Equilibrium occurs when the interest rate has risen to 7 percent, at which point the new smaller real money stock of $2 million is willingly held.

The Bank of Canada in Action

All this sounds nice in theory, but does it really happen? Indeed, it does, and sometimes with dramatic effect. Let's look at two episodes in the life of the Bank of Canada, one from the turbulent years of the early 1980s and the other from the period after the stock market crash of 1987.

Gerald Bouey's Fight Against Inflation As the 1980s opened, Canada was locked in the grips of double-digit inflation. The governor of the Bank of Canada, Gerald Bouey, with help from Paul Volcker of the United States' Federal Reserve System, reduced that inflation. He did so by forcing interest rates sharply upward in the early 1980s. This increase in interest rates resulted from open market operations by the Bank of Canada (and the Federal Reserve). These operations kept the banks short of reserves, which in turn held back the growth in the supply of loans and of money relative to the growth in their demand. Interest rates increased sharply. Let's relive the episode with the help of some economic analysis.

As we saw in Fig. 28.7(b), to increase interest rates, the Bank of Canada has to cut the real money supply. In practice, because the economy is growing and because prices are rising, a slowdown in nominal

Table 28.8 Growth Rates of the Money Supply, 1981–1982

Monetary aggregate	Growth rate (Percent per annum)	
	1981	1982
M1	3.3	−0.1
M2	15.1	9.4
M3	13.2	4.3
M2+	14.4	8.0

Source: Bank of Canada Review, December 1989, Table A1.

money supply growth is enough to increase interest rates. It is not necessary actually to cut the nominal money supply.

In 1982, money supply growth rates were slashed, as you can see from the numbers in Table 28.8. As a result of this slowdown in money supply growth, interest rates increased sharply. The treasury bill rate — the rate at which the government borrows on a three-month basis — increased from 12 percent to almost 18 percent. Mortgage rates — the rate at which homebuyers borrow — increased to more than 20 percent. The economy went into recession. The money supply growth slowdown and interest rate hike cut back the growth of aggregate demand. Real GDP fell and the inflation rate slowed down.

John Crow's Bank John Crow became governor of the Bank of Canada in January 1987. In the years preceding his appointment, money supply growth rates had been held steady and so had inflation. Crow, like his predecessor, is a fierce inflation fighter and was intent on holding the money supply growth rate steady. In October 1987, however, before Crow had been in the job for a full year, he was faced with one of the most severe crises that any central banker can be faced with — a stock market crash. The Bank of Canada, in the company of other central banks around the world, feared the recession potential that might be signalled by the stock market crash. In order to avoid any hint of financial tightness that might exacerbate a recessionary situation, the Bank of Canada permitted the money supply to grow quickly. Its growth rate for 1987 edged upward from its 1986 level, and short-term interest rates fell slightly.

As the months passed and it became increasingly clear that the October 1987 stock market crash was not signalling a recession, unemployment continued to fall, real GDP continued to be strong, and fears of recession were replaced by fears of a re-emergence of inflation.

Seeking to avoid such an event, the Bank of Canada again slowed down the money supply growth rate, just as Gerald Bouey had done eight years earlier, forcing interest rates upward again. Open market operations were targeted towards creating a shortage of reserves in the banking system to slow down the growth rate of the money supply. As a consequence, during 1988, the growth rates of all the monetary aggregates were substantially below what they had been in 1987.

Profiting by Predicting the Bank of Canada

Day by day, even minute by minute, the Bank of Canada can use open market operations to influence interest rates and the money supply. By increasing the supply of money, it can lower interest rates; by lowering the supply of money, it can increase interest rates. Holders of financial assets know about the powers of the Bank of Canada. They also know about another relationship that we have worked out: the higher the interest rate, the lower is the price of a bond and the lower the interest rate, the higher is the price of a bond. By putting these two things together they also know that if they can predict changes in monetary policy, then they can predict future interest rates and future bond prices. Predicting future bond prices is a potentially profitable activity. Predicting that interest rates are going to fall is the same as predicting that bond prices are going to rise — a good time to buy bonds. Predicting that interest rates are going to rise is the same as predicting that bond prices are going to fall — a good time to sell bonds.

Because predicting the Bank of Canada is profitable, a good deal of effort goes into that activity. But *if* people do correctly anticipate the Bank of Canada's monetary policy changes, then bond prices and interest rates will change as soon as the Bank's actions are foreseen. By the time the Bank of Canada actually takes its actions, they will have no effect. The effect will have occurred in anticipation of the Bank of Canada's actions. Only changes in the money supply that are not foreseen will change the interest rate at the time that those money supply changes occur.

At any given moment, the interest rate is determined by the demand for and the supply of money. The interest rate makes the quantity of money demanded equal to the quantity of money supplied. Changes in the interest rate occur as a result of changes in the money supply. When the money supply change is not predicted, interest rates will change at the same time as the change in the money supply. If a change in the money supply is foreseen, interest rates will start to change ahead of the change in the money supply.

■ In this chapter we've studied the determination of interest rates and discovered how the Bank of Canada can "fiddle with the knobs" to influence interest rate levels as well as the quantity of money and the volume of bank lending. In the next chapter, we're going to look at the effects of the Bank's actions on that other crucial barometer of the nation's financial health — the foreign exchange value of our dollar.

SUMMARY

The Bank of Canada

The Bank of Canada is the central bank of Canada. It is headed by a governor, aided by a staff of senior economists and other advisors, and directed by a board of directors representing a variety of regional and other interests. The Bank's main instrument for influencing the economy is its open market operations. By buying government securities in the market (an open market purchase), the Bank of Canada is able to increase the monetary base and the reserves available to banks. As a result, there is an expansion of bank lending and a fall in interest rates. By selling government securities, the Bank is able to decrease the monetary base and the reserves of banks and other financial institutions, thereby curtailing loans and putting upward pressure on interest rates. The overall effect of a change in the monetary base on the money supply is determined by the money multiplier, which in turn depends on the ratio of currency to deposits held by households and firms and the ratio of reserves to deposits held by banks and other financial institutions. (pp. 747-758)

The Demand for Money

The quantity of money demanded is the amount of currency, demand deposits, and other chequing accounts that people hold on the average. The quantity of money demanded is proportional to the price level, and the quantity of real money demanded depends on the interest rate and real GDP. A higher level of real GDP induces a larger quantity of real money demanded. A higher interest rate induces a smaller quantity of real money demanded. Fluctuations in the ratio of real GDP to real money (the velocity of circulation) are correlated with fluctuations in the interest rate. Technological change in the financial sector has also reduced the demand for money over the years. (pp. 758-765)

Interest Rate Determination

Changes in interest rates achieve stock equilibrium in the markets for money and financial assets. There is an inverse relationship between the interest rate and the price of a financial asset. The higher the interest rate, the lower is the price of a financial asset. Money market equilibrium achieves an interest rate that makes the quantity of real money available willingly held. If the quantity of real money is increased by the actions of the Bank of Canada, the interest rate falls and the prices of financial assets rise.

People attempt to profit by predicting the actions of the Bank of Canada. To the extent that they can predict the Bank actions, interest rates and the price of financial assets move in anticipation of the Bank's actions rather than in response to them. As a consequence, interest rates change when the Bank of Canada changes the money supply only if it catches people by surprise. Anticipated changes in the money supply produce interest rate changes by themselves. (pp. 765-770)

KEY ELEMENTS

Key Terms

Bank of Canada, 747
Bank rate, 750
Central bank, 747
Demand for real money, 761
Fixed exchange rate, 750
Flexible exchange rate, 766
Flow equilibrium, 766
Managed exchange rate, 750
Monetary base, 752
Monetary policy, 747
Money multiplier, 753
Nominal quantity of money, 759
Nonconvertible note, 752
Open market operations, 751
Perpetuity, 765
Required reserves, 750
Stock equilibrium, 766

Key Figures and Tables 

REVIEW QUESTIONS

1 What are the three main elements in the structure of the Bank of Canada?

2 What are the three kinds of exchange rate regimes?

3 In which exchange rate regime does the central bank not intervene at all?

4 What are the three policy tools of the Bank of Canada? Which of these is the main tool?

5 If the Bank of Canada wants to cut the quantity of money, does it buy or sell government of Canada securities in the open market?

6 Describe the events that take place when banks have excess reserves.

7 What is the money multiplier?

8 Why has the money multiplier in Canada been so constant in recent years?

9 Distinguish between nominal money and real money.

10 What do we mean by the demand for money?

11 What determines the demand for real money?

12 What is the opportunity cost of holding money?

13 What happens to the interest rate on a bond if the price of the bond increases?

14 How does equilibrium come about in the money market?

15 What happens to the interest rate if real GDP and the price level are constant and there is an increase in the money supply?

16 Explain why it pays people to try to predict the Bank of Canada's actions.

PROBLEMS

1 You are given the following information about a hypothetical economy. The banks have deposits of $300 million. Their reserves are $15 million, two-thirds of which are in deposits with the central bank. The monetary base is $40 million. This economy has no coins.

a) Set out the balance sheet of the chartered banks. Supply any missing numbers using your knowledge of the fact that total assets equal total liabilities.

b) What is the amount of currency in circulation?

c) What is the money supply?

d) What is the money multiplier?

2 Suppose that the central bank in the economy of problem 1 undertakes an open market purchase of securities of $1 million. What happens to the money supply? Explain why the money supply changes by more than the change in the monetary base.

3 You are given the following information about another imaginary economy: For each $1 increase in real GDP, the demand for real money increases by one-third of a dollar, other things being equal. Also, if the interest rate increases by 1 percentage point (for example, from 4 percent to 5 percent), the quantity of real money demanded falls by $40. If the price level is 1, real GDP is $1,000, and the real money supply is $133, what is the interest rate?

4 Suppose that the central bank in the economy of problem 3 wants to change the interest rate to 4 percent. By how much will it have to change the real money supply to achieve that objective?

CHAPTER 29

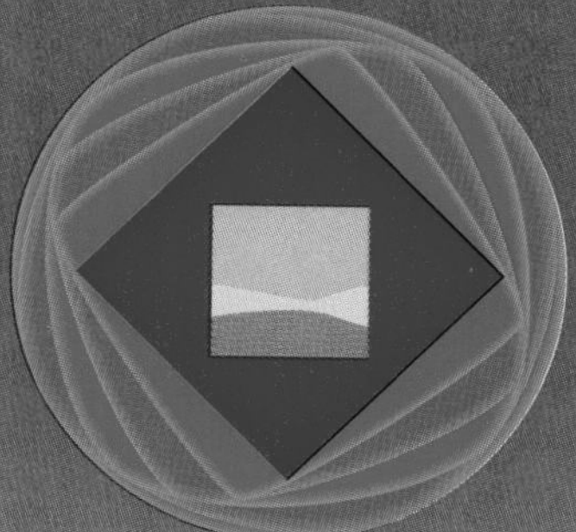

International Finance and the Exchange Rate

After studying this chapter, you will be able to:

- Explain how the foreign exchange value of the dollar is determined.
- Explain why the foreign exchange value of the dollar fluctuated in the 1980s.
- Explain the effects of changes in the exchange rate.
- Explain what determines interest rates and why they vary so much from one country to another.
- Explain why a fixed exchange rate ties interest rates and inflation rates together.
- Explain why a flexible exchange rate brings monetary independence.

Canada's Financial Insulator

"WHEN AMERICA SNEEZES, the rest of the world catches a cold." This saying from the Great Depression years of the early 1930s, reminds us that when the U.S. economy goes into recession, as it did in 1981, the rest of the world, to some degree, goes with it. And when the world's largest economy experiences booming conditions, some of the associated prosperity spills over its borders into enhanced export sales by almost every other country. But is there nothing that a country such as Canada can do to insulate itself from the U.S. economic seesaw? In particular, how does the nation's financial and monetary policy and its international monetary policy act to moderate the influence on Canada of the United States and the rest of world? ■ One potential cushion that we can place between ourselves and the rest of the world is the value of our dollar. How do fluctuations in the value of the Canadian dollar affect the economic lives of Canadians and do they protect Canadians from economic fluctuations originating in other countries? ■ Our dollar does indeed fluctuate considerably in value. In 1973, one Canadian dollar exchanged for exactly one U.S. dollar. At its lowest point, in 1986, it took C$1.45 to buy US$1 (the symbol US$ stands for the U.S. dollar and C$ stands for the Canadian dollar). Our exchange rate has returned from that low point, and at the end of 1989, US$1 could be bought for approximately C$1.17. Our dollar has fluctuated not only against the U.S. dollar but against all the other major currencies of the world. Against some, such as the Japanese yen, it has persistently declined in value. In 1970, C$1 would buy 340 Japanese yen. By the end of 1989, our dollar was worth only 121 yen. ■ What does the value of the dollar have to do with the prices of the things that we buy — the price of an English tweed coat, a Korean VCR, a Japanese car, or a foreign vacation? Do Eddie Bauer mountain jackets sold in Canada cost the same as the identical jacket sold in the United States? What makes our dollar fluctuate in value against other currencies? Why does our dollar decline against some currencies but at the same time increase against others? Why have the fluctuations been particularly extreme in recent years? Is there anything we can do to stabilize the value of the dollar? ■ The world is becoming ever more integrated. In October 1987, when the American stock market crashed, so did the stock markets of Canada, Japan, and Western Europe. But despite the fact that the world is getting smaller, there are enormous differences in the interest rates at which people borrow and lend around the world. For example, at the close of 1989, the Canadian government was paying almost 10 percent per year on its long-term borrowing. At that same time, the governments of Australia and Spain were paying more than 13 percent. But the government of the United States was paying only 8 percent, of West Germany only 6 percent, and of Japan and Switzerland barely more than 4 percent. How can interest rates around the world diverge so widely? Why don't loans dry up in low-interest-rate countries with all the money flooding to countries where interest rates are high? Why aren't interest rates made the same everywhere by the force of such movements? ■ In recent history, we have sometimes maintained a fixed value for the Canadian dollar against other currencies. The last time we did this was in the 1960s. At other times, we have allowed the Canadian dollar to find its own value in the world market for foreign exchange. Does it matter whether the Canadian dollar exchange rate is fixed or flexible? How do we keep the exchange rate fixed? What determines the value of a flexible exchange rate? Is the exchange rate regime something that only affects specialists who deal in foreign exchange or does it affect more broadly the economic lives of all Canadians?

■ During the 1980s, the issues of international economics have become important matters for all Canadians. We're going to study these issues in this chapter. We're going to discover why the Canadian dollar fluctuates so much against the values of other currencies, and why interest rates in Canada are so high compared with those in the United States, Japan, Germany, and Switzerland but still relatively low compared with those in many other countries. We're going to study the market forces that link countries together and that determine the values of their currencies, as well as the international transmission of interest rate and price changes.

Foreign Exchange

When Canadians buy foreign goods or invest in another country, they have to obtain some of that country's currency to make the transaction. When foreigners buy Canadian-produced goods or invest in Canada, they have to obtain some Canadian dollars. Canadians get foreign currency and foreigners get Canadian dollars in the foreign exchange market.

The **foreign exchange market** is the market in which the currency of one country is exchanged for the currency of another. The foreign exchange market is not a place like a downtown flea market or produce market. The market is made up of thousands of people — importers and exporters, banks, and specialists in the buying and selling of foreign exchange. They are called foreign exchange brokers. The sun never sets on the foreign exchange market. It opens on Monday morning in Tokyo, which is still Sunday evening in Montreal. As the day advances, markets open in Zurich, London, Montreal, New York, and finally, Vancouver, Los Angeles, and San Francisco. Before the West Coast markets have closed, Tokyo is open again for the next day of business. Dealers around the world are continually in contact using computers linked by telephone. On any given day, billions of dollars change hands.

The rate at which one currency exchanges for another is called a **foreign exchange rate**. For example, on September 27, 1989, one Canadian dollar bought 121.47 Japanese yen. The exchange rate between the Canadian dollar and the Japanese yen was 121.47 yen per dollar. Exchange rates can be expressed either way. We've just expressed the exchange rate between the yen and the dollar as a number of yen per dollar. Equivalently, we could express that exchange rate in terms of dollars per yen. That exchange rate, on September 27, 1989, was $0.008232 per yen. (In other words, a yen was worth slightly less than a penny).

The actions of the foreign exchange brokers make the foreign exchange market highly efficient. Exchange rates are almost identical no matter where in the world the transaction is taking place. If Canadian dollars were cheap in London and expensive in Tokyo, within a flash someone would have placed a buy order in London and a sell order in Tokyo, thereby increasing demand in one place and increasing supply in another, moving the prices to equality.

Foreign Exchange Regimes

Foreign exchange rates are of critical importance for millions of people. They affect the costs of our foreign vacations and our imported cars. They affect the number of dollars that we end up getting for the apples and wheat that we sell to Japan. Because of their importance, governments pay a great deal of attention to what is happening in foreign exchange markets and, more than that, take actions designed to achieve what they regard as desirable movements in exchange rates. As we noted in Chapter 28, there are three ways in which the government and the Bank of Canada can operate in the foreign exchange market — three foreign exchange market regimes. They are:

- Fixed exchange rate
- Flexible exchange rate
- Managed exchange rate

A *fixed exchange rate* regime is one in which the value of the dollar is pegged by the Bank of Canada. A *flexible exchange rate* regime is one in which the value of the dollar is determined by market forces with no intervention by the Bank of Canada. A *managed exchange rate* regime is one in which the Bank of Canada intervenes in the foreign exchange market to smooth out fluctuations in the value of the dollar but does not seek to maintain the dollar at an absolutely constant value for a long period of time. Also, under a managed exchange rate regime, the Bank of Canada does not announce the value of the dollar that it wishes to achieve.

Recent Exchange Rate History

Towards the end of World War II, the major countries of the world set up the International Monetary Fund (IMF). The **International Monetary Fund** is an international organization that monitors balance of payments and exchange rate activities. The IMF, located in Washington, D.C., came into being during World War II. In July 1944, at Bretton Woods, New Hampshire, 44 countries signed the Articles of Agreement of the IMF. The centrepiece of those agreements was the establishment of a worldwide system of fixed exchange rates between currencies. The anchor for this fixed exchange rate system was gold. One ounce of gold was defined to be worth US$35. All other currencies were pegged to the U.S. dollar at a fixed exchange rate. For example, the Japanese yen was set at 360 yen per U.S. dollar; the British pound was set at US$4.80.

Canada's participation in the IMF fixed exchange rate system was more limited than that of most other countries. From the creation of the system until 1962, Canada maintained a good deal of exchange rate independence. From 1962 to 1970 however, Canada operated a fixed exchange rate. Since 1970, Canada has allowed the foreign exchange value of its dollar to fluctuate. Sometimes those fluctuations have been almost completely freely determined by market forces, but most of the time we have had a managed exchange rate regime.

It was not only Canada that encountered problems with the fixed exchange rate regime of the international monetary system in the early 1970s. Although that system had served the world well during the 1950s and early 1960s, it came under increasing strain in the late 1960s and, by 1971, the order had almost collapsed. In the period since 1971, the world has operated with a variety of flexible and managed exchange rate arrangements. Some currencies have increased in value, and others have declined. The Canadian dollar is among the currencies that have declined. The Japanese yen is the currency that has had the most spectacular increase in value.

Figure 29.1(a) shows what has happened to the exchange rate of Canadian dollars in terms of Japanese yen since 1970. As you can see, the value of our dollar has fallen — the dollar has depreciated. **Currency depreciation** is the fall in the value of one currency in terms of another currency.

Just as the dollar has fallen in value in terms of the yen, so the yen has risen in value in terms of the dollar. The increase in the value of one currency in terms of another currency is called **currency appreciation**. You can see the appreciation of the yen and the depreciation of the dollar as the mirror images of each other in parts (a) and (b) of Fig. 29.1.

There are as many exchange rates for the Canadian dollar as there are currencies for which it can be exchanged. The Canadian dollar falls in value against some currencies (as we've just seen in the case of the Japanese yen) and increases against others. To measure the average movement in the value of the Canadian dollar, the Bank of Canada calculates the Canadian dollar index against the currencies of a group of industrialized countries called the Group of Ten (G-10). The **Canadian dollar index against the G-10 currencies** is an index that measures the value of the Canadian dollar in terms of its ability to buy a basket of currencies of the G-10 of countries, where the weight placed on each currency is related to its

Figure 29.1 Exchange Rates

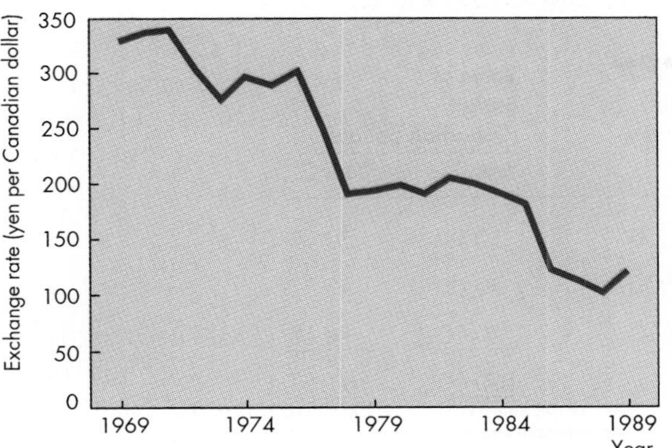

(a) The depreciating dollar

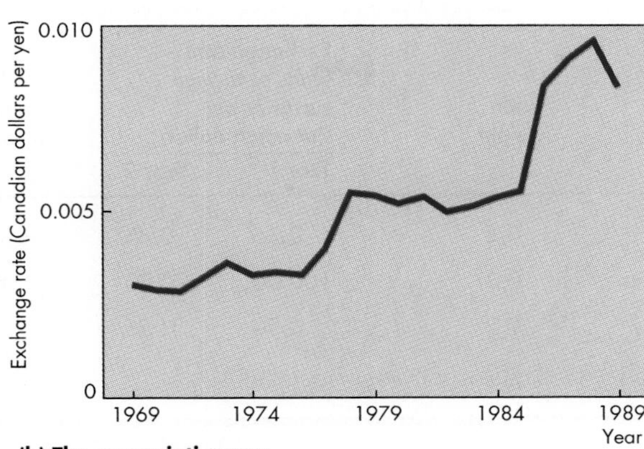

(b) The appreciating yen

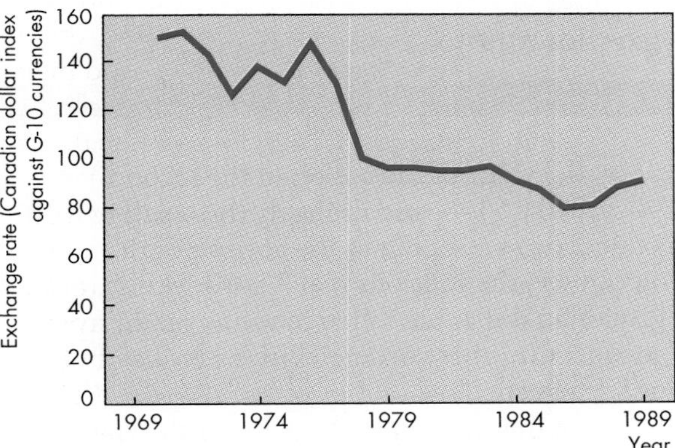

(c) The Canadian dollar against the other G-10 currencies

The exchange rate is the price at which two currencies can be traded. Part (a) shows the yen-dollar exchange rate expressed as yen per dollar. The dollar has fallen in value — depreciated — against the yen. Part (b) shows the yen-dollar exchange rate as dollars per yen. The price of yen in terms of Canadian dollars has increased — the yen has appreciated against the dollar. An index of the value of the Canadian dollar against the other G–10 currencies is shown in part (c). The Canadian dollar has depreciated on the average against all G–10 currencies although it appreciated slightly in 1974, 1976, and from 1987 through 1989.

Source: *Bank of Canada Review*, CANSIM series B3407 and B3418.

importance in Canada's international trade. The G-10 currencies are as follows:

- U.S. dollar
- U.K. pound
- French franc
- German mark
- Italian lira
- Japanese yen
- Swiss franc
- Dutch guilder
- Belgian franc
- Canadian dollar

An example of the calculation of the Canadian dollar index is set out in Table 29.1. In this example, we suppose that Canada trades only with three countries: the United States, Japan, and Britain. We also suppose that 50 percent of the trade is with the United States, 30 percent with Japan, and 20 percent with Britain. In year 1, the Canadian dollar is worth 0.75 U.S. dollars, 100 Japanese yen, or 0.50 British pounds.

Imagine putting these three foreign currencies into a "basket" worth 100 Canadian dollars, where 50 percent of the value of the basket is in U.S. dollars, 30 percent in Japanese yen, and 20 percent in British pounds. The table lists the contents of the basket: US$37.50, ¥3000, and £10. Converting these amounts of the three foreign currencies to Canadian dollars at the prevailing exchange rates results in a basket worth C$100. Fifty dollars worth of the basket is in U.S. dollars, $30 worth in

Table 29.1 Calculation of the Canadian Dollar Index

Currency	Trade weight	Exchange rate (units of foreign currency per Canadian dollar)		Contents of basket	Value of Basket (Canadian dollars)	
		Year 1	Year 2		Year 1	Year 2
U.S. dollar	0.5	0.75	0.75	US$37.50	50.00	50.00
Japanese yen	0.3	100.00	90.00	¥3000	30.00	33.33
British pound	0.2	0.50	0.55	£10	20.00	18.18
Total	1.0				100.00	101.51

Canadian dollar index:

Year 1: 100.00

Year 2: (100 ÷ 101.51) × 100 = 98.51

Japanese yen, and $20 worth in British pounds. In year 1, the index number for the basket is 100 by definition.

Suppose that in year 2, the exchange rates change in the way shown in the table. The U.S. dollar stays constant, the Japanese yen goes up in value so that only 90 Japanese yen can be bought for one Canadian dollar, and the British pound goes down in value so that one Canadian dollar buys 0.55 British pounds. What is the change in the value of the basket?

The change is calculated in the final column of the table. Because the U.S. dollar exchange rate is unchanged, the Canadian-dollar value of the U.S. dollars in the basket remains constant at C$50. Because the Japanese yen has appreciated in value, more Canadian dollars are now required to buy ¥3000. Thus the Canadian-dollar value of the Japanese yen in the basket is increased to C$33.33. Because the British pound has decreased in value, fewer Canadian dollars are required to buy the £10 in the basket. Thus the £10 is now worth C$18.18. The total number of Canadian dollars required to buy the basket that was initially worth C$100 is now C$101.51.

Because more Canadian dollars are now required to buy the basket of currency, the Canadian dollar has decreased in value. To calculate the index number for the Canadian dollar, we take the value of the basket in the first year — C$100 — divide it by the value of the basket in the second year — C$101.51 — and multiply the result by 100. This calculation is set out at the bottom of the table; as you can see, the index in year 2 is 98.51. That is, the Canadian dollar has fallen in value, on the average, against the other currencies in the basket, by about 1.5 percent.

Notice that the fall in the value of the Canadian dollar against the Japanese yen is 10 percent — a fall of ¥10 on ¥100. Notice also that the increase in value of the Canadian dollar against the British pound is also 10 percent — an increase of 5 British pence on an initial value of 50 British pence. Why, if the Canadian dollar has fallen in value by 10 percent against the Japanese yen and increased in value by 10 percent against the British pound, has it fallen in value on the average? The answer is that the Japanese yen has a bigger weight in the basket than does the British pound. As a result, the fall in value against the Japanese yen gets a bigger weight in the calculation of the index. The result is that the index for the Canadian dollar falls.

In these calculations we used hypothetical numbers. How the Canadian dollar has actually fluctuated against other currencies on the average in recent years is shown in Fig. 29.1(c). As you can see, it fluctuated around a constant level until 1976, and then it depreciated for three years. It then remained steady against other G-10 currencies until 1983; from 1983 to 1986 it depreciated; and after 1986 it appreciated.

Exchange Rate Determination

What determines the foreign currency value of the dollar? Why has the dollar depreciated against the yen since 1970? Why was that depreciation particularly spectacular after 1985? Why did the dollar temporarily appreciate against the yen in 1982?

The foreign exchange value of the dollar is a price and, like any other price, is determined by demand and supply. But what exactly do we mean by the demand for and supply of dollars? There are, in fact, three different senses in which we can speak of the supply of and demand for dollars and all three have featured, at various times, in the theories of the determination of the foreign exchange rate. These theories are:

- Flow theory
- Monetary theory
- Portfolio balance theory

Let's consider each of these in turn.

Flow Theory

The **flow theory of the exchange rate** is the proposition that the exchange rate adjusts to make the flow supply of dollars equal to the flow demand for dollars. The flow supply of dollars in any given period depends on the value of Canadian imports. Canadian residents supply dollars in exchange for foreign currency in order to be able to buy imports. The flow demand for dollars in any given period depends on the value of Canadian goods (exports) that foreigners plan to buy during that period of time. In addition to the flow demand and supply resulting from imports and exports, there is also a net flow demand or supply resulting from international borrowing and lending. According to the flow theory of the exchange rate, the value of the exchange rate adjusts to keep the flow demand for a currency equal to its flow supply.

The flow theory of the foreign exchange rate has a serious shortcoming. It does not explain how the net flows associated with international borrowing and lending are determined. In fact, those flows result from people's decisions about which assets to hold. People have to choose whether to hold domestic or foreign assets; they also have to choose the currency in which their assets will be denominated. But these choices are choices about stocks, not flows. The decision to *change* the stocks of assets held results in *flows*, but those *flows are the consequence of decisions about stocks*. Thus in considering the determination of the exchange rate, even if we approach the matter from the point of view of the flow supply and demand for a currency, we cannot avoid considering the demand for a currency as a stock to hold, rather than as a flow. The emphasis on the demand for a stock of currency gives rise to the other two theories of the exchange rate. Let's now turn to them.

Monetary Theory

The **monetary theory of the exchange rate** is the proposition that the exchange rate adjusts to make the stock of a currency demanded equal to the stock supplied. The stock of a currency is identical to the *quantity of money*. In Chapter 28, we saw how the quantity of money in Canada — the quantity of Canadian-dollar money — is determined by the behaviour of the banking system and the actions of the Bank of Canada. The quantity of money in Japan — the quantity of yen money — is determined by similar actions of the Bank of Japan; the quantity of U.S.- dollar money is determined by similar actions of the Federal Reserve Board in the United States; and so on. According to the monetary theory, the exchange rate adjusts to ensure that the quantity of money in each currency supplied equals the quantity demanded.

Most international finance economists regard the monetary theory of the exchange rate as too narrow and suggest that a broader asset aggregate should be considered. This consideration gives rise to the portfolio balance theory.

Portfolio Balance Theory

The **portfolio balance theory of the exchange rate** is the proposition that the exchange rate adjusts to make the stock demanded of financial assets denominated in units of that currency equal to the stock supplied. For example, the quantity of Canadian dollars supplied is the quantity of Canadian-dollar-denominated assets. This total includes Canadian-dollar securities issued by the government and by firms. It also includes Canadian-dollar bank notes issued by the Bank of Canada and Canadian-dollar bank deposits — the Canadian money supply. But the money supply is just one part of the total quantity of Canadian-dollar-denominated assets. The exchange rate adjusts to make the total quantity of Canadian-dollar-denominated assets demanded equal to the quantity supplied.

In studying the forces that determine the exchange rate, we'll work with this third and broadest theory — the portfolio balance theory. Let's now examine the forces that influence the quantity of dollar-denominated assets demanded and supplied.

The Demand for Canadian-Dollar Assets

The law of demand applies to dollar assets just as it does to anything else that people value. The quantity of dollar assets demanded increases when the price of dollars in terms of foreign currency falls and decreases when the price of dollars in terms of foreign currency rises. The law of demand applies to dollars for two separate reasons. First, there is a transactions demand. The lower the value of the dollar, the larger is the demand for Canadian exports and the smaller is our demand for imports. Hence the larger also is the amount of trade financed by dollars. Foreigners demand more dollars to buy Canadian exports, and we demand fewer units of foreign currency and more dollars as we switch from importing to buying Canadian-produced goods.

Second, there is a demand arising from expected capital gains. Other things being equal, the lower the value of the dollar today, the higher is its expected rate of appreciation (or the lower is its expected rate of depreciation). Hence the higher is the expected gain from holding dollar assets relative to the expected gain from holding foreign currency assets. Suppose that today the dollar is worth 120 Japanese yen, but you expect it to be worth 110 yen at the end of one year. That is, you're expecting the dollar to depreciate by 10 yen. Other things being equal, you will not plan to hold dollar assets in this situation. Instead, you will plan to hold yen assets. But if today's value of the dollar is 100 yen and you expect it to go 110 yen, then you're expecting the dollar to appreciate by 10 yen. In this situation, you will plan to hold dollar assets and take advantage of the expected rise in their value. Holding assets in a particular currency in anticipation of a gain in their value arising from a change in the exchange rate is one of the most important influences on the quantity demanded of dollar assets and of foreign currency assets. The more a currency is expected to appreciate, the greater is the quantity of assets in that currency that people want to hold.

Figure 29.2 shows the relationship between the foreign currency price of the Canadian dollar and the quantity of dollar assets demanded — the demand curve for dollar assets. When the foreign exchange rate changes, other things being equal, there is a movement along the demand curve.

Any other influence on the quantity of dollar assets that people want to hold results in a shift in the demand curve. Demand either increases or decreases. These other influences are:

- The volume of dollar-financed trade
- The Canadian price level
- The interest rates on dollar assets
- The interest rates on foreign currency assets
- The expected future value of the dollar

Figure 29.2 The Demand for Canadian-Dollar Assets

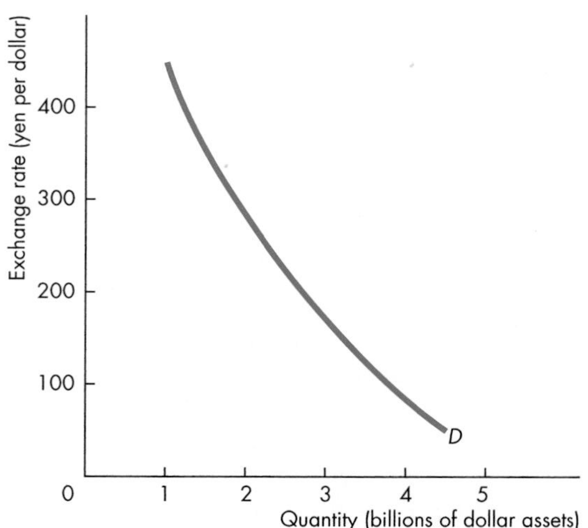

The quantity of Canadian-dollar assets that people demand, other things being held constant, depends on the foreign exchange rate. The lower the foreign exchange rate (the smaller the number of yen per dollar), the larger is the quantity of dollar assets demanded. The increased quantity demanded arises from an increase in the volume of dollar trade (the Japanese buy more Canadian goods and Canadians buy fewer Japanese goods) and an increase in the expected appreciation or decrease in the expected depreciation of dollar assets.

1. The Volume of Dollar-Financed Trade The demand for dollar assets depends on the volume of dollar-financed trade. The volume of trade is the real amount of trade undertaken. Other things remaining the same, the larger the volume of dollar-financed trade, the larger is the demand for dollar assets. The reason for this connection between the demand for dollar asssets and the volume of dollar-financed trade is identical to the reason for the connection between the demand for money and real expenditure that we studied in Chapter 28. By holding an inventory of dollar assets, people can avoid transactions costs of converting assets in other currencies into dollars each time they require dollars to undertake a purchase of goods or services.

2. The Canadian Price Level The demand for dollar assets is proportional to the Canadian price level, other things being equal. The reason for this relationship is that the dollar value of any given volume of transactions is proportional to the price level and so the amount of money required to finance a given real transaction is proportional to the price level at which the transaction takes place. In other words, the demand for dollar assets is a real demand, just like the demand for money in Chapter 28.

3. The Interest Rate on Dollar Assets Other things remaining the same, the higher the interest rate that can be earned on dollar assets, the larger the quantity of those assets that will be held. Canadians will switch out of foreign-currency assets into Canadian-dollar assets and foreigners will switch from holding their own domestic assets to Canadian-dollar assets.

4. The Interest Rates on Foreign Currency Assets The effect of interest rates on foreign-currency assets is opposite to that of the interest rate on Canadian-dollar assets. If a higher interest rate can be earned on foreign-currency assets, then both Canadians and foreigners will switch from Canadian-dollar assets to foreign-currency assets.

5. The Expected Future Value of the Dollar If the dollar is expected to appreciate against other currencies people will hold more dollars and fewer foreign-currency assets, other things being equal.

Table 29.2 summarizes the discussion of the influences on the quantity of dollar assets that people demand.

Table 29.2 The Demand for Dollar Assets 

The law of demand

The quantity of dollar assets demanded

Increases if	*Decreases if*
• The foreign-currency value of the dollar falls	• The foreign-currency value of the dollar rises

Changes in demand

The demand for dollar assets

Increases if	*Decreases if*
• Dollar-financed trade increases	• Dollar-financed trade decreases
• The price level rises	• The price level falls
• Interest rates on dollar assets rise	• Interest rates on dollar assets fall
• Interest rates on foreign currency assets fall	• Interest rates on foreign currency assets rise
• The dollar is expected to strengthen	• The dollar is expected to weaken

The Supply of Canadian-Dollar Assets

The supply of Canadian-dollar assets is determined primarily by the actions of the Bank of Canada. The supply also depends crucially on the foreign exchange rate regime in operation. Under a fixed exchange rate regime, the supply curve of dollar assets is horizontal at the chosen exchange rate. The government and the Bank of Canada stand ready to supply whatever quantity of dollar assets is demanded at the fixed exchange rate. Under a managed exchange rate regime, the Bank of Canada smooths fluctuations in the exchange rate, so the supply curve of dollar assets is upward sloping. The higher the foreign exchange rate, the larger is the quantity of dollar assets supplied. Under a flexible exchange rate regime, the Bank of Canada does not intervene in the foreign exchange market, so a fixed quantity of dollar assets is supplied, regardless of their price. As a consequence, the supply curve of dollar assets is vertical.

The supply of Canadian-dollar assets changes over time as a result of the following:

- The government's budget
- The Bank of Canada's monetary policy

The Government's Budget If the government has a budget deficit, the supply of Canadian-dollar assets increases. If the government has a budget surplus, the supply of dollar assets decreases. It is important to notice that the supply of Canadian-dollar assets increases when the government has a budget deficit, regardless of how the government finances that deficit. One way of financing the deficit is for the government to sell bonds to the Bank of Canada. This method of financing a deficit results in an immediate increase in the money supply. In such a situation, the supply of Canadian-dollar assets increases. But even if the government finances its deficit by selling bonds to households, firms, or foreigners, so long as those bonds are denominated in Canadian dollars, the total supply of Canadian-dollar assets increases.

It is possible for the government of Canada or the governments of any of the provinces to finance a deficit by issuing bonds denominated in currencies other than the Canadian dollar. For example, the government of Canada issues bonds denominated in U.S. dollars. It has even issued bonds denominated in German marks. When the government finances its deficit by selling bonds denominated in the currency of some other country, then the supply of Canadian dollar denominated assets does not increase.

The Bank of Canada's Monetary Policy The total supply of Canadian-dollar-denominated assets can also increase as a result of the Bank of Canada's monetary policy. If the Bank of Canada buys foreign currency or foreign-currency-denominated assets using newly created Canadian dollar bank deposits, the Canadian money supply increases, and there is an increase in the total quantity of Canadian-dollar-denominated assets supplied. If the Bank of Canada sells foreign securities or foreign currency, when it does so, it takes in existing Canadian dollar bank deposits or notes and the Canadian money supply as well as the total supply of Canadian-dollar-denominated assets decreases.

The above discussion is summarized in Table 29.3.

Table 29.3 The Supply of Dollar Assets 

Supply

Fixed exchange rate regime

The supply curve of dollar assets is horizontal at the fixed exchange rate.

Managed exchange rate regime

In order to smooth fluctuations in the foreign exchange value of the dollar, the quantity of dollar assets supplied by the Bank of Canada increases if the foreign exchange value of the dollar rises and decreases if the foreign exchange value of the dollar falls. The supply curve of dollar assets is upward sloping.

Flexible exchange rate regime

The supply curve of dollar assets is vertical.

Changes in supply

The supply of dollar assets

Increases if	*Decreases if*
• The government of Canada has a deficit	• The government of Canada has a surplus
• The Bank of Canada increases the money supply	• The Bank of Canada decreases the money supply

The Market for Canadian-Dollar Assets

Let's now bring together the demand and supply sides of the market for Canadian dollar assets and determine the exchange rate. Figure 29.3 illustrates the analysis.

Fixed Exchange Rate First, consider a fixed exchange rate regime, as illustrated in Fig. 29.3(a). The supply curve of dollar assets is horizontal at the fixed exchange rate of 200 yen per dollar. If the demand curve is D_0, the quantity of dollar assets is Q_0. An increase in demand to D_1 results in an increase in the quantity of dollar assets from Q_0 to Q_1 but no change in the yen price of dollars.

Flexible Exchange Rate Next look at Fig. 29.3(b), which shows what happens under a flexible exchange rate regime. In this case, the quantity of dollar assets supplied is fixed at Q_0, so the supply curve of dollar assets is vertical. If the demand curve for dollars is D_0, the exchange rate is 200 yen per dollar. If the demand for dollars increases from D_0 to D_1, the exchange rate increases to 300 yen per dollar.

Figure 29.3 Three Exchange Rate Regimes

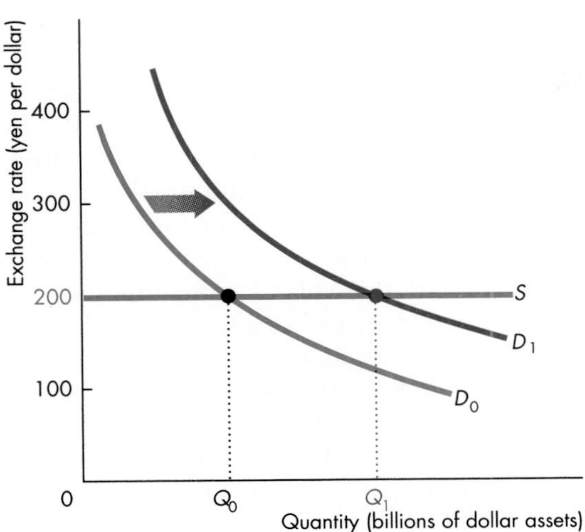

(a) Fixed exchange rate

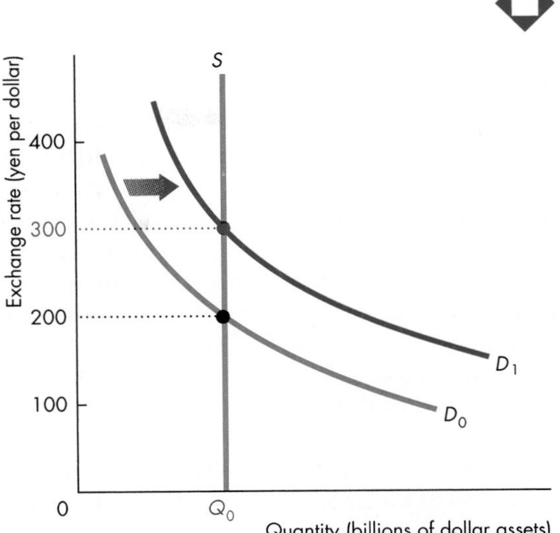

(b) Flexible exchange rate

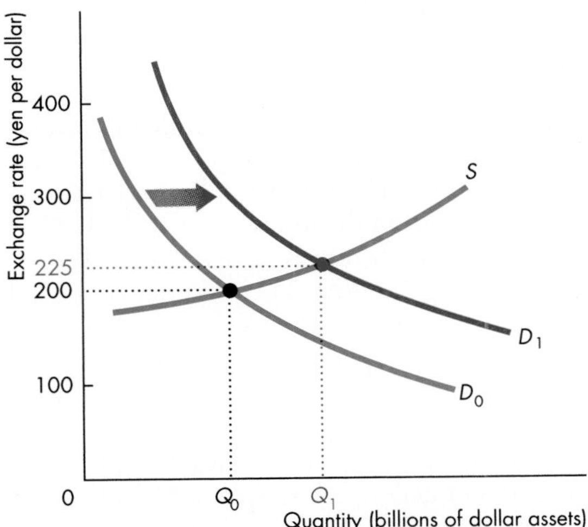

(c) Managed exchange rate

Under a fixed exchange rate regime (part a), the Bank of Canada stands ready to supply dollar assets or to take dollar assets off the market (supplying foreign currency in exchange) at a fixed exchange rate. The supply curve for dollar assets is horizontal. Fluctuations in demand lead to fluctuations in the quantity of dollar assets outstanding and to fluctuations in the nation's official holdings of foreign exchange. If demand increases from D_0 to D_1, the quantity of dollar assets increases from Q_0 to Q_1; the exchange rate does not change.

Under a flexible exchange rate regime (part b), the Bank of Canada fixes the quantity of dollar assets so that the supply curve of dollar assets is vertical. An increase in the demand for dollar assets from D_0 to D_1 results only in an increase in the value of the dollar — the exchange rate rises from 200 to 300 yen per dollar. The quantity of dollar assets remains constant at Q_0.

Under a managed exchange rate regime (part c), the supply curve of dollar assets is upward sloping, so if demand increases from D_0 to D_1, the dollar appreciates but the quantity of dollar assets supplied also increases — from Q_0 to Q_1. The Bank of Canada moderates the rise in the value of the dollar by increasing the quantity of dollar assets supplied but it does not completely prevent the exchange rate rise as it does in the case of fixed exchange rates.

Managed Exchange Rate Finally, consider a managed exchange rate regime, which appears in Fig. 29.3(c). Here, the supply curve is upward sloping. When the demand curve is D_0, the exchange rate is 200 yen per dollar. If demand increases to D_1, the yen value of the dollar rises but only to 225 yen per dollar. Compared with the flexible exchange rate case, the same increase in demand results in a smaller increase in the exchange rate when it is managed. The reason is that the Bank of Canada increases the quantity supplied in the managed exchange rate case so as to moderate the increase in the exchange rate.

The Exchange Rate Regime and Foreign Exchange Reserves

There is an important connection between the foreign exchange rate regime and the country's foreign exchange reserves — the country's official holdings (by the government and the Bank of Canada) of assets denominated in foreign currencies. Under fixed exchange rates (as shown in Fig. 29.3(a)), every time there is a change in the demand for dollar assets, the Bank of Canada must change the quantity of dollar assets supplied to match it. When the Bank of Canada has to increase the quantity of dollar assets supplied, it does so by offering dollar assets (bank deposits) in exchange for foreign currency (foreign bank deposits). In this case, the official holdings of foreign exchange increase. If the demand for dollar assets decreases, the Bank of Canada has to decrease the quantity of dollar assets supplied. The Bank of Canada does so by buying dollars back and using its foreign exchange holdings to do so. In this case, official holdings of foreign exchange decrease. Thus with a fixed exchange rate, fluctuations in the demand for dollar assets result in fluctuations in official holdings of foreign exchange.

Under a flexible exchange rate regime, there is no Bank of Canada intervention in the foreign exchange market. Regardless of what happens to the demand for dollar assets, no action is taken to change the quantity of dollar assets supplied. Therefore there are no changes in the country's official holdings of foreign exchange.

With a managed exchange rate, official holdings of foreign exchange are adjusted to meet fluctuations in the demand for dollar assets but in a manner less extreme than under fixed exchange rates. As a consequence, fluctuations in the official holdings of foreign exchange are smaller under a managed exchange rate regime than under a fixed exchange rate regime.

Why Is the Exchange Rate so Volatile?

We've seen times, especially recently, when the dollar-yen exchange rate has moved dramatically. On most of these occasions, the dollar has depreciated spectacularly, but on some occasions it has appreciated strongly.

The main reason the exchange rate fluctuates so remarkably is that fluctuations in the supply and the demand for dollar assets are not always independent of each other. Sometimes a change in supply will trigger a change in demand that reinforces the effect of the change in supply. Let's see how these effects work by looking at two episodes.

1981 to 1982 From 1981 to 1982, the Canadian dollar appreciated against the yen, rising from 194 to 201 yen per dollar. Figure 29.4(a) explains why this happened. In 1981, the demand and supply curves were those labelled D_{81} and S_{81}. The foreign exchange value of the dollar was 194 yen — the point at which the supply and demand curves intersect. By 1982, Canada was experiencing a severe recession. This recession was brought about in part by the Bank of Canada (and the Federal Reserve Board in the United States), which pursued very restrictive monetary policies. The Bank of Canada forced interest rates upward, cutting back on the supply of dollar assets. The direct effect was a shift in the supply curve from S_{81} to S_{82} — a decrease in the supply of dollars. But higher Canadian interest rates induced an increase in demand for Canadian dollar assets to take advantage of those higher interest rates. As a result, the demand curve shifted from D_{81} to D_{82}. These two shifts reinforced each other, increasing the yen price of the dollar to 201 yen.

1985 to 1986 There was a spectacular depreciation of the Canadian dollar in terms of yen from 173 yen per dollar in 1985 to 120 yen per dollar in 1986. This fall came about in the following way. In 1985, the demand and supply curves were those labelled D_{85} and S_{85} in Fig. 29.4(b). The yen price of the dollar — the exchange rate at which these two curves intersect — was 173 yen per dollar. From 1982 to 1985, the Canadian economy had been on a recovery. But it was a recovery through which a government of Canada budget deficit persisted. With a large government deficit, the supply of Canadian dollar assets was increasing. The Bank of Canada was also loosening up its monetary policy, permitting money supply growth rates to be rapid enough to keep the recovery going. The direct effect of these actions was an increase in the supply of dollar assets from S_{85} to S_{86}. But interest rates in Canada began to fall, and expectations of future declines in the value of the dollar also became widely held. As a consequence, the demand for dollar assets decreased from D_{85} to D_{86}. The result of this combined increase in supply and decrease in demand was a dramatic fall in the value of the dollar to 120 yen.

Figure 29.4 Why the Exchange Rate Is So Volatile

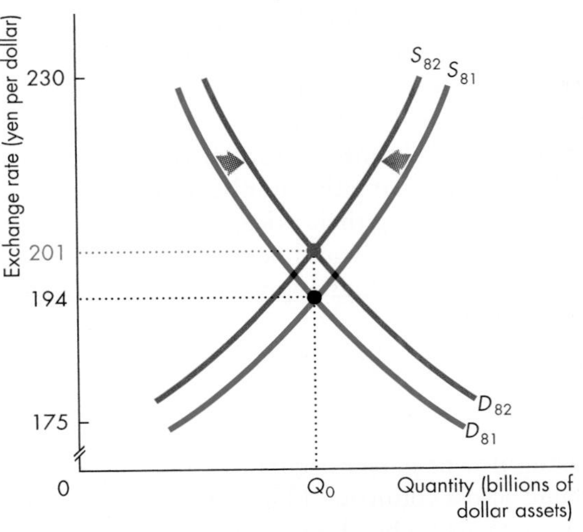

(a) 1981 to 1982

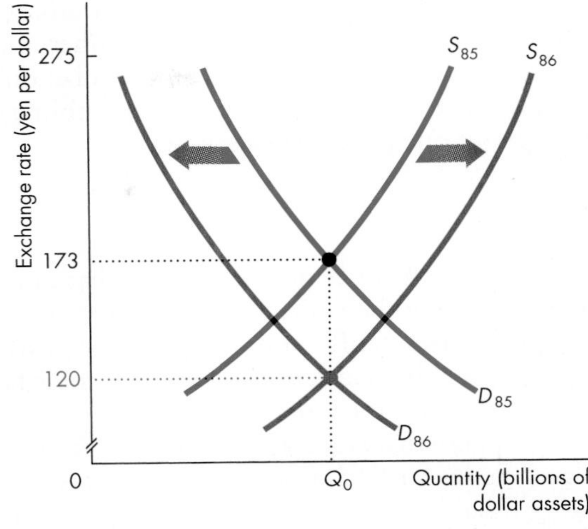

(b) 1985 to 1986

The exchange rate is volatile because shifts in the demand and supply curves for dollar assets are not independent of each other. From 1981 to 1982 (part a), the dollar appreciated from 194 to 201 yen per dollar. This appreciation arose because the supply curve of dollar assets shifted to the left, and higher interest rates induced an increase in demand for dollars assets, shifting the demand curve to the right. The result was a large increase in the foreign exchange value of the dollar. From 1985 to 1986 (part b), the Bank of Canada permitted the quantity of dollar assets to increase to sustain the long economic recovery. The supply curve shifted to the right. At the same time, interest rates decreased and expectations of further declines in the value of the dollar shifted the demand curve to the left. The result was a steep fall in the exchange rate, from 173 yen to 120 yen per dollar.

REVIEW

There are three possible foreign exchange rate regimes: fixed, flexible, and managed. Under a fixed exchange rate regime, the Bank of Canada pegs the exchange rate, but the foreign exchange reserves have to carry the burden of holding the exchange rate constant. A decrease in the demand for Canadian dollar assets or an increase in the demand for foreign currency assets has to be met by lowering Canada's official holdings of foreign currency. Under a flexible exchange rate regime, the Bank of Canada does not intervene in the foreign exchange markets. Canada's official holdings of foreign currency remain constant. Under a managed exchanged rate regime, the Bank of Canada smooths exchange rate fluctuations to a degree but less strongly than under fixed exchange rates. Under a flexible or a managed exchange rate regime, the exchange rate is determined by the demand for and supply of dollar assets. Fluctuations in supply often induce reinforcing fluctuations in demand, bringing severe fluctuations in the exchange rate. ■

Arbitrage, Prices, and Interest Rates

Arbitrage is the activity of buying low and selling high in order to make a profit on the margin between the two prices. Arbitrage has important effects on exchange rates, prices, and interest rates. An increase in the quantity of purchases forces the buying price up. A decrease in the quantity of sales forces the selling price down. The prices move until they are equal and there is no arbitrage profit available. An implication of arbitrage is the law of one price. The **law of one price** states that any given commodity will be available at a single price.

The law of one price has no respect for national borders or currencies. If the same commodity is being bought and sold on either side of the Detroit River, it doesn't matter that one of these transactions is being undertaken in Canada and the other in the United States and that one is using Canadian dollars and the other U.S. dollars. The forces of arbitrage bring about one price. Let's see how.

Arbitrage

Let's consider the price of a floppy disk that can be bought in either the United States or Canada. We will ignore taxes, tariffs, and transportation costs in order to keep the calculations simple, for these factors do not affect the fundamental issue.

Suppose that you can buy floppy disks in the United States for US$10 a box, and that this same box of disks is available in Canada for C$15 a box. Where would it pay to buy disks — in Canada or in the United States? The answer depends on the exchange rate between the Canadian and U.S. dollars. If a U.S. dollar cost C$1.50, then it is clear that the price of the disks is the same in both countries. Americans can buy a box of disks in the United States for US$10 or they can use US$10 to buy C$15 and then buy the disks in Canada. The cost is the same either way. The same is true for Canadians. Canadians can use C$15 to buy a box of disks in Canada, or they can use C$15 to buy US$10 and then buy the disks in the United States. Again, there is no difference in the price of the disks.

Suppose, however, that a U.S. dollar is less valuable than in the above example. In particular, suppose that a U.S. dollar costs C$1.40. In this case, it will pay to buy the disks in the United States. Canadians can buy US$10 for C$14, and therefore they can buy the disks in the United States for C$14 a box compared with C$15 in Canada. The same comparison holds for Americans. Americans can use US$10 to buy C$14, but that would not be enough to buy the disks in Canada since the disks cost C$15 there. Therefore it also pays Americans to buy the disks in the United States.

If the situation described above did prevail, there would be an advantage in switching the purchases of disks from Canada to the United States. Canadians would cross the border to buy their disks in the United States and keep on doing so until the Canadian price had fallen to C$14. Once that had happened, Canadians would be indifferent between buying their disks in Canada and in the United States. Arbitrage would have eliminated the difference in prices in the two countries.

Perhaps you are thinking that this is a pretty crazy example since we don't rush down to the United States every time we want to buy a box of floppy disks. But the fact that there is a profit to be made means that it would pay someone to organize the importing of disks into Canada from the United States, thereby increasing the number of disks available there and lowering their price. The incentive to undertake such a move would be present as long as disks were selling for a higher price in Canada than in the United States.

Purchasing Power Parity

Purchasing power parity occurs when money has equal value across countries. (The word "parity" simply means equality. The phrase "purchasing power" refers to the "value of money." Thus "purchasing power parity" directly translates to "equal value of money.") Purchasing power parity is an implication of arbitrage and of the law of one price. In the floppy disk example, when US$1 is worth C$1.40, US$10 will buy the same box of floppy disks that C$14 will buy. The value of money, when converted to common prices, is the same in both countries. Purchasing power parity thus prevails in that situation.

Purchasing power parity theory predicts that purchasing power parity applies to all goods and to price indexes, not just to a single good such as the floppy disk. That is, if any goods are cheaper in one country than in another, it will pay to convert money into the currency of that country, buy the goods in that country, and sell them in another. By such an arbitrage process, all prices are brought to equality.

One test of the purchasing power parity theory that has been proposed is to calculate what is called the real exchange rate between two countries. The **real exchange rate** is the ratio of the price index in one country to the price index in another. The prices in the second country are converted to prices in the first, using the exchange rate between the two currencies. For example, the real exchange rate between the Canadian dollar and the Japanese yen, expressed in units of Japanese goods per unit of Canadian goods, is calculated using the following formula:

$$\text{Real exchange rate between Canadian dollar and Japanese yen} = \frac{\text{GDP deflator in Canada} \times \text{Yen per dollar}}{\text{GDP deflator in Japan}}.$$

To measure the real exchange rate between the Canadian dollar and all other currencies, we calculate an index that is a weighted average of the real exchange rates between the Canadian dollar and every other currency; the weights reflect the importance of each other currency in Canadian international trade. This calculation is similar to that of the Canadian dollar index (of the nominal exchange rate) illustrated in Table 29.1.

There are large movements in the real exchange rate, and these movements lead some economists to conclude that the purchasing power parity theory is wrong. They argue that if the purchasing power parity theory were correct, the real exchange rate index would remain close to 100. Any increase in the GDP deflator in Canada not matched by an equal percentage increase in the GDP deflator in Japan would be accompanied by a depreciation of the Canadian dollar against the Japanese yen. The result would be an equal percentage change in Canadian prices and in Japanese prices, when both were valued in Japanese yen. Thus the real exchange rate index would remain at 100.

But there is a simple reason why real exchange rates do change that does not mean that the purchasing power parity theory is wrong; the existence of nontraded goods. A **nontraded good** is a good (or service) that cannot be traded over long distances. Sometimes it would be technically possible to undertake such a trade but prohibitively costly. In other cases, it would simply not be possible to undertake the trade. Doughnuts are an example of a nontraded good. It's lunchtime in Saskatoon, you are hungry, and doughnuts are your thing. You don't have much choice but to buy your doughnut right there. You can't take advantage of the fact that doughnuts are cheaper in Windsor and begin an arbitrage operation. Does this fact mean that purchasing power parity does not hold between Saskatoon and Windsor? No. It means that a doughnut in Saskatoon is a different good from a doughnut in Windsor. One of the dimensions of a nontraded good is its location.

There are many examples of goods that are nontraded internationally and it is the existence of these goods (and services) that give rise to movements in real exchange rates even though purchasing power parity holds. One of the most important examples is the public services provided by the government. You can't buy cheap street-sweeping services in Vietnam and sell them at a profit in Vancouver. Many location-specific services, such as fast food, are also in this category. When goods cannot be traded over long distances, the goods are strictly different goods. A fresh doughnut in Saskatoon is as different from a fresh doughnut in Windsor as it is from a pancake across the street.

Arbitrage operates to bring about equality in prices of identical goods, not different goods. It does not operate to bring about equality between prices of similar-looking goods in widely differing locations. For this reason, tests of the purchasing power parity theory based on real exchange rates are faulty. In fact, for real exchange rates to stay constant every time the exchange rate changes, the prices of all goods would also have to change — the dollar would have to fall against all currencies and the doughnut! (See Reading Between the Lines, pp. 788-789.)

"On the foreign-exchange markets today, the dollar fell against all major currencies and the doughnut."

An additional factor that influences the real exchange rate is the existence of taxes and restrictions on international trade. Such restrictions weaken the forces of arbitrage and prevent the same price from arising for the same commodity in different countries.

Arbitrage does not only occur in markets for goods and services. It also occurs in markets for assets. As a result, it brings about another important equality or parity — interest rate parity.

Interest Rate Parity

Interest rate parity occurs when interest rates are equal across countries once the differences in risk are taken into account. Interest rate parity is a condition brought about by arbitrage in the markets for

Big Mac Currencies

On the hamburger standard

Depressing though it may be to gourmets, the "Big Mac" hamburger sold by McDonald's could well oust the basket of currencies as an international monetary standard. After all, it is sold in 41 countries, with only the most trivial changes of recipe. That ought to say something about comparative prices. Think of the hamburger as a medium-rare guide to whether currencies are trading at the right exchange rates.

Big-Mac-watchers will rely on the theory of purchasing-power parity (PPP) for currencies. This argues that an exchange rate between two currencies is in equilibrium (i.e., at PPP) when it equates the prices of a basket of goods and services in both countries — or, in this case, that rate of exchange which leaves hamburgers costing the same in each country. Comparing actual exchange rates with PPPs is one indication of whether a currency is under- or over-valued.

The *Economist's* correspondents around the world have been gorging themselves in a bid to test Mac-PPPs. In Washington, a Big Mac costs $1.60; in Tokyo, our *Makudonarudo* correspondent had to fork out ¥370 ($2.40). Dividing the yen price by the [U.S.] dollar price yields a Mac-PPP of $1=¥231; but on September 1st, the [U.S.] dollar's actual exchange rate stood at ¥154. The same method gives a Mac-PPP against the D-mark of DM2.66, compared with a current rate of DM2.02. Conclusion: on Mac-PPP grounds, the dollar looks undervalued against the yen and the D-mark.

Sterling is different. The Mac-PPP for the pound is $1.45 (69p to the dollar), within a whisker of the actual rate of around $1.49.

The hamburger standard provides the United States with strong evidence for its contention that Asian NICs (newly industrialising countries) ought to upvalue their currencies; they are more or less tied to the [U.S.] dollar, so their exchange rates have barely budged during the past 18 months. A hamburger costs 64% more in Washington than in Hong Kong — i.e., on Mac-PPP grounds the [U.S.] dollar is 64% overvalued against the Hong Kong dollar. It is also 23% too high against the Singapore dollar.

Big Mac Currencies: Hamburger prices around the World

Country	Price* in local currency	Implied** purchasing power parity of the dollar	Actual exchange rate Sept. 1st	% over (+) or under (–) valuation of U.S. $
Australia	A$1.75	1.09	1.64	+50
Belgium	BFr90	56	42	–25
Britain	£1.10	0.69	0.67	–3
Canada	C$1.89	1.18	1.39	+18
France	FFr16.4	10.30	6.65	–35
Hong Kong	HK$7.60	4.75	7.80	+64
Ireland	IR£1.18	0.74	0.74	–1
Japan	¥370	231	154	–33
Holland	F14.35	2.7	22.28	–16
Singapore	S$2.80	1.75	2.15	+23
Spain	Ptas280	163	133	–18
Sweden	Skr16.5	10.30	6.87	–33
United States	$1.60	—	—	—
West Germany	DM4.25	2.66	2.02	–24

Source: McDonald's.
*Prices may vary slightly between branches.
**Foreign price divided by [U.S.] dollar price.

Caveat hamburger

The hamburger standard has its limitations. Using purchasing-power parities to forecast movements in exchange rates can produce misleading results. For instance, price differences between countries can be distorted by taxes, transport costs, property costs or such things as the famously high retail mark-ups in Japan and West Germany.

A more serious objection is that a PPP simply indicates where exchange rates should be in the long run if price levels were the only difference between countries. In fact, there are many other differences. So even though PPPs are handy for converting living standards (GDP per person) into a common currency, they are not necessarily the best way to judge the exchange rate needed to bring the current account of the balance of payments into "equilibrium". Confused? Some economics can be hard to digest.

***The Economist*, September 6, 1988.**

The Essence of the Story

- The Big Mac hamburger is sold in 41 countries but local prices vary, as shown in the table in the article for 14 countries.
- Purchasing power parity theory (PPP) predicts that Big Macs will cost the same in each country—when the prices are converted to a common currency.
- Equivalently, PPP predicts that the ratio of prices in local currencies will equal the exchange rate between the currencies.
- The ratios of local prices to the U.S. price are shown in the table (in column headed "Implied Purchasing Power Parity of the Dollar").

If PPP holds, each ratio should equal the actual currency exchange rate.

- The price of a Big Mac varies from 35 percent more than in the United States (France) to 64 percent less than in the United States (Hong Kong), implying that the French franc is 35 percent undervalued and the Hong Kong dollar is 64 percent overvalued.
- Cost differences might lead to departures from PPP.
- PPP is a long-run theory.

Background and Analysis

- The Big Mac is a non-traded good. Although its food content is almost identical everywhere, that is only a small part of the total product.
- The Big Mac is a fast meal that includes food, location, and service.
- In the United States, less than one-quarter of the total value of a Big Mac is food and more than three-quarters is the cost of the location and delivery of the service.
- Prices of non-traded goods vary according to local demand and supply. The prices of a Big Mac on September 1, 1986, expressed in U.S. dollars, are set out in the table.
- In France, Japan, and Sweden—the highest priced countries—Big Macs are sold only in the high-rent, high-density central city areas. Rent costs are high. These are also high wage countries. In Singapore, Australia, and Hong Kong, the labour cost of producing hamburgers is lower than in Canada and so is the rent cost.
- Although the food components are potentially traded goods, international restrictions on trade, especially in meat products, prevent the price equalization of even that part of a Big Mac.
- Exchange rates are determined by the demand for and supply of assets denominated in the various currencies.
- To assess whether arbitrage is working to produce the law of one price, traded goods whose transport costs are negligible must be compared.

Table 1

Country	Price in local currency	Exchange rate (Sept. 1, 1986)	Local price in dollars	Ratio of local price to U.S. price
France	FF16.4	6.65	2.47	1.54
Japan	¥370	154	2.40	1.50
Sweden	SKr16.5	6.87	2.40	1.50
Belgium	BFr90	42	2.14	1.34
West Germany	DM4.25	2.02	2.10	1.31
Spain	Ptas260	133	1.95	1.22
Holland	Fl4.35	2.28	1.91	1.19
Britain	£1.1	0.67	1.64	1.03
United States	$1.16	1	1.60	1.00
Ireland	IR£1.18	0.74	1.59	1.00
Canada	C$1.89	1.39	1.36	0.85
Singapore	S$2.8	2.15	1.30	0.81
Australia	A$1.75	1.64	1.07	0.67
Hong Kong	HK$7.6	7.8	0.97	0.61

Conclusion

- The hamburger standard exercise is a good idea but it is applied here to the wrong type of good.

assets — markets in which borrowers and lenders operate.

At the beginning of this chapter, we noted some facts about interest rates in different countries. Those facts seem to suggest that interest rates are *not* equal in different countries. To make things concrete, let's look at a specific example. On November 15, 1988, it was possible to borrow money from a bank in Tokyo at an interest rate of 3.4 percent a year. On that same day, banks in New York were accepting three-month deposits at an interest rate of 9 percent per year. Aren't these unequal interest rates? Isn't it possible for someone to borrow, say, a million U.S. dollars in Tokyo at an interest rate of 3.4 percent and put that money on deposit in a bank in New York, earning an interest rate of 9 percent and thereby profiting from the 5.6 percentage point difference between the two interest rates? Such a transaction, done for a year, would produce a profit of US$56,000, not bad for a few minutes work! It is also, apparently, an outcome that violates interest rate parity!

In fact, as you're about to discover, interest rates in Japan and the United States are almost equal — at least close enough to equality that you could not profit from the transactions just described.

The key to understanding why the interest rates are equal is to realize that when you borrow in Japan you are borrowing *yen.* You are committing yourself to repaying a certain number of *yen* when the loan is due. When you lend money in the United States — such as by placing it on deposit in a bank — you are lending *U.S. dollars* and the bank is obliged to repay *U.S. dollars.* It's a bit like borrowing apples and lending oranges. If you're borrowing apples and lending oranges, you've got to convert the apples to oranges. And when the loan becomes due, you've got to convert oranges back into apples. The prices at which you do these transactions affect the interest rates that you pay and receive.

Let's look a bit more closely at the $1 million borrowing and lending operation that you might have done on November 15, 1988 and see how much you would have made (or lost) on the deal. Table 29.4 summarizes the events. Part (a) lists data from November 15, 1988. It shows banks in Tokyo lending at an interest rate of 3.4 percent and banks in New York taking three-month deposits at an interest rate of 9 percent. (These are annual interest rates.) On the same day, yen sold on the foreign exchange market at 122 yen per U.S. dollar. That's the price at which you could convert the yen that you borrowed into the U.S. dollars that you were going to lend.

Table 29.4 International Borrowing and Lending

(a) Data on November 15, 1988

Bank lending rate in Tokyo	3.4 percent per year
Bank 3-month deposit rate in New York	9.0 percent per year
Price at which Japanese yen can be sold	122 yen per U.S. dollar
Price at which Japanese yen can be bought for delivery in three months	120 yen per U.S. dollar

(b) Transactions on November 15, 1988

Borrow	122	million yen in Tokyo
Sell	122	million yen in exchange for US$1 million
Deposit	US$1	million in a 3-month deposit account in New York
Buy	123.04	million yen for delivery in 3 months at 120 yen per U.S. dollar (no money needed now)

(c) Transactions on February 15, 1989

Receive	US$1.0225	million from bank —deposit plus interest
Pay	US$1.0253	million for forward yen contract
Loss	$0.0028	million (US$2,800)

(Like the price at which you can sell oranges for apples.)

At the end of three months, you have to convert dollars back into yen to repay your bank loan and the interest on it. There are two ways in which you can do that transaction. You can wait until February 15, 1989 and take your chances on the exchange rate between the U.S. dollar and the yen that prevails on that day. If you choose to do that, you will certainly be taking some risks. If the U.S. dollar appreciates in that three-month period, you will stand to gain. If the U.S. dollar depreciates, you will stand to lose.

But there is another way in which you can get the yen that you need to repay your bank loan on February 15. You can enter into a contract on November 15, 1988 at a price agreed on that day to buy a certain number of yen to be delivered on February

15, 1989. Such a contract is called a forward contract. A **forward contract** is a contract entered into at an agreed price to buy or sell a certain quantity of any commodity (including currency) at a specified future date. Forward contracts are traded on markets, and their prices are determined by supply and demand in the same manner that any actual commodity is traded. There are forward markets in most agricultural products and in raw materials, as well as currencies and stocks and bonds. The exchange rate in a forward contract is called a **forward exchange rate**. On November 15, 1988, the foreign exchange rate at which Japanese yen could be bought in the forward market for delivery three months in the future (on February 15, 1989) was 120 yen per U.S. dollar.

Part (b) of Table 29.4 sets out the transactions that you could undertake on November 15, 1988. You borrow 122 million yen in Tokyo and sell those yen at 122 yen per U.S. dollar in exchange for US$1 million. You deposit that US$1 million in a bank in New York on a three-month deposit account. That's the end of your cash transactions on that day. At the same time, you enter into a forward contract, buying enough yen for delivery on February 15, 1989 to repay your bank loan and the interest on it. At an interest rate of 3.4 percent per year, you'll need 123.04 million yen on February 15, 1989. So you enter into a contract now to buy those 123.04 million yen at an agreed price of 120 yen per U.S.dollar.

Part (c) tells us what happens on February 15, 1989. You receive your million U.S. dollars back from the bank together with a quarter of a year's interest (US$22,500). The total amount of dollars you have is US$1.0225 million. You pay for your forward yen contract, which costs you US$1.0253 million. (Divide the 123.04 million yen that you need by 120 yen per U.S. dollar, the price that you agreed to in the forward market back in November, and you'll see that the answer is US$1.0253 million.) Notice that you have paid out a bit more than you received. You have actually lost US$2,800 on this transaction — about a quarter of 1 percent of the total amount involved.

Now suppose that the interest rates in Tokyo and New York and the exchange rate and the forward exchange rate on November 15, 1988 were slightly different. Suppose that instead of making a loss, this set of transactions will turn a profit. How long will the profit opportunity exist? You and millions of people like you will be borrowing from banks in Japan, converting yen into U.S. dollars, depositing the money in New York, and taking out forward contracts to get the yen back to repay the yen loans at the end of the transaction period. Even if you can make only a few thousand dollars on a US$1 million contract, there is nothing to stop you from entering into a US$10 million or a US$100 million contract, making a large profit in the process.

But now think about what is going to happen to interest rates and exchange rates as you and everyone else attempt to profit. With an increased demand for loans from banks in Japan, the interest rate there is going to increase. With an increased supply of deposits to the banks in New York, the interest rate there is going to decrease. As more people offer yen in exchange for dollars, the exchange rate is going to increase — more yen will have to be offered for a U.S. dollar. And as more people try to buy yen in the forward market, the number of yen per U.S. dollar in that market will decline. Every one of these changes reduces the possibility of making a profit by borrowing in Tokyo and lending in New York, and these forces will operate until that profit opportunity is wiped out. They will not operate to reverse the profit — that is, to make it profitable to borrow in New York and lend in Tokyo. In such a situation, the reverse forces will be at work, again removing profit from international borrowing and lending actions.

In the situation that we've just described, interest rate parity prevails. The interest rate in Tokyo — when the expected change in the price of the yen between November and February is taken into account — is almost identical to that in New York. It costs 3.4 percent per year to borrow yen in Tokyo, but it costs 9 percent per year to borrow yen, convert them into U.S. dollars, and then convert them back into yen at a later date. It is in this sense that interest rates are equal. The dollar interest rate in Tokyo is the same as the dollar interest rate in New York. The yen interest rate in New York is the same as the yen interest rate in Tokyo.

A World Market

Arbitrage in asset markets operates on a worldwide scale and keeps the world capital markets linked in a single global market. This market is an enormous one. It involves borrowing and lending through banks, in bond markets, and in stock markets. The scale of this international business was estimated by Salomon Brothers, an investment bank, at more than $1 trillion in 1986. It is because of international arbitrage in asset markets that the fortunes of the stock markets around the world are so closely linked. A stock market crash in New York makes its new low-priced stocks look attractive compared with high-priced stocks in Montreal, Toronto, Tokyo, Hong Kong, Zurich, Frankfurt, and London. As a consequence, investors make plans to sell high in these other markets and buy low in New York. But before many such transactions can be put through, the prices in the other markets fall to match those in New York. Conversely, if the Tokyo market experiences rapid price increases and markets in the rest of the world stay constant, investors seek to sell high in Tokyo and buy low in the rest of the world. Again, these trading plans will induce movements in the prices in the other markets to bring them into line with the Tokyo market. The action of selling high in Tokyo will lower the prices there and the action of buying low in Frankfurt, London, New York, and Toronto will raise the prices there.

Monetary Independence

With what you have just learned about arbitrage and its effects on prices and interest rates, you can see why fixed exchange rates make one economy completely interdependent with another and why flexible exchange rates bring monetary and financial independence. Let's explore these issues.

Interdependence with a Fixed Exchange Rate

Suppose that Canada fixes its exchange rate against the U.S. dollar and that through Bank of Canada actions in the foreign exchange market, it manages to hold the Canadian dollar absolutely steady against the U.S. dollar. Also suppose that the Bank of Canada has large enough reserves of U.S. dollars to be able to withstand any pressures that might make the exchange rate move.

The forces of arbitrage bring the prices of traded goods into line with each other on both sides of the Canada-U.S. border. Where there are no tariffs or other trade restrictions, the prices are exactly the same regardless of whether a good is paid for in Canadian dollars or U.S. dollars — as in the example of disks that we reviewed earlier in this chapter. If there is an increase in prices in the United States, there is an increase of the same percentage in Canada, other things being constant. But other things are not necessarily constant and there may be a difference between the inflation rates in the United States and Canada. Nevertheless, a *change* in the inflation rate in the United States brings about a *change* in the inflation rate in Canada of an equal percentage magnitude. That is,

$$\text{Inflation rate in Canada} = \text{Inflation rate in United States} + \text{Other Influences}.$$

Similarly, arbitrage in asset markets brings the interest rates in the two countries into equality for assets having identical risks and other characteristics. For example, a major international firm such as Olympia and York, operated by the Reichmann brothers of Toronto, is able to borrow at a similar rate from the Bank of Montreal in Canadian dollars or from the First National City Bank in New York in U.S. dollars. If cheaper loans can be obtained in New York than in Montreal, the Reichmanns will move their borrowing to New York, thereby decreasing the demand for loans in Montreal and increasing the demand for loans in New York. Interest rates will increase in New York and decrease in Montreal. Until the two rates are equal, there remains an incentive to keep shifting the source of borrowing.

For assets of differing risk, interest rates will differ both within Canada and between Canada and the United States. For example, when a bank makes a loan to the Reichmann brothers, that loan is less risky than one made to a small firm that is taking a highly speculative position in the market for some new computer software. The small software company pays a higher interest rate than the Reichmanns regardless of whether it borrows in U.S. dollars or Canadian dollars. But, the software company pays the same interest rate regardless of whether it borrows in Montreal or New York.

Because the average riskiness of loans in Canada may differ from that in the United States, there may be a difference between the average interest rate here and south of the border. That difference reflects the difference in the average amount of risk in the two countries. Thus

$$\text{Interest rate in Canada} = \text{Interest rate in United States} + \text{Risk differential}.$$

Let's now work out what happens in Canada if the Federal Reserve System expands the rate at which money is created in the United States. Suppose that the Federal Reserve undertakes policies that speed up the growth of the money supply from 5 percent a year to 10 percent a year. This action eventually brings an increase in inflation in the United States of 5 percent a year. The higher inflation rate results in higher interest rates in the United States — by 5 percentage points. With higher inflation and higher interest rates in the United States and holding everything else constant, the forces of international commodity price and interest rate arbitrage that we have just considered bring higher inflation and higher interest rates to Canada. But other factors may change. Setting aside those other possible forces, the increased money supply growth in the United States increases Canada's interest rates and inflation rates by amounts equal to the increases in those same variables in the United States.

Fixed Exchange Rates in Action How do fixed exchange rates work in practice? They work exactly like the theoretical description you have just reviewed. During the 1960s, when the Canadian dollar was fixed in value against the U.S. dollar and other currencies, and most other currencies were also fixed in value against the U.S. dollar, inflation rates were remarkably similar around the world. So were interest rates. In recent times, the major countries of Western Europe (excluding the United Kingdom) have joined what is known as the European Monetary System (EMS). The **European Monetary System** is a fixed exchange rate system involving most of the members of the European Community — the most important being Germany, France, and Italy. Since these countries have locked the values of their currencies together, their inflation and interest rates have come into closer alignment.

You can think of interest rates and inflation rates *within* a country as being a special case of fixed exchange rates. The British Columbian dollar and the Newfoundland dollar are the same as the Ontario dollar. The exchange rate between these dollars is fixed at 1. Anything that changes the inflation rate in British Columbia, other things being equal, also changes the inflation rate in Newfoundland and in Ontario. Similarly, interest rates across Canada are linked through the forces of arbitrage that we have described.

We've seen how fixed exchange rates bring financial interdependence between countries. Let's now see how flexible exchange rates break that interdependence and enable a country to insulate itself from financial shocks stemming from the rest of the world.

Independence with a Flexible Exchange Rate

The existence of a flexible exchange rate does not render the forces of international arbitrage ineffective. Instead, by making it possible for the value of one money to change in terms of another, it enables dollar prices (and interest rates) to change in one country and not change in another, while respecting the laws and forces of arbitrage. To see how, let's first consider how flexible exchange rates insulate a country from inflation in another country.

We know that the basic forces of arbitrage ensure that

$$\text{Price in \$C} = \text{Price in \$US} \times \text{Exchange rate (\$C per \$US)}.$$

Consider again the case of disks. If disks cost $10 a box in the United States and if the Canadian-U.S. exchange rate is C$1.25 per $US1, then the price of that same box of disks in Canadian dollars is $12.50. Now suppose that prices of all goods increase in the United States by 10 percent. The price of a box of disks rises to $11. Suppose at the same time, for reasons that we'll examine in a moment, that the Canadian dollar appreciates against the U.S. dollar by 10 percent. The exchange rate changes to approximately C$1.14 per US$1. At this new exchange rate and new U.S. dollar price, what is the Canadian-dollar price of the box of disks that is brought about by the forces of arbitrage? The answer is $12.50, the same as before.

But there are factors other than U.S. prices and the exchange rate that can bring about price changes in Canada. Changes in tariffs, taxes, or other nonmonetary factors can influence the prices of goods in Canada relative to prices in the United States. Nevertheless, other things being equal, a change in the inflation rate in the United States does not translate into a change in the inflation rate in Canada unless the Canadian dollar stays constant against the U.S. dollar. In general, since the exchange rate changes when the U.S. inflation rate changes, there is some insulation of the Canadian inflation rate from the U.S. inflation rate. Inflation in the two countries is linked by the following equation:

$$\text{Inflation rate in Canada} = \text{Inflation rate in United States} - \text{Percentage appreciation of Canadian dollar} + \text{Other influences}.$$

If the U.S. inflation rate increases and the Bank of

Canada wants to insulate Canadians from that U.S. inflation, it must take steps that ensure that the Canadian dollar appreciates in value to offset the increase in U.S. inflation.

Next, consider asset markets and the determination of interest rates. As we saw earlier, when one currency is expected to change in value against another currency, there is a difference between the levels of interest rates in two countries. That difference equals the expected rate of change in the value of the currency. If the Canadian dollar is expected to depreciate against the U.S. dollar by 1 percent a year, Canadian interest rates are higher than U.S. interest rates by that same 1 percent a year. They may be even higher still because of risk differentials. That is,

$$\text{Expected interest rate in Canada} = \text{Interest rate in United States} - \text{Percentage appreciation of Canadian dollar} + \text{Risk differential}.$$

If interest rates rise in the United States and the Bank of Canada wants to protect Canadians from higher interest rates, it must take steps that produce the expected appreciation of the Canadian dollar.

How does the Bank of Canada achieve financial insulation with a flexible exchange rate? It does so by ensuring that Canadian monetary policy is geared towards Canadian objectives and does not respond to changes in U.S. monetary policy. Suppose, for example, that the same events that we analysed earlier in the case of fixed exchange rates occur. The Federal Reserve System increases the growth rate of the money supply in the United States by 5 percentage points (for example, from 3 to 8 percent a year). Inflation increases by 5 percentage points a year in the United States, and U.S. interest rates also increase by 5 percentage points. At the same time, the Bank of Canada makes no changes in its monetary policy; it holds Canada's money supply growth rate steady at its previous level. With no increase in the growth rate of the Canadian money supply, there can be no increase in the Canadian inflation rate. Prices in Canada continue to inflate at the same pace as before, and interest rates remain constant. But with higher inflation in the United States than in Canada, the Canadian dollar appreciates. It appreciates by the difference between the two inflation rates. Also, with an inflation rate differential that is plain for everyone to see, people expect the appreciation of the Canadian dollar to continue. As a consequence, the gap between interest rates in the United States and in Canada equals the expected rate of appreciation of the Canadian dollar.

Flexible Exchange Rates in Practice There is an enormous amount of evidence from the operation of flexible exchange rates that they do indeed provide financial independence. Countries such as Japan, West Germany, and Switzerland have persistently, year in and year out, achieved lower inflation rates and lower interest rates than any other countries. They have done so by keeping the growth rate of the money supply in their own economies close to the growth rate of real GDP. As a consequence, they have achieved low inflation. Their currencies have appreciated against other currencies and the expectation of continuing appreciation has kept their interest rates below those in other countries. In contrast, there are countries that have created money at a rapid pace — at an annual rate far in excess of the growth rate of real GDP. Examples are the United Kingdom, the Netherlands, Italy, and, to a degree, Canada. In these countries, a rapid rate of money supply growth has brought a higher-than-average inflation rate and currency depreciation. The expectation of continuing depreciation has resulted in interest rates that are higher than those in other countries.

A Paradox? From time to time, many people complain that the Bank of Canada pursues too tight a monetary policy, thereby forcing Canadian interest rates too high. These critics say that if the Bank permitted the money supply to grow at a faster pace, it could bring interest rates down. You have now learned that this conclusion is incorrect. If the Bank of Canada increased the Canadian money supply, it could indeed bring about a temporary decrease in interest rates. But if the Bank persistently increased the Canadian money supply at a more rapid pace, once this monetary policy became correctly anticipated, interest rates in Canada would rise and the foreign exchange value of the Canadian dollar would fall. Slack monetary policy would have brought higher interest rates, not lower interest rates. To achieve low interest rates, the Bank of Canada would have to slow down the growth rate of the Canadian money supply and maintain a lower average growth rate over several years. The consequence of this action would be lower inflation in Canada, an appreciating Canadian dollar, and lower interest rates in Canada than those in other countries.

Is this a paradox? Not really. A once-and-for-all (and unexpected) increase in the money supply brings a temporary decrease in interest rates. An ongoing and anticipated increase in the money supply brings higher interest rates, higher inflation, and a depreciating currency.

■ You've now discovered what determines the foreign exchange value of a country's currency. That value is determined by the demand for and supply of assets denominated in that currency and is strongly influenced by monetary policy actions. A rapid increase in the supply of assets denominated in that currency will result in a decline in its value relative to other currencies.

You've also learned how international arbitrage links prices and interest rates together in different countries. International arbitrage does not occur in markets for nontraded goods, so there are variations in real exchange rates. But arbitrage operates in markets for traded goods, and it is especially powerful in markets for assets. Arbitrage in asset markets keeps interest rates equal around the world. Differences in national interest rates reflect the expectations of changes in exchange rates. Once these differences in exchange rates are taken into account, interest rates are equal across countries.

You've also discovered that fixed exchange rates lock inflation and interest rates across countries in step with each other and that flexible exchange rates, in contrast, bring the possibility of an independent monetary policy and insulation from monetary shocks stemming from the rest of the world.

In the following chapters, we're going to look at some broader macroeconomic issues. In particular, we're going to see how monetary and fiscal policy actions lead to fluctuations in aggregate demand and how these fluctuations, in turn, lead to changes in inflation and unemployment and create booms and recessions.

SUMMARY

Foreign Exchange

Foreign currency is obtained in exchange for domestic currency in the foreign exchange market. The foreign exchange market operates 24 hours a day around the world. Central banks often intervene in foreign exchange markets. There are three types of foreign exchange rate regimes: fixed, flexible, and managed. When the exchange rate is fixed, the government declares a value for the currency in terms of some other currency and the central bank takes actions to ensure that that value of the exchange rate is maintained. To fix the value of the Canadian-dollar exchange rate, the Bank of Canada has to stand ready to supply Canadian-dollar assets and take in foreign currency assets or to remove Canadian-dollar assets from circulation in exchange for foreign currency assets. The country's foreign currency reserves fluctuate to maintain the fixed exchange rate.

A flexible exchange rate is one in which the central bank takes no actions to influence the value of its currency in the foreign exchange market. The country's foreign reserves remain constant and fluctuations in the demand for and supply of assets denominated in the domestic currency lead to fluctuations in the exchange rate.

A managed exchange rate is one in which the central bank takes actions to smooth fluctuations that would otherwise arise but does so less strongly than under a fixed exchange rate regime. (pp. 775-778)

Exchange Rate Determination

In a flexible or managed exchange rate regime, the exchange rate is determined by the demand for and supply of dollar assets. The demand for Canadian-dollar assets depends on the volume of Canadian-dollar trade financed, the price level in Canada and in other countries, the interest rates on Canadian-dollar assets, the interest rates on foreign currency assets, and expected changes in the foreign exchange value of the Canadian dollar.

The supply of Canadian-dollar assets depends on the exchange rate regime. Under fixed exchange rates, the supply curve is horizontal; under flexible exchange rates, the supply curve is vertical; under managed exchange rates, the supply curve is upward sloping. The position of the supply curve depends on the government's budget and the Bank of Canada's monetary policy. The larger the budget deficit and the more rapidly the Bank of Canada permits the money supply to grow, the further to the right is the supply curve. Fluctuations in the exchange rate occur because of fluctuations in the demand for and supply of Canadian-dollar assets; sometimes these fluctuations are large. Large fluctuations arise from changes in demand and supply that are interdependent. A shift in the supply curve often produces an induced change in the demand curve that reinforces the effect on the exchange rate. (pp. 779-785)

Arbitrage, Prices, and Interest Rates

Arbitrage — buying low and selling high — keeps the prices of goods and services that are traded internationally close to equality across all countries. Arbitrage also keeps interest rates in line with each other.

Some goods are not traded internationally — they are nontraded goods. International arbitrage does not bring the prices of such goods into equality. For this reason, there are fluctuations in a country's real exchange rate — the purchasing power of the dollar at home compared with its purchasing power abroad.

Interest rates around the world look unequal, but the appearance arises from the fact that loans are contracted in different currencies in different countries. To compare interest rates across countries, we have to take into account changes in the values of currencies. Countries whose currencies are appreciating have low interest rates; countries whose currencies are depreciating have high interest rates. If the rate of currency depreciation is taken into account, interest rates are equal for loans of equal risk. (pp. 785-792)

Monetary Independence

With a fixed exchange rate, a country is unable to use monetary policy to control its inflation rate and interest rates. A change in inflation in the rest of the world, other things being equal, changes inflation in the domestic economy. It also changes interest rates.

With a flexible exchange rate, a country can insulate itself from inflation and interest rate shocks coming from the rest of the world. If, in the face of a higher inflation rate in the rest of the world, domestic monetary policy is held steady, the domestic inflation rate stays constant. The currency appreciates and interest rates in the domestic economy stay below those in the rest of the world.

To achieve lower inflation and lower interest rates than those of other countries, the Bank of Canada must maintain an average growth rate of the Canadian money supply lower than the money supply growth rates that prevail in other countries. (pp. 792-795)

KEY ELEMENTS

Key terms

Arbitrage, 758
Canadian dollar index against the G-10 currencies, 776
Currency appreciation, 776
Currency depreciation, 776
European Monetary System, 793
Flow theory of the exchange rate, 779
Foreign exchange market, 775
Foreign exchange rate, 775
Forward contract, 791
Forward exchange rate, 791
Interest rate parity, 787
International Monetary Fund, 776
Law of one price, 785
Monetary theory of the exchange rate, 779
Nontraded good, 787
Portfolio balance theory of the exchange rate, 779
Purchasing power parity, 786
Real exchange rate, 786

Key Figures and Tables 

REVIEW QUESTIONS

1 Distinguish among the three exchange rate regimes: fixed, flexible, and managed.

2 Review the main influences on the quantity of dollar assets that people demand.

3 Review the influences on the supply of dollar assets.

4 How does the supply curve of dollar assets differ under the three exchange rate regimes?

5 Why does the foreign exchange value of the Canadian dollar fluctuate so much?

6 What is arbitrage?

7 How does arbitrage lead to purchasing power parity?

8 Why do real exchange rates fluctuate?

9 What is interest rate parity?

10 How does interest rate parity come about?

11 Why do fixed exchange rates limit independent monetary policy?

12 How do flexible exchange rates insulate an economy from changes in inflation in the rest of the world?

PROBLEMS

1 The interest rate on bank loans in Pioneerland is 11 percent a year. The interest rate on bonds in Ecoland is 4 percent a year. The currency of Pioneerland is the choo and the currency of Ecoland is the turky. In the foreign exchange market, turkies can be bought for choos at a rate of 8 choos per turky. In the forward market, turkies can be bought for delivery in one year at a rate of 9 choos per turky.

   a) How much would you gain or lose if you borrowed 1 million choos and invested the proceeds of the loan in Ecoland bonds, covering your transaction in the forward market?

   b) In which direction will the choo-turky exchange rate and the interest rates in Pioneerland and Ecoland be moving?

2 All the goods and services that are bought and sold in Pioneerland are also bought and sold in Ecoland and there are no nontraded goods. There are no tariffs or other impediments to trade between the two economies. Prices are rising in Pioneerland at 7 percent a year. Given the information presented in problem 1 about interest rates and foreign exchange rates, what is the inflation rate in Ecoland?

3 Do Ecoland and Pioneerland have a fixed exchange rate or a flexible exchange rate? Explain why.

4 Suppose that the exchange rate between the turky and the choo is fixed and that Ecoland does not change its monetary policy but Pioneerland does. What happens to inflation rates and to interest rates in the two economies?

PART 11

Macroeconomic Problems

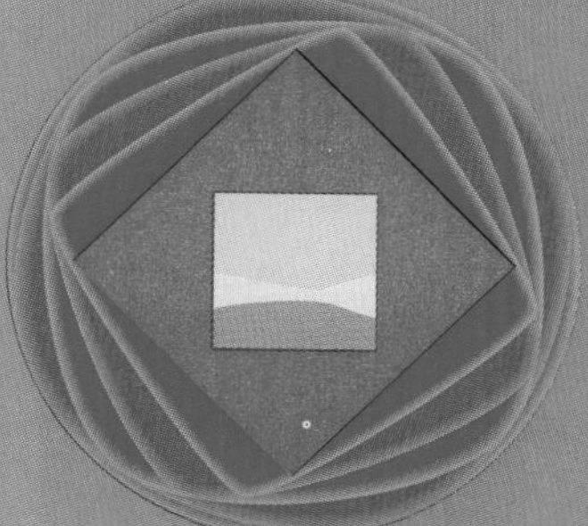

TALKING WITH
ROBERT E. LUCAS, JR.

Robert E. Lucas, Jr. is closely associated with the development of rational expectations macroeconomics. A professor of economics at the Universiy of Chicago, Lucas first applied his ideas about rational expectations to the Phillips curve. Michael Parkin spoke with Professor Lucas about rational expectations macroeconomics, his views on other approaches to economics, and his views of economic policy.

"People aren't reacting to every monetary contraction as if it's the first time."

You applied the idea of rational expectations to macroecomics and to expectations about inflation. How has that hypothesis changed the way we think about things?

It ties down a loose end that shouldn't have been there. Any important economic decision depends upon what you think about the future. Rational expectations is just a way of dealing with that.

What do you see as the chief criticisms of rational expectations hypothesis?

Here's the genuine difficulty people have with the idea. You would never discover the idea of rational expectations by introspection. Rational expectations describes something that has to be true of the outcome of a much more complicated underlying process. But it doesn't describe the actual thought process people use in trying to figure out the future. Our behaviour is adaptive. We try some mode of behaviour. If it's successful, we do it again. If not, we try something else. Rational expectations describes the situation when you've got it right.

Can you give an example?

In economics we're mostly concerned about repetitive events and decisions of some consequence. Our capitalist economy has been operating under pretty much the same laws for 200 years now. People aren't reacting to every monetary contraction as if it's the first time it ever happened. It's just inconceivable. I think people have developed certain ways of living with regular events as best they can.

What do you now think of the first rational expectations model that you proposed?

Rational expectations can be used in combination with a wealth of other assumptions to produce all kinds of different models. The particular models of business cycles that Tom Sargent and I, among others, advanced in the 1970s have run into hard times. In my case, I put a lot of emphasis on people having inadequate information about the quantity of money, and I think a lot of economists now feel that that's just too thin a reed to hang a theory of business cycles on. That it's just not that hard to get accurate information on the quantity of money, which, in the United States, is published every Friday. That's a criticism of a very specific model.

One of the most significant contributions of the 1980s has been real business cycle theory. How do you evaluate this approach?

Real business cycle theory asks what the time path of the economy's GNP or employment would be under the best possible macroeconomic policy. The early authors of this approach asked themselves what fraction of actual variation in GNP you could account for if you restrict yourself to the fluctuations in the rate of technological change. Their answer was, all of it. There's nothing left over for traditional macroeconomic theory to acount for. I don't think that can be right.

Why can't that be right?

Because you can't account for something like the events of 1929 to 1933 when real output fell by a quarter in four years, as if it resulted from the changes in the rate at which technology was decaying. The Depression didn't occur because production techniques got worse. Real business cycle theory suggests that real forces are much more important than we had thought and that the questions addressed by traditional macroeconomics are not as important as we once thought. That's the message.

How can we introduce monetary forces into a macroeconomic model that at the same time pays serious attention to real forces, one that shows fluctuations in price as well as in output?

I think that's a central unsolved problem that my 1972 paper on rational expectations, which we discussed earlier, addressed, only there I used deficiencies in people's information.

There's also the approach that looks at fixed wage contracts, work done by John Taylor or Stanley Fischer. I'm much more sympathetic to that line of thought than I was 10 years ago. Why is it that people commit themselves to agreements to buy and sell at fixed nominal prices in a world where the value of a dollar is fluctuating all the time? Why would you tie your future decisions to some unit when you have no way of knowing what that unit is going to mean later on? That's a great question. No one yet knows the answer to it.

Some economists suggest that even at the level of pricing goods, not just labour and contracts, we should think of a rigidity that arises from "menu costs." The idea that you've got to publish your prices, to label the shelves, jars, and bottles. And this is costly, so you won't change the price every minute. What do you think of this approach?

I think there's some truth to it. But it's criticized; It seems like a slim reed. People ask, do you mean to tell me that the Great Depression occurred because it was too much of a bother for supermarket clerks to put new price tags on the goods on their shelves? There's no question that there's something to this approach, but there's a question of how important it is. I think the details of individual price setting are very poorly understood. So when people adopt an assumption like rigid prices, I don't think we can afford to look down our noses at them.

You were a student of Milton Friedman, the architect of the movement called monetarism. How do you distinguish this approach from the kind of macroeconomics that you are responsible for creating?

I'm not that big on the distinction. I'm a monetarist. But the term does refer to several things. One aspect of what people call monetarism is just emphasis on the quantity of some monetary

"We can't afford to look down our noses at people who assume rigid prices."

"We don't want to manage the U.S. economy. And don't think anybody should take the job either."

aggregate as a determinant of prices and of economic activity. In some ways, I think that the revolution has been so successful that it doesn't seem like a revolution any more. In this day and age, no one talks about the price level, exchange rates, or interest rates without talking about the quantity of money. In that sense, we're all monetarists. The second aspect of monetarism is a hostility toward government's continual management of the economy. The role of government, in a monetarist perspective, is to make its own behaviour on fiscal or monetary policy simple and predictable and then just to let the system operate without fine-tuning. That view, I think, is absolutely right.

In recent years, we've experienced the biggest peacetime government budget deficit ever. How have you viewed the deficit over the years?

That's an embarrassing question for me because the deficit is not having the immediate unpleasant consequences I had predicted. My handle on the deficit is this. If you think of an economy in some kind of smooth, steady state, running a deficit year in and year out, what has to make up that deficit are changes in the monetary base. So I see large deficits that occur regularly as equivalent to a large rate of growth in the monetary base, which means inflation. I don't like deficits because they signal inflation. There's not a tight year to year connection, because you can issue bonds to cover the deficit, which are a promise either to raise taxes later or to print money later. But sooner or later it's the monetary base that fills the gap between government spending and tax revenues.

At the start of the Reagan administration, Tom Sargent and I wrote newspaper articles saying that the deficit would be inflationary. Well, that just hasn't happened. I'm in the process of re-thinking about deficits. I'm sympathetic to people like Larry Kotlikoff, who suspect that the deficit might be an illusion as a result of inadequate accounting. That it just doesn't measure anything since things like future social security liabilities are arbitrarily excluded or included.

What is the context of your well-known debate with James Tobin?

Tobin views the role of macroeconomics to be to provide principles for guiding monetary and fiscal policy in order to keep the economy near what he thinks of as full employment. And he thinks if this isn't done, we'll have the Depression again. People like Sargent or Friedman or myself basically come and poke holes, saying "Look, these principles you have for managing the economy are useless." Our opponents in this debate tried to discredit us as economic managers, asking, "Would you trust the management of the U.S. economy to Lucas?" We're not asking them to. We don't want the job, and we don't think anybody else should take it either.

CHAPTER 30

Aggregate Demand Management

After studying this chapter, you will be able to:

- Explain the interest rate transmission channel of monetary policy.
- Describe the other transmission channels of monetary policy—real balance effect, wealth effect, and exchange rate.
- Describe the time lags in the operation of monetary policy.
- Define and explain crowding out.
- Explain why crowding out weakens the effects of fiscal policy actions on aggregate demand.
- Explain the effects of fiscal policy on the exchange rate and net exports.
- Describe the time lags in the operation of fiscal policy.
- Describe the Keynesian-monetarist controversy about aggregate demand.
- Explain how the Keynesian-monetarist controversy about aggregate demand was settled.

Sparks Fly in Ottawa

EACH YEAR THE Federal Parliament and the provincial legislatures approve budgets that determine the level of government expenditure on goods and services. In 1989, that total exceeded $130 billion — about one-fifth of gross domestic product (GDP). These same legislative assemblies also determine the scale of social programs and the transfer payments associated with them as well as the rules governing the taxes that we all have to pay. In 1989, transfer payments were a further $130 billion and taxes approached $260 billion — two-fifths of GDP. Government expenditure, taxes, and transfer payments are the levers of fiscal policy. How do these levers of fiscal policy influence the economy? In particular, how do they affect aggregate demand? How do they affect other variables that influence aggregate demand, such as interest rates and the exchange rate? ■ Not far from Parliament Hill, on Sparks Street, is the home of the Bank of Canada. Here the Bank pulls the nation's monetary policy levers. At times, such as in 1981 and 1990, the Bank has used those levers to slow down the economy — increasing interest rates, slowing money growth, and slowing the growth of aggregate demand. At other times, such as in the mid-1980s, the Bank has used its monetary policy levers to speed up the economy — lowering interest rates, speeding up money growth, and increasing aggregate demand. We've seen how the Bank of Canada's policy levers influence interest rates and the exchange rate. But how do the effects of the Bank's actions ripple from interest rates and the exchange rate to the rest of the economy? How do they affect aggregate demand? ■ Standing between Parliament and the Bank of Canada is the Department of Finance, headed by the minister of finance. Under our system of government, the cabinet is ultimately responsible for all fiscal and monetary policy and the minister of finance is a key player in the cabinet's deliberations on these policies. There are times when the monetary policies being pursued by the Bank of Canada and the fiscal policies- set by the government and by Parliament are in harmony with each other. There are other times when they come into conflict — creating sparks on Sparks Street! Conflicts are at their worst when the government is running a large deficit (as it has been doing for the past decade or more) and the Bank of Canada is seeking to prevent inflationary pressures from arising, pushing interest rates high, as it did in 1990. ■ Since both the fiscal actions of Parliament and the monetary actions of the Bank of Canada can increase or decrease aggregate demand, are these two methods of changing aggregate demand equivalent? Does it matter whether a recession is avoided by having the Bank loosen its monetary policy or by getting Parliament to implement a tax cut? Do changes in taxes and government expenditure and changes in the money supply have to reinforce each other or can they offset each other? For example, when the Bank of Canada under governor John Crow slowed money growth and increased interest rates in 1990 to keep the lid on inflation, could Parliament have offset the Bank's actions by taking actions of its own — cutting taxes or increasing government expenditure? Alternatively, if Parliament cuts government expenditure, creating fears of recession, could the Bank increase the money supply and keep GDP up, thereby avoiding recession?

■ We are going to answer these important questions in this chapter. You already know that the effects of monetary and fiscal policy are determined by the interaction of aggregate demand and aggregate supply. And you already know quite a lot about these two concepts. But this chapter gives you an even deeper understanding of aggregate demand and the way it is affected by the monetary policy actions of the Bank of Canada and the fiscal policy actions of the federal government. ■ Although this chapter is about policy issues, it is not about the *conduct* of policy. It is a chapter about the *theory* of policy. It's important to get the theoretical foundations straight so that when we do come to study the conduct of policy, in Chapters 34 and 35, we will have a firm foundation on which to build.[1]

[1]It is possible to study stabilization policy in Chapters 34 and 35 without having previously studied the present chapter. But if you take the time and effort to study this chapter, you will find that you have a deeper understanding of the discussion of policy issues in those later chapters.

Money, Interest, and Aggregate Demand

Before embarking on our study of the influence of monetary and fiscal policy on aggregate demand, we need to remind ourselves of the place occupied by aggregate demand in our broader macroeconomic model.

Aggregate Demand and Aggregate Supply

Our focus in this chapter is on the effects of monetary and fiscal policy actions on the level of *aggregate demand.* Of course, our ultimate concern is not aggregate demand but real GDP, inflation, and unemployment. We want to know how policy affects these variables. As you know, real GDP and the price level are determined by the interaction of *aggregate demand* and *aggregate supply.* We've seen how these forces work in Chapter 24. By focussing on the aggregate demand side of the economy, we are not denying the importance of the aggregate supply side of the economy. We are simply isolating the demand side so that we can study it in greater detail.

Because we are studying aggregate demand, we ignore changes in the price level. Instead, we study the influences on the entire aggregate demand curve. In other words, we study how monetary and fiscal policy affect the position of the aggregate demand curve. In effect, we freeze the price level and ask questions about the directions and magnitudes of the shifts in the aggregate demand curve at a given price level. This approach does not mean we are assuming that the price level is actually constant. On the contrary, it is determined in exactly the manner analysed in Chapter 24. Each point on the aggregate demand curve represents an expenditure equilibrium — a point of intersection of the aggregate expenditure curve and the 45° line — with the aggregate expenditure curve reflecting spending plans at a given price level, (see Fig. 26.8). Because of this connection between aggregate demand and aggregate expenditure we can study the influences on aggregate demand in greater detail by using the aggregate expenditure model. That's what we do here.

Spending Decisions, Interest, and Money

We discovered in Chapter 26 that equilibrium expenditure depends on the level of autonomous expenditure. We also discovered that one of the components of autonomous expenditure — investment — varies

Figure 30.1 The Equilibrium Interest Rate and Real GDP

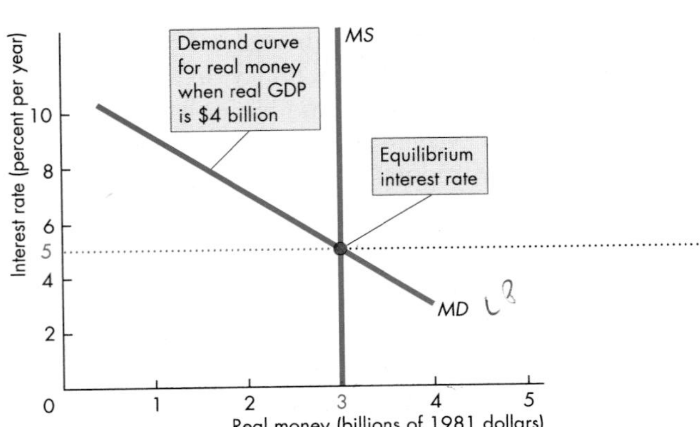

(a) Money and interest rate

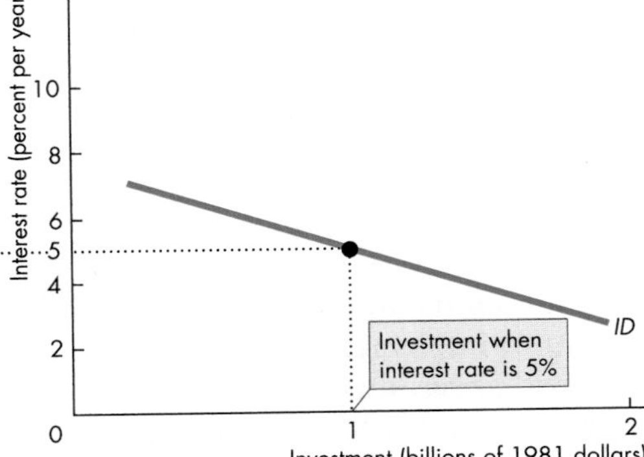

(b) Investment and interest rate

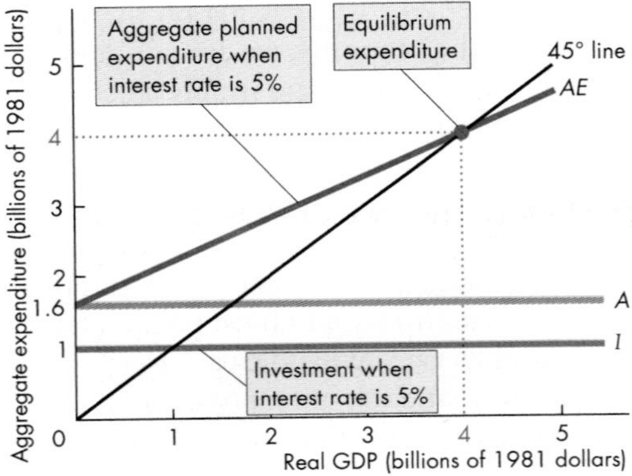

(c) Expenditure and real GDP

Equilibrium in the money market (part a) determines the interest rate. The money supply curve is *MS*. The demand curve for real money is *MD*. The position of the demand curve for real money is determined by real GDP. The demand curve for real money is *MD* when real GDP is $4 billion. The investment demand curve, (*ID*) in part (b) determines investment at the equilibrium interest rate determined in the money market. Investment is part of autonomous expenditure and its level determines the position of the aggregate expenditure curve (*AE*) shown in part (c). Where the aggregate expenditure curve intersects the 45° line, equilibrium expenditure and real GDP are determined. An equilibrium occurs when real GDP and the interest rate are such that the quantity of real money demanded equals the quantity of real money supplied and aggregate planned expenditure equals real GDP.

with the interest rate. The higher the interest rate, other things held constant, the lower is investment and hence the lower is autonomous expenditure and equilibrium expenditure. In Chapter 28, we saw that the interest rate is determined by equilibrium in the money market. By increasing the quantity of money, the Bank can lower interest rates.

We're now going to bring these two sets of results together and see how the Bank's actions influence aggregate demand.

The Interest Rate Transmission Channel

To study the interest rate transmission channel of monetary policy, let's see how we can link the money market, where the interest rate is determined, and the market for goods and services, where equilibrium expenditure is determined. First we'll study the economy at a given point in time and see how equilibrium expenditure and interest rates are determined. Then we'll disturb that equilibrium by changing the money supply and work out the consequences of the change.

Equilibrium Expenditure and the Interest Rate The determination of equilibrium expenditure and the interest rate is illustrated in Fig. 30.1. The figure has three parts: part (a) illustrates the money market;

part (b) shows investment demand; and part (c) shows aggregate planned expenditure and the determination of equilibrium expenditure. Let's begin by looking at part (a).

The curve labelled *MD* is the demand curve for real money. The position of that demand curve depends on the level of real GDP. For a given level of real GDP, there is a given demand curve for real money. Suppose that the demand curve shown in the figure is the one that describes the demand for real money when real GDP is $4 billion. If real GDP is more than $4 billion, the demand curve for real money is to the right of the one shown; if real GDP is less than $4 billion, the demand curve for real money is to the left of the one shown.

The curve labelled *MS* is the supply curve of real money. Its position is determined by the monetary policy actions of the Bank of Canada, the behaviour of the banking system, and the price level. At a given point in time, all these influences determine a quantity of money supplied that is independent of the interest rate. Hence the supply curve for real money is vertical.

The equilibrium interest rate is determined at the point of intersection of the demand and supply curves for real money. In the economy illustrated in Fig. 30.1, that interest rate is 5 percent.

Next, let's look at Fig. 30.1(b) where investment is determined. The investment demand curve is *ID*. The position of the investment demand curve is determined by profit expectations and, as those expectations change, the investment demand curve shifts accordingly. For given expectations, there is a given investment demand curve. This curve tells us the level of planned investment at each interest rate. But we already know the interest rate from equilibrium in the money market. When the investment demand curve is *ID* and the interest rate is 5 percent, the level of planned investment is $1 billion.

Fig. 30.1(c) shows the determination of equilibrium expenditure. (Notice that this diagram is similar to Fig. 26.4.) The aggregate expenditure curve (*AE*) shows the aggregate planned expenditure at each level of real GDP. Aggregate planned expenditure is made up of autonomous expenditure and induced expenditure. Investment is part of autonomous expenditure. In this example, total autonomous expenditure is $1.6 billion. That is, investment is $1 billion and the other components of autonomous expenditure are $0.6 billion. These amounts of investment and autonomous expenditure are shown by the horizontal lines in part (c). Investment is *I* and total autonomous expenditure is *A*. Induced expenditure in this example (the induced part of consumption expenditure minus imports) equals 0.6 multiplied by real GDP. In other words, the marginal propensity to spend on real GDP is 0.6.

Equilibrium expenditure is determined at the point of intersection of the *AE* curve and the 45° line. Equilibrium occurs when aggregate planned expenditure and real GDP are each $4 billion. That is, the level of aggregate demand is $4 billion.

The Money Market Again Recall that the demand curve *MD*, in Fig. 30.1(a), is the demand curve for real money when real GDP is $4 billion. We've just determined in Fig. 30.1(c) that at the expenditure equilibrium, real GDP is also $4 billion. What happens if the level of real GDP that we discover in part (c) differs from the value that we assumed when drawing the demand curve for real money in part (a)? Let's perform an experiment to answer this question.

Suppose, when drawing the demand curve for real money, we assumed that real GDP was $3 billion. In this case, the demand curve for real money would be to the left of the *MD* curve in part (a). The interest rate would be less than 5 percent. With an interest rate of less than 5 percent, investment would not be $1 billion as determined in part (b), but a larger amount. If investment were more than $1 billion, autonomous expenditure would be larger and the *AE* curve would be higher than the one shown in part (c). But if the aggregate expenditure curve were higher than *AE*, equilibrium expenditure and real GDP would be larger than $4 billion. Thus if we started with the demand curve for real money for a level of real GDP of less than $4 billion, expenditure equilibrium would occur at a level of real GDP of more than $4 billion. There is an inconsistency. The real GDP assumed in drawing the demand curve for real money was too low.

Next, let's reverse the experiment. Assume a level of real GDP of $5 billion. In this case, the demand curve for real money would be to the right of the *MD* curve in Fig. 30(a). The interest rate would be more than 5 percent. With an interest rate of more than 5 percent, investment would be less than $1 billion and the *AE* curve would be lower than the one shown in Fig. 30.1(c). In this case, expenditure equilibrium would occur at a level of real GDP that was less than $4 billion. Again, there is an inconsistency. If we assumed a level of real GDP of more than $4 billion to determine the position of the demand

Figure 30.2 The Effect of a Change in the Money Supply

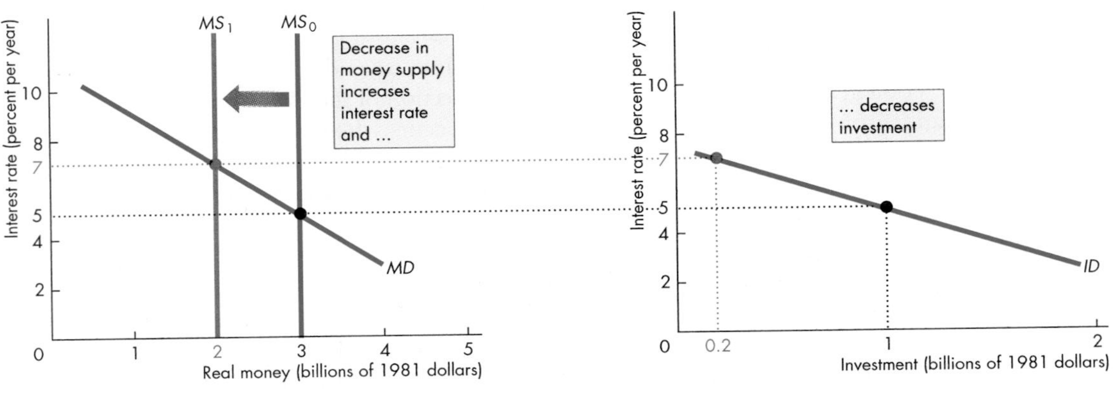

(a) Change in money supply

(b) Change in investment

A decrease in the money supply shifts the supply curve of real money from MS_0 to MS_1 (part a). Equilibrium in the money market is achieved by an increase in the interest rate from 5 percent to 7 percent. At the higher interest rate, investment decreases (part b).

curve for real money, expenditure equilibrium would occur at a level of real GDP that was less than $4 billion.

Only if we use a real GDP of $4 billion to determine the position of the demand curve for real money do we get a result that is consistent in the three parts of this figure. If the demand curve for real money is based on a real GDP of $4 billion, the interest rate determined (5 percent) delivers investment of $1 billion that, in turn, generates an expenditure equilibrium at the same level of real GDP that determines the position of the demand curve for real money. The situation described in Fig. 30.1 is one of stock and flow equilibrium. There is stock equilibrium in the money market and flow equilibrium in the market for goods and services.

The Effects of a Change in the Money Supply Suppose that the economy is in the situation illustrated in Fig. 30.1. The interest rate is 5 percent, investment is $1 billion, and real GDP is $4 billion. Also suppose that the Bank of Canada is concerned that the economy is overheating and that inflation is about to take off. To dampen the economy, the Bank decides to attempt to reduce aggregate demand by conducting an open market operation. It sells government securities, thereby decreasing reserves in the banking system and cutting the money supply.

Suppose that the Bank of Canada cuts the real money supply by $1 billion, from $3 billion to $2 billion. The real money supply curve shifts to the left from MS_0 to MS_1 in Fig. 30.2(a). The immediate effect of this action in the money market is an increase in the interest rate from 5 percent to 7 percent. The higher interest rate leads to a fall in investment, from $1 billion to $0.2 billion, as shown in Fig. 30.2(b).

The fall in investment lowers autonomous expenditure and so lowers aggregate planned expenditure. The fall in aggregate planned expenditure lowers the expenditure equilibrium and decreases real GDP, and the fall in real GDP decreases the demand for real money. The decrease in the demand for real money, in turn, has further effects on the interest rate. To keep track of all these simultaneous events, it's a good idea to break up the process and study it in two parts. That's what we'll do. First, we'll see what happens to equilibrium expenditure and real GDP if the interest rate stays at its new higher level of 7 percent. Then we'll study the adjustment process that follows as the interest rate and real GDP respond to the decreased money supply.

Equilibrium Expenditure at a Constant Interest Rate Recall that in Fig. 30.2(a) the real money supply decreased from $3 billion to $2 billion, and the real money supply curve shifted to the left from MS_0 to MS_1. The interest rate increased to 7 percent. The higher interest rate lowered investment from $1 billion to $0.2 billion, as shown in Fig. 30.2(b). Let's work out what happens to equilibrium expenditure and real GDP if the interest rate remains at its new higher level of 7 percent. With the interest rate at 7 percent, investment falls to $0.2 billion, autonomous expenditure falls by the same amount as the fall in investment, and so does aggregate planned expenditure. Figure 30.3 shows the downward shift of the aggregate expenditure curve from AE_0 to AE_1. That is, the *AE* curve shifts downward by $0.8 billion, the amount of the decrease in investment. When the aggregate expenditure curve is AE_1, equilibrium expenditure and real GDP are $2 billion.

The economy does not immediately jump from an equilibrium real GDP of $4 billion to one of $2 billion. Equilibrium real GDP has changed from $4 billion to $2 billion, so the economy *begins* to move in the direction of the new equilibrium. But that process takes time. During the adjustment process other

Figure 30.3 The Effect of a Change in the Money Supply on Equilibrium Real GDP

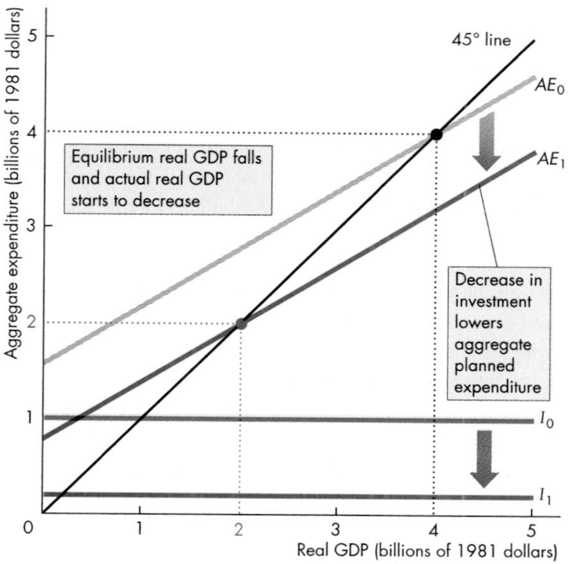

A decrease in the money supply increases the interest rate, lowers investment, and results in a fall in aggregate planned expenditure. The *AE* curve shifts downward from AE_0 to AE_1. Equilibrium real GDP falls from $4 billion to $2 billion. Actual real GDP starts to decrease.

changes take place that affect equilibrium real GDP so that the economy never actually gets to the point shown in Fig. 30.3. Let's now look at those other forces and see what course the economy actually takes.

The Adjustment Process

When investment decreases, the resulting decrease in aggregate planned expenditure sets up a multiplier process that gradually lowers the level of actual expenditure and real GDP. We described this process in Chapter 26.

When aggregate planned expenditure decreases, it falls below real GDP. But actual expenditure equals real GDP. There is, therefore, a gap between actual expenditure and planned expenditure — a gap filled by unplanned expenditure. The unplanned expenditure is an increase in inventories. An increase in inventories is part of investment. Thus, although planned investment decreases, as shown in Fig. 30.2(b), actual investment does not initially decrease by as much because of the unplanned increase in inventories.

With an unplanned increase in inventories, firms are anxious to restore inventories to their desired levels. To achieve this objective, firms cut back their production. As they do so, real GDP begins to fall.

So far, we've worked out two effects of a monetary policy action that increases interest rates. The first of these effects is a decrease in *equilibrium* expenditure and real GDP. We illustrated this effect in Fig. 30.3. The second effect, the one we have just described, is an unplanned increase in inventories that initiates a process of falling *actual* aggregate expenditure and real GDP. To understand what happens next, it is important to be clear about the distinction between actual real GDP and equilibrium real GDP. Actual real GDP is determined by actual expenditure — the sum of planned and unplanned expenditure. Equilibrium real GDP is determined by planned expenditure alone — by the *AE* curve. As the economy continues to adjust to a decrease in the money supply, actual real GDP continues to fall but equilibrium real GDP increases. The falling actual real GDP and rising equilibrium real GDP converge at a new equilibrium, which we're about to discover.

The fall in actual real GDP decreases the demand for real money. As a consequence, the demand curve for real money shifts to the left and the interest rate falls. A lower interest rate increases planned investment and makes the *AE* curve start to shift upward. As the *AE* curve shifts upward, equilibrium expenditure and equilibrium real GDP increase. Let's see how the interest rate changes induced by falling real GDP bring about the new equilibrium.

Induced Interest Rate Changes Suppose the Bank of Canada has decreased the money supply. Interest rates are 7 percent, and planned investment has fallen, but unplanned inventories are accumulating. Equilibrium real GDP has fallen to $2 billion, and actual real GDP, which started out at $4 billion, is falling. Figure 30.4 illustrates where this process ends.

Figure 30.4 The Convergence to a New Expenditure Equilibrium

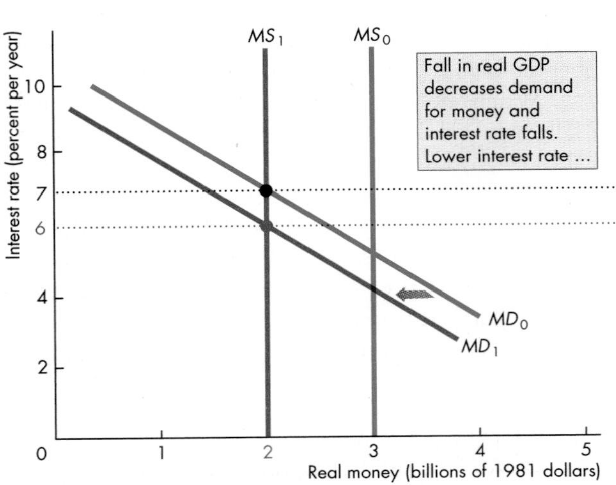

(a) Decrease in demand for money

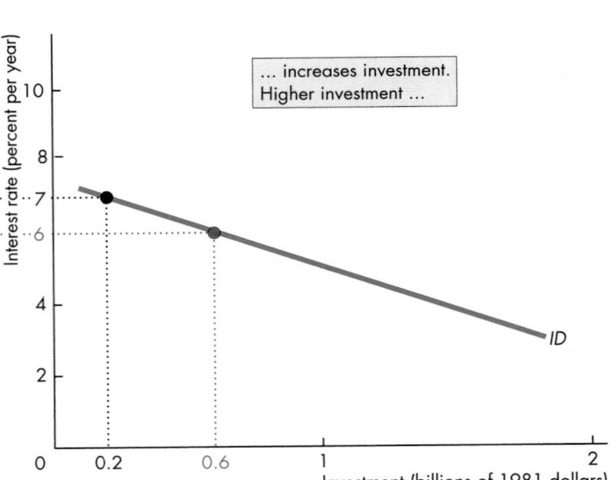

(b) Increase in investment

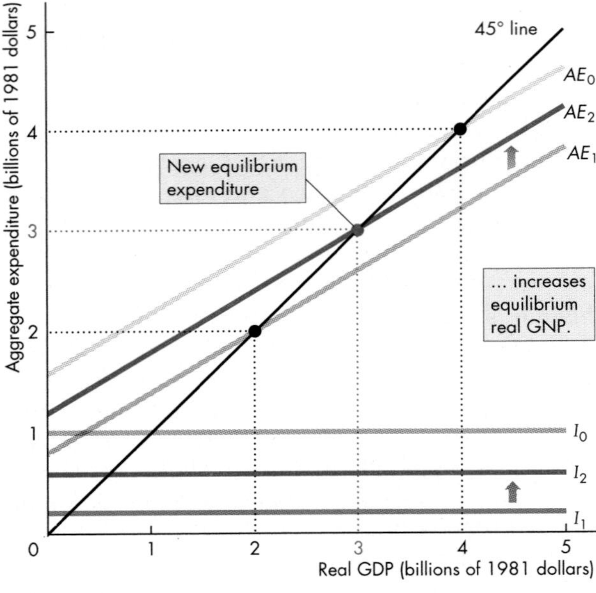

(c) New equilibrium real GDP

As real GDP falls, the demand curve for real money shifts to the left, from MD_0 to MD_1 (part a). The decrease in the demand for real money lowers the interest rate. As the interest rate falls, planned investment increases (part b). The increase in planned investment shifts the *AE* curve upward to AE_2 (part c). During the process of adjustment, actual real GDP falls and aggregate planned expenditure increases. A new expenditure equilibrium occurs when real GDP and aggregate planned expenditure have converged to the same value. In the figure, the new expenditure equilibrium occurs at a real GDP of $3 billion (part c). That level of real GDP makes the demand curve for real money MD_1 (part a), which generates an interest rate of 6 percent. At that interest rate, investment is $0.6 billion (part b), which in turn makes the aggregate expenditure curve AE_2 (part c).

Let's begin with part (a), which shows money market equilibrium.

Actual real GDP begins to fall. Falling real GDP shifts the demand curve for real money to the left of MD_0. Suppose that GDP has fallen to $3 billion and that the demand curve for real money, when real GDP is $3 billion, is MD_1. With this demand curve and the supply curve at MS_1, the equilibrium interest rate is 6 percent.

When the interest rate is 6 percent, investment is $0.6 billion, as shown in Fig. 30.4(b). Thus the fall in the interest rate from 7 percent to 6 percent increases planned investment from $0.2 billion to $0.6 billion.

The increase in planned investment from $0.2 billion to $0.6 billion shifts the *AE* curve upward from AE_1 to AE_2 in Fig. 30.4(c). When the aggregate expenditure curve is AE_2, equilibrium expenditure and equilibrium real GDP are $3 billion. But this level of real GDP is precisely the level that makes the demand curve for real money MD_1. When actual real GDP has fallen to $3 billion, the demand curve for real money has shifted to MD_1 and the interest rate has fallen to 6 percent. Investment has increased to $0.6 billion ($I_2$) and aggregate planned expenditure has increased, so that equilibrium expenditure and equilibrium real GDP are also $3 billion. In this situation, there is a new stock and flow equilibrium. The level of aggregate demand is $3 billion.

You may find it interesting to work out what would be happening in this economy if we had not picked a new equilibrium level of real GDP to start the story described in Fig. 30.4. Let's rerun the economic video and hit the pause button at a different point.

Starting from the initial decrease in the money supply, let's freeze the picture when real GDP has fallen by only $0.5 billion and is at $3.5 billion. The demand curve for real money has not shifted as far to the left as MD_1, and the interest rate has not yet fallen to 6 percent — it lies somewhere between 6 and 7 percent. Planned investment is increasing but has not yet increased to $0.6 billion — it lies somewhere between $0.2 billion and $0.6 billion. The aggregate expenditure curve is shifting upward, but it is below AE_2, lying somewhere between AE_1 and AE_2. Aggregate planned expenditure is less than actual expenditure and real GDP, so real GDP is falling.

But if real GDP is falling, the demand curve for real money is shifting to the left, the interest rate is falling, planned investment is increasing, and the *AE* curve is shifting upward. Equilibrium real GDP is increasing. Inventories are accumulating and actual real GDP is decreasing. Equilibrium real GDP and actual real GDP meet at some point in this process. The point at which they meet is that shown in Fig. 30.4(c).

R E V I E W

To lower aggregate demand, the Bank of Canada undertakes an open market operation. It sells Canadian government securities. This action sets up the following sequence of events:

- The quantity of money decreases and the money supply curve shifts to the left.
- The interest rate increases.
- Planned investment decreases.
- Aggregate planned expenditure decreases.
- Equilibrium expenditure and equilibrium real GDP decrease.
- Unplanned inventories accumulate.
- Actual real GDP begins to fall.
- Falling real GDP shifts the demand curve for real money to the left.
- The shifting demand curve for real money decreases the interest rate.
- The falling interest rate increases planned investment.
- Increasing planned investment increases equilibrium expenditure and equilibrium real GDP.
- Falling actual real GDP and rising equilibrium real GDP converge and meet at a new stock and flow equilibrium.
- In such an equilibrium, the real GDP and the interest rate that make the quantity of real money demanded equal to the quantity supplied also make aggregate planned expenditure equal to real GDP. ■

We've now seen how a change in the money supply sets up a chain of events that results in a change in investment and other components of aggregate expenditure. In the example that we have just worked through, the change in aggregate expenditure and the change in the money supply happen to be equal — a $1 billion change in the money supply produces a $1 billion change in aggregate demand. Such an outcome is not at all inevitable. It arises simply from the numbers used in the model economy that we studied. The actual effect of the money supply on aggregate demand could be much larger or much smaller. What determines the potency of a change in the money supply?

Figure 30.5 The Potency of Monetary Policy

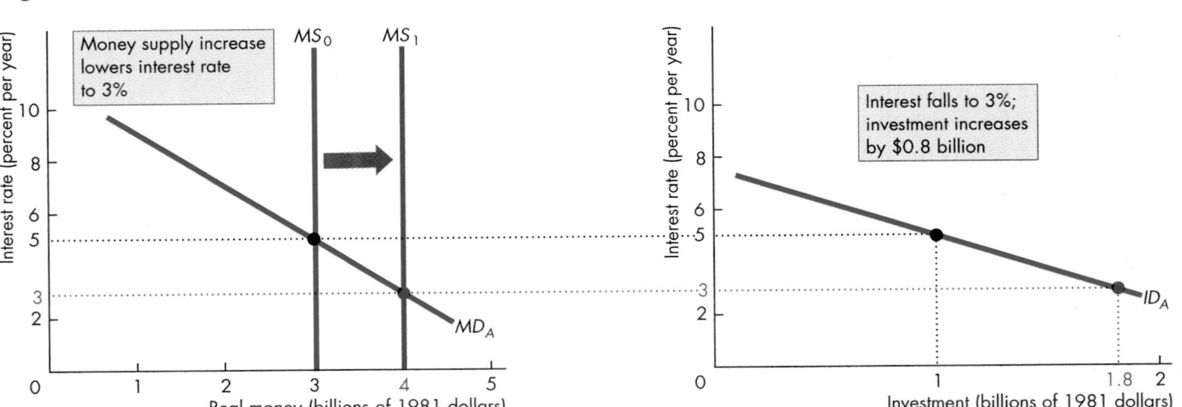

(a) Monetary policy is effective

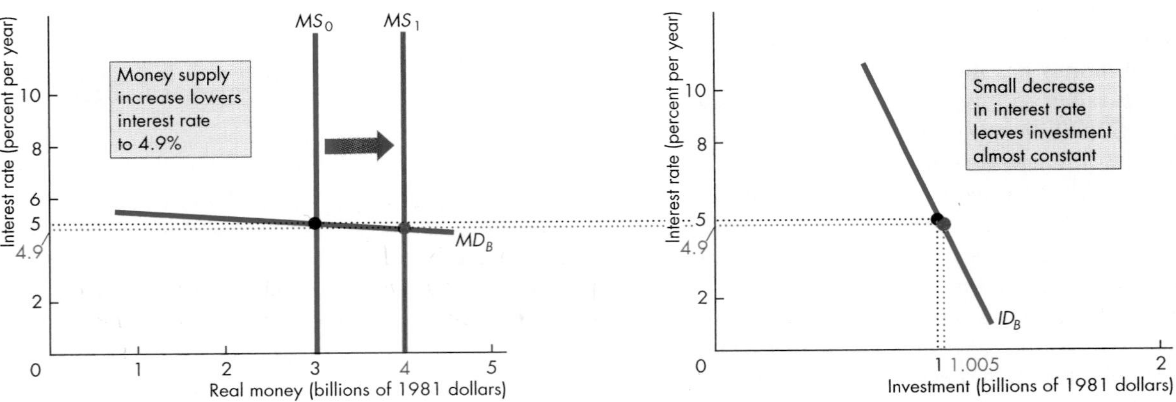

(b) Monetary policy is ineffective

Monetary policy is effective when a change in the money supply changes interest rates and a change in interest rates changes investment, as shown in part (a). Monetary policy is ineffective when a change in the money supply has virtually no effect on interest rates and/or when the change in interest rates has almost no effect on investment, as shown in part (b). The steeper the demand curve for real money and the flatter the investment demand curve, the more powerful is the effect of a change in the money supply on the level of aggregate planned expenditure.

How Potent Is Monetary Policy?

The potency of monetary policy depends on two key factors:

- The sensitivity of the demand for real money to the interest rate
- The sensitivity of investment demand to the interest rate

Let's contrast two cases, one in which a change in the money supply has a large effect on aggregate demand (that is, monetary policy is effective) and another in which it has almost no effect (monetary policy is ineffective). Figure 30.5 illustrates the two cases. First look at part (a). Here the demand curve for real money is MD_A and the investment demand curve is ID_A. Initially, the money supply is MS_0 and the equilibrium interest rate is 5 percent. At that interest rate, investment is $1 billion. An increase in the money supply shifts the supply curve of real money to the right from MS_0 to MS_1. The interest rate falls to 3 percent. The lower interest rate causes a movement along the investment demand curve and investment increases to $1.8 billion. This increase in investment increases equilibrium expenditure and aggregate demand.

Now look at Fig. 30.5(b). The demand curve for real money is MD_B and the investment demand curve is ID_B. The initial situation is the same as before. The supply curve of real money is MS_0, the interest rate is 5 percent, and at that interest rate investment is $1 billion. The money supply increases, shifting the supply curve of real money to the right, exactly as in part (a), to MS_1. But now the interest rate barely changes. It falls to 4.9 percent. This tiny decrease in the interest rate has an even tinier effect on investment — it increases by only $0.005 billion — $5 million. With almost no change in investment, there is almost no change in equilibrium expenditure and aggregate demand.

Why does investment increase by $0.8 billion in part (a) and by almost nothing in part (b)? It is because of the two key factors identified above. First, in part (a), the demand for real money is less sensitive to the interest rate in part (a) than it is in part (b). That is, for a given change in the quantity of real money, the interest rate has to change by more in part (a) than in part (b) to increase the quantity of real money demanded so as to restore money market equilibrium. Second, investment demand is more sensitive to the interest rate in part (a) than it is in part (b). That is, for a given fall in the interest rate, investment increases by more in part (a) than it does in part (b).

The less sensitive the demand for real money to the interest rate and the more sensitive investment demand to the interest rate, the larger is the effect of a change in the quantity of money on equilibrium expenditure and aggregate demand.

What determines how sensitive the demand for real money and investment demand are to changes in interest rates? The answer is the degree of substitutability between money and other financial assets and the sensitivity of the timing of investment decisions to changes in interest rates. Because money performs a unique function that other assets do not perform — it facilitates the exchange of goods and services — other financial assets are an imperfect substitute for money. Because of this, we hold money even though it has an opportunity cost. But the amount that we hold decreases as its opportunity cost — the interest rate — increases. The degree to which a change in the interest rate brings a decrease in the quantity of real money held depends on how close a substitute for money are other assets that do not directly serve as a medium of exchange.

The sensitivity of investment to changes in interest rates depends on how willing people are to vary the timing of their investment. Some investment activities can be easily postponed or brought forward in time at low cost. Others cannot. To the extent that people do not care much about the timing, investment is highly sensitive to changes in interest rates. To the extent that timing is of crucial importance, investment is insensitive to changes in interest rates.

In the two situations illustrated in Fig. 30.5, a change in the money supply has some effect on investment. In Fig. 30.5(b) the effect is tiny but not zero. But there is a special, extreme case in which monetary policy actually has no effect at all on investment. This case occurs when the demand curve for real money is horizontal or the investment demand curve is vertical. With a horizontal demand curve for real money, a change in the quantity of money has no effect on the interest rate. With a vertical investment demand curve, a change in the interest rate has no effect on investment and, therefore, no effect on aggregate expenditure. These cases are extreme and hypothetical, but they do serve to illustrate the key proposition that we have established in this section: the more sensitive the demand for real money to a change in the interest rate and the less sensitive investment demand to a change in the interest rate, the smaller is the effect of a change in the money supply on equilibrium expenditure and, therefore, on aggregate demand.

Time Lags of Monetary Policy

Monetary policy actions do not have an instantaneous effect on aggregate demand. Instead they operate with a time lag. That is, their effects are spread out over time. There are two important time lags:

- An autonomous expenditure lag
- An induced expenditure lag

Let's examine each in turn.

Autonomous Expenditure Lag Stock equilibrium in the market for money and other assets is achieved by continuous movements in interest rates. But the effects of interest rate changes on investment plans take some time to operate. This delay is the autonomous expenditure lag. Most of the investment that is being undertaken at any given moment is the result of decisions that have been made months and sometimes years in the past. For example, when a power company decides to increase its generating capacity, it knows that the decision that it is taking now will result in a stream of investment that runs five to seven years into the future. But not all investment plans have to be made so far in advance. Decisions to buy off-the-shelf items, such as automobiles, consumer durable goods, a wide variety of machine tools, computers, and a host of other equipment, can be implemented within a short period.

The fact that some investment is based on long-past decisions while other investment is based on more recent decisions means that the response of investment to a change in interest rates is spread out over time. For example, if interest rates increase, the purchase of a new automobile or piece of earth-moving equipment can be delayed easily and quickly. The purchase of a new electric power generating station is already under way and cannot be stopped at a reasonable cost. So investment falls, at first by a modest amount. The fall in investment gradually becomes larger, the longer interest rates stay high.

Induced Expenditure Lag A fall in investment induces a fall in consumption expenditure and in equilibrium expenditure. This induced change is the multiplier effect that we studied in Chapter 26. But the multiplier effect takes time to operate, so there is a second time lag. We described the elements of this lag in Chapter 26. Let's briefly recall them here. The chain of events begins with a change in firms' inventories. Only when firms adjust output to restore their inventories to their desired levels does real GDP change. And not until real GDP has changed is there a change in induced expenditure. A change in induced expenditure changes real GDP yet further. Eventually, the multiplier process comes to an end when aggregate planned expenditure is once again equal to real GDP.

The two time lags that we have just considered are those in the response of aggregate *demand* to policy actions. There are two other important lags of monetary policy:

- A price adjustment lag
- A policy formation lag

Let's briefly examine these lags.

Price Adjustment Lag The effect of a change in aggregate demand on real GDP and the price level depends on the short-run aggregate supply curve. If aggregate demand increases, the aggregate demand curve shifts to the right and the price level and real GDP increase. At first, the increase in the price level is small. Later, as higher prices induce an increase in wages, the short-run aggregate supply curve starts to shift upward. Prices then start to increase more quickly and the effects on real GDP of the increase in aggregate demand begin to diminish.

Policy Formation Lag We have described the time lags involved in the response of the economy to actions taken by the Bank of Canada. But the Bank responds to the state of the economy, and there is a lag in that process too. When the Bank sees inflation increasing, its reaction is to tighten the monetary reins, holding back on the growth rate of the money supply and permitting interest rates to nudge upward. When the Bank sees a recession on the horizon, it seeks to stimulate aggregate demand by increasing the money supply and lowering interest rates. But the Bank of Canada cannot reach decisions instantaneously on the basis of the current performance of the economy. The current and recent performance of the economy has to be assessed carefully and a consensus established on its most likely future course. Agreement must also be reached on the Bank's goals and the best actions to take for achieving them.

Also, because the effects of the Bank of Canada's actions operate with long time lags, the Bank must forecast the state of the economy at the time when all the effects of its current actions will have been realized. That is, the Bank of Canada has to behave like the electric power company. The power company knows that if it is to meet the demand for electric power in 1997, it must set into action some plans here and now, for building additional generating capacity that will come on stream in that year. If the time lag from the Bank's open market operation to a change in the inflation rate takes two years, the Bank's monetary policy actions in 1990 must be geared to the best available forecasts of the state of the economy in 1992. That is, the Bank, like the electric power company, must take actions today that will put in place the correct level of aggregate demand to maintain stable prices not today but two years from today.

So far, we have restricted our analysis of the effects of monetary policy to studying one channel of transmission — the interest rate channel. Let's now broaden our vision and look at some other channels whereby monetary policy influences aggregate demand.

Other Transmission Channels

There are three other important transmission channels of monetary policy:

- The real balance effect
- The wealth effect
- The exchange rate effect

Let's look at each of these in turn.

The Real Balance Effect The *real balance effect* is the effect of a change in the quantity of real money on the quantity of real GDP demanded. We first studied the real balance effect briefly in Chapter 24. Let's see how it works.

An increase in the quantity of money at a given price level increases the amount of real money in the economy. With additional holdings of real money, households and firms plan to reallocate their holdings of assets of all types. They want to lower their holdings of real money and increase their holdings of other assets. Some of these other assets are real assets — capital goods. To the extent that households convert their additional real money holdings into real assets, there is an increase in investment. This increase in investment is separate from the increase that results from a lower interest rate. Even if the interest rate does not change, a larger holding of real money balances will, in general, trigger an asset reallocation involving some additional spending on goods and services.

For example, the Bank of Canada may buy $100 million worth of government bonds from Petro-Canada. That is an open market operation that increases the monetary base and increases Petro-Canada's real money holdings. Let's suppose, to keep things simple, that no change in the interest rate has occurred at this time. Petro-Canada is not going to sit on this extra $100 million for very long. It's going to put these financial resources to work acquiring profitable assets. Some of the money may be used to take over other firms, and some of it may be used directly to buy new gas stations. To the extent that Petro-Canada buys new capital goods, there is an immediate increase in investment. If they take over other firms, these other firms have more real money and are able to increase their own investment. Gradually, investment increases as firms spend the extra real money balances that the open market operation created.

The Wealth Effect The effect of a change in real wealth on aggregate planned expenditure is the **wealth effect**. An increase in the money supply can lead to an increase in wealth mainly by its effect on stock prices. To see how this effect operates, let's go back to the previous example. Suppose that when Petro-Canada sells some government securities to the Bank of Canada, it uses the $100 million proceeds from the sale to buy shares of stock in other corporations. Petro-Canada's action increases the demand for the stock of some companies. That increase in demand shifts the demand curve for stock to the right and increases stock prices. Higher stock prices mean that all the existing shareholders are now wealthier. The paper assets that they are holding can now be sold for more than before. With greater wealth, some of these shareholders will sell some of their stock and buy additional consumer durable goods. To the extent that greater wealth stimulates consumption expenditure, it increases aggregate demand.

The increase in stock market prices in the 1980s provides a good example of how increasing stock prices can lead to increased consumption expenditure. And the stock market crash of 1987 shows how people can quickly reduce their spending when they are no longer as wealthy as they thought they were. The steady increase in the demand for BMWs and Jaguars during a stock market boom and the trailing off in the demand for such cars as a result of a stock market crash are examples of this transmission channel at work.

The Exchange Rate Effect An increase in the money supply can lead to a depreciation of the dollar and to an increase in net exports. Since net exports are part of aggregate expenditure, this *exchange rate effect* is a further channel through which monetary policy can influence aggregate demand. And this channel of monetary policy is especially important in an economy that has a large foreign trade sector, such as the Canadian economy. This effect works in the following way.

An increase in the money supply lowers interest rates. With lower interest rates, there is a tendency for international investment flows to occur. If interest rates fall in Canada but do not fall in Japan and Western Europe, international investors will sell the now lower-yielding Canadian-dollar assets and buy the relatively higher-yielding foreign currency assets. As they undertake these transactions, the demand for Canadian-dollar assets decreases and the demand for foreign-assets currency increases. The result is a lower foreign exchange value of the Canadian dollar relative to the values of other currencies. (This channel is discussed in greater detail in Chapter 29.)

With the Canadian dollar worth less, foreigners can now buy Canadian goods at a lower price and Canadians have to pay a higher price for the foreign goods that they buy. The result is a net increase in the demand for Canadian-made goods as Canadians switch from buying expensive imports to cheaper domestically produced goods and foreigners switch from buying their expensive home-produced goods to cheaper imports from Canada.

This process operates in the opposite direction if the Bank of Canada undertakes a monetary policy action that lowers the money supply and increases interest rates.

Time Lags Again Like the interest rate transmission channel, all these additional transmission channels for the effects of monetary policy on aggregate demand do not operate instantaneously. They all operate with time lags, and the same factors that influence the time lags in the interest rate channel operate in these cases as well.

The effects of monetary policy on the interest rate and the exchange rate just described are only the initial effects of a once-and-for-all change in the money supply. A change in the money supply growth rate that persists has the effects on inflation and interest rates described in Chapter 29 but leaves real interest rates, the real exchange rate, and aggregate demand unchanged.

R E V I E W

A change in the money supply affects aggregate demand by changing interest rates, real money balances, wealth, and the foreign exchange rate. An increase in the money supply leads to an increase in aggregate demand, and a decrease in the money supply leads to a decrease in aggregate demand. The potency of the effect of a change in the money supply depends on two main factors: the sensitivity of the demand for real money to changes in interest rates and the sensitivity of investment demand to changes in interest rates. Other things being equal, the less sensitive the demand for real money and the more sensitive investment demand to changes in interest rates, the greater is the effect of a change in the money supply on equilibrium expenditure and aggregate demand. Monetary policy actions operate with a time lag. Interest rate changes occur fairly quickly, but other changes — the change in investment and the induced change in consumption expenditure — occur more slowly. The Bank of Canada reacts to the state of the economy so aggregate demand is influenced by monetary policy actions that are themselves being influenced by the evolution of the economy. ■

Let's now turn to an examination of the effects of fiscal policy on aggregate demand.

Fiscal Policy and Aggregate Demand

We studied the effects of fiscal policy on aggregate planned expenditure and aggregate demand in Chapter 26. But the model economy that we used in that chapter was one in which the interest rate was fixed. The model that we are now studying is one in which interest rates are determined by money market equilibrium. In this model, a change in government expenditure on goods and services or a change in taxes has an effect not only on aggregate planned expenditure and real GDP but also on interest rates. When we take these effects into account, it turns out that the multipliers that we calculated in Chapter 26 overstate the change in equilibrium expenditure and real GDP that is brought about by a fiscal policy action. Let's see why.

Crowding Out

When the government increases its purchases of goods and services, autonomous expenditure increases and the increased equilibrium expenditure brought about by the subsequent multiplier process increases real GDP. This increase in real GDP leads to an increase in the demand for real money. Figure 30.6 illustrates the effects of this increase in the demand for real money. In part (a), with the money supply constant at $3 billion, the change in real income shifts the demand curve for real money from MD_0 to MD_1 and the interest rate increases from 5 to 6 percent.

As you can see by looking at Fig. 30.6(b), the higher interest rate lowers investment. Because

Figure 30.6 Fiscal Policy and Crowding Out

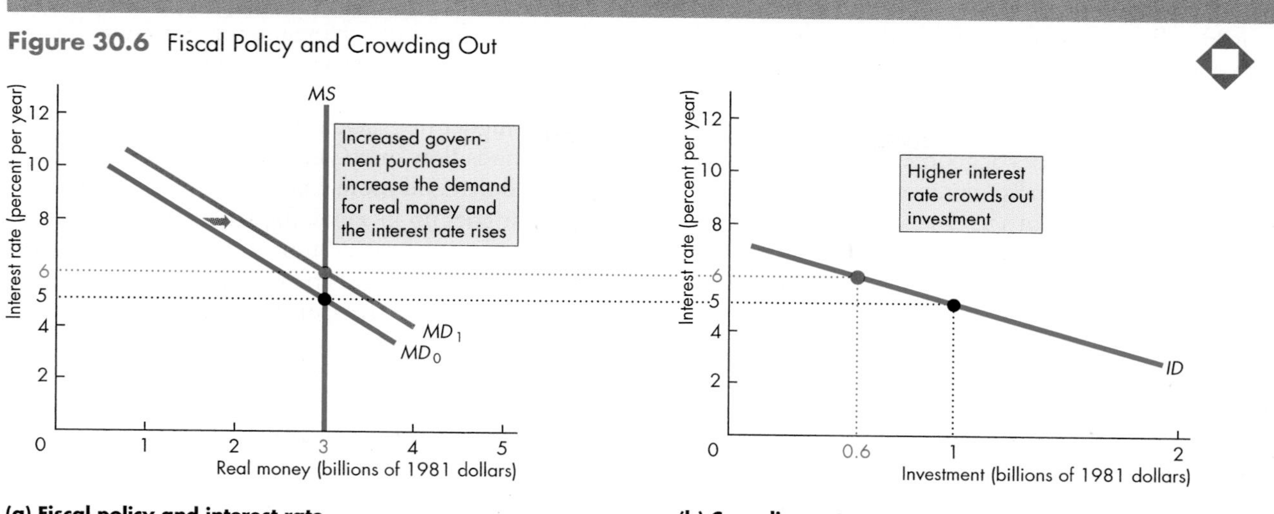

An increase in government purchases of goods and services or a tax cut increases aggregate planned expenditure, and real GDP rises. Rising real GDP increases the demand for money, and the demand curve for real money shifts from MD_0 to MD_1. The interest rate rises. A higher interest rate leads to a decrease in investment (part b). The decrease in investment offsets, to some extent, the initial increase in government purchases. The steeper the demand curve for real money and the flatter the investment demand curve, the larger is the crowding out effect.

investment is part of autonomous expenditure, the higher interest rate reduces autonomous expenditure. But recall that the experiment we are conducting is one in which autonomous expenditure has increased because of an increase in government purchases of goods and services. What we have now discovered is that an increase in government purchases of goods and services increases autonomous expenditure but generates a decrease in investment, which reduces autonomous expenditure. This phenomenon is called "crowding out." **Crowding out** is the tendency for an increase in government purchases of goods and services to increase interest rates, thereby reducing investment. The increase in government purchases of goods and services crowds out investment.

Crowding out may be partial or complete. Partial crowding out occurs when the decrease in investment is less than the increase in government purchases of goods and services. This is the normal case. Increased government purchases of goods and services increase real GDP, which increases the demand for real money, and so interest rates rise. Higher interest rates decrease investment. But the effect on investment is small relative to the initial change in government purchases.

Complete crowding out occurs if the decrease in investment equals the initial increase in government purchases. For complete crowding out to occur, a small change in the demand for real money must lead to a large change in the interest rate and the change in the interest rate must lead to a large change in investment. Although complete crowding out does not occur in practice, such an interesting extreme case serves to highlight the importance of the interaction between fiscal policy and monetary policy.

Influencing the Composition of Aggregate Demand

If aggregate demand is to be increased, there is a choice of methods for increasing it. Either the money supply can be increased or fiscal policy can be expansionary (by increasing government purchases or cutting taxes). If there is an increase in the money supply, as we have seen, increased aggregate demand follows lower interest rates. Lower interest rates, in turn, result in a higher level of investment. However, if aggregate demand is stimulated by fiscal policy, the increased aggregate demand comes along with higher interest rates. Higher interest rates lead to lower investment. Thus the method used to stimulate aggregate demand has an important effect on its *composition.*

An increase in aggregate demand, resulting from an increase in the money supply, leads to an increase in both investment and consumption expenditure while government purchases of goods and services are unchanged. If aggregate demand rises due to an increase in government purchases of goods and services, consumption expenditure also increases but investment decreases. If the increase in aggregate demand is brought about by a tax cut, consumption expenditure increases and investment decreases while government purchases remain constant.

Politics of Monetary and Fiscal Policy

Because monetary and fiscal policies affect the *composition* of aggregate expenditure in different ways, the two sets of policies have different effects on long-run economic growth. Also, the choice of the mix of the two policies generates political controversy and tension between the Bank of Canada and the federal and provincial governments. Usually, the federal and provincial governments do not want the Bank of Canada to tighten monetary policy, thereby increasing interest rates. Instead, they want to see the Bank steadily expanding the money supply, keeping interest rates as low as possible.

The Bank, on the other hand, frequently points to the importance of keeping government purchases of goods and services under control and keeping taxes sufficiently high to pay for those goods and services. It argues that unless the government of Canada increases taxes or cuts its expenditure, a more expansionary monetary policy cannot be pursued. Some of this tension in the current debate can be seen in Reading Between the Lines (pp. 820-821).

The choice of monetary or fiscal policy affects our long-term growth prospects because the long-term capacity of the economy to produce goods and services depends on the rate at which capital is accumulated and that, in turn, depends on the level of investment. Expansionary fiscal policies lead to a decrease in investment and a slowdown in the economy's long-term growth.

So far, we have concentrated on one channel through which fiscal policy affects the level of aggregate demand and its composition. There is another important channel — the exchange rate.

Fiscal Policy and the Exchange Rate

We've seen that an increase in government purchases or a decrease in taxes leads to higher interest rates. We've also seen that a change in interest rates affects the exchange rate. Higher interest rates make the foreign exchange value of the dollar increase. With interest rates higher in Canada than in the rest of the world, funds flow into Canada and people around the world demand more Canadian-dollar assets. As the dollar goes up in value, foreigners find Canadian-made goods and services more expensive and Canadians find imports less expensive. Exports fall and imports rise. These changes in net exports offset, to some degree, the initial increase in expenditure brought about by the expansionary fiscal policy.

In contrast, this effect is reversed if aggregate demand is increased by an expansion of the money supply. A larger money supply lowers interest rates. The lower interest rate makes the dollar weak and makes its foreign exchange value fall. With a weaker dollar, our exports fall in price and imports from the rest of the world increase in price. Exports rise and imports fall. (We studied these exchange rate effects in Chapter 24 and again in Chapter 29.)

The effects of fiscal policy, both on the level and composition of aggregate demand, do not occur instantaneously. Like monetary policy, fiscal policy operates with a time lag. Let's examine these time lags and see how they compare with those of monetary policy.

Time Lags of Fiscal Policy

Some fiscal policy actions have an immediate effect on aggregate demand. For example, a change in government purchases of goods and services has an immediate impact on the markets in which the government is buying the additional goods and services. A tax cut also has an immediate effect on disposable income, but its effect on consumption expenditure is more drawn out. There is a further delayed effect of fiscal policy. Rising incomes lead to an increase in the demand for real money and interest rates rise. Higher interest rates cause some crowding out of investment — investment decreases — but this effect is subject to the same time lags as the effects of monetary policy.

There is an important difference between the time lags of fiscal policy and those of monetary policy. Fiscal policy has an immediate effect on aggregate expenditure followed by a long drawn-out effect as interest rates change and other components of aggregate expenditure adjust in response to the changing interest rates. In contrast, monetary policy has no immediate effect on aggregate demand. The effect gradually builds up as more and more firms and households respond to the changing interest rates and other money and financial market conditions.

Fiscal policy has important policy formation lags that are longer than those of monetary policy. To implement changes in taxes or in government expenditure on goods and services, the entire legislative process must be completed. This process, which involves cabinet and Parliament, as well as many committees, interest groups, and lobbies, operates on a time frame that makes it virtually impossible to fine tune fiscal policy for macroeconomic stabilization purposes. Nevertheless, fiscal policy has important long-term effects, especially those arising from its influence on the composition of output, as discussed above.

R E V I E W

To increase aggregate demand, government purchases of goods and services may be increased or taxes may be decreased. Such actions set up the following sequence of events:

- Autonomous expenditure increases.
- Higher expenditure induces higher disposable income and consumption expenditure increases.
- A multiplier effect increases equilibrium expenditure and real GDP.
- Higher real GDP increases the demand for real money.
- An increase in the demand for real money raises interest rates.
- Higher interest rates lead to a cutback in investment and a partial offsetting of the initial effects of the increased autonomous expenditure arising from the fiscal policy action.
- The foreign exchange value of the Canadian dollar increases.
- Exports are cut and imports are stimulated.
- The changes in foreign trade flows partially offset the initial increase in autonomous expenditure brought about by the fiscal policy action.
- The net effect of fiscal stimulation depends on the relative strengths of the initial effects of the increase in autonomous expenditure and of the offsetting effects that result from higher interest rates and the higher exchange rate.

Fiscal policy time lags differ from those of monetary policy. A fiscal policy change has a large initial effect on aggregate demand, but the subsequent offsetting effects induced by higher interest rates and a higher exchange rate are spread out over time. Also, the lags in formulating and implementing fiscal policy are longer than those of monetary policy. ■

The analysis of the effects of monetary and fiscal policy on aggregate demand presented in this chapter was extremely controversial for several years in the 1950s and 1960s. It was at the heart of what was called the Keynesian-monetarist controversy. The Keynesian-monetarist controversy of today differs from that of the 1950s and 1960s; it's a controversy about how labour markets work, and we'll study it in Chapter 31. The earlier Keynesian-monetarist controversy was an interesting and important episode in the development of modern macroeconomics. Let's take a look at the essentials of the dispute and see how it was resolved.

The Keynesian-Monetarist Controversy

The Keynesian-monetarist controversy is an on going dispute in macroeconomics between two groups of economists. **Keynesians** are macroeconomists whose views about the functioning of the economy represent an extension of the theories of John Maynard Keynes published in his *General Theory*. Keynesians regard the economy as being inherently unstable and as requiring active government intervention to achieve stability. They assign a low degree of importance to monetary policy and a high degree of importance to fiscal policy. **Monetarists** are macroeconomists who assign a high degree of importance to variations in the quantity of money as the main determinant of aggregate demand and who regard the economy as inherently stable. The founder of modern monetarism is Milton Friedman. (Keynes and Friedman feature in Our Advancing Knowledge, pp. 662-664).

The nature of the Keynesian-monetarist debate has changed over the years. In the 1950s and 1960s, the debate and controversy focused almost exclusively on the relative effectiveness of fiscal policy and monetary policy in changing aggregate demand.

Conflict Between Monetary and Fiscal Policy

Rising rates shatter Tory deficit forecast

The sharp run-up in interest rates has left Finance Minister Michael Wilson's two-month-old budget forecast in tatters and will drive up this year's budget deficit by between $2 billion and $4 billion, economists say.

Without further spending cuts or tax increases, the mounting charges on the federal debt will eat up all the spending cuts in February's budget and leave the shortfall closer to $31.5 billion than the projected $28.5 billion, they say.

The Bank of Canada rate rose yesterday to 13.77% from 13.61%—for an increase since early January of 133 basis points (1 1/3 percentage points).

The Bank of Canada added cash to the market before and after yesterday's bill auction in an attempt to slow the rise in rates, traders said.

Economists who originally found Wilson's budget forecast reasonable now give him next to no chance of meeting his deficit target.

Short-term rates now are 2 1/2 percentage points higher than the 11.1% average Wilson counted on and long-term rates are almost two points higher than the 10 1/2% forecast.

"I think there's virtually no chance they're going to make [their deficit projection] unless there were a sea-change in attitudes in the financial markets," said Bank of Montreal chief economist Lloyd Atkinson.

With the three-month commercial paper rate averaging 13% so far this year, Atkinson noted rates would have to "fall like a rock" soon and stay there to reach an average of 11.1%.

"I think we're going to end up with a weaker economy than Wilson wants, short-term interest rates on average about 150 to 200 basis points higher, and what that adds up to is a budget deficit anywhere from $3 billion to $4 billion worse than $28.5 billion."...

Wilson said in Toronto yesterday he stands by his budget projections.

"We're only three weeks into the fiscal year so let's not jump to conclusions," he said.

Wilson defended the Bank of Canada's interest rate policy as critical to lowering inflation.

"Surely it's important for us to get the problem of inflation solved now before we get into that mess we had in 1982," he said.

But...[a senior Finance] official said interest rates have remained high because the economy is stronger than expected.

The Financial Post,
April 20, 1990
By Greg Ip
with files from Geoffrey Scotton

The Essence of the Story

- In the spring of 1990, Canadian interest rates were rising sharply and in April traders said the Bank of Canada had been adding cash to the market in an attempt to slow the rise in interest rates.
- By April 1990, rates were 2 to 2 1/2 percentage points higher than Finance Minister Wilson had assumed in his budget, and economists were forecasting an increase in the federal government's budget deficit of between $2 billion and $4 billion in 1990.
- The finance minister stood by his budget projections and defended the Bank of Canada's high interest rate policy as critical to lowering inflation.
- Bank of Montreal chief economist Lloyd Atkinson predicted that we would end up with a weaker economy than the finance minister wanted.
- A Senior Department of Finance official said interest rates have remained high because the economy is stronger than expected.

Background and Analysis

- The news item contains two conflicting interpretations of the interest rate increase in the spring of 1990. It results from:
  - The pursuit of tight anti-inflationary policies by the Bank of Canada.
  - A strong economy with the Bank of Canada acting as a moderating influence.
- The first interpretation is illustrated in Fig. (a). The bank of Canada decreases the money supply from MS_0 to MS_1 and interest rates increase from 11 percent to 13 percent.
- The second interpretation is illustrated in Fig. (b). An increase in real GDP leads to an increase in the demand for money from MD_0 to MD_1 and interest rates increase from 11 percent to 13 percent.
- The table below gives data on the growth rate of the real money supply—the growth rate of the quantity of money *less* the inflation rate.
- The interpretations are not mutually exclusive. Each factor could have contributed to the interest rate increase and the importance of each factor could change from month to month. To determine the factor at work, we need to look at real money supply growth and real GDP growth during the first part of 1990.
- Real GDP growth in the first quarter of 1990 was running at a 2 percent annual rate. This growth rate is below the average real GDP growth rate and is not a sign of a strong economy.

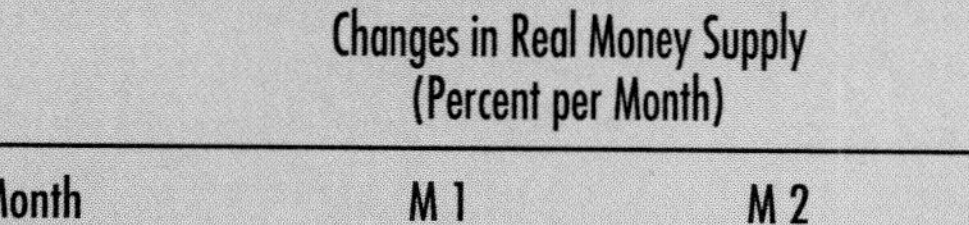

Changes in Real Money Supply (Percent per Month)

Month	M 1	M 2	M 3
Jan 1990	–1.1	0.1	0.1
Feb 1990	1.2	0.7	0.1
Mar 1990	–4.8	–0.5	–0.6
Apr 1990	1.7	0.6	0.6

Source: The Bank of Canada Review

Conclusion

- High and rising interest rates in the first quarter of 1990 resulted mainly from the actions of the Bank of Canada. Especially in March 1990, the Bank pursued very tight monetary policy, similar to that illustrated in Fig. (a).
- The Bank permitted faster money growth in April 1990, and it is possible that an increase in borrowing and investment spending in the month led to an increase in the demand for money as illustrated in Fig. (b). This possibility is consistent with the findings of Statistics Canada's investment intentions survey reported in April 1990 (see Reading Between the Lines, pp. 672-673).
- The news item contains two conflicting assessments of the effects of higher interest rates on the federal budget deficit in 1990. High interest rates with a slowing economy increase the deficit. High interest rates with a strong economy will not increase the deficit, provided the growth in the economy is strong enough to increase tax revenue by more than the increased interest burden. As of April, 1990, it was impossible to predict which of these situations would arise during the balance of 1990.

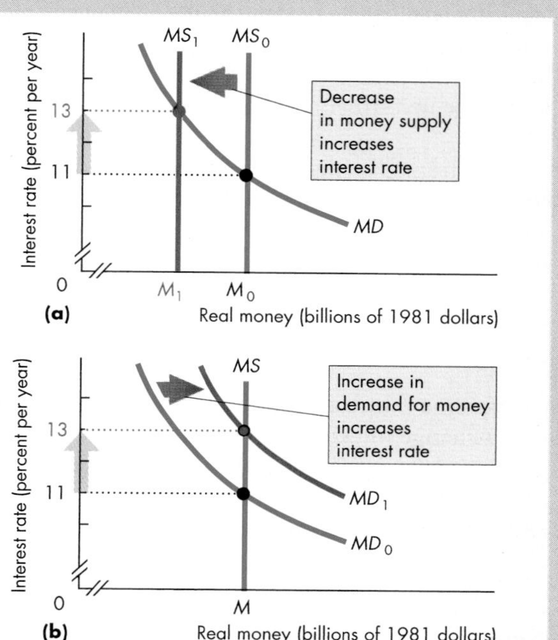

Ignoring non-central issues we can see the essence of the controversy if we distinguish three views:

- Extreme Keynesianism
- Extreme monetarism
- Intermediate position

Extreme Keynesianism

An extreme Keynesian is an economist who believes that a change in the money supply has no effect on the level of aggregate demand, and that a change in government purchases of goods and services or in taxes has a large and predictable effect on aggregate demand.

We saw earlier in this chapter that there are two circumstances in which a change in the money supply has no effect on aggregate demand. They are:

- A vertical investment demand curve
- A horizontal demand curve for real money

If the investment demand curve is vertical, investment is completely insensitive to changes in interest rates. In that situation, even if monetary policy changes interest rates, those changes do not affect aggregate planned expenditure and monetary policy is impotent. A horizontal demand curve for real money means that people are willing to hold any amount of money at a given interest rate — a situation called a **liquidity trap**. In a liquidity trap, a change in the quantity of money affects only the amount of money held. It does not affect interest rates. Therefore in a liquidity trap, even if investment does not respond to interest rate changes, monetary policy is impotent because it is unable to change interest rates in order to change investment and aggregate planned expenditure.

Extreme Keynesians believe that both of these conditions prevail. Though either circumstance would be sufficient on its own, extreme Keynesians suppose that both exist in reality.

Extreme Monetarism

An extreme monetarist is an economist who believes that a change in taxes or in government purchases of goods and services has no effect on aggregate demand and that a change in the money supply has a large and predictable effect on aggregate demand. There are two circumstances giving rise to the predictions of an extreme monetarist:

- A horizontal investment demand curve
- A vertical demand curve for real money

These conditions characterize the logical possibility of complete crowding out that we described previously. If an increase in government purchases of goods and services induces an increase in interest rates that is large enough to reduce investment by the same amount as the initial increase in government purchases, then fiscal policy has no effect on aggregate demand. For this result to occur, either the demand curve for real money must be vertical — a fixed amount of money is held regardless of the interest rate — or the investment demand curve must be horizontal — any amount of investment will be undertaken at a given interest rate.

The Intermediate Position

The intermediate position is that both monetary and fiscal policy affect aggregate demand. Crowding out is not complete, so that fiscal policy does have an effect. There is no liquidity trap and investment does respond to interest rates, so monetary policy does indeed affect aggregate demand. This position is the one that now appears to be correct. Let's see how economists came to this conclusion.

Sorting Out the Competing Claims

The dispute between monetarists, Keynesians, and those taking an intermediate position has two components. The first is a disagreement about the magnitudes of two economic parameters:

- The sensitivity of investment demand to changes in interest rates
- The sensitivity of the demand for real money to changes in interest rates

The second is a disagreement as to whether the economy is inherently stable or unstable.

Let's first consider the disagreement about the magnitude of the two economic parameters. If investment demand is highly sensitive to interest rates and the demand for real money is hardly sensitive at all, then monetary policy is powerful and fiscal policy is relatively ineffective and the world works in the manner claimed by extreme monetarists. If the demand for real money is highly sensitive to interest rate changes and investment demand is very insensitive, then fiscal policy is powerful and monetary policy is relatively ineffective and the world works in the manner claimed by extreme Keynesians.

Using statistical methods to study the demand for real money and investment demand and using data from a wide variety of historical and national experiences, economists were able to settle this dispute. Neither extreme position turned out to be supported by the evidence. The intermediate position was the strongest.

An intermediate position does not always win in scientific matters. Indeed, scientific progress is most exciting when logically possible situations are shown empirically not to occur. But in this particular dispute that outcome did not arise. The demand curve for real money does slope downward. So does the demand curve for investment. Neither of these demand curves is vertical nor horizontal, a finding that ruled out the positions adopted by both extreme Keynesians and extreme monetarists.

This particular controversy in macroeconomics is behind us, but other controversies still exist. One concerns the relative magnitudes of the multiplier effects of monetary and fiscal policy. Another concerns the time lags of those effects. But the major outstanding controversy that divides modern Keynesians and monetarists is whether or not the economy is inherently stable or unstable. That disagreement turns crucially on a disagreement about how the labour market works. We'll examine this controversy in the next chapter.

■ We have now studied the determination of aggregate demand and the way in which fluctuations in aggregate demand can be offset or produced by policy actions taken by the government and the Bank of Canada. Our next task is to turn to the aggregate supply side of the economy and to study the determination of long-run and short-run aggregate supply, employment, and unemployment.

The appendix to this chapter, although optional, offers a more comprehensive framework for this discussion.

SUMMARY

Money, Interest, and Aggregate Demand

The main transmission channel by which a change in the money supply affects aggregate demand is the interest rate. A decrease in the money supply increases the interest rate. The higher interest rate decreases investment, and lower investment reduces aggregate planned expenditure. A decrease in aggregate planned expenditure causes real GDP to fall. A fall in real GDP decreases the demand for real money. The demand curve for real money shifts to the left, and interest rates fall. Falling interest rates lead to an increase in investment, and aggregate planned expenditure starts to rise. Falling real GDP and rising aggregate planned expenditure converge at a new stock and flow equilibrium. Such an equilibrium is a situation in which real GDP and the interest rate take on values that make the quantity of real money demanded equal the quantity supplied and aggregate planned expenditure equal real GDP.

The effects of a change in the money supply on aggregate demand depend on two factors: the responsiveness of the demand for real money to the changes in interest rate and the responsiveness of investment demand to the changes in interest rate. The less responsive the demand for real money and the more responsive investment demand is to changes in the interest rate, the larger is the effect of a change in the money supply on aggregate demand.

Monetary policy operates with time lags. A change in the money supply has an immediate effect on interest rates, but its effect on expenditure plans is long term. Once expenditure has changed, a multiplier effect follows as induced expenditure gradually changes. Higher aggregate expenditure and real GDP eventually bring faster-rising prices. After a further lag, the Bank of Canada reacts to the state of the economy and makes further changes in its monetary policy.

Other transmission channels for monetary policy are the real balance effect, the wealth effect, and the exchange rate effect. A change in the quantity of real money has a direct effect on aggregate expenditure. A change in wealth also has a direct effect on aggregate expenditure. A change in the exchange rate changes both Canadian demand for foreign-made goods and services and foreign demand for Canadian-made goods and services. (pp. 805-816)

Fiscal Policy and Aggregate Demand

A change in government purchases of goods and services has a direct effect on aggregate demand. A change in taxes has an effect on aggregate demand through its effect on disposable income. But fiscal policy changes both real GDP and interest rates. Therefore fiscal policy has an indirect effect on investment. An increase in government purchases of goods and services that increases aggregate planned expenditure makes real GDP begin to rise. Rising real GDP increases the demand for real money and shifts the demand curve for real money to the right. An increase in the demand for real money increases interest rates. Higher interest rates lower investment. The fall in investment resulting from an increase in government purchases offsets the expansionary effect of the initial fiscal policy action. In an extreme situation, the offset would be total. That is, the decrease in investment would be sufficient to offset the entire increase in government purchases. In practice, such extreme crowding out does not seem to occur.

The mix of monetary and fiscal policy influences the composition of aggregate demand. If aggregate demand is increased as a result of an increase in the money supply, interest rates fall and investment increases. If aggregate demand is increased by an increase in government expenditure on goods and services, interest rates rise and investment falls. The different effects of monetary and fiscal policy on aggregate demand lead to political tensions. To keep aggregate demand in check and to moderate interest rates, the level of taxes must be high enough in relation to the level of government purchases.

Fiscal policy influences aggregate demand through the exchange rate. An increase in government purchases of goods and services tends to increase interest rates and to make the dollar appreciate. When the dollar strengthens, Canadians buy more imports and foreigners buy fewer Canadian-made goods, so Canadian exports decline. The operation of fiscal policy has time lags but they differ from those of monetary policy. In general, fiscal policy has a greater immediate effect than monetary policy, although it, too, has long drawn-out effects. Also, the decision lags in fiscal policy are much longer than those in monetary policy. (pp. 816-819)

The Keynesian-Monetarist Controversy

The Keynesian-monetarist controversy concerns the relative effectiveness of monetary and fiscal actions in influencing aggregate demand. The extreme Keynesian position is that only fiscal policy affects aggregate demand and that monetary policy is impotent. The extreme monetarist position is the converse — that only changes in the money supply affect aggregate demand and that fiscal policy is impotent. This was the central controversy in macroeconomics in the 1950s and 1960s. As a result of statistical investigations, we now know that neither extreme position is correct and that both monetary and fiscal actions influence aggregate demand. Controversy remains about the relative effectiveness of the two types of policy and the precise timing of their effects. (pp. 819-823)

KEY ELEMENTS

Key Terms

Crowding out, 817
Keynesians, 819
Liquidity trap, 822
Monetarists, 819
Wealth effect, 815

Key Figures

Figure 30.1 The Equilibrium Interest Rate and Real GDP, 806
Figure 30.4 The Convergence to a New Expenditure Equilibrium, 810
Figure 30.5 The Potency of Monetary Policy, 812
Figure 30.6 Fiscal Policy and Crowding Out, 817

REVIEW QUESTIONS

1 List the alternative transmission channels through which a change in the money supply leads to a change in real GDP.

2 Set out the main steps in the interest rate transmission channel of monetary policy.

3 Explain why a change in the money supply has a large effect on aggregate demand if investment is highly responsive to changes in interest rates.

4 Explain why monetary policy has a small effect on aggregate demand if the demand for real money is highly sensitive to changes in interest rates.

5 Explain how a change in stock prices is triggered by a change in the money supply.

6 Describe the time lags in the operation of monetary policy.

7 What is crowding out?

8 Why does an increase in government purchases on goods and services lead to higher interest rates?

9 What is a Keynesian?

10 What is a monetarist?

11 What were the main elements in the Keynesian-monetarist controversy about the relative effectiveness of stimulating aggregate demand by monetary policy and fiscal policy?

PROBLEMS

1 In the economy described in Fig. 30.1, suppose the money supply increases by $1 billion.

a) Work out the immediate effects of this change on the interest rate.

b) What is the effect on investment?

c) What is the immediate effect on aggregate planned expenditure?

d) What is the immediate effect on equilibrium real GDP?

e) What happens to inventory accumulation?

f) At what interest rate and level of real GDP is there a new stock and flow equilibrium?

2 Two economies are identical in every way except the following. In economy A, a change in the interest rate of 1 percentage point (for example, from 5 percent to 6 percent) results in a $100 million change in the quantity of real money demanded. In economy B, the same change in the interest rate leads to a $1 billion change in the quantity of real money demanded.

a) In which economy does a change in the quantity of real money have a larger effect on equilibrium real GDP?

b) In which economy does an increase in government expenditure on goods and services have a larger effect on real GDP?

c) In which economy is the crowding out effect the weakest?

3 The federal government wants to increase aggregate demand, stimulate exports, and increase investment. Explain whether it should seek to achieve this objective by increasing government purchases of goods and services, by cutting taxes, or by increasing the money supply. Explain the mechanisms at work under the alternative policies that lead to your policy recommendation. What are the time lags in the effectiveness of the alternative policies?

Appendix to Chapter 30

The *IS-LM* Model of Aggregate Demand

This appendix presents the *IS-LM* model of aggregate demand. This model provides an explicit account of the derivation of the aggregate demand curve and of the effects of monetary and fiscal policy on aggregate demand.

Because we are studying the determination of *aggregate demand*, we ignore aggregate supply and its interaction with aggregate demand to determine the price level and real GDP. Our focus is on a point on the aggregate demand curve at a given price level. This focus does not imply that the price level is constant. It is simply that the analysis that we are about to conduct is valid at *any* price level, so we will work out what happens at a particular price level.

The material is not inherently difficult but it is of a higher level than the presentation in the chapter and is optional. Nevertheless, after studying this appendix, you will emerge with a deeper and clearer understanding of aggregate demand and how it is influenced by monetary and fiscal policy.

Chapters 25, 26, and 28 contain the ingredients of the *IS-LM* model. First, let's refresh our memories about equilibrium expenditure and real GDP flows. Second, we'll look at money market equilibrium. Then we'll study these two elements together.

Equilibrium Expenditure and Real GDP

Aggregate planned expenditure depends on real GDP because consumption, the biggest component of aggregate expenditure, increases as real GDP increases. The equilibrium flows of aggregate planned expenditure and real GDP occur when aggregate planned expenditure equals real GDP. But aggregate planned expenditure also depends on the interest rate. The higher the interest rate, the lower is planned investment. Thus the higher the interest rate, the lower is aggregate planned expenditure.

These ideas, which were discussed in greater detail in Chapters 25 and 26, are summarized in Fig. A30.1. Let's work through this figure carefully, starting with its table.

Begin by looking at the two columns headed "Interest rate" and "Autonomous expenditure." Recall that investment is part of autonomous expenditure and that investment decreases as the interest rate rises. The table shows us how autonomous expenditure varies as the interest rate varies. For example, when the interest rate is 6 percent, autonomous expenditure is $1.2 billion. When the interest rate falls to 5 percent, autonomous expenditure rises to $1.6 billion.

Next, look at the last two rows of the table labelled "Induced expenditure" and "Real GDP." Recall

Figure A30.1 Aggregate Planned Expenditure, Flow Equilibrium, and the *IS* Curve

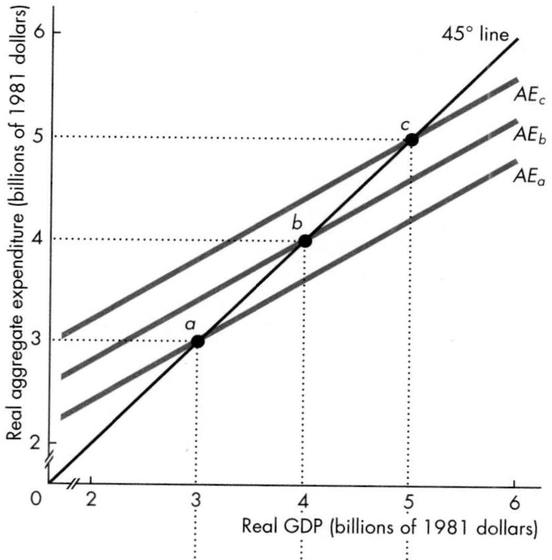

(a) Aggregate expenditure and real GDP

The table shows the aggregate planned expenditure — the sum of autonomous expenditure and induced expenditure — that occurs at various combinations of the interest rate and real GDP. For example, if the interest rate is 6 percent and real GDP is $5 billion, aggregate planned expenditure is $4.2 billion (top right number). Flow equilibrium — equality of aggregate planned expenditure and real GDP — is shown by the green squares. Each row *a*, *b*, and *c* represents an aggregate expenditure schedule and these are plotted as the aggregate expenditure curves AE_a, AE_b, and AE_c, respectively, in part (a). Equilibrium expenditure positions are shown in part (a), where these *AE* curves intersect the 45° line and are marked *a*, *b*, and *c*. Part (b) shows these same equilibrium positions but highlights the combinations of the interest rate and real GDP at which they occur. The line connecting those points is the *IS* curve.

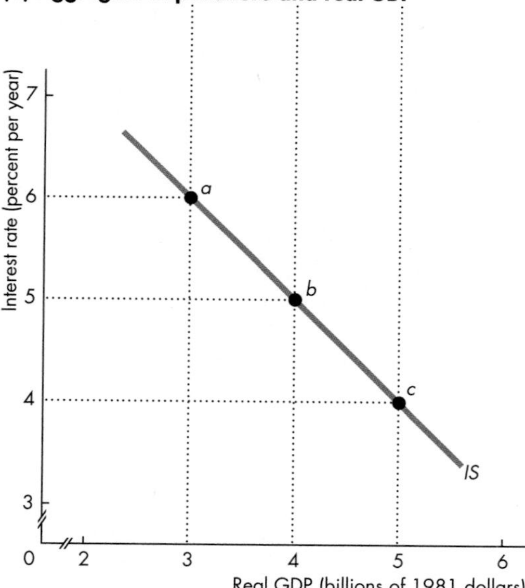

(b) The *IS* curve

	Interest rate (percent per year)	Autonomous expenditure (billions of 1981 dollars)	Aggregate planned expenditure (billions of 1981 dollars)		
a	6	1.2	3.0	3.6	4.2
b	5	1.6	3.4	4.0	4.6
c	4	2.0	3.8	4.4	5.0
	Induced expenditure		1.8	2.4	3.0
	Real GDP (billions of 1981 dollars)		3.0	4.0	5.0

that induced expenditure is expenditure that depends on real GDP. It is that part of consumption expenditure that depends on real GDP minus imports. The numbers here tell us how induced expenditure varies as real GDP varies. For example, if real GDP is $3 billion, induced expenditure is $1.8 billion. If real GDP increases to $4 billion, induced expenditure rises to $2.4 billion.

Finally, look at the section of the table labelled "Aggregate planned expenditure." Each number in this block tells us the level of aggregate planned expenditure at a specific combination of the interest rate and the level of real GDP. For example, row *b* tells us that when the interest rate is 5 percent and real GDP is $3 billion, aggregate planned expenditure is $3.4 billion — the sum of autonomous expenditure of $1.6 billion and induced expenditure of $1.8 billion. The other numbers in the top right section of the table are arrived at in the same way. Check that you can calculate them as the sum of autonomous expenditure and induced expenditure at the appropriate interest rate and real GDP.

The green squares in the table indicate positions of equilibrium expenditure. For example, look again at row *b*. It tells us that when the interest rate is 5 percent, equilibrium expenditure is $4 billion. At that interest rate, autonomous expenditure is $1.6 billion. At a real GDP of $4 billion, induced expenditure is $2.4 billion. Therefore aggregate planned expenditure is $4 billion, which equals real GDP. This is an expenditure equilibrium. When aggregate planned expenditure exceeds real GDP, real GDP increases. At an interest rate of 5 percent, if real GDP is $3 billion, aggregate planned expenditure is $3.4 billion — real GDP increases. When aggregate planned expenditure is less than real GDP, real GDP falls. At an interest rate of 5 percent, if real GDP is $5 billion, aggregate planned expenditure is $4.6 billion — real GDP falls. At an interest rate of 5 percent, aggregate planned expenditure is equal to real GDP only when real GDP is $4 billion. The two other green squares show equilibrium expenditure at interest rates of 6 percent and 4 percent.

The *IS* Curve

The *IS curve* shows combinations of real GDP and the interest rate at which aggregate planned expenditure equals real GDP. The name "*IS* curve" was suggested by the curve's inventor, the great English economist John Hicks. The letter *I* stands for investment and *S* stands for saving. When Hicks invented the *IS* curve, he used a model economy in which there was no government and no foreign sector, so flow equilibrium occurs when investment equals saving. The label *IS* tells us that along that curve planned investment is equal to saving in such an economy. In an economy with a government and foreign sector, the points on the *IS* curve are points at which planned injections into the circular flow of expenditure and income equal the planned leakages from the circular flow.

Figure A30.1 derives the *IS* curve. Part (a) looks familiar. It is similar to Fig. 26.4. The 45° line shows all the points at which aggregate planned expenditure equals real GDP. Curves AE_a, AE_b, and AE_c are aggregate planned expenditure curves. Curve AE_a represents aggregate planned expenditure when the interest rate is 6 percent (row *a* of the table). Curve AE_b shows aggregate planned expenditure when the interest rate is 5 percent (row *b*), and AE_c shows aggregate planned expenditure when the interest rate is 4 percent (row *c*).

There is just one expenditure equilibrium on each of these three aggregate planned expenditure curves. On curve AE_a, the expenditure equilibrium is at point *a*, where real GDP is $3 billion. The expenditure equilibrium on curve AE_b occurs at point *b*, where real GDP is $4 billion. The expenditure equilibrium on AE_c occurs at point *c*, where real GDP is $5 billion.

Figure A30.1(b) shows each expenditure equilibrium again but highlights the relationship between the interest rate and real GDP at the expenditure equilibrium. The horizontal axis in Fig. A30.1(b), like that of Fig. A30.1(a), measures real GDP. The vertical axis measures the interest rate. Point *a* in part (b) illustrates the expenditure equilibrium at point *a* in part (a) of the figure (or in row *a* of the table). It tells us that if the interest rate is 6 percent, the expenditure equilibrium occurs at a real GDP of $3 billion. Points *b* and *c* in the figure illustrate the expenditure equilibrium at points *b* and *c* of part (a). The continuous line through these points is the *IS* curve.

It is often helpful to think of the relationships between two variables as one of "cause and effect." For example, the investment demand curve tells us the level of investment (effect) at a particular interest rate (cause). The *IS* curve is *not* a "cause and effect" relationship. Rather, it is a relationship that can be read in two ways. The *IS* curve that we have just derived tells us that if the interest rate is 6 percent, then aggregate planned expenditure equals real GDP only if real GDP is $3 billion. But we can turn things around: if real GDP is $3 billion, the interest rate at which aggregate planned expenditure equals real GDP is 6 percent.

The *IS* curve shows combinations of the interest rate and real GDP at which there is an expenditure equilibrium. To determine the interest rate and real GDP, we need an additional relationship between those two variables. The second relationship between interest rates and real GDP comes from equilibrium in the money market.

Money Market Equilibrium

The quantity of money demanded depends on the price level, real GDP, and the interest rate. The quantity of money demanded is proportional to the price level. If the price level doubles,

Figure A30.2 The Money Market, Stock Equilibrium, and the *LM* Curve

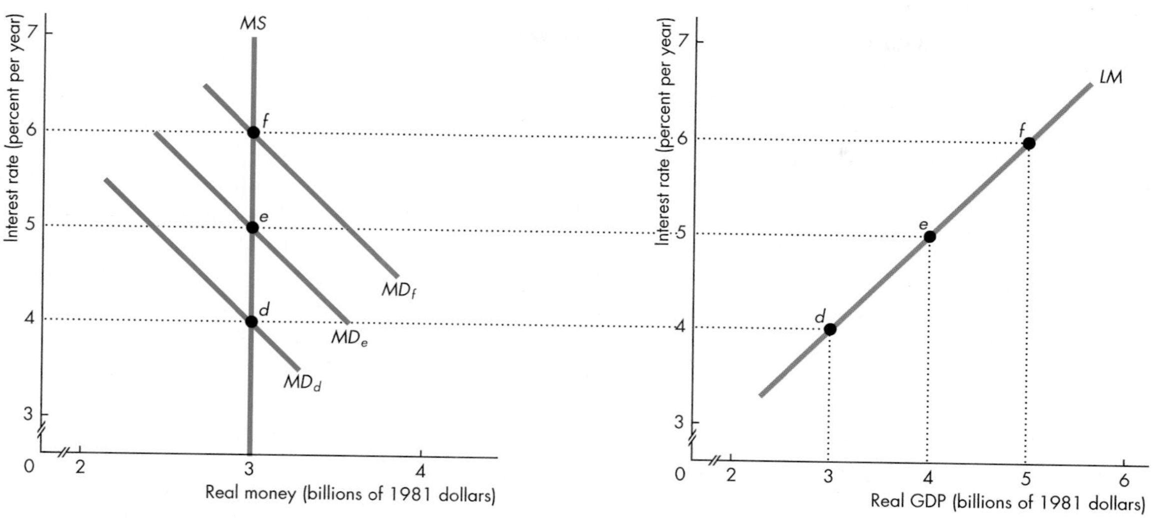

(a) Money market equilibrium

(b) The *LM* curve

The table shows the quantity of real money demanded at different combinations of the interest rate and real GDP. For example, if the interest rate is 6 percent and real GDP is $3 billion, the quantity of real money demanded is $2 billion (top left number). Stock equilibrium — equality between the quantity of real money demanded and supplied — is shown by the green squares. Each of columns *d*, *e*, and *f* represents a demand schedule for real money, and these are plotted as the demand curves for real money MD_d, MD_e, and MD_f, respectively in part (a). Money market equilibrium positions are shown in part (a), where these (*MD*) curves intersect the supply curve of real money *MS*, and are marked *d*, *e*, and *f*. Part (b) shows these same equilibrium positions but highlights the combinations of the interest rate and real GDP at which they occur. The line connecting these points is the *LM* curve.

Interest rate (percent per year)	**Quantity of real money demanded (billions of 1981 dollars)**		
6	2.0	2.5	3.0
5	2.5	3.0	3.5
4	3.0	3.5	4.0
Real GDP	3.0	4.0	5.0
Real money supply (billions of 1981 dollars)	3.0	3.0	3.0
	d	*e*	*f*

so does the quantity of money demanded. Real money is the ratio of the quantity of money to the price level. The quantity of real money demanded increases as real GDP increases and decreases as the interest rate increases.

The supply of money is determined by the actions of the Bank of Canada, the banks, and other financial intermediaries. For a given set of their actions and for a particular price level, the quantity of real money in existence is fixed. Money market equilibrium occurs when the quantity of real money supplied is equal to the quantity demanded. Equilibrium in the money market is a stock equilibrium. Figure A30.2 contains a numerical example that enables us to study money market equilibrium. Suppose that the quantity of money supplied is $3 billion. Also suppose that the GDP deflator is 100, so the quantity of real money supplied is also $3 billion. The real money supply is shown in the last row of the table. Money market equilibrium occurs when the quantity of real money demanded equals the quantity supplied — $3 billion. The quantity of real money demanded depends on real GDP and the interest rate. The table tells us about the demand for real money. Each row tells us how much real money is demanded at a given interest rate as real GDP varies, and each column tells us how much is demanded at a given real GDP as the interest rate varies. For example, at an interest rate of 6 percent and real GDP of $3 billion, the quantity of real money demanded is $2 billion. Alternatively, at an interest rate of 5 percent and real GDP of $4 billion, the quantity of real money demanded is $3 billion. The rest of the numbers in the table are read in a similar way.

Money market equilibrium occurs when the quantity of real money demanded equals the quantity supplied — $3 billion. The green squares in the table highlight the combinations of the interest rate and real GDP at which money market equilibrium occurs. If real GDP is $3 billion, the quantity of real money demanded is $3 billion when the interest rate is 4 percent. Thus at a real GDP of $3 billion and an interest rate of 4 percent, the money market is in equilibrium. The other two green squares tell us the interest rate at which the quantity of real money demanded is $3 billion when real GDP is $4 billion and $5 billion respectively. That is, they are interest rates at which the money market is in equilibrium.

The LM Curve

The *LM curve* shows the combinations of real GDP and the interest rate at which the quantity of real money demanded equals the quantity of real money supplied. The name "*LM* curve", like the name "*IS* curve", was invented by John Hicks. The quantity of money demanded used to be called *liquidity preference.* The label *LM,* when first used, meant that liquidity preference (*L*) is equal to the quantity of money supplied (*M*).

Figure A30.2 derives the *LM* curve. Part (a) shows the demand and supply curves for real money. The quantity supplied is fixed at $3 billion so the supply curve *MS* is vertical. Each of the table columns labelled *d, e,* and *f* is a demand schedule for real money — a schedule that tells us how the quantity of real money demanded rises as the interest rate falls. There is a different schedule for each level of real GDP. These three demand schedules for real money are graphed as demand curves for real money in part (a) of the figure as MD_d, MD_e, and MD_f. For example, when real GDP is $3 billion, the demand curve for real money is MD_d. Money market equilibrium occurs at the intersection of the supply curve and the demand curves for real money at points *d, e,* and *f* in part (a).

Figure A30.2(b) shows each money market equilibrium again but highlights the relationship between the interest rate and real GDP at which an equilibrium occurs. Points *d, e,* and *f* in part (b) illustrate the money market equilibrium represented by the green squares in the table and by those similarly labelled points in part (a). The continuous line through these points is the *LM* curve. The *LM* curve shows the interest rate and real GDP at which money market equilibrium occurs when the real money supply is $3 billion.

Like the *IS* curve, the *LM* curve does not have a "cause and effect" interpretation. The *LM* curve illustrated in Fig. A30.2(b) tells us that if the quantity of real money supplied is $3 billion and real GDP is $3 billion, then for money market equilibrium the interest rate is 4 percent. It also tells us that if the quantity of real money supplied is $3 billion and the interest rate is 4 percent, then for money market equilibrium real GDP is $3 billion. That is, the *LM* curve shows combinations of the interest rate and real GDP at which there is money market equilibrium.

The Equilibrium Interest Rate and Real GDP

We now have two relationships between the interest rate and real GDP. The first — the *IS* curve — tells us the relationship between those two variables when aggregate planned expenditure equals real GDP. The second — the *LM* curve — tells us the relationship between real GDP and the interest rate when the quantity of real money demanded equals the quantity supplied. But neither of these two relationships, on its own, determines the interest rate or real GDP. Yet together they determine both real GDP and the interest rate (at a given price level). Let's see how. Figure A30.3 brings together the *IS* curve and the *LM* curve to determine equilibrium real GDP and the interest rate. This equilibrium is the point of intersection of the *IS* curve and *LM* curve. Point *b* on the *IS* curve is a point of expenditure equilibrium. The interest rate and real GDP are such that aggregate planned expenditure equals real GDP. Point *e* on the *LM* curve is a point of money market equilibrium. The interest rate and real GDP are such that the

Figure A30.3 *IS-LM* Equilibrium

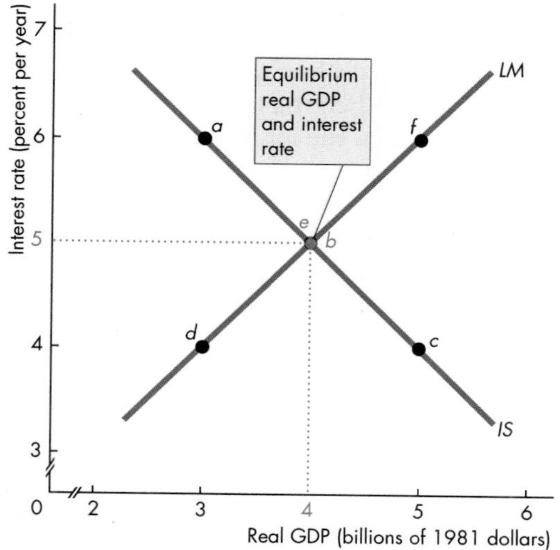

All points on the *IS* curve are points at which aggregate planned expenditure equals real GDP. All points on the *LM* curve are points at which the quantity of real money demanded equals the quantity of real money supplied. The intersection of the *IS* curve and the *LM* curve determines the equilibrium interest rate and real GDP — 5 percent and $4 billion. At this interest rate and real GDP, there is flow equilibrium in the goods market and stock equilibrium in the money market.

quantity of real money demanded equals the quantity of real money supplied. At this intersection point, there is both flow equilibrium in the goods market and stock equilibrium in the money market. The equilibrium interest rate is 5 percent and real GDP is $4 billion.

At all other points, there is either no expenditure equilibrium or the money market is not in equilibrium or both. At a point such as *a*, the economy is on its *IS* curve but off its *LM* curve. With real GDP at $3 billion and the interest rate at 6 percent, the interest rate is too high or real GDP is too low for money market equilibrium. Interest rates adjust quickly and would fall to 4 percent to bring about money market equilibrium, putting the economy at point *d*, a point on the *LM* curve. But point *d* is off the *IS* curve. At point *d*, with the interest rate at 4 percent and real GDP at $3 billion, aggregate planned expenditure exceeds real GDP. By checking back to the table in Fig. A30.1, you can see that aggregate planned expenditure is $3.8 billion, which exceeds real GDP of $3 billion. With aggregate planned expenditure larger than real GDP, real GDP will increase. But as real GDP increases, so does the demand for real money and so does the interest rate. Real GDP and the interest rate would rise and continue to do so until the point of intersection of the *IS* and *LM* curves is reached.

The account that we have just given, of what *would* happen if the economy was at a point like *a* or *d*, tells us that the economy cannot be at such points. The forces that operate in such situations would be so strong that they would always push the economy to the intersection of the *IS* and *LM* curves.

The Aggregate Demand Curve

The *aggregate demand curve* traces the relationship between the quantity of real GDP demanded and the price level (the GDP deflator), holding everything else constant. Let's see how we can derive the aggregate demand curve from the *IS-LM* model. To derive the aggregate demand curve, we vary the price level and work out how equilibrium real GDP varies as we do so.

The price level enters the *IS-LM* model to determine the quantity of real money supplied. The Bank of Canada determines the money supply as a certain number of current dollars. The higher the price level, the lower is the real value of those dollars. Because the price level affects the quantity of real money supplied, it also affects the *LM* curve.[1] Let's see how.

The Effects of a Change in Price Level on the *LM* Curve

Let's begin by asking what happens if the price level, instead of being 100, is 120 — 20 percent higher than before. The money supply is $3 billion. With a GDP deflator of 100, the real money supply is also $3 billion. But if the GDP deflator is 20 percent higher, the real money supply is 20 percent lower — $2.5 billion. (The real money supply is $3 billion divided by 1.2, which equals $2.5 billion.) We can see in the table in Fig. A30.2 that the quantity of real money demanded is $2.5 billion if real GDP is

[1] In a more general version of the *IS-LM* model, the price level also affects the *IS* curve. Its effects are the result of the real balance effect on expenditure and the international substitution effect. In this appendix, we'll ignore those effects. In the real world, those effects reinforce the effects that we are studying here.

\$4 billion and the interest rate is 6 percent. Thus with a GDP deflator of 120, an interest rate of 6 percent, and real GDP of \$4 billion this becomes a point on the *LM* curve. You can see it as point *g* in Fig. A30.4(a).

Next, suppose that the GDP deflator is lower than the original case — 86 instead of 100. Now the real money supply becomes \$3.5 billion (the real money supply is \$3 billion divided by 0.86, which equals \$3.5 billion). Again for money market equilibrium, we can see in the table of Fig. A30.2 what happens to the interest rate at a real GDP of \$4 billion. With a GDP deflator of 86, the interest rate falls to 4 percent in order to increase the quantity of real money demanded to \$3.5 billion — to make it equal to the real money supply. Thus with a GDP deflator of 86, an interest rate of 4 percent, and real GDP of \$4 billion this becomes a point on the *LM* curve — point *h* in Fig. A30.4(a).

The *LM* Curve Shift The example that we have worked through tells us that there is a different *LM* curve for each price level. Figure A30.4(a) illustrates the *LM* curves for the three price levels we have considered. The initial *LM* curve has the GDP deflator equal to 100. This curve has been relabelled as LM_0 in Fig. A30.4(a). When the GDP deflator is 120 and real GDP is \$4 billion, the interest rate that achieves equilibrium in the money market is 6 percent. This equilibrium is shown as point *g* on curve LM_1 in Fig. A30.4(a). The entire *LM* curve shifts up to LM_1 in order to pass through point *g*. When the GDP deflator is 86 and real GDP is \$4 billion, the interest rate that achieves equilibrium in the money market is 4 percent. This equilibrium is shown as point *h* on the curve LM_2 in Fig. A30.4(a). The entire *LM* curve shifts downward to LM_2 in order to pass through point *h*.

Figure A30.4 Deriving the Aggregate Demand Curve

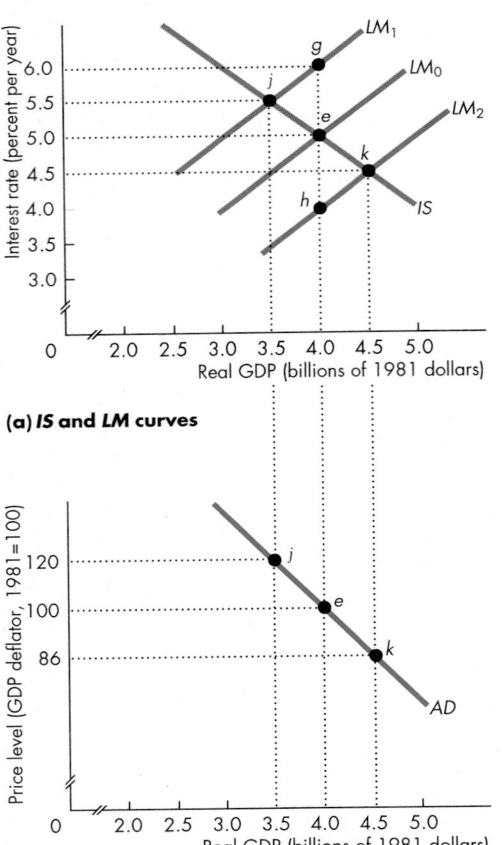

The position of the *LM* curve depends on the price level. In part (a), if the GDP deflator is 100, the *LM* curve is LM_0. If the GDP deflator increases to 120, the *LM* curve shifts to the left to LM_1. For money market equilibrium, a lower real money supply requires a higher interest rate at each level of real GDP. For example, if real GDP is \$4 billion, the interest rate has to increase from 5 percent to 6 percent (point *g*). If the price level falls, the real money supply increases and the *LM* curve shifts to the right to LM_2. If real GDP is \$4 billion, the interest rate falls to 4 percent (point *h*) to maintain money market equilibrium.

When the GDP deflator is 100, the *IS* and *LM* curves intersect at point *e* — at an interest rate of 5 percent and real GDP of \$4 billion. This equilibrium is shown again in part (b) as a point on the aggregate demand curve — point *e*. This point tells us that when the GDP deflator is 100, the quantity of real GDP demanded is \$4 billion. If the GDP deflator is 120, the *LM* curve is LM_1. The equilibrium interest rate at point *j* is 5.5 percent and real GDP is \$3.5 billion. A second point on the aggregate demand curve is point *k*. If the GDP deflator is 86, the *LM* curve is LM_2, the interest rate is 4.5 percent, and real GDP is \$4.5 billion. Joining points *j*, *e*, and *k* gives the aggregate demand curve.

Now that we have worked out the effects of a change in the price level on the position of the *LM* curve, we can derive the aggregate demand curve.

The Aggregate Demand Curve Derived

The aggregate demand curve shows how aggregate expenditure varies as the price level varies. We can derive the aggregate demand curve from the *IS-LM* model. Equilibrium in the *IS-LM* model determines real GDP for a given price level such that the money market is in equilibrium and there is an expenditure equilibrium. Since there is an expenditure equilibrium, the equilibrium real GDP determined by the *IS-LM* model is also aggregate expenditure. Therefore we can derive the aggregate demand curve by determining the equilibrium real GDP in the *IS-LM* model for a variety of different price levels. Let's derive the aggregate demand curve.

Figure A30.4(a) shows the *IS* curve and the three *LM* curves associated with the three different price levels (GDP deflators of 86, 100, and 120). When the GDP deflator is 100, the *LM* curve is LM_0. Equilibrium is at point *e*, where real GDP is \$4 billion and the equilibrium interest rate is 5 percent. If the GDP deflator is 120, the *LM* curve is LM_1. Equilibrium is at point *j*, where real GDP is \$3.5 billion and the interest rate is 5.5 percent. If the GDP deflator is 86, the *LM* curve is LM_2. Equilibrium is at point *k*, where real GDP is \$4.5 billion and the interest rate is 4.5 percent. At each price level there is a different equilibrium real GDP and interest rate.

Figure A30.4(b) traces the aggregate demand curve. The price level is measured on the vertical axis and real GDP on the horizontal axis. When the GDP deflator is 100, equilibrium real GDP is \$4 billion (point *e*). When the GDP deflator is 120, equilibrium real GDP is \$3.5 billion (point *j*). And when the GDP deflator is 86, real GDP demanded is \$4.5 billion (point *k*). Each of these points corresponds to the same point in Fig. A 30.4(a). The line joining these points in Fig. A30.4(b) is the aggregate demand curve.

Now that we have derived the aggregate demand curve and seen how it depends on flow equilibrium in the goods market and stock equilibrium in the money market, we can work out the effects on aggregate demand of changes in government expenditure on goods and services, in taxes, and in the money supply. To perform this analysis we return to considering what happens at a particular price level. Let's begin with fiscal policy and work out its effects on aggregate demand.

Fiscal Policy and Aggregate Demand

A change in government purchases or in taxes shifts the *IS* curve and the aggregate demand curve. In Chapter 26, we worked out the magnitude of the change in aggregate planned expenditure resulting from a change in government purchases or in taxes when the interest rate is constant. In terms of the *IS-LM* model, these multiplier effects tell us how far the *IS* curve shifts. But a change in aggregate planned expenditure at a given interest rate is not the same thing as a change in aggregate demand. When aggregate planned expenditure changes, the interest rate usually changes as well, and that has further effects on expenditure plans.

Figure A30.5 illustrates three different effects of a change in fiscal policy. In all three parts of the figure, the same fiscal policy action takes place. Either a rise in government purchases or a cut in autonomous taxes shifts the *IS* curve from IS_0 to IS_1. In part (a), the normal case, the *LM* curve is upward-sloping (LM_N) . When the *IS* curve shifts, the interest rate increases and so does real GDP. But the increase in real GDP is smaller than the magnitude of the rightward shift in the *IS* curve. The reason is that the higher interest rate leads to a decrease in investment, and that decrease in investment partially offsets the initial increased expenditure resulting from the fiscal policy action.

In Fig. A30.5(b), the *LM* curve is horizontal (LM_H). The *LM* curve is horizontal only if there is a liquidity trap — a situation in which people are willing to hold any quantity of money at a given interest rate. When the *IS* curve shifts to the right, real GDP increases by the same amount as the rightward shift of the *IS* curve. Interest rates stay constant. In this case, the multiplier effect of Chapter 26 still operates.

In Fig. A30.5(c), the *LM* curve is vertical (LM_V). Although the *IS* curve shifts to the right by exactly the same amount as in Figs. A30.5(a) and A30.5(b), real GDP stays constant. Here, the interest rate increases. The higher interest rate leads to a decrease in investment that exactly offsets the initial increase in expenditure resulting from the fiscal policy.

Figure A30.5 Fiscal Policy and Aggregate Demand

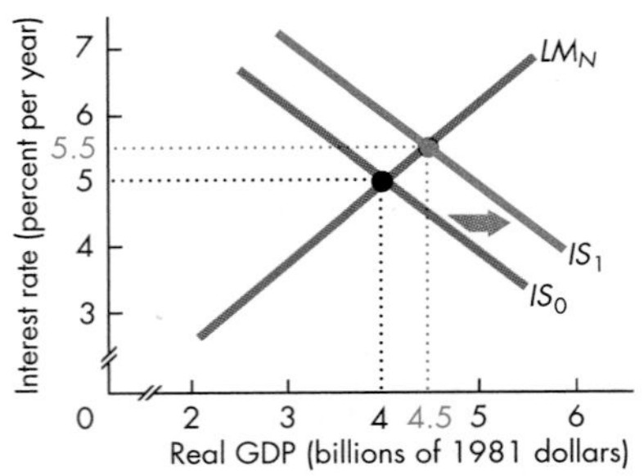

(a) Fiscal policy: normal case

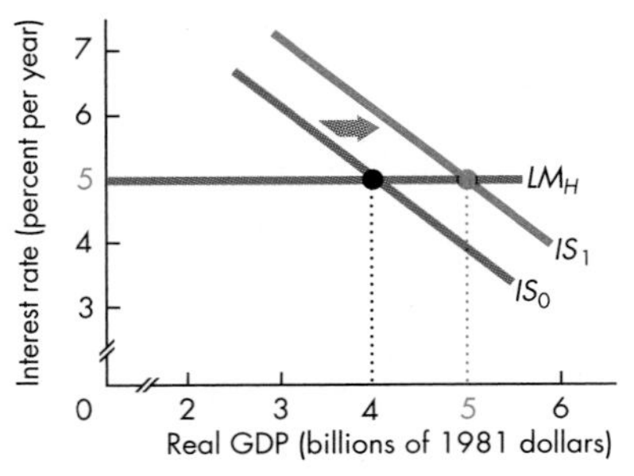

(b) Fiscal policy: maximum effect on GDP

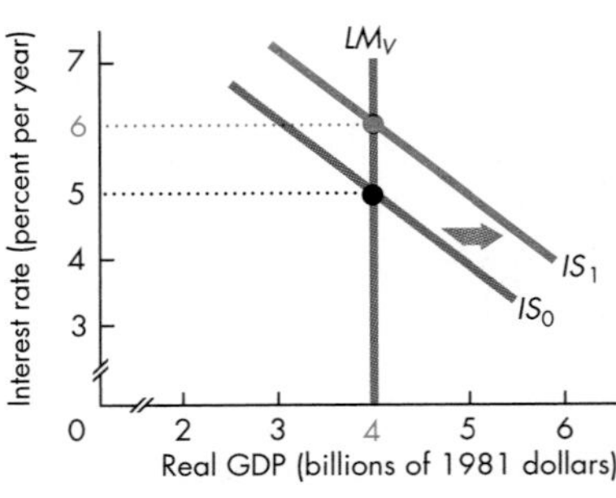

(c) Fiscal policy: no effect on GDP

An increase in government purchases or an autonomous tax cut shifts the *IS* curve to the right. The effects of fiscal policy on real GDP and the interest rate depend on the slope of the *LM* curve. In the normal case (part a), interest rates and real GDP rise. If there is a liquidity trap, the *LM* curve is horizontal (part b) and real GDP increases but interest rates stay constant. If the demand for money is insensitive to changes in interest rates, the *LM* curve is vertical (part c) and interest rates rise but real GDP stays constant. In this case, there is complete crowding out. The higher interest rate leads to a cut in investment that exactly offsets the initial fiscal policy action.

There is complete crowding out. Complete crowding out occurs if the demand for real money is completely insensitive to changes in interest rates. No matter what the interest rate, the quantity of real money demanded is a constant portion of real GDP.

Figure A30.5(b) corresponds to the extreme Keynesian prediction, Fig. A30.5(c) to the extreme monetarist prediction, and Fig. A30.5(a) to the intermediate position.

Next, let's consider monetary policy.

Monetary Policy and Aggregate Demand

We saw earlier in this appendix that when the *LM* curve shifts because of a change in the price level, equilibrium real GDP changes and there is a movement along the aggregate demand curve. But a change in the money supply also shifts the *LM* curve. If the *LM* curve shifts because there is a change in the nominal money supply, then the aggregate demand curve shifts. The magnitude of the change in aggregate demand — the shift in the aggregate demand curve — depends on two factors: the size of the shift of the *LM* curve and the slope of the *IS* curve. Figure A30.6 shows three possible cases. In each, the *LM* curve shifts to the right by the same amount, from LM_0 to LM_1. In part (a), the normal case, the *IS* curve is downward-sloping (IS_N). When the money supply increases, the interest rate falls and real GDP rises. The rise in real GDP results from increased investment induced by the lower interest rate.

In Fig. A30.6(b), the *IS* curve is horizontal (IS_H). This situation arises if people re-time their investment whenever the interest rate rises above or falls below 5 percent. If the interest rate rises above 5 percent, all investment stops; if the interest rate falls below 5 percent, there is no limit to the amount of investment that people try to undertake. At 5 percent, any amount of investment will be undertaken. In this case, a change in the money supply shifts the *LM* curve and increases real GDP but leaves the interest rate unchanged.

In Fig A30.6(c), the *IS* curve is vertical (IS_V). This case arises if investment is completely insensitive to interest rates. People plan to undertake a given level of investment regardless of the interest cost involved. In this case, when the *LM* curve shifts, interest rates fall but the lower interest rate does not stimulate additional expenditure, so real GDP stays constant.

Figure A30.6(c) corresponds to the predictions

Figure A30.6 Monetary Policy and Aggregate Demand

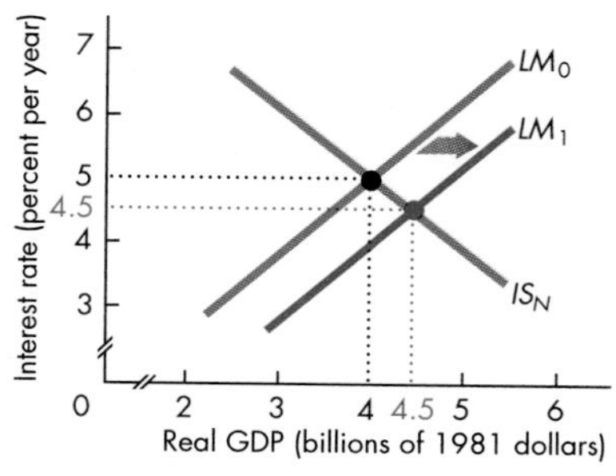

(a) Monetary policy: normal case

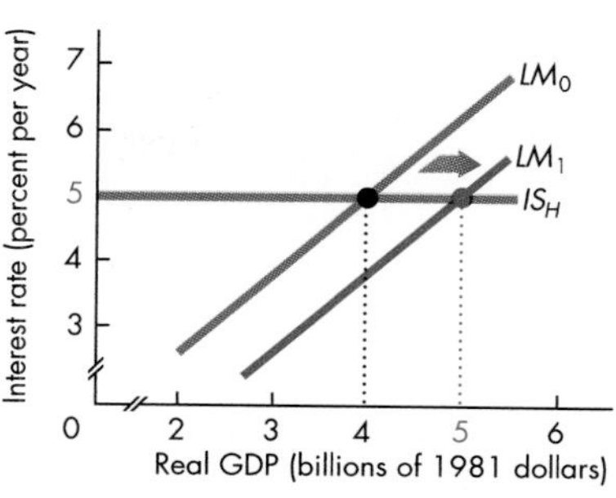

(b) Monetary policy: maximum effect on GDP

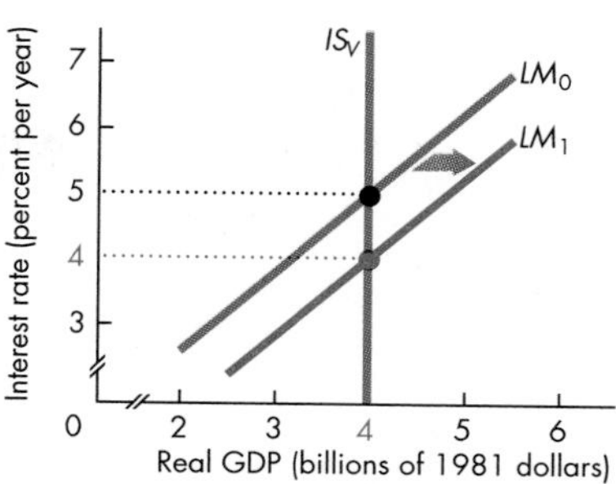

(c) Monetary policy: no effect on GDP

An increase in the money supply shifts the *LM* curve to the right. The effect of the monetary action on interest rates and real GDP depends on the slope of the *IS* curve. In one normal case (part a) interest rates fall and real GDP rises. The lower interest rates stimulate investment. In one special case (part b), the *IS* curve is horizontal. People don't care *when* they undertake their investment and will undertake any amount at an interest rate of 5 percent. The change in the money supply changes real GDP but leaves the interest rate constant. In the other special case (part c), investment demand is completely insensitive to interest rates. The *IS* curve is vertical, and a change in the money supply lowers interest rates but leaves real GDP unchanged. In this case, the lower interest rate has no effect on investment, so there is no initial injection of additional expenditure.

of extreme Keynesians: a change in the money supply has no effect on real GDP. Figure A30.6(b) corresponds to the predictions of extreme monetarists: a change in the money supply has a large and powerful effect on real GDP. Figure A30.6(a) is the intermediate position.

CHAPTER 31

Unemployment and Aggregate Supply

After studying this chapter, you will be able to:

- Explain why real GDP and employment fluctuate together.
- Explain how firms decide how much labour to employ.
- Explain how households decide how much labour to supply.
- Explain how wages, employment, and unemployment are determined if wages are flexible.
- Explain how wages, employment, and unemployment are determined if wages are "sticky".
- Derive the short-run and long-run aggregate supply curves.
- Explain the influences that shift the aggregate supply curves.

Jobs and Incomes

As OUR ECONOMY ebbs and flows through the business cycle, employment and unemployment march in close step with real gross domestic product (GDP). Sometimes the Canadian economy is in a state of deep recession — real GDP has fallen and the unemployment rate is high. Such a situation prevailed in the winter of 1982. More than 12 percent of the labour force was without a job. And although one-third of those unemployed had been without jobs for only four weeks or less, another one-third had lacked jobs for one to three months, and one-sixth had gone without work for more than six months. By 1989, the economy had experienced six years of continuous recovery and unemployment had fallen to 7.5 percent. Why does unemployment occur? Why, at times, are more than one in eight people of working age looking unsuccessfully for a job? What makes the unemployment rate rise and fall? ■ A few years ago, Massey Ferguson announced it was going to close its farm equipment plant in Brantford, Ontario. The workers and the mayor of Brantford reacted angrily. Instead of laying off its workers, why didn't Massey Ferguson cut back on each worker's hours and negotiate a pay cut to keep the plant working? ■ The opposite of unemployment is overtime work. Many firms routinely have labour working overtime — when the economy is booming most firms are in that situation. But even while some firms are paying overtime to their workers, other people are still without jobs. Why? Why don't the unemployed get jobs and the employed work normal hours for normal wages?

■ In this chapter we'll take a close look at the Canadian labour market. We'll attempt to discover why the unemployment rate is sometimes unusually high and what brings high unemployment rates down. Our study of labour markets will take us to the heart of the current controversy in macroeconomics — the controversy over whether the economy is inherently stable or inherently unstable. Eonomists disagree about how flexible the labour market is as an instrument for bringing about changes in wages to equate the quantity of labour supplied and the quantity demanded. Some economists see the labour market as a highly flexible and sophisticated instrument that maintains equality between the quantities of labour demanded and supplied on a continuous basis. In the view of these economists, unemployment arises mainly from frictions and from the fact that it takes time for labour to be reallocated from one sector to another or from one region of the country to another. That is, they explain fluctuations in unemployment as fluctuations in the natural rate of unemployment. ■ Another group of macroeconomists believe that wages do not adjust quickly enough to maintain equality between the quantity of labour supplied and the quantity demanded. Sometimes, in the view of these economists, wages are "too high" and, as a consequence, the quantity of labour demanded is less than the quantity supplied and unemployment is above its natural rate. ■ The alignment of macroeconomists in this controversy is similar to that in the older Keynesian-monetarist controversy that we discussed in the previous chapter. Monetarists tend to take the view that wages are flexible and that unemployment is frictional or "natural." Keynesians take the view that wages are "sticky" and that some unemployment arises from insufficient wage flexibility. Unlike the old Keynesian-monetarist controversy, this one is still not settled. We have not yet found the acid test that would enable economists on both sides of the debate to set out a research agenda that could, in principle, settle their differences. Given this current state of knowledge, all we can do is to set out the competing views and work out their implications. That's what we'll do in this chapter. ■ Our study of the labour market will complete a further block in the macroeconomic jigsaw puzzle — the aggregate supply block. We'll return to the short-run and long-run aggregate supply curves that you studied in Chapter 24 and see how those curves are related to the labour market. We'll discover that along the long-run aggregate supply curve, the quantity of labour demanded equals the quantity supplied, and we'll see how the levels of employment and unemployment change as the economy slides along its short-run aggregate supply curve. But to understand these connections, we must first study the relationship between employment and real GDP.

The Short-Run Aggregate Production Function

A **production function** shows how output varies as the employment of inputs is varied. A **short-run production function** shows how output varies when the quantity of labour employed varies, holding constant the quantity of capital and the state of technology. Although production functions exist for every kind of economic activity — building dams, baking cakes, or performing musicals — the production function we will study in this chapter is the *aggregate* production function. The **short-run aggregate production function** shows how real GDP varies as the quantity of labour employed is varied, holding the capital stock and state of technology constant.

The table in Fig. 31.1 records part of an economy's short-run aggregate production function. (The economy is an imaginary one. We'll look at the Canadian economy's production function later in this section.) In that table, we look at the aggregate quantity of labour, measured in millions of hours a year, over the range 100 to 200. Through that range of employment, real GDP varies between $3.7 billion and $4.1 billion a year (measured in 1981 dollars). The short-run aggregate production function is illustrated in the graph in Fig. 31.1. The labour input is measured on the horizontal axis and real GDP on the vertical axis. The short-run production function (*PF*) slopes upward, indicating that more labour input produces more real GDP.

The Marginal Product of Labour

The **marginal product of labour** is the additional real GDP produced by one additional hour of labour input, holding all other inputs and technology constant. We calculate the marginal product of labour as the change in real GDP divided by the change in the quantity of labour employed. Let's do such a calculation, using the data in Fig. 31.1.

When the labour input increases by 25 million from 100 to 125 million hours, real GDP increases from $3.7 billion to $3.9 billion — an increase of $0.2 billion. The marginal product of labour over this range is $8 an hour ($0.2 billion ÷ 25 million). Next, look at what happens at a higher level of labour input. When the labour input increases again by 25 million hours, from 175 million to 200 million

Figure 31.1 The Short-Run Aggregate Production Function

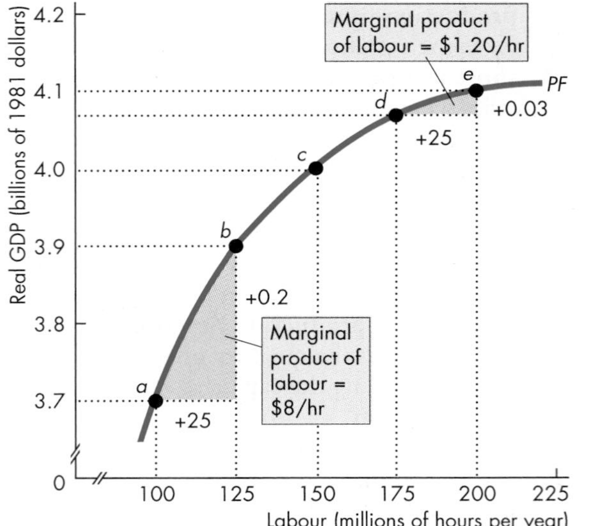

	Labour (millions of hours per year)	Real GDP (billions of 1981 dollars per year)
a	100	3.70
b	125	3.90
c	150	4.00
d	175	4.07
e	200	4.10

The short-run aggregate production function shows the level of real GDP at each quantity of labour input, holding constant the stock of capital equipment and state of technology. The table lists five points on a short-run aggregate production function. Each row tells us the amount of real GDP that can be produced by a given labour input. Points *a* through *e* in the graph correspond to the rows in the table. The curve passing through these points traces the economy's short-run aggregate production function. The marginal product of labour is highlighted in the diagram. As the labour input increases, real GDP also increases but by successively smaller amounts. For example, a 25 million hour increase in labour from 100 to 125 million increases real GDP by $0.2 billion — a marginal product of $8 per hour. But a 25 million hour increase in labour from 175 to 200 million hours increases real GDP by only $0.03 billion — a marginal product of $1.20 per hour.

hours, real GDP increases but by much less than in the previous case — by only $0.03 billion. Now the marginal product of labour is only $1.20 an hour ($0.03 billion ÷ 25 million).

The most important fact about the marginal product of labour — apparent from the calculations that we've just performed and visible in the figure — is that it declines as the labour input increases. This phenomenon is called the diminishing marginal product of labour. The **diminishing marginal product of labour** is the tendency for the marginal product of labour to decline as the labour input increases, holding everything else constant. The diminishing marginal product of labour is a feature of almost every production process. It arises because we are dealing with a *short-run* production function. As the quantity of labour employed is varied, all other inputs are held constant. Thus, although more labour can produce more output, the additional labour operates the same capital equipment — machines and tools — as a smaller labour force would. As more people are hired, the capital equipment is worked closer and closer to its physical limits and output cannot be increased in proportion to the increased labour input. This feature is present in almost all production processes. It is also present in the relationship between aggregate employment and aggregate output — real GDP.

The fact that the marginal product of labour diminishes has an important influence on the demand for labour, as we shall see shortly. But first, let's look at some of the things that make the production function shift.

Economic Growth and Technological Change

Economic growth is the expansion of the economy's productive capacity. Every year some of the economy's resources are devoted to developing new technologies to achieve greater output from a given amount of labour input. Also, resources are devoted to building new capital equipment that incorporates the most productive technologies available. Because capital accumulates and technology advances, the short-run aggregate production function shifts upward over time. Figure 31.2 illustrates such a shift. The curve labelled PF_{90} is the same as the production function in Fig. 31.1. During 1990, capital accumulates and new technologies are incorporated into new and more productive capital equipment. Some old and less productive capital wears out and is retired to the scrap heap. The net result is an increase

Figure 31.2 The Growth of Output

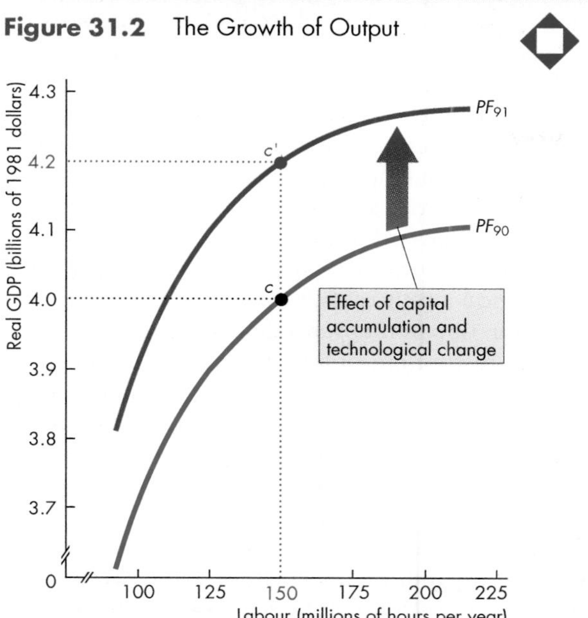

Output grows over time. The accumulation of capital and the adoption of more productive technologies makes it possible to achieve a higher level of real GDP for any given labour input. For example, between 1990 and 1991 the production function shifts upward from PF_{90} to PF_{91}. A labour input of 150 million hours produces $4.0 billion of real GDP in 1990 (point *c*) and $4.2 billion in 1991 (point *c'*).

in the productivity of the economy that results in an upward movement of the short-run aggregate production function to PF_{91}. When 150 million hours of labour are employed in 1990, the economy can produce a real GDP of $4 billion (point *c*). By 1991, that same quantity of labour can produce $4.2 billion (point *c'*) . Each level of labour input produces more output in 1991 than in 1990.

Variable Growth Rates

Capital accumulation and technological change do not proceed at a constant pace. Sometimes they are rapid and at other times they are very slow. Also, there are times when a lot of new things are being discovered but have not yet been put into practice through innovation in production techniques. In other words, there may be periods of rapid invention but slow innovation. **Invention** is the discovery of a new technique. **Innovation** is the act of putting a new technique into operation.

Although the short-run aggregate production function usually shifts upward over time, it occasionally shifts downward — lowering the economy's production potential. Examples of negative influences, or shocks, that make the aggregate production function shift downward are widespread drought, major disruptions to international trade, major civil unrest, and war. A serious disruption of international trade occurred in 1974 when the Organization of Petroleum Exporting Countries (OPEC) placed an embargo on oil exports. This deprived the industrialized world of one of its most crucial natural resources. Firms could not obtain all the fuel they needed, and as a result, the labour force could not produce as much output as it normally would. As a consequence of that embargo, the short-run aggregate production function shifted downward in 1974.

Let's take a closer look at the short-run aggregate production function in Canada.

The Canadian Short-Run Aggregate Production Function

We can examine the short-run aggregate production function in Canada by looking at the relationship between real GDP and aggregate employment.

Figure 31.3 measures real GDP on the vertical axis and the quantity of labour on the horizontal axis. The values of these two variables are plotted for each year between 1975 and 1989. For example, in 1975 labour hours were 18.9 billion and real GDP was $283 billion; in 1989 labour hours were 25.6 billion and real GDP was $460 billion. These two points and the other points in the figure do not all lie on the same short-run aggregate production function. Instead, each lies on its own short-run aggregate production function. Each year the stock of capital equipment and the state of technology change, so the economy's productive potential is usually higher than in the year before. The production function for 1975 is PF_{75} and that for 1989 is PF_{89}.

The 1989 short-run aggregate production function is 35 percent higher than the 1975 short-run aggregate production function. This fact means that if employment in 1989 had been the same as it was in 1975, real GDP in 1989 would have been only $390 billion. Equivalently, if employment in 1975 had been the same as it was in 1989, real GDP in 1975 would have been $340 billion.

The difference between real GDP in 1989 and in 1975 is partly accounted for by an increase in capital stock and technological change, which shifted the short-run aggregate production function

Figure 31.3 The Canadian Short-Run Aggregate Production Function

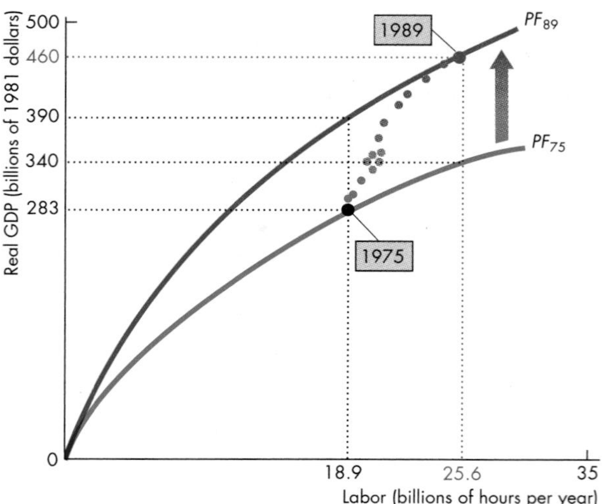

The points in the figure show real GDP and aggregate hours of labour employed in Canada for each year between 1975 and 1989. In 1975, for example, labour input was 18.9 billion hours and real GDP was \$283 billion. In 1989, labour input was 25.6 billion hours and real GDP was \$460 billion. The points do not lie on one short-run aggregate production function. Instead, the short-run aggregate production function shifts from year to year as capital accumulates and technologies change. The figure shows the short-run aggregate production functions for 1975 and 1989 — PF_{75} and PF_{89}. The 1989 production function is 35 percent higher than that for 1975. For example, the 18.9 billion hours of labour that produced \$283 billion of real GDP in 1975 would have produced \$390 billion of real GDP in 1989. Similarly, the 25.6 billion hours of labour that produced \$460 billion of real GDP in 1989 would have produced only \$340 billion of real GDP in 1975.

Sources: Real GDP: see Fig. 22.5. Labour hours: actual hours worked per week multiplied by number of people employed (annual averages), Statistics Canada, *The Labour Force*, catalogue no. 71-529.

upward, and partly by an increase in employment from 18.9 billion hours to 25.6 billion hours, which produced a movement along the new short-run aggregate production function.

REVIEW

A production function tells us how the output that can be produced varies as inputs are varied. A short-run production function tells us how the output that can be produced varies as the employment of labour varies, holding everything else constant. The short-run aggregate production function tells us how real GDP varies as total labour hours vary. The marginal product of labour — the increase in real GDP resulting from a one-hour increase of labour input — diminishes as the labour input increases.

The short-run aggregate production function usually shifts upward from year to year, but on occasion it shifts downward. Capital accumulation and technological advances shift the short-run aggregate production function upward. Shocks, such as droughts, disruptions of international trade, and civil and political unrest, shift the production function downward. The short-run aggregate production function in Canada shifted upward by 35 percent between 1975 and 1989. ■

We've just seen that the level of output in any given year depends on the position of the short-run aggregate production function and on the quantity of labour employed. Even if the production function shifts upward, it is still possible for output to fall because of a fall in employment. For example, in 1982 employment fell by almost 1 billion hours from its 1981 level, and real GDP fell by \$11 billion. To determine the level of output, we need to understand not only the influences on the short-run aggregate production function, but also those on the level of employment. To determine the level of employment, we need to study the demand for and supply of labour and how the market allocates labour to jobs. We'll begin by studying the demand for labour.

The Demand for Labour

The **quantity of labour demanded** is the number of labour hours hired by all the firms in an economy. The **demand for labour** is a schedule or curve that shows the quantity of labour demanded at each level of the real wage rate. The **real wage rate** is the wage per hour expressed in *constant dollars* — for example, the wage per hour expressed in 1981 dollars. The wage rate expressed in *current dollars* is called the **money wage rate**. The real wage rate is the money wage rate divided by the GDP deflator × 100. A real wage rate expressed in 1981 dollars tells us what today's money wage rate would buy if prices today were the same as in 1981. For example, if today the money wage rate is \$13.50 and the

GDP deflator is 141, the real wage rate is $9.57 ($13.50 ÷ 141 × 100).

An example of a demand for labour schedule is shown in the table of Fig. 31.4. Row *a* tells us that at a real wage rate of $9 an hour, 100 million hours of labour (per year) are demanded. The other rows of the table are read in a similar way. The demand for labour schedule is graphed as the demand for labour curve (*LD*). Each point on the curve corresponds to the row identified by the same letter in the table.

Why is the quantity of labour demanded influenced by the *real* wage rate? Why isn't it the *money* wage rate that affects the quantity of labour demanded? Also, why does the quantity of labour demanded increase as the real wage rate decreases? That is, why does the demand for labour curve slope downward? Let's answer these questions.

Diminishing Marginal Product and the Demand for Labour

Firms are in business to maximize profits. Each worker a firm hires adds to its costs and increases its output. Up to a point, the extra output produced by the worker is worth more to the firm than the wages it has to pay. But each additional hour of labour hired produces less output than the previous hour — the marginal product of labour diminishes. As the amount of labour employed increases and the capital equipment employed is constant, more workers have to work the same machines and the plant operates closer and closer to its physical limits. Output increases, but it does not increase in proportion to the increase in labour input. As the firm hires more workers, it eventually reaches the point at which the revenue from selling the extra output produced by an additional hour of labour equals the hourly wage rate. If the firm hires even one more hour of labour, the extra cost incurred will exceed the revenue brought in from selling the extra output. The firm will not employ that additional hour of labour. It will stop at the point at which the revenue brought in by the last hour of labour input equals the wage rate.

To see why the real wage, rather than the money wage, affects the quantity of labour demanded, let's consider an example. A pop factory employs 400 hours of labour. The additional output produced by the last hour hired is 11 bottles of pop. That is, the marginal product of labour is 11 bottles of pop per hour. Pop sells for 50 cents a bottle, so the revenue brought in from selling these 11 bottles is $5.50. Suppose the money wage rate is also $5.50 an hour. The last hour of labour hired brings in as much revenue as the wages paid out, so it just pays the firm to hire that hour of labour. The firm is paying a real wage rate that is exactly the same as the marginal

Figure 31.4 Demand for Labour

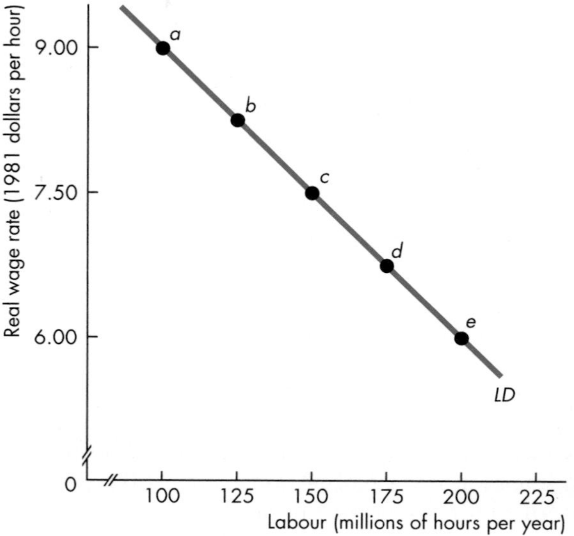

	Real wage rate (1981 dollars per hour)	Quantity of labour demanded (millions of hours per year)
a	9.00	100
b	8.25	125
c	7.50	150
d	6.75	175
e	6.00	200

The quantity of labour demanded increases as the real wage rate decreases, as illustrated by the labour demand schedule in the table and the demand for labour curve (*LD*). Each row in the table tells us the quantity of labour demanded at a given real wage rate and corresponds to a point on the labour demand curve. For example, when the real wage rate is $7.50 an hour, the quantity of labour demanded is 150 million hours a year (point *c*). The demand for labour curve slopes downward because it pays firms to hire workers so long as their marginal product is greater than or equal to the real wage. The lower the real wage rate, the larger is the number of workers whose marginal product exceeds that real wage.

product of labour — 11 bottles of pop. That is, the real wage rate is equal to the money wage rate of $5.50 an hour divided by the price of pop, 50 cents a bottle.

To see why the money wage rate does not affect the quantity of labour demanded, suppose that the money wage rate and all prices double. The money wage rate increases to $11 an hour and the price of pop increases to $1 a bottle. The pop factory is in the same real situation as before. It pays $11 for the last hour of labour employed and sells the output produced by that labour for $11. The money wage rate has doubled from $5.50 to $11 an hour, but nothing *real* has changed. The real wage rate is still 11 bottles of pop. As far as the firm is concerned, 400 hours is still the right quantity of labour to hire. The money wage rate has changed, but the real wage rate and the quantity of labour demanded have remained constant.

To see why the real wage affects the quantity of labour demanded, let's work out what happens if the money wage rate increases to $11 an hour while the price of pop remains constant at 50 cents a bottle. The real wage rate has now increased to 22 bottles of pop (the money wage of $11 an hour ÷ 50 cents, the price of a bottle of pop). The last hour of labour hired now costs $11, but it brings in only $5.50 of extra revenue. It does not pay the firm to hire this hour of labour. The firm cuts back its labour input until its marginal product brings in $11 of revenue. That occurs when the marginal product of labour is 22 bottles an hour (22 bottles × 50 cents a bottle = $11). The marginal product is again equal to the real wage rate. But to make the marginal product of labour equal to the real wage rate, the firm has to decrease the quantity of labour employed. Thus when the real wage rate increases, the quantity demanded decreases.

In the example that we've just worked through, the real wage increased because the money wage increased with a constant output price. But the same outcome occurs if the money wage remains constant and the output price decreases. For example, if the wage rate remains at $5.50 an hour while the price of pop falls to 25 cents a bottle, the real wage is 22 bottles of pop. The pop bottling factory hires that amount of labour that makes the marginal product of labour equal to 22 bottles an hour.

Thus the quantity of labour demanded depends on the real wage, not the money wage, and the higher the real wage, the lower is the quantity of labour demanded.

We now know why the quantity of labour demanded depends on the real wage and why the demand curve for labour curve slopes downward. But what makes the curve shift?

Shifts in the Demand for Labour Curve

When the marginal product of each hour of labour changes, the demand for labour curve shifts. The accumulation of capital and the development of new technologies are constantly increasing the marginal product of each hour of labour. We've already seen one effect of such changes. They shift the short-run aggregate production function upward, as shown in Fig. 31.2. At the same time, they make the short-run aggregate production function steeper. Anything that makes the short-run production function steeper increases the marginal product of each hour of labour — increases the extra output obtained from one additional hour of labour. At a given real wage rate, firms increase the amount of labour they hire until the revenue brought in from selling the extra output produced by the last hour of labour input equals the hourly wage. Thus as the short-run aggregate production function shifts upward, the demand for labour curve also shifts to the right.

In general, the demand for labour curve shifts to the right over time. But there are fluctuations in the pace at which it shifts, fluctuations that match those in the short-run aggregate production function. Fluctuations in the production function produce changes in the demand for labour, which in turn produce fluctuations in employment, real GDP, and the real wage rate.

Let's look at the demand for labour in Canada and see how it has changed over the period since 1969.

The Canadian Demand for Labour

Figure 31.5 shows the real wage rate and the quantity of labour employed in each year between 1975 and 1989. For example, in 1989 the real wage was $9.75 an hour (in 1981 dollars) and 25.6 billion hours of labour were employed. The figure also shows two demand curves for labour, one for 1975 and the other for 1989. Between 1975 and 1989, the production function shifted upward and the marginal product of labour increased. If the quantity of labour employed in 1989 had been the same as it was

Figure 31.5 The Canadian Demand for Labour

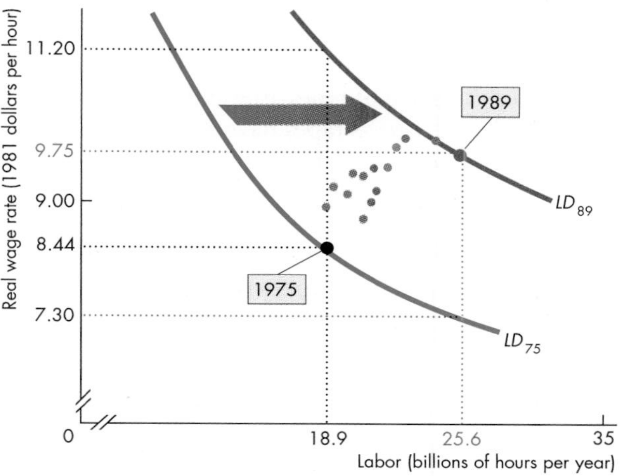

The figure shows the quantity of labour employed and real wages in Canada from 1975 to 1989. For example, in 1975 the real wage was $8.44 per hour and 18.9 billion hours of labour were employed. In 1989, the real wage was $9.75 per hour and 25.6 billion hours of labour were employed. These two points (and the points for the years between them) do not lie on a single demand for labour curve. The demand for labour curve has shifted as a result of shifts in the short-run aggregate production function. The figure shows the demand curves for 1975 and 1989 — LD_{75} and LD_{89}. Over time, the demand for labour curve has shifted to the right.

Sources: Labour hours: see Fig. 31.3. Real wage rate: wages, salaries, and supplementary labour income (CANSIM series D20002) deflated by the GDP Deflator (CANSIM series D20337), divided by labour hours.

in 1975, 18.9 billion hours, the real wage rate would have been $11.20 per hour. If the quantity of labour employed in 1975 had been as high as that in 1989 (25.6 billion hours) the real wage rate in that year would only have been $7.30 per hour.

R E V I E W

The quantity of labour demanded by firms depends on the real wage rate. For an individual firm, the real wage rate is the money wage rate paid to the worker divided by the price for which the firm's output sells. For the economy as a whole, the real wage rate is the money wage rate divided by the price level. The lower the real wage rate, the greater is the quantity of labour demanded. The demand for labour curve slopes downward.

The demand for labour curve shifts because of shifts in the short-run aggregate production function. An increase in the capital stock or advances in technology embodied in the capital stock shift the short-run aggregate production function upward and increase the marginal product of labour. The demand for labour curve shifts to the right, but at an uneven pace. ■

Let's now turn to the other side of the labour market and see how the supply of labour is determined.

The Supply of Labour

The **quantity of labour supplied** is the number of hours of labour services that households supply to firms. The **supply of labour** is a schedule or curve that shows how the quantity of labour supplied varies as the real wage varies.

A supply of labour schedule appears in the table in Fig. 31.6. Row *a* tells us that at a real wage rate of $6 an hour, 100 million hours of labour (per year) are supplied. The other rows of the table are read in a similar way. The supply of labour schedule is graphed as the supply of labour curve (*LS*). Each point on the *LS* curve represents the row identified by the same letter in the table. As the real wage increases, the quantity of labour supplied increases. The supply of labour curve slopes upward.

But why does the quantity of labour supplied increase when the real wage increases? There are two reasons:

- Hours per worker increase.
- The labour force participation rate increases.

The Determination of Hours per Worker

In choosing how many hours to work, a household has to decide how to allocate its time between work and other activities. If a household chooses not to work for an hour, it does not get paid for that hour. The real hourly wage rate that the household gives up is the opportunity cost of an hour of not working. What the household really gives up by not working is all the goods and services that it could buy with the hourly money wage. So the opportunity cost of an

Figure 31.6 The Supply of Labour

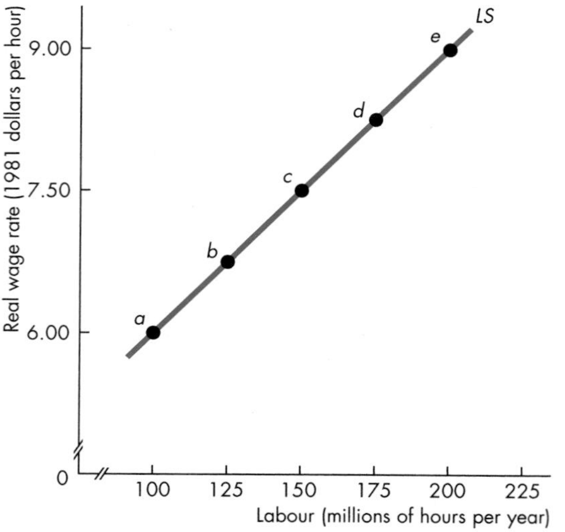

	Real wage rate (1981 dollars per hour)	Quantity of labour supplied (millions of hours per year)
a	6.00	100
b	6.75	125
c	7.50	150
d	8.25	175
e	9.00	200

The quantity of labour supplied increases as the real wage rate increases, as illustrated by the labour supply schedule in the table and the supply of labour curve (*LS*). Each row of the table tells us the quantity of labour supplied at a given real wage rate and corresponds to a point on the labour supply curve. For example, when the real wage rate is $7.50 per hour, the quantity of labour supplied is 150 million hours per year (point *c*). The supply of labour curve slopes upward because households work longer hours, on the average, at higher wages and more households participate in the labour force. These responses are reinforced by intertemporal substitution — the re-timing of work to take advantage of temporarily high wages.

hour of time spent not working is the real hourly wage rate.

What happens to people's willingness to work if the real wage rate increases? Does a higher wage lead to more work or less? Such a change has two opposing effects:

- A substitution effect
- An income effect

Substitution Effect The substitution effect of a change in the real wage rate works in exactly the same way as a change in the price of tapes affects the quantity of tapes demanded. Just as tapes have a price, so does time. As we've just noted, the real hourly wage rate is the opportunity cost of an hour spent not working. A higher real wage rate increases the opportunity cost of time and makes time itself a more valuable commodity. This higher opportunity cost of not working encourages people to reduce their nonwork time and increase the time spent working. Thus as the real wage rate increases, more hours of work are supplied.

Income Effect But a higher real wage rate also increases people's incomes. As you know, the higher a person's income, the greater is that person's demand for all the different types of goods and services. One such "good" is leisure — the time to do pleasurable things that don't generate an income. Thus a higher real wage rate also makes people want to enjoy longer leisure hours and supply fewer hours of work.

Which of these two effects dominates depends on the individual's attitude towards work and also on the real wage rate. Attitudes towards work, though varying among individuals, do not change much, on the average, over time. But the real wage rate does change, bringing changes in the quantity of labour supplied. At a very low real wage rate, the substitution effect is stronger than the income effect. That is, the inducement to substitute working time for leisure time is stronger than the inducement to spend part of a larger income on longer leisure hours. As a consequence, as the real wage rate increases, the quantity of labour supplied also increases.

At a high enough real wage rate, the income effect becomes stronger than the substitution effect. The inducement to spend more of the additional income on leisure time is stronger than the incentive to economize on leisure time, now that its opportunity cost has increased.

Some people enjoy such a high real wage that a further increase would reduce their hours of work. But for most of us a higher real wage coaxes us to work more. Thus, on the average, the higher the real wage rate, the more hours each person works.

The Participation Rate

The **labour force participation rate** is the proportion of the working age population that is in the labour force — that is, either employed or unemployed (but seeking employment). For a variety of reasons, people differ in their willingness to work. Some people have better productive opportunities at home and so need a bigger inducement to quit those activities and work for someone else. Other individuals place a very high value on leisure, and they require a high real wage to induce them to do any work at all. These considerations suggest that each person has a reservation wage. A **reservation wage** is the lowest wage at which a person will supply any labour. Below that wage, a person will not work.

Those people who have a reservation wage less than or equal to the actual real wage will be in the labour force, and those with a reservation wage greater than the actual real wage will not be in the labour force. The higher the real wage rate, the larger is the number of people whose reservation wage falls below the real wage. Hence, the higher the real wage rate, the higher is the labour force participation rate.

Reinforcing and strengthening the increase in hours worked per household and the labour force participation rate is an intertemporal substitution effect on the quantity of labour supplied.

Intertemporal Substitution

Households have to decide not only whether to work but *when* to work. This decision is based not just on the current real wage but on the current real wage relative to expected future real wages. Suppose that the wage rate is higher today than it is expected to be later on. How does this information affect a person's labour supply decision? It encourages more work today and less in the future. Thus the higher the real wage relative to what is expected in the future (other things being constant), the larger is the quantity of labour supplied.

Temporarily high real wages are similar to a high rate of return. When wages are temporarily high, people can obtain a higher rate of return on their work effort by enjoying a smaller amount of leisure and supplying more labour. By investing in some work now and taking the return in more leisure time later, they can obtain a higher overall level of consumption of goods and services and of leisure.

We've now seen why, as the real wage rate increases, the quantity of labour supplied increases — why the supply of labour curve slopes upward. Let's now bring the two sides of the labour market together and study the determination of wages and employment.

Wages and Employment

We have discovered that as the real wage rate increases, the quantity of labour demanded declines and the quantity of labour supplied increases. We now want to study how the two sides of the labour market interact to determine the real wage, employment, and unemployment.

Economists disagree about how the labour market works. In fact, this disagreement is the main source of current controversy in macroeconomics. There are two leading theories about the labour market:

- The flexible wage theory
- The sticky wage theory

The flexible wage theory is built on the assumption that labour is traded in markets that operate much like the markets for ordinary goods and services, with the real wage continuously and freely adjusting to keep the quantity demanded equal to the quantity supplied. The sticky wage theory is based on the assumption that the dominant form of trading in the labour market is a wage contract that specifies a fixed money wage for a fixed period of time — hence the name "sticky wages." If money wages are sticky, real wages do not continuously adjust to keep the quantity of labour demanded equal to the quantity supplied. Let's look at these two theories, beginning with the simplest — the flexible wage theory.

The Flexible Wage Theory

The flexible wage theory of the labour market emphasizes the possibility that wages adjust to achieve a continuous balance between the quantities of labour supplied and demanded. The theory is illustrated in Fig. 31.7. The demand for labour curve is *LD* and the supply of labour curve is *LS*. This market determines an equilibrium real wage rate of $7.50 an hour and a quantity of labour employed of 150 million hours. If the real wage rate is below its equilibrium level of $7.50 an hour, the quantity of labour demanded exceeds the quantity supplied. In such a situation, wages rise since firms are willing to offer higher and higher wages in order to overcome their

Figure 31.7 Equilibrium with Flexible Wages

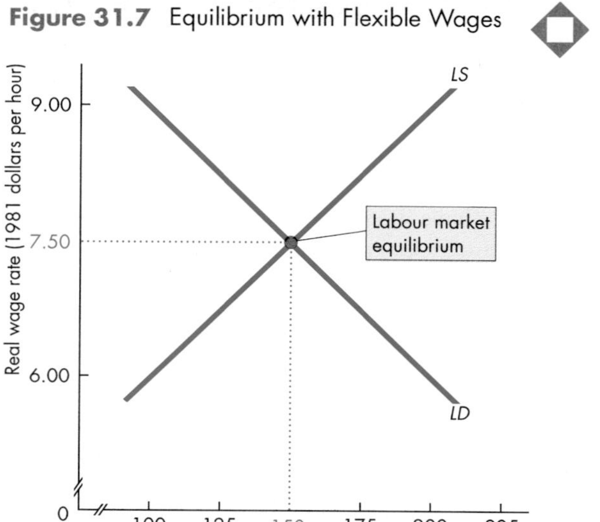

Equilibrium occurs when the real wage makes the quantity of labour demanded equal to the quantity supplied. This equilibrium occurs at a real wage of $7.50 per hour. At that real wage rate, 150 million hours of labour are employed. At real wage rates of less than $7.50 per hour, the quantity of labour demanded exceeds the quantity supplied and the real wage rate rises. At real wage rates of more than $7.50 per hour, the quantity of labour supplied exceeds the quantity of labour demanded and the real wage rate falls.

labour shortages. The real wage rate continues to rise until it reaches $7.50 an hour, at which point there is no shortage of labour.

If the real wage rate is higher than its equilibrium level of $7.50 an hour, the quantity of labour supplied exceeds the quantity demanded. In this situation, households are not able to get all the work that they want and firms find it easy to hire labour. Firms have an incentive to cut the wage, and households will accept the lower wage to get a job. The real wage rate falls until it reaches $7.50 an hour. At that point every household is satisfied with the quantity of labour that it is supplying.

Changes in Wages and Employment The flexible wage theory makes predictions about wages and employment that are identical to the predictions of the demand and supply model that we studied in Chapter 4. An increase in the demand for labour shifts the demand for labour curve to the right and increases both the real wage rate and the quantity of labour employed. An increase in the supply of labour shifts the supply of labour curve to the right, lowering the real wage rate and increasing employment.

The demand for labour increases over time because capital accumulation and technological change increase the marginal product of labour. The supply of labour increases over time because the working age population is steadily growing. Rightward shifts of the demand for labour curve are generally larger than shifts of the supply of labour curve so, over time, both the quantity of labour employed and the real wage rate increase. But real wages do not increase steadily each and every year, and there are examples of prolonged periods, such as the 1980s, when real wages remained relatively steady or even, on occasion, declined.

Aggregate Supply With Flexible Wages In Chapter 24, we studied the concept of aggregate supply and the long-run and short-run aggregate supply curves. What does the flexible wage theory of the labour market tell us about aggregate supply?

Recall the definitions of the short-run aggregate supply curve and the long-run aggregate supply curve. The short-run aggregate supply curve tells us how the quantity of real GDP supplied varies as the price level varies, holding input prices constant. The long-run aggregate supply curve tells us how the quantity of real GDP varies as the price level varies when all input prices have adjusted by the same percentage as the price level.

According to the flexible wage theory of the labour market, the money wage rate adjusts to determine a real wage that brings equality between the quantity of labour demanded and the quantity supplied. If the prices of all other inputs behave in the same way, then all input prices change to preserve equilibrium in the various input markets. The aggregate supply curve generated by the flexible wage model of the labour market is the same as the long-run aggregate supply curve. It is vertical. Let's see why.

Figure 31.8 illustrates the derivation of the long-run aggregate supply curve. Part (a) shows the aggregate labour market. The demand and supply curves shown are exactly the same as those in Fig. 31.7. And the equilibrium, a real wage of $7.50 an hour and employment of 150 million hours, is exactly the same equilibrium as was determined in that figure.

Figure 31.8(b) shows the short-run aggregate

Figure 31.8 Aggregate Supply with Flexible Wages

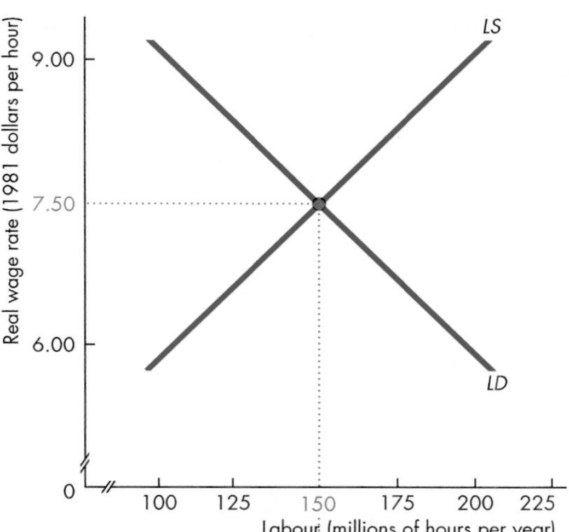

(a) Labour market

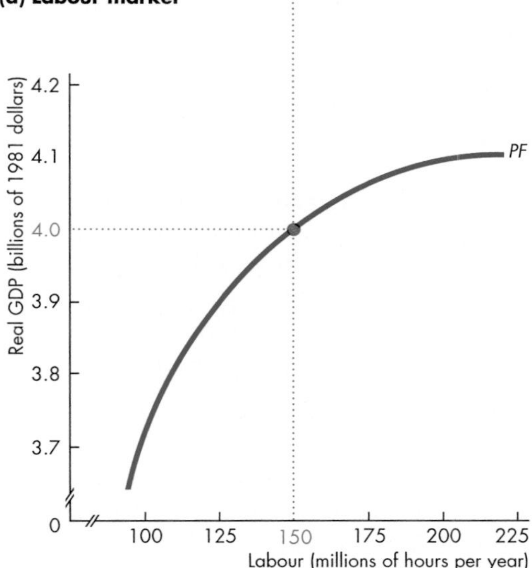

(b) Short-run aggregate production function

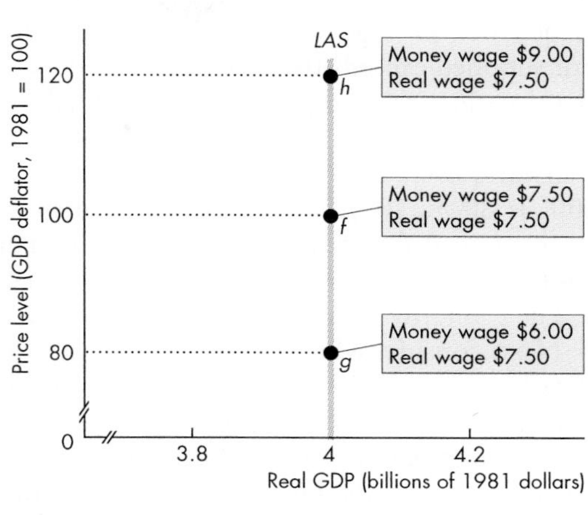

(c) Long-run aggregate supply curve

Labour market equilibrium determines the real wage and employment. The demand for labour curve (*LD*) intersects the supply of labour curve (*LS*) at a real wage of $7.50 per hour and 150 million hours of employment (part a). The short-run aggregate production function (*PF*) and employment of 150 million hours determine real GDP at $4 billion (part b). Real GDP supplied is $4 billion regardless of the price level. The long-run aggregate supply curve is the vertical line (*LAS*) in part (c). If the GDP deflator is 100, the economy is at point *f*. If the GDP deflator is 120, money wages rise to keep real wages constant at $7.50 per hour, employment remains at 150 million hours, and real GDP is $4 billion. The economy is at point *h*. If the GDP deflator is 80, money wages fall to keep real wages constant at $7.50 per hour, employment remains at 150 million hours, and real GDP is $4 billion. The economy is at point *g*.

production function. This production function is exactly the same as the one shown in Fig. 31.1. We know from the labour market in Fig. 31.8(a) that 150 million hours of labour are employed. Fig. 31.8(b) tells us that when 150 million hours of labour are employed, real GDP is $4 billion.

Figure 31.8(c) shows the long-run aggregate supply curve. That curve tells us that real GDP is $4 billion regardless of the price level. Let's examine the aggregate supply curve more closely and convince ourselves that it really is vertical.

Suppose that the price level, measured by the GDP deflator, is 100. In this case, the economy is at point *f* in Fig. 31.8(c). That is, the GDP deflator is 100 and real GDP is $4 billion. We've determined, in Fig. 31.8(a), that the real wage rate is $7.50. With a

GDP deflator of 100, the money wage (the wage in current dollars) is also $7.50.

Let's now ask what happens to real GDP at two different price levels — a lower one and a higher one. First, suppose that the GDP deflator is not 100 but 80. If the money wage rate remains at its initial level of $7.50, the real wage rate rises and the quantity of labour supplied exceeds the quantity demanded. In such a situation, the money wage rate will fall. It falls to $6.00 an hour. With a money wage of $6.00 and a GDP deflator of 80, the real wage rate is still $7.50 ($6.00 ÷ 80 × 100). With the lower money wage but a constant real wage rate, employment remains at 150 million hours and real GDP is constant at $4 billion. The economy is at point *g* in Fig. 31.8(c).

Next, consider what happens to real GDP if the GDP deflator is not 100 but 120 (a 20 percent higher price level). If the money wage rate stays at $7.50 an hour, the real wage rate falls and the quantity of labour demanded exceeds the quantity supplied. In such a situation, the money wage rate rises. It keeps rising until it reaches $9.00 an hour. At that money wage rate, the real wage is $7.50 ($9.00 ÷ 120 ÷ 100) and the quantity of labour demanded equals the quantity supplied. Employment remains at 150 million hours, so real GDP remains at $4 billion, which means that the economy is at point *h* in Fig. 31.8(c).

Points *f*, *g*, and *h* all lie on the long-run aggregate supply curve. We have considered only three price levels. We could have considered any price level and reached the same conclusion: a change in the price level generates a proportionate change in the money wage rate and leaves the real wage rate unchanged. Employment and real GDP are also unchanged. The long-run aggregate supply curve is vertical.

Fluctuations in Real GDP According to the flexible wage theory of the labour market, fluctuations in real GDP arise from shifts in the long-run aggregate supply curve. Technological change and capital accumulation shift the short-run aggregate production function upward and also shift the demand for labour curve to the right. Population growth shifts the supply of labour curve to the right. These changes in economic conditions change equilibrium employment and real GDP and also shift the long-run aggregate supply curve. Most of the time these changes result in a shift of the long-run aggregate supply curve to the right — increasing real GDP. But the pace at which the long-run aggregate supply curve shifts to the right varies, leading to fluctuations in the growth rate of real GDP. Occasionally, the short-run aggregate production function shifts downward. When it does so, the demand for labour curve shifts to the left, employment falls, and the long-run aggregate supply curve shifts to the left, producing a recession.

R E V I E W

The flexible wage theory of the labour market maintains that the real wage rate adjusts freely enough to maintain continuous equality between the quantity of labour demanded and the quantity of labour supplied. In such an economy, there is only one aggregate supply curve — the vertical long-run aggregate supply curve. Fluctuations in employment, money wages, and real GDP occur because of fluctuations in the supply of labour and in the short-run aggregate production function, which, in turn, lead to fluctuations in the demand for labour. The most important source of fluctuations is the uneven pace of technological change and other occasional negative influences on the short-run aggregate production function. ■

The labour market analysis that we have just studied leaves out one feature of real world labour markets that some economists regard as important — money wage rates are fixed by wage contracts and do not adjust quickly. Let's now examine how the labour market works when money wages are sticky.

The Sticky Wage Theory

The sticky wage theory of the labour market emphasizes that money wage rates are fixed by contracts and that they are not free to adjust minute by minute to enable changes in the real wage rate to maintain a balance between the aggregate quantity of labour demanded and supplied. Economists who regard the flexible wage theory as the appropriate one argue that there are many ways in which money wages, even those that are fixed by contracts, can and do adjust upward or downward and that they do so quickly enough to maintain labour market equilibrium. Bonus payments and the mix of overtime and normal work time (overtime being paid at a higher wage rate) are the two principal means whereby wage flexibility is achieved. But most economists, while recognizing the scope for flexibility in wages from bonuses and overtime rates, believe that they are insufficient to keep the quantity of labour supplied equal to the quantity of labour demanded. Basic money wage rates, they point out, rarely adjust more frequently than once a year, so money wage rates are fairly rigid. Real wage rates change more frequently than do money wage rates because of changes in the price level, but not with sufficient flexibility to achieve continuous full employment.

The starting point for the sticky wage theory of the labour market is a theory of the determination of the money wage rate — the wage that is "sticky."

Money Wage Determination Firms naturally like to pay as low a wage as possible. Workers like as high a wage as possible. But workers want to get hired and firms want to be able to find labour. Firms recognize that if they offer too low a wage, there will be a labour shortage. Workers recognize that if they try to achieve too high a wage, there will be a shortage of jobs — excessive unemployment. The wage that balances these opposing forces is the equilibrium wage — the wage that makes the quantity of labour demanded equal to the quantity supplied. But if money wages are set for a year or more in advance, it is impossible to achieve a continuous balance between the quantity of labour demanded and the quantity supplied. In such a situation, how is the wage determined? It is set at a level designed to achieve an expectation or belief that, on the average, the quantity of labour demanded will equal the quantity supplied. Let's work out what that money wage rate is.

If the labour demand and supply curves are the same as those that we used in Fig. 31.7, the real wage that achieves balance between the quantity demanded and quantity supplied is $7.50, as shown in Fig. 31.9. The money wage that this real wage translates into depends on the price level. If the GDP deflator is 100 and the real wage is $7.50, then the money wage is $7.50 (point *c* in the figure). When firms and workers agree to a money wage rate for a future contract, they do not know what the price level is going to be. All they can do is base the contract on their best forecast of future prices. Let's suppose that firms and their workers all have the same expectations about the future. In our example, we suppose that they *expect* the GDP deflator for the coming year to be 100. That being the case, firms and workers are ready to agree to a money wage rate of $7.50 per hour.

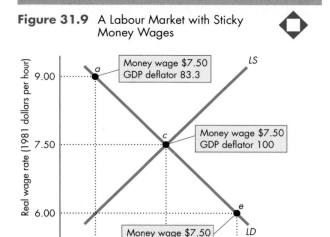

Figure 31.9 A Labour Market with Sticky Money Wages

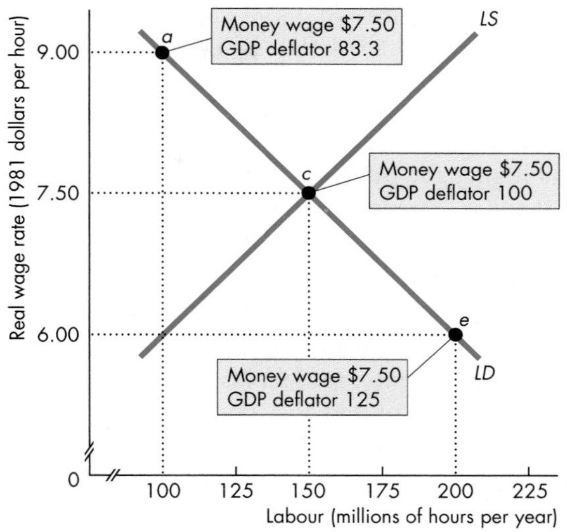

The labour demand curve is *LD* and the labour supply curve is *LS*. The money wage is set to achieve an expected balance between the quantity of labour demanded and the quantity supplied. If the GDP deflator is expected to be 100, the money wage rate is set at $7.50 per hour. The labour market is expected to be at point *c*. The quantity of labour employed is determined by the demand for labour. If the GDP deflator turns out to be 100, then the real wage is equal to $7.50 and the economy operates at point *c*, employing 150 million hours of labour. If the GDP deflator turns out to be 83.3, then the real wage is $9.00 per hour and the quantity of labour demanded falls to 100 million hours. The economy operates at point *a*. If the GDP deflator is 125, then the real wage is $6.00 per hour and employment increases to 200 million hours — the economy operates at point *e*.

Real Wage Determination The real wage rate that actually emerges depends on the *actual* price level. If the GDP deflator turns out to be 100, as expected, then the real wage rate is $7.50, as expected. In this case, employment is 150 million hours — the quantity determined at the intersection of the labour demand and labour supply curves. But many other outcomes are possible. Let's consider two of them, one in which the price level turns out to be higher than expected and one in which it turns out to be lower.

First, suppose that the GDP deflator turns out to be 125. In this case, the real wage is $6. That is, with a money wage of $7.50 and a GDP deflator of 125, people can buy the same goods that a money wage of $6 buys when the GDP deflator is 100. Next, suppose that the GDP deflator turns out to be 83.3 instead of 100. In this case, the real wage is $9. A money wage of $7.50 with a GDP deflator of 83.3 buys the same quantity of goods that a real wage of $9 buys when the GDP deflator is 100. Points *a*, *c*, and *e* in Fig. 31.9 illustrate the relationship between the price level, the money wage, and the real wage. The money wage is constant at $7.50 and the higher the price level, the lower is the real wage. If the real wage is different from $7.50, how is the level of employment determined?

Employment with Sticky Wages The sticky wage theory assumes that the quantity of labour demanded determines employment. Households agree to supply whatever labour firms demand, provided firms pay the agreed wage. This means that the labour supply curve *LS* is used to calculate the money wage rate but does not represent a constraint on the amount of labour that firms can employ. At the money wage of $7.50, households willingly supply whatever labour firms demand for the duration of the wage contract. Since the quantity of labour demanded at the actual real wage determines employment, actual employment is determined from the demand for labour curve in Fig. 31.9. Thus when the money wage is $7.50 and the GDP deflator is 83.3, the real wage is $9 and the quantity of labour demanded and employment are 100 million hours (point *a* in the figure). When the money wage is $7.50 and the GDP deflator is 125, the real wage is $6 and the quantity of labour demanded and employment are 200 million hours (point *e* in the figure).

Short-Run Aggregate Supply With Sticky Wages When money wages are sticky, the short-run aggregate supply curve — like the one that we examined in Chapter 24 — slopes upward. Figure 31.10 illustrates why this is so. First, look at the table in that figure. The first column lists three values of the GDP deflator — those that we have just considered. With the money wage fixed at $7.50, the next column shows us the real wage at these three price levels. The third column shows us how much labour will be employed at each real wage rate, and the final column shows us how much real GDP that level of employment can produce. (The numbers used in this table come from the short-run aggregate production function shown in Fig. 31.1.)

First, let's consider row *c*, where the GDP deflator is 100. Recall that this was the expected value of the GDP deflator when the $7.50 wage rate was set. In this case, the real wage is $7.50 and the quantity of labour demanded equals the quantity supplied — 150 million hours. Real GDP is $4 billion. This situation is shown as point *c* in the figure. If the money wage rate always adjusts to keep the real wage constant at $7.50 an hour, real GDP will remain constant at $4 billion and the economy will be on its long-run aggregate supply curve, which is shown in the figure as *LAS*. This is the aggregate supply curve generated by the flexible wage model.

Next look at row *a*. In this situation, the GDP deflator is below its expected level and the real wage turns out to be $9 an hour. At that real wage, only 100 million hours of labour are demanded and real GDP is $3.7 billion. It is shown as point *a* in the figure. Next look at row *e*. Here the GDP deflator turns out to be higher than expected, so the real wage is lower than expected. Employment is 200 million hours and real GDP $4.1 billion — point *e* in the figure. The points *a*, *c*, and *e* lie on the short-run aggregate supply curve (*SAS*).

The short-run aggregate supply curve cuts the long-run aggregate supply curve at the expected price level — where the GDP deflator is 100. At a price level higher than the one expected, the quantity of real GDP supplied exceeds its long-run level. When the GDP deflator is below the one expected, the quantity of real GDP supplied falls short of its long-run level.

All the factors that lead to fluctuations in long-run aggregate supply in the flexible wage theory apply to the long-run aggregate supply curve of the sticky wage theory. In addition, employment and real GDP can fluctuate because of movements along the short-run aggregate supply curve. These movements occur because of changes in real wages. Real wages can change in the sticky wage theory when the price level moves but the contractually determined money wage rate stays constant.

REVIEW

The sticky wage theory emphasizes the importance of labour market contracts that fix the money wage rate, making it insensitive in the short run to price level changes. The money wage is set on the basis of expectations about the price level over the course of the wage contract. If the price level turns out to be the same as expected, the real wage is the same as it

Figure 31.10 Aggregate Supply with Sticky Wages

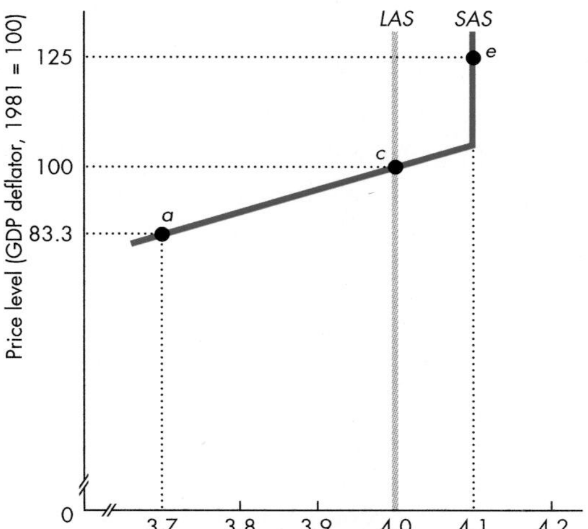

	Price level (GDP deflator)	Real wage rate (1981 dollars per hour)	Labour (millions of hours per year)	Real GDP (billions of 1981 dollars per hour)
a	83.3	9.00	100	3.70
c	100.0	7.50	150	4.00
e	125.0	6.00	200	4.10

The table shows the effects of changes in the price level on real GDP supplied when the expected GDP deflator is 100 and the contracted money wage is fixed at $7.50 per hour. If the GDP deflator is 100, the real wage is also $7.50 per hour. Employment is 150 million hours and real GDP is $4 billion. The economy is producing at point *c* on its long-run aggregate supply curve (*LAS*). At a lower price level (row *a*), the real wage rate increases, employment falls, and real GDP falls. This price level and real GDP are shown as point *a* on the graph. At a higher price level (row *e*), the real wage rate falls, employment increases, and real GDP increases. Point *e* on the graph corresponds to row *e* of the table. The short-run aggregate supply curve (*SAS*) passes through points *a*, *c*, and *e*.

would be if wages were flexible. If the price level turns out to be lower than expected, the real wage is higher than in the flexible wage case. If the price level is higher than expected, the real wage is lower than in the flexible wage case.

The level of employment is determined by the demand for labour. When the real wage is higher than expected, employment falls; when the real wage is lower than expected, employment increases. These movements in the level of employment result in changes in the level of real GDP and are represented as movements along the short-run aggregate supply curve. A price level above that expected lowers the real wage, increases employment, and increases real GDP; a price level below that expected increases the real wage, lowers employment, and lowers real GDP. ■

So far, although we have been examining models of the labour market, we have used those models to determine the level of employment and wages but have ignored unemployment. How is unemployment determined?

Unemployment

In the labour market models that we have just been studying, we have determined the real wage rate and aggregate hours of labour employed but have not said anything about *who* supplies the hours. Unemployment arises when some members of the labour force are working zero hours — they are seeking work but have not found work. Why does unemployment exist? Why does its rate vary?

There are four main reasons why unemployment arises. They are:

- It pays firms to vary the number of workers employed rather than the number of hours per worker when they seek to vary employment.
- Firms have imperfect information about people looking for work.
- Households have incomplete information about available jobs.
- Wage contracts prevent the wage adjustments that

would be needed to keep the quantity of labour demanded equal to the quantity supplied.

The flexible wage theory emphasizes the first three of these sources of unemployment. The sticky wage theory acknowledges the importance of these factors but regards the fourth factor as the most significant cause of unemployment and of variations in its rate. First, we'll examine the sources of unemployment that everyone agrees are present regardless of whether wages are flexible or sticky. Then we'll see how wage stickiness generates yet more unemployment.

Indivisible Labour

If firms found it profitable to do so, they would vary the amount of labour they employ by varying the hours worked by each person on their payrolls. For example, suppose that a firm employs 400 hours of labour each week and has 10 workers, each working 40 hours. If the firm decides to cut back its production and reduce employment to 360 hours, it can either lay off one worker or cut the hours of each of its 10 workers to 36 a week. In most production processes, however, the profitable reaction for the firm is to lay off one worker and keep the remaining workers' hours constant. There is an optimum or efficient number of hours for each worker. Work hours in excess of the optimum result in decreased output per hour as workers become tired. Employing a large number of workers for a small number of hours each also lowers output per hour since workers take time to get started up and workers' leaving and arriving causes disruptions to the production process. For these reasons, labour is an economically indivisible factor of production. That is, taking account of the output produced per hour, it pays firms to hire labour in indivisible lumps. As a consequence, when the demand for labour changes, what happens is a change in the number of people employed, rather than the number of hours per worker.

Being fired or laid off would not be important if workers could find equally good jobs right away. But finding a job takes time and effort — it has an opportunity cost. Firms are not fully informed about all the potential workers available to them, and households are not fully informed about all the potential jobs available to them. As a consequence, both firms and workers have to search for a profitable match. Let's examine this source of unemployment.

Job Search and Unemployment

Because households are incompletely informed about available jobs, they find it efficient to devote resources to searching for the best available job. Time spent searching for a job is part of unemployment. Let's take a closer look at this source of unemployment by examining the labour market decisions that people make and the flows that arise from those decisions. Fig. 31.11 provides a schematic summary of this discussion.

Labour Market Decisions and Flows The working age population is divided into two broad groups: those in the labour force and those not in the labour force. Those not in the labour force are the three groups identified at the top of the figure: full-time students, specialists in household production (homemakers), and retirees. The labour force consists of two broad groups: the employed and the unemployed.

Decisions made by the demanders of labour and the suppliers of labour result in nine types of flows that change the numbers of people employed and unemployed. These flows are shown by the arrows in the figure. Let's look at each of these decisions and see how the flow that results from it affects the amount of unemployment and employment.

There are two ways in which a person not in the labour force can become unemployed. Full-time students can decide to quit school, enter the labour force, and search for a job; and specialists in household production can decide to change their activities by entering or re-entering the labour force and seeking a job. When such people enter the labour force, they are initially unemployed.

There are three ways in which employed workers can become unemployed: an employer may lay off workers temporarily; an employer may fire workers; and workers may decide to quit their current jobs to find better ones. Each of these decisions results in a fall in employment and a rise in unemployment.

There are four ways in which people can leave the pool of unemployment. They may decide to withdraw from the labour force temporarily (to bring up children, become homemakers, or go back to school); they may quit work altogether and retire; they may be recalled from temporary layoff; and they may be hired in a new job.

At any one moment, there is a stock of employment and unemployment, and over any given

Figure 31.11 Labour Market Flows

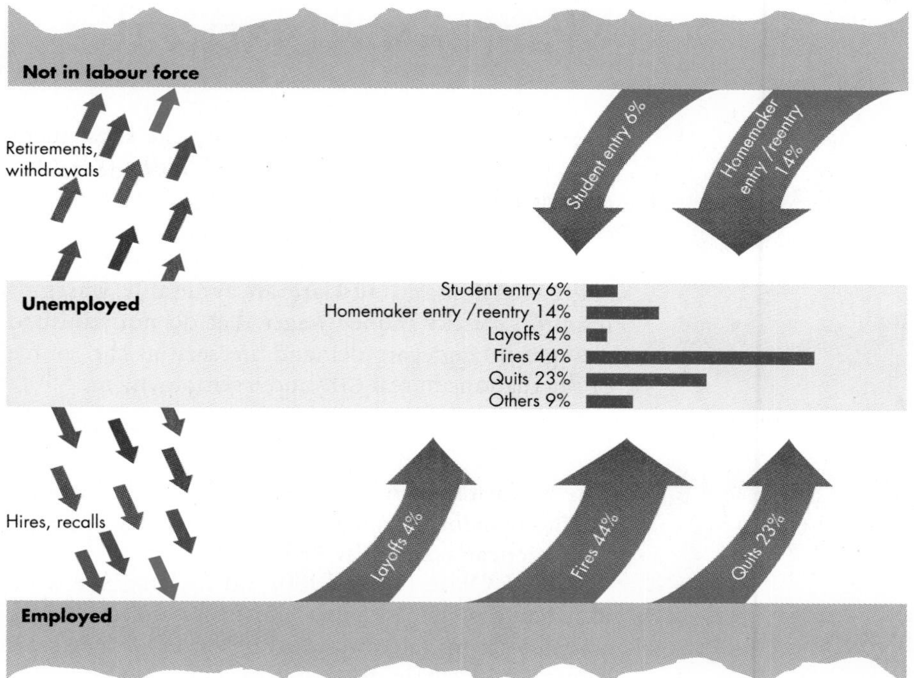

The working age population is divided into two groups: those in the labour force and those not in the labour force. The labour force, in turn, is divided into those employed and those unemployed. The figure shows the flows between the labour force and the rest of the population and between the employed and the unemployed. New entrants from full-time schooling flow into the unemployment pool. As these new entrants are hired, they flow out of the unemployment pool. Flows from employed to unemployed occur as a result of fires, quits, and layoffs. Flows in the opposite direction occur as a result of hires and recalls. Workers sometimes withdraw temporarily from the labour force to become homemakers or to go back to school. Other workers retire. Those who have temporarily withdrawn from the labour force re-enter and search for a job. They flow in through the unemployment pool. The quantity of unemployment depends on the scale of the flows and on the length of time that people remain in the unemployed category. The greater the entry flow and the greater the rate of fires, quits, and layoffs, the higher is the average rate of unemployment.

Source: Statistics Canada, *The Labour Force*, September, 1989 catalogue no. 71-001.

period, there are flows between the labour force and the rest of the population and between employment and unemployment. In September 1989, for example, there were 13.5 million people in the labour force — 66.8 percent of the population aged 15 years and over. Of these, 0.9 million (6.7 percent of the labour force) were unemployed, and 12.6 million (93.3 percent of the labour force) were employed. Of the 0.9 million unemployed, 44 percent had been fired from their previous jobs and 23 percent had quit their previous jobs. Fourteen percent had re-entered the labour force after a period of specializing in household production. The rest of the unemployed were in the other three categories — new entrants (6 percent), layoffs (4 percent), and others, such as newly arrived immigrants (9 percent).

Unemployment with Flexible Wages

If real wages are flexible, all the unemployment that exists arises from the sources that we have just reviewed. Furthermore, fluctuations in unemployment are caused by fluctuations in labour market flows.

OUR ADVANCING KNOWLEDGE

Unemployment: Waste or "Natural"?

Arthur Okun

Edward Prescott

Ever since the Great Depression and the subsequent publication of Keynes' General Theory (see Our Advancing Knowledge, pp. 662-664), most macroeconomists have believed that fluctuations in unemployment have been caused by fluctuations in aggregate demand and are an avoidable waste of resources. Sticky money wages that do not adjust to changes in aggregate demand are seen as the source of fluctuations in real GDP and unemployment.

Okun's Law

The quantitative relationship between output and unemployment is called "Okun's Law," named after the American economist Arthur Okun.

Arthur Okun (1929-1980) did his graduate work in economics at Columbia University and taught for several years at Yale. But most of Okun's professional career was spent in Washington, D.C. He became a member of President John F. Kennedy's Council of Economic Advisors in 1964. He became chairman of the Council in 1968 and so became President Lyndon B. Johnson's senior economic advisor. After he left the CEA, he spent the rest of his life as a research economist at the Brookings Institution. Okun was a compassionate and articulate exponent of Keynesian macroeconomics.

The relationship that intrigued Arthur Okun is illustrated in the figure below.

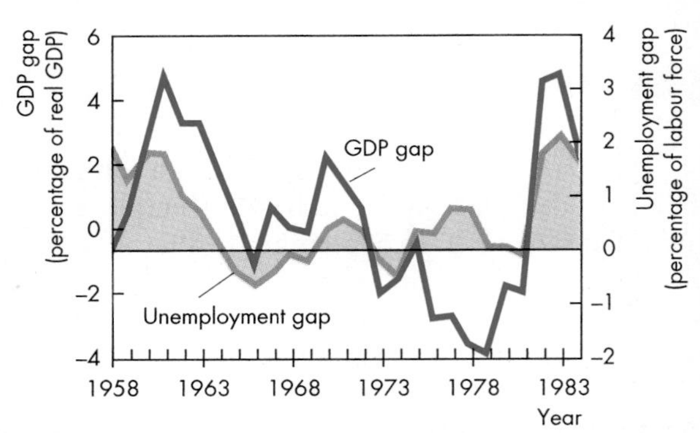

The deviations of real GDP from trend is the GDP gap measured on the left-hand scale. The "natural" rate of unemployment is based on the assumptions of Chapter 22 (see Fig. 22.4). The actual unemployment rate minus its natural rate is the unemployment gap measured on the right-hand scale. The two gaps track each other closely, a finding that led Okun and other economists to conclude that fluctuations in aggregate demand produce fluctuations in real GDP that lead to fluctuations in unemployment. This cause-and-effect relationship is Okun's Law.

This consensus has been challenged in recent years by real business cycle theorists and by those economists focusing on sectoral shifts as sources of cyclical unemployment.

Real Business Cycle Theory

Real business cycle theory is a new branch of macroeconomics developed by Edward Prescott of the University of Minnesota, Finn Kydland of Carnegie-Mellon University, and John Long and Charles Plosser of the University of Rochester. Real business cycle theory explains aggregate fluctuations as the consequence of fluctuations in the pace of technological change. According to real business cycle theory, fluctuations in employment and real GDP are the best possible response to real changes affecting the economy.

The concept of indivisible labour, discussed in this chapter has been incorporated into real business cycle theories by Richard Rogerson of the University of Rochester. Gary Hansen of the University of California at Los Angeles has shown that an artificial economy incorporating these ideas, that can be run on a computer, produces fluctuations in output, employment, and unemployment similar to those observed in the U.S. economy.

Sectoral Shifts

The possible importance of sectoral shifts as a cause of unemployment has been suggested by David Lilien of the University of Southern California. Lucy Samson, of Université Laval, applied Lilien's ideas to Canada. She calculated the scale of sectoral shifts by measuring the amount of labour turnover across major sectors of the Canadian economy. She discovered that this measure of labour turnover was strongly correlated with the actual unemployment rate and was able to explain most of the rise in unemployment in the 1970s. The figure below illustrates Samson's findings for the period of her study—1958 to 1982.

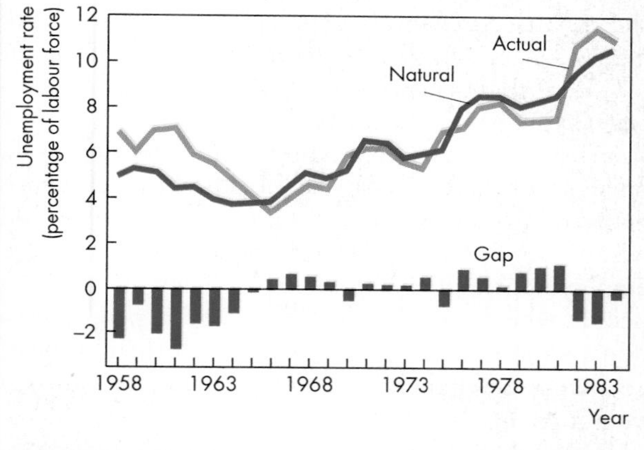

One curve plots the actual unemployment rate; and the other Samson's calculation of the natural rate produced by variations in the extent of worker's switching jobs across sectors of the economy. The unemployment gap, possibly resulting from fluctuations in aggregate demand, is also plotted in the figure.

Lilien found patterns in the U.S. data similar to those that Samson found for Canada. However, Lilien's results and interpretation have been challenged by Katharine Abraham (of the Brookings Institution and MIT) and Lawrence Katz (of the University of California, Berkeley) who show that sectoral shifts are correlated with aggregate demand. They argue that Arthur Okun's original conclusion —that unemployment is caused primarily by aggregate demand fluctuations—is broadly correct.

OUR ADVANCING • KNOWLEDGE •

The Keynesian Resurgence

In recent years, there has been a burst of research activity aimed at providing a theoretical foundation for the Keynesian idea that unemployment is wasteful. Carl Shapiro of Princeton University and Joseph Stiglitz of Stanford University have suggested the efficiency wage hypothesis. The central idea of this hypothesis is that firms can get greater effort from their workers by paying them a higher wage. But a higher wage results in unemployment — an excess of the quantity of labour supplied over the quantity demanded. Indeed, it is the threat and fear of unemployment that generates the greater effort from workers who are paid an efficiency wage.

Assar Lindbeck (see Talking with Assar Lindbeck, pp. 1-4), of the University of Stockholm, and Dennis Snower, of the University of London, have developed what they call the "insider-outsider" theory of employment and unemployment. Their idea is that people who have jobs don't care about people who don't, so worker's negotiate wages with their employers that preserve their own employment level but that do not enable "outsiders" to get in.

Peter Diamond of MIT and Peter Howitt and Preston McAfee of the University of Western Ontario have suggested that job search, of the type discussed in this chapter, can create "multiple equilibrium" levels of unemployment. If a large number of firms are looking for a large number of workers, the chances that each group will find good matches are high and unemployment is low. If a small number of firms are looking for a small number of workers, the chances of finding good matches are much lower and unemployment is high. Diamond's ideas have been used to explain the difference between European unemployment (persistently high) and U.S. unemployment (falling through the 1980s).

The significance of the debate among economists about the causes of unemployment is not just of academic interest and importance. It is crucial for the design and conduct of macroeconomic stabilization policy. If real wages are flexible enough to ensure that all unemployment is natural unemployment and fluctuations in actual unemployment are fluctuations in natural unemployment, then aggregate demand policy has no role to play. There is only one aggregate supply curve — the vertical long-run aggregate supply curve. Fluctuations in real GDP, employment, and unemployment are all associated with shifts in this vertical aggregate supply curve. Monetary and fiscal policy can be used to influence aggregate demand and shift the aggregate demand curve. But these shifts will not affect real GDP, employment, and unemployment. They will only affect the price level and inflation rate.

On the other hand, if wages are not sufficiently flexible and if some unemployment results from sticky wages, the short-run aggregate supply curve slopes upward and a role exists for managing the level of aggregate demand to achieve full employment. A fall in aggregate demand can produce a fall in real GDP and an increase in unemployment. That fall in aggregate demand can, in principle at least, be offset by an appropriate increase in the money supply, an increase in government purchases of goods and services, or a tax cut.

Economists remain a long way from agreement about the causes of unemployment and the reasons for its sometimes high and constantly fluctuating rate.

For example, a bulge in the birth rate, such as that in the 1950s, leads, after a time lag, to a bulge in new entrants in the labour force. Such a bulge occurred in the 1970s. This bulge in new entrants produced a rise in unemployment.

Cycles in unemployment arise from the fact that the scale of hiring, firing, and job-quitting ebbs and flows with the fluctuations in real GDP — with the business cycle. These labour market flows and the resulting unemployment are also strongly influenced by the pace and direction of technological change and by changes in prices determined in the rest of the world. When some sectors of the economy are expanding quickly and others are contracting quickly, labour turnover increases. This means large flows between employment and unemployment. The pool of people temporarily unemployed increases at such a time.

Canada's recent macroeconomic history offers many important examples of this kind of phenomenon. For example, in 1973 through 1975, massive increases in the world price of oil resulted in an economic boom in the oil-producing western provinces and an economic slump in the oil-using provinces of central Canada. When oil prices collapsed in 1982, the reverse occurred. The booming conditions of industrial sectors through most of the 1980s led to a relative decline in the economies of western Canada and the Maritimes and rapid expansion in central Canada. The flows of labour and the changes in employment and unemployment in the Canadian economy during the 1970s and 1980s were strongly influenced by these events.

According to the flexible wage model of the labour market, the unemployment rate is always equal to the natural rate of unemployment. There is a balance between the quantity of labour demanded and the quantity of labour supplied. But the quantity of labour supplied is the number of hours available for work at a given moment without further search for a better job. And the quantity of labour demanded is the number of hours that firms wish to hire at a given moment, given their knowledge of the individual skills and talents available. In addition to supplying hours for work, households also supply time for job search. Those people who devote no time to working and specialize in job search are the ones who are unemployed.

According to the sticky wage model of the labour market, there is another source of unemployment in addition to the natural rate of unemployment that occurs in a flexible wage labour market. Let's see what it is.

Unemployment with Sticky Wages

We've already studied an economy with sticky money wages and seen how the level of employment and real GDP are determined in such an economy. Such an economy generates unemployment over and above that arising from the frictions we have just considered. If the price level is lower than expected, real wages are above their equilibrium level and the quantity of labour employed is less than the quantity supplied. Unemployment increases above its natural rate. Figure 31.12 shows why.

Suppose that the expected GDP deflator is 100 and money wages are set at \$7.50 an hour. The labour market is expected to be in equilibrium with 150 million hours of employment. Now suppose that the price level turns out to be lower than expected. In particular, suppose that the GDP deflator is 83.3. As we have just seen in Fig. 31.9, this level of the GDP deflator increases the real wage to \$9 an

Figure 31.12 Unemployment with Sticky Money Wages

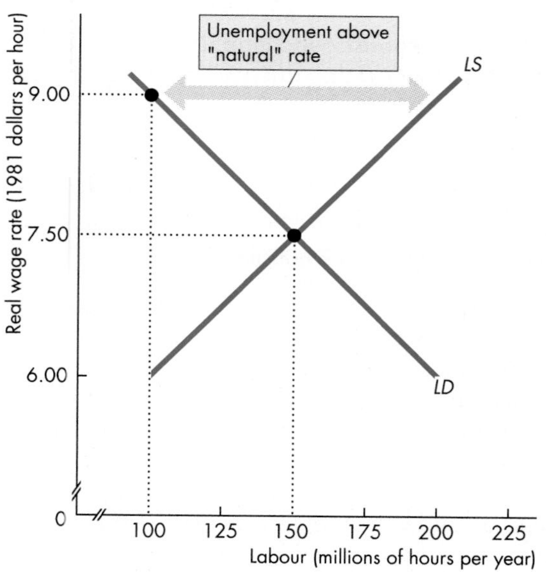

Money wages are set at \$7.50 per hour in anticipation that the GDP deflator will be 100. The deflator turns out to be 83.3, so real wages are \$9.00 per hour. At this higher real wage rate, the quantity of labour demanded falls short of the quantity of labour supplied. The horizontal gap between the demand curve (*LD*) and the supply curve (*LS*) represents unemployment in excess of the natural rate. With sticky money wages, fluctuation in the price level cause fluctuations in the level of unemployment.

hour. At that real wage, the quantity of labour demanded falls substantially short of the quantity of labour supplied. The gap between these two magnitudes is unemployment in excess of that occurring in a flexible wage model — unemployment above its natural rate. In the situation depicted in Fig. 31.12, the economy has moved down its short-run aggregate supply curve and is at the position marked *a* in Figs. 31.9 and 31.10.

If the price level turns out to be higher than expected, the real wage falls below $7.50. In this case, the quantity of labour demanded exceeds the quantity of labour supplied. But workers have contracted to work whatever hours the firm requires at the agreed money wage. Hence the level of employment rises and unemployment falls below its natural rate. In this situation, the economy has moved up its short-run aggregate supply curve and is at a position such as point *e* in Fig. 31.10.

According to the sticky wage theory, fluctuations in unemployment arise primarily from the mechanism that we have just described. Changes in the real wage rate arising from sticky money wages and a changing price level result in movements along the labour demand curve and movements along the short-run aggregate supply curve.

Those economists who emphasize the role of sticky wages in generating fluctuations in unemployment usually regard the natural rate of unemployment as constant or slowly changing. Fluctuations in the actual unemployment rate are fluctuations around the natural rate. Notice that this interpretation of fluctuations in unemployment contrasts with that of the flexible wage theory. A flexible wage model predicts that *all* changes in unemployment are fluctuations in the natural rate of unemployment.

If most of the fluctuations in unemployment do arise from sticky wages, managing aggregate demand can moderate the size of the fluctuations in unemployment. By keeping aggregate demand steady so that the price level stays close to its expected level, the economy can be kept close to full employment.

The controversy about unemployment, and some recent attempts to improve our understanding of the phenomenon, are presented in Our Advancing Knowledge on pp. 856-858.

■ We have now studied the labour market and the determination of long-run and short-run aggregate supply, employment, wages, and unemployment. Our next task is to bring together the aggregate demand and aggregate supply sides of the economy again and to see how they interact to determine inflation and business cycles. We are going to pursue these tasks in the next two chapters.

S U M M A R Y

The Short-Run Aggregate Production Function

The short-run aggregate production function tells us how real GDP varies as the aggregate quantity of labour employed varies with a given stock of capital equipment and given state of technology. As the labour input increases, real GDP increases but by diminishing marginal amounts. The short-run aggregate production function shifts as a result of capital accumulation and technological change. These factors cause the short-run aggregate production function to shift upward over time. Occasionally the production function shifts downward because of negative influences, such as restrictions on international trade and drought. The Canadian short-run aggregate production function shifted upward by 35 percent between 1975 and 1989. (pp. 839-842)

The Demand for Labour

Firms choose how much labour to demand. The lower the real wage rate, the larger is the quantity of labour hours demanded. In choosing how much labour to hire, firms aim to maximize their profits. They achieve this objective by ensuring that the revenue brought in by an additional hour of labour equals the hourly wage rate. The more hours of labour that are employed, the lower the revenue brought in by the last hour of labour. Firms can be induced to increase the quantity of labour hours demanded either by a decrease in the price of labour — a drop in the wage rate — or by an increase in the revenue brought in — a rise in the price of output. Both a decrease in wages and an increase in prices result in a lower real wage. Thus the lower the real wage, the higher is the quantity of labour demanded.

The relationship between the real wage and the quantity of labour demanded is summarized in the demand for labour curve, which slopes downward. The demand for labour curve shifts as a result of shifts in the short-run aggregate production function. (pp. 842-845)

The Supply of Labour

Households choose how much labour to supply. They also choose the timing of their labour supply. The higher the real wage rate, the more hours each worker supplies up to some maximum. The higher this participation rate, the higher is the quantity of labour currently supplied. Given the effects of all these forces, the higher the real wage rate, the greater is the quantity of labour supplied. (pp. 845-847)

Wages and Employment

Economists offer two theories of labour market equilibrium: one based on the assumption that wages are flexible, and the other based on the assumption that wages are sticky. Under the flexible wage theory, the real wage rate adjusts to ensure that the quantity of labour supplied equals the quantity demanded.

With flexible wages, the aggregate supply curve is vertical — it is the long-run aggregate supply curve. The quantity of real GDP supplied is independent of the price level. The long-run aggregate supply curve shifts as a result of shifts in the supply of labour curve and shifts in the short-run aggregate production function that lead to shifts in the demand for labour curve.

With sticky money wages, real wages do not adjust to balance the quantity of labour supplied and the quantity demanded. Money wages are set to make the expected quantity of labour demanded equal to the expected quantity supplied. The real wage depends on the money wage contracted and the price level. The level of employment is determined by the demand for labour, with households agreeing to supply the quantity demanded. Fluctuations in the price level relative to what was expected generate fluctuations in the quantity of labour demanded and in employment and real GDP. The higher the price level relative to what was expected, the lower is the real wage. The lower the real wage, the greater is the quantity of labour demanded and the greater is employment and real GDP.

With sticky money wages, the aggregate supply curve slopes upward — it is the short-run aggregate supply curve. The higher the price level, the higher is the quantity of real GDP supplied. (pp. 847-853)

Unemployment

The labour market is in a constant state of change — of labour turnover. Labour turnover creates unemployment. New entrants to the labour force and workers re-entering after a period of household production take time to find a job. Some people quit an existing job to seek a better one. Some are laid off, and others are fired and forced to find another job. The pace of labour turnover is not constant. When technological change leads to an expansion of one sector and a contraction of another, labour turnover increases. Finding new jobs and moving takes time, and the process of adjustment may create overtime and unfilled vacancies in the expanding sector but unemployment in the contracting sector.

Even if wages are flexible, unemployment arising from labour-market turnover cannot be avoided. The rate of unemployment arising from this source is the natural rate of unemployment. In labour markets with flexible wages, all the fluctuations in unemployment are fluctuations in the natural rate arising from changes in the rate of labour turnover.

If wages are sticky, unemployment arises for all the same reasons. In addition, with sticky wages, the real wage may not move quickly enough to keep the quantity of labour demanded equal to the quantity supplied. In such a case, if the real wage rate is "too high," the level of employment is below full employment and unemployment rises above its natural rate. If the real wage rate is "too low," the quantity of labour demanded and employed rises and unemployment falls below its natural rate. (pp. 853-860)

KEY ELEMENTS

Key Terms

Demand for labour, 842
Diminishing marginal product of labour, 840
Innovation, 841
Invention, 841
Labour force participation rate, 847
Marginal product of labour, 839
Money wage rate, 842
Production function, 839
Quantity of labour demanded, 842

Key Figures 

REVIEW QUESTIONS

1 What is the relationship between output and labour input in the short run? Why does the marginal product of labour diminish?

2 If the short-run aggregate production function shifts from 1990 to 1991 by the amount shown in Fig. 31.2, what happens to the marginal product of labour between 1990 and 1991?

3 Explain why the demand for labour curve slopes downward.

4 Given your answer to question 2, does the demand for labour curve shift between 1990 and 1991? If so, in what direction and by how much?

5 Why does the labour force participation rate rise as the real wage rate rises?

6 How is the quantity of labour currently supplied influenced by wages today relative to those expected in the future?

7 Explain what happens in a labour market with flexible wages when the marginal product of labour for each unit of labour input rises.

8 For the situation described in question 7, explain what happens to the long-run aggregate supply curve.

9 What are sticky wages?

10 Explain what happens in a labour market with sticky wages when the marginal product of labour for each unit of labour input rises.

11 For the situation described in question 10, explain what happens to the short-run aggregate supply curve.

12 Explain how unemployment can arise if wages are flexible.

13 Explain how unemployment fluctuates above its natural rate.

PROBLEMS

1 You are given the following information about the economy of Miniland:

Labour hours:	Real GDP:
1	10
2	19
3	27
4	34
5	40
6	45
7	49
8	52

a) Draw a graph of Miniland's short-run aggregate production function.

b) Calculate, at each level of employment, the marginal product of labour.

c) Draw a graph of Miniland's demand curve for labour.

d) Calculate the level of employment in Miniland (hours) if the real wage rate is $6 an hour.

2 Economic growth in Miniland results in a shift in its short-run aggregate production to the following:

Labour hours	Real GDP
1	20
2	38
3	54
4	68
5	80
6	90
7	98
8	104

Its demand and supply schedules for labour are:

Real wage rate	Labour hours demanded	Labour hours supplied
6	8	2
8	7	3
10	6	4
12	5	5
14	4	6
16	3	7
18	2	8
20	1	9

a) If real wages are flexible, how much labour is employed and what is the real wage rate?

b) If the GDP deflator is 120, what is the money wage rate?

c) If real wages are flexible, what is the aggregate supply curve in this economy?

d) If money wages are sticky and if the GDP deflator is expected to be 100, what is the money wage rate in this economy?

e) Find three points on the short-run aggregate supply curve of this economy.

f) Calculate the real wage rate at each of the three points that you have used in your answer to *e*).

3 There are two economies, each with constant unemployment rates but with a great deal of labour market turnover. In economy A, there is a rapid pace of technological change. Twenty percent of the work force is either fired or quits its job every year and 20 percent is hired every year. In economy B, only 5 percent is fired or quits and 5 percent is hired. Which economy has the higher unemployment rate? Why?

4 There are two economies, Flexiland and Fixland. These economies are identical in every way except that in Flexiland, wages are flexible and maintain equality between the quantities of labour demanded and supplied. In Fixland, money wages are sticky but *set* so that, on the average, the quantity of labour demanded equals the quantity supplied.

a) Explain which economy has the higher average unemployment rate.

b) Explain which economy has the largest fluctuations in unemployment.

CHAPTER 32

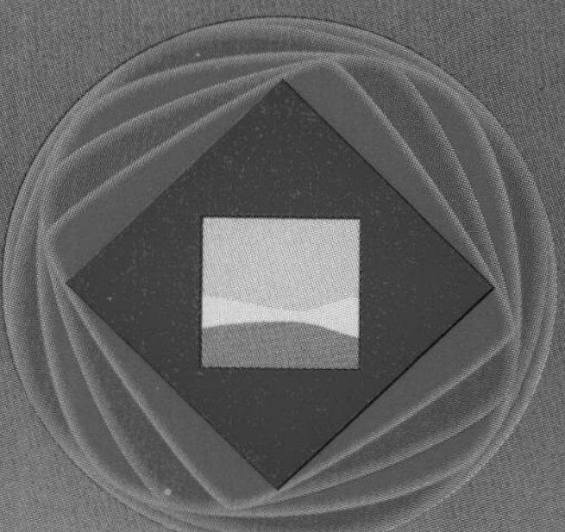

Expectations and Inflation

After studying this chapter, you will be able to:

- Describe the features of macroeconomic equilibrium.
- Explain the costs of wrong expectations about inflation.
- Explain how expectations of inflation affect *actual* inflation.
- Explain the concept of macroeconomic rational expectations.
- Calculate the rational expectation of the price level.
- Explain how inflation is determined.
- Explain how inflation expectations affect interest rates.

Wanted: A Crystal Ball

WHILE FIRMS AND labour unions haggled about wages in 1973, they all agreed about one thing: inflation in 1974 would be about 7 percent. Pay settlements came in at 11 percent. In other words, taking inflation out of the picture, they expected pay raises of 4 percent. But the unexpected happened. In 1974, inflation surged to 11 percent — equalling the average pay raise. Real wages were stationary. In effect, unanticipated inflation had socked workers with the equivalent of an unexpected 4 percent pay cut. ■ What causes inflation? Why do the best made plans often go awry when it comes to inflation? How do people form expectations about inflation? How do those expectations influence the economy? ■ Suppose that by a supreme effort of self-discipline you have saved $100 for a rainy day. On January 1, 1988, you put your $100 in a 30-year government of Canada bond, with an annual yield of 13 ¾ percent. If you reinvest the interest income each year, you will have $4770 to spend on January 1, 2020. Is that a good deal? Should you run out and buy bonds? That depends on what $4770 buys in the year 2020. With no inflation, your $100 will have grown into enough to buy a modest car or a fairly fancy audio-video system. If inflation averages 13 percent, however, $4779 in the year 2020 will buy the same amount of goods as $100 did in 1990. If inflation averages 20 percent, a pizza that today costs $20 will cost $4779 in 2020. No matter how much you like pizza, it will not be a good deal, over 30 years, to shrink $100 into today's equivalent of $20. How do expectations of inflation affect interest rates? Are bondholders any better than labour unions at forecasting inflation rates?

■ This book will not tell you whether government of Canada bonds are a good deal today. To do that, we would need a crystal ball. But this chapter will help you to understand what people in the real world do in the absence of crystal balls. We will discover that the actual levels of real gross domestic product (GDP), the GDP deflator, and interest rates all depend on inflation expectations. We're also going to discover that when expectations turn out to be wrong (as they almost always do), the forecasting errors themselves have an important influence on real GDP, employment and unemployment, and inflation.

Macroeconomic Equilibrium

There are two ways in which we can describe an economy in macroeconomic equilibrium. One is in terms of the various demand and supply curves that we have studied in the previous chapters. The other is in terms of what each individual in the economy is doing. Let's first describe macroeconomic equilibrium using the analysis of the earlier chapters on the markets for goods, money, and labour.

Equilibrium in the Markets for Goods, Money, and Labour

When the economy is in *macroeconomic equilibrium*; four conditions are satisfied:

- Real GDP demanded equals real GDP supplied.
- Aggregate planned expenditure equals real GDP.
- Real money demanded equals real money supplied.
- Quantity of labour demanded equals quantity of labour supplied.

The first condition for macroeconomic equilibrium requires that the price level be such that the aggregate demand curve intersects the short-run aggregate supply curve. In such a situation, real GDP demanded equals real GDP supplied (see Chapter 24). The second condition requires that real GDP be at the level at which the aggregate expenditure curve intersect the 45° line (see Chapter 26). The third condition requires that the interest rate be such that the quantity of money demanded equals the quantity of money supplied (see Chapter 28). The fourth condition requires that the quantity of labour employed be determined by the demand for labour curve and that households supply the quantity of labour that they wish to supply, given the wages that prevail, the information that they have about available jobs, and the wage and employment contracts that they have accepted (see Chapter 31).

Macroeconomic equilibrium does not imply full employment. *Full-employment equilibrium*, a situation in which the level of unemployment equals the *natural rate of unemployment*, is one possible macroeconomic equilibrium. At such an equilibrium, the economy produces its capacity output. But macroeconomic equilibrium can occur at an output level above capacity (with unemployment below its natural rate) or an output level below capacity (with unemployment above its natural rate).

Lets' expand our understanding of macroeconomic equilibrium by describing the actions of the people in the economy.

Individuals in a Macroeconomic Equilibrium

Macroeconomic equilibrium is a state in which no one wants to change his or her actions under the current circumstances, given all the information and options available. That is, no one finds it profitable to take different actions. The amount of consumption and investment, the quantity of money held, and the quantity of labour employed seem to each individual to be the best available, given current conditions and existing contracts. Such a situation is not necessarily one in which everyone is satisfied. Some people may well feel disappointed or even cheated. The most likely source of disappointment is that inflation has turned out to be different from what was expected when contracts of various kinds were entered into. Workers and lenders feel cheated when inflation is higher than expected. Employers and borrowers feel cheated when inflation is lower than expected. But none of these groups can, in the circumstances they face, do any better than they are currently doing.

This description of macroeconomic equilibrium in terms of what people are doing is equivalent to the more formal definition. If anyone wants to behave differently, the price level, the interest rate, wages, and income cannot balance the quantities demanded and supplied in the economy.

Our main goal in this chapter is to discover how the price level, inflation, expectations of future inflation, and interest rates are determined. We are going to approach this goal by studying a model economy in macroeconomic equilibrium. We are going to discover how expectations of inflation affect actual inflation and how errors in forecasting inflation affect real GDP in the model economy. We are then going to see how the predictions that we can obtain in a model economy help us understand the actual forces generating inflation in Canada today.

The Effects of Price Level Expectations

Let's begin by studying the simplest possible economy: one in which no one expects inflation and none occurs. Such an economy is illustrated in Fig. 32.1. The long-run aggregate supply curve (*LAS*) tells us that capacity real GDP is $4 billion. With no inflation expected, the GDP deflator is expected to be 100. The short-run aggregate supply curve is *SAS*. We discovered in Chapter 31 that the short-run aggregate supply curve intersects the long-run aggregate supply curve at the expected price level. The short-run aggregate supply curve in Fig. 32.1 intersects *LAS* at the expected price level of 100, at point *a*. With no actual inflation, the aggregate demand curve is *AD*.

Figure 32.1 Equilibrium with a Given Price Level Expectation

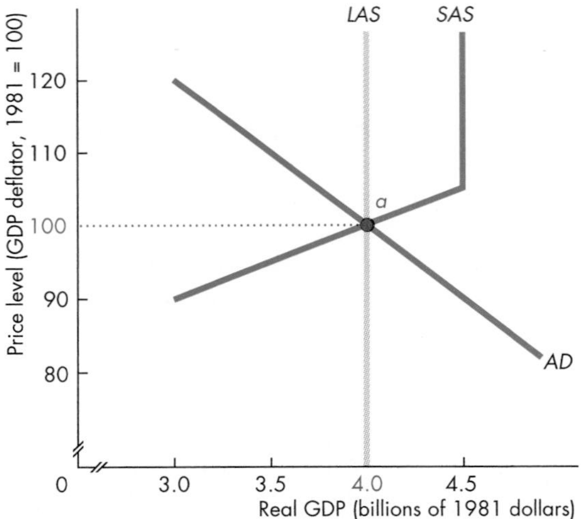

The long-run aggregate supply curve (*LAS*) and the short-run aggregate supply curve (*SAS*) intersect at the expected price level, which is 100. When aggregate demand is *AD*, equilibrium occurs at point *a*. The price level is equal to the expected price level, the GDP deflator is 100, and real GDP is equal to its capacity level of $4 billion.

This curve intersects the short-run aggregate supply curve at point *a* — where the GDP deflator is 100 and real GDP is $4 billion. This macroeconomic equilibrium is a full-employment equilibrium. The economy is producing its capacity level of real GDP. The GDP deflator is expected to be 100, and it actually turns out to be 100.

What happens if the people in this economy expect inflation? The answer is that the economy gets some inflation but not as much as was expected. In other words, expectations of inflation are partially self-fulfilling. To see why, let's examine how the equilibrium shown in Fig. 32.1 is disturbed when some inflation is expected.

Let's suppose that everyone expects 15 percent inflation, which means that the GDP deflator is expected to rise to 115. Figure 32.2(a) shows the effects of this expectation. The short-run aggregate supply curve shifts upward to SAS_1. Pay attention to the magnitude of the shift. The vertical distance between SAS_0 and SAS_1 is the percentage increase in the price level that people are expecting. The new *SAS* curve (SAS_1) intersects the *LAS* curve at the expected price level of 115.

The new equilibrium occurs at point *b*, where SAS_1 intersects *AD*. Real GDP is $3.5 billion and the GDP deflator is 110. The increase in the actual price level is less than the increase in the expected price level. Fifteen percent inflation was expected, but actual inflation turns out to be 10 percent. Real GDP falls below its capacity level — economy goes into a recession.

You may be able to understand these results more clearly if we turn to an example in one small part of the economy. Let's examine the effects of an increase in the expected inflation rate on one small pop bottling plant in Halifax. The firm and its workers agree that inflation is going to be 15 percent next year, so they agree to raise wages by 15 percent. With higher wages, the firm's costs increase and the supply curve of bottled pop shifts to the left. In agreeing to higher wages, the firm expects to be able to sell its output for 15 percent higher prices.

In order to isolate the effects of the change in inflation expectations, we must hold everything else constant. In particular, we must keep demand constant. Nothing has happened to aggregate demand and nothing has happened to the demand for pop. The firm's supply curve of pop has shifted to the left, but the demand curve for pop is unchanged. As a result, the price of pop rises and the quantity of pop sold falls. The firm cuts back on its employment,

Figure 32.2 The Effects of Price Level Expectations

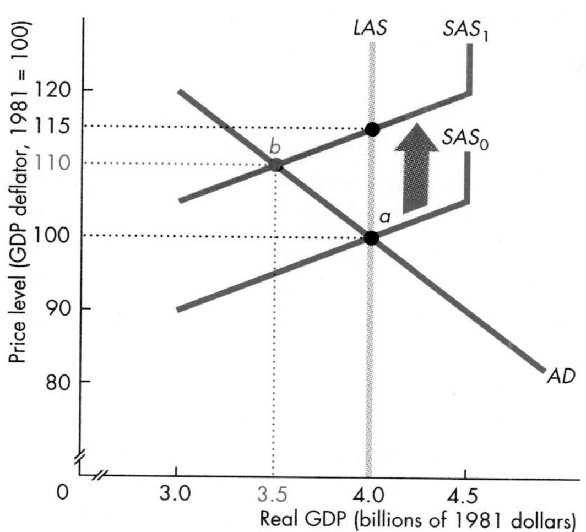

(a) Price level expected to rise by 15 percent

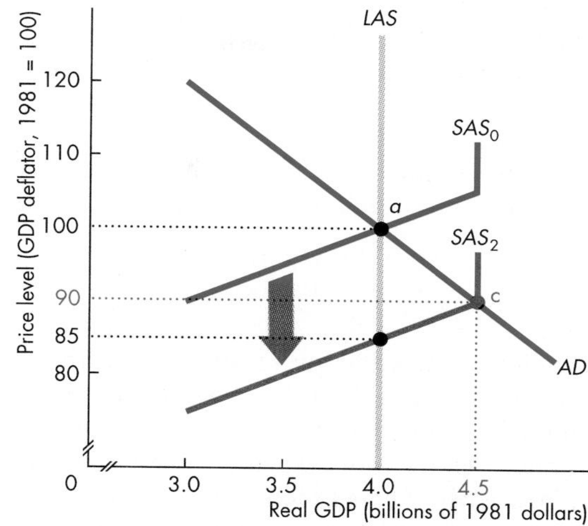

(b) Price level expected to fall by 15 percent

Long-run aggregate supply is *LAS* and aggregate demand is *AD*. Three possible expected price levels are analysed. First, as in Fig. 32.1, the expected price level is 100, the short-run aggregate supply curve is SAS_0, and the actual price level equals the expected price level. That is, macroeconomic equilibrium is at point *a* in both parts. Second, if the expected price level is 115, the short-run aggregate supply curve becomes SAS_1 in part (a). The actual price level rises to 110 and real GDP falls to $3.5 billion — macroeconomic equilibrium is at point *b* in part (a). Third, if the expected price level is 85, the short-run aggregate supply curve becomes SAS_2, in part (b). The actual price level falls to 90 and real GDP rises to $4.5 billion — macroeconomic equilibrium is at point *c* in part (b). A change in the expected price level with aggregate demand constant changes the actual price level in the same direction as the change in the expected price level, but the actual price level changes by a smaller amount than does the expected price level.

laying off some of its workers. For the pop producer, the increase in the expected price level increases its labour costs by the same percentage as prices are expected to increase. But actual prices increase by less than expected, so output and employment fall.

Next, let's work out what happens if the price level is expected to fall by 15 percent, which means that the GDP deflator is expected to fall from 100 to 85. We can see the effect in Fig. 32.2(b). With an expected price level of 85, the short-run aggregate supply curve becomes SAS_2. It intersects the long-run aggregate supply curve at the expected price level. The new equilibrium is where *AD* intersects SAS_2, at point *c*, where output is $4.5 billion and the GDP deflator is 90. At this equilibrium, real GDP is above its capacity level. The price level falls but not by as much as was expected. A 15 percent expected fall in the price level has resulted in a 10 percent actual fall in the price level and an increase in real GDP. The economy goes into a boom.

Again, let's look at what happens at the pop bottling plant. With the price level expected to fall, the firm and the unions agree to lower wages. Again, we're isolating the effects of a change in expectations about prices, so let's suppose that nothing happens to aggregate demand or the demand for pop. Lower wages mean lower costs, so the firm's supply curve of pop shifts to the right. The price of pop falls, but the quantity traded increases. The firm has to hire additional workers and work its plant overtime. Extra costs are incurred to produce the extra output, so the price of pop falls by less than the price level is expected to fall.

You have now seen how variations in the expected price level lead to variations in the actual performance of the economy. The higher the expected price level, other things being equal, the higher is the actual price level and the lower is real GDP. But a rise in the expected price level induces a smaller rise in the actual price level than was expected. Only when the price level equals the expected price level is the economy producing its capacity real GDP. When price level expectations are wrong, real GDP is either above or below capacity. If price level expectations are higher than the actual price level, real GDP is below capacity; if price level expectations are lower than the actual price level, real GDP is above capacity.

The Cost of Wrong Forecasts

Our inability to know the future combined with our need to make forecasts about it inevitably imposes costs on us. The more wrong we are in assessing the future price level, the more expensive our mistake will be. To see why errors in forecasting the price level are expensive, let's return to the example of the pop bottling plant.

Wages In the first case we looked at, the firm and its workers expected more inflation (15 percent) than occurred (10 percent). That outcome imposes costs on both the firm and the workers. Wages increase by a larger percentage than prices. But faced with higher real labour costs, the firm cuts back on employment. Workers are laid off or given only part-time work. At the higher real wage, they would like more work but can't get it. With lower output and with costs that have increased by a bigger percentage than prices, the firm makes a smaller profit.

In the second case, the firm and its workers expected a 15 percent fall in prices. They were wrong again. Prices actually fell by 10 percent. In this case, real wages fall and the firm increases its output. But to do so, it has to operate its plant at an output level above its capacity and incurs a very high rate, incurring overtime and other costs associated with operating the plant at its physical limits. The workers in this situation feel cheated. They've worked overtime to produce the extra output, but when they come to spend their wages, they discover that prices have not fallen by as much as was expected, so they can buy only a smaller quantity of goods and services than anticipated. Their real wage has fallen.

Interest Rates Just as firms and workers incur costs from wrong forecasts of the price level, so do borrowers and lenders. Interest rates are agreed to on the basis of some expectation of the future value of money — an expectation that, in turn, depends on the future course of the price level. If inflation turns out to be unexpectedly high, borrowers gain and lenders lose. But what borrowers gain is less than what lenders lose. Both groups regret the scale of borrowing and lending that took place. Borrowers wish they had borrowed more and lenders wish they'd lent less. The situation is symmetric. If inflation turns out to be lower than expected, lenders gain and borrowers lose. Again both groups regret the scale of borrowing and lending. In this case, lenders wish they'd lent more and borrowers wish they'd borrowed less. Again the gains of the lenders are not sufficient to match the losses of the borrowers.

Costs occur regardless of whether price expectations turn out to be wrong on the up side or the down side. Wrong expectations impose costs on firms and households, and the larger the forecasting error, the larger are those costs. The costs of wrong forecasts, like any other costs, are something to be minimized. These costs arise from scarcity just as all other costs arise from scarcity. In this case, what is scarce is crystal balls. Nevertheless, although the costs of wrong forecasts cannot be entirely avoided, they can at least be made as small as possible.

Minimizing the Losses from Wrong Expectations

Without crystal balls, people cannot be right all the time. But they can use all the information available to them to minimize their forecasting errors. That is, they can form a rational expectation. A **rational expectation** is a forecast based on all the available information, so that the expected forecast error is zero and the range of error is as small as possible. A rational expectation has two features. First, the range of the forecast error is as small as possible. No information that might narrow the range of uncertainty has been wasted. Given what is known, the range of uncertainty cannot be made smaller. Second, a rational expectation is correct on the average. This means neither that a rational expectation is an accurate forecast nor that it will ever be exactly correct. Rather, it means that there is as much chance that the forecast will be too high as it will be too low, and by the same amounts. By making a forecast that consciously errs on one side or the other, people will avoid being wrong in one direction. But the cost of doing so is being *more* wrong in the other direction. Since the costs of wrong forecasts occur regardless of whether expectations are too high or too low, the best that can be done is to make a forecast that has an equal chance of being too high or too low.

Now let's turn to the task of determining the rational expectation of the price level.

The Rational Expectation of the Price Level

How do people form expectations of the price level? In particular, how do they form a rational expectation?

How People Form Expectations in the Real World

Different people devote different amounts of time and effort to forming expectations. Some people specialize in forecasting and even make a living by selling their forecasts. For example, investment advisors forecast the future prices of stocks and bonds. Banks, large stock and commodity brokers, government agencies, and private forecasting firms make macroeconomic forecasts about inflation.

Specialist forecasters stand to lose a great deal by making wrong forecasts. They have a strong incentive, therefore, to make their forecasts as accurate as possible — minimizing the range of error and at least getting them correct on the average. Furthermore, organizations that stand to lose by having wrong forecasts invest a good deal of effort in checking the forecasts of the professionals. For example, all the large banks, all the major labour unions, government departments, and most large private-sector producers of goods and services devote a lot of effort not only to making their own forecasts but also to checking their forecasts and comparing them with the forecasts of others. But most people devote little time and effort to making forecasts. Instead, they get their forecasts either by buying them from specialists or by mimicking people who appear to have been successful.

How Economists Predict People's Forecasts

Economics is sometimes called the science of choice. It is the science that tries to predict the choices that people make in the face of scarcity. But if an important determinant of people's choices is their expectations of such phenomena as inflation, then predicting people's choices requires predicting their expectations of inflation. How do economists set about that task?

Economists assume that people are as rational in their use of information and in forming expectations as they are in all their other economic actions. This idea leads economists to the rational expectations hypothesis (whose origin is described in Our Advancing Knowledge on page 873). The **rational expectations hypothesis** is the proposition that the forecasts that people make are the same as the forecasts made by an economist using the relevant economic theory together with all the information available at the time the forecast is made. For example, to predict people's expectations of the price of orange juice, economists use the economic model of demand and supply, together with all the available information about the positions of the demand and supply curves for orange juice.

To make a prediction about people's expectations of the price level and inflation, economists use the economic model of aggregate demand and aggregate supply. Let's see how we can use the model of aggregate demand and aggregate supply to work out the rational expectation of the price level.

Calculating a Rational Expectation of the Price Level

To calculate a rational expectation of the price level, we use the aggregate demand and aggregate supply model to forecast the state of the economy in much the same way that meteorologists use a model of the atmosphere to forecast the weather. But there is an important difference between the meteorologist's model of the atmosphere and the economist's model of aggregate demand and aggregate supply. Tomorrow's weather will not be affected by our forecast of it. Whether we forecast a sunny day or a torrential downpour, the outcome is independent of that forecast. The consensus forecast of the price level does, however, affect the actual price level. If the price level is expected to rise, the actual price level is higher than it would be otherwise. We must take this fact into account when working out a rational expectation of the price level.

We'll now calculate a rational expectation of the price level. We will use Fig. 32.3 to guide our analysis. The aggregate demand and aggregate supply model predicts that the price level is at the point of

Figure 32.3 The Rational Expectation of the Price Level

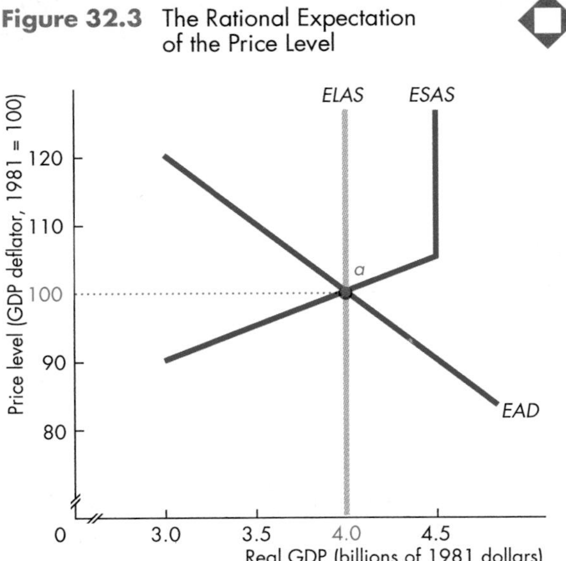

The rational expectation of the price level is the best available forecast. That forecast is constructed by forecasting the expected aggregate demand curve (*EAD*) and the expected long-run aggregate supply curve (*ELAS*). The rational expectation of the price level occurs at the point of intersection of curves *EAD* and *ELAS*. The expected short-run aggregate supply curve (*ESAS*) is such that it too passes through the intersection of curves *ELAS* and *EAD*.

intersection of the aggregate demand and short-run aggregate supply curves. To forecast the price level, therefore, we have to forecast the positions of these curves.

Let's begin with aggregate demand. Suppose that we have forecasted all the things that influence aggregate demand. We then have a forecast of the position of the aggregate demand curve. This forecast is given by the expected aggregate demand curve (*EAD*).

Our next task is to forecast the position of the short-run aggregate supply curve, but this poses a problem. We know that the position of the short-run aggregate supply curve is determined by two things:

- Long-run aggregate supply
- The expected price level

The short-run aggregate supply curve intersects the long-run aggregate supply curve at the expected price level. Can you see the problem? We're trying to forecast the price level. The price level is determined at the intersection of the aggregate demand curve and short-run aggregate supply curve, but we don't know where the short-run aggregate supply curve is until we know the expected price level.

The problem is solved by finding a forecast of the price level that makes our forecast of both the aggregate demand and short-run aggregate supply curves intersect at that same forecasted price level. So the next step in that process is to forecast long-run aggregate supply.

Suppose that we have made the best forecast we can of capacity real GDP and that we expect long-run aggregate supply to be $4 billion. Our expectation, then, is that the long-run aggregate supply curve will be *ELAS* in Fig. 32.3. We're now ready to forecast the price level. At the same time, we're going to forecast the position of the short-run aggregate supply curve. Our forecast is that the price level will be 100 and that the short-run aggregate supply curve will be *ESAS*.

REVIEW

The rational expectation of the price level is calculated by using

- Expected aggregate demand (*EAD*).
- Expected long-run aggregate supply (*ELAS*).

The point of intersection of the expected short-run aggregate demand curve and the expected long-run aggregate supply curve determines the rational expectation of the price level. The expected short-run aggregate supply curve (*ESAS*) passes through the point of intersection of the expected aggregate demand and expected long-run aggregate supply curves. ■

Theory and Reality

The analysis that we have just conducted leads to the question: do real people form expectations of the price level by using that same analysis? We can imagine that graduates of economics might, but it seems unrealistic to attribute such calculations to most people. Does this fact make the whole idea of rational expectations invalid?

The answer is no! In performing our calculations, we have been building an economic model. That model does not seek to describe the thought

Expectations

It is only in the last 20 years that economists have developed a satisfactory way of incorporating expectations into economic models.

In earlier times, three alternative assumptions about expectations were used:

- Perfect foresight
- Static expectations
- Adaptive expectations

ECONOMETRICA

JOURNAL OF THE ECONOMETRIC SOCIETY

An International Society for the Advancement of Economic Theory in its Relation to Statistics and Mathematics

CONTENTS

VOL. 29, NO. 3—July, 1961

With perfect foresight, the people in an economic model have complete knowledge of the future. Using this assumption, economists make predictions about what would happen if forecasts were always accurate. Such predictions can be useful concerning very long-term tendencies.

Using adaptive expectations, the people in an economic model change their forecast in proportion to the extent to which their previous forecast was wrong. Here's an example: You forecast inflation to be 2 percent and it turns out to be 5 percent. You have made a 3 percentage point error. Suppose you always adjust your forecast by a half of your error. Your next forecast is a 3.5 percent inflation rate. But inflation is 5 percent again. Now your error is 1.5 percentage points. You revise your forecast again to 4.25 percent. If inflation stays at 5 percent, eventually, your forecast will approach 5 percent. The adaptive expectations assumption has some intuitive appeal, but it implies that people waste information. They forecast inflation only on the basis of its current level and their prior expectations of that current level. Any knowledge that they have about the mechanisms generating inflation is ignored.

The modern theory of expectations — the rational expectations theory — was first suggested in 1961 by John F. Muth,[1] at the time a Ph.D. student at Carnegie-Mellon University in Pittsburg. Muth's idea was to assume that the people in an economic model have knowledge of the model economy and use that knowledge to make forecasts. The idea was revolutionary but it was ignored for almost a decade. Then, in the early 1970s, Robert E. Lucas, Jr., began to apply Muth's ideas to macroeconomics and, in the process, revolutionized the subject. Lucas's work inspired such scholars as Thomas Sargent and Robert Barro to undertake statistical investigations of aggregate fluctuations, incorporating the rational expectations hypothesis. The rational expectations assumption is now used by almost all macroeconomists.

[1] John F. Muth, "Rational Expectations and the Theory of Price Movements," Econometrica (1961), vol. 29, pp. 315-335.

processes of real people. Its goal is to make predictions about *behaviour*, not mental processes. The *rational expectations hypothesis* states that the forecasts that people make, regardless of how they make them, are on average the same as the forecasts that an economist makes using the relevant economic theory. In using the rational expectations hypothesis, economists do not deny that in reality people make decisions in very complicated ways, possibly in ways that the decision maker couldn't even describe. To forecast that behaviour, economists assume that people are rational, seeking to get as much as possible out of their scarce resources. By building models that incorporate this assumption and then making predictions using these models, economists seek to understand and predict actual behaviour. Assuming that people's expectations are rational is just another application of the central theme of economics: if expectations are rational, they can only be improved by incurring a cost. In such a situation, the cost of a better forecast has to be offset against its benefits.

Now that we know what macroeconomic rational expectations are and how rational expectations of the price level and output are calculated, let's go on to see how actual real GDP and the actual price level are determined and to compare them with their rational expectations.

Rational Expectations Equilibrium

We have done two things in this chapter. First, we have discovered how macroeconomic equilibrium is affected by changes in the expected price level. Second, we have worked out a rational expectation of the price level. Our next task is to bring these two things together to work out a macroeconomic equilibrium when the expected price level is a rational expectation — that is, when it is the best forecast of the price level that is available.

We're going to illustrate and summarize our analysis in Fig. 32.4. The figure has three parts. Part (a) contains people's forecasts of the economy and parts (b) and (c) show two alternative outcomes that differ from the forecast. The forecast in part (a) is exactly the same as the one seen in Fig. 32.3. The forecasted or expected price level is 100. In part (b), we work out what happens when aggregate demand turns out to be different from expected aggregate demand. The long-run aggregate supply curve (*LAS*) and the short-run aggregate supply curve (*SAS*) in part (b) are identical to the expected long-run aggregate supply curve (*ELAS*) and the expected short-run aggregate supply curve (*SAS*) in part (a).

Figure 32.4 Rational Expectations Equilibrium

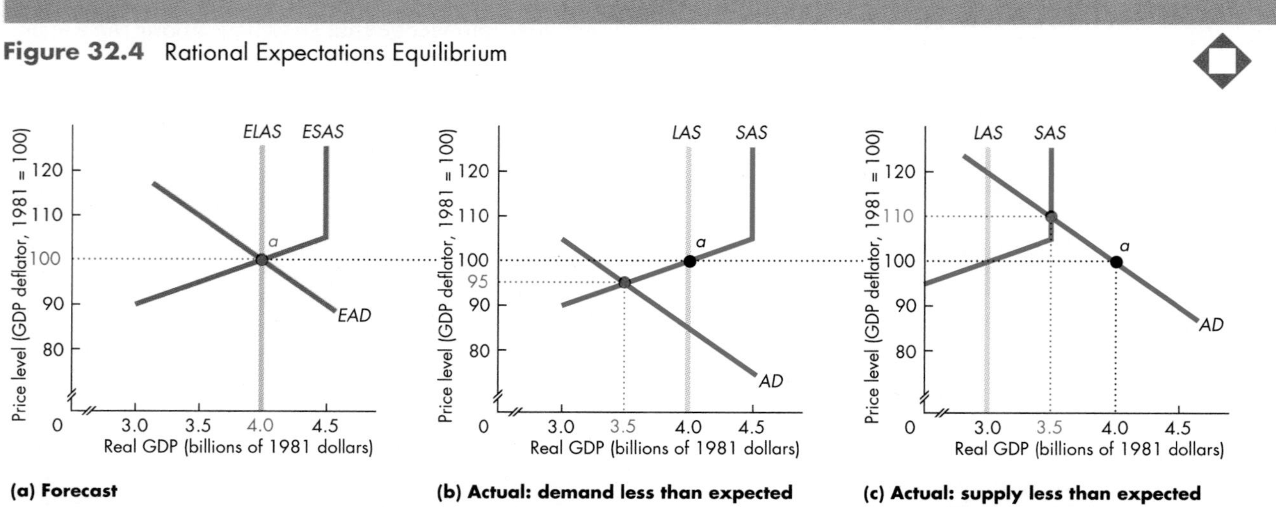

The rational expectation of the price level is calculated in part (a). It occurs at the intersection of curves *EAD* and *ELAS* (point *a*). If long-run aggregate supply turns out to be as expected but aggregate demand is lower than expected, as in part (b), real GDP falls below capacity and the price level falls below its expected level. If aggregate demand turns out to be as expected but aggregate supply is lower than expected, as in part (c), the price level rises above its expected level and real GDP falls.

The point at which these curves intersect — point *a* — is the same in each part of the figure and occurs when the GDP deflator is 100 and real GDP is $4 billion.

Part (b) shows what happens when actual aggregate demand turns out to be lower than expected. Such an outcome might arise from an *unexpected* slowdown in the rate at which the Bank of Canada is creating money, an *unexpected* fall in foreign demand for Canadian exports, an *unexpected* tax increase, or an *unexpected* reduction in government purchases of goods and services. The actual aggregate demand curve is *AD*. Equilibrium is determined where the actual aggregate demand curve intersects the short-run aggregate supply curve. The GDP deflator is 95 and real GDP $3.5 billion. With actual aggregate demand below its expected level, the price level is below its expected level and real GDP is below capacity.

Part (c) shows what happens when aggregate supply turns out to be less than expected but aggregate demand is the same as expected. The aggregate demand curve (*AD*) in part (c) is identical to the expected aggregate demand curve in part (a). But the aggregate supply curves are farther to the left in part (c) than in part (a). Such a situation could arise because of an *unexpected* slowdown in capacity growth, perhaps because of *unexpectedly* slow technological change or capital accumulation. Again, the equilibrium occurs where the aggregate demand curve intersects the short-run aggregate supply curve. In this case, that equilibrium is at a GDP deflator of 110 and real GDP of $3.5 billion. The actual price level is higher than expected because short-run aggregate supply is lower than expected. With the price level higher than expected, real GDP is above its capacity level. In this particular case, the capacity level of real GDP has fallen compared with its expected value; real GDP itself has also fallen but by less than the fall in capacity GDP.

The two equilibrium positions shown in parts (b) and (c) are examples of a rational expectations equilibrium. A **rational expectations equilibrium** is a macroeconomic equilibrium based on expectations that are the best available forecasts. In a rational expectations equilibrium, the actual values of real GDP and the GDP deflator are not always those forecasted, but they are affected by those forecasted. For example, in Fig. 32.4(b), both the GDP deflator and real GDP are lower than expected. This outcome occurs when aggregate demand turns out to be lower than expected. In Fig. 32.4(c), the GDP deflator is higher than expected and real GDP is lower than expected. This outcome occurs when aggregate supply turns out to be lower than expected. In both cases, the outcome depends on the actual as well as the expected levels of aggregate demand and aggregate supply. If the forecasted price level had been lower, real GDP would have been higher and the actual price level (inflation rate) lower than what occurred. If the forecasted price level had been higher, real GDP would have been lower and the actual price level (inflation rate) higher than what occurred.

Once the events that we've just described have occurred and the economy has been observed, people are aware of what has happened and they know that their expectations were wrong. But by then it is too late to do anything about it. Time has passed on and people are forming expectations for the future.

Other rational expectations equilibrium positions can occur — those that occur when aggregate supply is at or above, rather than below, its expected level and aggregate demand is at or above, rather than below, its expected level. For example, if long-run aggregate supply turns out to be higher than expected, real GDP is above its expected level and the price level and inflation are below their expected levels. If aggregate demand turns out to be higher than expected, real GDP is above its expected level and the price level and inflation are higher than expected. (Actually there are nine possible combinations. Aggregate demand and aggregate supply can each be below, at, or above its expected level.)

Individuals in a Rational Expectations Equilibrium

The key characteristic of any economic equilibrium is that all the people in the economy, all of whom are trying to do the best they can for themselves, have reached a situation in which they cannot make a reallocation of their resources that they regard as superior to the one they have chosen.

Each household or firm sees itself as a small part of the overall economy. Those firms and households that have sufficient market power to influence prices have exerted that influence to their maximum possible advantage. But most households and firms are not able to exert a significant effect on the prices that they face. Each household and firm does its best to forecast those prices relevant to its own actions.

Armed with its best forecasts — rational expectations — each household works out how many chickens, microwave ovens, and suits to buy, how much to spend on cars and plumbing, how much money to have in the bank, and how many hours a week to work. These decisions are expressed not as fixed quantities but as demand and supply schedules. On the other side of the markets, firms, also armed with their rational expectations, determine how much new capital equipment to install (investment), how much output to supply, and how much labour to demand. Like households, firms don't express their decisions as fixed quantities. Instead they express them as demand schedules for factors of production and supply schedules of output.

Prices, wages, and interest rates are determined in the markets for goods and services, labour, and money, at levels that ensure the mutual consistency of all the plans of individual households and firms trading in these markets. The quantities demanded and supplied in each market balance.

In a rational expectations equilibrium, each person is satisfied that there is no better action he or she could currently take. But such an equilibrium is not static. The economy constantly changes. You can imagine the economy at each point as a freeze-frame in a video: in the frame, the supply and demand curves in the markets for the various goods, services, and factors of production all intersect, determining their prices and quantities at that moment. Economists try to understand what is happening by stopping the video to take a closer look at it.

Inflation

We're now going to use our macroeconomic model of aggregate demand and aggregate supply to study the causes of inflation. First, recall that inflation is the percentage rise in the price level. That is,

$$\text{Inflation rate} = \frac{\text{Current year's price level} - \text{Last year's price level}}{\text{Last year's price level}} \times 100$$

Let's write this equation in symbols. We'll call this year's price level P_1 and last year's price level P_0. So

$$\text{Inflation rate} = \frac{P_1 - P_0}{P_0} \times 100 .$$

This equation shows that there is a connection between the inflation rate and the price level. For a given price level last year, the higher the inflation rate, the higher is the price level this year. Let's begin our analysis of the causes of inflation by focusing on an inflation that is anticipated.

Anticipated Inflation

Let's suppose that last year the GDP deflator was 100 and real GDP was $4 billion. Let's also suppose that the economy's capacity output last year was $4 billion, as the economy was at full employment. Figure 32.5 illustrates the economy last year. The aggregate demand curve last year was AD_0, the aggregate supply curve was SAS_0, and the long-run aggregate supply curve was LAS. Since the economy was in equilibrium at capacity real GDP, the actual price level equalled the expected price level.

Figure 32.5 Anticipated Inflation

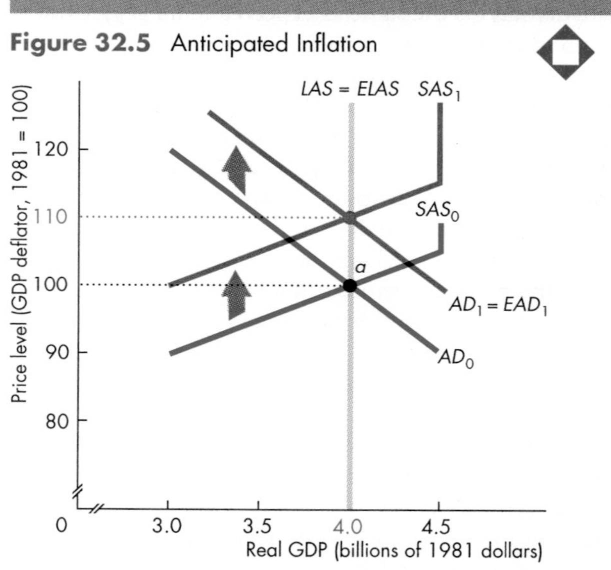

The actual and expected long-run aggregate supply curve (LAS) is at a real GDP of $4 billion. Last year, aggregate demand was AD_0 and the short-run aggregate supply curve SAS_0. The actual price level was the same as that expected — a GDP deflator of 100. This year aggregate demand is expected to rise to EAD_1. The rational expectation of the GDP deflator changes from 100 to 110. As a result, the short-run aggregate supply curve shifts up to SAS_1. Anticipated inflation is 10 percent. If aggregate demand actually increases as expected, the actual aggregate demand curve AD_1 is the same as the expected aggregate demand curve EAD_1. Equilibrium occurs at a real GDP of $4 billion and an actual GDP deflator of 110. Inflation is 10 percent, as anticipated.

To simplify our analysis, let's suppose that at the end of last year capacity real GDP was not expected to change, so that this year's expected long-run aggregate supply is the same as last year's. Let's also suppose that aggregate demand was expected to increase, so the expected aggregate demand curve for this year is EAD_1. We can now calculate the rational expectation of the price level for this year. It is a GDP deflator of 110, the price level at which the new expected aggregate demand curve cuts the expected long-run aggregate supply curve. Wages increase as a result of the expected increase in the price level, and the short-run aggregate supply curve shifts upward. In particular, given that the expected price level has increased by 10 percent, the short-run aggregate supply curve for next year (SAS_1) shifts upward by the same percentage and passes through the long-run aggregate supply curve (LAS) at the expected price level.

If aggregate demand actually increases by exactly the amount expected, then the actual aggregate demand curve AD_1 is the same as EAD_1. The intersection point of AD_1 and SAS_1 determines the actual price level — where the GDP deflator is 110. Between last year and this year, the economy experienced an increase in the GDP deflator from 100 to 110 or, equivalently, an inflation rate of 10 percent. There was no change in real GDP, so the economy's growth rate was zero.

In this example, inflation was anticipated. The price level was expected to rise from 100 to 110 — there was an expected inflation rate of 10 percent. The price level did exactly what it was expected to do, so there was an actual inflation rate of 10 percent.

What caused the inflation? The immediate answer is the anticipated and actual rise in aggregate demand. Because aggregate demand was expected to rise from AD_0 to EAD_1, the short-run aggregate supply curve shifted up from SAS_0 to SAS_1. Because aggregate demand actually did increase by the amount that was expected, the aggregate demand curve shifted up from AD_0 to AD_1. The combination of the anticipated and actual upward shift in the aggregate demand curve produced a rise in the price level that was anticipated.

For prices to keep rising year after year — for inflation to be an ongoing phenomenon — something must be making the aggregate demand curve continue to shift upward year after year. What makes the aggregate demand curve continue to shift upward year after year? The answer is the quantity of money. Growth in the quantity of money makes the aggregate demand curve shift upward. An anticipated increase in the quantity of money shifts the aggregate demand curve upward, increases the expected price level, thereby shifting the short-run aggregate supply curve upward, increasing the price level, and leaving real GDP constant. That is, for the growth of the quantity of money to cause anticipated inflation, the money supply growth itself must be anticipated. Only in this case will the economy follow the course described in Fig. 32.5. If the expected growth rate in the money supply differs from the actual growth rate so that the expected aggregate demand curve shifts by an amount different from the actual aggregate demand curve, the inflation rate will depart from its expected level and, to some extent, there will be unanticipated inflation.

Unanticipated Inflation

The events described in Fig. 32.5 involve an increase in aggregate demand of exactly the amount expected. The consequence is a fully anticipated inflation. But fully anticipated inflation is a rare phenomenon. There are some years in which errors in forecasting inflation are especially large. For example, from 1969 to 1970, inflation accelerated in a way that was completely unforeseen in 1968. In those years, the economy boomed and real GDP rose above its capacity level. And in 1982 and 1983, the inflation rate fell by magnitudes that were completely unforeseen in 1981. In those years, the economy went into a severe recession. Let's take a closer look at unanticipated movements in prices, dealing first with a case in which inflation is higher than anticipated.

We'll begin with the same situation as that in Fig. 32.5. Last year the GDP deflator was 100 and real GDP was \$4 billion. Capacity real GDP was also \$4 billion. In Fig. 32.6, the economy is on its long-run aggregate supply curve (LAS) and at the point of intersection of the aggregate demand curve AD_0 and the short-run aggregate supply curve SAS. Now let's suppose that this year people expect aggregate demand to be the same as it was last year. In other words, the expected aggregate demand curve is AD_0 (remember the aggregate demand curve AD_0 has been labelled $AD_0 = EAD_1$). Because aggregate demand is expected to remain constant at AD_0, the expected price level does not change and the short-run aggregate supply curve stays at SAS.

Despite people's expectations that aggregate demand will be unchanged, let's suppose that in fact

Figure 32.6 An Unanticipated Rise in the Price Level

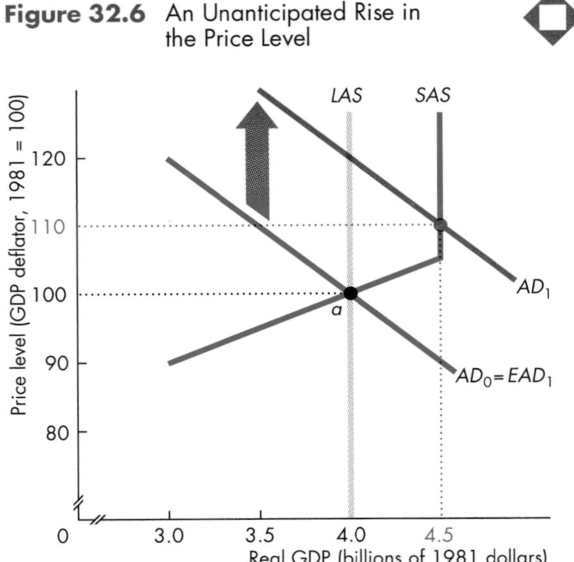

The long-run aggregate supply curve is *LAS*. Last year, the aggregate demand curve was AD_0, a level of aggregate demand that was expected, and the short-run aggregate supply curve was *SAS*. The actual price level was the same as that expected — a GDP deflator of 100. This year, people do not expect aggregate demand to rise, so expected aggregate demand is EAD_1, which is the same as AD_0. The expected GDP deflator remains at 100, so the short-run aggregate supply curve remains at *SAS*. No inflation is expected. Aggregate demand actually rises to AD_1, so the price level rises to 110 and real GDP rises to $4.5 billion. The 10 percent rise in the price level is unanticipated.

aggregate demand increases to AD_1. Such a situation might arise if the Bank of Canada had for several years pursued a tight monetary policy that kept the price level constant and then, without warning, suddenly started to permit the money supply to increase at a rapid rate. The point where the aggregate demand curve AD_1 intersects the short-run aggregate supply curve (*SAS*) determines the price level and real GDP. The GDP deflator increases to 110 and real GDP increases to $4.5 billion. The economy experiences 10 percent inflation (a GDP deflator of 110 compared with 100 in the previous year). But because the expected inflation rate is zero, that inflation is unanticipated.

To understand what is going on in the individual parts of the economy, keep the Halifax pop bottling firm in mind. In the situation that we have just analysed, with no inflation expected, wages are held steady and the firm's costs stay constant. Households are happy with no wage increase because, like the firm that employs them, they expect no increases in prices. When demand actually increases and prices rise, real wages fall. The firm scrambles to hire more labour and increase its output. The bottling plant is worked at its physical limits.

The situation that developed in the Canadian economy at the end of the 1960s is a good example of the process that we have just described. In 1969 and 1970, aggregate demand increased at a faster pace than was anticipated. As a consequence, inflation increased and real GDP moved above its capacity level.

Now let's consider the case in which inflation turns out to be lower than expected. We'll begin in the same place, with a GDP deflator of 100 and real GDP of $4 billion. This initial equilibrium is shown in Fig. 32.7 at the point of intersection of the aggregate demand curve AD_0 and the short-run aggregate supply curve SAS_0.

Aggregate demand is expected to increase from AD_0 to EAD_1. As a result, the price level is expected to rise from 100 to 115. Therefore the short-run aggregate supply curve shifts up from SAS_0 to SAS_1.

Now suppose that although aggregate demand is expected to increase, it stays constant at AD_0. Such a situation would arise if the Bank of Canada had been permitting the money supply to increase at a rapid rate for several years and then, without warning, kept the money supply constant. The aggregate demand curve, AD_1, is the same as that of the previous year, AD_0. The point of intersection of the aggregate demand curve and the short-run aggregate supply curve determines real GDP and the price level. The GDP deflator increases from 100 to 110, an inflation rate of 10 percent. The GDP deflator was expected to increase from 100 to 115, an expected inflation rate of 15 percent. The actual inflation rate is less than anticipated. Real GDP is $3.5 billion, which is below its capacity level. Thus when aggregate demand is expected to increase and it doesn't, actual inflation is below its expected level and actual GDP is below capacity.

The situation we have just described is similar to the one that occurred in 1982 and 1983. In those years, after several years of rapid money growth, the Bank of Canada tightened the reins on the money supply, slowing down the growth rate of aggregate demand. As a consequence, the inflation rate slowed down more quickly than anticipated, and real GDP went below capacity.

We've focused on the relationship between

Figure 32.7 An Unanticipated Fall in Inflation

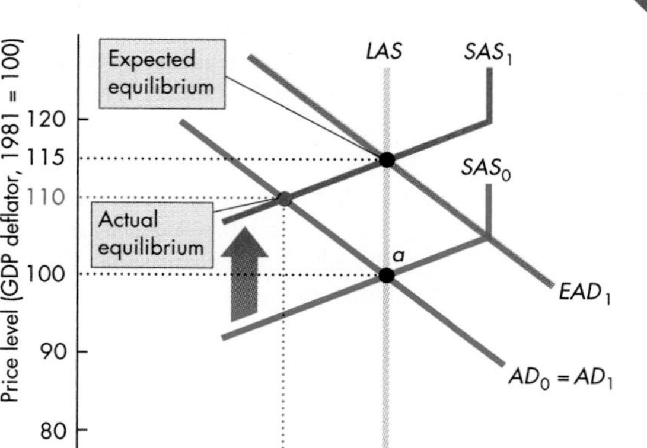

Initially, the actual and expected GDP deflator is 100 and real GDP is \$4 billion — the point of intersection of AD_0, *LAS*, and SAS_0. Aggregate demand is expected to rise to EAD_1. The rational expectation is that the GDP deflator will increase by 15 percent to 115. The short-run aggregate supply curve shifts upward to SAS_1. Actual aggregate demand does not rise but remains at AD_0. That is, AD_1 is the same as AD_0. The new equilibrium occurs at the intersection of AD_1 and SAS_1. The GDP deflator increases to 110 and real GDP falls to \$3.5 billion. Inflation was expected to be 15 percent but turns out to be 10 percent. Real GDP falls below its capacity level.

unanticipated inflation and real GDP. But we know that as real GDP fluctuates, so does unemployment. Thus there is also a relationship between unanticipated inflation and unemployment. That relationship is part of what is known as Phillips curve theory (see Our Advancing Knowledge, pp. 884-885).

The Quantity Theory of Money

When we looked at the relationship between money supply growth and inflation in Chapter 27, we discovered that there is a correlation between inflation and the growth rate of the money supply, both historically in Canada and in the experience of other countries. We also discovered, however, that the correlation is not perfect. There are some important departures of the inflation rate from the growth rate of the money supply.

The analysis that we have conducted in this chapter explains these deviations. For an increase in the money supply to produce an increase in the price level with no change in real GDP, that increase must be anticipated. An unanticipated increase in the money supply increases the price level and real GDP. An unanticipated slowdown in money growth lowers inflation but also lowers real GDP. It is because money supply growth in the real world is partly anticipated and partly unanticipated that the correlation between inflation and money growth is an imperfect one.

In addition, as we have seen in this chapter, changes in aggregate supply also affect the price level, independently of changes in the money supply. This is another reason for the less-than-complete correlation between inflation and money supply growth. Let's look at the actual relationship between inflation and money growth in Canada since 1969.

Canadian Inflation and Money Growth Since 1969

Figure 32.8 looks at the relation between inflation and money growth in Canada between 1969 and 1989. The money supply growth rate shown is that of M2 — the aggregate to which the Bank of Canada pays most attention. Looking at that figure, you can perhaps see why the Bank of Canada pays a good deal of attention to the growth rate of the M2 measure of the money supply: fluctuations in the growth rate of M2 and fluctuations in the inflation rate are remarkably close. There are, nevertheless, particular years or periods during which the relationship is less strong. Let's examine more closely two periods in which inflation and money growth moved apart from each other.

First, look at the period in the early 1980s when both inflation and money growth were falling. The decline in the money supply growth rate preceded the decline in inflation. According to the rational expectations theory, this pattern emerged because the slowdown in money supply growth was at first not expected to persist and, therefore, was not built into the assumptions people made when agreeing on wages. The short-run aggregate supply curve continued to move upward at a steady pace despite the fact that the aggregate demand curve was moving upward at a slower pace. Real GDP fell below its capacity level, and inflation began to decline but not as quickly, at first, as the decline in the growth rate of the money supply.

Figure 32.8 Inflation and Money Growth

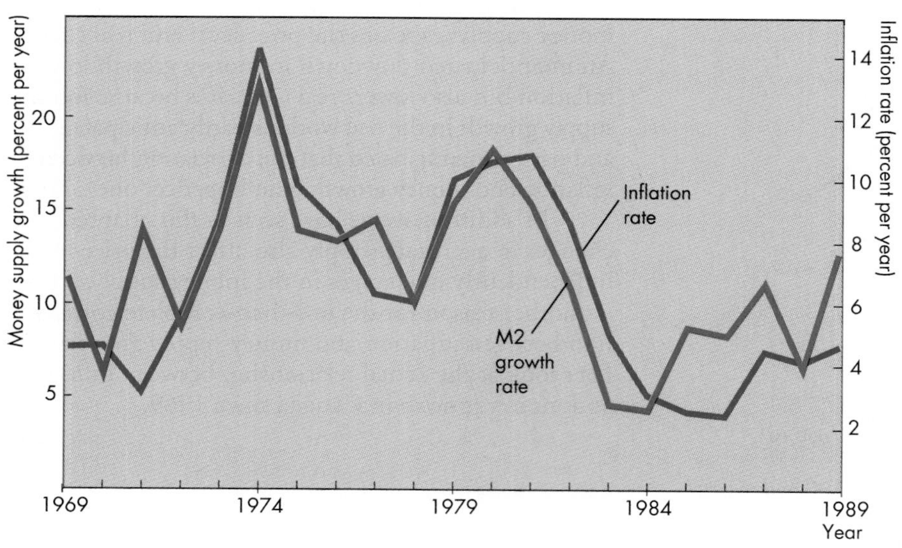

Sources: Inflation: Chapter 22. Money supply growth: *Bank of Canada Review*, CANSIM series B1630.

The inflation rate and the money supply growth rate are plotted alongside each other for the years 1969 to 1989. The money supply is M2. Fluctuations in the inflation rate closely follow fluctuations in the growth rate of M2. There is a tendency for the M2 growth rate to change slightly ahead of the inflation rate, especially when a large change occurs, as in the early 1980s. This phenomenon occurs when the slowdown of money growth is not expected to persist. In such a situation, wages continue to increase at their old rate and the short-run aggregate supply curve shifts upward at a faster pace than the aggregate demand curve. Real GDP declines as the inflation rate declines. On other occasions, when the economy is growing strongly, the money supply growth rate can increase without triggering an increase in inflation. Such an event took place during the second half of the 1980s.

Next, consider the second half of the 1980s. During this period, the inflation rate remained fairly steady, but the money supply growth rate accelerated somewhat. This was a period in which rapid capital accumulation and strong growth in long-run aggregate supply were increasing capacity output at a rate roughly equal to the pace at which aggregate demand was increasing as a result of more rapid money supply growth. As a consequence, despite the more rapid money supply growth, inflation remained steady. You can see, nevertheless, the delayed effects of more rapid money supply growth in the form of slightly higher inflation in 1987 through 1989.

Despite many influences on inflation — influences such as those just described that sometimes dominate the picture — the clear fact remains that money supply growth generally leads to inflation and that most of the ups and downs in the inflation rate are brought about by fluctuations in money supply growth rates. Reading Between the Lines, pp. 882-883, examines the controversy at the beginning of 1990, concerning the Bank of Canada's attempts to lower the money supply growth rate in order to bring inflation down and maintain a "zero inflation" target.

R E V I E W

When aggregate demand increases by the amount that is expected, a fully anticipated inflation occurs. If aggregate demand increases unexpectedly, the price level rises and unanticipated inflation occurs. If aggregate demand fails to increase by as much as expected, the price level may still rise but not by as much as expected; inflation is lower than expected.

Anything that shifts the aggregate demand curve changes the price level. Unanticipated changes in aggregate demand produce unanticipated changes in the price level. Anticipated changes in aggregate demand produce anticipated changes in the price level. The source of *persistent* increases in aggregate demand is increases in the money supply. Anticipated increases in the money supply bring an increase in the price level with no effect on real GDP. Unanticipated increases in the money supply affect both the price level and real GDP. Because actual money supply changes are partly anticipated and partly unanticipated, there is a less-than-perfect correlation between inflation and money supply growth. ■

So far, we've studied the causes of inflation — both anticipated and unanticipated. We are now going to look at the relationship between inflation and interest rates.

Interest Rates and Inflation

The Canadian economy has seen massive fluctuations in interest rates in recent years. In the early 1960s, corporations could raise long-term capital at interest rates of 5 percent a year. By the end of the 1960s, that interest rate had almost doubled to 8 percent a year. During the 1970s, the interest rates paid by firms for long-term loans fluctuated between 8 and 11 percent. During the early 1980s, interest rates hit close to 20 percent. Why have interest rates fluctuated so much? Why were they so high in the late 1970s and early 1980s?

To answer these questions, it is necessary to distinguish between nominal interest rates and real interest rates. **Nominal interest rates** are those actually paid and received in the marketplace. *Real interest rates* are the rates that nominal interest rates translate into when the effects of inflation are taken into account. If the nominal interest rate is 15 percent a year and prices are rising by 10 percent a year, the real interest rate is only 5 percent a year. If you make a one-year loan of $100 on January 1, 1989, it's true you have $115 to spend on January 1, 1990. But you need $110 to buy the same goods that $100 would have bought a year earlier. All you've really made is $5 — the difference between the $110 you need to buy $100 worth of goods and the $115 that you've got.

When we studied how interest rates are determined in Chapter 28, we analysed an economy with no inflation. In such an economy, there is no difference between the nominal and real interest rate. There's just one interest rate, and its level ensures that the quantity of money demanded equals the quantity of money supplied. But we know that in the real world, the price level is rarely constant, and most of the time it is increasing. What are the effects on interest rates of a rising price level and of expectations that the price level will continue to rise? These are the questions to which we now turn.

Expectations of Inflation and Interest Rates

Let's begin our exploration of the relationship between inflation expectations and interest rates by imagining two economies that are identical in every way except for one: one of the economies has no inflation and the other has a 10 percent inflation rate. In each case, people correctly anticipate the behaviour of the price level. That is, in the first economy, no inflation is expected and none occurs. In the second economy, 10 percent inflation is expected and 10 percent inflation occurs. What is the difference in the interest rates in these two economies?

Suppose that in the zero-inflation economy the interest rate is 5 percent a year. What will the interest rate be in the second economy? The answer is 15.5 percent a year. Why?

First, let's look at things from the point of view of lenders. People who make loans recognize that the value of the money that they have lent is falling at a rate of 10 percent a year. Each year the money buys 10 percent less than it would have bought the year before. Lenders want to protect themselves against such a loss in the value of money so they ask for a higher interest rate on the loans that they make.

Now let's look at the situation from the point of view of borrowers. People who borrow recognize that in an economy that is inflating at 10 percent a year the money they use to repay what they have borrowed will be worth 10 percent less each year than it was worth the year before. They recognize that lenders need to be protected against the falling value of money, so they willingly agree to a higher interest rate.

But how much higher is that interest rate? First, borrowers and lenders agree to add 10 percentage points because the value of the money borrowed and lent is expected to fall at an annual rate of 10 percent. Second, they recognize that even the interest payment will buy less at the end of the year than at the beginning of the year. To allow for that factor, they add 10 percent of the interest rate. Since the interest rate is 5 percent when there is zero inflation, 10 percent of the interest rate is half a percentage point. So the total amount that they agree to add is 10.5 percentage points (10 + 0.5). When they add this total amount to the real interest rate of 5 percent, the interest rate they agree on is 15.5 percent (10.5 + 5). Thus the nominal interest rate equals the real interest rate plus an allowance for the expected rate of inflation that is slightly higher than that expected inflation rate. The higher the expected inflation rate, the higher is the nominal interest rate. When inflation and interest rates are low, the nominal interest rate approximately equals the sum of the real interest rate and the expected inflation rate.

Anti-Inflation Strategy

Looking for alternatives to Crow's losing battle

...In the two years since the Bank of Canada governor [John Crow] announced what amounted to zero inflation as his central goal,...inflation has actually worsened....

While most economists support Crow, some wonder whether cutting inflation will be worth the costs of evaporating export markets and permanently higher unemployment in the future....

But judging the efficacy of monetary policy is complicated by trying to determine just how much inflation has actually responded.

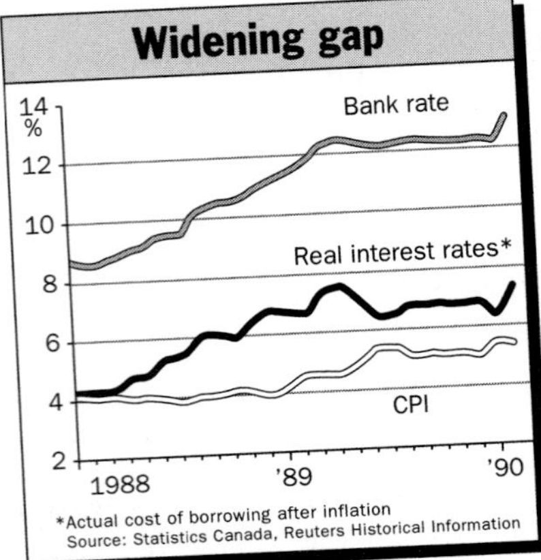

"To compare what's happening to monetary policy one year and the outcome the same year is not legitimate—there's a couple years' lag in there," said David Laidler, a monetary economist and scholar in residence at the C.D. Howe Institute and contributor to the institute's recent study, Zero Inflation.

"The inflation we had last year was the result of what the Bank was doing in 1987. They were frightened of a recession. They were printing money."

As a result, Crow has had to make up for his looseness of 1987 with tightness now, Laidler said, to keep inflation from rising in 1991 and beyond. And unlike many pessimists, including Crow, Laidler...is cautiously optimistic that monetary policy is about tight enough that if it was maintained forever, it could achieve inflation in the zero-to-2% range.

"That does not mean tight monetary policy forever," he stressed, adding the tightness will disappear and interest rates will fall if inflation does drop to that level.

But many economists still believe the monetarist solution is too expensive.

"Monetary policy has been very successful in the last 30 years only after creating financial crises," said Pierre Fortin, head of the Centre for Research on Economic Policy at the Université de Québec à Montréal....

Although he considers himself "ambivalent" toward the use of controls, Fortin said they are still more efficient at bringing down inflation than high interest rates.

Fortin sees more promise in trying to "talk" down inflation through co-operation between government, business and labor....

The Financial Post,
April 9, 1990
By Greg Ip

The Essence of the Story

- In the two years since the Bank of Canada governor John Crow announced his zero inflation goal, inflation has actually increased.
- Most economists support Crow's goal, but some believe the cost of achieving it is too high.
- Pierre Fortin, head of the Centre for Research on Economic Policy at the Université de Québec à Montréal said:
  - Monetary policy only lowers inflation after creating financial crises.
  - We should try to "talk" down inflation through co-operation between government, business, and labour.
- David Laidler, of the C.D. Howe Institute [and professor at the University of Western Ontario] says:
  - Judging monetary policy is complicated: there is a two-year lag from a change in monetary policy to a response of inflation.
  - With steady money growth, tightness will disappear and interest rates will fall as inflation falls.

Background and Analysis

- Figure (a) illustrates David Laidler's observation that inflation does not respond instantly to a change in the money supply growth rate. Inflation and money supply growth trended upward through 1988 and 1989 but the upturn in inflation lagged behind that in money supply growth.
- Figure (a) also illustrates the severity with which the Bank of Canada hit the monetary brake in the first quarter of 1990.
- Using Fig. (b) we can analyze the consequences of the Bank of Canada's policy and make sense of the observations of David Laidler and Pierre Fortin.
- In mid-1990, the long-run aggregate supply curve was *LAS*, the short-run aggregate supply curve was SAS_0, and the aggregate demand curve was AD_0. The GDP deflator was 150 and real GDP was $470 billion (1981 dollars).
- Assume that real GDP growth was zero (a useful approximation that keeps the figure simple) so that the long-run aggregate supply curve in both 1990 and 1991 was *LAS*.
- Assume that wages were rising at 5 percent per year so that the short-run aggregate supply curve in 1991 was SAS_1.

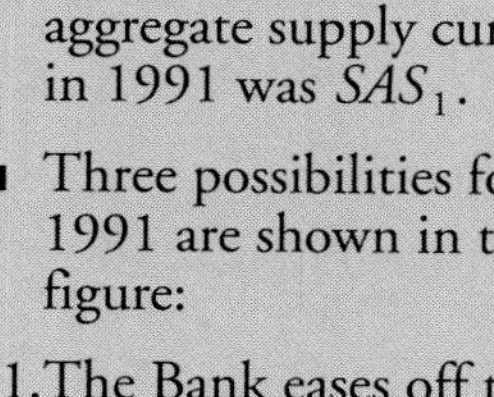

- Three possibilities for 1991 are shown in the figure:

1. The Bank eases off the monetary brake and permits the money supply to start growing more quickly. In this case, aggregate demand increases and the aggregate demand curve is AD_1. The price level rises to 157.5—an inflation rate of 5 percent per year and real GDP remains constant.
2. The Bank of Canada sticks to its tight monetary policy. In this case the aggregate demand curve is AD_0. The price level rises to 155—an inflation rate of just over 3 percent per year and real GDP declines to $460 billion. The economy experiences a recession and inflation declines. As the slower inflation starts to affect wages, the short-run aggregate curve begins to shift upward less quickly, inflation decreases still further, and gradually real GDP returns to its long-run full-employment level. But this process takes time. This is David Laidler's scenario.
3. The Bank of Canada sticks to its tight monetary policy so the aggregate demand curve is AD_0 but the government successfully "talks down" the inflation rate persuading everyone to moderate wage and price increases. Wages do not increase and the short-run aggregate supply curve is SAS_0. Inflation is eradicated and there is no recession. This is Pierre Fortin's scenario.

- There is disagreement as to whether the government could in fact "talk down" the inflation rate or restrict it with controls on wages and prices. Therefore this policy is unlikely to be pursued.
- The Bank of Canada has never, in its entire history, pursued a policy of keeping the money supply growing at a steady non-inflationary rate. Instead, when inflation increases, the Bank steps on the brake. When inflation subsides and the economy goes into recession, the Bank steps on the gas pedal. The Bank will likely continue to behave in this way and in 1991 inflation will continue and money supply growth and aggregate demand growth will keep pace with it.

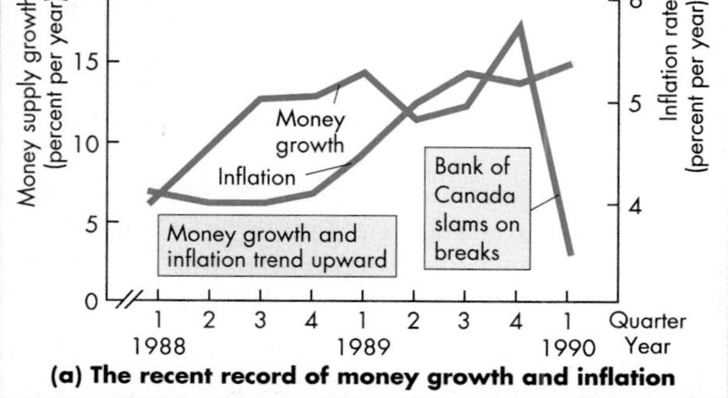

(a) The recent record of money growth and inflation

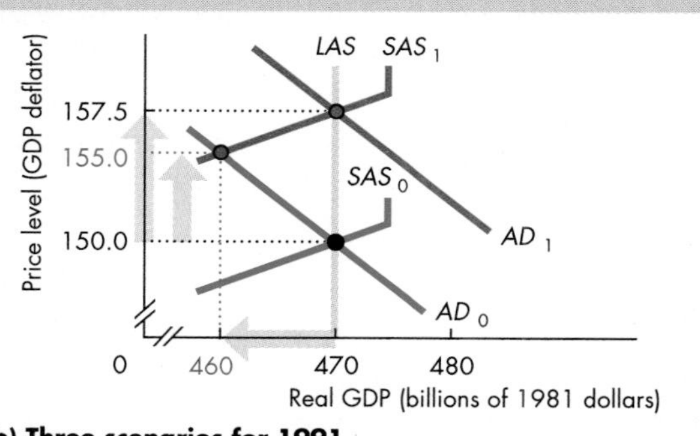

(b) Three scenarios for 1991

The Phillips Curve

A.W. Phillips

In 1958, an electrical engineer turned economist, A. W. (Bill) Phillips, (1914-1975), became a household name among economists. In that year, Phillips, a native of New Zealand working at the London School of Economics, published an article displaying what is now called the Phillips curve — a curve that shows a negative relationship between the unemployment rate and the inflation rate.[1] Remarkably, that relationship, which had prevailed, on the average, over a period of 100 years, fit the experience of the 1950s almost exactly. Perhaps equally remarkably, Bill Phillips was not the first to discover the relationship that now bears his name. A similar relationship had been proposed a decade or so earlier by Lawrence R. Klein[2] (of the University of Pennsylvania), a quarter century before that by Irving Fisher[3], and, sixty years before that by Karl Marx.[4] So, perhaps the Phillips curve should be called the Marx curve!

Phillips Curve Theory

The central proposition of the Phillips curve theory is that, other things remaining constant, the higher the unemployment rate, the lower is the inflation rate. The figure illustrates the Phillips curve, *PC*. Along the Phillips curve, the higher the unemployment rate, the lower is the inflation rate. At *a*, unemployment is 6 percent and inflation is 10 percent a year.

Phillips' original idea was that the unemployment rate indicates the state of demand pressure in the economy. When unemployment is low, real GDP is above capacity, bottlenecks arise, and inflation accelerates. When unemployment is high, real GDP is below capacity, and inflation diminishes.

In the early 1960s, the Phillips curve became a central element of macroeconomics. At that time, most economists worked with the following model:

- Real GDP is determined by aggregate expenditure — at the point at which the *AE* curve cuts the 45° line, as in Fig. 26.3(a) on page 690.
- For a given GDP, unemployment is determined by Okun's Law (pp. 856-858).
- For a given amount of unemployment, inflation is determined by the Phillips curve.

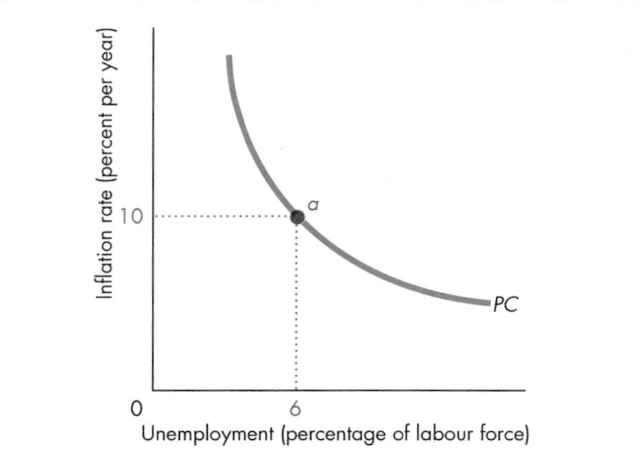

The Phillips curve was regarded as a menu for policy choice—a list of options for policymakers. They could opt for low unemployment at the price of high inflation, or they could opt for low inflation at the price of high unemployment.

Natural Rate Hypothesis

The natural rate hypothesis was proposed independently, in the mid-1960s, by Edmund Phelps (now at Columbia University but then a young professor at the University of Pennsylvania) and by Milton Friedman.

The Phelps-Friedman natural rate hypothesis states that:

- For a given expected inflation rate, the higher the unemployment rate, the lower is the inflation rate—a short-run Phillips curve.
- When the inflation rate equals the expected inflation rate, there is a unique unemployment rate, the natural rate of unemployment—a long-run Phillips curve.

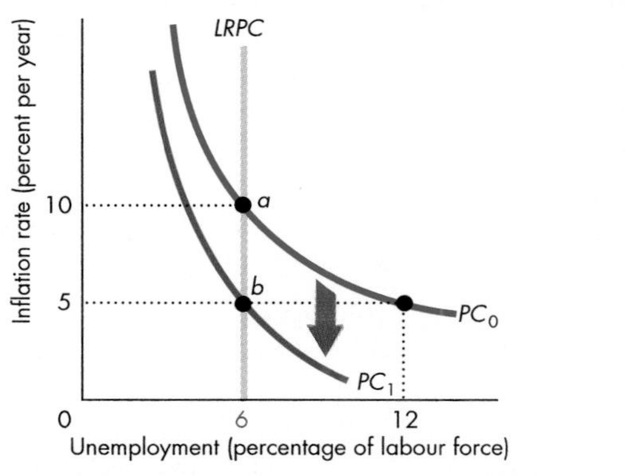

The figure above illustrates the short-run and long-run Phillips curves. If the expected inflation rate is 10 percent a year, the short-run Phillips curve is PC_0. If the expected inflation rate falls to 5 percent, the short-run Phillips curve shifts downward to PC_1. At points *a* and *b*, inflation is equal to its expected rate and unemployment is equal to its natural rate. The distance by which the short-run Phillips curve shifts downward when the expected inflation rate falls is equal to the change in the expected inflation rate. Points *a* and *b* lie on the long-run Phillips curve (*LRPC*). This curve tells us that any inflation rate is possible at the natural rate of unemployment so long as that inflation is expected.

Phelps' and Friedman's theorizing led them to the conclusion that the Phillips curve could not be a menu for policy choice. They predicted that increases in expected inflation in the late 1960s would shift the Phillips curve upward.

Variable Natural Rate of Unemployment

Until the 1970s, the natural rate of unemployment was regarded as a constant. In recent years, however, it has become clear that the natural rate of unemployment varies. Some of these variations arise from changes in the amount of labour market turnover resulting from technological change, which leads to job switching from sector to sector and region to region. A change in the natural rate of unemployment shifts both the short-run and the long-run Phillips curve (see the figure below). If the natural rate of unemployment increases from 6 percent to 8 percent, the long-run Phillips curve shifts from $LRPC_0$ to $LRPC_1$, and if expected inflation is constant at 5 percent a year, the short-run Phillips curve shifts from PC_1 to PC_2. Because the expected inflation rate is constant, the short-run Phillips curve PC_1 intersects the long-run curve $LRPC_0$ (point *b*) at the same inflation rate as the short-run Phillips curve PC_2 intersects the long-run curve $LRPC_1$ (point *c*).

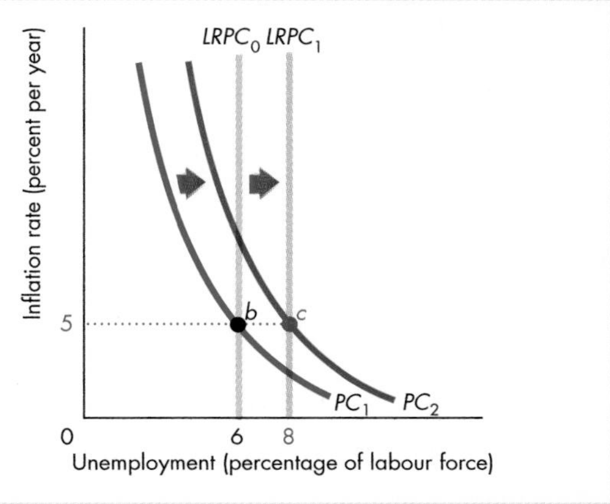

OUR ADVANCING • KNOWLEDGE •

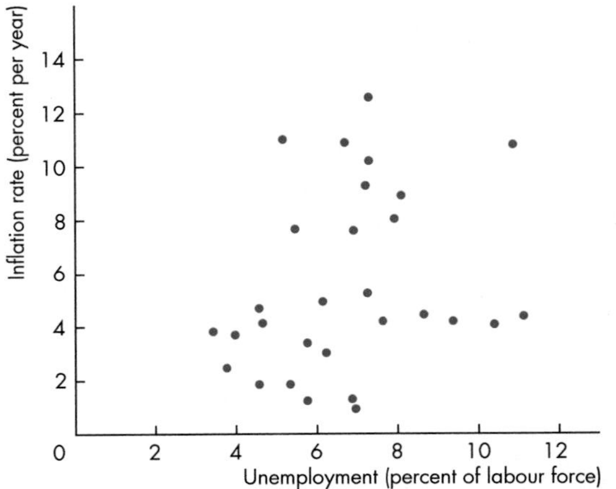

(a) The time sequence

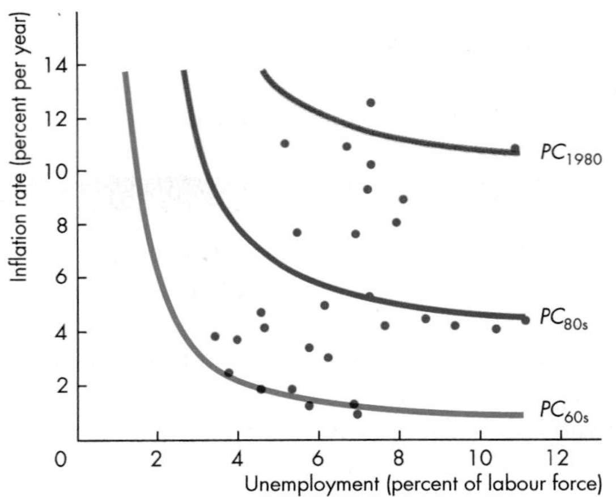

(b) Three Phillips curves

The Phillips Curve in Canada

Let's look at the relationship between inflation and unemployment in Canada to see how we can interpret that relationship using the Phillips curve theory. Begin by looking at part(a) of the adjacent figure. It is a scatter diagram of inflation and unemployment since 1960. Each dot in the figure represents a combination of inflation and unemployment for a particular year. As you can see, there does not appear to be any clear relationship between inflation and unemployment. We certainly cannot see a Phillips curve similar to that shown in the figure on p. 884.

But we can interpret the data in terms of a shifting short-run Phillips curve. Part(b) provides such an interpretation. Three short-run Phillips curves appear there. The first is that for the 1960s, PC_{60s}. Increasing inflation expectations and an increasing natural rate of unemployment shifted the short-run Phillips curve upward and to the right. It reached its highest level in 1980, when it was PC_{1980}. Since 1980, inflation expectations have fallen strongly and, to some degree, the natural rate of unemployment has probably also fallen. By the late 1980s, the Phillips curve had shifted to PC_{80s}.

---

[1] A.W. Phillips, "The Relation Between Unemployment and the Rate of Change of Money Wages in the United Kingdom", 1861-1957, *Economica* 25 (November 1988): 283-99.

[2] *Economic Fluctuations in the United States: 1921-1941*, Cowles Commission Monograph 11, New York: John Wiley and Sons, 1950.

[3] A Statistical Relation Between Unemployment and Price Changes" originally published in the *International Labor Review*, and which can be found most conveniently as "I Discovered the Phillips Curve," *Journal of Political Economy*, vol. 81(2), pt.1, Mar./Apr. 1973, pp.496-502.

[4] According to Ronald Bodkin (of the University of Ottawa), who cites Paolo Sylos-Labini, a noted Italian scholar of macroeconomics at the University of Rome, Marx suggested a kind of Phillips curve in *Das Kapital*. first published in 1867.

By considering the behaviour of borrowers and lenders, you can see that it makes sense for the nominal interest rate to rise above the real interest rate by an amount slightly larger than the expected inflation rate. But when we studied the determination of interest rates in Chapter 28, we discovered that it is the demand for real money and the supply of real money that determine interest rates. But which interest rate — the nominal interest rate or the real interest rate — is it that equates the quantity of real money demanded with the quantity supplied? In Chapter 28, these two interest rates were the same because there was no inflation.

To answer this question, we need to determine the opportunity cost of holding money. The opportunity cost of holding money has two components. One is the fall in the value of money that results from inflation. The other is the real interest rate that could have been earned by reducing money holding and making loans or investing in real capital — plant and equipment. Thus

$$\text{Opportunity cost of holding money} = \text{Expected inflation rate} + \text{Real interest rate}.$$

But we know the nominal interest rate is also approximately equal to the expected inflation rate plus the real interest rate. We've discovered, therefore, that the opportunity cost of holding money is the nominal interest rate. It is the nominal interest rate that adjusts in the money market to ensure that the quantity of money demanded equals the quantity available. The higher the expected inflation rate, the higher is the opportunity cost of holding money and the lower is the quantity of money people plan to hold.

Inflation and Interest Rates in Canada

What is the actual relationship between inflation and interest rates in Canada? That relationship is illustrated in Fig. 32.9. The interest rate, measured on the vertical axis, is that paid by the government of Canada on three-month loans — the three-month treasury bill rate. Each point on the graph represents a year in Canadian macroeconomic history between 1969 and 1989. The upward-sloping line shows the relationship between the interest rate and the inflation rate if the real interest rate had been constant at its average value for the 1969-1989 period. As you can see, there is a clear correlation between the inflation rate and the interest rate. That correlation arises

Figure 32.9 Inflation and the Interest Rate

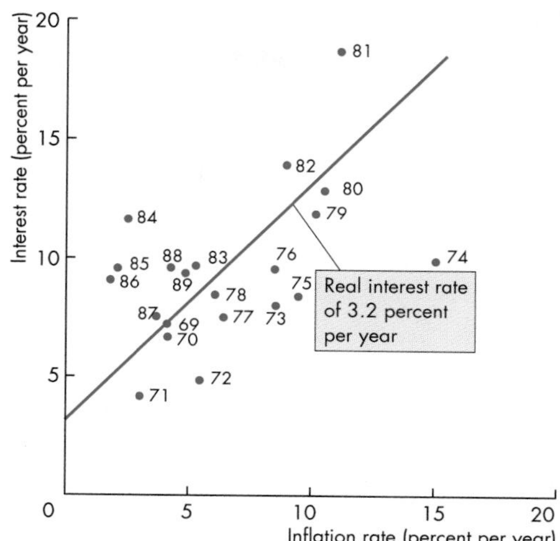

Other things being equal, the higher the expected inflation rate, the higher is the interest rate. A graph showing the relationship between interest rates and the actual inflation rates reveals that the influence of inflation on interest rates is a powerful one. Here, the interest rate is that paid by the government of Canada on three-month loans — the three-month treasury bill rate. Each point represents a year in Canadian macroeconomic history between 1969 and 1989.

Sources: Inflation rate: Fig. 22.1. Interest rate: *Bank of Canada Review*, CANSIM series B14007.

from the relationship that you have just studied. To the extent that a higher inflation rate is anticipated, it results in higher interest rates.

During the 1960s, both actual and expected inflation were moderate and so were interest rates. In the early 1970s, inflation began to increase, but it was not expected to increase much and certainly not to persist. As a result, interest rates did not rise very much at that time. By the mid-1970s, there was a burst of unexpectedly high inflation. Interest rates increased somewhat but not by nearly as much as the inflation rate. During the late 1970s and early 1980s, inflation of close to 10 percent a year came to be expected as an ongoing and highly persistent phenomenon. As a result, interest rates increased to about 15 percent a year. Then in 1984 and 1985, the inflation rate fell — at first unexpectedly. Interest rates began to fall, but not nearly as quickly as the inflation rate. Short-term interest rates fell more quickly than long-term interest rates because, at that time, it was expected that inflation would be lower in the short term but not so low in the long term.

The relationship between inflation and interest rates is even more dramatically illustrated by international experience. For example, Chile has recently been experiencing an inflation rate of about 30 percent a year with interest rates of about 40 percent a year. Brazil has experienced inflation rates of more than 200 percent a year with interest rates also above 200 percent a year. At the other extreme, such countries as Japan and Belgium have low inflation and low nominal interest rates.

The Money Supply and Interest Rates Again

We have seen that high nominal interest rates and high expected inflation rates go together. We have also seen that high expected inflation is the product of a high anticipated money supply growth rate. Thus a high anticipated growth rate of the money supply brings not only a high anticipated inflation rate but also high interest rates.

In Chapter 28, when we studied the effects of the Bank of Canada's actions on interest rates, we concluded that an increase in the quantity of money lowers interest rates. How can both of these conclusions be correct? How can an increase in the anticipated growth rate of the money supply increase interest rates while an increase in the quantity of money lowers them?

The answer lies in the time scale of the adjustments of interest rates to a change in the money supply. If the Bank of Canada takes an unexpected action that increases the quantity of money, the immediate effect of that action is to lower interest rates. Lower interest rates are needed to make the quantity of money demanded equal to the quantity supplied. But if the Bank of Canada continues to increase the money supply and keeps on increasing it year after year at a pace faster than real GDP is growing, people will come to expect that increase in the money supply and the inflation that goes with it. In these circumstances, they will not be willing to make loans unless they obtain a return on them that sufficiently compensates them for the loss in the value of money resulting from inflation.

Thus it is an unanticipated increase in the money supply that brings a fall in interest rates. An anticipated and ongoing increase in the money supply increases interest rates. The decrease in interest rates following an increase in the money supply is an immediate but temporary response. The increase in interest rates associated with an increase in the growth rate of the money supply is a long-run response.

■ We have now completed our study of inflation and the relationship between the inflation rate and the interest rate. Our next task, which we'll pursue in Chapter 33, is to see how the same aggregate demand and aggregate supply model that we have used to study inflation also helps us to explore and interpret fluctuations in real GDP and explain recessions and depressions.

SUMMARY

Macroeconomic Equilibrium

When an economy is in macroeconomic equilibrium, four conditions are satisfied:

- Real GDP demanded equals real GDP supplied.
- Aggregate planned expenditure equals real GDP.
- Real money demanded equals real money supplied.
- Quantity of labour demanded equals quantity of labour supplied.

Stated another way, macroeconomic equilibrium is a state in which no one wishes to act differently under current circumstances, given the information and options available. Macroeconomic equilibrium is not necessarily full-employment equilibrium. The higher the level of aggregate demand, the higher are real GDP and the price level. The higher the expected price level, the lower is real GDP and the higher is the price level. When the actual price level equals the expected level, real GDP is at capacity output. If the price level is higher than expected, real GDP is above capacity. If the price level is lower than expected, real GDP is below capacity. Wrong price expectations are costly. Losses from wrong expectations can be minimized by minimizing forecasting errors. The expectations that minimize those errors are rational expectations. (pp. 867-871)

The Rational Expectation of the Price Level

Different people devote different amounts of attention to forming expectations — some specialize in the activity, and others simply follow someone else's forecast. The rational expectation of the price level can be found by using the theory of aggregate demand and aggregate supply to forecast the state of the economy. But people do not explicitly use the theory of aggregate demand and aggregate supply to make their forecasts of the price level. They use a variety of methods. The rational expectations hypothesis states that regardless of how people actually go about calculating their expectations, on the average, the expectations that they form are the same as the forecast that an economist would make using the relevant economic theory. (pp. 871-874)

Rational Expectations Equilibrium

A rational expectations equilibrium is a macroeconomic equilibrium based on expectations that are the best available forecasts. The rational expectations equilibrium occurs at the intersection of the aggregate demand and short-run aggregate supply curves. A rational expectations equilibrium may be a full-employment equilibrium, but other possibilities exist. Aggregate demand and aggregate supply may be higher or lower than expected. The combination of these possibilities means that output may be higher or lower than capacity and the price level higher or lower than expected. Regardless of which situation the economy experiences, in a rational expectations equilibrium no one would have acted differently given the state of affairs in which they made their choices. (pp. 874-876)

Inflation

Inflation is the percentage rise in the price level from one year to another. When changes in aggregate demand and aggregate supply are correctly anticipated, there is anticipated inflation. Any unanticipated changes in aggregate demand or aggregate supply produce unanticipated inflation. An unanticipated increase in aggregate demand leads to an unanticipated rise in the inflation rate and raises output above capacity. If aggregate demand rises by less than expected, there is an unanticipated fall in the inflation rate and output falls below capacity.

The inflation rate depends on all the factors that influence aggregate demand and aggregate supply. But one of those factors dominates the path of the price level. It is the money supply. Growth in the money supply and increases in the price level are closely related to each other. However, the other influences on aggregate demand and aggregate supply also have effects, so examining annual money supply growth rates and inflation rates reveal considerable independence of inflation from money supply growth from year to year. (pp. 876-881)

Interest Rates and Inflation

Expectations of inflation affect nominal interest rates. The higher the expected inflation rate, the higher is the nominal interest rate. Borrowers will willingly pay more and lenders will successfully demand more as the anticipated rate of inflation rises. Borrowing and lending and asset-holding plans are made consistent with each other by adjustments in the real interest rate — the difference between the nominal interest rate and the expected inflation rate. (pp. 881-888)

K E Y E L E M E N T S

Key Terms

Nominal interest rates, 881
Rational expectation, 870
Rational expectations equilibrium, 875
Rational expectations hypothesis, 871

Key Figures 

Figure 32.3 The Rational Expectation of the Price Level, 872
Figure 32.4 Rational Expectations Equilibrium, 874
Figure 32.5 Anticipated Inflation, 876
Figure 32.6 An Unanticipated Rise in the Price Level, 878
Figure 32.7 An Unexpected Fall in Inflation, 879

R E V I E W Q U E S T I O N S

1 What are the conditions that are satisfied in a macroeconomic equilibrium?

2 Describe and illustrate the calculation of a rational expectation of the price level.

3 Why are wrong price expectations costly? Suggest some of the losses that an individual will suffer as a result of transactions that incorporate wrong price expectations in labour markets as well as in asset markets.

4 For a given price level expectation, analyse the effects on real GDP and the price level of the following:

a) An increase in the money supply

b) An increase in government purchases of goods and services

c) A rise in income taxes

d) An increase in investment demand

e) A fall in long-run aggregate supply

f) A rise in the expected price level

5 Draw a diagram to illustrate a rational expectations equilibrium in which real GDP is below capacity.

6 How does anticipated inflation come about?

7 What is the main factor leading to changes in aggregate demand that produce ongoing and persistent increases in the price level?

8 Review the relationship between inflation and money supply growth in Canada since 1969.

a) In which years was inflation particularly high compared with money supply growth? Why?

b) In which years was inflation particularly low compared with money supply growth? Why?

9 What is the connection between the expected inflation rate and interest rates?

PROBLEMS

1 An economy has the following aggregate demand and short-run aggregate supply:

Price level (GDP deflator)	Real GDP demanded (billions of 1981 dollars)	Real GDP supplied (billions of 1981 dollars)
80	4	1
100	3	3
120	2	5
140	1	5

The expected price level is 100.

a) What is capacity real GDP?

b) What is actual real GDP?

c) What is the price level?

2 In the economy of problem 1, the expected price level increases to 120.

a) What is the new short-run aggregate supply schedule?

b) What is the level of real GDP?

c) What is-the price level?

d) Is GDP above or below capacity?

3 In 1990, the expected aggregate demand for 1991 is as follows:

Price level (GDP deflator)	Expected real GDP demanded (billions of 1981 dollars)
120	4.0
121	3.9
122	3.8
123	3.7
124	3.6

In 1990, the level of capacity real GDP expected for 1991 is $3.8 billion. Calculate the 1990 rational expectation of the price level for 1991.

4 The economy in problem 3 has the following short-run aggregate supply schedule:

Price level (GDP deflator)	Real GDP supplied (billions of 1981 dollars)
120	3.2
121	3.5
122	3.8
123	4.1
124	4.4

a) Explain why this short-run aggregate supply schedule is consistent with your answer to problem 3.

b) Calculate the actual and expected inflation rate if the aggregate demand curve is expected to shift upward by 10 percent and if it actually does shift upward by that amount.

CHAPTER 33

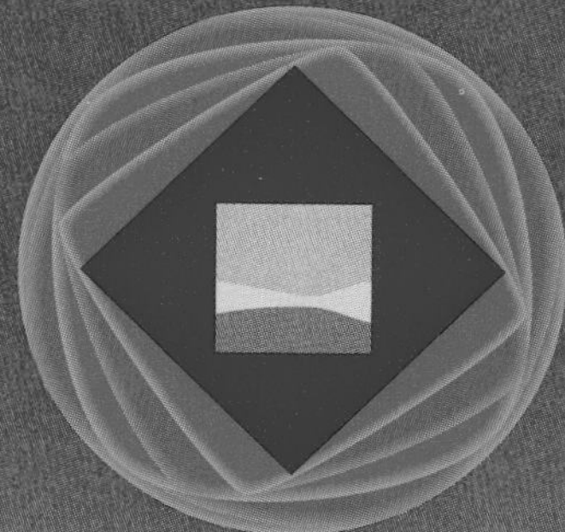

Recessions and Depressions

After studying this chapter, you will be able to:

- Describe the origins of the worldwide recession of the 1980s.
- Describe the course of money, interest rates, and expenditure as the economy contracts.
- Describe the labour market in recession.
- Compare and contrast the flexible and sticky wage theories of the labour market in recession.
- Describe the economy in the contraction phase of the Great Depression between 1929 and 1933.
- Compare the economy of the 1930s with that of the 1980s and assess the likelihood of another Great Depression.

What Goes Up Must Come Down

THE 1920S WERE years of unprecedented prosperity for Canadians — indeed, for the citizens of all the major industrial countries. After the horrors of World War I, the economic machine was back at work, producing such technological marvels as cars and airplanes, telephones and vacuum cleaners. Houses and apartments were being built at a frantic pace. Then, almost without warning in October 1929, came an unprecedented stock market crash. Overnight, the values of stocks and shares trading on Wall Street and Bay Street and in London, Paris, and Berlin fell by as much as 30 percent. During the four succeeding years, there followed the worst economic contraction in recorded history. By 1933, world output had fallen to only two-thirds of its 1929 level. In Canada, real gross domestic product (GDP) fell by 30 percent; unemployment increased to a fifth of the labour force; and prices were down 22 percent. The cost of the Great Depression, in terms of human suffering, will never be fully known. But the cost went far beyond the hardship faced by those who had no jobs. Families were unclothed, hungry, and homeless. Social tensions and crime increased, and the political attitudes that were to dominate the next 40 years of Canadian history were formed. What caused the Great Depression? ■ In October 1987, stock markets in Canada and throughout the world crashed. The crash was so steep and so widespread that it has been dubbed a stock market "meltdown" — conjuring up images of Three Mile Island and Chernobyl. This severe and widespread stock market crash caused some commentators to draw parallels between 1987 and 1929 — the eve of the greatest economic depression in history. Are there similar forces at work in the Canadian and world economies today that might bring about a Great Depression of the 1990s? ■ Although not in the same league as the Great Depression, we experienced a severe recession in 1982. In that year real GDP fell by 3.2 percent and unemployment increased to more than 12 percent. What caused the 1982 recession? Are all recessions triggered in the same way, or are there a variety of causes?

■ In this chapter we'll use the macroeconomic tools that we studied in the previous chapters to interpret the dramatic events that we have just reviewed. We're going to unravel some of the mysteries of recession and depression and assess the likelihood of a serious depression such as that of the 1930s occurring again. We'll begin by examining the two most recent recessions in Canadian economic history.

The 1982 Recession

The most recent recession in Canada occurred in 1982. We're going to examine the mechanisms at work during this episode of Canadian macroeconomic history, paying special attention to the labour market and to the central disagreement among economists about how the labour market works during an economic contraction.

The Origin of the 1982 Recession

We'll begin by examining the forces that initiated the 1982 recession. Then we'll study the mechanisms whereby the effect of those forces was worked out.

The Canadian economy in 1981 had a fairly good year. Real GDP grew by almost 4 percent and unemployment held steady at 7.5 percent. But there was a black cloud hanging over the Canadian economy — and the U.S. economy as well. That cloud was the continuation of two-digit inflation. Both the Federal Reserve Board in the United States (often called "the Fed") and the Bank of Canada took severe measures in 1981 aimed at squeezing inflation out of the system. But the inflation had become so deeply ingrained that few people had confidence in the likely success of the anti-inflation war that was about to be waged.

Let's see what happened in 1982 as the tough anti-inflation policies of governor Gerald Bouey of the Bank of Canada and chairman Paul Volcker of the Fed came into conflict with stubborn inflationary expectations here and in the United States.

Because the United States is the larger of the two economies and because it has such a profound influence on our own economic fortunes, let's begin by seeing what happened there.

The U.S. Recession in 1981 The years 1979 to 1981 were not outstanding ones for the U.S. economy. To begin with, in 1979 the economy had to endure yet another series of increases in the price of a barrel of oil — to $15 in April, to $19 in June, and finally, to $26 by the year's end. Oil prices went on increasing through 1980 and 1981, and by October 1981, crude oil cost $37 a barrel. These large and continued increases in the price of oil put great strain on the U.S. economy. Energy-intensive production activities declined, and research efforts were devoted to finding more energy-efficient methods of production, transportation, and home heating.

Along with these energy shocks was a massive revolution in the electronics sector of the economy. Microprocessors of all kinds became cheaper and affordable computing power found more widespread applications.

The combination of these two processes — continued increases in the price of energy and expanded applications for microprocessors — generated an unusually large reallocation of resources in the U.S. economy. Traditionally strong sectors began to grow more slowly or even to decline, and new sectors emerged with rapid growth.

What came to be called the Rust Belt (the once-strong steel-producing and manufacturing areas of the Ohio Valley and the Great Lakes) was the scene of relative decline, and the Sun Belt (Texas and the southwest), Silicon Valley (in California), and other areas specializing in electronics and related products became focal points for expansion and growth.

The years 1979 through 1981 were also times of high inflation in the United States. The price level increased by close to 10 percent during each of these years. There was a widely held belief that inflation was so entrenched that it could be anticipated to continue at this level into the foreseeable future. This, then, was the scene for the 1982 recession.

The origin of that recession and its magnitude

are illustrated in Fig. 33.1.[1] U.S. aggregate demand and short-run aggregate supply in 1980 are shown by AD_{80} and SAS_{80}. Real GDP was \$3.2 trillion and the GDP deflator was 85. In the two years preceeding 1982, aggregate demand was expected to continue increasing at the same pace as it had in the late 1970s, and the expected aggregate demand curve for 1982 was EAD_{82}. If expectations had been correct, the economy would have moved to point *a* with real GDP continuing to grow at its trend rate and inflation remaining at about 10 percent a year. With a widespread expectation that inflation was going to continue at 10 percent a year, wages and other input prices increased, shifting the short-run aggregate supply curve upward to SAS_{82}.

Events did not turn out as expected. Instead of permitting aggregate demand to continue growing, the Federal Reserve Board, under chairman Paul Volcker, applied a severe dose of monetary restraint. The Fed permitted interest rates to increase and slowed down the pace of investment. Instead of shifting to EAD_{82} the aggregate demand curve only moved up to AD_{82}. By slowing the growth of aggregate demand down to below the pace at which the short-run aggregate supply curve was shifting upward, the Fed put the economy into recession. Real GDP fell to \$3.1 trillion, and the inflation rate began to slow down.

The Canadian Recession The course of events in Canada was similar to that in the United States and is illustrated in Fig. 33.2. Let's begin the story in 1981. In that year, the aggregate demand curve was AD_{81} and the short-run aggregate supply curve was SAS_{81}. Real GDP was \$356 billion and the price level was 100. (Recall that 1981 is the base year for Canada's real GDP calculations, see Chapter 23).

With firmly held expectations of continuing two-digit inflation, people expected that aggregate demand would increase in 1982 to EAD_{82}. Continued inflation of more than 10 percent a year meant that wage adjustments also ran at substantially more than 10 percent a year. As a result, the short-run aggregate supply curve shifted upward to SAS_{82}. If all the expectations had been fulfilled, macroeconomic equilibrium in 1982 would have occurred where the aggregate demand curve EAD_{82} intersects the short-run aggregate supply curve, SAS_{82}. Real GDP would have grown by about 3 percent and inflation would have continued at about 11 percent.

Figure 33.1 The U.S. Recession in 1981

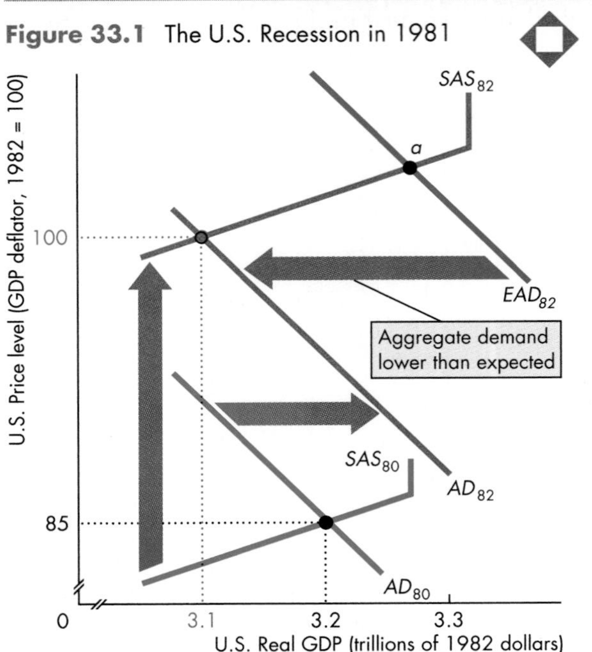

In 1980, the U.S. economy was on its aggregate demand curve AD_{80} and its short-run aggregate supply curve SAS_{80}, with real GDP at \$3.2 trillion and a GDP deflator of 85. Inflation was raging, and wages and other input prices were increasing at a rapid rate to reflect the strong inflationary expectations. The short-run aggregate supply curve shifted upward, and by 1982 it was SAS_{82}. If aggregate demand continued to increase at the pace of the late 1970s, as it was expected to do, the aggregate demand curve would have moved to EAD_{82} and the economy would have gone to point *a* — a steady increase in real GDP and a continuation of inflation at around 10 percent per year. But 1982 was not a normal year — the unexpected happened. The Fed slowed down money growth and forced interest rates up. The aggregate demand curve shifted to AD_{82}. The combination of continuing high inflation expectations, shifting the *SAS* curve upward, and a slowdown of aggregate demand growth put the economy into recession. Real GDP fell and inflation moderated.

[1] In this figure, as well as in Figs. 33.2 and 33.6, we use the aggregate demand-aggregate supply model to determine equilibrium real GDP and the price level. These figures omit the long-run aggregate supply curve. There are two reasons for this omission. First, it is the intersection point of the short-run aggregate supply curve and aggregate demand curve that determines the actual level of real GDP and the price level. The long-run aggregate supply curve is needed only to determine if an economy is operating above or below capacity. Since we're studying recessions in this chapter, the economy is always, in some sense, falling below its capacity output level. But there is some uncertainty about how far below capacity the economy has gone — in other words, there is some disagreement about the exact position of the long-run aggregate supply curve.

Figure 33.2 The 1982 Recession in Canada

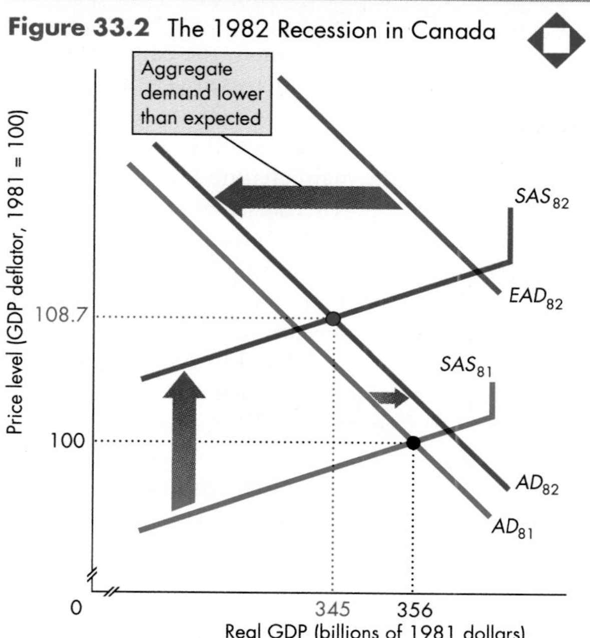

In 1981, real GDP was \$356 billion and the price index was 100, at the intersection of AD_{81} and SAS_{81}. Expectations of continuing inflation led to expectations of an increase in aggregate demand for 1982 of EAD_{82}. Wage increases, consistent with these same expectations, made the short-run aggregate supply curve move upward to SAS_{82}. A slowdown in the growth rate of money supply, both in the United States and in Canada, made actual aggregate demand increase by less than expected to AD_{82}. The economy moved to the point of intersection of AD_{82} and SAS_{82} with a higher price level and a fall in real GDP.

But events did not turn out that way. The contractionary monetary policy in the United States decreased U.S. demand for Canadian output, thereby causing aggregate demand in Canada to grow less quickly than it had been expected to. The Bank of Canada's own contractionary monetary policy reinforced these effects. Aggregate demand grew but not nearly by as much as it had been expected to. The *AD* curve shifted from AD_{81} to AD_{82}. The difference between the curves EAD_{82} and AD_{82} is the unexpected negative shock to aggregate demand that resulted from the pursuit of tough anti-inflationary monetary policies in the United States and Canada. The economy moved to its 1982 equilibrium at the intersection of AD_{82} and SAS_{82}. The price level increased by 8.7 percent and real GDP fell from \$356 billion to \$345 billion.

Notice the similarity between the patterns of events in the United States and Canada. In both cases, the *SAS* curve shifts upward by an amount based on expectations of a continuation of two-digit inflation. The *AD* curve shifted upward by much less than was expected. The result was a continuation of inflation but at a pace slower than expected and a fall in aggregate output.

Let's now take a closer look at the recession mechanism.

Recession Mechanism

In studying the recession mechanism, we'll focus our attention on the Canadian economy. Events similar to those that we analyse here also occurred in the United States.

The markets in which things happen first and move fastest are the markets for money and financial assets. We're going to begin our examination of the recession mechanism by examining the money market.

Money and Interest Rates A general feature of a recession is that before it begins and in its early stages, interest rates increase. But once the recession is under way, interest rates fall. By the time real GDP has reached its trough, interest rates have fallen, sometimes to levels lower than those at the onset of the recession. Why do interest rates behave in this manner? To find out, let's study the money market in the early 1980s. Figure 33.3 contains the relevant analysis.

The real money supply in 1980 (M2 valued in constant 1981 dollars) was about \$122 billion. Thus the supply curve of real M2 was the one labelled *MS* in Fig. 33.3. The demand curve for real M2 in 1980 was MD_{80}. Interest rates in 1980 were determined at the intersection point of MD_{80} and *MS* at about 13 percent a year.

During 1981, the GDP deflator increased by about 11 percent. The Bank of Canada permitted M2 to grow at approximately that same 11 percent rate. Thus the real quantity of M2 remained unchanged. The supply curve of real M2 in 1981 was *MS*, the same curve as it had been in 1980.

Two forces shifted the demand curve for real M2 in 1981. They were:

- Real GDP growth
- Higher interest rates on savings deposits

With real GDP growing and with interest rate competition pushing financial institutions to offer

Figure 33.3 Interest Rates and Money in Recession

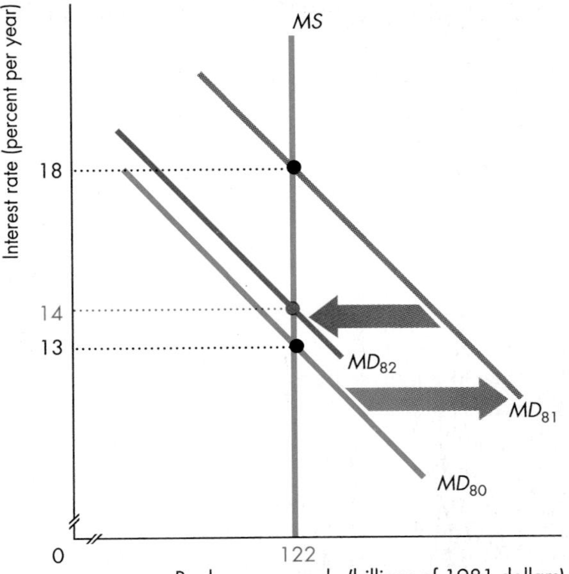

As the economy went into the 1982 recession, interest rates increased but as the recession deepened, interest rates began to fall. From 1980 to 1982, the Bank of Canada held the real money supply (M2 definition) almost constant at $122 billion. The real money supply curve was *MS*. In 1980, the demand curve for real money was MD_{80}. The interest rate, determined at the intersection of MD_{80} and *MS*, was 13 percent per year. An increase in real GDP and an increase in interest rates on savings deposits shifted the demand curve for real money to the right in 1981 to MD_{81}. Interest rates increased sharply to 18 percent per year. High interest rates brought lower spending and the economy went into recession. Lower real GDP brought a decrease in the demand for real money and the demand curve shifted to MD_{82}. Interest rates fell to 14 percent per year.

better terms for savings accounts, the demand curve for real M2 shifted to the right in 1981.[2] The shift is illustrated as the movement from MD_{80} to MD_{81}. With a higher demand for real money but no increase in the supply of real money, the equilibrium interest rate increased. And it increased very sharply — to 18 percent a year.

It was the very high interest rates of 1982 that constituted one of the main channels whereby the restrictive monetary policy translated itself into lower spending. Interest rates of 18 percent a year combined with inflation of about 10 percent a year to give real interest rates of 8 percent a year. Such real interest rates limited the amount of households' expenditure on consumer durables and firms' spending on new structures and plant and machinery. Expenditure began to decline, and equilibrium real GDP declined with it.

We can see the effects of recession in the money market by continuing to review the events that are unfolding in Fig. 33.3. In 1982, the demand curve for real money shifted from MD_{81} to MD_{82}. The demand for real money decreased. The decrease in the demand for real money resulted from the decrease in real GDP. At the same time as real GDP was declining, the Bank of Canada's monetary policy was holding the growth rate of M2 very close to the inflation rate. In other words, real M2 was being kept constant. For yet a further year, therefore, the supply curve of real money remained at *MS*. With a constant real money supply and a decrease in the demand for real money, interest rates fell to 14 percent a year.

Notice the pattern of events in the money market just before the recession begins and once it gets under way. At first, interest rates rise because an increase in the demand for real money is met by no increase in the supply of real money. Once the recession is under way, interest rates fall because the decrease in real GDP brings a decrease in the demand for real money. In the Canadian case, interest rates fell during the recession but not to a level lower than that from which they had started. If the recession had been more severe, it is possible that at its depth interest

[2]Why do higher interest rates on savings accounts lead to a shift in the demand curve for M2? Don't changes in interest rates lead to a movement along the demand for money curve? To answer these questions, remember that the demand curve for real money is plotted against the interest rate on non-money assets that might be held instead of money. For example, if the interest rate on Canada savings bonds or government of Canada treasury bills changes, there is a change in the opportunity cost of holding money. In such a situation, people will change the quantity of money they hold and there will be a movement along the demand curve for money. However, holding constant interest rates on other non-money assets, any other factors that influence the quantity of money held do lead to a shift in the demand curve for money. One such influence is the interest rate on the money assets themselves. Thus a change in the interest rate on savings deposits, with interest rates on non-money assets held constant, leads to a shift in the demand curve for M2. Keep in mind that the interest rate against which we draw a demand curve for real money is not the interest rate on bank deposits and other assets that are part of the money supply itself. It is the interest rate on other assets that are alternative ways of holding wealth to money itself.

Table 33.1 Expenditure in the 1982 Contraction

	Real GDP		Components of aggregate expenditure (billions of 1981 dollars)								
	Y	=	*C*	+	*I*	+	*G*	+	*EX*	-	*IM*
1981	356	=	196	+	78	+	78	+	97	-	93
1982	345	=	191	+	58	+	80	+	95	-	79
Change	–11	=	–5	+	–20	+	2	+	–2	-	–14
Percentage change	–3		–3		–26		3		–2		–15

Source: Statistics Canada, *National Income and Expenditure Accounts,* 1989 catalogue no. 13-001.

rates could have fallen to levels lower than those that prevailed previously.

As we have just noted, it is the behaviour of interest rates that gives rise to the fall in aggregate expenditure. Let's look more closely at how aggregate expenditure changed during the 1982 recession.

Changes in Expenditure When the economy is in a recession, real GDP falls and real aggregate expenditure also falls. (Recall that real GDP and real aggregate expenditure are equal to each other.) But the main component of aggregate expenditure that falls is investment — see Table 33.1. Investment falls for two reasons. First, an increase in real interest rates — in interest rates relative to expected inflation — increases the opportunity cost of buying new capital equipment. Second, expectations of recession lead to a revision downward of profit expectations, and that too lowers investment. For these two reasons, investment falls. During the 1982 recession in Canada, investment (in 1981 dollars) fell from $78 billion in 1981 to $58 billion in 1982.

A decrease in investment has two effects. First, it decreases aggregate expenditure and aggregate demand. Second, it results in a slowdown in the growth rate of the capital stock and thus in a slowdown in the pace of innovation of new technologies. This aspect of the investment slowdown feeds back to slow down the growth of aggregate supply. But it is the effect of decreased investment on aggregate demand that dominates.

As you can see from Table 33.1, the decrease in other components of aggregate expenditure was much smaller than the decrease in investment. On that particular occasion, the decrease in exports was really quite small — only 2 percent. The other large change was spending on imports, which fell by 15 percent. There is a connection between the decrease in imports and the decrease in investment. Much of Canada's investment consists of specialized equipment made in other countries. When investment declines, the demand for Boeing airplanes and Caterpillar earthmovers from the United States, for high-tech instruments from Germany, and for electronic components from Japan declines.

The fact that our exports did not decline by much does not mean that the Canadian recession was not strongly influenced by events in the rest of the world. The climate of pessimism generated by a worldwide recession has an effect on investment independent of its direct effect on Canadian exports in any given year. It is the prospect of future business, rather than the fact of current business, that influences firms' investment spending.

We've now reviewed the events of the 1982 recession in terms of the aggregate demand-aggregate supply model and in terms of events that occurred in the money market and of the components of aggregate expenditure. Next, we're going to examine the labour market.

One of the main reasons people fear recession is because it is associated with a high unemployment rate. What happens in the labour market during a recession? Why does unemployment increase during a recession? Let's examine these questions.

The Labour Market in Recession

Figure 33.4 provides a summary and analysis of the main events. The demand curve for labour in both

1981 and 1982 was *LD*. That is, there was no change in the demand for labour between 1981 and 1982. Recall that the demand for labour curve is derived from the economy's short-run aggregate production function. The short-run aggregate production function shows the level of real GDP that can be produced for a given labour input. Canada's short-run aggregate production function did not move between 1981 and 1982. In a normal year, the short-run aggregate production function shifts upward. But in 1982, the forces making for an increase in the production function — the accumulation of capital and technological change — were offset by other forces that prevented growth in the economy's productive capacity. These other forces are not well understood. But they probably include large changes in the composition of output arising in part from changes in relative prices — most notably, the relative price of energy.

Regardless of the specific underlying causes, the fact that Canada's short-run aggregate production function did not move during 1982 meant that the demand for labour curve also stayed put.

The supply curve of labour, however, shifted to the right — there was an increase in the supply of labour of about 1.5 percent as a result of an increase in the population aged 15 years and over. Thus the supply of labour curve shifted to the right by that percentage amount — not a large shift, but a definite shift to the right.

There is controversy about how the labour market works and about its ability to act as a coordination mechanism to bring about equality between the quantities of labour demanded and supplied. Let's see how we can interpret the events occurring in the Canadian labour market in 1982, using both the sticky wage theory and the flexible wage theory and see why economists continue to be unable to agree on how the labour market functions.

Figure 33.4 The Labour Market in Recession: Sticky Wage Theory

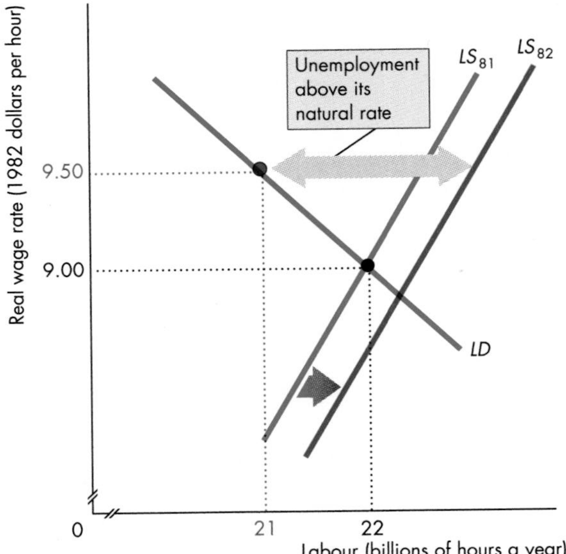

The demand for labour curve in 1981 and 1982 was *LD*. The supply curve in 1981 was LS_{81}, and it shifted to LS_{82} in 1982. Wages and employment in 1981 were at the intersection of *LD* and LS_{81} with a real wage rate of $9 per hour and 22 billion hours of labour being demanded and supplied. In 1982, higher money wages combined with lower-than-expected inflation increased the real wage rate to $9.50 per hour. Employment decreased to 21 billion hours. The difference between the quantity of labour demanded and the quantity supplied is the unemployment gap — the extent to which unemployment exceeds its natural rate.

The Sticky Wage Theory The sticky wage theory of the labour market is illustrated in Fig. 33.4. In 1981, the labour market operated at the point of intersection of *LD* and LS_{81}. The quantity of labour supplied and demanded was 22 billion hours at a wage rate of $9 an hour. There was some unemployment but it was frictional and the unemployment rate was equal to the natural rate.

During 1981, money wages increased at a pace consistent with expectations that inflation would continue at about 10 percent a year. Inflation actually slowed down so real wages increased unexpectedly — up to about $9.50 an hour. With higher real wages, the quantity of labour demanded declined — there was a movement along the demand curve. Also, with higher real wages, the quantity of labour supplied increased — there was a movement along the supply curve. The difference between the quantity of labour supplied and the quantity demanded at the higher real wage rate represents the extent to which unemployment exceeds its natural rate. To achieve full employment in 1982, the real wage rate would have actually had to decline since the supply of labour increased.

This account of the labour market is the most conventional one, the one that most economists regard as probably being correct.

Flexible Wage Theory Although most economists accept the sticky wage theory, an increasing number are questioning that interpretation of the labour market

Figure 33.5 The Labour Market in Recession: A Flexible Wage Theory

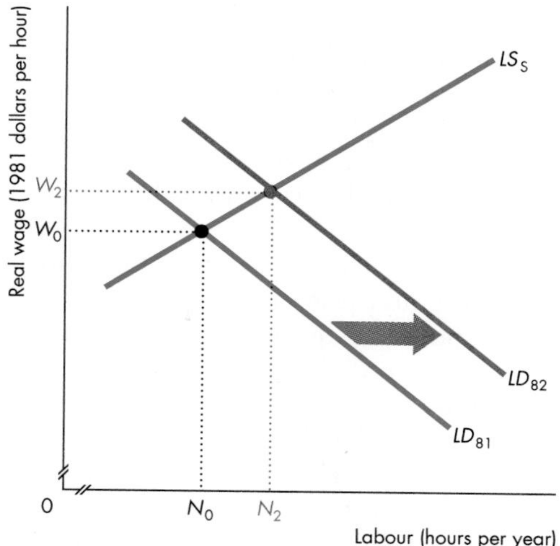

(a) Skilled labour

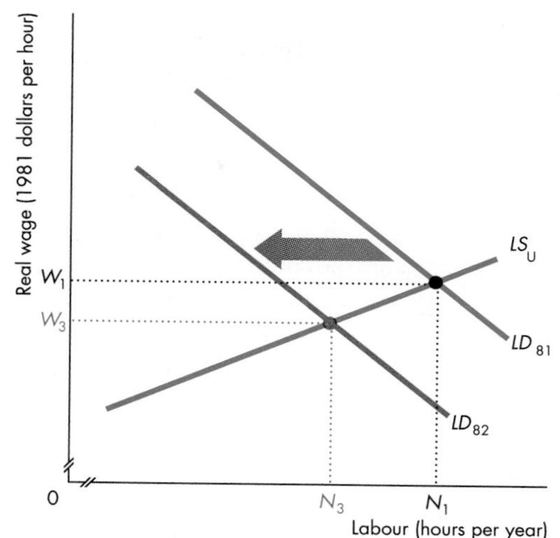

(b) Unskilled labour

The labour market is divided into two categories of labour — skilled and unskilled. In part (a), the supply curve of skilled labour is LS_S, and in part (b), the supply curve of unskilled labour is LS_U. The demand curves for skilled and unskilled labour in 1981 are LD_{81} (in both parts). In 1981, the wages of skilled labour are W_0 and the employment level N_0, and the wages of unskilled labour are W_1 and the employment level N_1. In 1982 there is an increase in the demand for skilled labour and a decrease in the demand for unskilled labour. Skilled employment increases to N_2 and wages increase to W_2. Unskilled employment decreases to N_3 and wages decrease to W_3. Aggregate employment is the sum of the employment of the skilled and unskilled, and this aggregate declines since the decrease in the employment of the unskilled exceeds the increase in the employment of the skilled. The average wage rate is a weighted average of the wage rates of the two groups. The average wage rate increases because the wage rate of skilled workers increases and the proportion of jobs held by them also increases.

in recession. There are a wide variety of flexible wage models of the labour market; the one that we'll examine here is just an example. It is an example, nevertheless, that fits the broad facts of the 1982 recession very closely.

The theory is illustrated with the model economy displayed in Fig. 33.5. The labour force is divided into two groups — one group skilled, and the other unskilled. The market for skilled labour is shown in part (a) and for unskilled labour in part (b). Focus first on the supply curves. The supply curve of skilled labour is LS_S and of unskilled labour LS_U. Notice how these supply curves differ from each other. The supply curve of skilled labour lies above that for unskilled labour. That is, for a given quantity of labour supplied, a higher wage rate is required to call forth an hour of skilled labour than that to call forth an hour of unskilled labour. The difference in wage rates at which skilled and unskilled workers are willing to supply their labour reflects the costs of acquiring skills — costs of schooling and of experience. In this model economy, we'll suppose that the supply of labour remains constant.

The demand for labour curves are shown as LD_{81} and LD_{82} in the two parts of the figure. Focus first on the situation prevailing in 1981. In the market for skilled labour, the wage rate is W_0 and the level of employment N_0 — determined at the point of intersection of LS_S and LD_{81}. In the market for unskilled labour, the wage rate is W_1 and the employment level is N_1 — at the intersection point of LD_{81} and LS_U. There are more unskilled workers than skilled workers, but unskilled workers are paid a lower wage than skilled workers. Aggregate employment is the sum of the employment of skilled workers and unskilled workers, and average wages are an average of the wage rates of the skilled (W_0) and the unskilled (W_1) where the average is weighted by the proportions of the two kinds of labour.

Now look at what happens in 1982. There is an increase in the demand for skilled labour and a decrease in the demand for unskilled labour. The wages of skilled labour increase to W_2 and their employment level increases to N_2. The wages of unskilled workers decrease to W_3 and their employment decreases to N_3. Aggregate employment falls because the decrease in employment of the unskilled exceeds the increase in employment of the skilled. The average wage rate increases because the wage rates of skilled workers increase and the proportion of workers earning the higher skilled wage also increases. There is an increase in unemployment as the unskilled workers whose labour demand declines become unemployed or start to look for better jobs. But the change in employment is a change in the natural rate of unemployment. There is no gap between the quantity of labour supplied and the quantity demanded. The labour market is in equilibrium and the plans of demanders and suppliers of labour are completely coordinated.

Which Theory of the Labour Market is Correct? What exactly do economists disagree about concerning the labour market and why? The essence of the controversy is summarized in Figs. 33.4 and 33.5. First, everyone agrees about the facts. Real wages in 1981 were \$9 an hour, on the average. In 1982, they increased to \$9.50, on the average. Employment in 1981 was 22 billion hours, and it fell to 21 billion hours in 1982.

In addition, there is not much disagreement about the demand for labour. Most economists agree that the quantity of labour actually employed is determined by the profit-maximizing decisions of firms. That quantity depends on the real wage. This means that the level of employment and the real wage in any particular year are a point on the demand for labour curve. If we agree that the employment level and real wage are a point on the demand for labour curve, we can figure out the position of the curve and work out what makes it shift. Thus there is little disagreement among economists about the slope and position of the demand for labour curve.

Where economists disagree is on the supply of labour and the forces at work in achieving a labour market equilibrium. Because a large amount of labour is supplied on long-term contracts with wages and other terms fixed for the duration of the contract, most economists believe that households do not normally operate on their supply of labour curve. Furthermore, most economists believe, on the basis of evidence from variations in hours of work and wages, that the quantity of labour supplied does not respond much to changes in real wages. They believe that the situation is like the one shown in Fig. 33.4.

Other economists believe that the combination of the real wage rate and the level of employment represents not only a point on the demand for labour curve but also a point on the supply of labour curve. But to rationalize the aggregate data, it is necessary to study a model economy that distinguishes between the various types of labour. Economists who regard the flexible wage model as being the appropriate one emphasize not only its ability to explain the facts about average wages and aggregate employment, but also its consistency with other evidence about the structure of the labour market.

For example, during 1982, the employment rate among young men (aged 15 to 24 years) decreased by 13 percent and that for young women (the same age group) decreased by 7.5 percent. In contrast, the employment rate of men aged 25 years and over decreased by only 2 percent, and the employment rate of women in that age group actually increased by 1 percent. By virtue of their job experience and longer training, older workers are generally more skilled and, therefore, more productive than younger workers. We can think of the skilled labour of Fig. 33.5(a), therefore, as being workers aged 25 years and over and the unskilled labour of Fig. 33.5(b) as being workers aged 15 to 25 years. In sectors of the economy that did not decline much or even expanded during the recession, the productivity of the older and more skilled workers increased. These sectors were government, construction, services, and agriculture. In sectors that declined most sharply, the productivity of the less skilled workers declined more than that of the skilled workers. These sectors were logging and forestry, the manufacture of durables, retail trade, and transportation.

These facts about changes in the composition of output and employment do not demonstrate that the flexible wage theory is correct. They are, however, consistent with that theory.

The fundamental problem remains. No one has

yet suggested a test that is sufficiently clear for all economists to agree on. The Keynesian-monetarist controversy about aggregate demand was eventually settled when economists were able to agree on tests of the effects of interest rates on the demand for real money and aggregate expenditure. The modern controversy among Keynesians, monetarists, and real business cycle theorists will be settled only when economists can agree on and implement a test of their competing views about how the quantity of labour supplied responds to a change in the real wage rate. Once such a test has been implemented, we shall be able to put this controversy behind us. Until then, professional economists and students of economics have to live with the fact that there are many unanswered questions about this large and important issue at the heart of macroeconomics.

Determining which of the two theories is correct is not just a matter of academic curiosity. It is a matter of enormous importance in designing an appropriate anti-recessionary policy. We discovered in Chapter 31 that if the flexible wage theory is true, the aggregate supply curve is vertical. This fact means that any attempt to bring the economy out of recession by increasing aggregate demand — for example, by lowering interest rates and increasing the money supply or by fiscal policy measures — is doomed to failure and can result only in a higher price level (more inflation). Conversely, if the sticky wage theory is correct, the labour market looks like the one depicted in Fig. 33.4, and the short-run aggregate supply curve looks like that shown in Figs. 33.1 and 33.2; thus an increase in aggregate demand, although increasing the price level somewhat, will also increase real GDP and bring the economy out of a recession.

Another Great Depression?

Following the 1982 recession the Canadian economy moved into a period of sustained recovery. In fact, that recovery has been one of the longest and strongest on record. It resulted from developments on both the demand and supply sides of the economy. On the supply side, a steady accumulation of capital and technological change, together with growth of population, increased capacity real GDP by about 33 percent between 1982 and 1989. In the first of these years, the economy was operating below capacity, but by 1989 real GDP was at or perhaps slightly above capacity. As the recovery got under way, inflation fell. At first, the drop in inflation was unanticipated, and it was that fact that led to the 1982 recession. Wage rates were set at too high a level, given what happened to prices. But lower inflation gradually came to be anticipated and, as it did so, real GDP approached its capacity level. Throughout the recovery, interest rates eased, which helped to stimulate additional investment.

Although the recovery continued, there was, by the fall of 1987, widespread fear that the good times were coming to an end, at least for a while. In October 1987, these fears were strengthened by the biggest stock market crash to hit the Canadian economy (and, indeed, the world economy) since that of 1929, which had heralded the Great Depression. On Wall Street, the magnitude of the 1987 crash was almost identical to the 1929 crash — the range between the high and the low was 34 percent. This similarity was so striking that many commentators concluded that the closing years of the 1980s and the early 1990s would resemble the Great Depression of the early 1930s. A book that fed such fears, one that otherwise might have passed almost unnoticed, became a bestseller.[3]

Is there going to be another Great Depression? Of course, the answer to this question is that no one knows. But we can try to assess the likelihood of such an event. Let's begin by first asking some questions. What was the Great Depression like? Just how bad did things get in the early 1930s? What would the Canadian economy look like in the 1990s if it had a rerun of those events? Once we've charted the broad anatomy of the Great Depression, we'll examine why it happened and consider the question of whether it could happen again and how likely such an event would be.

What the Great Depression Was Like

At the beginning of 1929, the Canadian economy was operating at capacity output and unemployment was only 2.9 percent of the labour force. But as that eventful year unfolded, increasing signs of economic weakness began to appear. The most dramatic events

[3]Ravi Batra, *The Great Depression of 1990* (New York: Simon and Schuster) 1987.

occurred in October when the stock market collapsed, losing more than one-third of its value in only two weeks. The four years that followed were years of monstrous economic depression — depression so severe that the episode came to be called the Great Depression.

The dimensions of the Great Depression can be seen in Fig. 33.6. That figure shows the situation on the eve of the Great Depression in 1929, when the economy was on its aggregate demand curve (AD_{29}) and short-run aggregate supply curve (SAS_{29}). Real GDP was $42 billion and the GDP deflator was 15. (Real GDP at the end of the 1980s was some 11 times its 1929 level, and the GDP deflator approached 10 times its 1929 level).

In 1930, there was widespread expectation that prices would fall, so wages fell. With lower wages, the short-run aggregate supply curve shifted downward. But aggregate demand fell by a larger amount than expected. In 1930, the economy went into recession. Real GDP fell by about 7 percent and the price level fell by a similar amount. It was not unusual at that time for prices occasionally to fall. When the price level is falling the economy is experiencing *deflation.*

If the normal course of events had ensued in 1930, the economy might have remained in its depressed state for several months and then started a recovery. But 1930 was not a normal year. During it and the next three years, the economy was further bombarded with huge negative demand shocks (the sources of which we'll look at in a moment). The aggregate demand curve shifted to the left, all the way to AD_{33}. With a depressed economy, the price level was expected to fall, and wages fell in line with those expectations. Money wages fell. As a result of lower wages, the aggregate supply curve shifted downward, from SAS_{29} to SAS_{33}. But the size of the downward shift of the short-run aggregate supply curve was much less than the drop in aggregate demand. As a result, the aggregate demand curve and the short-run aggregate supply curve in 1933 intersected at a real GDP of $30 billion and a GDP deflator of 12. Real GDP had fallen from its 1929 level by almost 30 percent, and the price level had fallen by 20 percent.

Although the Great Depression brought enormous hardship, the distribution of that hardship was very uneven. One-fifth of the labour force had no jobs at all. And at that time, there were virtually no organized social security and unemployment programs in place. So, for many families, there was virtually no income. But the pocketbooks of the other 80 percent of the labour force barely noticed the

Figure 33.6 The Great Depression

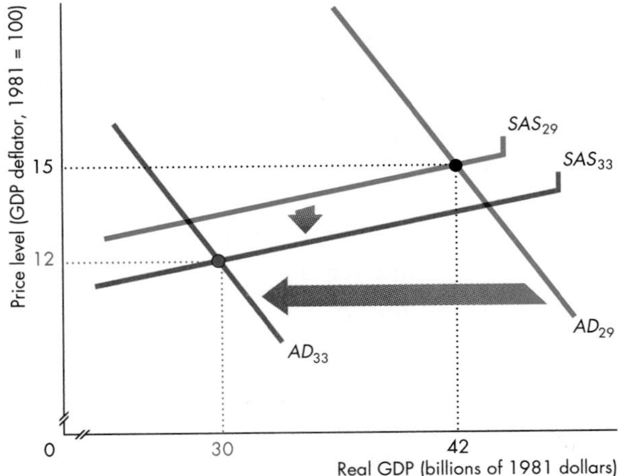

In 1929, real GDP was $42 billion and the GDP deflator was 15 — at the intersection of AD_{29} and SAS_{29}. In 1930, increased pessimism and uncertainty resulted in a drop in investment and in the demand for durables, resulting in a fall in aggregate demand. During the next three years, demand continued to fall. By 1933, aggregate demand had shifted down to AD_{33}. To some degree, the fall in aggregate demand was anticipated, so wages fell and the short-run aggregate supply curve moved down to SAS_{33}. By 1933, real GDP had fallen to $30 billion (about 70 percent of its 1929 level) and the GDP deflator had fallen to 12 (80 percent of its 1929 level).

Great Depression. It's true that wages fell. But at the same time, the price level fell by even more. Hence, real wages for those who had jobs increased, even through the contraction years of the Great Depression.

You can begin to appreciate the magnitude of the Great Depression if you compare it with the 1982 recession. From 1981 to 1982, real GDP fell by 3 percent. In comparison, from 1929 to 1933, real GDP fell by close to 30 percent. A 1990s Great Depression of the same magnitude would lower GDP to its mid-1970s level.

Why the Great Depression Happened

The late 1920s were years of economic boom. New houses and apartments were built on an unprecedented scale, new firms were created, and the capital stock of the nation expanded. But these were also years of increasing uncertainty. The uncertainty was rooted in the international economy. The main source of that increased uncertainty was international. The world economy was going through tumultuous times. The patterns of world trade were changing as Britain, the traditional economic powerhouse of the world, began its period of relative economic decline, and new economic powers, such as Germany and Japan, as well as Canada, began to emerge. International currency fluctuations and the introduction of restrictive trade policies by many countries (see Chapter 36) further increased the uncertainty faced by firms. There was also domestic uncertainty arising from the fact that there had been such a strong boom in recent years, especially in the capital goods sector and housing. No one believed that that boom could continue, but there was great uncertainty as to when it would end and how the pattern of demand would change.

This environment of uncertainty led to a slowdown in consumer spending, especially on new homes and household appliances. By the fall of 1929, the uncertainty had reached a critical level and contributed to the stock market crash. The stock market crash, in turn, heightened people's fears about economic prospects in the foreseeable future. Fear fed fear. Investment collapsed. The building industry almost disappeared. An industry that had been operating flat out just two years earlier was now building virtually no new houses and apartments. It was this drop in investment plus a drop in consumer spending on durables that led to the initial decrease in aggregate demand.

The Deepening Depression At this stage, what became the Great Depression was no worse than many previous recessions had been. What distinguished the Great Depression from other previous recessions (and subsequent ones) were the events that followed between 1930 and 1933. Even to this day, economists have not come to agreement on how to interpret those events. One view, argued by Peter Temin,[4] is that spending continued to fall for a wide variety of reasons — including a continuation of increasing pessimism and uncertainty. According to Temin's view, the continued contraction resulted from a decrease in investment demand and a fall in autonomous expenditure. Milton Friedman and Anna J. Schwartz have argued that the continuation of the contraction was almost exclusively the result of the subsequent worsening of financial and monetary conditions.[5] In their view, it was a severe cut in the money supply that lowered aggregate demand, prolonging the contraction and deepening the depression.

Although there is argument about the causes of the contraction phase of the Great Depression, the disagreement is not about the elements at work but the degree of importance attached to each. Everyone agrees that increased pessimism and uncertainty lowered investment demand, and everyone agrees that there was a massive contraction of the real money supply. Temin and his supporters assign primary importance to the fall in autonomous expenditure and secondary importance to the fall in the money supply, while Friedman and Schwartz and their supporters assign primary responsibility to the money supply and regard the other factors as of limited importance.

The Components of Expenditure Let's look at the contraction of aggregate demand a bit more closely. The key facts about the composition of aggregate expenditure are shown in Table 33.2. As you can see, just as in the case of the 1982 recession, the major decline in spending came from investment. During the Great Depression, the decline in investment was a near-total collapse — a 90 percent decline. It is this decline in investment expenditure that Peter Temin emphasizes in his interpretation of the events. But monetary actions were also important. Let's examine these, beginning with a look at monetary forces in the U.S. economy.

Monetary Forces in the United States In the United States between 1930 and 1933, there was a massive 20 percent contraction in the nominal money supply. This fall in the money supply was not directly induced by the actions of the Fed. The monetary base hardly fell at all. But the bank deposits component of the money supply suffered an enormous collapse, primarily because a large number of banks failed. The primary source of bank failure was unsound lending by the banks in the boom running up to the onset of the Great Depression. Fuelled by increasing stock prices and booming business conditions, bank loans had expanded. After the stock market crash and the downturn, many borrowers found themselves in hard economic times. They could not pay the interest on

[4]Peter Temin, *Did Monetary Forces Cause the Great Depression?* (New York: W. W. Norton, 1976).

[5]Milton Friedman and Anna J. Schwartz, *A Monetary History of the United States 1867-1960* (Princeton: Princeton University Press, 1963), Chapter 7.

Table 33.2 Expenditure in the Contraction Phase of the Great Depression

	Real GDP		Components of aggregate expenditure (billions of 1981 dollars)								
	Y	=	*C*	+	*I*	+	*G*	+	*EX*	–	*IM*
1929	42	=	27	+	10	+	7	+	9	–	11
1933	29	=	22	+	1	+	6	+	7	–	7
Change	–13	=	–5	+	–9	+	–1	+	–2	–	–4
Percentage change	–31		–19		–90		–14		–22		–36

Source: F.H. Leacy, *Historical Statistics of Canada*, 2nd ed. (Ottawa: Statistics Canada and Social Science Federation of Canada, 1982).

their loans, and they could not meet the agreed repayment schedules. Banks had deposits that exceeded the realistic value of the loans that they had made. When depositors withdrew funds from the banks, the banks lost reserves, and many of them simply couldn't meet their depositors' demands to be repaid.

Bank failures create uncertainty and this growing uncertainty leads to additional failures. Seeing banks fail, people become anxious to protect themselves and so take their money out of the banks. Such were the events of 1930. The quantity of notes and coins in circulation increased, and the volume of bank deposits declined. But the very action of individuals' taking money out of the bank to protect their wealth accentuated the process of banking failure. Banks were increasingly short of cash and unable to meet their obligations.

Bank failure and the massive contraction of the money supply had two effects on the economy. First, the bank failures themselves brought financial hardship to many producers, increasing the business failure rate throughout the economy. At the same time, a sharp drop in the money supply kept interest rates high. Not only did nominal interest rates stay high; real interest rates increased sharply. The real interest rate is (approximately) the difference between the nominal interest rate and the expected inflation rate. During the Great Depression, inflation was negative — the price level was falling. Thus the real interest rate equalled the nominal interest rate plus the expected rate of deflation. With high real interest rates, investment remained low.

Monetary Forces in Canada Monetary contraction also occurred in Canada although on a less serious scale than in the United States. Our money supply declined in each of the contraction years of the Great Depression — but at a steady 5 percent a year in contrast to the whopping 20 percent in the United States. Also, no chartered bank in Canada failed, while bank failure was a severe problem in the United States.

The Stock Market Crash What role did the stock market crash of 1929 play in producing the Great Depression? It certainly created an atmosphere of fear and panic, and it probably also contributed to the overall air of uncertainty that dampened investment spending. It also reduced the wealth of shareholders, encouraging them to cut back on their consumption expenditure. But the direct effect of the stock market crash on consumption expenditure, although a factor contributing to the Great Depression, was not the major source of the drop in aggregate demand. It was the collapse in investment arising from increased uncertainty that brought the 1930 decline in aggregate demand.

But the stock market crash was a predictor of severe recession. It reflected the expectations of shareholders concerning future profit prospects. As those expectations became pessimistic, the prices of shares were bid lower and lower. That is, the behaviour of the stock market was a consequence of expectations about future profitability and those expectations were lowered as a result of increased uncertainty.

Can It Happen Again?

Since, even today, we have an incomplete understanding of the causes of the Great Depression, we are not able to predict such an event or to be sure that one cannot occur again. But some important differences between the economy of the 1990s and that of the 1930s make a severe depression much less likely today than it was 60 years ago. The most important features of the economy that make severe depression less likely today are:

- Taxes and government spending
- Bank deposit insurance
- The Bank of Canada's role as lender of last resort
- Multi-income families

Let's examine these in turn.

Taxes and Government Spending

The government sector was a much less important part of the economy in 1929 than it has become today. On the eve of that earlier recession, government purchases of goods and services were 15 percent of GDP. In contrast, today they are more than 20 percent. Government transfer payments were around 5 percent of GDP in 1929. These items have grown to 20 percent of GDP today.

A larger level of government purchases of goods and services means that when recession hits, a large component of aggregate demand does not decline. It is government transfer payments, however, that are the most important economic stabilizer. When the economy goes into recession and depression, more people qualify for unemployment compensation and social security. As a consequence, although disposable income decreases, the extent of the decrease is moderated by the existence of such programs. Consumption expenditure, in turn, does not decline by as much as it would in the absence of such government programs. But limited decline in consumption expenditure further limits the overall decrease in aggregate expenditure, thereby limiting the magnitude of an economic downturn.

Bank Deposit Insurance In 1967, the government of Canada established the Canada Deposit Insurance Corporation (CDIC). The CDIC insures bank deposits up to $60,000 per deposit so that most depositors have no fear about the consequences of a bank failure. If a bank fails, the CDIC pays the deposit holders. Similar arrangements have been introduced in the United States, where deposits up to $100,000 are insured by the Federal Deposit Insurance Corporation. With government-insured bank deposits, one of the key events that turned a fairly ordinary recession into the Great Depression in the United States is most unlikely to occur. It was the fear of bank failure that caused people to withdraw their deposits from banks. The aggregate consequence of these individually rational acts was to cause the very bank failures that were feared. With deposit insurance, most depositors have nothing to lose if a bank fails and so have no incentive to take actions that are likely to give rise to that failure.

Although bank failure was not a severe problem in Canada during the Great Depression, it clearly was an important factor in intensifying the depression in the United States. And the severity of the U.S. recession certainly had an impact on Canada and the rest of the world.

Lender of Last Resort The Bank of Canada is the lender of last resort in the Canadian economy. If a single bank is short of reserves, it can borrow reserves from other banks. If the entire banking system is short of reserves, banks can borrow from the Bank of Canada. By making reserves available (at a suitable interest rate), the Bank is able to make the quantity of reserves in the banking system respond flexibly to the demand for those reserves. Bank failure can be prevented or at least contained to cases in which bad management practices are the source of the problem and widespread failures of the type that occurred in the Great Depression prevented.

It is interesting to note that during the weeks following the October 1987 stock market crash, Fed chairman Alan Greenspan and Bank of Canada governor John Crow used every opportunity available to remind the world banking and financial community of their ability and readiness to maintain calm financial conditions.

Multi-Income Families At the time of the Great Depression, families with more than one wage earner were much less common than they are today. The labour force participation rate in 1929 was about 55 percent. Today, it is 67 percent. Thus even if the unemployment rate increased to 20 percent today, 54 percent of the adult population would actually have jobs. During the Great Depression, only 44 percent of the adult population had work. Multi-income

A Repeat of 1981-1982?

Repeat of 1981-82 recession not in the cards, analysts say

BANKRUPTCIES are soaring, consumers are carrying record debt loads and interest rates have climbed to heights unseen since the 1981-82 recession....

It's not hard to see the recessionary signals but are they the signals of a repeat of 1981-82?....

While many economists agree the economy is weakening, with some predicting a recession, most believe enough has changed since 1981 that a repeat of that catastrophe is not in the cards.

The turmoil of 1981-82 left deep scars on many Canadians and businesses. It was the deepest downturn since the Great Depression.

In an effort to break the back of inflation, running at more than 12%, the Bank of Canada followed the lead of the U.S. Federal Reserve Board. In the spring of 1981, the Bank of Canada began jacking interest rates to record highs. In the process, thousands of businesses went bankrupt, others chopped their workforces, the housing market collapsed and unemployment soared to almost 13% from 7%. The number of jobless almost doubled to 1.5 million while employment fell.

Eight years later, consumers and businesses have watched nervously as interest rates have again started climbing. Real interest rates—the difference between the nominal interest rate and inflation—are now almost at the level they peaked at in 1981....

It may come as small comfort that despite all these danger signs, economists do not forecast a severe recession. They didn't forecast the last one. Even as that recession was under way, many were calling for 3% real growth in 1982. (The economy shrank 3.4% that year.)

The difference this time, economists say, is that inflation, though rising, is not out of control as it was nine years ago and should not require the same level of interest rates.

"I don't think anyone is looking for 1981-82 to happen again," says Paul Dearby, associate director of forecasting at the Conference Board of Canada.... Real interest rates have returned to their 1981 level, and that will hurt investment and the auto and housing markets, Dearby says. But he says it was high nominal rates that drove so many businesses into bankruptcy and wrecked the housing market in 1981-82....

Another important difference between then and now is that Canada's high real interest rates are not following the U.S., says John Clinkard, senior economist at Canadian Imperial Bank of Commerce. While maintaining interest rates at their current level will hurt, in 1981 both countries were suffering, he says. "That's really the key. We have never had a recession in Canada without having one in the U.S."

***The Financial Post*, March 12, 1990**

By Greg Ip

The Essence of the Story

- In 1981-82, Canada experienced a severe recession—real GDP declined by 3.4 percent—that resulted from record high interest rates.
- In the spring of 1990, real interest rates—the difference between the nominal interest rate and inflation—were almost as high as they had been in 1981. Was a repeat of the 1981-82 recession going to occur?
- Economists believed a repeat of the 1981-82 recession unlikely.
- Paul Dearby, associate director of forecasting at the Conference Board of Canada, said it was high nominal rates that lead to recession in 1981-82.
- John Clinkard, senior economist at Canadian Imperial Bank of Commerce, said that Canada has never had a recession without the United States having one and in 1990 recession in the United States did not appear likely.
- Economists failed to forecast the 1981-82 recession, predicting a 3 percent growth rate for real GDP in 1982.

Background and Analysis

Interest Rates in Canada and the United States: 1981 and 1990

	Canada		United States	
	1981	1990	1981	1990
Banks' prime lending rate	21.3*	14.8**	20.5*	10.0**
Inflation rate	12.5#	4.9##	10.4#	5.7##
Real lending rate	8.8	9.9	10.1	4.3

*Third quarter peak. **June 1990.
Annual average. ### Three months ended May 1990 (annual rate).

Sources: Canada, *The Bank of Canada Review*
United States, *Economic Report of the President*

- The table shows interest rates in Canada and the United States in 1981 and 1990.
- In 1981, real interest rates in the two countries were close to 10 percent per year.
- In 1990, the real interest rate in Canada appears to be 5 percent points higher than that in the United States.
- The apparent difference in real interest rates is accounted for by the fact that in mid-1990, the Canadian dollar was expected to fall in value against the U.S. dollar by about 5 percent. (See Chapter 29).
- Since Canadian dollars borrowed in mid-1990 were expected to fall by 5 percent in value, the real interest rate in Canada was really the same as that in the United States—and about one half of its 1981 level.
- Recessions can arise from two sources:
  - A sharp decrease in aggregate supply
  - A sharp decrease in aggregate demand
- In 1981, the main influences on investment and aggregate demand in Canada were:
  - Tight monetary policy in Canada
  - Tight monetary policy in the United States
  - An unusual degree of pessimism concerning profit prospects from new investment
- All three influences reinforced each other and produced a severe decrease in aggregate demand and recession.
- In 1990, the main influences on investment and aggregate demand were:
  - Tight monetary policy in Canada
  - Optimism about profit prospects from investment resulting from the continued strength of the world economy, (see Reading Between the Lines, pp. 1054-1055)
- Tight monetary policy in Canada is the only negative influence on investment and it is not as severe an influence as it was in 1981. It is counteracted by the other positive influence and is unlikely to be strong enough to push the Canadian economy into recession in 1991. This is the conclusion reached by John Clinkard, senior economist at the Canadian Imperial Bank of Commerce.
- Paul Dearby, associate director of forecasting at the Conference Board of Canada is reported in the news item to have said it was high *nominal* interest rates that led to recession in 1981-82.
- High nominal interest rates on their own do not cause recession. As long as expectations of inflation are in line with nominal interest rates, firms and households will willingly borrow and lend independently of the level of the nominal interest rate.
- There are some spectacular examples of countries that have had no recession but have had nominal interest rates far higher than those experienced by Canada in 1981.
- These examples show that it is the level of real interest rates, not nominal interest rates, that influence investment and aggregate demand.
- The prediction that 1991 will not be like 1982 appears to be a sensible one. It will turn out to be wrong only if the United States and world economies go into recession in the second half of 1990.

Country	Interest Rate	Real GDP Growth Rate
Brazil, 1984	215%	4.5%
Israel, 1984	823%	1.7%

families have greater security than single-income families. The chance that both (or all) income earners in a family will lose their jobs simultaneously is much lower than the chance that a single earner will lose work. With greater family income security, family consumption is likely to be less sensitive to fluctuations in family income that are seen as temporary. Thus when aggregate income falls, it does not induce a cut in consumption. For example, during the 1982 recession, as real GDP fell by 3 percent, personal consumption expenditure fell by only 2 percent.

For the four reasons we have just reviewed, it appears the economy has better shock-absorbing characteristics today than it had in the 1920s and 1930s. Even if there is a collapse of confidence leading to a fall in investment, the recession mechanism that is now in place will not translate that initial shock into the large and prolonged fall in real GDP and rise in unemployment that occurred 60 years ago.

Because the economy is now more immune to severe recession than it was 60 years ago, even a stock market crash of the magnitude that occurred in 1987 had barely noticeable effects on spending. A crash of a similar magnitude in 1929 resulted in the near collapse of investment (especially in housing) and consumer durable purchases. In the period following the 1987 stock market crash, investment and spending on durable goods hardly changed.

None of this is to say that there might not be a deep recession or even a great depression in the 1990s. But it would take a very severe shock to trigger one. And at the beginning of 1990, the consensus was that there was not even the prospect of a recession of the magnitude of the 1981-82 recession —see Reading Between the Lines, pp. 906-907.

■ We have now completed our study of the working of the macroeconomy. We've studied the macroeconomic model of aggregate demand and aggregate supply, and we've learned a great deal about the workings of the markets for goods and services, labour, and money and financial assets. We have applied our knowledge to explaining and understanding the problems of unemployment, inflation, and business cycle fluctuations.

In the next part of the book, we will study two aspects of macroeconomic policy — the policies that governments can take to stabilize the economy and the policy towards the government's budget deficit.

S U M M A R Y

The 1982 Recession

The 1982 recession resulted from a fall in the growth of aggregate demand, triggered by the monetary policies of the U.S. Federal Reserve Board and the Bank of Canada. In their attempt to beat inflation, the central banks unexpectedly slowed the growth of aggregate demand. Wages had increased on the presumption that inflation would continue at 10 percent a year, and those wage changes shifted the short-run aggregate supply curve upward. But the upward shift of the short-run aggregate supply curve was much larger than that of the aggregate demand curve. As a consequence, real GDP declined, but inflation moderated. Before the recession, real interest rates had increased but, as the recession intensified, they declined.

There is controversy about the behaviour of the labour market during a recession. According to the sticky wage interpretation of events, real wages do not adjust to bring equality between the quantities of labour demand and supplied. When the economy goes into recession, the quantity of labour supplied exceeds the quantity demanded and unemployment is higher than its natural rate. According to the flexible wage interpretation of events, real wages do adjust to maintain continuous equality between the quantities of labour demanded and supplied.

Changes in demand for different types of labour result in a change in the skill composition of the employed and a change in the average wage rate. The individuals losing jobs are primarily the unskilled. The increase in unemployment that occurs during the recession arises from increased job search activity associated with a high degree of labour turnover resulting from changes in the relative productivities of the skilled and the unskilled. Macroeconomists have not yet devised an acid test that would enable them to resolve their dispute about the labour market mechanism in recession. (pp. 893-901)

Another Great Depression?

The Great Depression that began in 1929 lasted

longer and was more severe than any before it or since. The Great Depression started with increasing uncertainty and pessimism, which brought a fall in investment (especially in housing) and purchases of consumer durables. Increased uncertainty and pessimism also brought on the stock market crash. The crash added to the pessimistic outlook, and further spending cuts occurred. In the United States, the financial system nearly collapsed. Banks failed and the money supply fell, resulting in a continued fall in aggregate demand. The Canadian financial system held up better, but the chaos in the United States hurt north of the border and throughout the world. Expectations of falling prices led to falling wages, although the fall in aggregate demand continued to exceed expectations and real GDP continued to decline.

The Great Depression itself produced a series of reforms that make a repeat of such a depression much less likely. The creation of the Bank of Canada as lender of last resort and the introduction of federal deposit insurance, both reduced the risk of bank failure and financial collapse. Higher taxes and government spending have given the economy greater resistance against depression, and the increased labour force participation rate provides a greater measure of security, especially for families with more than one wage earner. For these reasons, even a large initial change in aggregate demand or aggregate supply is much less likely to translate into an accumulative depression than it did in the early 1930s. Thus even a stock market crash as severe as the one that occurred in 1987 does not lead to a collapse in aggregate demand. (pp. 901-909)

KEY ELEMENTS

Key Figures 

REVIEW QUESTIONS

1 What triggered the 1982 recession?

2 What was the path of interest rates as the economy went into the 1982 recession?

3 Can the events of the 1982 recession be explained by a flexible wage theory? Explain why or why not.

4 Describe the changes in employment and real wages in the 1982 recession. With which theory of the labour market are these changes in real wages and unemployment consistent?

5 Describe the changes in real GDP, employment and unemployment, and the price level that occurred during the Great Depression years of 1929 to 1933.

6 What were the main causes of the onset of the Great Depression in 1929?

7 What events in 1931 and 1933 led to the continuation and increasing severity of the fall in real GDP and the rise in unemployment?

8 What four features of today's economy make a severe depression less likely now than in 1929?

PROBLEMS

1 Analyse the changes in the interest rate during the 1982 recession by drawing a diagram of the money market that shows shifts in the demand and supply curves for real money. What policy changes could have prevented interest rates from rising? What would the effects of such actions have been on real GDP and the price level?

2 During the 1982 recession, real wages and employment decreased. How can these events be explained by the sticky wage theory? By the flexible wage theory?

3 Compare and contrast the events that took place between 1929 and 1933 with those of 1982.

4 List all of the features of the Canadian economy in 1990 and 1991 that you can think of that are consistent with a pessimistic outlook for the 1990s.

5 List all of the features of the Canadian economy in 1990 and 1991 that you can think of that are consistent with an optimistic outlook for the 1990s.

6 How do you think the Canadian economy is going to evolve over the next year or two? Explain your predictions, drawing on the pessimistic and optimistic factors that you have listed in the previous two questions and on your knowledge of macroeconomic theory.

PART 12

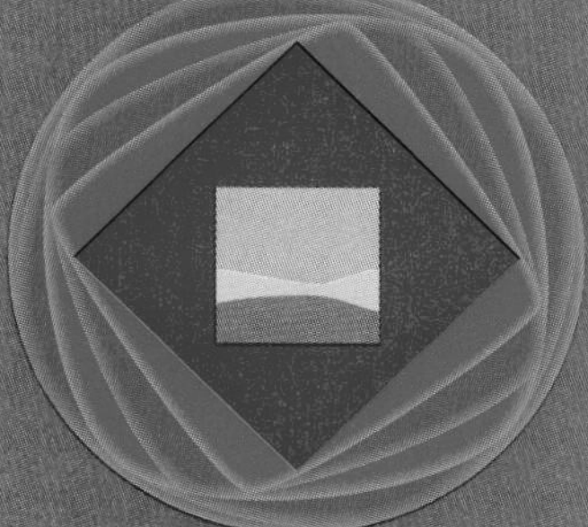

Macroeconomic Policy

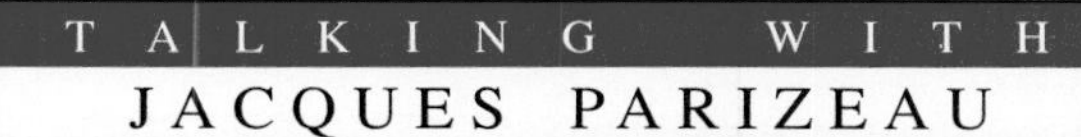

Jacques Parizeau obtained his bachelor's degree at Ecole des Hautes Etudes Commerciales, Universite de Montreal and his PHD at the London School of Economics. He also studied at the Universite de Paris and at the Institut d'Etudes Politiques in Paris. Before entering politics, Dr. Parizeau had a distinguished academic career at the Universite de Montreal and a public service career as economic advisor to successive premiers of Quebec. He was minister of finance in the Parti Québécois government and is now chef du Parti Québécois and leader of the opposition in the Quebec National Assembly. Michael

"In a small country, you must know constantly where you are in relation to the rest of the world."

Parkin spoke with Jacques Parizeau about his career and about the economic problems and challenges facing Canada and Quebec at the beginning of the 1990s.

Mr. Parizeau, does being an economist make you a better politician?

It's not necessarily a help. Politics is heavily loaded with fads. The wind blows in one direction and then in the opposite direction. If you understand economics, there are fads that you refuse to follow because you're convinced they're wrong.

Can you give an example?

Privatization. Many politicians in Canada jumped into promoting it simply because it was the fashion of the day. I didn't.

You were, though, the architect of the deregulation of Quebec's financial sector.

Yes, but *specifically* of that sector. There you have another example of a fad. Deregulation was the order of the day—everything had to be deregulated. But I wasn't interested in deregulation at large. I wanted to look at the merits of each case. I wanted to build financial elephants—financial institutions large enough to go beyond our borders and start buying and expanding in the United States. It had nothing to do with the religion of deregulation.

What principles of economics have you found yourself using most frequently?

Nothing has been as useful to me as the theory of international trade. It's strange how the more abstract aspects of international trade theory have had an enormous bearing on what I've been doing here. In a small country, you must know constantly where you are in relation to the rest of the world. You start from there. Even when you're facing problems that seem to be strictly domestic—minimum wage levels, social justice—you constantly relate them to where you are in competitive terms with the rest of world.

In 1967, you took a three-day train trip to Banff that's been called your "road to damascus." What happened on that trip?

I had to speak in Banff at one of these high-level conferences with all kinds of luminaries from the universities, governments, senators, what-have-you. I was supposed to deliver a speech on Canadian federalism, but I hadn't had a chance to write it. I decided to take the CPR out and write my paper on the train. I rented a small salon and on the train, had my meals delivered, and I had a marvellous trip. I started my paper as a federalist and concluded it as a sovereignist. Here's why.

During the previous half dozen years, there had been a remarkable shift of financial resources from the federal government to Quebec and to the other provinces. The provinces had become the real big spenders in terms of public investment. Quebec alone or Ontario alone had capital expenditures larger than those of the federal government. Quebec had withdrawn from 27 shared-cost programs. We were the only province to exercise that right, but all the others had it too. From the point of view of developing Canadian priorities, the situation was a horror. There was no policy of public capital expenditure in Canada. I developed what I called the theory of the 12 bastards—12 Crown corporations, departments, and large cities that invested as they wanted at the level they wanted, never talked to each other and went in completely opposite directions. One couldn't see any way in which any order could be put in there.

Canada had become unmanageable. For it to become manageable, what would it mean? Quebec would have to give back to Ottawa—and I started to list the things. I thought, "Quebec will never accept giving that back!" And I knew that if no one in Quebec would accept that and if there wasn't a real government any more in Ottawa, then we should have a real government in Quebec.

The result of that speech in Banff was horrid. I lost more friends in two hours than at any other time in my life!

How would you characterize the economic program of the PQ?

There are two main thrusts. One stems from the fact that an independent Quebec must be in a position to earn its keep in global markets. That explains why we were so much in favour of the Canada-United States Free Trade Agreement. It also explains why we attach so much importance to that winning combination of public and private enterprise that has developed in Quebec. At the same time—and this is the second thrust—the PQ doesn't shun the objectives of social justice in any way. It is a social democratic party.

How do these thrusts translate into macroeconomic and monetary policy? For example, would having a real government in Quebec require establishing its own currency and central bank?

No. As an economist, I've never had problems with the idea of a separate Quebec currency with a floating exchange rate. On the other hand, I recognize that it would be convenient and comforting, both for Quebeckers and for other Canadians, to maintain the same currency. The trend in Western Europe is towards a common currency. We already have a common currency, so let's keep it. The creation of a common currency for the entire North American trading bloc would, I think, be a good idea, but that's for tomorrow—it will take a long time.

So you're willing to let Ottawa make the decisions about monetary policy—about interest rates?

Insofar as Quebec has only about a third of the population of the rest of Canada, we can't imagine that we're going to run monetary policy from day to day. Therefore there must be a framework in which the Bank of Canada operates. If the Bank needed to go beyond that framework there would be a mechanism for talking about such things.

". . . an independent Quebec must be in a position to earn its keep in global markets. That explains why we were so much in favour of the Canada-United States Free Trade Agreement."

"we're at the stage of experiments. Canada doesn't know what stabilization policies are."

After the experience of 1981 and of the last 18 months, I don't think I'd be alone in Canada in trying to limit the spread between short-term interest rates in Canada and short-term rates in the United States. A six-percentage-point spread is just too much. It's taking an awful risk with the employment level for any additional inroad on inflation that it might make.

Does the government of Quebec have a responsibility to maintain full employment in Quebec?

That question brings out my Jacobin reflexes. I feel that government must govern, and yes, the responsibility for employment in Quebec is that of the Quebec government. I don't want quarrels between governments on policies for professional training. Ten percent of the population is unemployable. We're in the midst of a major industrial shift away from the "soft" sectors: textiles, clothing, furniture, shoes, that sort of thing. It's useless to imagine that we're going to settle anything long term by just funnelling social welfare cheques in that direction.

Do you see a need for macroeconomic stabilization policy?

We've never had stabilization policies in Canada! Look at 1982: the worst recession year since the 1930s. To fight the effects of high interest rates, the federal government tried to be expansionist in its fiscal policy. However, because the recession was so strong, the credit ratings of all the provinces were in jeopardy.

So all of us increased taxes and cut expenditures—for an amount three times greater than the expansion that the federal government was trying to induce.

As minister of finance at that time, I did start a few experiments. One was called Corvée-Habitation. Because of high interest rates, housing investment had collapsed. We decided to guarantee all purchasers of new houses a mortage rate set at four points below the going rate. That difference was not a subsidy from taxpayers. We sat around a table with representatives of all the employers, unions, private lenders, and professions in the construction industry and said, "You will all pitch in." Only the chartered banks refused, and I *taxed* them so they'd contribute like the others. Construction of housing shot up. When the accounts were settled, it hadn't cost the treasury one cent. And now the unions are fighting over the $12 million left in the pot!

Another experiment encouraged the acceleration of investment projects. We offered companies 20 percent of the cost of a project, no strings attached, if they would begin it immediately. Why 20 percent? Input-output studies told us that if most of the work was done in Quebec, the provincial treasurer would get a 20 percent return on the cost of the project in sales and income taxes. So the subsidy didn't change the deficit and it enormously increased investment in a matter of two years. There again, marvellous results and a reduced deficit!

So I experimented a great deal. But we're at the stage of experiments. Canada doesn't know what stabilization policies are.

CHAPTER 34

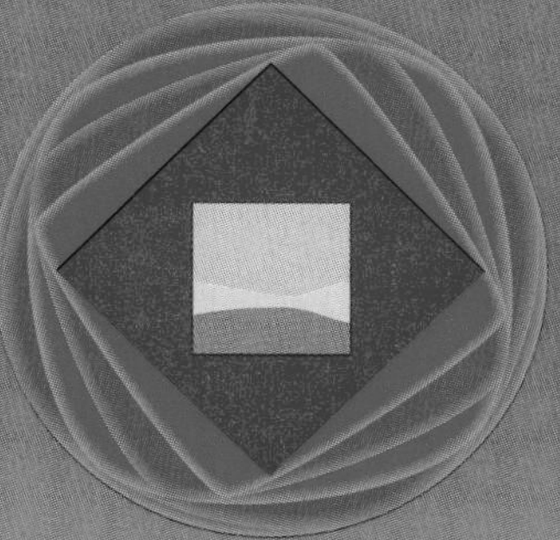

Stabilizing the Economy

After studying this chapter, you will be able to:

- Describe the goals of macroeconomic stabilization policy.
- Describe the key players whose actions influence economic stability.
- Explain how the state of the economy affects the popularity of the government.
- Explain how the government and the Bank of Canada can influence the economy.
- Distinguish between fixed rules and feedback rules for stabilization policy.
- Explain the debate among economists between fixed rules and feedback rules.
- Review the stabilization successes and failures of the recent past and the challenges of the present and future.

Who's in Charge?

PEOPLE PANIC WHEN things go very wrong and turn to their political leaders for reassurance and action. Thus it was, in the depths of the Great Depression, that our grandparents turned to the conservative government of Richard Bennett to deliver them from that economic holocaust and establish an economic order that would banish such horrors forever. When, by 1935, the government's program appeared to be having only limited success, a large swing in voter sentiment swept Mackenzie King's Liberals into office. Almost fifty years later, when Brian Mulroney's Conservatives arrived in Ottawa, their political agenda was to unleash the forces of competition, enabling free people in free markets to find their own economic progress and prosperity. But when the Canadian, U.S., and world stock markets crashed on a mild and sunny October Monday in 1987, after five consecutive years of economic expansion, the cry went out again — "Who's in charge?" Who *is* in charge of the Canadian economy? When the stock market crashes, what can and what does government do about it? What does the government do about less dramatic macroeconomic ills such as high inflation, high unemployment, and slow and variable real GDP growth? ■ In 1979, after two years with unemployment at more than 8 percent and inflation high by historical standards, the electorate rejected the Liberal government of Pierre Trudeau, which had been in power for more than a decade, and elected Progressive Conservative Joe Clark as prime minister. Less than a year later, with unemployment not much lower and inflation climbing again, the electorate dismissed Joe Clark and re-elected Pierre Trudeau. In 1984, with unemployment higher than ever before but with inflation having fallen dramatically, the electorate again rejected the Liberals (now with John Turner the prime minister) and returned the Progressive Conservatives (under Brian Mulroney) to power in a landslide election. How important was the economy in determining these election outcomes? What aspects of the economy do voters care about? Do they mainly fear unemployment, worrying little about inflation? Or is inflation the source of nightmares and unemployment less important? ■ Although we all want security — security of employment, security of lifetime savings that will not be wiped out — how much security can the government actually provide? And how much insecurity is induced by our political system and the stabilization policies that it pursues? ■ The second half of the 1980s was a period of unimagined prosperity and macroeconomic stability. How was this stability and prosperity achieved? What was the price that had to be paid to achieve it? And what are the stabilization policy challenges that face Canada as we move forward into the 1990s?

■ In this chapter, we're going to study the problems of stabilizing the Canadian economy — of avoiding inflation, high unemployment, and wildly fluctuating levels and growth rates of economic activity summarized in real GDP. At the end of the chapter, you will have a clearer and deeper understanding of the macroeconomic policy problems facing Canada today and of the political debate that surrounds us concerning those problems.

The Stabilization Problem

The stabilization problem is how to deliver a macroeconomic performance that is as smooth and predictable as possible. Solving this problem involves specifying targets to be achieved and then devising policies that result in getting as close as possible to those targets.

Macroeconomic Policy Targets

The targets of stabilization policy are the specific values of macroeconomic variables that policymakers seek to achieve. There are five main variables that macroeconomic policy targets. They are:

- Unemployment
- Real GDP Growth
- Inflation
- Foreign exchange rate
- International trade balance

Unemployment One goal of macroeconomic policy is to keep the unemployment rate as close as possible to its *natural rate*. Keeping unemployment close to its natural rate avoids, on the one side, the costs of excessive unemployment and, on the other side, the costs of excessive bottlenecks in the economy. When unemployment is above its natural rate, output is lost, there is a slowdown in the accumulation of human capital, and if unemployment is high and prolonged, serious psychological and social problems arise for the unemployed workers and their families. When unemployment falls below its natural rate, labour and other resources do not move to their highest value uses as quickly as they otherwise would.

Real GDP Growth A second target of macroeconomic policy is to keep real GDP growth steady. It is the upward trend in real GDP that brings ever improving living standards. So a growth rate that is too low results in a smaller volume of goods and services being available. It also might result in the growth in the demand for labour not keeping up with the supply of labour so that unemployment rises above its natural rate. Thus this target of policy interacts with the first one. But a growth rate that is too high also brings problems. It can lead to congestion, pollution, overcrowding, and bottlenecks in production processes that lead to inflation.

Inflation A third target of macroeconomic policy is a low and predictable rate of inflation. When inflation proceeds at a low and predictable rate, the usefulness of money is greatly enhanced. It becomes a more effective measuring rod for conducting transactions, especially those that are spread out over time, such as borrowing and lending and working on a long-term contract for an agreed wage.

Foreign Exchange Rate The fourth target of macroeconomic policy is the maintenance of stable exchange rates between the dollar and other foreign currencies. This is a goal not only of Canadian stabilization policy but of world stabilization policy. By achieving stable and predictable foreign exchange rates, money becomes a more effective medium of exchange not only for domestic transactions but also for international transactions.

International Trade Balance The fifth target of macroeconomic policy is also an international target. It is the attainment of balanced trade with the rest of the world. When we have a trade deficit with the rest of the world, we have to borrow and pay the interest on our loans and political pressures mount to introduce measures that will curtail our imports. When we have a trade surplus with the rest of the world, some other countries have deficits and political pressures develop in those countries to curtail our exports. Achieving balanced international trade over the long-run avoids these pressures and creates an environment in which relatively free international trade may take place.

Links Among the Targets

The five targets of macroeconomic stabilization policy are not independent of each other. We saw in Chapter 22 that unemployment and real GDP fluctuate in sympathy with each other. Other things being equal, the faster the growth rate of real GDP, the lower is the unemployment rate. Inflation and the foreign exchange value of the dollar also move together. Although, as we saw in Chapter 29, movements in these two variables are not as precisely linked as those of real GDP and unemployment. Nevertheless, other things being equal, if the inflation rate goes up by 1 percentage point, the dollar loses 1 percent of its value against the currencies of other countries. Finally, the international trade balance fluctuates with the state of the economy, although its movements depend on a large number of other factors, including the state of the world economy.

The links between the five macroeconomic policy targets make it useful, for many purposes, to divide them into two groups:

- Real targets
- Nominal targets

The **real targets** of macroeconomic policy are unemployment at its natural rate, steady growth in real GDP, and balanced international trade. The **nominal targets** of macroeconomic policy are low and predictable inflation and stable foreign exchange rates.

Macroeconomic Performance Indexes

Macroeconomic performance can be summarized in a variety of ways. The ones that we'll consider are indexes that combine, in some way, the real targets and the nominal targets of macroeconomic policy. All the indexes can be stated in terms of a combination of unemployment (real target) and inflation (nominal target). The different indexes place different weights on these two variables. Let's begin by considering one of the best known indexes, although one that has absolutely no scientific basis — the misery index.

Misery Index The **misery index** (MI) is an index of macroeconomic performance equal to the sum of the inflation rate and the unemployment rate. That is,

$$\text{MI} = \text{Inflation rate} + \text{Unemployment rate}$$

An increase in the misery index is "bad," and a decrease in the misery index is "good." This index attaches equal weights to inflation and unemployment. That is, an increase in the inflation rate of 1 percentage point is just as bad as an increase in the unemployment rate of 1 percentage point. The misery index was devised as a political slogan by the Democrats in the United States in 1975 during the Ford administration. It was subsequently used by the Republicans themselves against President Jimmy Carter. Since then it has become part of the conventional wisdom on how economies are performing and has even appeared, from time to time, in *The Economist* magazine.

The idea behind the misery index is that it provides a measure of the extent to which the real and nominal macroeconomic policy targets have been missed. The higher the inflation rate, the less is the success in achieving low and predictable inflation and a stable dollar. The higher the unemployment rate, the less is the success in keeping unemployment close to its natural rate and in keeping real GDP growth steady.

A second index of macroeconomic performance, one that does have some scientific basis, is based on voter behaviour.

Voter Behaviour The effects of economic performance on voter behaviour have been studied most thoroughly by Ray Fair of Yale University, using data on U.S. presidential elections. By examining the outcome of all the presidential elections between 1916 and 1984, Fair discovered the following:

- For each 1 percentage point increase in the real GDP growth rate, the incumbent political party gets a 1 percentage point increase in voter share.
- For each 3 percentage point increase in the inflation rate, the incumbent political party gets a 1 percentage point decrease in voter share.

Thus real GDP growth is three times as important as inflation in its effects on votes.

There are no studies of the relationship between Canadian voting behaviour and the state of the Canadian economy that lead to such clear-cut conclusions as those discovered by Fair concerning U.S. voters. The effects of the economy on Canadian elections seem to be more unpredictable than the effects of the U.S. economy on the U.S. presidential elections. Nevertheless, it is clear that the state of the economy affects the popularity of the government. We can use such links between the state of the economy and voter behaviour to construct a voter unpopularity index (UPI). By way of example, let's use Fair's numbers. The unpopularity index is:

$$\text{UPI} = \begin{matrix}\text{Inflation}\\ \text{rate}\end{matrix} - \left(3 \times \begin{matrix}\text{Real GDP}\\ \text{growth}\\ \text{rate}\end{matrix}\right).$$

Politicians seek to make the UPI as low as possible — that is, they seek to avoid unpopularity. The idea behind this index is similar to that of the misery index. It combines the real and nominal aspects of macroeconomic performance into a single index that tells us whether that performance is better or worse as indicated by its effects on voter behaviour. The higher the inflation rate and the lower the real GDP growth rate, the more unpopular is the government. Real GDP growth is three times as important as inflation in determining voter behaviour.

In order to compare the unpopularity index with the misery index, we need a relationship between unemployment and real GDP growth. We saw such a relationship — Okun's Law — in Our Advancing Knowledge, pp. 856-858. Okun's Law states that for each 3 percentage points that real GDP falls relative to trend, the unemployment rate increases by 1 percentage point, other things being equal. Using Okun's law together with Fair's voter popularity findings, an unpopularity index becomes

$$\text{UPI} = \begin{matrix}\text{Inflation}\\ \text{rate}\end{matrix} + \left(9 \times \begin{matrix}\text{Unemployment}\\ \text{rate}\end{matrix}\right).$$

What this equation tells is that, on the average, voters care nine times as much about unemployment of a given percentage as they do about inflation of that same percentage, other things being equal. This means that if the unemployment rate increases by 1 percentage point, a government seeking to maintain its popularity must find a way of lowering the inflation rate by 9 percentage points. Thus unemployment matters a great deal for electoral popularity. If inflation increases by 1 percentage point, the government must find a way of lowering the unemployment rate by one-ninth of one percentage point in order to maintain its popularity.

A third index of macroeconomic performance is based on nominal GDP.

Nominal GDP Target James Tobin of Yale University and John Taylor of Stanford University have suggested that a useful operating goal for macroeconomic policy is keeping the growth rate of nominal GDP steady. Many Canadian economists accept this as a useful operating goal. Nominal GDP is the current dollar value of the final goods and services produced. Thus nominal GDP increases when real GDP increases and when prices increase. The following simple equation tells us the connection between nominal GDP, real GDP, and inflation:

$$\begin{matrix}\text{Nominal}\\ \text{GDP}\\ \text{growth rate}\end{matrix} = \begin{matrix}\text{Real GDP}\\ \text{growth rate}\end{matrix} + \begin{matrix}\text{Inflation}\\ \text{rate.}\end{matrix}$$

If the inflation rate increases by 1 percentage point and only if real GDP growth rate falls by 1 percentage point, nominal GDP growth will remain steady. Thus the goal of stabilizing the growth rate of nominal GDP puts equal weight on inflation and real GDP growth. The nominal GDP target, then, is a bit like Fair's voter unpopularity index, except that the weight placed on real GDP growth is not three times that placed on inflation but equal to that placed on inflation. We can use Okun's Law to compare a nominal GDP target with the misery index. Using Okun's law with a nominal GDP target gives the following stabilization policy index (SPI):

$$\text{SPI} = \begin{matrix}\text{Inflation}\\ \text{rate}\end{matrix} + \left(3 \times \begin{matrix}\text{Unemployment}\\ \text{rate}\end{matrix}\right).$$

A comparison of SPI and MI shows that a nominal GDP target places twice as much importance on unemployment as does the misery index. But like the misery index, a higher value of the SPI indicates a worsening of economic performance.

Performance Indexes 1960–1989 The macroeconomic performance of Canada from 1960 to 1989, as measured by the three performance indexes that we have just reviewed, is set out in Fig. 34.1. (All the indexes have been scaled to have the same average values.) As you can see, all three indexes tell the same broad story. Macroeconomic performance improved between 1961 and 1966. It then started to deteriorate

Figure 34.1 Indexes of Macroeconomic Performance

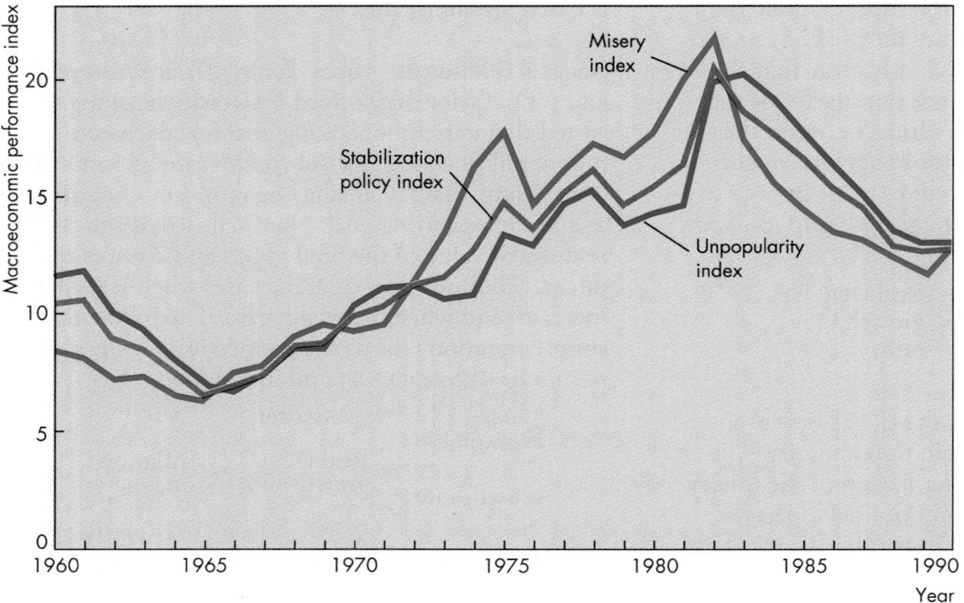

The voter popularity of a government depends in part on macroeconomic performance. The more strongly the economy grows and the lower the inflation rate, the more popular is the government. Three indexes of performance are graphed here. The misery index, which was invented for political purposes, is simply the sum of the inflation rate and the unemployment rate. The unpopularity index, which is based on election results, measures voter unpopularity. The stabilization policy index measures the closeness with which nominal GDP targets are achieved.

and continued to do so all the way through 1975. In 1976, there was a brief period of improvement, but this was followed by a further severe deterioration through 1982. After 1982, the macroeconomic performance of Canada improved according to all three indexes.

Of course, indexes such as those just reviewed have limitations. They tell us nothing about the distribution of economic misery or prosperity. They also do not take into account variations in the natural rate of unemployment. There are times when unemployment is high because an unusually large amount of reallocation of labour and other resources is taking place. At such times, the high unemployment rate reflects the fact that a larger number of people are voluntarily relocating to their highest value jobs. Such indexes also do not take into account the extent to which inflation is anticipated or unanticipated. As we've seen, this distinction makes a crucial difference to the costs of inflation and the people on whom those costs fall.

REVIEW

There are five main targets of macroeconomic policy that fall into two groups, real and nominal.

1. Real targets are:

- Keeping unemployment close to its natural rate
- Keeping the growth rate of real GDP steady
- Keeping international trade balanced.

2. Nominal targets are:

- Keeping inflation low and predictable
- Keeping the foreign exchange value of the dollar stable

The targets are linked together. Other things being equal, the faster real GDP grows, the lower is the unemployment rate and the larger is the international trade deficit. Also, other things being equal, the higher the inflation rate, the faster the dollar loses value against foreign currencies. Macroeconomic performance can be summarized in a variety of indexes that combine the policy targets and that place differing weights on real and nominal variables. ■

We have now reviewed the targets of macroeconomic policy and seen how we can summarize macroeconomic performance in a variety of performance indexes. Although the indexes that we've studied are crude, they all point in a similar direction. And the state of the economy, as summarized in such indexes, has an important effect on the actions of policymakers.

But who are the policymakers?

The Key Players

There are two key players that formulate and execute macroeconomic stabilization policy. They are:

- The Bank of Canada
- The government of Canada

The Bank of Canada

The *Bank of Canada* is the nation's central bank. The main features of the Bank of Canada are described in Chapter 28. The Bank influences the economy by trading in markets in which it is a major participant. The two most important such markets are those for government debt and for foreign currency. The Bank's decisions to buy and sell in these markets influence interest rates, the value of the dollar in terms of foreign currencies, and the amount of money in the economy. These variables, which the Bank of Canada can directly influence, in turn affect the conditions on which the millions of firms and households in the economy undertake their own economic actions. But the Bank of Canada itself operates under severe constraints — constraints imposed by the spending and taxing decisions made by the government of Canada.

The Government of Canada

The government of Canada implements the nation's fiscal policy. Fiscal policy has three elements:

- Spending plans
- Tax laws
- The federal deficit (or surplus)

All three elements of fiscal policy are brought together in the federal budget. The **federal budget** is a statement of the federal government's financial plan, itemizing programs and their costs, revenues, and the proposed deficit or surplus. The expenditure side of the budget is a list of programs, together with the amount that the government plans to spend on each and a forecast of the total amount of government expenditure. Some expenditure items in the federal budget are directly controlled by government departments. Others arise from decisions to fund particular programs whose total cost depends on actions that the government can forecast but not directly control. For example, social welfare expenditure depends on the state of the economy and on how many people qualify for support. Assistance payments to farmers (subsidies) depend on farm costs and market prices.

Parliament makes decisions about government revenue by enacting tax laws. As in the case of some important items of government expenditure, the government cannot control with precision the amount of tax revenue that it will receive. Parliament makes the tax laws, but the amount of tax paid is determined by the actions of millions of people and firms, who make their own choices about how much to work, spend, and save.

The difference between the expenditure on government programs and the taxes received is the government deficit or surplus. Every year since 1975, the federal government has spent more than it has received, and in the early 1980s, an unusually large gap between outlays and revenues arose. (We will discuss the deficit of the 1980s in detail in Chapter 35.)

One way of balancing the federal budget is to increase government revenue. But there is disagreement about how this objective might be achieved. There are two competing views. One, associated with the "supply side" views of former U.S. President Ronald Reagan, is that tax reform and lower tax rates will increase revenue by stimulating economic activity, increasing the incomes on which taxes are paid by enough to ensure that lower tax rates, combined with higher incomes, bring in higher revenue. The other view is that revenue can be increased only by increasing tax rates and introducing new taxes.

We've now reviewed the effects of macroeconomic performance on political popularity and have also described the key players in the policymaking game. Let's now turn our attention to the methods used for stabilizing the economy.

Alternative Means of Stabilizing the Economy

There are obviously many different monetary and fiscal policies that can be pursued. To understand the policies that *are* adopted, it is convenient to classify all possible policies into two broad categories:

- Fixed rules
- Feedback rules

Fixed Rules and Feedback Rules

A **fixed rule** specifies an action to be pursued independently of the state of the economy. Everyday life offers many examples of fixed rules. Perhaps the best known is the one that keeps the traffic flowing by having us all drive on the right. The best-known fixed rule for stabilization policy is one that has long been advocated by Milton Friedman. He proposes setting the growth rate of money supply at a constant rate year in and year out, regardless of the state of the economy. As we have seen, inflation persists because continual increases in the money supply raise aggregate demand. Friedman proposes allowing the money supply to grow at a rate that would hold the *average* inflation rate at zero.

A **feedback rule** specifies the policy response to changes in the state of the economy. An everyday example of a feedback rule is the one that governs your actions in choosing what to wear and whether or not to carry an umbrella. You base those actions on the best available forecast of the day's temperature and rainfall. (With a fixed rule, you would either always or never carry an umbrella.) A stabilization policy feedback rule is one that changes policy instruments, such as the money supply, interest rates, or even taxes, in response to the state of the economy. For example, the Bank of Canada is pursuing a feedback rule if an increase in unemployment causes it to engage in an open market operation aimed at increasing the money supply growth rate and lowering interest rates. The Bank is also pursuing a feedback rule if an increase in the inflation rate triggers an open market operation aimed at cutting the money supply growth rate and raising interest rates.

The key distinction between a fixed rule and a feedback rule is that with a fixed rule, policy instruments are set without regard to whether the economy is depressed, booming, or moving into recession or recovery, while with a feedback rule, policy instrument settings are changed in direct response to the state of the economy.

Expectations and Policy Rules

We saw in Chapter 32 that inflation expectations play an important role in determining the actual inflation rate and the level of real GDP. Expectations of inflation, in turn, depend partly on expectations about changes in aggregate demand. These expectations, in turn, depend on expectations about stabilization policy. But expectations about stabilization policy obviously depend on the stabilization policy rules that are being pursued. If the Bank of Canada pursues a fixed rule, such as Friedman's constant money supply growth rate rule, people will expect the Bank to keep aggregate demand growing at its average rate. (They might expect other factors to speed up or slow down the growth rate of aggregate demand, but they will not expect the Bank of Canada's own actions to have such an effect.) Alternatively, if the Bank always lowers interest rates and speeds up the growth of aggregate demand when unemployment rises to some trigger point and always increases interest rates and slows the growth of aggregate demand when inflation rises to some trigger point, then forecasts about the future growth of aggregate demand will incorporate the effects of the forecasted change in the Bank's monetary actions.

Let's study the effects of a fixed rule and a feedback rule for the conduct of stabilization policy by examining how real GDP (and employment and unemployment, which move with real GDP) and the price level behave under two alternative rules.

The Two Rules Compared

We'll study a model economy that starts out at full employment and has no inflation. Figure 34.2 illustrates this situation. The economy is on aggregate demand curve AD_0 and short-run aggregate supply curve *SAS*. These curves intersect at a point on the long-run aggregate supply curve (*LAS*). The GDP deflator is 100 and real GDP is $4 billion. Now let's see what happens if there is a change in aggregate demand.

Suppose that there is an unexpected and temporary fall in aggregate demand. Perhaps a wave of pessimism about the future results in a fall in investment demand, or perhaps a recession in the rest of the world leads to

Figure 34.2 A Fall in Aggregate Demand

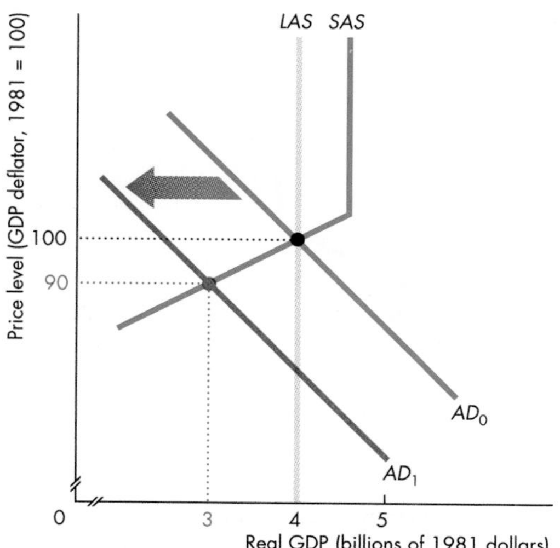

The economy starts out at full employment on aggregate demand curve AD_0 and short-run aggregate supply curve *SAS*, with the two curves intersecting on the long-run aggregate supply curve *LAS*. Real GDP is \$4 billion and the GDP deflator is 100. A fall in aggregate demand (resulting from pessimism about future profits, for example) unexpectedly shifts the aggregate demand curve to AD_1. Real GDP falls to \$3 billion, and the GDP deflator falls to 90. The economy is in a depressed state.

a fall in exports. Regardless of the origin of the fall in aggregate demand, the aggregate demand curve shifts to the left, to AD_1 in the figure. Because the fall in aggregate demand is unanticipated, expected aggregate demand remains at AD_0, so the expected GDP deflator remains at 100. The short-run aggregate supply curve stays at *SAS*. Aggregate demand curve AD_1 intersects the short-run aggregate supply curve *SAS* at a GDP deflator of 90 and a real GDP of \$3 billion. The economy is in a depressed state. Real GDP is below its long-run level, and unemployment is above its natural rate.

The fall in aggregate demand from AD_0 to AD_1 is not permanent. But, at the same time, it is not purely temporary — aggregate demand only gradually increases back to its original level of AD_0. That is, as confidence in the future improves, firms' investment picks up, or as economic recovery proceeds in the rest of the world, exports gradually rise, and so the aggregate demand curve gradually returns to AD_0, but it takes a good deal of time to do so.

We are going to work out how the economy responds during the period in which aggregate demand gradually increases to its original level. We will examine the economy's response under two alternative monetary policies: a fixed-rule policy with the money supply constant, and a feedback-rule policy that stimulates aggregate demand by increasing the money supply. Figure 34.3 illustrates the analysis.

First, we'll consider what happens with a fixed rule.

Fixed Rule When aggregate demand falls to AD_1, the money supply growth rate is held constant. (It remains constant because in this example, the growth rate of the money supply is zero.) No special measures are taken to bring the economy back to full employment. But recall that we are assuming that aggregate demand gradually increases because of other factors, and it eventually returns to AD_0. As it does so, real GDP and the GDP deflator gradually increase. The GDP deflator gradually returns to 100 and real GDP to its long-run level of \$4 billion, as shown in Fig. 34.3(a). Throughout this process, the economy experiences more rapid growth than usual, but it is beginning from a state of excess capacity. Unemployment remains high until the aggregate demand curve has returned to AD_0.

Let's contrast this adjustment with what occurs under a feedback-rule monetary policy.

Feedback Rule Under the feedback rule that we are analysing, the money supply increases whenever there is a fall in aggregate demand and decreases whenever there is a rise in aggregate demand. When aggregate demand falls to AD_1, the Bank of Canada increases the money supply to shift the aggregate demand curve back to AD_0, as shown in Fig. 34.3(b). As the other forces that increase aggregate demand kick in, the Bank of Canada gradually cuts back on the money supply, holding the aggregate demand curve steady at AD_0. Real GDP jumps back to its full-employment level and the GDP deflator jumps back to 100.

Under the fixed-rule policy, the economy goes into a recession and stays there for as long as it takes the aggregate demand curve to return to its original position. Under the feedback-rule policy, the economy is pulled out of its recession quickly by the policy action. The price level and real GDP fall and rise by exactly the same amounts in the two cases, but real GDP stays below its long-run level longer with a fixed rule than it does with a feedback rule.

Figure 34.3 Two Monetary Policies

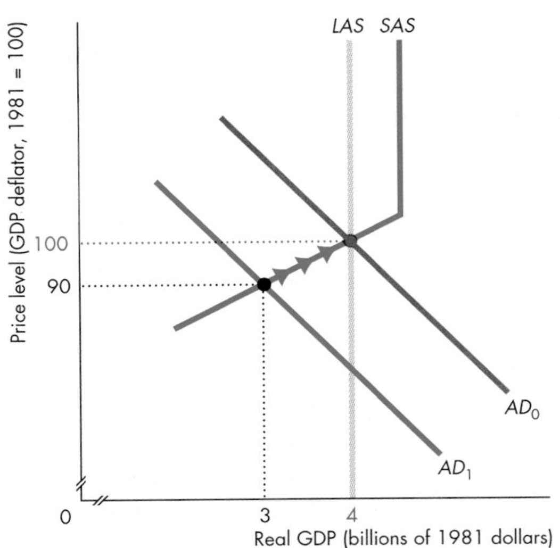

(a) Fixed rule

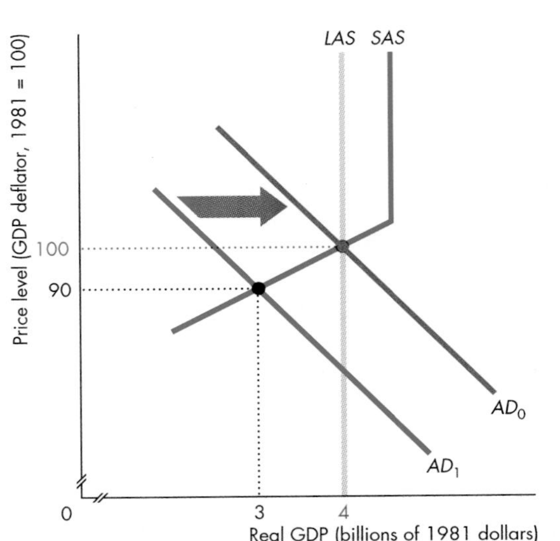

(b) Feedback rule

The economy is in a depressed state with a GDP deflator of 90 and real GDP of $3 billion. The short-run aggregate supply curve is *SAS*. A fixed-rule monetary policy (part a) leaves the aggregate demand curve initially at AD_1, so the GDP deflator remains at 90 and real GDP at $3 billion. As other influences on aggregate demand gradually increase, the aggregate demand curve shifts back to AD_0. As it does, real GDP rises back to $4 billion and the GDP deflator increases to 100. A feedback-rule monetary policy (part b) increases the money supply, shifting the aggregate demand curve instantly from AD_1 to AD_0. Real GDP returns to $4 billion and the GDP deflator returns to 100. The money supply is then gradually decreased as the other influences on aggregate demand increase its level. As a result, the aggregate demand curve is kept steady at AD_0 and real GDP stays at $4 billion.

So Feedback Rules Are Better?

Isn't it obvious that a feedback rule is better than a fixed rule? Can't the Bank of Canada use a feedback rule to keep the economy close to full employment with a stable price level? Of course, unforecasted changes — such as the fall in aggregate demand in our example — will hit the economy from time to time. But by responding with an active change in the quantity of money, can't the Bank of Canada minimize the damage from such a shock? Most economists believe so.

Despite the apparent superiority of a feedback rule, some economists believe that a fixed rule works best. These economists assert the following:

- Feedback rules require greater knowledge of the economy than we have.
- Feedback rules introduce unpredictability.
- Feedback rules generate bigger fluctuations in aggregate demand.
- Aggregate supply shocks, not aggregate demand shocks, cause most economic fluctuations.

We'll look briefly at the first three assertions. Then, in the next section, we'll look at greater length at the fourth.

Knowledge of the Economy Although the aggregate demand-aggregate supply model of the economy provides us with a useful tool for both understanding and predicting aggregate fluctuations, it is not a precise tool. We can predict the general direction in which the economy will move following a change in one of the factors that influence aggregate demand or aggregate supply. But we cannot predict with any certainty either the magnitude of a change or its precise timing. The multiplier effects of monetary and fiscal policy actions take place over a prolonged period of time and are influenced by far more factors than can be kept track of. Also, we have a limited knowledge of the precise way in which the labour market works. The degree of wage flexibility and the economy's capacity level of real GDP and natural rate of unemployment are all magnitudes that can only be estimated and about which there is uncertainty and disagreement.

Lacking a precise model of the economy that makes exact predictions about the quantitative effects of policy actions and of other exogenous influences, we are not able to design feedback rules that can be guaranteed to smooth out fluctuations. We may easily end up designing rules that make fluctuations more severe. For example, suppose that whenever the inflation rate increases, the money supply growth rate is decreased. If it takes one to two years for the change in the money supply growth rate to have its full effects on real GDP and the price level, by the time those effects are being felt the economy may already have moved into a contraction phase of the business cycle. If that is so, the slowdown in money supply growth will accentuate the contraction, making the recession more severe than it otherwise would have been.

The second problem with the feedback rules is that they can introduce unpredictability. Let's see how.

Predictability of Feedback Rules To make decisions about long-term contracts for employment (wage contracts) and about borrowing and lending, people have to anticipate the future course of prices — the future inflation rate. To make a forecast of inflation, it is necessary to forecast aggregate demand. Suppose that people anticipate that aggregate demand is going to rise less quickly next year. In view of this anticipation, firms and workers agree to a slower rate of wage increase. The short-run aggregate supply curve shifts upward less quickly as a result of the expectation of slower growth in aggregate demand. If aggregate demand actually slows down, as anticipated, inflation also slows, but firms continue to produce at their capacity output levels and there is full employment. A correctly anticipated slowdown in the growth of aggregate demand has resulted in a slowdown in inflation but no slowdown in output growth and no increase in unemployment.

Contrast this case with one in which there is an unanticipated slowdown in aggregate demand. Aggregate demand is expected to continue growing at its current rate, but, in fact, it slows down. Given their anticipation, firms and workers agree to keep money wages rising at their current rate. As a consequence, the short-run aggregate supply curve shifts upward. When aggregate demand fails to increase at the expected rate, real GDP falls below its capacity level, unemployment rises above its natural rate, and there is a slowdown in inflation. The economy goes into recession because money wages have been set too high for the level of aggregate demand that has actually come about.

Why might aggregate demand growth slow down unexpectedly? One reason is that the Bank of Canada unexpectedly slows down the growth rate of the money supply, forcing interest rates up and lowering investment. Such an action by the Bank of Canada slows inflation but also pushes real GDP below its capacity level and increases unemployment. If the Bank sticks to a rock-steady, fixed rule for increasing the money supply, then the Bank itself cannot contribute to unexpected fluctuations in aggregate demand. To the extent that the Bank of Canada's actions are unpredictable, they lead to unpredictable fluctuations in aggregate demand. These fluctuations, in turn, produce fluctuations in real GDP, employment, and unemployment.

There is more scope for the Bank of Canada's actions to be unpredictable when it is pursuing a feedback rule, rather than a fixed rule, for in such a situation the future values of the variables to which the Bank reacts will also have to be predicted. Consequently, a feedback rule for monetary policy can create more unpredictable fluctuations in aggregate demand than a fixed rule. Economists disagree whether those bigger fluctuations offset the potential stabilizing influence of the predictable changes the Bank of Canada makes. No agreed measurements have been made to settle this dispute. Nevertheless, the unpredictability of the Bank's actions is an important fact of economic life.

It is not surprising that the Bank of Canada seeks to keep some of its actions behind a smokescreen. First, the Bank wants to maintain as much freedom of action as possible, so it does not want to state too precisely the rules that it will follow in any given circumstances. Second, the Bank of Canada is part of a political process; it is not immune to political influence. For at least these two reasons, the Bank of Canada does not specify feedback rules that are as precise as the one that we have analysed in this chapter, so it cannot deliver an economic performance that has the stability we generated in the model economy.

If it is difficult for the Bank of Canada to pursue a predictable, feedback stabilization policy, it is probably impossible for the government to do so. Since stabilization policy is formulated in terms of spending programs and tax laws, and since those programs and laws themselves are the outcome of a political process, there can be no effective way in which a government can adhere to a predictable feedback fiscal policy.

Variability of Aggregate Demand with Feedback Rules

Some economists argue that a feedback rule will not only make aggregate demand more unpredictable but will also make it fluctuate more. The main thrust of the argument is that stabilization policies affect aggregate demand with a time lag that is long and impossible to predict. As a consequence, any policy action taken today will be inappropriate for the state of the economy at that uncertain future date when the policy's effects will be felt.

For example, when the Bank of Canada puts on the monetary brake, the first response is an increase in interest rates. Some time later, the higher interest rates produce a slowdown in investment and the purchases of consumer durable goods. Some time later still, this fall in expenditure reduces income, which, in turn, induces lower consumption expenditure. The sectors in which the spending cuts occur vary, and so does the impact on employment. It can take anywhere from nine months to two years for the Bank's initial action to cause a change in employment, real GDP, and the inflation rate. Thus to smooth the fluctuations in aggregate demand, the Bank needs to take actions today that are based on a forecast of what will be happening over a period stretching more than a year into the future. It is no use taking actions a year from today to influence the situation that then prevails. It's too late. Any actions taken then will have their effect yet one or two additional years into the future.

If the Bank of Canada were good at economic forecasting and based its policy actions on its forecasts, it is possible that it could deliver the type of ideal smoothing of aggregate demand that we assumed in the model economy earlier in this chapter. But if the Bank takes policy actions based on today's economy rather than on the forecasted economy a year in the future, then those actions will often be inappropriate ones. When unemployment is high and the Bank puts its foot on the accelerator, it speeds the economy back to full employment. But the Bank is not able to ease off the accelerator and gently tap the brake, holding the economy at its full-employment point. Instead, the accelerator pedal is left down as the economy races through the full-employment point and starts to experience shortages and inflationary pressures. Eventually, when inflation increases and unemployment falls below its natural rate, the Bank steps on the brake, pushing the economy back below full employment. The Bank's own reactions to the current state of the economy become one of the major sources of fluctuations in aggregate demand and the major factor that people have to forecast in order to make their own economic choices.

Earlier we noted a fourth reason for economists' disagreement on monetary policy: they do not agree about the sources of aggregate fluctuations. Those advocating feedback rules believe most fluctuations come from aggregate demand. Those advocating fixed rules believe that fluctuations in aggregate supply are the dominant ones. Let's now analyse how aggregate supply fluctuations affect the economy under a fixed rule and a feedback rule for monetary policy, and see why those economists who believe that aggregate supply fluctuations are dominant favour a fixed rather than a feedback rule.

Stabilization Policy and Aggregate Supply

There are two reasons why aggregate supply fluctuations can cause problems for a stabilization feedback rule. They are:

- Cost-push inflation
- A slowdown in capacity growth

In either of these situations, the economy experiences stagflation. **Stagflation** is a situation in which real GDP stops growing or even declines and inflation accelerates. Let's study the effects of alternative policies to deal with this problem.

Cost-Push Inflation

Cost-push inflation is inflation that has its origin in cost increases. The two most important potential sources of cost-push inflation are wage increases and increases in raw material prices (such as the increases in the price of oil that occurred in the 1970s and the early 1980s). To proceed, a cost-push inflation must be accommodated by an increase in the

Figure 34.4 Monetary Policy and Aggregate Supply: A Wage Increase

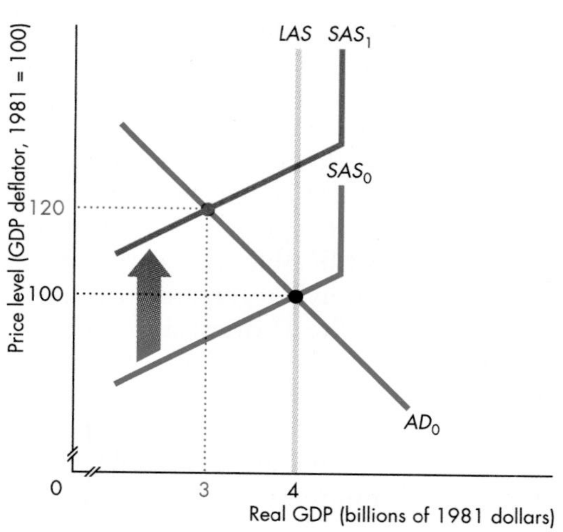

(a) Fixed rule

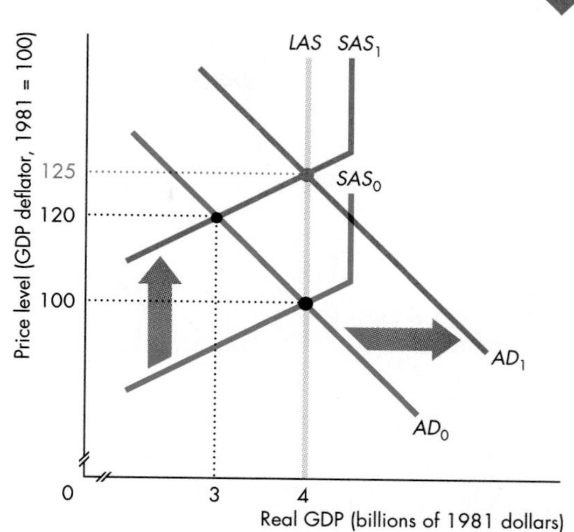

(b) Feedback rule

The economy starts out on AD_0 and SAS_0, with a GDP deflator of 100 and real GDP of \$4 billion. A labour union (or the key suppliers of an important raw material) forces up wages (or the price of the raw material), shifting the short-run aggregate supply curve to SAS_1. Real GDP falls to \$3 billion and the GDP deflator increases to 120. With a fixed rule for the money supply (part a), the Bank of Canada makes no change to aggregate demand. The economy stays depressed until wages (or raw material prices) fall again, and the economy returns to its original position. With a feedback rule (part b), the Bank injects additional money, increasing aggregate demand to AD_1. Real GDP returns to \$4 billion (full employment), but the GDP deflator increases to 125. The economy is set for another round of cost-push inflation.

money supply — which in turn increases aggregate demand. A monetary policy feedback rule makes cost-push inflation possible. A fixed rule makes such inflation impossible. Let's see why.

Consider the economy shown in Fig. 34.4. Aggregate demand is AD_0, short-run aggregate supply is SAS_0, and long-run aggregate supply is LAS. Real GDP equals its capacity level of \$4 billion and the GDP deflator is 100.

Now suppose that a number of labour unions or the key suppliers of an important raw material, such as oil, try to gain a temporary advantage by increasing the price at which they are willing to sell their labour services — by increasing wages — or by increasing the price of the raw material. To make the exercise more interesting, let's suppose that the people in question control a significant portion of the economy, so that when they increase the wage rate or the price of oil, the short-run aggregate supply curve shifts upward from SAS_0 to SAS_1.

A Fixed Rule Figure 34.4(a) shows what happens in a model economy if the Bank of Canada follows a fixed rule for monetary policy. With a fixed rule, the Bank pays no attention to the fact that there has been an increase in wages or raw material prices. The money supply growth rate does not change. (In this example with a zero money supply growth rate, the money supply itself remains constant.) The short-run aggregate supply curve has shifted upward to SAS_1, and aggregate demand stays at AD_0. The price level rises to a GDP deflator of 120, and real GDP falls to \$3 billion. The economy is experiencing stagflation. It is depressed, and until those responsible for the increased wages or raw material prices reverse their action, the economy remains depressed. This decrease in wages or raw material prices may take a long time to come about. Eventually, however, the low level of real GDP and associated high level of unemployment will bring about a lowering of wages — of those very wages whose increase caused the initial problem.

Eventually, the short-run aggregate supply curve will shift back downward to SAS_0. The GDP deflator will fall to 100 and real GDP will increase to $4 billion.

A Feedback Rule Figure 34.4(b) shows what happens if the Bank of Canada is operating with a monetary feedback rule. The starting point is the same as before — the economy is on SAS_0 and AD_0 with a GDP deflator of 100 and real GDP of $4 billion. Wages are increased, and the short-run aggregate supply curve shifts upward to SAS_1. The economy goes into a recession with real GDP falling to $3 billion and the price level increasing to 120. The Bank's monetary feedback rule is to increase the money supply growth rate and to increase aggregate demand whenever real GDP is below capacity. So, with real GDP at $3 billion, the Bank pumps up the money supply growth rate and shifts the aggregate demand curve to AD_1. The price level increases to 125 and real GDP returns to $4 billion. The economy moves back to full employment but at a higher price level. The unionized workers or raw material suppliers who saw an advantage in forcing up their wages or prices before will see the same advantage again. Thus the short-run aggregate supply curve will shift up once more, and the Bank will chase it with an increase in aggregate demand. The economy will be in a free-wheeling inflation.

Incentives to Push up Costs You can see that there are no checks on the incentives to push up costs if the Bank of Canada pursues a feedback rule of the type that we've just analysed. If some group sees a temporary gain from pushing up the price at which they are selling their own resources and if the Bank always accommodates the rise to prevent unemployment and slack business conditions from emerging, then cost-push elements will have a free rein. But if the Bank pursues a fixed-rule policy, the incentive to attempt to steal a temporary advantage by increasing wages or prices is severely weakened. The cost of higher unemployment and lower output is a consequence that each group has to recognize.

Thus a fixed rule is capable of delivering a steady inflation rate (or even zero inflation), while a feedback rule, in the face of cost-push pressures, will leave the inflation rate free to rise and fall at the whim of whichever group believes it can gain a temporary advantage from pushing up its wage or price.

A Slowdown in Capacity Growth

Some economists believe that fluctuations in real GDP (and in employment and unemployment) are caused not by fluctuations in aggregate demand but by fluctuations in the growth rate of long-run aggregate supply. These economists have developed a new theory of aggregate fluctuations called real business cycle theory (see Our Advancing Knowledge, pp. 856-858). **Real business cycle theory** is a theory of aggregate fluctuations based on the existence of flexible wages and random shocks to the economy's aggregate production function. The word "real" draws attention to the idea that it is random shocks to real things — the economy's real production possibilities — rather than nominal things — the money supply and its rate of growth — that are, according to the theory, the most important sources of aggregate fluctuations.

According to real business cycle theory, there is no useful distinction to be made between the long-run aggregate supply curve and the short-run aggregate supply curve. Because wages are flexible, the labour market is always in equilibrium at the natural rate of unemployment. The vertical long-run aggregate supply curve is also the short-run aggregate supply curve. Fluctuations occur because of shifts in the long-run aggregate supply curve. Normally, the long-run aggregate supply curve shifts to the right — the economy expands. But the pace at which that curve shifts to the right varies. Also, on occasion, the long-run aggregate supply curve shifts to the left, bringing a decrease in aggregate supply and a fall in real GDP.

Economic policy that influences the aggregate demand curve has no effect on real GDP. But it does affect the price level. However, if the real business cycle theory is correct and if a feedback monetary policy is used to increase aggregate demand every time real GDP falls, that policy will make price level fluctuations more severe than they otherwise would be. To see why, consider Fig. 34.5.

Imagine that the economy starts out on aggregate demand curve AD_0 and long-run aggregate supply curve LAS_0 at a GDP deflator of 100 and real GDP of $4 billion. Now suppose that the long-run aggregate supply curve shifts to LAS_1. (An actual fall in long-run aggregate supply could occur as a result of a severe drought or other natural catastrophe or perhaps as the result of a disruption of international trade, such as the OPEC embargo of the 1970s.)

Figure 34.5 Monetary Policy and Aggregate Supply: A Capacity Decrease

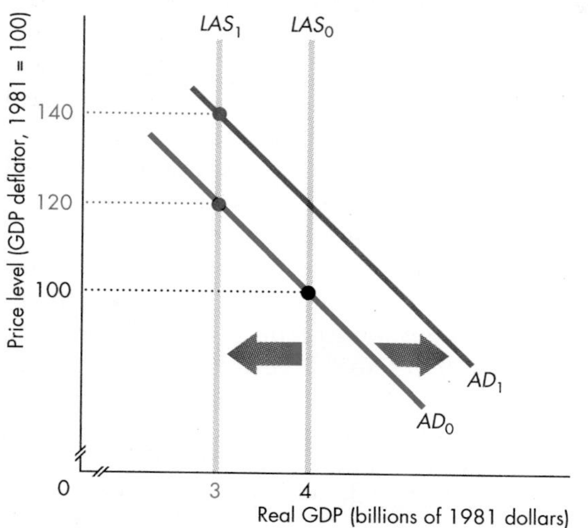

A fall in capacity output shifts the long-run aggregate supply curve from LAS_0 to LAS_1. Real GDP falls to \$3 billion and the GDP deflator rises to 120. With a fixed money supply rule, aggregate demand stays at AD_0, and that is the end of the matter. With a feedback rule, the Bank of Canada increases the money supply, intending to increase real GDP. Aggregate demand moves to AD_1, but the long-run result is an increase in the price level — the GDP deflator rises to 140 — with no change in real GDP.

A Fixed Rule With a fixed rule for the money supply, the fall in the long-run aggregate supply has no effect on the Bank of Canada and no effect on aggregate demand. The aggregate demand curve remains AD_0. Real GDP falls to \$3 billion and the GDP deflator increases to 120.

A Feedback Rule Now suppose that the Bank of Canada uses a feedback rule. In particular, suppose that when real GDP falls, the Bank increases the money supply to increase aggregate demand. In the example then, the Bank increases the money supply and shifts the aggregate demand curve to AD_1. The Bank's goal is to bring real GDP back to \$4 billion. But the long-run aggregate supply curve has shifted, so capacity output has fallen to \$3 billion. The increase in aggregate demand cannot bring forth an increase in output if the economy does not have the capacity to produce that output. So, real GDP stays at \$3 billion, but the price level rises still further — the GDP deflator goes to 140.

You can see that in this case the attempt to stabilize real GDP using a feedback rule for monetary policy has no effect on real GDP but generates a substantial price level increase.

We've now seen some of the shortcomings of using a feedback rule for monetary policy. Some economists believe that these shortcomings are serious and urge the Bank to implement a fixed rule. Others, regarding the potential advantages of a feedback rule as greater than its costs, urge the Bank to continue to pursue such policies.

Controlling Inflation by Announcing Monetary Policy

Those who favour feedback rules often argue that the Bank of Canada should not only seek to vary its actions in light of current economic conditions but should also seek to minimize the damage it does by clearly announcing the policy actions that it intends to follow. This argument has a special appeal when applied to slowing down inflation. When the Bank, in fact, slowed down inflation in 1982, we all paid a very high price. The Bank's monetary policy action was unpredicted. As a result, it occurred in the face of wages that had been set at too high a level to be consistent with the growth of aggregate demand that the Bank subsequently allowed. The consequence was high unemployment.

Couldn't the Bank have lowered inflation without causing unemployment by telling people far enough ahead of time that it did indeed plan to slow down the growth rate of aggregate demand? Wouldn't wages then have increased less quickly, enabling inflation to be cured at much lower cost in terms of increased unemployment? Couldn't the Bank, by announcing its intentions, have led people to form a rational expectation that inflation would slow down, thereby making the short-run aggregate supply curve shift upward by the same amount as the Bank intended to shift the aggregate demand curve upward, keeping the two curves intersecting along the long-run aggregate supply curve? The Bank of Canada tried just such an approach in the 1970s. In the following section we'll see how such a policy worked out.

The Quantity Theory and Monetarism

David Hume

The quantity theory of money has had a long and checkered history. Its first statement — that a change in the quantity of money brings about a proportional change in the price level — was made by the French philosopher Jean Bodin in the early seventeenth century. Its first clear statement in the English language was by David Hume. Hume was an extraordinary philosopher and economist who lived in Edinburgh, Scotland, from 1711 to 1776. He died in the year Adam Smith's *Wealth of Nations* was published. Hume was a close friend of Adam Smith and had enormous influence on him.

A milestone in the development of the quantity theory of money was the contribution of Henry Thornton, a British monetary economist and legislator who lived in London from 1760 to 1815. While a member of the British parliament, Thornton wrote his impressive *An Enquiry into the Nature and Effects of the Paper Credit of Great Britain*. In this book, he developed the notions of the quantity of money and its velocity of circulation, the two key elements in the modern statement of the quantity theory of money.

The first major American contribution to the development of the quantity theory was that by Irving Fisher (see Our Advancing Knowledge, pp. 662-664). Born in 1867, Fisher studied and spent his entire professional career at Yale University. His book, *The Purchasing Power of Money*, published in 1911, provided extensive evidence on the long-run proportionality between the quantity of money and the general level of prices.

The quantity theory of money was never popular with everyone. It was particularly unpopular with John Maynard Keynes (see Our Advancing Knowledge, pp. 662-664). Keynes argued that there is but the loosest connection between the quantity of money and the price level. He described the lack of a connection with the ancient proverb, "There's many a slip twixt cup and lip." Keynes' views on the lack of a connection between money and the price level were so forcefully expressed that he was able to attract a very large following, and his views became the dominant ones in the 1950s and early 1960s.

Throughout the postwar years, the University of Chicago's Milton Friedman (see Our Advancing Knowledge, pp. 662-664) had been quietly working away on his version of the quantity theory of money. In a monumental work with Anna J. Schwartz, *A Monetary History of the United States 1867-1960*, published in 1963, the role and importance of money in explaining fluctuations in the U.S. economy was argued and established. Then, in 1967, Friedman published what was to become a landmark paper, "The Quantity Theory of Money: A Restatement." In that paper, Friedman argued that the quantity theory of money, in its modern form, is a theory about the demand for money. There is, argued Friedman, a stable demand curve for real money, and the demand for real money depends on the interest rate (the opportunity cost of holding money) and real income. Variations in the nominal money supply can produce short-run variations in real GDP and interest rates, but, in the long run, all their effects are felt only on the price level.

From his views about the importance of money in influencing aggregate expenditure, Friedman formulated what has become a famous rule — the "*k* percent rule." Friedman said, pick a number *k* equal to the average growth rate of real GDP and make the money supply grow steadily year after year at that rate. On the average, inflation will be zero. The economy will fluctuate but the fluctuations will be as small as they can possibly be made and smaller than those that would arise from active attempts to stabilize aggregate demand. Friedman's views were given the name "monetarism" by Karl Brunner, a proponent of Friedman's version of monetary theory and another advocate of steady money supply growth rules.

Today, monetarism has a large following among economists working in central banks and advising governments in Canada, the United States, and around the world.

The quantity theory of money has always had its dissenters. Modern critics of the quantity theory of money include Thomas Sargent of Stanford's Hoover Institution, Bruce Smith of Cornell University, and Neil Wallace of the University of Minnesota. These scholars argue that the quantity of money is not the important variable for determining the general price level except in special circumstances. Only because there are legal tender laws and legal restrictions on bank reserve holdings does the quantity of money take on a special significance. More generally, they argue, it is the total value of outstanding government debt that is the important nominal magnitude for determining the general price level. Tests of their views remain controversial, and more will have to be undertaken before it can be said that the foundations of the quantity theory of money have been destroyed.

Constraints on Stabilization Policy

Dollar's dive shackles Ottawa's economic policy

....A strong consensus has emerged among economists that Canada's two top economic policy makers — Finance Minister Michael Wilson and Bank of Canada governor John Crow — have few options left open to them. Their limited choices range from harder to hardest.

"I think we are very severely constrained," said Sylvia Ostry, chairman of the Centre for International Studies at the University of Toronto and a former top federal policy adviser.

As economic experts see it, both domestic and international events have shackled Ottawa's fiscal and monetary policies.

At home, the federal deficit hamstrings Ottawa's freedom to use its spending and taxing powers to influence the economy. The deficit may force Mr. Wilson to cut spending in his budget next month even though the economy is slowing.

Internationally, the central bank is hemmed in by the fact that Canada's financial markets are so vulnerable to the rivers of money flowing across national boundaries. Those flows can change course the moment a bulletin flashes across a money trader's news screen.

When Mr. Crow tried to reduce interest rates this month by a mere quarter of a percentage point, the inflows of money that had been pushing up the dollar abruptly reversed. In just two weeks, the Canadian dollar lost everything it had gained in the previous seven months....

While the spotlight has exposed the limits of monetary policy for the past two weeks, it will shift to Mr. Wilson as budget day draws near.

As the economy flirts with recession, there seems to be little Ottawa can do in a budget to ease a recession's impact.

"I don't think there is any room on the fiscal side to do anything positive for the economy," said Douglas Peters, chief economist at the Toronto-Dominion Bank.

A year ago, Ottawa used tax rebates from the first stage of tax reform to put money into the economy. Now, the federal government is tightening its fiscal policy.

The latest round of indirect tax increases on Jan. 1 means that Ottawa will siphon more than $9 billion (Canadian) or 1.5 per cent of gross domestic product out of the economy this year, said Michael Manford, chief economist at Scotia McLeod Inc. of Toronto.

And Ernest Stokes, chief economist at the WEFA Group of Toronto, an economic forecasting company, warned that if Mr. Wilson were to tighten further fiscally, it would "make a bad situation worse."....

Lloyd Atkinson, chief economist at the Bank of Montreal, said a tough budget would bolster confidence, strengthen the dollar and open the door to interest rate reductions....

***The Globe and Mail,* January 27, 1990**
By James Rusk

The Essence of the Story

- Economists are in strong agreement that Canada's monetary and fiscal policy options are severely constrained.
- The federal deficit limits the use of fiscal policy to influence the economy.
- A high degree of international capital mobility limits the use of monetary policy to influence the economy.
- A high interest rate spread with the United States has resulted in a strong dollar.
- There is a variety of opinions about what fiscal policy can and should do:
  - Douglas Peters, chief economist at the Toronto-Dominion Bank and Ernest Stokes, chief economist at a Toronto economic forecasting company, believe there is no fiscal action that can improve the economy.
  - Lloyd Atkinson, chief economist at the Bank of Montreal, believes a tough budget would strengthen the dollar and lower interest rates.

Background and Analysis

- This story was written in January 1990, before the budget of that year. At the time of the story, the economy was experiencing an increase in inflation and there was growing concern that a recession was just around the corner.

Fiscal Policy

- What were the fiscal policy options facing the Minister of Finance?
- There were three broad alternatives:
  - *Expansionary*: Increase taxes and/or cut spending and reduce the deficit.
  - *Contractionary*: Cut taxes and/or increase spending and increase the deficit.
  - *Neutral*: Keep taxes, spending, and the deficit steady.
- An *expansionary* fiscal policy would:
  - Increase aggregate demand.
  - Increase the demand for money and put upward pressure on interest rates.
  - Strenghten the dollar on foreign exchange markets.
- A *contractionary* fiscal policy would:
  - Decrease aggregate demand.
  - Decrease the demand for money and put downward pressure on interest rates.
  - Weaken the dollar on foreign exchange markets.
- Fear of higher interest rates and a stronger dollar (from expansionary fiscal policy) and fear of recession (from contractionary fiscal policy) make both options look unattractive to many observers.
- But the actual changes in interest rates and the strength of the dollar depend on the monetary policy that accompanies the fiscal policy.

Monetary Policy

- The Bank of Canada's monetary policy actions are constrained by the market forces that bring about *interest rate parity* (see Chapter 29).
- *Interest rate parity* is a situation in which interest rates are equal across countries once expectations of changes in exchange rates and differences in risk are taken into account.
- Suppose that U.S. government treasury bills have an interest rate of 10 percent per year, Canadian government treasury bills have an interest rate of 15 percent per year, and these two types of treasury bill are equally risky.
- Question: Why would anyone put their money into U.S. government treasury bills when they can make 5 percent per year more on Canadian treasury bills?
- Answer: Because they expect the Canadian dollar to fall in value by 5 percent per year. Market forces achieve interest rate parity.
- If Bank of Canada policy maintains a fixed exchange rate with the U.S. dollar, Canada must accept interest rate levels and an inflation rate determined in the United States.
- If the Bank of Canada pursues a policy of maintaining a lower inflation rate in Canada than that in the United States, the Canadian dollar will *appreciate* against the U.S. dollar and our interest rates will be lower than those in the United States.
- If the Bank of Canada pursues a policy of maintaining a higher inflation rate in Canada than that in the United States, the Canadian dollar will *depreciate* against the U.S. dollar and our interest rates will be higher than those in the United States.
- If the Bank of Canada pursues a *temporary* policy of aiming for a lower inflation rate in Canada than that in the United States, the Canadian dollar will *temporarily appreciate* against the U.S. dollar but be *expected to depreciate* in the future and our interest rates will be higher than those in the United States. This was the situation in the first half of 1990.
- To achieve lower interest rates in Canada, the Bank of Canada would have to establish credibility that its pursuit of a "zero inflation" target is a permanent commitment.
- Many economists, and, more importantly, many financial market specialists, believe that such a credible commitment is only possible if the federal government deficit is reduced. This is the view expressed in the story by Lloyd Atkinson of the Bank of Montreal.

R E V I E W

Attempts to stabilize the economy may use either fixed rules or feedback rules. A fixed rule sets policy instruments independently of the state of the economy and a feedback rule makes policy instruments react to the state of the economy. The policy rule employed influences expectations. Economists do not agree on which type of rule works best. Feedback rules require greater knowledge of the way the economy works than fixed rules and a more accurate diagnosis of whether the source of a disturbance is on the demand side or the supply side of the economy. If negative shocks to aggregate supply are the major source of macroeconomic disturbance, a feedback rule results in inflation. If aggregate demand fluctuations are the major source of macroeconomic disturbance, a feedback rule can moderate its influence on unemployment and real GDP fluctuations. It is not possible to use policy announcements to influence expectations if those announcements are out of line with previous policy. ■

Let's now turn to an examination of the Bank of Canada's attempts to stabilize the Canadian economy in the 1970s and 1980s.

Stabilizing the Canadian Economy

So far in this chapter, we've studied the theory of stabilization policy. It is now time to turn to an examination of stabilization policy in practice. We'll begin this examination by studying the Bank of Canada's monetary targeting policies of the 1970s and early 1980s.

The Bank of Canada's Monetary Targeting

From 1975 through 1982, the Bank of Canada pursued a policy of announcing ahead of time its target range for the growth rate of the M1 definition of the money supply. When the Bank embarked on this

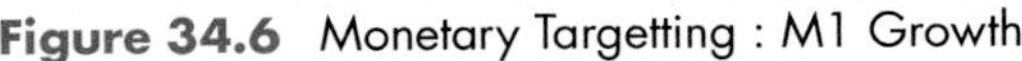

Figure 34.6 Monetary Targetting : M1 Growth

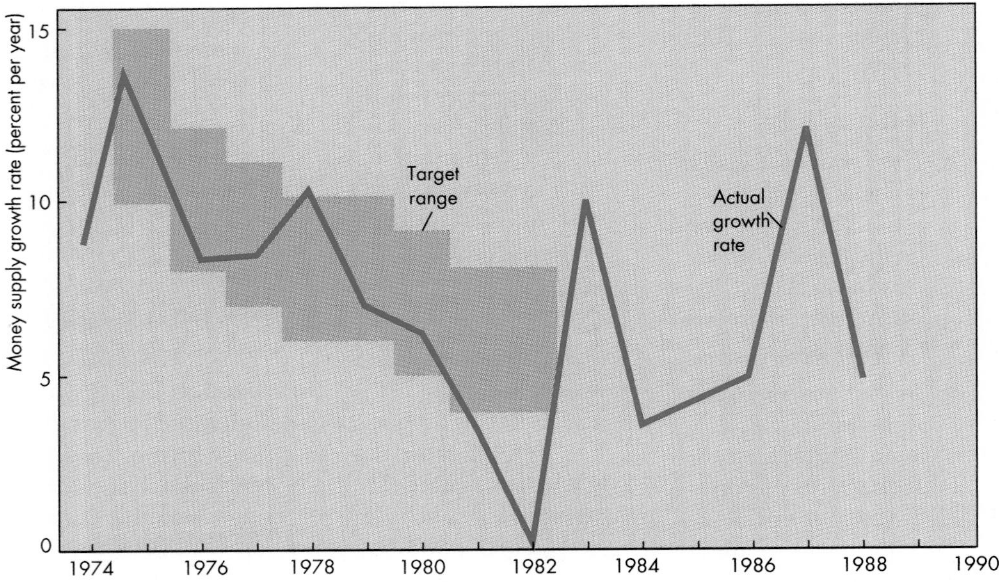

From 1975 to 1982, the Bank of Canada announced a target range for the growth rate of the M1 definition of the money supply. The figure shows this target range. The actual growth rate of M1 remained inside the target range with a small exception in 1978 and a large and important exception in 1982. In 1982, the Bank effectively abandoned its targeting by tightening its monetary policy much more severely than it had announced. Since targeting was abandoned in 1982, M1 growth has been highly volatile.

Figure 34.7 M2 Growth and Inflation

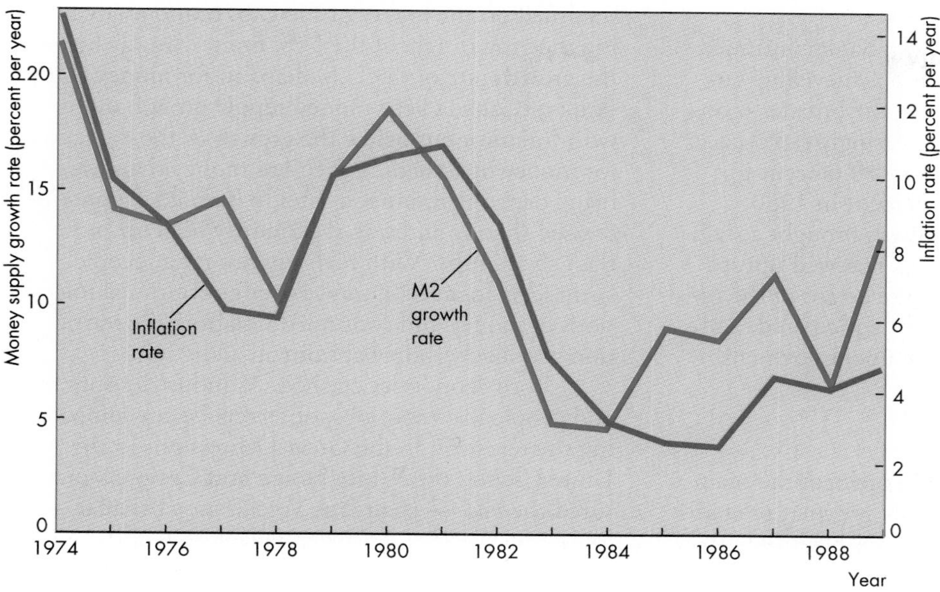

From 1975 through 1978, the growth rates of all the monetary aggregates declined. So did the inflation rate. From 1978 to 1981, the growth rate of M1 declined (see Fig. 34.6), but the growth rate of M2 and other broader aggregates increased. So did the inflation rate. Inflation eventually came under control when the growth rate of M2 was brought under control in the early 1980s.

policy, inflation was running at more than 10 percent a year. The Bank's plan was to squeeze the inflation out of the economy gradually by gently slowing the growth rate of the money supply. It announced a target range for a period of about a year into the future. Approximately each year, a new target was announced for a lower average growth rate.

The Bank's target range for the growth rate of M1 is illustrated in Fig. 34.6. As you can see, in the first year of monetary targeting, the Bank planned the money supply to grow at 10 to 15 percent a year. By the time targeting was abandoned in 1982 the target was for a growth rate of 4 to 8 percent a year.

The actual growth rate of M1 is also shown in the figure. As you can see, with the brief and tiny exception of 1978, the actual growth rate of M1 remained inside the target range until 1982. In 1982, however, the money supply growth rate collapsed. The M1 definition of the money supply stopped growing altogether. Since 1982 there has been a series of huge swings in the growth rate of M1.

During the 1975 to 1982 period, it appears that the Bank of Canada was pursuing a serious policy of inflation reduction by not only announcing the slowdown in money supply growth but also delivering such a slowdown. In the face of such a policy, why did expectations of inflation not moderate and the actual inflation rate not decline? The answer is to be found in the performance of the growth rate of other monetary aggregates.

M2 Growth In particular, the growth rate of M2 — the definition of money that includes personal savings accounts — grew at an increasing rate during the period that the growth rate of M1 was decreasing. In effect, the Bank of Canada was squeezing the growth rate of M1 by forcing interest rates up, but it was not keeping the overall growth rate of the money supply in check. As M1 growth declined, more and more of our money supply took the form of chequable savings deposits, and the actual money supply growth rate was increasing. Figure 34.7 shows what was happening. Between 1975 and 1978, the growth rate of M2, like the growth rate of M1, was declining. So was the inflation rate. Thus for the three-year period during which the Bank of Canada pursued a policy of announcing and delivering a slowdown in the growth rate of the money supply, the inflation rate did decline. Furthermore, this decline in the inflation rate was achieved with a modest increase in the unemployment rate and a modest slowdown in the growth rate of real GDP.

From 1978 through 1981, the Bank continued to target the growth rate of M1 and achieved its targets. But it eased off and permitted the broader monetary aggregates to grow at an increasingly rapid pace. The M2 growth rate increased from 10 percent to 16 percent in 1979 and to 18.5 percent in 1980. This rapid acceleration of M2 growth brought a swift increase in aggregate demand and a renewed upturn in the inflation rate. To a degree, the extent of the increase in aggregate demand was not anticipated, and real GDP growth increased and the unemployment rate decreased in its wake.

Unexpected Deflation As the 1980s opened, the main stabilization problem facing Canada was that of eradicating a double digit inflation that was beginning to look like a permanent feature of life.

By 1981, concerned with the persistence of double-digit inflation, the Bank of Canada continued to announce a target growth range for M1, but it actually abandoned its monetary targeting and instead pursued a policy of tight money. In an unrelenting war on inflation, the Bank pushed interest rates up to more than 20 percent and took the money supply growth rate through the floor. Let's look a bit more closely at this episode.

The Bank of Canada's Finest Hour?

The Canadian economy in early 1981 could be compared to an overweight jogger: it was running in agony. While the economy was growing at a good pace, interest rates and inflation were high. Worst of all, people had resigned themselves to expect that prices would rise by about 10 percent a year forever.

By the fall of 1980, the U.S. Federal Reserve had already put its foot firmly on the monetary brake, forcing interest rates up to more than 20 percent a year. By December of 1980, the Bank of Canada followed the Fed, hiking its bank rate up more than 4 points to 17¼ percent. From January to April 1981, the Fed eased off the brake and gently touched the gas pedal; so did the Bank of Canada, but more gently. Then, in May 1981, both central banks slammed on the brakes again. It was at this time that the war on inflation was declared. Foremost in the decision was Fed chairman Paul Volcker. Volcker's bank slammed on the brakes of the U.S. economy by holding the growth rate of the U.S. money supply below the growth rate of the U.S. demand for money. The Bank of Canada kept money supply growth in line with inflation but below the growth in the demand for money in Canada. Given less money than was being demanded, interest rates in both economies increased sharply and stayed extremely high for more than six months. With high interest rates, people spent less. To an economy expecting continual injections of money and continued inflation, the restriction was like withdrawal from an addiction.

Both economies crashed. As industries suffered and people lost their jobs, observers began comparing the recession to the Great Depression. In the United States, the White House and Congress pressured the Fed — chairman Volcker in particular — to ease up. Volcker, however, talked only of the importance of beating inflation. In Canada, politicians and commentators of most shades of opinion berated the governor of the Bank of Canada, Gerald Bouey, for following the Fed with restrictive policies and high interest rates.

The tremendous shock inflicted by the Bank of Canada and the Fed knocked most of the inflation — and inflationary expectations — out of the Canadian and U.S. economies (see Chapter 33). That done, the central banks stepped on the gas again, allowing the money supply to grow fast enough to keep interest rates falling and the economy growing. Both economies enjoyed a powerful recovery with surprisingly low inflation from 1982 through 1989. Bouey and Volcker had put their economies on a course that was to lead to the longest peacetime period of sustained expansion in Canadian and U.S. economic history.

The Bank of Canada and the Fed became villains to some. But to many more, even to farmers and to housebuyers who were hurt by their policies, they became heroes.

Many economists now say that the Bank of Canada achieved its goals. But while some economists believe that the economy needed governor Bouey's strong-arm methods, others feel that the Bank inflicted unnecessary pain. With delicate monetary tools at its disposal, critics claim that the Bank of Canada dropped the scalpel in favour of the hatchet.

Whatever the pros and cons of the particular episode, monetary policy did lower the inflation rate in the early 1980s, and the economy was put on its longest sustained peacetime recovery path ever. It is keeping that recovery going and preventing a renewed inflation that constitutes the major challenge of the 1990s. Let's now look at that challenge.

The Bank of Canada on a Tightrope

Although the Bank of Canada is not a circus act, it is a very experienced tightrope walker. Unable to see the future, it is a blindfold tightrope walker. Unable to act independently of Ottawa's fiscal policy and international constraints, it walks with its hands tied behind its back! (See Reading Between the Lines, pp. 928-929). Let's look at the bank's balancing act during the recovery years of the 1980s.

Throughout this period, the Bank was trying to promote the two broad policy goals of steady, sustained real GDP growth and low inflation. Having gone through an agonizing recession to snuff out inflation in the early 1980s, the Bank did not want to see prices again climbing out of control. But keeping inflation under control requires keeping the growth of aggregate demand in check and thereby running the risk of killing the recovery and touching off recession.

So the Bank of Canada's tightrope act through the recovery years of the 1980s was to keep aggregate demand growing at a pace that balanced the needs of the growing economy and the fears of rekindling inflation. If the money supply grew too slowly, the recovery would be snuffed out; if it grew too fast, inflation would increase.

To balance on its tightrope, the Bank of Canada leaned first in one direction and then the other. During the early years of the recovery, from 1982 to 1987, the Bank leaned in the direction of permitting the money supply and aggregate demand to grow fast enough to take up the slack in the economy. But throughout this period, it kept money growth on a steady growth path. That is, the money supply grew, but at a moderate rate.

By the fall of 1987, when the stock market crashed, the Bank of Canada, fearing an impending recession, was ready to ease its control on money supply growth. However, as the months passed and the feared recession kept failing to arrive, the Bank's concerns slowly turned from recession to inflation. With unemployment continuing to fall and with signs of an upturn in inflation, the Bank became more and more convinced that it was about to fall off the tightrope into inflation. It started leaning, gently and tentatively, in the opposite direction. It became more willing to risk falling off the tightrope into recession to avoid what it saw as the larger risk of falling off into inflation.

By the spring of 1990, the Bank was more convinced than ever that the risks all lay on the inflation side of the tightrope. In an attempt to slow down the growth in aggregate demand and limit inflation, it pushed interest rates ever higher, opening a 4 percentage point spread between short-term interest rates in Canada and comparable rates in the United States. The dollar continued to strengthen.

Unlike the circus tightrope walker, the Bank of Canada will probably never become completely surefooted. The tightrope which the Bank has to walk is one that is constantly changing: the tension on the rope changes without warning, and the winds that blow around it are constantly shifting in force and direction, also without warning. Although not much is certain in the world of economics, one of the things about which we can be sure is that there will be many more recessions and inflationary upturns. The Bank will, from time to time, fall off that tightrope.

■ We've now examined the main issues of stabilization policy. We've seen how fixed and feedback rules operate under differing assumptions about the behaviour of the economy and why economists take different views on using these rules. Finally, we have looked at recent stabilization policy.

In the next chapter, we examine what many people believe is our economy's single most serious problem — the government's budget deficit.

S U M M A R Y

The Stabilization Problem

The targets of macroeconomic policy fall into two categories: real and nominal. The real targets are to keep unemployment at its natural rate, to achieve steady and sustained growth in real GDP, and to maintain balanced international trade. The nominal targets are to achieve low and predictable inflation and to maintain stable exchange rates between the dollar and foreign currencies. Indexes of macroeconomic performance combine the real and nominal targets into a single measure. Three such measures are the misery index, an unpopularity index based on voter behaviour, and a stabilization policy index based on a nominal GDP growth target. All three indexes paint a similar picture of Canadian macroeconomic performance: steady improvement through 1965; continued deterioration through 1975; a slight improvement in 1976; continued deterioration through 1982; and finally steady and persistent improvement from 1983 to 1989. (pp. 917-921)

The Key Players

The key players in the formulation and execution of macroeconomic policy are the Bank of Canada and the government of Canada. The Bank of Canada makes the nation's monetary policy. The government of Canada makes the fiscal policy. (p. 921)

Alternative Means of Stabilizing the Economy

There are two broad types of stabilization policy: fixed rules and feedback rules. Since expectations about aggregate demand affect wages and other costs and therefore affect short-run aggregate supply, expectations about policy, as well as actual policy actions, influence the course of the economy.

Fixed-rule policy permits the aggregate demand curve to fluctuate as a result of all the independent forces that influence demand. As a result, there are fluctuations in real GDP and the price level. Feedback-rule policy adjusts the money supply to offset the effects of other influences on aggregate demand. An ideal feedback rule would keep the economy at full employment with stable prices.

Some economists argue that feedback rules require greater knowledge of the economy than we have, introduce unpredictability, generate bigger fluctuations in aggregate demand, and are ineffective in the face of the most prominent type of shock — an aggregate supply shock. Feedback rules are unpredictable because it is not possible for the Bank of Canada or the government of Canada to specify with great clarity and precision ahead of time exactly how its policies will react to the state of the economy. Feedback rules induce greater variability in aggregate demand because actions are based on the current state of the economy; they have their effects only many months later, when the economy is in a different state from that which triggered the policy action. (pp. 922-926)

Stabilization Policy and Aggregate Supply

Two types of aggregate supply shock generate stabilization problems. They are cost-push inflation and changes in capacity real GDP. A fixed rule minimizes the threat of cost-push inflation and the problems associated with it. A feedback rule validates cost-push inflation and leaves the price level and inflation rate free to pursue whatever course they are pushed in. If capacity real GDP falls (or its growth rate slows down), a fixed rule results in lower output (and higher unemployment) and a higher price level. A feedback rule that increases the money supply to stimulate aggregate demand results in an even higher price level and higher inflation. Output (and unemployment) follows the same course as with a fixed rule. (pp. 926-934)

Stabilizing the Canadian Economy

During the 1975 to 1982 period, the Bank of Canada pursued a policy of announcing its money supply growth target and gradually slowing down that target growth rate with a view to squeezing out inflation without causing serious unemployment or recession. At first, the policy worked and the growth rates of all the monetary aggregates were in line with each other. By the late 1970s, however, the policy failed as the Bank paid exclusive attention to M1, permitting M2 growth to accelerate.

The main stabilization problem in 1980 was the elimination of severe inflation. To reduce inflation, the Bank of Canada engineered a severe slowdown in the growth rate of aggregate demand by generating a sharp rise in interest rates. The result was an unanticipated fall in aggregate demand and a severe recession. The main problem as the Canadian economy entered the 1990s was to ensure a continuation of moderate inflation and sustained growth that characterized the 1980s. (pp. 934-937)

KEY ELEMENTS

Key Terms

Cost-push inflation, 926
Federal budget, 921
Feedback rule, 922
Fixed rule, 922
Misery index, 918
Nominal targets, 918
Real business cycle theory, 928
Real targets, 918
Stagflation, 926

Key Figures 

Figure 34.3 Two Monetary Policies, 924
Figure 34.4 Monetary Policy and Aggregate Supply: A Wage Increase, 927
Figure 34.5 Monetary Policy and Aggregate Supply: A Capacity Decrease, 929

REVIEW QUESTIONS

1 What are the goals of macroeconomic stabilization policy?

2 Describe three ways of measuring macroeconomic performance.

3 What are the main institutions that formulate and execute macroeconomic policy in Canada?

4 What is the distinction between a fixed rule and a feedback rule?

5 Analyse the effects of a decrease in aggregate demand that is temporary if a fixed money supply rule is employed.

6 Analyse the behaviour of output and the price level in the face of a permanent decrease in aggregate demand under a fixed monetary rule and a feedback monetary rule.

7 Why do economists disagree with each other on the appropriateness of fixed and feedback rules?

8 Analyse the effects of a rise in the price of oil on real GDP and the price level if the Bank of Canada employs a fixed monetary rule.

9 What is stagflation? Explain how it might arise.

PROBLEMS

1 The economy is experiencing 10 percent inflation and 7 percent unemployment. Set out policies for the Bank of Canada and the government of Canada that will lower both inflation and unemployment. Explain how and why your proposed policies will work.

2 The economy is booming and inflation is beginning to rise, but it is widely agreed that a massive recession is just around the corner. Weigh the advantages and disadvantages of the Bank's pursuing a fixed-rule monetary policy and a feedback-rule monetary policy.

3 You have been hired by the prime minister to draw up a plan that will maximize the chance of his being re-elected.

a) What are the macroeconomic stabilization policy elements in that plan?

b) What do you have to make the economy do in an election year?

c) How important is it to keep inflation in check?

d) How important is it to prevent unemployment from rising?

e) What policy actions will help achieve the prime minister's objectives? (In dealing with this problem, be careful to take into account the effects of your proposed policy on expectations and the effects of those expectations on actual economic performance.)

4 The economy of Miniland has the following aggregate demand and aggregate supply schedules:

Aggregate demand: Price level (GDP deflator)	Real GDP demanded (billions of 1981 dollars)
120	3.0
110	3.5
100	4.0
90	4.5
80	5.0

Short-run aggregate supply Price level (GDP deflator)	Real GDP supplied (billions of 1981 dollars)
90	3.0
95	3.5
100	4.0
105	4.5
110	4.5

Long-run aggregate supply equals $4.0 billion.

a) Find the equilibrium levels of real GDP and the price level (GDP deflator).

b) Calculate the deviation of real GDP from its capacity level.

5 A world recession results in a decrease in aggregate demand in Miniland. Compared with the situation set out in problem 4, the aggregate quantity of real GDP demanded decreases by $1.5 billion at each price level.

a) Calculate the new level of real GDP.

b) Calculate the new price level.

c) Calculate the amount by which real GDP is below its capacity level.

6 If the govenor of the Minibank (the central bank of Miniland) was Milton Friedman, and if Miniland was in the situation described in your answers to problem 5, what monetary policy would be adopted by the Minibank and what would its effects be?

7 If the Minibank pursues a feedback policy designed to maintain full-employment, and if Miniland is in the situation described in your answers to problem 5, what actions would the central bank take? If the bank increased aggregate demand by the same amount as the world recession (described in problem 5) had decreased it, if the world recession persisted, and if there were no other changes in the influences on aggregate demand and aggregate supply, what would happen to the price level and real GDP in Miniland?

8 If the Minibank increased aggregate demand by the same amount as the world recession (described in problem 5) had decreased it, if the world recession ended, and if there were no changes in any other influences on aggregate demand and aggregate supply, what would happen to the price level and real GDP in Miniland?

9 Miniland is in the situation described by the aggregate demand and short-run aggregate supply schedules of problem 4. An economy-wide labour union forces an increase in wages that shifts the short-run aggregate schedule upward by 33 ⅓ percent.

a) What is the effect of this action on real GDP and the price level if Milton Friedman is the governor of the Minibank?

b) What is the effect of this action on real GDP and the price level if the Minibank successfully pursues a policy of changing aggregate demand to maintain full employment?

CHAPTER 35

The Federal Deficit

After studying this chapter, you will be able to:

- Explain why the federal government of Canada has spent more each year since 1975 than it has raised in revenue.
- Distinguish between federal government debt and the federal deficit.
- Distinguish between the *nominal* deficit and the *real* deficit.
- Explain why the federal deficit appears to be larger than it really is.
- Describe the various means available for financing the federal deficit.
- Explain why the federal deficit makes the Bank of Canada's job harder.
- Explain why a federal deficit can cause inflation.
- Explain why a federal deficit can be a burden on future generations.
- Describe the measures that can be taken to eliminate the federal deficit.

Ottawa Spendthrifts

EVERY YEAR SINCE 1975, the government of Canada has spent more than it has raised in revenue. On occasion the gap has grown to more than \$30 billion. This enormous gap between government spending and revenue, called the federal deficit, is now a larger proportion of the Canadian economy than ever except in time of war. Why do we have a federal deficit? Why is the deficit *so* large? ■ The deficit is in fact, so large that the total debt of the federal government increased by more in the past 15 years than it did in the entire period since Confederation. But is the deficit *really* so large? How can we gauge the scale of the deficit when there is so much inflation? How big is the deficit when we adjust for changes in the value of money? ■ Some countries, such as Bolivia, Chile, Brazil, and Israel, have had large government deficits and runaway inflations. Following World War I, Germany suffered an enormous budget deficit as a result of being required to pay France compensation for damage inflicted during the war. That deficit produced a hyperinflation — an inflation of more than 50 percent per month. The fact that deficits have, at other times and places, produced extraordinary inflations raises the question for us today: will Canada's federal deficit lead to a renewed outburst of inflation? Does the deficit somehow make it harder or even impossible for the Bank of Canada to control the money supply and keep inflation in check? ■ When we incur a personal debt, that debt has to be repaid. That is, we incur a self-imposed burden to repay the debt with interest. This fact leads to worries that when the nation incurs a debt as a result of a government deficit, a burden is being placed not just on ourselves but on our children and grandchildren. Does a federal deficit create a burden on future generations? ■ There are two ways in which we can approach any problem. We can pretend it doesn't exist, or we can try to identify its nature and solve it. How are we approaching the federal deficit? Are we sticking our heads in the sand like ostriches, or are we taking steps that are calculated to eliminate the deficit in a reasonably short time span? What are the prospects for the future of the deficit?

■ In this chapter, we're going to study what became perhaps the hottest economic topic of the 1980s. We're going to examine the origins of the federal deficit, gauge its true scale, and explain why deficits are feared and why they constitute a problem. We'll also discuss some of the measures that are being taken to eliminate the deficit. Because the deficit is a hot economic and political topic, the public debate on it has generated more heat and smoke than light. In this chapter, we'll clear away some of the rhetorical smoke, lower the temperature, and try to answer the questions posed. By the time you're through with this chapter, you'll be able to explain what the deficit is all about.

The Sources of the Deficit

What exactly is the deficit? The **budget surplus or budget deficit** of the federal government is the difference between the revenue it receives and its total expenditure over a given period of time — usually a year. The federal government's total expenditure is the sum of government purchases of goods and services, transfer payments and subsidies, and interest on the government's debt. If tax revenue exceeds expenditure, the federal government has a surplus. If expenditure exceeds revenue, the federal government has a deficit. Thus we can define the budget surplus or deficit as follows:

$$\text{Surplus or deficit} = \text{Revenue} - \text{Expenditure}.$$

If the surplus or deficit is zero — in other words if revenue and expenditure are equal — the government's budget is balanced. A **balanced budget** is a government budget that is in neither surplus nor deficit.

Federal government debt is the total amount of borrowing that the federal government has undertaken and the total amount that it owes to households, firms, and foreigners. Government debt is a *stock*. It is the accumulation of all the past deficits minus all the past surpluses. The federal deficit is a *flow*. It is the flow that adds to the stock of outstanding debt. Thus if the federal government has a deficit, its debt is increasing. If the federal government has a surplus, its debt is decreasing. If the federal government has a balanced budget, its debt is constant.

The Federal Budget 1969-1989

The federal deficit, measured as a percentage of gross domestic product (GDP), is shown in Fig. 35.1. The deficit is shown as a percentage of GDP, rather than in billions of dollars, so that we can see its importance in relation to the scale of the economy.

Figure 35.1 Revenue, Expenditure, and the Deficit

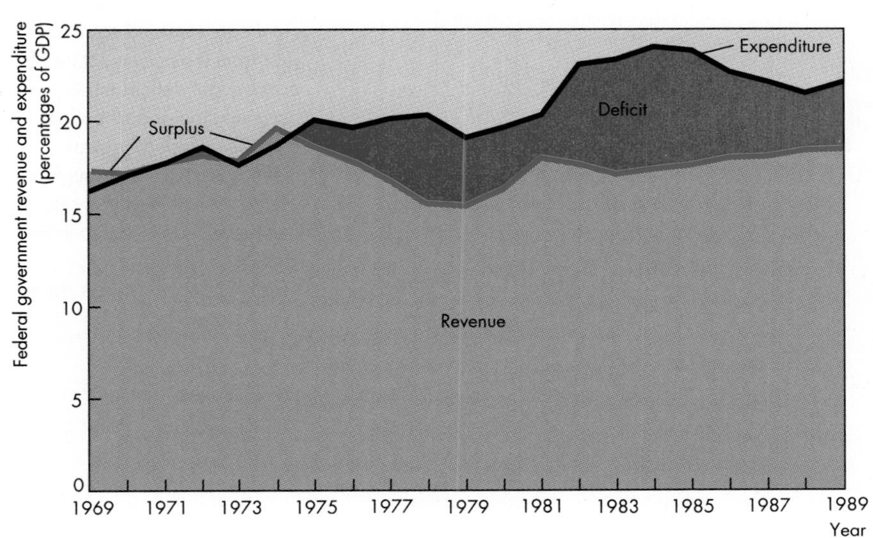

The figure records the federal government's revenue (blue area), expenditure (black line), and deficit (red area) from 1969 to 1989. The deficit that first emerged in 1975 has persisted since that time.

Source: *Bank of Canada Review*, October 1989, Table G1.

(Because of economic growth and inflation, GDP in 1988 was almost eight times what it was in 1969.)

As Fig. 35.1 illustrates, the last time the federal government had a budget surplus was in 1974. Since that time, the federal government has had a budget deficit. The deficit climbed to 4.5 percent of GDP by 1978 and then slackened off through 1981. It grew again to a new peak of 6.8 percent of GDP in 1984. As a percentage of GDP, the deficit declined from 1984 through 1988, but it averaged more than 3 percent through the entire decade.

The effect of the deficit on the government's debt is shown in Fig. 35.2. As you can see, federal government debt as a percentage of GDP declined through 1976, when it reached its lowest point after World War II. It then remained basically constant through 1981. In the recession year of 1982 and the years 1983 through 1985, government debt as a percentage of GDP persistently increased. From 1986 to 1989, government debt was a stable percentage of GDP — about 45 percent. Such a ratio of government debt to GDP is not unusually high and, as you can see, is about the same as we had in 1972, before the federal government's current deficit emerged.

Why does the federal government have a deficit? Where did the deficit come from? The immediate source of the deficit can be seen by glancing back to Fig. 35.1. That figure shows that when the deficit first arose, in the second half of the 1970s, its main origin was a persistent decrease in the government's revenue. Expenditure did increase, but only slightly. It also shows that the further increase in the deficit during the 1980s came mainly from an increase in expenditure, with revenue more or less constant.

Why did government revenue fall in the 1970s? Which elements of government expenditure increased most sharply in the 1980s? And why haven't government revenue and expenditure stayed in line? Let's answer these questions by looking at the federal government's revenue and expenditure in a bit more detail.

Federal Government Revenue

There are three broad categories of federal government revenue:

- Investment income
- Indirect taxes
- Income taxes

These three elements of federal government revenue are illustrated in Fig. 35.3. Let's look at each of them.

Investment Income Investment income is the revenue received by the federal government from Crown corporations. Some Crown corporations incur a loss, but

Figure 35.2 The Federal Government Debt

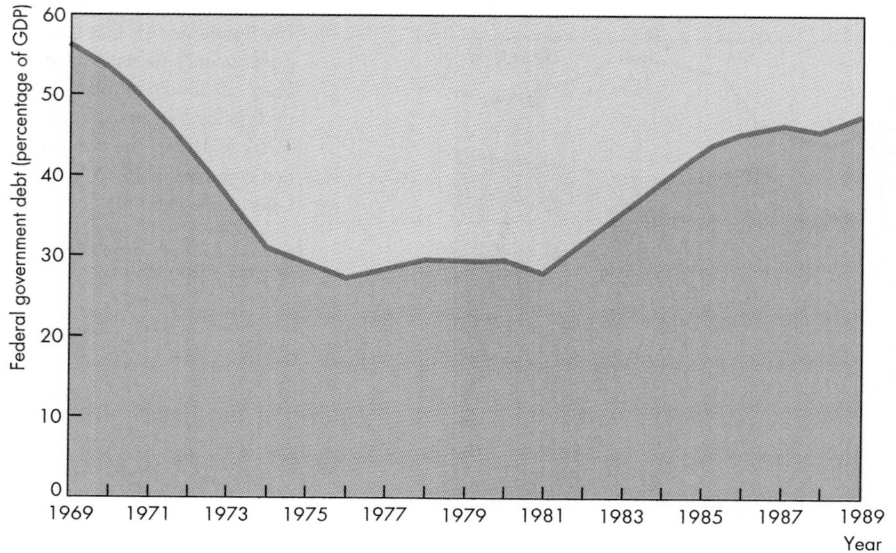

Federal government debt is the total amount of federal government debt outstanding. It results from the accumulation of past budget deficits minus the accumulation of past budget surpluses. Federal government debt declined through 1976. It remained fairly stable through 1981 but then increased sharply through 1985. It became stable again in the second half of the 1980s.

Source: *Bank of Canada Review*, October 1989, Table G4.

Figure 35.3 Federal Government Revenue

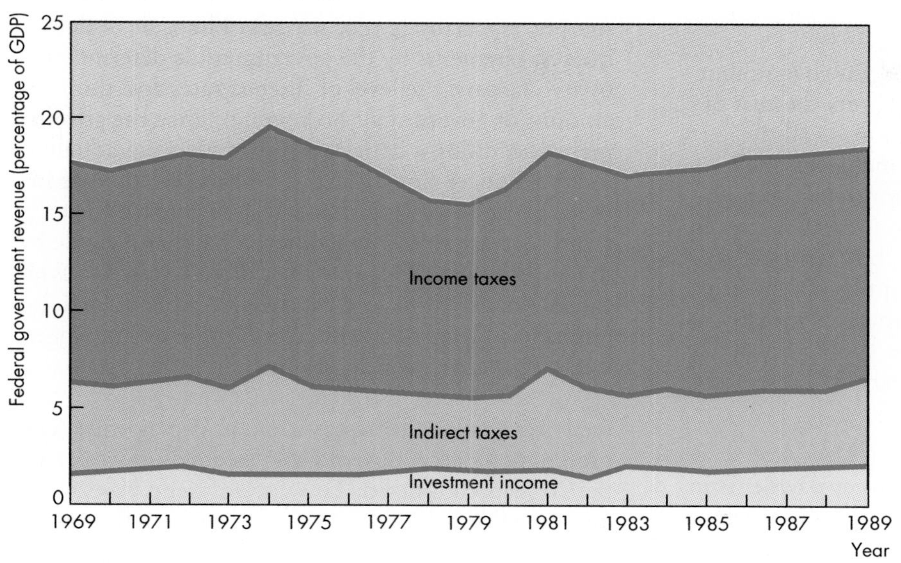

The three categories of federal government revenue are: investment income, indirect taxes, and income taxes. Investment income (the income from Crown corporations) is a steady fraction of GDP. Indirect taxes fluctuate slightly, and they increased temporarily in 1974 and 1981. The largest item of government revenue and the one that fluctuates most is income taxes. There is no overall trend in federal government revenue, but it fluctuates between 16 and 20 percent of GDP.

Source: Bank of Canada Review, October 1989, Table G1.

others, such as Petro-Canada and Air Canada, which are now partly privatized, make a profit. This source of government income is not large but it is steady.

Indirect Taxes Indirect taxes are taxes on the goods and services that we buy. An example of an indirect tax is the goods and services tax (GST). These taxes also include the customs duties that we pay when we import goods from other countries. Federal government receipts from indirect taxes have been a fairly stable percentage of GDP over the years. However, a sharp boost in indirect taxes in 1974 and 1981 temporarily increased the importance of this source of federal government revenue. The introduction of the GST in 1990 did not increase the government's revenue from indirect taxes. Instead, it replaced revenue previously raised by the manufacturer's sales tax. However, because the GST is a tax levied at a lower rate and on a broader range of items than the now-abolished manufacturer's sales tax, it is possible (and some believe likely) that the GST rate will be increased and revenue from this tax, therefore, increased.

Income Taxes Income taxes include the taxes paid by individuals on their labour and capital incomes, taxes paid by companies on their profits, and taxes paid by foreigners on incomes earned in Canada. These taxes have fluctuated much more than the other components of federal government revenue. It was the steady decline in income taxes in 1976 through 1979 that was the immediate cause of the onset of the federal government's deficit. Taxes decreased because the federal income tax code was indexed to the cost of living. Higher inflation, which brought higher prices, also brought higher personal deductions from taxable income. Also, the income levels at which higher tax brackets became effective were increased.

Increases in tax rates in the early 1980s boosted the government's income tax receipts, and continued steady increases in rates through the 1980s led to a gentle but persistent increase in federal government revenue as a percentage of GDP.

Total Revenue When all three of the components of the federal government revenue are added together, we find that their total has fluctuated between 16 and 20 percent of GDP, and there are no discernible trends in total revenue.

Next, let's consider expenditure.

Federal Government Expenditure

We will examine federal government expenditure by dividing it into three categories:

- Purchases of goods and services
- Transfer payments and subsidies
- Debt interest

Figure 35.4 shows the behaviour of these items of expenditure over the 20 years between 1969 and 1989. Let's examine each in turn.

Purchases of Goods and Services Federal government expenditure on goods and services covers the cost of the federal government administration — all the main federal departments of state, including such items as national defence and environmental protection. The total resources devoted to these activities increased substantially over the years, but expressed as a percentage of GDP, the amount spent by the government on goods and services was remarkably steady. It even declined somewhat during the 1980s. This source of government activity is clearly not responsible for the current deficit situation.

Transfer Payments and Subsidies Transfer payments include social security and welfare benefits and unemployment insurance benefits. Subsidies include payments to farmers and other producers under a variety of price-support and income maintenance programs. This item of federal expenditure is the largest and the one that grew strongly throughout the period shown. It grew especially quickly during the early 1980s, but the general trend throughout the 20 years shown in Fig. 35.4 was an upward one.

Debt Interest Debt interest is the smallest of the three categories of government expenditure that we are considering. But it is the one that increased most sharply, especially in recent years. The scale of debt interest payments by the government is determined by two factors: the level of interest rates and the amount of government borrowing. Since the government is running a deficit, its borrowing is gradually increasing over time. It is the continuous increase in the scale of borrowing that is responsible for the trend increase in the debt-interest payments made by the government. This source of increased expenditure causes the deficit to feed on itself — a bigger deficit results in a bigger debt which, in turn, results in bigger interest payments which, in turn, add to the deficit.

Total Expenditure Total government expenditure, expressed as a percentage of GDP, trended upward over the 20 years considered. This upward trend was strongest in the first half of the 1970s and again in the first half of the 1980s. After 1984, there was a gradual decline in the percentage of GDP spent by the government.

The Story of the Deficit

The story of the deficit can now be told in simple and straightforward terms. Until 1975, the federal government collected in taxes pretty much the same

Figure 35.4 Federal Government Expenditure

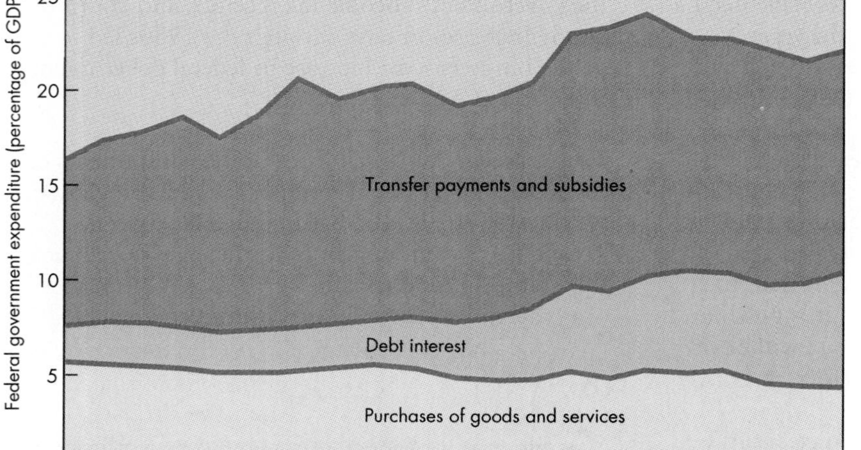

Source: *Bank of Canada Review*, October 1989, Table G1.

The three categories of federal government expenditure are: purchases of goods and services, transfer payments and subsidies, and debt interest. Expenditure on goods and services (the operation of the federal government, including national defence) was a steady and slightly declining percentage of GDP. Debt interest increased most — causing the deficit to feed on itself. Transfer payments and subsidies increased most strongly and fluctuated most. It was the steady increase in transfer payments and subsidies combined with the sharp increase in debt interest that increased government expenditure.

amount as it spent on goods and services, transfer payments and subsidies, and debt interest. Then, in 1975, there was a sharp increase in transfer payments and subsidies and a decrease in tax revenue. A deficit emerged.

But why did tax revenue fall and transfer payments and subsidies increase in 1975? What event triggered these changes? The event that provoked this transformation of the government's budget was the energy crisis facing Canada and the world in the mid-1970s. The Canadian government did not permit the large increase in world energy prices to flow through into energy prices in Canada. Instead, the government cut its own taxes on energy and increased its subsidies to those dependent on more costly energy. With the deficit in place, gradual decreases in income taxes, resulting mainly from the indexation of personal taxes, resulted in an ongoing deficit. It was given a further boost in 1982 when a surge in transfer payments (mainly unemployment insurance payments) increased the deficit yet further. The ongoing deficit, resulting in increasing federal government debt, has resulted in increasing interest payments that have further fed the deficit. This has been the story of the deficit since the mid-1970s.

A Personal Analogy Perhaps you can see more clearly why the deficit feeds on itself if you think in personal terms. Suppose that each year, you spend more than you earn and you keep on doing this. Your debt, let's say at the bank, rises each year. Therefore each year you owe the bank more in interest as a result of having a bigger debt outstanding. The government is in exactly the same situation. But the government doesn't just borrow from banks. It borrows from everyone who buys the bonds that it issues — households, firms, chartered banks and trust companies, the Bank of Canada, and foreigners. The government has been running a deficit continuously since 1975, so its outstanding debt has been rising and the interest payments on that debt have also been rising.

The Deficit and the Business Cycle

There is an important relationship between the size of the deficit and the stage of the business cycle through which the economy is passing. We defined the business cycle, in Chapter 22, as the ebbs and flows of economic activity measured by the percentage deviation of real GDP from trend. We also saw that fluctuations in the deviation of real GDP from trend match very closely fluctuations in the deviation of unemployment from the natural rate.

To see the connection between the deficit and the business cycle, look at Fig. 35.5. This figure shows the federal government deficit (as a percentage of GDP) and the unemployment rate for the 20 years between 1969 and 1989. As you can see, there is a remarkably close relationship between these two variables. When the unemployment rate increases, so does the deficit; when the unemployment rate decreases, so does the deficit. A change in the unemployment rate of 1 percentage point changes the deficit by an amount equal to somewhat more than 1 percent of GDP.

Why does the deficit become larger when the unemployment rate increases and the economy goes into recession? Why does the deficit recede as unemployment falls and the economy recovers? Part of the answer lies on the expenditure side and part on the revenue side of the government's account.

The federal government's expenditure and revenue depends on the state of the economy. The government passes tax laws defining tax *rates*, not *dollars* to be paid in taxes. As a consequence, the revenue that the government collects from taxes depends on the level of income: if the economy is in a recovery phase of the business cycle, tax collections rise; if the economy is in a recession phase, tax collections fall.

Spending programs behave similarly. Many government programs are related to the state of well-being of individual citizens and firms. For example, when the economy is in a recession, unemployment is high, economic hardship from poverty increases, and a larger number of firms and farms experience hard times. Transfer payments and subsidies increase as the government responds to the increased economic hardship. When the economy experiences boom conditions, expenditure on programs to compensate for economic hardship declines. In light of both these factors, the deficit rises when the economy is in a depressed state and falls when the economy is in a state of boom.

The Deficit in Recovery

From 1983 to 1989, the economy was in a prolonged and strong recovery. With a recovery under way and unemployment declining, we would expect the deficit to decline. Our expectations are in line with what happened. But the deficit did not decline as strongly as one would expect, given the strong recovery of the economy. It is the persistence of a large deficit, even in the face of strong economic recovery, that leads some observers to express grave concern about the potential effects of an ongoing deficit on

Figure 35.5 Unemployment and the Federal Deficit

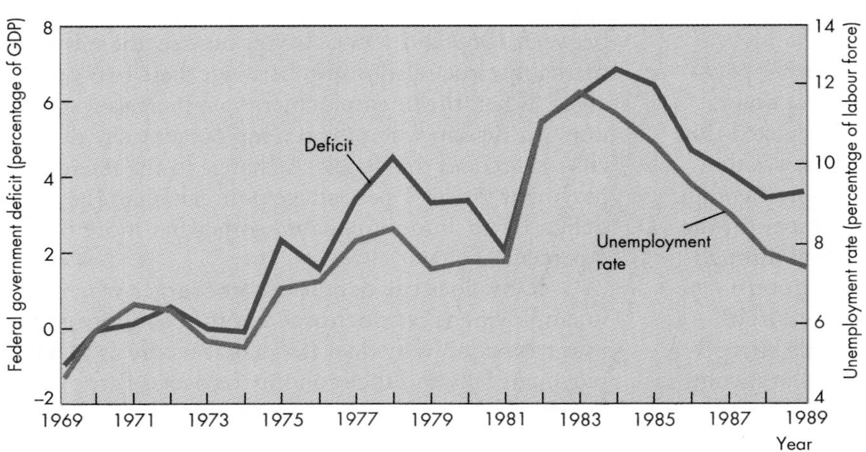

Recession leads to higher unemployment and recovery leads to lower unemployment. There is a close connection between the business cycle and the deficit: when the unemployment rate increases, so does the deficit; when the unemployment rate decreases, so does the deficit.

Source: Fig. 22.3 and Fig. 35.1

the long-term health of the economy. In 1989 the deficit was about 3 percent of GDP with the economy in a boom condition. Any recession that hits us in the early 1990s will increase the deficit sharply. To figure out roughly by how much, we can use the relationship visible in Fig. 35.5. Other things being equal, if the unemployment rate increases by 1 percentage point, the deficit increases by about 1.25 percent of GDP. Thus if the economy goes into a recession in the early 1990s and unemployment climbs to 10 percent — an increase of 3 percentage points — the deficit will climb to 8 percent of GDP — an increase of 4 percentage points.

R E V I E W

The federal deficit emerged in 1975 because the world oil shock resulted in a decrease in federal government revenue. The deficit remained in place because revenue continued to decline while expenditure rose only slightly. The deficit increased further in the early 1980s as a result of a sharp increase in government expenditure. The deficit fed on itself. A higher deficit led to higher borrowing, which in turn led to higher interest payments and a yet higher deficit.

The deficit is related to the business cycle. Other things being equal, the stronger the economy, the lower is the deficit. In the economic recovery of the 1980s, the relationship between the state of the economy and the deficit was broken — the deficit remained large with the economy in a strong recovery. If a deep recession occurs in the early 1990s, the deficit will climb to perhaps 8 percent of GDP. ■

We've now seen where the deficit came from and how it relates to the business cycle. We've also seen that the deficit is large and that it persisted despite strong and prolonged recovery. But is the deficit really as bad as it looks? Can it really be true that in eight years the federal government debt increased by more than in the entire previous history of the nation? These are important questions to which we'll now turn our attention.

The Real Deficit

Inflation distorts many things, not the least of which is the deficit. To remove the inflationary distortion from the measured deficit, we need a concept of the real deficit. The **real deficit** is the change in the real value of government debt in a year. The real value of government debt is equal to the market value of the debt divided by the price level. We are going to see how we can calculate the real deficit and how such a calculation changes our view of the size of the government's deficit. But before we do that, let's consider real deficits in more personal terms by examining the real deficit of a family.

The Real Deficit of a Family

In 1960, a young couple (perhaps your parents) ran a

deficit to buy a new house. That deficit took the form of a mortgage. The amount borrowed to cover the deficit — the difference between the cost of the house and what the family had available to put down as a deposit — was $30,000. Today, the children of that couple are buying their first house. To do so, they also are incurring a deficit. But they're borrowing $120,000 to buy their first house. Is the $120,000 deficit (mortgage) of the 1990 house-buyer really four times as big as the deficit (mortgage) of the 1960 house-buyer? In dollar terms, the 1990 borrowing is indeed four times as big as the 1960 borrowing. But in terms of what money will buy, these two debts are almost equivalent to each other. Inflation in the years between 1960 and 1990 has raised the prices of most things to about four times what they were in 1960. Thus a mortgage of $120,000 in 1990 is really the same as a mortgage of $30,000 in 1960.

When a family buys a new home and finances it with a mortgage, it has a deficit in the year in which it buys the home. But in all the following years, until the loan has been paid off, the family has a surplus. That is, each year the family pays to the lender a sum of money, part of which covers the interest on the outstanding debt but part of which *reduces* the outstanding debt. The reduction in the outstanding debt is the household's surplus. Inflation has another important effect here. Because inflation brings higher prices, it also brings a lower *real* value of the outstanding debt. Thus the real value of the mortgage declines by the amount paid off each year plus the amount wiped out by inflation. Other things being equal, the higher the inflation rate, the faster the mortgage is really paid off and the larger is the household's real surplus.

The Federal Government's Real Deficit

This line of reasoning applies with equal force to the federal government. Because of inflation, the government's deficit is not *really* as big as it appears. To see how we can measure the deficit and correct for the distortion of inflation, we'll work through a concrete numerical example. First, look at Case A in Table 35.1 — a situation in which there is no inflation. Government expenditure, excluding debt interest, is $17 billion and revenue is $20 billion. Thus if the government didn't have interest to pay, it would have a surplus of $3 billion. But the government has debt of $50 billion, and interest rates are running at 4 percent a year. Thus the government must pay $2 billion of debt interest (4 percent of $50 billion).

When we add the $2 billion of debt interest to the government's other spending, we see that the government's total expenditure is $19 billion, so the government has a $1 billion surplus. The government's debt falls to $49 billion — the $50 billion at the beginning of the year is reduced by the surplus that the government has run.

Next, let's look at this same economy with exactly the same spending, revenue, and debt but in a situation in which the inflation rate is 10 percent a year — Case B in Table 35.1. With 10 percent inflation, the market interest rate will not be 4 percent a year but 14 percent. The reason the interest rate is higher by 10 percentage points is that the real value of government debt declines by 10 percent a year.

Table 35.1 How Inflation Distorts the Deficit

	Case A	Case B
Government expenditure (excluding debt interest)	$17 billion	$17 billion
Revenue	$20 billion	$20 billion
Government debt	$50 billion	$50 billion
Market interest rate	4% per year	14% per year
Inflation rate	0% per year	10% per year
Real interest rate	4% per year	4% per year
Debt interest paid	$ 2 billion	$ 7 billion
Surplus (+) or deficit (–)	+ $ 1 billion	– $ 4 billion
Government debt at end of year	$49 billion	$54 billion
Real government debt at end of year	$49 billion	$49 billion
Real surplus (+) or deficit (–)	+$ 1 billion	+$ 1 billion

Inflation distorts the measured deficit by distorting the debt interest payments made by the government. In this example, the real interest rate is 4 percent per year and government debt is $50 billion, so debt interest in real terms is $2 billion. With no inflation, Case A, the actual debt interest paid is also $2 billion. At 10 percent inflation, Case B, interest rates rise to 14 percent per year (in order to preserve a real interest rate of 4 percent per year), and debt interest increases to $7 billion. The deficit increases by $5 billion from a surplus of $1 billion to a deficit of $4 billion. This deficit is apparent, not real. With 10 percent inflation, the real value of the government's debt falls by $5 billion, offsetting the deficit of $4 billion and resulting in a real surplus of $1 billion.

Lenders — the households, firms, and foreigners who buy government debt — know that the money they will receive in repayment of the loans they make to the government will be worth less than the money they lend out. The government also recognizes that the money it will use to repay its debt will have a lower value than the money it borrows. Thus the government and the people from whom it borrows readily agree to a higher interest rate that compensates for these foreseen changes in the value of money. So, with a 14 percent interest rate, the government has to pay $7 billion in debt interest — 14 percent of $50 billion. When the $7 billion of debt interest is added to the government's other spending, total expenditure is $24 billion — $4 billion more than revenue. Therefore the government has a deficit of $4 billion. At the end of one year, the government's debt will have increased from $50 billion to $54 billion.

The difference between the two situations that we've just described is a 10 percent inflation rate. Nothing else is changed. What the government is actually spending and receiving is the same in the two cases, and the real interest rate is the same. At the end of one year, government debt has increased to $54 billion in Case B and has fallen to $49 billion in Case A. But the real debt is the same in the two cases. You can see that equality by keeping in mind that although government debt increases to $54 billion in Case B, the prices of all things have increased by 10 percent. If we deflate the government debt in Case B to express it in constant dollars instead of current dollars, we see that real government debt has actually fallen to $49 billion. ($54 billion divided by 1.1 — 1 plus the proportionate inflation rate — equals $49 billion.) Thus even in Case B, the real situation is that there is a surplus of $1 billion. Inflation makes it appear that there is a $4 billion deficit when really there is a $1 billion surplus.

The numbers in Table 35.1 are, of course, hypothetical. They deal with two imaginary situations. But the calculations we've just done provide us with a method of adjusting the federal government deficit to eliminate the effects of inflation and reveal the real deficit. How important is it to adjust the Canadian deficit for inflation in order to obtain an inflation-free view of the deficit?

The Real and Nominal Federal Deficit in Canada

Figure 35.6 provides an answer to the above question. The nominal and the real deficits (or surpluses) of Canada are plotted alongside each other. As you can see, although a nominal deficit emerged in 1975, a real deficit did not emerge until 1977. Even then, when the nominal deficit climbed to almost 5 percent of GDP, the real deficit barely hit 3 percent of GDP. By 1981, the federal government had a real surplus again, although only briefly. Through the 1980s, the nominal and real deficits increased up to 1984 and thereafter declined. By 1989, the real deficit was

Figure 35.6 The Real Deficit and the Nominal Deficit

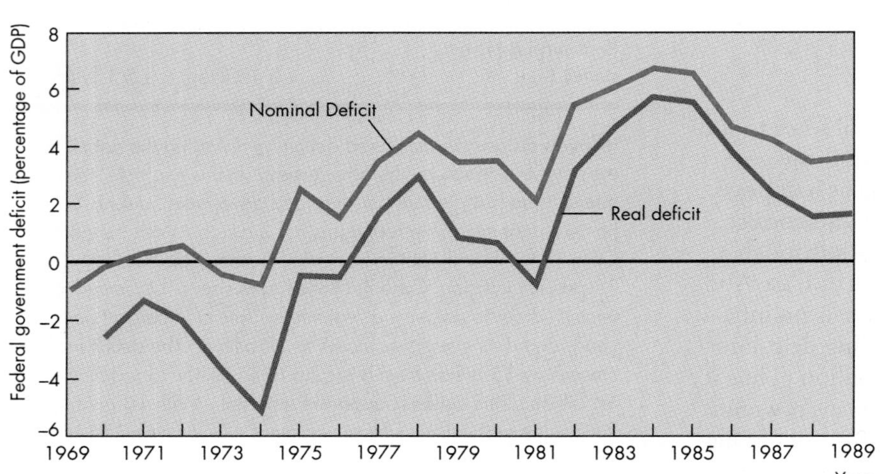

We obtain the real deficit by removing the effects of inflation from interest rates and from the value of government debt. The real deficit and the nominal deficit follow similar paths, but the real deficit is lower than the nominal deficit (or the real surplus is higher than the nominal surplus). Only when real interest rates became high in the 1980s did a serious and persistent real deficit arise.

less than 2 percent of GDP, although the nominal deficit was more than 3 percent of GDP.

The reason the large nominal deficits of the late 1970s were not real deficits is that inflation was high during those years. Only when inflation declined in the mid-1980s, while interest rates remained high, did a large and persistent real deficit emerge.

You can see then that the distinction between the real and nominal deficits is an important practical distinction. Taking the distinction into account dramatically changes our view of the scale and seriousness of the deficit in Canada today. But it does not remove our concern. Looking at the deficit in real terms tells us that the emergence of a deficit is a relatively recent phenomenon. It is also, however, a serious phenomenon. From 1982 to 1989, the real deficit averaged close to 3 percent of GDP.

Let's now go on to examine some of the effects of a deficit.

Deficits and Inflation

Many people fear federal government deficits because they believe deficits lead to inflation. Do deficits cause inflation? That depends on how the government finances the deficit.

Financing the Deficit

To finance its deficit, the federal government sells bonds. But the effects of bond sales depends on who buys the bonds. If they are bought by the Bank of Canada, they bring an increase in the money supply. If they are bought by anyone else, they do not bring a change in the money supply. When the Bank buys government bonds they pay for them by creating new money (see Chapter 28). We call such financing of the deficit money financing. **Money financing** is the financing of the federal deficit by the sale of bonds to the Bank of Canada, which results in the creation of additional money. All other financing of the federal deficit is called debt financing. **Debt financing** is the financing of the federal deficit by selling bonds to anyone other than the Bank of Canada (households, firms, or foreigners).

Let's look at the consequences of these two ways of financing the deficit.

Debt Financing First, suppose that the federal government borrows money by selling bonds to households and firms. In order to sell a bond, the government must offer the potential buyer a sufficiently attractive deal. In other words, the government must offer a high enough rate of return to convince people to lend their money.

Let's suppose that the going interest rate is 10 percent a year. In order to sell a bond worth $100 to cover its deficit of $100, the government must promise not only to pay back the $100 at the end of the year but also to pay the interest of $10 accumulated on that debt. Thus to finance a deficit of $100 today, the government must pay $110 a year from today. At that time, in order simply to stand still, the government would have to borrow $110 to cover the cost of repaying, with interest, the bond that it sold a year earlier. Two years from today the government will have to pay $121 — the $110 borrowed plus 10 percent interest ($11) on that $110. The process continues with the total amount of debt and total interest payments mushrooming year after year.

Money Financing Next, consider what happens if instead of selling bonds to households, firms, and foreigners, the government sells bonds to the Bank of Canada. This case compared with that of debt financing has two important differences. First, the government winds up paying no interest on its bonds; second, additional money gets created.

The government ends up paying no interest on the bonds bought by the Bank of Canada because the Bank, although an independent agency, pays its residual profits to the government. Thus other things being equal, if the Bank receives an extra million dollars from the government in interest payments on government bonds held by the Bank, the Bank's profits increase by that same million dollars and flow back to the government. Second, when the Bank buys bonds from the government, it uses newly created money to do so. This newly created money flows into the banking system in the form of an increase in the monetary base and enables the banks to create yet additional money by making additional loans. (See Chapters 27 and 28.)

As we studied in Chapter 24 and Chapter 32, an increase in the money supply causes an increase in aggregate demand. Higher aggregate demand eventually brings a higher price level. Persistent money financing leads to continuous increases in aggregate demand and to inflation.

Debt Financing Versus Money Financing

Figure 35.7 illustrates the extent to which debt financing and money financing have been used to cover the federal deficit in Canada over the past 20 years. As you can see, money financing has been used in a very limited way. It is true that in the 1970s and early 1980s, money financing increased, but there were times in the 1980s when the total amount of bond financing even exceeded the deficit itself. Thus in Canada, the large federal deficit has not, as yet, brought a large amount of money financing.

What are the pros and cons of financing a deficit by issuing debt or creating money?

In comparing these two methods of covering the deficit, it is clear that debt financing leaves the government with an ongoing obligation to pay interest — an obligation that gets bigger each year if the government keeps running deficits. When the government uses money financing, it pays its bills and that is the end of the matter. (The government pays interest to the Bank of Canada, but the Bank pays its profits to the government, so the government has no ongoing interest obligation.) Thus there is a clear advantage from the government's point of view to covering its deficit by money financing rather than by debt financing. Unfortunately, this solution causes inflationary problems for everybody else.

But the alternative, debt financing, is not problem-free. Financing the deficit through bond sales to households, firms, and foreigners causes a mushrooming scale of debt and interest payments. The larger the scale of debt and interest payments, the bigger the deficit problem becomes and the greater is the temptation to end the process of debt financing and begin to finance the deficit by selling bonds to the Bank of Canada — money financing. This ever-present temptation is what leads many people to fear that deficits are inflationary even when they are not immediately money financed. It has even been suggested recently that debt financing is more inflationary than money financing. Let's examine this proposition more closely.

Unpleasant Arithmetic

To study the effects of financing a federal deficit with debt issue versus money creation, suppose that the government has a deficit of a given size that it plans to maintain indefinitely. Initially, the government covers its deficit by creating money. Consequently, the economy experiences inflation. The inflation rate depends on the deficit's size. The larger the deficit, the larger is the sum of money that has to be created and the faster aggregate demand increases. The faster aggregate demand increases, other things being equal, the higher is the inflation rate.

Suppose the economy is experiencing steady inflation as a result of a money-financed deficit, and the government tries to slow the inflation by slowing the growth rate of the money supply and covering its deficit by selling bonds to the public. It makes no changes in its spending and taxing policies, so the deficit, excluding debt interest, remains constant. The deficit, including debt interest, begins to grow. Furthermore, everyone understands this fact. The

Figure 35.7 Debt Financing Versus Money Financing

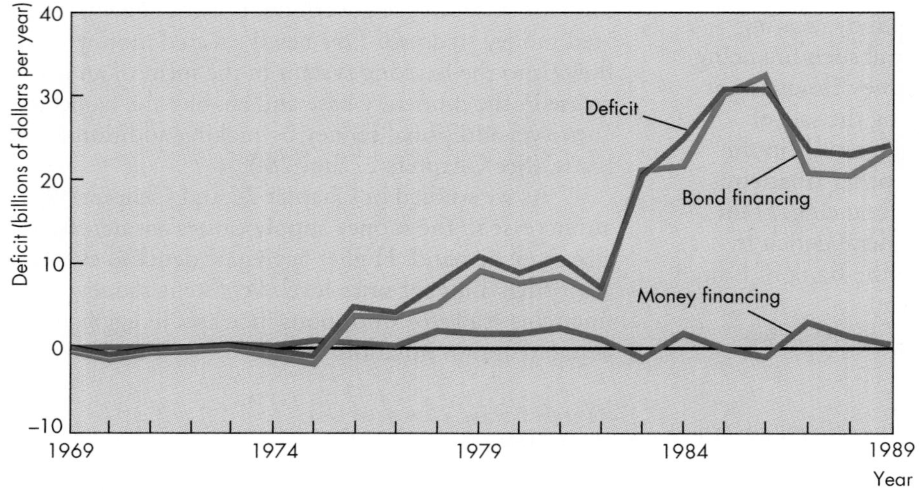

As the federal deficit has mushroomed through the 1970s and 1980s, so also has the financing of that deficit by issuing debt. The use of money financing has been kept under tight control and in some years, such as 1983 and 1986, the amount of debt issued even exceeded the deficit.

Source: Fig. 35.1 and *Bank of Canada Review*, CANSIM series B201.

people to whom the government wants to sell bonds fully realize that with an ongoing deficit financed by bond sales, the government's borrowing will have to increase to cover the additional interest payments arising from the growing federal government debt. They will also reason that at some point, the amount of government debt will have grown so large that the interest burden on it will be larger than the government is willing to pay. At that point, they continue to reason, the government will do what it can do here and now — cover its deficit by money financing. But the key difference is that to cover the deficit by money financing requires only that the deficit, excluding debt interest, be money financed. The longer the government attempts to cover its deficit by debt financing, the larger is the deficit (the original deficit plus the additional interest burden) that will ultimately have to be paid for by creating money.

Thus, people continue to reason, at some future time the federal government will resort to creating money and there will be rapid inflation. At that time, the government bonds that are being bought today will lose value at a rate so rapid as to make them almost worthless. Hence, if government bonds are going to be bought today, the interest rate on them must be sufficient to compensate for the anticipated future loss in their value resulting from the inflation that will eventually arise. And, in anticipation of a fall in the value of money, people will reduce the amount of money that they plan to hold here and now. This reduction in the demand for money will lead to an increase in the demand for goods and so to rising prices.

This argument was first advanced by Thomas Sargent, of the Hoover Institution at Stanford University, and Neil Wallace, of the University of Minnesota. They called their calculations "unpleasant monetarist arithmetic." It is unpleasant arithmetic because deferring the date at which a deficit is financed by money creation worsens the inflation that will ensue. It is unpleasant *monetarist* arithmetic because it constitutes a direct attack on the central proposition of monetarism — that inflation is caused by the growth rate of the money supply. If the money supply growth rate is contained, inflation will not erupt. The unpleasant monetarist arithmetic calculations point out that the deficit must be small enough to provide confidence in the ability and willingness of the government and the central bank to continue to keep money supply growth in line with growth in the economy's capacity to produce goods and services. A deficit that is too large to reinforce that expectation will be inflationary.

But for the deficit to be the problem that Sargent and Wallace say it is, it must be a truly persistent phenomenon. A deficit that is large and lasts even for a decade does not inevitably have to produce inflation. If there are widely held expectations that the deficit is going to be brought under control at some reasonably near future date, then the unpleasant arithmetic, although correct, is not relevant.

We have now reviewed the relationship between deficits and inflation. Deficits are not inevitably inflationary. But the larger the deficit and the longer it persists, the greater the pressure and the temptation to cover the deficit by creating money, thereby generating inflation.

Another common view about the deficit is that it places a burden on future generations. Let's now examine that view.

A Burden on Future Generations?

A common and popular cry is "We owe it to our children to control the deficit." Is this view correct? How will a deficit burden future generations?

We've already examined one way in which the deficit might leave a burden on future generations — the burden of inflation. But when people talk about the deficit as a burden on future generations, they usually mean something other than inflation.

For example, somebody has to pay the interest on the huge federal government debt that the deficit creates. The government will pay the interest with money it takes from the people as taxes. Taxes will have to be raised. Won't those taxes burden future generations?

Wait, though. Don't the people who pay the taxes also receive the interest? If so, how can the deficit be a burden to future generations? It might be a burden to some members of the future generation, but it must be a benefit to others, so in the aggregate it evens out.

Although in the aggregate the interest paid equals the taxes collected, there may be important redistribution effects. For example, one feature of our present deficit is that some government debt is being bought not by Canadians but by European and Japanese investors. So part of the future burden of the current deficit is that future Canadian taxpayers will have to provide the resources with which to pay interest to foreign holders of Canadian government debt.

Also, today's deficit can make people poorer tomorrow by slowing today's pace of investment and reducing the stock of productive capital equipment available for future generations. This phenomenon is called crowding out.

Crowding Out

Crowding out is the tendency for an increase in government purchases of goods and services to bring a decrease in investment (see Chapter 30). If crowding out occurs, and if government purchases of goods and services are financed by government debt, the result is that the economy has a larger stock of government debt and a smaller stock of real capital. Unproductive government debt replaces productive real capital.

Whether or not crowding out actually occurs is a controversial issue. Let's see why it might be important. In order for crowding out to occur, a deficit has to result in lower investment, so that future generations have a smaller real capital stock than they otherwise would have had. This drop in investment will lower their income and, in a sense, be a burden to them. (They will still be richer than we are but not as rich as they would have been if they had a larger stock of productive machines.) Let's examine how the deficit might be a burden to future generations as a result of lowering investment today.

As we studied in Chapter 25, the scale of investment depends on its opportunity cost. That opportunity cost is the real interest rate. Other things being equal, the higher the real interest rate, the less firms will want to invest in new plant and equipment. For a government deficit to crowd out investment, it must cause interest rates to rise. Some people believe that a deficit does increase interest rates because the government's own borrowing represents an increase in the demand for loans with no corresponding increase in the supply of loans. Figure 35.8 shows what happens in this case. Part (a) shows the demand and supply curves for loans. Initially, the demand for loans is D_0 and the supply of loans is S_0. The real interest rate is 3 percent, and the quantity of loans

Figure 35.8 The Deficit, Borrowing, and Crowding Out

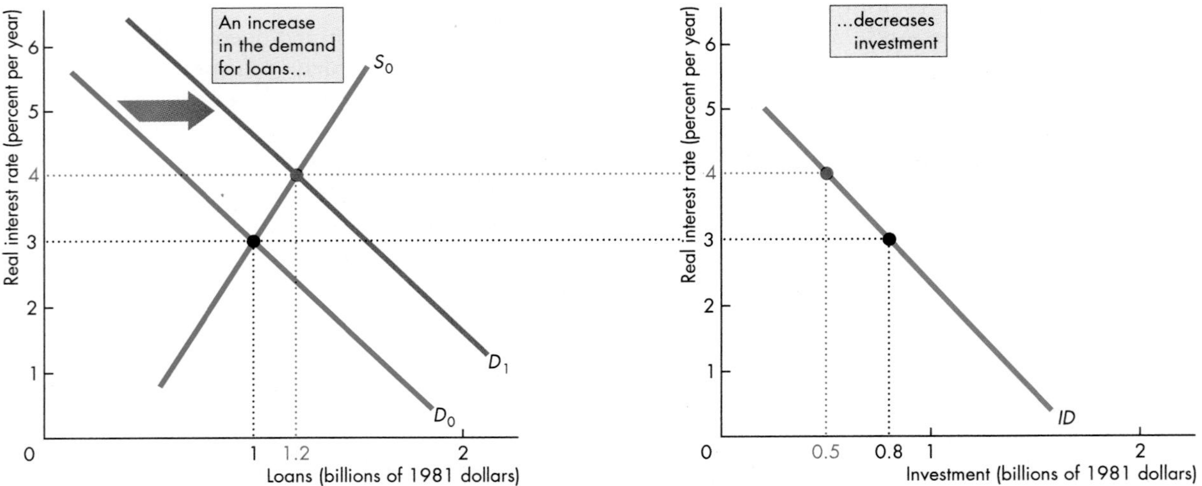

(a) The market for loans **(b) Investment**

Part (a) shows the market for loans. The demand for loans is D_0 and the supply is S_0 The quantity of loans outstanding is $1 billion and the real interest rate is 3 percent. Part (b) shows the determination of investment. At an interest rate of 3 percent, investment is $0.8 billion. The government runs a deficit and finances the deficit by borrowing. The government's increase in demand for loans shifts the demand curve to D_1. The interest rate rises to 4 percent and the equilibrium quantity of loans increases to $1.2 billion. The higher interest rate leads to a decrease in investment in part (b). The government deficit crowds out capital accumulation.

outstanding is \$1 billion. Part (b) shows investment. At a real interest rate of 3 percent, investment is \$0.8 billion.

Now suppose that the government runs a deficit. To finance its deficit, the government borrows. There is an increase in the demand for loans. The demand curve for loans shifts from D_0 to D_1. There is no change in the supply of loans, so the real interest rate increases to 4 percent and the quantity of loans increases to \$1.2 billion. Notice that the increase in loans that occurs in equilibrium is smaller than the increase in the demand for loans. That is, the demand curve shifts to the right by an amount larger than the increase in loans that actually occurs. The higher interest rate brings a decrease in investment and a lower capital stock. Thus the increased stock of government debt crowds out some productive capital.

Does a deficit make real interest rates rise as shown in Fig. 35.8? Many economists believe so, and they have some strong evidence to point to. Real interest rates in Canada in the 1980s — precisely the years in which we had a large real deficit — were higher than at any time in history. Furthermore, there is a general tendency for real interest rates and the real deficit to fluctuate in sympathy with each other.

It is this relationship in the data that leads some economists to predict that a higher real deficit means higher real interest rates, lower investment, and a smaller scale of capital accumulation. Because of the effects on real interest rates, the real deficit and the accumulation of paper debt crowds out the accumulation of productive physical capital. As a consequence, future output will be lower than it otherwise would have been, so the deficit burdens future generations.

Ricardian Equivalence

Some economists do not believe that deficits crowd out capital accumulation. On the contrary, they argue, debt financing and paying for government spending with taxes are equivalent. The level of purchases of goods and services matters, but not the way in which it is financed.

This idea is known as Ricardian equivalence after the first economist to advance it, the great English economist David Ricardo (see Our Advancing Knowledge, pp. 958-959). Recently, Ricardo's idea has been given a forceful restatement by Robert Barro of Harvard University. Barro argues as follows: if the government increases its purchases of goods and services but does not increase taxes, people are smart enough to recognize that higher taxes are going to have to be paid later to cover the higher spending and interest payments on the debt that is being issued today. In recognition of having to pay higher taxes later, people will cut their consumption now, increasing their saving so as to ensure that when the government finally levies higher taxes, they will have accumulated sufficient wealth to meet those tax liabilities without a further cut in consumption. The scale of increased saving matches the scale of increased government spending.

Figure 35.9 illustrates this case. Initially the demand for loans is D_0 and the supply of loans S_0. The real interest rate is 3 percent and the quantity of loans outstanding is \$1 billion. The government runs a deficit and finances that deficit by borrowing. The demand curve for loans shifts to the right to D_1. At the same time, according to the reasoning of Ricardo and Barro, there is a cut in consumption and an increase in the supply of loans. The supply curve shifts to the right to S_1. The quantity of loans increases from \$1 to \$1.3 billion and the real interest rate stays constant at 3 percent. With no change in the real interest rate, there is no crowding out of investment.

Figure 35.9 Ricardian Equivalence

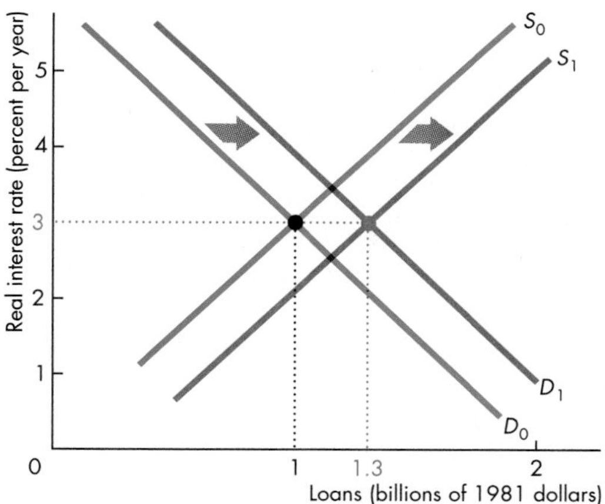

Initially, the demand for loans is D_0 and the supply of loans is S_0. The equilibrium quantity of loans is \$1 billion and the real interest rate is 3 percent. An increase in the government deficit, financed by borrowing, increases the demand for loans and shifts the demand curve to D_1. Households, recognizing that the increased government deficit will bring increased future taxes to pay the additional interest charges, cut their consumption and increase their saving. The supply curve of loans also shifts to the right to S_1. The equilibrium quantity of loans increases to \$1.3 billion, but the real interest rate stays constant at 3 percent. There is no crowding out of investment.

Some economists argue that Ricardian equivalence breaks down because people take into account only future tax liabilities that will be borne by themselves, and not those to be borne by their children and their grandchildren. Proponents of the Ricardian equivalence proposition argue that it makes no difference whether future tax liabilities are going to be borne by people currently alive or by their descendants. If the taxes are going to be borne by future generations, the current generation takes account of those future taxes and adjusts its own consumption so that it can make bequests on a scale large enough to enable those taxes to be paid.

Setting out the assumptions necessary for Ricardian equivalence leaves most economists convinced that the proposition cannot be empirically relevant. Yet there is a perhaps surprising amount of evidence in its support. In order to interpret the evidence, it is important to be clear that Ricardian equivalence does *not* imply that real interest rates are not affected by the level of government purchases of goods and services. A higher level of government purchases, other things being equal, brings a higher real interest rate. The Ricardian equivalence proposition implies only that real interest rates are not affected by the way in which a given level of government purchases is financed. Regardless of whether it is financed by taxes or by borrowing, real interest rates will be the same.

Whether the deficit does affect real interest rates remains unclear. If people do take into account future tax burdens (and not just their own but their children's and grandchildren's), then saving will respond to offset the deficit and the deficit itself will have little or no effect on real interest rates and capital accumulation. If people ignore the implications of the deficit for their own and their descendants' future consumption possibilities, the deficit will indeed increase real interest rates. The jury remains out on this question.

The Future of the Deficit

The future of the deficit depends on what happens to government expenditure and revenue. There are two basic ways of eliminating a deficit:

- Reducing expenditure
- Increasing revenue

Reducing Expenditure

Throughout modern history, government expenditure has tended to increase not only in total but as a percentage of GDP. The government of Canada has done better than most governments to contain the growth of its expenditure. In some European countries, governments spend close to 50 percent of GDP. At its peak, that figure increased to more than 53 percent in the Netherlands in 1983.

Many components of government expenditure have a built-in tendency to increase. Two such components are education and health care. People with high incomes spend a larger fraction of income on these items than do those with low incomes. If the government plays a significant role in the provision of these two goods, it is inevitable that government purchases and transfer payments, expressed as a percentage of GDP, will gradually rise. Only by removing certain responsibilities from the domain of government can the government's share of GDP be effectively contained. Thus in many European countries the government is getting out of a wide variety of activities involving the provision of services. In Britain, for example, the Thatcher government is even trying to get out of the health care business or at least to limit its involvement in that sector. There is less scope for such privatization in Canada, for we have not taken the route of the Europeans in this regard.

Thus there is little scope for significant cuts in government expenditure as long as we maintain our obligations under programs such as social insurance, education, welfare, and health maintenance for the poor and the elderly.

It is because of the difficulty of making significant inroads into government spending that many take the view that the only way to eliminate the deficit is to increase government revenue. Let's examine that option.

Increasing Revenue

Two approaches to increasing revenue have been proposed:

- Increase tax rates.
- Decrease tax rates.

Does that sound paradoxical? Not really, when you remember that what the government wants to do is to increase its tax *revenue*. **Tax revenue** is the product of the tax rate and the tax base. A **tax rate** is the percentage rate of tax levied on a particular activity.

The **tax base** is the activity on which a tax is levied. For example, the tax base for personal income tax is total income minus some specified allowances. The federal income tax rates for 1989 were 17, 26, and 29 percent (depending on income level).

There is ambiguity and disagreement about whether an increase in tax rates increases or decreases tax revenues. The source of the disagreement is something called the Laffer curve. The **Laffer curve**, named after Arthur Laffer, who first proposed it, is a curve that relates tax revenue to the tax rate. Figure 35.10 illustrates a hypothetical Laffer curve. The tax rate ranges between 0 and 100 percent on the vertical axis. Tax revenue, measured in billions of dollars, is shown on the horizontal axis. If the tax rate is zero, then no taxes are raised. That is why the curve begins at the origin. As the tax rate increases, tax revenue also increases but only up to some maximum — *m* in the figure. In this example, once the tax rate has reached 40 percent, the tax revenue is at its maximum. If the tax rate increases above 40 percent, tax revenue falls. Why does this happen?

Revenue falls because there is a fall in the scale of the activity that is being taxed. Suppose that the item in question is gasoline. With no tax, lots of people drive gas-guzzling cars and consume billions of litres a week. If gasoline is taxed, its price increases and the quantity bought declines. At first, the quantity bought falls by a smaller percentage than the percentage increase in tax, and the tax revenue rises. But there comes a point at which the fall in the quantity demanded rises by a bigger percentage than the rise in tax. At that point, tax revenue begins to decline. People sell their gas-guzzlers, buy smaller cars, join car pools, and use public transport. The tax rate goes up, but the tax base goes down and tax revenue declines.

You can now see that whether a cut in the *tax rate* increases or decreases *tax revenue* depends on where we are on the Laffer curve. If we're at a point such as *a* in Fig. 35.10, a decrease in the tax rate results in an increase in tax revenue. But if we're at point *b*, a decrease in the tax rate results in a decrease in tax revenue. To increase tax revenue from point *b*, we have to increase the tax rate.

Economists and other observers argue about where we are on the Laffer curve for each of the various taxes. Some people suspect that for the very highly taxed commodities, such as gasoline, tobacco products, and alcohol, we are on the backward-bending part of the Laffer curve, so that an increase in the tax rate would decrease tax revenue. But hardly anyone believes this to be the case for the big revenue-raising taxes, such as personal income taxes and sales taxes. It is much more likely, in the case of those taxes, that an increase in tax rates would increase tax revenue.

Figure 35.10 The Laffer Curve

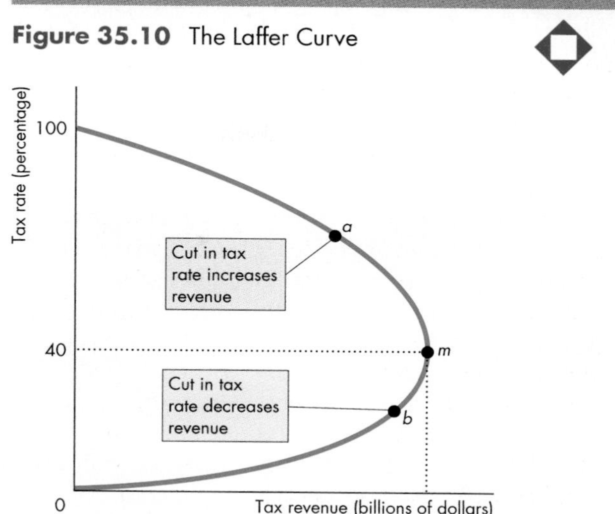

The Laffer curve shows the relationship between a tax rate and tax revenue. If the tax rate is 0 percent, the government collects no tax revenue. As the tax rate increases, the government's tax revenue also increases, but up to some maximum (*m*). As the tax rate continues to increase, tax revenue declines. At a tax rate of 100 percent, the government collects no revenue. Higher taxes act as a disincentive. The more heavily taxed an activity, the less that activity is undertaken. When the percentage decrease in the activity is less than the percentage increase in the tax rate, we are at a point such as *b* and tax revenue rises. When the percentage decrease in the activity exceeds the percentage increase in the tax rate, we are at a point such as *a* and tax revenue decreases.

The second approach to increasing revenue is to reform taxes, lowering high marginal tax rates and perhaps introducing new taxes at low rates on activities not previously taxed. The GST is an example of such a change in the tax structure. By replacing the manufacturer's sales tax, a tax on a limited range of manufactured goods at a high rate, by the goods and services tax, a tax on almost all goods and services at a lower rate, the government aims to bring in a similar amount of total tax revenue while imposing a smaller overall tax burden and distortion on the economy. Once such a new tax is in place, however, the temptation to use it as a source of additional revenue by increasing its rate will be strong.

David Ricardo and the Deficit

David Ricardo

The economic landscape of England at the end of the eighteenth century was an exciting and rapidly changing one. Britain had left the gold standard in 1797, and by 1799, the price of gold was rising rapidly; equivalently, the value of paper money was falling rapidly. That same year, a 27-year-old stockbroker, on a weekend visit to Bath, happened upon a copy of *The Wealth of Nations* (see Our Advancing Knowledge, pp. 20-21), a book of which he was to become "a great admirer." The young man in question was David Ricardo (1772-1832), possibly the greatest economist of his time.

Born in London in 1772 into a devout Jewish family, Ricardo began his career at the age of 14, working for his father, a wealthy stockbroker. At 21, Ricardo displeased his father in the extreme by marrying a Quaker and was banished from the family business and disinherited. Continuing to work on his own as a stockbroker, Ricardo demonstrated real brilliance, amassing a fortune of £775,000—equivalent to $46 million in today's money.

Ricardo made important contributions to a host of economic problems and issues, ranging from the value of money to the theory of value, exchange, and international trade, and laid the foundations of modern public finance theory. His most significant work was *On the Principles of Political Economy*, published in 1817. Despite being a practical man, this book and much of his other writing, dealt with abstract and difficult matters of theory—matters that remain controversial even today among historians of economic thought.

Theoretical though it is, much of Ricardo's work has practical consequences. His contribution that has the most relevance for us today is that on public debt and on what has come to be called Ricardian equivalence. The idea of Ricardian equivalence was set out in a brief paper titled "Funding System" that was first published in the relatively obscure *Supplement to the Fourth, Fifth, and Sixth Editions of the Encyclopaedia Britannica.*

Ricardo's interest in public debt and government deficits was sparked by the enormous deficit incurred by Great Britain during the Napoleonic Wars which ended in 1815. At its peak, in 1815, the British government's budget deficit was £35 million, almost one-half its annual revenue from taxes. Thus it was in the context of a discussion of the appropriate way in which to finance a war that Ricardo offered his thoughts on debt and taxes. Although the words he used are open to several interpretations, Ricardo is usually held to have asserted that if people take full account of the future tax burden that will have to be imposed in order to pay the interest on public debt, then financing government purchases with current taxes is equivalent to financing it with debt and paying interest on that debt in perpetuity. But Ricardo also expressed a belief that people do not in fact make such rational calculations when making decisions on whether to consume or save.[1] As a consequence, tax financing of government expenditure leads to lower private consumption and lower interest rates than does debt financing.

Interest in Ricardo's work was revived in the middle 1970s by Robert Barro[2] (then at the University of Chicago and now at Harvard University). Using a model economy in which each generation takes account of the effects of its own actions on the consumption possibilities of the succeeding generation, Barro showed some of the conditions under which Ricardo's equivalence theorem holds. But, as Barro pointed out, almost every other model in use at that time assumed that debt and taxes were not equivalent.

The issue of Ricardian equivalence took on an extremely practical note when, during the early 1980s in the face of an already large deficit, U.S. President Ronald Reagan proposed cutting taxes. Some economists claimed that Ricardian equivalence was a valid description of the American economy and that a tax cut that increased the deficit would have no adverse effects. Interest rates would *not* increase and private saving would increase to finance the increased amount of government debt outstanding. Others (the majority) claimed that Ricardian equivalence was an abstract idea of little or no practical relevance and that a tax cut would stimulate aggregate demand, resulting in a deficit that would create a debt that would be a burden on future generations. In the majority, and among Barro's most vocal critics were Martin Feldstein, Chairman of President Reagan's Council of Economic Advisers, and Nobel Laureate James Buchanan (see Our Advancing Knowledge, pp. 516-517).

A whole series of studies of the issue, undertaken during the 1980s, failed to come to a decisive conclusion, although one of the most recent of these studies, by Paul Evans[3] of Ohio State University, suggests that U.S. consumers are indeed Ricardian — that Ricardian equivalence is a "reasonable approximation." But the issue has not been settled.

---

[1] Gerald P. O'Driscoll, Jr., "The Ricardian Nonequivalence Theorem," *Journal of Political Economy* 85 (1977): 207-10.

[2] Robert J. Barro, "Are Government Bonds Net Worth?" *Journal of Political Economy* 82, 6 (1974): 1095-117.

[3] Paul Evans, "Are Consumers Ricardian? Evidence for the United States," *Journal of Political Economy* 96, 5 (1988): 983-1004.

The search for changes in taxes that will bring higher tax revenue is a permanent feature of our economic life and will always be with us, regardless of whether or not there is a deficit. But in a deficit situation, that search takes on a much greater urgency.

■ We have now completed our study of macroeconomics and of the challenges and problems of stabilizing the economy. In this study, our main focus has been the economy of Canada. We have taken into account the linkages between Canada and the rest of the world, but international economic relations have not been our main concern. In the remaining chapters we are going to shift our focus and study some vital international issues. First, in Chapter 36, we examine the international exchange of goods and services. Second, in Chapter 37, we study the financing of international trade and the determination of our balance of payments. Third, in Chapter 38, we turn our attention to the problems of the developing countries of the Third World. Finally, in Chapter 39, we examine economic systems different from our own, such as those employed in the Soviet Union and China, and look at the momentous events taking place in Eastern Europe.

SUMMARY

The Sources of the Deficit

Until 1975, the federal government collected in taxes about the same amount as it spent. Then, in 1975, there was a sharp increase in transfer payments and a decrease in tax revenue, and a deficit emerged. The event that transformed the government's budget was the energy crisis of the mid-1970s. A large increase in world energy prices led the government of Canada to cut taxes on energy and increase subsidies to energy-dependent sectors. The deficit was worsened by decreases in income tax revenues resulting from the indexation of personal taxes in the 1970s and by a surge in transfer payments (mainly unemployment insurance payments) in the early 1980s. The deficit increased the federal government debt and resulted in increased interest payments that further fed the deficit.

The deficit fluctuates in sympathy with the business cycle. When the economy is in a recovery, taxes increase and transfer payments decrease as a percentage of GDP. The deficit declines. When the economy goes into recession, taxes decrease and transfer payments increase as a percentage of GDP, and so the deficit increases.

Even taking account of the effects of the cycle on the deficit, the federal government deficit is still large. That is, the deficit is large despite the fact that the economy had a long, strong recovery. It is this fact that makes the current deficit a serious problem. (pp. 943-948)

The Real Deficit

Inflation distorts the deficit by overstating the real interest burden carried by the government. Adjusting the deficit for this fact measures the real deficit. It reveals that the real deficit became a persistent problem only in 1981. The cycles in the deficit remain the same, whether measured in real or current dollar terms. (pp. 948-951)

Deficits and Inflation

If deficits are money financed, they cause inflation. If they are debt financed, whether they cause inflation or not depends on how permanent they are. A temporary debt-financed deficit has no inflationary effects. A permanent debt-financed deficit leads to inflation. It does so because the buildup of debt leads to a buildup of interest payments and a yet higher deficit. At some future date, the deficit will be money financed; the longer the deficit persists and the more debt the government issues, the larger is the amount of money that it will create at that time. Fear of future inflation leads to a demand here and now for less government debt and less money. As a consequence, interest rates and inflation increase in anticipation of a future (perhaps a distant future) increase in money creation to finance the deficit. (pp. 951-953)

A Burden on Future Generations?

Whether the deficit is a burden on future generations is a controversial issue. Some economists believe that the deficit causes real interest rates to rise, thereby lowering investment and the amount of capital that we accumulate. As a consequence, future output will be lower than it otherwise would have been and future generations will be burdened with the effects of the deficit.

Other economists argue that government expenditure affects interest rates but the way in which that expenditure is financed does not. They suggest that if government spending is financed by borrowing, people will recognize that future taxes will have to increase to cover both the spending and the interest payments on the accumulated debt. In anticipation of those higher future taxes, saving will increase and consumption will decrease in the present. Thus the burden of increased government expenditure — not the burden of the deficit — is spread across all generations. (pp. 953-956)

The Future of the Deficit

The future of the deficit depends on the future of government expenditure and taxes. Decreasing expenditure would be difficult and is unlikely to occur. Increasing revenue could result from either increasing tax rates (if we are on the upward-sloping part of the Laffer curve) or decreasing tax rates (if we are on the backward-bending part of the Laffer curve). If the deficit is to be eliminated, it is likely to result from increased tax rates. (pp. 956-960)

KEY ELEMENTS

Key Terms

Balanced budget, 943
Budget surplus or budget deficit, 943
Debt financing, 951
Federal government debt, 943
Laffer curve, 957
Money financing, 951
Real deficit, 948
Tax base, 957
Tax rate, 956
Tax revenue, 956

Key Figures 

Figure 35.1 Revenue, Expenditure, and the Deficit, 943
Figure 35.5 Unemployment and the Federal Deficit, 948
Figure 35.6 The Real Deficit and the Nominal Deficit, 950
Figure 35.10 The Laffer Curve, 957

REVIEW QUESTIONS

1 What were the main changes in taxes and government spending associated with the emergence of the federal government deficit?

2 Starting in 1980, trace the events that resulted in a continued increase in the federal government's deficit.

3 Distinguish between the real deficit and the nominal deficit.

4 In calculating the real deficit, which of the following would you do:

a) Value the interest payments in real terms and take into account the change in the real value of government debt?

b) Calculate the interest payments in nominal terms and take into account the change in the real value of government debt?

c) Calculate the interest payments in real terms but ignore the change in the real value of outstanding government debt?

5 Explain how using debt financing to cover a deficit results in mushrooming interest payments.

6 Explain how, in a modern financial system such as Canada's, the government finances its deficit by creating money.

7 Review the ways in which the deficit could be a burden on future generations.

8 Why do some economists argue that taxes and government debt are equivalent to each other so that the deficit does not matter?

9 Why do some economists think that government revenue can be increased by cutting tax rates?

PROBLEMS

1 You are given the following information about an economy. When unemployment is at its natural rate (5 ½ percent) government spending and taxes are each 20 percent of GDP. There is no inflation. For each 1 percentage point increase in the unemployment rate, government spending increases by 1 percentage point of GDP and taxes fall by 1 percentage point of GDP. Suppose that the economy experiences a cycle in which the unemployment rate takes the following values:

Year	Unemployment rate
1	5
2	6
3	7
4	6
5	5
6	4
7	5

a) Calculate the actual deficit (as a percentage of GDP) for each year.

b) Is the actual deficit related to the business cycle?

2 Government expenditure, excluding debt interest, in an economy is $8.5 billion. Revenue is $10 billion. The government debt is $25 billion. Interest rates are 24 percent a year and there is a 20 percent inflation rate. Calculate the following:

a) The debt interest that the government pays

b) The government's budget surplus or deficit

c) The value of government debt at the end of the year

d) The government's real deficit

e) The real value of the government debt at the end of the year

3 In Lafferland, the only tax is one on labour income. The wage rate (before-tax wage rate) is $10 an hour. The quantity of labour employed depends on the tax rate: the higher the tax rate, the smaller the quantity of labour employed. The following schedule sets out this relationship:

Tax rate (percent)	Quantity of labour employed
0	5,000
10	4,500
20	4,000
30	3,500
40	3,000
50	2,500
60	2,000
70	1,500
80	1,000
90	500
100	0

a) Find the Laffer curve for this economy and draw a graph of it.

b) At what tax rate is tax revenue maximized?

c) What is the maximum amount of tax revenue that the government of Lafferland can raise with its tax on labour income?

d) If the tax rate was 70 percent and the government wanted to increase tax revenue, would it increase or decrease the tax rate?

e) If the tax rate was 30 percent and the government wanted to increase tax revenue, would it increase or decrease the tax rate?

4 Ricardiana is a country whose citizens care as much about the economic wellbeing of their children as they do about their own. The government of Ricardiana increases taxes, decreases borrowing, and keeps its level of purchases of goods and services constant. What happens to interest rates, saving, and investment in Ricardiana?

PART 13

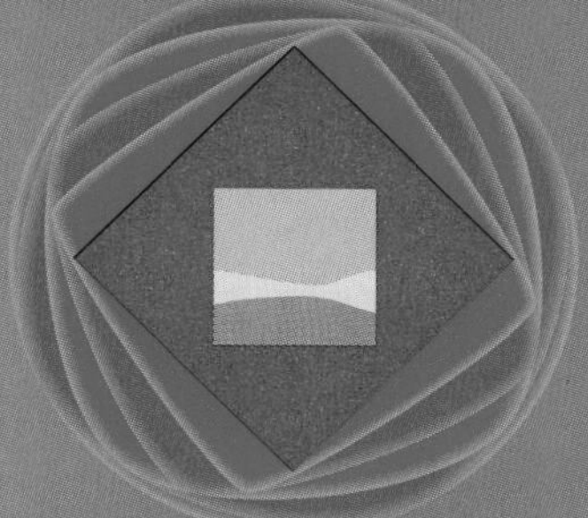

The World Economy

TALKING WITH JUDITH MAXWELL

Judith Maxwell earned her BComm from Dalhousie University and then went to the London School of Economics for graduate work. She has had a distinguished career as a journalist (for the *Financial Times of Canada*), a researcher, and a director of research. Since 1985, she has chaired the Economic Council of Canada. Michael Parkin talked with Judith Maxwell about her career and the economic challenges confronting Canada in the global economy of the 1990s.

"Women have a lot to bring to economics . . . it's surprising that more of them are not drawn to the subject."

Mrs Maxwell, when did you decide to become an economist?

When I went to university, I didn't want to take science because that meant standing up in labs all day, and I didn't want to take arts because that meant writing too many essays. So I took a BComm. The fact that economics was part of that degree was an accident. But I got very engaged with the subject. Then I kept on learning as a journalist. Having to write every week about, say, why the unemployment rate had gone up or the inflation rate wouldn't move meant that I learned from the real world almost as much economics as I had from a textbook.

Why don't more women work as economists?

I don't know. Women have a lot to bring to economics. Given their interest in the other social sciences, it's surprising that more of them are not drawn to the subject. Actually, there are quite a few women—Caroline Pestieau, Wendy Dobson, Maureen Farrow, Gail Cook, and Sylvia Ostry—in the forefront of public policy debates on economics. But there are too few women behind them. It's not the usual pyramid.

What excites you about economics?

For me economics is about the well-being of real people. I always feel most comfortable when I connect economic analysis to policy decisions that influence the distribution of income or the quality of life of real individuals.

How do you see the world economy of the 1990s and Canada's place in it?

What's emerging are three big trading areas: North America, the Pacific Rim, and Europe. Canada fits into this global economy as a highly developed but slow-growing, middle-sized power that's going to have to adapt to competition of new types and from new sources. It's going to be a testing but exciting decade for Canadians.

What's your assessment of the first year of the operation of the Canada-United States Free Trade Agreement?

The Council's projection was that free trade would bring a small but significant increase in living standards for Canadians. But it's hard to figure out what's been going on in the past year because we've had not only the new trading structure but also a high exchange rate, high interest rates, and a high degree of capacity utilization. There is no question that a lot of new investment and restructuring is going on. We just don't know how much of it can be attributed to the free trade agreement.

What are the implications for Canada of a trade agreement between the United States and Mexico? Should Canada be a player in the discussions?

Canada and the United States together will be neither the largest nor the most diversified of the three big trading areas. So they should certainly be looking at Latin America for a wider trading area in this hemispere. But building a formal trade area with such diverse countries is no easy matter. The Canada-United States trade agreement is a consolidation of a relationship that evolved over 50 years. In the case of Mexico I suspect that what we're talking about is the gradual construction of a more intimate relationship among the three countries. I don't think Canada should leave that purely to the United States. There are all kinds of potential Canada-Mexico linkages. So I think we should be a player, either on our own or in conjunction with the U.S.-Mexico discussions.

What about the rest of this hemisphere?

Think of what would happen if Brazil or Mexico takes off. Both were looking very promising in the 1970s. Debt burdens held them back through the 1980s, but they have tremendous potential. Mexico has been getting its house in order, and Brazil recently took some important initiatives that could make a big difference to its capacity to grow internally and play internationally.

What are the implications for Canada of Europe's 1992 economic unification?

Production systems in Europe are being integrated through a tremendous wave of merger and acquisition activity. Larger companies are being organized, and cross-border alliances are being forged. To compete, Canadians are going to need production facilities inside Europe in many industries. The process of integration will make a faster-growing market, creating more opportunities for Canadians. But the Europeans will end up with a lot of stronger companies. As they reach out to compete inside the North American market, there may be stronger competition in certain areas.

What about developments in Eastern Europe?

What's interesting is whether the deepening of the European common market through the 1992 process is compatible with the broadening of the market, which is where the Eastern European countries come in. Some people argue that the opening of Eastern Europe will accelerate integration in Western Europe. But others argue that the process of unifying Germany and building links between Western and Eastern Europe will be a distraction that's destabilizing for Europe in the short run. The European economy is relatively fully utilized, so shifting resources into Eastern Europe will mean that something has to be given up. Whether that's going to be managed in a way that is not inflationary and not destabilizing to European currency arrangements is an open question.

How will these developments affect Canada?

The first impact, which appears to be unavoidable, is that world demand for savings will increase, and therefore, world interest rates will be higher in the 1990s than they would otherwise have been. As a debtor country, Canada will therefore face higher debt service costs. Another impact will be a sort of

"All the countries of Eastern Europe have to modernize their telephone systems . . . There are great opportunities there."

"Get a really solid degree in economics, and make sure you have strong computer and writing skills."

trade creation effect on specific markets. For example, all the countries of Eastern Europe have to modernize their telephone systems. Canada has a very well-developed communications system, and one of our most successful exporting companies is Northern Telecom. There are great opportunities there. But also there's potential trade diversion effects. The Soviet Union exports grain, oil, and natural gas, which are two of our key products, and so its entry into the world market may well be unfavourable for Canada.

Let's turn to the Pacific. Postwar Japan has been amazingly successful. What lessons does it offer us?

Canada cannot transplant Japanese institutions, but we should try to develop Japan's capacity for consensus and its social cohesion. These areas have been our stumbling blocks for decades. Given the frictions that we now see on the federal-provincial front and that are emerging in management-labour relationships, during the 1990s we have to try to build stronger institutions in Canada for the resolution of conflicts and for reaching consensus before conflicts emerge.

You've had a very distinguished career, doing economics and communicating it to the general public and to policymakers. Many students would love to pursue such a career. What advice can you give?

Get a really solid degree in economics, and make sure you have strong computer and writing skills. The best way to hone all these skills is to work in economics with researchers or other users of economics. When you are applying for jobs later, you should be able to demonstrate that you've used economics in a project situation, either during your summers or in a couple of selected areas immediately after you finish your degree. I hope that we will generate more and more economists who have all the technical skills, which are important, but who also see economics as a means to understanding people and who understand that the end result is the quality of life and the well-being of individuals in society.

Unlike you, few people are good economics writers. Is there something a student can do to develop good writing skills, other than just practice?

Writing was an acquired skill for me. I got a job as a research assistant at a newspaper and gradually moved into writing. I kept getting stuff thrown back on me, all marked up. Eventually I got the hang of it. There's no substitute for deliberate effort. Take a course in how to structure your message. Also, let's face it: what makes a good writer is being a clear thinker.

CHAPTER 36

Trading with the World

After studying this chapter, you will be able to:

- Describe the trends and patterns in international trade.
- Explain comparative advantage.
- Explain why all countries can gain from international trade.
- Explain how prices adjust to bring about balanced trade.
- Explain how economies of scale and diversity of taste lead to gains from international trade.
- Explain why trade restrictions lower the volume of imports and exports, and lower our consumption possibilities.
- Explain why we have trade restrictions even though they lower our consumption possibilities.

Silk Routes and Rust Belts

SINCE ANCIENT TIMES, people have striven to expand their trading as far as technology allowed. The maritime nations of southern Europe, the Middle East, and north Africa had flourishing trades in the Mediterranean 5000 years ago. Roman coins have been found in the ruins of ancient Indian cities. Marco Polo opened up the silk route between Europe and China in the thirteenth century. Merchants of Venice imported goods from the entire known world in the fifteenth century. Adventurers such as Christopher Columbus paved the way for the beginnings of t rade between Europe and the Americas. Today, container ships laden with cars and machines and Boeing 747s stuffed with fresh fruit, New Zealand lamb, and French cheeses ply sea and air routes, carrying billions of dollars worth of goods and services. Why do people go to such great lengths to trade with those in other nations? What does the pattern of international trade look like today? And what have been the recent trends in international trade? ■ International trade obviously brings enormous benefits. It enables us to consume fresh tropical fruit that doesn't grow here, to use raw materials such as chromium that are not found here, to buy a wide range of manufactured goods such as cars, VCRs, TVs, and textiles that are available at lower prices from other countries. It also enables producers — workers and the firms that employ them — in export industries to earn more by expanding the markets for their products. ■ But international trade also has its costs. In recent years, a massive increase in the penetration of the Japanese, European, and Korean car industries into North America has brought about a severe contraction of our own car-producing sector. Jobs in Windsor, Detroit, and other car-producing cities have disappeared, creating what has come to be called the Rust Belt. Do the benefits of international trade make up for the cost of jobs displaced by foreign competition? Could we, as politicians often claim, improve our economy by restricting imports? ■ The rich countries of the European Community, Japan, and the United States import vast quantities of raw materials from Third World countries and from resource-rich developed countries such as Australia and Canada. To pay for these raw materials, the importing countries sell manufactured goods to the resource suppliers. Do resource suppliers become poorer when they sell their bauxite, coal, and copper to other countries and buy farm combines and commercial jets in return? ■ The wages earned by the workers in the textile and electronics factories of Singapore, Taiwan, and Hong Kong are incredibly low compared with wages in Canada. Obviously, these countries can make manufactured goods much more cheaply than we can. How can we possibly compete with countries that pay their workers a fraction of Canadian wages? Are there any industries, besides perhaps real estate development, where we have an advantage? ■ As every Canadian school child is taught, the centrepiece of Canadian economic policy from the very foundation of our nation has been the tariff — a tax on imported goods from abroad. Wide-ranging protective tariffs were introduced by Sir John A. Macdonald in his National Policy of 1879. Although Canada, along with other countries, has been a part of the long process of trade liberalization that has taken place since World War II, even today we remain a heavily protected nation. In 1988, Canada signed a free trade agreement with the United States. By the time this agreement comes into full force, towards the end of this decade, the barriers to international trade between Canada and the United States will virtually have been eliminated. What are the effects of trade restrictions? Does Canada need trade restrictions in order to be economically strong? Will the trade liberalization brought about by the Canada-United States Free Trade Agreement lead to Canada's ruin?

■ In this chapter, we're going to learn about international trade. We'll begin by looking at some facts about international trade, examining the patterns of imports and exports and trends in the main items that Canada buys from and sells to other countries. Then we will discover how *all* nations can gain by specializing in producing the goods and services at which they have an advantage compared with other countries and by exchanging some of their output with each other. We'll discover that all countries can compete, no matter how high their wages. We will also explain why countries restrict trade, despite the fact that international trade brings benefits to all. We'll discover who suffers and who benefits when international trade is restricted.

Patterns and Trends in International Trade

The goods and services we buy from people in other countries are called **imports**. The goods and services we sell to people in other countries are called **exports**. What are the most important things that we import and export? Most people would probably guess that a resource-rich nation such as Canada imports manufactured goods and exports raw materials. Although that is one feature of Canada's international trade, it is not its most prominent feature. The vast bulk of exports and imports is manufactured goods. We sell automobiles, earthmoving equipment, aircraft, and electronic equipment, as well as raw materials and lumber products. We also import and export a huge volume of services — such as travel and freight and shipping services. Let's take a closer look at Canada's international trade in a recent year.

Canada's International Trade

Figure 36.1 provides a quick overview of the main components of Canada's exports (part a) and imports (part b).

By far the biggest item in Canada's international trade is motor vehicles (including motor vehicle parts). Most of this trade crosses the border between Canada and the United States and is the result of an agreement, known as the Auto Pact, between the two countries. Automobiles and automobile parts are permitted to cross the border without any restriction; in return for this freedom of movement, automobile manufacturers agree to undertake a sizeable amount of their manufacturing in Canada. Our second biggest export is, perhaps predictably, the products of the forestry industry — lumber and other forestry products, including pulp and newsprint.

Motor vehicles are also our largest import. Other big import items are consumer goods, electronic equipment, machinery, and other equipment. But we also import a great deal of travel — Canadians travelling abroad buy the tourism services of other countries.

Trade in Services Perhaps you are wondering why we call travel an export and an import. After all, travel is not the same as moving goods across the border, as we do when we import or export a car. How do we

Figure 36.1 Canadian Exports and Imports

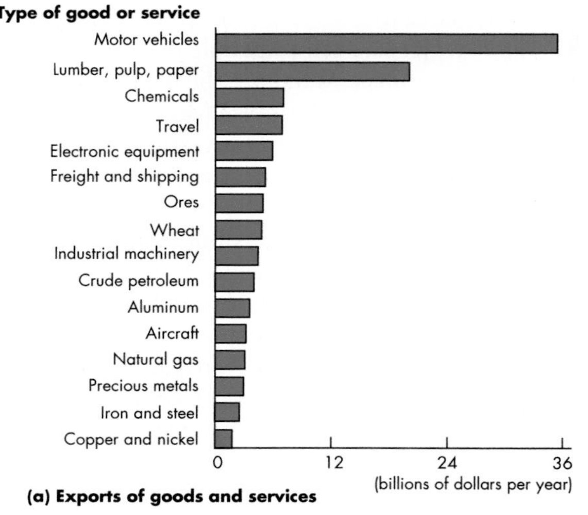

(a) Exports of goods and services

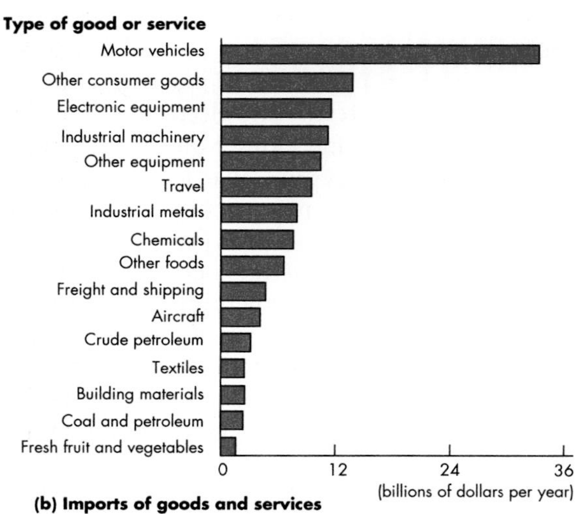

(b) Imports of goods and services

Canada exports and imports more motor vehicles and motor vehicle parts than any other individual category of goods or services. Lumber, pulp and paper, chemicals, and travel are also important exports, and consumer goods, electronic equipment, and industrial machinery and other equipment, as well as travel, are important imports.

Source: *Bank of Canada Review*, October 1989, Tables J6 and J7.

export and import travel and other services? Let's look at some examples.

Suppose that you decided to vacation in France, travelling there on an Air France flight from Toronto. What you buy from Air France is not a good but a transportation service. Although the concept may sound odd at first, in economic terms you are importing that service from France. Since you pay Canadian money to a French company in exchange for a service, it doesn't matter that most of your flight time is over the Atlantic Ocean. For that matter, the money you spend in France on hotel bills, restaurant meals, and other things is also classified as the import of services. Similarly, the vacation taken by a French student in Canada counts as an export of services from Canada to France.

When we import TV sets from South Korea, the owner of the ship that carries those TV sets may be Greek and the company that insures the cargo may be British. The payments that we make for the transportation and insurance to the Greek and British companies are also payments for the import of services. Similarly, when a Canadian shipping company transports newsprint to Tokyo, the transportation cost is an export of a service to Japan.

Geographical Patterns Canada has important trading links with almost every part of the world except Eastern Europe — which includes the Soviet giant — where trade is almost nonexistent. With the amazing developments that are taking place in the Soviet Union and the rest of Eastern Europe, this situation might very well change dramatically in the early 1990s. Nevertheless, at the end of the 1980s, there was little trade with the Eastern European bloc.

Figure 36.2 gives a quick overview of the geographical pattern of Canada's international trade. As you can see, the vast bulk of that trade takes place across the U.S. border. Our trade with the countries of the European Community (the most important members being the United Kingdom, France, West

Figure 36.2 The Geographical Pattern of Canada's International Trade

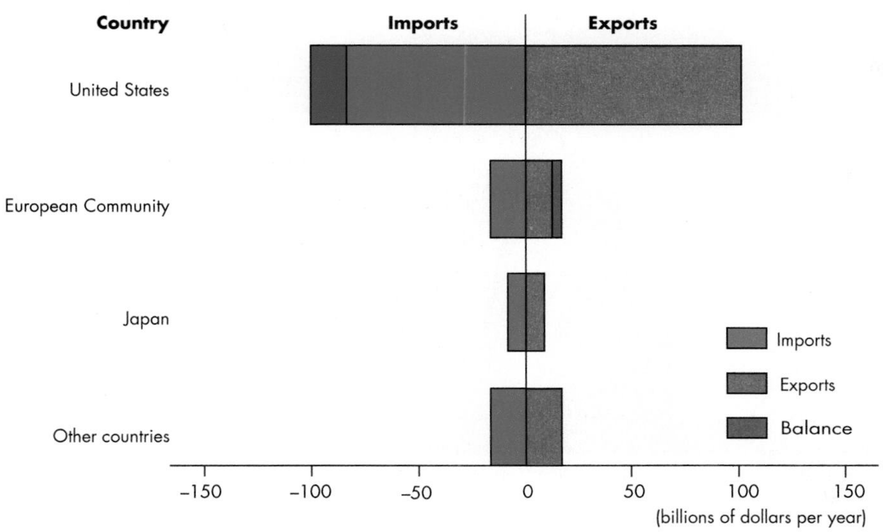

The vast bulk of Canada's international trade is with the United States. We have a net export surplus with the United States, a net export deficit with the European Community, and balanced trade with Japan and other countries.

Source: *Bank of Canada Review,* October 1989, Table J4.

Germany, and Italy) is tiny in comparison and that with Japan is even smaller.

Figure 36.2 not only shows the volume of our exports and imports. It also illustrates our balance of trade. The **balance of trade** is the value of exports minus the value of imports. If the balance is positive, then the value of exports exceeds the value of imports and Canada is a **net exporter**. If the balance is negative, the value of imports exceeds the value of exports and Canada is a **net importer**.

As you can see from Fig. 36.2, Canada exports more to the United States than it imports from that country. We are, therefore, a net exporter to the United States. Our balance of trade with the European Community is in the opposite direction. We are a net importer from that region. Our trade with Japan and other countries is almost exactly balanced.

Trends in the Balance of Trade International trade has become an increasingly important part of our economic life. We now both export and import much larger quantities of almost all goods and services than we did even a decade ago. There have also been important trends in the balance of our international trade. The balance of trade is shown in Fig. 36.3. As you can see, in the period between 1964 and 1989, that balance was usually positive — Canada was a net exporter — but there were four years in which we were a net importer. The years in which we were most heavily a net importer were those immediately following the huge increase in world oil prices in the mid-1970s. The increased cost of imported oil temporarily threw our balance of trade into a deficit in those years.

The Balance of Trade and International Borrowing

When people buy more than they sell, they have to finance the difference by borrowing. When they sell more than they buy, they can use the surplus to make loans to others. This simple principle, which governs the income and expenditure and borrowing and lending of individuals and firms, is also a feature of our balance of trade. If we import more than we export, we have to finance the difference by borrowing from foreigners. When we export more than we import, we make loans to foreigners to enable them to buy goods in excess of the value of the goods they have sold to us.

This chapter does *not* cover the factors that determine the balance of trade and the scale of international borrowing and lending that finance that balance.[1] It is concerned with understanding the volume, pattern, and directions of international trade, rather than its balance. To help us keep our focus on

[1]These matters are dealt with in Chapter 37.

Figure 36.3 Canada's Balance of Trade

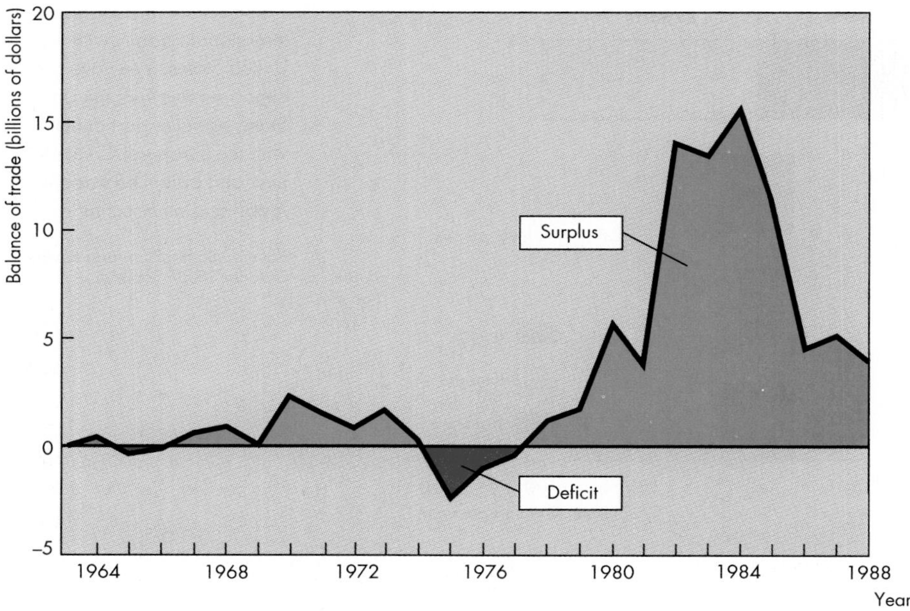

Canada's balance of trade fluctuates, but it usually is positive — we are a net exporter. The last time we had a deficit was in the mid-1970s when the world price of oil products swelled our import bill.

Source: *Bank of Canada Review*, October 1989, Table J2.

these topics, we'll build a model in which there is no international borrowing and lending — just international trade in goods and services. We'll find that we are able to understand what determines the volume, pattern, and direction of international trade and also establish its benefits and the costs of trade restrictions within this framework. This model could be expanded to include international borrowing and lending, but such an extension would not change the conclusions that we'll reach here about the factors that determine the volume, pattern, and directions of international trade.

Let's now begin to study those factors.

Opportunity Cost and Comparative Advantage

Let's apply the lessons that we learned in Chapter 3, about the gains from trade between Jane and Joe, to the trade between nations. We'll begin by recalling how we can use the production possibility frontier to measure opportunity cost.

Opportunity Cost in Pioneerland

Pioneerland (a fictitious country) can produce grain and cars at any point inside or along the production possibility frontier shown in Fig. 36.4. (We're holding constant the output of all the other goods that Pioneerland produces.) The Pioneers, the people of Pioneerland, consume all the grain and cars that they produce, and they operate at point *a* in the figure. That is, Pioneerland is producing and consuming 15 billion bushels of grain and 8 million cars each year. What is the opportunity cost of a car in Pioneerland?

We can answer that question by calculating the slope of the production possibility frontier at point *a*. For, as we discovered in Chapter 3, the slope of the frontier measures the opportunity cost of one good in terms of the other. To measure the slope of the frontier at point *a*, place a straight line tangential to the frontier at point *a* and calculate the slope of that line. Recall that the formula for the slope of a line is the change in *y* divided by the change in *x* as we move along the line. Here, *y* is billions of bushels of grain and *x* is millions of cars. So

Figure 36.4 Opportunity Cost in Pioneerland

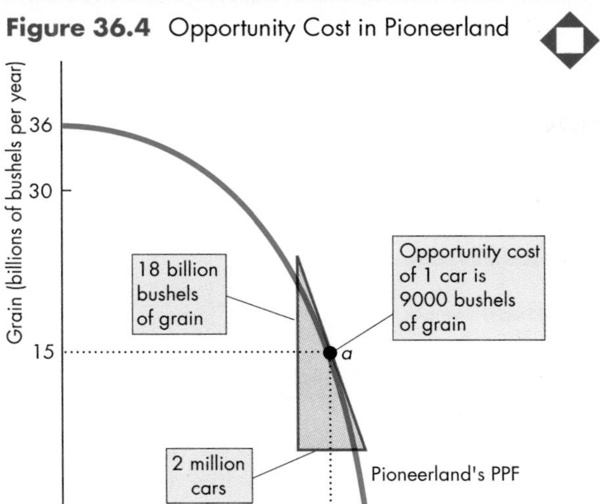

Pioneerland produces and consumes 15 billion bushels of grain and 8 million cars a year. That is, it produces and consumes at point *a* on its production possibility frontier. Opportunity cost is measured as the slope of the production possibility frontier. At point *a*, 2 million cars cost 18 billion bushels of grain. Equivalently, 1 car costs 9,000 bushels of grain or 9,000 bushels cost 1 car.

the slope (opportunity cost) is the change in the number of bushels of grain divided by the change in the number of cars. As you can see from the red triangle in the figure, at point *a*, if the number of cars produced increases by 2 million, grain production decreases by 18 billion bushels. Therefore the slope is 18 billion divided by 2 million, which equals 9,000. To get one more car, the people of Pioneerland must give up 9,000 bushels of grain. Thus the opportunity cost of 1 car is 9,000 bushels of grain. Equivalently, 9,000 bushels of grain cost 1 car.

Opportunity Cost in Magic Empire

Now consider the production possibility frontier in Magic Empire (the only other country in our model world). Figure 36.5 illustrates its production possibility frontier. Like the Pioneers, the Magicians consume all the grain and cars that they produce. Magic Empire consumes 18 billion bushels of grain a year and 4 million cars, at point *a'*.

We can do the same kind of calculation of opportunity cost for Magic Empire as we have just done for Pioneerland. At point *a'*. 1 car costs 1,000 bushels of grain, or, equivalently, 1,000 bushels of grain costs 1 car.

Comparative Advantage

The opportunity cost of cars and grain in Pioneerland and Magic Empire are summarized in Table 36.1. As you can see, cars are cheaper in Magic Empire than in Pioneerland. One car costs 9,000 bushels of grain in Pioneerland but only 1,000 bushels of grain in Magic Empire. But grain is cheaper in Pioneerland than in Magic Empire — 9,000 bushels of grain costs only 1 car in Pioneerland while that same amount of grain costs 9 cars in Magic Empire.

Magic Empire has a comparative advantage in car production. Pioneerland has a comparative advantage in grain production. A country has a **comparative advantage** in producing a good if it can produce that good at a lower opportunity cost than any other country. Let's see how opportunity cost differences and comparative advantage generate gains from international trade.

Figure 36.5 Opportunity Cost in Magic Empire

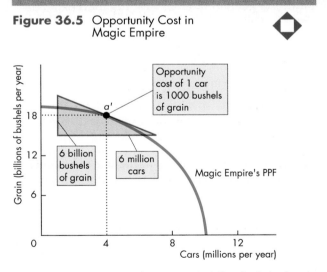

Magic Empire produces and consumes 18 billion bushels of grain and 4 million cars a year. That is, it produces and consumes at point *a'* on its production possibility frontier. Opportunity cost is measured as the slope of the production possibility frontier. At point *a'*, 6 million cars cost 6 billion bushels of grain. Equivalently, 1 car costs 1,000 bushels of grain or 1,000 bushels cost 1 car.

Table 36.1 Opportunity Costs of Cars and Grain in Pioneerland and Magic Empire

Country	Opportunity Costs	
	Cars	Grain
Pioneerland	1 car costs 9,000 bushels	9,000 bushels cost 1 car
Magic Empire	1 car costs 1,000 bushels	1,000 bushels cost 1 car

Cars cost more in Pioneerland and grain costs more in Magic Empire. Pioneerland has a comparative advantage in grain and Magic Empire has a comparative advantage in cars.

The Gains from Trade

If Magic Empire can buy grain for what it costs Pioneerland to produce it, then Magic Empire can buy 9,000 bushels of grain for 1 car. That is much lower than the cost of growing grain in Magic Empire, where it costs 9 cars to produce 9,000 bushels of grain. If the Magicians buy at the low Pioneerland price, they will reap some gains.

If the Pioneers can buy cars for what it costs Magic Empire to produce them, they can obtain a car for 1,000 bushels of grain. Since it costs 9,000 bushels of grain to produce a car in Pioneerland, the Pioneers will gain from such an activity.

In this situation, it makes sense for Magicians to buy their grain from Pioneers and for Pioneers to buy their cars from Magicians. Let's see how such profitable international trade comes about.

Reaping the Gains from Trade

We've seen that the Pioneers would like to buy their cars from the Magicians and that the Magicians would like to buy their grain from the Pioneers. Let's see how the two groups do business with each other, concentrating attention on the international market for cars.

Figure 36.6 illustrates such a market. The quantity of cars traded internationally is measured on the horizontal axis. On the vertical axis we measure the price of a car, but it is expressed as its opportunity cost — the number of bushels of grain that a car costs. If no international trade takes place, that price in Pioneerland is 9,000 bushels of grain, indicated by point *a* in the figure. Again, if no trade takes place, that price is 1,000 bushels of grain in Magic Empire, indicated by point *a′* in the figure. (The points *a* and *a′* in Fig. 36.6 correspond to the points identified by those same letters in Figs. 36.4 and 36.5.) The lower the price of a car (in terms of bushels of grain), the greater is the quantity of cars that the Pioneers import from the Magicians. This fact is illustrated in the downward-sloping curve that shows Pioneerland's import demand for cars.[2]

The Magicians respond in the opposite direction. The higher the price of cars (in terms of bushels of grain), the greater is the quantity of cars that Magicians export to Pioneers. This fact is reflected in Magic Empire's export supply of cars — the upward-sloping line in the figure.[3]

The international market in cars determines the equilibrium price and quantity traded. This equilibrium occurs where the import demand curve intersects the export supply curve. In this case, the equilibrium price of a car is 3,000 bushels of grain. Four million cars a year are exported by Magic Empire and imported by Pioneerland. Notice that the price at which cars are traded is lower than the initial price in Pioneerland but higher than the initial price in Magic Empire.

Balanced Trade

Notice that the number of cars exported by Magic Empire — 4 million a year — is exactly equal to the number of cars imported by Pioneerland. How does Pioneerland pay for its cars? By exporting grain. How much grain does Pioneerland export? You can find

[2]The slope of Pioneerland's import demand curve for cars depends partly on the country's production possibility frontier and partly on the preferences of the citizens of Pioneerland.

[3]The slope of Magic Empire's export supply curve of cars depends on that country's production possibility frontier and on the preferences of the citizens of Magic Empire.

Figure 36.6 International Trade in Cars

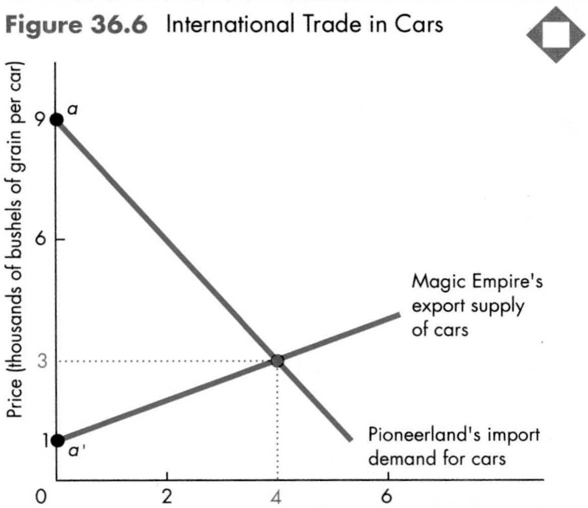

As the price of a car decreases, the quantity of imports demanded by Pioneerland increases — Pioneerland's import demand curve for cars is downward sloping. As the price of a car increases, the quantity of cars supplied by Magic Empire for export increases — Magic Empire's export supply curve of cars is upward sloping. Without international trade, the price of a car is 9,000 bushels of grain in Pioneerland (point *a*) and 1,000 bushels of grain in Magic Empire (point *a'*). With free international trade, the price of a car is determined at the intersection of the export supply curve and the import demand curve — a price of 3,000 bushels of grain. At that price, 4 million cars per year are imported by Pioneerland and exported by Magic Empire. The value of grain exported by Pioneerland and imported by Magic Empire is 12 billion bushels per year, the quantity required to pay for the cars imported.

the answer by noticing that for 1 car Pioneerland has to pay 3,000 bushels of grain. Hence, for 4 million cars it has to pay 12 billion (3,000 × 4 million) bushels of grain. Thus Pioneerland's exports of grain are 12 billion bushels a year. Magic Empire imports this same quantity of grain.

Magic Empire exchanges 4 million cars for 12 billion bushels of grain each year, and Pioneerland does the opposite, exchanging 12 billion bushels of grain for 4 million cars. Trade is balanced between these two countries. The value received from exports equals the value paid out for imports.

Changes in Production and Consumption

We've seen that international trade makes it possible for the Pioneers to buy cars at a lower price than they can produce them for themselves. It also enables the Magicians to sell their cars for a higher price, which is equivalent to saying that the Magicians can buy grain for a lower price. Thus everybody seems to gain. Magicians buy grain at a lower price and Pioneers buy cars at a lower price. How is it possible for everyone to gain? What are the changes in production and consumption that accompany these gains?

The consumption possibilities of an economy that does not trade internationally are identical to its production possibilities. Without international trade, the economy can only consume what it produces. But with international trade, an economy can consume quantities of goods that differ from those that it produces. The production possibility frontier describes the limit of what a country can produce, but it does not describe the limits to what it can consume. Figure 36.7 will help you to see the distinction between production possibilities and consumption possibilities when a country trades internationally.

First, notice that the figure has two parts, part (a) for Pioneerland and part (b) for Magic Empire. The production possibility frontiers that you saw in Figs. 36.4 and 36.5 are reproduced here. The slopes of the two black lines in the figure represent the opportunity costs in the two countries when there is no international trade. Pioneerland produces and consumes at point a and Magic Empire produces and consumes at *a'*. Cars cost 9,000 bushels of grain in Pioneerland and 1,000 bushels of grain in Magic Empire.

With international trade, Magic Empire can sell cars to Pioneerland for 3,000 bushels of grain each. Pioneerland can buy cars from Magic Empire for that price. Thus both countries can exchange cars for grain or grain for cars at a price of 3,000 bushels of grain per car. These trading possibilities are illustrated by the (identical) red lines in both parts of Fig. 36.7.

With international trade, the producers of cars in Magic Empire can now get a higher price for their output. As a result, they increase the quantity of car production. At the same time, grain producers in Magic Empire get a lower price for their grain and so they reduce production. Producers in Magic Empire adjust their output until the opportunity cost in Magic Empire equals the opportunity cost in the world market. Opportunity cost in the world market is identical for both countries and is determined as the slope of the red lines in Fig. 36.7 — 1 car costs 3,000 bushels of grain. For Magic Empire, the opportunity cost of producing a car equals the world opportunity cost at point *b'* in Fig. 36.7(b).

Figure 36.7 Expanding Consumption Possibilities

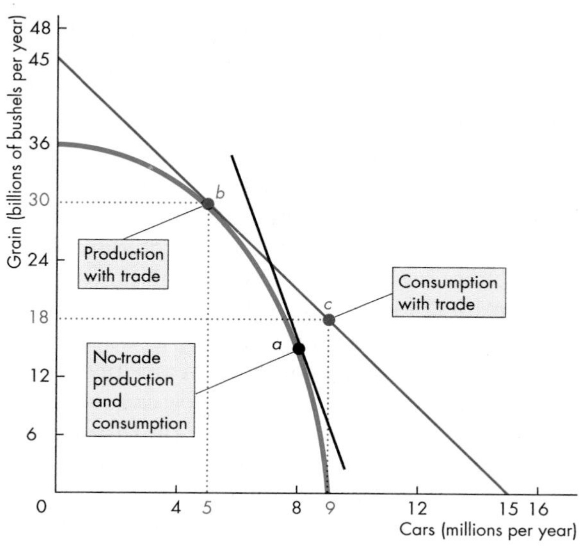

(a) Pioneerland

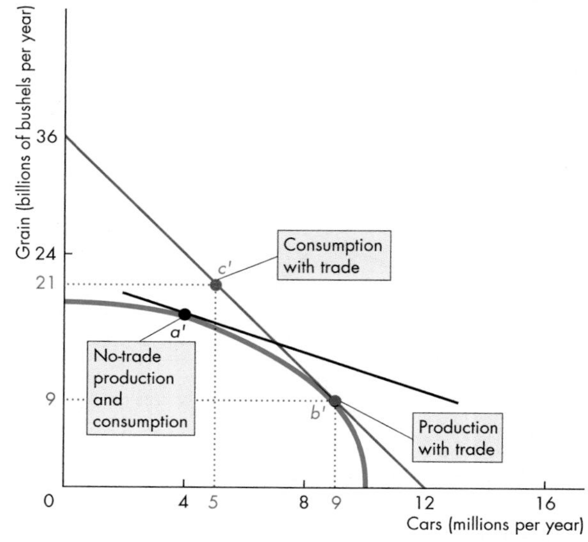

(b) Magic Empire

With no international trade, the Pioneers produce and consume at point *a* and the opportunity cost of a car is 9,000 bushels of grain (the slope of the black line in part a). Also with no international trade, the Magicians produce and consume at point *a′* and the opportunity cost of 1,000 bushels of grain is 1 car (the slope of the black line in part b).

Goods can be exchanged internationally at a price of 3,000 bushels of grain for 1 car along the red line. In part (a). Pioneerland decreases its production of cars and increases its production of grain, moving from *a* to *b*. It exports grain and imports cars, and it consumes at point *c*. The Pioneers have more of both cars and grain than they would if they produced all their own consumption goods (at point *a*).

In part (b), Magic Empire increases car production and decreases grain production, moving from *a′* to *b′*. Magic Empire exports cars and imports grain, and it consumes at point *c′*. The Magicians have more of both cars and grain than they would if they produced all their own consumption goods (at point *a′*).

But the Magicians do not consume at point *b′*. That is, they do not increase their consumption of cars and decrease their consumption of grain. They sell some of their car production to Pioneerland in exchange for some of Pioneerland's grain. To see how that works out, we first need to check in with Pioneerland to see what's happening there.

In Pioneerland, cars are now less expensive and grain more expensive than before. As a consequence, producers in Pioneerland decrease car production and increase grain production. They do so until the opportunity cost of a car in terms of grain equals the cost on the world market. They move to point *b* in part (a). But the Pioneers do not consume at point *b*. They exchange some of their additional grain production for the now cheaper cars from Magic Empire.

The figure shows us the quantities consumed in the two countries. We saw in Fig. 36.6 that Magic Empire exports 4 million cars a year and Pioneerland imports those cars. We also saw that Pioneerland exports 12 billion bushels of grain a year and Magic Empire imports that grain. Thus Pioneerland's consumption of grain is 12 billion bushels a year less than it produces and its consumption of cars is 4 million a year more than it produces. Pioneerland consumes at point *c* in Fig. 36.7(a).

Similarly, we know that Magic Empire consumes 12 billion bushels of grain more than it produces and

4 million cars fewer than it produces. Thus Magic Empire consumes at c' in Fig. 36.7(b).

Calculating the Gains from Trade

You can now literally "see" the gains from trade in Fig. 36.7. Without trade, Pioneers produce and consume at *a* (part a) — a point on Pioneerland's production possibility frontier. With international trade, Pioneers consume at point *c* (in part a) — a point *outside* the production possibility frontier. At point *c*, Pioneers are consuming 3 billion bushels of grain a year and 1 million cars a year more than before. These increases in consumption of cars and grain, beyond the limits of the production possibility frontier, are the gains from international trade.

But Magicians also gain. Without trade, they consume at point a' (part b) — a point on Magic Empire's production possibility frontier. With international trade, they consume at point c' — a point outside the production possibility frontier. With international trade, Magicians consume 3 billion bushels of grain a year and 1 million cars a year more than without trade. These are the gains from international trade for Magic Empire.

Gains for All

When Pioneers and Magicians trade with each other, potentially everyone can gain. Domestic sellers add the net demand of foreigners to their domestic demand, so their market expands. Buyers are faced with domestic supply plus net foreign supply, so they have a larger total supply available to them. As you know, prices increase when there is an increase in demand and they decrease when there is an increase in supply. Thus the increased demand (from foreigners) for exports increases their price and the increased supply (from foreigners) of imports decreases their price. Gains in one country do not bring losses in another. Everyone, in this example, gains from international trade.

Absolute Advantage

Suppose that in Magic Empire, fewer workers are needed to produce any given output of either grain or cars than in Pioneerland. In this situation, Magic Empire has an absolute advantage over Pioneerland. A country has an **absolute advantage** if its output per unit of inputs of all goods is higher than that of another country. With an absolute advantage, can't Magic Empire outsell Pioneerland in all markets? If Magic Kingdom can produce all goods using fewer factors of production than Pioneerland, why does it pay Magic Empire to buy *anything* from Pioneerland?

The answer is that the cost of production in terms of the factors of production employed is irrelevant for determining the gains from trade. It does not matter how much labour, land, and capital are required to produce 1,000 bushels of grain or a car. What matters is how many cars must be given up to produce more grain or how much grain must be given up to produce more cars. That is, what matters is the opportunity cost of one good in terms of the other good. Magic Empire may have an absolute advantage in the production of all things, but it cannot have a comparative advantage in the production of all goods. The statement that the opportunity cost of cars in Magic Empire is lower than in Pioneerland is identical to the statement that the opportunity cost of grain is higher in Magic Empire than in Pioneerland. Thus *whenever opportunity costs diverge, everyone has a comparative advantage in something.* All countries can potentially gain from international trade.

R E V I E W

When countries have divergent opportunity costs, they can gain from international trade. Each country can buy goods and services from another country at a lower opportunity cost than it can produce them for itself. Gains arise when each country increases its production of those goods and services in which it has a comparative advantage (of goods and services that it can produce at an opportunity cost that is lower than that of other countries) and exchanges some of its production for that of other countries. All countries gain from international trade. Everyone has a comparative advantage at something. ■

Gains from Trade in Reality

The gains from trade between Pioneerland and Magic Empire in grain and cars, take place in a model economy, an economy that we have imagined. But the same phenomena occur every minute of every day in real world economies. We buy cars made in Japan and Canadian producers of grain sell large amounts of their output to Japanese households and firms. We buy airplanes and vegetables from U.S. producers and sell natural gas and forest products to Americans in return. We buy shirts and fashion goods from the people of Hong Kong and sell them machinery in return. We buy TV sets and VCRs from South Korea and Taiwan and sell them financial and other services as well as manufactured goods in return.

Thus much of the international trade that we see in the real world takes precisely the form of the trade that we studied in our model economy. But as we discovered earlier in this chapter, a great deal of world trade is heavily concentrated among industrial countries and primarily involves the international exchange of manufactured goods. Thus the type of trade we have just analysed — exchanging cars for grain — although an important and clearly profitable type of trade, is not the most prominent type. Why do countries exchange manufactured goods with each other? Can our model of international trade explain such exchange?

A Puzzle

At first thought, it seems puzzling that countries would trade manufactured goods. Consider, for example, Canada's trade in cars and auto parts. Why does it make sense for Canada to produce cars for export and at the same time to import large numbers of cars from the United States, Japan, Korea, and Western Europe? Wouldn't it make more sense to produce in Canada all the cars that we buy here? After all, we have access to the best technology available for producing cars. Auto workers in Canada are surely as productive as their fellow workers in the United States, Western Europe, and the Pacific countries. Capital equipment, production lines, robots, and the like used in the manufacture of cars are as available to Canadian car producers as they are to any others. This line of reasoning leaves a puzzle concerning the sources of international exchange of similar commodities produced by similar people using similar equipment. Why does it happen?

Diversity of Taste The first part of the answer to the puzzle is that people have a tremendous diversity of taste. Let's stick with the example of cars. Some people prefer a sports car, some prefer a limousine, some a regular full-size car, and some a compact. In addition to size and type, cars vary in many other dimensions. Some have low fuel consumption, some have high performance, some are spacious and comfortable, some have a large trunk, some have four-wheel drive, some have front-wheel drive, some have manual transmission, some have automatic transmission, some are durable, some are flashy, some have a radiator grill that looks like a Greek temple, others look like a wedge. People's preferences across these many dimensions vary.

The tremendous diversity in tastes for cars means that people would be dissatisfied if they were forced to consume from a limited range of standardized cars. People value variety and are willing to pay for it in the marketplace.

Economies of Scale The second part of the answer to the puzzle is economies of scale. *Economies of scale* are the tendency, present in many production processes, for the average cost of production to be lower, the larger the scale of production. In such situations, larger and larger production runs lead to ever lower average production costs. Many manufactured goods, including cars, experience economies of scale. For example, if a car producer makes only a few hundred (perhaps even a few thousand) cars of a particular type and design, it has to use production techniques that are much more labour-intensive and much less automated than those actually employed to make hundreds of thousands of cars in a particular model. With low production runs and labour-intensive production techniques, costs are high. With very large production runs and automated assembly lines, production costs are much lower. But to obtain lower costs, the automated assembly lines have to produce a large number of cars.

It is the combination of diversity of taste and economies of scale that produces such a large amount of international trade in similar commodities. Diversity of taste and the willingness to pay for variety does not guarantee that variety will be available. It could simply be too expensive to provide a highly diversified range of different types of cars, for example. If every car bought in North America today were made in North America and if the present range of diversity were available, production runs would be remarkably short. Car producers would not be able to reap economies of scale. Although the current variety of cars could be made available, it would be at a very high price, perhaps a price that no one would be willing to pay.

But with international trade, each manufacturer of cars has the whole world market to serve.

Each producer specializes in a limited range of products and then sells its output to the entire world market. This arrangement enables large production runs for the most popular cars and feasible production runs for even the most customized cars demanded by only a handful of people.

The situation in the market for cars is present in many other industries, especially those producing specialized machinery and specialized machine tools. Thus international exchange of similar but slightly differentiated manufactured products is a highly profitable activity.

This type of trade can be understood with exactly the same model of international trade we studied earlier. Although we normally think of cars as a single commodity, we simply have to think of sports cars and sedans and so on as different goods. By specializing in a few of these "goods", different countries are able to enjoy economies of scale and, therefore, a comparative advantage in their production.

Transportation Costs Although the combination of diversity of taste and economies of scale produces a large amount of international trade in similar commodities such as automobiles, it does not explain all the two-way trade in similar commodities. If you glance back at Fig. 36.1, you may be struck by the fact that Canada both imports and exports large amounts of chemicals and crude petroleum. It is perhaps easy to understand why we both import and export a category of goods as broad as chemicals. After all, there are many different individual chemicals, some of which we export and others of which we import. But crude petroleum is crude petroleum — there are various grades of the product but otherwise it does not differ all that much. Why do we import and export crude petroleum? The main part of the answer has to do with transportation costs. It is less costly to move petroleum in large tankers across the oceans than it is to transport it overland. Thus the petroleum consumed in Eastern Canada is imported along the Atlantic seaboard while much of the petroleum used in the Western United States is imported from Alberta (and is therefore a Canadian export of crude petroleum).

Adjustment Costs

You can see that comparative advantage and international trade bring gains regardless of the goods being traded. When the rich countries of the European Community, Japan, and the United States import raw materials from the Third World and from Australia and Canada, the importing countries gain and so do the exporting countries. When we buy cheap TV sets, VCRs, shirts, and other goods from low-wage countries, both we and the exporters gain from the exchange. It's true that if we increase our imports of cars and produce fewer cars ourselves, jobs in our car-producing sector will disappear. But jobs in other sectors, sectors in which we have a comparative advantage and supply to other nations, will expand. After the adjustment is completed, those whose jobs have been lost find employment in the expanding sectors, sometimes even at higher wages than they had previously. They buy goods produced in other countries at even lower prices than those at which they were available before. The long-run gains from international trade are not gains for some people at the expense of losses for others.

But changes in comparative advantage that lead to changes in international trade patterns can take a long time to adjust to. For example, the increase in automobile imports and the corresponding relative decline in domestic car production has not immediately brought increased wealth for displaced auto workers. Better jobs take time to find, and often people go through a period of prolonged search, putting up with inferior jobs and lower wages than they had before. Thus only in the long run can everyone gain from international specialization and exchange. Short-run adjustment costs, which can be large and relatively prolonged, may be borne by groups that have lost their comparative advantage.

Partly because of the costs of adjustment to changing international trade patterns but also for other reasons, governments intervene in international trade, restricting its volume. Let's examine what happens when governments restrict international trade. We'll contrast restricted trade with free trade. We'll see that free trade brings the greatest possible benefits. We'll also see why, in spite of the benefits of free trade, governments sometimes restrict trade.

Trade Restrictions

Governments restrict international trade in order to protect domestic industries from foreign competition. The restriction of international trade is called **protectionism**. Governments employ two main protectionist methods:

- Tariffs
- Nontariff barriers

A **tariff** is a tax that is imposed by the importing

country when a good crosses an international boundary. A **nontariff barrier** is any action other than a tariff that restricts international trade. Examples of nontariff barriers are quantitative restrictions and licensing regulations limiting imports. We'll consider nontariff barriers in more detail below. First, let's look at tariffs.

Canadian Tariffs

The Canadian economy has always been protected by tariffs. The history of those tariffs, from Confederation to 1989, is illustrated in Fig. 36.8. The figure shows tariffs as a percentage of total imports — the average tariff rate. As you can see, the average tariff rate climbed from the early 1870s to more than 20 percent by the 1890s. The rate fluctuated but then steadily declined through the 1930s. After World War II, there was a stronger trend decline in tariff rates.

Today, average tariffs are less than 5 percent of total imports, and because of an historic agreement between Canada and the United States — the Canada-United States Free Trade Agreement — this average is going to decline during this decade. Let's take a look at the free trade agreement.

The Canada-United States Free Trade Agreement

In 1987, the governments of Canada and the United States agreed to create a free trade area encompassing their two countries and resulting in the eventual elimination of tariffs and most other impediments to free trade and capital movements between Canada and the United States. The agreement came into effect on January 1, 1989, following a period of intense political activity. The general election of 1988 was, in effect, a referendum on the free trade agreement.

The agreement between Canada and the United States is one that will gradually reduce tariff barriers on trade between the two countries through 1998. When the agreement first came into effect, tariffs were eliminated on 15 percent of all goods traded between the two countries, including such items as computers, whisky, and motorcycles. More tariff cuts occurred on January 1, 1990, and more are scheduled for January 1 in each of the years through 1998.

Even after January 1, 1998, some trade between Canada and the United States will be subject to temporary tariffs. Fresh fruits and vegetables will be protected on a seasonal basis for yet a further decade.

In addition to eliminating tariff barriers to trade in goods and services between Canada and the United States, the free trade agreement seeks to establish predictable rules, to secure access for both Canadian and American producers to each other's markets, and to establish fair competition — what is popularly called "a level playing field." Crucial to the agreement is the establishment of procedures and institutions for the administration of the agreement and the resolution of disputes.

Figure 36.8 Canadian Tariffs: 1867–1989

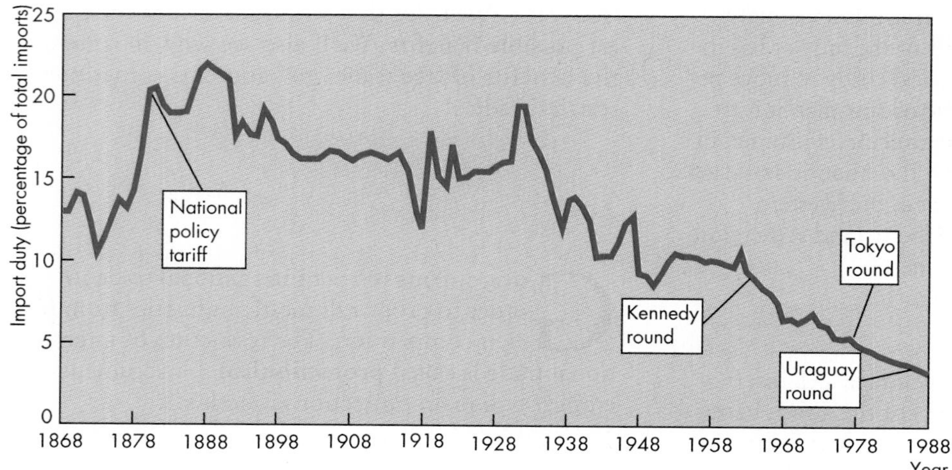

Average Canadian tariffs increased steadily from Confederation through the 1890s, but then declined at a gentle pace until the 1930s. After World War II, tariffs declined more rapidly.

Source: 1868-1975: *Historical Statistics of Canada*, Series G485. 1976-1988: *Bank of Canada Review*.

The pros and cons of the free trade agreement involve technical economic issues, political issues, and emotional issues. In what follows, we will study the effects of protection from a narrowly economic perspective. Adopting such an economic perspective does not mean that political and emotional factors are unimportant. It is simply a reflection of the fact that economists have no special expertise in those areas.

Before analysing the effects of protectionism and its removal, let's briefly consider the current state of Canadian tariffs as they affect our trade with countries other than the United States.

Contemporary Tariffs

Even though our average tariffs are now much lower than they were in earlier Canadian history, some sectors still have high tariffs. For example, if you want to buy a shirt from Hong Kong, you pay a 25 percent duty on that import. Shoes from Brazil cost you an extra 23 percent in duty. A pearl ring or necklace from Japan costs you 13 percent in duty. Import duties on automobiles from Japan run at 9.2 percent.

Because of the free trade agreement, tariffs on imports from the United States are somewhat lower than those from other countries and, through the 1990s, that gap is going to get ever wider. In 1990, for example, while a Japanese car has a 9.2 percent duty, a U.S.-produced car has a duty of only 7.2 percent. A pair of blue jeans made in Hong Kong has a 25 percent duty, but a similar pair of blue jeans made in San Francisco has a duty of only 18 percent.

International Agreements

The temptation for governments to impose tariffs is a strong one. First, tariffs provide revenue to the government. Second, they enable the government to satisfy special interest groups in import-competing industries. But, as we've seen, free international trade brings enormous benefits. Because free trade brings benefits and because the temptation to restrict trade is so great, countries have entered into various multilateral agreements whose goal is the enhancement of free international trade. The largest and probably the most important is the General Agreement on Tariffs and Trade (GATT). The **General Agreement on Tariffs and Trade** is an international agreement designed to limit government intervention that restricts international trade. The GATT was negotiated immediately following World War II and was signed in October 1947. Its goal is to liberalize trading activity and to provide an organization to administer more liberal trading arrangements. The GATT secretriat is a small organization located in Geneva, Switzerland.

Since the formation of GATT, several rounds of negotiations have taken place, resulting in general tariff reductions. The Kennedy Round, which began in the early 1960s, resulted in large tariff cuts. Yet further tariff cuts resulted from the Tokyo Round, which took place between 1973 and 1979. The most recent GATT tariff round, the Uruguay Round, which began in 1986 is attempting to achieve less restricted trade in services and agricultural products but made limited progress.

Another important multilateral arrangement is Europe 1992. **Europe 1992** is the process of creating an integrated, single-market economy among the member nations of the European Community. After 1992, the European Community will be the largest single integrated economy in the world, larger even than the United States.

In addition to the multilateral agreements under the GATT, some important bilateral trade agreements have been put in place. From the point of view of Canada, the most important of these is the Canada-United States Free Trade Agreement that became effective on January 1, 1989 (see Reading Between the Lines, pp. 984-985). Under this agreement, barriers to international trade between Canada and the United States will be virtually eliminated after a 10-year phasing-in period.

How Tariffs Work

To determine the effects of tariffs and the effects of eliminating them — such as the process under way as a result of the Canada-United States Free Trade Agreement — we need to know how tariffs work. To analyse how tariffs work, we're going to return to the example of trade between Pioneerland and Magic Empire. We're going to work with this model economy rather than the real economy for two reasons. First, we'll find it easier to understand the basic principles involved in the working of tariffs and their elimination. Second, we are less emotionally involved in the affairs of the Pioneers and Magicians than we are in our own affairs. Thus we shall be better able to focus clear-headedly on the purely economic aspects of the tariff issue.

Let's return, then, to Pioneerland and Magic Empire. Suppose that these two countries are trading cars and grain in exactly the same way that we analysed before. Magic Empire exports cars and Pioneerland exports grain. The volume of car imports into Pioneerland is 4 million a year, and cars are selling on the world market for 3,000 bushels of grain. Let's suppose that grain costs one dollar a bushel so, equivalently, cars are selling for $3,000. Figure 36.9 illustrates this situation. The volume of trade in cars and their price are determined at the point of intersection of Magic Empire's export supply curve of cars and Pioneerland's import demand curve for cars.

Now suppose that the government of Pioneerland, perhaps under pressure from car producers, decides to impose a tariff on imported cars. In particular, suppose that a tariff of $4,000 per car is imposed. (This is a huge tariff, but the car producers of Pioneerland are fed up with competition from Magic Empire). What happens?

The first part of the answer is obtained by studying the effects on the supply of cars in Pioneerland. Cars are no longer available at the Magic Empire export supply price. To that price must be added the tariff of $4,000 — the amount paid to the government of Pioneerland on each car imported. As a consequence, the supply curve in Pioneerland shifts in the manner shown in Fig. 36.9. The new supply curve becomes that labelled "Magic Empire's export supply of cars plus tariff." The vertical distance between Magic Empire's export supply curve and the new supply curve is the tariff imposed by the government of Pioneerland.

The next part of the answer is found by determining the new equilibrium. Imposing a tariff has no effect on the demand for cars in Pioneerland, so it has no effect on Pioneerland's import demand for cars. The new equilibrium occurs where the new supply curve intersects Pioneerland's import demand curve for cars. That equilibrium is at a price of $6,000 a car, with 2 million cars a year being imported. Imports fall from 4 million to 2 million cars a year. At the higher price of $6,000 a car, domestic car producers increase their production. Domestic grain production decreases to free up the resources for the expanded car industry.

The Pioneers' total spending on imported cars is $12 billion ($6,000 a car × 2 million cars imported). But not all of that money goes to the Magicians. They receive $2,000 a car, or $4 billion for the 2 million cars. The difference — $4,000 a car, or a total of $8 billion for the 2 million cars — is collected by the government of Pioneerland as tariff revenue.

Obviously, the government of Pioneerland is happy with this situation. It is now collecting $8 billion that it didn't have before. But what about the

Figure 36.9 The Effects of a Tariff

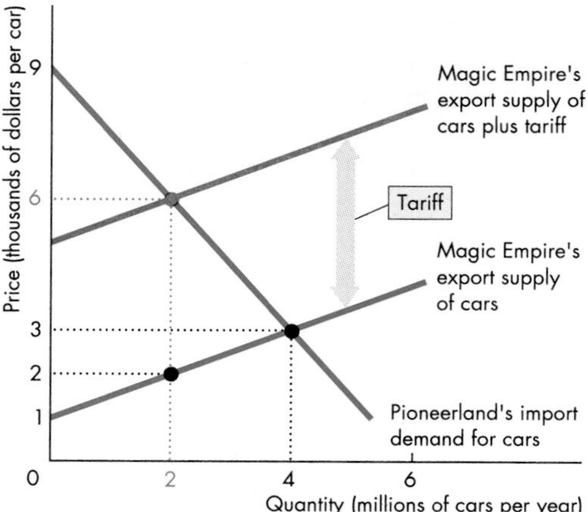

Pioneerland imposes a tariff on cars imported from Magic Empire. The tariff increases the price that Pioneers have to pay for cars. It shifts the supply curve of cars in Pioneerland upward. The distance between the original supply curve and the new one is the amount of the tariff. The price of cars in Pioneerland increases and the quantity of cars imported decreases. The government of Pioneerland collects a tariff revenue of $4,000 per car — a total of $8 billion on the 2 million cars imported. Pioneerland's exports of grain decrease since Magic Empire now has a lower income from its exports of cars.

Pioneers? How do they view the new situation? The demand curve tells us the maximum price that a buyer is willing to pay for one more unit of a good. As you can see from Pioneerland's import demand curve for cars, if one more car could be imported, someone would be willing to pay almost $6,000 for it. Magic Empire's export supply curve of cars tells us the minimum price at which additional cars are available. As you can see, one additional car would be supplied by Magic Empire for a price only slightly more than $2,000. Thus since someone is willing to pay almost $6,000 for a car and someone is willing to supply one for little more than $2,000, there is obviously a gain to be had from trading an extra car. In fact, there are gains to be had — willingness to pay exceeds the minimum supply price — all the way up to 4 million cars a year. Only when 4 million cars are being traded is the maximum price that a Pioneer is willing to pay equal to the minimum price that is acceptable to a Magician. Thus restricting international trade reduces the gains from international trade.

It is easy to see that the tariff has lowered Pioneerland's total import bill. With free trade, Pioneerland was paying $3,000 a car and buying 4 million cars a year from Magic Empire. Thus the total import bill was $12 billion a year. With a tariff, Pioneerland's imports have been cut to 2 million cars a year and the price paid to Magic Empire has fallen to only $2,000 a car. Thus the import bill has been cut to $4 billion a year. Doesn't this fact mean that Pioneerland's balance of trade has changed? Is Pioneerland now importing less than it is exporting?

To answer that question, we need to figure out what's happening in Magic Empire. We've just seen that the price that Magic Empire receives for cars has fallen from $3,000 to $2,000 a car. Thus the price of cars in Magic Empire has decreased. But if the price of cars has fallen, the price of grain has increased. With free trade, the Magicians could buy 3,000 bushels of grain for one car. Now they can buy only 2,000 bushels for a car. With a higher price of grain, the quantity demanded by the Magicians decreases. As a result, Magic Empire's import of grain declines. But so does Pioneerland's export of grain. In fact, Pioneerland's grain industry suffers from two sources. First, there is a decrease in the quantity of grain sold to Magic Empire. Second, there is increased competition for inputs from the now-expanded car industry. Thus the tariff leads to a contraction in the scale of the grain industry in Pioneerland.

It seems paradoxical at first that a country, by imposing a tariff on cars, would hurt its own export industry, lowering its exports of grain. It may help to think of it this way. Foreigners buy grain with the money they make from exporting cars. If they export fewer cars, they cannot afford to buy as much grain. In fact, in the absence of any international borrowing and lending, Magic Empire has to cut its imports of grain by exactly the same amount as the loss in revenue from its export of cars. Grain imports into Magic Empire will be cut back to a value of $4 billion, the amount that can be covered by the new lower revenue from Magic Empire's car exports. Thus trade is still balanced in this post-tariff situation. Although the tariff has cut imports, it has also cut exports, and the cut in the value of exports is exactly equal to the cut in the value of imports. The tariff, therefore, has no effect on the balance of trade — it simply reduces the volume of trade.

The result that we have just derived is perhaps one of the most misunderstood aspects of international economics. On countless occasions, politicians and others have called for tariffs in order to remove a balance of trade deficit or have argued that lowering tariffs would produce a balance of trade deficit. They have drawn this conclusion by failing to work out all the implications of a tariff. Because a tariff raises the price of imports and cuts imports, the easy conclusion is that the tariff strengthens the balance of trade. But a tariff also changes the *volume* of exports. The equilibrium effects of a tariff are to reduce the volume of trade in both directions, by the same value on each side of the equation. The balance of trade itself is left unaffected.

Learning the Hard Way Although the analysis that we have just worked through leads to the clear conclusion that tariffs cut both imports and exports and make everyone worse off, Canadians have not found that conclusion easy to accept. Time and again in our history we have imposed high tariff barriers on international trade (as Fig. 36.8 illustrates). Whenever tariff barriers are increased, the volume of trade declines. The most vivid historical example of this interaction occurred during the Great Depression years of the early 1930s when the world's largest trading nation, the United States, increased its tariffs, setting up a retaliatory round of tariff changes in many countries. The consequence of these very high tariffs was an almost complete disappearance of world trade.

Let's now turn our attention to the other range of protectionist weapons — nontariff barriers.

Nontariff Barriers

There are three important forms of nontariff barriers:

- Quotas
- Voluntary export restraints
- Product standards regulations

A **quota** is a quantitative restriction on the import of a particular good. It specifies the maximum amount of the good that may be imported in a given period of time. A **voluntary export restraint** is an agreement between two governments in which the government of the exporting country agrees to restrain the volume of its own exports. Voluntary export restraints are often called VERs.

Product standards regulations are legally defined standards of product design, and quality content (usually based on health or safety considerations) that have an effect on the ease with which foreign products can be sold in a domestic market. An example of this type of regulation acting as a nontariff barrier is that of electric stoves. In Canada, but

Free Trade

What's free about free trade?

The value of the year-old North American agreement is still being debated

....[A] year after the Canada-U.S. Free Trade Agreement [FTA] went into force, taking the two countries a giant step toward becoming the world's largest tariff-free zone, the benefits are by no means visible to everyone. While U.S. businessmen and analysts pronounce themselves satisfied with the pact, in Canada a spirited debate is still being waged over the FTA's effectiveness—or lack thereof—in promoting the national interest.

The controversy might be more muted if the Canadian economy was showing greater pep. But twelve months after the FTA took effect, economic growth had fallen from 2.9% last year to a projected 2% this year. The shrinkage was largely due to high Canadian interest rates and a steep climb in the value of the Canadian dollar, to about 85¢ in U.S. terms. That increase, to the highest level since 1980, has cut deeply into Canadian exports—74% of which go to the U.S.....

Canadian detractors of the FTA have loudly blamed the agreement for...any attendant woe. The leading labor federation, the Canadian Labour Congress, charges that the accord has caused U.S. multinational companies to prune Canadian subsidiary firms, thereby pulling jobs back to the U.S. The C.L.C. blames the trade treaty for virtually every major plant closing last year—more than 50 in all, with a loss of 70,000 jobs. Says union trade analyst Bruce Campbell: "The FTA is propelling the Canadian branch-plant economy into a warehouse economy."

Treaty defenders dispute the claim. "By far the most decisive factor this year has been the strong Canadian dollar," says Gary Hufbauer, a professor of international financial diplomacy at Washington's Georgetown University. Moreover, businessmen on both sides of the border appear to embrace the pact wholeheartedly. Owing to a flood of business petition, Washington and Ottawa have agreed to speed up the phasing out of tariffs, worth an estimated $5 billion annually, on 400 additional items ranging from antibiotics to snowshoes. Says Charles Roh, U.S. assistant trade representative for North America: "There is an enthusiasm that the agreement is working as we intended."...

The pace of the merger wave in Canada has been extraordinary. Over the first nine months of 1989 $10.8 billion worth of buyouts and acquisitions by foreign firms were carried out. According to the anti-treaty Pro-Canada Council, 80% of the deals were struck by U.S. firms, moving significant chunks of the Canadian economy south of the border. Without the FTA, only $2.6 billion worth of takeovers were consummated in 1988.

But Canadian firms have also used the pact as a springboard to enter the vast U.S. market, albeit on a smaller scale. For example Artopex, an Montreal-based furniture maker, is spending some $4.3 million building a factory near Albany.

Time,
January 29, 1990
Reported by James L. Graff/Ottawa
and John F. McDonald/Washington

The Essence of the Story

- One year after the Canada-United States Free Trade Agreement went into force there was disagreement as to whether the agreement was promoting Canada's national interest.
- Canadian economic growth had fallen from 2.9 percent in 1989 to a projected 2 percent in 1990—attributed to high interest rates and a sharp rise in the value of the Canadian dollar.
- The Canadian Labour Congress blames the free trade agreement for major plant closings—more than 50—and job losses—70,000—during 1989.
- Treaty defenders claim that Canada's economic problems during 1989 result from the strong dollar.
- There have been a large number of petitions from firms in both Canada and the United States requesting a speed up of the phasing out of tariffs.
- Foreign investment in Canadian firms and Canadian investment in foreign firms has increased.

Background and Analysis

- In 1989-1990, the Canadian economy was responding to and anticipating several forces that will have long-lasting and far-reaching effects on Canada's comparative advantage. Some of the more important of these forces, together with their predicted effects are set out below.

- The gradual elimination of tariffs under the provisions of the Canada-United States Free Trade Agreement that came into effect on January 1, 1989. Predicted effects:

  - Increased specialization in both Canada and the United States and an increased volume of trade between them.
  - A contraction in Canada and an expansion in the United States of those industries in which the United States has a comparative advantage. For example, machine tools, chemical processing plants, and earthmoving equipment.
  - An expansion in Canada and a contraction in the United States of those industries in which Canada has a comparative advantage. For example, electronic communication systems, computer programs, and paper products.
  - A loss of some jobs and the creation of new jobs on both sides of the border.
  - Mergers and acquisitions as firms rationalize their production processes to take maximum advantage of the new trading arrangements.

- The imminent (1992) unification of the economies of Western Europe to form the world's largest single market. Predicted effect:

  - Acquisitions by Canadian firms of European firms and mergers of Canadian and European firms to enable Canadians to sell more effectively in the enlarged European market and to enable European firms, exploiting economies of scale in their production processes, to sell more effectively in the Canadian market.

- The emergence of the countries of Eastern Europe from communism. Predicted effects:

  - Canadian investment in, and joint ventures with, firms in Eastern Europe.
  - Increased Canadian trade with Eastern Europe.

- Also, in 1990, the Canadian economy was responding to some short-term, but powerful influences:

  - A steady rise in the value of the Canadian dollar against the U.S. dollar.
  - A steady rise in Canadian interest rates.

- Isolating the effects of the Canada-United States Free Trade Agreement is difficult and will only be possible sometime after its implementation and as a result of careful and costly economic research.

- It is virtually certain that the slowdown of the Canadian economy in 1990 was entirely unrelated to the free trade agreement and, as claimed by some in the story, resulted mainly from the behaviour of Canadian interest rates and the dollar.

- The longer term influences set out above will continue to have an effect on the relative prosperity of Canadians for many years and it is likely that there will be an unusually large scale of plant closings and job losses as well as plant openings and job gains.

- Those who gain will not be very vocal. They will attribute their gains to their own hard work and skill.

- Those who lose will be vocal. They will attribute their losses to, among other things, the free trade agreement.

- Some losses will result from the free trade agreement. But most economic studies predict that the gains from increased international specialization and exchange will outweigh these losses.

not in the United States, product standard regulations require that each heating element be independently fused. This Canadian safety regulation has the effect of keeping U.S. stoves out of Canada and protects domestic manufacturers. Similar regulations affect such goods as television sets, automobiles, furniture, and toys.

Since World War II, nontariff barriers have become important features of international trading arrangements, and there is now general agreement that nontariff barriers are a more severe impediment to international trade than tariffs.

Although it is difficult to quantify the effects of nontariff barriers in a way that makes them easy to compare with tariffs, some studies have attempted to do just that. Such studies attempt to assess the tariff rate that would restrict trade by the same amount as the nontariff barriers do. With such calculations, nontariff barriers and tariffs can be added together to assess the total amount of protection. When we add nontariff barriers to tariffs for Canada, the overall amount of protection increases more than threefold. Even so, Canada is one of the least protectionist countries in the world. The incidence of total protection is higher in the European Community and is higher still in other developed countries and Japan. The less developed countries and the newly industrializing countries have the highest protection rates of all.

Quotas are especially important in the textile industries, where an international agreement called the Multifibre Arrangement establishes quotas on a wide range of textile products. Agriculture is also subject to extensive quotas. Voluntary export restraints are particularly important in regulating the international trade in cars between Japan and North America.

Figure 36.10 The Effects of a Quota

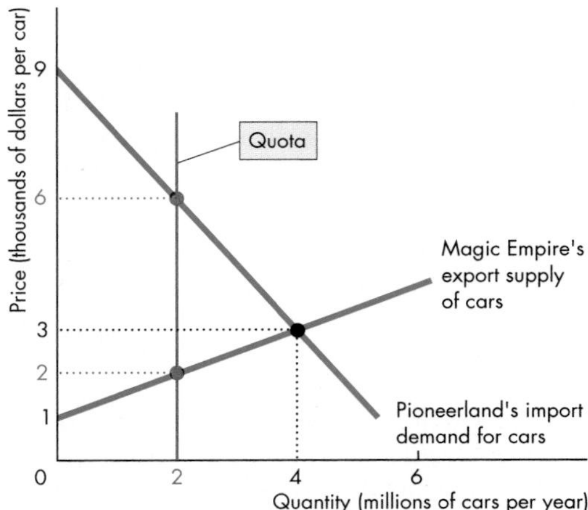

Pioneerland imposes a quota of 2 million cars per year on car imports from Magic Empire. That quantity appears as the vertical line marked "Quota." Since the quantity of cars supplied by Magic Empire is restricted to 2 million, the price at which those cars will be traded increases to $6,000. Importing cars is profitable since Magic Empire is willing to supply cars at $2,000 each. There is competition for import quotas — rent seeking.

How Quotas and VERs Work

To understand how nontariff barriers affect international trade, let's return to the example of trade between Pioneerland and Magic Empire. Suppose that Pioneerland imposes a quota on car imports. Specifically, suppose that the quota restricts imports to not more than 2 million cars a year. What are the effects of this action?

The answer is found in Fig. 36.10. The quota is shown by the vertical red line at 2 million cars a year. Since it is illegal to import more than that number of cars in total, car importers buy only that quantity from Magic Empire producers. They pay $2,000 a car to the Magic Empire producer. But what do they sell their cars for? The answer is $6,000 each. Since the import supply of cars is restricted to 2 million cars a year, people with cars for sale will be able to get $6,000 each for them. The quantity of cars imported equals the quantity determined by the quota.

Importing cars is now obviously a profitable business. An importer gets $6,000 for an item that costs only $2,000. Thus there is severe competition among car importers for the available quotas. It is the pursuit of the profits from quotas that economists call "rent seeking."

The value of imports — the amount paid to Magic Empire — declines to $4 billion, exactly as in the case of the tariff. Thus with lower incomes from car exports and with a higher price of grain, Magicians cut back on their imports of grain in exactly the same way as they did under a tariff.

The key difference between a quota and a tariff lies in who gets the profit represented by the difference between the import supply price and the domestic selling price. In the case of a tariff, that difference goes to the government. In the case of a quota, that difference goes to the person who has the right to import under the quota regulations.

A voluntary export restraint is like a quota

arrangement where a quota is allocated to each exporting country. The effects of VERs are similar to those of quotas but differ from them in that the gap between the domestic price and the export price is captured not by domestic importers but by the foreign exporter. The government of the exporting country has to establish procedures for allocating the restricted volume of exports among its producers.

R E V I E W

When a country opens itself up to international trade and trades freely at world market prices, it expands its consumption possibilities. When trade is restricted, some of the gains from trade are lost. A country may be better off with restricted trade than with no trade, but not as well off as it could be if it engaged in free trade. A tariff reduces the volume of imports, but it also reduces the volume of exports. Under both free trade and restricted trade (without international borrowing and lending), the value of imports equals the value of exports. With restricted trade, both the total value of exports and the total value of imports are lower than under free trade, but trade is still balanced. ■

Why Quotas and VERs Might Be Preferred to Tariffs

At first sight, it seems puzzling that countries would ever want to use quotas and even more puzzling that they would want to use VERs. We have seen that the same domestic price and the same quantity of imports can be achieved by using any of the three devices for restricting trade. However, a tariff provides the government with a source of revenue, while a quota provides domestic importers with a profit, and a VER provides the foreigner with a profit. Why then would a country use a quota or a voluntary export restraint rather than a tariff?

There are two possible reasons. First, a government can use quotas to reward its political supporters. Under a quota, licences to import become tremendously profitable. So the government bestows riches on the people to whom it gives licences to import. Second, quotas are more precise instruments for holding down imports. As demand fluctuates, the domestic price of the good fluctuates but not the quantity of imports. You can see this implication of a quota by going back to Fig. 36.10. Suppose that the demand for imports fluctuates. With a quota, these demand fluctuations simply produce fluctuations in the domestic price of the import but no change in the volume of imports. With a tariff, fluctuations in demand lead to no change in the domestic price but to large changes in the volume of imports. Thus if for some reason the government wants to control the quantity of imports and does not care about fluctuations in the domestic price, it will use a quota.

Why would a government use a voluntary export restraint rather than a tariff or quota? The government may want to avoid a tariff or quota war with another country. If one country imposes a tariff or a quota, that might encourage another country to impose a similar tariff or quota on the exports of the first country. Such a "war" would result in a much smaller volume of trade and a much worse outcome for both countries. A voluntary export restraint can be viewed as a way of achieving trade restrictions to protect domestic industries, while giving some kind of compensation to encourage the foreign country to accept that situation and not retaliate with its own restrictions. Finally, VERs are often the only form of trade restriction that can be entered into legally under the terms of the General Agreement on Tariffs and Trade.

Dumping and Countervailing Duties

Dumping is the selling of a good in a foreign market for a lower price than in the domestic market or for a lower price than its cost of production. Such a practice can arise from a discriminating monopoly that is seeking to maximize profit. Under GATT, dumping is illegal. A country may impose antidumping duties on foreign producers if domestic producers can show that they have been injured by dumping.

Countervailing duties are tariffs that are imposed to enable domestic producers to compete with government-subsidized foreign producers. Under current U.S. law, if American producers can show that a foreign subsidy has damaged their market, a countervailing duty can be imposed. Governments often subsidize some of their domestic industries, but defining what is a subsidy and what is a legitimate form of government aid (or simply a different government approach) can be a problem. The Canadian lumber industry offers an example. American producers say it is subsidized. Canadian governments, which own much of our timberland, say their method of renting it to producers simply differs from the American method.

Why is International Trade Restricted?

Historically, tariffs were imposed not to restrict international trade — although they did have that effect — but to provide revenue for the government. Since governments control the extent of their political and legal influence, it is relatively easy to collect a tax on goods that cross their borders. So the tariff was the most easily collected tax and the one most relied on. As other taxes, such as income taxes, became more easy to collect and as the economic rationale for free international trade became better understood, tariffs were gradually reduced. You've seen that downward trend in the Canadian tariff in Fig. 36.8. The downward trend is also going to continue as the Canada-United States Free Trade Aggreement comes into greater effect through the 1990s. Despite the general tendency for tariffs to decline, there remains a great deal of intervention in international trade and protection from foreign competition. Why, when free international trade increases our consumption possibilities, do we continue to restrict such trade with the types of barriers that we've just described?

The key reason is that with free trade consumption possibilities increase *on the average*, but not everyone shares in the gain and some people even lose. Free trade brings benefits to some and costs to others, with total benefits exceeding total costs. It is the uneven distribution of costs and benefits that is the principal source of impediment to achieving more liberal international trade.

Returning to our example of international trade in cars and grain between Pioneerland and Magic Empire, the benefits from free trade accrue to all the producers of grain and those producers of cars who do not have to bear the costs of adjusting to a smaller car industry. The costs of free trade are borne by the car producers and their employees who have to move and become grain producers. Compared with the number of people who lose, the number who gain is, in general, enormous. The gain per person will, therefore, be rather small. The loss per person to those who bear the loss is large. Since the loss that falls on those who bear it is large, it pays those people to incur considerable expense in order to lobby against free trade. On the other hand, it does not pay those who gain to organize to achieve free trade. The gain from trade for any one individual is too small for him or her to spend much time or money on a political organization to achieve free trade. The loss from free trade is seen as being so great by those bearing that loss that they *do* find it profitable to join a political organization to prevent free trade. Each group is optimizing — weighing benefits against costs and choosing the best action for themselves. The anti-free-trade group will, however, undertake a larger quantity of political lobbying than the pro-free-trade group.

Compensating Losers

If, in total, the gains from free international trade exceed the losses, why don't those who gain compensate those who lose so that everyone is in favour of free trade? To some degree, such compensation does take place. It also takes place indirectly as a consequence of unemployment compensation arrangements. But, as a rule, only limited attempts are made to compensate those who lose from free international trade. The main reason full compensation is not attempted is that the costs of identifying the losers would be enormous. Also, it would never be clear whether or not a person who has fallen on hard times is suffering because of free trade or for other reasons, perhaps reasons largely under the control of the individual. Furthermore, some people who look like losers at one point in time may, in fact, wind up gaining. The young auto worker who loses his job in Windsor and becomes a computer assembly worker in Ottawa resents the loss of work and the need to move. But a year or two later, looking back on events, he counts himself fortunate. He's made a move that has increased his income and given him greater job security.

It is because we do not, in general, compensate the losers from free international trade that protectionism is such a popular and permanent feature of our national economic and political life.

Political Outcome

The political outcome that emerges from the activity that we've just examined depends on a balance of forces. There are clear *net* gains from free international trade. When a political party believes that it can capture those gains and distribute them to the voters in a way that makes at least 50 percent of the voters feel better off, it will push for free trade. The support for the Canada-United States Free Trade Agreement by the Progressive Conservate government of Brian Mulroney is an example of such an outcome. But the constituencies pressing for the protection that we've described and analysed are always present, and politicians react to these constituencies as well. The producers of protected goods are far more vocal and much more sensitive swing-voters than the consumers of those goods. The political outcome, therefore, although occasionally delivering a breakthrough, leans in the direction of maintaining protection. Even if all tariffs were eliminated, the nontariff barriers remaining in place would severely restrict international trade

■ You've now seen how free international trade enables everyone to gain from increased specialization and exchange. By producing goods at which we have a comparative advantage and exchanging some of our own production for that of others, we expand our consumption possibilities. Placing impediments on that exchange when it crosses national borders restricts the extent to which we can gain from specialization and exchange. By opening our country up to free international trade, the market for the things that we sell expands and their prices rise. The market for the things that we buy also expands and their prices fall. All countries gain from free international trade. As a consequence of price adjustments (in the absence of international borrowing and lending), the value of imports adjusts to equal the value of exports.

In the next chapter, we're going to study the ways in which international trade is financed and also learn why international borrowing and lending that permits unbalanced international trade arises. We'll discover the forces that determine the Canadian balance of payments.

SUMMARY

Patterns and Trends in International Trade

Large flows of trade take place between rich and poor countries. Resource-rich countries exchange natural resources for manufactured goods, and resource-poor countries import their resources in exchange for their own manufactures. However, by far the biggest volume of trade is in manufactures exchanged among the rich industrialized countries. The biggest single Canadian export item is automobiles and automobile parts. These goods are also our biggest imports. Trade in services has grown in recent years. Total trade has also grown over the years. The Canadian balance of trade fluctuates but is usually positive — Canada is a net exporter. (pp. 969-972)

Opportunity Cost and Comparative Advantage

When opportunity costs differ between countries, the country with the lowest opportunity cost of producing a good is said to have a comparative advantage in that good. Comparative advantage is the source of the gains from international trade. A country can have an absolute advantage, but not a comparative advantage, in the production of all goods. Every country has a comparative advantage in something. (pp. 972-974)

The Gains from Trade

Countries can gain from trade if their opportunity costs differ. Through trade, each country can obtain goods at a lower opportunity cost than it could if it produced all goods at home. Trading allows consumption to exceed production. By specializing in producing the good in which it has a comparative advantage and then trading some of that good for imports, a country can consume at points outside its production possibility frontier. Each country can consume at such a point.

In the absence of international borrowing and lending, trade is balanced as prices adjust to reflect the international supply and demand for goods. The world price is established at the level that balances the production and consumption plans of the trading parties. At the equilibrium price, trade is balanced, and domestic consumption exactly matches a combination of domestic production and international trade. (pp. 974-977)

Gains from Trade in Reality

Comparative advantage explains the enormous volume and diversity of international trade that takes place in the world. But much trade takes the form of exchanging similar goods for each other — for example, one type of car for another. Such trade arises because of economies of scale in the face of diversified tastes. By specializing in producing a few goods, having long production runs, and then trading those goods internationally, consumers in all countries can enjoy greater diversity of products at lower prices. (pp. 977-979)

Trade Restrictions

A country can restrict international trade by imposing tariffs or nontariff barriers — quotas, voluntary export restraints, and product standards regulations.

All trade restrictions raise the domestic price of imported goods, lower the volume of imports, and reduce the total value of imports. They also reduce the total value of exports by the same amount as the reduction in the value of imports.

All trade restrictions create a gap between the domestic price and the foreign supply price of an import. In the case of a tariff, that gap is the tariff revenue collected by the government. But the government raises no revenue from a quota. Instead, domestic importers who have a licence to import increase their profit. A voluntary export restraint resembles a quota except that the foreign exporter receives a higher price.

Governments restrict trade because restrictions help the producers of the protected commodity and the workers employed by those producers. Because their gain is sufficiently large and the loss per consumer sufficiently small, the political equilibrium favours restricted trade. Politicians pay more attention to the vocal and active concerns of the few who stand to lose than to the quieter and less strongly expressed views of the many who stand to gain. But there are net gains from free trade and when a political party believes that it can reap those gains and distribute them so that a majority of voters benefit, it will run against the tide of protectionism. The Canada-United States Free Trade Agreement and the general downward trend in tariffs are important examples illustrating cases in which the forces of protectionism have been resisted and displaced. (pp. 979-989)

KEY ELEMENTS

Key Terms

Absolute advantage, 977
Balance of trade, 971
Comparative advantage, 973
Countervailing duties, 987
Dumping, 987
Exports, 969
Europe 1992, 981
Exports, 969
General Agreement on Tariffs and Trade, 981
Imports, 969
Net exporter, 971
Net importer, 971
Nontariff barrier, 980
Product standards regulation, 983
Protectionism, 979
Quota, 983
Tariff, 979
Voluntary export restraint, 983

Key Figures 

Figure 36.1 Canadian Exports and Imports, 970
Figure 36.4 Opportunity Cost in Pioneerland, 973
Figure 36.5 Opportunity Cost in Magic Empire, 973
Figure 36.6 International Trade in Cars, 975
Figure 36.7 Expanding Consumption Possibilities, 976
Figure 36.9 The Effects of a Tariff, 982
Figure 36.10 The Effects of a Quota, 986

REVIEW QUESTIONS

1 What are Canada's main exports and imports?

2 How does Canada trade services internationally?

3 Which items of international trade have been growing the most quickly in recent years?

4 What is comparative advantage? Why does it lead to gains from international trade?

5 Explain why international trade brings gains to all countries.

6 Distinguish between comparative advantage and absolute advantage.

7 Explain why all countries have a comparative advantage in something.

8 Explain why we import and export such large quantities of certain similar goods — cars, for example.

9 What are the main ways in which we restrict international trade?

10 What are the effects of a tariff?

11 What are the effects of a quota?

12 What are the effects of a voluntary export restraint?

13 Describe the main trends in tariffs and nontariff barriers.

14 Which countries have the largest restrictions on their international trade?

15 Why do countries restrict international trade?

PROBLEMS

1 a) Using Fig. 36.4, calculate the opportunity cost of a car in Pioneerland at the point on the production possibility frontier at which 4 million cars are produced.

b) Using Fig. 36.5, calculate the opportunity cost of a car in Magic Empire when it produces 8 million cars.

c) With no trade, Pioneerland produces 4 million cars and Magic Empire produces 8 million cars. Which country has a comparative advantage in the production of cars?

d) If there is no trade between Pioneerland and Magic Empire, how much grain is consumed and how many cars are bought in each country?

2 Suppose that the two countries in problem 1 start to trade freely.

a) Which country exports grain?

b) What adjustments will be made to the amount of each good produced by each country?

c) What adjustment will be made to the amount of each good consumed by each country?

d) What can you say about the price of a car under free trade?

3 Compare the total production of each good produced in problems 1 and 2.

4 Compare the situation in problems 1 and 2 with that analysed in this chapter. Why does Magic Empire export cars in the chapter analysis but import them in problem 2?

5 What are the gains from trade for

a) Pioneerland?

b) Magic Empire?

6 The following figure depicts the international market for soybeans.

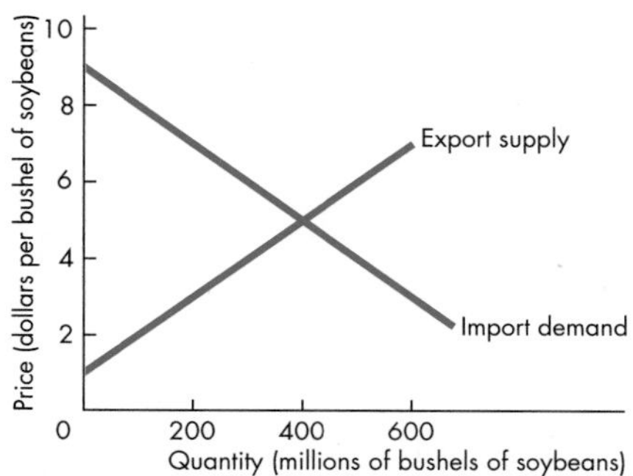

a) What is the world price of soybeans if there is free trade between these countries?

b) If the country that imports soybeans im poses a tariff of $2 per bushel, what is the world price of soybeans and what quantity of soybeans gets traded internationally? What is the price of soybeans in the importing country? Calculate the tariff revenue.

7 If the importing country in problem 5(a) imposes a quota of 300 million bushels, what is the price of soybeans in the importing country? What is the revenue from the quota and who gets this revenue?

8 If the exporting country in problem 5(a) imposes a VER of 300 million bushels of soybeans, what is the world price of soybeans? What is the revenue of soybean growers in the exporting country? Which country gains from the VER?

9 Suppose that the exporting country in problem 5(a) subsidizes production by paying its farmers $1 a bushel for soybeans harvested.

a) What is the price of soybeans in the importing country?

b) What action might soybean growers in the importing country take? Why?

CHAPTER 37

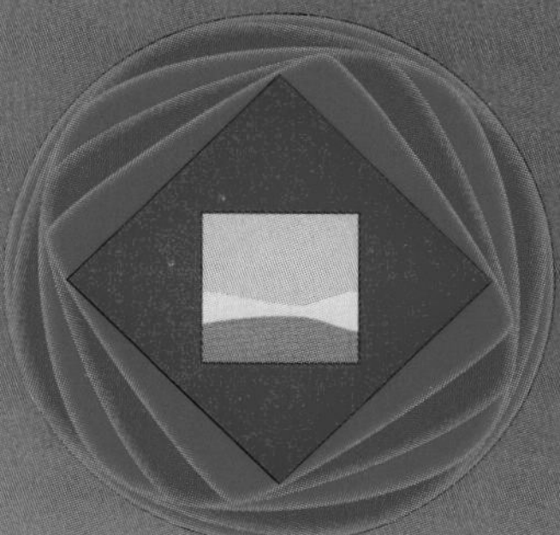

The Balance of Payments and the Dollar

After studying this chapter, you will be able to:

- Explain how international trade is financed.
- Describe a country's balance of payments accounts.
- Explain what determines the amount of international borrowing and lending.
- Explain why Canada is an international borrower.
- Explain the links between the exchange rate and the balance of payments.

The Global Economy

FOR MOST OF US, economic life centres on the city and country in which we live. But for an increasing number of chief executive officers, marketing managers, accountants, lawyers, and many other professionals, the economy is the world — there is a truly global economy. ■ For example, foreigners are buying U.S. assets at an astonishing rate. In recent years, Carnation Foods, the canned concentrated milk producer, was bought by Swiss business interests for $3 billion and Doubleday, the publisher, was bought by Germans for $0.5 billion. Allied Stores, which owns Brooks Brothers, was bought by Canadians for $3.5 billion. Smith and Wesson, that most American of gun manufacturers, was bought by a British firm for $0.1 billion. Sohio gasoline stations were bought out by British Petroleum for $7.6 billion. Chesebrough-Pond's, the makers of cleansing cream and Q-tips, was bought by a Dutch and British firm for $3.1 billion. Dunes Hotel and Country Club, one of Las Vegas's best known gambling and entertainment centres, is now owned by Japanese. Tycoons such as Britain's Gordon White, Germany's Mark Wossner, Australia's George Herscu, and Japan's Shigeru Kobayashi are roaming the United States with a giant shopping cart, loading it up with everything in sight, from high-rise buildings in Manhattan to shopping malls in Los Angeles. What is causing this foreign invasion of the United States? ■ There are many Canadian multinational giants. The name Ellis-Don is visible on high-rise buildings ascending over London, England, and many other parts of the world. Olympia and York, controlled by the Reichmann brothers of Toronto, is also responsible for massive urban development projects around the globe. Why do Canadian firms undertake so much of their business in other countries? ■ Of course, the traffic is not all one way. Foreigners are investing in Canada on a massive scale too. Vancouver's property boom in the late 1980s was to a large degree the result of a massive injection of investment from the other side of the Pacific Ocean — from Hong Kong and Japan. New car factories springing up in Ontario are almost exclusively financed by the Japanese. Why are foreigners investing so much in Canada? And do we invest more in other countries than foreigners invest here? ■ "Exporters Feel Stronger Dollar's Pinch" read a headline in the *Calgary Herald* in April 1987. The story went on to say, "While a stronger dollar is a boon to travellers, importers, consumers, and companies with debts in U.S. funds, it's pinched the pocketbooks of exporters — 80 percent of whose goods go to American markets." Why is a strong dollar a boon to travellers and importers but a problem for exporters? Does the strength of the dollar affect our balance of trade with the rest of the world? ■ "Dollar Plunges on News of Trade Deficit" or "Dollar Surges on News of Trade Surplus." Headlines such as these are commonplace. They seem to be telling us that the strength of our dollar depends on the balance of our international trade. Does the balance of international trade affect the strength of the dollar? Or is it the other way around — that is, does the strength of the dollar affect our international trade balance?

■ In this chapter, we investigate the questions that have just been posed. We begin by reviewing the way in which international trade is financed and study the structure of the accounts in which our international activities are recorded — the balance of payments accounts. We study the forces that determine the balance of our international trade and the scale of our international borrowing and lending. We also study the links between the balance of trade and the exchange rate.

Financing International Trade

When Eatons imports Toshiba television sets from Japan, it does not pay for those TVs with Canadian dollars — it uses Japanese yen. When Benetton imports designer sweaters from Italy, it pays for them using Italian lire, and when a French power company buys a Candu reactor, it pays for it with Canadian dollars. Whenever we buy goods from another country, we use the currency of that country in order to make the transaction. It doesn't make any difference what the item being traded is — it can be a consumer good or a capital good, a service, a building, or even a firm.

We're going to study the markets in which transactions in different types of currency take place. But first we're going to look at the scale of international trading, and borrowing and lending, and at the way in which we keep our records of these transactions. Such records are called the balance of payments accounts.

Balance of Payments Accounts

A country's **balance of payments accounts** records its international trading, borrowing, and lending. There are in fact three balance of payments accounts:

- Current account
- Capital account
- Official settlements account

Current Account The **current account** records three items:

- Net exports
- Net interest payments
- Other transfers

Net exports is the difference between the value of goods and services exported to foreigners and value of goods and services imported from foreigners. We studied this item in Chapter 25 and in Chapter 36. **Net interest payments** are the payments of interest received by Canadians on their investments abroad minus the payments of interest made by Canadians to foreigners on their investments here in Canada. Other transfers are gifts and other money, such as foreign aid payments, received from and paid to foreigners. By far the largest item in the current account is the balance of trade. Interest payments are also important. Other transfers are a small item.

Capital Account The **capital account** records all the international borrowing and lending transactions. The capital account balance records the difference between the amount that a country lends to the rest of the world and the amount it borrows from the rest of the world.

Official Settlements Account The **official settlements account** shows the net increase or decrease in a country's holdings of official foreign exchange reserves.

Canada's Balance of Payments Accounts

Table 37.1 shows the Canadian balance of payments accounts for 1988. As you can see from the table,

Table 37.1 Canada's Balance of Payments Accounts for 1988

	Billions of dollars
Current account	
Import of goods and services	–153
Export of goods and services	157
Net transfers	–14
Current account balance	–10
Capital account	
Foreign investment in Canada less Canadian investment abroad	22
Official settlements account	
Increase in Canada's official foreign exchange	12

Source: Bank of Canada Review, October 1989, Table J1.

Canada had a current account deficit of $10 billion in 1988. That deficit arose from the fact that our net transfers to foreigners — transfers to foreigners minus foreign transfers to Canadians — exceeded our net exports. Our net exports — the difference between our exports and imports of goods and services — was positive. But this positive item was not sufficient to offset the negative net transfers.

How do we pay for our current account deficit? We pay by borrowing from abroad. The capital account tells us by how much. In 1988, we borrowed $22 billion from the rest of the world. The difference between our net borrowing from abroad and our current account deficit is the change in Canada's official foreign exchange reserves. **Official foreign exchange reserves** are the federal government's holdings of gold and foreign currency denominated assets. In 1988, those reserves increased by $12 billion. This amount is the difference between the current account deficit and the capital account surplus.

The numbers in Table 37.1 give you a snapshot of the balance of payments accounts in 1988. In that year, Canada had a balance of trade surplus but a current account deficit and a large capital account surplus. It also had a large surplus on the official settlements account. Was 1988 a typical year?

This question is answered in Fig. 37.1, which shows the history of Canada's balance of payments accounts going back to 1970. As you can see in part (a), the current account balance is almost a mirror image of the capital account balance. Changes in our foreign currency holdings (part b) are normally quite small compared with the balances on these other two accounts. Thus 1988 was an unusual year in the scale of the official settlements balance. It was also unusual in the sense that the current account deficit was almost as large as it has ever been.

Let's try to deepen our understanding of the balance of payments accounts and the way in which they are linked together by considering the income and expenditure, borrowing and lending, and the bank account of an individual.

Individual Analogy An individual's current account records the income from supplying the services of factors of production and the expenditure on goods and services. Consider, for example, Joanne. She earned an income in 1989 of $25,000. Joanne has $10,000 worth of investments, which earned her an income of $1,000. Joanne's current account shows an income of $26,000. Joanne spent $18,000 buying goods and services for consumption. She also bought a new house, which cost her $60,000. So Joanne's total expenditure was $78,000. The difference between her expenditure and income was $52,000 ($78,000 – $26,000). This amount was Joanne's current account deficit.

To pay for the expenditure of $52,000 in excess of her income, Joanne either has to use the money that she has in the bank or take out a loan. In fact, Joanne took a mortgage of $50,000 to help buy her house. This was the only borrowing that Joanne did, so her capital account surplus was $50,000. With a current account deficit of $52,000 and a capital account surplus of $50,000, Joanne was still $2,000 short. She got that $2,000 from her own bank account. Her cash holdings decreased by $2,000.

Joanne's supply of factors of production is analogous to a country's supply of exports. Her purchases of goods and services, including her

Figure 37.1 The Balance of Payments, 1970 – 1988

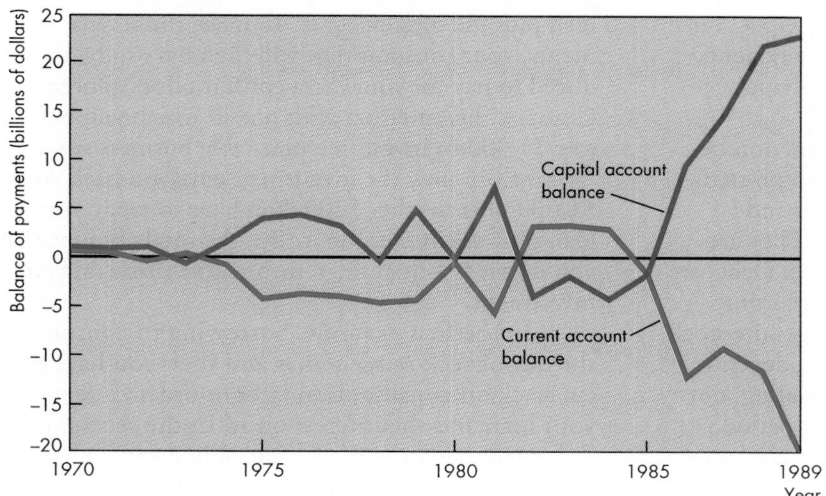

(a) Current and capital account balances

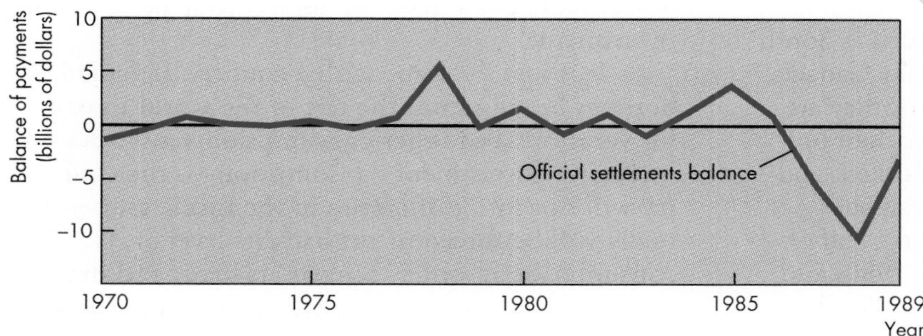

(b) Official settlements balance

Part (a) shows the capital and current account balances. The current account balance was slightly positive (exports were greater than imports) between 1970 and 1973. The balance was negative from 1974 on, except in 1982 to 1984. The capital account balance mirrors the current account balance. When the current account balance is positive, the capital account balance is usually negative — we lend to the rest of the world — and when the current account balance is negative, the capital account balance is usually positive — we borrow from the rest of the world. Part (b) shows the changes in the country's official holdings of foreign currency. Fluctuations in these holdings are small compared with fluctuations in the current account balance and the capital account balance.

Source: *Bank of Canada Review*, October 1989, Table J1.

purchase of a house, are analogous to a country's imports. Joanne's mortgage — borrowing from someone else — is analogous to a country's foreign borrowing. Joanne's purchase of the house is analogous to a country's foreign investment. The change in her own bank account is analogous to the change in the country's official reserves.

What determines a country's current account balance and its scale of international borrowing or lending?

International Borrowing and Lending

A country's past and present international current account balance and borrowing and lending determine whether that country is a

- Net borrower
- Net lender
- Debtor nation
- Creditor nation

A country that is borrowing more from the rest of the world than it is lending to it is called a **net borrower**. Similarly, a **net lender** is a country that is lending more to the rest of the world than it is borrowing from it. A net borrower may be going deeper into debt or may simply be reducing its net assets held in the rest of the world. In contrast, the total stock of foreign investment determines whether a country is a debtor or creditor. A **debtor nation** is a country that during its entire history has borrowed more from the rest of the world than it has lent to it. It has a stock of outstanding debt to the rest of the world that exceeds the stock of its own claims on the rest of the world. A **creditor nation** is a country that has invested more in the rest of the world than other countries have invested in it. Canada is a debtor nation. A debtor nation is one whose net receipts of interest on debt are negative — that is, the payments made by the country exceed its interest receipts.

Stocks and Flows At the heart of the distinction between a net borrower/net lender and a debtor/creditor nation is the distinction between flows and stocks. Borrowing and lending are flows. They are amounts borrowed or lent per unit of time. Debts are stocks. They are amounts owed at a point in time. The flow of borrowing and lending changes the stock of debt. But the outstanding stock of debt depends mainly on past flows of borrowing and lending, not on the current period's flows. The current period's flows determine the *change* in the stock of debt outstanding.

Canada is not the only net borrower nation. It is in the company of poorer countries that are at an earlier stage of economic development, such as South Korea, the Philippines, and Singapore. Like Canada, these countries not only are net borrowers, they are also debtor nations. That is, their total stock of borrowing from the rest of the world exceeds their lending. The debt of these developing countries has grown from less than a third to more than a half of their gross domestic products during the 1980s and has given rise to what has been called the "Third World debt crisis."

The majority of countries, in fact, are net borrowers, including, in recent years, the United States. But a small number of countries are huge net lenders. Examples of net lenders are the oil-rich countries, such as Saudi Arabia and Venezuela, and developed economies such as Japan and West Germany.

Borrowing to Consume or to Invest

Should Canada be concerned about being a net borrower? The answer to this question depends on what we do with the borrowed money. If we borrow to consume, then we do have a problem. If we borrow to invest in additional capital equipment, provided that investment generates a high enough return, we do not have a problem — in fact, we reap benefits from our international borrowing.

It's easy to see why borrowing to consume leads to problems while borrowing to invest does not by considering the case of an individual. Suppose you borrow $1,000 to take a Caribbean vacation in your final year of school. When you quit school and start working, you're going to have to repay that $1,000 loan plus the interest on it. To make those repayments, your consumption will then have to be reduced to pay for your extra consumption splurge. Contrast this situation with one in which you borrow $1,000 to invest in a profitable business venture. A year from now the investment pays you back your $1,000 plus another $200. You have to repay your loan plus the interest on it. But the total amount that you owe is less than the return you've made on your investment.

In the first example, borrowing to consume, the day of reckoning comes and then you have to cut back on consumption later in order to repay your loan and the interest on it. In the second case, you put the loan to work; not only do you not have to cut back on future consumption, but you can actually consume more in the future as a result of having taken a loan and used it to make a sound investment.

It is just the same with a country. If Canada borrows heavily from the rest of the world to pay for vacations and other consumption activities — including government consumption — the country will run into difficulties in the future and eventually will be forced to cut back its level of consumption in order to repay its loans and pay the interest on them. If, on the other hand, Canada borrows huge amounts of funds from the rest of the world to develop and profit from its vast human and physical resource base, then by generating more rapid economic growth than would otherwise been possible, Canadians become richer, are able to repay their international debts and the interest on them, and still wind up with more consumption than before.

Canada's International Borrowing

Is Canada borrowing from the rest of the world to finance consumption or investment? Until 1981, Canada had a scale of capital accumulation that exceeded its private saving and international borrowing. But since 1981, our capital accumulation has been smaller than domestic saving plus foreign borrowing. In the peak year, 1985, we borrowed close to $25 billion to finance public and private consumption in excess of what our income could sustain. Since 1985, our consumption of foreign loans has declined, and by 1988, we were almost back in the situation that had prevailed before 1981 and were borrowing mainly to invest and accumulate profitable capital assets.

Let's now turn to an examination of the factors that determine the scale of our international borrowing and lending and the size of our current account balance.

R E V I E W

When we buy goods from the rest of the world or invest in the rest of the world, we use foreign currency. When foreigners buy goods from us or invest in Canada, they use Canadian currency. We record international transactions in the balance of payments accounts. The current account shows our exports and imports of goods and services and net transfers to the rest of the world. The capital account shows our net foreign borrowing or lending. The official settlements account shows the change in the country's holdings of a foreign currency. In the late 1980s, the Canadian current account moved into a large deficit and the capital account moved into a large surplus — Canada was a net borrower. ■

Current Account Balance

What determines the current account balance and the scale of a country's net foreign borrowing or lending? To answer that question, we need to begin by recalling some of the things that we learned about the national income accounts in Chapter 23.

Sector Balances

Table 37.2 is going to refresh your memory and summarize the necessary calculations for you. Part (a) lists the national income variables that are needed, with their symbols. Their values in Canada in 1988 are also shown. Part (b) presents two key national income equations.

First, equation (1) reminds us that gross domestic product (GDP) is the sum of consumption expenditure, investment, government purchases of goods and services, and net exports (the difference between exports and imports). Equation (2) reminds us that aggregate income is used in three different ways: consumption expenditure, saving, and payment to the government in the form of taxes (net of transfer payments). Equation (1) tells us how our expenditure generates our income. Equation (2) tells us how we dispose of that income.

Table 37.2(c) takes you into some new territory. It examines surpluses and deficits. We'll look at three surpluses or deficits — net exports, the government sector, and the private sector. To obtain these surpluses and deficits, first subtract equation (2) from equation (1). The result is equation (3). By rearranging equation (3), we obtain a relationship for net exports — exports minus imports — that appears as equation (4) in the table.

Notice that in equation (4) net exports has two components. The first is taxes minus government spending, and the second is saving minus investment. These items are the surpluses or deficits of the government and private sectors.

The **government sector surplus or deficit** is the difference between taxes (net of all transfer payments including debt interest) and government sector purchases of goods and services. If taxes (net of transfer payments) exceed government sector purchases of goods and services, the government sector has a surplus. If government sector purchases of goods and services exceed taxes (net of transfer payments) the government sector has a deficit. Notice that the government sector deficit differs from the federal deficit examined in Chapter 35. The government sector includes the federal government, the provincial governments, and local governments.

The **private sector surplus or deficit** is the difference between saving and investment. If saving exceeds investment, the private sector has a surplus to lend to other sectors. If investment exceeds saving, the private sector has a deficit that has to be financed by borrowing from other sectors.

Part (d) of Table 37.2 sets out the connection between net exports and the current account balance (the current account is set out in Table 37.1). We start with net exports, subtract net interest payments made by Canadians to the rest of the world, and add back net transfers from the rest of the world. The result is the current account balance. This is the amount that has to be financed by international borrowing or a change in the nation's official foreign exchange reserves.

Table 37.2 Determination of the Current Account Balance and Net Foreign Borrowing

	Symbols and equations	Canada, 1988 (billions of dollars)
(a) Variables		
Gross domestic product (GDP)	Y	602
Consumption expenditure	C	353
Investment	I	119
Government purchases of goods and services	G	126
Exports of goods and services	EX	157
Imports of goods and services	IM	153
Saving	S	143
Taxes, net of transfer payments	T	106
(b) National income and expenditure		
Aggregate expenditure	(1) $Y = C + I + G + EX - IM$	
Uses of income	(2) $Y = C + S + T$	
Difference between (1) and (2)	(3) $0 = I - S + G - T + EX - IM$	
(c) Surpluses and deficits		
Net exports	(4) $EX - IM = (T - G) + (S - I)$	157 – 153 = 4
Government sector	$T - G$	106 – 126 = –20
Private sector	$S - I$	143 – 119 = 24
(d) Net exports and the current account		
Net exports	$EX - IM$	4
less net interest paid abroad		–18
plus net transfers from the rest of the world		4
Current account balance		–10

Bookkeeping and Behaviour

The calculations that we've just performed are really nothing more than bookkeeping. We've simply manipulated the national income and balance of payments accounts. We've discovered that the current account balance equals net exports plus net transfer payments from the rest of the world less net interest paid abroad. We've also discovered that net exports are equal to the sum of the deficits of the government and private sectors. But what determines those other two deficits? Why, for example, isn't the private sector in a surplus equal to the government sector deficit, so that the current account deficit is zero? Does an increase in the government sector deficit always bring an increase in the current account deficit?

Figure 37.2 The Three Deficits

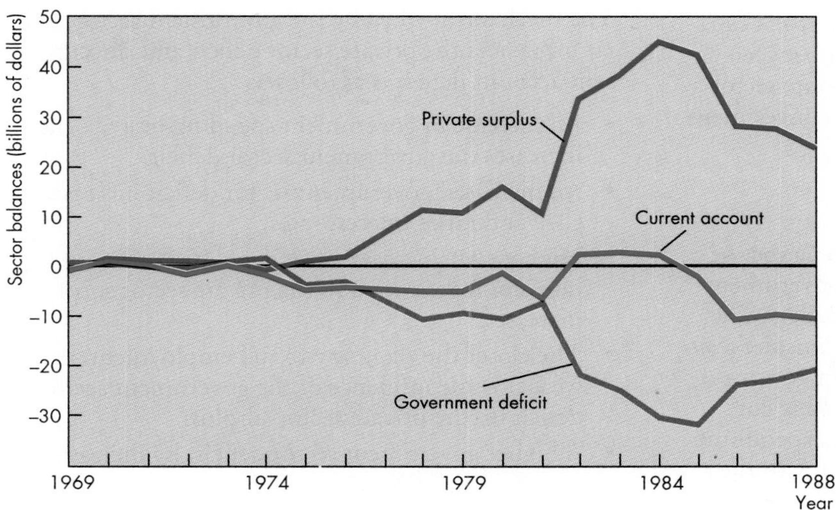

Source: Current account, CANSIM series D71002; Government deficit, CANSIM series D20193: Private surplus calculated to be consistent. *Bank of Canada Review*, November, 1989.

The current account balance fluctuates in sympathy with fluctuations in the sum of the private sector (saving minus investment) and the government sector deficit (government spending minus taxes). The relationship between these three balances is illustrated here. Through 1976, the current account deficit and the government sector deficit moved in close harmony with each other. Between 1977 and 1987, a large private sector surplus emerged. By 1982, this surplus more than offset the government sector deficit and there was a current account surplus. After 1985, the private sector surplus, although large, began to decline and the current account moved into a deficit again.

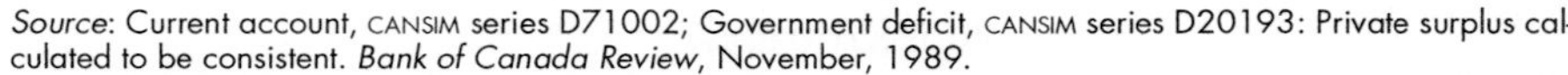

Government Sector Deficit and the Current Account You can see the answers by looking at Fig. 37.2. That figure shows the government sector deficit, the private sector surplus, and the current account balance. As you can see, up to 1976, the current account deficit and the government sector deficit moved in close sympathy with each other: there was a clear tendency for the current account deficit to become larger when the government sector deficit became larger. But between 1977 and 1987, these two variables moved a long way apart. A huge private sector surplus emerged. For a few years this private sector surplus more than offset the government sector deficit, so the current account was in surplus. After 1988, the current account moved into a deficit, and an increasingly large one. Accompanying this development in the current account, the private sector surplus declined.

What causes the relationship among the three deficits that we can see in Fig. 37.2? Let's begin to answer this question by looking at the effects of the government sector deficit on the private sector surplus.

Effects of Government Sector Deficit on Private Sector Surplus It is not surprising that there are fluctuations in the private sector surplus or deficit. As we've just seen, that variable is the gap between saving and investment. As we learned in Chapter 25, one of the main influences on the level of saving is disposable income. Anything that increases disposable income increases saving and increases the private sector surplus, other things being equal. In that same chapter, we learned that investment depends on the interest rate and on expectations of future profits. Again other things being equal, anything that lowers interest rates or increases future profit expectations increases investment and decreases the private sector surplus.

But when the government sector changes its taxes or spending — thereby changing its deficit — there are some effects on income and interest rates that, in turn, influence private sector saving and investment and the private sector surplus or deficit. An increase in government purchases of goods and services or a tax cut — either of which will increase the government sector deficit — tends to increase GDP and the interest rate. The higher GDP stimulates additional saving, but the higher interest rate dampens investment plans. Thus to some degree, an increased government sector deficit induces an increased private sector surplus. But the government sector deficit has this effect on the private sector surplus only if the government's actions do indeed stimulate higher income and higher interest rates.

When the economy is operating close to capacity, as it is most of the time, the higher government sector deficit does not produce a higher level of real GDP. Also, internationally mobile capital lessens the effect of increased government spending on interest rates.

Thus the two mechanisms by which an increase in the government sector deficit can increase the private sector surplus can be relatively weak.

When the economy has substantial excess capacity, as it had in the 1980s, the weak link between the government sector deficit and the private sector deficit is broken and a low level of private investment results in a large private sector surplus.

Effects of a Government Sector Deficit on the Current Account Deficit How does a change in the government sector deficit affect the current account deficit? The easiest way of seeing what happens is to consider a situation of full employment. An increase in government purchases of goods and services or a tax cut leads to an increase in aggregate planned expenditure and an increase in aggregate demand. But with the economy at full employment, there is no spare capacity to generate a comparable increase in output. Part of the increased demand for goods and services, therefore, spills over into the rest of the world and imports increase. Also, part of the domestic production going for export is diverted to satisfy domestic demand. Exports decrease. The rise in imports and the fall in exports increase the current account deficit. The excess of imports over exports leads to a net increase in borrowing from the rest of the world.

But the economy does not operate at precisely full employment. Nor does foreign capital flow in at a fixed interest rate. Thus the linkage between government sector deficit and the current account deficit is not a precise one. Some of the main factors during 1989 that influenced the largest components of Canada's current account balance, its exports and imports of goods and its balance of trade, are examined in Reading Between the Lines, pp. 1004-1005.

Spreading Risks Although foreign investors are lending to Canada to finance the government sector deficit, they are not simply buying government bonds. Furthermore, although our own private sector saving is almost equal to investment, we are not the only people buying new capital equipment in Canada. Foreigners lend to the government and they buy private sector firms and open new firms. We use some of our savings to pay for the purchase of new capital equipment but we also use some savings to lend to the government. It is for these reasons that the incredible volume of international investment described in the chapter opener is taking place.

R E V I E W

The mechanism whereby the government sector deficit influences the private sector deficit and the current account deficit is as follows:

- An increase in government spending or a tax cut increases the government sector deficit.
- An increased government sector deficit increases GDP and raises interest rates.
- Higher GDP increases saving and higher interest rates cut investment, so the private sector surplus increases.
- The closer the economy to full employment, the weaker is the influence of the government sector deficit on the private sector surplus.
- A higher government sector deficit, by increasing domestic aggregate demand, increases the demand for imports and diverts goods destined for export to domestic uses.
- Net exports fall, so the current account deficit increases. ■

Net Exports and the Dollar

Exporters don't like a strong dollar and importers don't like a weak dollar. Why? Does the strength of the dollar affect the volume of our exports and imports? And does it affect the balance of trade — our net exports? Or does causation run the other way? That is, is the strength of the dollar itself determined by the balance of trade? Does a balance of trade surplus lead to a strengthening of the dollar and a balance of trade deficit to a weakening of the dollar? These are the questions that we are going to tackle in this section. We'll begin by looking at the connection between Canadian dollar prices and the foreign exchange rate.

Prices and the Exchange Rate

In order to understand the relationship between prices and the exchange rate, let's first refresh our memory about the important distinction between two concepts of price — *relative price* and *money price*. Relative price, recall, is the price of one good in terms of another. In Chapter 36, we studied a model economy in which there are just two goods — grain and cars. In that economy, the relative price is the number of bushels of grain that exchanges for a car. The money price of a good or service is the number of dollars for which it trades. The money price depends on the price level or, equivalently, on the value of money. The value of money is, in turn, determined by the amount of money supplied relative to the amount demanded.

Relative prices are determined by demand and supply and, in the case of goods and services that are traded internationally, by demand and supply in the world market, not the domestic market of any individual country. Money prices are determined partly by relative prices and partly by the value of money in an individual country. Each country has its own money prices that depend on the value of that country's money.

Let's consider an example in a model economy similar to the one that we studied in Chapter 36. As in that earlier model, there are two goods: grain and cars. Suppose that one car exchanges for 1,000 bushels of grain on the world market. That is the relative price of cars and grain. The price of a car in terms of grain is 1,000 bushels, and the price of 1,000 bushels of grain is 1 car.

The dollar price of cars and grain is going to depend on the value of money. If the value of money is such that $1 buys 1 bushel of grain, then $1 is the money price of a bushel of grain. The money price of a car is $1,000. That is, the ratio of the two money prices equals the relative price. If the value of money is such that 1 bushel of grain costs $4, then a car costs $4,000.

Money Prices in Two Countries

Money prices can differ from one country to another because of differences in the value of money. The example set out in Table 37.3 shows the connection between the prices in two countries and the exchange rate between the two currencies. In this example, we continue to use grain and cars and the two countries in question are Canada and the United States. Suppose that the world relative price of cars and grain is the same as in the previous section — 1 car costs 1,000 bushels of grain. And suppose that the value of money in the United States is such that 1 bushel of grain costs $4. One car costs $4,000. These are the world market prices expressed in U.S. dollars. The world market prices expressed in Canadian dollars depend on the exchange rate between the Canadian dollar and the U.S. dollar. Three examples are set out in the table. At an exchange rate of C$1.75 per US$1 (an exchange rate that is much lower than we have ever experienced), the bushel of grain that costs $4 in the United States costs $7 in Canada, and the car that costs $4,000 in the United States costs $7,000 in Canada. The other two examples give the prices in Canada, expressed in Canadian dollars, at exchange rates of C$1.25 per US$1 and C$0.75 per US$1.

Table 37.3 Canadian and U.S. Dollar Prices and the Exchange Rate

World market prices in U.S. dollars

Grain	$4 a bushel
Cars	$4,000 each

World market prices in Canadian dollars

	Canadian dollar price	
Exchange rate	Grain (bushel)	Cars (each)
C$1.75 per $US1	$7	$7,000
C$1.25 per $US1	$5	$5,000
C$0.75 per $US1	$3	$3,000

The key message from Table 37.3 is that prices in Canada, expressed in Canadian dollars, depend on world market prices and on the value of the Canadian dollar in terms of other currencies. The higher foreign exchange value of the Canadian dollar against other currencies, the lower is the Canadian dollar price of a good.

Prices of Exports and Imports

You can see now why exporters like a weak dollar and importers like a strong dollar. If the dollar is weak, the price received by an exporter, in Canadian dollars, is high. If the dollar is strong, the price received by an exporter is low. For example, suppose we export grain. With a strong dollar at C$0.75 per US$1, the grain exporter receives only $3 a bushel. With a weak Canadian dollar, at, say, C$1.75 per US$1, the exporter receives $7 a bushel. The importer likes a strong dollar for the same reason. With a strong dollar — say C$0.75 per US$1 — a car costs only C$3,000. But with a weak dollar, at C$1.75 per US$1, that same car costs C$7,000.

The Dollar and the Balance of Trade

An important connection between the dollar and the balance of trade arises from the relationship that

Trade Balance and the Dollar

Trade balance back in the black for November

The merchandise trade balance was back in the black in November after Canadians cut back sharply on their purchases from the rest of the world and marginally increased export sales.

Statistics Canada said the trade balance went from a revised deficit of $356-million in October to a surplus of $679-million in November as imports fell $1-billion to $10.8-billion and exports edged up $58-million to $11.5-billion. The October deficit was revised from the previous figure of $421-million.

Economists said the significant drop in imports was yet another indication that high interest rates and a high dollar are curtailing economic growth and dampening consumer demand. There has been a spate of economic indicators recently telling the same story, including labor force figures released last week that showed a drop in employment and a rise in unemployment...

Imports of automotive products, a category that includes cars, trucks and parts, fell to $2.4-billion in November from $2.9-billion in October. Imports of machinery and equipment, a measure of business investment, were down to $3.5-billion from $3.8-billion the previous month...

On the export side, the largest increase was in wheat exports, which rose to $304-million from $203-million in October as a result of a better harvest last fall. Statscan [Statistics Canada] noted that wheat exports seem to be returning to 1986 levels after sharp declines because of the 1988 drought...

With figures in for 11 months of the year, Canadian exports ... were $128 billion and imports $123.3-billion, leaving an over-all surplus of $4.7-billion. That is considerably lower than the surplus of $9.2-billion for the same period in 1988.

Exporters have been begging the Bank of Canada to loosen its grip on monetary policy and allow interest rates and the dollar to drop. There are indications that the central bank may be easing slightly, although no one expects rates to plummet overnight...

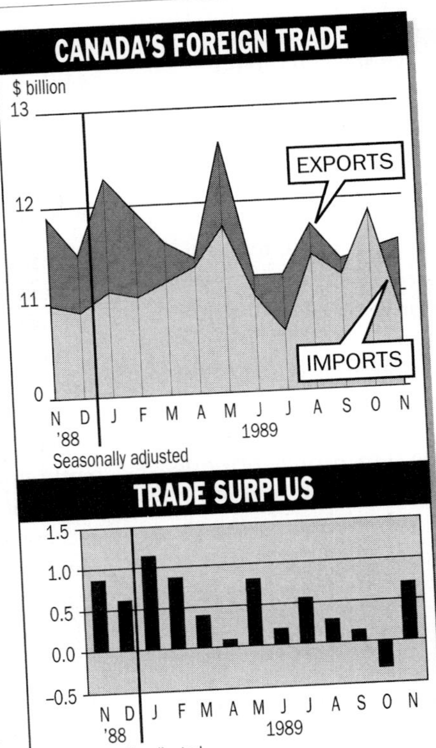

***The Globe and Mail,* January 18, 1990**
By Madelaine Drohan

The Essence of the Story

- Canada's trade balance went from a deficit of $356 million in October 1989 to a surplus of $679 million in November 1989. Imports fell $1 billion and exports increased by $58 million.
- Economists said the drop in imports was an indication that high interest rates and a high dollar were slowing economic growth. Labour force figures showed a drop in employment and a rise in unemployment.
- Imports of automotive products fell to $2.4 billion in November from $2.9 billion in October. Imports of machinery and equipment fell to $3.5 billion from $3.8 billion the previous month.
- On the export side, the largest increase was in wheat exports, which rose to $304 million from $203 million in October due to a good harvest.
- Exports for the first 11 months of 1989 were $128 billion and imports were $123.3 billion, leaving an over-all surplus of $4.7 billion down from a surplus of $9.2 billion for the same period in 1988.
- Exporters pleaded with the Bank of Canada to lower interest rates and let the dollar drop.

Background and Analysis

November 1989

- Figure (a) illustrates the events in November 1989. It shows the import function (see Chapter 26), exports, and the trade balance.
- Exports were virtually constant at \$11.5 billion in both October and November. They are shown by the horizontal line *EX*.
- The import function shown has a *marginal propensity to import* (see Chapter 25) of 0.2. Each additional dollar of GDP brings in an additional 20 cents of imports—an assumption.
- In October, the import function was IM_{Oct}, GDP was \$50 billion (an approximation) and imports were \$11.8 billion. There was a deficit of \$0.3 billion.
- In November, the import function shifted downward to IM_{Nov}, attributed in the story to the slowing of economic growth in Canada. GDP remained at its October level (approximately) and imports decreased to \$10.8 billion giving a surplus of \$0.7 billion.
- From one month to another, there are many random influences on both exports and imports and it is impossible to say with any certainty that the decline in imports in November 1989 was caused by the slowing of economic growth. The explanation seems implausible because the slow-down was very moderate, despite high interest rates and the strong dollar.

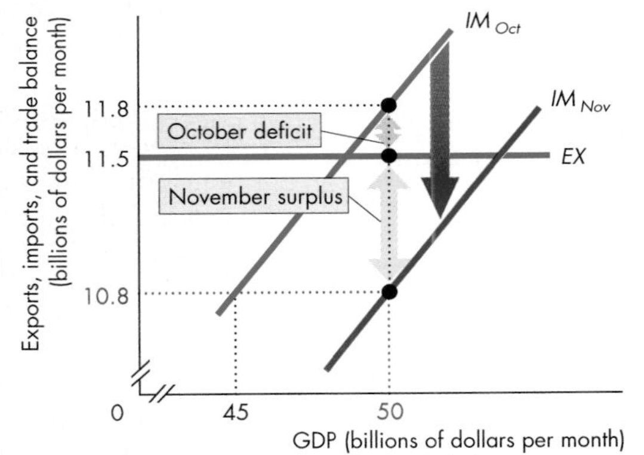

(a) The decrease in imports in November 1989

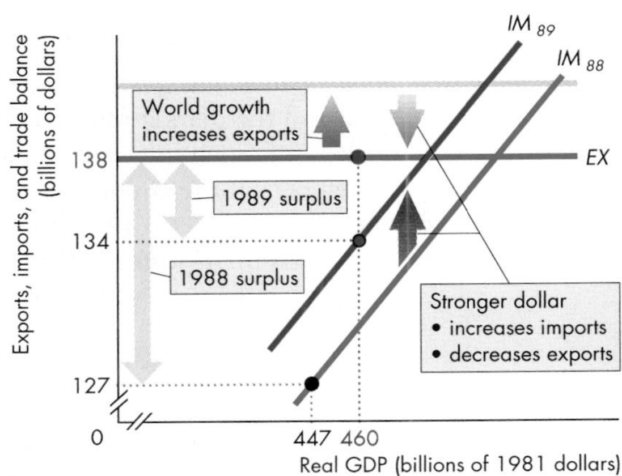

(b) The trade balance, 1988 and 1989

1988 and 1989 compared

- In 1988 there was a trade surplus of \$11 billion. (In the story, the numbers given are for only the first 11 months of 1988.) That surplus decreased to \$4 billion in 1989. Figure (b) explains why.
- The steady strengthening of the Canadian dollar made our imports cheaper and our exports more expensive. This led to an upward shift in the imports function and to a downward shift in the exports line.
- World economic growth produced a steady increase in the demand for our exports, leading to an upward shift in the exports line.
- The two influences on exports offset each other and there was no net change in exports.
- Imports increased for two reasons: the stronger dollar shifted the import function upward and higher real GDP led to a movement along the import function. As a result, the surplus declined.

Other influences

- The balance of trade is just one component of the current account balance, although an important one.
- The balance of trade and the current account balance are influenced by many factors not considered above. The most important of these is the federal government deficit. This influence did not change much in 1989, hence it was not responsible for the *changes* in the trade balance in that year.

we've just studied between prices and the value of the dollar. Canadian demand and supply for the goods that we export and import depend on their prices in Canada. Other things being equal, the higher the price of any good, the more of it will be produced and the less of it consumed. Equivalently, the higher the price of a good, the larger is the quantity supplied and the smaller is the quantity demanded. Let's study the connection between prices, the exchange rate, and the balance of trade by returning to our model economy. That model economy produces and consumes two goods: grain and cars. It exports grain and it imports cars, but it produces and consumes some of each of the goods. The markets for the two goods are illustrated in Fig. 37.3. Focus first on part (a) of the figure. In the market for grain (left part) the supply curve is S_x and the demand curve is D_x. In the market for cars (right part) the demand curve is D_m and the supply curve is S_m. The relative price of cars and grain, determined on the world market, is 1,000 bushels of grain per car, as before. Suppose that the price of these goods on the world economy is US$4 a bushel for grain and US$4,000 each for cars. Also, suppose that the exchange rate between the Canadian dollar and the U.S. dollar is C$1.75 per US$1 (the first example of Table 37.3). In this situation, the price of grain in Canadian dollars is $7, so that the quantity of grain demanded in Canada is 3 million bushels and the quantity supplied is 8 million bushels. Five million bushels are exported and total exports are $35 million (5 million bushels × $7 per bushel). Also the price of a car in Canadian dollars is $7,000, so that the quantity of cars demanded is 5,000 and the quantity of cars supplied is 4,000. Canada imports 1,000 cars and its total imports are $7 million (1,000 cars × $7,000 per car). In this situation, Canada has a balance of trade surplus or positive net exports.

Next, look at part (b) of Fig. 37.3. This part illustrates what happens if the Canadian dollar is more valuable than the U.S. dollar — for example, C$0.75 equals US$1. In this case, the Canadian dollar price of grain is $3 a bushel and of a car is $3,000. At $3 a bushel, the quantity of grain supplied by Canadian growers is 6 million bushels a year and the quantity demanded is 5 million bushels a year. One million bushels a year are exported and total exports are $3 million. At a price of $3,000 a car, the quantity of cars demanded in Canada is 7,000 a year, and the quantity supplied is 2,000 a year. Five thousand cars a year are imported at $3,000 a car, so imports are $15 million. In this situation, Canada has a balance of trade deficit or negative net exports.

We've established that with a high value for the dollar, we import more than we export, and with a low value for the dollar, we export more than we import. In between these two situations is one in which exports and imports are equal in value. This case is illustrated in Fig. 37.3(c). Here, C$1.25 equals US$1, so that the prices in Canadian dollars are $5 a bushel for grain and $5,000 for each car. At these prices, the quantity of grain supplied by Canadians is 7,000 bushels and the quantity demanded is 4,000 bushels. Canada exports 3,000 bushels of grain at $5 a bushel, so total exports are $15 million. At $5,000 a car, the quantity of cars supplied in Canada is 3,000 a year and the quantity of cars demanded is 6,000 a year. Canada imports 3,000 cars a year at $5,000 a car, so the total imports are $15 million. In this situation, the balance of trade is zero, and so are net exports.

Equilibrium Exchange Rate

How is the exchange rate determined? What is the equilibrium exchange rate? We answered these questions in Chapter 29, where we studied the forces that determine the exchange rate. The exchange rate is determined to make the quantity of Canadian-dollar assets demanded equal to the quantity of Canadian-dollar assets supplied. It is not determined by the balance of trade. Indeed, causation goes the other way around. The exchange rate is determined in asset markets — markets for Canadian-dollar assets. Given the exchange rate that is determined in those markets, the Canadian-dollar prices of the goods Canada exports and imports are determined. And given those prices, its balance of trade is determined.

That balance has to be consistent with the analysis that we conducted above where we discovered that the balance of trade is equal to the sum of the private sector deficit and the government sector deficit. This consistency is achieved because of some important interdependencies between the demand and supply curves in the markets for goods and services that are imported and exported and the market for Canadian-dollar assets. Let's explore one such interdependency by working out what happens if the government cuts its tax receipts and increases its transfer payments, thereby increasing the government sector deficit.

Government Sector Deficit, lNet Exports, and the Exchange Rate

Let's look back to the early 1970s when both the government sector deficit and net exports were close to

Figure 37.3 Exports, Imports, and the Dollar

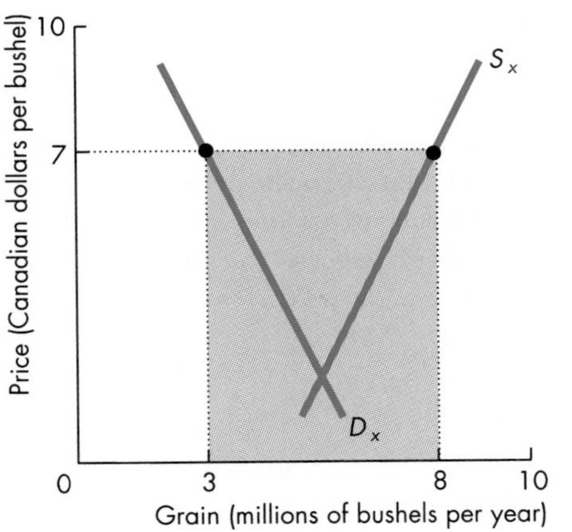

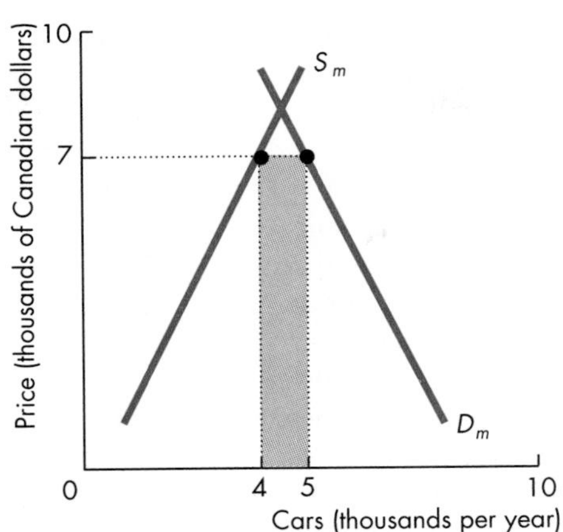

(a) Exports greater than imports

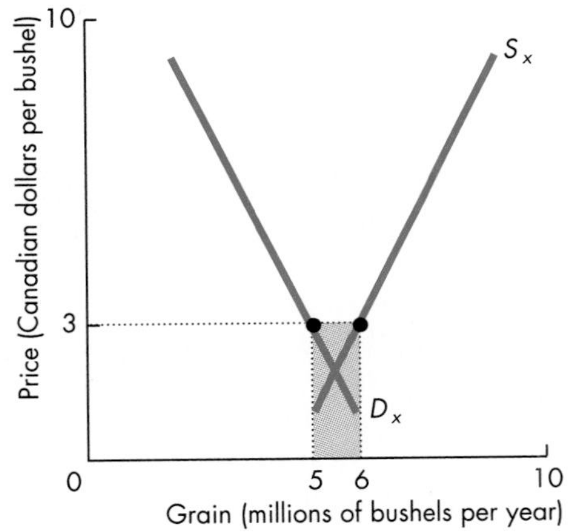

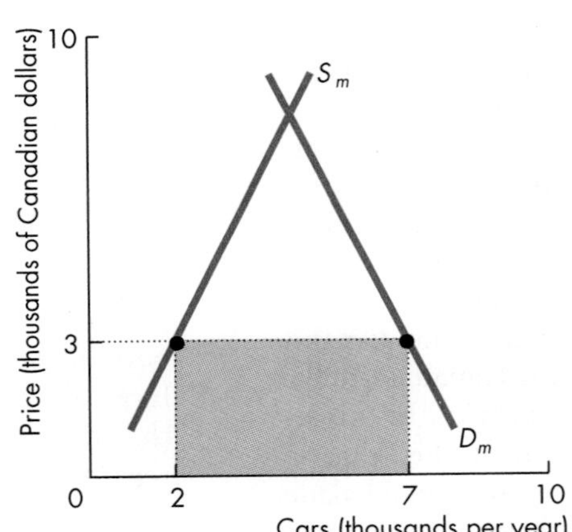

(b) Imports greater than exports

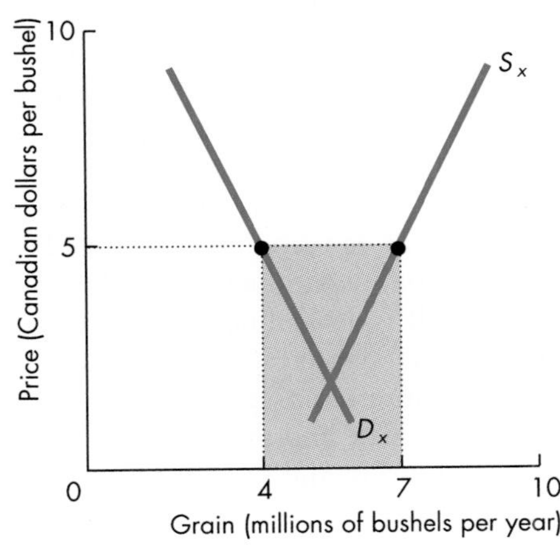

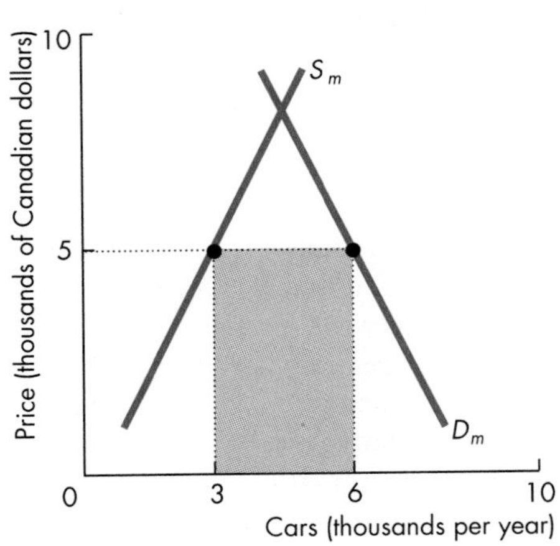

(c) Exports equal imports

The foreign exchange value of the Canadian dollar influences Canadian dollar prices. Other things being equal, the higher the Canadian dollar price of a good, the lower is the quantity demanded by Canadians and the larger is the quantity supplied by Canadians. The figure illustrates two goods: grain, which is exported, and cars, which are imported.

When the exchange rate is C$1.75 per US$1, the price of grain is C$7 per bushel and the price of a car is C$7,000. The demand curve for grain is D_x and the supply curve is S_x. The demand curve for cars is D_m and the supply curve is S_m. At the exchange rate of C$1.75 per US$1 (part a), Canada has an excess of exports over imports (compare the shaded areas in the two parts of the figure).

When the exchange rate is C$0.75 per US$1, the Canadian dollar prices are $3 per bushel for grain and $3,000 for a car. In this situation (part b), imports are greater than exports. When the exchange rate is C$1.25 per US$1, the Canadian dollar price of grain is $5 per bushel and of cars is $5,000. The value of exports and the value of imports are equal (part c).

zero. At that time, the Canadian dollar was just about equal in value to the U.S. dollar. Soon after, the Canadian dollar declined in value against the U.S. dollar and a large government sector deficit emerged. What was the cause of the decline in the value of our dollar, and how did the government sector deficit influence the balance of trade and the value of the dollar?

Let's begin with the cause of the government sector deficit and its initial effects. A government sector deficit occurred in the mid-1970s because of a fall in tax revenue and an increase in transfer payments and subsidies. Lower taxes and higher transfer payments bring higher levels of disposable incomes. With higher disposable incomes, Canadians increased their demand for all goods and services — consumption goods and services, capital goods, domestic goods and services that might otherwise have been exported, and goods and services produced in other countries. The private sector moved into a deficit, as did the government sector. The supply of exports declined, the demand for imports increased, and there was a balance of trade deficit. With an increased government sector and private sector deficit, there was an increase in the supply of Canadian-dollar assets — in the form of government bonds and private bonds and other securities. The increased supply of Canadian-dollar assets relative to the demand for them lowered their value — the Canadian-dollar declined in value against other currencies. In this sequence of events, there was a decline in the value of the dollar, net exports became negative and a balance of trade deficit arose. These two developments were a consequence of the initial change in the balance of the government sector's budget. It is not that a deteriorating balance of payments caused a decline in the value of the dollar. It is that some third force caused both the balance of trade deficit and the falling value of the dollar.

Could the balance of trade deficit be corrected by forcing the value of the dollar down even further? From the analysis that we conducted in Fig. 37.3, you might be tempted to conclude that it could. There we discovered that the lower the value of the dollar, the larger the value of net exports. But such a conclusion would be incorrect, for it would mean holding constant too many other things that could not in fact be constant. It's important to recognize that the curves that appear in Fig. 37.3 assume that all influences (other than the price of the good in question) on the quantities demanded and supplied are held constant. To force the value of the dollar down, the Bank of Canada would have to increase the supply of Canadian-dollar assets at an even faster pace — it would have to conduct open market operations, making more money available in Canada. In so doing, it would not only lower the value of the dollar but also increase the prices of all goods and services in Canada. The prices of exports and imports relative to the prices of other, nontraded goods and relative to wages and other production costs would not change, so the balance of trade would not change.

Stabilizing the Exchange Rate

We've seen that permitting the value of the Canadian dollar to decline even further than it did could not have prevented the balance of trade deficit that emerged in the mid-1970s. But could the decline in the value of the Canadian dollar itself have been prevented? The answer is yes. It could have been prevented if the Bank of Canada had adopted a tight monetary policy, decreasing the supply of Canadian-dollar assets so as to preserve the foreign exchange value of the dollar. However, to have achieved a constant foreign exchange value of the dollar, the Canadian price level would have had to rise at a much slower pace than it did — perhaps not at all. Slowing the rise of prices quickly would have created a recession, bringing costs that the government and Bank of Canada did not regard as appropriate ones to bear for the benefit of a stable foreign exchange value of the dollar.

The Real-Nominal Distinction

The distinction between real and nominal variables is a crucial one in the whole study of economics. It is especially important for the topic that we have just been studying. The balance of trade is a real phenomenon. It is determined by the demands and supplies for exports and imports that, in turn, are determined by the factors of production, technologies, and preferences. The volume of trade is determined by the forces that we described in Chapter 36. The balance of trade is determined by intertemporal choices — by decisions both in the private and the government sector concerning consumption and saving. The exchange rate, like the price level, is a nominal magnitude. Its value is determined by the supply and demand of nominal quantities — of money and financial assets.

There is the connection between the government sector deficit — a real variable — and the supply of Canadian-dollar assets and money — a nominal variable. But that connection does not give rise to any inevitable links between the balance of payments and the dollar. The links and correlations that have arisen historically are not the only possible ones. A different monetary policy and the same fiscal policy would have produced the same behaviour of the balance of payments but a different behaviour of the exchange rate. The same monetary policy with a different fiscal policy would have produced a similar movement in the exchange rate but a different course for the balance of payments.

■ You've now discovered what determines a country's current account balance. The most important influence on the current account balance is the government sector deficit. A country in which taxes are less than government spending is likely to be one that has a deficit in its trade with the rest of the world.

In the final two chapters, we're going to look at some further global economic issues. In Chapter 38, we'll examine the problems faced by developing countries as they seek to grow. In Chapter 39, we'll look at countries that operate with economic systems that differ from our own — the command economies of the Soviet Union, Eastern Europe, and the People's Republic of China and the economy of Japan.

SUMMARY

Financing International Trade

International trade, borrowing, and lending are financed using foreign currency. A country's international transactions are recorded in its balance of payments accounts. The current account records receipts and expenditures connected with the sale and purchase of goods and services, as well as net transfers to the rest of the world. The capital account records international borrowing and lending transactions. The official settlements account shows the increase or decrease in the country's foreign currency holdings. (pp. 995-997)

International Borrowing and Lending

A country that borrows more from the rest of the world than it lends to it is a net borrower; a country that lends more to the rest of the world than it borrows from it is a net lender. Borrowing and lending are flows. Debts are stocks. Borrowing increases debt, and a debtor nation is one that has borrowed more than it has lent throughout its entire history. A creditor nation is one that has lent more than it has borrowed throughout its history. Historically, Canada has been a net borrower from the rest of the world and is a debtor nation. Canada has used its international borrowing to develop its economic resources and increase its level of income. (pp. 997-999)

Current Account Balance

The current account balance is equal to net exports less interest paid abroad plus net transfers from the rest of the world. Net exports is equal to the sum of the government sector balance and the private sector balance. Before 1977, the current account balance and the government deficit moved in sympathy with each other. Between 1977 and 1984, a large private sector surplus emerged which more than offset the government deficit and there was a current account surplus. The private sector surplus declined after 1985 and the current account again moved into a deficit. (pp. 999-1002)

Net Exports and the Dollar

The higher the foreign exchange value of the dollar, the lower are the prices, in Canadian dollars, received by exporters and paid by importers. Other things being equal, the higher the foreign exchange value of the dollar, the smaller the volume of exports and the larger the volume of imports. Although the foreign exchange value of the dollar affects imports and exports and the balance of trade, the value of the dollar itself is only indirectly influenced by the balance of payments. It is determined by the demand and supply of Canadian-dollar assets in the world economy. But there are important linkages between the demand for and supply of Canadian dollars and the balance of payments. An increase in the government sector deficit brings an increase in the supply of Canadian-dollar assets and a decrease in the value of the Canadian dollar. It also brings an increase in demand for goods and an increase in the balance of trade deficit (or a decrease in the balance of trade surplus). (pp. 1002-1009)

KEY ELEMENTS

Key Terms

Balance of payments accounts, 995
Capital account, 995
Creditor nation, 998
Current account, 995
Debtor nation, 997
Government sector surplus or deficit, 999
Net borrower, 997
Net interest payments, 995
Net lender, 997
Official foreign exchange reserves, 996
Official settlements account, 995
Private sector surplus or deficit, 999

Key Figures 

REVIEW QUESTIONS

1 What are the transactions recorded in a country's current account? in its capital account? in its official settlements account?

2 What is the relationship among the balances on the current account, the capital account, and the official settlements account?

3 Distinguish between a country that is a net borrower and one that is a creditor. Are net borrowers always creditors? Are creditors always net borrowers?

4 What is the connection between a country's current account balance and the government sector deficit and the private sector deficit?

5 Why do fluctuations in the government sector deficit lead to fluctuations in the current account balance?

PROBLEMS

1 The citizens of Pioneerland, whose currency is the choo, conduct the following transactions in 1990:

Variable	Billions of choos
Imports of goods and services	250
Exports of goods and services	397
Borrowing from the rest of the world	80
Lending to the rest of the world	20
Increase in official holdings of foreign currency	3

a) Set out Pioneerland's current account and calculate its current account balance.

b) Set out Pioneerland's capital account and calculate its capital account balance.

c) Is Pioneerland operating a flexible exchange rate for the choo?

2 You are told the following about Ecoland, a country whose currency is the turky and whose exchange rate is flexible:

Variable	Billions of turkies
GDP	50
Consumption expenditure	30
Government purchases of goods and services	12
Investment	11
Exports of goods and services	10
Government budget deficit	2

Calculate the following for Ecoland:

a) Imports of goods and services

b) Current account balance

c) Capital account balance

d) Taxes (net of transfer payments)

e) Private sector deficit or surplus

PART 14

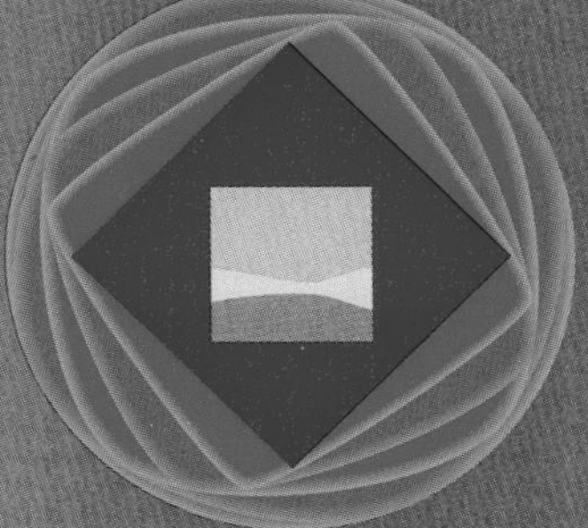

Growth, Development, and Comparative Systems

TALKING WITH

JANOS KORNAI

Janos Kornai is professor of economics at Harvard University and department head of the Institute of Economics and the Hungarian Academy of Sciences. Professor Kornai divides his time between Cambridge and Budapest. His books and publications have been translated into 17 languages and include *Over-centralization in Economic Administration*, *Economics Of Shortage*, and *Contradictions and Dilemmas*. Michael Parkin spoke with Dr. Kornai about how socialist economies work and the changes that are taking place in the socialist world.

"The maximal state associated with classical socialism is not sustainable."

Professor Kornai, why did you become an economist?

My interest in economics started very early and has always been part of my concern for political and social issues. When I was younger, I was attracted to the ideals and goals of socialism, and my research reflected that. Since then I have become more critical of socialist political economy and have become interested in alternative economic theories and in the kind of economics practised in the West.

We're observing remarkable changes in socialist countries—Hungary, China, the Soviet Union, Poland, in both political and economic spheres. What do you think is driving these changes?

On the surface, events like the death of a leader can trigger the desire to reform the system. But more fundamentally, it's because of deep dissatisfaction with the system—dissatisfaction of the party apparatus and leadership as well as popular discontent. But these changes won't be finished overnight. Yugoslavia, for example, has been moving away from what I call classical socialism—the traditional socialism associated with Lenin, Stalin, and Mao—for 40 years!

Do you see any connection between these reforms and the deregulation and privatization that's occurring in the United States and Europe?

They're not totally distinct. They're parallel in that they are both movements in the direction to what political philosophy calls the minimal state. But of course they're not starting at the same point and that makes quite a difference. Reforming socialist countries are moving away from a highly centralized, bureaucratic society—what I like to call a maximal state. By contrast, Britain under Labour governments was very far from a maximal state, so privatization under Conservative governments in Britain is different from reforms in Eastern Bloc countries.

Do you see any long-term patterns of socialist economies tending to go from maximal to minimal state?

It is still early to know that. But my impression is that the maximal degree associated with classical socialism is not sustainable for many reasons. I'll mention just a few. It's terribly expensive for a society to monitor everyone's activity. Next, growth gives rise to increasing complexity—not only producing more goods, but more differentiated products. For example, in Maoist China, everyone wore the same blue uniform, so it was easy to plan their production.

But in a modern economy there are billions of goods and services. That makes complete centralization hopeless. The economy just can't keep up and there are shortages of many goods. I agree with F. A. Hayek, who argued that you need a market with free enterprise just to make use of decentralized human knowledge.

Some Western economists emphasize the role of the rational central planner in classical socialist economies, but does this ideal exist in the real world?

First let's consider whether this planner is just a single person. In fact, it never is just one individual, but the whole hierarchy of party officals, civil servants, and managers of state-owned firms. The huge apparatus is not a monolithic group, with uniform preferences, but a set of people with conflicting interests. The conflicts are revealed in the fights among interest groups, lobbies, and in various factions of the party.

As for the idea of a *rational* central planner, rationality includes the notion of stable preferences. But if you look, for example, at the history of socialist China, you'll immediately observe that Mao's own policy goals changed radically several times. His preferences were clearly *not* stable. Finally let's emphasize *planner*—I can speak about this from my personal experience in designing some of the models that were used to make plans. Planning theory assumes that you use the full information available to make the best possible calculations.

But the planner is a human being with certain bureaucratic and personal interests who may not disclose certain information if it's not in his or her best interest. That planner, again, is part of a multilevel hierarchy, and may have to bargain with a superior about how ambitious the plan will be. In short, planning is a complicated social process, rather than a few wise people with well-defined goals and preferences constructing an ideal plan.

Shortages of consumer goods are quite common in centralized socialist economies. What is the effect of chronic shortages on the economy?

There are immediate effects on the lives of people in their capacity as consumers. You can't spend your income according to your preferences. If you want pork, but it's chronically unavailable, you're forced to buy herring instead. This kind of forced substitution leads to a decrease in consumer welfare. If you've ever experienced a seller's market—at an airline ticket counter, for example—you know how it feels to be at the seller's mercy. Turning to production, there's no incentive to improve quality, no competition to drive innovation. Shortages have a very serious effect, therefore, in reducing efficiency.

Does the concept of forced substitution change the practical definition of "demand" in shortage economies?

Yes, indeed. There's an assumption underlying the textbook concept of demand familiar to most North American college students, namely, that goods are available. But what if you want to buy apples and you can't find them anywhere in the city, or only on Mondays?

"Planning is a complicated social process, rather than a few wise people constructing an ideal plan."

Sooner or later, a consumer who grows up in a shortage economy gets used to these supply constraints and stops demanding apples. You have to take these supply constraints and consumer expectations into account when figuring out the demand for apples.

"The time is ripe for a wider synthesis in methodology."

Market economies coordinate the plans of buyers and sellers, demanders and suppliers, through prices. How is this coordination achieved in socialist economies?

Price is still an important factor in the choices consumers make. Supply may constrain purchases, but households are very sensitive to the prices of meat or milk, for example. Households are also sensitive to wage differentials in their supply of labour. It's in the supply of goods that price is much less important. Instead, the instructions of central planners determine which goods are produced and how much. Other centralized mechanisms that are used as signals include rationing and licensing. An important decentralized signal is inventories and back-orders. If you're used to having a two-year waiting list for cars, for example, and it suddenly shoots up to four years, then you know you have more customers than you're used to supplying. Finally, there's the concept—introduced by Albert Hirschman—of *voice*. In a market economy, if you don't like a certain shop, well, you can take your business elsewhere. But you can also use your *voice* to complain. The latter is an important signal in socialist economies as well. Except if your voice is too loud!

You have been trained in both Marxian and Neoclassical economic theory. What principles guide your work?

My goal has always been to understand the deep answers to important questions about how economic systems work, not just to find a comfortable analytic framework. Marxian economics frequently gives the wrong answers but to important questions. Neoclassical economics, on the other hand, can give you very precise answers, but the questions themselves may or may not be important. Young economists, working with the conventional Neoclasssical toolkit do not get from the underlying theory a good guide for choosing the right research strategy. They may easily miss the point and be tempted to use this powerful intellectual appparatus for addressing irrelevant issues, with a good chance that they can still impress their colleagues. They should instead start to use the Neoclassical analytical methods only *after* having identified the problem, the situation, the economic actors' motivations, and the social constraints. The time is ripe for a wider synthesis in methodology.

CHAPTER 38

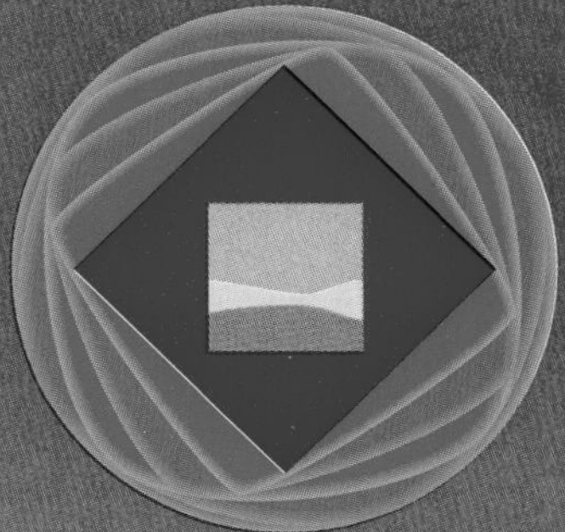

Growth and Development

After studying this chapter, you will be able to:

- Describe the international distribution of income.
- Explain the importance of economic growth.
- Explain how the accumulation of capital and technological progress bring higher per capita incomes.
- Describe the impediments to economic growth in poor countries.
- Explain the possible effects of population control, foreign aid, free trade, and demand stimulation on economic growth and development.
- Evaluate policies designed to stimulate economic growth and development.

Feed the World

IN 1984, PEOPLE ALL OVER Canada saw images of starving Ethiopian children on their television screens. In a surge of sympathy, they donated millions of dollars, most visibly through a rock concert benefit called Live Aid. The people of many other countries also responded generously. While the flow of aid didn't eliminate the hunger, it saved many thousands of lives. ■ A success? Only in the short run, sadly. Three years later, Ethiopia was as poor as ever, and it again suffered a devastating famine. The *average* person in Ethiopia has an income that is equivalent to about $2 a week. And Ethiopia, like all other countries, has an unequal distribution of income, so the poorest people in that country have much less than $2 a week. These poorest of the world's people have no shelter, they wear rags for clothes, and they spend most of their lives in hunger. Why are so many countries, like Ethiopia, chained to poverty? Why are there such differences in income between the poorest and richest countries? Does foreign aid help these countries? Why hasn't it alleviated their poverty? ■ As World War II ended, Hong Kong emerged from occupation by the Japanese as a poor colony of Britain. Occupying a cluster of overcrowded rocky islands with few natural resources, Hong Kong today is a city of vibrant, hard-working, and increasingly wealthy people. Its exports flow through the world, and with astonishing speed, its people are bootstrapping themselves out of poverty. A similar story can be told of Singapore. Two and a half million people crowded into an island city-nation have, by their dynamism, transformed their economy, increasing their average income sixfold since 1960. How do some countries manage to unshackle themselves from poverty? What do they have that other poor countries lack? Can their lessons be applied elsewhere? ■ Rich countries are not all equally wealthy. At the end of World War II, per capita income in Japan was a mere 17 percent of that in the United States; France's was 47 percent and Germany's 40 percent of the U.S. levels. Yet today per capita income — income per person — in these three countries is almost the same as that of the United States.

How did countries like Canada, the United States, Japan, France, and West Germany get to be wealthy? Why have Japan and several European countries grown so quickly and caught up to the United States in the past few decades? ■ The world's population has passed 5 billion inhabitants. These billions of people are unevenly distributed over the earth's surface. More than 4 billion live in the world's poor countries and only 1 billion in the rich industrial countries. It is estimated that by the year 2020, world population will exceed 8 billion, with close to 7 billion living in the poor countries and only 1.4 billion in the industrial countries. The governments of poor countries are constantly seeking new and more effective methods of containing their population growth rates, though with limited success. In 1988, China revised its forecasts of its own population, predicting that by the turn of the century, population targets would have been exceeded by an amount equal to more than five times the population of Canada. Why is the population growth rate so rapid in poor countries? What are the effects of rapid population growth on economic growth and development? ■ In a typical year in the mid-1980s, rich countries gave developing countries $85 billion worth of aid. Canada is a generous donor, and the United States provided more than one-third of all foreign aid. Other large donors were Japan, France, West Germany, the United Kingdom, and Belgium. The recipients of this aid were the poor countries of Africa, Latin America, and Asia. What are the effects of foreign aid on economic growth and development? ■ Some poor countries try to encourage growth and development by protecting their domestic industries from international trade and foreign competition. Other countries adopt an outward-looking orientation, engaging in free trade with the rest of the world. What kind of international trade policy gives a developing country the best chance of rapid and sustained economic growth?

■ In this chapter, we'll study the questions just posed. They are all aspects of one of those big questions posed in Chapter 1: what causes differences in wealth among nations, making the people in some countries rich and in others poor? We don't fully know the answer to this question. But there are some things that we do understand. We'll review that knowledge in this chapter. We'll also review some of the ideas people have advanced about what can be done to speed up the growth of poor countries. Some strategies can truly help poor countries, but others have mixed results and may even hurt their development.

The International Distribution of Income

There is a great deal of inequality in the distribution of income in Canada. In 1982, the poorest 20 percent of the population earned 5 percent of total income while the richest 20 percent of the population earned 43 percent. As we will see, such differences in income within a country, large though they are, look insignificant when compared with the differences among the nations. Let's see how income is distributed among the nations of the world.

The Poorest Countries

The poorest countries are sometimes called underdeveloped countries. An **underdeveloped country** is a country in which there is little industrialization, limited mechanization of the agricultural sector, very little capital equipment, and low per capita income. In many underdeveloped countries, large numbers of people live on the edge of starvation. Such people devote their time to producing the meagre supplies of food and clothing required for themselves and their families. They have no surplus to trade with others or to invest in new tools and capital equipment. One of the most publicized of the poor countries is Ethiopia, where thousands of people spend their lives trekking across parched landscapes in search of meagre food supplies.

Just how poor are the poorest countries? We'll use the United States as a reference point. Those countries, whose per capita incomes range between 4 and 9 percent of those in the United States, contain 27 percent of the world's people, who earn only 6 percent of world income. These poorest of countries are located mainly in Asia and Africa. Examples are Burma, Laos, Somalia, Ethiopia, and Ghana.

Developing Countries

A **developing country** is one that is poor but is accumulating capital and developing an industrial and commercial base. The developing countries have a large and growing urban population and steadily growing incomes. The per capita income level in such countries ranges between 10 and 30 percent of that in the United States. These countries are located in all parts of the world, but many are found in Asia, the Middle East, and in Central America. Examples are India, Egypt, and Mexico. The 17 percent of the world's people who live in these countries earn 11 percent of world income.

Newly Industrialized Countries

Newly industrialized countries (often called NICs) are countries in which there is a rapidly developing, broad industrial base and per capita income is growing quickly. Today their per capita income levels approach 50 percent of those in the United States. Examples of such countries are Trinidad, Israel, and South Korea. The 3 percent of the world's people who live in newly industrialized countries earn 3 percent of world income.

Industrial Countries

Industrial countries are countries that have a large amount of capital equipment and in which people undertake highly specialized activities, enabling them to earn high per capita incomes. These are the countries of Western Europe, Canada and the United States, Japan, and Australia and New Zealand. The 17 percent of the world's people who live in these countries earn 49 percent of world income.

Oil-Rich Countries

A small number of oil-rich countries have very high per capita incomes despite the fact that they are, in most other respects, similar to the poorest countries or developing countries. These countries have little industry and, indeed, little of anything of value to sell to the world except oil. The 4 percent of the world's people who live in these countries earn 4 percent of world income. But that income is very unequally distributed within these countries — most of the people have incomes similar to those in the poorest countries, but a small number are among the richest people in the world.

Communist Countries

Close to 33 percent of the world's people live in communist countries, and they earn 28 percent of world income. A **communist country** is a country in which there is limited private ownership of productive capital and of firms and limited reliance on the market as a means of allocating resources. Rather, government agencies plan and direct the production and distribution of most goods and services. Rapid changes are taking place in many of these countries as a result of the freedom movement unleashed in 1989. We describe the economies of these countries and the changes that are taking place there in Chapter 39.

Per capita incomes in the communist countries vary enormously. In China, per capita income is about 15 percent of that in the United States. China is a developing country. Per capita income in the German Democratic Republic (East Germany), an industrial country, is almost 70 percent of that of the United States. Other industrial communist countries are Czechoslovakia, Poland, Hungary, and the Soviet Union. Some communist countries, such as Romania, Yugoslavia, and Bulgaria, have per capita incomes similar to those of the newly industrialized countries. Thus within the communist countries, there is a great deal of variety in income levels and the degree of economic development.

The World Lorenz Curve

A **Lorenz curve** plots the cumulative percentage of income against the cumulative percentage of population. If income is equally distributed, the Lorenz curve is a 45° line running from the origin. The degree of inequality is indicated by the extent to which the Lorenz curve departs from the 45° line of equality. Fig. 38.1 shows two Lorenz curves: one curve depicts the distribution of income among families in Canada, and the other the distribution of average per capita income across countries.

As you can see, the distribution of income among countries is more unequal than the distribution of income among families within Canada. Forty percent of the world's people live in countries whose incomes account for less than 10 percent of the world's total. The richest 20 percent of the people live in countries whose incomes account for 55 percent of the world's total income. Inequality in income is even more severe than that apparent in Fig. 38.1, for the world Lorenz curve tells us only how unequal average incomes are among countries. It does not reveal inequality within countries.

Figure 38.1 The World Lorenz Curve, 1980 

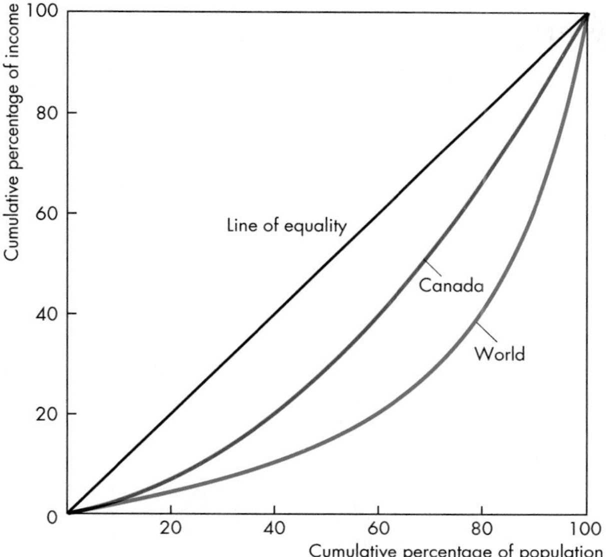

The cumulative percentage of income is plotted against the cumulative percentage of population. If income were distributed equally across countries, the Lorenz curve would be a straight diagonal line. The distribution of per capita income across countries is even more unequal than the distribution of income across families in Canada.

Source: Robert Summers and Alan Heston, "Improved International Comparison of Real Product and Its Composition: 1950 –1980," *Review of Income and Wealth*, series 30 (June 1984): 207- 62.

Such numbers provide a statistical description of the enormity of the world's poverty problem. To better appreciate the severity of the problem, imagine that your family has an income of 30 cents a day for each person. That 30 cents has to buy housing, food, clothing, transportation, and all the other things consumed. Such is the lot of more than a quarter of the world's people.

Although there are many poor people in the world, there are also many whose lives are undergoing dramatic change. They live in countries in which rapid economic growth is taking place. As a result of economic growth and development, millions of people now enjoy living standards undreamt of by their parents and inconceivable to their grandparents. Let's look at the connection between income level and the rate of economic growth.

Growth Rates and Income Levels

Poor countries can and do grow into rich countries. Poor countries become rich countries by achieving high growth rates of real per capita income over prolonged periods of time. Like compound interest, a small increase in the growth rate pays large dividends over the years. A slowdown in the growth rate maintained over a number of years can result in a huge loss of real income.

The importance of economic growth and its effects on income levels are vividly illustrated by our own recent experience. In Canada in the early 1970s, aggregate income, measured by real gross domestic product (GDP), was growing at more than 5 percent a year. After 1974, that slowed down. The path actually followed by Canadian GDP growth is shown in Fig. 38.2(a). The path that would have been followed if the pre-1974 growth trend had been maintained is also shown in that figure. By 1989, Canadian real GDP was $460 billion — 26 percent — less than it would have been if the 1974 growth rate had been maintained.

When poor countries have a slow growth rate and rich countries a fast growth rate, the gap between the rich and the poor widens. Figure 38.2(b) shows how the gap between real GDP in Canada and in many poor countries, such as Ethiopia, has widened over the years.

For a poor country to catch up to a rich country, its growth rate must exceed that of the rich country. How long would it take a poor country, such as China, to achieve an income level equal to that in the United States? In 1980, per capita income in China was 14 percent of that in the United States. In the 1980s, the United States experienced an average per capita income growth rate of 1.5 percent a year. If that growth rate is maintained and if per capita income in China also grows at 1.5 percent a year, China will remain at 14 percent of U.S. income levels forever. The gap will remain constant. If per capita income in the United States were to grow at 1.5 percent and if China could maintain a per capita income growth rate at twice that level — 3 percent per year — China's per capita income would catch up to the United States' in the first part of the twenty-second century, about 2115. If China could do twice as well as that — maintaining a 6 percent per year growth rate in per capita incomes — the people of China would have income levels as high as those in the United States within your own lifetime — in the

Figure 38.2 Growth Rates and Income Levels

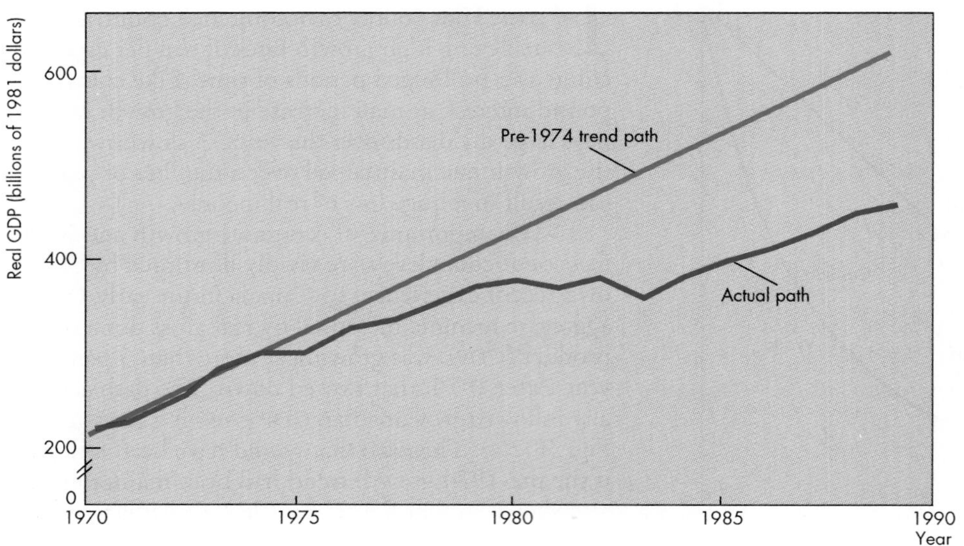

(a) Canadian output loss from growth slowdown

Real GDP per capita (thousands of 1975 dollars)

8, 6, 4, 2, 0

Canada

Widening gap between rich and poor

Ethiopia

1950 1955 1960 1965 1970 1975 1980 Year

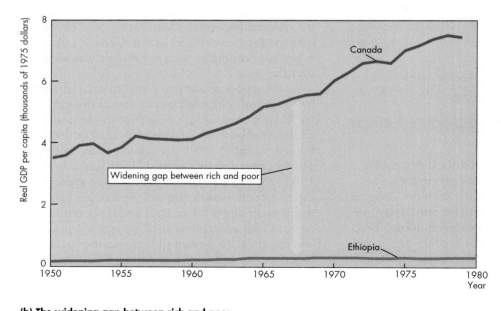

(b) The widening gap between rich and poor

A fall in the growth rate of real income in Canada after 1974 (part a) has resulted in GDP that is $160 billion (26 percent) less than what it would have been if the pre-1974 trend had continued. Small changes in the growth rate, maintained over a long period of time, produce large differences in income levels. Steady growth in Canada, compared with almost none in Ethiopia (part b), results in a gradually widening gap between the rich and the poor.

Sources: Part (a), Statistics Canada, CANSIM series D20031. Part (b) Robert Summers and Alan Heston, "Improved International Comparisons of Real Product and its Composition: 1950 –1980", *The Review of Income and Wealth*, Series 30, No. 2, June 1984, pp. 207- 62.

mid-2030s. If China could pull off a miracle and make per capita income grow at 12 percent a year, it would take just 20 years to catch up to the United States.

Growth rates as high as 10 or 12 percent are not unknown. Japan grew in excess of 10 percent a year, on the average, for almost 20 years following World War II. Recently China has indeed experienced per capita income growth of 12 percent a year, a rate that, if sustained, doubles per capita income every six years. Even the poorest countries in the world — countries with per capita incomes of only 4 percent of those of the United States — would catch the United States in a matter of 30 or 40 years if they could achieve and maintain growth rates of this level.

The key then to achieving high per capita income is to attain and maintain a high economic growth rate. That is how today's rich countries attained their high living standards. The poor countries of today will join the rich countries of tomorrow only if they can find ways of attaining and maintaining rapid growth.

Clearly, the question of what determines a country's economic growth rate is a vital one. Let's turn to an examination of this crucial question.

Inputs, Technological Progress, and Economic Growth

In the aggregate, income equals the value of output. Thus to increase average income, a country has to increase its output. A country's output depends on its resources or inputs and on the techniques it employs for transforming inputs into outputs. This relationship between inputs and outputs is the *production function.* There are three inputs:

- Land
- Labour
- Capital

Land includes all the natural, nonproduced inputs, such as land itself, the minerals under it, and all other nonproduced inputs. The quantity of these inputs is determined by nature, and countries have no choice but to put up with whatever natural resources they happen to have. Countries cannot achieve rapid and sustained economic growth by increasing their stock of natural resources. But countries can and do experience fluctuations in income as a result of fluctuations in the prices of their natural resources. Furthermore, there are times when those prices are rising quickly, and such periods bring temporary income growth. The late 1970s was an example of a period in which resource-rich countries experienced rapid income growth as a result of rising commodity prices. But to achieve long-run, sustained income growth, countries have to look beyond their natural resources.

One such source of increased output is a sustained increase in *labour* inputs. That is, a country can produce more output over the years simply because its population of workers grows. But for each successively larger generation of workers to have a higher *per capita* income than the previous generation, per capita output must increase. Population growth, on its own, does not lead to higher per capita output.

The input most responsible for rapid and sustained economic growth is capital. There are two broad types of capital — physical and human. *Physical capital* includes such things as highways and railways, dams and irrigation systems, tractors and ploughs, factories, trucks and cars, and buildings of all kinds. *Human capital* is the accumulated knowledge and skills of the working population. As individuals accumulate more capital, their incomes grow. As nations accumulate more capital per worker, labour productivity and output per capita grow.

To study the behaviour of per capita output, we use the per capita production function. The **per capita production function** shows how per capita output varies as the per capita stock of capital varies in a given state of knowledge about alternative technologies. Figure 38.3 illustrates the per capita production function. Per capita output is measured on the vertical axis and the per capita stock of capital on the horizontal axis. Curve *PF* shows how per capita output varies as the amount of per capita capital varies. A rich country such as Canada has a large amount of per capita capital and a large per capita output. A poor country such as Ethiopia has hardly any capital and very low per capita output.

Capital Accumulation

By accumulating capital, a country can grow and move along its per capita production function. The greater the amount of capital (per capita), the greater is output (per capita). But the fundamental *law of diminishing returns* applies to the per capita production function. That is, as capital per capita increases, output per capita also increases but by decreasing increments. Thus there is a limit to the extent to which a country can grow merely by accumulating capital. Eventually, the country will reach the point at which the extra output from extra capital is simply not worth the effort of accumulating more capital. At

Figure 38.3 The Per Capita Production Function

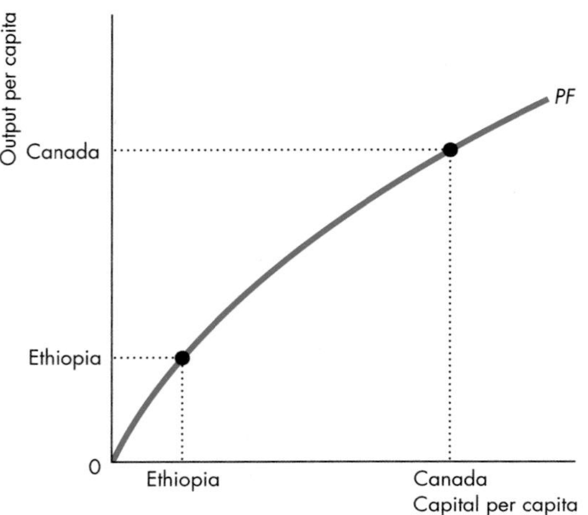

The per capita production function (*PF*) traces how per capita output varies as the stock of per capita capital varies. If two countries use the same technology but one of them has a larger capital stock, that country will also have a higher per capita income level. For example, suppose that Ethiopia and Canada each use the same technology. Ethiopia has a low per capita capital stock and a low level of output per capita. Canada has a large per capita capital stock and a large per capita output rate.

such a point, it will pay the country to consume rather than to increase its capital stock.

No country has yet reached such a point because the per capita production function is constantly shifting upward as a result of improvements in technology. Let's see how technological change affects output and economic growth.

Technological Change

Although rich countries have much more capital per capita than poor countries, that is not the only difference between them. Typically, rich countries use more productive technologies than do poor countries. That is, even if two countries have the same per capita capital, the rich country produces more output than the poor country. For example, a farmer in a rich country might use a ten-horsepower tractor, whereas a farmer in a poor country might use literally ten horses. Each has the same amount of "horsepower," but the output achieved by using the tractor is considerably more than that produced by using ten horses. The combination of better technology and more per capita capital accentuates still further the difference between the rich and poor countries.

Figure 38.4 illustrates the importance of the difference that technological advance makes. Imagine that the year is 1867 and both Canada and Ethiopia (then called Abyssinia) use the same techniques of production and have the same per capita production function, PF_{1867}. With a larger per capita stock of capital, Canada produces a higher level of per capita output in 1867 than does Ethiopia. By 1990, technological advances adopted in Canada, but not in Ethiopia, enable Canada to produce more output from given inputs. The per capita production function in Canada shifts upward to PF_{1990}. Output per capita in Canada in 1990 is much higher than it was in 1867 for two reasons. First, the per capita stock of capital equipment has increased dramatically; second, the techniques of production have improved, resulting in an upward shift in the production function.

The faster the pace of technological advance, the faster the production function shifts upward. The faster the pace of capital accumulation, the more quickly a country moves along its production function. Both

Figure 38.4 Technological Change

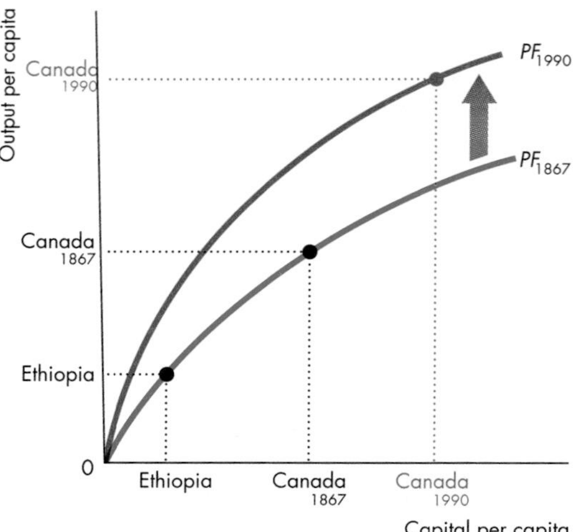

In 1867, Canada and Ethiopia have the same production function, PF_{1867}. By 1990, technological change has shifted the production function upward in Canada to PF_{1990}. Per capita income in Canada has increased from $Canada_{1867}$ to $Canada_{1990}$, partly because of an increase in the per capita capital stock and partly because of an increase in productivity arising from the adoption of better technology.

Figure 38.5 Investment Trends

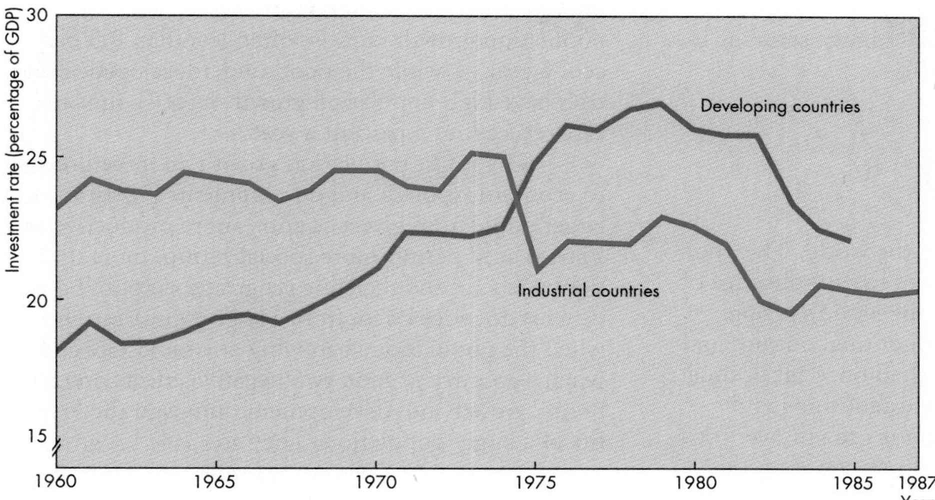
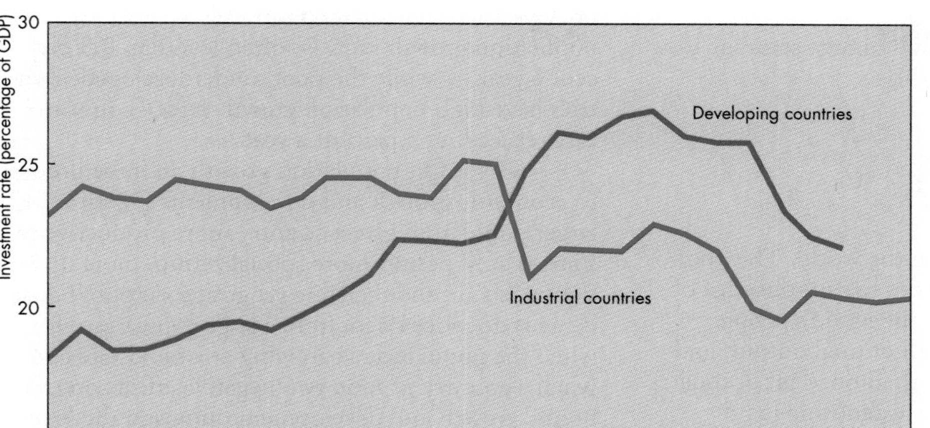

(a) Investment rates in Industrial and developing countries

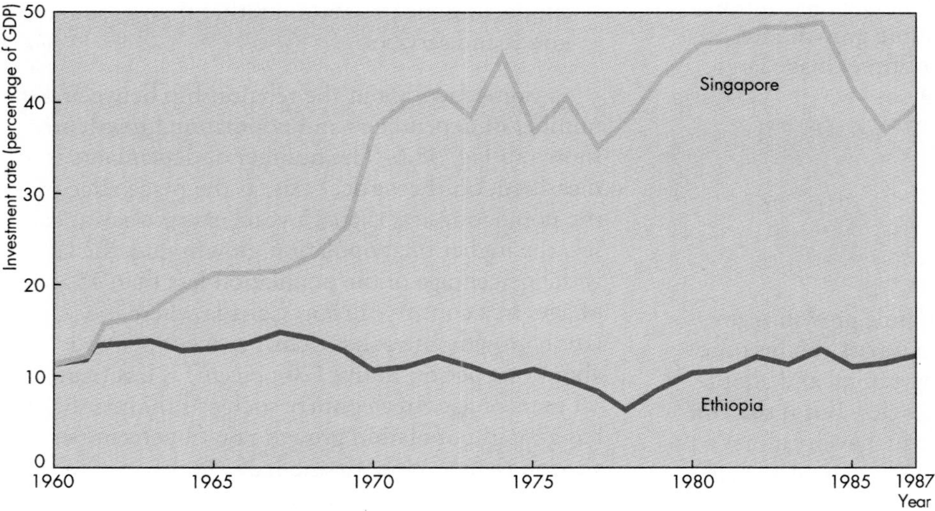

(b) Investment rates in Ethiopia and Singapore

The rate of investment in developing countries (including NICs) increased from 1960 to 1977 and subsequently decreased. Investment in industrial countries was steady during the 1960s and early 1970s but fell after 1974 (part a). Investment in Singapore has increased dramatically while that in Ethiopia has been almost constant (part b). High investment in Singapore has led to rapid growth, while low investment in Ethiopia has led to slow growth.

Source: International Monetary Fund, *International Financial Statistics*, (1988).

forces lead to increased per capita output. A poor country becomes a rich country partly by moving along its production function and partly by adopting better technology, thereby shifting its production function upward.

The importance of the connection between capital accumulation and output growth is illustrated in Fig. 38.5. Capital accumulation is measured by the percentage of output represented by investment. (Recall that investment is the purchase of new capital equipment.) The figure shows what has been happening to investment over time in developing countries (including NICs) and industrial countries and in two extreme cases of developing countries — Singapore and Ethiopia. As you can see in part (a), the developing countries have been steadily increasing the percentage of output invested, while in industrial countries that percentage has declined slightly. Fast-growing Singapore invests more than 40 percent of its output. Slow-growing Ethiopia invests less than 15 percent of its output. The source of Singapore's dramatic growth and of Ethiopia's almost static income level can be seen in part (b).

R E V I E W

There is enormous inequality in the world. The poorest people in the poorest countries live on the edge of starvation. The poorest fifth of the world's people consume less than one-twentieth of total output, and the richest fifth consume more than one-half of total output. Nations become rich by establishing and maintaining high rates of economic growth over prolonged periods. Economic growth results from the accumulation of capital and the adoption of increasingly efficient technologies. The more rapidly capital is accumulated and the more rapid is the pace of technological change, the higher is the rate of economic growth. Small changes in economic growth rates, maintained over a long period of time, make large differences to income levels. ■

Obstacles to Economic Growth

The prescription for economic growth seems straightforward: poor countries can become wealthy by accumulating capital and adopting the most productive technologies. But if the cure for abject poverty is so simple, why haven't more poor countries become rich? Why are there so many poor people in the world today?

We do not know the answers to all these questions. If we did, we would be able to solve the problem of economic underdevelopment and there wouldn't be any poor countries. But we do understand some of the reasons for poverty and underdevelopment. Let's see what they are.

Rapid Population Growth

One of the impediments to economic development and rapid and sustained growth in per capita income is rapid population growth. In the past 20 years, world population has been growing at an average rate of 2 percent per year. At a population growth rate this high, world population doubles every 37 years. That population stood at more than 5 billion at the end of 1988. But the pattern of population growth is uneven. Rich industrial countries have relatively low population growth rates — often less than 0.5 percent a year — while the poor, underdeveloped countries have high population growth rates — in some cases exceeding 3 percent a year.

Why is fast population growth an impediment to economic growth and development? Doesn't a larger population give a country more productive resources amd permit more specialization, more division of labour, and therefore yet greater output? These benefits do indeed stem from a large population. But when the population is growing at a rapid rate and when a country is poor, two negative effects on economic growth and development outweigh the benefits of a larger population. They are:

- An increase in the proportion of dependants to workers
- An increase in the amount of capital devoted to supporting the population rather than producing goods and services

Some facts about the relationship between the number of dependants and population growth are shown in Fig. 38.6. The number of dependants is measured, on the vertical axis, as the percentage of the population less than 15 years of age. As you can see, the higher the population growth rate, the larger is the percentage of the population less than 15 years of age. In a country such as Canada where the population growth rate is less than 1 percent per year, about one person in five (20 percent) is less than 15 years of age. In a country such as Ethiopia that has a rapid population growth rate (3 percent per year or higher), close to one-half (50 percent) of the population is less than 15 years of age.

Let's see why there is a connection between the population growth rate and the percentage of young people in the population. A country may have a steady population because it has a high birth rate and an equally high death rate. But the same steady population growth rate can occur with a low birth rate and a low death rate. Population growth rates increase when either the birth rate increases or the death rate decreases. Historically, it has been a fall in the death rate with a relatively constant birth rate that has led to population explosions. The fall in the death rate has mainly taken the form of a fall in the infant mortality rate, and it is this phenomenon that

Figure 38.6 Population Growth and Number of Dependants

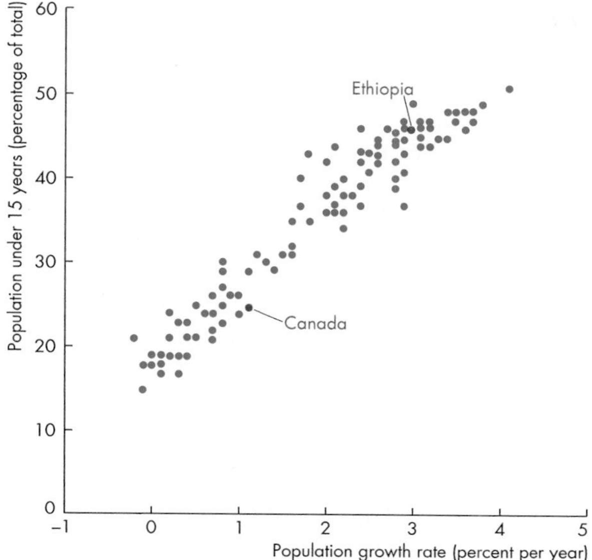

Each point in the scatter graph represents a country. It marks the percentage of the population that is under 15 years of age (measured on the vertical axis) and the population growth rate (measured on the horizontal axis). The number of young people in the population is strongly influenced by the population growth rate. In slow-growing countries such as Canada, about 20 percent of the population is under 15 years of age, while in fast-growing countries such as Ethiopia, more than 40 percent of the population is under 15 years of age.

Source: Population Reference Bureau Inc., World Population Data Sheet (Washington, D.C., 1988).

results in an enormous increase in the proportion of young people in the population.

In a country with a large number of young people, capital resources are directed towards providing schools, hospitals, roads, and housing, rather than irrigation schemes and industrial capital projects. Such a use of scarce capital resources is obviously not wasteful and does bring great benefits, but it does not add to the economy's capacity to produce goods and services out of which yet additional capital accumulation can be provided.

Low Saving Rate

There is a further obstacle to rapid and sustained economic growth and development. Poor people have such a low level of income that they consume most of it, undertaking only a tiny volume of saving. Saving is the source of finance for capital accumulation, and as we have seen, capital accumulation is itself one of the main engines of economic growth. Let's investigate the connection between capital accumulation and saving.

As we saw in Chapter 23, there are just three things that people can do with their income: consume it, save it, or pay it in taxes. That is,

$$\text{Income} = \text{Consumption} + \text{Saving} + \text{Taxes} .$$

We also saw in Chapter 23 that, in aggregate, the value of output equals income. An economy's output consists of consumption goods, capital goods, goods and services bought by the government, and net exports (exports minus imports). Expenditure on capital goods is investment, and expenditure on goods and services bought by the government is called government purchases of goods and services. Thus

$$\begin{aligned}\text{Income} = {} & \text{Consumption} + \text{Investment} + \\ & \text{Government purchases} + \text{Net exports} .\end{aligned}$$

The first of the above equations tells us that income minus consumption is equal to saving plus taxes. The second equation tells us that income minus consumption is equal to investment plus government purchases plus net exports. Using these two equations then, we see that

$$\begin{aligned}\text{Saving} + \text{Taxes} = {} & \text{Investment} + \\ & \text{Government purchases} + \\ & \text{Net exports} .\end{aligned}$$

The difference between government purchases and taxes is the government sector deficit. We can rearrange the last equation, therefore, as

$$\begin{aligned}\text{Investment} = {} & \text{Saving} - \text{Net exports} \\ & - \text{Government sector deficit} .\end{aligned}$$

This equation tells us that there are three influences on the pace at which a country can accumulate capital (can invest): saving, the government sector deficit, and net exports. If net exports are negative — imports exceed exports — they are financed by borrowing from the rest of the world. Thus we can rewrite the above equation as

$$\text{Investment} = \text{Saving} + \begin{matrix}\text{Borrowing} \\ \text{from the} \\ \text{rest of} \\ \text{the world}\end{matrix} - \begin{matrix}\text{Government} \\ \text{sector} \\ \text{deficit} .\end{matrix}$$

Other things being equal, the larger the volume of saving, the smaller the government sector deficit (the larger the government sector surplus), and the larger the borrowing from the rest of the world, the faster is the pace of capital accumulation.

The fraction of income that people save depends on their income level. Very poor people save nothing. As income rises, some part of income is saved. The higher the income level, the higher is the proportion of income saved. These patterns in the relationship between income and saving crucially affect the pace at which a country can grow.

Saving is by far the most important component of the sources of financing investment. But in general, the larger the amount of saving, the larger also is the amount of resources available from the rest of the world through the country's current account deficit (negative net exports). Furthermore, the government in a country with few resources often runs a deficit, thereby restricting yet further the amount available for capital accumulation through investment.

Let's now look at a third impediment to rapid growth and development, the burden of international debt.

International Debt

Poor countries often go into debt with the rest of the world. Loans have to be repaid and interest has to be paid on the loans outstanding. To make debt repayments and interest payments, poor countries need a net export surplus. That is, a country needs a current account surplus. Yet as we have just seen, when a country's net exports are negative, the current account deficit provides additional financial resources to domestic saving, which enable the country to accumulate capital at a faster pace than would otherwise be possible. A country that has a current account surplus is one that is accumulating capital at a slower pace than its domestic saving permits. Such a country uses part of its saving to accumulate capital — and thereby increases productivity — and uses the other part to pay interest on or repay loans from the rest of the world.

A poor country that borrows heavily from the rest of the world and uses the borrowing to invest in productive capital will not become overburdened by debt provided the growth rate of income exceeds the interest rate on the debt. In such a situation, debt interest can be paid out of the higher income and there is still some additional income left over for additional domestic consumption or capital accumulation. Countries that borrow from the rest of the world and use the resources for consumption or for investment in projects that have a low rate of return — a rate lower than the interest rate on the debt — are the ones that become overburdened by debt.

The burden of international debt became particularly onerous for many developing countries during the 1980s. For example, the Latin American countries accumulated international debts of almost $0.5 trillion. Many of these debts were incurred during the 1970s when raw material prices were rising quickly. From 1973 to 1980, the prices of most raw materials increased, on the average, by close to 20 percent per year — a rate much higher than the interest rates on the international debt being accumulated. In such a situation, raw-material-producing countries, hungry for capital, borrowed on an enormous scale. The rate of return seemed high enough to permit repayment easily. But in the early years of the 1980s, raw material prices collapsed. The revenue with which to repay the huge international debts was not coming in. To add a further burden, interest rates increased sharply during the 1980s. Today, because of the combination of sagging raw material prices and higher interest rates, many poor countries have a crippling burden of international debt.

The Underdevelopment Trap

The obstacles to economic development are so severe that some economists have suggested that there is a kind of poverty trap that applies to countries — the underdevelopment trap. The **underdevelopment trap** is a situation in which a country is locked into a low per capita income situation that reinforces itself. A low level of capital (both physical and human) per worker results in low output per worker. Low productivity, in turn, produces low per capita income. Low per capita income results in low saving. With low saving, there is a low rate of capital accumulation. Capital accumulation can barely keep up with population growth, so the stock of capital per worker remains low, and the cycle repeats itself.

Overcoming the Obstacles to Economic Development

To disturb an equilibrium, some external force has to be applied. A variety of forces have been suggested to help poor countries break out of the equilibrium underdevelopment trap.

They are:

- Population control
- Foreign aid
- Removal of trade restrictions
- Demand stimulation

Let's look at each of these in turn.

Population Control

Almost all developing countries use population control methods as part of their attempt to break out of the underdevelopment trap. Population control programs have two key elements: the provision of low-cost birth control facilities and the provision of incentives encouraging people to have a small number of children. These methods have met with some limited success. One of the most highly publicized programs of population control is that employed in China. In that country, families are strongly discouraged from having more than one child. Despite this policy, the population of China continues to grow, and forecasts released in 1989 suggest that by the year 2000 the population will have grown above its target level by an amount equal to five times the entire population of Canada.

Thus important though it is, population control is not the method most likely to yield success in the fight against underdevelopment and poverty.

Foreign Aid

The idea that foreign aid helps economic development arises from a simple consideration. If a country is poor because it has too little capital, then with foreign aid, it can accumulate more capital and achieve a higher per capita output. Repeated applications of foreign aid year after year can enable a country to grow much more quickly than it could if it had to rely exclusively on its own domestic saving. On this line of reasoning, the greater the flow of foreign aid to a country, the faster it will grow.

Some economists suggest that foreign aid will not necessarily make a country grow faster. They argue that such aid consolidates the position of corrupt and/or incompetent politicians and that these politicians and their policies are two of the main impediments to economic development. Most people who administer foreign aid do not take this view. The consensus is that foreign aid does indeed help economic development. But it is also agreed that foreign aid is not a major factor in influencing the pace of development of poor countries. Its scale is simply too small to make a decisive difference.

A factor that has made a decisive difference in many countries is international trade policy. Let's now turn to an examination of the effects of international trade on growth and development.

Trade and Development

There is a continual cry in the rich countries for protection from imports produced with "cheap labour" in the underdeveloped countries. Other people complain that buying from underdeveloped countries "exploits" low-wage workers. As a consequence, countries introduce tariffs, quotas, and voluntary restrictions on trade (see Chapter 36). How do such restrictions affect underdeveloped countries, and how does the removal of such restrictions affect their growth and development? To answer this question, consider the following example, which is illustrated in Fig. 38.7. Imagine a situation (such as that prevailing in the 1950s) in which the United States produces virtually all the cars sold there. The U.S. automobile market is shown in part (a). The demand for cars is shown by curve D_{US} and the supply by curve S_{US}. The price of cars is P_{US} and the quantity produced and bought is Q_{US}.

Suppose that Mazda builds an automobile production plant in Mexico. The supply curve of cars produced in Mexico is shown in Fig. 38.7(b) as the curve S_M. What happens in the United States depends on U.S. international trade policy.

First, suppose that the United States restricts the import of cars from Mexico. To make things as clear as possible, let's suppose that there is a complete ban on such imports. In this case, Mexico produces no cars for export to the United States. The price of cars in the United States remains at P_{US} and the quantity traded remains at Q_{US}.

In contrast, let's see what happens if the United States engages in free trade with Mexico. (A trade accord between the United States and Mexico has, in fact, recently been negotiated). To determine the price of cars and the quantities produced and consumed in the United States and the quantity produced in Mexico for export to the United States, we need to consider Fig. 38.7(c). The demand curve for cars in the United States remains D_{US} but the supply curve becomes S_W. This supply curve is made up of the sum of the quantities supplied both in the United States and Mexico at each price. Equilibrium is achieved in the U.S. market at a price of P_W and a

Figure 38.7 International Trade and Economic Development

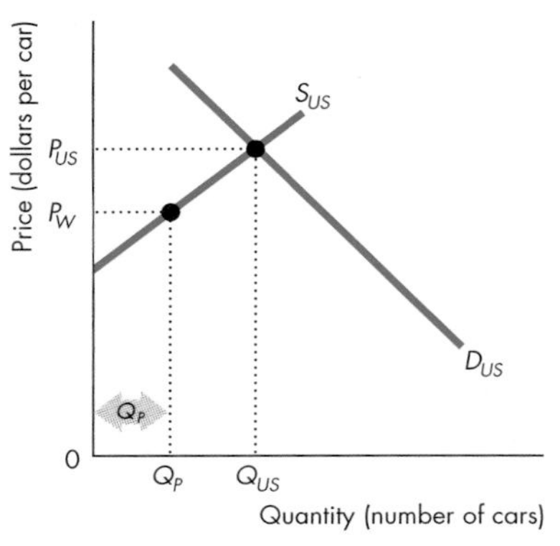

(a) U.S. production and demand

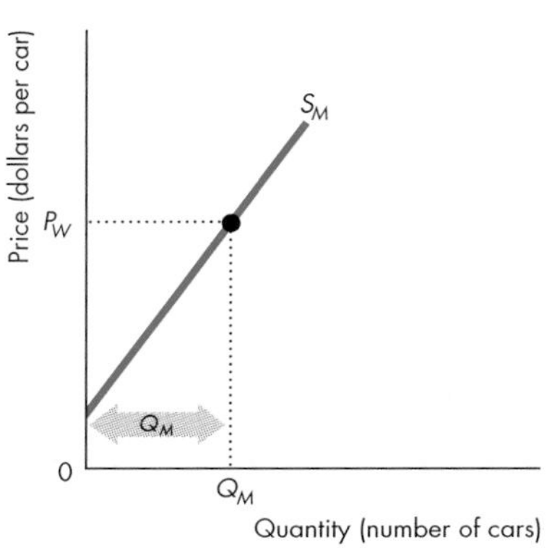

(b) Mexican production

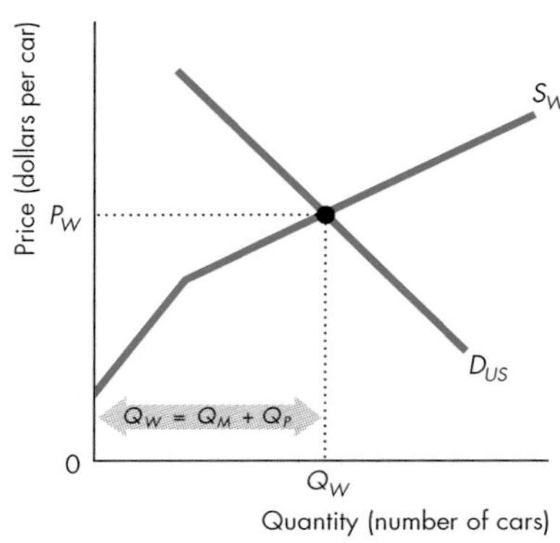

(c) U.S. car market with free trade

The U.S. market for cars (part a) has demand curve D_{US} and supply curve S_{US}. The price of cars is P_{US} and the quantity produced and bought is Q_{US}. Mazda builds an automobile plant in Mexico and the supply curve of cars from that plant is S_M (part b). If the United States prohibits the import of cars from Mexico, the U.S. automobile market remains unchanged and Mexican output is zero. If the United States permits free international trade in cars with Mexico, the price in the U.S. market is P_W (part c) and the total quantity of cars bought in the United States is Q_W (W stands for "with trade"). Parts (a) and (b) show that at price P_W, Q_M cars are produced in Mexico and Q_P (P stands for "production") in the United States. Free international trade permits poor countries to sell their output for a price higher than they would otherwise receive and rich countries to buy goods for a price lower than they would otherwise pay.

quantity traded of Q_W. To see where these cars are produced, go back to parts (a) and (b) of the figure. Mexico produces Q_M, the United States produces Q_P, and these two production levels sum to Q_W.

Mazda's Mexican plant increases its output of cars and its workers generate income. The output of cars is decreased in the United States. By permitting unrestricted trade with underdeveloped countries, rich countries gain by being able to consume goods that are imported at lower prices than would be possible if only domestic supplies were available. Developing countries gain by being able to sell their output for a higher price than would prevail if they had only the domestic market available to them.

Some of the most dramatic economic growth and development success stories have been based on reaping the gains from relatively unrestricted international trade. Countries such as Hong Kong and Singapore have opened their economies to free trade with the rest of the world and dramatically increased their living standards by specializing and producing goods and services in which they have a *comparative advantage* — which they can produce at a lower opportunity cost than other countries.

Aggregate Demand Stimulation and Growth

It is often suggested that growth and development can be stimulated by expanding aggregate demand. The suggestion takes two forms. Sometimes it is suggested that if the rich countries stimulate their own aggregate demand, their economies will grow more quickly and, as a consequence, commodity prices will remain high. High commodity prices help poor countries and so stimulate their income growth and economic development. (Reading Between the Lines, pp. 1004-1005 provides a recent example of this line of reasoning.) It is also often suggested that poor countries can make themselves grow faster by stimulating their own level of aggregate demand.

Can stimulating aggregate demand in the rich countries help the poor countries? Can aggregate demand stimulation in poor countries help them grow? The answers to both of these questions are almost certainly no, but let's see why. As we discovered when we studied the theory of aggregate demand and aggregate supply in Chapter 24, changes in aggregate income can occur as a result of either a change in aggregate demand or a change in aggregate supply.

But aggregate demand changes affect output and income in the short run only. That is, when wages and other input prices are fixed, a change in aggregate demand changes both output and the price level. But in the long run, a change in aggregate demand leads to a change in the prices of goods and services and of factors of production. Once input prices have adjusted in response to a change in aggregate demand, income returns to its capacity level. Changes in per capita capacity income can be brought about only by changes in per capita productivity — which, in turn, is brought about by changes in the stock of per capita capital and in the state of technology.

This macroeconomic model of aggregate demand and aggregate supply applies to all countries, rich and poor alike. If rich countries stimulate aggregate demand by persistently permitting aggregate demand to grow at a pace faster than capacity growth, they will generate inflation. If they hold aggregate demand growth to a pace similar to the growth of capacity, prices will be stable. In recent history, we have seen rich countries generating both rapid inflation and moderate inflation. The 1970s was a decade of rapid inflation. During that decade, commodity prices also increased quickly, enabling many developing countries to increase the pace of capital accumulation and income growth. The 1980s were a decade of moderate inflation. It was this decade that brought falling raw material prices and the burden of large international debt to many developing countries.

Developing countries can make aggregate demand grow at a rapid or moderate rate. The more rapidly aggregate demand grows, relative to the growth of capacity, the higher is the inflation rate. Some developing countries inflate quickly and others slowly. But there is virtually no connection between the pace of their development and the inflation rate. As Fig. 38.8 illustrates, fast-growing Singapore, which invests more than 40 percent of its output in capital equipment each year, has had a moderate inflation rate, while average-growing Ghana has had the highest inflation rate of the developing countries — more than 100 percent a year. Slow-growing Ethiopia, which invests only 10 percent of its output, has had a moderate inflation rate. Each blue dot in the figure shows the investment percentage and inflation rate in a developing country. As you can see, the dots do not form a clear relationship between these variables. Thus the pace at which a developing country stimulates aggregate demand, although affecting its inflation rate, has no appreciable effect on the growth rate of real income or the pace of economic development.

Figure 38.8 Inflation and Economic Growth

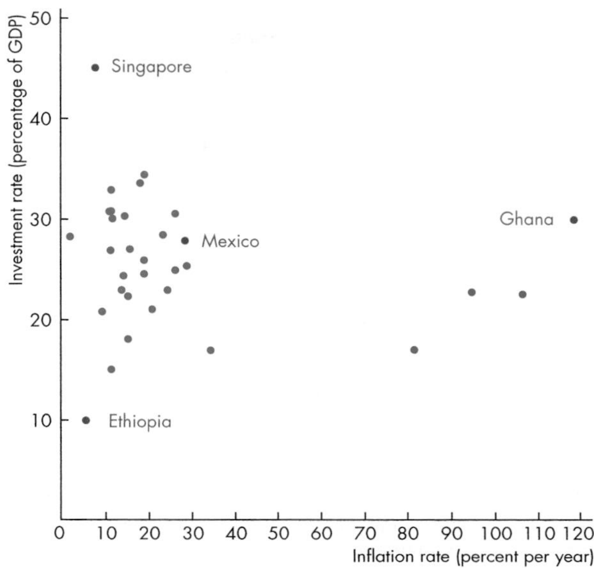

Each point in the figure represents a country. It shows the country's investment level (as a percentage of GDP) plotted against the annual inflation rate. The data are for 1960 to 1985. There is no discernible connection between a country's inflation rate and its pace of investment and economic growth. Fast-growing Singapore has had a low inflation rate, as has slow-growing Ethiopia. Medium-growing Ghana has had the highest inflation rate in the developing world.

Source: International Monetary Fund, *International Financial Statistics* (1988).

We've seen that to grow quickly, a country must accumulate capital at a rapid pace. To do so, it must achieve a high saving rate and undertake foreign borrowing that is used in high-return activities. The most rapidly growing developing countries have a high pace of capital accumulation and obtain a high return on their capital by pursuing a free trade policy, thereby ensuring that they produce those goods and services in which they have a comparative advantage.

Deflation and Development

Concerted effort urged to raise world trade

A United Nations report has urged industrial nations to promote worldwide growth by coordinating their economic policies without delay and said deflation is now the biggest threat to prosperity.

"The defeat of inflation is a major achievement," Kenneth Dadzie, head of the UN Conference on Trade and Development, said in a foreword to the Geneva-based body's annual report on the state of the world economy.

But resulting deflation has now become a menace to stability, the Ghanaian UN official said. Deflationary forces now constitute "the single most pervasive threat to world prosperity."

While welcoming a trend toward increased co-ordination of industrialized countries' economic strategies over the past year, Mr. Dadzie said not all accepted the need to stimulate global growth and cut real interest rates.

The recent collapse in oil and tin prices is the latest manifestation of deflation. Real non-oil commodity prices as a whole, despite a recent increase for coffee, had plunged to the lowest level since the Great Depression of the 1930s.

Deflation was "sapping the vitality of much of the world economy, developing countries in particular, and eroding the fabric of international trade and finance, leaving in its trail widespread unemployment, protectionism and insolvency."

Mr. Dadzie cautioned against relying on prospective cuts in the United States' record budget deficit, the oil price decline and the depreciation of the U.S. dollar to remedy the situation.

"The combined impact of these factors is unlikely to raise the momentum of growth in the world economy," he said. Lower crude prices, for one, would help net importers but sharply strain debtor countries heavily dependent on energy exports.

"As a whole, developing countries are net oil exporters and will lose $50-billion (U.S.) in net export revenues in 1986."

The 171-page report forecast a 2.9 percent growth in output among developed market-economy countries next year, up only marginally over 1986.

It said Japan and North America would lead the way with growth rates of 3.5 percent next year, with Western Europe and others lagging behind with 2.5 percent next year.

Third World growth was expected to average 2.7 percent, slightly above 1986, ranging from South Asia's 4.9 percent to a fall of 0.6 percent among the least developed African states.

Only the Communist economies of Eastern Europe would enjoy a significant gain of 4.2 percent, compared with 3.2 last year. China, which posted an exceptionally rapid 13 percent in 1985, would slide progressively back to 7 percent in 1987.

Mr. Dadzie called for multilateral development finance institutions to step up net lending.

The report said Third World nations had borne the brunt of deflation, with low commodity prices severely damaging export earnings, debt-servicing ability and growth.

The Globe and Mail
August 12, 1986

The Essence of the Story

- The United Nations' Conference on Trade and Development (UNCTAD) has issued its annual report on the state of the world economy in 1986:
- It predicted that world output growth 1987 would be 2.9 percent.
- It asserted that deflation in the industrial countries had damaged the developing countries by lowering:
  - Commodity prices
  - Export earnings
  - Ability to pay debt interest
  - Output growth
- It urged the industrial countries to embark on a program of co-ordinated aggregate demand expansion.
- UNCTAD's head, Kenneth Dadzie, said:
  - Inflation had been defeated.
  - Real commodity prices were at historically low levels.
  - Deflation was blocking output growth and causing reduced international trade and investment, unemployment, protectionism, and bankruptcy.
- The combined effects of a cut in the U.S. budget deficit, a lower value for the U.S. dollar, and a lower oil price would not raise world output growth.
- Output growth would be stimulated only if real interest rates were cut.

Background and Analysis

Facts

- During the years before the news article was written, inflation was cut significantly in industrial countries:

	1990	1991
U.S.	13.5	4.3
Canada	10.2	4.3
U.K.	18.0	5.0
Japan	8.0	2.3

- Inflation was also cut in some developing countries, but in most countries it increased:

	1980	1984
Africa	14.2	20.1
Asia	12.5	7.1
Europe	35.5	33.9
Middle East	17.2	16.2
Latin America	55.1	146.3

- Commodity prices fell in the early 1980s. Some prices in 1984, expressed as a percentage of their 1980 levels, were:

Food	73.6
Beverages	98.4
Agricultural Raw Materials	88.8
Metals	73.1
Oil	99.3
All commodities	82.2

Assertions

- Low real commodity prices hurt developing countries by lowering their export earnings, hampering their ability to repay their debts, and slowing their output growth.

Correct:

- Commodities form a large part of the output of developing countries. Low real commodity prices, therefore, lower the value of the output of these countries and lower the volume of capital and other imports that they can buy with a given volume of exports. Lower export earnings slow down growth and make it harder to service debts.
- Real commodity prices were low because of deflation in the developed countries. A new, concerted effort to stimulate aggregate demand would raise real commodity prices again.

Conclusion

Probably wrong:

- Output growth was low in the developed countries and unemployment was high. But output and employment are determined by aggregate demand and aggregate supply. Only the unanticipated fluctuations in aggregate demand have real effects. Much of the depressed state of the developed countries is likely associated with aggregate supply-side disturbances. In any case, real commodity prices are not well correlated with the business cycle. As the figure illustrates, when the industrial countries were booming in the 1960s and early 1970s, real commodity prices were falling. The recession of the mid-1970s saw commodity prices rise very high. Only in the 1980s did real commodity prices fall in line with the drop in output in the rich countries.
- Real commodity prices are altered by supply and demand for individual commodities. Some commodity prices rise and some fall even when the average prices are steady. For example, over the past 25 years, the price of zinc (commonly used in computers and electronic technology) has steadily increased, while the price of iron has steadily declined. There is no simple connection between real commodity prices and the state of aggregate demand in developed countries. In fact, correctly anticipated demand expansion in the developed countries would raise prices (and inflation) in those countries and have minimal effects on the developing countries.
- Coordinated aggregate demand expansion in the rich countries would lower real interest rates and stimulate development throughout the world.

Certainly wrong:

- Aggregate demand stimulation using fiscal policy would almost certainly raise real interest rates. Aggregate demand expansion using monetary policy might lower real interest rates temporarily but would have no lasting effect on real interest rates and, if associated with higher inflation, would raise nominal interest rates.

- In 1986, the policy advocated by UNCTAD is aggregate demand stimulation. Pursuing such a policy would certainly produce higher prices and perhaps renewed inflation in the developed countries, and it would do little to help the plight of the developing world.

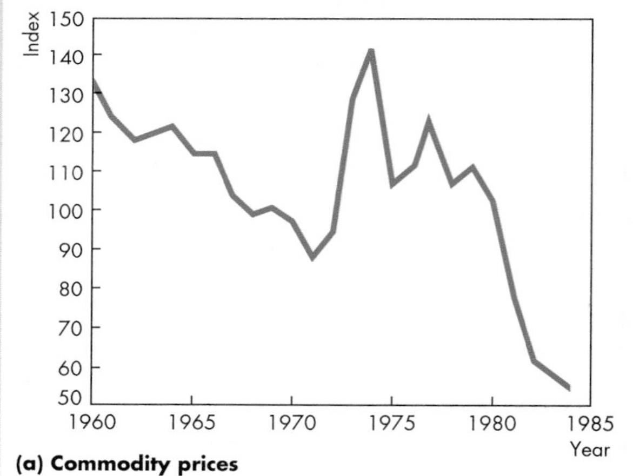

(a) Commodity prices

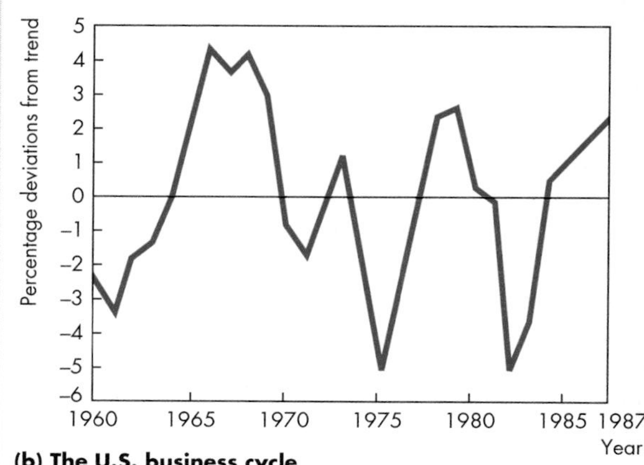

(b) The U.S. business cycle

SUMMARY

The International Distribution of Income

There is enormous inequality in the international distribution of income. The poorest countries have average per capita income levels of 4 to 9 percent of that in the United States. Half of the world's population earns only 15 percent of world income and the richest 20 percent earns 55 percent of income. (pp. 1017-1019)

Growth Rates and Income Levels

Poor countries become rich by achieving and maintaining high rates of per capita income growth for prolonged periods. Rich countries grow at about 1.5 percent per year. Poor countries that have a slower growth rate than that fall further behind. Poor countries that achieve a growth rate higher than 1.5 percent per year gradually close the gap with the rich countries. High and sustained growth can make a dramatic difference in a relatively short time span. If China can maintain a per capita income growth rate of 6 percent per year, its per capita income will catch up with that of the United States by the mid-2030s. (pp. 1019-1021)

Inputs, Technological Progress, and Economic Growth

Per capita income growth results from the growth in per capita capital and in technological change. The greater the fraction of income invested in new capital equipment and the faster the pace of technological change, the higher is the rate of economic growth. (pp. 1021-1024)

Obstacles to Economic Growth

There are three major obstacles to sustained economic growth and development: rapid population growth, a low saving rate, and a large international debt burden. Rapid population growth results in a large proportion of young dependants in the population. Low saving results in a low rate of capital accumulation. A large international debt burden results in some savings having to be used to pay debt interest rather than to accumulate capital and improve productivity.

Low income results in low saving, which in turn results in low investment and thus low income growth. Many poor countries are caught in what appears to be an underdevelopment trap. (pp. 1024-1026)

Overcoming the Obstacles to Economic Development

The main techniques for overcoming the obstacles to economic development are the implementation of population control measures, foreign aid, and the removal of trade restrictions. Of these, the most dramatic success stories have almost always involved rapid expansion of international trade.

The stimulation of aggregate demand, by either rich or poor countries, cannot in the long run contribute to economic growth and development. If aggregate demand grows at the same rate as capacity, prices are stable; if aggregate demand grows at a faster rate than capacity, prices rise — there is inflation. The inflation rate does not appear to have a major influence on the rate of economic growth and development. (pp. 1026-1029)

KEY ELEMENTS

Key Terms

Communist country, 1018
Developing country, 1017
Industrial Countries, 1018
Lorenz curve, 1018
Newly industrialized countries, 1018
Per capita production function, 1021
Underdeveloped country, 1017
Underdevelopment trap, 1026

Key Figures

Figure 38.1 The World Lorenz Curve, 1980, 1019
Figure 38.4 Technological Change, 1022
Figure 38.5 Investment Trends, 1023
Figure 38.6 Population Growth and Number of Dependants, 1025

REVIEW QUESTIONS

1 Describe the main differences between the richest and the poorest countries of the world.

2 Compare the distribution of income among families in Canada with the distribution of income among countries in the world. Which distribution is more unequal?

3 How long will it take a poor country such as China to catch up with a rich country such as the United States if per capita income in the United States grows at 1.5 percent per year and per capita income in China grows at the following rates:

a) 1.5 percent per year?

b) 3 percent per year?

c) 6 percent per year?

d) 12 percent per year?

4 What determines a country's per capita income level? What makes the per capita income level change?

5 Give an example of a country in which rapid economic growth has occurred and of one in which slow economic growth has occurred. Which of these countries had the higher investment rate?

6 Review the obstacles to economic growth.

7 Why is rapid population growth an obstacle to economic growth?

8 Describe the underdevelopment trap.

9 What are the main ways in which poor countries try to overcome their poverty?

10 Why does free trade stimulate economic growth and development?

11 Why does aggregate demand stimulation not improve a country's rate of economic growth and its development?

PROBLEMS

1 A poor country has 10 percent of the per capita income of a rich country. The rich country is growing at 5 percent per year. The poor country achieves a growth rate of 10 percent per year. How many years will it take per capita income in the poor country to catch up with that of the rich country?

2 Siliconia is a poor country with no natural resources except sand. Per capita income is $500 a year, and this entire income is consumed. Per capita income is constant — there is no economic growth. The government sector has a balanced budget and there are no exports or imports. Suddenly the price of silicon increases, and Siliconia is able to export sand at a huge profit. Exports soar from zero to $400 (per capita). Per capita income increases to $1,000 a year and per capita consumption increases to $600 a year. There are still no imports, and Siliconia has a current account surplus of $400 per capita.

a) What happens to investment and the growth rate in Siliconia?

b) If Siliconia imports capital goods equal in value to its exports, what will be its investment? What will be its current account balance?

c) If the government sector of Siliconia runs a budget deficit of $100 (per capita), what will be its investment?

CHAPTER 39

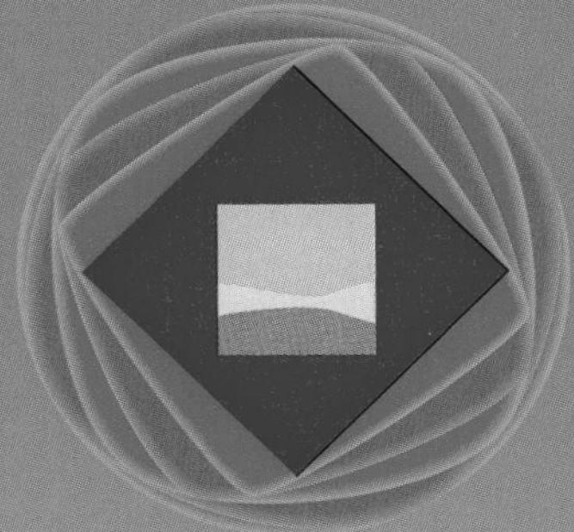

Comparing Economic Systems

After studying this chapter, you will be able to:

- Explain why the economic problem of scarcity is common to all economic and political systems.
- Describe various political systems that have been proposed to deal with the economic problem.
- Explain the difference between capitalism and socialism.
- Describe the varieties of capitalism in the United States, Japan, and Western Europe.
- Describe the main features of the economy of the Soviet Union.
- Explain the economic restructuring—or *Perestroika*—being undertaken in the Soviet Union.
- Describe the economic reforms being undertaken in China.
- Assess the efficiency of alternative economic systems.

Momentous Economic Change

WE LIVE IN A TIME of momentous economic change. Throughout Eastern Europe —in Bulgaria, Czechoslvakia, East Germany, Hungary, Poland, Romania, the Soviet Union, and Yugoslavia —communism and socialism are being rejected and some form of capitalism is being introduced in its place. This process of economic transformation in Eastern Europe began, quietly, in the summer of 1987 at a meeting of the Central Committee of the Communist Party of the Soviet Union when Mikhail Gorbachev presented his model for the "radical restructuring of economic management" of the Soviet economy —*Perestroika.* He preached his message in meeting with ordinary Russians, and proclaimed the virtues of "working an extra bit harder" with an almost religious intensity. In his book, *Perestroika,* which became a best seller even in North America and Western Europe, he described the steps being taken to implement his "*perestroika* revolution." ■ But the pace of the process accelerated in 1989 when, one by one, the countries of Eastern Europe embraced an open democratic political system. With democracy came political demands for improved economic performance. ■ The world's biggest communist country is China. Even there, and despite the bloody crackdown on the Tiananmen Square democracy movement in the summer of 1989, widespread economic reforms are being implemented. In that country, the goal declared by the architect of the modern Chinese economy, Deng Xiaoping, is to build "a socialist nation with Chinese characteristics" that will embody "one country and two systems." The two systems are the communist system developed in China and the Soviet Union, and the capitalist system of the United States, Western Europe, and Japan. ■ Although less dramatic, changes in government economic management are also taking place in Canada, the United States, Western Europe, and Japan. In Canada, that change has taken the form of deregulation and of privatization of Crown corporations, both federal and provincial, such as Air Canada, Petro-Canada, and the Saskatchewan Oil and Gas Corporation. In Britain and many other Western European countries, deregulation has also been accompanied by the selling of state-operated businesses, such as railways, telecommunications, and public utilities, to private enterprise. In the United States, which has never had a great deal of state-owned enterprise, change has taken the form of a steady process of deregulation, a process begun during the years when Jimmy Carter was president and given greater momentum during the Reagan years. In Japan, the change that is taking place is resulting in a greater liberalization of the Japanese economy and of its international trading and financial relations. ■ What are the main differences between the economic system that the Eastern European countries and the Soviet Union are now abandoning, and the economic system of Canada, the United States, Western Europe, and Japan? What exactly are capitalism, socialism, and communism? Why are the Soviet Union and other countries of Eastern Europe implementing such massive changes in their methods of economic management? Why are countries in Western Europe and Japan privatizing large parts of their economies? How do the alternative economic systems of capitalism and communism perform? Can a single country successfully combine the two different economic systems?

■ In this chapter, we're going to describe some of the key differences in the economic systems of the world. We will learn how capitalist and communist economies operate. We'll examine some of the diversity among the capitalist economies of Canada, the United States, Japan, and Western Europe. We'll study the economic system of the Soviet Union before its current reforms. We'll see why *perestroika* is taking place and what its effects may be. We'll examine the economic reforms in China and describe its economic goals. Finally, we'll compare the performances of the alternative economic systems.

The Fundamental Economic Problem

The first thing that we learn when we begin to study economics is that the source of all economic problems is the universal fact of *scarcity*. In embarking on a study of comparative economic systems, it is worthwhile reviewing and reinforcing our understanding of the implications of scarcity.

Scarcity

Scarcity arises because we all want to consume more goods and services than the available resources make possible. The *production possibility frontier* describes the limits to what we can produce — it separates the attainable from the unattainable (see Chapter 3). Our consumption possibilities are maximized if we arrange our economic affairs in such a way that we produce at a point on our production possibility frontier. The first aspect of solving the economic problem, therefore, involves getting onto the frontier.

Getting onto the Production Possibility Frontier

If we operate at a point on the production possibility frontier rather than at some point inside it, we produce more of all goods. We cannot take it for granted, however, that we will automatically operate on the frontier. We may waste resources. For example, resources are wasted if we produce more of some perishable commodity at a given moment than can be quickly consumed. Some of the commodity rots and may as well not have been produced. Therefore the resources used to produce that commodity are wasted.

Another more subtle, yet more important form of waste arises if productive resources are combined in a way that makes the cost of production higher than it needs to be. For example, electricity can be generated by using water power, coal, oil, or nuclear power as the energy source. If the cost of producing a megawatt of electricity is lowest using nuclear power, but hydro power or oil is used instead, then productive resources are wasted. Don't lose sight, however, that in economics the word "cost" includes *all* costs. In the case of power production, the costs include environmental costs such as pollution, the hazard of nuclear accident and contamination, and many other costs not borne by the producer of electricity.

Different economic systems use different methods to get the economy to a point on its production possibility frontier. We will look at those methods in the next section. Once the economy is on its production possibility frontier, no more of any one good can be produced without producing less of some other good. It is this fact that gives rise to the concept of *opportunity cost.* The opportunity cost of producing one more unit of any particular good is the amount of some other good or goods foregone. Because it is possible to produce more of one good only by producing less of another good, a second aspect of solving the economic problem involves getting to the right point on the frontier.

Producing the Right Quantities of Goods and Services

Determining how much of each of the various goods and services to produce requires that people's preferences of the alternatives be taken into account. For example, if people placed a high value on clean air and a low value on quick and convenient transportation, we would produce fewer cars and highways and have more stringent methods of controlling exhaust emission. If people valued vacations on the moon highly and placed little or no value at all on any of the other things that we currently produce and consume, then we would use an enormous amount of our resources to build lunar transportation systems and holiday resorts! If we all became addicted to fruit and ice cream and refused to eat meat, Burger King and McDonald's fast-food outlets would either go out of business or radically change their mix of products. Baskin Robbins would be booming.

The way in which individual preferences influence the quantities of goods and services produced varies from one economic system to another. As we'll see shortly, our own economic system takes individual consumers' preferences as the dominant force in determining what is produced. In other systems, individual preferences play a limited role and those of the government's planning agency are dominant.

Getting onto the production possibility frontier and choosing the right point on it are two aspects of solving the economic problem. There is a third aspect — determining the distribution of economic well-being.

The Distribution of Economic Well-Being

An economy could be at a point on its production possibility frontier and that point could exactly reflect consumers' preferences concerning the values of the various goods. At that point, production of more of any one good and less of any other good would make somebody worse off. There are, however, many such points, each of which is associated with a different distribution of economic well-being. One such point is where everyone is equally well off. Another is where 90 percent of the population are almost starving and the other 10 percent are living in enormous luxury. In effect, economic systems make decisions about who gets what. Some economic systems favour, in principle at least, considerable equality in the distribution of economic well-being. Other systems favour equality of opportunity but pay little attention to the distribution that results from equal opportunities.

R E V I E W

The best we can do in the face of scarcity is to get ourselves onto the production possibility frontier. The point on the frontier that we go to depends on whose preferences determine which goods and services the economy produces and on how the economic system distributes well-being. No economic system can abolish the economic problem. At best, each system can only help people cope with scarcity. ■

Let's see how different economic systems cope with the fundamental economic problem.

Alternative Economic Systems

Economic systems differ in a number of detailed and subtle ways. There are, however, two main dimensions along which economic systems vary. They are:

- Who owns capital and land.
- Who allocates resources.

Figure 39.1 summarizes the possibilities. Capital and land may be owned entirely by individuals, entirely by the state, or by a mixture of the two. Resources may be allocated entirely by markets, entirely by government economic planners, or by a mixture of the two. The blue and red corners of the figure represent two idealized extreme cases: capitalism and socialism.

Capitalism is an economic system based on private ownership of capital and land and on market allocation of resources. **Socialism** is an economic system based on state ownership of capital and land and on a centrally planned allocation of resources. **Central planning** is a method of allocating resources by command. It involves a central planning authority that makes the plans and then communicates them to the country's various production and distribution

Figure 39.1 Alternative Economic Systems

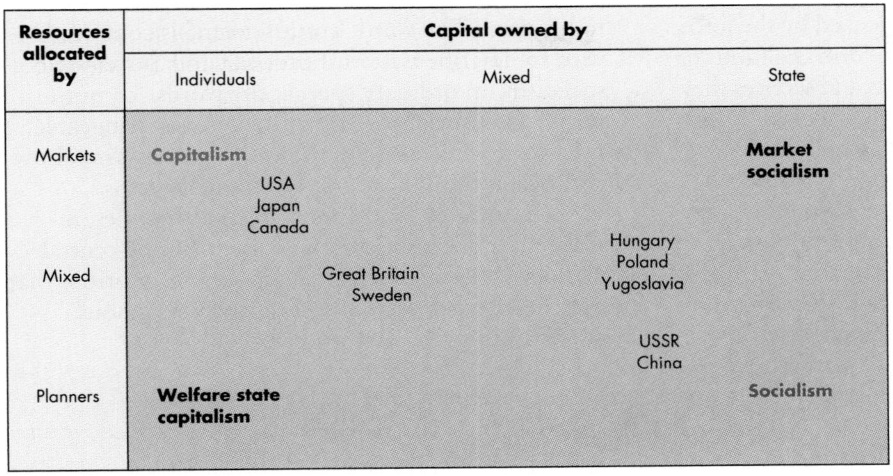

Resources allocated by	Capital owned by		
	Individuals	Mixed	State
Markets	**Capitalism** USA Japan Canada		**Market socialism**
Mixed		Great Britain Sweden	Hungary Poland Yugoslavia
Planners	**Welfare state capitalism**		USSR China **Socialism**

Under capitalism, individuals own capital and land — farms and factories, plant and equipment — and resources are allocated by markets. Under socialism, the state owns capital and land and resources are allocated by a planning and command system. Market socialism combines state ownership of capital and land with a market allocation of resources. Welfare state capitalism combines private capital and land ownership with a high degree of state intervention in the allocation of resources.

organizations. The plans are monitored by a large team of bureaucrats. No country has ever used an economic system that precisely corresponds to one of these extreme types, but Canada, the United States, and Japan come close to being capitalist economies and the Soviet Union and China to being socialist economies.

Some countries combine private and state ownership and market allocation and planning. **Market socialism** or **decentralized planning** is an economic system that combines socialism's state ownership of capital and land with capitalism's market allocation of resources. Yugoslavia and Hungary are examples of market socialist economies. In such economies, the planners communicate a set of prices to the country's production and distribution organizations and then leave those organizations free to produce whatever quantities they choose at those prices. Another combination is welfare state capitalism. **Welfare state capitalism** combines capitalism's private ownership of capital and land with a heavy degree of state intervention in the allocation of resources. Sweden, the United Kingdom, and other Western European countries provide examples of welfare state economies.

Because of the extraordinary changes that are taking place today, especially in Eastern Europe, the position occupied by each country in Fig. 39.1 is undergoing change. The Soviet Union and other Eastern European countries are moving away from central planning towards market socialism and, to a lesser degree, towards capitalism. The capitalist countries themselves are moving in the direction of even greater reliance on the unregulated market as the means of allocating resources.

Since the economic systems of the countries shown in Fig. 39.1 are made up of a combination of capitalism and socialism, let's examine these two extreme types a bit more closely.

Capitalism

Let's describe a country that has a pure (hypothetical) form of capitalism. Such a country is one in which a concern for individual liberty is paramount. Its foundation is the establishment and enforcement of individual property rights. Each individual owns what he or she has produced or legitimately acquired. Resources are legitimately acquired as a result of buying them from a willing seller or receiving them as a gift. These are the only ways in which resources can be transferred between individuals. Any other method of transferring resources is illegal.

Preventing illegal transfers is the only proper role of the state. No other economic action by any individual or group of individuals may be blocked by the force of the state. All individuals are free to form coalitions or groups to buy and sell whatever goods and services they choose and in whatever quantities they choose.

Governments may be viewed as coalitions among individuals that provide certain types of goods and services. Furthermore, if a government can offer better terms than any other coalition, so that people choose to trade with it rather than with some other group, then a government may legitimately undertake economic actions. A government may not, however, coerce individuals in any way other than to prevent them from attempting to violate other people's property rights.

In capitalist economies, the allocation of resources is determined by individual choices expressed through markets. *What* is produced is determined by consumers' preferences; *how* goods are produced is determined by profit-maximizing firms; *for whom* goods are produced is determined by individual decisions on the supply of factors of production and by the market-determined prices at which those factors of production trade.

Socialism

Socialism is an economic system based on the political philosophy that the private ownership of capital and land enables the rich (owners of capital and land) to exploit the poor (workers who have no capital and land). To avoid such exploitation, capital and land are owned by the state. Individuals are permitted to own only their *human capital* and capital equipment used for consumption purposes, such as consumer durable goods. All other capital is owned by the state. Thus the state owns all factories and farms and the plant and equipment to operate them. All labour works for the state and all consumption goods and services are produced by and bought from the state.

Under socialism, some people are wealthier (and have higher incomes than others), but gross inequalities of wealth arising from the ownership of massive industrial and commercial complexes are not permitted. The principle governing the distribution of income is: from each according to his ability, to each according to his contribution. That is, the state pays each individual a wage that reflects the state's own opinion of the value of the output of the individual.

A variant of socialism is communism. **Communism** is an economic system based on the state ownership of capital and land, on central planning, and on distributing income in accordance with the rule: from each according to his ability, to each according to his need. The word "communism" is commonly used to describe Eastern European and Soviet-style socialism. In ordinary speech, the words "communism" and "socialism" are virtually interchangeable. It is worthwhile keeping the two words distinct, however, when thinking about economic systems.

In socialist (and communist) economies, resources are allocated not by markets but by central planners, and it is their preferences and priorities that determine *what*, *how*, and *for whom* the various goods and services are produced.

The Pros and Cons of Capitalism

Advantages of Capitalism The major advantages of capitalism arise because each individual's judgement about his or her own well-being is paramount in determining what economic actions take place. Each individual decides how much work to do and for whom to work, how to spend time away from work, and how to dispose of the income made from selling his or her resources. Individual incentives are strong. Adam Smith wrote:

> As every individual . . . endeavors as much as he can both to employ his capital in the support of domestic industry and so to direct that industry that its produce be of the greatest value; every individual necessarily labors to render the annual revenue of society as great as he can . . . He intends only his own gain, and he is in this, as in many other cases, led by an invisible hand to promote an end which was no part of his intention. [1]

Adam Smith went on to reject any detailed state intervention in economic life:

> The statesman, who should attempt to direct private people in what manner they ought to employ their capitals, would not only load himself with a most unnecessary attention, but assume an authority which could safely be trusted, not only to no single person, but to no counsel or senate whatever, and which would nowhere be so dangerous as in the hands of a man who had the folly and presumption enough to fancy himself fit to exercise it.[2]

[1] Adam Smith, *The Wealth of Nations* (New York: Random House, 1937), p. 423.

[2] Ibid.

Disadvantages of Capitalism A major disadvantage of capitalism is seen, even by those who support this economic system, as arising from the fact that the historical distribution of endowments is arbitrary and indeed is the result of illegitimate transfers. For example, the European colonizers of North America took land from the native people of this continent. Because illegitimate transfers — violations of private property rights — have occurred in the past, the current distribution of wealth has no legitimacy. If there were no large inequality in the distribution of wealth, its historical origins would not be a matter of much concern. But the fact that wealth is distributed very unequally leads most people to the conclusion that there is a role for state intervention to redistribute income and wealth.

A further disadvantage of capitalism arises from the belief that some people do not know what is good for them and will, if left to their own devices, make the wrong choices. We all agree that children should not be permitted to exercise complete freedom of choice. Most people would also extend some restrictions to the mentally ill, the senile, and to those who are addicted to or users of dangerous drugs. Some advocates of socialism go further, arguing that planners are able to make better choices than people would make for themselves.

We have reviewed some arguments against capitalism that might be used to persuade people that such a system is not desirable. But there is a more fundamental problem with capitalism: it has an inherent contradiction.

The Contradiction The inherent contradiction of capitalism is that private property rights can be enforced only if the state has a monopoly on coercion. If the state were simply competing with others to enforce property rights, then every time a disagreement arose between two parties, each would hire its own enforcers to settle the dispute. Battles would ensue. Only when a single supplier of coercive power has emerged victorious can private property rights be enforced without indulging in a process of open physical violence and conflict. The state is the monopolist in the provision of coercion for enforcing property rights. But once the state has achieved that monopoly position, there is no way of preventing it from expanding its coercive activities. There is no check on those individuals who hold offices of state and who exercise the state's powers. Furthermore, there is no way of preventing private individuals and coalitions of them from attempting to persuade the state to use its powers in a broader manner.

Whether it is because of the persuasiveness of the arguments against capitalism or because of the fundamental internal contradiction in the system, capitalism is a hypothetical rather than an actual economic system. No country ever has or ever will experience that pure form of economic organization. It is a philosophical ideal or reference point against which to compare actual systems. If we could have such a system and if we could remedy the historical violations of property rights, then many people would agree that we would have done the best we could to solve the economic problem. But such a solution is simply not available to us. It is for this reason that most capitalist economies include some element of state ownership and control of economic activity.

Varieties of Capitalism

There is no unique model of capitalism. Most of this book illustrates and elaborates the principles of economics using examples drawn from our own capitalist economy, Canada, and that of our neighbour, the United States. But not all capitalist economies follow the North American model. In this section, we take a quick look at some of the key differences among the capitalist economies and some of the trends that are emerging in those countries.

Japan

Japan's economic performance since World War II is known as the "Japanese economic miracle." Emerging from the war with a per capita income less than one-fifth of that in the United States, Japan has transformed itself into an economic giant whose per capita income now approaches that of North America. The most spectacular growth period occurred in the 25 years from 1945 to 1970, when its per capita income increased eightfold. Today, the Japanese have a dominant position in world markets for cars and computers, audio and video equipment and a wide range of high-tech commodities. The Japanese tourist is now as common a sight in London, Paris, and Rome as the North American tourist. And there are many more Japanese visitors to North America than North Americans visiting Japan. What has led to this transformation of Japan into one of the world's most powerful and richest economies?

There are four features of the Japanese economy that appear to be responsible for its dramatic success. They are:

- Reliance on free-market, capitalist methods
- Self-disciplined, hardworking, loyal, and cooperative people
- Small scale of government
- Pro-business government intervention

The economic system in Japan is similar to that in Canada. People are free to pursue their ideas, to own firms, to hire labour and other inputs, and to sell their outputs in relatively free markets.

The Japanese people have a long tradition of loyalty and a strong work ethic. As a consequence, Japanese workers are loyal to their employers and firms are loyal to their workers. This cooperative atmosphere is one that results in hard work and high productivity.

The Japanese government is the smallest in the capitalist world. The total scale of government is less than one-fifth of the economy. That is, average taxes and government spending account for slightly less than one-fifth of gross domestic product (GDP). This contrasts with a government sector that accounts for more than 40 percent of GDP in Canada. The relatively small scale of government in Japan means that taxes are low and are not, therefore, a major discouragement to work, to saving, and to accumulating capital. To the extent that the Japanese government does intervene in the economy, that intervention is pro-business.

The main vehicle of government intervention is the **Ministry of International Trade and Industry** (MITI) — a government agency responsible for stimulating Japanese industrial development and international trade. In the years immediately following World War II, MITI encouraged the development of basic industries such as coal, electric power, shipbuilding, and steel. It used tariffs and quotas to protect these industries in their early stages of development, subsidized them, and ensured that capital resources were abundantly available for them. The agency is almost entrepreneurial in its activities. During the 1960s, with the basic industries in place, MITI turned its attention to helping the chemical and lighter manufacturing industries. In the 1980s, it helped Japanese industry to dominate the world computer market.

But MITI is active not only in fostering the growth and development of certain industries; it also helps speed the decline of those industries that are not contributing to rapid income growth. For example, in the mid-1970s when the price of oil increased dramatically, the smelting of bauxite to create aluminum became inefficient in Japan. Within two years, the country's bauxite-smelting industry had been closed down, and Japan was importing all its aluminium from Australia. By identifying industries for profitable growth and those for profitable decline, MITI helps speed the adjustment process in reallocating resources to take maximum advantage of technological change and trends in prices.

The result of Japan's economic system and government economic intervention has been a high rate of capital accumulation. There has also been a high rate of accumulation of human capital, especially in the applied sciences. Going along with a high rate of capital accumulation — both physical and human — has been a high rate of technological advance and a lack of inhibitions about using the best technologies available, wherever in the world they might have been developed.

Welfare State Capitalism

Capitalism in Western Europe is more heavily tinged with socialism than in Canada, the United States, or Japan. It is welfare state capitalism. The countries of Western Europe, many of which now belong to the European Community, are basically capitalist market economies in the sense that most productive resources are owned by private individuals and most resources are allocated by individuals trading freely in markets for both goods and services and factors of production. But the scale of government and the degree and direction of government intervention are larger in these countries than in Canada and much larger than in the United States and Japan.

In European countries, government expenditure and taxes range between 40 to 50 percent of GDP. These high tax rates create disincentives that result in less work effort and lower saving rates than in countries with lower taxes. Many Western European countries also have a large, nationalized industry sector. A **nationalized industry** is an industry owned and operated by a publicly owned authority that is directly responsible to the government. In Canada, a nationalized firm is a Crown Corporation. Railways, airlines, gas provision, electricity, telephones, radio and television broadcasting, coal production, steel making, banking and finance, and even automobile manufacture are among the list of industries that are either wholly or partly publicly owned in some European countries. Nationalized industries are often managed on a command rather than market principle and usually are less efficient than privately owned competitive firms.

Increasingly in recent years, European governments have been selling state-owned enterprises. The process of selling state-owned enterprises is called **privatization**. Some countries have also retreated from very high tax rates.

European countries have noticed the economic success of Japan, Canada, and the United States and, right or wrong, have concluded the greater reliance on capitalism in those economies is, in part, responsible for their economic success. That conclusion is reinforced by a widespread belief that the socialist methods employed by the Soviet Union and China are no longer serving those countries well. Let's take a closer look at socialism — first in the Soviet Union and then in China.

The Soviet Union

The Soviet Union, or the Union of Soviet Socialist Republics, was founded in 1917 following the Bolshevik revolution led by Vladimir Ilyich Lenin. The Soviet Union is a vast, resource-rich, and diverse nation. Its land area is 2.5 times that of Canada; its population is approaching 300 million; it has vast reserves of coal, oil, iron ore, natural gas, timber, and almost every other mineral resource. It is a nation of enormous ethnic diversity, with Russians making up only 50 percent of the population; the remaining population includes many European, Asian, and Arabic ethnic groups.

History

A compact economic history of the Soviet Union appears in Table 39.1. Although the nation was founded in 1917, its modern economic management system was not put in place until the 1930s. The architect of this system was Joseph Stalin. The financial, manufacturing, and transportation sectors of the economy were taken into state ownership and control by Lenin. Stalin added the farms to this list. He abolished the market and introduced a command planning mechanism, initiating a series of five-year plans that placed their major emphasis on setting and attaining goals for the production of capital goods. The production of consumer goods was given a secondary place and personal economic conditions were harsh. With emphasis on the production of capital goods, the Soviet economy grew quickly.

After Stalin's death in 1953, steady economic growth continued, but the emphasis in economic planning gradually shifted away from capital goods towards consumer goods production. In the 1960s, the growth rate began to sag, and by the 1970s and early 1980s, the Soviet economy was running into serious problems. Productivity was actually declining, especially in agriculture but also in some industries. Growth slowed to a lower rate than was being achieved in western capitalist countries and the Soviet Union began to fall further behind its superpower rival — the United States. It was in this situation that Mikhail Gorbachev came to power with plans to restructure the Soviet economy, based on the idea of increased individual accountability and rewards based on performance.

Because the Soviet economy is currently undergoing a major restructuring process, it is impossible to give an up-to-date description of its economic organization. But it is possible to describe the economic organization from which the modern Soviet Union economy is evolving. That organization was established in the 1930's by Stalin. Let's examine its main features.

Table 39.1 A Compact Summary of Key Periods in the Economic History of the Soviet Union

Period	Main economic events/characteristics
1917–1921 (Lenin)	• Bolshevik Revolution • Nationalization of banking, industry, and transportation • Forced requisitioning of agricultural output
1921–1924 (Lenin)	• New Economic Policy (NEP), 1921 • Market allocation of most resources
1928 –1953 (Stalin)	• Abolition of market • Introduction of command planning and five-year plans • Collectivization of farms • Emphasis on capital goods and economic growth • Harsh conditions
1953–1970 (Khrushchev to Brezhnev	• Steady growth • Increased emphasis on consumer goods
1970 –1985 (Brezhnev to Chernenko)	• Deteriorating productivity in agriculture and industry • Slowdown in growth
1985 – (Gorbachev)	• *Perestroika* — reforms based on increased acountability and decentralization including the beginning of private ownership

Figure 39.2 Organization Chart of the Soviet Union

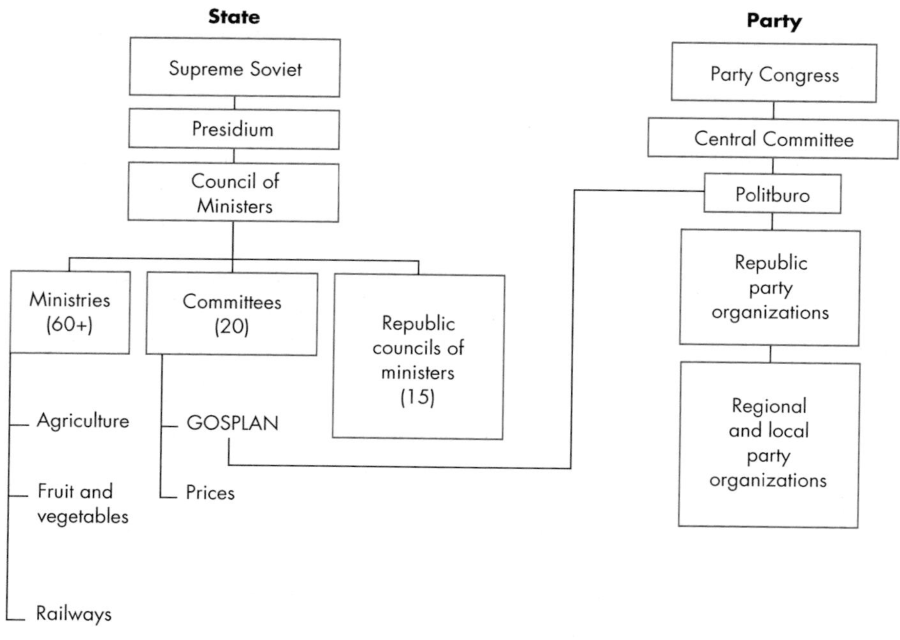

Two parallel organizations — the state and the party — manage the Soviet economy. Although the two organizations are parallel, the party is the dominant partner. The State Committee for Economic Planning — GOSPLAN — has direct links to the Politburo, the chief organ of party power. Economic plans are administered by ministries that deal with each sector of the economy. Plans are also monitored by regional and local party organizations. This chart shows only the tip of a bureaucratic iceberg. Each of the 15 republics of the Soviet Union has an organization similar to that shown here, and each local region within each republic has yet another similar organization.

Planning and Command System

There are two parallel organizations in the system established by Stalin for the economic management of the Soviet Union: the state and the Communist Party. Power resides in the Communist Party. The most important policy-making body in the Soviet Union is the Politburo, a small group of party officials appointed by the Central Committee of the Communist Party, in turn appointed by the Party Congress, as shown in Fig. 39.2. The Party Congress, made up of delegates from all levels of the Party and all regions of the country, exercises only nominal control over the Central Committee and the Politburo.

These organs of the Communist Party parallel the state institutions. The Soviet parliament is the Supreme Soviet. This body meets infrequently and appoints a Presidium to conduct work between sessions. The Council of Ministers is the government bureaucracy. This bureaucracy controls 60 ministries responsible for detailed aspects of production. The figure provides a sample of the names and responsibilities of some of the 60 ministries. Twenty committees report to the Council of Ministers; of these, two play a central role in economic planning and control. The first of these is the State Committee for Economic Planning, whose acronym in Russian is GOSPLAN. **GOSPLAN** is the committee responsible for drawing up and implementing the state's economic plans. The second important economic committee is one that determines prices. Also reporting to the Council of Ministers are the Councils of Ministers of the 15 republics of the Soviet Union.

The organization chart shown in Fig. 39.2 is just the tip of a bureaucratic iceberg, for each of the 15 republics of the Soviet Union has a set of institutions that almost exactly parallels the institutions of the central government just described. This organizational form is also replicated at the regional level and yet again at the local level. Thus there are ministries and party organizations whose influence stretches deep into the most detailed aspects of economic life in the Soviet Union.

The Communist Party of the Soviet Union exercises control over the state by three main methods:

- GOSPLAN reports to the Politburo.
- The party approves all major projects.
- The party controls appointments.

The detailed plans for economic activity, drawn up by GOSPLAN (and described below), are reported to and approved by the Politburo. The party exercises detailed day-to-day control over all major projects and production activities through its regional and local organizations. The Communist party's most powerful tool for influencing the Soviet economy is its control over all major appointments in the state bureaucracy, in industry, and in the military.

State Enterprises The basic production unit in the Soviet economy is the **state enterprise**. An enterprise is run by a state-appointed director, who is in charge of all the enterprise's operations but is required to follow the instructions imposed by the state's economic plans. State enterprises operate in both the industrial and agricultural sectors of the economy, and the enterprise manager plays a key role in the fulfilment of plans. Soviet managers are rewarded through a complex system of performance-related payments.

Planning at GOSPLAN Every five years, GOSPLAN draws up a five-year plan. The **five-year plan** is a broad outline of the general economic targets and directions set for a period of five years. Each year GOSPLAN also draws up an annual plan. The **annual plan** is a month-by-month set of targets for output, prices, inputs, investment, and money and credit flows. The plans are approved by the Politburo and the Council of Ministers and then communicated to the individual enterprises — farms and factories — that produce the goods and services. Enterprises are overseen both by the ministries that are responsible for the various industries and by local party organizations.

The annual plan is organized around five basic balances:

1 Consumer goods
2 Labour
3 Credit
4 Capital goods
5 Materials

1. Consumer Goods Balance Consumer goods balance is the achievement of a balance between the quantities supplied and demanded for each category of consumer goods and services. Soviet planners have three ways of achieving consumer goods balance: changing output, changing incomes, and changing prices. Figure 39.3 illustrates these three possibilities. The demand for some good — say, shoes — is D_0; the quantity of shoes that the planners intend to produce is Q_0; the supply curve is S_0; and the cost of producing shoes is C. If the price of shoes is set by the planners at C, there will be an excess of the quantity demanded over the quantity supplied — an amount equal to Q_1 minus Q_0. The planners will not have achieved consumer goods balance in the market for shoes. From the diagram, you can see three ways in which they can achieve a balance. First they can increase production to Q_1, in which case the supply curve will shift to the right to S_1 (part a). Second, they can impose higher income taxes, thereby reducing after-tax income and lowering the demand for shoes (part b). They will have to increase taxes by enough to shift the demand curve to the left from D_0 to D_1. At a price of C, the quantity of shoes demanded equals the quantity supplied (Q_0).

In practice, although these two methods of achieving consumer goods balance are available to the Soviet planners, they are not the main methods used. The easiest way of achieving consumer goods balance (and the one most frequently used) is to adjust the price. Soviet planners adjust prices by imposing turnover taxes. The **turnover tax** in the Soviet Union is a tax on a consumer good designed to make its market price high enough to achieve a balance between the quantity demanded and quantity supplied. In this example (Fig. 39.3c), a turnover tax sufficient to increase the price to P ensures consumer goods balance in the market for shoes.

2. Labour Balance Labour balance is the achievement of a balance between the quantities supplied and demanded for each category of labour services. It is achieved, in the short run, by adjusting wage rates. Large differentials in wages — larger than those common in Canada — are necessary to achieve labour balance. In the long run, labour balance is also influenced by the planners' ability to direct resources allocated to education and training, favouring the acquisition of skills in short supply.

3. Credit Balance Credit balance is the achievement of a balance between the quantities of credit supplied and demanded. The banking system in the Soviet Union is owned and controlled by the state. Credit balance is achieved by having the state banking system make available the credit that the planners have decided is required.

Figure 39.3 Consumer Goods Balance

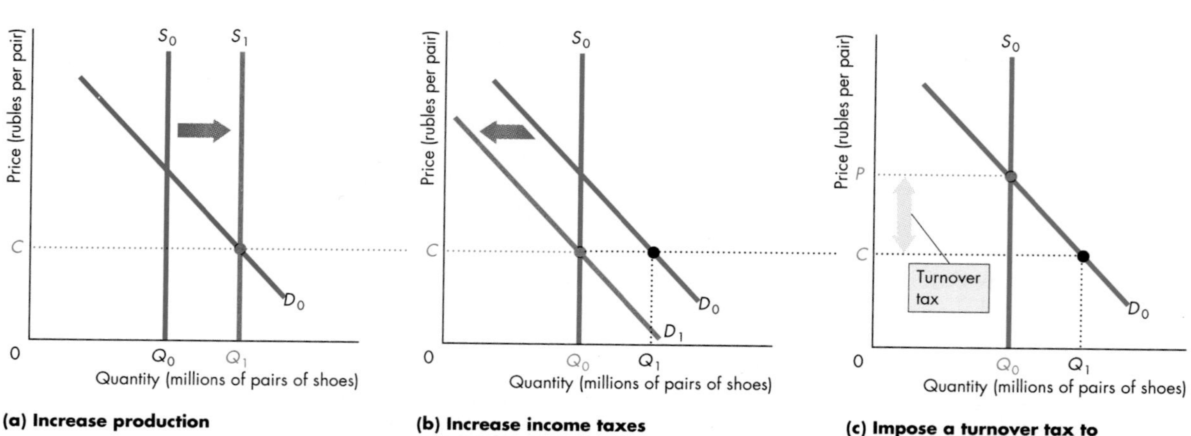

The cost of producing shoes is C. The demand for shoes is D_0, and the quantity produced is Q_0. Three ways of achieving consumer goods balance are available. In part (a), the decision to increase output results in a shift in the supply curve to S_1. When the price is C and the quantity of shoes produced and consumed is Q_1, consumption goods balance is achieved. In part (b), income taxes are increased, reducing after-tax income. The demand for shoes decreases and the demand curve shifts to the left to D_1. The price is C and the quantity of shoes produced and consumed is Q_0. In part (c), the planners impose a turnover tax on shoes. A tax equal to the difference between P and C is imposed, raising the price of shoes to P. The quantity demanded decreases to Q_0 and consumer goods balance is achieved. Soviet planners use the turnover tax more frequently than the other two methods for achieving consumer goods balance.

4. Capital Goods Balance Capital goods balance is the achievement of a balance between the quantities supplied and demanded of each type of capital good. The central planners decide how to allocate the scarce capital goods available and, through their control of credit, influence the demand for capital goods by individual production enterprises.

5. Materials Balance Materials balance is the achievement of a balance between the quantities demanded and supplied for each and every raw material and intermediate good used in the production of final consumer goods and capital goods. This balancing exercise is the most complex aspect of Soviet planning. There are literally billions of raw materials and intermediate goods, and the detailed plans for the material balances fill 70 volumes — 12,000 pages — each year.

An example of a simplified materials balance schedule is set out in Table 39.2. For this example, there are just three materials. (The actual Soviet plans consider more than 30,000 separate materials at the central planning level and a further 50,000 at the regional and local levels.) Any material used in the production process has three possible sources: production, inventories, and imports. Any raw material or produced input can be put to three broad categories of use: as an intermediate input into the production of other goods, as a final domestic product for consumption or investment purposes, and as an export. For each material, a detailed plan showing the balance between the quantity supplied and quantity demanded is drawn up. For example, the first row of the table shows that 490 tonnes of coal are produced and 10 tonnes are taken from inventory. The quantity supplied is 500 tonnes of coal. The quantity demanded is made up of 50 tonnes as inputs to the coal industry itself, 300 tonnes to produce electric power, 50 tonnes to extract chemicals that are converted into nylon, 75 tonnes for domestic heating, and 25 tonnes to be exported. The total

Table 39.2 Materials Balance

	Quantity supplied			Quantity demanded				
				Intermediate goods			Final goods	
Material	**Production**	**Inventories**	**Imports**	**Coal**	**Electric power**	**Nylon**	**Domestic**	**Foreign**
Coal (tonnes)	490	10	0	50	300	50	75	25
Electric power (kilowatt hours)	10,000	0	0	2,000	1,000	1,500	5,500	0
Nylon (metres)	20,000	200	2,000	0	0	0	22,200	0

Materials can be supplied from production, inventories, or imports. They are demanded as an input into the production of intermediate goods, for final domestic consumption, or for export. Plans are drawn up to ensure that the quantity supplied equals the quantity demanded. To achieve materials balance, Soviet planners can increase production, decrease inventories, increase imports, decrease the quantity demanded as an intermediate good, decrease final demand, or decrease exports. Reductions in final domestic demand are the main method employed for achieving materials balance.

quantity demanded is 500 tonnes. The plan for coal balances. The second row of the table shows the plan for electric power and the third row shows that for nylon.

Table 39.2 shows a balance between the quantity demanded and the quantity supplied of each material. Suppose that there is an excess of the quantity demanded over the quantity supplied of electric power. What can the Soviet planners do in such a situation? They can plan to produce more electric power, or they can plan to produce less coal and less nylon, thereby reducing the amount of electric power demanded, or they can reduce the quantity of electric power for final domestic use. The Soviet planners usually choose the last of these options. If they were to increase the output of electric power, there would be an increase in the quantity of coal demanded in the electric power industry. That increase would result in a shortage in the coal sector that would require further adjustments in that sector. To balance the quantity supplied and quantity demanded of electric power by reducing the amount going to some other industry would result in the failure of that industry to achieve its targets.

The Market Sector Although the economy of the Soviet Union is a planned one, a substantial amount of economic activity takes place outside the planning and command economy, and the market sector is expanding under Gorbachev's reforms. The most important component of the market sector is in agriculture. It is estimated that rural households work 35 million private plots. These private plots constitute less than 3 percent of the agricultural land of the Soviet Union, but they produce close to a quarter of total agricultural output and a third of all the meat and milk produced. Some estimates suggest that the productivity on private plots is forty times that of state enterprise farms and collective farms.

There are other economic activities undertaken by Soviet citizens outside the planning systems. Many of these are legal but some are not. Many of the illegal ones involve the buying and selling of goods brought in illegally from abroad.

Perestroika

At the June 1987 meeting of the Central Committee of the Communist Party, Mikhail Gorbachev announced the first step in his reform plan, now universally known as *perestroika*. The key elements in this plan are:

- Increased independence for state enterprises
- Reform of accounting methods to calculate enterprises' full cost, revenue, and profit

- Requirement that each enterprise achieve the "highest end results" (maximum profits)
- Establishment of a direct link of income to performance
- Reduction in the power of central planners, relieving them of "interference in day-to-day activities"
- Reform of planning and pricing
- Decreased reliance on the command system of management and an increased role for individual incentives

Gorbachev spoke of the need to "create a powerful system of motives and stimuli [to] encourage workers to reveal their capability, work fruitfully [and] use productive resources most effectively." Remarkably, he declared that "there is only one criterion of justice [in the distribution of income]: whether or not it is earned."[3] Gorbachev even talked of abolishing job security and of closing down unprofitable state enterprises.

In the period since the initiation of *perestroika*, the Soviet Union and many of the other Eastern European socialist countries (Hungary, Czechoslovakia, Poland, East Germany, Bulgaria, and Romania) have experienced enormous political change. Those political changes are also bringing more rapid economic reorganization in their wake. Perhaps the most remarkable change is the introduction of privately owned firms in the Soviet Union.

By the standards that have prevailed previously in the Soviet Union, Gorbachev's plans are revolutionary. They call for a redistribution of economic power, so it is not surprising that they are meeting a great deal of resistance. But to the extent that they contain the basis for improved economic performance, they also have a large number of supporters. How quickly and how far the Soviet Union will be able to travel along the road charted by Mikhail Gorbachev, we cannot yet say. But the direction that the Soviet economy is now taking is exciting and at least holds out the promise of a more efficient, productive, and prosperous Soviet Union.

We'll assess the performance of the Soviet economy and compare its performance with that of capitalist economies later in this chapter. But first, let's look at the other socialist giant, China.

[3]Mikhail Gorbachev, *Perestroika: New Thinking for Our Country and the World* (New York: Harper and Row, 1987).

China

China is the world's largest nation with a population of more than a billion people. Chinese civilization is ancient and has a splendid history, but the modern nation — the People's Republic of China — dates only from 1949. A compact summary of key periods in the economic history of the People's Republic is presented in Table 39.3.

Modern China was created when a revolutionary Communist movement, led by Mao Zedong, captured control of the country, forcing its previous leader, Chiang Kai-shek onto the island of Formosa (now Taiwan). Like the Soviet Union, China is a socialist country. But unlike the Soviet Union, China is largely nonindustrialized — it is a developing country.

During the early years of the People's Republic, the country followed the Soviet model of economic planning and command. Urban manufacturing industry was taken over and operated by the state, and the farms were collectivized. Also following the Stalin

Table 39.3 A Compact Summary of Key Periods in the Economic History of the People's Republic of China

Period	Main economic events/characteristics
1949	• People's Republic of China established under Mao Zedong
1949-1952	• Economy centralized under a new communist government
	• Emphasis on heavy industry and "socialist transformation"
1952-1957	• First five-year plan
1958-1960	• The Great Leap Forward: an economic reform plan based on labour-intensive production methods
	• Massive economic failure
1966	• Cultural Revolution: revolutionary zealots
1976	• Death of Mao Zedong
1978	• Reforms of Deng Xiaoping: liberalization of agriculture and introduction of individual incentives
	• Growth rates accelerated
1989	• Democracy movement; government crackdown

model of the 1930s, primary emphasis was placed on the production of capital equipment.

The Great Leap Forward

In 1958, Mao Zedong set the Chinese economy on a path sharply divergent from the one the Soviet Union had followed. Mao called his new path "the Great Leap Forward". The **Great Leap Forward** was an economic plan based on small-scale, labour-intensive production. It paid little or no attention to linking individual pay to individual effort. Instead, it relied on a revolutionary commitment to the success of collective plans.

The Great Leap Forward was an economic failure. Productivity increased, but so slowly that living standards hardly changed. In the agricultural sector, massive injections of modern, high-yield seeds, improved irrigation, and chemical fertilizers were insufficient to enable China to feed its population. The country became the world's largest importer of grains, edible vegetable oils, and even raw cotton.

Within China, the popular explanation for poor performance, especially in agriculture, was that the country had reached the limits of its arable land and that its population explosion was so enormous that agriculture was being forced to use substandard areas for farming. The key problem was that the revolutionary and ideological motivation for the Great Leap Forward degenerated into what came to be called the Cultural Revolution. Revolutionary zealots denounced productive managers, engineers, scientists and scholars, and banished them to the lives of peasants. Schools and universities were closed, and the accumulation of human capital was severely disrupted.

1978 Reforms

In 1978, two years after the death of Mao Zedong, the new Chinese leader, Deng Xiaoping, proclaimed major economic reforms. Collectivized agriculture was abolished. Agricultural land was distributed among households on long-term leases in a system that is still used. In exchange for a lease, a household agrees to pay a fixed tax and contracts to sell part of its output to the state. The household makes its own decisions on cropping patterns and the quantity and types of fertilizers and other inputs to use; it also hires its own workers. Private farm markets were liberalized, and since then farmers have received a higher price for their produce. Also, the state increased the price that it paid to farmers, especially for cotton and other nongrain crops.

The results of the reforms of Deng Xiaoping have been astounding. Annual growth rates of output of cotton and oil-bearing crops increased a staggering fourteenfold. Soybean production, which had been declining at an annual rate of 1 percent between 1957 and 1978, now started to grow at 4 percent a year. The growth rates of yields per hectare also increased dramatically. By 1984, a country that six years earlier had been the world's largest importer of agricultural products became a food exporter.

The reforms have not only produced massive expansion in the agricultural sector. Increased rural incomes have brought an expanding rural industrial sector that, by the middle 1980s, was employing a fifth of the rural population.

Reform of the manufacturing sector has provided stronger incentives for enterprise managers and a greater degree of independence for making production decisions. These reforms, similar to those now being proposed by Gorbachev in the Soviet Union, have resulted in rapid growth in industrial output. China has gone even further and is encouraging foreign investment and joint ventures. In addition, it is experimenting with formal capital markets and now has a stock market.

Motivated partly by political considerations, China is proclaiming the virtues of what it calls the "one country, two systems" approach to economic management. The political source of this movement is the existence of two capitalist enclaves in which China has a close interest — Taiwan and Hong Kong. China claims sovereignty over Taiwan. And it wants to create an atmosphere in which it becomes possible for China to be reunified at some future date. Hong Kong, is currently leased by Britain from China, but that lease terminates in 1997. When it expires, Hong Kong will become part of China. Anxious not to damage the economic prosperity of Hong Kong, China is proposing that Hong Kong continue operating as a capitalist economy. With Hong Kong and Taiwan as part of the People's Republic of China, the stage will be set for the creation of other capitalist "islands" in such dynamic cities as Shanghai.

It is too early to say whether China has invented a new economic system — one country, two systems. And the violent suppression of the democracy movement in Tiananmen Square in the summer of 1989 further clouds our view of where China is heading. But the experiment in comparative economic systems currently in progress in China is one of the most exciting that the world has seen. Economists of all political shades of opinion are watching it closely, and its lessons will be of enormous value for future generations — whatever those lessons turn out to be.

Comparing Capitalism and Socialism

We have now defined capitalist and socialist economic systems and have described the economic organization of some of the leading examples of these systems. In this final section, we'll use some of the economic models that we have studied to analyse the workings of capitalist and socialist economic systems. We'll also compare the performances of the two systems in practice.

To make our comparison of the working of a capitalist and socialist economy as clear as possible, we're going to work with a model economy. The model economy under capitalism will have perfect competition and no external economies or diseconomies. We'll study the same economy under socialism.

Capitalism

Under capitalism, individual households choose the quantities of productive resources to supply and the quantities of goods and services to demand. Each firm seeks to make the biggest possible profit and to produce at the lowest possible cost. The demand for a good or service is summarized by its market demand curve. That curve also shows the value placed on each extra unit of the good. The supply of the good is summarized by the market supply curve. The supply curve also shows the marginal cost of producing each unit of the good. The equilibrium price and quantity are determined by the point at which the supply and demand curves intersect.

Figure 39.4 illustrates a market in a perfectly competitive capitalist economy — the market for shoes. The demand curve for shoes (D) and the supply curve of shoes (S) intersect at quantity Q_C and price P_C. At this price and quantity, the perfectly competitive capitalist economy achieves *allocative* efficiency. The value placed on the last pair of shoes produced (P_C) is the same as the marginal cost of producing them.

What happens under socialism?

Socialism

Now imagine that the economy whose market for shoes is depicted in Fig. 39.4 is taken over by a socialist government. It is now operated under centralized socialist planning. Let's see how the shoe market will perform under this new system of economic control. Figure 39.5 illustrates the shoe market in a socialist economy.

Consumers still have their views about the value they place on goods and services, so the demand for shoes is represented by the same demand curve. There is a difference, however, on the supply side. Under socialism, firms do not own the means of production, so the individual manager of a plant has no incentive to maximize profit and minimize cost. The manager's income is determined by the central planner; the manager receives a bonus if the firm achieves its target output, but there is no incentive for output to be produced in the most efficient possible way. On the contrary, the manager has an incentive to produce inefficiently. To see this, we need to consider how production targets are determined under socialism.

The central planner sets targets for total output

Figure 39.4 Prices and Quantities Under Capitalism

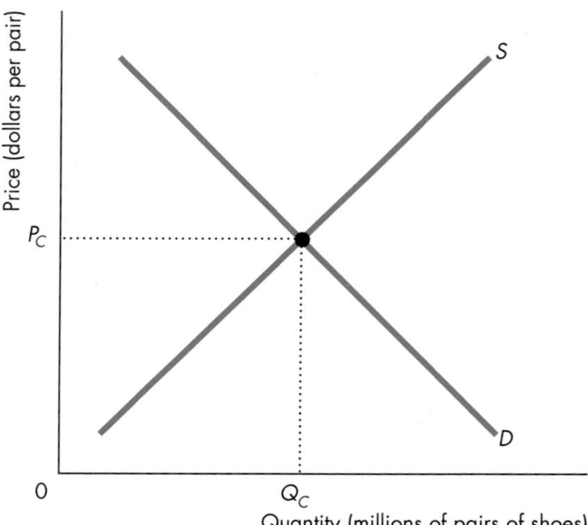

The preferences and choices of households determine the demand for shoes (curve D). The profit-maximization decisions of firms determine the supply of shoes (curve S). With a perfectly competitive shoe market, capitalism produces quantity Q_C at price P_C. If there are no external costs and benefits, this outcome achieves allocative efficiency.

Figure 39.5 Prices and Quantities Under Socialism

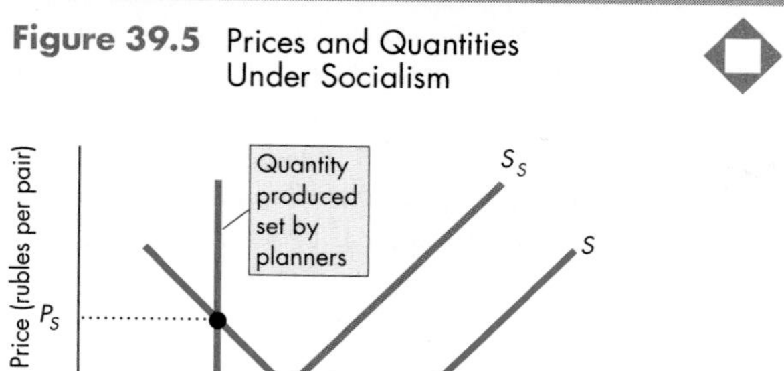

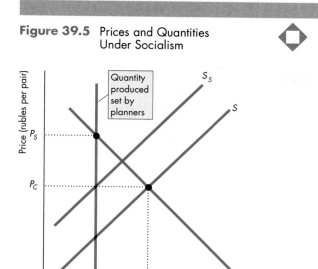

Consumers determine the demand for shoes (curve D). Socialist managers determine the supply of shoes (curve S_S). Socialist managers have less incentive than capitalist entrepreneurs to supply goods at least cost, so the supply curve S_S lies to the left of the capitalism supply curve S. The central planning process sets a target output of shoes for the economy at Q_S. To achieve a balance of the quantity demanded and the quantity supplied, a tax is imposed on shoes to raise the price to P_S. Socialism delivers a lower quantity of shoes traded and a higher price of shoes than does capitalism.

and allocates those targets to the various production plants. The target output rate for any individual plant depends on what that plant has historically been able to produce. Therefore it always pays for a manager of a plant to pretend that his plant can produce less than it in fact can. Thus the supply curve under socialism is, in general, to the left of the supply curve under capitalism. The line labelled S_S in Fig. 39.5 is a possible supply curve for shoes under socialism, given the supply curve S under capitalism.

The gap between the socialist and capitalist supply curves is waste or inefficiency. The gap arises because the manager of the socialist factory has little incentive to produce the target output at minimum cost and a high incentive to hide the true potential of his plant so that he will be assigned an easier production target.

The next big difference between capitalism and socialism concerns the way in which prices and quantities are determined. The quantity supplied is determined partly by the plans of the central planners and partly by the actions of the individual enterprises and the incentives that they face. Suppose that the outcome of the planning process is a quantity of shoes produced of Q_S. To achieve a balance between the quantity demanded and quantity supplied, the socialist planners will have to introduce a tax on shoes, raising their price to P_S. At this price, there is a balance between the quantity demanded and quantity supplied.

Central planning with state ownership produces a smaller quantity of shoes, Q_S compared with Q_C, at a higher price, P_S compared with P_C, than the perfectly competitive capitalist economy. This inferior performance has arisen from two sources: inefficient production resulting in higher average cost and production of the wrong quantity. Part of this problem is addressed by market socialism, but part is not. Let's see the difference that market socialism makes.

Market Socialism

We will continue to look at the same economy and its shoe market. The demand for shoes remains as before and is shown again in Fig. 39.6. Again, the socialist manager has less incentive than the capitalist manager to maximize profit and produce at least cost so his supply curve is S_S rather than the capitalist supply curve S. But the price is now determined in a decentralized manner in the market for shoes. The supply curve S_S and the demand curve D intersect at the price P_{MS} and at quantity Q_{MS}. This price is higher than the competitive capitalist price and the quantity is smaller, but more shoes are produced and sold at a lower price under market socialism than under centrally planned socialism (as in Fig. 39.5).

To get the economy to produce the capitalist quantity of shoes at the capitalist price, incentives have to be put in place at the individual firm level to encourage socialist factory managers to produce at least cost and to be as efficient as capitalist managers.

Perestroika in the Model Economy

We can interpret *perestroika* in this model economy. Under the central planning methods of Stalin, the Soviet economy produces too few shoes at too high a price. It is the situation depicted in Fig. 39.5. By moving to the decentralized planning that countries such as Hungary and Yugoslavia have employed for some years, the socialist economy can do better,

Figure 39.6 Prices and Quantities Under Market Socialism

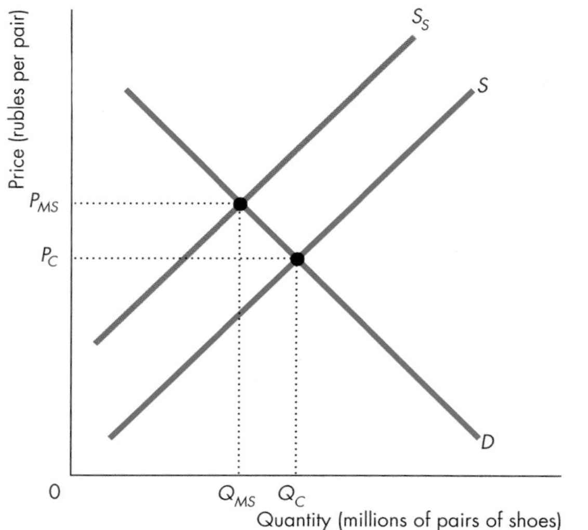

The market socialist demand and supply curves are the same as they are under socialism. The price of shoes is set in a decentralized way, so the quantity demanded and the quantity supplied are equal. If the price is set too low, the central planner will gradually increase it. If the price is set too high, the central planner will gradually decrease it. On the average, the price is P_{MS} and the quantity traded is Q_{MS}. A smaller quantity of shoes is traded and at a higher price than in a perfectly competitive capitalist economy. But more shoes are traded and at a lower price than under socialism.

lowering the price and increasing the quantity produced as shown in Fig. 39.6. Such a move is one part of *perestroika.* But the socialist economy can do better still, provided it can make incentives at the production plant level strong enough to achieve maximum profits and produce efficiently. If that does prove to be possible, the socialist economy will be able to lower the price and increase the quantity produced to equal the competitive capitalist levels.

Most economists believe that to achieve incentives strong enough for efficient production at the individual production plant level, the private ownership of firms is essential. If this belief is correct, it will take some time for socialist economies to achieve the efficiency levels that are routinely achieved in the capitalist West.

There is a further potential problem facing socialist economies as they seek to move closer to the capitalist methods of economic allocation and control. The problem is that *perestroika* appears to be a piecemeal and somewhat undirected process. Some sectors of the economy are moving towards a market allocation while others are not. Central planning mechanisms are breaking down before they have been fully replaced with an alternative decentralized market mechanism. In the actual process of change, there is the possibility that economic conditions for the average consumer will deteriorate before they improve. The problem of managing *perestroika* is made even more difficult by the rapid changes in political institutions that are taking place simultaneously.

Regardless of how the Soviet Union and other socialist economies evolve over the coming few years, the opportunities that are available and the lessons that can be learned are of historic importance.

Inefficiencies in Capitalism

In the model economies we just looked at, we ignored elements of inefficiency in capitalism. That does not mean that they are not present in the real world. Capitalist economies do not function like the perfectly competitive ideal. There are external costs and benefits, monopoly elements, and taxes and subsidies, all of which move the economy away from the competitive ideal. But these problems are present in socialist economies as well. They do not directly enter into an evaluation of the two systems. But we cannot compare the performance of capitalist and socialist economies merely by looking at an idealized, perfectly competitive model.

The ultimate test of capitalism and socialism comes in a comparison not of models but of actual performance. How have socialist economies performed and how does that performance compare with that of capitalist economies?

Economic Growth and Average Living Standards

One way of comparing the success of alternative economic systems is to look at their capacity to deliver economic growth and high standards of living. Table 39.4 tells us what has happened in the United States, Japan, and the Soviet Union over 140 years of history. As you can see, throughout this period, the United States has experienced steady and sustained economic growth rates of between 3 and 4 percent a year. This growth rate has produced a living standard for Americans that is the highest in the world. Impressive though the

U.S. growth performance has been, Japan, another capitalist economy, has done better. By growing in excess of 10 percent a year in many of the postwar years, it has transformed itself from a war-devastated country in 1945 into one of the richest industrial giants in the world today.

Compare these performances with that of the Soviet Union. The Soviet Union was a capitalist country until the revolution in 1917. It was, however, a very poor country, and most of its people worked in the agricultural sector. Eleven years after the Revolution, in 1928, the Soviet Union instituted central planning and established its first five-year plan. Since that date, Soviet economic growth has been impressive. As you can see, in Table 39.4, Soviet growth rates have been larger than those of the United States except in the 1980s. They have not been as high as those of Japan. Nevertheless, the result is that per capita income in the Soviet Union reached one-half that of the United States by the late 1970s.

The Soviet Union achieved its rapid growth primarily by squeezing consumption and focusing on capital accumulation and investment. In the United States, consumption and investment have grown at roughly the same rate over the long term. In the Soviet Union, consumption has grown at approximately half the pace of the growth rate of investment. During the first two five-year plans (the period from 1928 to 1937), consumption grew by only 0.7 percent a year while income grew by 5.4 percent a year and investment by 14.5 percent a year. Not until the late 1960s did consumption and investment in the Soviet Union grow at a similar pace. Thus although the Soviet Union has grown quickly, it has done so at enormous cost — Soviet planners have squeezed consumption to a point that capitalist countries would not have tolerated.

Table 39.4 Annual Growth Rates in the United States, Japan, and the Soviet Union

	Annual growth rate (percentage)		
Years	**United States**	**Japan**	**Soviet Union**
1840 – 1885	4.4		
1885 – 1905	3.7	5.7	3.3 (1885 – 1913)
1905 – 1929	3.4	7.4	
1929 – 1950	2.8		5.4 (1928 – 1937)
1950 – 1960	3.2	11.5	5.7 (1940 – 1960)
1960 – 1970	4.0		5.1
1970 – 1979	3.1		3.2
1980 – 1986	3.1		2.0

Source: 1840 –1950: Paul R. Gregory and Robert C. Stuart, *Soviet Economic Structure and Performance*, 2nd ed. (New York: Harper & Row, 1981); 1850 –1986: U.S. Central Intelligence Agency, *USSR: Measures of Economic Growth and Development, 1950 – 80*, U.S. Congress, Joint Economic Committee (Washington, D.C.: U.S. Government Printing Office, 1982,); and U.S. Central Intelligence Agency,: "Gorbachev's Economic Program," Report to U.S. Congress, Subcommittee on National Security Economics (April 13, 1988).

Figure 39.7 Income per Person in 1987 in Ten Countries

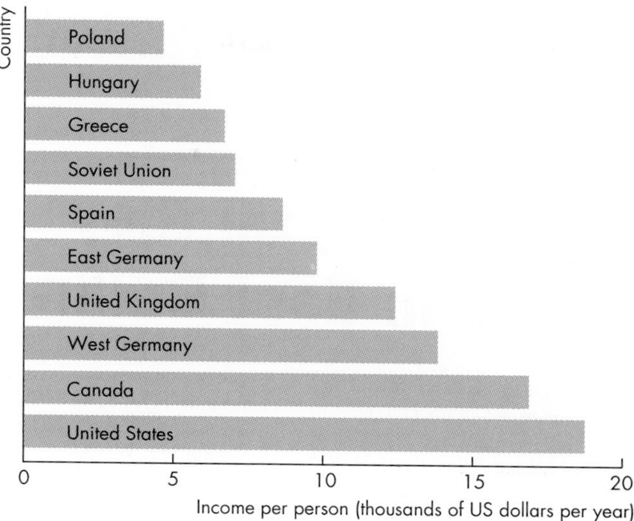

Income per person in the Soviet Union is similar to that in Greece and Spain. It is higher than that in Poland and Hungary but lower than that in East Germany. Poland, Hungary, and East Germany were formerly planned economies. The difference between the income levels of East Germany and West Germany gives the clearest indication of the comparative performance of planned and market economies.

Despite the fact that the Soviet Union has had some periods of rapid growth in the past, its recent growth performance is poor and the average level of income that it has managed to achieve is far below that of Canada and the United States. In fact, as Figure 39.7 shows, average income in the Soviet Union is similar to such countries as Greece and Spain and less than one half of Canadian and U.S. average income levels.

The growth performance of China also provides interesting evidence on the performance of a

Capitalism Comes to East Germany

Shopping till they drop in East Berlin

Only days before they plunge into another revolution, East Germans have turned their capital city [East Berlin] into a sprawling bazaar.

They are buying and selling everywhere—in improvised stalls, out of the back of vans, on upturned cartons on the sidewalk...

In theory, the market economy was not going to arrive in East Germany until next Monday [July 2, 1990]. That is the day when the apparatus of the Communist economy is dismantled and East Germany is merged in an economic union with West Germany.

The West German Deutschmark will become the common currency and, on Monday, there will be nothing to stop East Germans buying anything money can buy...

For the more than 40 years that East Germany was ruled by Communist economic theory, the dazzlingly prosperous economy of West Germany was right next door...

Depending on whether you ran the state or the state ran you, West Germany was either a capitalist nightmare or an unattainable dream.

But the collapse of the old Communist regime and the destruction of the Berlin Wall has changed all that. West Germany is coming East.

Typical is Dieter Fuerstenau. For 24 years, he has been selling East German stoves and refrigerators from a surprisingly attractive store on Karl Liebknecht plaza.

With the changes in recent months, he has started to import West German models to let his customers have their choice.

It has required complex price adjustments because the old East German regime subsidized stoves and made money on refrigerators. Stoves were deemed a necessity, fridges were not...

The same thinking decreed that East German industry should not bother producing things such as dishwashers, microwave ovens and clothes dryers. Needless luxuries, they said.

So now Mr. Fuerstenau is managing a dwindling showroom of East German products and an expanding stock from the West—including microwaves, dishwashers and dryers...

***The Globe and Mail,* June 28, 1990**

By John Gray

The Essence of the Story

- On Monday, July 2, 1990 the communist economy of East Germany, which had been in place for more than 40 years, was replaced by a market economy. The West German Deutschmark became the common currency and the two parts of Germany formed an economic union.
- A few days before German economic unification, East Berlin became a "sprawling bazaar."
- Under the communist regime, stoves, deemed to be a necessity, were subsidized and refrigerators, deemed unnecessary, where heavily taxed. Dishwashers, microwave ovens, and clothes dryers, regarded as needless luxuries, were not produced at all.
- In June 1990, Dieter Fuerstenau, the manager of a store selling stoves and refrigerators, allowed his inventory of East German products to decline and started selling West German models including microwave ovens, dishwashers, and clothes dryers.

Background and Analysis

- In the socialist (or communist) State of East Germany, many goods considered necessities by the State were subsidized. Examples are stoves, potatoes, bread, housing, public transportation, and children's clothing.
- The situation in the market for such goods is illustrated in Fig. (a) (i). Households' preferences determine the demand curve, D_{Stoves}, and technology and factor prices determine the supply curve, S_{Stoves}. The State sets the price to reflect its own judgement about how necessary stoves are and pays a subsidy to ensure a quantity supplied equal to the quantity demanded. If the State sets the price at a level such that the quantity demanded exceeds the quantity supplied, waiting lines and black markets develop.
- The State regards some goods as unnecessary luxuries and sets their prices at a high level—in effect, making a positive economic profit or raising a tax on them. Examples are refrigerators, coffee, and colour television sets.

- Figure (a) (ii) illustrates this case. The State sets the price of refrigerators above their cost of production, making a positive economic profit.
- Some goods are not available at all in the socialist economy, except illegally on a black market. Examples are microwave ovens.
- Figure (a) (iii) illustrates this case. A quantity, Q_B, is illegally brought into the country and traded on the black market for the highest price it can command—P_B.
- Figure (b) shows what happens in these three types of markets when socialism is abandoned and replaced with a market economy. There is a perfectly elastic supply of goods to East Germany at West German prices, *WPG*. The prices of subsidized items increase and the quantity traded decreases. The prices of taxed items decrease and the quantity traded increases. The prices of items traded on black markets decrease dramatically and there is a large increase in the quantity of such items.
- In the case of Germany, there is a perfectly elastic supply of manufactured goods from West Germany at the prices prevailing in that part of Germany. Thus the East Germans cannot experience increases in *all* prices. Some prices rise but some fall as more goods and services become available.

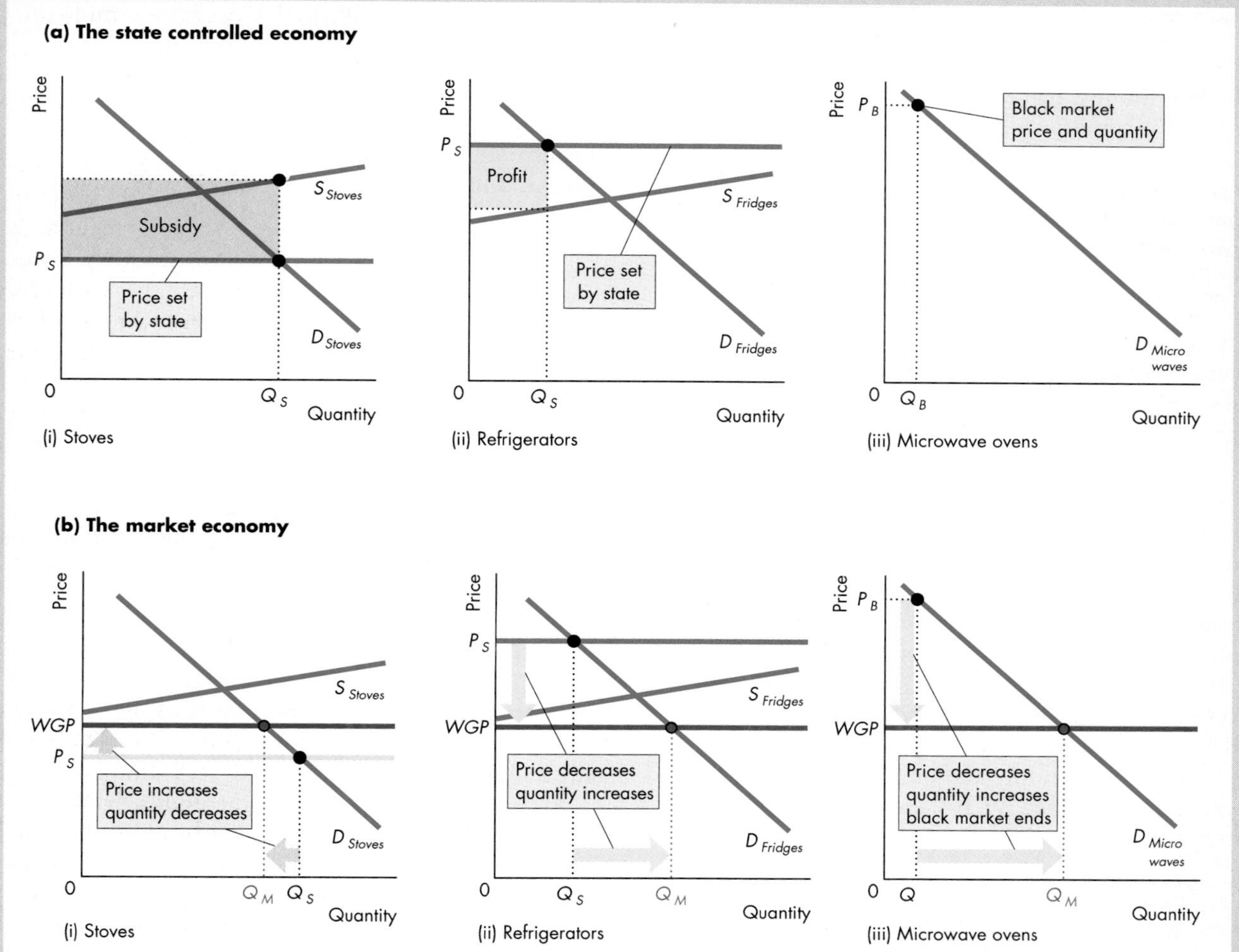

Figure 39.8 Economic Growth in China

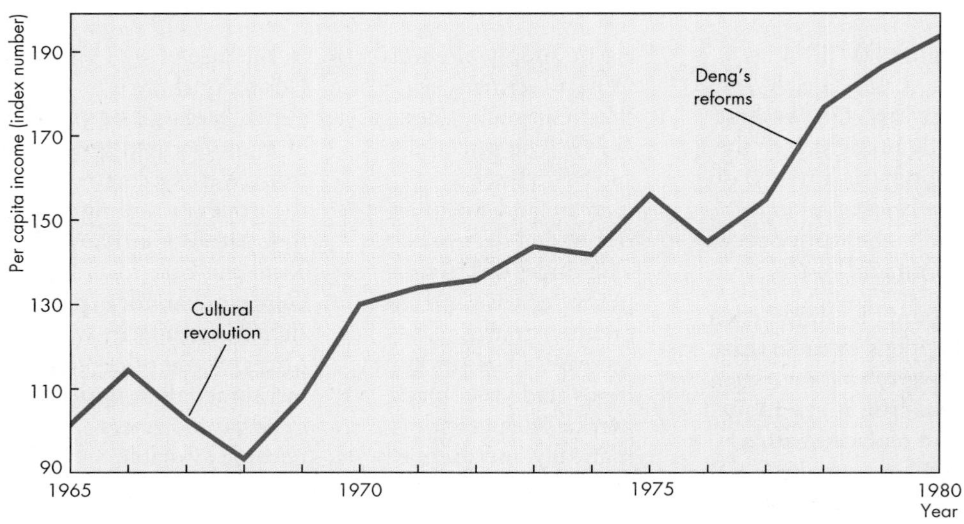

The growth of per capita income in China has been strongly influenced by the economic system. During the Cultural Revolution, per capita income fell. Under a central planning and command mechanism in the early 1970s, per capita income grew at a moderate pace. Under capitalist methods of production in agriculture following the 1978 reforms, per capita income growth increased dramatically.

Source: International Monetary Fund, *International Financial Statistics* (1988).

socialist economy. Figure 39.8 illustrates the rise in per capita income since 1965. During the Cultural Revolution of the mid-1960s, per capita income actually fell. The growth rate increased quickly in the late 1960s, but it then became modest until Deng's reforms of the late 1970s. Following those reforms, per capita income began to grow at a rate that, if maintained, will double the standard of living every ten years. Thus when China has relied most heavily on socialist methods, its growth rate has been negative or slow, and when it has relied on capitalist methods, its growth rate has increased.

Productivity

How productive are the socialist economies? We have noted that managers under socialism have less incentive to use the least-cost method of production and be efficient than do managers under capitalism. Calculations by Soviet experts suggest that the aggregate income per unit of productive resources used in the Soviet Union is slightly less than 50 percent of what it is in the U.S. economy and only 65 percent of the productivity of France, West Germany, and the United Kingdom.[4]

[4]Paul R. Gregory and Robert C. Stuart, *Soviet Economic Structure and Performance*, 2nd ed. (New York: Harper and Row, 1981).

From the available evidence, it appears that socialism is substantially less successful than capitalism at producing high living standards. Does it, however, produce greater equality in the distribution of income?

Income Inequality Under the Two Systems

There is considerable inequality of income and wealth in our own economy. Is the same true of the socialist economies of Eastern Europe and the Soviet Union? The answer seems to be yes. The Soviet Union has not published much data on the distribution of income among individuals and families. But, from the evidence that is available, it appears that the distribution of wage income in the Soviet Union is about the same as that in the capitalist economies of Western Europe and North America. But the overall distribution of income also depends on the distribution of income from the ownership of capital. Comparing this overall distribution of income is possible only in approximate terms, as Fig. 39.9 shows. The broad conclusion emerging from the studies that have been done is that the overall distribution of after-tax income in the Soviet Union is about as equal as the distribution in the welfare state economies of Western Europe, such as the United Kingdom, and more equal than

Figure 39.9 Socialist and Capitalist Lorenz Curves

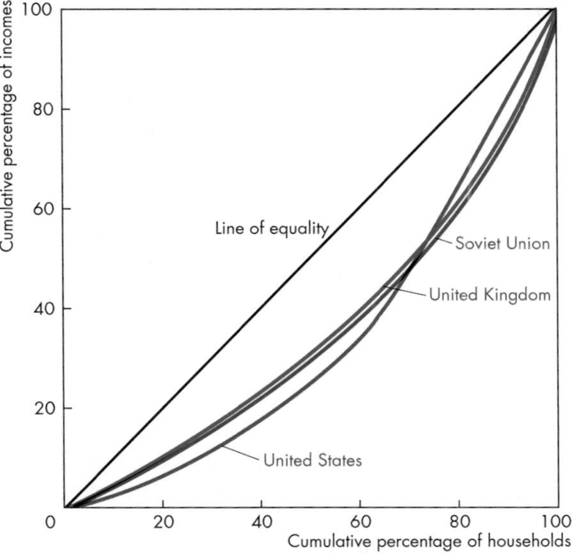

The degree of income inequality is illustrated by the Lorenz curve. If a given percentage of households have that same percentage of income, incomes are distributed equally. The further the Lorenz curve is from the line of equality, the greater the degree of inequality. The Lorenz curves for the Soviet Union and the United Kingdom show that those two countries have an almost identical distribution of income, one that is more equal than that in the United States.

the distribution in other capitalist economies, such as the United States.

Ceteris Paribus

Making comparisons between countries is a bit like trying to compare apples and oranges. They differ in so many respects that it is hardly clear whether we have been able to isolate the factors responsible for differences in their performances. One important difference between nations is their cultural history and the customs and habits of their people. Ideally, we'd like to be able to compare the performances of countries in which these historical and cultural factors are similar. That is, we'd like to be able to hold all these other things constant — to maintain the *ceteris paribus* condition.

We do have available a few comparisons between socialist and capitalist economies that do almost satisfy this *ceteris paribus* condition. Examples are East Germany and West Germany, North Korea and South Korea. Some of the recent exciting developments in East and West Germany are dealt with in Reading Between the Lines, on pp. 1054-1055. These two parts of Germany had almost identical incomes at the end of World War II. West Germany became a capitalist economy and East Germany a socialist one. Today, per capita income in West Germany exceeds that in East Germany by a margin of three to one. At the end of the Korean War, in 1953, North Korea and South Korea embarked upon opposite roads. North Korea adopted the socialist model and South Korea the capitalist one. South Korea had fewer resources than North Korea, but today South Korea, a capitalist country, dominates socialist North Korea in per capita income and wealth.

We've seen that socialist economies can achieve rapid growth rates by choosing a resource allocation that favours the production of capital equipment and holds the growth of consumer goods production in check. We've also seen, however, that capitalist economies can achieve prolonged and sustained growth. Also, capitalist economies appear to achieve a greater measure of economic and allocative efficiency. The degree of inequality is less pronounced in the Soviet Union than in Canada and the United States but similar to that of the welfare state capitalist economies of Western Europe.

■ This comparison of the economic performance of socialist and capitalist economies seems to favour capitalism. A practical consequence of this comparison is the universal movement now taking place towards greater reliance on private enterprise and market mechanisms and less emphasis on government intervention, regulation, and control. For the moment, right or wrong, the view is increasingly widely held that capitalism works and socialism does not. The evidence generated by the variety of real world experiments conducted since World War II appears to support that conclusion. But it is the hallmark of a good scientist to maintain an open and sceptical mind even in the face of strong evidence. A great deal of work is required, and no doubt more will be done before the final verdict on the superiority of one economic system over another is delivered.

SUMMARY

The Fundamental Economic Problem

No economic system can abolish the fundamental economic problem of scarcity. Each system attempts to get the economy onto its production possibility frontier, choose a point on the frontier, and distribute the gains from economic activity. (pp. 1037-1038)

Alternative Economic Systems

Economic systems vary in two dimensions — who owns capital and land and who allocates resources. Under capitalism, capital and land are privately owned and resources are allocated by markets. Under socialism, capital and land are owned by the state and resources are allocated by a command planning system.

Capitalism is based on the political philosophy that individual liberty is paramount. Individual preferences guide the production of goods and services. Socialism is an economic system based on the political philosophy that the private ownership of capital and land enables the wealthy to exploit the poor. The goods and services produced under socialism reflect the preferences of central planners, not individual consumers.

Welfare state capitalism combines private ownership of capital and land with a large degree of state intervention. Market socialism combines state ownership of capital with market-determined prices.

All countries employ economic systems that contain some elements of capitalism and socialism. Canada, the United States, and Japan come closest to being capitalist economies, and the Soviet Union and China are examples of socialist economies. The countries of Western Europe employ welfare state capitalism, while some Eastern European countries such as Hungary and Yugoslavia employ market socialism. (pp. 1038-1041)

Varieties of Capitalism

The capitalist economy whose performance has been most spectacular is Japan. Its performance has been based on a strong reliance on the free market and capitalist methods of production, a small scale of government and low taxes, and pro-business government intervention. Japan's Ministry of International Trade and Industry (MITI) has taken an active and entrepreneurial role in protecting and subsidizing industries identified as priority growth areas and fostering the decline of inefficient industries.

Capitalism in Western Europe has larger elements of socialism than capitalism in Japan, Canada, or the United States. Government expenditure and taxes are higher and many industries are publicly owned or nationalized. In recent years, European welfare states have been retreating from state ownership and high taxes. (pp. 1041-1043)

The Soviet Union

The Soviet Union is a vast, resource-rich nation that uses a socialist economic system with a central planning and command mechanism. Soviet planning, managed by GOSPLAN, is based on a series of detailed plans for consumer goods, labour, credit, capital goods, and materials. Targets are specified for production enterprises, and enterprises are encouraged to achieve their targets by a complex system of incentives. They are also monitored by local officials of the Communist party and of state ministries. Since 1987, the Soviet Union has embarked upon a process of economic restructuring called *perestroika.* This restructuring involves a move away from central planning and command towards decentralized incentives and market prices. (pp. 1043-1048)

China

Since the foundation of the People's Republic of China, economic management has been through turbulent changes. At first, China used the Soviet system of central planning. It then introduced the Great Leap Forward, which in turn degenerated into the Cultural Revolution. China at first grew quickly with heavy reliance on state planning and capital accumulation, but growth slowed and, at times, per capita income actually fell. In 1978, China revolutionized its economic management, placing greater emphasis on private incentives and markets. As a consequence, productivity grew at a rapid rate and per capita income increased.

When Hong Kong becomes part of China at the end of this century, the island will be permitted to remain capitalist. So will Taiwan if it is reunified with China, as the Chinese wish. Furthermore, what are, in effect, capitalist zones are being established within China. Recent political events cast a serious shadow across the Chinese economy and raise doubts about its future course. But if the Chinese experiment continues, it will become an exciting real world test of alternative economic systems. (pp. 1048-1050)

Comparing Capitalism and Socialism

The historical records of capitalism and socialism show that socialism is capable of achieving high growth rates of per capita income. But it does so at the cost of squeezing consumption to levels below those that would be tolerated in capitalist economies. The most spectacular growth performance has been achieved by capitalist economies or by socialist economies when they have relaxed their central planning and command mechanisms and relied on decentralized incentives and markets. Productivity is higher in capitalist economies than in socialist economies. The distribution of income is more equal in socialist economies than in some capitalist economies, but it is similar to that in welfare state capitalist countries. (pp. 1050-1057)

K E Y E L E M E N T S

Key Terms

Annual plan, 1045
Capitalism, 1038
Central planning, 1038
Communism, 1040
Decentralized planning, 1039
Five-year plan, 1045
GOSPLAN, 1044
Great Leap Forward, 1049
Market socialism or decentralized planning, 1039
Ministry of International Trade and Industry (MITI), 1042
Nationalized industry, 1042
Privatization, 1043
Socialism, 1038
State enterprise, 1045
Turnover tax, 1045
Welfare state capitalism, 1039

Key Figures and Tables

Figure 39.1 Alternative Economic Systems, 1039
Figure 39.2 Organization Chart of the Soviet Union, 1044
Figure 39.3 Consumer Goods Balance, 1046
Figure 39.5 Prices and Quantities Under Socialism, 1051
Figure 39.6 Prices and Quantities Under Market Socialism, 1052
Table 39.1 A Compact Summary of Key Periods in the Economic History of the Soviet Union, 1043
Table 39.3 A Compact Summary of Key Periods in the Economic History of the People's Republic of China, 1048

R E V I E W Q U E S T I O N S

1 What are the three aspects of the economic problem that any economic system has to tackle?

2 What are the main economic systems? Set out the key features of each.

3 How does capitalism solve the economic problem? What determines how much of each good to produce?

4 How does socialism solve the economic

problem? What determines how much of each good to produce?

5 How does market socialism determine the price and quantity of each good?

6 Give examples of countries that are capitalist, socialist, market socialist, and welfare state capitalist. (Do not cite those countries that appeared in Fig. 39.1.)

7 Describe the capitalist economy of Japan. What are the sources of its dramatic success?

8 Describe the role of the Ministry of International Trade and Industry (MITI) in Japan. Compare and contrast capitalism in Western Europe with that in Canada and Japan. Describe the planning and command system in the Soviet Union.

9 How does GOSPLAN achieve consumer goods balance?

10 How does GOSPLAN achieve materials balance?

11 What are the main components of *perestroika*?

12 Review the main episodes in China's economic management since 1949.

13 Compare the economic growth performance of the United States, the Soviet Union, and Japan. What do we learn from this comparison?

14 Compare the degree of income inequality in socialist and capitalist economies. Why is the distribution of income more unequal in the United States than in the Soviet Union?

15 What might we learn from the "one-country, two-systems" experiment that is going on in China?

GLOSSARY

Above full-employment equilibrium A situation in which macroeconomic equilibrium occurs at a level of real GDP above long-run aggregate supply.

Absolute advantage A person has an absolute advantage if he is more productive than another person in the production of all goods. A country has an absolute advantage if its output per unit of inputs of all goods is higher than that of another country.

Acceleration principle A principle stating the effect of a speed-up or slowdown in the growth rate of real GDP on investment demand. When the growth rate of real GDP speeds up (slows down) the investment demand curve shifts to the right (left).

Agent A person who works for a principal and performs various activities, some of which are not observable by the principal.

Aggregate consumption function The relationship between real consumption expenditure and real GDP.

Automatic stabilizer A mechanism that decreases the fluctuations in aggregate expenditure resulting from fluctuations in some component of aggregate expenditure.

Aggregate demand The entire relationship between the aggregate quantity of goods and services demanded — real GDP demanded — and the price level — the GDP deflator — holding everything else constant.

Aggregate demand curve A curve showing real GDP demanded at each price level, holding everything else constant.

Aggregate demand schedule A list showing the quantity of real GDP demanded at each price level, holding everything else constant.

Aggregate expenditure curve A graph of the aggregate expenditure schedule.

Aggregate expenditure schedule A list of the level of aggregate planned expenditure at each level of real GDP.

Aggregate quantity of goods and services demanded The sum of the quantities of consumption goods and services demanded by households, of investment goods demanded by firms, of goods and services demanded by governments, and of net exports demanded by foreigners.

Aggregate quantity of goods and services supplied The sum of the quantities of all the final goods and services produced by all the firms in the economy.

Allocative efficiency The situation that occurs when no resources are wasted — when no one can be made better off without making someone else worse off.

Annual plan A plan of the Soviet government specifying month by month targets for output, prices, inputs, investment, and money and credit flows.

Anticipated inflation An inflation rate that has been, on the average, correctly forecast.

Anti-combine law A law prohibiting certain kinds of market activity, such as monopoly and monopolistic practices.

Arbitrage The activity of buying low and selling high in order to make a profit on the margin between the two prices.

Asset Anything of value that a household, firm, or government owns.

Assortative mating Marrying within one's own socioeconomic group.

Assumptions The foundation on which a model is built.

Autonomous expenditure The sum of those components of aggregate planned expenditure that are not influenced by real GDP.

Autonomous expenditure multiplier or the multiplier The amount by which a change in autonomous expenditure is multiplied to calculate the change in equilibrium expenditure and real GDP.

Automatic stabilizer A mechanism that decreases the fluctutations in aggregate expenditure resulting from fluctuations in some component of aggregate expenditure.

Autonomous tax multiplier The magnitude by which a change in autonomous taxes is multiplied to determine the change in equilibrium expenditure and real GDP that it generates.

Autonomous taxes Taxes that do not vary directly with real GDP.

Average cost pricing rule A rule that sets the price equal to average total cost.

Average fixed cost Total fixed cost per unit of output — total fixed cost divided by output.

Average product Total product per unit of variable input.

Average propensity to consume The ratio of consumption expenditure to disposable income.

Average propensity to save The ratio of saving to disposable income.

Average revenue Total revenue divided by the quantity sold. Average revenue also equals price.

Average revenue product Total revenue divided by the quantity of the factor hired.

Average revenue product curve A curve that shows the average revenue product of a factor at each quantity of the factor hired.

Average total cost Total cost per unit of output — total cost divided by output.

Average variable cost Total variable cost per unit of output — total variable cost divided by output.

Axes The scale lines on a graph.

Balanced budget A government budget that is in neither surplus nor deficit.

Balanced budget multiplier The amount by which changes in government purchases of goods and services and taxes of equal amounts are multiplied to determine the change in equilibrium expenditure that they generate.

Balance of payments accounts A country's record of international trading, borrowing, and lending.

Balance of trade The value of exports minus the value of imports.

Balance sheet A list of assets and liabilities.

Bank of Canada Canada's central bank.

Bank rate The interest rate at which the Bank of Canada stands ready to lend reserves to the chartered banks.

Barriers to entry Restrictions on the entry of new firms into an industry.

Barter The direct exchange of goods for goods.

Base period The period against which the current period is compared in a price index.

Bequest A gift from one generation to the next.

Bilateral monopoly A market structure in which a single buyer and a single seller confront each other.

Binding arbitration A process in which a third party — an arbitrator — determines wages and other employment conditions.

Black market An illegal trading arrangement in which buyers and sellers do business at a price higher than the legally imposed price ceiling.

Bond A legally enforceable obligation to pay specified sums of money at specified future dates.

Bond market The market in which the bonds issued by firms and governments are traded.

Bond yield The interest on a bond, expressed as a percentage of the price of the bond.

Break-even point An output rate at which total revenue equals total cost (and at which profit is zero).

Budget equation An equation that states the maximum possible consumption of one good, given income, prices, and consumption of other goods.

Budget line The limits to a household's consumption choices.

Budget surplus or budget deficit The difference between revenue and expenditure in a given period of time. If revenue exceeds expenditure, the government has a budget surplus. If expenditure exceeds revenue, the government has a budget deficit.

Bureaucrats Appointed officials who work at various levels in government departments.

Business cycle The periodic but irregular up and down movement in economic activity measured by fluctuations in real GDP and other macroeconomic variables.

Canadian dollar index against the G-10 currencies An index that measures the value of the Canadian dollar in terms of its ability to buy a basket of currencies of the G-10 countries, where the weight placed on each currency is related to its importance in Canada's international trade.

Capacity The output rate at which a plant's average total cost is at a minimum.

Capacity output The output at which the firm's cost per unit produced is minimized.

Capital The real assets — the equipment, buildings, tools and other manufactured goods used in production — owned by a household, firm, or government.

Capital account A record of a country's international borrowing and lending transactions.

Capital accumulation The growth of capital resources.

Capital goods Goods that can be used many times before they eventually wear out. Examples of capital goods are buildings, plant and equipment, automobiles, and telephones.

Capital stock The stock of plant, equipment, and buildings (including residential housing).

Capital-intensive technique A method of production that uses a relatively large amount of capital and a relatively small amount of labour to produce a given quantity of output.

Capitalism An economic system based on the private ownership of capital and land used in production and on market allocation of resources.

Capture theory of intervention A theory of regulation that states that the regulations that exist are those that maximize producer surplus.

Cartel A group of producers who enter a collusive agreement to restrict output in order to raise prices and profits.

Central bank A public authority charged with regulating and controlling a country's monetary and financial institutions and markets.

Central planning A method of allocating resources by command.

Ceteris paribus Other things being equal, or other things remaining constant.

Change in demand A shift of the entire demand curve that occurs when some influence on buyers' plans, other than the price of the good, changes.

Change in supply A shift in the entire supply curve that occurs when some influence on producers' plans, other than the price of the good, changes.

Change in the quantity demanded A movement along a demand curve that results from a change in the price of the good.

Change in the quantity supplied A movement along the supply curve that results from a change in the price of the good.

Chartered bank A private firm, chartered under the Bank Act to receive deposits and make loans.

Chequable deposit A loan by a depositor to a bank, the ownership being transferable from one person to another by writing an instruction to the bank — a cheque — asking the bank to alter its records.

Choke price The price at which it no longer pays to use a natural resource.

Closed economy An economy that has no links with any other economy.

Closed shop A plant or firm in which all the employees are required to join the labour union.

Collective bargaining A process of negotiation between employers (or their representatives) and a union on wages and other employment conditions.

Collusive agreement An agreement between two (or more) producers to restrict output in order to raise prices and profits.

Command mechanism A method of determining *what, how,* and *real* goods and services are produced, based on the authority of a ruler or ruling body.

Commission A compensation rule based on the value of sales.

Commodity money A physical commodity valued in its own right and also used as a medium of exchange.

Common stock Stock that entitles its holder to vote at shareholders' meetings, but gives a claim to dividends only if the directors vote to pay one. Such a dividend is paid at a variable rate, determined by the directors and varying according to the firm's profits.

Communism An economic system based on state ownership of capital and land, on central planning, and on distributing income in accordance with the rule: from each according to his ability, to each according to his need.

Communist country A country in which there is limited private ownership of productive capital and of firms, limited reliance placed on the market as a means of allocating resources, and in which government agencies plan and direct the production and distribution of most goods and services.

Comparative advantage A person has a comparative advantage in producing a good if he or she can produce that good at a lower opportunity cost than anyone else. A country has a comparative advantage in producing a good if it can produce that good at a lower opportunity cost than any other country.

Compensation rule A formula for calculating a person's income.

Competition A contest for command over scarce resources.

Complement A good that is used in conjunction with another good.

Constant returns to scale Technological conditions under which the percentage change in a firm's output is equal to the percentage change in its inputs.

Consumer equilibrium A situation in which a consumer has allocated his or her income in a manner that maximizes total utility.

Consumer Price Index An index that measures the average level of the prices of the basket of goods and services typically consumed by an urban Canadian family.

Consumer surplus The difference between the value of a good and its price.

Consumption The process of using up goods and services.

Consumption expenditure The aggregate expenditure by households on consumption goods and services.

Consumption function The relationship between consumption expenditure and disposable income.

Consumption goods Goods that can be used just once. Examples are dill pickles and toothpaste.

Contraction A business cycle phase in which there is a slowdown in the pace of economic activity.

Convertible paper money A paper claim to a commodity (such as gold) that can be converted into the commodity at a guaranteed price. The paper claim circulates as a medium of exchange.

Convertible stock Stock that entitles its holder to receive a fixed coupon payment, as a bondholder does, and to convert the stock into a fixed number of shares of common stock.

Cooperation People working with others to achieve a common end.

Cooperative A firm owned by a group of people who have a common objective and who collectively bear the risks of the enterprise and share in its profits.

Cooperative equilibrium An equilibrium that results when each player responds rationally to the credible threat of the other player to inflict heavy damage if the agreement is broken.

Coordinates Lines running from a point on a graph perpendicularly to the axes.

Coordination mechanism A mechanism that makes the choices of one individual compatible with the choices of others.

Corporation A firm owned by one or more limited liability shareholders.

Cost-push inflation Inflation that has its origin in cost increases.

Countervailing duty A tariff that is imposed to enable domestic producers to compete with subsidized foreign producers.

Coupon payment The amount paid each year to the holder of a bond.

Craft union A group of workers who have a similar range of skills but work for different firms and industries.

Creditor nation A country that during its entire history has invested more in the rest of the world than other countries have invested in it.

Cross elasticity of demand The percentage change in the quantity demanded of a good divided by the percentage change in the price of a substitute or complement.

Crowding out The tendency for an increase in government purchases of goods and services to increase interest rates, thereby reducing—crowding out—investment expenditure.

Crown corporation A publicly owned corporation—some are federal and some are provincial.

Currency Bank notes and coins.

Currency appreciation The increase in the value of one currency in terms of another currency.

Currency depreciation The fall in the value of one currency in terms of another currency.

Currency drain The tendency for some of the funds lent by banks and financial institutions to remain outside the banking system and circulate as currency in the hands of the public.

Current account A record of receipts from the sale of goods and services to foreigners, the payments for goods and services bought from foreigners, and gifts and other transfers (such as foreign aid payments) received from and paid to foreigners.

Current account balance The value of all the goods and services that we sell to other countries minus the value of goods and services that foreigners buy from us.

Curve Any relationship between two variables plotted on a graph, even a linear relationship.

Deadweight loss A measure of allocative inefficiency— the reduction in consumer and producer surplus resulting from restricting output below its efficient level.

Debt financing The financing of the federal deficit by selling bonds to anyone (households, firms, or foreigners) other than the Bank of Canada.

Debtor nation A country that during its entire history has borrowed more from the rest of the world than it has lent to it. It has a stock of outstanding debt to the rest of the world that exceeds the stock of its own claims on the rest of the world.

Decentralized planning or **market socialism** An economic system that combines socialism's state ownership of capital and land with capitalism's market allocation of resources.

Decision maker Any person or organized group of persons that make economic choices.

Decreasing returns to scale (or diseconomies of scale) Technological conditions under which the percentage change in a firm's output is less than the percentage change in the scale of inputs.

Deflation A downward movement in the average level of prices.

Demand The entire relationship between the quantity demanded of a good and its price.

Demand curve A graph showing the relationship between the quantity demanded of a good and its price, holding everything else constant.

Demand for labour A schedule or curve showing the quantity of labour demanded at each level of the real wage rate.

Demand for real money The relationship between the quantity of real money demanded and the interest rate, holding constant all other influences on the amount of money that people wish to hold.

Demand schedule A list of the quantities demanded at different prices, holding everything else constant.

Depreciation The fall in the value of capital or the value of a durable input resulting from its use and from the passage of time.

Depression A deep business cycle trough.

Deregulation The removal of rules restricting prices, product standards and types, and entry conditions.

Derived demand Demand for an input not for its own sake but in order to use it in the production of goods and services.

Desired reserve ratio The ratio of reserves to deposits that banks regard as necessary in order to be able to conduct their business.

Developing country A country that is poor but is accumulating capital and developing an industrial and commercial base.

Diminishing marginal product of labour The tendency for the marginal product of labour to decline as the labour input increases, holding everything else constant.

Diminishing marginal rate of substitution The general tendency for the marginal rate of substitution to diminish as the consumer moves along an indifference curve, increasing the consumption of good **x** and decreasing the consumption of good **y**.

Diminishing marginal returns A situation in which the marginal product of the last worker hired falls short of the marginal product of the second last worker hired.

Diminishing marginal utility The decline in marginal utility that occurs as more and more of the good is consumed.

Discounting The conversion of a future sum of money to its present value.

Discouraged workers People who do not have jobs and would like to work, but have stopped seeking work.

Disposable income Income plus transfer payments minus taxes.

Dissaving Negative saving; a situation in which consumption expenditure exceeds disposable income.

Distribution after taxes and transfers The income distribution that takes account of taxes levied and transfers made by the government.

Dominant strategy A game strategy that is a player's unique best action regardless of the action taken by the other player.

Dominant strategy equilibrium A Nash equilibrium in which there is a dominant strategy for each player in a game.

Double coincidence of wants A situation that occurs when person A wants to buy what person B is selling, and person B wants to buy what person A is selling.

Double counting Counting the expenditure on both the final good and the intermediate goods and services used in its production.

Dumping The sale of a good in a foreign market for a lower price than in the domestic market or for a lower price than its cost of production.

Duopoly A market structure in which two producers of a commodity compete with each other.

Durable input A factor of production that is not entirely used up in a single production period.

Economic activity What people do to cope with scarcity.

Economic depreciation The change in the market price of a durable input over a given period. Economic depreciation over a year is calculated as the market price of the input at the beginning of the year minus its market price at the end of the year.

Economic efficiency A state in which the cost of producing a given output is as low as possible.

Economic growth The persistent expansion of our production possibilities.

Economic model An artificial or imaginary economy, or part of an economy.

Economic rent An income received by the owner of a factor over and above the amount required to induce that owner to offer the factor for use.

Economic theory A generalization that enables us to understand and predict economic choices.

Economics The study of how people use their limited resources to try to satisfy unlimited wants.

Economies of scale Reductions in the cost of producing a unit of a good that occur as the scale of output increases.

Economies of scope Decreases in average total cost made possible by increasing the number of different goods produced.

Economizing Making the best use of scarce resources.

Economy A mechanism that allocates scarce resources among competing uses.

Efficient market A market in which the actual price embodies all currently available relevant information.

Elastic demand Demand with an elasticity greater than 1; the quantity demanded of a good drops by a larger percentage than its price rises.

Elasticity of demand The short name for price elasticity of demand.

Elasticity of supply The percentage change in the quantity supplied of a good divided by the percentage change in its price.

Employment The number of adult workers (aged 16 and older) who have jobs.

Endowment The resources that people have.

End-state theory of distributive justice A theory of distributive justice that examines the fairness of the outcome of economic activity.

Entry The act of setting up a new firm in an industry.

Equation of exchange An equation that states that the quantity of money multiplied by the velocity of circulation of money equals the price level multiplied by real GDP.

Equal pay for work of equal value The payment of equal wages for different jobs that are judged to be of comparable worth.

Equilibrium A situation in which everyone has economized — that is, all individuals have made the best possible choices in the light of their own preferences and given their endowments and the available technologies — and in which those choices have been co-ordinated and made compatible with the choices of everyone else. Equilibrium is the solution or outcome of an economic model.

Equilibrium expenditure Aggregate planned expenditure that equals real GDP.

Equilibrium price The price at which the quantity demanded equals the quantity supplied. At this price, opposing forces exactly balance each other.

Equity or equity capital The owner's stake in a business.

Europe 1992 The process of creating an integrated single-market economy among the member nations of the European Community.

European monetary system A fixed exchange rate system involving most of the members of the European Community.

Excess capacity A state in which output is less than that at which average total cost is a minimum.

Excess reserves The difference between a bank's actual reserves and desired reserves.

Excise tax A tax on the sale of a particular commodity. The tax may be set as a fixed dollar amount per unit of the commodity, in which case it is called a *specific tax*. Alternatively, the tax may be set as a fixed percentage of the value of the commodity, in which case it is called an *ad valorem tax*.

Exhaustible natural resources Natural resources that can be used only once and that cannot be replaced once used.

Exit The act of closing down a firm and leaving an industry.

Expansion A business cycle phase in which there is a speedup in the pace of economic activity.

Expected inflation rate The rate at which people, on the average, believe that the price level will rise.

Expenditure approach A measure of GDP obtained by adding together consumption expenditure, investment, government purchases of goods and services, and net exports.

Exports The goods and services that we sell to people in other countries.

External benefits Those benefits from a good accruing to people other than its buyer.

External costs Those costs of a good borne by people other than its producer.

External diseconomies Factors outside the control of a firm that raise its costs as industry output rises.

External economies Factors beyond the control of a firm that lower its costs as industry output rises.

Externality A cost or benefit arising from an economic transaction that falls on a third party and that is not taken into account by those who undertake the transaction.

Factor cost The cost of all the factors of production used to produce a good or service.

Factor incomes approach A measure of GDP obtained by adding together all the incomes paid by firms to households for the services of the factors of production they hire — wages, interest, rent, and profits.

Factor market A market in which factors of production are bought and sold.

Factors of production The economy's productive resources — land, labour, and capital.

Federal budget A statement of the federal government's financial plan, itemizing programs and their costs, revenues, and the proposed deficit or surplus.

Federal government debt The total amount of borrowing that the federal government has undertaken and the total amount that it owes to households, firms, and foreigners.

Feedback rule A rule that states which policy instruments will be used and how each instrument will respond to the state of the economy.

Fiat money An intrinsically worthless or almost worthless commodity that serves the functions of money.

Final goods and services Goods and services that are not used as inputs in the production of other goods and services but are bought by their final user.

Financial asset A paper claim of the holder against another household or firm.

Financial innovation The development of new financial products and methods of borrowing and lending.

Financial intermediary A firm that takes deposits from households and firms and makes loans to other households and firms.

Firm An institution that buys or hires factors of production and organizes them to produce and sell goods and services.

Fiscal policy The government's attempt to vary its purchases of goods and services and its taxes to smooth the fluctuations in aggregate expenditure.

Five-year plan A plan of the Soviet government specifying in broad outline the general economic targets and directions for a period of five years.

Fixed cost A cost that is independent of the output level.

Fixed exchange rate An exchange rate, the value of total which is pegged by the country's central bank.

Fixed inputs Those inputs whose quantity used cannot be varied in the short run.

Fixed rule A rule put in place and maintained regardless of the state of the economy.

Flexible exchange rate An exchange rate, the value of which is determined by market forces in the absence of central bank intervention.

Flow A quantity measured over a period of time.

Flow equilibrium A situation in which the quantity of goods or services supplied per unit of time equals the quantity demanded per unit of time.

Flow theory of the exchange rate The proposition that the exchange rate adjusts to make the flow supply of dollars equal to the flow demand for dollars.

Foreign exchange market The market in which the currency of one country is exchanged for the currency of another.

Foreign exchange rate The rate at which one country's money exchanges for another's.

Forward contract A contract entered into at an agreed price to buy or sell a certain quantity of any commodity (including currency) at a specified future date.

Forward exchange rate The exchange rate in a forward contract.

Four-firm concentration ratio The percentage of the value of sales accounted for by the largest four firms in an industry.

Free rider Someone who consumes a good without paying for it.

Free-rider problem The tendency for the scale of provision of a public good to be too small — to be allocatively inefficient — if it is privately provided.

Frictional unemployment Unemployment arising from new entrants into the labour market and job turnover caused by technological change.

Full employment A situation in which all unemployment is frictional.

Full-employment equilibrium A macroeconomic equilibrium in which actual real GDP equals capacity real GDP.

Game theory A method of analysing strategic behaviour.

General Agreement on Tariffs and Trade An agreement that limits government taxes and restrictions on international trade.

GDP deflator A price index that measures the average level of the prices of all the goods and services that make up GDP. It is calculated as nominal GDP divided by real GDP, multiplied by 100.

Goods and services All the valuable things that people produce. Goods are tangible and services are intangible.

Goods and services tax A tax on the value added in all sectors of the economy to almost all goods and services. (The exceptions are health and dental services, day-care services, most educational and financial services, and long-term residential rents.)

Goods market A market in which goods and services are bought and sold.

GOSPLAN The Soviet planning committee responsible for drawing up and implementing the state's economic plans.

Government An organization that provides goods and services and redistributes income and wealth.

Government deficit The total expenditure of the government sector less the total revenue of that sector.

Government licence A licence that controls entry into a particular occupation, profession, or industry.

Government purchases multiplier The amount by which a change in government purchases of goods and services is multiplied to determine the change in equilibrium expenditure that it generates.

Government sector surplus or deficit The difference between taxes (net of transfer payments) and government sector purchases of goods and services. If taxes exceed purchases, the government sector has a surplus. If purchases exceed taxes, the government sector has a deficit.

Great Leap Forward An economic plan for postrevolutionary China based on small-scale, labour-intensive production motivated by revolutionary zeal.

Gresham's Law The tendency for bad money to drive out good money. Bad money is debased money; good money is that which has not been debased.

Gross domestic product The value of output produced in Canada in a year.

Gross investment The value of new capital equipment purchased in a given time period. It is the amount spent on replacing depreciated capital and on making net additions to the capital stock.

Historical cost Cost that values factors of production at the prices actually paid for them.

Hotelling Principle The proposition that the market for a stock of a natural resource is in equilibrium, when the price of that resource is expected to rise at a rate equal to the interest rate.

Household Any group of people living together as a decision-making unit.

Household production The production of goods and services for consumption within the household.

Human capital The accumulated skill and knowledge of human beings. It is the value of a person's education and acquired skills.

Implications The outcome of a model that follows logically from its assumptions.

Implicit rental rate The rent that a firm implicitly pays to itself for the use of the durable inputs that it owns.

Imports The goods and services that we buy from people in other countries.

Imputed cost An opportunity cost that does not involve an actual expenditure of cash.

Incentive An inducement to an agent to behave in a particular way.

Incidence of low income The percentage of households whose income falls below a low-income cutoff.

Income The amount received by households in payment for the services of factors of production.

Income effect The effect of a change in income on the quantity consumed.

Income elasticity of demand The percentage change in the quantity demanded divided by the percentage change in income.

Increasing marginal returns A situation in which the marginal product of the last worker hired exceeds the marginal product of the second last worker hired.

Increasing returns to scale (or economies of scale) Technological conditions under which the percentage change in a firm's output exceeds the percentage change in its inputs.

Indexing A technique that links payments made under a contract to the price level.

Indifference curve A line showing all possible combinations of two goods among which the consumer is indifferent.

Indirect tax A tax on the production or sale of a good or service. Indirect taxes are included in the price paid for the good or service by its final purchaser.

Individual demand The relationship between the quantity demanded by a single individual and the price of a good.

Induced expenditure The sum of those components of aggregate planned expenditure that do vary as real GDP varies.

Induced taxes Taxes that vary directly with real GDP.

Industrial country A country that has a large amount of capital equipment, and in which people undertake highly specialized activities, enabling them to earn high per capita incomes.

Industrial union A group of workers who have a variety of skills and job types but who work for the same firm or industry.

Inelastic demand Demand with an elasticity between zero and 1; the quantity demanded of a good drops by a smaller percentage than its price rises.

Inferior good A good, the demand for which decreases when income increases.

Inflation An upward movement in the average level of prices.

Inflation rate The percentage change in the price level.

Inflationary gap The difference between actual real GDP and capacity real GDP when actual exceeds capacity.

Injections Expenditures that add to the circular flow of expenditure and income — investment, government purchases of goods and services, and exports.

Innovation The act of putting a new technique into operation.

Insurance company A financial intermediary that takes in households' savings and provides life insurance and pensions.

Intellectual property The intangible product of creative effort, protected by copyrights and patents. This type of property includes books, music, computer programs, and inventions of all kinds.

Interest rate parity A situation in which interest rates are equal across all countries once the differences in risk are taken into account.

Intermediate goods and services Goods and services that are used as inputs into the production of another good or service.

International monetary fund An international organization that monitors the balance of payments and exchange rate activities.

International substitution The substitution of domestic goods for foreign goods or of foreign goods for domestic goods.

Intertemporal substitution The substitution of goods now for goods later or of goods later for goods now.

Invention The discovery of a new technique.

Inventories The stocks of raw materials, semifinished products, and unsold final goods held by firms.

Investment The purchase of new plant, equipment, and buildings, and additions to inventories in a given time period.

Investment demand The relationship between the level of investment and the real interest rate.

Investment demand curve A curve showing the relationship between the real interest rate and the level of planned investment, holding everything else constant.

Investment demand schedule The list of quantities of planned investment at each interest rate, holding everything else constant.

Isocost equation An equation that states the relationship between the quantities of inputs that can be hired at given input prices for a given total cost.

Isocost line A line that shows all the combinations of capital and labour that can be hired at given input prices for a given total cost.

Isocost map A map that shows a series of isocost lines, each for a different total cost.

Isoquant A curve that shows the different combinations of labour and capital required to produce a fixed quantity of output.

Isoquant map A map that shows a series of isoquants, each for a different level of output.

Joint unlimited liability The liability of each and every partner for the full debts of a partnership.

Keynesian A macroeconomist whose beliefs about the functioning of the economy represent an extension of the theories of John Maynard Keynes. A Keynesian regards the economy as being inherently unstable, and as requiring active government intervention to achieve stability. A Keynesian assigns a low degree of importance to monetary policy and a high degree of importance to fiscal policy.

Labour The brain-power and muscle-power of human beings.

Labour force The total number of employed and unemployed workers.

Labour force participation rate The proportion of the working age population that is either employed or unemployed (but seeking employment).

Labour-intensive technique A method of production that uses a relatively large amount of labour and a relatively small amount of capital to produce a given quantity of output.

Labour union A group of workers organized for the purpose of increasing wages and influencing other job conditions.

Laffer curve A curve that relates tax revenue to the tax rate.

Land Natural resources of all kinds.

Law of diminishing marginal rate of substitution A general tendency for the marginal rate of substitution of capital for labour to fall as the amount of capital decreases and the amount of labour increases.

Law of diminishing returns The general tendency for marginal product to eventually diminish as more of the variable input is employed, holding the quantity of fixed inputs constant.

Law of one price A law stating that any given commodity will be available at a single price.

Leakages Income that is not spent on domestically produced goods and services — savings, taxes (net of transfer payments), and imports.

Least-cost technique The combination of inputs that minimizes the total cost of producing a given output, given the input prices.

Legal monopoly A monopoly that occurs when a law, licence, or patent restricts competition by preventing entry.

Liability A debt — something that a household, firm, or government owes.

Limited liability The limitation of liability of the firm's owners for debts only up to the value of their financial investment.

Linear relationship The relationship between two variables depicted by a straight line on a graph.

Liquid asset An asset that is instantly convertible into a medium of exchange with virtually no uncertainty about the price at which it can be converted.

Liquidity The degree to which an asset is instantly convertible into cash at a known price.

Liquidity trap A situation in which the demand curve for real money is horizontal at a given interest rate, and people are willing to hold any amount of money at that interest rate.

Loan A commitment of a fixed amount of money for an agreed period of time.

Lobbying The activity of bringing pressure to bear on government agencies or institutions through a variety of informal mechanisms.

Lockout The refusal by a firm to operate its plant and employ its workers.

Long run A period of time in which the quantities of all inputs can be varied.

Long-run aggregate supply The relationship between the aggregate quantity of final goods and services (real GDP) supplied and the price level (the GDP deflator) when all factor prices are adjusted in step with changes in the price level so that *real* factor prices are constant.

Long-run aggregate supply curve A curve showing the relationship between the quantity of real GDP supplied and the price level when all factor prices have changed by the same percentage as the change in the price level so that *real* factor prices are constant.

Long-run average cost curve A curve that traces the relationship between the lowest attainable average total cost and output when all inputs can be varied.

Long-run cost The cost of production when a firm uses the economically efficient plant size.

Long-run demand curve The demand curve that describes the change in the quantity demanded in response to a change in price after buyers have made all possible adjustments to their buying plans.

Long-run demand for labour The relationship between the wage rate and the quantity of labour demanded when all inputs can be varied.

Long-run elasticity of demand for labour The percentage change in the quantity of labour demanded divided by the percentage change in the wage rate when all inputs are varied.

Long-run supply curve The supply curve that describes the response of the quantity supplied to a change in price after *all* technologically possible adjustments to supply have been made.

Lorenz curve A curve that shows the cumulative percentage of income or wealth against the cumulative percentage of population.

Loss The difference between a firm's total revenue and total cost when cost exceeds revenue.

Low-income cutoff An income level used to determine the incidence of low income, such that families with incomes below this level normally spend more than 58.5 percent of their income on food, clothing, and shelter.

M1 A measure of money that sums currency held outside banks and privately held demand deposits at chartered banks.

M2 A measure of money that sums M1, savings deposits at chartered banks, and nonpersonal notice deposits at chartered banks.

M3 A measure of money that sums M2 and nonpersonal, fixed term deposits of residents booked in Canada.

M2+ measure of money that sums M2, deposits at trust and mortgage companies, and deposits and shares at caisses populaires and credit unions.

Macroeconomic equilibrium A situation in which the quantity of real GDP demanded equals the quantity of real GDP supplied.

Macroeconomics The branch of economics that studies the economy as a whole. It is concerned with aggregates and averages of behaviour rather than with detailed individual choices.

Managed exchange rate An exchange rate, the value of which is influenced by the central bank's intervention in the foreign exchange market.

Marginal benefit The increase in total benefit resulting from a one-unit increase in the scale of provision of a public good.

Marginal cost The increase in total cost resulting from a unit increase in output.

Marginal cost pricing rule The rule that sets price equal to marginal cost. It maximizes total surplus in the regulated industry.

Marginal private cost The marginal cost directly incurred by the producer of a good.

Marginal product The change in total product resulting from a unit increase in a variable input.

Marginal product of capital The change in total product resulting from a one-unit increase in the quantity of capital employed, holding the quantity of labour constant.

Marginal product of labour The change in total product (output) resulting from a one-unit increase in the quantity of labour employed, holding the quantity of all other inputs constant.

Marginal propensity to consume The fraction of the last dollar of disposable income that is spent on consumption goods and services.

Marginal propensity to import The fraction of the last dollar of real GDP spent on imports.

Marginal propensity to save The fraction of the last dollar of disposable income that is saved.

Marginal propensity to spend on domestic goods and services or marginal propensity to spend The fraction of the last dollar of real GDP spent on domestic goods and services.

Marginal rate of substitution The rate at which a person will give up one good in order to get more of another good and, at the same time, remain indifferent.

Marginal rate of substitution of capital for labour The decrease in capital per unit increase in labour that keeps output constant.

Marginal revenue The change in total revenue resulting from a one-unit increase in the quantity sold.

Marginal revenue product The change in total revenue resulting from employing one more unit of a factor.

Marginal revenue product curve A curve that shows the marginal revenue product of a factor at each quantity of the factor hired.

Marginal social benefit The dollar value of the benefit from one additional unit of consumption, including the benefit to the buyer and any indirect benefits accruing to any other member of society.

Marginal social cost The cost of producing one additional unit of output, including both the costs borne by the producer and any other costs indirectly incurred by any other member of society. It is the marginal cost incurred by the producer of a good, together with the marginal cost imposed as an externality on others.

Marginal tax rate The fraction of the last dollar of income paid to the government in taxes (net of transfer payments by the government.)

Marginal utility The additional total utility or change in total utility resulting from the last unit of a good consumed.

Marginal utility per dollar spent The marginal utility obtained from the last unit of a good consumed divided by the price of the good.

Market Any arrangement that facilitates buying and selling (trading) of a good, service, factor of production or future commitment.

Market activity The same thing as supplying labour.

Market constraints The conditions under which a firm can buy its inputs and sell its output.

Market demand The relationship between the total quantity of a good demanded and its price.

Market distribution The distribution of income that would prevail in the absence of government policies.

Market failure The inability of an unregulated market to achieve allocative efficiency in all circumstances.

Market mechanism A method of determining *what, how,* and *for whom* goods and services are produced, based on individual choices co-ordinated through markets.

Market price The price that people actually pay for a good or service. Such prices include indirect taxes but are net of subsidies.

Market socialism or decentralized planning An economic system that combines socialism's state ownership of capital and land with capitalism's market allocation of resources.

Maturity structure The distribution of future dates on which bonds are to be redeemed.

Median voter theorem The proposition that political parties will pursue policies that maximize the net benefit of the median voter.

Medium of exchange Anything that is generally acceptable in exchange for goods and services.

Merger The combining of the assets of two (or more) firms to form a single new firm.

Microeconomics The branch of economics that studies the decisions of individual households and firms, and the way in which individual markets work. Microeconomics also studies the way in which taxes and government regulation affect our economic choices.

Minimum wage law A regulation making it illegal to trade labour below a specified wage.

Ministry of International Trade and Industry A Japanese government agency responsible for stimulating Japanese industrial development and international trade.

Misery index An index of macroeconomic performance equal to the sum of the inflation rate and the unemployment rate.

Mixed economy An economy that relies partly on the market mechanism and partly on a command mechanism to co-ordinate economic activity.

Mixed good A good that lies between a private good and a public good.

Momentary supply curve The supply curve that describes the immediate response of the quantity supplied to a change in price.

Monetarist A macroeconomist who assigns a high degree of importance to variations in the quantity of money as the main determinant of aggregate demand and who regards the economy as inherently stable.

Monetary base The sum of the Bank of Canada notes in circulation, chartered banks' deposits at the Bank, and coins in circulation.

Monetary exchange A system in which some commodity or token serves as the medium of exchange.

Monetary policy The attempt to control inflation and the foreign exchange value of the domestic currency and to moderate the business cycle by changing the quantity of money in circulation and adjusting interest rates.

Monetary theory of the exchange rate The proposition that the exchange rate adjusts to make the stock of a currency demanded equal to the stock supplied.

Money A medium of exchange.

Money financing The financing of the federal deficit by the sale of bonds to the Bank of Canada which results in the creation of additional money.

Money multiplier The amount by which a change in the monetary base is multiplied to determine the resulting change in the quantity of money.

Money wage rate The wage rate expressed in current dollars.

Monitoring The observation of the actions of an agent by a principal.

Monitoring costs The costs of observing the actions of an agent.

Monopolistic competition A market type in which a large number of firms compete with each other by making similar but slightly different products.

Monopoly The sole supplier of a good, service, or resource that has no close substitutes and there is a barrier preventing the entry of new firms into the industry.

Monopsony A market structure in which there is just a single buyer.

Mortgage A loan secured by the value of land and buildings.

Multiplier The change in equilibrium real GDP divided by the change in autonomous expenditure.

Nash equilibrium The outcome of a game in which the strategy chosen by player A is the best possible response to the strategy of player B and when player B's strategy is the best possible response to the strategy of player A.

Nationalization The act of placing a corporation under public ownership.

Nationalized industry An industry owned and operated by a publicly owned authority directly responsible to a government.

Natural monopoly A monopoly that occurs when there is a unique source of supply of a raw material or when one firm can supply the entire market at a lower price than two or more firms can.

Natural rate of unemployment The unemployment rate when the economy is at full employment and the only unemployment is frictional.

Natural resources Nonproduced factors of production with which we are endowed.

Negative relationship A relationship between two variables that move in opposite directions.

Net benefit Total benefit minus total cost.

Net borrower A country that is borrowing more from the rest of the world than it is lending to it.

Net domestic income at factor cost The sum of all factor incomes — compensation of employees, rental income, corporate profits, net interest, and proprietors' income.

Net domestic product at market prices The sum of all factor incomes plus indirect taxes minus subsidies.

Net exports The expenditure by foreigners on Canadian-produced goods and services minus the expenditure by Canadian residents on foreign-produced goods and services.

Net exporter A country whose value of exports exceeds its value of imports.

Net export function The relationship between net exports and Canadian real GDP, holding constant real GDP in the rest of the world, prices, and the exchange rate.

Net financial assets Financial assets minus financial liabilities.

Net importer A country whose value of imports exceeds its value of exports.

Net interest payments Interest payments received by Canadians on their investments abroad minus the payments of interest made by Canadians to foreigners on their investments in Canada.

Net investment Net additions to the capital stock — gross investment minus depreciation.

Net lender A country that is lending more to the rest of the world than it is borrowing from it.

Net present value The sum of the present values of payments spread over several years.

Net present value of an investment The present value of a stream of marginal revenue product generated by the investment minus the cost of that investment.

Newly industrialized country A country in which there is a rapidly developing broad industrial base and per capita income is growing quickly.

Nominal GDP The output of final goods and services valued at current prices.

Nominal interest rate The interest rate actually paid and received in the marketplace.

Nominal quantity of money The quantity of money measured in current dollars.

Nominal targets Macroeconomic policy targets of low and predictable inflation and stable foreign exchange rates.

Nonconvertible note A bank note that is not convertible into any commodity and that obtains its value by government fiat.

Nonexhaustible natural resources Natural resources that can be used repeatedly without depleting what is available for future use.

Nonmarket activity Leisure and nonmarket production activities, including education and training.

Nontariff barrier Any action other than a tariff that restricts international trade.

Nontraded good A good that cannot be traded over long distances.

Normal good A good, the demand for which increases when income increases.

Normative statement A statement about what *ought* to be. An expression of an opinion that cannot be verified by observation.

Not-for-profit firm An organization that chooses or is required to have equal total costs and total revenue.

Official foreign exchange reserves The federal government's holdings of gold and foreign- currency denominated assets.

Official settlements account An account showing the net increase or decrease in a country's official holdings of foreign exchange reserves.

Oligopoly A market type in which a small number of producers compete with each other.

Open economy An economy that has economic links with other economies.

Open market operation The purchase or sale of government securities by the Bank of Canada.

Opportunity cost The best forgone alternative.

Optimizing Balancing benefits against costs to do the best within the limits of what is possible.

Origin The zero point that is common to both axes on a graph.

Output approach A measure of GDP obtained by summing the value added of each firm in the economy.

Overutilized capacity When a plant produces more than the output at which average total cost is a minimum.

Paradox of thrift The fact that an increase in saving leads to an increase in the income of an individual but may lead to a decrease in aggregate expenditure and real GDP. The paradox arises because an increase in saving occurs with no increase in investment.

Partnership A firm with two or more owners who have unlimited liability.

Patent An exclusive right granted by the government to the inventor of a product or service.

Payoff The score of each player in a game.

Payoff matrix A table that shows the payoffs resulting from every possible action by each player for every possible action by each other player.

Peak The upper turning point of a business cycle — the point at which the economy is turning from expansion to contraction.

Per capita production function A curve showing how per capita output varies as the per capita stock of capital varies, with a given technology.

Perfect competition A state that occurs in markets in which the following conditions exist: a large number of firms sell an identical product; there are many buyers; there are no restrictions on entry; existing firms have no advantage over potential new entrants; and all firms and buyers are fully informed about the prices of each and every firm.

Perfect price discrimination The practice of charging each consumer the maximum price that he or she is willing to pay for each unit bought.

Perfectly competitive firm's supply curve A curve that shows how a perfectly competitive firm's output varies as the market price varies.

Perfectly elastic demand Demand with an elasticity of infinity; the quantity demanded becomes zero if the price rises by the smallest amount and the quantity demanded becomes infinite if the price falls by the smallest amount.

Perfectly inelastic demand Demand with an elasticity of zero; the quantity demanded does not change as the price rises.

Perpetuity A bond that promises to pay a certain fixed amount of money each year forever.

Physical limits The maximum output that a plant can produce.

Piece rate A compensation rule based on the output of a worker.

Planned expenditure The expenditure that economic agents (households, firms, governments, and foreigners) plan to undertake in given circumstances.

Political equilibrium A situation in which the choices of voters, politicians, and bureaucrats are all compatible and in which no one group of agents will be better off by making a different choice.

Politicians Elected officials in federal and state government — from chief executives (the president, state governor, or mayor) to members of the legislatures (state and federal senators and representatives).

Portfolio balance theory of the exchange rate The proposition that the exchange rate adjusts to make the stock of financial assets denominated in units of that currency demanded equal to the stock supplied.

Portfolio choice A choice concerning which assets and liabilities to hold.

Positive relationship A relationship between two variables that move in the same direction.

Positive statement A statement about what *is*. Something that can be verified by careful observation.

Preferences A ranking of likes and dislikes and the intensity of those likes and dislikes.

Preferred stock Stock that conveys no voting rights but gives a prior claim on dividends at a fixed rate, regardless of the profit level.

Present value The value in the present of a future sum of money. It is equal to the amount that, if invested today, will grow as large as that future sum, taking into account the interest that it will earn.

Price discrimination The practice of charging a higher price to some customers than to others for an identical good or of charging an individual customer a higher price on a small purchase than on a large one.

Price-earnings ratio The current price of a share divided by the current profit per share.

Price effect The effect of a change in the price on the quantity of a good consumed.

Price elasticity of demand The percentage change in the quantity demanded of a good divided by the percentage change in its price.

Price index A measure of the average level of prices in one period as a percentage of their level in an earlier period.

Price level The average level of prices as measured by a price index.

Price stability A situation in which the average level of prices is moving neither up nor down.

Price taker A firm that cannot influence the price of its product.

Principal An individual who sets a compensation rule to motivate an agent to choose activities advantageous to the principal.

Principle of minimum differentiation The tendency for competitors to make themselves almost identical in order to appeal to the maximum number of clients or voters.

Private debt money A loan that a borrower promises to repay in currency on demand.

Private enterprise An economic system that permits individuals to decide on their own economic activities.

Private good A good or service, each unit of which is consumed by only one individual.

Private property right Legally established title to the sole ownership of a scarce resource.

Private sector surplus or deficit The difference between saving and investment. If saving exceeds investment, the private sector has a surplus. If investment exceeds saving, the private sector has a deficit.

Privatization The process of selling a publicly owned corporation to private shareholders.

Process theory of distributive justice A theory of distributive justice that examines the fairness of the *mechanism* or *process* that results in a given distribution.

Producer surplus The difference between a producer's total revenue and the opportunity cost of production.

Product differentiation Making a product slightly different from that of a competing firm.

Product standards regulation Legally defined standards of product design, materials and ingredients, and quality, usually based on health or safety considerations, but having an effect on the ease with which foreign products can be sold in a domestic market.

Production The conversion of natural, human, and capital resources into goods and services.

Production function A relationship showing how output varies as the employment of inputs is varied.

Production possibility frontier The boundary between attainable and unattainable levels of production.

Productivity The output per unit of input. For example, labour productivity is output per hour of labour.

Professional association An organized group of professional workers, such as lawyers, dentists, or doctors, that seeks to influence the compensation and other labour market conditions affecting its members.

Profit The difference between a firm's total revenue and total cost when revenue exceeds cost.

Profit maximization Making the largest possible profit.

Profit-sharing A compensation rule that allocates a certain fraction of a firm's profit to its employees.

Progressive income tax An income tax at a marginal rate that rises with the level of income.

Property Anything of value.

Property rights Social arrangements that govern the ownership, use, and disposal of property.

Proportional income tax An income tax that is at a constant rate regardless of the level of income.

Protectionism The restriction of international trade.

Public choice theory A theory predicting the behaviour of the government sector of the economy as the outcome of the individual choices made by voters, politicians, and bureaucrats interacting in a political marketplace.

Public franchise An exclusive right granted to a firm to supply a good or service.

Public good A good of which each unit is necessarily consumed by everyone and from which no one can be excluded.

Public interest theory A theory predicting that government action will take place to eliminate waste and achieve an efficient allocation of resources.

Public interest theory of intervention A theory that intervention is supplied to satisfy the demand of consumers and producers for the maximization of total surplus — or the attainment of allocative efficiency.

Purchasing power parity A situation that occurs when money has equal value across countries.

Quantity demanded The amount of a good or service that consumers plan to buy in a given period of time.

Quantity of labour demanded The number of labour hours hired by all the firms in an economy.

Quantity of labour supplied The number of hours of labour services that households supply to firms.

Quantity of money The quantity of currency, bank deposits, and deposits at other types of financial institutions such as trust companies, held by households and firms.

Quantity supplied The amount of a good or service that producers plan to sell in a given period of time.

Quantity theory of money The proposition that an increase in the quantity of money leads to an equal percentage increase in the price level.

Quantity traded The quantity actually bought and sold.

Quota A restriction on the quantity of a good that a firm is permitted to sell or that a country is permitted to import.

Rand formula A rule making it compulsory for all workers in a unionized plant to contribute to the union whether or not they belong to the union.

Rank-tournament compensation rule A compensation rule under which the payment to the agent depends on the agent's rank in a tournament.

Rate of return regulation A regulation that sets the price at a level that enables the regulated firm to earn a specified target percentage return on its capital.

Rational choice The best possible course of action from the point of view of the individual making the choice.

Rational expectation The best forecast that can be made on the basis of all the available and relevant information. A rational expectation is one in which the expected forecast error is zero and the range of error is as small as possible.

Rational expectations equilibrium A macroeconomic equilibrium based on expectations that are the best available forecasts.

Rational expectations hypothesis The hypothesis that the forecasts people make, regardless of how they make them, are on the average the same as the forecasts that an economist makes using the relevant economic theory.

Rational ignorance The decision not to acquire information, because the cost of doing so is greater than the benefit derived from having it.

Rawlsian theory of fairness A theory of distributive justice that gives the biggest income possible to the least well-off.

Real assets Physical things, such as buildings, plant and equipment, inventories, and consumer durable goods.

Real balance effect The influence of a change in the quantity of real money on the quantity of real GDP demanded.

Real business cycle theory A theory of aggregate fluctuations based on the existence of flexible wages and random shocks to the economy's aggregate production function.

Real deficit The change in the real value of government debt in a year.

Real exchange rate The ratio of the price index in one country to the index in another.

Real GDP The output of final goods and services valued at prices prevailing in the base period.

Real income Income expressed in units of goods. Real income in terms of a particular good is income divided by the price of that good.

Real interest rate The interest rate minus the expected inflation rate.

Real money The quantity of goods that a given amount of money will buy.

Real targets Macroeconomic policy targets of unemployment at its natural rate, steady growth in real GDP, and balanced international trade.

Real wage rate The wage rate expressed in constant dollars.

Recession A contraction in the level of economic activity in which real GDP declines in two successive quarters.

Recession gap The difference between capacity real GDP and actual real GDP when actual is less than capacity.

Redemption date The date on which the final payment on a bond is made.

Redemption value The amount paid to a bondholder on the redemption date of a bond.

Regressive income tax An income tax at a marginal rate that falls with the level of income.

Regulation Rules enforced by a government agency to restrict economic activity by determining prices, product standards and types, and the conditions under which new firms may enter an industry.

Relative price The ratio of the price of one good to the price of another. It is expressed as the number of units of one good that one unit of another good will buy.

Rent ceiling A regulation making it illegal to charge a rent higher than a specified level.

Rent seeking The activity of attempting to create a monopoly.

Required reserves The minimum reserves that a bank is permitted to hold.

Reservation wage The lowest wage rate at which a person or household will supply any labour to the market. Below that wage, a person will not work.

Reserve ratio The fraction of a bank's total deposits that are held in reserves.

Reserves Cash holdings in a bank's vault plus the bank's deposits with the Bank of Canada.

Residual claimant The agent who receives the firm's profits and is responsible for its losses.

Returns to scale The change in output relative to the change in inputs when all the inputs are changed by the same percentage.

Royalty A compensation rule based on the value of sales.

Saving Income minus consumption. Saving is measured in the national income accounts as disposable income (income less taxes) minus consumption expenditure.

Saving function The relationship between saving and disposable income.

Scarcity The universal state in which wants exceed resources.

Scatter diagram A diagram that plots the value of one economic variable associated with the value of another.

Search activity The time and effort spent in searching for someone with whom to do business.

Security A marketable, financial asset that a bank, household, or firm can sell but at a price that fluctuates. For example, a government of Canada long-term bond.

Self-sufficiency A state that occurs when each individual consumes only what he or she produces.

Share A fraction of the stock of a corporation.

Short run A period of time in which the quantities of some inputs are fixed and others can be varied.

Short-run aggregate production function The relationship showing how real GDP varies as the quantity of labour employed, holding the capital stock and state of technology constant.

Short-run aggregate supply The relationship between the aggregate quantity of final goods and services (real GDP) supplied and the price level (the GDP deflator), holding constant the prices of the factors of production.

Short-run aggregate supply curve A curve showing the relationship between the quantity of real GDP supplied and the price level, holding everything else constant.

Short-run aggregate supply schedule A list showing the quantity of real GDP supplied at each price level, holding everything else constant.

Short-run demand curve The demand curve that describes the initial response of buyers to a change in the price of a good.

Short-run demand for labour The relationship between the wage rate and the quantity of labour demanded when the firm's capital input is fixed and labour is the only variable input.

Short-run elasticity of demand for labour The percentage change in the quantity of labour demanded divided by the percentage change in the wage rate when labour is the only variable input.

Short-run industry supply curve A curve that shows how the total quantity supplied in the short run by all firms in an industry varies as the market price varies.

Short-run production function The relationship showing how the maximum output attainable varies as the quantity of the variable input varies, holding the quantity of the fixed input and the state of technology constant.

Short-run supply curve The supply curve that describes the response of the quantity supplied to a change in price when only *some* of the technologically possible adjustments to the production process have been made.

Shutdown point The point at which a firm's maximum profit is the same regardless of whether it produces a positive amount of output or produces nothing—temporarily shuts down.

Simple money multiplier The amount by which an increase in bank reserves is multiplied to calculate the effect of the increase in reserves on total bank deposits, when there are no losses of currency from the banking system.

Single-price monopoly A monopoly that charges the same price for each unit of output.

Slope The change in the value of the variable measured on the y-axis divided by the change in the value of the variable measured on the x-axis.

Socialism An economic system based on state ownership of capital and land and on a centrally planned allocation of resources.

Sole proprietorship A firm with a single owner who has unlimited liability.

Specialization The production of only one good or a few goods.

Stagflation A situation in which real GDP stops growing or even declines and inflation accelerates.

Standard of deferred payment An agreed measure in which contracts for future receipts and payments are written.

State enterprise The basic production unit of the Soviet economy.

Stock A quantity measured at a point in time.

Stock equilibrium A situation in which all the available stock of an asset is willingly held.

Stock exchange An organized market for trading in stock.

Stock market The market in which the equities of firms are traded.

Stock yield The income from a share in the stock of a firm, expressed as a percentage of the price of the share.

Store of value Any commodity that can be held and sold at a later time.

Strategic interaction Acting in a way that takes into account the expected behaviour of others and the mutual recognition of interdependence.

Strategies All the possible actions of each player.

Strike The refusal of a group of workers to work under the prevailing conditions.

Subsidy A payment made by the government to producers of goods and services, such as subsidies paid to grain growers and dairy farmers.

Substitute A good that may be used in place of another good.

Substitution effect The effect of a change in price on the quantities consumed when the consumer remains indifferent between the original and the new combinations of goods consumed.

Sunk costs The historical cost of buying plant and machinery that have no current resale value.

Supply The entire relationship between the quantity supplied of a good and its price.

Supply curve A graph showing the relationship between the quantity supplied and the price of a good, holding everything else constant.

Supply of labour A schedule or curve showing how the quantity of labour supplied varies as the real wage varies.

Supply schedule A list of quantities supplied at different prices, holding everything else constant.

Takeover The purchase of the stock of one firm by another firm.

Tariff A tax on an import by the government of the importing country.

Tax base The activity on which a tax is levied.

Tax rate The percentage rate at which a tax is levied on a particular activity.

Tax revenue The product of the tax rate and the tax base.

Team production A production process in which a group of individuals each specializes in mutually supportive tasks.

Technique Any feasible way of converting inputs into output.

Technological efficiency A state in which it is not possible to increase output without increasing inputs.

Technological progress The development of new and better ways of producing goods and services.

Technology The method for converting resources into goods and services.

Theory of distributive justice A set of principles against which one can test whether a particular distribution of economic well-being is fair.

Time-series consumption function The relationship between real consumption expenditure and real disposable income over time.

Time-series graph A graph showing the value of a variable on the y-axis plotted against time on the x-axis.

Time rate A compensation rule based on the number of hours an individual works.

Tit-for-tat strategy A strategy in which a player cooperates in the current period if the other player cooperated in the previous period but cheats if the other player cheated in the previous period.

Total benefit The total dollar value that people place on a given level of provision of a public good.

Total cost The sum of the costs of all the inputs used in production.

Total expenditure The amount spent for the purchase of a good. It equals the price of the good multiplied by the quantity bought.

Total fixed cost The cost of all the fixed inputs.

Total product The total quantity produced by a firm in a given period of time.

Total product curve A graph showing the maximum output attainable with a given amount of capital as the amount of labour employed is varied.

Total revenue The amount received from the sale of a good. It equals the price of the good multiplied by the quantity sold.

Total surplus The sum of consumer surplus and producer surplus.

Total utility The total benefit or satisfaction that a person gets from consumption of goods and services.

Total variable cost The cost of variable inputs.

Transactions costs The costs arising from finding a trading partner, negotiating an agreement about the price and other aspects of the exchange, and of ensuring that the terms of the agreement are fulfilled.

Transfer earnings The income required to induce the supply of a factor of production.

Transfer payment A payment made by the government to households in the form of social benefits.

Transfer payments multiplier The amount by which a change in transfer payments is multiplied to determine the change in equilibrium expenditure that it generates.

Trend A general tendency for a variable to rise or fall.

Trend real GDP A measure of the general upward tendency or drift of real GDP that ignores its fluctuations.

Trigger strategy A strategy in which a player cooperates if the other player cooperates but plays the Nash equilibrium strategy forever thereafter if the other player cheats.

Trough The lower turning point of a business cycle — the point at which the economy turns from contraction to expansion.

Trust company A financial intermediary that takes in households' savings and makes loans in the form of mortgages for the purchases of houses and consumer loans to finance purchases of consumer durable goods.

Turnover tax A Soviet tax on a consumer good designed to make its market price high enough to achieve a balance between the quantity demanded and the quantity supplied.

Unanticipated inflation Inflation that catches people by surprise.

Underdeveloped country A country in which there is little industrialization, limited mechanization of the agricultural sector, very little capital equipment, and low per capita income.

Underdevelopment trap A situation in which a country is locked into a low per capita income situation that reinforces itself.

Underground economy All economic activity that is legal but unreported.

Unemployment The number of adult workers who are not employed and who are seeking jobs.

Unemployment equilibrium A situation in which macroeconomic equilibrium occurs at a level of real GDP below capacity real GDP and there is a recessionary gap.

Unemployment rate Unemployment expressed as a percentage of the labour force.

Unit elastic demand An elasticity of 1; the quantity demanded of a good and its price change in equal proportions.

Unit of account An agreed measure for stating the prices of goods and services.

Unlimited liability The legal responsibility for all debts incurred by a firm up to an amount equal to the entire wealth of its owner.

Utilitarian theory The theory that the fairest outcome is the one that maximizes the sum of all individual utilities in society.

Utility The benefit or satisfaction that a person obtains from the consumption of a good or service.

Utility maximization The attainment of the greatest possible total utility, given the consumer's income and the prices of goods.

Value The maximum amount that a person is willing to pay for a good.

Value added The value of a firm's output minus the value of the inputs bought from other firms.

Value of money The amount of goods and services that can be bought with a given amount of money.

Variable cost A cost that varies with the output level.

Variable inputs Those inputs whose quantity used can be varied in the short run.

Velocity of circulation The average number of times a dollar is used annually to buy the goods and services that make up GDP.

Voluntary export restraint A self-imposed restriction by an exporting country on the volume of its exports of a particular good. Voluntary export restraints are often called VERs.

Voters The consumers of the outcome of the political process.

Wants The unlimited desires or wishes that people have for goods and services.

Wealth The total assets of a household, firm, or government minus its total liabilities.

Wealth effect The effect of a change in real wealth on aggregate planned expenditure.

Welfare state capitalism An economic system combining capitalism's private ownership of capital and land with a heavy degree of state intervention in the allocation of resources.

x-axis The horizontal scale on a graph.

x-coordinate A line running from a point on a graph horizontally to the y-axis. It is called the x-coordinate because its length is the same as the value marked off on the x-axis.

y-axis The vertical scale on a graph.

y-coordinate A line running from a point on a graph vertically to the x-axis. It is called the y-coordinate because its length is the same as the value marked off on the y-axis.

INDEX

Key concepts and pages where they are defined appear in boldface.
Page references followed by the letter n refer to footnotes.

PHOTO CREDITS

Michael Parkin and ***Robin Bade*** (p.iii): Jeremy Jones Photography. ***Adam Smith*** (p.20): Archiv fur Kunst und Geschichte. ***Antoine-Augustin Cournot*** (p.84): Historical Pictures Service, Chicago. ***Alfred Marshall*** (p.84): Historical Pictures Service, Chicago. ***Jeremy Bentham*** (p.194): Mary Evans Picture Library. ***Jacob Viner*** (p.250): Published with permission of Princeton University Libraries. ***Joan Robinson*** (p.318): Peter Lofts. ***John von Neumann*** (p.356): Historical Pictures Service, Chicago. ***Kenneth Arrow*** (p.516): UPI/Bettmann. ***James Buchanan*** (p.516): George Mason University, Center for Public Choice. ***Jean-Baptiste Say*** (p.634): Courtesy Library of Congress. ***Irving Fisher*** (p.662): Irving Fisher Papers. Manuscripts and Archives Department, Yale University Library. ***John Maynard Keynes*** (p.662): UPI/Bettmann. ***Franco Modigliani*** (p.663): The MIT Museum. ***Milton Friedman*** (p.664): UPI/Bettmann Newsphotos. ***Arthur Okun*** (p.856): John Neubauer. ***Edward Prescott*** (p.857): Edward Prescott. ***Econometrica cover*** (p.875): Reprinted by permission of The Econometric Society. ***A.W. Phillips*** (p.884): The MIT Museum. ***David Hume*** (p.930): The Bettmann Archive. ***David Ricardo*** (p.958): Courtesy Claire Friedland, University of Chicago, Center for the Study of the Economy and the State, engraving by T. Hodgetts, from a painting by Thomas Phillips.

INTERVIEW PHOTOS

Assar Lindbeck (pp.1–4), Christopher Green (pp.203–206), Curtis Eaton (pp.277–280), Morley Gunderson (pp.375–378), Peter Lougheed (pp.489–492), Gerald Bouey (pp.713–716), Jacques Parizeau (pp.911–914), Judith Maxwell (pp.963–966): Robin Bade. Milton Friedman (pp.97–100), Gary Becker (pp.151–154), James Tobin (pp.561–564), Paul Volcker (pp.645–648), Robert E. Lucas Jr. (pp.799–802), Janos Kornai (pp.1011–1014): Marshall Henrichs.